A+ Guide to Hardware: Managing, Maintaining, and Troubleshooting
SIXTH EDITION

Jean Andrews, Ph.D.

Australia • Canada • Mexico • Singapore • Spain • United Kingdom • United States

A+ Guide to Hardware, Sixth Edition, Managing, Maintaining, and Troubleshooting, International Student Edition
Jean Andrews

Vice President, Careers & Computing: Dave Garza

Executive Editor: Stephen Helba

Acquisitions Editor: Nick Lombardi

Director, Development – Careers & Computing: Marah Bellegarde

Product Development Manager: Juliet Steiner

Senior Product Manager: Michelle Ruelos Cannistraci

Developmental Editor: Jill Batistic/Deb Kaufmann

Editorial Assistant: Sarah Pickering

Brand Manager: Kristin McNary

Senior Market Development Manager: Mark Linton

Senior Production Director: Wendy Troeger

Production Manager: Andrew Crouth

Senior Content Project Manager: Andrea Majot

Art Director: GEX

Technology Project Manager: Joseph Pliss

Media Editor: William Overocker

Cover image: ©Pavelk/Shutterstock

© 2014 Course Technology, Cengage Learning

ALL RIGHTS RESERVED. No part of this work covered by the copyright herein may be reproduced, transmitted, stored or used in any form or by any means graphic, electronic, or mechanical, including but not limited to photocopying, recording, scanning, digitizing, taping, Web distribution, information networks, or information storage and retrieval systems, except as permitted under Section 107 or 108 of the 1976 United States Copyright Act, without the prior written permission of the publisher.

> For permission to use material from this text or product,
> submit all requests online at **cengage.com/permissions**
> Further permissions questions can be emailed to
> **permissionrequest@cengage.com**

Library of Congress Control Number: 2012951194

ISBN-13: 978-1-133-13537-1

ISBN-10: 1-133-13537-4

Cengage Learning International Offices

Asia
www.cengageasia.com
tel: (65) 6410 1200

Brazil
www.cengage.com.br
tel: (55) 11 3665 9900

Latin America
www.cengage.com.mx
tel: (52) 55 1500 6000

**Represented in Canada by
Nelson Education, Ltd.**
www.nelson.com
tel: (416) 752 9100/(800) 668 0671

Australia/New Zealand
www.cengage.com.au
tel: (61) 3 9685 4111

India
www.cengage.co.in
tel: (91) 11 4364 1111

UK/Europe/Middle East/Africa
www.cengage.co.uk
tel: (44) 0 1264 332 424

Cengage Learning is a leading provider of customized learning solutions with office locations around the globe, including Singapore, the United Kingdom, Australia, Mexico, Brazil, and Japan. Locate your local office at: **www.cengage.com/global**

For product information and free companion resources: **www.cengage.com/international**

Visit your local office: **www.cengage.com/global**

Visit our corporate website: **www.cengage.com**

AVAILABILITY OF RESOURCES MAY DIFFER BY REGION. Check with your local Cengage Learning representative for details.

Printed in the United States of America
1 2 3 4 5 6 7 16 15 14 13 12

Table of Contents

**CompTIA A+ 220-801 Exam,
2012 Edition Examination Objectives
Mapped to Chapters** . . . . **vii**

**CompTIA A+ 220-802 Exam,
2012 Edition Examination Objectives
Mapped to Chapters** . . . . **xx**

CHAPTER 1

**First Look at Computer Parts
and Tools** **1**

What's Inside the Case 2
   Form Factors Used by Computer Cases, Power
      Supplies, and Motherboards 9
   Drives, Their Cables, and Connectors 18
Protecting Yourself and the Equipment
   against Electrical Dangers 23
   Measures and Properties of Electricity 24
   Protect Yourself against Electrical
      Shock and Burns 28
   Protect the Equipment against Static
      Electricity or ESD 29
Tools Used by a PC Repair Technician 33
   POST Diagnostic Cards 35
   Power Supply Tester 37
   Multimeter 37
   Loopback Plugs 37
   Proper Use of Cleaning Pads and Solutions . . . 39
   Managing Cables 40
   Lifting Heavy Objects 40

CHAPTER 2

Working Inside a Computer **45**

How to Work Inside a Computer Case 46
   Step 1: Plan and Organize Your Work 46
   Step 2: Open the Computer Case
      and Examine the System 47
   Step 3: Remove Expansion Cards 52
   Step 4: Remove the Motherboard,
      Power Supply, and Drives 55
   Steps to Put a Computer Back Together 60
Cooling Methods and Devices 67
   Processor Coolers, Fans, and Heat Sinks 67

   Case Fans and Other Fans and Heat Sinks 69
   Liquid Cooling Systems 71
   Dealing with Dust 72
Selecting a Power Supply 73
   Types and Characteristics of
      Power Supplies 74
   How to Calculate Wattage Capacity 75

CHAPTER 3

All About Motherboards **81**

Motherboard Types and Features 82
   Motherboard Form Factors 82
   Processor Sockets 84
   The Chipset 89
   Buses and Expansion Slots 94
   On-board Ports and Connectors 104
Configuring a Motherboard 106
   Using Jumpers to Configure a
      Motherboard 108
   Using Setup BIOS to Configure a
      Motherboard 110
Maintaining a Motherboard 122
   Updating Motherboard Drivers 122
   Flashing BIOS 124
   Replacing the CMOS Battery 125
Installing or Replacing a Motherboard 126
   How to Select a Motherboard 126
   How to Install or Replace a Motherboard . . . 127

CHAPTER 4

**Supporting Processors
and Upgrading Memory** **137**

Types and Characteristics of Processors 138
   How a Processor Works 140
   Intel Processors 142
   AMD Processors 145
Selecting and Installing a Processor 146
   Select a Processor to Match System Needs . . . 146
   Install a Processor 147
Memory Technologies 162
   DIMM Technologies 165
   RIMM Technologies 171
   Memory Technologies and Memory
      Performance 172

How to Upgrade Memory................................. 173
   How Much Memory Do I Need and
      How Much Is Currently Installed?........ 173
   How Many and What Kind of Memory
      Modules Are Currently Installed?........ 175
   How Many and What Kind of Modules
      Can Fit on My Motherboard?............. 176
   How Do I Select and Purchase the
      Right Memory Modules?................. 180
   How Do I Install the New Modules?........ 182

CHAPTER 5

Supporting Hard Drives 189

Hard Drive Technologies and Interface
   Standards... 190
   Technologies Used Inside a Hard Drive..... 190
   Interface Standards Used by a Hard Drive... 193
How to Select and Install Hard Drives................ 204
   Selecting a Hard Drive 204
   Steps to Install a Serial ATA Drive 205
   Steps to Configure and Install a Parallel
      ATA Drive.. 214
   Setting Up Hardware RAID 220
About Tape Drives and Floppy Drives 228
   Installing Tape Drives and Selecting
      Tape Media.. 228
   Installing a Floppy Drive................ 230

CHAPTER 6

Supporting I/O and Storage Devices............... 237

Basic Principles for Supporting Devices 238
   Using the Action Center and
      Device Manager..................................... 238
   Ports and Wireless Connections Used
      by Peripheral Devices................. 244
Installing I/O Peripheral Devices 250
   Mouse or Keyboard..................... 251
   Barcode Readers........................ 252
   Biometric Devices...................... 253
   Digital Cameras and Camcorders........... 254
   Webcams............................... 255
   Graphics Tablets....................... 256
   MIDI Devices 257

   Touch Screens 258
   KVM Switches 259
Installing and Configuring Adapter Cards 260
   Sound Cards and Onboard Sound 265
   TV Tuner and Video Capture Cards 266
Supporting the Video Subsystem 268
   Monitor Technologies and Features 268
   Video Cards and Connectors.............. 272
   Changing Monitor Settings 277
   Video Memory and Windows 7/Vista....... 280
Supporting Storage Devices............................ 282
   File Systems Used by Storage Devices...... 282
   Standards Used by Optical Drives and Discs...284
   Installing an Optical Drive............... 288
   Solid-State Storage..................... 290

CHAPTER 7

Satisfying Customer Needs.........301

Job Roles and Responsibilities........................... 302
   Certification and Professional
      Organizations 303
   Record-keeping and Information Tools..... 305
What Customers Want: Beyond
   Technical Know-how....................................... 306
Planning for Good Service............................... 310
   Initial Contact with a Customer 311
   Interview the Customer................. 312
   Set and Meet Customer Expectations 314
   Working with a Customer on Site......... 315
   Working with a Customer on the Phone.... 316
   Dealing with Difficult Customers 318
   The Customer Decides When the
      Work Is Done 321
   Sometimes You Must Escalate a Problem.... 322
   The Job Isn't Finished until the
      Paperwork Is Done.............................. 322
   Working with Co-workers 323
Dealing with Prohibited Content and Activity.... 328
Customizing Computer Systems 329
   Graphics or CAD/CAM Workstation........ 330
   Audio and Video Editing Workstation...... 332
   Virtualization Workstation................ 333
   Gaming PC............................ 334
   Home Theater PC 335
   Home Server PC 337
   Thick Client and Thin Client 338

CHAPTER 8

Troubleshooting Hardware Problems 345

How to Approach a Hardware Problem 346
Troubleshooting the Electrical System 352
    Problems That Come and Go 355
    Power Problems with the Motherboard 356
    Problems with Overheating 357
Troubleshooting POST before Video Is Active 363
Troubleshooting Error Messages during
    the Boot 364
Troubleshooting the Motherboard,
    Processor, and RAM 366
    Problems with Installations 373
Troubleshooting Hard Drives 376
Troubleshooting Monitors and Video 380
Protecting a Computer and the Environment 388
    Physically Protect Your Equipment 388
    Document Preventive Maintenance 392
    How to Dispose of Used Equipment 393

CHAPTER 9

Connecting to and Setting Up a Network 401

Understanding TCP/IP and Windows
    Networking 402
    Layers of Network Communication 402
    How IP Addresses Get Assigned 406
    How IPv4 IP Addresses Are Used 407
    How IPv6 IP Addresses Are Used 412
    View IP Address Settings 414
    Character-Based Names Identify
        Computers and Networks 415
    TCP/IP Protocol Layers 417
Connecting a Computer to a Network 423
    Connect to a Wired Network 423
    Connect to a Wireless Network 428
    Connect to a Wireless WAN (Cellular)
        Network 434
    Create a Dial-up Connection 439
Setting Up a Multifunction Router for a
    SOHO Network 441
    Functions of a SOHO Router 442
    Install and Configure the Router on
        the Network 444

CHAPTER 10

Networking Types, Devices, and Cabling 463

Network Types and Topologies 464
    Network Technologies Used for Internet
        Connections 467
Hardware Used by Local Networks 476
    Wired and Wireless Network Adapters 476
    Dial-up Modems 482
    Switches and Hubs 482
    Wireless Access Points and Bridges 484
    Other Network Devices 485
    Ethernet Cables and Connectors 486
Setting Up and Troubleshooting Network Wiring . . . 491
    Tools Used by Network Technicians 492
    How Twisted-pair Cables and
        Connectors Are Wired 496

CHAPTER 11

Supporting Notebooks 513

Special Considerations when Supporting
    Notebooks 514
    Warranty Concerns 516
    Service Manuals and Other Sources
        of Information 517
    Diagnostic Tools Provided by
        Manufacturers 519
    The OEM Operating System Build 520
Maintaining Notebooks and Notebook
    Components 523
    Special Keys, Buttons, and Input
        Devices on a Notebook 524
    PCMCIA and ExpressCard Slots 527
    Updating Port or Slot Drivers 530
    Power and Electrical Devices 531
    Power Management 533
    Port Replicators and Docking Stations 536
Replacing and Upgrading Internal Parts 539
    Three Approaches to Dealing with
        a Broken Internal Device 539
    Upgrading Memory 540
    Replacing a Hard Drive 544
    Disassembling and Reassembling a
        Notebook Computer 546
    Working Inside an All-in-one Computer 567

Troubleshooting Notebooks 571
    Problems Logging onto Windows 571
    No Wireless Connectivity 571
    Power or Battery Problems 573
    No Display 574
    Flickering, Dim, or Otherwise Poor Video ... 575

CHAPTER 12

Supporting Printers 581

Printer Types and Features 582
    Printer Languages 582
    Types of Printers 583
Using Windows to Install, Share, and
    Manage Printers 591
    Installing a Local or Network Printer 593
    Sharing an Installed Printer 602
    Installing a Shared Printer 604
    Managing Printer Features and
        Add-on Devices 605
    Managing the Printer Queue 607
Printer Maintenance and Upgrades 608
    Online Support for Printers 608

    Cleaning a Printer 610
    Printer Maintenance Kits 612
    Upgrade the Printer Memory or
        Hard Drive 617
    Print Servers and the Print
        Management Tool 619
Troubleshooting Printers 622
    Printer Does Not Print 623
    Poor Print Quality 634

APPENDIX A

Keystroke Shortcuts in Windows 643

APPENDIX B

CompTIA A+ Acronyms 647

Glossary 657

Index 677

CompTIA A+ 220-801 Exam, 2012 Edition Examination Objectives Mapped to Chapters

A+ Guide to Hardware and *A+ Guide to Software* when used together fully meet all of the CompTIA A+ exams objectives. If the A+ exam objective is covered in the corresponding textbook, it is referenced in the Page Numbers column.

DOMAIN 1.0 PC HARDWARE

1.1 Configure and apply BIOS settings.

OBJECTIVES	CHAPTER	PAGE NUMBERS
▲ Install firmware upgrades – flash BIOS	3	106–126
▲ BIOS component information	3	106–126
• RAM	3	106–126
• Hard drive	3	106–126
• Optical drive	3	106–126
• CPU	3	106–126
▲ BIOS configurations	3	106–126
• Boot sequence	3	106–126
• Enabling and disabling devices	3	106–126
• Date/time	3	106–126
• Clock speeds	3	106–126
• Virtualization support	3	106–126
▪ BIOS security (passwords, drive encryption: TPM, lo-jack)	3	106–126
▲ Use built-in diagnostics	3	106–126
▲ Monitoring	3	106–126
• Temperature monitoring	3	106–126
• Fan speeds	3	106–126
• Intrusion detection/notification	3	106–126
• Voltage	3	106–126
• Clock	3	106–126
• Bus speed	3	106–126

1.2 Differentiate between motherboard components, their purposes, and properties.

OBJECTIVES	CHAPTER	PAGE NUMBERS
▲ Sizes	3	82–106, 125–131
• ATX	3	82–106, 125–131
• Micro-ATX	3	82–106, 125–131
• ITX	3	82–106, 125–131
▲ Expansion slots	3	82–106, 125–131
• PCI	3	82–106, 125–131
• PCI-X	3	82–106, 125–131
• PCIe	3	82–106, 125–131
• miniPCI	3	82–106, 125–131
• AGP2x, 4x, 8x	3	82–106, 125–131
▲ RAM slots	4	162–184
▲ CPU sockets	3	82–106, 125–131
▲ Chipsets	3	82–106, 125–131
• North Bridge	3	82–106, 125–131
• South Bridge	3	82–106, 125–131
• CMOS battery	3	82–106, 125–131

▲ Jumpers	3	82–106, 125–131
▲ Power connections and types	3	82–106, 125–131
▲ Fan connectors	3	82–106, 125–131
▲ Front panel connectors	2	46–67
• USB	2	46–67
• Audio	2	46–67
• Power button	2	46–67
• Power light	2	46–67
• Drive activity lights	2	46–67
• Reset button	2	46–67
▲ Bus speeds	3	82–106, 125–131

1.3 Compare and contrast RAM types and features.

OBJECTIVES	CHAPTER	PAGE NUMBERS
▲ Types	4	162–184
• DDR	4	162–184
• DDR2	4	162–184
• DDR3	4	162–184
• SDRAM	4	162–184
• SODIMM	4	162–184
• RAMBUS	4	162–184
• DIMM	4	162–184
• Parity vs. non-parity	4	162–184
• ECC vs. non-ECC	4	162–184
• RAM configurations	4	162–184
▪ Single channel vs. dual channel vs. triple channel	4	162–184
• Single sided vs. double sided	4	162–184
▲ RAM compatibility and speed	4	162–184

1.4 Install and configure expansion cards.

OBJECTIVES	CHAPTER	PAGE NUMBERS
▲ Sound cards	6	260–282
▲ Video cards	6	260–282
▲ Network cards	10	476–482
▲ Serial and parallel cards	6	260–282
▲ USB cards	6	260–282
▲ Firewire cards	6	260–282
▲ Storage cards	5	220–227
▲ Modem cards	10	476–482
▲ Wireless/cellular cards	10	476–482
▲ TV tuner cards	6	260–282
▲ Video capture cards	6	260–282
▲ Riser cards	3	101

1.5 Install and configure storage devices and use appropriate media.

OBJECTIVES	CHAPTER	PAGE NUMBERS
▲ Optical drives	6	238–293
• CD-ROM	6	238–293
• DVD-ROM	6	238–293
• Blu-Ray	6	238–293

▲ Combo drives and burners	6	238–293
• CD-RW	6	238–293
• DVD-RW	6	238–293
• Dual Layer DVD-RW	6	238–293
• BD-R	6	238–293
• BD-RE	6	238–293
▲ Connection types	6	238–293
• External	6	238–293
▪ USB	6	238–293
▪ Firewire	6	238–293
▪ eSATA	5	190–232
▪ Ethernet	6	238–293
• Internal SATA, IDE and SCSI	5	190–232
▪ IDE configuration and setup (Master, Slave, Cable Select)	5	190–232
▪ SCSI IDs (0 – 15)	5	190–232
• Hot swappable drives	5	190–232
▲ Hard drives	5	190–232
• Magnetic	5	190–232
• 5400 rpm	5	190–232
• 7200 rpm	5	190–232
• 10,000 rpm	5	190–232
• 15,000 rpm	5	190–232
▲ Solid state/flash drives	5	190–232
• Compact flash	6	238–293
• SD	6	238–293
• Micro-SD	6	238–293
• Mini-SD	6	238–293
• xD	6	238–293
• SSD	5	190–232
▲ RAID types	5	190–232
• 0	5	190–232
• 1	5	190–232
• 5	5	190–232
• 10	5	190–232
▲ Floppy drive	5	190–232
▲ Tape drive	5	190–232
▲ Media capacity	6	238–293
• CD	6	238–293
• CD-RW	6	238–293
• DVD-RW	6	238–293
• DVD	6	238–293
• Blu-Ray	6	238–293
• Tape	5	190–232
• Floppy	5	190–232
• DL DVD	6	238–293

1.6 Differentiate among various CPU types and features and select the appropriate cooling method.

OBJECTIVES	CHAPTER	PAGE NUMBERS
▲ Socket types	3	84–89
• Intel: LGA, 775, 1155, 1156, 1366	3	84–89
• AMD: 940, AM2, AM2+, AM3, AM3+, FM1, F	3	84–89

OBJECTIVES	CHAPTER	PAGE NUMBERS
▲ Characteristics	4	138–162
• Speeds	4	138–162
• Cores	4	138–162
• Cache size/type	4	138–162
• Hyperthreading	4	138–162
• Virtualization support	4	138–162
• Architecture (32-bit vs. 64-bit)	4	138–162
• Integrated GPU	4	138–162
▲ Cooling	2	67–73
• Heat sink	2	67–73
• Fans	2	67–73
• Thermal paste	2	67–73
• Liquid-based	2	67–73

1.7 Compare and contrast various connection interfaces and explain their purpose.

OBJECTIVES	CHAPTER	PAGE NUMBERS
▲ Physical connections		
• USB 1.1 vs. 2.0 vs. 3.0 speed and distance characteristics	6	238–293
▪ Connector types: A, B, mini, micro	6	238–293
• Firewire 400 vs. Firewire 800 speed and distance characteristics	6	238–293
• SATA1 vs. SATA2 vs. SATA3, eSATA, IDE speeds	5	190–204
• Other connector types	1	2–5
▪ Serial	1	2–5
▪ Parallel	1	2–5
▪ VGA	1	2–5
▪ HDMI	1	2–5
▪ DVI	1	2–5
▪ Audio	1	2–5
▪ RJ-45	1	2–5
▪ RJ-11	1	2–5
• Analog vs. digital transmission	1	2–5
▪ VGA vs. HDMI	1	2–5
▲ Speeds, distances and frequencies of wireless device connections	6	238–293
• Bluetooth	6	238–293
• IR	6	238–293
• RF	6	238–293

1.8 Install an appropriate power supply based on a given scenario.

OBJECTIVES	CHAPTER	PAGE NUMBERS
▲ Connector types and their voltages	1	2–23
• SATA	1	2–23
• Molex	1	2–23
• 4/8-pin 12v	1	2–23
• PCIe 6/8-pin	1	2–23
• 20-pin	1	2–23
• 24-pin	1	2–23
• Floppy	1	2–23
▲ Specifications	2	73–77
• Wattage	2	73–77

• Size	2	73–77
• Number of connectors	2	73–77
• ATX	1	2–23
• Micro-ATX	1	2–23
▲ Dual voltage options	1	2–23

1.9 Evaluate and select appropriate components for a custom configuration, to meet customer specifications or needs.

OBJECTIVES	CHAPTER	PAGE NUMBERS
▲ Graphic / CAD / CAM design workstation	7	329–339
• Powerful processor	7	329–339
• High-end video	7	329–339
• Maximum RAM	7	329–339
▲ Audio/Video editing workstation	7	329–339
• Specialized audio and video card	7	329–339
• Large fast hard drive	7	329–339
• Dual monitors	7	329–339
▲ Virtualization workstation	7	329–339
• Maximum RAM and CPU cores	7	329–339
▲ Gaming PC	7	329–339
• Powerful processor	7	329–339
• High-end video/specialized GPU	7	329–339
• Better sound card	7	329–339
• High-end cooling	7	329–339
▲ Home Theater PC	7	329–339
• Surround sound audio	7	329–339
• HDMI output	7	329–339
• HTPC compact form factor	7	329–339
• TV tuner	7	329–339
▲ Standard thick client	7	329–339
• Desktop applications	7	329–339
• Meets recommended requirements for running Windows	7	329–339
▲ Thin client	7	329–339
• Basic applications	7	329–339
• Meets minimum requirements for running Windows	7	329–339
▲ Home Server PC	7	329–339
• Media streaming	7	329–339
• File sharing	7	329–339
• Print sharing	7	329–339
• Gigabit NIC	7	329–339
• RAID array	7	329–339

1.10 Given a scenario, evaluate types and features of display devices.

OBJECTIVES	CHAPTER	PAGE NUMBERS
▲ Types	6	238–293
• CRT	6	238–293
• LCD	6	238–293
• LED	6	238–293
• Plasma	6	238–293
• Projector	6	238–293
• OLED	6	238–293

▲ Refresh rates	6	238–293
▲ Resolution	6	238–293
▲ Native resolution	6	238–293
▲ Brightness/lumens	6	238–293
▲ Analog vs. digital	6	238–293
▲ Privacy/antiglare filters	6	238–293
▲ Multiple displays	6	238–293

1.11 Identify connector types and associated cables.

OBJECTIVES	CHAPTER	PAGE NUMBERS
▲ Display connector types	6	268–282
• DVI-D	6	268–282
• DVI-I	6	268–282
• DVI-A	6	268–282
• Displayport	1	2–5
• RCA	6	268–282
• DB-15	1	2–5
• BNC	10	476–490
• miniHDMI	6	268–282
• RJ-45	10	476–506
• miniDin-6	6	268–282
▲ Display cable types	6	268–282
• HDMI	6	268–282
• DVI	6	268–282
• VGA	6	268–282
• Component	6	268–282
• Composite	6	268–282
• S-video	6	268–282
• RGB	6	268–282
• Coaxial	10	476–490
• Ethernet	10	476–490
▲ Device connectors and pin arrangements	5	190–204
• SATA	5	190–204
• eSATA	6	238–293
• PATA	5	190–204
■ IDE	5	190–204
■ EIDE	5	190–204
• Floppy	5	228–232
• USB	6	238–293
• IEE1394	1	2–5
• SCSI	5	190–204
• PS/2	1	2–5
• Parallel	1	2–5
• Serial	1	2–5
• Audio	1	2–5
• RJ-45	10	476–506
▲ Device cable types		
• SATA	5	190–204
• eSATA	6	238–293
• IDE	5	190–204

• EIDE	5	190–204
• Floppy	5	228–232
• USB	6	238–293
• IEE1394	6	238–293
• SCSI	5	190–204
▪ 68pin vs. 50pin vs. 25pin	5	190–204
• Parallel	12	596–602
• Serial	6	238–293
• Ethernet	10	476–506
• Phone	10	476–490

1.12 Install and configure various peripheral devices.

OBJECTIVES	CHAPTER	PAGE NUMBERS
◢ Input devices	6	238–282
• Mouse	6	238–282
• Keyboard	6	238–282
• Touch screen	6	238–282
• Scanner	6	238–282
• Barcode reader	6	238–282
• KVM	6	238–282
• Microphone	6	238–282
• Biometric devices	6	238–282
• Game pads	6	238–282
• Joysticks	6	238–282
• Digitizer	6	238–282
◢ Multimedia devices	6	238–282
• Digital cameras	6	238–282
• Microphone	6	238–282
• Webcam	6	238–282
• Camcorder	6	238–282
• MIDI enabled devices	6	238–282
◢ Output devices	6	238–282
• Printers	12	591–608
• Speakers	6	238–282
• Display devices	6	238–282

DOMAIN 2.0 NETWORKING

2.1 Identify types of network cables and connectors.

OBJECTIVES	CHAPTER	PAGE NUMBERS
◢ Fiber	10	476–506
• Connectors: SC, ST and LC	10	476–506
◢ Twisted Pair	10	476–506
• Connectors: RJ-11, RJ-45	10	476–506
• Wiring standards: T568A, T568B	10	476–506
◢ Coaxial	10	476–506
• Connectors: BNC, F-connector	10	476–506

2.2 Categorize characteristics of connectors and cabling.

OBJECTIVES	CHAPTER	PAGE NUMBERS
▲ Fiber	10	476–490
• Types (single-mode vs. multi-mode)	10	476–490
• Speed and transmission limitations	10	476–490
▲ Twisted pair	10	476–490
• Types: STP, UTP, CAT3, CAT5, CAT5e, CAT6, plenum, PVC	10	476–490
• Speed and transmission limitations	10	476–490
▲ Coaxial	10	476–490
• Types: RG-6, RG-59	10	476–490
• Speed and transmission limitations	10	476–490

2.3 Explain properties and characteristics of TCP/IP.

OBJECTIVES	CHAPTER	PAGE NUMBERS
▲ IP class	9	402–415
• Class A	9	402–415
• Class B	9	402–415
• Class C	9	402–415
▲ IPv4 vs. IPv6	9	402–415
▲ Public vs. private vs. APIPA	9	402–415
▲ Static vs. dynamic	9	402–415
▲ Client-side DNS	9	402–415
▲ DHCP	9	402–415
▲ Subnet mask	9	402–415
▲ Gateway	9	402–415

2.4 Explain common TCP and UDP ports, protocols, and their purpose.

OBJECTIVES	CHAPTER	PAGE NUMBERS
▲ Ports	9	415–423
• 21 – FTP	9	415–423
• 23 – TELNET	9	415–423
• 25 – SMTP	9	415–423
• 53 – DNS	9	415–423
• 80 – HTTP	9	415–423
• 110 – POP3	9	415–423
• 143 – IMAP	9	415–423
• 443 – HTTPS	9	415–423
• 3389 – RDP	9	415–423
▲ Protocols	9	415–423
• DHCP	9	415–423
• DNS	9	415–423
• LDAP	9	415–423
• SNMP	9	415–423
• SMB	9	415–423
• SSH	9	415–423
• SFTP	9	415–423
▲ TCP vs. UDP	9	415–423

2.5 Compare and contrast wireless networking standards and encryption types.

OBJECTIVES	CHAPTER	PAGE NUMBERS
▲ Standards	9	452–456
• 802.11 a/b/g/n	9	452–456
• Speeds, distances, and frequencies	9	452–456
▲ Encryption types	9	452–456
• WEP, WPA, WPA2, TKIP, AES	9	452–456

2.6 Install, configure, and deploy a SOHO wireless/wired router using appropriate settings.

OBJECTIVES	CHAPTER	PAGE NUMBERS
▲ MAC filtering	9	441–456
▲ Channels (1 – 11)	9	441–456
▲ Port forwarding, port triggering	9	441–456
▲ SSID broadcast (on/off)	9	441–456
▲ Wireless encryption	9	441–456
▲ Firewall	9	441–456
▲ DHCP (on/off)	9	441–456
▲ DMZ	9	441–456
▲ NAT	9	441–456
▲ WPS	9	441–456
▲ Basic QoS	9	441–456

2.7 Compare and contrast Internet connection types and features.

OBJECTIVES	CHAPTER	PAGE NUMBERS
▲ Cable	10	464–476
▲ DSL	10	464–476
▲ Dial-up	10	464–476
▲ Fiber	10	464–476
▲ Satellite	10	464–476
▲ ISDN	10	464–476
▲ Cellular (mobile hotspot)	10	464–476
▲ Line of sight wireless internet service	10	464–476
▲ WiMAX	10	464–476

2.8 Identify various types of networks.

OBJECTIVES	CHAPTER	PAGE NUMBERS
▲ LAN	10	464–476
▲ WAN	10	464–476
▲ PAN	10	464–476
▲ MAN	10	464–476
▲ Topologies	10	464–476
• Mesh	10	464–476
• Ring	10	464–476
• Bus	10	464–476
• Star	10	464–476
• Hybrid	10	464–476

2.9 Compare and contrast network devices their functions and features.

OBJECTIVES	CHAPTER	PAGE NUMBERS
▲ Hub	10	476–490
▲ Switch	10	476–490
▲ Router	10	476–490
▲ Access point	10	476–490
▲ Bridge	10	476–490
▲ Modem	10	476–490
▲ NAS	10	476–490
▲ Firewall	10	476–490
▲ VoIP phones	10	476–490
▲ Internet appliance	10	476–490

2.10 Given a scenario, use appropriate networking tools.

OBJECTIVES	CHAPTER	PAGE NUMBERS
▲ Crimper	10	491–506
▲ Multimeter	10	491–506
▲ Toner probe	10	491–506
▲ Cable tester	10	491–506
▲ Loopback plug	10	491–506
▲ Punchdown tool	10	491–506

DOMAIN 3.0 LAPTOPS

3.1 Install and configure laptop hardware and components.

OBJECTIVES	CHAPTER	PAGE NUMBERS
▲ Expansion options	11	523–571
• Express card /34	11	523–571
• Express card /54	11	523–571
• PCMCIA	11	523–571
• SODIMM	11	523–571
• Flash	11	523–571
▲ Hardware/device replacement	11	523–571
• Keyboard	11	523–571
• Hard Drive (2.5 vs. 3.5)	11	523–571
• Memory	11	523–571
• Optical drive	11	523–571
• Wireless card	11	523–571
• Mini-PCIe	11	523–571
• screen	11	523–571
• DC jack	11	523–571
• Battery	11	523–571
• Touchpad	11	523–571
• Plastics	11	523–571
• Speaker	11	523–571
• System board	11	523–571
• CPU	11	523–571

3.2 Compare and contrast the components within the display of a laptop.

OBJECTIVES	CHAPTER	PAGE NUMBERS
▲ Types	11	564–567
• LCD	11	564–567
• LED	11	564–567
• OLED	11	564–567
• Plasma	11	564–567
▲ Wi-Fi antenna connector/placement	11	564–567
▲ Inverter and its function	11	564–567
▲ Backlight	11	564–567

3.3 Compare and contrast laptop features.

OBJECTIVES	CHAPTER	PAGE NUMBERS
▲ Special function keys	11	514–538
• Dual displays	11	514–538
• Wireless (on/off)	11	514–538
• Volume settings	11	514–538
• Screen brightness	11	514–538
• Bluetooth (on/off)	11	514–538
• Keyboard backlight	11	514–538
▲ Docking station vs. port replicator	11	514–538
▲ Physical laptop lock and cable lock	11	514–538

DOMAIN 4.0 PRINTERS

4.1 Explain the differences between the various printer types and summarize the associated imaging process.

OBJECTIVES	CHAPTER	PAGE NUMBERS
▲ Laser	12	582–591
• Imaging drum, fuser assembly, transfer belt, transfer roller, pickup rollers, separate pads, duplexing assembly	12	582–591
• Imaging process: processing, charging, exposing, developing, transferring, fusing and cleaning	12	582–591
▲ Inkjet	12	582–591
• Ink cartridge, print head, roller, feeder, duplexing assembly, carriage and belt	12	582–591
• Calibration	12	582–591
▲ Thermal	12	582–591
• Feed assembly, heating element	12	582–591
• Special thermal paper	12	582–591
▲ Impact	12	582–591
	12	582–591
• Print head, ribbon, tractor feed	12	582–591
• Impact paper	12	582–591

4.2 Given a scenario, install, and configure printers.

OBJECTIVES	CHAPTER	PAGE NUMBERS
▲ Use appropriate printer drivers for a given operating system	12	591–608
▲ Print device sharing	12	591–608
• Wired	12	591–608
▪ USB	12	591–608
▪ Parallel	12	591–608
▪ Serial	12	591–608
▪ Ethernet	12	591–608
• Wireless	12	591–608
▪ Bluetooth	12	591–608
▪ 802.11x	12	591–608
▪ Infrared (IR)	12	591–608
• Printer hardware print server	12	591–608
▲ Printer sharing	12	591–608
• Sharing local/networked printer via Operating System settings	12	591–608

4.3 Given a scenario, perform printer maintenance.

OBJECTIVES	CHAPTER	PAGE NUMBERS
▲ Laser	12	608–619
• Replacing toner, applying maintenance kit, calibration, cleaning	12	608–619
▲ Thermal	12	608–619
• Replace paper, clean heating element, remove debris	12	608–619
▲ Impact	12	608–619
• Replace ribbon, replace print head, replace paper	12	608–619

DOMAIN 5.0 OPERATIONAL PROCEDURES

5.1 Given a scenario, use appropriate safety procedures.

OBJECTIVES	CHAPTER	PAGE NUMBERS
▲ ESD straps	1	24–33, 39–40
▲ ESD mats	1	24–33, 39–40
▲ Self-grounding	1	24–33, 39–40
▲ Equipment grounding	1	24–33, 39–40
▲ Personal safety	1	24–33, 39–40
• Disconnect power before repairing PC	2	46–67
• Remove jewelry	2	46–67
• Lifting techniques	1	24–33, 39–40
• Weight limitations	1	24–33, 39–40
• Electrical fire safety	1	24–33, 39–40
• CRT safety – proper disposal	1	24–33, 39–40
• Cable management	1	24–33, 39–40
▲ Compliance with local government regulations	8	388–395

5.2 Explain environmental impacts and the purpose of environmental controls.

OBJECTIVES	CHAPTER	PAGE NUMBERS
▲ MSDS documentation for handling and disposal	1	24–33, 39–40
▲ Temperature, humidity level awareness and proper ventilation	8	388–395

	Chapter	Page Numbers
▲ Power surges, brownouts, blackouts	8	388–395
• Battery backup	8	388–395
• Surge suppressor	1	24–33, 39–40
▲ Protection from airborne particles	8	388–395
• Enclosures	8	388–395
• Air filters	8	388–395
▲ Dust and debris	8	388–395
• Compressed air	8	388–395
• Vacuums	8	388–395
▲ Component handling and protection	1	24–33, 39–40
• Antistatic bags	1	24–33, 39–40
▲ Compliance to local government regulations	8	388–395

5.3 Given a scenario, demonstrate proper communication and professionalism.

OBJECTIVES	CHAPTER	PAGE NUMBERS
▲ Use proper language – avoid jargon, acronyms, slang when applicable	7	302–328
▲ Maintain a positive attitude	7	302–328
▲ Listen and do not interrupt the customer	7	302–328
▲ Be culturally sensitive	7	302–328
▲ Be on time (if late contact the customer)	7	302–328
▲ Avoid distractions	7	302–328
• Personal calls	7	302–328
• Talking to co-workers while interacting with customers	7	302–328
• Personal interruptions	7	302–328
▲ Dealing with difficult customer or situation	7	302–328
• Avoid arguing with customers and/or being defensive	7	302–328
• Do not minimize customer's problems	7	302–328
• Avoid being judgmental	7	302–328
• Clarify customer statements (ask open ended questions to narrow the scope of the problem, restate the issue or question to verify understanding)	7	302–328
▲ Set and meet expectations/timeline and communicate status with the customer	7	302–328
• Offer different repair/replacement options if applicable	7	302–328
• Provide proper documentation on the services provided	7	302–328
• Follow up with customer/user at a later date to verify satisfaction	7	302–328
▲ Deal appropriately with customers confidential materials	7	302–328
• Located on a computer, desktop, printer, etc.	7	302–328
	7	

5.4 Explain the fundamentals of dealing with prohibited content/activity.

OBJECTIVES	CHAPTER	PAGE NUMBERS
▲ First response	7	328–329
• Identify	7	328–329
• Report through proper channels	7	328–329
• Data/device preservation	7	328–329
▲ Use of documentation/documentation changes	7	328–329
▲ Chain of custody	7	328–329
• Tracking of evidence/documenting process	7	328–329

CompTIA A+ 220-802 Exam, 2012 Edition Examination Objectives Mapped to Chapters

A+ Guide to Hardware and *A+ Guide to Software* when used together fully meet all of the CompTIA A+ exams objectives. If the A+ exam objective is covered in the corresponding textbook, it is referenced in the Page Numbers column.

DOMAIN 1.0 OPERATING SYSTEMS

1.1 Compare and contrast the features and requirements of various Microsoft Operating Systems.

OBJECTIVES	CHAPTER	PAGE NUMBERS
▲ Windows XP Home, Windows XP Professional, *Windows XP Media Center, Windows XP 64-bit* Professional		See *A+ Guide to Software*
▲ Windows Vista Home Basic, Windows Vista Home Premium, Windows Vista Business, Windows Vista Ultimate, Windows Vista Enterprise		See *A+ Guide to Software*
▲ Windows 7 Starter, Windows 7 Home Premium, Windows 7 Professional, Windows 7 Ultimate, Windows 7 Enterprise		See *A+ Guide to Software*
▲ Features:		See *A+ Guide to Software*
• 32-bit vs. 64-bit		See *A+ Guide to Software*
• Aero, gadgets, user account control, bit-locker, shadow copy, system restore, ready boost, sidebar, compatibility mode, XP mode, easy transfer, adminisrative tools, defender, Windows firewall, security center, event viewer, file structure and paths, category view vs. classic view		See *A+ Guide to Software*
▲ Upgrade paths – differences between in place upgrades, compatibility tools, Windows upgrade OS advisor		See *A+ Guide to Software*

1.2 Given a scenario, install and configure the operating system using the most appropriate method.

OBJECTIVES	CHAPTER	PAGE NUMBERS
▲ Boot methods		See *A+ Guide to Software*
• USB		See *A+ Guide to Software*
• CD-ROM		See *A+ Guide to Software*
• DVD		See *A+ Guide to Software*
• PXE		See *A+ Guide to Software*
▲ Type of installations		See *A+ Guide to Software*
• Creating image		See *A+ Guide to Software*
• Unattended installation		See *A+ Guide to Software*
• Upgrade		See *A+ Guide to Software*
• Clean install		See *A+ Guide to Software*
• Repair installation		See *A+ Guide to Software*
• Multiboot		See *A+ Guide to Software*
• Remote network installation		See *A+ Guide to Software*
• Image deployment		See *A+ Guide to Software*

- Partitioning — See A+ *Guide to Software*
  - Dynamic — See A+ *Guide to Software*
  - Basic — See A+ *Guide to Software*
  - Primary — See A+ *Guide to Software*
  - Extended — See A+ *Guide to Software*
  - Logical — See A+ *Guide to Software*
- File system types/formatting — See A+ *Guide to Software*
  - FAT — See A+ *Guide to Software*
  - FAT32 — See A+ *Guide to Software*
  - NTFS — See A+ *Guide to Software*
  - CDFS — See A+ *Guide to Software*
  - Quick format vs. full format — See A+ *Guide to Software*
- Load alternate third party drivers when necessary — See A+ *Guide to Software*
- Workgroup vs. Domain setup — See A+ *Guide to Software*
- Time/date/region/language settings — See A+ *Guide to Software*
- Driver installation, software, and windows updates — See A+ *Guide to Software*
- Factory recovery partition — See A+ *Guide to Software*

1.3 Given a scenario, use appropriate command line tools.

OBJECTIVES	CHAPTER	PAGE NUMBERS
Networking		See A+ *Guide to Software*
• PING		See A+ *Guide to Software*
• TRACERT		See A+ *Guide to Software*
• NETSTAT		See A+ *Guide to Software*
• IPCONFIG		See A+ *Guide to Software*
• NET		See A+ *Guide to Software*
• NSLOOKUP		See A+ *Guide to Software*
• NBTSTAT		See A+ *Guide to Software*
OS		See A+ *Guide to Software*
• KILL		See A+ *Guide to Software*
• BOOTREC		See A+ *Guide to Software*
• SHUTDOWN		See A+ *Guide to Software*
• TLIST		See A+ *Guide to Software*
• MD		See A+ *Guide to Software*
• RD		See A+ *Guide to Software*
• CD		See A+ *Guide to Software*
• DEL		See A+ *Guide to Software*
• FDISK		See A+ *Guide to Software*
• FORMAT		See A+ *Guide to Software*
• COPY		See A+ *Guide to Software*
• XCOPY		See A+ *Guide to Software*
• ROBOCOPY		See A+ *Guide to Software*
• DISKPART		See A+ *Guide to Software*
• SFC		See A+ *Guide to Software*
• CHKDSK		See A+ *Guide to Software*
• [command name] /?		See A+ *Guide to Software*

1.4 Given a scenario, use appropriate operating system features and tools.

OBJECTIVES	CHAPTER	PAGE NUMBERS
▲ Recovery console		See A+ *Guide to Software*
• Fixboot		See A+ *Guide to Software*
• Fixmbr		See A+ *Guide to Software*
▲ Administrative		
• Computer management		See A+ *Guide to Software*
• Device manager		See A+ *Guide to Software*
• Users and groups		See A+ *Guide to Software*
• Local security policy		See A+ *Guide to Software*
• Performance monitor		See A+ *Guide to Software*
• Services		See A+ *Guide to Software*
• System configuration		See A+ *Guide to Software*
• Task scheduler		See A+ *Guide to Software*
• Component services		See A+ *Guide to Software*
• Data sources		See A+ *Guide to Software*
• Print management	12	619–622
• Windows memory diagnostics		See A+ *Guide to Software*
• Windows firewall		See A+ *Guide to Software*
• Advanced security		See A+ *Guide to Software*
▲ MSCONFIG		See A+ *Guide to Software*
• General		See A+ *Guide to Software*
• Boot		See A+ *Guide to Software*
• Services		See A+ *Guide to Software*
• Startup		See A+ *Guide to Software*
• Tools		See A+ *Guide to Software*
▲ Task Manager		See A+ *Guide to Software*
• Applications		See A+ *Guide to Software*
• Processes		See A+ *Guide to Software*
• Performance		See A+ *Guide to Software*
• Networking		See A+ *Guide to Software*
• Users		See A+ *Guide to Software*
▲ Disk management		See A+ *Guide to Software*
• Drive status		See A+ *Guide to Software*
• Mounting		See A+ *Guide to Software*
• Extending partitions		See A+ *Guide to Software*
• Splitting partitions		See A+ *Guide to Software*
• Assigning drive letters		See A+ *Guide to Software*
• Adding drives		See A+ *Guide to Software*
• Adding arrays		See A+ *Guide to Software*
▲ Other		See A+ *Guide to Software*
• User State Migration tool (USMT), File and Settings Transfer Wizard, Windows Easy Transfer		See A+ *Guide to Software*
▲ Run line utilities		See A+ *Guide to Software*
• MSCONFIG		See A+ *Guide to Software*
• REGEDIT		See A+ *Guide to Software*

- CMD | | See *A+ Guide to Software*
- SERVICES.MSC | | See *A+ Guide to Software*
- MMC | | See *A+ Guide to Software*
- MSTSC | | See *A+ Guide to Software*
- NOTEPAD | | See *A+ Guide to Software*
- EXPLORER | | See *A+ Guide to Software*
- MSINFO32 | | See *A+ Guide to Software*
- DXDIAG | 6 | 280–282

1.5 **Given a scenario, use Control Panel utilities** (the items are organized by "classic view/large icons" in Windows).

OBJECTIVES	CHAPTER	PAGE NUMBERS
▲ Common to all Microsoft Operating Systems		
• Internet options		See *A+ Guide to Software*
▪ Connections		See *A+ Guide to Software*
▪ Security		See *A+ Guide to Software*
▪ General		See *A+ Guide to Software*
▪ Privacy		See *A+ Guide to Software*
▪ Programs		See *A+ Guide to Software*
▪ Advanced		See *A+ Guide to Software*
• Display	6	272–282
▪ Resolution	6	272–282
• User accounts		See *A+ Guide to Software*
• Folder options		
▪ Sharing		See *A+ Guide to Software*
▪ View hidden files		See *A+ Guide to Software*
▪ Hide extensions		See *A+ Guide to Software*
▪ Layout		See *A+ Guide to Software*
• System		
▪ Performance (virtual memory)		See *A+ Guide to Software*
▪ Hardware profiles	11	537–538
▪ Remote settings		See *A+ Guide to Software*
▪ System protection		See *A+ Guide to Software*
• Security center		See *A+ Guide to Software*
• Windows firewall		See *A+ Guide to Software*
• Power options	11	533–536
▪ Hibernate	11	533–536
▪ Power plans	11	533–536
▪ Sleep/suspend	11	533–536
▪ Standby	11	533–536
▲ Unique to Windows XP		
• Add/remove programs		See *A+ Guide to Software*
• Network connections	9	423–441
• Printers and faxes	12	622–633
• Automatic updates		See *A+ Guide to Software*
• Network setup wizard		See *A+ Guide to Software*

- Unique to Vista
  - Tablet PC settings — 11 — 524–526
  - Pen and input devices — 11 — 524–526
  - Offline files — See *A+ Guide to Software*
  - Problem ports and solutions — See *A+ Guide to Software*
  - Printers — 12 — 622–633
- Unique to Windows 7
  - HomeGroup — See *A+ Guide to Software*
  - Action center — See *A+ Guide to Software*
  - Remote applications and desktop applications — See *A+ Guide to Software*
  - Troubleshooting — See *A+ Guide to Software*

1.6 Setup and configure Windows networking on a client/desktop.

OBJECTIVES	CHAPTER	PAGE NUMBERS
▲ HomeGroup, file/print sharing		See *A+ Guide to Software*
▲ WorkGroup vs. domain setup		See *A+ Guide to Software*
▲ Network shares/mapping drives		See *A+ Guide to Software*
▲ Establish networking connections		
• VPN		See *A+ Guide to Software*
• Dialups	9	402–415, 423–441
• Wireless	9	402–415, 423–441
• Wired	9	402–415, 423–441
• WWAN (Cellular)	9	402–415, 423–441
▲ Proxy settings		See *A+ Guide to Software*
▲ Remote desktop		See *A+ Guide to Software*
▲ Home vs. Work vs. Public network settings		See *A+ Guide to Software*
▲ Firewall settings		See *A+ Guide to Software*
• Exceptions		See *A+ Guide to Software*
• Configuration		See *A+ Guide to Software*
• Enabling/disabling Windows firewall		See *A+ Guide to Software*
▲ Configuring an alternative IP address in Windows	9	402–415, 423–441
• IP addressing	9	402–415, 423–441
• Subnet mask	9	402–415, 423–441
• DNS	9	402–415, 423–441
• Gateway	9	402–415, 423–441
▲ Network card properties		
• Half duplex/full duplex/auto	10	476–481
• Speed	10	476–481
• Wake-on-LAN	10	476–481
• PoE	10	476–481
• QoS	10	476–481

1.7 Perform preventive maintenance procedures using appropriate tools.

OBJECTIVES	CHAPTER	PAGE NUMBERS
▲ Best practices		See *A+ Guide to Software*
• Schedules backups		See *A+ Guide to Software*
• Scheduled check disks		See *A+ Guide to Software*

• Scheduled defragmentation		See *A+ Guide to Software*
• Windows updates		See *A+ Guide to Software*
• Patch management		See *A+ Guide to Software*
• Driver/firmware updates	6	238–243
• Antivirus updates		See *A+ Guide to Software*
▲ Tools		See *A+ Guide to Software*
• Backup		See *A+ Guide to Software*
• System restore		See *A+ Guide to Software*
• Check disk		See *A+ Guide to Software*
• Recovery image		See *A+ Guide to Software*
• Defrag		See *A+ Guide to Software*

1.8 **Explain the differences among basic OS security settings.**

OBJECTIVES	CHAPTER	PAGE NUMBERS
▲ User and groups		See *A+ Guide to Software*
• Administrator		See *A+ Guide to Software*
• Power user		See *A+ Guide to Software*
• Guest		See *A+ Guide to Software*
• Standard user		See *A+ Guide to Software*
▲ NTFS vs. Share permissions		See *A+ Guide to Software*
• Allow vs. deny		See *A+ Guide to Software*
• Moving vs. copying folders and files		See *A+ Guide to Software*
• File attributes		See *A+ Guide to Software*
▲ Shared files and folders		See *A+ Guide to Software*
• Administrative shares vs. local shares		See *A+ Guide to Software*
• Permission propagation		See *A+ Guide to Software*
• Inheritance		See *A+ Guide to Software*
▲ System files and folders		See *A+ Guide to Software*
▲ User authentication		See *A+ Guide to Software*
• Single sign-on		See *A+ Guide to Software*

1.9 **Explain the basics of client-side virtualization.**

OBJECTIVES	CHAPTER	PAGE NUMBERS
▲ Purpose of virtual machines		See *A+ Guide to Software*
▲ Resource requirements		See *A+ Guide to Software*
▲ Emulator requirements		See *A+ Guide to Software*
▲ Security requirements		See *A+ Guide to Software*
▲ Network requirements		See *A+ Guide to Software*
▲ Hypervisor		See *A+ Guide to Software*

DOMAIN 2.0 SECURITY

2.1 **Apply and use common prevention methods.**

OBJECTIVES	CHAPTER	PAGE NUMBERS
▲ Physical security		See *A+ Guide to Software*
• Lock doors		See *A+ Guide to Software*
• Tailgating		See *A+ Guide to Software*

- Securing physical documents/passwords/shredding — See A+ *Guide to Software*
- Biometrics — See A+ *Guide to Software*
- Badges — See A+ *Guide to Software*
- Key fobs — See A+ *Guide to Software*
- RFID badge — See A+ *Guide to Software*
- RSA token — See A+ *Guide to Software*
- Privacy filters — See A+ *Guide to Software*
- Retinal — See A+ *Guide to Software*
- Digital security — See A+ *Guide to Software*
  - Antivirus — See A+ *Guide to Software*
  - Firewalls — See A+ *Guide to Software*
  - Antispyware — See A+ *Guide to Software*
  - User authentication/strong passwords — See A+ *Guide to Software*
  - Directory permissions — See A+ *Guide to Software*
- User education — See A+ *Guide to Software*
- Principle of least privilege — See A+ *Guide to Software*

2.2 Compare and contrast common security threats.

OBJECTIVES	CHAPTER	PAGE NUMBERS
Social engineering		See A+ *Guide to Software*
Malware		See A+ *Guide to Software*
Rootkits		See A+ *Guide to Software*
Phishing		See A+ *Guide to Software*
Shoulder surfing		See A+ *Guide to Software*
Spyware		See A+ *Guide to Software*
Viruses		See A+ *Guide to Software*
• Worms		See A+ *Guide to Software*
• Trojans		See A+ *Guide to Software*

2.3 Implement security best practices to secure a workstation.

OBJECTIVES	CHAPTER	PAGE NUMBERS
Setting strong passwords		See A+ *Guide to Software*
Requiring passwords		See A+ *Guide to Software*
Restricting user permissions		See A+ *Guide to Software*
Changing default usernames		See A+ *Guide to Software*
Disabling guest account		See A+ *Guide to Software*
Screensaver required password		See A+ *Guide to Software*
Disable autorun		See A+ *Guide to Software*

2.4 Given a scenario, use the appropriate data destruction/disposal method.

OBJECTIVES	CHAPTER	PAGE NUMBERS
Low level format vs. standard format		See A+ *Guide to Software*
Hard drive sanitation and sanitation methods		See A+ *Guide to Software*
• Overwrite		See A+ *Guide to Software*
• Drive wipe		See A+ *Guide to Software*

- ▲ Physical destruction
  - Shredder
  - Drill
  - Electromagnetic
  - Degaussing tool

See A+ *Guide to Software*
See A+ *Guide to Software*
See A+ *Guide to Software*
See A+ *Guide to Software*
See A+ *Guide to Software*

2.5 Given a scenario, secure a SOHO wireless network.

OBJECTIVES	CHAPTER	PAGE NUMBERS
▲ Change default usernames and passwords	9	442–456
▲ Changing SSID	9	442–456
▲ Setting encryption	9	442–456
▲ Disabling SSID broadcast	9	442–456
▲ Enable MAC filtering	9	442–456
▲ Antenna and access point placement	9	442–456
▲ Radio power levels	9	442–456
▲ Assign static IP addresses	9	442–456
	9	442–456

2.6 Given a scenario, secure a SOHO wired network.

OBJECTIVES	CHAPTER	PAGE NUMBERS
▲ Change default usernames and passwords	9	442–456
▲ Enable MAC filtering	9	442–456
▲ Assign static IP addresses	9	442–456
▲ Disabling ports	9	442–456
▲ Physical security	9	442–456

DOMAIN 3.0 MOBILE DEVICES

3.1 Explain the basic features of mobile operating systems.

OBJECTIVES	CHAPTER	PAGE NUMBERS
▲ Android vs. iOS		See A+ *Guide to Software*
• Open source vs. closed source/vendor specific		See A+ *Guide to Software*
• App source (app store and market)		See A+ *Guide to Software*
• Screen orientation (accelerometer/gyroscope)		See A+ *Guide to Software*
• Screen calibration		See A+ *Guide to Software*
• GPS and geotracking		See A+ *Guide to Software*

3.2 Establish basic network connectivity and configure email.

OBJECTIVES	CHAPTER	PAGE NUMBERS
▲ Wireless/cellular data network (enable/disable)		See A+ *Guide to Software*
▲ Bluetooth		See A+ *Guide to Software*
• Enable Bluetooth		See A+ *Guide to Software*
• Enable pairing		See A+ *Guide to Software*
• Find device for pairing		See A+ *Guide to Software*
• Enter appropriate pin code		See A+ *Guide to Software*
• Test connectivity		See A+ *Guide to Software*
▲ Email configuration		See A+ *Guide to Software*
• Server address		See A+ *Guide to Software*
■ POP3		See A+ *Guide to Software*

- IMAP — See *A+ Guide to Software*
- Port and SSL settings — See *A+ Guide to Software*
- Exchange — See *A+ Guide to Software*
- Gmail — See *A+ Guide to Software*

3.3 Compare and contrast methods for securing mobile devices.

OBJECTIVES	CHAPTER	PAGE NUMBERS
Passcode locks		See *A+ Guide to Software*
Remote wipes		See *A+ Guide to Software*
Locator applications		See *A+ Guide to Software*
Remote backup applications		See *A+ Guide to Software*
Failed login attempts restrictions		See *A+ Guide to Software*
Antivirus		See *A+ Guide to Software*
Patching/OS updates		See *A+ Guide to Software*

3.4 Compare and contrast hardware differences in regards to tablets and laptops.

OBJECTIVES	CHAPTER	PAGE NUMBERS
No field serviceable parts		See *A+ Guide to Software*
Typically not upgradeable		See *A+ Guide to Software*
Touch interface		See *A+ Guide to Software*
• Touch flow		See *A+ Guide to Software*
• Multitouch		See *A+ Guide to Software*
Solid state drives		See *A+ Guide to Software*

3.5 Execute and configure mobile device synchronization.

OBJECTIVES	CHAPTER	PAGE NUMBERS
Types of data to synchronize		See *A+ Guide to Software*
• Contacts		See *A+ Guide to Software*
• Programs		See *A+ Guide to Software*
• Email		See *A+ Guide to Software*
• Pictures		See *A+ Guide to Software*
• Music		See *A+ Guide to Software*
• Videos		See *A+ Guide to Software*
Software requirements to install the application on the PC		See *A+ Guide to Software*
Connection types to enable synchronization		See *A+ Guide to Software*

DOMAIN 4.0 TROUBLESHOOTING

4.1 Given a scenario, explain the troubleshooting theory.

OBJECTIVES	CHAPTER	PAGE NUMBERS
Identify the problem		See *A+ Guide to Software*
• Question the user and identify user changes to computer and perform backups before making changes		See *A+ Guide to Software*
Establish a theory of probable cause (question the obvious)		See *A+ Guide to Software*
Test the theory to determine cause		See *A+ Guide to Software*
• Once theory is confirmed determine next steps to resolve problem		See *A+ Guide to Software*

• If theory is not confirmed re-establish new theory or escalate		See *A+ Guide to Software*
▲ Establish a plan of action to resolve the problem and implement the solution		See *A+ Guide to Software*
▲ Verify full system functionality and if applicable implement preventive measures		See *A+ Guide to Software*
▲ Document findings, actions and outcomes		See *A+ Guide to Software*

4.2 Given a scenario, troubleshoot common problems related to motherboards, RAM, CPU, and power with appropriate tools.

OBJECTIVES	CHAPTER	PAGE NUMBERS
▲ Common symptoms	8	346–376
• Unexpected shutdowns	8	346–376
• System lockups	8	346–376
• POST code beeps	8	346–376
• Blank screen on bootup	8	346–376
• BIOS time and settings resets	8	346–376
• Attempts to boot to incorrect device	8	346–376
• Continuous reboots	8	346–376
• No power	8	346–376
• Overheating	8	346–376
• Loud noise	8	346–376
• Intermittent device failure	8	346–376
• Fans spin – no power to other devices	8	346–376
• Indicator lights	8	346–376
• Smoke	8	346–376
• Burning smell	8	346–376
• BSOD	8	346–376
▲ Tools	1	33–38
• Multimeter	1	33–38
• Power supply tester	1	33–38
• Loopback plugs	1	33–38
• POST card	1	33–38

4.3 Given a scenario, troubleshoot hard drives and RAID arrays with appropriate tools.

OBJECTIVES	CHAPTER	PAGE NUMBERS
▲ Common symptoms		
• Read/write failure		See *A+ Guide to Software*
• Slow performance		See *A+ Guide to Software*
• Loud clicking noise	8	376–380
• Failure to boot	8	376–380
• Drive not recognized		See *A+ Guide to Software*
• OS not found		See *A+ Guide to Software*
• RAID not found	8	376–380
• RAID stops working	8	376–380
• BSOD		See *A+ Guide to Software*
▲ Tools	8	376–380
• Screwdriver	8	376–380
• External enclosures	8	376–380
• CHDKS	8	376–380

OBJECTIVES	CHAPTER	PAGE NUMBERS
• CHKDSK	8	376–380
• FORMAT		See A+ *Guide to Software*
• FDISK		See A+ *Guide to Software*
• File recovery software		See A+ *Guide to Software*

4.4 **Given a scenario, troubleshoot common video and display issues.**

OBJECTIVES	CHAPTER	PAGE NUMBERS
▲ Common symptoms	8	380–387
• VGA mode	8	380–387
• No image on screen	8	380–387
• Overheat shutdown	8	380–387
• Dead pixels	8	380–387
• Artifacts	8	380–387
• Color patterns incorrect	8	380–387
• Dim image	8	380–387
• Flickering image	8	380–387
• Distorted image	8	380–387
• Discoloration (degaussing)	8	380–387
• BSOD	8	380–387

4.5 **Given a scenario, troubleshoot wired and wireless networks with appropriate tools.**

OBJECTIVES	CHAPTER	PAGE NUMBERS
▲ Common symptoms		See A+ *Guide to Software*
• No connectivity		See A+ *Guide to Software*
• APIPA address		See A+ *Guide to Software*
• Limited connectivity		See A+ *Guide to Software*
• Local connectivity		See A+ *Guide to Software*
• Intermittent connectivity		See A+ *Guide to Software*
• IP conflict		See A+ *Guide to Software*
• Slow transfer speeds		See A+ *Guide to Software*
• Low RF signal		See A+ *Guide to Software*
▲ Tools		See A+ *Guide to Software*
• Cable tester		See A+ *Guide to Software*
• Loopback plug		See A+ *Guide to Software*
• Punch down tools	10	491–506
• Toner probes	10	491–506
• Wire strippers	10	491–506
• Crimper	10	491–506
• PING		See A+ *Guide to Software*
• IPCONFIG		See A+ *Guide to Software*
• TRACERT		See A+ *Guide to Software*
• NETSTAT		See A+ *Guide to Software*
• NBTSTAT		See A+ *Guide to Software*
• NET		See A+ *Guide to Software*
• Wireless locator		See A+ *Guide to Software*

4.6 **Given a scenario, troubleshoot operating system problems with appropriate tools.**

OBJECTIVES	CHAPTER	PAGE NUMBERS
▲ Common symptoms		
• BSOD		See A+ *Guide to Software*
• Failure to boot		See A+ *Guide to Software*

- Improper shutdown — See A+ *Guide to Software*
- Spontaneous shutdown/restart — See A+ *Guide to Software*
- RAID not detected during installation — See A+ *Guide to Software*
- Device fails to start — See A+ *Guide to Software*
- Missing dll message — See A+ *Guide to Software*
- Services fails to start — See A+ *Guide to Software*
- Compatibility error — See A+ *Guide to Software*
- Slow system performance — See A+ *Guide to Software*
- Boots to safe mode — See A+ *Guide to Software*
- File fails to open — See A+ *Guide to Software*
- Missing NTLDR — See A+ *Guide to Software*
- Missing Boot.ini — See A+ *Guide to Software*
- Missing operating system — See A+ *Guide to Software*
- Missing Graphical Interface — See A+ *Guide to Software*
- Graphical Interface fails to load — See A+ *Guide to Software*
- Invalid boot disk — See A+ *Guide to Software*

▲ Tools — See A+ *Guide to Software*
- Fixboot — See A+ *Guide to Software*
- Recovery console — See A+ *Guide to Software*
- Fixmbr — See A+ *Guide to Software*
- Sfc — See A+ *Guide to Software*
- Repair disks — See A+ *Guide to Software*
- Pre-installation environments — See A+ *Guide to Software*
- MSCONFIG — See A+ *Guide to Software*
- DEFRAG — See A+ *Guide to Software*
- REGSRV32 — See A+ *Guide to Software*
- REGEDIT — See A+ *Guide to Software*
- Event viewer — See A+ *Guide to Software*
- Safe mode — See A+ *Guide to Software*
- Command prompt — See A+ *Guide to Software*
- Emergency repair disk — See A+ *Guide to Software*
- Automated system recovery — See A+ *Guide to Software*

4.7 **Given a scenario, troubleshoot common security issues with appropriate tools and best practices.**

OBJECTIVES	CHAPTER	PAGE NUMBERS
▲ Common symptoms		See A+ *Guide to Software*
• Pop-ups		See A+ *Guide to Software*
• Browser redirection		See A+ *Guide to Software*
• Security alerts		See A+ *Guide to Software*
• Slow performance		See A+ *Guide to Software*
• Internet connectivity issues		See A+ *Guide to Software*
• PC locks up		See A+ *Guide to Software*
• Windows updates failures		See A+ *Guide to Software*
• Rogue antivirus		See A+ *Guide to Software*
• Spam		See A+ *Guide to Software*
• Renamed system files		See A+ *Guide to Software*
• Files disappearing		See A+ *Guide to Software*
• File permission changes		See A+ *Guide to Software*
• Hijacked email		See A+ *Guide to Software*
• Access denied		See A+ *Guide to Software*

- Tools — See A+ *Guide to Software*
  - Anti-virus software — See A+ *Guide to Software*
  - Anti-malware software — See A+ *Guide to Software*
  - Anti-spyware software — See A+ *Guide to Software*
  - Recovery console — See A+ *Guide to Software*
  - System restore — See A+ *Guide to Software*
  - Pre-installation environments — See A+ *Guide to Software*
  - Event viewer — See A+ *Guide to Software*
- Best practices for malware removal — See A+ *Guide to Software*
  - Identify malware symptoms — See A+ *Guide to Software*
  - Quarantine infected system — See A+ *Guide to Software*
  - Disable system restore — See A+ *Guide to Software*
  - Remediate infected systems — See A+ *Guide to Software*
    - Update anti-virus software — See A+ *Guide to Software*
    - Scan and removal techniques (safe mode, pre-installation environment) — See A+ *Guide to Software*
  - Schedule scans and updates — See A+ *Guide to Software*
  - Enable system restore and create restore point — See A+ *Guide to Software*
  - Educate end user — See A+ *Guide to Software*

4.8 Given a scenario, troubleshoot and repair common laptop issues while adhering to the appropriate procedures.

OBJECTIVES	CHAPTER	PAGE NUMBERS
Common symptoms	11	539–576
• No display	11	539–576
• Dim display	11	539–576
• Flickering display	11	539–576
• Sticking keys	11	539–576
• Intermittent wireless	11	539–576
• Battery not charging	11	539–576
• Ghost cursor	11	539–576
• No power	11	539–576
• Num lock indicator lights	11	539–576
• No wireless connectivity	11	539–576
• No Bluetooth connectivity	11	539–576
• Cannot display to external monitor	11	539–576
Disassembling processes for proper re-assembly	11	539–576
• Document and label cable and screw locations	11	539–576
• Organize parts	11	539–576
• Refer to manufacturer documentation	11	539–576
• Use appropriate hand tools	11	539–576

4.9 Given a scenario, troubleshoot printers with appropriate tools

OBJECTIVES	CHAPTER	PAGE NUMBERS
Common symptoms	12	622–637
• Streaks	12	622–637
• Faded prints	12	622–637
• Ghost images	12	622–637
• Toner not fused to the paper	12	622–637
• Creased paper	12	622–637

• Paper not feeding	12	622–637
• Paper jam	12	622–637
• No connectivity	12	622–637
• Garbled characters on paper	12	622–637
• Vertical lines on page	12	622–637
• Backed up print queue	12	622–637
• Low memory errors	12	622–637
• Access denied	12	622–637
• Printer will not print	12	622–637
• Color prints in wrong print color	12	622–637
• Unable to install printer	12	622–637
• Error codes	12	622–637
◢ Tools	12	622–637
• Maintenance kit	12	622–637
• Toner vacuum	12	622–637
• Compressed air	12	622–637
• Printer spooler	12	622–637

Introduction A+ Guide to Hardware

A+ Guide to Hardware, Sixth Edition was written to be the very best tool on the market today to prepare you to support personal computers. Updated to include the most current hardware technologies, this book takes you from the just-a-user level to the I-can-fix-this level for PC hardware matters. This book achieves its goals with an unusually effective combination of tools that powerfully reinforce both concepts and hands-on, real-world experiences. It also provides thorough preparation for the hardware content on the new 2012 CompTIA A+ Certification exams. (The software content on the 2012 A+ Certification exams is covered in the companion book, *A+ Guide to Software, Sixth Edition*.) Competency in using a computer is a prerequisite to using this book. No background knowledge of electronics is assumed. An appropriate prerequisite course for this book would be a general course in microcomputer applications.

This book includes:

- **Several in-depth, hands-on projects** are spaced throughout each chapter that invite you to immediately apply and reinforce skills and are designed to make certain that you not only understand the material, but also execute procedures and make decisions on your own.
- **Comprehensive review and practice end-of-chapter material**, including a chapter summary, key terms, review questions that focus on A+ content, critical thinking questions, and real-world problems to solve.
- **Step-by-step instructions** on installation, maintenance, optimization of system performance, and troubleshooting.
- **Online video clips** featuring Jean Andrews illustrating key points from the text to aid your understanding of the material.
- **A wide array of photos, drawings, and screen shots** support the text, displaying in detail the exact software features you will need to understand how to manage and maintain your PC.

In addition, the carefully structured, clearly written text is accompanied by graphics that provide the visual input essential to learning. For instructors using the book in a classroom, instructor resources are available online and on the Instructor Resources CD.

Coverage is balanced—while focusing on new hardware and software, the text also covers the real work of PC repair, where some older technology remains in widespread use and still needs support. For example, the book now covers virtualization, quad-channel memory, home theater systems, and cellular connections, but also addresses using PCI expansion slots, DDR2 memory, and impact printers because many individuals and businesses still use these older technologies. To rein in the physical size and weight of the book, most of the content on less significant and older technologies has been placed on the web site that accompanies the book. There you will find content on Linux, Mac OS, Windows 2000/XP, SCSI, the hexadecimal number system, electricity, multimeters, and legacy motherboards, hard drives, and processors.

This book provides thorough preparation for the hardware portions of CompTIA's A+ 2012 Certification examinations. The software portions of the A+ 2012 exams are covered in the companion book, *A+ Guide to Software*. Both books together map completely to these new exam objectives.

This certification credential's popularity among employers is growing exponentially, and obtaining certification increases your ability to gain employment and improve your salary. To get more information on A+ certification and its sponsoring organization, the Computing Technology Industry Association, see their web site at *www.comptia.org*.

FEATURES

To ensure a successful learning experience, this book includes the following pedagogical features:

- **Learning Objectives:** Every chapter opens with a list of learning objectives that sets the stage for you to absorb the lessons of the text.
- **Comprehensive Step-by-Step Troubleshooting Guidance:** Troubleshooting guidelines are included in almost every chapter. In addition, Chapter 8 gives insights into general approaches to troubleshooting that help apply the specifics detailed in each chapter for different hardware and software problems. There you'll also find troubleshooting procedures for many hardware subsystems integrated into overall troubleshooting strategies.
- **Step-by-Step Procedures:** The book is chock-full of step-by-step procedures covering subjects from hardware installation and maintenance to troubleshooting the boot process.
- **Art Program:** Numerous detailed photographs, three-dimensional art, and screen shots support the text, displaying hardware and software features exactly as you will see them in your work.
- **CompTIA A+ Table of Contents:** This table of contents gives the page that provides the primary content for each certification objective on the A+ 2012 exams. This is a valuable tool for quick reference.
- **Hands-on Projects:** These sections give you practice using the skills you have just studied so that you can learn by doing and know you have mastered a skill.
- **Applying Concepts:** These sections offer practical applications for the material being discussed. Whether outlining a task, developing a scenario, or providing pointers, the Applying Concepts sections give you a chance to apply what you've learned to a typical PC problem.

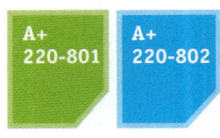

A+ Icons: All of the content that relates to CompTIA's 2012 A+ 220-801 and A+ 220-802 Certification exams, whether it's a page or a sentence, is highlighted with an A+ icon. The icon notes the exam name and the objective number. This unique feature highlights the relevant content at a glance, so that you can pay extra attention to the material.

Notes: Note icons highlight additional helpful information related to the subject being discussed.

A+ Exam Tip Boxes: These boxes highlight additional insights and tips to remember if you are planning to take the CompTIA A+ Exams.

Caution Icons: These icons highlight critical safety information. Follow these instructions carefully to protect the PC and its data and to ensure your own safety.

Video Clips: Short video passages reinforce concepts and techniques discussed in the text and offer insight into the life of a PC repair technician.

End-of-Chapter Material: Each chapter closes with the following features, which reinforce the material covered in the chapter and provide real-world, hands-on testing:

- **Chapter Summary:** This bulleted list of concise statements summarizes all major points of the chapter.
- **Key Terms:** The content of each chapter is further reinforced by an end-of-chapter key term list. The definitions of all terms are included at the end of the book in a full-length glossary.
- **Review Questions:** You can test your understanding of each chapter with a comprehensive set of review questions. The "Reviewing the Basics" questions check your understanding of fundamental concepts focused on A+ content, while the "Thinking Critically" questions help you synthesize and apply what you've learned and also focus on A+ content.
- **Real Problems, Real Solutions:** Each comprehensive problem allows you to find out if you can apply what you've learned in the chapter to a real-life situation.

CertBlaster Test Prep Resources: *A+ Guide to Hardware, Sixth Edition* includes CertBlaster test preparation questions that mirror the look and feel of CompTIA's A+220-801 certification exam.

Companion web site: The free companion web site includes video clips that feature Jean Andrews illustrating key concepts in the text and providing advice on the real world of PC repair. Also included is less significant and older content that still might be important in some PC repair situations. The content includes the following: The Hexademical Number System and Memory Addressing, Supporting Windows XP, Introducing the Mac OS, Introducing Linux, Electricity and Multimeters, Facts about Legacy Motherboards, How an OS Uses System Resources, Facts about Legacy Processors, All about SCSI, Behind the Scenes with DEBUG, FAT Details, and Selecting and Installing Hard Drives Using Legacy Motherboards. Other helpful online tools include Frequently Asked Questions, Sample Reports, Computer Inventory and Maintenance form, Troubleshooting Flowcharts, and an electronic Glossary.

CompTIA A+ and PC Repair: For additional content and updates to this book and information about our complete line of CompTIA A+ and PC Repair topics, please visit our web site at *www.cengage.com/pcrepair*.

WHAT'S NEW IN THE SIXTH EDITION

Here's a summary of what's new in the *Sixth Edition*:

- Maps to the hardware content on the CompTIA's 2012 A+ Exams.
- More focus on A+, with non-A+ content moved online to the companion web site or eliminated.
- New content added (all new content was also new to the A+ 2012 exams).
  - Windows 7 is added. Operating systems covered are now Windows 7, Vista, and XP.
  - Supporting TCP/IP version 6 is added to Chapter 9.

- New content on making network cables, network wiring (T568A and T568B), and troubleshooting networks is added to Chapter 10.
- Disassembling an all-in-one computer is added to Chapter 11.
- New content on how printers work and how to support them is added to Chapter 12.
- How to configure motherboards and processors to support virtualization.
- Third Generation (Ivy Bridge) and Second Generation (Sandy Bridge) processor and chipset architectures by Intel are covered in Chapter 4.
- Connecting a computer to a cellular network.
- Enhanced content on supporting RAID and NAS.
- Designing customized systems for virtualization workstations, CAD/CAM workstations, gaming PCs, home theater systems, home servers, video editing workstations, thick clients, and thin clients are covered in Chapter 7.

ANATOMY OF A PC REPAIR CHAPTER

This section is a visual explanation of the components that make up a PC Repair chapter. The figures identify some of our traditional instructional elements as well as the enhancements and new features we have included for the sixth edition.

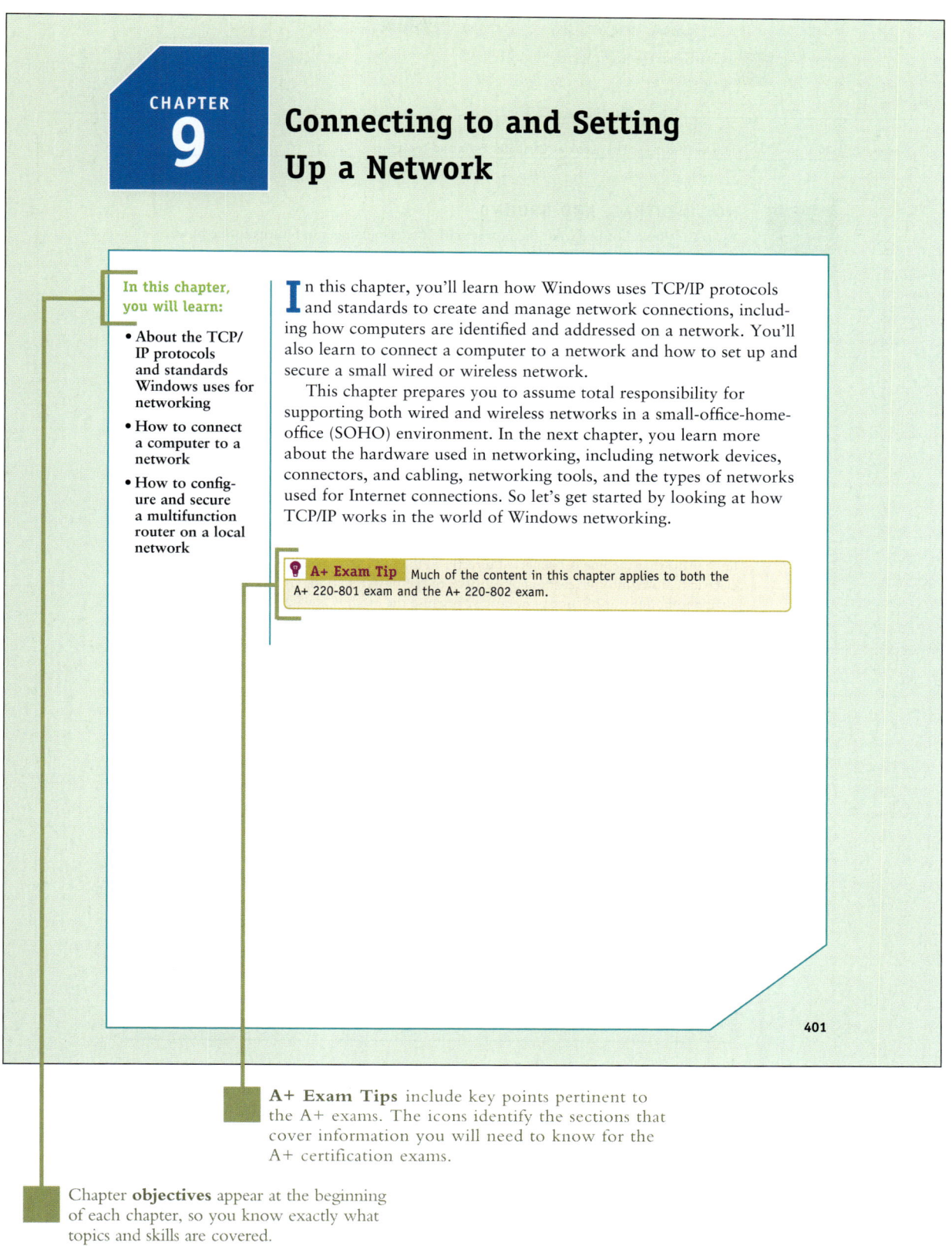

CHAPTER 9

Connecting to and Setting Up a Network

In this chapter, you will learn:

- About the TCP/IP protocols and standards Windows uses for networking
- How to connect a computer to a network
- How to configure and secure a multifunction router on a local network

In this chapter, you'll learn how Windows uses TCP/IP protocols and standards to create and manage network connections, including how computers are identified and addressed on a network. You'll also learn to connect a computer to a network and how to set up and secure a small wired or wireless network.

This chapter prepares you to assume total responsibility for supporting both wired and wireless networks in a small-office-home-office (SOHO) environment. In the next chapter, you learn more about the hardware used in networking, including network devices, connectors, and cabling, networking tools, and the types of networks used for Internet connections. So let's get started by looking at how TCP/IP works in the world of Windows networking.

> **A+ Exam Tip** Much of the content in this chapter applies to both the A+ 220-801 exam and the A+ 220-802 exam.

401

A+ Exam Tips include key points pertinent to the A+ exams. The icons identify the sections that cover information you will need to know for the A+ certification exams.

Chapter **objectives** appear at the beginning of each chapter, so you know exactly what topics and skills are covered.

Cautions identify critical safety information.

---

26   **CHAPTER 1**   First Look at Computer Parts and Tools

A+
220-801
5.1, 5.2

HOT, NEUTRAL, AND GROUND

AC travels on a hot line from the power station to a building and returns to the power station on a neutral line. When the two lines reach the building and enter an electrical device, such as a lamp, the device controls the flow of electricity between the hot and neutral lines. If an easier path (one with less resistance) is available, the electricity follows that path. This can cause a short, a sudden increase in flow that can also create a sudden increase in temperature—enough to start a fire and injure both people and equipment. Never put yourself in a position where you are the path of least resistance between the hot line and ground!

> ⚡ **Caution** It's very important that PC components be properly grounded. Never connect a PC to an outlet or use an extension cord that doesn't have the third ground plug. The third line can prevent a short from causing extreme damage. In addition, the bond between the neutral and ground helps eliminate electrical noise (stray electrical signals) within the PC that is sometimes caused by other electrical equipment sitting very close to the computer.

To prevent uncontrolled electricity in a short, the neutral line is grounded. Grounding a line means that the line is connected directly to the earth, so that, in the event of a short, the electricity flows into the earth and not back to the power station. Grounding serves as an escape route for out-of-control electricity because the earth is always capable of accepting a flow of current. With computers, a surge suppressor can be used to protect a computer and its components against power surges.

> ⚡ **Caution** Beware of the different uses of black wire. In PCs and in DC circuits, black is used for ground, but in home wiring and in AC circuits, black is used for hot!

The neutral line to your house is grounded many times along its way (in fact, at each electrical pole) and is also grounded at the breaker box where the electricity enters your house. You can look at a three-prong plug and see the three lines: hot, neutral, and ground (see Figure 1-31).

To verify that a wall outlet is wired correctly for hot, neutral, and ground, use a simple receptacle tester, as shown in Figure 1-32. Even though you might have a three-prong outlet in your home, the ground plug might not be properly grounded. To know for sure, you can test the outlet with a receptacle tester.

> 📝 **Notes** House AC voltage in the United States is about 110–120 V, but know that in other countries, this is not always the case. In many other countries, the standard is 220 V. Outlet styles also vary from one country to the next.

Now that you know about electricity and how to protect a computer from surges and out-of-control electricity, let's turn our attention to protecting yourself against the dangers of electricity.

Notes indicate additional content that might be of student interest or information about how best to study.

Video icons indicate content shown with video online. Videos illustrate key concepts.

What's Inside the Case 5

A+ 220-801 1.7, 1.8, 1.11

Port	Description
[25-pin parallel port image] © Cengage Learning 2014	A parallel port is a 25-pin female port used by older printers. This older port has been replaced by USB ports.
[modem/network port image] © Cengage Learning 2014	A modem port, also called an RJ-11 port, is used to connect dial-up phone lines to computers. A modem port looks like a network port, but is not as wide. In the photo, the right port is a modem port and the left port is a network port, shown for comparison.

Table 1-1 Ports used with laptop and desktop computers (continued)

© Cengage Learning 2014

A+ 220-801 1.8

▶ **Video** Looking inside a PC

I know you're eager to open a case and work inside it, but first let's get familiar with the major components in the case and how to work with them safely so you don't fry a motherboard or bend delicate connectors. Figure 1-2 shows the inside of a computer case.

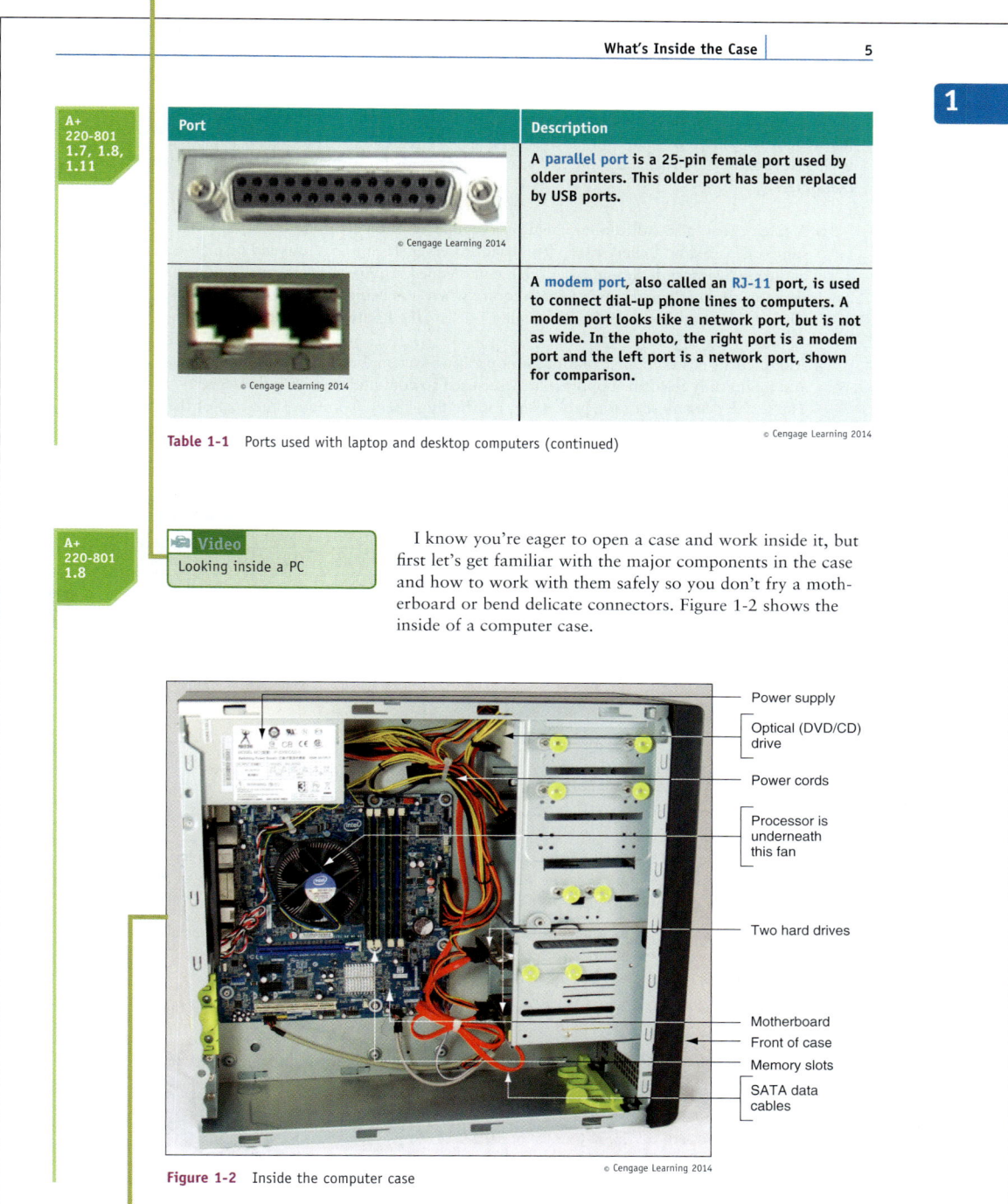

Figure 1-2 Inside the computer case

© Cengage Learning 2014

Full-color photos and screen shots accurately depict computer hardware and software components.

xli

A+ Exam Objectives are highlighted with an icon identifying the exam and objective number to help you identify information tested on the exams. The A+ 220-801 and A+ 220-802 exams are mapped.

Customizing Computer Systems | 339

A+
220-801
1.9

These VM clients that receive the virtual desktop from the server can be a thick client, thin client, or zero client. You might be called on to customize a thick client or thin client computer for a customer. (A zero client, also called a dumb terminal, is built by the manufacturer. It does not have an OS and is little more than an interface to the network with a keyboard, monitor, and mouse.) Here are the details for a thick client and thin client computer:

▲ A thick client, also called a fat client, is a regular desktop computer or laptop that is sometimes used as a client by a virtualization server. It can be a low-end or high-end desktop or laptop. It should meet the recommended requirements to run Windows 7 and any applications the user might require when it is being used as a stand-alone computer rather than a VM client. Table 7-1 lists the hardware requirements for Windows 7.

▲ A thin client is a computer that has an operating system, but has little computer power and might only need to support a browser used to communicate with the server. The server does most of the processing for the thin client. To reduce the cost of the computer, configure it to meet only the minimum requirements for Windows.

Hardware	For 32-bit Windows 7	For 64-bit Windows 7
Processor	1 GHz or faster	1 GHz or faster
Memory	1 GB	2 GB
Free hard drive space	16 GB	20 GB
Video device and driver	Direct X 9 device with WDDM 1.0 or higher driver	Direct X 9 device with WDDM 1.0 or higher driver

© Cengage Learning 2014

Table 7-1 Minimum and recommended hardware requirements for Windows 7

Hands-on | Project 7-7 Research a Customized System

Working with a partner, design a gaming PC or a Home Theater PC by doing the following:

1. Search the web for a prebuilt system that you like. Print or save the web page showing the detailed specifications for the system and its price. Which parts in the system do you plan to use for your system? Which parts would you not use or upgrade for your own system?

2. Search the web for the individual parts for your system. Save or print web pages showing all the parts you need to build this computer. Don't forget the case, power supply, motherboard, processor, RAM, hard drive, and other specialized components.

3. Make a list of each part with links to the web page that shows the part for sale. What is the total cost of all parts?

4. Exchange your list and web pages with a partner and have your partner check your work to make sure each part is compatible with the entire system and nothing is missing. Do the same for your partner's list of parts.

5. After you are both convinced your list of parts is compatible and nothing is missing, submit your work to your instructor.

Hands-on Projects provide practical exercises throughout each chapter so that you can practice the skills as they are learned.

A+ 220-801 1.6

APPLYING CONCEPTS   SELECT A PROCESSOR

Your friend, Alice, is working toward her A+ certification. She has decided the best way to get the experience she needs before she sits for the exam is to build a system from scratch. She has purchased an Asus motherboard and asked you for some help selecting the right processor. She tells you that the system will later be used for light business needs and she wants to install a processor that is moderate in price to fit her budget. She says she doesn't want to install the most expensive processor the motherboard can support, but neither does she want to sacrifice too much performance or power.

The documentation on the Asus web site (*support.asus.com*) for the ASUS P8Z68-V LX motherboard gives this information:

▲ The ATX board contains the Z68 chipset and socket LGA1155 and uses DDR3 memory.

▲ CPUs supported include a long list of Second Generation Core i3, Core i5, and Core i7 processors and Celeron and Pentium processors. Here are five processors found in this list:

- Intel Core i7-2600, 3.4 GHz, 8 MB cache
- Intel Core i5-3450, 3.1 GHz, 6 MB cache
- Intel Core i3-2120, 3.3 GHz, 3 MB cache
- Intel Celeron G540, 2.5 GHz, 2 MB cache
- Intel Pentium G860, 3.0 GHz, 3 MB cache

Based on what Alice has told you, you decide to eliminate the most expensive processors (the Core i7) and the least-performing processors (the Celerons and Pentiums). That decision narrows your choices down to the Core i3 and Core i5. Before you select one of these processors, you need to check the list on the Asus site to make sure the specific Core i3 or Core i5 processor is in the list. Look for the exact processor number, for example, the Core i3-2120. Also double-check and make sure the processor uses the correct socket and is a Second Generation processor.

You will also need a cooler assembly. If your processor doesn't come boxed with a cooler, select a cooler that fits the processor socket and gets good reviews. You'll also need some thermal compound if it is not included with the cooler.

INSTALL A PROCESSOR

Now let's look at the details of installing a processor in an Intel LGA1155, LGA1366, LGA775, and AMD AM2+ sockets.

Video — Installing a Processor

INSTALLING AN INTEL PROCESSOR IN SOCKET LGA1155

We're installing the Intel Core i5-2320 processor in Socket LGA1155 shown in Figure 4-8. In the photo, the socket has its protective cover in place.

Applying Concepts sections provide practical advice or pointers by illustrating basic principles, identifying common problems, providing steps to practice skills, and encouraging creating solutions.

Key Terms are defined as they are introduced and listed at the end of each chapter. Definitions can be found in the Glossary and online.

Reviewing the Basics | 341

▲ A thick client needs to meet recommended requirements for Windows and applications, and a thin client is a low-end computer that only needs to meet the minimum requirements for Windows.

>> KEY TERMS

For explanations of key terms, see the Glossary near the end of the book.

- 10-foot user interface
- A+ Certification
- call tracking
- chain of custody
- copyright
- escalate
- expert system
- hardware-assisted virtualization (HAV)
- Home Theater PC (HTPC)
- HTPC case
- hypervisor
- license
- site license
- software piracy
- technical documentation
- thick client
- thin client
- ticket
- virtualization server

>> REVIEWING THE BASICS

1. Name five job roles that can all be categorized as a PC technician.
2. Of the five jobs in Question 1, which one job might never include interacting with the PC's primary user?
3. Assume that you are a customer who wants to have a PC repaired. List five main characteristics that you would want to see in your PC repair person.
4. What is one thing you should do when you receive a phone call requesting on-site support, before you make an appointment?
5. You make an appointment to do an on-site repair, but you are detained and find out that you will be late. What is the best thing to do?
6. When you arrive for an on-site service call, how important is your greeting? What would be a good greeting to start off a good business relationship?
7. When making an on-site service call, what should you do before making any changes to software or before taking the case cover off a computer?
8. What should you do after finishing your PC repair?
9. What is a good strategy to follow if a conflict arises between you and your customer?
10. If you are about to make an on-site service call to a large financial organization, is it appropriate to show up in shorts and a T-shirt? Why or why not?
11. You have exhausted your knowledge of a problem and it still is not solved. Before you escalate it, what else can you do?
12. If you need to make a phone call while on a customer's site and your cell phone is not working, what do you do?
13. When someone calls your help desk, what is the first thing you should do?
14. What is one thing you can do to help a caller who needs phone support and is not a competent computer user?

Reviewing the Basics sections check understanding of fundamental concepts.

Thinking Critically sections require you to analyze and apply what you've learned.

---

398 | CHAPTER 8 | Troubleshooting Hardware Problems

>> THINKING CRITICALLY

1. You upgrade a faulty PCIe video card to a recently released higher-performing card. Now the user complains that Windows 7 hangs a lot and gives errors. Which is the most likely source of the problem? Which is the least likely source?

   a. Overheating

   b. Windows does not support the new card.

   c. The drivers for the card need updating.

   d. Memory is faulty.

2. What should you immediately do if you turn on a PC and smell smoke or a burning odor?

   a. Unplug the computer.

   b. Dial 911.

   c. Find a fire extinguisher.

   d. Press a key on the keyboard to enter BIOS setup.

3. When you boot up a computer and hear a single beep, but the screen is blank, what can you assume is the source of the problem?

   a. The video card or onboard video

   b. The monitor or monitor cable

   c. Windows startup

   d. The processor

4. You suspect that a power supply is faulty, but you use a power supply tester to measure its voltage output and find it to be acceptable. Why is it still possible that the power supply may be faulty?

5. Someone asks you for help with a computer that hangs at odd times. You turn it on and work for about 15 minutes, and then the computer freezes and powers down. What do you do first?

   a. Replace the surge protector.

   b. Replace the power supply.

   c. Wait about 30 minutes for the system to cool down and try again.

   d. Install an additional fan.

>> REAL PROBLEMS, REAL SOLUTIONS

REAL PROBLEM 8-1: Using Event Viewer to Troubleshoot a Hardware Problem

Just about anything that happens in Windows is recorded in Event Viewer (Eventvwr.msc). You can find events such as a hardware or network failure, OS error messages, or a device that has failed to start. When you first encounter a Windows, hardware, application, or security problem, get in the habit of checking Event Viewer as one of your first steps toward investigating the problem. To save time, first check the Administrative Events log because it filters out all events except Warning and Error events, which are the most useful for troubleshooting. Do the following to practice using Event Viewer:

Real Problems, Real Solutions allow you to apply what you've learned in the chapter to a real-life situation.

STATE OF THE INFORMATION TECHNOLOGY (IT) FIELD

Computers and information technology are absolutely essential for businesses to thrive, or perhaps even exist, in today's world. In addition, the Internet makes it possible for a local or national business to go global and reach customers, suppliers, and other businesses anywhere on the planet. As technology continues to change, how we do business must also continually change. These fundamental changes in business practices have created an ongoing need for skilled and certified IT workers across industries. IT workers have flooded out of traditional IT businesses into various IT-dependent industries such as banking, government, insurance, and healthcare.

Millions of individuals are self-employed in this country. Among them are the computer specialists who must keep their skills sharp as they navigate an ever-changing employment and technological landscape.

Without skilled workers in IT, businesses will struggle with the ever-changing technologies. With such a quick product life cycle, IT workers must strive to keep up with these changes to continue to bring value to their employers.

CERTIFICATIONS

Companies increasingly rely on technical certifications to identify the skills a particular job applicant possesses. Traditional degrees and diplomas are no longer sufficient to identify the education and skills needed for the many jobs in the IT industry. Technical certifications are a way for employers to ensure the quality and skill qualifications of their computer professionals, and they can offer job seekers a competitive edge. In most careers, salary and compensation are determined by experience and education, but in IT, the number and type of certifications an employee earns also factor into salary and wage increases.

As you look at certifications, note that there are two types: vendor neutral and vendor specific. Vendor-neutral certifications are those that test for the skills and knowledge required in specific industry job roles and do not subscribe to a specific vendor's technology solution. Vendor-neutral certifications include all of the Computing Technology Industry Association's (CompTIA) certifications, Project Management Institute's certifications, and Security Certified Program certifications. Vendor-specific certifications validate the skills and knowledge necessary to be successful when using a specific vendor's technology solution. Some examples of vendor-specific certifications include those offered by Microsoft, IBM, Novell, and Cisco.

Certifications provide job applicants with more than just a competitive edge over their noncertified counterparts who apply for the same IT positions. Some institutions of higher education grant college credit to students who successfully pass certification exams, moving them further along in their degree programs. Certifications also give individuals who are interested in careers in the military the ability to move into higher positions more quickly. And many advanced certification programs accept, and sometimes require, entry-level certifications as part of their exams. For example, Cisco and Microsoft accept some CompTIA certifications as prerequisites for their certification programs.

CAREER PLANNING

Finding a career that fits a person's personality, skill set, and lifestyle is challenging and fulfilling, but can often be difficult. What are the steps individuals should take to find that dream career? Is IT interesting to you? Chances are that if you are reading this book, this question has been answered. What about IT do you like? To find out, ask yourself some questions: Are you a person who likes to work alone, or do you like to work in a group? Do you like speaking directly with customers or do you prefer to stay behind the scenes? Is your lifestyle conducive to a lot of travel, or do you need to stay in one location? All of these factors influence your decision when faced with choosing the right job. A variety of web sites offer assistance with career planning and assessing an inventory of your interests, work values, and abilities.

WHAT'S NEW WITH COMPTIA A+ CERTIFICATION

In the spring of 2012, CompTIA (*www.comptia.org*) published the objectives for the 2012 CompTIA A+ Certification exams. These exams went live in the fall of 2012. However, you can still become CompTIA A+ certified by passing the older 2009 exams that are to remain available until the summer of 2013.

The A+ 2012 exams include two exams, and you must pass both to become A+ certified. The two exams are the A+ 220-801 exam and the A+ 220-802 exam.

Here is a breakdown of the domain content covered on the two A+ 2012 exams:

CompTIA A+ 220-801 Exam	
PC Hardware	40%
Networking	27%
Laptops	11%
Printers	11%
Operational Procedures	11%
Total	100%

CompTIA A+ 220-802 Exam	
Operating Systems	33%
Security	22%
Mobile Devices	9%
Troubleshooting	36%
Total	100%

HOW TO BECOME COMPTIA CERTIFIED

This training material can help you prepare for and pass a related CompTIA certification exam or exams. In order to achieve CompTIA certification, you must register for and pass a CompTIA certification exam or exams. For information on becoming CompTIA certified, please visit *http://certification.comptia.org/Training/testingcenters*.

CompTIA is a nonprofit information technology (IT) trade association. CompTIA's certifications are designed by subject matter experts from across the IT industry. Each CompTIA certification is vendor neutral, covers multiple technologies, and requires demonstration of skills and knowledge widely sought after by the IT industry.

To contact CompTIA with any questions or comments, please visit *http://certification.comptia.org/contact* or call (866) 835-8020, ext. 2.

A+ TEST PREPARATION MATERIALS

A+ Guide to Hardware, Sixth Edition includes CertBlaster test preparation questions that mirror the look and feel of CompTIA's A+ 220-801 certificate exam. For additional information on the CertBlaster test preparation questions, go to *http://www.dtipublishing.com*. To log in and access the CertBlaster test preparation questions for *A+ Guide to Hardware, Sixth Edition*, please go to *http://www.certblaster.com/cengage.htm*.

TO INSTALL CERTBLASTER:

1. Click the title of the CertBlaster test prep application you want to download.
2. Save the program (.EXE) file to a folder on your C: drive. (Warning: If you skip this step, your CertBlaster will not install correctly.)
3. Click **Start** and choose **Run**.
4. Click **Browse** and then navigate to the folder that contains the .EXE file. Select the .EXE file and click **Open**.
5. Click **OK** and then follow the on-screen instructions.
6. When the installation is complete, click **Finish**.
7. Click **Start**, choose **All programs**, and click **CertBlaster**.

TO REGISTER CERTBLASTER:

1. Open the CertBlaster test you want by double-clicking it.
2. In the menu bar, click **File > Register Exam** and enter the access code when prompted. Use the access code provided inside the card placed in the back of this book.

TO USE THIS BOOK TO PREPARE FOR A+ EXAMS

This book, *A+ Guide to Hardware, 6th Edition*, covers the hardware portions on the A+ 220-801 and A+ 220-802 exams. The software portions on the exam can be found in the *A+ Guide to Software, 6th Edition*. In addition, the *A+ Guide to Managing and Maintaining Your PC, 8th Edition*, covers content on both exams. Diagram 1 shows you three paths you can take to prepare for the A+ exams by using these books.

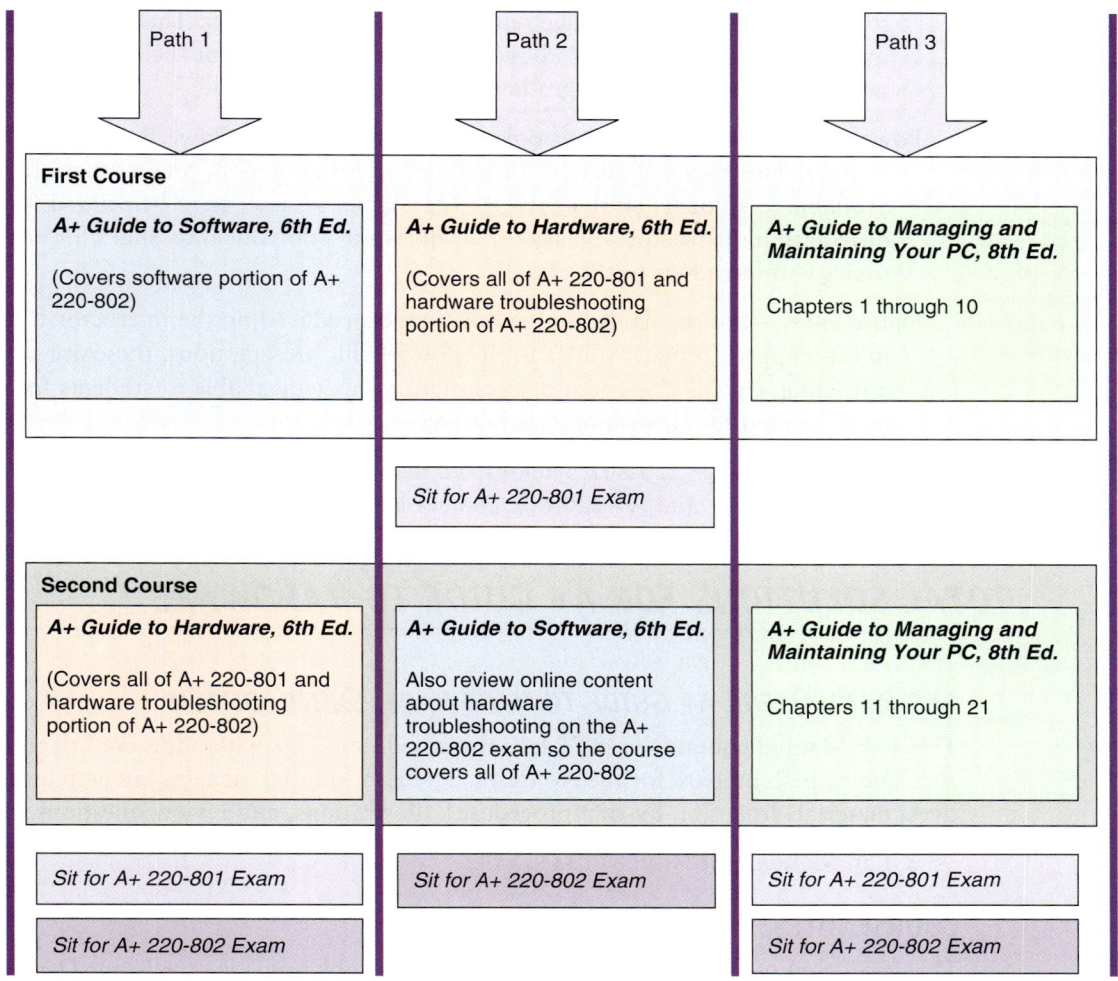

© Cengage Learning 2014

INSTRUCTOR RESOURCES CD (ISBN: 9781133135296)

Please visit *login.cengage.com* and log in to access instructor-specific resources. To access additional course materials, please visit *www.cengagebrain.com*. At the *CengageBrain.com* home page, search for the ISBN of your title (from the back cover of your book) using the search box at the top of the page. This will take you to the product page where these resources can be found.

The following supplemental materials are available when this book is used in a classroom setting. All of the supplements available with this book are provided to the instructor on a single CD-ROM.

Electronic Instructor's Manual: The *Instructor's Manual* that accompanies this textbook includes additional instructional material to assist in class preparation, including suggestions for classroom activities, discussion topics, and additional projects.

Solutions: Answers to the end-of-chapter material are provided. These include the answers to the Review Questions and to the Hands-on Projects (when applicable).

ExamView®: This textbook is accompanied by ExamView, a powerful testing software package that allows instructors to create and administer printed, computer (LAN-based), and Internet exams. ExamView includes hundreds of questions that correspond to the topics covered in this text, enabling students to generate detailed study guides that include page references for further review. The computer-based and Internet testing components allow students to take exams at their computers, and also save the instructor time by grading each exam automatically.

PowerPoint Presentations: This book comes with Microsoft PowerPoint slides for each chapter. These are included as a teaching aid for classroom presentation, to make available to students on the network for chapter review, or to be printed for classroom distribution. Instructors, please feel at liberty to add your own slides for additional topics you introduce to the class.

Figure Files: All of the figures in the book are reproduced on the Instructor Resource CD, in bit-mapped format. Similar to the PowerPoint presentations, these are included as a teaching aid for classroom presentation, to make available to students for review, or to be printed for classroom distribution.

A+ 220-801 and A+ 220-802 Syllabus: To help prepare for class, a sample syllabus for the A+ 220-801 and A+ 220-802 courses is provided.

TOTAL SOLUTIONS FOR A+ GUIDE TO HARDWARE

LAB MANUAL FOR A+ GUIDE TO HARDWARE, SIXTH EDITION

This Lab Manual contains over 75 labs to provide students with additional hands-on experience and to help prepare for the A+ exam. The Lab Manual includes lab activities, objectives, materials lists, step-by-step procedures, illustrations, and review questions.

- Lab Manual (ISBN: 9781133135142)

COURSENOTES

This laminated quick reference card reinforces critical knowledge for CompTIA's A+ exam in a visual and user-friendly format. CourseNotes will serve as a useful study aid, supplement to the textbook, or as a quick reference tool during the course and afterward.

- A+ Exam# 220-801 CourseNotes (ISBN: 9781133135234)
- A+ Exam# 220-802 CourseNotes (ISBN: 9781133135241)

WEB-BASED LABS

Using a real lab environment over the Internet, students can log on anywhere, anytime via a web browser to gain essential hands-on experience using labs from *A+ Guide to Software, Sixth Edition.*

- Web-Based Labs for A+: Software Labs (To Accompany A+ Guide to Managing and Maintaining Your PC, 8e and A+ Guide to Software, 6e) (ISBN: 9781133135203)
- Web-Based Labs for A+ Guide to Software (ISBN: 9781133135227)

dtiMETRICS

dtiMetrics is an online testing system that automatically grades students and keeps class and student records. dtiMetrics tests against Cengage's textbook as well as against the CompTIA A+ certification exam, including a quiz for each chapter in the book along with a midterm and final exam. dtiMetrics is managed by the classroom instructor, who has 100 percent of the control, 100 percent of the time. It is hosted and maintained by dtiPublishing.

- dtiMetrics for A+ Guide to Hardware (ISBN: 9781133135180)

LABCONNECTION

LabConnection provides powerful computer-based exercises, simulations, and demonstrations for hands-on, skills courses such as this. It can be used as both a virtual lab and as a homework assignment tool, and provides automatic grading and student record maintenance. LabConnection maps directly to the textbook and provides remediation to the text and to the CompTIA A+ certification exam. It includes the following features:

- **Enhanced comprehension**—Through LabConnection's guidance while in the virtual lab environment, learners develop skills that are accurate and consistently effective.
- **Exercises**—Lab Connection includes dozens of exercises that assess and prepare the learner for the virtual labs, establishing and solidifying the skills and knowledge required to complete the lab.
- **Virtual labs**—Labs consist of end-to-end procedures performed in a simulated environment where the student can practice the skills required of professionals.
- **Guided learning**—LabConnection allows learners to make mistakes but alerts them to errors made before they can move on to the next step, sometimes offering demonstrations as well.
- **Video demonstrations**—Video demonstrations guide the learners step-by-step through the labs while providing additional insights to solidify the concepts.
- **SCORM-compliant grading and record keeping (for online version)**—LabConnection will grade the exercises and record the completion status of the lab portion, easily porting to, and compatible with, distance learning platforms.
- **LabConnection Online for A+ Guide to Hardware** (ISBN: 9781133703778)
- **LabConnection On DVD for A+ Guide to Hardware** (ISBN: 9781133703747)

COURSEMATE

To access additional materials (including CourseMate, described in the next section), please visit *www.cengagebrain.com*. At the CengageBrain.com home page, search for the ISBN of your title (from the back cover of your book) using the search box at the top of the page. This will take you to the product page for your book, where you will be able to access these resources.

A+ Guide to Hardware, Sixth Edition offers CourseMate, a complement to your textbook. CourseMate includes the following:

- An interactive eBook, with highlighting, note taking, and search capabilities.
- Interactive learning tools, including Quizzes, Flash cards, PowerPoint slides, Glossary, and more!
- Engagement Tracker, a first-of-its-kind tool that monitors student engagement in the course.

Go to *login.cengage.com* to access these resources.

- CourseMate Printed Access Code with eBook (ISBN: 9781133135500)
- CourseMate Instant Access Code with eBook (ISBN: 9781133135494)

PC TROUBLESHOOTING POCKET GUIDE

This compact and portable volume is designed to help students and technicians diagnose any computer problem quickly and efficiently. Up to date and current for today's technologies. (ISBN: 9781133135166)

COMPTIA A+ PC REPAIR FLASHCARDS

Use the PC Repair flashcards to test knowledge of PC repair concepts and to help prepare for CompTIA's A+ 220-801 and 220-802 exams. (ISBN: 9781133278771)

ACKNOWLEDGMENTS

Thank you to the wonderful people at Cengage Course Technology who continue to give their best and to go the extra mile to make the books what they are: Nick Lombardi, Michelle Ruelos Cannistraci, and Andrea Majot. I'm grateful for all you've done. Thank you, Deb Kaufmann and Jill Batistick, Developmental Editors, for your careful attention to detail and your awesome commitment to excellence, to Nancy Lamm, our excellent copy editor and to Christine Clark, our patient and careful proofreader. Thank you, Ashlee Welz Smith and Teresa Storch, for your careful attention to the technical accuracy of the book. Thank you Abigail Reip for your research efforts. Thank you to Joy Dark and Jill West who were here with me taking many photographs, researching, and helping with the many other details of the writing process.

Thank you to all the people who took the time to voluntarily send encouragement and suggestions for improvements to the previous editions. Your input and help is very much appreciated. The reviewers of this edition all provided invaluable insights and showed a genuine interest in the book's success. Thank you to:

> Keith Conn – Cleveland Institute of Electronics/World College
> Lee Cottrell – Bradford School, Pittsburgh, PA
> Humberto Hilario – PC AGE Career Institute
> Jeff McDowell – United Tribes Technical College
> Carlos Miranda – Mount San Antonio College
> Alicia Pearlman – Baker College
> Jonathan Weissman – Finger Lakes Community College
> June West – Spartanburg Community College

When planning this edition, Course Technology sent out a survey to A+ and PC Repair instructors for their input to help us shape the edition. Many instructors responded, for which I am grateful. I spent much time poring over their answers to our questions, their comments, and their suggestions. You'll find many of your ideas fleshed out in the pages of this book. Thank you so much for your help!

To the instructors and learners who use this book, I invite and encourage you to send suggestions or corrections for future editions. Please write to me at *jean.andrews@cengage.com*. I never ignore a good idea! And to instructors, if you have ideas for how to make a class in PC Repair or A+ Preparation a success, please share your ideas with other instructors! You can find me on Facebook at *http://www.facebook.com/JeanKnows*, where you can interact with me and other instructors.

This book is dedicated to the covenant of God with man on earth.

Jean Andrews, Ph.D.

ABOUT THE AUTHOR

Jean Andrews has more than 30 years of experience in the computer industry, including more than 13 years in the college classroom. She has worked in a variety of businesses and corporations designing, writing, and supporting application software; managing a PC repair help desk; and troubleshooting wide area networks. She has written numerous books on software, hardware, and the Internet, including the bestselling *A+ Guide to Managing and Maintaining Your PC, Eighth Edition* and *A+ Guide to Software: Managing, Maintaining and Troubleshooting, Sixth Edition*. She lives in northern Georgia.

READ THIS BEFORE YOU BEGIN

The following hardware, software, and other equipment are needed to do the Hands-on Projects in each chapter:

- You need a working PC that can be taken apart and reassembled. Use a Pentium or higher computer.
- Troubleshooting skills can better be practiced with an assortment of nonworking expansion cards that can be used to simulate problems.
- Windows 7, Vista, or XP is needed for all chapters. Internet access is needed for most chapters.
- Equipment required to work on hardware includes a grounding mat and grounding strap and flathead and Phillips head screwdrivers. In addition, a power supply tester, cable tester, and can of compressed air are useful. Network wiring tools needed for Chapter 10 include a wire cutter, wire stripper, and crimper.
- Before undertaking any of the lab exercises, starting with Chapter 1, please review the safety guidelines in the next section.

Follow these instructions carefully for your own safety.

PROTECT YOURSELF, YOUR HARDWARE, AND YOUR SOFTWARE

When you work on a computer, it is possible to harm both the computer and yourself. The most common accident that happens when attempting to fix a computer problem is erasing software or data. Experimenting without knowing what you are doing can cause damage. To prevent these sorts of accidents, as well as the physically dangerous ones, take a few safety precautions. The text below describes the potential sources of damage and danger and how to protect against them.

POWER TO THE COMPUTER

To protect both yourself and the equipment when working inside a computer, turn off the power, unplug the computer, press the power button to drain residual power, and always use a grounding bracelet as described in Chapter 1. Consider the monitor and the power supply to be "black boxes." Never remove the cover or put your hands inside this equipment unless you know about the hazards of charged capacitors. Both the power supply and the monitor can hold a dangerous level of electricity even after they are turned off and disconnected from a power source.

PROTECT AGAINST ESD

To protect the computer against electrostatic discharge (ESD), commonly known as static electricity, always ground yourself before touching electronic components, including the hard drive, motherboard, expansion cards, processors, and memory modules. Ground yourself and the computer parts, using one or more of the following static control devices or methods:

- *Ground bracelet or static strap:* A ground bracelet is a strap you wear around your wrist. To protect components against ESD, the other end is attached to a grounded conductor such as the computer case or a ground mat.

- *Ground mats:* Ground mats can come equipped with a cord to plug into a wall outlet to provide a grounded surface on which to work. Remember, if you lift the component off the mat, it is no longer grounded and is susceptible to ESD.
- *Static shielding bags:* New components come shipped in static shielding bags. Save the bags to store other devices that are not currently installed in a PC.

The best solution to protect against ESD is to use a ground bracelet together with a ground mat. Consider a ground bracelet to be essential equipment when working on a computer. However, if you find yourself in a situation without one, touch the computer case before you touch a component. When passing a component to another person, touch the other person first so that ESD is discharged between you and the other person before you pass the component. Leave components inside their protective bags until ready to use. Work on hard floors, not carpet, or use antistatic spray on the carpets. Generally, don't work on a computer if you or the computer just came inside from the cold.

For today's computers, always unplug the power cord before working inside a computer. Even though the power switch is turned off, know that power is still getting to the system when the computer is plugged in. After you've unplugged the power, press the power button to drain the system of power. Then and only then is it safe to open the case without concern for damaging a component. And don't forget to use that ground bracelet.

There is an exception to the ground-yourself rule. Inside a monitor case, laser printer, or power supply, there is substantial danger posed by the electricity stored in capacitors. When working inside these devices, you *don't* want to be grounded because you would provide a conduit for the voltage to discharge through your body. In this situation, be careful *not* to ground yourself.

When handling motherboards and expansion cards, don't touch the chips on the boards. Don't stack boards on top of each other, which could accidentally dislodge a chip. Hold cards by the edges, but don't touch the edge connections on the card.

Don't touch a chip with a magnetized screwdriver. When using a multimeter to measure electricity, be careful not to touch a chip with the probes. Don't touch the chips on the bottom of hard drives.

After you unpack a new device or software that has been wrapped in cellophane, remove the cellophane from the work area quickly. Don't allow anyone who is not properly grounded to touch components. Do not store expansion cards within one foot of an old CRT monitor because the monitor can discharge as much as 29,000 volts of ESD onto the screen.

Hold an expansion card by the edges. Don't touch any of the soldered components on a card. If you need to put an electronic device down, place it on a grounded mat, inside a static shielding bag, or on a flat, hard surface. Keep components away from your hair and clothing.

PROTECT HARD DRIVES AND DISKS

Always turn off a computer before moving it, to protect the hard drive, which might be spinning. Never jar a computer while the hard disk is running. Avoid placing a PC on the floor, where the user can accidentally kick it. To keep a computer well ventilated and cool, don't place it on thick carpet.

Follow the usual precautions to protect CD, DVD, and Blu-ray discs. Keep optical discs away from heat, direct sunlight, and extreme cold, and protect them from scratches. Treat discs with care and they'll generally last for years.

CHAPTER 1

First Look at Computer Parts and Tools

In this chapter, you will learn:

- About the various parts inside a computer case and how they connect together and are compatible
- How to protect yourself and the equipment against the dangers of electricity when working inside a computer case
- About tools you will need as a PC hardware technician and safety precautions when working around computer equipment

Like many other computer users, you have probably used your personal computer to play games, update your Facebook profile, write papers, or build Excel worksheets. This book takes you from being an end user of your computer to becoming a PC support technician. The only assumption made here is that you are a computer user—that is, you can turn on your machine, load a software package, and use that software to accomplish a task. No experience in electronics is assumed.

As a PC support technician, you'll want to become A+ certified, which is the industry standard certification for PC support technicians. This book prepares you to pass the A+ 220-801 exam by CompTIA (*www.comptia.org*). This exam is primarily about hardware. The A+ 220-801 exam and the A+ 220-802 exam are required by CompTIA for A+ Certification. The A+ 220-802 exam is primarily about software and also includes troubleshooting both software and hardware. Even though troubleshooting hardware is covered on the A+ 220-802 exam, this book includes hardware troubleshooting so that you learn in this book all you need to know about PC hardware for A+ certification. The software portions of the A+ 220-802 exam are covered in the companion book, *A+ Guide to Software, Managing and Troubleshooting*, 6th edition. This book and the *A+ Guide to Software, Managing and Troubleshooting* fully prepare you for both exams needed for CompTIA A+ certification.

In this chapter, you learn to recognize various hardware components you'll find inside a computer case and about the tools you'll need to work inside the case. In the next chapter, you'll learn to take a computer apart and reassemble it. Consider these two chapters your one-two punch toward becoming a hardware technician.

WHAT'S INSIDE THE CASE

A+ 220-801 1.7, 1.8, 1.11

Before we discuss the parts inside a computer case, let's take a quick look at the case and the ports and switches on it. The computer case, sometimes called the chassis, houses the power supply, motherboard, processor, memory modules, expansion cards, hard drive, optical drive, and other drives. A computer case can be a tower case, a desktop case that lies flat on a desk, an all-in-one case used with an all-in-one computer, or a mobile case used with laptops and tablet PCs. A **tower case** (see Figure 1-1) sits upright and can be as high as two feet and has room for several drives. Often used for servers, this type of case is also good for PC users who anticipate upgrading, because tower cases provide maximum space for working inside a computer and moving components around. A **desktop case** lies flat and sometimes serves double-duty as a monitor stand. In this chapter and the next, you learn how to work inside a tower or desktop case, and in Chapter 11, you learn how to work inside a laptop case and all-in-one case.

© Courtesy of IN WIN Development Inc.

Figure 1-1 This slimline tower case supports a MicroATX motherboard

> **Notes** When a computer using a desktop case is in use, don't sit the case on its end that is designed to lie flat because the CD or DVD drive might not work properly.

Table 1-1 lists ports you might find on a laptop or desktop computer. Consider this table your introduction to these ports so that you can recognize them when you see them. Later in the book, you learn more about the details of each port.

> **A+ Exam Tip** The A+ 220-801 exam expects you to know how to identify the ports shown in Table 1-1.

What's Inside the Case 3

A+ 220-801
1.7, 1.8, 1.11

Port	Description
	A **VGA (Video Graphics Array) port**, also called a **DB-15 port**, is a 15-pin female port that transmits analog video. (Analog means a continuous signal with infinite variations as compared to digital, which is a series of binary values—1s and 0s.) All older monitors use VGA ports.
	An **S-Video port** is a 4-pin or 7-pin round video port sometimes used to connect to a television. The 7-pin port is shown on the left. The 4-pin port is missing the extra pins in the middle and is the more common type.
	A **DVI (Digital Video Interface) port** transmits digital or analog video. Three types of DVI ports exist, which you learn about in Chapter 6.
	An **HDMI (High-Definition Multimedia Interface) port** transmits digital video and audio (not analog transmissions) and is often used to connect to home theater equipment.
	A **DisplayPort** transmits digital video and audio (not analog transmissions) and is slowly replacing VGA and DVI ports on personal computers.
	A **Thunderbolt** port transmits both video and data on the same port and cable. The port is shaped the same as the DisplayPort and is compatible with DisplayPort devices.
	A **network port**, also called an **Ethernet port**, or an **RJ-45** port, is used by a network cable to connect to the wired network. Fast Ethernet ports run at 100 Mbps (megabits per second), and Gigabit Ethernet runs at 1,000 Mbps or 1 Gbps (gigabit per second). A megabit is one million bits and a gigabit is one billion bits. A bit is a binary value of one or zero.

© Cengage Learning 2014

Table 1-1 Ports used with laptop and desktop computers (continues)

A+ 220-801
1.7, 1.8, 1.11

Port	Description
	A system usually has three or more round audio ports, also called sound ports, for a microphone, audio in, audio out, and stereo audio out. If you have one audio cable to connect to a speaker or ear buds, plug it into the lime green sound port in the middle of the three ports.
	An S/PDIF (Sony-Philips Digital Interface) sound port connects to an external home theater audio system, providing digital audio output and the best signal quality.
	A USB (Universal Serial Bus) port is a multi-purpose I/O port used by many different devices, including printers, mice, keyboards, scanners, external hard drives, and flash drives. Some USB ports are faster than others. Hi-Speed USB 2.0 is faster than regular USB, and Super-Speed USB 3.0 is faster than USB 2.0.
	A FireWire port (also called an IEEE1394 port, pronounced "I-triple-E 1394 port") is used for high-speed multimedia devices such as digital camcorders.
	An external SATA (eSATA) port is used by an external hard drive using the eSATA interface. eSATA is faster than FireWire.
	A PS/2 port, also called a mini-DIN port, is a round 6-pin port used by a keyboard or mouse. The ports look alike but are not interchangeable. On a PC, the purple port is for the keyboard, and the green port is for the mouse. Newer computers use USB ports for the keyboard and mouse rather than the older PS/2 ports.
	An older serial port, sometimes called a DB9 port, is a 9-pin male port used on older computers. It has been mostly replaced by USB ports.

Table 1-1   Ports used with laptop and desktop computers (continues)

What's Inside the Case

A+ 220-801
1.7, 1.8, 1.11

Port	Description
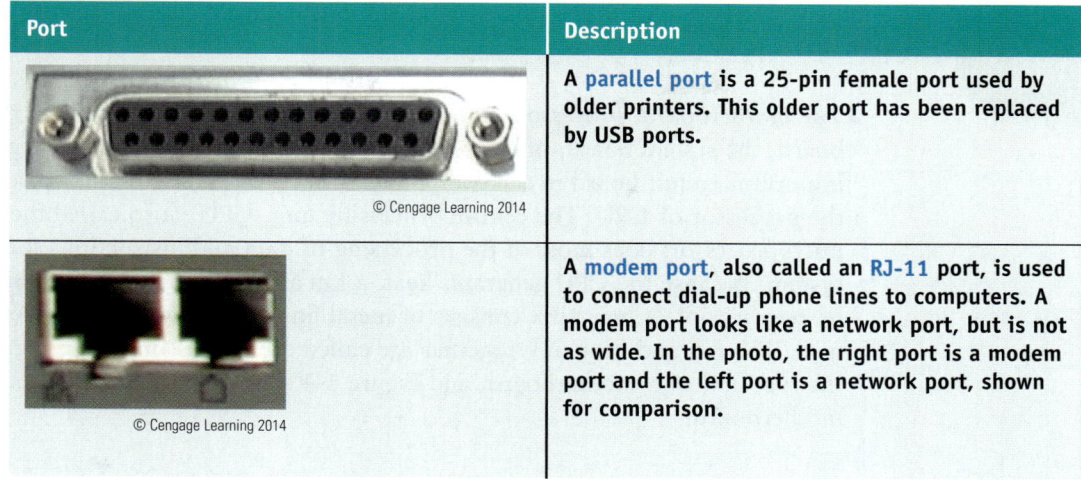	A **parallel port** is a 25-pin female port used by older printers. This older port has been replaced by USB ports.
	A **modem port**, also called an **RJ-11** port, is used to connect dial-up phone lines to computers. A modem port looks like a network port, but is not as wide. In the photo, the right port is a modem port and the left port is a network port, shown for comparison.

Table 1-1 Ports used with laptop and desktop computers (continued)

© Cengage Learning 2014

A+ 220-801
1.8

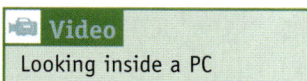
Video
Looking inside a PC

I know you're eager to open a case and work inside it, but first let's get familiar with the major components in the case and how to work with them safely so you don't fry a motherboard or bend delicate connectors. Figure 1-2 shows the inside of a computer case.

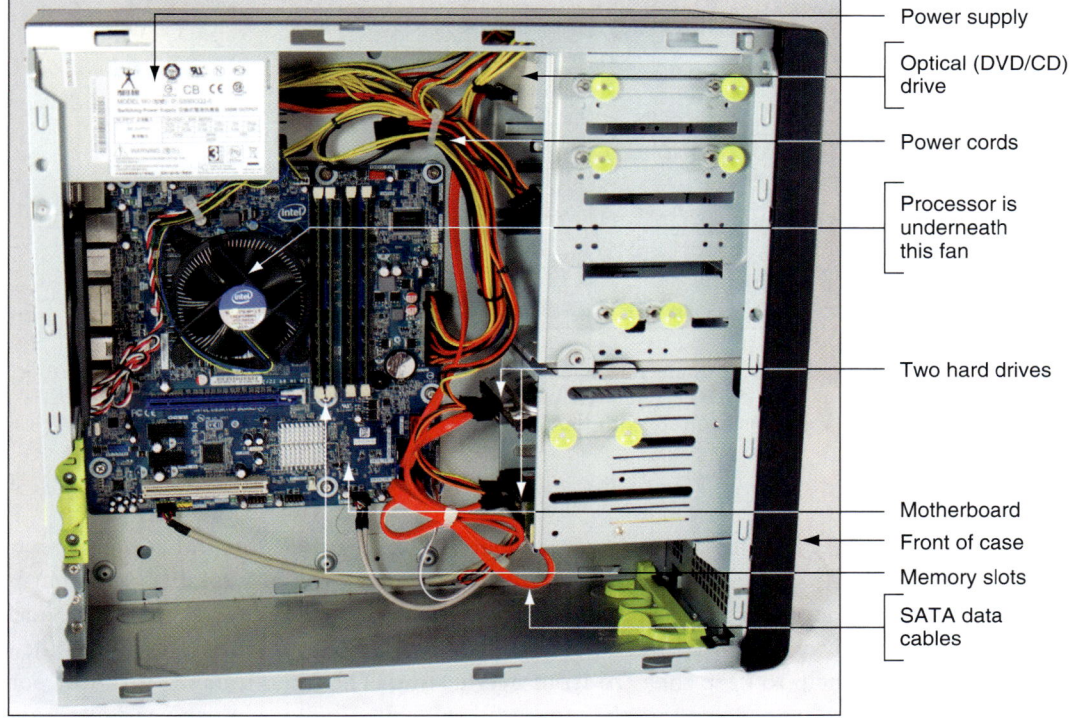

Figure 1-2 Inside the computer case

Here is a quick explanation of the main components installed in the case, which are called **internal components**:

- *The motherboard, processor, and cooler.* The **motherboard**, also called the **main board**, the **system board**, or the techie jargon term, the mobo, is the largest and most important circuit board in the computer. The motherboard contains a socket to hold the processor or CPU. The **central processing unit (CPU)**, also called the **processor** or **microprocessor**, does most of the processing of data and instructions for the entire system. Because the CPU generates heat, a fan and heat sink might be installed on top to keep it cool. A **heat sink** consists of metal fins that draw heat away from a component. The fan and heat sink together are called the processor cooler. Figure 1-3 shows the top view of a motherboard, and Figure 1-4 shows the ports on the side of a motherboard.

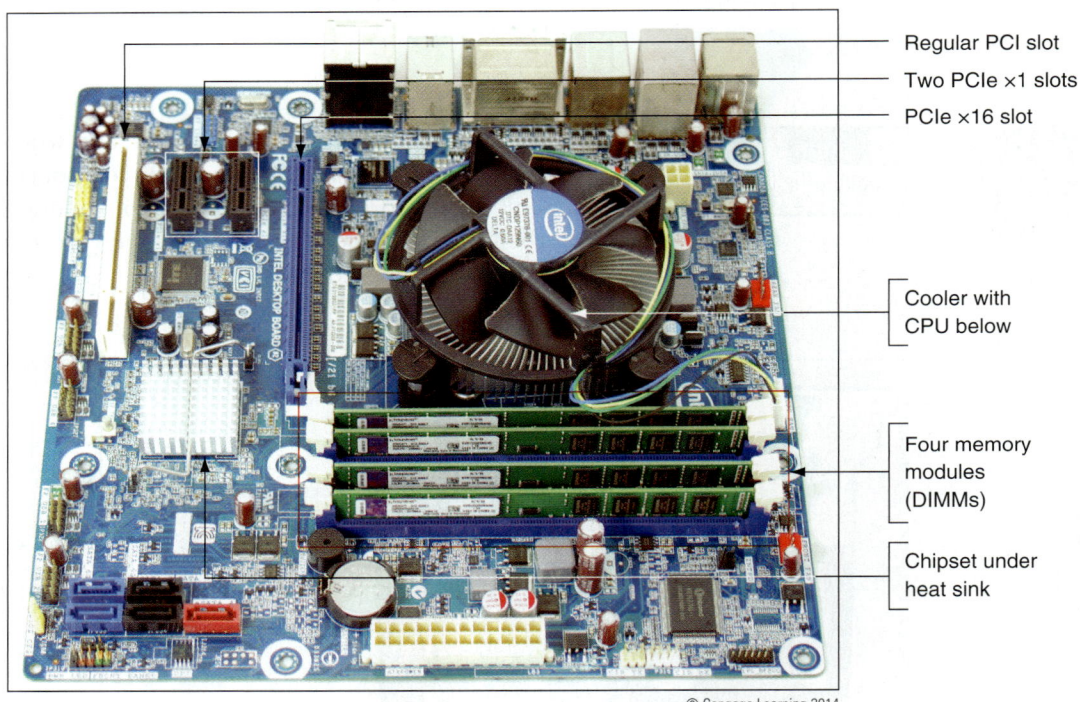

Figure 1-3 All hardware components are either located on the motherboard or directly or indirectly connected to it because they must all communicate with the CPU

- *Expansion cards.* A motherboard has expansion slots to be used by expansion cards. An **expansion card**, also called an adapter card, is a circuit board that provides more ports than those provided by the motherboard. Figure 1-5 shows a video card that provides three video ports. Notice the cooling fan and heat sink on the card, which help to keep the card from overheating. The trend today is for most ports in a system to be provided by the motherboard (called onboard ports) and less use of expansion cards.

What's Inside the Case

Figure 1-4 Ports provided by a motherboard

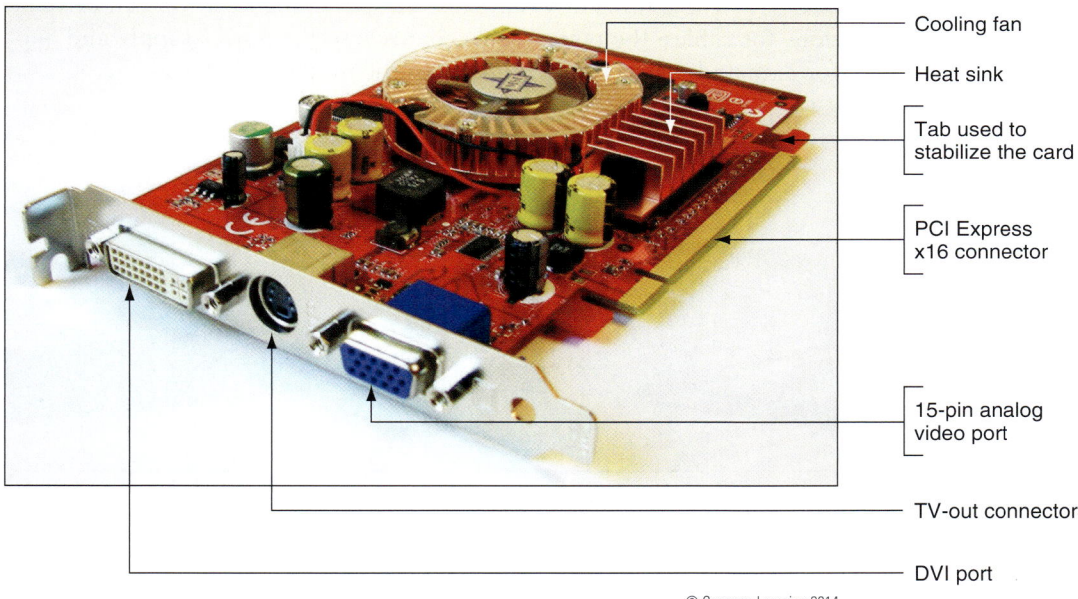

Figure 1-5 The easiest way to identify this video card is to look at the ports on the end of the card

▲ *Memory modules.* A motherboard has memory slots, called **DIMM (dual inline memory module)** slots, to hold memory modules. Figure 1-6 shows a memory module installed in one DIMM slot and three empty DIMM slots. Memory, also called **RAM (random access memory)**, is temporary storage for data and instructions as they are being processed by the CPU. The memory module shown in Figure 1-6 contains several RAM chips. Video cards also contain some embedded RAM chips for **video memory**.

Figure 1-6 A DIMM holds RAM and is mounted directly on a motherboard

▲ *Hard drives and other drives.* A system might have one or more hard drives, an optical drive, a tape drive, or, for really old systems, a floppy drive. A **hard drive**, also called a **hard disk drive (HDD)**, is permanent storage used to hold data and programs. For example, the Windows 7 operating system and applications are installed on the hard drive. All drives in a system are installed in a stack of drive bays at the front of the case. The system shown in Figure 1-2 has two hard drives and one optical drive installed. These three drives are also shown in Figure 1-7. Each drive has two connections for cables: the power cable connects to the power supply and another cable, used for data and instructions, connects to the motherboard.

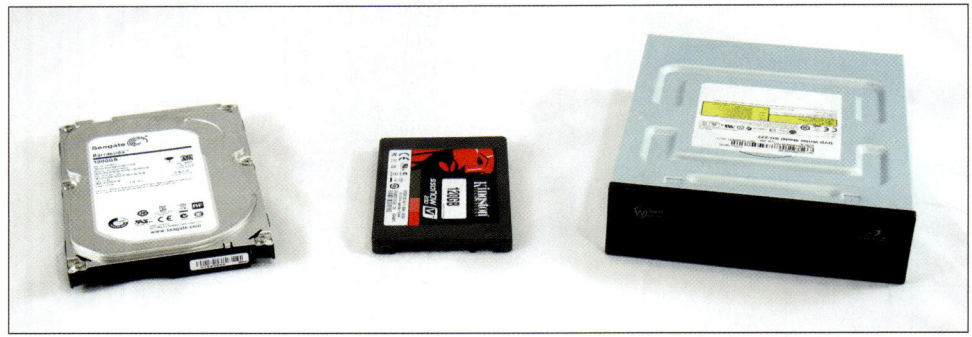

Figure 1-7 Two types of hard drives (larger magnetic drive and smaller solid-state drive) and a DVD drive

▲ *Power supply.* A computer **power supply**, also known as a **power supply unit (PSU)**, is a box installed in a corner of the computer case (see Figure 1-8) that receives and converts the house current so that components inside the case can use it. Most power supplies have a **dual-voltage selector switch** on the back of the computer case where you can switch the input voltage to the power supply to 115 V used in the United States or 220 V used in other countries. See Figure 1-9. The power cables can connect to and supply power to the motherboard, expansion cards, and drives.

> **Notes** If you ever need to change the dual-voltage selector switch, be sure you first turn off the computer and unplug the power supply.

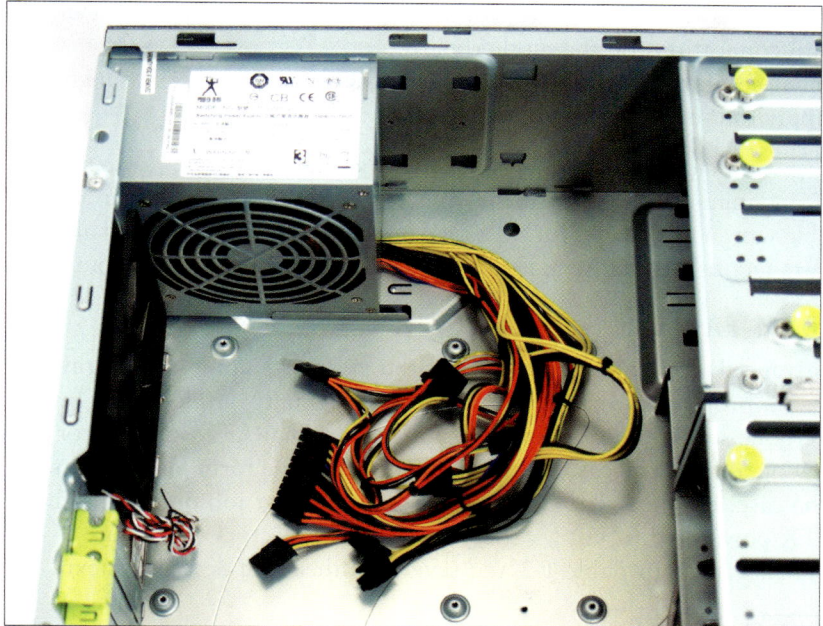

Figure 1-8 Power supply with attached power cables

© Cengage Learning 2014

Figure 1-9 The dual-voltage selector switch sets the input voltage to the power supply

© Cengage Learning 2014

FORM FACTORS USED BY COMPUTER CASES, POWER SUPPLIES, AND MOTHERBOARDS

The computer case, power supply, and motherboard must all be compatible and fit together as an interconnecting system. The standards that describe the size, shape, screw hole positions, and major features of these interconnected components are called **form factors**. Using a matching form factor for the motherboard, power supply, and case assures you that:

- The motherboard fits in the case.
- The power supply cords to the motherboard provide the correct voltage, and the connectors match the connections on the board.
- The holes in the motherboard align with the holes in the case for anchoring the board to the case.
- The holes in the case align with ports coming off the motherboard.

A+ 220-801 1.8

- For some form factors, wires for switches and lights on the front of the case match up with connections on the motherboard.
- The holes in the power supply align with holes in the case for anchoring the power supply to the case.

The two form factors used by most desktop and tower computer cases and power supplies are the ATX and mini-ATX form factors. Motherboards use these and other form factors that are compatible with ATX or mini-ATX power supplies and cases. You learn about other motherboard form factors in Chapter 3. Following are the important details about ATX and mini-ATX.

ATX FORM FACTOR

ATX (Advanced Technology Extended) is the most commonly used form factor today. It is an open, nonproprietary industry specification originally developed by Intel in 1995, and has undergone several revisions since then. The original ATX form factor for cases had case fans blowing air into the case, but early revisions to the form factor had fans blowing air out of the case. Blowing air out of the case does a better job of keeping the system cool.

An ATX power supply has a variety of power connectors (see Figure 1-10). The power connectors are listed in Table 1-2 and several of them are described next.

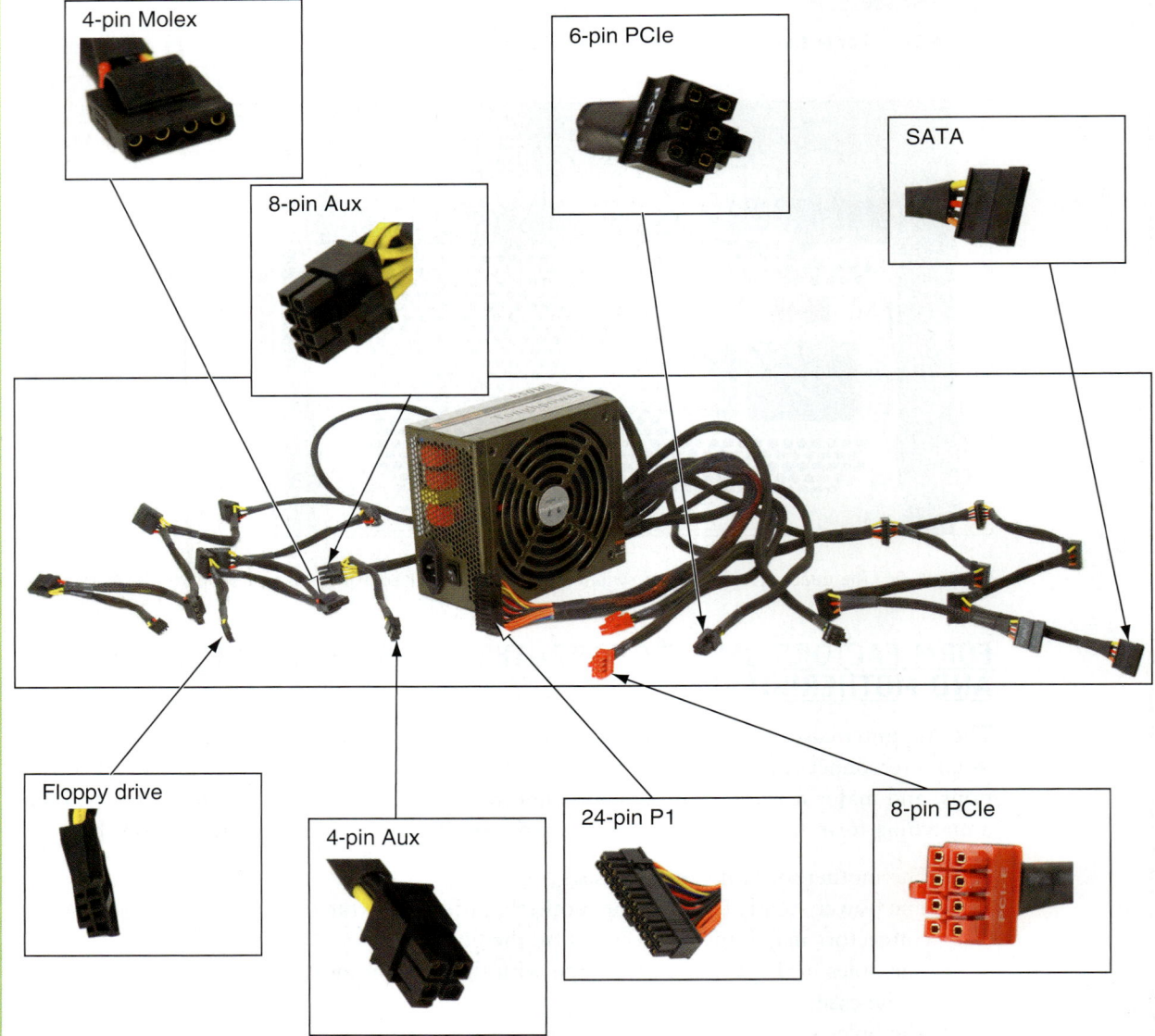

Figure 1-10 ATX power supply with connectors

What's Inside the Case

A+ 220-801 1.8

Connector	Description
	20-pin P1 connect is the main motherboard power connector used in the early ATX systems
	24-pin P1 connector, also called the 20+4 pin connector, is the main motherboard power connector used today
	20+4 pin P1 connector with four pins removed so the connector can fit into a 20-pin P1 motherboard connector
	4-pin auxiliary motherboard connector used for extra 12-V power to the processor
	8-pin auxiliary motherboard connector used for extra 12-V power to the processor, providing more power than the older 4-pin auxiliary connector
	4-pin Molex connector is used for IDE (PATA) drives
	15-pin SATA connector used for SATA drives
	4-pin Berg connector used by a floppy disk drive (FDD)

Table 1-2 Power supply connectors (continues)

© Cengage Learning 2014

A+ 220-801 1.8

Connector	Description
© Cengage Learning 2014	6-pin PCIe connector provides an extra +12 V for high-end video cards using PCI Express, Version 1 standard
© Cengage Learning 2014	8-pin PCIe connector provides an extra +12 V for high-end video cards using PCI Express, Version 2
© Cengage Learning 2014	6-pin plus 2-pin +12 V PCIe connector is used by high-end video cards using PCIe ×16 slots to provide extra voltage to the card. To get the 8-pin connector, combine both the 6-pin and 2-pin connectors.

© Cengage Learning 2014

Table 1-2 Power supply connectors (continued)

> **A+ Exam Tip** The A+ 220-801 exam expects you to know about each connector listed in Table 1-2.

Power connectors have evolved because components using new technologies require more power. As you read about the following types of power connectors and why each came to be, you'll also learn about the evolving expansion slots and expansion cards that drove the need for more power:

- ▲ *20-pin P1 connector.* The first ATX power supplies and motherboards used a single power connector called the P1 connector that had 20 pins. Figure 1-11 shows an ATX case with an ATX power supply installed, and Figure 1-12 shows the P1 connector on an ATX motherboard. The **20-pin P1 connector** used by the power supply and motherboard provided +3.3 volts, +5 volts, +12 volts, -12 volts, and an optional and rarely used -5 volts. This 20-pin power connector was sufficient for powering expansion cards installed in **PCI (Peripheral Component Interconnect)** expansion slots on the motherboard (see Figure 1-13). Several versions of PCI slots evolved over time, which you learn about in Chapter 3.
- ▲ *4-pin and 8-pin auxiliary connectors.* When processors began to require more power, the ATX Version 2.1 specifications added a **4-pin motherboard auxiliary connector** near the processor socket to provide an additional 12 V of power (see Figure 1-14). A power supply that provides this 4-pin 12-volt power cord is called an **ATX12V power supply**. Later boards replaced the 4-pin 12-volt power connector with an **8-pin motherboard auxiliary connector** that provided more amps for the processor.

Figure 1-11 ATX power supply with connections

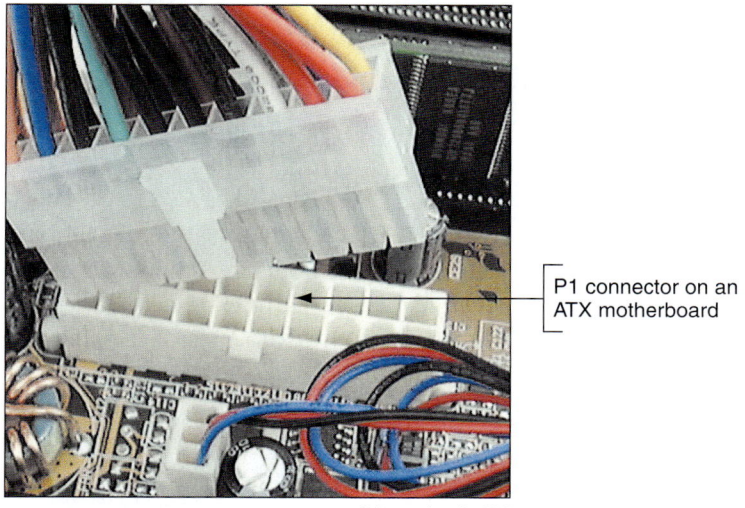

Figure 1-12 The first ATX P1 power connector used 20 pins

▲ *24-pin or 20+4-pin P1 connector.* Later, when faster **PCI Express (PCIe)** slots were added to motherboards, more power was required and a new ATX specification (ATX Version 2.2) allowed for a **24-pin P1 connector**, also called the 20+4 power connector. The 20-pin power cable will still work in the new 24-pin connector. Looking back at Figure 1-3, you can see one long blue PCIe ×16 slot (16 lanes for 16-bit transfers on this slot) that can be used by a video card and two short black PCIe ×1 slots (for 1-bit transfers) that can be used for other expansion cards that fit this type slot.

Figure 1-13 A PCI expansion card about to be installed in a PCI slot

Figure 1-14 The 4-pin 12-volt auxiliary power connector on a motherboard with power cord connected

The extra 4 pins on the 24-pin P1 connector provide +12 volts, +5 volts, and +3.3 volts pins. Motherboards that support PCI Express and have the 24-pin P1 connector are sometimes called Enhanced ATX boards. Figure 1-15 shows a 20-pin P1 power cord from the power supply and a 24-pin P1 connector on a motherboard. Figure 1-16 shows the pinouts for the 24-pin power cord connector, which is color-coded to wires from the power supply. The 20-pin connector is missing the lower four pins, which are listed in the photo and diagram.

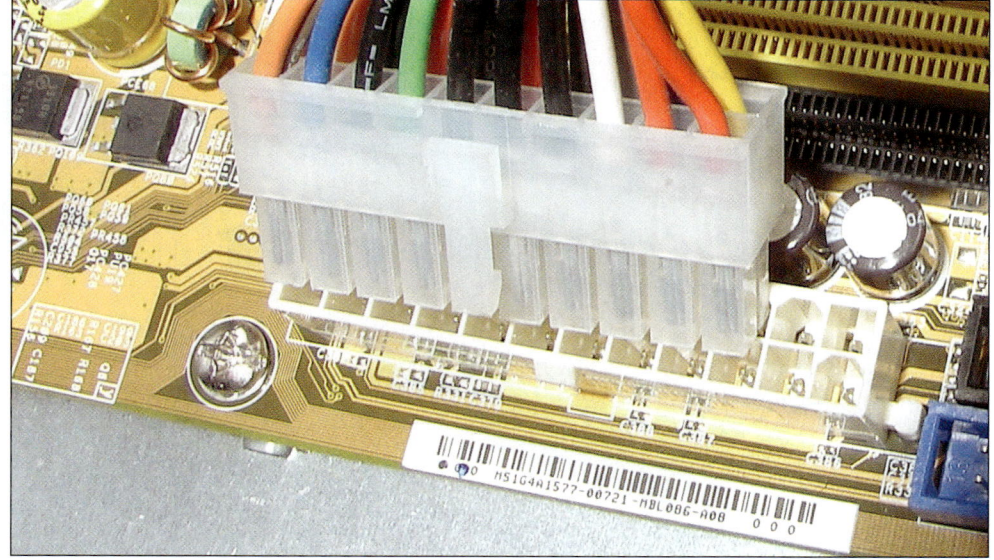

Figure 1-15 A 20-pin power cord ready to be plugged into a 24-pin P1 connector on an ATX motherboard

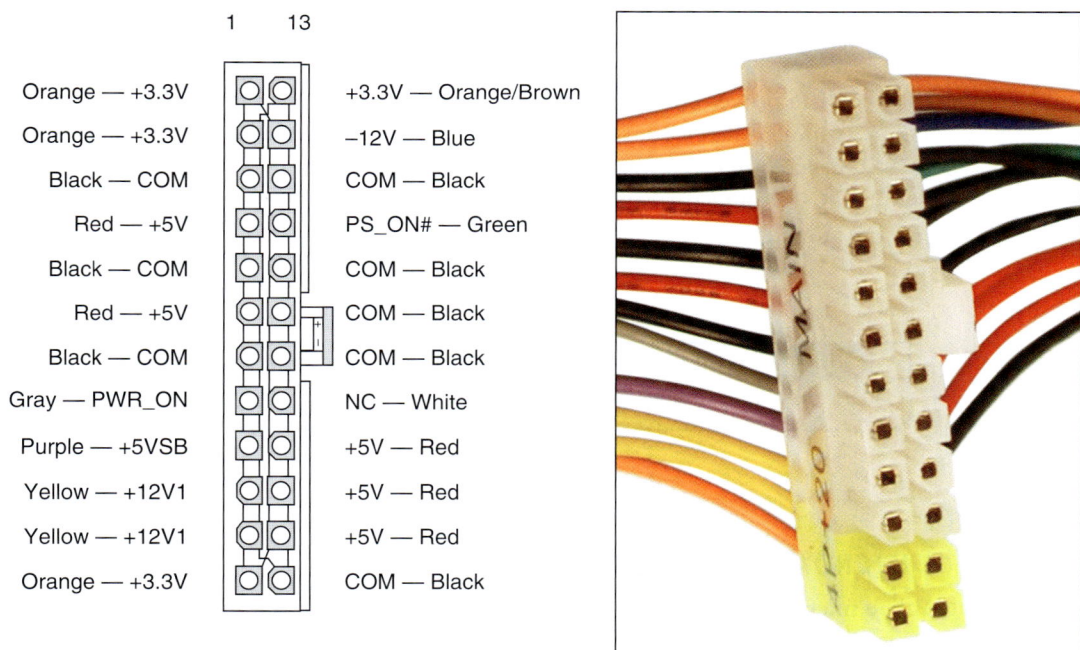

Figure 1-16 P1 24-pin power connector follows ATX Version 2.2 and higher standards

Figure 1-17 shows a PCIe ×16 video card. The edge connector has a break that fits the break in the slot. The tab at the end of the edge connector fits into a retention mechanism at the end of the slot, which helps to stabilize a heavy video card.

16 | **CHAPTER 1** First Look at Computer Parts and Tools

A+ 220-801 1.8

Figure 1-17 This PCIe ×16 video card has a 6-pin PCIe power connector to receive extra power from the power supply

▲ *6-pin and 8-pin PCIe connectors.* Video cards draw the most power in a system, and ATX Version 2.2 provides for power cables to connect directly to a video card to provide it additional power than comes through the PCIe slot on the motherboard. The **PCIe power connector** might have 6 or 8 pins. PCI Express, Version 1, defined the 6-pin connector, and PCI Express, Version 2, defined the 8-pin connector. The video card shown in Figure 1-17 has a 6-pin connector on the top of the card. A 6- or 8-pin PCIe connector can also be located on the motherboard to supply extra power for the video card.

> **Notes** For more information about all the form factors discussed in this chapter, check out the form factor web site sponsored by Intel at *www.formfactors.org*.

MICROATX FORM FACTOR

The **microATX (MATX)** form factor is a major variation of ATX and addresses some technologies that have emerged since the original development of ATX. MicroATX reduces the total cost of a system by reducing the number of expansion slots on the motherboard, reducing the power supplied to the board, and allowing for a smaller case size. A microATX motherboard (see Figure 1-18) will fit into a case that follows the ATX 2.1 or higher standard. A microATX power supply uses a 24-pin P1 connector and is not likely to have as many extra wires and connectors as those on an ATX power supply.

A+ 220-801 1.8

Figure 1-18 This MicroATX motherboard by Biostar is designed to support an AMD processor

> **A+ Exam Tip** The A+ 220-801 exam expects you to recognize and know the more important features of the ATX and micro-ATX form factors used by power supplies.

Hands-on | Project 1-1 Identify Ports and Parts

Do the following to identify computer ports and parts that your instructor might have on display:

1. Look on the front and back of your computer case and list the type of ports the computer offers.
2. For a power supply, list the number and type of power connectors.
3. For a motherboard, list the number and type of expansion slots on the board. Does the board have a 20-pin or 24-pin P1 connector? What other power connectors are on the board? How many memory slots does the board have?
4. For expansion cards, examine the ports on the back of the card. Can you tell by the ports the purpose of the card? What type slot does the card use?

> **Caution** Later in the chapter, you learn that you can damage a computer component with static electricity if you touch the component when you are not grounded. Before you touch a sensitive computer component, you first need to dissipate any static electricity on your body. You learn how to do that later in the chapter. For now, to protect a working component your instructor has on display, don't touch; just look.

A+ 220-801 1.8

Hands-on Project 1-2: Examine the Power Supply, Motherboard, and Expansion Cards Inside a Case

If you have access to a computer with the case cover removed, examine its components and answer the following questions. As you look, remember to not touch anything inside the case unless you are properly grounded.

1. Identify the power supply, motherboard, and any expansion cards that might be installed on the motherboard. Remember: Don't touch a component unless you are properly grounded. If the case is plugged into a power source, don't touch inside the case even if you are grounded.
2. Identify the cooler that is installed on top of the processor. This cooler is likely to have a fan on top and a heat sink that you cannot see. The processor is hidden under the cooler.
3. Identify the memory modules and memory slots. How many memory slots are there? How many of these slots are populated?
4. If an expansion card is installed, what type of ports does the card provide at the rear of the case? Find the one screw that is used to attach the expansion card to the case.
5. Locate the screws that are attaching the motherboard to the case. How many screws are used? Do you see screw holes in the motherboard that are not being used? As a general rule of thumb, up to nine screws can be used to attach a motherboard to a case.
6. How many power cables are coming from the power supply? How many of these cables are connected to the motherboard? To other devices inside the computer? Identify each type of power cable the system is using.
7. Find the screws or clips that are attaching the power supply to the case. Is the power supply attached using screws, clips, or both screws and clips?

Now let's learn about the drives you might find installed inside a system.

DRIVES, THEIR CABLES, AND CONNECTORS

A computer might have one or more hard drives, an optical drive (CD, DVD, or Blu-ray), tape drive, floppy drive, or some other type of drive. A drive receives power by a power cable from the power supply, and communicates instructions and data through a cable attached to the motherboard. Two standards that hard drives, optical drives, and tape drives use for both types of connections are the faster **serial ATA (SATA)** standard and the slower and older **parallel ATA (PATA)** standard. Both standards are published by the American National Standards Institute (ANSI, see *www.ansi.org*). Most drives today use the faster SATA interface. Figure 1-19 shows a SATA cable connecting a hard drive and motherboard. SATA cables can only connect to a SATA connector on the motherboard in one direction (see Figure 1-20). SATA drives get their power from a power cable that connects to the drive using a **SATA power connector** (refer back to the photo in Table 1-2).

What's Inside the Case   19

A+
220-801
1.8

Serial ATA cable

Power cord

Figure 1-19 A hard drive subsystem using the SATA data cable

Figure 1-20 A SATA cable connects to a SATA connector in only one direction; use red connectors on the motherboard first

The PATA interface, also called the IDE interface, uses a wide 40-pin ribbon cable and connector. The standard allows for only two connectors on a motherboard for two data cables (see Figure 1-21). Each IDE ribbon cable has a connection at the other end for an IDE drive and a connection in the middle of the cable for a second IDE drive. See Figure 1-22. Using this interface, a motherboard can accommodate up to four IDE or PATA drives in one system.

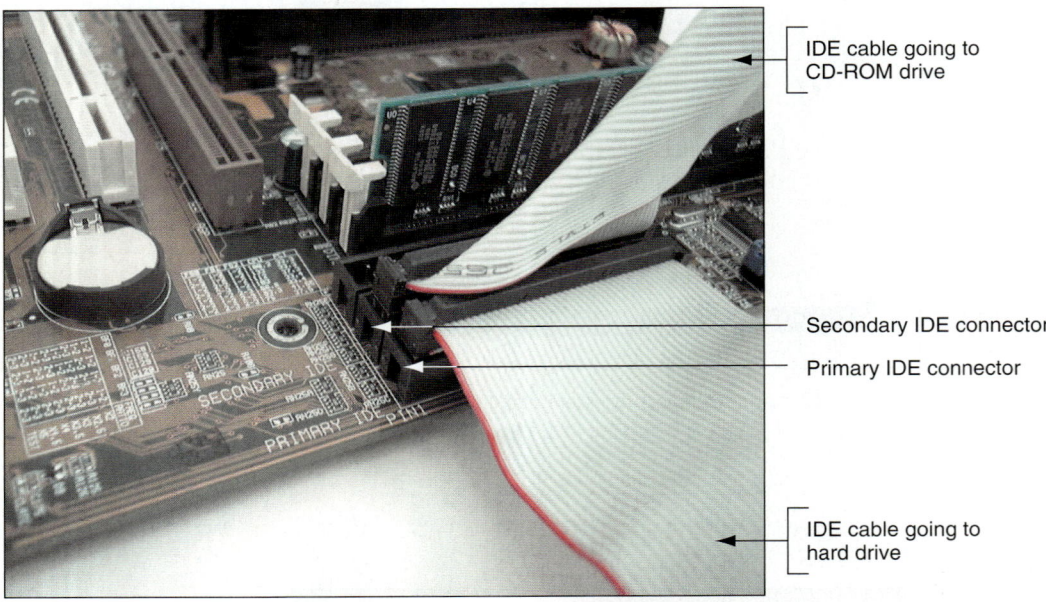

Figure 1-21 Using a parallel ATA interface, a motherboard has two IDE connectors, each of which can accommodate two devices; a hard drive usually connects to the motherboard using the primary IDE connector

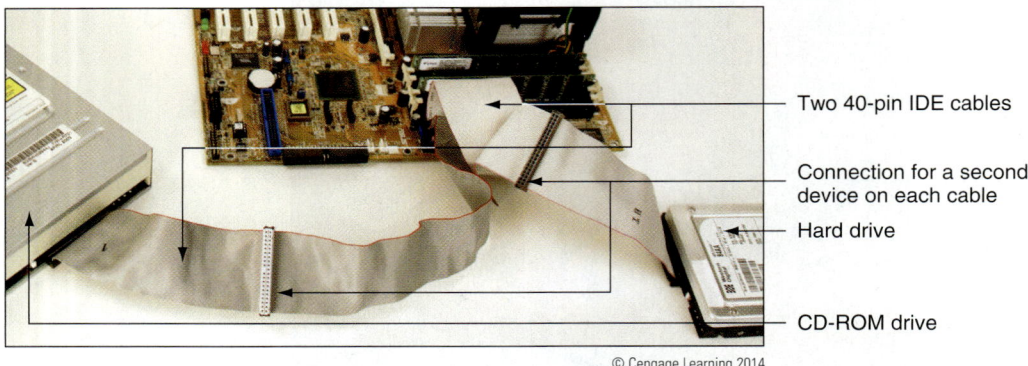

Figure 1-22 Two IDE devices connected to a motherboard using both IDE connections and two cables

PATA drives use a 4-pin power connector called a **Molex power connector**. A Molex connector is shaped so it connects in only one direction (see Figure 1-23).

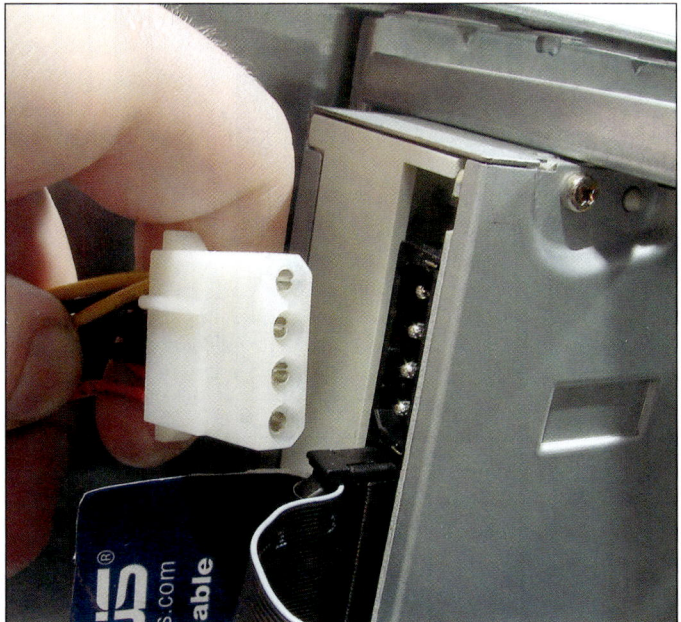

Figure 1-23 Molex power connector to a drive is shaped so that it orients in only one direction

Older motherboards provide a connection for a floppy drive data cable (see Figure 1-24). A **floppy drive**, also called a **floppy disk drive (FDD)**, can hold 3.5-inch disks containing up to 1.44 MB of data. The floppy drive cable has 34 pins and a twist in the cable and can accommodate one or two drives (see Figure 1-25). The drive at the end of the cable is drive A, which is the drive that follows the twist in the cable. If another drive were connected to the middle of the cable, it would be drive B in a computer system, which is the drive before the twist. The 4-pin **Berg power connector** used by floppy drives is smaller than a Molex connector (see the photo in Table 1-2).

Figure 1-24 An older motherboard usually provides a connection for a floppy drive cable

Cables used by PATA drives might be a 40-pin conductor IDE cable or a higher-quality 80-conductor IDE cable used by the Enhanced IDE (EIDE) standards. (An 80-conductor cable has 80 thin wires connected to 40 pins.) Figure 1-26 shows the two IDE cables on the right and a floppy drive cable on the left. IDE and floppy drive cables have a red

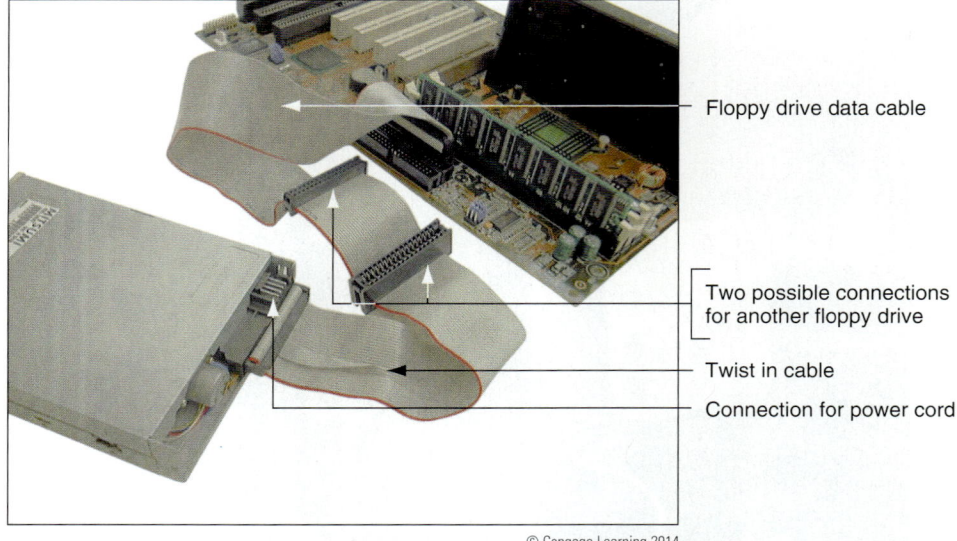

Figure 1-25 One floppy drive connection on a motherboard can support one or two floppy drives

color or stripe down one side of the cable. This edge color marks this side of the cable as pin 1. Pin 1 is labeled on the connector so that you can orient the cable in the connector (see Figure 1-27). The EIDE cables and some floppy drive cables have a covered pinhole and a notch in the motherboard connector, so these cables can connect in only one direction. See Figure 1-28.

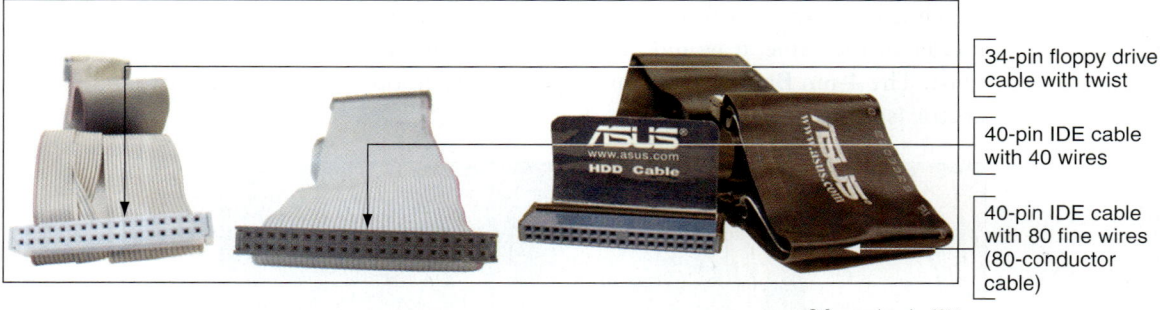

Figure 1-26 A system might have up to three types of ribbon cables

Figure 1-27 Pin 1 for this IDE connection is clearly marked

Figure 1-28 The notch on the side of this floppy drive connector allows the floppy drive cable to connect in only one direction

Hands-on | Project 1-3 Identify Drives and Their Connectors

If your instructor has provided a display of drives, for each drive identify the purpose of the drive (for example, a hard drive or optical drive) and the type of interface the drive uses (for example, IDE or SATA). If you have access to a computer with the case cover removed, answer the following questions:

1. List the drives installed, the purpose of each drive and the type of interface and power connector it uses.

2. How many connectors does the motherboard have for drives? Identify each type of connector (SATA, IDE, or floppy drive connector).

And this brings us to the fact that you need to know about electricity, how a computer uses it, and how to protect yourself and the equipment against electrical dangers.

PROTECTING YOURSELF AND THE EQUIPMENT AGAINST ELECTRICAL DANGERS

By the end of the next chapter, you will know how to take a working desktop computer apart and put the computer back together. When you're done, it's expected the computer will still work! That might not be the case, however, if you don't understand electricity and how to protect yourself and the equipment against it. In this part of the chapter, you learn how to keep from getting a shock or damaging a component. Let's begin with a discussion of the basics of electricity.

MEASURES AND PROPERTIES OF ELECTRICITY

A+ 220-801 5.1, 5.2

In our modern world, we take electricity for granted, and we miss it terribly when it's cut off. Nearly everyone depends on it, but few really understand it. A successful PC support technician is not one who tends to encounter failed processors, fried motherboards, smoking monitors, or frizzed hair. To avoid these excitements, you need to understand how to measure electricity and how to protect computer equipment from its damaging power.

Let's start with the basics. To most people, volts, ohms, joules, watts, and amps are vague terms that simply mean electricity. All these terms can be used to measure some characteristic of electricity, as listed in Table 1-3.

Unit	Definition	Computer Example
Volt (for example, 115 V)	A measure of electrical force measured in volts. The symbol for volts is V.	A power supply steps down the voltage from the 115-volt house current to 3.3, 5, and 12 volts that computer components can use.
Amp or ampere (for example, 1.5 A)	An amp is a measure of electrical current. The symbol for amps is A.	An LCD monitor requires about 5 A to operate. A small laser printer uses about 2 A. A CD-ROM drive uses about 1 A.
Ohm (for example, 20 Ω)	An ohm is a measure of resistance to electricity. The symbol for ohm is Ω.	Current can flow in typical computer cables and wires with a resistance of near zero Ω (ohm).
Joule (for example, 500 joules)	A measure of work or energy. One joule (pronounced "jewel") is the work required to push an electrical current of one amp through a resistance of one ohm.	A surge suppressor (see Figure 1-29) is rated in joules—the higher the better. The rating determines how much work it can expend before it can no longer protect the circuit from a power surge.
Watt (for example, 20 W)	A measure of electrical power. One watt is one joule per second, and measures the total electrical power needed to operate a device. Watts can be calculated by multiplying volts by amps. The symbol for watts is W.	The power consumption of an LCD computer monitor is rated at about 14 W. A DVD burner uses about 25 W when burning a DVD.

© Cengage Learning 2014

Table 1-3   Measures of electricity

Figure 1-29   A surge suppressor protects electrical equipment from power surges and is rated in joules

A+
220-801
5.1, 5.2

> **Notes** To learn more about how volts, amps, ohms, joules, and watts measure the properties of electricity, see the content "Electricity and Multimeters" in the online content that accompanies this book at *cengagebrain.com*. To find out how to access this content, see the Preface to this book.

Now let's look at how electricity gets from one place to another and how it is used in house circuits and computers.

AC AND DC

Electricity can be either AC, alternating current, or DC, direct current. **Alternating current (AC)** goes back and forth, or oscillates, rather than traveling in only one direction. House current in the United States is AC and oscillates 60 times in one second (60 hertz). Voltage in the system is constantly alternating from positive to negative, which causes the electricity to flow first in one direction and then in the other. Voltage alternates from +115 V to -115 V. AC is the most economical way to transmit electricity to our homes and workplaces. By decreasing current and increasing voltage, we can force alternating current to travel great distances. When alternating current reaches its destination, it is made more suitable for driving our electrical devices by decreasing voltage and increasing current.

Direct current (DC) travels in only one direction and is the type of current that most electronic devices require, including computers. A **rectifier** is a device that converts AC to DC, and an **inverter** is a device that converts DC to AC. A **transformer** is a device that changes the ratio of voltage to current. The power supply used in computers is both a rectifier and a transformer.

Large transformers reduce the high voltage on power lines coming to your neighborhood to a lower voltage before the current enters your home. The transformer does not change the amount of power in this closed system; if it decreases voltage, it increases current. The overall power stays constant, but the ratio of voltage to current changes, as illustrated in Figure 1-30.

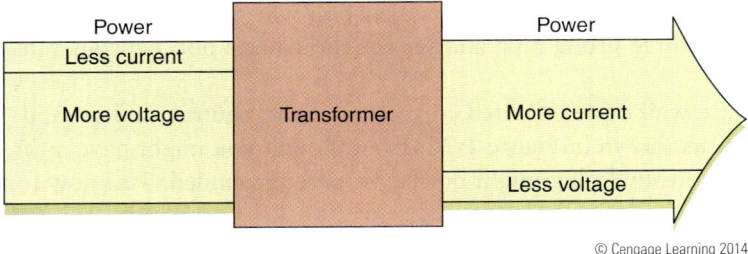

Figure 1-30 A transformer keeps power constant but changes the ratio of current to voltage

Direct current flows in only one direction. Think of electrical current like a current of water that flows from a state of high pressure to a state of low pressure or rest. Electrical current flows from a high-pressure state (called hot) to a state of rest (called ground or neutral). For a power supply, a power line may be either +5 or −5 volts in one circuit, or +12 or −12 volts in another circuit. The positive or negative value is determined by how the circuit is oriented, either on one side of the power output or the other. Several circuits coming from the power supply accommodate different devices with different power requirements.

HOT, NEUTRAL, AND GROUND

AC travels on a hot line from the power station to a building and returns to the power station on a neutral line. When the two lines reach the building and enter an electrical device, such as a lamp, the device controls the flow of electricity between the hot and neutral lines. If an easier path (one with less resistance) is available, the electricity follows that path. This can cause a short, a sudden increase in flow that can also create a sudden increase in temperature—enough to start a fire and injure both people and equipment. Never put yourself in a position where you are the path of least resistance between the hot line and ground!

> **Caution** It's very important that PC components be properly grounded. Never connect a PC to an outlet or use an extension cord that doesn't have the third ground plug. The third line can prevent a short from causing extreme damage. In addition, the bond between the neutral and ground helps eliminate electrical noise (stray electrical signals) within the PC that is sometimes caused by other electrical equipment sitting very close to the computer.

To prevent uncontrolled electricity in a short, the neutral line is grounded. Grounding a line means that the line is connected directly to the earth, so that, in the event of a short, the electricity flows into the earth and not back to the power station. Grounding serves as an escape route for out-of-control electricity because the earth is always capable of accepting a flow of current. With computers, a surge suppressor can be used to protect a computer and its components against power surges.

> **Caution** Beware of the different uses of black wire. In PCs and in DC circuits, black is used for ground, but in home wiring and in AC circuits, black is used for hot!

The neutral line to your house is grounded many times along its way (in fact, at each electrical pole) and is also grounded at the breaker box where the electricity enters your house. You can look at a three-prong plug and see the three lines: hot, neutral, and ground (see Figure 1-31).

To verify that a wall outlet is wired correctly for hot, neutral, and ground, use a simple receptacle tester, as shown in Figure 1-32. Even though you might have a three-prong outlet in your home, the ground plug might not be properly grounded. To know for sure, you can test the outlet with a receptacle tester.

> **Notes** House AC voltage in the United States is about 110–120 V, but know that in other countries, this is not always the case. In many other countries, the standard is 220 V. Outlet styles also vary from one country to the next.

Now that you know about electricity and how to protect a computer from surges and out-of-control electricity, let's turn our attention to protecting yourself against the dangers of electricity.

A+ 220-801 5.1, 5.2

Figure 1-31 A polarized plug showing hot and neutral, and a three-prong plug showing hot, neutral, and ground

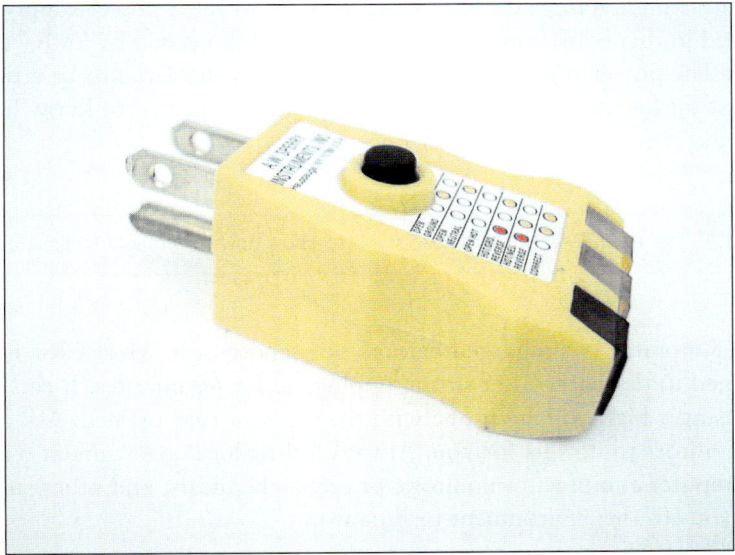

Figure 1-32 Use a receptacle tester to verify that hot, neutral, and ground are wired correctly

A+ 220-801 5.1, 5.2

PROTECT YOURSELF AGAINST ELECTRICAL SHOCK AND BURNS

To protect yourself against electrical shock, when working with any electrical device, including computers, printers, scanners, and network devices, disconnect the power if you notice a dangerous situation that might lead to electrical shock or fire. When you disconnect the power, do so by pulling on the plug at the AC outlet. To protect the power cord, don't pull on the cord itself. Also, don't just turn off the on/off switch on the device; you need to actually disconnect the power. Note that any of the following can indicate a potential danger:

- The power cord is frayed or otherwise damaged in any way.
- Water or other liquid is on the floor around the device or spilled on it.
- The device has been exposed to excess moisture.
- The device has been dropped or you notice physical damage.
- You smell a strong electronics odor.
- The power supply or fans are making a whining noise.
- You notice smoke coming from the computer case or the case feels unusually warm.

When working inside computers, printers, and other electrical devices, remove your jewelry that might come in contact with components. Jewelry is made of metal and might conduct electricity if it touches a component.

Power supplies and CRT monitors (the old-fashioned monitors that have a large case with a picture tube) contain capacitors. A capacitor holds its charge even after the power is turned off and the device is unplugged. A ground is the easiest possible path for electricity to follow. If you are grounded and touch a charged capacitor, its charge can flow through you to the ground, which can shock you! Therefore, if you ever work inside one of these devices, be careful that you are not grounded. Later in the chapter, you will learn that being grounded while working on sensitive low-voltage electronic equipment such as a motherboard or processor is a good thing, and the best way to ground yourself is to wear an antistatic grounding bracelet connected to ground. However, when working on a CRT monitor, power supply, or laser printer, *don't* wear the anti-static bracelet because you don't want to be ground for these high-voltage devices. How to work inside a power supply or CRT monitor is not covered in this book and is not considered a skill needed by an A+ certified support technician. The power supply and monitor are both considered to be a **field replaceable unit (FRU)**. That means, as a support technician, you are expected to know how to replace one when it breaks, but not how to repair one.

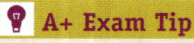 **A+ Exam Tip** The A+ 220-801 exam expects you to know how to properly dispose of a CRT monitor.

Be sure a CRT monitor is discharged before you dispose of it. Most CRT monitors today are designed to discharge after sitting unplugged for 60 minutes. It can be manually discharged by using a high-voltage probe with the monitor case opened. Ask a technician trained to fix monitors to do this for you. Always follow local government regulations when disposing of computer equipment, monitors, printers, chemicals, and other substances that might be dangerous to the environment or humans.

Notes Go to *www.youtube.com* and search on "discharge a CRT monitor" to see some interesting videos that demonstrate the charge inside a monitor long after the monitor is turned off and unplugged. As for proper procedures, I'm not endorsing all these videos; just watch for fun.

A+ 220-801 5.1, 5.2

Never use water to put out a fire fueled by electricity because water is a conductor and you might get a severe electrical shock. A computer lab needs a fire extinguisher that is rated to put out electrical fires. Fire extinguishers are rated by the type of fires they put out:

- Class A extinguishers can use water to put out fires caused by wood, paper, and other combustibles.
- Class B extinguishers can put out fires caused by liquids such as gasoline, kerosene, and oil.
- **Class C fire extinguishers** use nonconductive chemicals to put out a fire caused by electricity. See Figure 1-33.

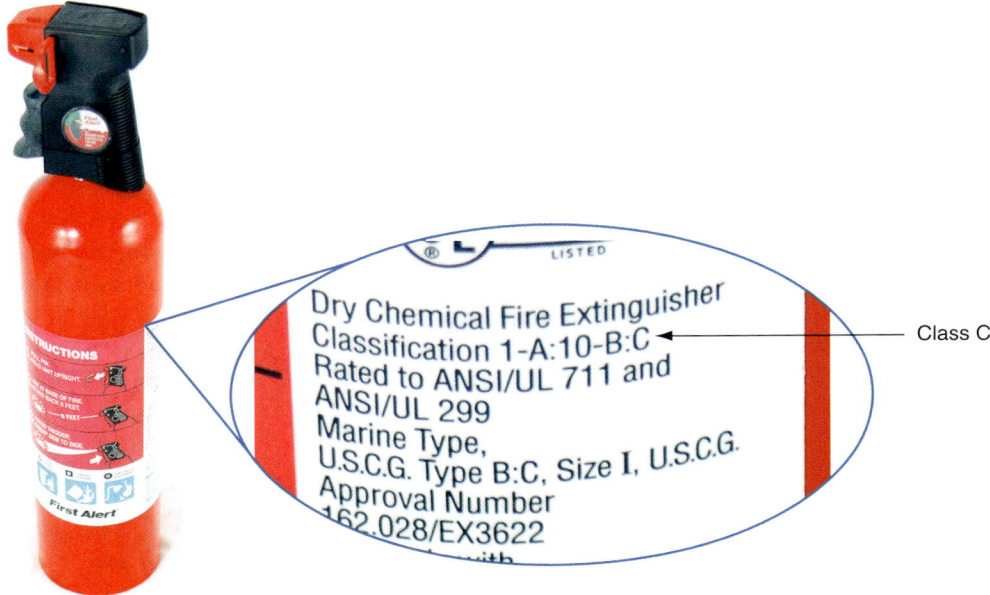

Figure 1-33 A Class C fire extinguisher is rated to put out electrical fires

PROTECT THE EQUIPMENT AGAINST STATIC ELECTRICITY OR ESD

Suppose you come indoors on a cold day, pick up a comb, and touch your hair. Sparks fly! What happened? Static electricity caused the sparks. **Electrostatic discharge (ESD)**, commonly known as **static electricity**, is an electrical charge at rest. When you came indoors, this charge built up on your hair and had no place to go. An ungrounded conductor (such as wire that is not touching another wire) or a nonconductive surface (such as your hair) holds a charge until the charge is released. When two objects with dissimilar electrical charges touch, electricity passes between them until the dissimilar charges become equal.

To see static charges equalizing, turn off the lights in a room, scuff your feet on the carpet, and touch another person. Occasionally, you can see and feel the charge in your fingers. If you can feel the charge, you discharged at least 1,500 volts of static electricity. If you hear the discharge, you released at least 6,000 volts. If you see the discharge, you released at least 8,000 volts of ESD. A charge of only 10 volts can damage electronic components! *You can touch a chip on an expansion card or motherboard, damage the chip with ESD, and never feel, hear, or see the electrical discharge.*

ESD can cause two types of damage in an electronic component: catastrophic failure and upset failure. A catastrophic failure destroys the component beyond use. An upset failure damages the component so that it does not perform well, even though it may still function to some degree. Upset failures are more difficult to detect because they are not consistent and not easily observed. Both types of failures permanently affect the device. Components are easily damaged by ESD, but because the damage might not show up for weeks or months, a technician is likely to get careless and not realize the damage he or she is doing.

> **Caution** Unless you are measuring power levels with a multimeter, never, ever touch a component or cable inside a computer case while the power is on. The electrical voltage is not enough to seriously hurt you, but more than enough to permanently damage the component.

Before touching or handling a component (for example, a hard drive, motherboard, expansion card, processor, or memory modules), to protect it against ESD, always ground yourself first. You can ground yourself and the computer parts by using one or more of the following static control devices or methods:

▲ *Ground bracelet.* A **ground bracelet**, also called an **ESD strap**, **antistatic wrist strap**, or ESD bracelet, is a strap you wear around your wrist. The strap has a cord attached with an alligator clip on the end. Attach the clip to the computer case you're working on, as shown in Figure 1-34. Any static electricity between you and the case is now discharged. Therefore, as you work inside the case, you will not damage the components with static electricity. The bracelet also contains a resistor that prevents electricity from harming you.

Figure 1-34 A ground bracelet, which protects computer components from ESD, can clip to the side of the computer case and eliminate ESD between you and the case

Protecting Yourself and the Equipment against Electrical Dangers | 31

▲ *Ground mats.* A ground mat, also called an ESD mat, dissipates ESD and is commonly used by bench technicians (also called depot technicians) who repair and assemble computers at their workbenches or in an assembly line. Ground mats have a connector in one corner that you can use to connect the mat to ground (see Figure 1-35). If you lift a component off the mat, it is no longer grounded and is susceptible to ESD, so it's important to use a ground bracelet with a ground mat.

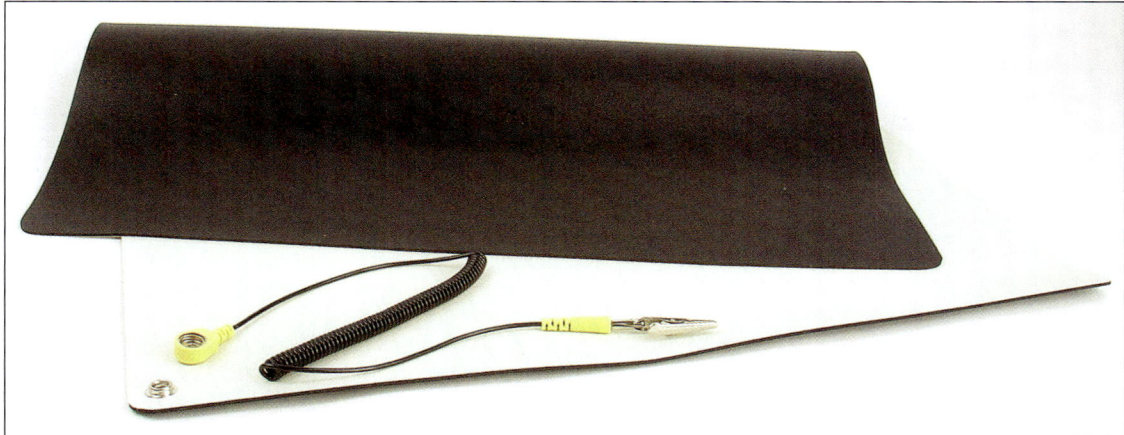

Figure 1-35 A ground mat dissipates ESD and should be connected to ground

▲ *Static shielding bags.* New components come shipped in static shielding bags, also called antistatic bags. These bags are a type of Faraday cage, named after Michael Faraday, who built the first cage in 1836. A Faraday cage is any device that protects against an electromagnetic field. Save the bags to store other devices that are not currently installed in a PC. As you work on a computer, know that a device is not protected from ESD if you place it on top of the bag; the protection is inside the bag (see Figure 1-36).

Figure 1-36 Static shielding bags help protect components from ESD

▲ *Antistatic gloves.* Wear **antistatic gloves**, also called **ESD gloves**, designed to prevent an ESD discharge between you and a device, as you pick it up and handle it (see Figure 1-37). The gloves can be substituted for an antistatic bracelet, and are good for moving, packing, or unpacking sensitive equipment. Even through these gloves tend to get in the way when working inside computer cases, Intel recommends you wear them when handling a processor.

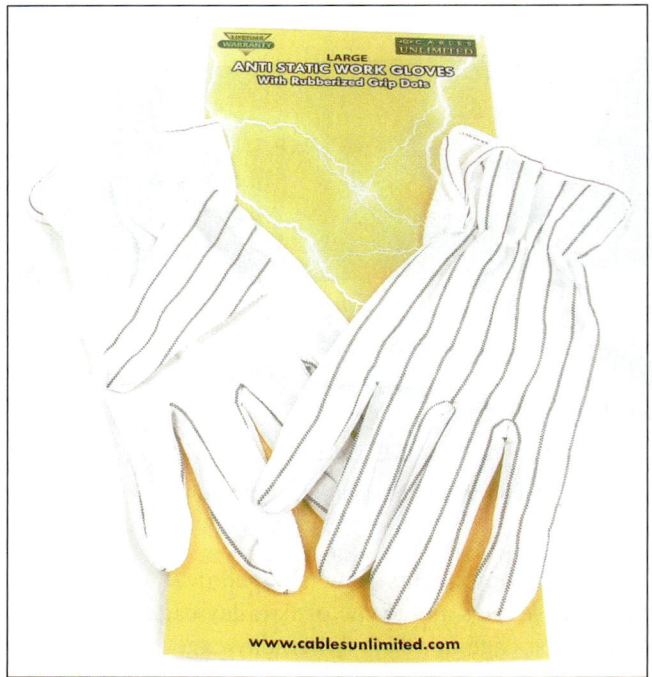

Figure 1-37 Use antistatic gloves to prevent static discharge between you and the equipment you are handling

> ⚡ **Caution** A CRT monitor can also damage components with ESD. Don't place or store expansion cards on top of or next to a CRT monitor, which can discharge as much as 29,000 volts onto the screen.

The best way to guard against ESD is to use a ground bracelet together with a ground mat or wear antistatic gloves. Consider a ground bracelet or antistatic gloves essential equipment when working on a computer. However, if you are in a situation in which you must work without one, touch the computer case or the power supply before you touch a component in the case, which is called **self-grounding**. Self-grounding dissipates any charge between you and whatever you touch. Here are some rules that can help protect computer parts against ESD:

▲ *Rule 1:* When passing a circuit board, memory module, or other sensitive component to another person, ground yourself and then touch the other person before you pass the component.
▲ *Rule 2:* Leave components inside their protective bags until you are ready to use them.
▲ *Rule 3:* Work on hard floors, not carpet, or use antistatic spray on the carpets.
▲ *Rule 4:* Don't work on a computer if you or the computer have just come in from the cold because there is more danger of ESD when the atmosphere is cold and dry.

A+ 220-801 5.1, 5.2

▲ *Rule 5:* When unpacking hardware or software, remove the packing tape and cellophane from the work area as soon as possible because these materials attract ESD.
▲ *Rule 6:* Keep components away from your hair and clothing.

> **A+ Exam Tip** The A+ 220-801 exam emphasizes that you should know how to protect computer equipment as you work on it, including how to protect components against damage from ESD.

Hands-on | Project 1-4 Practice Handling Computer Components

Working with a partner, you'll need some computer parts and the antistatic tools you learned about in this part of the chapter. Practice touching, picking up, and passing the parts between you. As you do so, follow the rules to protect the parts against ESD. Have a third person watch as you work and point out any ways you might have exposed a part to ESD. As you work, be careful to not touch components on circuit boards or the gold fingers on the edge connector of an expansion card. When you are finished, store the parts in antistatic bags.

Now that you know about electrical dangers and ways to protect you and the equipment, let's discuss the tools you need.

TOOLS USED BY A PC REPAIR TECHNICIAN

A+ 220-802 4.2

Every PC repair technician needs a handy toolbox with a few essential tools. Several hardware and software tools can help you maintain a computer and diagnose and repair computer problems. The tools you choose depend on the amount of money you can spend and the level of PC support you expect to provide.

Essential tools for PC hardware troubleshooting are listed here, and several of them are shown in Figure 1-38. You can purchase some of these tools in a PC toolkit, although most PC toolkits contain items you really can do without.

Figure 1-38 Tools used by PC support technicians when maintaining, repairing, or upgrading computers

Here is a list of essential tools:

- Ground bracelet, ground mat, or antistatic gloves to protect against ESD when working inside the computer case
- Flathead screwdriver
- Phillips-head or crosshead screwdriver
- Torx screwdriver set, particularly size T15
- Tweezers, preferably insulated ones, for picking pieces of paper out of printers or dropped screws out of tight places
- Extractor, a spring-loaded device that looks like a hypodermic needle (When you push down on the top, three wire prongs come out that can be used to pick up a screw that has fallen into a place where hands and fingers can't reach.)
- Software, including recovery CD or DVD for any OS you might work on (you might need several, depending on the OSs you support), antivirus software on bootable CDs or USB flash drives, and diagnostic software

The following tools might not be essential, but they are very convenient:

- Cans of compressed air (see Figure 1-39), small portable compressor, or antistatic vacuum cleaner to clean dust from inside a computer case
- Cleaning solutions and pads such as contact cleaner, monitor wipes, and cleaning solutions for CDs, DVDs, tapes, and drives
- Multimeter to check cables and the power supply output
- Power supply tester
- Needle-nose pliers for removing jumpers and for holding objects (especially those pesky nuts on cable connectors) in place while you screw them in
- Cable ties to tie cables up and out of the way inside a computer case
- Flashlight to see inside the computer case
- AC outlet ground tester
- Network cable tester (You will learn to use this tool in Chapter 9.)

Figure 1-39　A can of compressed air is handy to blow dust from a computer case

- Loopback plugs to test ports
- Small cups or bags to help keep screws organized as you work
- Antistatic bags (a type of Faraday cage) to store unused parts
- Chip extractor to remove chips (To pry up the chip, a simple screwdriver is usually more effective, however.)
- Pen and paper for taking notes
- POST diagnostic cards

Keep your tools in a toolbox designated for PC troubleshooting. If you put discs and hardware tools in the same box, be sure to keep the discs inside a hard plastic case to protect them from scratches and dents. In addition, make sure the diagnostic and utility software you use is recommended for the hardware and software you are troubleshooting.

Now let's turn our attention to the details of several PC support technician tools, including diagnostic cards, power supply testers, and multimeters. Then we'll finish up the chapter with some additional safety procedures you need to be aware of.

POST DIAGNOSTIC CARDS

Although not an essential tool, a **POST diagnostic card**, also called a **POST card**, or motherboard test card, can be of great help to discover and report computer errors and conflicts that occur when you first turn on a computer and before the operating system (such as Windows 7) is launched. To understand what a POST card does, you need to know about the programs and data stored on the motherboard called the **BIOS (basic input/output system)**. Some adapter cards, such as a video card, also have BIOS programs embedded on the card.

The BIOS programs are stored on a special ROM (read-only memory) chip; because these embedded programs are so closely tied to the hardware, they are called **firmware**. Figure 1-40 shows an embedded firmware chip on a motherboard that contains the BIOS programs. When the computer is not receiving power, the firmware chip is powered by a battery nearby so it does not lose the data it holds in the memory on the chip, which is called CMOS RAM. CMOS RAM holds the motherboard configuration or settings and include the computer date and time, power-on passwords, and which devices to look to when the BIOS is searching for an operating system (OS) to launch.

Figure 1-40 This firmware chip contains flash ROM and CMOS RAM; CMOS RAM is powered by the coin battery located near the chip

The motherboard BIOS serves three purposes:

▲ **System BIOS** manages essential devices (such as the keyboard, mouse, hard drive, and monitor) before the OS is launched.
▲ **Startup BIOS** is used to start the computer.
▲ **BIOS setup** or **CMOS setup** is used to change the motherboard configuration or settings.

So now back to the usefulness of a POST card. The **POST (power-on self test)** is a series of tests performed by the startup BIOS when you first turn on a computer. These tests determine if startup BIOS can communicate correctly with essential hardware components required for a successful boot. If you have a problem that prevents the PC from booting that you suspect is related to hardware, you can install the POST card in an expansion slot on the motherboard and then attempt to boot. The card monitors the boot process and reports errors, usually as coded numbers on a small LED panel on the card. You then look up the number online or in the documentation that accompanies the card to get more information about the error and its source.

Examples of these cards are listed below. Some manufacturers make cards for either desktop or laptop computers. The Post Code Master card is shown in Figure 1-41.

▲ PC POST Diagnostic Test Card by Elston System, Inc. (*www.elstonsystems.com*)
▲ PCI POST Diagnostic Test Card by StarTech.com (*www.startech.com*)
▲ Post Code Master by Microsystems Development, Inc. (*www.postcodemaster.com*)

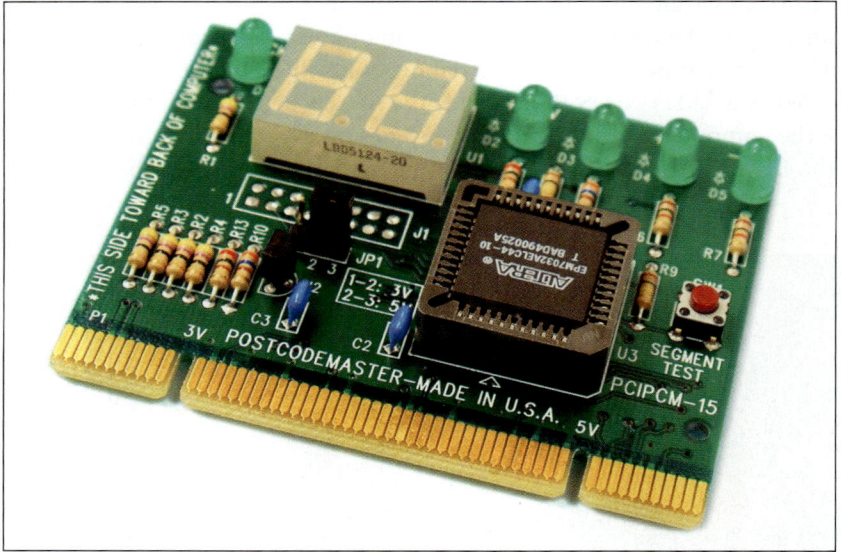

© Cengage Learning 2014

Figure 1-41 Post Code Master diagnostic card by Microsystems Developments, Inc. installs in a PCI slot

Before purchasing these or any other diagnostic tools or software, read the documentation about what they can and cannot do, and read some online product reviews. Try using Google.com and searching on "PC diagnostic card reviews."

> **Notes** Some Dell computers have lights on the case that blink in patterns to indicate a problem early in the boot before the OS loads. These blinking lights give information similar to that given by POST cards.

POWER SUPPLY TESTER

A **power supply tester** is used to measure the output of each connector coming from the power supply. You can test the power supply when it is outside or inside the case. As you saw earlier in Figure 1-8, the power supply provides several cables and connectors that power various components inside the computer case. A power supply tester has plugs for each type of cable. Connect a power cable to the tester, plug up the power supply, and turn on the tester. An LCD panel reports the output of each lead (see Figure 1-42). Later in the chapter, you learn about the various power supply cables and the voltages they supply.

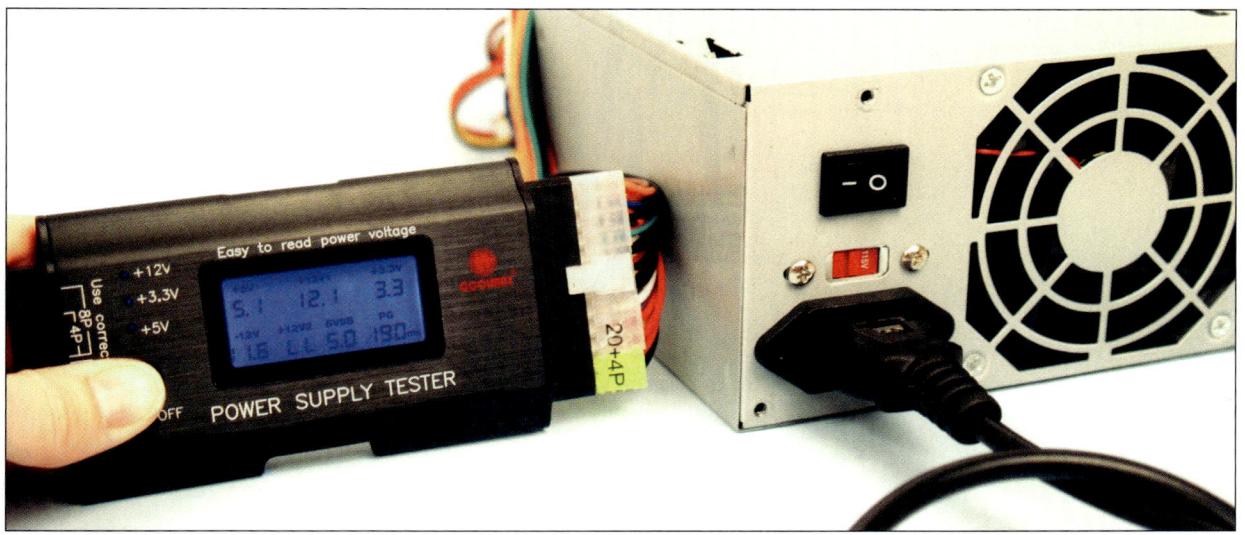

Figure 1-42 Use a power supply tester to test the output of each power connector on a power supply

MULTIMETER

A **multimeter** (see Figure 1-43) is a more general-purpose tool that can measure several characteristics of electricity in a variety of devices. Some multimeters can measure voltage, current, resistance, or continuity. (Continuity determines that two ends of a cable or fuse are connected without interruption.) When set to measure voltage, you can use it to measure output of each pin on a power supply connector. Set to measure continuity, a multimeter is useful to test fuses, to determine if a cable is good, or to match pins on one end of a cable to pins on the other end.

LOOPBACK PLUGS

A **loopback plug** is used to test a port in a computer or other device to make sure the port is working and might also test the throughput or speed of the port. Figure 1-44 shows a loopback plug testing a network port on a laptop. You know both the port and the network cable are good because the lights on either side of the port are lit. You can also buy a USB loopback plug to test USB ports.

38   **CHAPTER 1**   First Look at Computer Parts and Tools

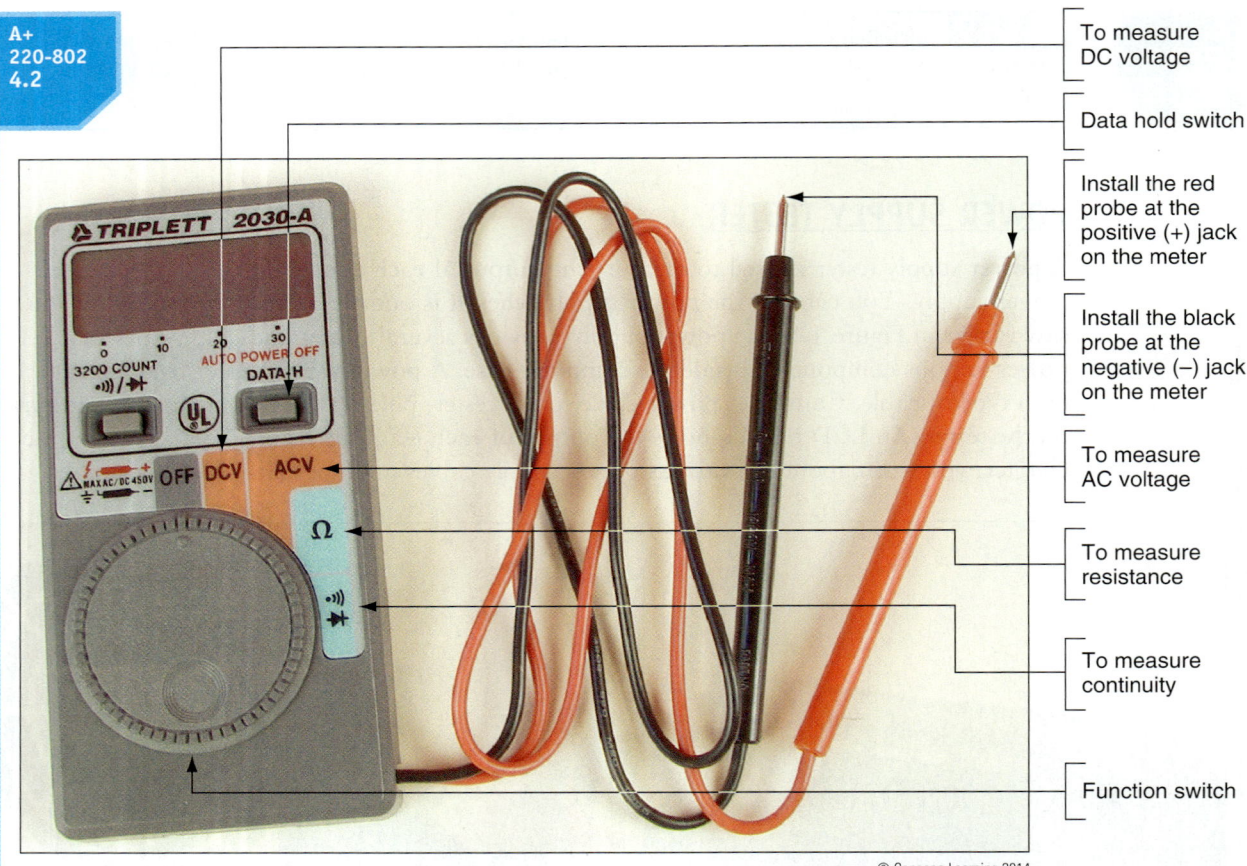

Figure 1-43   This digital multimeter can be set to measure voltage, resistance, or continuity

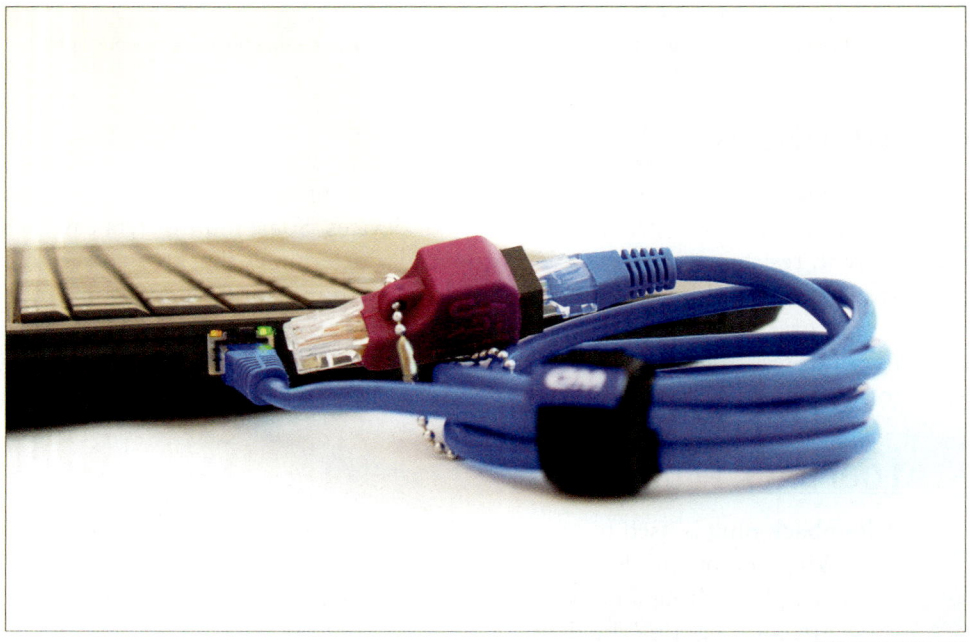

Figure 1-44   A loopback plug testing a network port and network cable

PROPER USE OF CLEANING PADS AND SOLUTIONS

A+ 220-801
5.1, 5.2

As a PC technician, you'll find yourself collecting different cleaning solutions and cleaning pads to clean a variety of devices, including the mouse and keyboard, CDs, DVDs, Blu-ray discs and their drives, tapes and tape drives, and CRT and LCD monitors. Figure 1-45 shows a few of these products. The contact cleaner in the figure is used to clean the contacts on the edge connectors of expansion cards; the cleaning can solve a problem with a faulty connection.

Figure 1-45 Cleaning solutions and pads

Most of these cleaning solutions contain flammable and poisonous materials. Take care when using them so that they don't get on your skin or in your eyes. To find out what to do if you are accidentally exposed to a dangerous solution, look on the instructions printed on the can or check out the material safety data sheet (see Figure 1-46). A **Material Safety Data Sheet (MSDS)** explains how to properly handle substances such as chemical solvents and how to dispose of them.

An MSDS includes information such as physical data, toxicity, health effects, first aid, storage, shipping, disposal, and spill procedures. It comes packaged with the chemical; you can order one from the manufacturer, or you can find one on the Internet (see *www.ilpi.com/msds*).

> **A+ Exam Tip** The A+ 220-801 exam expects you to know how to use MSDS documentation to find out how to dispose of chemicals so as to help protect the environment. You also need to know that you must follow all local government regulations when disposing of chemicals and other materials dangerous to the environment.

Figure 1-46 Each chemical you use should have available a material safety data sheet

If you have an accident with these or other dangerous products, your company or organization might require you to report the accident to your company and/or fill out an accident report. Check with your organization to find out how to handle reporting these types of incidents.

MANAGING CABLES

People can trip over cables or cords left on the floor, so be careful that cables are in a safe place. If you must run a cable across a path or where someone sits, use a cable or cord cover that can be nailed or screwed to the floor. Don't leave loose cables or cords in a traffic area where people can trip over them (called a **trip hazard**).

LIFTING HEAVY OBJECTS

Back injury, caused by lifting heavy objects, is one of the most common injuries that happen at work. Whenever possible, put heavy objects, such as a large laser printer, on a cart to move them. If you do need to lift a heavy object, follow these guidelines to keep from injuring your back:

1. Looking at the object, decide which side of the object to face so that the load is the most balanced.
2. Stand close to the object with your feet apart.
3. Keeping your back straight, bend your knees and grip the load.
4. Lift with your legs, arms, and shoulders, and not with your back or stomach.
5. Keep the load close to your body and avoid twisting your body while you're holding it.
6. To put the object down, keep your back as straight as you can and lower the object by bending your knees.

Don't try to lift an object that is too heavy for you. Because there are no exact guidelines for when heavy is too heavy, use your best judgment as to when to ask for help.

Now that you know about computer parts and their connections, the dangers and ways to protect you and the equipment against electricity, and the tools you need, you're ready to learn how to work inside a computer case. Have fun doing that in the next chapter, but don't forget to practice all the safety skills you learned about in this chapter.

>> CHAPTER SUMMARY

What's Inside the Case

- Video ports a computer might have include the VGA, S-Video, DVI, DisplayPort, and HDMI ports. Other ports include a network, sound, S/PDIF, USB, FireWire, eSATA, and PS/2 ports.
- Internal computer components include the motherboard, processor, expansion cards, DIMM memory modules, hard drive, optical drive, floppy drive, tape drive, and power supply.
- Form factors used by cases, power supplies, and motherboards are the ATX and micro-ATX form factors. The form factor determines how the case, power supply, and motherboard fit together and the cable connectors and other standards used by each.
- Power connectors used by the ATX and mini-ATX form factors include the 20-pin P1, 24-pin P1, 4-pin and 8-pin auxiliary motherboard, 4-pin Molex, 15-pin SATA, 4-pin FDD, 6-pin PCIe, and 8-pin PCIe connectors.
- Standards used by hard drives and other drives to interface with the motherboard and power supply are serial ATA (SATA) and parallel ATA (PATA). The PATA standard is also called the IDE standard.

Protecting Yourself and the Equipment against Electrical Dangers

- Units used to measure electricity include volts, amps, ohms, joules, and watts.
- Microcomputers require direct current (DC), which is converted from alternating current (AC) by the PC's power supply inside the computer case.
- A power supply and CRT monitor contain dangerous charges even when unplugged. PC support technicians consider them to be field replaceable units and you should not need to open one.
- Never use water to put out an electrical fire. Use a Class C fire extinguisher rated for electrical fires.
- Equipment to protect computer components against ESD includes a ground bracelet, ground mat, antistatic bags, and antistatic gloves.

Tools Used by a PC Repair Technician

- Special tools a PC support technician might need include a POST diagnostic card, power supply tester, multimeter, and loopback plugs.
- A Material Safety Data Sheet tells you how to handle chemicals and includes physical data, toxicity, health effects, first aid, storage, shipping, disposal, and spill procedures.
- Be careful to not lift a heavy object in a way you can hurt your back, and make sure cables are not trip hazards.

>> KEY TERMS

For explanations of key terms, see the Glossary near the end of the book.

> **A+ Exam Tip** To help you prepare for the A+ exams, the key terms in each chapter focus on the terms you need to know for the exams. Before you sit for the exams, be sure to review all the key terms in the Glossary.

4-pin motherboard auxiliary connector
8-pin motherboard auxiliary connector
20-pin P1 connector
24-pin P1 connector
alternating current (AC)
amp
antistatic bags
antistatic gloves
antistatic wrist strap
ATX (Advanced Technology Extended)
ATX12V power supply
audio port
Berg power connector
BIOS (basic input/output system)
BIOS setup
central processing unit (CPU)
Class C fire extinguisher
CMOS setup
DB-15 port
desktop case
DIMM (dual inline memory module)
direct current (DC)
DisplayPort
dual voltage selector switch
DVI (Digital Video Interface) port
electrostatic discharge (ESD)
ESD gloves
ESD mat
ESD strap
Ethernet port
expansion card

external SATA (eSATA)
field replaceable unit (FRU)
FireWire port
firmware
floppy disk drive (FDD)
floppy drive
form factors
ground bracelet
ground mat
hard disk drive (HDD)
hard drive
HDMI (High Definition Multimedia Interface) port
heat sink
IEEE1394 port
internal components
inverter
joule
loopback plug
main board
Material Safety Data Sheet (MSDS)
microATX (MATX)
microprocessor
modem port
Molex power connector
motherboard
multimeter
network port
ohm
parallel ATA (PATA)
parallel port
PCI (Peripheral Component Interconnect)
PCI Express (PCIe)
PCIe power connector

POST (power-on self test)
POST card
POST diagnostic card
power supply
power supply tester
power supply unit (PSU)
processor
PS/2 port
RAM (random access memory)
RJ-11
RJ-45
rectifier
S-Video port
S/PDIF (Sony Philips Digital Interface) sound port
SATA power connector
self-grounding
serial ATA (SATA)
serial port
startup BIOS
static electricity
surge suppressor
system BIOS
system board
Thunderbolt
tower case
transformer
trip hazard
USB (Universal Serial Bus) port
VGA (Video Graphics Array) port
video memory
volt
watt

>> REVIEWING THE BASICS

1. Which is faster, a Hi-Speed USB port or a SuperSpeed USB port?
2. What type of output does an S/PDIF port provide?
3. List five types of video ports.

4. What is the purpose of an expansion slot on a motherboard?
5. What should be the setting for a dual-voltage selector switch on a power supply when using the computer in the United States?
6. What unit of measure is used to describe the amount of work a surge suppressor can do before it stops protecting the circuit from an electrical surge?
7. Hot wires in home wiring are normally colored ____, and ground wires in computers are normally colored ____.
8. What is the difference between a transformer and a rectifier? Which are found in a PC power supply?
9. What device can you use to make sure a computer is protected against power surges?
10. A power supply receives 120 volts of ___ power from a wall outlet and converts it to 3.3, 5, and 12 volts of ____ power.
11. Why is a power supply dangerous even after the power is disconnected?
12. Which two tools can a PC support technician use when taking apart a computer to best protect computer components against ESD?
13. What is the purpose of a POST diagnostic card?
14. What are the three purposes accomplished by the motherboard BIOS?
15. How is the best way to determine if a cable inside a computer is a data and instruction cable or a power cable?
16. What technology standard provides for up to four drives installed in a system?
17. How many pins does the P1 connector have that uses the ATX Version 2.2 standard?
18. What device might require extra power so that it uses the 12V 6-pin power connector? In what two locations might you find the connector?
19. What is the purpose of the 4-pin auxiliary connector on a motherboard?
20. What is the purpose of the 4-pin Molex connector?

>> THINKING CRITICALLY

1. You purchase a new computer system that does not have wireless capability, and then you decide that you want to use a wireless connection to the Internet. What are the least expensive ways (pick two) to upgrade your system to wireless?
    a. Trade in the computer for another computer that has wireless installed.
    b. Purchase a second computer that has wireless.
    c. Purchase a wireless expansion card and install it in your system.
    d. Purchase a USB wireless adapter and connect it to your PC by way of a USB port.
2. How much power is consumed by a load drawing 5 A with 120 V across it?
3. When working on a computer, which of the following best protects against ESD? Why?
    a. Always touch the computer case before touching a circuit board inside the case.
    b. Always wear a ground bracelet clipped to the side of the case.

c. Always sit a computer on an antistatic mat when working on it.

d. Always work on a computer in a room without carpet.

4. When troubleshooting a computer hardware problem, which tool might help with each of the following problems?

   a. You suspect the network port on a computer is not functioning.

   b. The system fails at the beginning of the boot and nothing appears on the screen.

   c. A hard drive is not working and you suspect the Molex power connector from the power supply might be the source of the problem.

>> REAL PROBLEMS, REAL SOLUTIONS

REAL PROBLEM 1-1: Planning Your PC Repair Tool Kit

Research on the web to find the following tools for sale: ground bracelet, antistatic gloves, set of flathead and Phillips-head screwdrivers, can of compressed air, monitor cleaning wipes, multimeter, power supply tester, cable ties, flashlight, loopback plug to test an Ethernet port, POST diagnostic card, and toolbox.

Print or save the web page showing each tool and its price. What is the total cost of this set of tools? If you were building your own PC repair tool kit, which tools would you purchase first if you could not afford the entire set of tools? Which tools not listed would you add to your toolbox?

CHAPTER 2

Working Inside a Computer

In this chapter, you will learn:

- How to take a computer apart and put it back together
- About the methods and devices for keeping a system cool
- How to select a power supply to meet the power needs of a system

This chapter and Chapter 1 work together as a pair to show you how to safely work inside a computer. In Chapter 1, you learned about all the safety procedures you should follow when working inside a computer. In this chapter, you apply these skills as you learn how to open a computer case and disassemble and reassemble the components in a desktop computer system. You also learn about the fans, heat sinks, and other devices needed to keep a system cool. Finally, you learn how to select a power supply to meet the wattage needs of a system.

HOW TO WORK INSIDE A COMPUTER CASE

A+ 220-801 1.2, 5.1

In this part of the chapter, you'll learn how to take a computer apart and put it back together. This skill is needed in this and other chapters as you learn to add or replace computer parts inside the case and perhaps even build a system from scratch. As you read the following steps, you might want to perform the Hands-on Projects, which allow you to follow along by taking a computer apart. As you do so, be sure to follow all the safety precautions discussed in Chapter 1.

In the steps that follow, each major computer component is identified and described. You learn much more about each component later in the book. Take your time—*don't rush*—as you take apart a computer for the first time. It can be a great learning experience or an expensive disaster! As you work, pay attention to the details, and work with care.

STEP 1: PLAN AND ORGANIZE YOUR WORK

When you first begin to learn how to work inside a computer case, make it a point to practice good organization skills. If you keep your notes, tools, screws, and computer parts well organized, your work goes smoother and is more fun. Here are some tips to keep in mind:

- Make notes as you work so that you can backtrack later if necessary. (When you're first learning to take a computer apart, it's really easy to forget where everything fits when it's time to put it back together. Also, in troubleshooting, you want to avoid repeating or overlooking things to try.)
- Remove loose jewelry that might get caught in cables and components as you work.
- To stay organized and not lose small parts, keep screws and spacers orderly and in one place, such as a cup or tray.
- Don't stack boards on top of each other: You could accidentally dislodge a chip this way. When you remove a circuit board or drive from a computer, carefully lay it on an antistatic mat or in an antistatic bag in a place where it won't get bumped.
- When handling motherboards, cards, or drives, don't touch the chips on the device. Hold expansion cards by the edges. Don't touch any soldered components on a card, and don't touch the edge connectors unless it's absolutely necessary. All this helps prevent damage from static electricity. Also, your fingerprints on the edge connectors can later cause corrosion.
- To protect a microchip, don't touch it with a magnetized screwdriver.
- Never ever touch the inside of a computer that is turned on. The one exception to this rule is when you're using a multimeter to measure voltage output.
- Consider the monitor and the power supply to be "black boxes." Never remove the cover or put your hands inside this equipment unless you know about the hazards of charged capacitors and have been trained to deal with them. The power supply and monitor contain enough power to kill you, even when they are unplugged.
- As you work, remember to watch out for sharp edges on computer cases that can cut you.
- In a classroom environment, after you have reassembled everything, have your instructor check your work before you put the cover back on and power up.

Now that you've prepared your work area and tools, put on your ground bracelet and let's get started with opening the computer case.

STEP 2: OPEN THE COMPUTER CASE AND EXAMINE THE SYSTEM

A+
220-801
1.2, 5.1

Here are the steps to open a computer case:

1. **Back up important data.** If you are starting with a working computer, make sure important data is first backed up. Copy the data to an external storage device such as a flash drive or external hard drive. If something goes wrong while you're working inside the computer, at least your data will be safe.

2. **Power down the system and unplug it.** Unplug the power, monitor, mouse, and keyboard cables, and any other peripherals or cables attached and move them out of your way.

> **Caution** When you power down a computer and even turn off the power switch on the rear of the computer case, know that residual power is still on. Some motherboards even have a small light inside the case to remind you of this fact and to warn you that power is still getting to the system. Therefore, be sure to always unplug the power cord before opening a case.

3. **Press and hold down the power button for a moment.** After you unplug the computer, press the power button for about three seconds to completely drain the power supply (see Figure 2-1). Sometimes when you do so, you'll hear the fans quickly start and go off as residual power is drained. Only then is it safe to work inside the case.

© Cengage Learning 2014

Figure 2-1 Press the power button after the computer is unplugged

4. **Have a plastic bag or cup handy to hold screws.** When you reassemble the PC, you will need to insert the same screws in the same holes. This is especially important with the hard drive because screws that are too long can puncture the hard drive housing.

A+ 220-801 1.2, 5.1

5. **Open the case cover.** Sometimes I think figuring out how to open a computer case is the most difficult part of disassembling. If you need help figuring it out, check the user manual or web site of the case manufacturer. To remove the computer case cover, do the following:

   ▲ Many newer cases require you to start by laying the case on its side and removing the faceplate on the front of the case first. Other cases require you to remove a side panel first, and really older cases require you to first remove the entire sides and top as a single unit. Study your case for the correct approach.

   ▲ Most cases have panels on each side of the case that can be removed. It is usually necessary to only remove the one panel to expose the top of the motherboard. To know which panel to remove, look at where the ports are on the rear of the case. For example, in Figure 2-2, the ports on this motherboard are on the left side of the case, indicating the bottom of the motherboard is on the left. Therefore, you will want to remove the right panel to expose the top of this motherboard. Lay the case down to its left so that the ports and the motherboard are sitting on the bottom. Later, depending on how drives are installed, it might become necessary to remove the bottom panel in order to remove the screws that hold the drives in place.

Motherboard is mounted to this side of the case

© Cengage Learning 2014

Figure 2-2 Decide which side panel to remove

Locate the screws that hold the side panel in place. Be careful not to unscrew any screws besides these. The other screws probably are holding the power supply, fan, and other components in place (see Figure 2-3). Place the screws in the cup or bag used for that purpose. Some cases use clips on a side panel in addition to or instead of screws (see Figure 2-4).

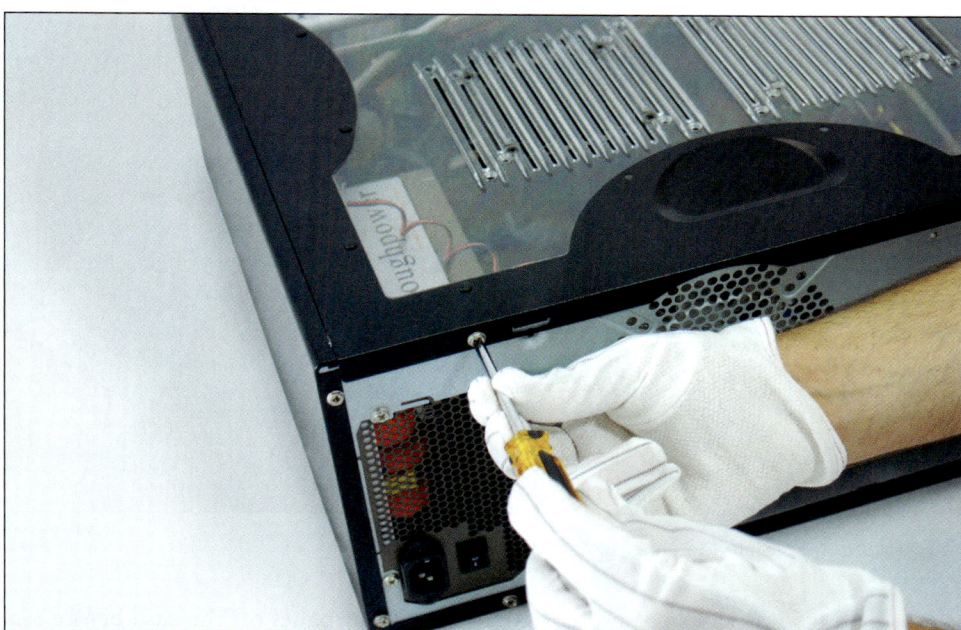

Figure 2-3 Locate the screws that hold the side panel in place

Figure 2-4 On this system, clips hold the side panel in place

▲ After the screws are removed, slide the panel toward the rear, and then lift it off the case (see Figure 2-5).

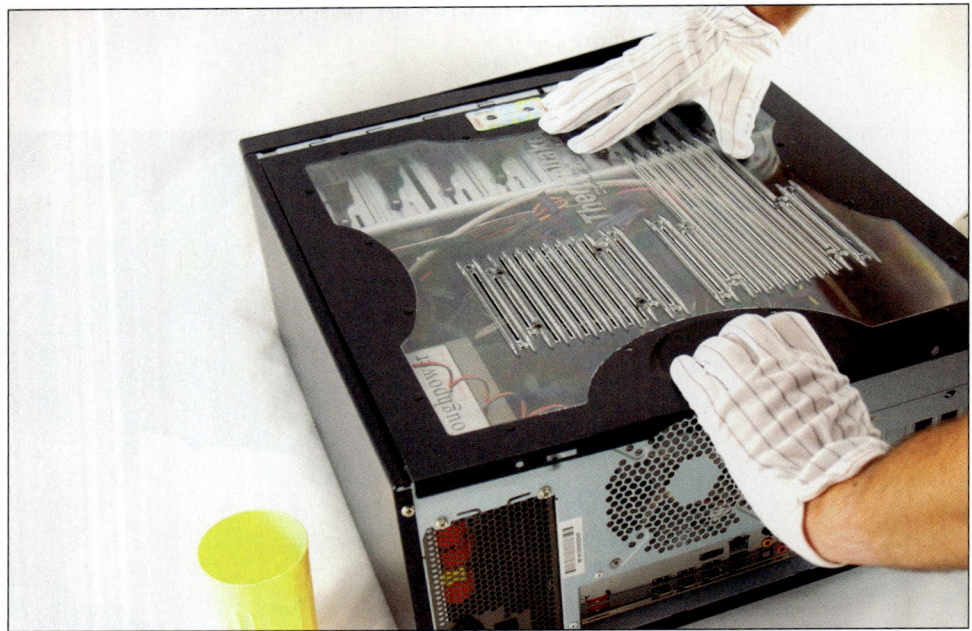

Figure 2-5 Slide the panel to the rear of the case

▲ Some cases require you to pop the front panel off the case before removing the side panels. Look for a lever on the bottom of the panel and hinges at the top. Squeeze the lever to release the front panel and lift it off the case (see Figure 2-6).

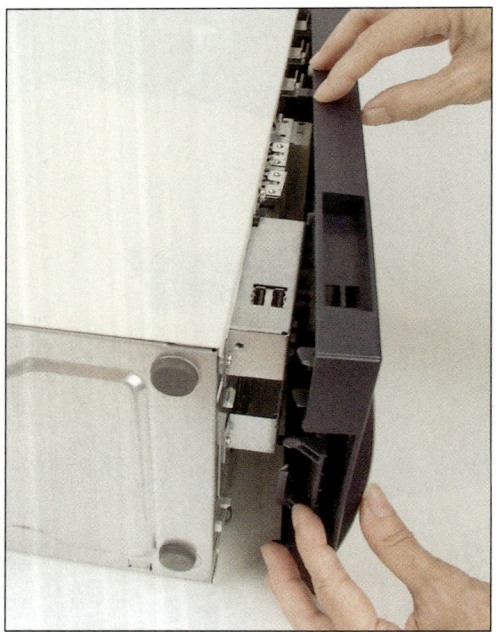

Figure 2-6 Newer cases require you to remove the front panel before removing the side panel of a computer case

Then remove a single screw (see Figure 2-7) and slide the side panel to the front and then off the case (see Figure 2-8).

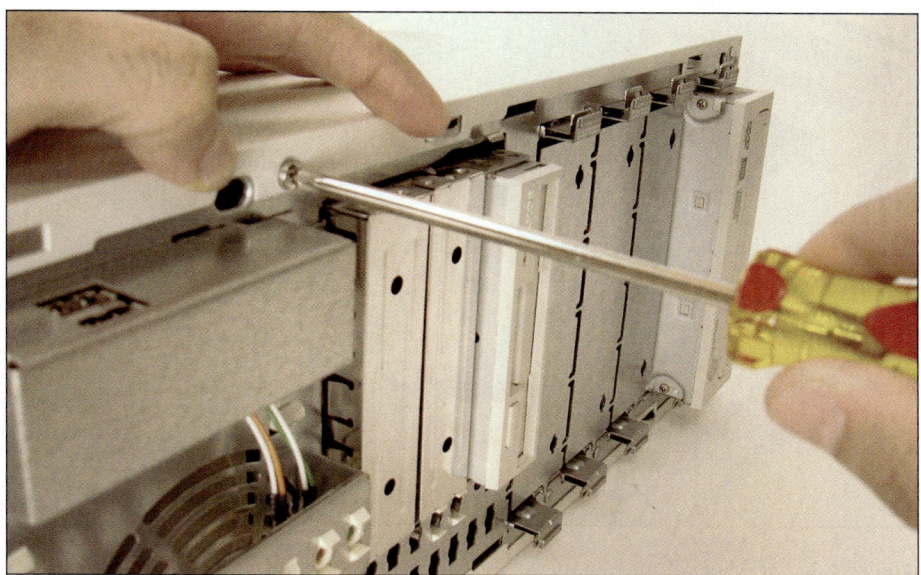

Figure 2-7 One screw holds the side panel in place

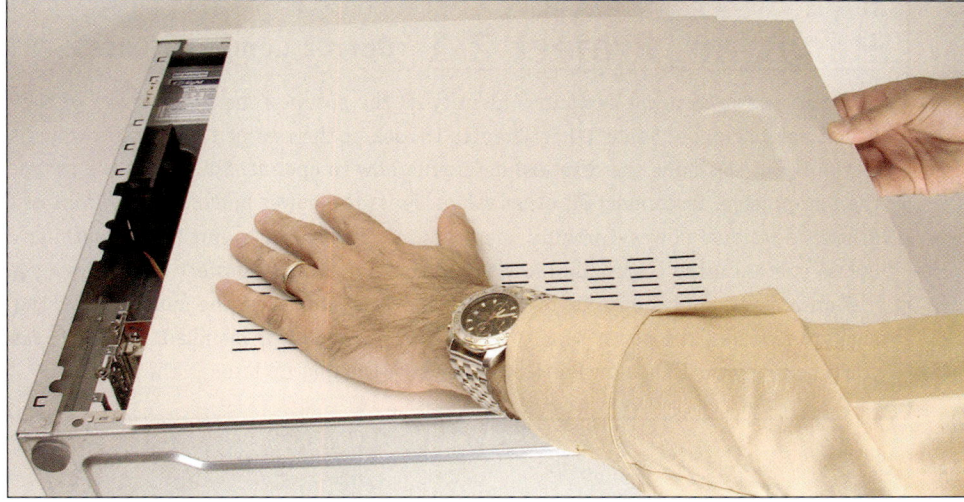

Figure 2-8 Slide the side panel to the front of the case and then lift it off the case

6. **Clip your ground bracelet to the side of the computer case.** To dissipate any charge between you and the computer, put on your ground bracelet if you have not already done so. Then clip the alligator clip on the ground bracelet to the side of the computer case (see Figure 2-9).

After you open a computer case, the main components you see inside are the power supply, motherboard, and drives installed in drive bays. You also see a lot of cables and wires connecting various components. These cables are power cables from the power supply to various components, or cables carrying data and instructions between components. The best way to know the purpose of a cable is to follow the cable from its source to destination.

Figure 2-9 Attach the alligator clip of your ground bracelet to the side of the computer case

Hands-on | Project 2-1 Open a Computer Case

Using a desktop or tower computer, identify all the ports on the front or rear of the case. If you need help, see Table 1-1 in Chapter 1. Look at the rear of the case. On which side is the motherboard? Examine the case and determine how to open it. Shut down the system, and unplug the power cable. Disconnect all other cables. Press the power button on the front of the case to discharge residual power. Carefully open the case. Remember to not touch anything inside the case unless you are using a ground bracelet or antistatic gloves to protect components against ESD.

Draw a diagram of the inside of the case and label all drives, the motherboard, the cooler, DIMM memory modules, the power supply, and any expansion cards installed. Leave the case open so you'll be ready for Hands-on Projects 2-2 and 2-3 coming up later in the chapter.

STEP 3: REMOVE EXPANSION CARDS

If you plan to remove several components, draw a diagram of all cable connections to the motherboard, expansion cards, and drives. You might need the cable connection diagram to help you reassemble. Note where each cable begins and ends, and pay particular attention to the small wires and connectors that connect the lights, switches, and ports on the front of the case to the motherboard. It's important to be careful about diagramming these because it is so easy to connect them in the wrong position later when you reassemble. If you want, use a felt-tip marker to make a mark across components, to indicate a cable connection, board placement, motherboard orientation, speaker connection, brackets, and so on, so that you can simply line up the marks when you reassemble. This method, however, probably won't work for the front case wires because they are so small. For these, consider writing down the color of the wires and their position on the pins (see Figure 2-10).

Figure 2-10 Diagram the pin locations of the color-coded wires that connect to the front of the case

> **Notes** A connector on a motherboard that consists of pins that stick up from the board is called a header. For example, the group of pins shown in Figure 2-10 is called the **front panel header**.

Computer systems vary in so many ways, it's impossible to list the exact order to disassemble one. Most likely, however, you need to remove the expansion cards first. Do the following to remove the expansion cards:

1. Remove any wire or cable connected to the card.
2. Remove the screw holding the card to the case (see Figure 2-11).

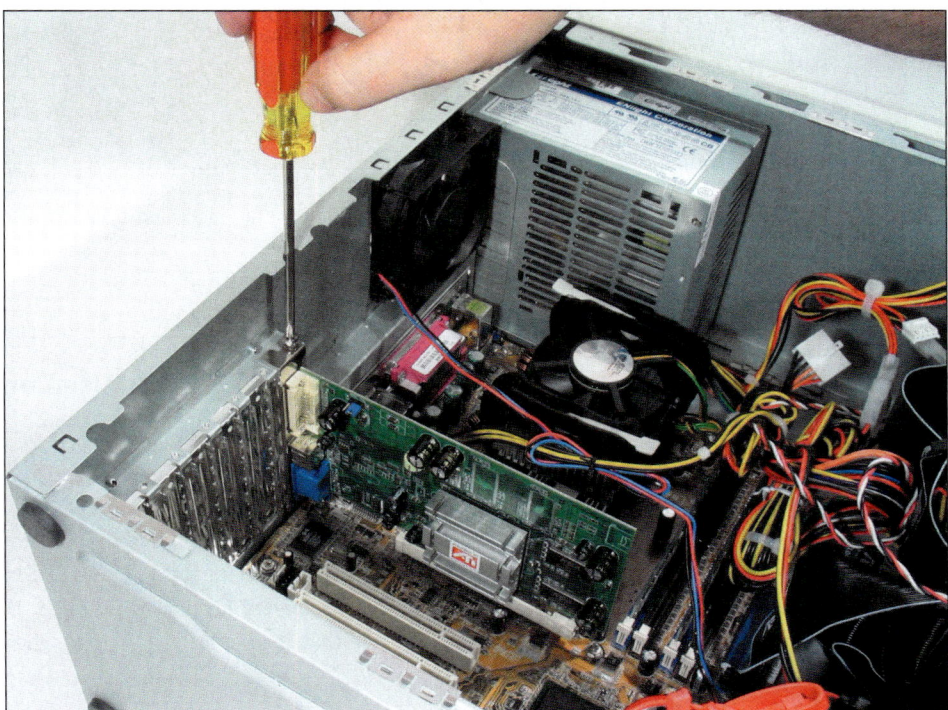

Figure 2-11 Remove the screw holding an expansion card to the case

A+ 220-801 1.2, 5.1

3. Grasp the card with both hands and remove it by lifting straight up. If you have trouble removing it from the expansion slot, you can *very slightly* rock the card from end to end (*not* side to side). Rocking the card from side to side might spread the slot opening and weaken the connection.

4. As you remove the card, don't put your fingers on the edge connectors or touch a chip, and don't stack the cards on top of one another. Lay each card aside on a flat surface, preferably in an antistatic bag.

> **Notes** Some video cards use a latch that helps to hold the card securely in the slot. To remove these cards, use one finger to hold the latch back from the slot, as shown in Figure 2-12, as you pull the card up and out of the slot.

© Cengage Learning 2014

Figure 2-12 Hold the retention mechanism back as you remove a video card from its expansion slot

Hands-on | Project 2-2 Identify Connectors Used on an Installed Motherboard

If necessary, remove the case cover to your desktop computer. Next, remove the expansion cards from your system. With the expansion cards out of the way, you can more clearly see the power cables and other cables and cords connected to the motherboard. Diagrams and notes are extremely useful when disassembling and reassembling a system. To practice this skill, draw a large rectangle that represents the motherboard. On the rectangle, label every header or connector that is used on the board. Include on the label the type of cable that is used and where the other end of the cable connects.

STEP 4: REMOVE THE MOTHERBOARD, POWER SUPPLY, AND DRIVES

A+ 220-801 1.2, 5.1

Depending on the system, you might need to remove the motherboard next or remove the drives next. My choice is to first remove the motherboard. It and the processor are the most expensive and easily damaged parts in the system. I like to get them out of harm's way before working with the drives. However, in some cases, you must remove the drives or the power supply before you can get to the motherboard. Study your situation and decide which to do first. To remove the motherboard, do the following:

1. Unplug the power supply lines to the motherboard. There might also be an audio wire from the optical drive to the motherboard. Disconnect it from the motherboard.

2. Unplug PATA, SATA, and floppy drive cables to the motherboard.

3. The next step is to disconnect wires leading from the front of the computer case to the motherboard, which are called the **front panel connectors**. If you don't have the motherboard manual handy, be very careful to diagram how these wires connect because they are never labeled well on a motherboard. Make a careful diagram and then disconnect the wires. Figure 2-13 shows five leads and the pins on the motherboard front panel header that receive these leads. The pins are color-coded and cryptically labeled on the board.

Figure 2-13 Five leads from the front panel connect to two rows of pins on the motherboard front panel header

4. Disconnect any other cables or wires connected to the motherboard. A case fan might be getting power by a small wire connected to the motherboard. In addition, USB ports on the front of the computer case might be connected by a cable to the motherboard.

5. You're now ready to remove the screws that hold the motherboard to the case. A motherboard is installed so that the bottom of the board does not touch the case. If the fine traces or lines on the bottom of the board were to touch the case, a short

would result when the system is running. To keep the board from touching the case, screw holes are elevated, or you'll see **spacers**, also called **standoffs**, which are round plastic or metal pegs that separate the board from the case. Carefully pop off these spacers and/or remove the screws (up to nine) that hold the board to the case (see Figure 2-14) and then remove the board. Set it aside in a safe place. Figure 2-15 shows a motherboard sitting to the side of these spacers. One spacer is in place and the other is lying beside its case holes. Also notice in the photo the two holes in the motherboard where screws are used to connect the board to the spacers.

Figure 2-14 Remove up to nine screws that hold the motherboard to the case

Figure 2-15 This motherboard connects to a case using screws and spacers that keep the board from touching the case

**A+
220-801
1.2, 5.1**

Notes When you're replacing a motherboard in a case that is not the same size as the original board, you can use needle-nose pliers to unplug a standoff so you can move it to a new hole.

6. The motherboard should now be free and you can carefully remove it from the case, as shown in Figure 2-16.

Figure 2-16 Remove the motherboard from the case © Cengage Learning 2014

Caution Some processors have heavy cooling assemblies installed on top of them. For these systems, it is best to remove the cooler before you take the motherboard out of the case because the motherboard is not designed to support this heavy cooler when the motherboard is not securely seated in the case. How to remove the cooler is covered in Chapter 3.

7. To remove the power supply from the case, look for screws that attach the power supply to the computer case, as shown in Figure 2-17. Be careful not to remove any screws that hold the power supply housing together. You do not want to take the housing apart. After you have removed the screws, the power supply still might not be free. Sometimes, it is attached to the case on the underside by recessed slots. Turn the case over and look on the bottom for these slots. If they are present, determine in which direction you need to slide the power supply to free it from the case.

8. Remove each drive next, handling the drives with care. Here are some tips:

   ▲ Some drives have one or two screws on each side of the drive attaching the drive to the drive bay. After you remove the screws, the drive slides to the front or to the rear and then out of the case.

Figure 2-17   Removing the power supply mounting screws

- Sometimes, there is a catch underneath the drive that you must lift up as you slide the drive forward.
- Some drive bays have a clipping mechanism to hold the drive in the bay. First release the clip and then pull the drive forward and out of the bay (see Figure 2-18). Handle the drives with care. Some drives have an exposed circuit board on the bottom of the drive. Don't touch this board.

Figure 2-18   To remove this CD drive, first pull the clip forward to release the drive from the bay

▲ Some cases have a removable bay for small drives (see Figure 2-19). These bays can hold narrow drives such as hard drives, floppy drives, and tape drives. The bay is removed first and then the drives are removed from the bay. To remove the bay, first remove the screws or release the clip holding the bay in place and then slide the bay out of the case. The drives are usually installed in the bay with two screws on each side of each drive. Remove the screws and then the drives (see Figure 2-20).

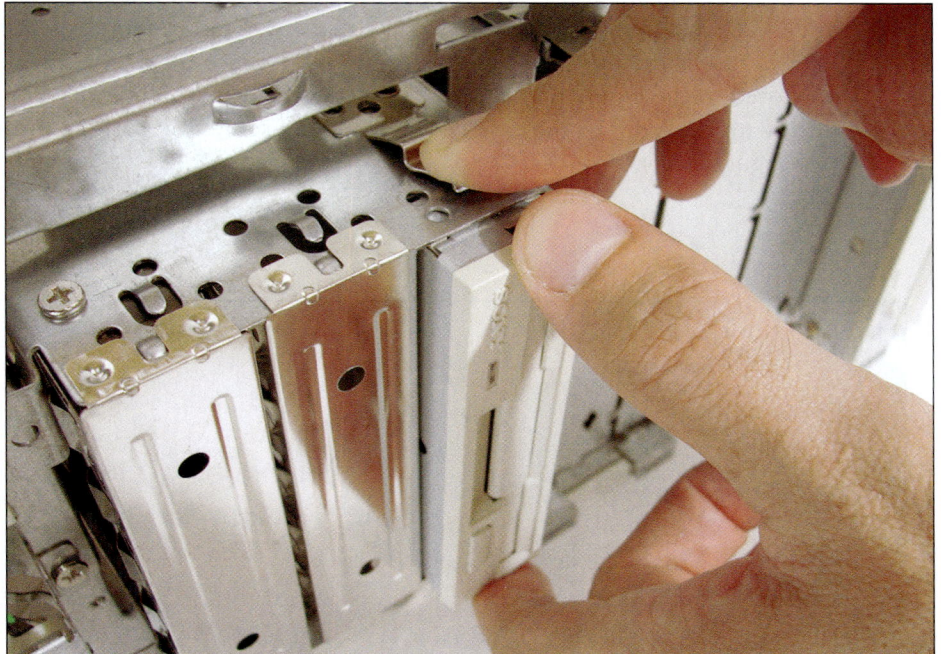

Figure 2-19 Push down on the clip and then slide the removable bay forward and out of the case

Figure 2-20 Drives in this removable bay are held in place with screws on each side of the bay

A+ 220-801 1.2, 5.1

STEPS TO PUT A COMPUTER BACK TOGETHER

To reassemble a computer, reverse the process of disassembling. Here is where your diagrams will be really useful and having the screws and cables organized will also help. In the directions that follow, we're also considering the possibility that you are installing a replacement part as you reassemble the system. Do the following:

1. Install components in the case in this order: power supply, drives, motherboard, and cards. When installing drives, know that for some systems, it's easier to connect data cables to the drives and then slide the drives into the bay. If the drive is anchored to the bay with screws or latches, be careful to align the front of the drive flush with the front of the case before installing screws or pushing in the latches (see Figure 2-21).

Figure 2-21 Align the front of the drive flush with the case front and then anchor with a screw

2. Place the motherboard inside the case. Make sure the ports stick out of the I/O shield at the rear of the case and the screw holes line up with screw holes on the bottom of the case. Figure 2-22 shows how you must align the screw holes on the motherboard with those in the case. There should be at least six screw sets, and there might be as many as nine. Use as many screws as there are holes in the motherboard. Figure 2-23 shows one screw being put in place.

How to Work Inside a Computer Case   61

Figure 2-22 Align screw holes in the case with those on the motherboard

Figure 2-23 Use one screw in each screw hole on the motherboard

3. Connect the power cords from the power supply to the motherboard. A system will always need the main P1 power connector and most likely will need the 4-pin auxiliary connector for the processor. Other power connectors might be needed depending on the devices you later install in the system. Here are the details:

   ▲ Connect the P1 power connector from the power supply to the motherboard (see Figure 2-24).

**A+
220-801
1.2, 5.1**

Figure 2-24 The 24-pin connector supplies power to the motherboard

▲ Connect the 4-pin auxiliary power cord coming from the power supply to the motherboard, as shown in Figure 2-25. This cord supplies the supplemental power required for the processor.

Figure 2-25 The auxiliary 4-pin power cord provides power to the processor

▲ A board might have a 6-pin or 8-pin PCIe power connector (see Figure 2-26). If the board has either connector, connect the 6-pin or 8-pin cord from the power supply to the connector. If a power supply doesn't have this connector, you can use an adapter to convert two Molex connectors to a PCIe connector.

A+
220-801
1.2, 5.1

Figure 2-26 8-pin PCIe Version 2.0 power connector

▲ Some boards designed to support multiple PCIe video cards will have additional power connectors on the board to power these wattage-hungry cards. For example, Figure 2-27(a) shows a Molex-style connector on one board that provides auxiliary power to PCIe graphics cards. This same board offers a SATA-style connector, shown in Figure 2-27(b). The motherboard documentation says to use just one of these auxiliary power connectors to provide additional wattage for PCIe video cards.

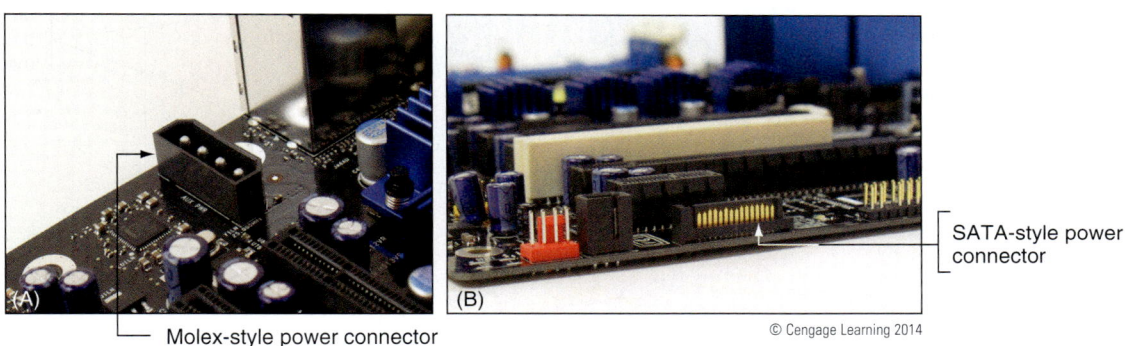

Figure 2-27 Auxiliary power connectors to support PCIe

▲ To power the case fan, connect the power cord from the fan to pins on the motherboard labeled Fan Header. Alternately, some case fans use a 4-pin Molex connector that connects to a power cable coming directly from the power supply.

▲ If a CPU and cooler are already installed on the motherboard, connect the power cord from the CPU fan to the pins on the motherboard labeled CPU Fan Header.

4. Connect the wire leads from the front panel of the case to the front panel header on the motherboard. These are the wires for the switches, lights, and ports on the front of the computer. Because your case and your motherboard might not have been made by the same manufacturer, you need to pay close attention to the source of the wires to determine where they connect on the motherboard. For example, Figure 2-28 shows a computer case that has seven connectors from the front panel that connect to the motherboard. Figure 2-29 shows the front panel header on the motherboard for these lights and switches. If you look closely at the board in Figure 2-29, you can see labels identifying the pins.

Figure 2-28 Seven connectors from the front panel connect to the motherboard

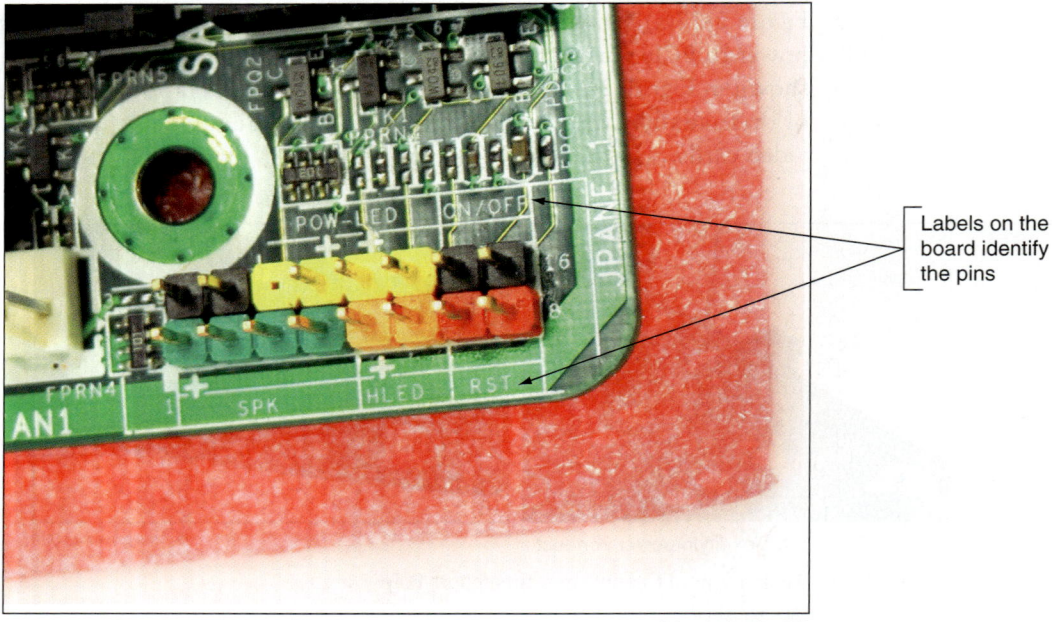

Figure 2-29 Front panel header uses color-coded pins and labels

The five connectors on the right side of Figure 2-28 from right to left are labeled as follows:

▲ *Power SW.* Controls power to the motherboard; must be connected for the PC to power up
▲ *HDD LED.* Controls the drive activity light on the front panel that lights up when any SATA or IDE device is in use (HDD stands for hard disk drive; LED stands for light-emitting diode; and an LED is a light on the front panel.)
▲ *Power LED+.* Positive LED controls the power light and indicates that power is on
▲ *Power LED−.* Negative LED controls the power light; the two positive and negative leads indicate that power is on
▲ *Reset SW.* Switch used to reboot the computer

Notes Positive wires connecting the front panel to the motherboard are usually a solid color, and negative wires are usually white or striped.

To help orient the connector on the motherboard pins, look for a small triangle embedded on the connector that marks one of the outside wires as pin 1 (see Figure 2-30). Look for pin 1 to be labeled on the motherboard as a small 1 embedded to either the right or the left of the group of pins. If the labels on the board are not clear, turn to the motherboard user guide for help. The diagram in Figure 2-31 shows what you can expect from one motherboard user guide. Notice pin 1 is identified as a square pin in the diagram, rather than round like the other pins.

Notes If the user guide is not handy, you can download it from the motherboard manufacturer's web site. Search on the brand and model number of the board, which is imprinted somewhere on the board.

Sometimes the motherboard documentation is not clear, but guessing is okay when connecting a wire to a front panel header connection. If it doesn't work, no harm is done. Figure 2-32 shows all front panel wires in place and the little speaker also connected to the front panel header pins.

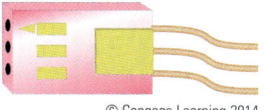

Figure 2-30 Look for the small triangle embedded on the wire lead connectors to orient the connector correctly to the motherboard connector pins

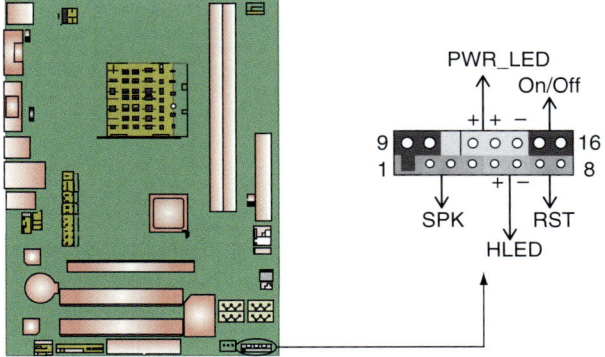

Pin	Assignment	Function	Pin	Assignment	Function
1	+5 V	Speaker connector	9	N/A	N/A
2	N/A		10	N/A	
3	N/A		11	N/A	N/A
4	Speaker		12	Power LED (+)	Power LED
5	HDD LED (+)	Hard drive LED	13	Power LED (+)	
6	HDD LED (−)		14	Power LED (−)	
7	Ground	Reset button	15	Power button	Power-on button
8	Reset control		16	Ground	

Figure 2-31 Documentation for front panel header connections

Figure 2-32 Front panel header with all connectors in place

5. Connect wires to ports on the front panel of the case. Depending on your motherboard and case, there might be cables to connect audio ports or USB ports on the front of the case to headers on the motherboard. Audio and USB connectors are the two left connectors shown in Figure 2-28. You can see these ports for audio and USB on the front of the case in Figure 2-33. Look in the motherboard documentation for the location of these connectors. The audio and USB connectors are labeled for one board in Figures 2-34(a) and (b).

Figure 2-33 Ports on the front of the computer case

Figure 2-34 Connectors for front panel ports

6. Install the video card and any other expansion cards.

7. Take a few minutes to double-check each connection to make sure it is correct and snug. Verify all required power cords are connected correctly and the video card is seated solidly in its slot. Also verify that no wires or cables are obstructing fans. You can use cable ties to tie wires up and out of the way.

8. Plug in the keyboard, monitor, and mouse.

9. In a classroom environment, have the instructor check your work before you close the case and power up.

10. Turn on the power and check that the PC is working properly. If the PC does not work, most likely the problem is a loose connection. Just turn off the power and go back and check each cable connection and each expansion card. You probably have not solidly seated a card in the slot. After you have double-checked, try again.

Now step back and congratulate yourself on a job well done! By taking a computer apart and putting it back together, you've learned much about how computer parts interconnect and work. So now you're ready to move on to study each subsystem or major component in the computer case and how to support it. Let's begin with the pieces and parts used to keep a system from overheating.

COOLING METHODS AND DEVICES

The processor, expansion cards, and other components in the case produce heat, and, if they get overheated, the system can get unstable and components can fail or be damaged. As a PC support technician, you need to know how to keep a system cool. Devices that are used to keep a system cool include CPU fans, case fans, coolers, heat sinks, liquid cooling systems, and dust-preventing tools.

In this part of the chapter, you learn about these several methods to keep the system cool. We begin with keeping the processor cool.

PROCESSOR COOLERS, FANS, AND HEAT SINKS

Because a processor generates so much heat, computer systems use a cooling assembly to keep temperatures below the Intel maximum limit of 185 degrees Fahrenheit/85 degrees Celsius. Good processor coolers maintain a temperature of 90–110 degrees F (32–43 degrees C). The cooler (see Figure 2-35) sits on top of the processor and consists of a fan and a heat sink. A heat sink uses fins that draw heat away from the processor. The fan can then blow the heat away.

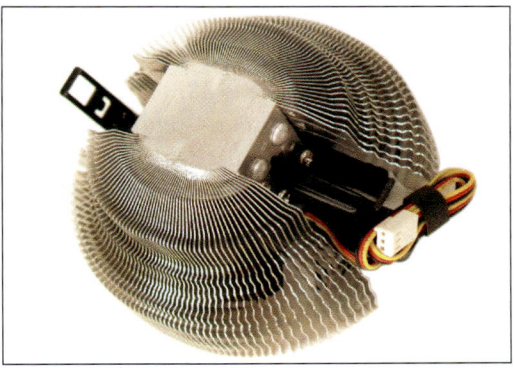

Figure 2-35 A cooler sits on top of a processor to help keep it cool

A+ 220-801 1.6

A cooler is made of aluminum, copper, or a combination of both. Copper is more expensive, but does a better job of conducting heat. For example, the Thermaltake (*www.thermaltake.com*) multisocket cooler shown in Figure 2-36 is made of copper and has an adjustable fan control.

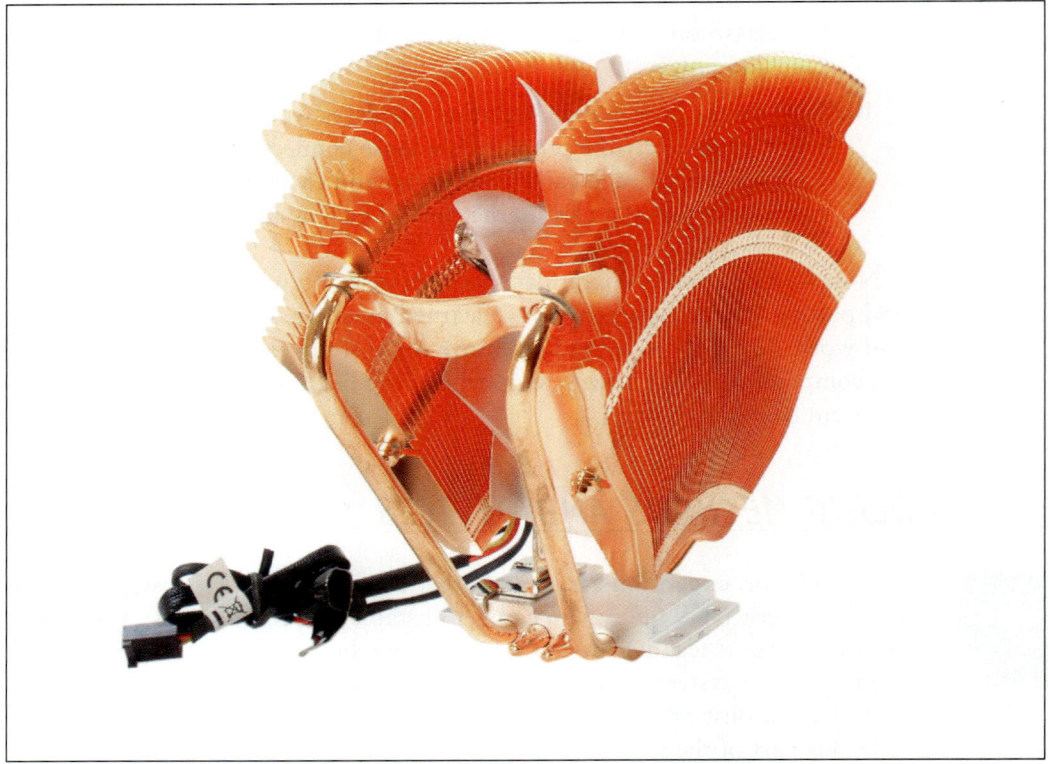

Figure 2-36 The Thermaltake V1 copper cooler fits Intel LGA1366 and LGA775 and AMD AM2 and AM2+ sockets

The cooler is bracketed to the motherboard using a wire or plastic clip. A creamlike **thermal compound** is placed between the bottom of the cooler heatsink and the top of the processor. This compound eliminates air pockets, helping to draw heat off the processor. The thermal compound transmits heat better than air and makes an airtight connection between the fan and the processor. When processors and coolers are boxed together, the cooler heatsink might have thermal compound already stuck to the bottom (see Figure 2-37).

To get its power, the fan power cord connects to a 4-pin fan header on the motherboard (see Figure 2-38). The fan connector will have three or four holes. A three-hole connector can fit onto a 4-pin header; just ignore the last pin. A 4-pin header on the motherboard supports pulse width modulation (PWM) that controls fan speed in order to reduce the overall noise in a system. If you use a fan power cord with three pins, know that the fan will always operate at the same speed. You learn how to install a processor and cooler in the next chapter.

Cooling Methods and Devices

Figure 2-37 Thermal compound is already stuck to the bottom of this cooler that was purchased boxed with the processor

Figure 2-38 A cooler fan gets its power from a 4-pin PWM header on the motherboard

CASE FANS AND OTHER FANS AND HEAT SINKS

To prevent overheating, you can also install additional case fans. Most cases have one or more positions on the case to hold a **case fan** to help draw air out of the case. Figure 2-39 shows holes on the rear of a case designed to hold a case fan.

A computer case might need as many as seven or eight fans mounted inside the case; however, the trend is to use fewer and larger fans. Generally, large fans tend to perform better and run quieter than small fans.

A+
220-801
1.6

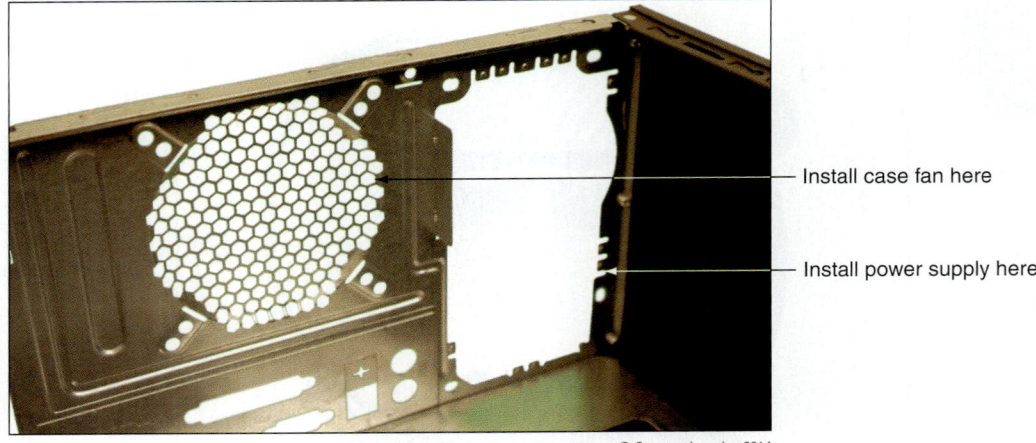

Figure 2-39 Install a case fan on the rear of this case to help keep the system cool

Processors and video cards, also called graphics cards, are the two highest heat producers in a system. Some graphics cards come with a fan on the side of the card. You can also purchase heat sinks and fans to mount on a card to keep it cool. Another solution is to use a fan card mounted next to the graphics card. Figure 2-40 shows a PCI fan card. Be sure you select the fan card that fits the expansion slot you plan to use, and make sure there's enough clearance beside the graphics card for the fan card to fit.

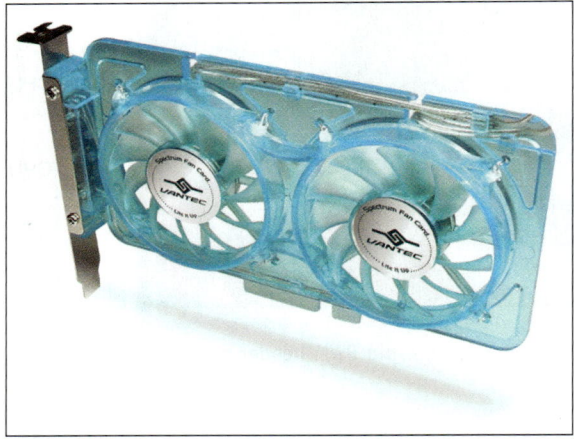

Figure 2-40 A PCI fan card by Vantec can be used next to a high-end graphics card to help keep it cool

For additional cooling, consider a RAM cooler such as the one in Figure 2-41. It clips over a DIMM memory module. A fan might be powered by a SATA power connector or 4-pin Molex power connector. The fan in Figure 2-41 uses a Molex connector. You can use an adapter to convert a SATA or Molex connector to whichever the power supply provides.

When selecting any fan or cooler, take into consideration the added noise level and the ease of installation. Some coolers and fans can use a temperature sensor that controls the fan. Also consider the guarantee made by the cooler or fan manufacturer.

Cooling Methods and Devices

A+ 220-801 1.6

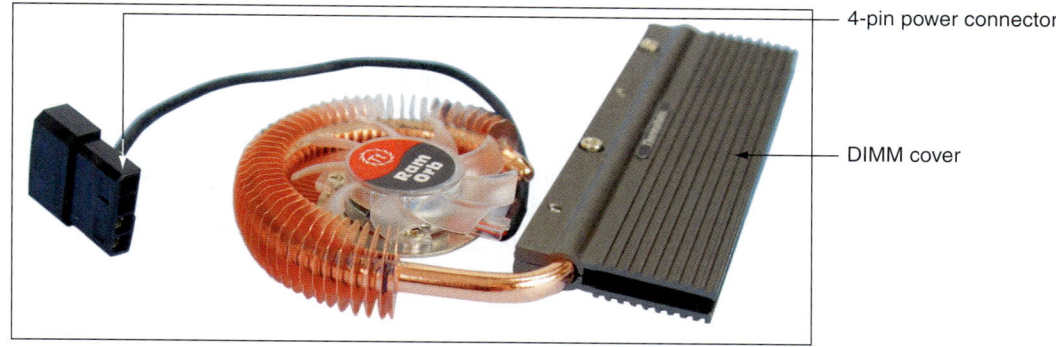

Figure 2-41 A RAM cooler keeps memory modules cool

© Cengage Learning 2014

LIQUID COOLING SYSTEMS

In addition to using fans, heat sinks, and thermal compound to keep a processor cool, a liquid cooling system can be used. For the most part, they are used by hobbyists attempting to overclock to the max a processor in a gaming computer. Recently, however, Intel has recommended using a liquid cooling system with its processors that use the LGA2011 socket on a motherboard. (You learn more about this socket in Chapter 4.) Liquid cooling systems tend to run quieter than other cooling methods. They might include a PCI card that has a power supply, temperature sensor, and processor to control the cooler.

Using liquid cooling, a small pump sits inside the computer case, and tubes move liquid around components and then away from them to a place where fans can cool the liquid, similar to how a car radiator works. Figure 2-42 shows one liquid cooling system where the liquid is cooled by fans sitting inside a large case. Sometimes, however, the liquid is pumped outside the case, where it is cooled.

Courtesy of Thermaltake (USA) Inc.

Figure 2-42 A liquid cooling system pumps liquid outside and away from components where fans can then cool the liquid

A+ 220-801 1.6

DEALING WITH DUST

Dust is not good for a PC because it insulates PC parts like a blanket, which can cause them to overheat. Dust inside fans can jam fans, and fans not working can cause a system to overheat (see Figure 2-43). Therefore, ridding the PC of dust is an important part of keeping a system cool and should be done as part of a regular preventive maintenance plan, at least twice a year. You can blow the dust out of the case using a can of compressed air, or you can vacuum out the dust using a special antistatic vacuum designed to be used around sensitive equipment. Whenever you open a computer case, take a few minutes to rid the inside of dust. And while you're cleaning up dust, don't forget to blow or vacuum out the keyboard.

© Cengage Learning 2014

Figure 2-43 This dust-jammed fan caused a system to overheat

> **Notes** When working in a customer's office or home, be sure you clean up any mess you create from blowing dust out of a computer case.

The motherboard BIOS records the temperatures of the processor and inside the case, and you can read this information on BIOS setup screens, which you learn to do in Chapter 3. In Chapter 8, you learn how to troubleshoot problems with overheating.

Hands-on | Project 2-3   Blow Dust Out of a Case

If necessary, open the case cover to your desktop computer. Using a can of compressed air, blow the dust away from all fans and other components inside the case. Be careful to not touch components unless you are properly grounded. When you're done, close the case cover.

Hands-on Project 2-4 | Identify Airflow Through a Case

Turn on a computer and feel the front and side vents to decide where air is flowing into and out of the case. Identify where you believe fans are working to produce the airflow. Power down the computer, unplug it, and press the power button to completely drain the power. Then open the computer case. Are fans located where you expected? Which fans were producing the strongest airflow through the case when the system was running? In which direction is each case fan drawing air, into the case or out of the case?

SELECTING A POWER SUPPLY

To finish up this chapter about working inside a computer, let's discuss what you need to consider when purchasing a power supply. Reasons you might need to purchase a power supply are when you are building a new system from scratch, a power supply in an existing system fails, or the power supply in an existing system is not adequate for the system.

When building a new system, you can purchase a computer case with the power supply already installed (see Figure 2-44), or you can purchase a power supply separate from the case.

Figure 2-44 This case comes with a power supply, power cord, and bag of screws

A+ 220-801 1.8

Let's now turn our attention to the features of a power supply.

TYPES AND CHARACTERISTICS OF POWER SUPPLIES

As you select the right power supply for a system, you need to be aware of the following power supply features:

- ▲ *ATX or Micro-ATX form factor.* The form factor of a power supply determines the size of the power supply and the placement of screw holes and slots used to anchor the power supply to the case.
- ▲ *Wattage ratings.* A power supply has wattage ratings, which are the amounts of power it can supply. These wattage capacities are listed in the documentation and on the side of a power supply, as shown in Figure 2-45. When selecting a power supply, pay particular attention to the capacity for the +12 V rail. (A rail is the term used to describe each voltage line of the power supply.) The +12 V rail is the most used, especially in high-end gaming systems. Sometimes you need to use a power supply with a higher-than-needed overall wattage to get enough wattage on this one rail. Also, a high-end PSU might have a second +12 V rail.

Figure 2-45 Consider the number and type of power connectors and the wattage ratings of a power supply

- ▲ *Number and type of connectors.* Consider the number and type of power cables and connectors the unit provides. Connector types are shown in Table 1-2 of Chapter 1. Some power supplies include detached power cables that you can plug into connectors on the side of the unit. By using only the power cables you need, extra power cables don't get in the way of airflow inside the computer case.

> **Notes** If a power supply doesn't have the connector you need, it is likely you can buy an adapter to convert one connector to another. For example, Figure 2-46 shows an adapter that converts two Molex cables to one 12 V 6-pin PCIe connector.

- ▲ *Fans inside the PSU.* Every power supply has a fan inside its case; some have two fans. The fan can be mounted on the back or top of the PSU. Fans range in size from 80mm to 150mm wide. The larger the fan, the better job it does and the quieter it runs. Some PSUs can automatically adjust the fan speed based on the internal temperature of the system.

> **Notes** Some power supplies are designed without fans so that they can be used in home theater systems or other areas where quiet operation is a requirement.

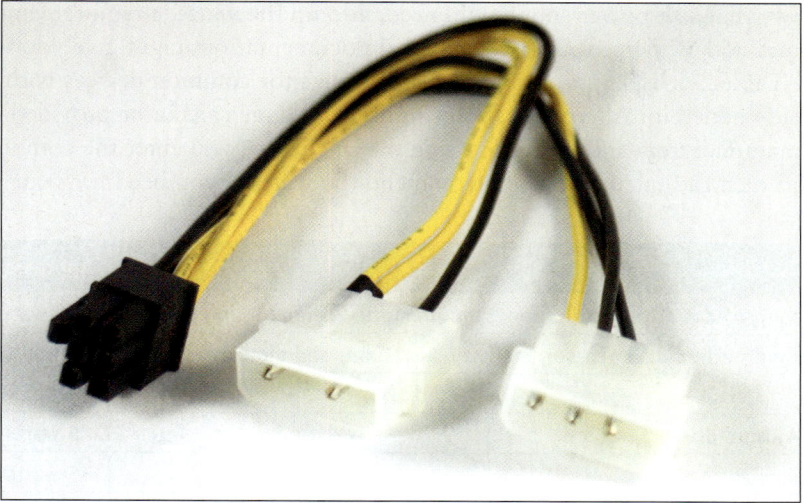

Figure 2-46 This adapter converts two Molex cables to a single 12 V 6-pin PCIe connector

▲ *Extra feature.* Consider the warranty of the power supply and the overall quality. Some power supplies are designed to support two video cards used in a gaming computer. Two technologies used for dual video cards are SLI by NVIDIA and Crossfire by AMD. If you plan to use dual video cards, use a PSU that supports SLI or Crossfire used by the video cards. Know that more expensive power supplies are quieter, last longer, and don't put off as much heat as less expensive ones. Also, expect a good power supply to protect the system against over voltage. Know that a power supply rated with Active PFC runs more efficiently and uses less electricity than other power supplies.

HOW TO CALCULATE WATTAGE CAPACITY

When deciding what wattage capacity you need for the power supply, consider the total wattage requirements of all components inside the case as well as USB and FireWire devices that get their power from ports connected to the motherboard.

> **A+ Exam Tip** The A+ 220-801 exam expects you to know how to select and install a power supply. You need to know how to decide on the wattage, connectors, and form factor of the power supply.

Keep these two points in mind when selecting the correct wattage capacity for a power supply:

▲ *Video cards draw the most power.* Video cards draw the most power in a system, and they draw from the +12 V output. If your system has a video card, pay particular attention to the +12 V rating. The trend nowadays is for the motherboard to provide the video components and video port, thus reducing the overall wattage needs for a system. Video cards are primarily used in gaming computers or other systems that require high-quality graphics.

▲ *The power supply should be rated about 30 percent higher than expected needs.* Power supplies that run at less than peak performance last longer and don't overheat. In addition, a power supply loses some of its capacity over time. Also, don't worry about a higher-rated power supply using too much electricity. Components only draw what they need.

A+ 220-801 1.8

To know what size power supply you need, add up the wattage requirements of all components, and add 30 percent. Device technical documentation might give you the information you need. Table 2-1 lists appropriate wattage ratings for common devices with the 30 percent extra already added in. Alternately, you can use a wattage calculator provided on the web site of many manufacturers and vendors. Using the calculator, you enter the components in your system and then the calculator will recommend the wattage you need for your power supply.

Devices	Approximate Wattage
Moderately priced motherboard, processor, memory, keyboard, and mouse	100 watts
High-end motherboard, processor, memory, keyboard, and mouse	100 to 150 watts
Fan	5 watts
IDE (PATA) hard drive	25 watts
SATA hard drive	35 watts
CD-RW drive or tape drive	25 watts
DVD-RW or Blu-ray drive	35 watts
Low-end PCI video card	40 watts
Moderately priced video card	100 watts
High-end PCIe x16 video card	150–300 watts
PCI card (network card, Firewire card, or other PCI card)	20 watts
PCIe x16 card other than a video card	100 watts
Liquid cooling system (used in high-end gaming computers that put off a lot of heat)	50–150 watts

© Cengage Learning 2014

Table 2-1 To calculate the power supply rating you need, add up total wattage

Notes Some Dell motherboards and power supplies do not use the standard P1 pinouts for ATX, although the power connectors look the same. For this reason, never use a Dell power supply with a non-Dell motherboard, or a Dell motherboard with a non-Dell power supply, without first verifying that the power connector pinouts match; otherwise, you might destroy the power supply, the motherboard, or both. PC Power and Cooling (www.pcpowerandcooling.com) makes power supplies modified to work with a Dell motherboard.

Table 2-2 lists a few case and power supply manufacturers.

Manufacturer	Web Site
Antec	www.antec.com
Cooler Master	www.coolermaster.com
ENlight Corporation	www.enlightcorp.com
PC Power and Cooling	www.pcpowerandcooling.com
Rosewill	www.rosewill.com
Silverstone	www.silverstonetek.com
Sunus Suntek	www.suntekgroup.com
Thermaltake	www.thermaltakeusa.com
Zalman	www.zalman.com

© Cengage Learning 2014

Table 2-2 Manufacturers of cases and power supplies for personal computers

Hands-on Project 2-5 Calculate Wattage Capacity for Your System

A+ 220-801 1.8

Do the following to compare the wattage capacity of the power supply installed in your computer to the recommended value:

1. Search the web for a power supply wattage calculator. Be sure the one you use is provided by a reliable web site. For example, the ones at *newegg.com* and *extreme.outervision.com* are reliable. (At *newegg.com*, click **Computer Hardware** and then click **Power Supply Wattage Calculator**. At *extreme.outervision.com*, click **eXtreme Power Supply Calculator**.)
2. Enter the information about your computer system. Print or save the web page showing the resulting calculations.
3. What is the recommended wattage capacity for a power supply for your system?
4. Look on the printed label on the power supply currently installed in your computer. What is its wattage capacity?
5. If you had to replace the power supply in your system, what wattage capacity would you select?

Hands-on Project 2-6 Shop for a Power Supply

Shop online for a power supply to meet the needs of each of the following systems. Print or save the web page showing the power supply, its features, and its price:

1. A regular desktop system for light computing has a moderately priced motherboard and processor, onboard video, two SATA hard drives, a DVD-RW drive, and two case fans. The system needs a Micro-ATX power supply rated at about 350 watts.
2. A file server has a high-end motherboard and processor, moderately priced PCIe ×16 video card, six SATA hard drives, DVD-RW drive, tape drive, PCI RAID card, and four fans. The system needs an ATX power supply rated at about 550 watts.
3. A gaming system has a high-end motherboard and processor, two high-end video cards using SLI technology, two SATA hard drives, a Blu-ray drive, and four fans. The system needs an ATX power supply rated at about 800 watts. (The two high-end video cards require about 275 watts each.)
4. Suppose the gaming system in Number 3 is generating extra heat because of overclocking and a liquid cooling system has been installed. (**Overclocking** is running a processor, motherboard, or video card at a higher frequency than the manufacturer recommends. Overclocking is not considered a best practice because it can cause a system to overheat, become unstable, or give intermittent errors. It might also void the warranty of a component.) To account for the needs of the liquid cooling system, the power supply needs to be upgraded to 1800 watts.

>> CHAPTER SUMMARY

How to Work Inside a Computer Case

- When a PC support technician is disassembling or reassembling a computer, it is important to stay organized, keep careful notes, and follow all the safety procedures to protect the computer equipment.
- Before opening a computer case, shut down the system, unplug it, disconnect all cables, and press the power button to drain residual power.
- An expansion card fits in a slot on the motherboard and is anchored to the case by a single screw or clip.

Cooling Methods and Devices

- Devices that are used to keep a processor and system cool include CPU coolers and fans, case fans, heat sinks, and liquid cooling. Also, clean out the dust inside a case because dust can cause a system to overheat.
- Liquid cooling systems use liquids pumped through the system to keep it cool and are sometimes used by hobbyists when overclocking a system.

Selecting a Power Supply

- Important features of a power supply to consider when purchasing it are its form factor, wattage capacity, number and type of connectors it provides, fan size, support for dual video cards, and warranty.
- To decide on the wattage capacity of a power supply, add up the wattage requirements for all components in a system and then increase that total by about 30 percent.

>> KEY TERMS

For explanations of key terms, see the Glossary near the end of the book.

case fan	front panel header	spacers
cooler	heat sink	standoffs
front panel connectors	overclocking	thermal compound

>> REVIEWING THE BASICS

1. When taking a computer apart, why is it important to not stack boards on top of each other?
2. Why is it important to remove loose jewelry before working inside a computer case?
3. When assembling a system, which do you install first, the drives or the motherboard?
4. What is the purpose of raised screw holes or standoffs installed between the motherboard and case?

5. When installing the front panel wires to the motherboard front panel header, how do you know which pins to use for each wire if the pins on the header are not labeled?

6. What are the two major components of a processor cooler assembly?

7. How many pins does the CPU fan header on a current motherboard have?

8. If the power connector from the CPU fan has only three pins, it can still connect to the 4-pin header, but what functionality is lost?

9. How do you determine the wattage capacity needed by a power supply?

10. Which one component in a high-end gaming computer is likely to draw the most power?

>> THINKING CRITICALLY

1. You disassemble and reassemble a computer. When you first turn it on, you see no lights and hear no sounds. Nothing appears on the monitor screen. What is the most likely cause of the problem? Explain your answer.

    a. A memory module is not seated properly in a memory slot.

    b. You forgot to plug up the monitor's external power cord.

    c. A wire in the case is obstructing a fan.

    d. Power cords to the motherboard are not connected.

2. How much power is consumed by a load drawing 5 A with 120 V across it?

3. What is a reasonable wattage capacity for a power supply to be used with a system that contains a DVD drive, three hard drives, and a high-end video card?

    a. 250 watts

    b. 1000 watts

    c. 700 watts

    d. 150 watts

4. When overclocking a system, what two problems are most likely to occur?

    a. "Low memory" errors

    b. An unstable system that causes intermittent errors

    c. Loss of hard drive space used by the overclocking virtual memory file

    d. Overheating

>> REAL PROBLEMS, REAL SOLUTIONS

REAL PROBLEM 2-1: Taking a Lab Computer Apart and Putting It Back Together

A PC technician needs to be comfortable with taking apart a computer and putting it back together. In most situations, the essential tools you'll need for the job are a ground bracelet, a Phillips-head screwdriver, a flat-head screwdriver, paper, and pen.

Working with a partner and using a lab computer designated to be disassembled, take a computer apart. It is not necessary to remove the processor or memory modules from the motherboard, but be very careful to properly support the motherboard and processor as you remove them from the case. Then reassemble the system. Don't replace the computer case panel until your instructor has inspected all cable connections. Then turn on the computer and verify all is working.

REAL PROBLEM 2-2: Replacing a Power Supply

Suppose you turn on a system and everything is dead—no lights, nothing on the monitor screen, and no spinning fan or hard drive. You verify the power to the system works, all power connections and power cords are securely connected, and all pertinent switches are turned on. You can assume the power supply has gone bad. It's time to replace it. To prepare for this situation in a real work environment, exchange power supplies with another student in your lab who is using a computer that has a power supply rated at about the same wattage as yours. Then verify that your system starts up and works.

CHAPTER 3
All About Motherboards

In this chapter, you will learn:

- About the different types and features of motherboards
- How to use setup BIOS and physical jumpers to configure a motherboard
- How to maintain a motherboard
- How to select, install, and replace a motherboard

In the last chapter, you learned how to work inside a computer and began the process of learning about each major component or subsystem in a computer case. In this chapter, we build on all that knowledge to learn about motherboards, which techies sometimes call the mobo. You'll learn about the many different features of a motherboard, including motherboard sockets, chipsets, buses, expansion slots, and onboard ports and connectors. Then you'll learn how to support a motherboard, and that includes configuring, maintaining, installing, and replacing it. A motherboard is considered a field replaceable unit, so it's important to know how to replace one, but the good news is you don't need to know how to repair one that is broken. Troubleshooting a motherboard works hand in hand with troubleshooting the processor and other components that must work to boot up a computer, so we'll leave troubleshooting the motherboard until Chapter 8, *Troubleshooting Hardware Problems*.

MOTHERBOARD TYPES AND FEATURES

A+ 220-801 1.2

A motherboard is the most complicated component in a computer. When you put together a computer from parts, generally you start with deciding on which processor and motherboard you will use. Everything else follows these two decisions. Take a look at the details of Figure 3-1, which shows a microATX motherboard by Intel that can hold an Intel Core i7, Core i5, or Core i3 processor in the LGA1155 processor socket. When selecting a motherboard, generally, you'd need to pay attention to the form factor, processor socket, chipset, buses and number of bus slots, and other connectors, slots, and ports. In this part of the chapter, we'll look at the details of each of these features so that you can read a mobo ad with the knowledge of a pro and know how to select the right motherboard when replacing an existing one or when building a new system.

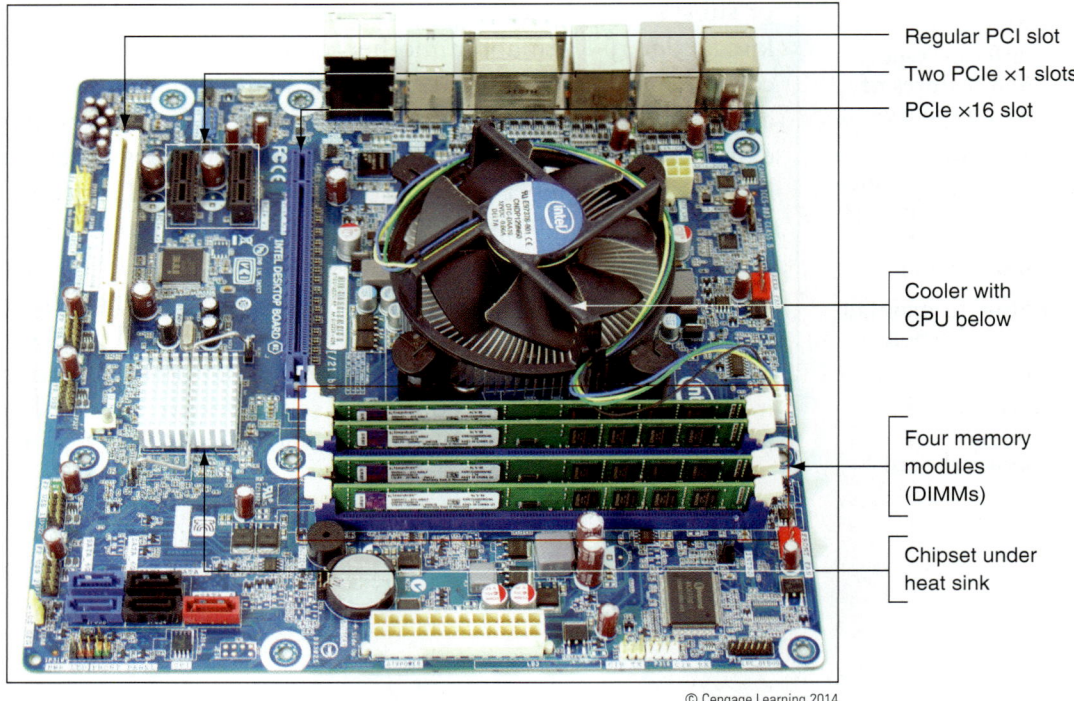

Figure 3-1 The Intel desktop motherboard DH67GD with processor, cooler, and memory modules installed

MOTHERBOARD FORM FACTORS

Recall from Chapter 1 that a motherboard form factor determines the size of the board and its features that make it compatible with power supplies and cases. The most popular motherboard form factors are ATX, microATX (a smaller version of ATX), and Mini-ITX (a smaller version of microATX). You saw a microATX motherboard in Figure 3-1. Figure 3-2 shows an ATX board, and a Mini-ITX board is shown in Figure 3-3. Also know that the Mini-ITX board is commonly referred to as an ITX board.

Table 3-1 lists the popular and not-so-popular form factors used by motherboards, and Figure 3-4 shows a comparison of the sizes and hole positions of the ATX, microATX, and Mini-ITX boards. Each of these three boards can fit into an ATX computer case and use an ATX power supply.

Motherboard Types and Features

Figure 3-2 Intel DX58SO motherboard is designed with the gamer in mind

Figure 3-3 A Mini-ITX motherboard

Form Factor	Motherboard Size	Description
ATX, full size	Up to 12" x 9.6" (305mm × 244mm)	This popular form factor has had many revisions and variations.
MicroATX	Up to 9.6" x 9.6" (244mm × 244mm)	Smaller version of ATX.
Mini-ITX (a.k.a. ITX)	Up to 6.7" x 6.7" (170mm x 170mm)	Small form factor used in low-end computers and home theater systems. The boards are often used with an Intel Atom processor and are sometimes purchased as a motherboard-processor combo unit.
FlexATX	Up to 9" x 7.5"	Smaller version of MicroATX.
BTX	Up to 12.8" wide	The BTX boards can have up to seven expansion slots, are designed for improved airflow, and can use an ATX power supply.

Table 3-1 Motherboard form factors (continues)

Form Factor	Motherboard Size	Description
MicroBTX	Up to 10.4" wide	Smaller version of BTX and can have up to four expansion slots.
PicoBTX	Up to 8" wide	Smaller than MicroBTX and can have up to two expansion slots.
NLX	Up to 9" x 13.6"	Used in low-end systems with a riser card.

Table 3-1 Motherboard form factors (continued)

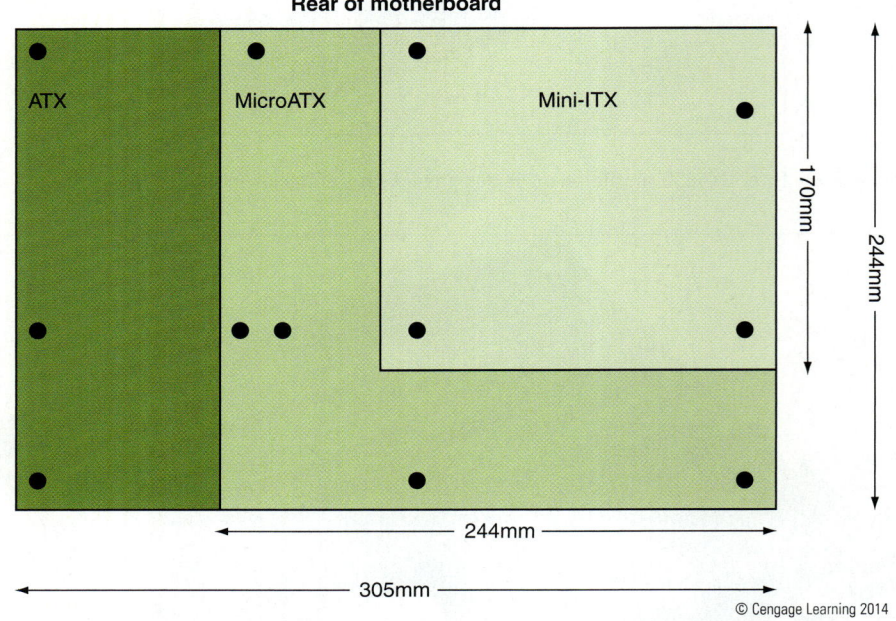

Figure 3-4 Sizes and hole positions for the ATX, microATX, and Mini-ITX motherboards

> **A+ Exam Tip** The A+ 220-801 exam expects you to know about the ATX, MicroATX, and ITX motherboard form factors.

PROCESSOR SOCKETS

Another important feature of a motherboard is the processor socket. This socket and the chipset determine which processors a board can support. A socket for a personal computer is designed to hold either an Intel processor or an AMD processor. Some older processors were installed on the motherboard in a long narrow slot, but all processors sold today use sockets. Now let's look at sockets for Intel and AMD processors.

SOCKETS FOR INTEL PROCESSORS

Table 3-2 lists the sockets used by Intel processors for desktop systems. The first two sockets are currently used by new Intel processors. The last six sockets in the table have been discontinued by Intel, but you still need to be able to support them because you might be called on to replace a processor or motherboard using one of these legacy sockets. The types of memory listed in the table that are used with these sockets are explained in detail in Chapter 4. Also know that Intel makes several Itanium and Xeon processors designed for servers. These server processors might use different sockets than those listed in the table. Mobile processor sockets are also not included in the table.

A+ 220-801
1.2, 1.6

Intel Socket Names	Used by Processor Family	Description
LGA2011	Second Generation (Sandy Bridge) Core i7 Extreme, Core i7, Core i5, Core i3, Pentium, and Celeron	▲ 2011 pins in the socket touch 2011 lands on the processor, which uses a flip-chip land grid array (FCLGA). ▲ Used in high-end gaming and server computers and might require a liquid cooling system.
LGA1155 and FCLGA1155	Third Generation (Ivy Bridge) Core i7, Core i5 Second Generation (Sandy Bridge) Core i7 Extreme, Core i7, Core i5, Core i3, Pentium, and Celeron	▲ 1155 pins in the socket touch 1155 lands on the processor. ▲ The LGA1155 is currently the most popular Intel socket and is shown in Figure 3-5. ▲ Works with DDR3 memory and was designed to replace the LGA1156 socket.
LGA1156 or Socket H or H1	Core i7, Core i5, Core i3, Pentium, and Celeron	▲ 1156 pins in the socket touch 1156 lands on the processor, which uses a flip-chip land grid array (FCLGA). ▲ Works with DDR3 memory.
LGA1366 or Socket B	Core i7, Core i7 Extreme	▲ 1366 pins in the socket touch 1366 lands on the processor. ▲ Works with DDR3 memory.
LGA771 or Socket J	Core 2 Extreme	▲ 771 pins in the socket touch 771 lands on the processor. ▲ Used on high-end workstations and low-end servers. ▲ Works with DDR2 memory on boards that have two processor sockets.
LGA775 or Socket T	Core 2 Extreme, Core 2 Quad, Core 2 Duo, Pentium Dual-Core, Pentium Extreme Edition, Pentium D, Pentium Pentium 4, and Celeron	▲ 775 pins in the socket touch 775 lands on the processor. ▲ Works with DDR3 and DDR2 memory.
Socket 478	Pentium 4, Celeron	▲ 478 holes in the socket are used by 478 pins on the processor. ▲ Uses a dense micro Pin Grid Array (mPGA).
Socket 423	Pentium 4	▲ 423 holes in the socket are used by 423 pins on the processor. ▲ 39 x 39 SPGA grid.

© Cengage Learning 2014

Table 3-2 Sockets for Intel processors used for desktop computers

> **A+ Exam Tip** The A+ 220-801 exam expects you to know about Intel LGA sockets, including the 775, 1155, 1156, and 1366 LGA sockets.

Figure 3-5 The LGA1155 socket is used by a variety of Intel processors

Sockets and processors use different methods to make the contacts between them. Here is a list of the more important methods:

- A **pin grid array (PGA)** socket has holes aligned in uniform rows around the socket to receive the pins on the bottom of the processor. Early Intel processors used PGA sockets, but they caused problems because the small delicate pins on the processor were easily bent as the processor was installed in the socket. Some newer Intel mobile processors, including the Second Generation Core i3, Core i5, and Core i7 processors use the PGA988 socket or the FCPGA988 socket in laptops.
- A **land grid array (LGA)** socket has blunt protruding pins on the socket that connect with lands or pads on the bottom of the processor. The first LGA socket was the LGA775 socket. It has 775 pins and is shown with the socket lever and top open in Figure 3-6. Another LGA socket is the LGA1366 shown in Figure 3-7. LGA sockets generally give better contacts than PGA sockets, and the processor doesn't have the delicate pins so easily damaged during an installation. You learn how to use both sockets in Chapter 4.

Figure 3-6 Socket LGA775 is the first Intel socket to use lands rather than pins

Figure 3-7 The LGA1366 socket with socket cover removed and load level lifted ready to receive a processor

Notes Figure 3-8 shows a close-up photo of the LGA775 socket and the bottom of a Pentium processor. Can you make out the pads or lands on the processor and the pins in the socket?

Figure 3-8 Socket LGA775 and the bottom of a Pentium processor

▲ Some sockets can handle a processor using a **flip-chip land grid array (FCLGA)** processor package or a **flip chip pin grid array (FCPGA)** package. The chip is flipped over so that the top of the chip is on the bottom and makes contact with the socket. The LGA1155 socket has a flip chip version, which is called the FCLGA1155 socket. The two sockets are not compatible.

▲ A **staggered pin grid array (SPGA)** socket has pins staggered over the socket to squeeze more pins into a small space.

▲ A **ball grid array (BGA)** connection is not really a socket. The processor is soldered to the motherboard, and the two are always purchased as a unit. For example, the little Atom processors often use this technology with a Mini-ITX motherboard in low-end computers or home theater systems.

When a processor is installed in a socket, extreme care must be taken to protect the socket and the processor against ESD and from damage caused by bending the pins or scratching the socket holes during the installation. Take care to not touch the bottom of the processor or the pins or holes of the socket, which can leave finger oil on the gold plating of the contact surfaces. This oil can later cause tarnishing and lead to a poor contact. So that even force is applied when inserting the processor in the socket, all current processor sockets have one or two levers on the sides of the socket. These sockets are called **zero insertion force (ZIF) sockets**, and this lever is used to lift the processor up and out of the socket. Push the levers down and the processor moves into its pin or hole connectors with equal force over the entire housing. Because the socket and processor are so delicate, know that processors generally should not be removed or replaced repeatedly.

SOCKETS FOR AMD PROCESSORS

Table 3-3 lists the AMD sockets for desktop systems. AMD has chosen to use the PGA socket architecture for its desktop processors. (Some of AMD's server processors use Socket F, which is an LGA socket.) Figure 3-9 shows the AM2+ socket. The lever on the

AMD Socket	Used by Processor Family	Description
FM2	Used with the Trinity line of AMD processors	▲ 904 holes for pins (PGA) ▲ Uses AMD Piledriver architecture with integrated graphics controller in the processor ▲ Works with DDR3 memory ▲ Soon to be released
FM1	AMD A4, A6, A8, E2, Athlon II	▲ 905 holes for pins (PGA) ▲ Works with DDR3 memory
AM3+	AMD FX	▲ 942 holes for pins (PGA) ▲ Uses Bulldozer architecture and is compatible with AM3 processors ▲ Works with DDR3 memory
AM3 or AMD3	Phenom II	▲ 941 holes for pins (PGA) ▲ Works with DDR3 or DDR2 memory
AM2+ or AMD2+	Phenom II, Phenom, and Athlon	▲ Works with DDR2 memory ▲ 940 holes for pins (PGA) ▲ Faster than AMD2
Socket F (1207) or F	Opteron, Athlon 64 FX	▲ 1207 pins for lands on the bottom of the processor ▲ Used with servers and high-end workstations
AM2, AMD2, or M2	Athlon 64, Athlon, Phenom, Sempron, Second Generation Opteron	▲ 940 holes for pins (PGA) ▲ Works with DDR2 memory
Socket 940	Athlon	▲ 940 holes for pins (PGA) ▲ Works with DDR memory
Socket 939	Athlon and Sempron	▲ 939 holes for pins (PGA) ▲ Works with DDR memory
Socket 754	Athlon and Sempron	▲ 754 holes for pins (PGA) ▲ Works with DDR memory
Socket A	Athlon, Sempron, and Duron	▲ 462 holes for pins (PGA) ▲ Works with DDR memory

Table 3-3 Sockets for AMD processors used for desktop computers

side of the socket is lifted, and an Athlon 64 processor is about to be inserted. If you look closely near the lower edge of the processor, you can see the small delicate pins that will seat into the holes of the socket.

Figure 3-9 AMD Athlon 64 processor to be inserted into an AM2+ socket

> **A+ Exam Tip** The A+ 220-801 exam expects you to know about these AMD sockets: 940, AM2, AM2+, AM3, AM3+, FM1, and F.

MATCH A PROCESSOR TO THE SOCKET AND MOTHERBOARD

As you glance over Tables 3-2 and 3-3, you'll notice the same processor family listed under several different sockets. For example, the AMD Athlon family of processors offers many versions of the Athlon. Among these are the Athlon X2 Dual-Core, the Athlon Neo, and the Athlon 64 X2 Dual-Core. Because these various processors within the same processor family use different sockets, you must be careful when matching a processor to a motherboard. To be certain you have a good match, search the Intel (*www.intel.com*) or AMD (*www.amd.com*) web site for the exact processor you are buying and make sure the socket it uses is the same as the socket on the motherboard you plan to use.

Also, look at the motherboard documentation for a list of processors that the motherboard supports. It is not likely to support every processor that uses its socket because the motherboard chipset is designed to work only with certain processors.

> **A+ Exam Tip** The A+ 220-801 exam expects you to be familiar with the desktop processor sockets in use today. You also need to know about notebook processor sockets, which are covered in Chapter 11.

THE CHIPSET

A **chipset** is a set of chips on the motherboard that works closely with the processor to collectively control the memory, buses on the motherboard, and some peripherals. The chipset must be compatible with the processor it serves. The major chipset manufacturers are Intel (*www.intel.com*), AMD (*www.amd.com*), NVIDIA (*www.nvidia.com*), SiS (*www.sis.com*), and VIA (*www.via.com.tw*).

Intel dominates the chipset market for several reasons: It knows more about its own Intel processors than other manufacturers do, and it produces the chipsets most compatible with the Intel family of processors.

INTEL CHIPSETS

Intel has produced far too many chipsets to list them here. To see a complete comparison chart of all Intel chipsets, start at the Intel link *ark.intel.com*.

Here is a list of the more significant chipset families by Intel:

▲ **North Bridge and South Bridge use a hub architecture.** Beginning with the release in 2006 of the Intel i800 series of chipsets, a hub using the Accelerated Hub Architecture is used to connect buses (see Figure 3-10). This hub has a fast and slow end, and each end is a separate chip on the motherboard. The fast end of the hub, called the **North Bridge**, contains the graphics and memory controller, and connects directly to the processor by way of a 64-bit bus, called the **Front Side Bus (FSB)**, **system bus**, or host bus. The slower end of the hub, called the **South Bridge**, contains the I/O controller hub (ICH). All I/O (input/output) devices, except video, connect to the hub by using the slower South Bridge. Notice that in Figure 3-10, the primary PCI Express slot, the

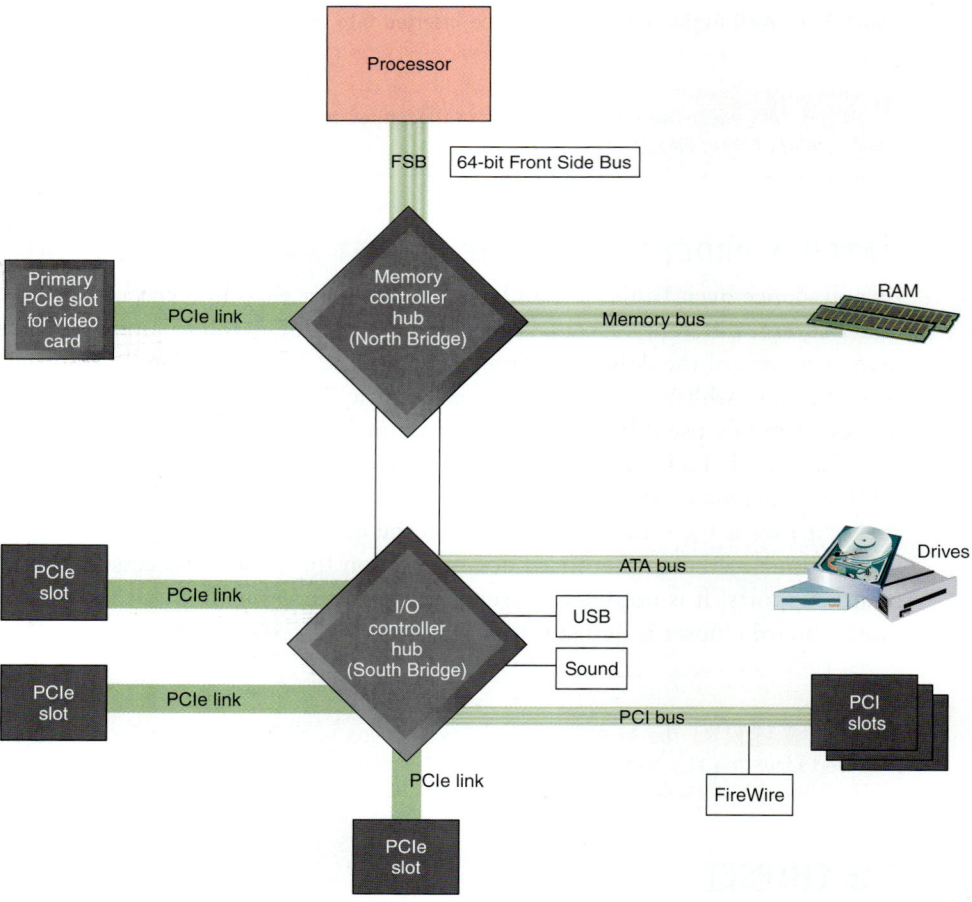

Figure 3-10 The chipset's North Bridge and South Bridge control access to the processor for all components

slot designated for the video card, has direct access to the North Bridge, but other PCI Express slots must access the processor by way of the slower South Bridge. On a motherboard, when you see two major chip housings for the chipset, one is controlling the North Bridge and the other is controlling the South Bridge (refer to Figure 3-2). Other chipset manufacturers besides Intel also use the North Bridge and South Bridge architecture for their chipsets.

▲ **Nehalem chipsets with the memory controller in the processor.** The release of the X58 chipset in 2008 was significant because, with previous chipsets, the memory controller was part of the North Bridge. But beginning with the X58, the memory controller was contained in the processor housing. For example, in Figure 3-11, the Core i7 processor contains the memory controller. Notice that memory connects directly to the processor rather than to the North Bridge. Another significant change is the 64-bit Front Side Bus was replaced with a technology called the **QuickPath Interconnect (QPI)**. The QPI has 16 lanes for data packets and works similar to how PCI Express works. All Intel chipsets since the X58 use QuickPath Interconnects. A motherboard using the X58 chipset is shown in Figure 3-12. The board comes with a fan that can be clipped to the top of the North Bridge to help keep the chipset cool.

Nehalem chipsets, which Intel has begun to call the previous generation of chipsets, support the Intel LGA1366 socket, the Core i7 processors, and PCI Express Version 2. They can also support either SLI or CrossFire technologies. (SLI and CrossFire are two competing technologies that allow for multiple video cards installed in one system.)

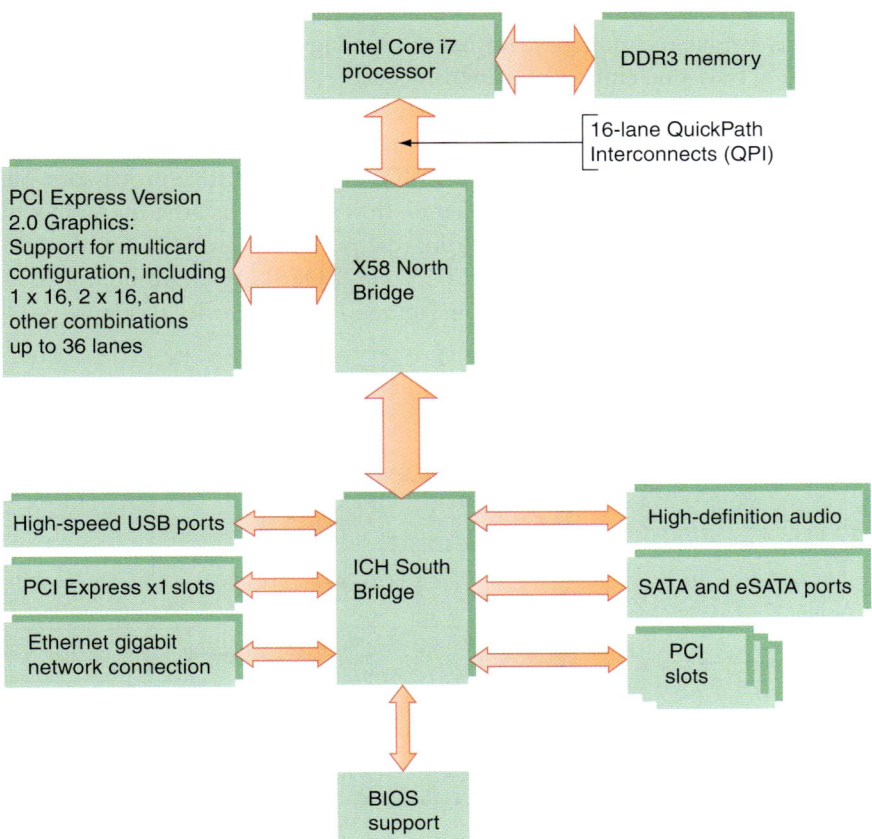

Figure 3-11 X58 chipset architecture

Figure 3-12 The X58 chipset uses heat sinks to stay cool

> **Notes** For an interesting white paper by Intel on QuickPath Interconnect, including a brief history of processor interfaces, go to *www.intel.com* and search on "An Introduction to the Intel QuickPath Interconnect."

▲ *Sandy Bridge chipsets with the memory and graphics controller in the processor.* In 2011, Intel introduced its second-generation chipsets and sockets, which it code-named Sandy Bridge technologies. Rather than using the traditional North Bridge and South Bridge, only one chipset housing is needed, which houses the Platform Controller Hub. The processor interfaces directly with the faster graphics PCI Express 2.0 bus as well as with memory (see Figure 3-13). Therefore, both the memory controller and graphics controller are contained within all Sandy Bridge processors. Sandy Bridge processors, such as the Second Generation Core i7, use the LGA1155 or the LGA2011 socket, and Sandy Bridge motherboards use DDR3 memory. Sandy Bridge chipsets for desktop computers include X79, P67, H67, Q65, Q67, and B65. The H67 chipset on an Intel motherboard is shown in Figure 3-14 and earlier in Figure 3-1.

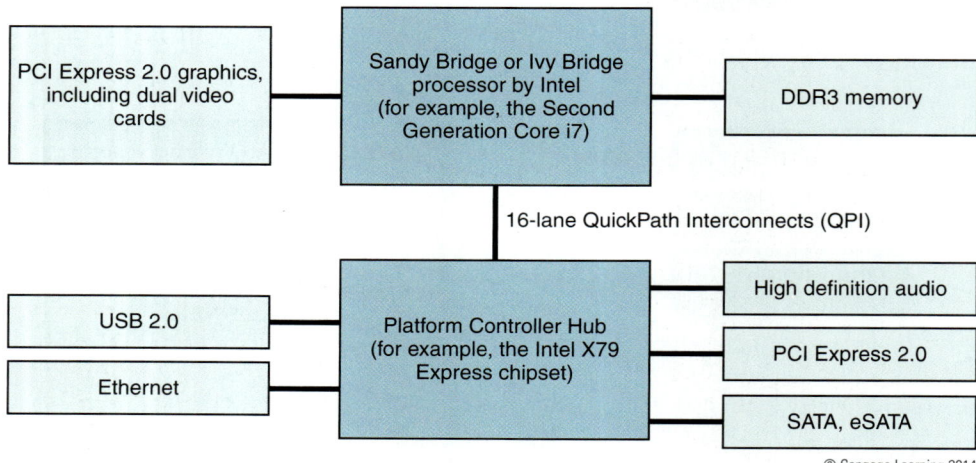

Figure 3-13 The Sandy Bridge architecture uses a single chipset hub, called the Platform Controller Hub

Figure 3-14 The Sandy Bridge H67 chipset on the Intel DH67GD motherboard sits under a heat sink to keep it cool

© Cengage Learning 2014

- *Ivy Bridge chipsets.* Third-generation processors and chipsets by Intel, released in 2012 and codenamed Ivy Bridge, use less power, squeeze more transistors into a smaller space, and perform better than earlier products. Ivy Bridge chipsets include B75, Q75, Q77, H77, Z75, and Z77. Several Ivy Bridge processors use the LGA1155 socket for backward compatibility with earlier motherboards. The Ivy Bridge chipset uses a single Platform Controller Hub.

AMD CHIPSETS

AMD purchased ATI Technologies, a maker of chipsets and graphics processors (called a graphics processor unit or GPU), in 2006, which increased AMD chipset and GPU offerings. Significant chipsets by AMD include the following:

- The AMD A-series chipsets (code named Trinity) are designed to compete with Ivy Bridge chipsets in the light notebook market.
- The AMD 9-series chipset supports AMD CrossFireX technologies.
- The AMD 9-series, 8-series, and 7-series chipsets are designed with the gamer, hobbyist, and multimedia enthusiast in mind. They focus on good graphics capabilities and support overclocking. The 9-series is the most current and supports 8-core AMD processors.
- The AMD 580X Crossfire chipset supports ATI CrossFire.
- The AMD 780V chipset is designed for business needs.
- The AMD 740G and 690 chipsets are designed for low-end, inexpensive systems.

NVIDIA, SIS, AND VIA CHIPSETS

NVIDIA, SiS, and VIA all make graphics processors and chipsets for both AMD and Intel processors. Recall that NVIDIA's method of connecting multiple video cards in the same system is called SLI. If you're planning a gaming computer with two video cards, check out a motherboard that supports SLI and uses the nForce chipset. In motherboard ads, look for the SLI and nForce logos.

Hands-on Project 3-1 Identify the Intel Chipset and Processor on Your Computer

Intel offers two utilities you can download and run to identify an installed Intel processor or chipset. If you are using a computer with an Intel processor, download and run the two utilities:

▲ The URL to the Processor Identification Utility is *www.intel.com/p/en_US/support/highlights/processors/toolspiu/*.

▲ The URL to the Chipset Identification Utility is *www.intel.com/support/chipsets/sb/CS-009266.htm*.

Web sites change often, so if these links don't work, try searching the Intel web site for each utility. What information does each utility provide about your processor and chipset?

Hands-on Project 3-2 Research the Intel ARK Database

Intel provides an extensive database of all its processors, chipsets, motherboards, and other products at *ark.intel.com*. Research the database and answer these questions:

1. List four Third Generation Core i7 processors. For each processor, list the Processor Number, the maximum memory it supports, and the socket it uses.

2. List three Intel motherboards: An ATX board, a microATX board, and a Mini-ITX board. For each motherboard, list the processor socket it provides, the chipset it uses, the maximum memory it supports, and the number of PCIe slots it has.

3. What are the launch dates for these chipsets: Q35 Express, Z77 Express, and B75 Express?

4. What is the latest chipset released by Intel? List five processors that can use this chipset.

BUSES AND EXPANSION SLOTS

When you look carefully at a motherboard, you see many fine lines on both the top and the bottom of the board's surface (see Figure 3-15). These lines, sometimes called **traces**, are circuits or paths that enable data, instructions, and power to move from component to component on the board. This system of pathways used for communication and the protocol and methods used for transmission are collectively called the **bus**. (A **protocol** is a set of rules and standards that any two entities use for communication.) The parts of the bus that we are most familiar with are the lines of the bus that are used for data; these lines are called the **data bus**. A bus can also carry electrical power (to power components on the motherboard), control signals (to coordinate activity), and memory addresses (for one program to tell another program where to find data or instructions).

All data and instructions inside a computer exist in binary, which means there are only two states: on and off. Binary data is put on a line of a bus by placing voltage on that line. We can visualize that bits are "traveling" down the bus in parallel, but in reality, the voltage placed on each line is not "traveling"; rather, it is all over the line. When one component

Figure 3-15 On the bottom of the motherboard, you can see bus lines terminating at the CPU socket

at one end of the line wants to write data to another component, the two components get in sync for the write operation. Then, the first component places voltage on several lines of the bus, and the other component immediately reads the voltage on these lines. The CPU or other devices interpret the voltage, or lack of voltage, on each line on the bus as binary digits (0s or 1s).

The width of a data bus is called the **data path size**. Some buses have data paths that are 8, 16, 32, 64, 128, or more bits wide. For example, a bus that has eight wires, or lines, to transmit data is called an 8-bit bus. Figure 3-16 shows an 8-bit bus between the CPU and memory that is transmitting the letter A (binary 0100 0001). All bits of a byte are placed on their lines of the bus at the same time: no voltage for binary zero and voltage for binary one. For every eight bits of a bus, a bus might use a ninth bit for error checking. Adding a check bit for each byte allows the component reading the data to verify that it is the same data written to the bus.

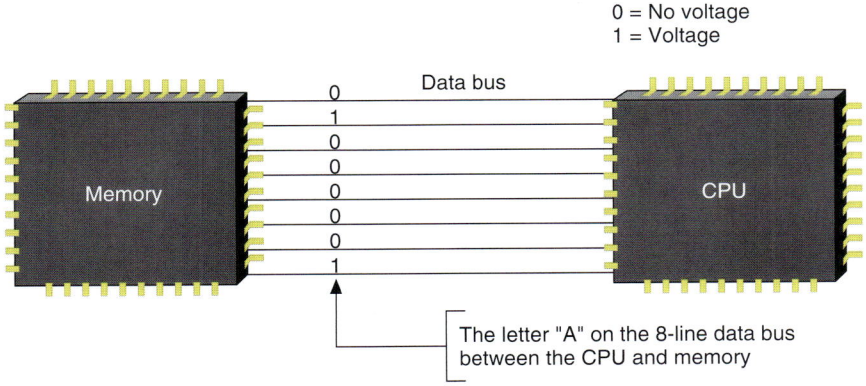

Figure 3-16 A data bus has traces or lines that carry voltage interpreted by the CPU and other devices as bits

One of the most interesting lines, or circuits, on a bus is the **system clock** or system timer, which is dedicated to timing the activities on the motherboard much like a metronome helps a musician with timing. The chipset sends out a continuous pulsating electrical signal on one line of the system bus. This one system clock line, dedicated to carrying the pulse, is read by other components on the motherboard (including the processor, bus slots, memory slots, and so forth) and ensures that all activities are synchronized. Remember that everything in a computer is binary, and this includes the activities themselves. Instead of continuously working to perform commands or move data, the CPU, bus, and other devices work in a binary fashion—do something, stop, do something, stop, and so forth. Each device works on a clock cycle or beat of the clock. Some devices, such as the CPU, do two or more operations on one beat of the clock, and others do one operation for each beat. Some devices might even do something on every other beat, but most components inside the system work according to these beats or cycles.

You can think of this as similar to children jumping rope. The system clock (child turning the rope) provides the beats or cycles, while devices (children jumping) work in a binary fashion (jump, don't jump). In the analogy, some children jump two or more times for each rope pass.

> **Notes** If the processor requests something from a slow device and the device is not ready, the device issues a **wait state**, which is a command to the processor to wait for slower devices to catch up.

The speed of memory, Front Side Bus, processor, or other component is measured in **hertz (Hz)**, which is one cycle per second; **megahertz (MHz)**, which is one million cycles per second; and **gigahertz (GHz)**, which is one billion cycles per second. Common ratings for memory are 1333 MHz and 1866 MHz. Common ratings for Front Side Buses are 2600 MHz, 2000 MHz, 1600 MHz, 1333 MHz, 1066 MHz, 800 MHz, 533 MHz, or 400 MHz. A CPU operates from 166 MHz to almost 4 GHz. The CPU can put data or instructions on its internal bus at a much higher rate than does the motherboard. Although we often refer to the speed of the CPU and memory, talking about the frequency of these devices is more accurate, because the term "speed" implies a continuous flow, while the term "frequency" implies a digital or binary flow: on and off, on and off.

> **Notes** Rather than measuring the frequency of a system bus, sometimes you see a system bus measured in performance such as the GA-990FXA-UD3 motherboard by GIGABYTE (see *www.gigabyte.us*). This system bus is rated at 5.2 GT/s or 5200 MT/s. One GT/s is one billion transfers per second, and one MT/s is one million transfers per second.

A motherboard can have more than one bus, each using a different protocol, speed, data path size, and so on. Table 3-4 lists the various buses used on motherboards today, in order of throughput speed from fastest to slowest. (Throughput is sometimes called bandwidth.) Looking at the second column of Table 3-4, you can see that a bus is called an expansion bus, local bus, local I/O bus, or local video bus. A bus that does not run in sync with the system clock is called an expansion bus. For chipsets that use a South Bridge, expansion buses always connect here. Most buses today are local buses, meaning they run in sync with the system clock. If a local bus connects to the slower I/O controller hub or South Bridge of the chipset, it is called a local I/O bus. Because the video card needs to run at a faster rate than other adapter cards, this one slot always connects to the faster end of the chipset,

Motherboard Types and Features

A+ 220-801 1.2

the North Bridge, or directly to the processor when using Sandy Bridge or Ivy Bridge technology. Older boards used AGP video slots, and today's boards use PCI Express x16 slots for video. These video buses that connect to the North Bridge or to the processor are called local video buses.

Bus	Bus Type	Data Path in Bits	Address Lines	Bus Frequency	Throughput
PCI Express Version 2	Local video and local I/O	Serial with up to 32 lanes	Up to 32 lanes	2.5 GHz	Up to 500 MB/sec per lane in each direction
PCI Express Version 1.1	Local video and local I/O	Serial with up to 16 lanes	Up to 16 lanes	1.25 GHz	Up to 250 MB/sec per lane in each direction
PCI Express Version 1	Local video and local I/O	Serial with up to 16 lanes	Up to 16 lanes	1.25 GHz	Up to 250 MB/sec per lane in each direction
PCI-X	Local I/O	64	32	66, 133, 266, or 533 MHz	Up to 8.5 GB/sec
PCI	Local I/O	32 or 64	32 or 64	33, 66 MHz	133, 266, or 532 MB/sec
AGP 1x, 2x, 3x, 4x, 8x	Local video	32	NA	66, 75, 100 MHz	266 MB/sec to 2.1 GB/sec
FireWire 400 and 800	Local I/O or expansion	1	Serial	NA	Up to 3.2 Gbps (gigabits per second)
USB 1.1, 2.0, and 3.0	Expansion	1	Serial	3 MHz	12 or 480 Mbps (megabits per second) or 5.0 Gbps (gigabits per second)

Table 3-4 Buses listed by throughput

The AGP buses were developed specifically for video cards, and the PCI buses are used for many types of cards, including video cards. We'll now look at the details of the PCI and AGP buses. The FireWire and USB buses are discussed in Chapter 6.

CONVENTIONAL PCI

The first PCI bus had a 32-bit data path, supplied 5 V of power to an adapter card, and operated at 33 MHz. It was the first bus that allowed adapter cards to run in sync with the CPU. PCI Version 2.x introduced the 64-bit, 3.3 V PCI slot, doubling data throughput of the bus. Because a card can be damaged if installed in the wrong voltage slot, a notch in a PCI slot distinguishes between a 5 V slot and a 3.3 V slot. A Universal PCI card can use either a 3.3 V or 5 V slot and contains both notches (see Figure 3-17). Conventional PCI

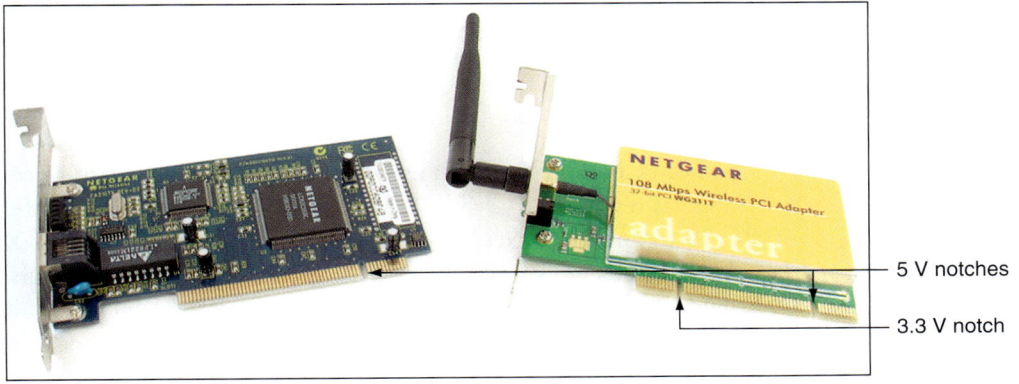

Figure 3-17 A 32-bit, 5 V PCI network card and a 32-bit, universal PCI wireless card show the difference in PCI notches set to distinguish voltages in a PCI slot

is no longer evolving and ended up with four types of slots and six possible PCI card configurations to use these slots. These slots and cards include 32-bit PCI and 64-bit PCI-X, all shown in Figure 3-18.

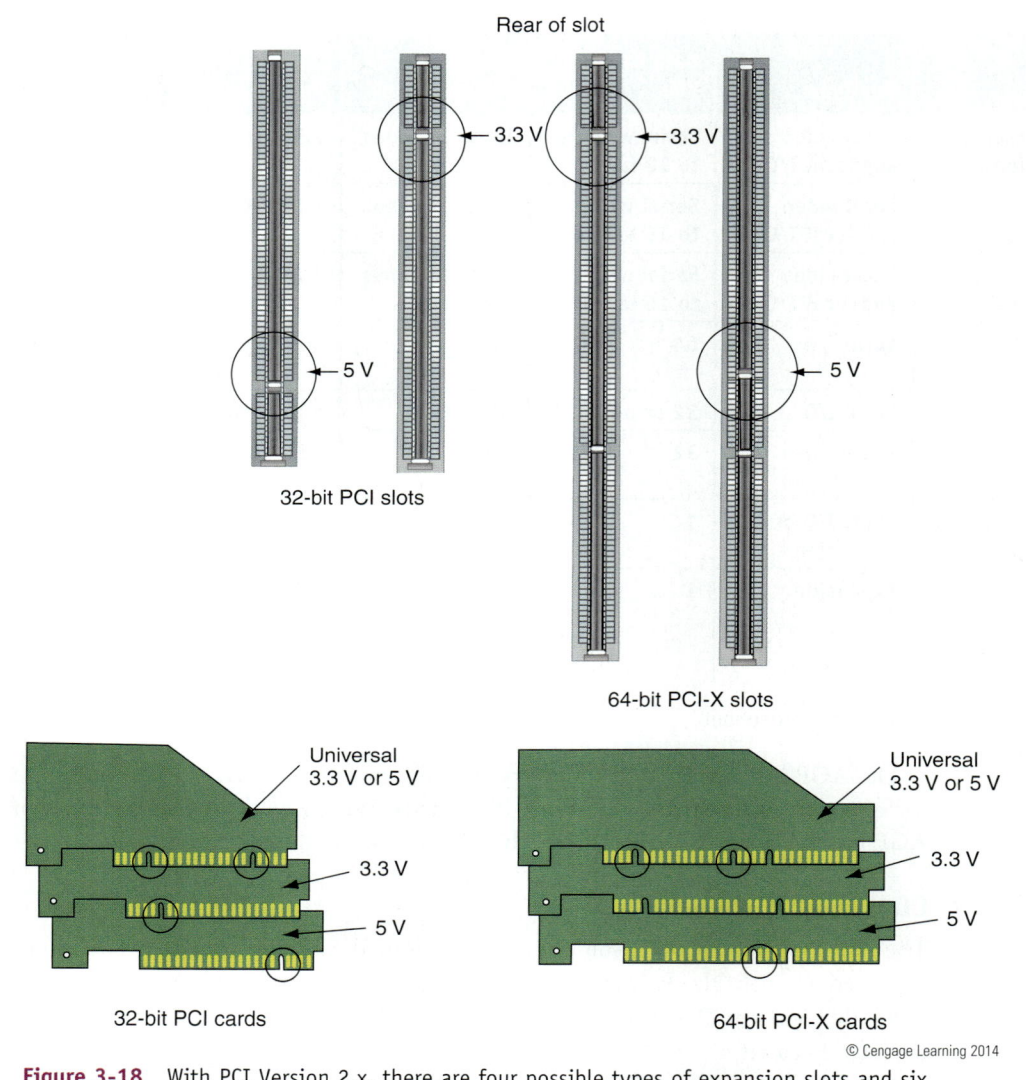

Figure 3-18 With PCI Version 2.x, there are four possible types of expansion slots and six differently configured PCI expansion cards to use these slots

> **Notes** The miniPCI bus and slot is used in laptops and is covered in Chapter 11.

PCI-X

The next evolution of PCI is PCI-X, which uses a 64-bit data path and had three major revisions; the last and final revision is PCI-X 3.0. All PCI-X revisions are backward compatible with conventional PCI cards and slots, except 5-V PCI cards are not supported. PCI-X focused on the server market; therefore, it's unlikely you'll see PCI-X slots in desktop computers. Motherboards that use PCI-X tend to have several different PCI slots with some 32-bit or 64-bit slots running at different speeds. For example, Figure 3-19 shows a server motherboard with three types of slots. The two long white slots are PCI-X; the two shorter white slots are PCI, and the two black slots are PCI-e. The two PCI-X slots can use most 32-bit and 64-bit PCI or PCI-X cards.

Courtesy of Super Micro Computer, Inc.

Figure 3-19 The two long white PCI-X slots can support PCI cards

PCI EXPRESS

PCI Express (PCIe) uses an altogether different architectural design than conventional PCI and PCI-X; PCIe is not backward compatible with either. PCI Express will ultimately replace both these buses as well as the AGP bus, although it is expected PCI Express will coexist with conventional PCI for some time to come (see Figure 3-20). Whereas PCI uses a 32-bit or 64-bit parallel bus, PCI Express uses a serial bus, which is faster than a parallel bus because it transmits data in packets similar to how an Ethernet network, USB, and FireWire transmit data. A PCIe expansion slot can provide one or more of these serial lanes.

© Cengage Learning 2014

Figure 3-20 Three PCI Express slots and three PCI slots on a motherboard

Another difference in PCI Express is how it connects to the processor. One or more PCI Express slots used for video cards have a direct link to the North Bridge or to the processor (using Sandy Bridge or Ivy Bridge architecture). Refer back to Figures 3-9, 3-10, and 3-12.

PCI Express currently comes in four different slot sizes called PCI Express ×1 (pronounced "by one"), ×4, ×8, and ×16. Figure 3-21 shows three of these slots. Notice in the photo how the PCIe slots are not as tall and the pins are closer together than the conventional PCI slot. A PCI Express ×1 slot contains a single lane for data; this lane is actually four wires. One pair of wires is used to send data and the other pair receives data, one bit at a time. The ×16 slot contains 16 lanes, with each lane timed independently of other lanes. The more lanes you have, the more data gets transmitted in a given time. Therefore, a ×16 slot is faster than a ×4 slot, which is faster than a ×1 slot. A shorter PCI Express card (such as a ×1 card) can be installed in a longer PCI Express slot (such as a ×4 slot).

Figure 3-21 Three types of PCIe slots and one conventional PCI slot

Revisions of PCIe include PCIe version 1.1, PCIe version 2.0 and 2.1, and PCIe version 3.0, which doubles the throughput of Version 2. Here are important facts about PCIe versions 1.0, 1.1, and 2.0:

- ▲ *PCIe version 1.0.* The original PCIe version 1.0 allowed for 150 W to PCIe cards. Pins on the expansion card provide 75 W, and a new 6-pin PCIe connector from the power supply provides an additional 75 W.
- ▲ *PCIe version 1.1.* PCIe version 1.1 allowed for more wattage to PCIe cards, up to 225 watts. The standard allows for two 6-pin PCIe connectors from the power supply to the card. Therefore, the total 225 W comes as 75 W from the slot and 150 W from the two connectors.
- ▲ *PCIe version 2.0.* PCIe version 2.0 doubled the frequency of the PCIe bus and allows for up to 32 lanes on one slot (though few motherboards or cards actually use 32 lane slots). The allowed wattage to one PCIe 2.0 card was increased to a total of 300 watts by using a new 8-pin PCIe power connector that provides 150 W (see Figure 3-22). The 300 watts to the card come from the slot (75 W), from the 8-pin connector (150 W), and an additional 75 W come from a second auxiliary connector on the motherboard. This second connector can be a 6-pin PCIe connector, a Molex-style connector, or a SATA-style connector. You'll see an example of these connectors later in the chapter.

Figure 3-22 8-pin PCIe Version 2.0 power connector

PCI RISER CARDS USED TO EXTEND THE SLOTS

Suppose you are installing a Mini-ITX or microATX motherboard into a low-profile or slimline case that does not give you enough room to install a PCI card standing up in an expansion slot. In this situation, a PCI riser card can solve the problem. The riser card installs in the slot and provides another slot at a right angle (see Figure 3-23). When you install an expansion card in this riser card slot, the card sits parallel to the motherboard, taking up less space. These riser cards come for all types of PCI slots, including PCIe, PCI-X, and conventional PCI.

Figure 3-23 PCI riser card provides a 3.3-V slot or 5-V slot depending on which direction the card is inserted in the PCI slot

THE AGP BUSES

Motherboard video slots and video cards used the Accelerated Graphics Port (AGP) standards for many years, but AGP has been replaced by PCI Express. Even though AGP is a dying technology, you still need to know how to support it in case you are ever called on to replace an AGP video card or a motherboard with an AGP slot.

AGP evolved over several years, and the different AGP standards can be confusing. AGP standards include three major releases (AGP 1.0, AGP 2.0, and AGP 3.0), one major change in the AGP slot length standard (AGP Pro), four different speeds (1x, 2x, 4x, and 8x) yielding four different throughputs, three different voltages (3.3 V, 1.5 V, and 0.8 V), and six different expansion slots (AGP 3.3 V, AGP 1.5 V, AGP Universal, AGP Pro 3.3 V, APG Pro 1.5 V, and AGP Pro Universal). To help you make sense of all this, Table 3-5 sorts it all out.

Standard	Speeds (Cycles Per Clock Beat)	Maximum Throughput	Voltage	Slots Supported
AGP 1.0	1x	266 MB/sec	3.3 V	Slot keyed to 3.3 V
AGP 2.0	1x, 2x, or 4x	533 MB/sec or 1.06 GB/sec	3.3 V or 1.5 V	Slot keyed to 1.5 V Slot keyed to 3.3 V Universal slot (for either 1.5 V or 3.3 V cards)
AGP Pro	Applies to all speeds	NA	3.3 V or 1.5 V	AGP Pro 3.3 V keyed AGP Pro 1.5 V keyed AGP Pro Universal (for either 1.5 V or 3.3 V cards)
AGP 3.0	4x or 8x	2.12 GB/sec	1.5 V and 0.8 V	Universal AGP 3.0 (4x/8x) slot Slot keyed to 1.5 V Slot keyed to AGP Pro 1.5 V

Table 3-5 AGP standards summarized

© Cengage Learning 2014

As you can see from Table 3-5, there are several different AGP slots and matching card connectors that apply to the different standards. When matching video cards to AGP slots, be aware of these several variations. For instance, the first two slots in Figure 3-24 are used by cards that follow the AGP 1.0 or AGP 2.0 standards. These slots have key positions so that you cannot put an AGP 3.3 V card in an AGP 1.5 V slot or vice versa. The third slot is a universal slot that can accommodate 3.3 V or 1.5 V cards. All three slots are 2.9 inches long and have 132 pins, although some pins are not used. Figure 3-25 shows a motherboard with an older AGP 3.3 V slot. Notice how the keyed 3.3 V break in the slot is near the back side of the motherboard where expansion cards are bracketed to the case.

Another AGP standard, AGP Pro, has provisions for a longer slot. This 180-pin slot has extensions on both ends that contain an additional 20 pins on one end and 28 pins on the other end, to provide extra voltage for an AGP card that consumes more than 25 watts of power. These wider slots might be keyed to 3.3 V or 1.5 V or might be a Universal Pro slot that can hold either 3.3 V or 1.5 V cards. Also, when using an AGP Pro video card, leave the PCI slot next to it empty to improve ventilation and prevent overheating.

The last AGP standard, AGP 3.0, runs at 8x or 4x speeds. AGP 3.0 cards can be installed in an AGP 1.5 V slot, but signals are put on the data bus using 0.8 V. It's best to install an AGP 3.0 card in a slot that is designed to support AGP 3.0 cards. However, if you install an AGP 3.0 card in an older AGP 1.5 V slot, the card might or might not work, but the card will not be damaged.

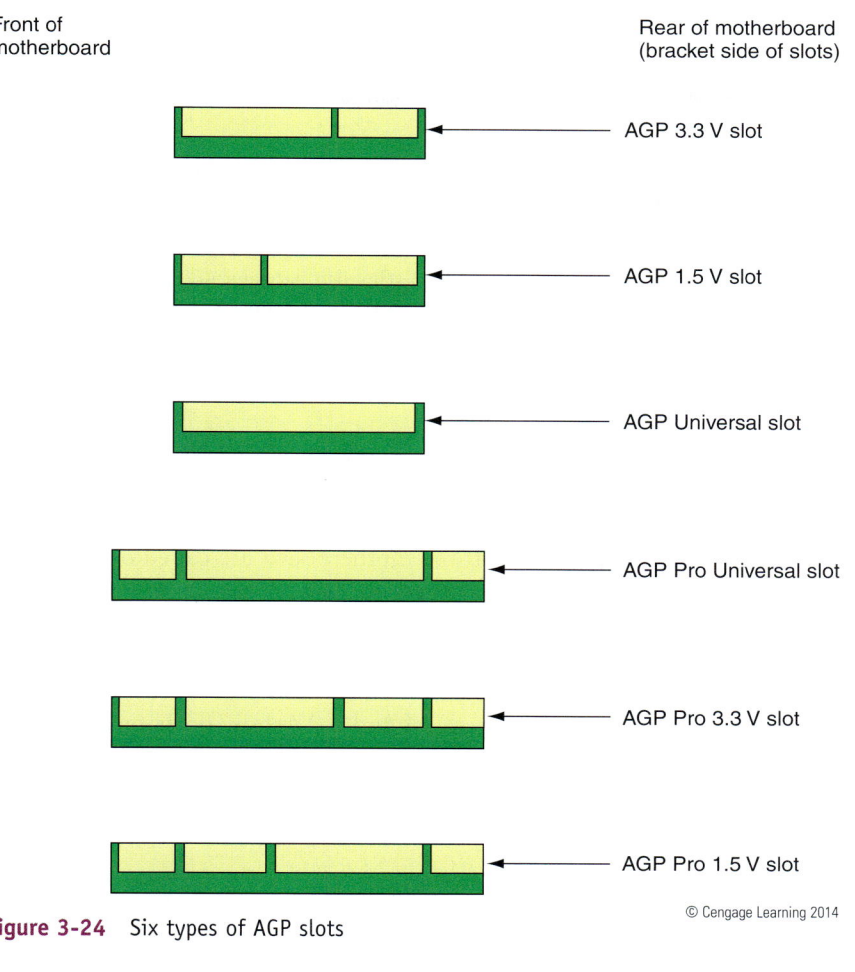

Figure 3-24 Six types of AGP slots

Figure 3-25 This motherboard uses an AGP 3.3 V slot, which accommodates an AGP 1.0 video card

An AGP video card will be keyed to 1.5 V or 3.3 V, or a universal AGP video card has both keys so that it can fit into either a 1.5 V keyed slot or a 3.3 V keyed slot. A universal AGP video card also fits into a universal AGP slot. If an AGP video card does not make

A+ 220-801 1.2

use of the extra pins provided by the AGP Pro slot, it can still be inserted into the AGP Pro slot if it has a registration tab that fits into the end of the Pro slot near the center of the motherboard. In Chapter 6, you'll learn about AGP video cards.

> **Notes** If you're trying to buy an AGP video card to match a motherboard slot, you have to be really careful. When reading an AGP ad, it's hard to distinguish between AGP 3.3 V and AGP 3.0, but there's a big difference in these standards, and they are not interchangeable.

ON-BOARD PORTS AND CONNECTORS

In addition to expansion slots, a motherboard might also have several ports and internal connectors. Ports coming directly off the motherboard are called **on-board ports** or integrated components. Almost all motherboards have two or more USB ports and sound ports. Boards might also offer a network port, FireWire (IEEE 1394) port, video port, one or more eSATA ports (for external SATA hard drives), and a port for a wireless antenna. Older motherboards might have mouse and keyboard ports (called PS/2 ports), modem port, parallel port, and serial port. Figures 3-26 and 3-27 show ports on older motherboards. Figure 3-28 shows ports on a current high-end motherboard.

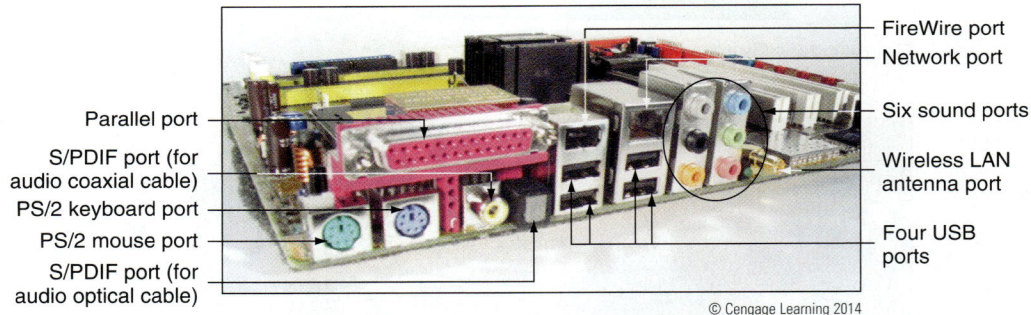

Figure 3-26 A motherboard provides ports for common I/O devices

Figure 3-27 Ports on a value Biostar motherboard

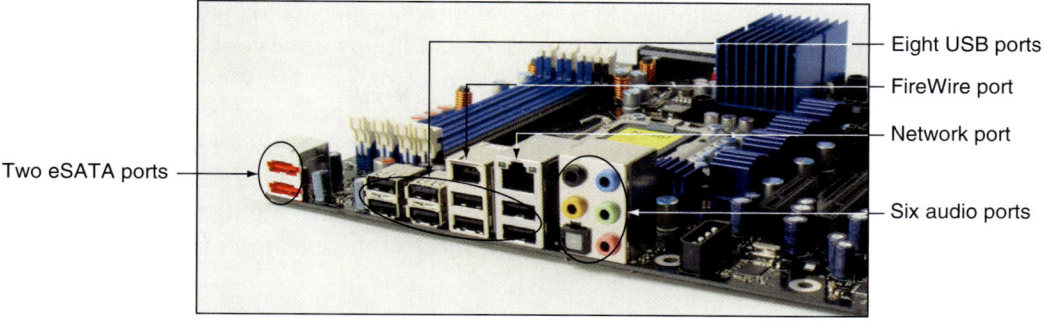

Figure 3-28 Intel DX58SO motherboard on-board ports

When you purchase a motherboard, the package includes an **I/O shield**, which is the plate that you install in the computer case that provides holes for these I/O ports. The I/O shield is the size designed for the case's form factor, and the holes in the shield are positioned for the motherboard ports (see Figure 3-29). When you first install a motherboard, you might need to install the drivers that come on the CD bundled with the board before some of the motherboard ports will work. How to install the motherboard drivers is covered later in the chapter.

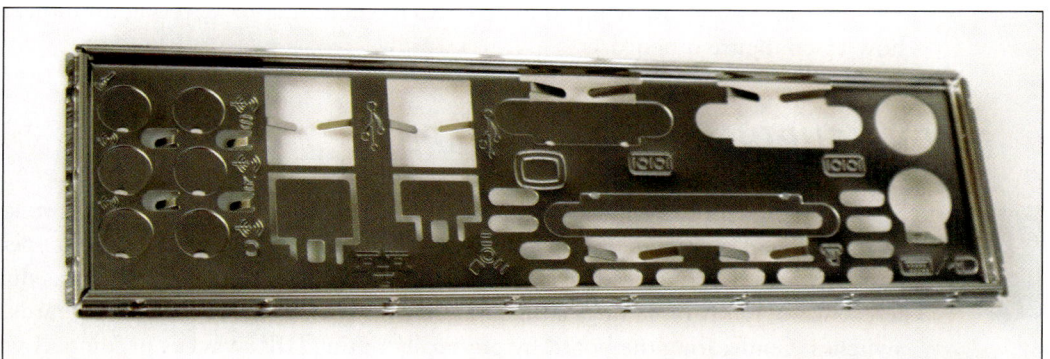

Figure 3-29 The I/O shield fits the motherboard ports to the computer case

Some motherboards come with connector modules that provide additional ports off the rear of the case. For example, Figure 3-30 shows three modules that came bundled with one motherboard. To use the ports on a module, you connect its cable to a connector on the motherboard and install the module in a slot on the rear of the case intended for an expansion card.

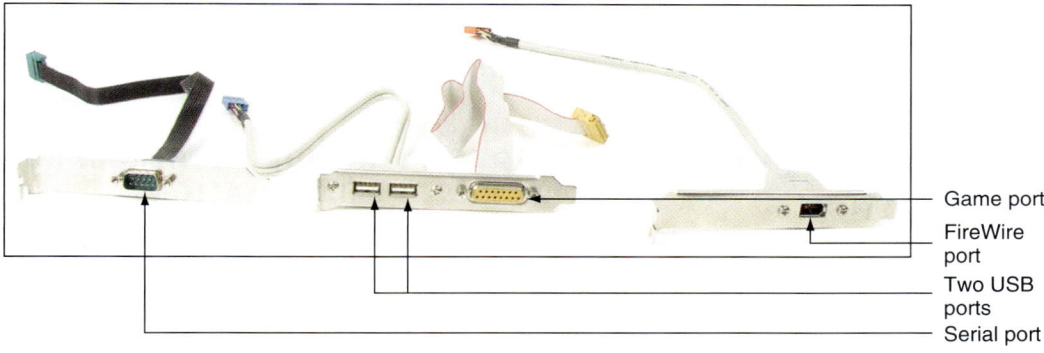

Figure 3-30 These modules provide additional ports off the rear of a computer case

A+ 220-801 1.2

A motherboard might have several internal connectors, including parallel ATA (PATA) connectors (also called IDE connectors), a floppy drive connector, serial ATA (SATA) connectors, SCSI connectors, a USB connector, or a FireWire (IEEE 1394) connector. When you purchase a motherboard, look in the package for the motherboard manual either printed or on CD. It will show a diagram of the board with a description of each connector. For example, the connectors for the motherboard in Figure 3-31 are labeled as the manual describes them. If a connector is a group of pins sticking up on the board, the connector is called a header. You will learn to use most of these connectors in later chapters.

Figure 3-31 Internal connectors on a motherboard for drives and ports on the front of the case

Now that you know what to expect when examining or selecting a motherboard, let's see how to configure a board.

CONFIGURING A MOTHERBOARD

A+ 220-801 1.1

Settings on the motherboard are used to enable or disable a connector or port, set the frequency of the CPU or Front Side Bus, control security features, and control what happens when the PC first boots. In the past, configuring these and other motherboard settings was done in three different ways: jumpers, settings stored in CMOS RAM, and, for really old boards, a bank of DIP switches. Configuring the board by physically setting DIP switches or jumpers was extremely inconvenient because you had to open the computer case to make a change.

A more convenient method is to store configuration data in CMOS RAM, and today's computers store almost all configuration data there. **CMOS (complementary metal-oxide semiconductor)** is a method of manufacturing microchips, and **CMOS RAM** is a small amount of memory stored on the motherboard used to hold motherboard settings. This CMOS RAM retains the data even when the computer is turned off because it is charged by a nearby battery. A program in BIOS, called BIOS setup or CMOS setup, can easily make changes to the settings stored in CMOS RAM.

Now let's see how to configure a motherboard using jumpers, setup BIOS, and motherboard drivers. (It's unlikely you'll see a board that still uses DIP switches.) The first step in the process of configuring a motherboard is to locate the motherboard documentation.

> **APPLYING CONCEPTS** — **FIND THE MOTHERBOARD DOCUMENTATION**
>
> To know how to configure a motherboard, you need access to the motherboard user guide, which explains all the settings and how to use them. This guide can be a PDF file stored on the CD or DVD that came bundled with the motherboard. If you don't have the CD, you can download the user guide from the motherboard manufacturer's web site.

To find the correct user guide online, you need to know the board manufacturer and model. If a motherboard is already installed in a computer, you can use the Windows System Information utility (msinfo32.exe) to report the brand and model of the board. To access the utility, click **Start**, type **msinfo32.exe** in the Search box, and press **Enter**. In the System Information window, click **System Summary**. In the System Summary information in the right pane, look for the motherboard information labeled as the System Manufacturer and System Model (see Figure 3-32).

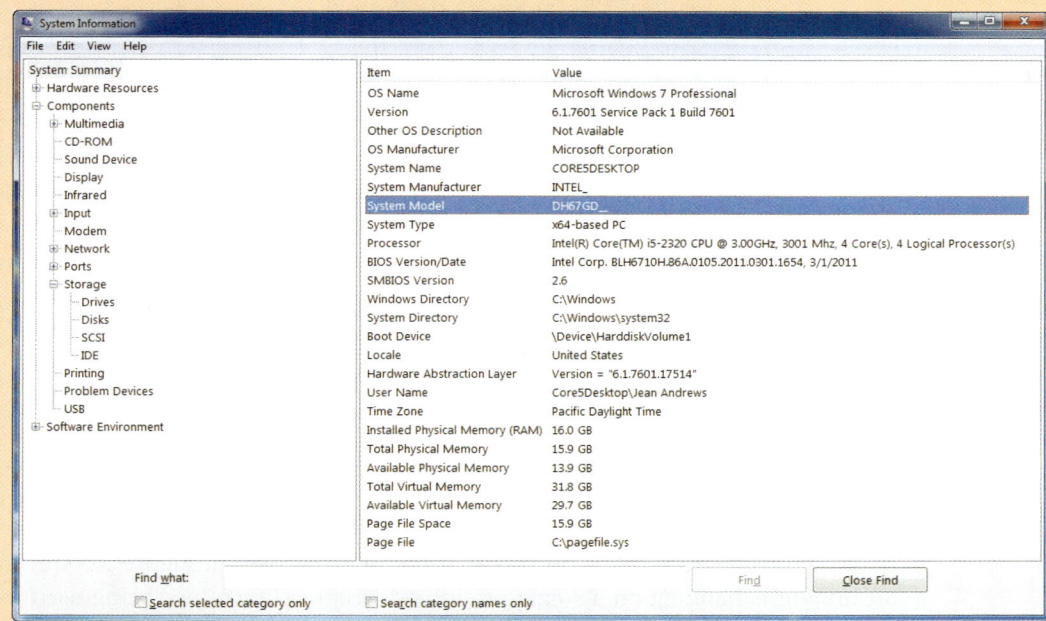

Source: Microsoft Windows 7

Figure 3-32 Use the System Information window to identify the motherboard brand and model

If the motherboard is not installed or the system is not working, look for the brand and model imprinted somewhere on the motherboard (see Figure 3-33). Next, go to the web site of the motherboard manufacturer and download the user guide. Web sites for several motherboard manufacturers are listed in Table 3-6. The diagrams, pictures, charts, and explanations of settings and components in the user guide will be invaluable to you when supporting this board.

© Cengage Learning 2014

Figure 3-33 The motherboard brand and model are imprinted somewhere on the board

Manufacturer	Web Address
ASUS	www.asus.com
BIOSTAR Group	www.biostar.com.tw
Evga	www.evga.com
ASRock	www.asrock.com
Gigabyte Technology Co., Ltd.	www.gigabyte.com
Intel Corporation	www.intel.com
Micro-Star International (MSI)	www.msicomputer.com
Super Micro Computer, Inc.	www.supermicro.com

Table 3-6 Major manufacturers of motherboards

USING JUMPERS TO CONFIGURE A MOTHERBOARD

Older motherboards relied heavily on jumpers to configure the board, and newer motherboards still use a few important jumpers. A **jumper** is two small posts or metal pins that stick up off the motherboard that is open or closed. An open jumper has no cover, and a closed jumper has a cover on the two pins (see Figure 3-34). On older boards, a group of jumpers might be used to tell the system at what speed the CPU is running, or to turn a power-saving feature on or off. Look at the jumper cover in Figure 3-34(b) that is "parked," meaning it is hanging on a single pin for safekeeping, but is not being used to turn a jumper setting on.

Figure 3-34 A 6-pin jumper group on a circuit board: (a) has no jumpers set to on, (b) has a cover parked on one pin, and (c) is configured with one jumper setting turned on

Most motherboards today allow you to set a supervisor password (to make changes in setup BIOS) or a power-on password (to get access to the system). Know that these passwords are not the same password that can be required by a Windows OS at startup. If both passwords are forgotten, you cannot use the computer. However, jumpers can be set to clear both passwords. Also, BIOS firmware might need updating (called flashing the BIOS) to solve a problem with the motherboard or to use a new motherboard feature. If flashing BIOS fails, a jumper can be set to undo the update.

For example, Figure 3-35 shows a group of three jumpers on one board. (The tan jumper cap is positioned on the first two jumper pins on the left side of the group.) Figure 3-36

A+ 220-801 1.1

shows the motherboard documentation on how to use these jumpers. When jumpers 1 and 2 are closed, which they are in the figure, normal booting happens. When jumpers 2 and 3 are closed, passwords to BIOS setup can be cleared on the next boot. When no jumpers are closed, on the next boot, the BIOS will recover itself from a failed update. Once set for normal booting, the jumpers should be changed only if you are trying to recover when a power-up password is lost or flashing BIOS has failed. To know how to set jumpers, see the motherboard documentation.

Figure 3-35 This group of three jumpers controls the BIOS configuration

Jumper Position	Mode	Description
1 — 3	Normal (default)	The current BIOS configuration is used for booting.
1 — 3	Configure	After POST, the BIOS displays a menu in CMOS setup that can be used to clear the user and supervisor power-on passwords.
1 — 3	Recovery	Recovery is used to recover from a failed BIOS update. Details can be found on the motherboard CD.

Figure 3-36 BIOS configuration jumper settings

Hands-on | Project 3-3 Examine a Motherboard in Detail

1. Look at the back of your computer. Without opening the case, list the ports that you believe come directly from the motherboard.
2. Remove the cover of the case, which you learned to do in Chapter 2. List the different expansion cards in the expansion slots. Was your guess correct about which ports come from the motherboard?
3. To expose the motherboard so you can identify its parts, remove all the expansion cards, as discussed in Chapter 2.

A+ 220-801 1.1

4. Draw a diagram of the motherboard and label these parts:
   - Processor socket
   - Chipset
   - RAM (each DIMM slot)
   - CMOS battery
   - Expansion slots (Identify the slots as PCI, PCIe x1, PCIe x4, PCIe x16, and AGP.)
   - Each port coming directly from the motherboard
   - Power supply connections
   - SATA or IDE drive connectors

5. Draw a rectangle on the diagram to represent each bank of jumpers on the board.

6. What is the brand and model of the motherboard?

7. Locate the manufacturer's web site. If you can find the motherboard manual on the site, download it.

8. You can complete the following activity only if you have the documentation for the motherboard: Locate the jumper on the board that returns BIOS setup to default settings and label this jumper on your diagram. It is often found near the battery. Some boards might have more than one, and some have none.

9. Reassemble the computer, as you learned to do in Chapter 2.

Hands-on | Project 3-4 Examine Motherboard Documentation

Using the motherboard brand and model installed in your computer, or another motherboard brand and model assigned by your instructor, download the user guide from the motherboard manufacturer and answer these questions:

1. What processors does the board support?
2. What type of RAM does the board support?
3. What is the maximum RAM the board can hold?
4. If the board has a PCIe slot, what version of PCIe does the board use?
5. What chipset does the board use?

USING SETUP BIOS TO CONFIGURE A MOTHERBOARD

The motherboard settings stored in CMOS RAM don't normally need to be changed except, for example, when there is a problem with hardware, or a power-saving feature or security feature (such as a power-on password) needs to be disabled or enabled. In this part of the chapter, you learn about motherboard settings that you can view or change using setup BIOS.

> **A+ Exam Tip** The A+ 220-801 exam expects you to know about BIOS settings regarding RAM, the hard drive, optical drive, CPU, boot sequence, system date and time, virtualization support, built-in diagnostics, monitoring temperature, fan speeds, intrusion detection, voltage, and clock and bus speeds. All these settings are covered in this part of the chapter.

A+ 220-801 1.1

ACCESS THE BIOS SETUP PROGRAM

You access the BIOS setup program by pressing a key or combination of keys during the boot process. The exact way to enter setup varies from one motherboard manufacturer to another. Table 3-7 lists the keystrokes needed to access BIOS setup for some common BIOS types.

BIOS	Key to Press During POST to Access Setup
AMI BIOS	Del
Award BIOS	Del
Older Phoenix BIOS	Ctrl+Alt+Esc or Ctrl+Alt+S
Newer Phoenix BIOS	F2, F1, or Del
Dell computers using Phoenix BIOS	Press Ctrl+Alt+Enter or press F2 every few seconds until the message *Entering Setup* appears.
Compaq computers	Press the F10 key while the cursor is in the upper-right corner of the screen, which happens just after the two beeps during booting. For older Compaq computers, press F1, F2, F10, or Del.

Table 3-7 How to access setup BIOS

© Cengage Learning 2014

For the exact method you need to use to enter setup, see the documentation for your motherboard. A message such as the following usually appears on the screen near the beginning of the boot:

`Press DEL to change Setup`

or

`Press F2 for Setup`

When you press the appropriate key or keys, a setup screen appears with menus and Help features that are often very user-friendly. Although the exact menus depend on the BIOS maker, the sample screens that follow will help you become familiar with the general contents of BIOS setup screens. Figure 3-37 shows a main menu for setup. On this menu, you can view information about the BIOS version, processor model and speed, memory speed, total memory, and the amount of memory in each memory slot. You can also change the system date and time.

Now let's examine setup screens that apply to the boot sequence, virtualization, built-in diagnostics, monitoring the system, and security.

A+
220-801
1.1

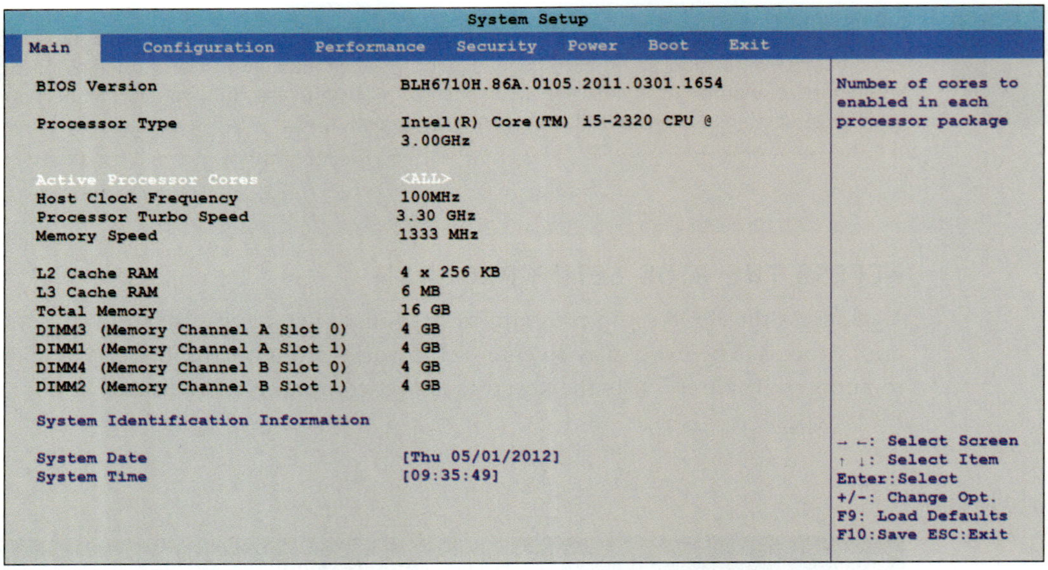

Source: Intel

Figure 3-37 BIOS setup main menu

CHANGE THE BOOT SEQUENCE

Figure 3-38 shows an example of a boot menu in BIOS setup. Here, you can set the order in which the system tries to boot from certain devices (called the boot sequence or boot priority). Most likely when you first install a hard drive or an operating system, you will want to have the BIOS attempt to first boot from a DVD so that you can install Windows from the setup DVD. After the OS is installed, to prevent accidental boots from a DVD or other media, change setup BIOS to boot first from the hard drive.

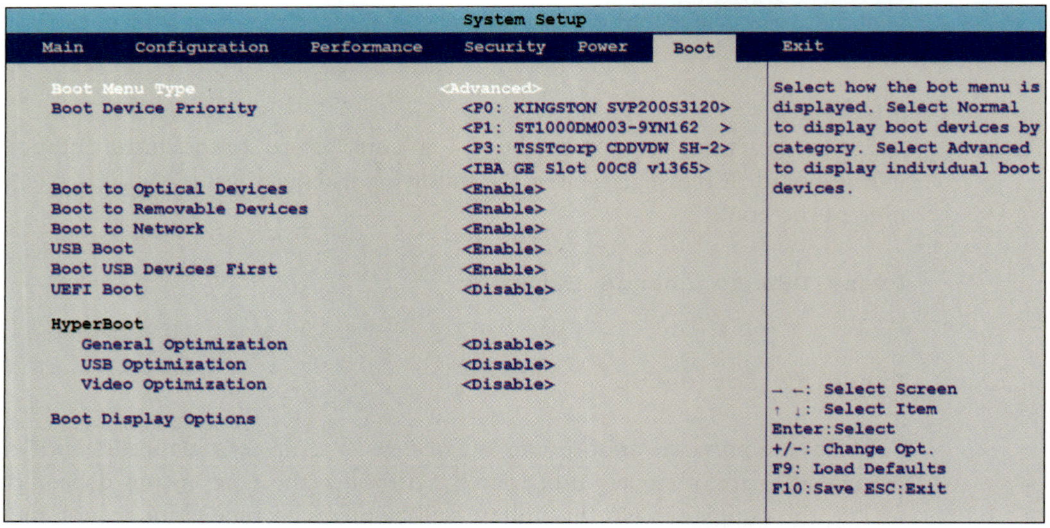

Source: Intel

Figure 3-38 Set the boot priority order in BIOS setup

Notice in Figure 3-38 the option to perform a UEFI Boot. **Unified Extensible Firmware Interface (UEFI)** is a new standard that is slowly replacing the BIOS standard. It is an interface between firmware on the motherboard and the operating system and improves

A+ 220-801 1.1

on processes for booting, handing over the boot to the OS, and loading device drivers and applications before the OS loads. The UEFI Boot must be enabled in order to boot from a hard drive that is larger than 2 TB (terabytes). For more information on UEFI, see the UEFI consortium at *www.uefi.org*.

Also, the BIOS setup boot screens might give you options regarding built-in diagnostics that occur at the boot. Recall from Chapter 1 that these tests are called the POST (Power-on Self Test). You can configure some motherboards to perform a quick boot and bypass the extensive POST. For these systems, if you are troubleshooting a boot problem, be sure to set BIOS to perform the full POST.

CONFIGURE ONBOARD DEVICES

You can enable or disable some onboard devices (for example, a network port, FireWire port, USB ports, or video ports) using setup BIOS. For one system, the Configuration screen shown in Figure 3-39 does the job. On this screen, you can enable or disable a port or group of ports, and you can configure the Front Panel Audio ports for Auto, High Definition audio, Legacy audio, or you can disable these audio ports. What you can configure on your system depends on the onboard devices the motherboard offers.

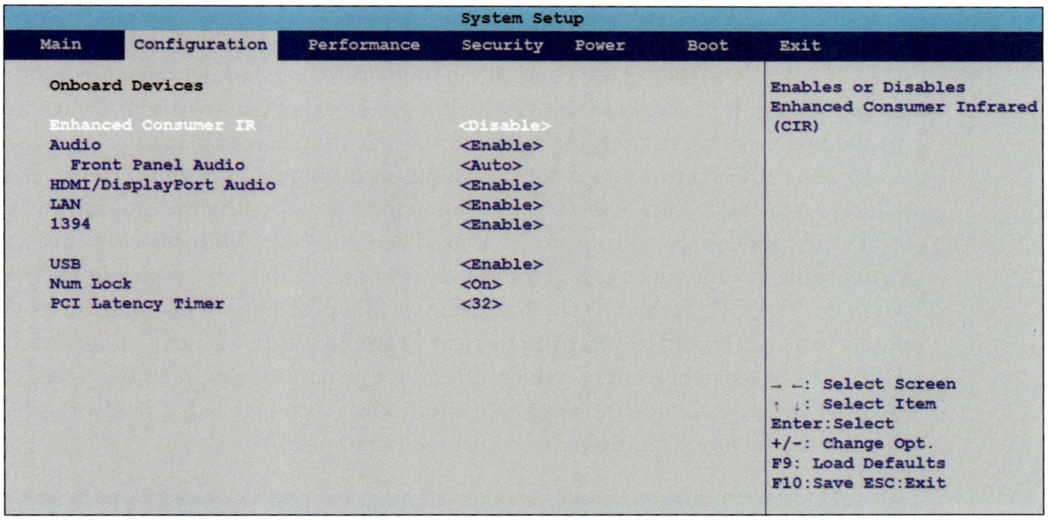

Figure 3-39 Enable and disable onboard devices

Source: Intel

> **Notes** You don't have to replace an entire motherboard if one port fails. For example, if the network port fails, use BIOS setup to disable the port. Then use an expansion card for the port instead.

VIEW HARD DRIVE AND OPTICAL DRIVE INFORMATION

Using setup BIOS, you can view information about installed hard drives and optical drives. For example, in Figure 3-40, one system shows five internal SATA and eSATA ports and one external eSATA port. One 120 GB hard drive is installed on SATA port 0, and another 1000 GB hard drive is installed on SATA port 1. Both ports are internal SATA connectors on the motherboard. Notice the optical drive is installed on SATA port 3, also an internal connector on the motherboard.

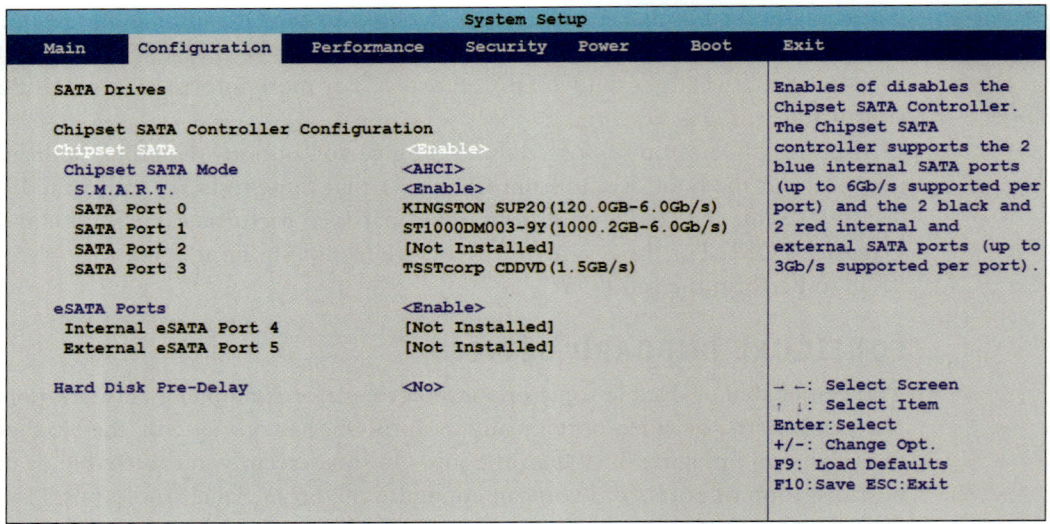

Figure 3-40 A BIOS setup screen showing a list of drives installed on the system

Source: Intel

PROCESSOR AND CLOCK SPEEDS

Recall from Chapter 1 that overclocking is running a processor, memory, motherboard, or video card at a higher speed than the manufacturer recommends. Some motherboards allow overclocking. If you decide to overclock a system, pay careful attention to the temperature of the processor so it does not overheat; overheating can damage the processor. Figure 3-41 shows one BIOS setup screen for adjusting performance. Notice on the screen the Host Clock Frequency. This is the basic system clock provided by the chipset, by which all other components synchronize activities. The Core Max Multiplier on this screen is 33. (This value is sometimes called the bus/core ratio.) When you multiple 100 MHz by 33, you get 3.30 GHz, which is the frequency of the processor. This board uses the QuickPath Interconnect. For older boards that use a Front Side Bus, you can change the speed of the FSB to overclock the system, which affects the processor and memory speeds. On some boards, you can change the processor multiplier to change the processor speed and/or change the memory multiplier to affect memory speed.

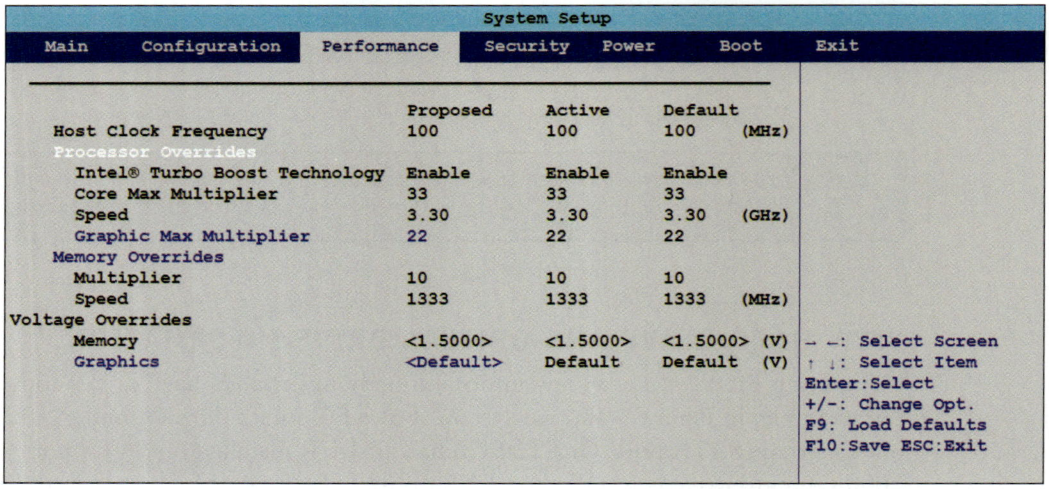

Figure 3-41 A motherboard might give options for changing the clock speed or multipliers for the processor and memory

Source: Intel

A+ 220-801 1.1

MONITOR TEMPERATURES, FAN SPEEDS, AND VOLTAGES

Using BIOS setup screens, you can monitor temperatures inside the case, fan speeds, and voltages. One BIOS screen that allows you to monitor these values and also control fan speeds is shown in Figure 3-42. Case and CPU fans on modern computers adjust their speeds based on the temperatures of the CPU, memory, and motherboard. You can also install software (for example, SpeedFan by Alfredo Comparetti at *www.almico.com/speedfan.php*) in Windows to monitor temperatures and control fan speeds. To use the software, you might need to change a BIOS setting to allow software to control the speeds. For this system, when you select Processor Temperature, you can set the threshold temperatures that software uses to create an alert.

```
                           System Setup
  Main   Configuration   Performance   Security   Power   Boot   Exit

  Fan Control & Real-Time Monitoring

  CPU Fan                              1008 RPM
  Front Fan                               0 RPM
  Rear Fan                              659 RPM

  Processor Temperature                  63  °C
  PCH Temperature                        53  °C
  Memory Temperature                     36  °C
  VR Temperature                         41  °C

  +12.0V                              11.96 V
  +5.0V                                5.07 V
  +3.3V                                3.36 V
  Memory Vcc                           1.54 V
  Processor Vcc                        1.20 V
  PCH Vcc                              1.07 V
  +3.3V Standby                        3.39 V
                                                       → ←: Select Screen
  Restore Default Fan Control Configuration            ↑ ↓: Select Item
                                                       Enter:Select
  Warning: Setting items on these screens to incorrect values may cause   +/-: Change Opt.
  system to overheat and/or produce undesired acoustics!                  F9: Load Defaults
                                                                          F10:Save ESC:Exit
```

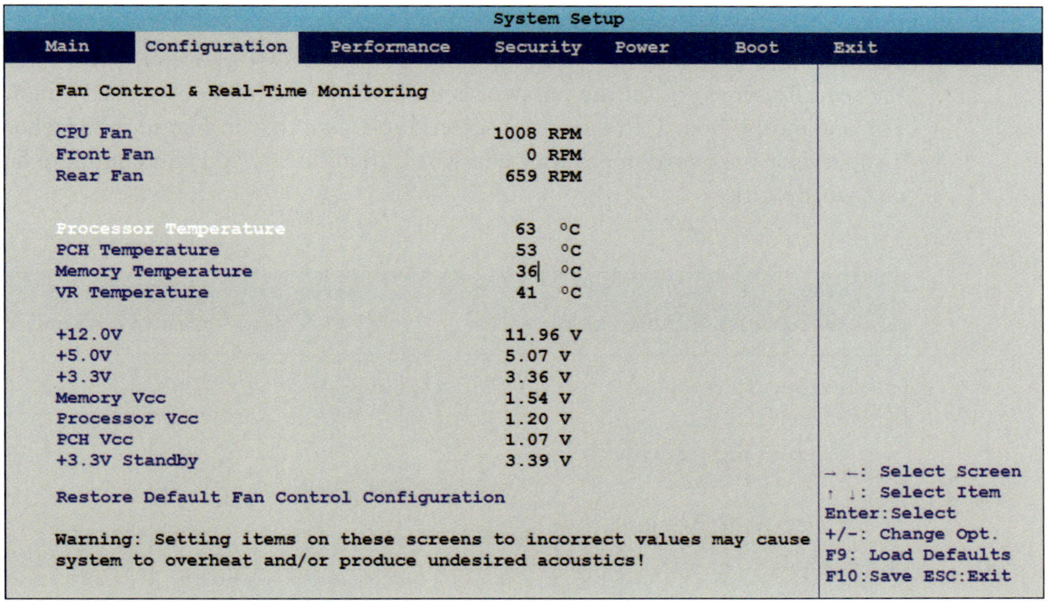

Source: Intel

Figure 3-42 Monitor temperatures, fan speeds, and voltages in a system

INTRUSION DETECTION

BIOS settings might offer several security features, and one of these is an intrusion-detection alert. For example, for the BIOS setup screen shown in Figure 3-43, you can enable event logging, which logs when the case is opened. To use the feature, you must use a cable to connect a switch on the case to a header on the motherboard.

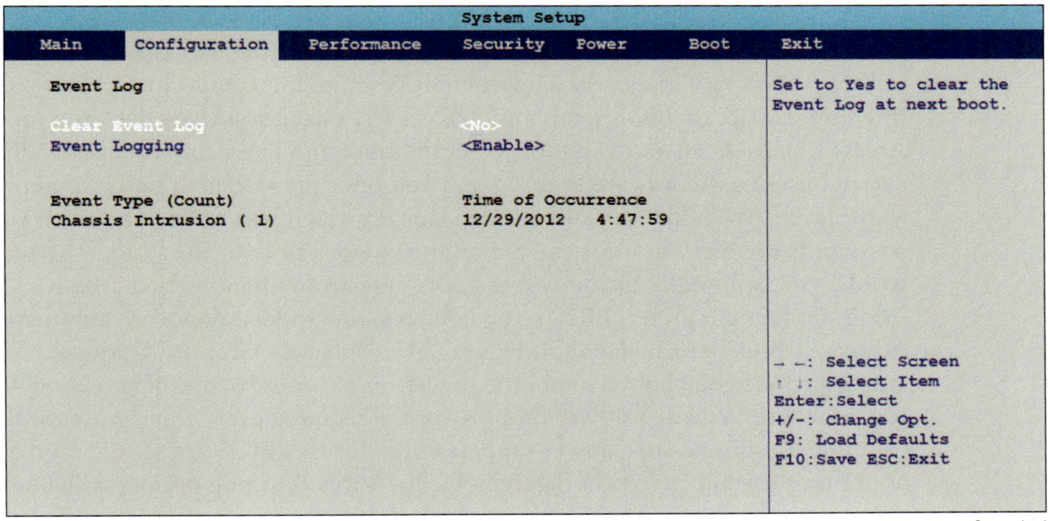

```
                           System Setup
  Main   Configuration   Performance   Security   Power   Boot   Exit

  Event Log                                              Set to Yes to clear the
                                                         Event Log at next boot.
  Clear Event Log                      <No>
  Event Logging                        <Enable>

  Event Type (Count)                   Time of Occurrence
  Chassis Intrusion ( 1)               12/29/2012   4:47:59




                                                       → ←: Select Screen
                                                       ↑ ↓: Select Item
                                                       Enter:Select
                                                       +/-: Change Opt.
                                                       F9: Load Defaults
                                                       F10:Save ESC:Exit
```

Source: Intel

Figure 3-43 BIOS is enabled to log a chassis intrusion

**A+
220-801
1.1**

When the security measure is in place and the case is opened, BIOS displays an alert the next time the system is powered up. For example, the alert message at startup might be "Chassis Intruded! System has halted." If you see this message, know that the case has been opened. Reboot the system and the system should start up as usual. To make sure the alert was not tripped by accident, verify that the case cover is securely in place. Also, sometimes a failed CMOS battery can trip the alert. Intrusion-detection devices are not a recommended best practice for security. False alerts are annoying, and criminals generally know how to get inside a case without tripping the alert.

POWER-ON PASSWORDS

Power-on passwords are assigned in BIOS setup and kept in CMOS RAM to prevent unauthorized access to the computer and/or the BIOS setup utility. Most likely, you'll find the security screen to set the passwords under the boot menu or security menu options. For one motherboard, this security screen looks like that in Figure 3-44, where you can set a supervisor password and a user password. In addition, you can configure how the user password works.

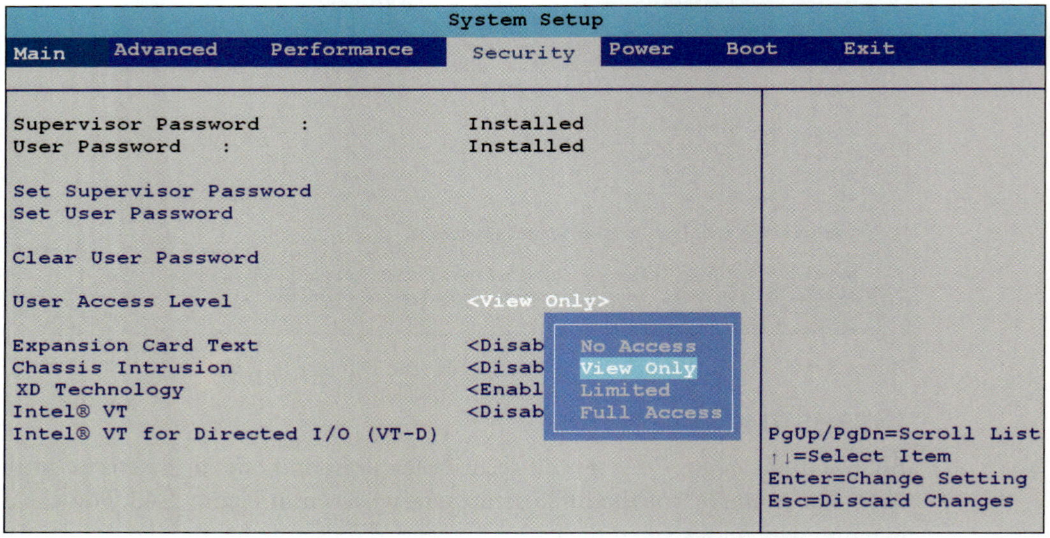

```
                              System Setup
 Main    Advanced    Performance    Security    Power    Boot    Exit

 Supervisor Password    :           Installed
 User Password          :           Installed

 Set Supervisor Password
 Set User Password

 Clear User Password

 User Access Level                  <View Only>

 Expansion Card Text                <Disab   No Access
 Chassis Intrusion                  <Disab   View Only
 XD Technology                      <Enabl   Limited
 Intel® VT                          <Disab   Full Access
 Intel® VT for Directed I/O (VT-D)                        PgUp/PgDn=Scroll List
                                                          ↑↓=Select Item
                                                          Enter=Change Setting
                                                          Esc=Discard Changes
```
Source: Intel

Figure 3-44 Set supervisor and user passwords in BIOS setup to lock down a computer

The choices under User Access Level are **No Access** (the user cannot access the BIOS setup utility), **View Only** (the user can access BIOS setup, but cannot make changes), **Limited** (the user can access BIOS setup and make a few changes such as date and time), and **Full Access** (the user can access the BIOS setup utility and make any changes). When supervisor and user passwords are both set and you boot the system, a box to enter a password is displayed. What access you have depends on which password you enter. Also, if both passwords are set, you must enter a valid password to boot the system. By setting both passwords, you can totally lock down the computer from unauthorized access.

For another computer, BIOS setup controls how to lock down a computer on the Advanced BIOS screen shown in Figure 3-45. Under the Security Option, choices are Setup and System. If you choose Setup, the power-on passwords control access only to BIOS setup. If you choose System, a power-on password is required every time you boot the system. (The supervisor and user power-on passwords for this BIOS are set on another screen.) Also notice on the setup screen in Figure 3-45, the Virus Warning option, which is enabled.

If an attempt to write to the boot sectors of the hard drive happens, a warning message appears on-screen and an alarm beeps. (The boot sector is the first few bytes at the beginning of a hard drive that contains information needed to boot from the drive.)

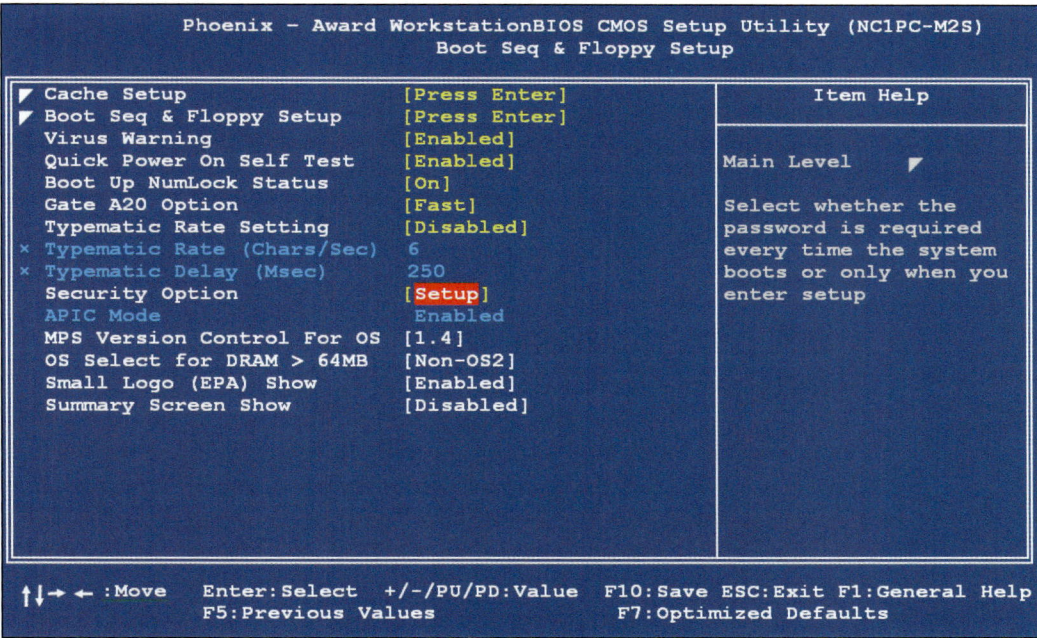

Figure 3-45 Change the way a user password functions to protect the computer

Source: Phoenix Award BIOS

A+ Exam Tip The A+ 220-801 exam expects you to know how to use BIOS setup to secure a workstation from unauthorized use.

Notes For added protection, configure the BIOS setup utility so that a user cannot boot from a removable device such as a CD, USB device, or floppy disk.

Caution In the event that passwords are forgotten, know that supervisor and user passwords to the computer can be reset by setting a jumper on the motherboard to clear all BIOS customized settings and return BIOS setup to its default settings. To keep someone from using this technique to access the computer, you can use a computer case with a lockable side panel and install a lock on the case.

LOJACK FOR LAPTOPS TECHNOLOGY

LoJack is a technology embedded in the BIOS of many laptops to protect a system against theft. When you subscribe to the LoJack for Laptops service by Absolute (*www.absolute.com*), the Computrace Agent software is installed. The software and BIOS work together to protect the system. The company can locate your laptop whenever it connects to the Internet, and you can give commands through the Internet to lock the laptop or delete all data on it.

DRIVE ENCRYPTION AND DRIVE PASSWORD PROTECTION

A+ 220-801 1.1

Some motherboards and hard drives allow you to set a password that must be entered before someone can access the hard drive. This password is kept on the drive and works even if the drive is moved to another computer. Some manufacturers of storage media offer similar products. For example, Seagate (*www.seagate.com*) offers Maxtor BlackArmor, a technology that encrypts an entire external storage media that is password protected.

> **Notes** Drive lock password protection might be too secure at times. I know of a situation where a hard drive with password protection became corrupted. Normally, you might be able to move the drive to another computer and recover some data. However, this drive asked for the password, but then could not confirm it. Therefore, the entire drive, including all the data, was inaccessible.

THE TPM CHIP AND HARD DRIVE ENCRYPTION

Many high-end computers have a chip on the motherboard called the **TPM (Trusted Platform Module) chip**. BitLocker Encryption in Windows 7/Vista is designed to work with this chip; the chip holds the BitLocker encryption key (also called the startup key). If the hard drive is stolen from the computer and installed in another computer, the data would be safe because BitLocker has encrypted all contents on the drive and would not allow access without the startup key stored on the TPM chip. Therefore, this method assures that the drive cannot be used in another computer. However, if the motherboard fails and is replaced, you'll need a backup copy of the startup key to access data on the hard drive.

> **A+ Exam Tip** The A+ 220-801 exam expects you to know about drive encryption and the TPM chip.

When you use Windows to install BitLocker Encryption, the initialization process also initializes the TPM chip. Initializing the TPM chip configures it and turns it on. After BitLocker is installed, you can temporarily turn off BitLocker, which also turns off the TPM chip. For example, you might want to turn off BitLocker to test the BitLocker recovery process. Normally, BitLocker will manage the TPM chip for you, and there is no need for you to manually change TPM chip settings. However, if you are having problems installing BitLocker, one thing you can do is clear the TPM chip. *Be careful!* If the TPM chip is being used to hold an encryption key to protect data on the hard drive and you clear the chip, the encryption key will be lost. That means all the data will be lost, too. Therefore, don't clear the TPM chip unless you are certain it is not being used to encrypt data.

APPLYING CONCEPTS | INITIALIZE OR CLEAR THE TPM CHIP

To initialize or clear the TPM chip, follow these steps:

1. Log onto Windows using an administrator account.
2. Click **Start**, type **tpm.msc**, and press **Enter**. Respond to the User Account Control box.

3. The TPM Management console opens. If there is no TPM chip present, the console displays a message that no TPM chip can be found. If your system has a TPM chip, the screen looks similar to the one in Figure 3-46.

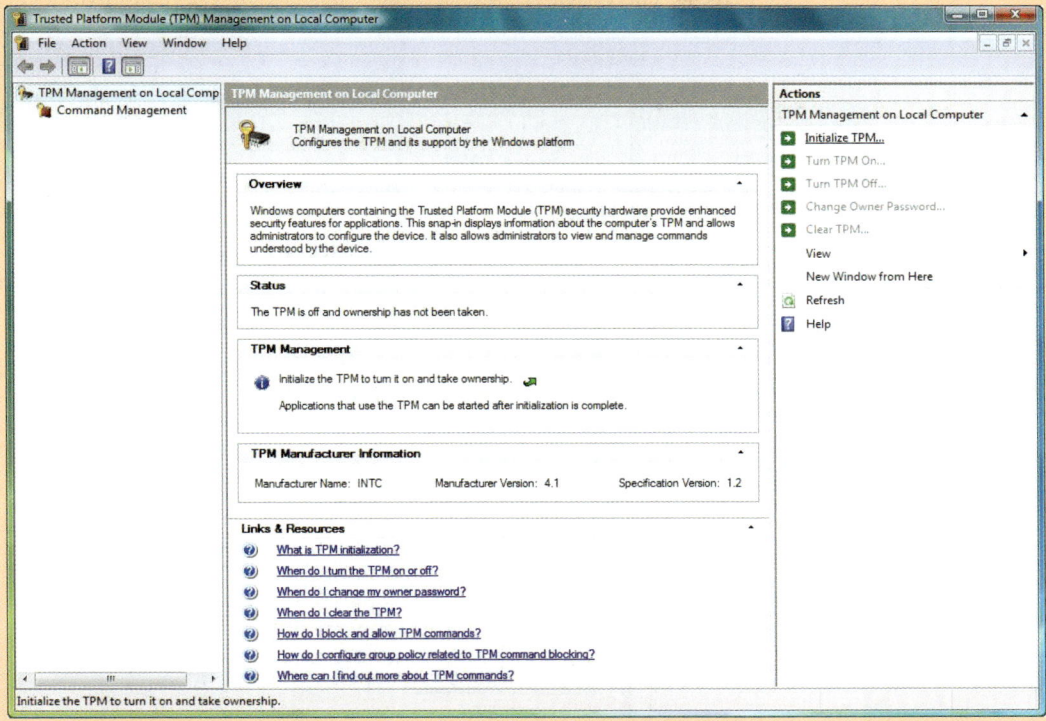

Figure 3-46 Use the TPM Management console to manage the TPM chip
Source: Microsoft Windows Vista

4. Notice in the right pane that Initialize TPM is not dimmed, which means that the TPM chip has not yet been initialized. To initialize it, click **Initialize TPM**. A dialog box (see Figure 3-47) appears, listing the steps to initialize the TPM chip, which includes shutting down and restarting the system.

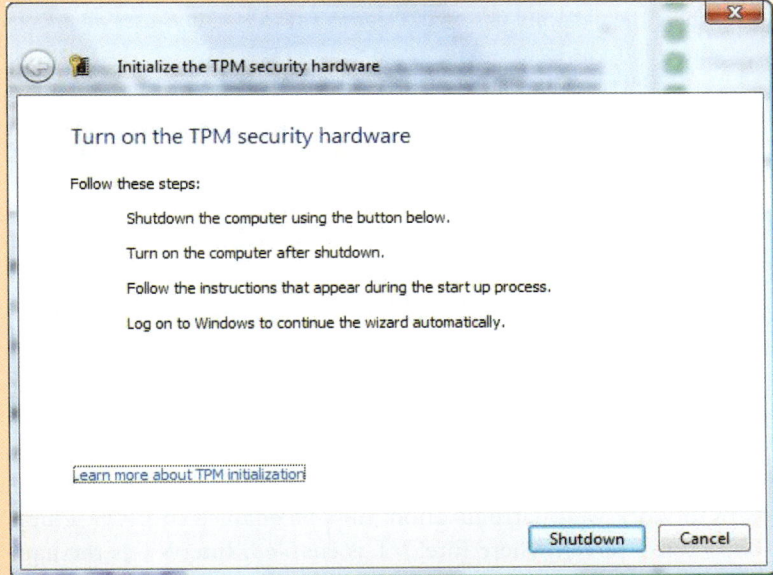

Figure 3-47 Steps to initialize the TPM chip
Source: Microsoft Windows Vista

A+ 220-801 1.1

5. After the restart, you are given the opportunity to create the TPM owner password, save the password to a removable media, and print the password (see Figure 3-48). These steps initialize the TPM chip and assign ownership. You can then use encryption software such as BitLocker Encryption or other software embedded on the hard drive to encrypt data on the drive.

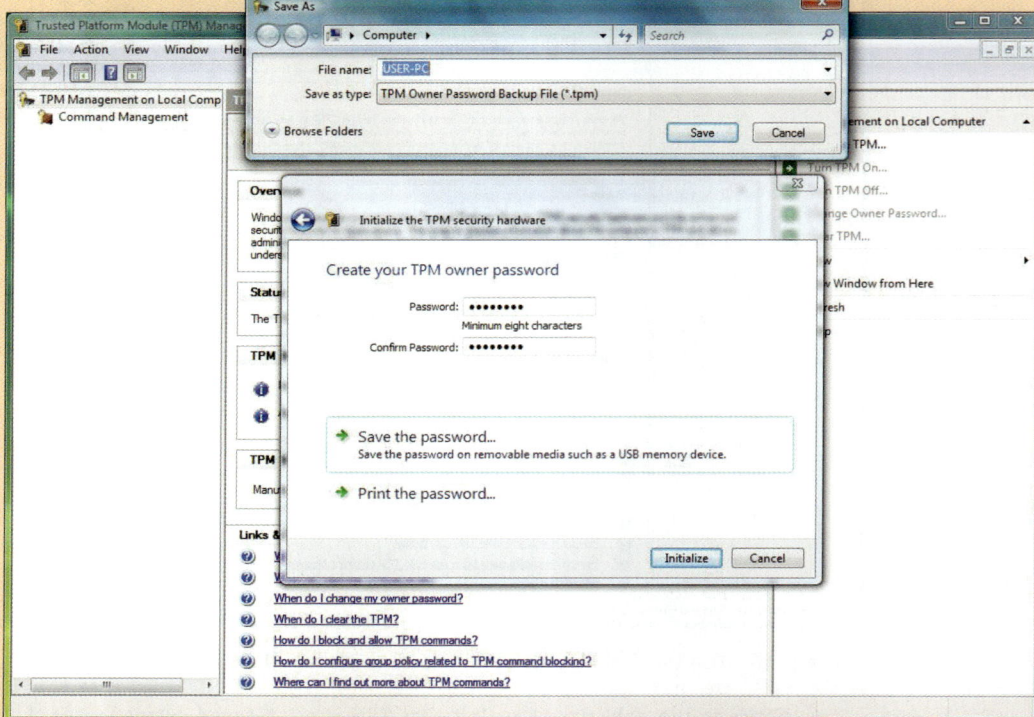

Figure 3-48 Create and save the TPM owner password

Source: Microsoft Windows Vista

6. To clear the TPM chip after it has been initialized, under Action, click **Clear TPM** and follow the directions on-screen. You will be asked to enter the owner password or provide the media where the password is stored. Clearing the TPM chip causes all encrypted data protected by the chip to be lost.

BIOS SUPPORT FOR VIRTUALIZATION

Virtualization is when one physical machine hosts multiple activities that are normally done on multiple machines. One type of virtualization is the use of virtual machines. A virtual computer or **virtual machine (VM)** is software that simulates the hardware of a physical computer. Each VM running on a computer works like a physical computer and is assigned virtual devices such as a virtual motherboard and virtual hard drive. Examples of VM software are Windows Virtual PC and Oracle Virtual Box. For VM software to work well, virtualization must be enabled in BIOS setup. Figure 3-49 shows one BIOS setup screen where Intel VT is enabled. Intel VT is the name that Intel gives to its virtualization technology.

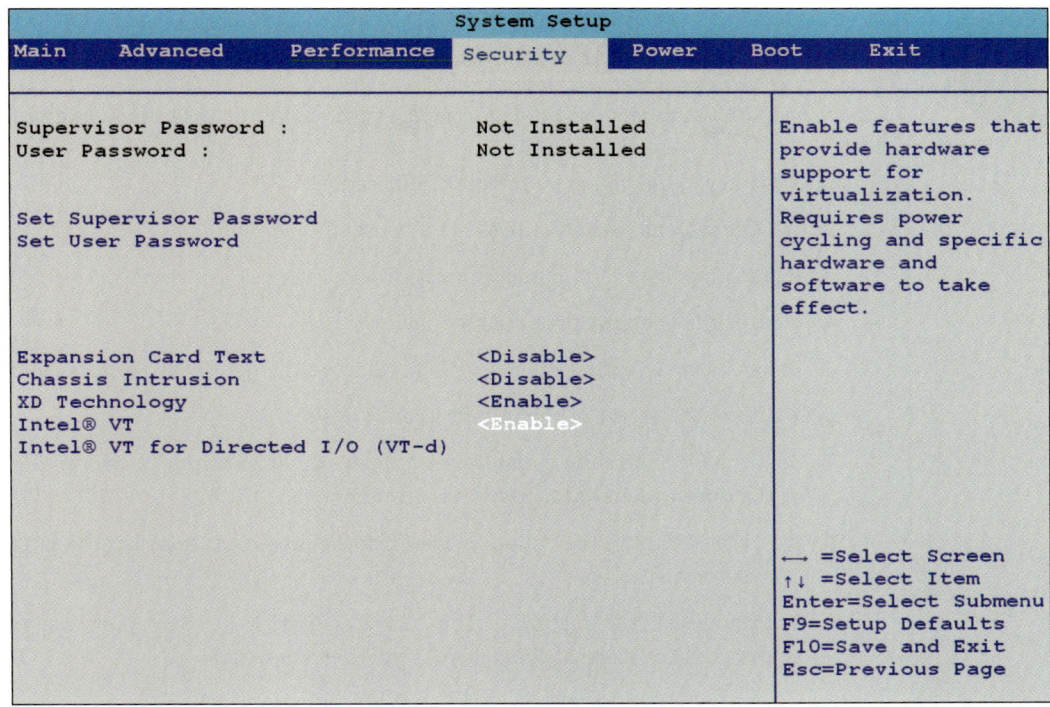

Figure 3-49 BIOS setup screen to enable hardware virtualization

EXITING THE BIOS SETUP MENUS

When you finish with BIOS setup, an exit screen such as the one shown in Figure 3-50 gives you various options, such as exit and save your changes or exit and discard your changes. Notice in the figure that you also have the option to load BIOS default settings. This option can sometimes solve a problem when a user has made several inappropriate changes to the BIOS settings.

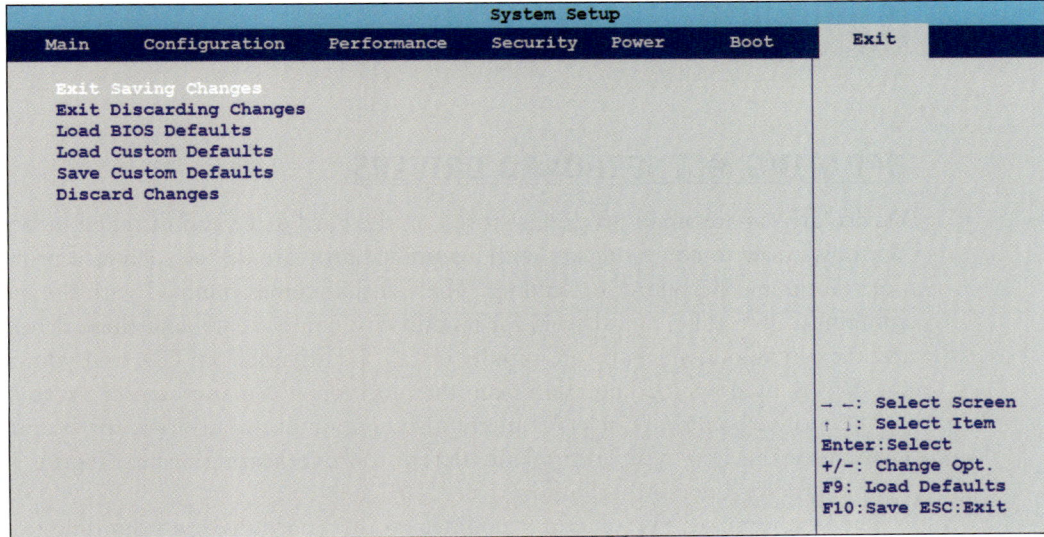

Figure 3-50 BIOS setup Exit menu

> **A+ 220-801 1.1**
>
> ## Hands-on Project 3-4 Examine BIOS Settings
>
> Access the BIOS setup program on your computer and answer the following questions:
>
> 1. What key(s) did you press to access BIOS setup?
> 2. What brand and version of BIOS are you using?
> 3. What is the frequency of your processor?
> 4. What is the boot sequence order of devices?
> 5. Do you have an optical drive installed? What are the details of the installed drive?
> 6. What are the details of the installed hard drive(s)?
> 7. Does the BIOS offer the option to set a supervisor or power-on password? What is the name of the screen where these passwords are set?
> 8. Does the BIOS offer the option to overclock the processor? If so, list the settings that apply to overclocking.
> 9. Can you disable the onboard ports on the computer? If so, which ports can you disable, and what is the name of the screen(s) where this is done?
> 10. List three BIOS settings that control how power is managed on the computer.

Now let's see what other tasks you might need to do when you are responsible for maintaining a motherboard.

MAINTAINING A MOTHERBOARD

To maintain a motherboard, you need to know how to update the motherboard drivers, flash BIOS, and replace the CMOS battery. All these skills are covered in this part of the chapter.

> **A+ Exam Tip** The A+ 220-801 exam expects you to know how to maintain a motherboard by updating drivers and firmware and replacing the CMOS battery.

UPDATING MOTHERBOARD DRIVERS

Device drivers are small programs stored on the hard drive and installed in Windows that tell Windows how to communicate with a specific hardware device such as a printer, network port on the motherboard, or scanner. The CD that comes bundled with the motherboard contains a user guide and drivers for its onboard components, and these drivers need to be installed in Windows. You can initially install the drivers from CD, and you can also update the drivers by downloading them from the motherboard manufacturer's web site.

The motherboard CD or DVD might also contain useful utilities, for example, a utility to monitor the CPU temperature and alert you if overheating occurs. Figure 3-51 shows the main menu for one motherboard driver CD.

The motherboard manufacturer updates motherboard drivers from time to time. For an unstable motherboard, you can try downloading and installing updated chipset drivers and other drivers for onboard components. Figure 3-52 shows the download page for one Intel

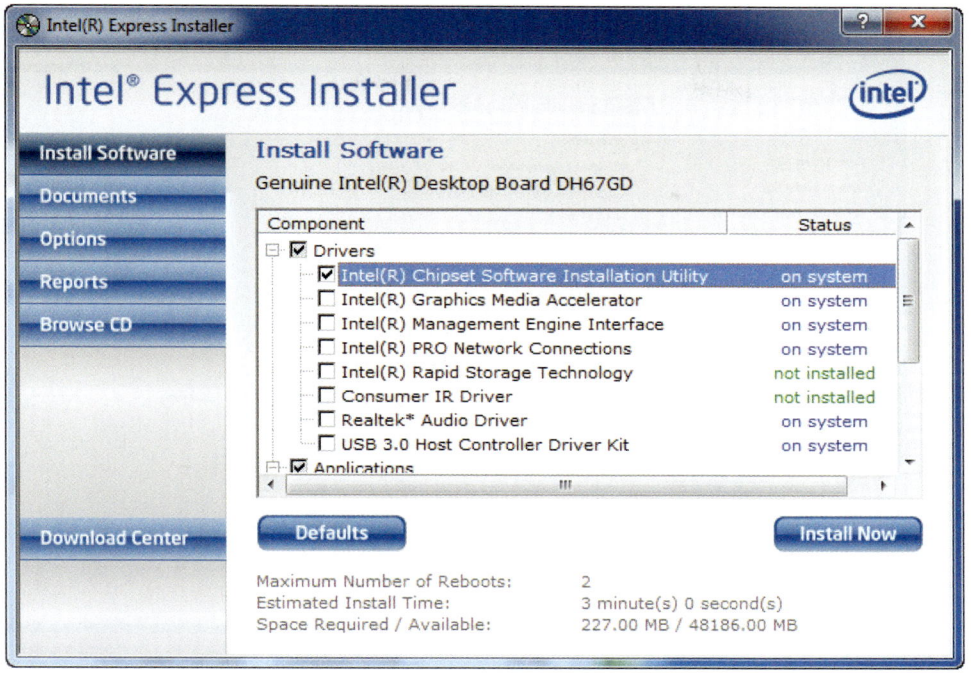

Figure 3-51 Main menu provided by the CD bundled with an Intel motherboard
Source: Intel.com

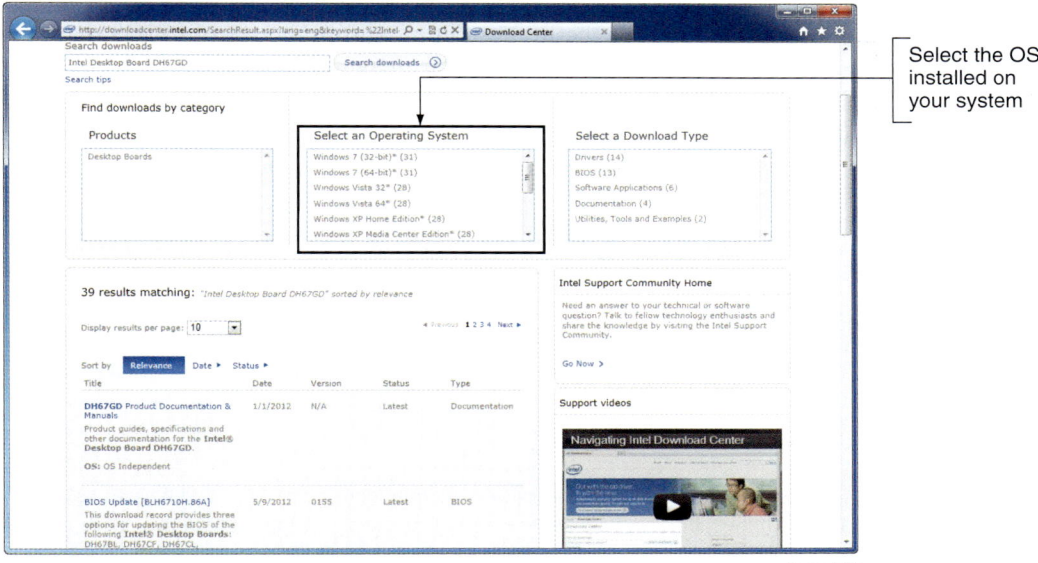

Figure 3-52 Download drivers, BIOS updates, documentation, utilities, and other help software from the motherboard manufacturer's web site
Source: Intel

motherboard where you can download drivers and BIOS updates. Notice in the figure the choices for operating systems.

Be sure to select the correct OS (for example, Windows 7) and the correct type (32 bit or 64 bit). Always use 32-bit drivers with a 32-bit OS and 64-bit drivers with a 64-bit OS. The bit number is the number of bits the driver or OS can process at one time, and you want that to match up. To know what edition and type of Windows you are using, click **Start**, right-click **Computer**, and select **Properties**. The System window appears, giving you details about the Windows installation (see Figure 3-53).

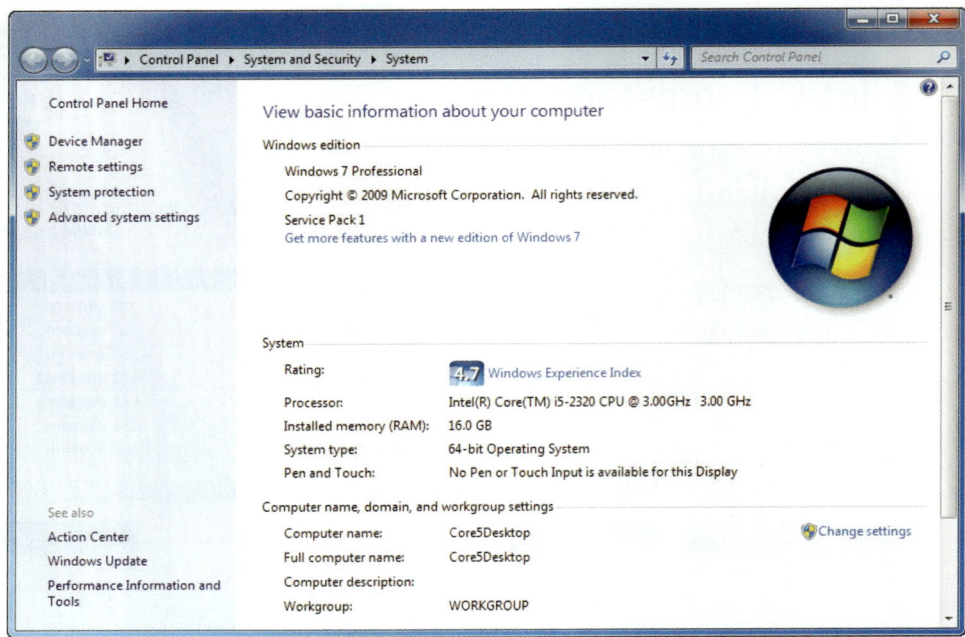

Figure 3-53 The System window reports the edition and type of OS installed

Source: Microsoft Windows 7

FLASHING BIOS

Recall that BIOS includes the BIOS setup program, the startup BIOS that manages the startup process, and the system BIOS that manages basic I/O functions of the system. All these programs are stored on a firmware chip. The process of upgrading or refreshing the programming stored on the firmware chip is called updating the BIOS or **flashing BIOS**. Here are some good reasons you might want to flash the BIOS:

- The system hangs at odd times or during the boot.
- Some motherboard functions have stopped working or are giving problems. For example, the onboard video port is not working.
- You want to incorporate some new features or component on the board. For example, a BIOS upgrade might be required before you upgrade the processor.

> **Caution** Be sure you use the correct motherboard brand and model when selecting the BIOS update on the manufacturer's web site. Trying to use the wrong update can cause problems.

The BIOS updates are downloaded from the motherboard manufacturer's web site (refer to Figure 3-52). To flash BIOS, always follow the directions that you can find in the user guide for your motherboard. Here are four methods that most motherboards can use:

- *Express BIOS update.* Some motherboards allow for an express BIOS update, which is done from Windows. Download the update file to your hard drive. Close all open applications. Double-click the file, which runs the update program, and follow the directions on-screen. The system will reboot to apply the update.

▲ *Update from a USB flash drive using setup BIOS.* Copy the downloaded update file to a USB flash drive. Then restart the system and press a key at startup that launches the BIOS update process. (For Intel motherboards, you press F7.) A screen appears where you can select the USB flash drive. BIOS finds the update file on the flash drive, completes the update, and restarts the system.

▲ *Update using a bootable CD.* You can download an ISO file from the motherboard manufacturer's web site that contains the BIOS update. An ISO file has an .iso file extension and contains an ISO image of a CD. You can use an ISO image to create a bootable CD with software and data on it. After you have created the bootable CD, boot from it and follow the directions on-screen to flash the BIOS.

> **Notes** To use Windows 7 to burn a CD from an ISO file, first insert a blank CD in the optical drive. Then right-click the .iso file, select **Burn disc image**, and follow the directions on-screen.

If the BIOS update is interrupted or the update gives errors, you are in an unfortunate situation. You might be able to revert to the earlier version. To do this, generally, you download the recovery file from the web site and copy the file to a USB flash drive. Then set the jumper on the motherboard to recover from a failed BIOS update. Reboot the system and the BIOS automatically reads from the device and performs the recovery. Then reset the jumper to the normal setting and boot the system.

> **Notes** To identify the BIOS version installed, look for the BIOS version number displayed on the main menu of BIOS setup. Alternately, you can use the System Information utility (Msinfo32.exe) in Windows to display the BIOS version.

Makers of BIOS code are likely to change BIOS frequently because providing the upgrade on the Internet is so easy for them. Generally, however, follow the principle that "if it's not broke, don't fix it." Update your BIOS only if you're having a problem with your motherboard or there's a new BIOS feature you want to use. Also, don't update the BIOS unless the update is a later version than the one installed. One last word of caution: it's very important the update not be interrupted while it is in progress. A failed update can make your motherboard totally unusable. Be sure you don't interrupt the update, and make sure there are no power interruptions.

> **Caution** Be very *careful* that you upgrade BIOS with the correct upgrade and that you follow the manufacturer's instructions correctly. Upgrading with the wrong file could make your system BIOS useless. If you're not sure that you're using the correct upgrade, *don't guess*. Check with the technical support for your BIOS before moving forward. Before you call technical support, have the information that identifies your BIOS and motherboard available.

REPLACING THE CMOS BATTERY

A small trickle of electricity from a nearby lithium coin-cell battery (see Figure 3-54) enables CMOS RAM to hold configuration data, even while the main power to the computer is off. If the CMOS battery is disconnected or fails, setup information is lost. An indication that the battery is getting weak is that the system date and time are incorrect after power has been disconnected to the PC. A message about a low battery can also appear at startup.

A+ 220-801 1.1, 1.2

Figure 3-54 The coin-cell battery powers CMOS RAM when the system is turned off

> **A+ Exam Tip** The A+ 220-801 exam expects you to know about the CMOS battery.

The CMOS battery on the motherboard is considered a field replaceable unit. The battery is designed to last for years and recharges when the motherboard has power. However, on rare occasions, you might need to replace one if the system loses BIOS settings when it is unplugged. Make sure the replacement battery is an exact match to the original or is one the motherboard manufacturer recommends for the board. Power down the system, unplug it, press the power button to drain the power, and remove the case cover. Use your ground bracelet to protect the system against ESD. The old battery can be removed with a little prying using a flathead screwdriver. The new battery pops into place. For more specific directions, see the motherboard documentation.

Now let's turn our attention to installing or replacing a motherboard.

INSTALLING OR REPLACING A MOTHERBOARD

A+ 220-802 4.2

A motherboard is considered a field replaceable unit, so you need to know how to replace one when it goes bad. In this part of the chapter, you learn how to select a motherboard and then how to install or replace one.

A+ 220-801 1.2

HOW TO SELECT A MOTHERBOARD

Because the motherboard determines so many of your computer's features, selecting the motherboard is, in most cases, your most important decision when you purchase a computer or assemble one from parts. Depending on which applications and peripheral devices you plan to use with the computer, you can take one of three approaches to selecting a motherboard. The first approach is to select the board that provides the most room for expansion, so you can upgrade and exchange components and add devices easily. A second approach is to select the board that best suits the needs of the computer's current configuration, knowing that when you need to upgrade, you will likely switch to new technology and a new motherboard. The third approach is to select a motherboard that meets your present needs with moderate room for expansion.

Ask the following questions when selecting a motherboard:

1. What form factor does the motherboard use?
2. Which brand (Intel or AMD) and model processors does the board support? Which chipset does it use? How much memory can it hold? What memory speeds does the board support?
3. What type and how many expansion slots are on the board (for example, PCI Express 2.0 or PCI)?
4. How many and what hard drive controllers and connectors are on the board (for example, SATA, eSATA, and IDE)?
5. What are the embedded devices on the board, and what internal slots or connections does the board have? (For example, the board might provide a network port, wireless antenna port, FireWire port, two or more USB ports, video port, and so forth.)
6. Does the board fit the case you plan to use?
7. What are the price and the warranty on the board? Does the board get good reviews?
8. How extensive and user-friendly is the documentation?
9. How much support does the manufacturer supply for the board?

Sometimes a motherboard contains an on-board component more commonly offered as a separate device. One example is support for video. The video port might be on the motherboard or might require a video card. The cost of a motherboard with an embedded component is usually less than the combined cost of a motherboard with no embedded component and an expansion card. If you plan to expand, be cautious about choosing a proprietary board that has many embedded components. Often such boards do not easily accept add-on devices from other manufacturers. For example, if you plan to add a more powerful video card, you might not want to choose a motherboard that contains an onboard video port. Even though you can likely disable the video port in BIOS setup, there is little advantage to paying the extra money for it.

> **Notes** If you have an embedded component, make sure you can disable it so you can use another external component if needed. Components are disabled in BIOS setup.

Table 3-6 shown earlier in the chapter lists some manufacturers of motherboards and their web addresses. For motherboard reviews, check out *www.motherboards.org* and *www.pcmag.com*, or do a general search of the web.

HOW TO INSTALL OR REPLACE A MOTHERBOARD

When you purchase a motherboard, the package comes with the board, I/O shield, documentation, drivers, and various screws, cables, and connectors (see Figure 3-55). When you replace a motherboard, you pretty much have to disassemble an entire computer, install the new motherboard, and reassemble the system, which you learned to do in Chapter 2. The following list is meant to be a general overview of the process and is not meant to include the details of all possible installation scenarios, which can vary according to the components and case you are using. The best place to go for detailed instructions on installing a motherboard is the motherboard user guide.

Video: Motherboard Installation

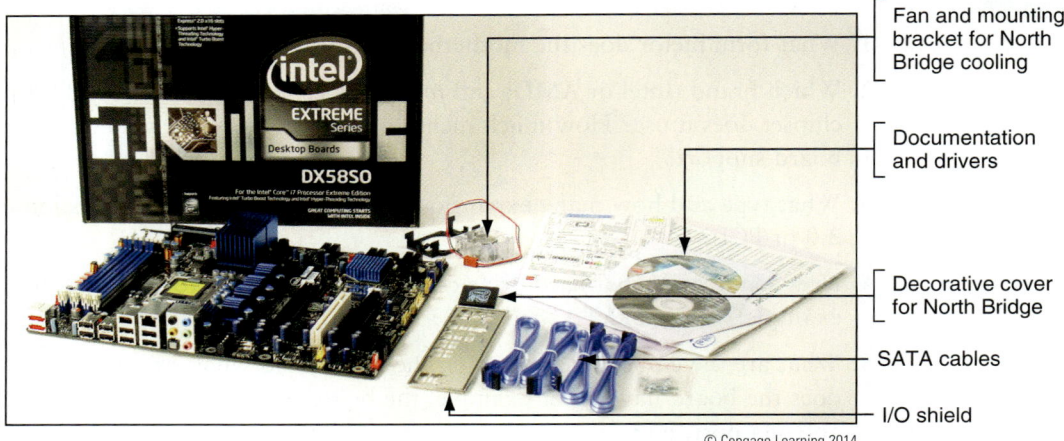

Figure 3-55 A new motherboard package

> **Caution** As with any installation, remember the importance of using a ground strap (ground bracelet) to ground yourself when working inside a computer case to protect components against ESD. Alternately, you can use antistatic gloves to protect components.

The general process for replacing a motherboard is as follows:

1. *Verify that you have selected the right motherboard to install in the system.* The new motherboard should have the same form factor as the case, support the RAM modules and processor you want to install on it, and have other internal and external connectors you need for your system.

2. *Get familiar with the motherboard documentation, features, and settings.* Especially important are any connectors and jumpers on the motherboard. It's a great idea to read the motherboard user guide from cover to cover. At the least, get familiar with what it has to offer and study the diagrams in it that label all the components on the board. Learn how each connector and jumper is used. You can also check the manufacturer's web site for answers to any questions you might have.

3. *Remove components so you can reach the old motherboard.* Use a ground bracelet. Turn off the system and disconnect all cables and cords. Press the power button to dissipate the power. Open the case cover and remove all expansion cards. Disconnect all internal cables and cords connected to the old motherboard. To safely remove the old motherboard, you might have to remove drives. If the processor cooler is heavy and bulky, you might remove it from the old motherboard before you remove the motherboard from the case.

4. *Set any jumpers on the new motherboard.* This is much easier to do before you put the board in the case. Verify the BIOS startup jumper is set for normal startup.

5. *Install the I/O shield.* The I/O shield is a metal plate that comes with the motherboard and fits over the ports to create a well-fitting enclosure for them. A case might come with a standard I/O shield already in place. Hold the motherboard up to the shield and make sure the ports on the board will fit the holes in the shield (see Figure 3-56). If the holes in the shield don't match up with the ports on the board, punch out the shield and replace it with the one that came bundled with the motherboard.

Figure 3-56 Make sure the holes in the I/O shield match up with the ports on the motherboard

6. *Install the motherboard.* Place the motherboard into the case and, using spacers or screws, securely fasten the board to the case. Because coolers are heavy, most processor instructions say to install the motherboard before installing the processor and cooler to better protect the board or processor from being damaged. On the other hand, some motherboard manufacturers say to install the processor and cooler and then install the motherboard. Follow the order given in the motherboard user guide. The easiest approach is to install the processor, cooler, and memory modules on the board and then place the board in the case (see Figure 3-57).

7. *Install the processor and processor cooler.* The processor comes already installed on some motherboards, in which case you just need to install the cooler. How to install a processor and cooler is covered in Chapter 4.

8. *Install RAM into the appropriate slots on the motherboard.* How to install RAM is covered in Chapter 4.

9. *Attach cabling that goes from the case switches to the motherboard, and from the power supply and drives to the motherboard.* Pay attention to how cables are labeled and to any information in the documentation about where to attach them. Chapter 1 can help you identify the types of power connectors. You'll need to connect the P1 connector, the fan connectors, and the processor auxiliary power connector. Position and tie cables neatly together to make sure they don't obstruct the fans and the air flow.

Figure 3-57 Motherboard with processor, cooler, and memory modules installed is ready to go in the case

10. *Install the video card on the motherboard.* This card should go into the primary PCI Express x16 slot. If you plan to install multiple video cards, install only one now and check out how the system functions before installing the second one.

11. *Plug the computer into a power source, and attach the monitor, keyboard, and mouse.* Initially install only the devices you absolutely need.

12. *Boot the system and enter BIOS setup.* Make sure settings are set to the default. If the motherboard comes new from the manufacturer, it will already be at default settings. If you are salvaging a motherboard from another system, you might need to reset settings to the default. You will need to do the following while you are in BIOS setup:

    ▲ Check the time and date.

    ▲ Make sure abbreviated POST (quick boot) is disabled. While you're installing a motherboard, you generally want it to do as many diagnostic tests as possible. After you know the system is working, you can choose to abbreviate POST.

    ▲ Set the boot order to the hard drive, and then a CD, if you will be booting the OS from the hard drive.

    ▲ Leave everything else at their defaults unless you know that particular settings should be otherwise.

    ▲ Save and exit.

13. *Observe POST and verify that no errors occur.*

14. *Verify Windows starts with no errors.* If Windows is already installed on the hard drive, boot to the Windows desktop. Use Device Manager to verify that the OS recognizes all devices and that no conflicts are reported.

15. *Install the motherboard drivers.* If your motherboard comes with a CD that contains

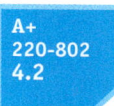
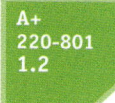

some motherboard drivers, install them now. You will probably need Internet access so that the setup process can download the latest drivers from the motherboard manufacturer's web site. Reboot the system one more time, checking for errors.

16. *Install any other expansion cards and drivers.* Install each device and its drivers, one device at a time, rebooting and checking for conflicts after each installation.

17. *Verify that everything is operating properly, and make any final OS and BIOS adjustments, such as setting power-on passwords.*

> **Notes** Whenever you install or uninstall software or hardware, keep a notebook with details about the components you are working on, configuration settings, manufacturer specifications, and other relevant information. This helps if you need to backtrack later and can also help you document and troubleshoot your computer system. Keep all hardware documentation for this system together with the notebook in an envelope in a safe place.

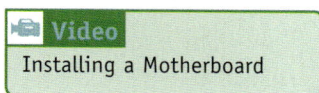
Installing a Motherboard

Hands-on | Project 3-6 Insert and Remove Motherboards

Using old or defective expansion cards and motherboards, practice inserting and removing expansion cards and motherboards. In a lab or classroom setting, the instructor can provide extra cards and motherboards for exchange.

>> CHAPTER SUMMARY

Motherboard Types and Features

- The motherboard is the most complicated of all components inside the computer. It contains the processor socket and accompanying chipset, firmware holding the BIOS, CMOS RAM, system bus, memory slots, expansion slots, jumpers, ports, and power supply connections. The motherboard you select determines both the capabilities and limitations of your system.

- The most popular motherboard form factors are ATX, microATX, and Mini-ITX.

- A motherboard will have one or more Intel sockets for an Intel processor or one or more AMD sockets for an AMD processor.

- Intel, AMD, NVIDIA, and SiS are the most popular chipset manufacturers. The chipset embedded on the motherboard determines what kind of processor and memory the board can support.

- Major advancements in Intel chipsets include the Accelerated Hub Architecture (using the North Bridge and South Bridge), Nehalem chipsets (using the memory controller on the processor), Sandy Bridge chipsets (using the memory and graphics controller on the processor) and the Ivy Bridge chipsets.
- Buses used on motherboards include conventional PCI, PCI-X, PCI Express, and AGP. AGP is used solely for video cards. PCI Express has been revised three times and is replacing all the other bus types.
- Some components can be built into the motherboard, in which case they are called on-board components. Other components can be attached to the system in some other way, such as on an expansion card.

Configuring a Motherboard

- The most common method of configuring components on a motherboard is BIOS setup. Some motherboards also use jumpers or DIP switches to contain configuration settings.
- Motherboard settings that can be configured using BIOS setup include changing the boot priority order, enabling or disabling onboard devices, support for virtualization, and security settings (for example, power-on passwords and intrusion detection). You can also view information about the installed processor, memory, and storage devices and temperatures, fan speeds, and voltages.

Maintaining a Motherboard

- Motherboard drivers might need updating to fix a problem with a board component or to use a new feature provided by the motherboard manufacturer.
- Sometimes ROM BIOS programming stored on the firmware chip needs updating or refreshing. This process is called updating BIOS or flashing BIOS. The CMOS battery that powers CMOS RAM might need replacing.

Installing or Replacing a Motherboard

- When selecting a motherboard, pay attention to the form factor, chipset, expansion slots, and memory slots used and the processors supported. Also notice the internal and external connectors and ports the board provides.
- When installing a motherboard, first study the motherboard and its manual, and set jumpers on the board. Sometimes the processor and cooler are best installed before installing the motherboard in the case. When the cooling assembly is heavy and bulky, it is best to install it after the motherboard is securely seated in the case.

>> **KEY TERMS**

For explanations of key terms, see the Glossary near the end of the book.

Accelerated Graphics Port (AGP)	CMOS RAM	hertz (Hz)
ball grid array (BGA)	data bus	I/O shield
bus	data path size	ISO image
chipset	device driver	jumper
CMOS (complementary metal-oxide semiconductor)	flashing BIOS	land grid array (LGA)
	Front Side Bus (FSB)	flip-chip land grid array (FCLGA)
CMOS battery	gigahertz (GHz)	

flip-chip pin grid array (FCPGA)
LoJack
megahertz (MHz)
North Bridge
on-board ports
PCI Express (PCIe)
pin grid array (PGA)
protocol

QuickPath Interconnect
riser card
South Bridge
staggered pin grid array (SPGA)
system bus
system clock
TPM (Trusted Platform Module) chip

traces
Unified Extensible Firmware Interface (UEFI)
virtual machine (VM)
virtualization
wait state
zero insertion force (ZIF) socket

>> REVIEWING THE BASICS

1. What are the three most popular form factors used for motherboards?
2. Which type of Intel chipset was the first to support the graphics controller to be part of the processor?
3. How many pins does the Intel Socket B have? What is another name for this socket?
4. What type of memory does the LGA1155 socket work with? Which socket was it designed to replace?
5. Does the Sandy Bridge chipset family use two chipset housings on the motherboard or a single chipset housing? The Nehalem chipset?
6. How many pins does the AMD socket AM2 have?
7. Which socket by AMD uses a land grid array rather than a pin grid array?
8. Which is a better performing Intel chipset, the X58 or the H67?
9. Which part of a Nehalem chipset connects directly to the processor, the North Bridge or the South Bridge?
10. What are the names of the two technologies used to install multiple video cards in the same system?
11. What are the two different voltages that a PCI slot can provide?
12. How does the throughput of PCI Express Version 1.1 compare to PCIe Version 1? How does PCIe Version 2 compare to Version 1?
13. What is the maximum wattage that a PCIe Version 2.0 expansion card can draw?
14. What new type of power connector on the motherboard was introduced with PCIe Version 1.0? How much power does this connector provide?
15. What new type of power connector was introduced with PCIe Version 2.0? How much power does this connector provide?
16. If you are installing an expansion card into a case that does not have enough clearance above the motherboard for the card, what device can you use to solve the problem?
17. What is the purpose of an AGP slot?
18. Which is faster, a PCI Express x16 bus or the latest AGP bus?

19. Which chip on the motherboard does Windows Bitlocker Encryption use to secure the hard drive?
20. How can you find out how many memory slots are populated on a motherboard without opening the computer case?
21. What are two reasons you might decide to flash BIOS?
22. What is the easiest way to obtain the latest software to upgrade BIOS?
23. What can you do if the power-on password and the supervisor password to a system have been forgotten?
24. Where is the boot priority order for devices kept?
25. How is CMOS RAM powered when the system is unplugged?
26. Describe how you can access the BIOS setup program.
27. If a USB port on the motherboard is failing, what is one task you can do that might fix the problem?
28. What might the purpose be for a SATA-style power connector on a motherboard?
29. What is the purpose of installing standoffs or spacers between the motherboard and the case?
30. When installing a motherboard, suppose you forget to connect the wires from the case to the front panel header. Will you be able to power up the system? Why or why not?

>> THINKING CRITICALLY

1. Why does a motherboard sometimes support more than one Front Side Bus speed?
2. Why don't all buses on a motherboard operate at the same speed?
3. When you turn off the power to a computer at night, it loses the date, and you must reenter it each morning. What is the problem and how do you solve it?
4. Why do you think the trend is to store configuration information on a motherboard in CMOS RAM rather than by using jumpers or switches?
5. Why do you think the trend is to put more control such as the graphics controller and the memory controller in the processor rather than in the chipset?
6. When troubleshooting a motherboard, you discover the network port no longer works. What is the best and least expensive solution to this problem? If this solution does not work, which solution should you try next?

    a. Replace the motherboard.

    b. Disable the network port and install a network card in an expansion slot.

    c. Use a wireless network device in a USB port to connect to a wireless network.

    d. Return the motherboard to the factory for repair.

    e. Update the motherboard drivers.

7. A computer freezes at odd times. At first, you suspect the power supply or overheating, but you have eliminated overheating and replaced the power supply without solving the problem. What do you do next?

   a. Replace the processor.

   b. Replace the motherboard.

   c. Reinstall Windows.

   d. Replace the memory modules.

   e. Flash BIOS.

>> REAL PROBLEMS, REAL SOLUTIONS

REAL PROBLEM 3-1: Labeling the Motherboard

Figure 3-58 shows a blank diagram of an ATX motherboard. Using what you learned in this chapter and in Chapter 1, label as many components as you can. If you would like to print the diagram, look for "Figure 3-58" in the online content that accompanies this book at *www.cengagebrain.com*. For more information on accessing this content, see the Preface.

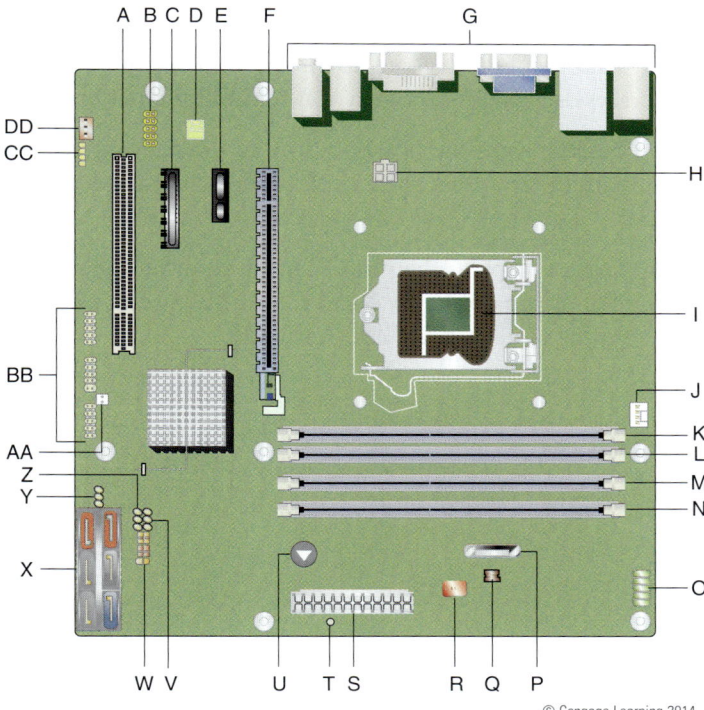

Figure 3-58 Label the motherboard

REAL PROBLEM 3-2: Selecting a Replacement Motherboard

When a motherboard fails, you can select and buy a new board to replace it. Suppose the motherboard in your computer has failed and you want to buy a replacement and keep your repair costs to a minimum. Try to find a replacement motherboard on the web that can use the same case, power supply, processor, memory, and expansion cards as your current system. If you cannot find a good match, what other components might have to be replaced (for example, the processor or memory)? What is the total cost of the replacement parts? Save or print web pages showing what you need to purchase.

REAL PROBLEM 3-3: Research Maintaining a Motherboard

Using the motherboard user guide that you downloaded in Hands-on Project 3-4, answer the following questions:

1. How many methods can be used to flash BIOS on the motherboard? Describe each method. What can you do to recover the system if flashing BIOS fails?
2. Locate the CMOS battery on the diagram of the motherboard. What are the steps to replace this battery?

Using a computer in your school lab, do the following to practice replacing the CMOS battery:

1. Locate the CMOS battery on your motherboard. What is written on top of the battery? Using the web, find a replacement for this battery. Print the web page showing the battery. How much does the new battery cost?
2. Enter BIOS setup on your computer. Write down any BIOS settings that are not default settings. You'll need these settings later when you reinstall the battery.
3. Turn off and unplug the PC, press the power button to drain the system of power, open the case, remove the battery, and boot the PC. What error messages appear? What is the system date and time?
4. Power down the PC, unplug it, press the power button to drain the power, replace the battery, and boot the PC. Close up the case and return BIOS settings to the way you found them. Make sure the system is working normally.

CHAPTER 4
Supporting Processors and Upgrading Memory

In this chapter, you will learn:

- About the characteristics and purposes of Intel and AMD processors used for personal computers
- How to install and upgrade a processor
- About the different kinds of physical memory and how they work
- How to upgrade memory

In the last chapter, you learned about motherboards. In this chapter, you'll learn about the two most important components on the motherboard, which are the processor and memory. You'll learn how a processor works, about the many different types and brands of processors, and how to match a processor to the motherboard.

Memory technologies have evolved over the years. When you support an assortment of desktop and notebook computers, you'll be amazed at all the different variations of memory modules used in newer computers and older computers still in use. A simple problem of replacing a bad memory module can become a complex research project if you don't have a good grasp of current and past memory technologies.

The processor and memory modules are considered field replaceable units (FRU), so you'll learn how to install and upgrade a processor and memory modules. Upgrading the processor or adding more memory to a system can sometimes greatly improve performance. How to troubleshoot problems with the processor or memory is covered in Chapter 8, *Troubleshooting Hardware Problems*.

TYPES AND CHARACTERISTICS OF PROCESSORS

A+ 220-801 1.6

The processor installed on a motherboard is the primary component that determines the computing power of the system (see Figure 4-1). Recall that the two major manufacturers of processors are Intel (*www.intel.com*) and AMD (*www.amd.com*).

Figure 4-1 An AMD Athlon 64 X2 installed in socket AM2+ with cooler not yet installed

In this chapter, you learn a lot of details about processors. As you do, try to keep these nine features of processors at the forefront. These features affect performance and compatibility with motherboards:

- *Feature 1: Clock speed the processor supports.* Current Intel and AMD processors work with system buses that run at 1.8 GHz up to more than 3.4 GHz. Recall from Chapter 3 that the smaller the processor multiplier, the faster the system bus runs in comparison to the processor speed.
- *Feature 2: Processor speed.* Processor core frequency is measured in gigahertz, such as 3.3 GHz.
- *Feature 3: Socket and chipset the processor can use.* Recall from Chapter 3 that important Intel sockets for desktop systems are the PGA988, LGA2011, LGA1155, LGA1156, LGA1366, and LGA775. AMD's important desktop sockets are AM3+, AM3, AM2+, AM2, FM1, F, and 940 sockets.
- *Feature 4: Processor architecture (32 bits or 64 bits).* All desktop and laptop processors sold today from either Intel or AMD are hybrid processors, which can process 64 bits or 32 bits at a time, but older processors handled only 32 bits. A hybrid processor can use a 32-bit operating system or a 64-bit OS. Most editions of Windows 7 come in either type.

- *Feature 5: Multiprocessing abilities*. The ability of a system to do more than one thing at a time is accomplished by several means:
  - *Multiprocessing*. Two processing units (called arithmetic logic units or ALUs) installed within a single processor (called **multiprocessing** and first used by Pentium processors). The Pentium was the first processor that could execute two instructions at the same time.
  - *Dual processors*. A server motherboard might have two processor sockets, called **dual processors** or a **multiprocessor platform** (see Figure 4-2). A processor (for example, the Xeon processor for servers) must support this feature.

Two processor sockets

Source: Intel

Figure 4-2 This motherboard for a server has two processor sockets, which allow for a multiprocessor platform

  - *Multi-core processing*. Multiple processors can be installed in the same processor housing (called **multi-core processing**). A processor package might contain up to eight cores (dual-core, triple-core, quad-core, and so forth).
  - *Multithreading*. Each processor or core processes two threads at the same time. When Windows hands off a task to the CPU it is called a **thread** and might involve several instructions. To handle two threads, the processor requires extra registers, or holding areas, within the processor housing that it uses to switch between threads. In effect, you have two logical processors for each physical processor or core. Intel calls this technology **Hyper-Threading** and AMD calls it **HyperTransport**. The feature must be enabled in BIOS setup.
- *Feature 6: Memory cache, which is the amount of memory included within the processor package*. Today's processors all have some memory on the processor chip (called a die). Memory on the processor die is called **Level 1 cache (L1 cache)**. Memory in the processor package, but not on the processor die, is called **Level 2 cache (L2 cache)**. Some processors use a third cache farther from the processor core, but still in the processor package, which is called **Level 3 cache (L3 cache)**. Memory used in a memory cache

is static RAM or SRAM (pronounced "S-Ram"). Memory used on the motherboard loses data rapidly and must be refreshed often. It is, therefore, called volatile memory or dynamic RAM or DRAM (pronounced "D-Ram"). SRAM is faster than DRAM because it doesn't need refreshing; it can hold its data as long as power is available.

▲ *Feature 7: The memory features on the motherboard that the processor can support.* Current types of DRAM memory modules used on a motherboard include DDR, DDR2, or DDR3. Besides the type of memory, a processor can support certain amounts of memory, memory speeds, and number of memory channels (single, dual, triple, or quad channels). All these characteristics of memory are discussed later in the chapter.

▲ *Feature 8: Support for virtualization.* Recall from Chapter 3 that a computer can use software to create and manage multiple virtual machines that contain virtual devices. Most processors sold today support virtualization, and the feature must be enabled in BIOS setup.

▲ *Feature 9: Integrated graphics.* A processor might include an integrated GPU. A graphics processing unit (GPU) is a processor that manipulates graphic data to form the images on a monitor screen. The GPU might be on a video card, on the motherboard, or embedded in the CPU package. When inside the CPU package, it is called integrated graphics. Many AMD processors and all the Intel second generation (Sandy Bridge) and third generation (Ivy Bridge) processors have integrated graphics.

> **A+ Exam Tip** The A+ 220-801 exam expects you to be familiar with the characteristics of processors. Know the purposes and characteristics of Hyper-threading, core processing, types of cache, virtualization, integrated GPU, and 32-bit versus 64-bit processing.

Let's now turn our attention to a discussion of how a processor works, including several of the processor features just listed. Then you'll learn about the families of Intel and AMD processors.

HOW A PROCESSOR WORKS

Although processors continue to evolve, they all have some common elements. These elements are diagrammed in Figure 4-3 for the Pentium processor. The Pentium made several major advances in processor technologies when it was first introduced. Because of its historical significance and the foundation it created for today's processors, it's a great place to start when learning how a processor works.

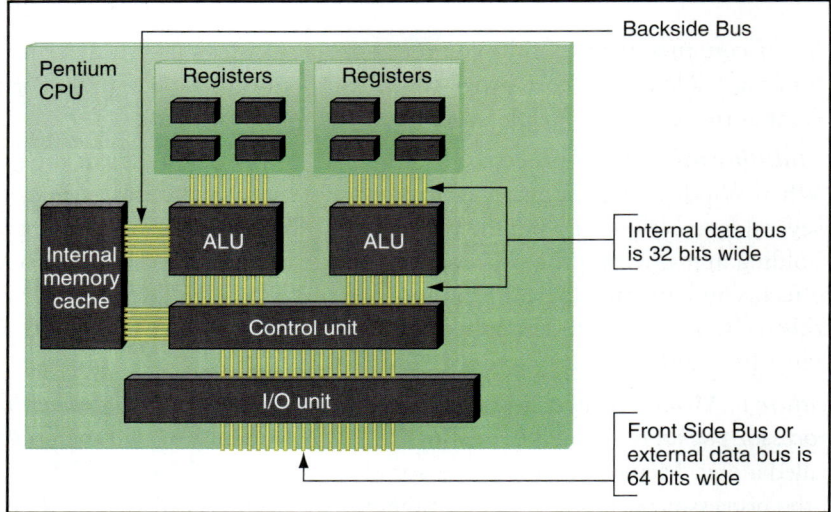

Figure 4-3 Since the Pentium processor was first released in 1993, the standard has been for a processor to have two arithmetic logic units so that it can process two instructions at once

A processor contains these basic components diagrammed in Figure 4-3 for the Pentium processor:

A+ 220-801 1.6

- An input/output (I/O) unit manages data and instructions entering and leaving the processor.
- A control unit manages all activities inside the processor itself.
- One or more arithmetic logic units (ALUs) do all logical comparisons and calculations inside the processor. All desktop and laptop processors sold today contain two ALUs in each processor core within the processor package.
- Registers, which are small holding areas on the processor chip, work much like RAM does outside the processor to hold counters, data, instructions, and addresses that the ALU is currently processing.
- Internal memory caches (L1, L2, and possibly L3) hold data and instructions waiting to be processed by the ALU.
- Buses inside the processor connect components within the processor housing. These buses run at a much higher frequency than the Front Side Bus (FSB) that connects the processor to the chipset and memory on the motherboard.

The speed at which the processor operates internally is called the **processor frequency**. For example, if the processor operates at 3.2 GHz internally but the Front Side Bus is operating at 800 MHz, the processor operates at four times the FSB speed. This factor is called the **multiplier**. As you learned in Chapter 3, you can view the actual processor frequency and the clock speed using the BIOS setup screens. You can also change the multiplier or the clock speed in order to overclock or throttle the processor.

In Figure 4-3, you can see the internal data bus for the Pentium was only 32 bits wide. More important, however, than the width of the internal bus is the fact that each ALU and register in the early Pentiums could process only 32 bits at a time. All desktop and laptop processors sold today from either Intel or AMD contain ALUs and registers that can process 32 bits or 64 bits at a time. To know which type of operating system to install, you need to be aware of three categories of processors currently used on desktop and laptop computers:

- *32-bit processors.* These older processors are known as **x86 processors** because Intel used the number 86 in the model number of these processors. If you are ever called on to install Windows on one of these old Pentium computers, you must use a 32-bit version of Windows. These processors can handle only 32-bit instructions from the OS.
- *Processors that can process 32 bits or 64 bits.* These hybrid processors are known as **x86-64 bit processors**. AMD was the first to produce one (the Athlon 64) and called the technology AMD64. Intel followed with a version of its Pentium 4 processors and called the technology Extended Memory 64 Technology (EM64T). Because of their hybrid nature, these processors can handle a 32-bit OS or a 64-bit OS. All desktop or laptop processors made after 2007 are of this type.
- *64-bit processors.* Intel makes several 64-bit processors for workstations or servers that use fully implemented 64-bit processing, including the Itanium and Xeon processors. Intel calls the technology IA64, but they are also called x64 processors. They require a 64-bit operating system and can handle 32-bit applications only by simulating 32-bit processing.

> **Notes** To know which type of operating system is installed (32-bit or 64-bit) and other information about the Windows installation, recall from Chapter 3 that you can use the System window. To open the System window, click **Start**, right-click **Computer**, and select **Properties**.

Each core in a processor has its own cache and can also share a cache. Figure 4-4 shows how quad-core processing can work if the processor uses an L3 cache and an internal memory controller. Each core within a processor has its own independent internal L1 and L2 caches. The L1 cache is on the die and the L2 cache is off the die. In addition, all the cores might share an L3 cache within the processor package. Recall from Chapter 3 that prior to the memory controller being in the processor package, it was part of the North Bridge chipset. Putting the controller inside the processor package resulted in a significant increase in system performance.

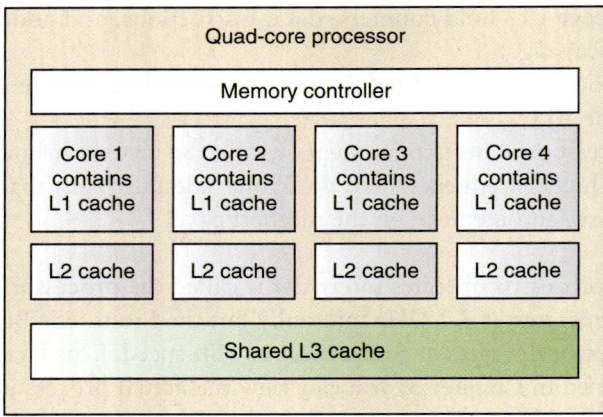

Figure 4-4 Quad-core processing with L1, L2, and L3 cache and the memory controller within the processor housing

INTEL PROCESSORS

Intel's current families of processors for the desktop include the Core, Atom, Celeron, and Pentium families of processors. In addition, Intel groups its processors into Third Generation, Second Generation, and Previous Generation processors. Each generation improves on how the processor and chipset are integrated in the system. Processors in each family are listed in Table 4-1. Some significant retired processors are also listed. Later in the chapter, I'll explain the memory technologies mentioned in the table.

Processor	Speed	Description
Third Generation (Ivy Bridge) Processors		
Core i7	Up to 3.9 GHz	8 MB cache, quad core 1333/1600 MHz DDR3 memory Dual channel memory
Core i5	Up to 3.8 GHz	6 MB cache, quad core 1333/1600 MHz DDR3 memory Dual channel memory

Table 4-1 Current Intel processors (continues)

A+ 220-801 1.6

Processor	Speed	Description
Second Generation (Sandy Bridge) Processors		
Core i7 Extreme	Up to 3.9 GHz	15 MB cache, six cores 1066/1333/1600 MHz DDR3 memory Quad channel memory
Core i7	Up to 3.9 GHz	8 to 12 MB cache, four or six cores 1066/1333/1600 MHz DDR3 memory Dual or quad channel memory
Core i5	Up to 3.8 GHz	3 to 6 MB cache, dual or quad core 1066/1333 MHz DDR3 memory Dual channel memory
Core i3	Up to 3.4 GHz	3 MB cache, dual core 1066/1333 MHz DDR3 memory Dual channel memory
Pentium	Up to 3.0 GHz	3 MB cache 1066/1333 MHz DDR3 memory Dual channel memory
Previous Generation Processors		
Core i7 Extreme	Up to 3.4 GHz	8 or 12 MB cache 1066 MHz DDR3 memory Triple channel memory
Core i7	Up to 3.3 GHz	8 or 12 MB cache, four or six cores 800/1066/1333 MHz DDR3 memory Dual or triple channel memory
Core i5	Up to 3.3 GHz	4 or 8 MB cache, dual or quad core 1066/1333 MHz DDR3 memory Dual channel memory
Core i3	Up to 3.3 GHz	Dual core, 4 MB cache 1066/1333 MHz DDR3 memory Dual channel memory
Atom	Up to 2.1 GHz	Up to 1 MB cache, some dual core 800/1066 MHz DDR3 memory 667/800 MHz DDR2 memory Single channel memory
Celeron, Celeron Desktop, Celeron D	1.6 to 3.6 GHz 533/667/800 MHz FSB	128 KB to 1 MB cache
Core 2 Extreme, Core 2 Quad, Core 2 Duo	Up to 3.2 GHz 533 to 1600 MHz FSB	2 to 12 MB cache Dual or quad core
Pentium Extreme, Pentium, Pentium 4, Pentium D	Up to 3.7 GHz	Up to 4 MB cache, some dual core

© Cengage Learning 2014

Table 4-1 Current Intel processors (continued)

An Intel Sandy Bridge Core i5 processor is shown in Figure 4-5. You can purchase a processor with or without the cooler. When it's purchased with a cooler, it's called a boxed processor. The cooler is also shown in the photo. If you purchase the cooler separately, make sure it fits the socket you are using.

A+ 220-801 1.6

Figure 4-5 The Intel Core i5 processor (processor number i5-2320) with boxed cooler

Each processor listed in Table 4-1 represents several processors that vary in performance and functionality. To help identify a processor, Intel uses a processor number. For example, two Core i7 processors are identified as i7-940 and i7-920. To find details about an Intel processor, search the Intel ARK database at *ark.intel.com* (see Figure 4-6).

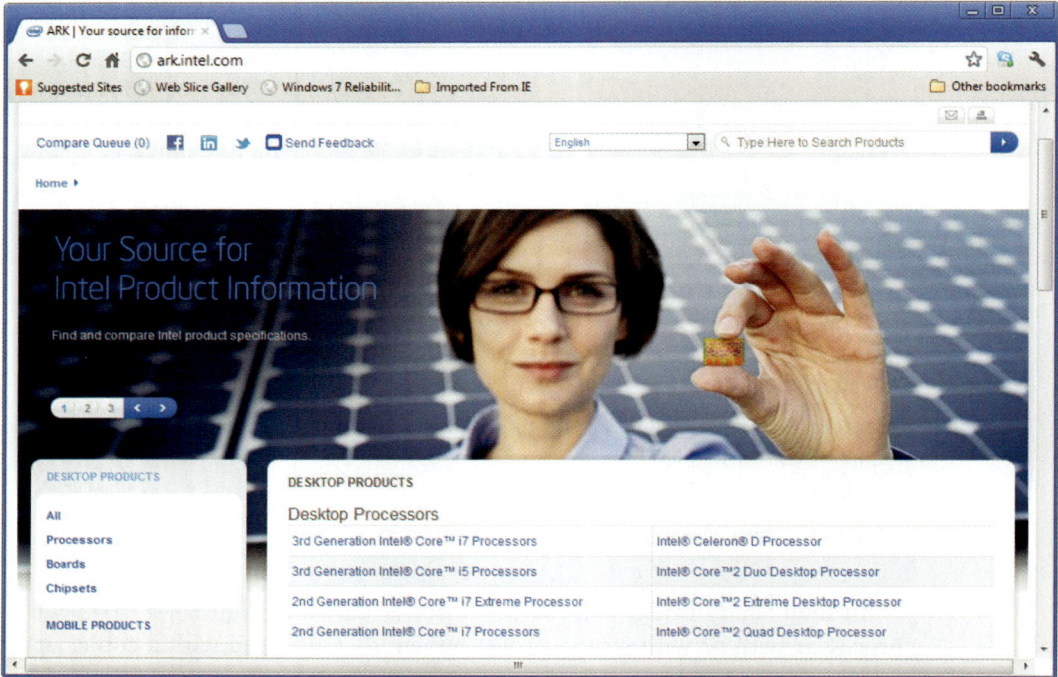

Figure 4-6 The Intel ARK database at *ark.intel.com* lists details about all Intel products

**A+
220-801
1.6**

Some of the Intel mobile processors are packaged in the Centrino processor technology. Using the **Centrino** technology, the Intel processor, chipset, and wireless network adapter are all interconnected as a unit, which improves laptop performance. Several Intel mobile processors have been packaged as a Centrino processor. You also need to be aware of the Intel Atom processor, which is Intel's smallest processor and is used in low-cost PCs, laptops, and netbooks.

AMD PROCESSORS

Processors by Advanced Micro Devices, Inc. or AMD (*www.amd.com*) are popular in the game and hobbyist markets, and are generally less expensive than comparable Intel processors. Recall that AMD processors use different sockets than do Intel processors, so the motherboard must be designed for one manufacturer's processor or the other, but not both. Many motherboard manufacturers offer two comparable motherboards—one for an Intel processor and one for an AMD processor.

The current AMD processor families are the FX, Phenom, Athlon, and Sempron for desktops and the Athlon, Turion, V Series, Phenom, and Sempron for laptops. Table 4-2 lists the current AMD processors for desktops. Figure 4-7 shows an FX processor by AMD.

Processor	Core Speed	Description
FX Black Edition Family		
FX 4-Core Black Edition	Up to 3.6 GHz	Quad-core uses AM3+ socket
FX 6-Core Black Edition	Up to 3.3 GHz	Six-core uses AM3+ socket
FX 8-Core Black Edition	Up to 3.6 GHz	Eight-core uses AM3+ socket
Phenom Family		
Phenom II X6	Up to 3 GHz	Six core uses AM3 socket
Phenom II X6 Black	Up to 3.2 GHz	Six core uses AM3 socket
Phenom II X4	Up to 3.2 GHz	Quad-core uses AM3 socket
Phenom II X3	Up to 2.5 GHz	Triple-core uses AM3 socket
Phenom II X2	Up to 3.1 GHz	Dual-core uses AM3 socket
Phenom X4	Up to 2.6 GHz	Quad-core uses AM2+ socket
Phenom X3	Up to 2.4 GHz	Triple-core uses AM2+ socket
Athlon Family		
Athlon II X2	Up to 3 GHz	Dual-core uses AM3 socket
Athlon X2	Up to 2.3 GHz	Dual-core uses AM3 socket
Athlon	Up to 2.4 GHz	Single-core uses AM2 socket
Sempron Family		
Sempron	Up to 2.3 GHz	Single-core uses AM2 socket

Table 4-2 Current AMD processors

A+ 220-801 1.6

Courtesy of AMD

Figure 4-7 The AMD FX processor can have up to eight cores

In the next part of the chapter, you'll learn the detailed steps to select and install a processor in several of the popular Intel and AMD sockets used by a desktop computer.

SELECTING AND INSTALLING A PROCESSOR

A PC repair technician is sometimes called on to assemble a PC from parts, exchange a processor that is faulty, add a second processor to a dual-processor system, or upgrade an existing processor to improve performance. In each situation, it is necessary to know how to match a processor for the system in which it is installed. And then you need to know how to install the processor on the motherboard for each of the current Intel and AMD sockets used for desktop and laptop systems. In this part of the chapter, you'll learn about selecting and installing processors in desktops. In Chapter 11, you'll learn about selecting and installing processors in laptops.

SELECT A PROCESSOR TO MATCH SYSTEM NEEDS

When selecting a processor, the first requirement is to select one that the motherboard is designed to support. Among the processors the board supports, you need to select the best one that meets the general requirements of the system and the user needs. To get the best performance, use the highest-performing processor the board supports. However, sometimes you need to sacrifice performance for cost.

APPLYING CONCEPTS — SELECT A PROCESSOR

Your friend, Alice, is working toward her A+ certification. She has decided the best way to get the experience she needs before she sits for the exam is to build a system from scratch. She has purchased an Asus motherboard and asked you for some help selecting the right processor. She tells you that the system will later be used for light business needs and she wants to install a processor that is moderate in price to fit her budget. She says she doesn't want to install the most expensive processor the motherboard can support, but neither does she want to sacrifice too much performance or power.

The documentation on the Asus web site (*support.asus.com*) for the ASUS P8Z68-V LX motherboard gives this information:

- The ATX board contains the Z68 chipset and socket LGA1155 and uses DDR3 memory.
- CPUs supported include a long list of Second Generation Core i3, Core i5, and Core i7 processors and Celeron and Pentium processors. Here are five processors found in this list:
  - Intel Core i7-2600, 3.4 GHz, 8 MB cache
  - Intel Core i5-3450, 3.1 GHz, 6 MB cache
  - Intel Core i3-2120, 3.3 GHz, 3 MB cache
  - Intel Celeron G540, 2.5 GHz, 2 MB cache
  - Intel Pentium G860, 3.0 GHz, 3 MB cache

Based on what Alice has told you, you decide to eliminate the most expensive processors (the Core i7) and the least-performing processors (the Celerons and Pentiums). That decision narrows your choices down to the Core i3 and Core i5. Before you select one of these processors, you need to check the list on the Asus site to make sure the specific Core i3 or Core i5 processor is in the list. Look for the exact processor number, for example, the Core i3-2120. Also double-check and make sure the processor uses the correct socket and is a Second Generation processor.

You will also need a cooler assembly. If your processor doesn't come boxed with a cooler, select a cooler that fits the processor socket and gets good reviews. You'll also need some thermal compound if it is not included with the cooler.

INSTALL A PROCESSOR

Now let's look at the details of installing a processor in an Intel LGA1155, LGA1366, LGA775, and AMD AM2+ sockets.

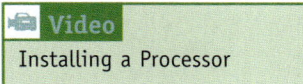

INSTALLING AN INTEL PROCESSOR IN SOCKET LGA1155

We're installing the Intel Core i5-2320 processor in Socket LGA1155 shown in Figure 4-8. In the photo, the socket has its protective cover in place.

A+ 220-801 1.6

Figure 4-8 Intel socket LGA1155 with protective cover in place

> **A+ Exam Tip** The A+ 220-801 exam expects you to know how to install a processor in these Intel processor sockets: LGA775, LGA1155, LGA1156, and LGA1366 sockets.

When building a new system, if the motherboard is not already installed in the case, follow the directions of the motherboard manufacturer to install the motherboard and then the processor or to install the processor and then the motherboard. The order of installation varies among manufacturers. When replacing a processor in an existing system, power down the system, unplug the power cord, press the power button to drain the system of power, and open the case. Follow these steps to install the processor and cooler using socket LGA1155:

1. Read all directions in the motherboard user guide and carefully follow them in order.
2. Use a ground bracelet or antistatic gloves to protect the processor, motherboard, and other components against ESD.
3. Open the socket by pushing down on the socket lever and gently pushing it away from the socket to lift the lever (see Figure 4-9).

Figure 4-9 Release the lever from the socket

Selecting and Installing a Processor | 149

A+ 220-801 1.6

4. As you fully open the socket lever, the socket load plate opens, as shown in Figure 4-10.

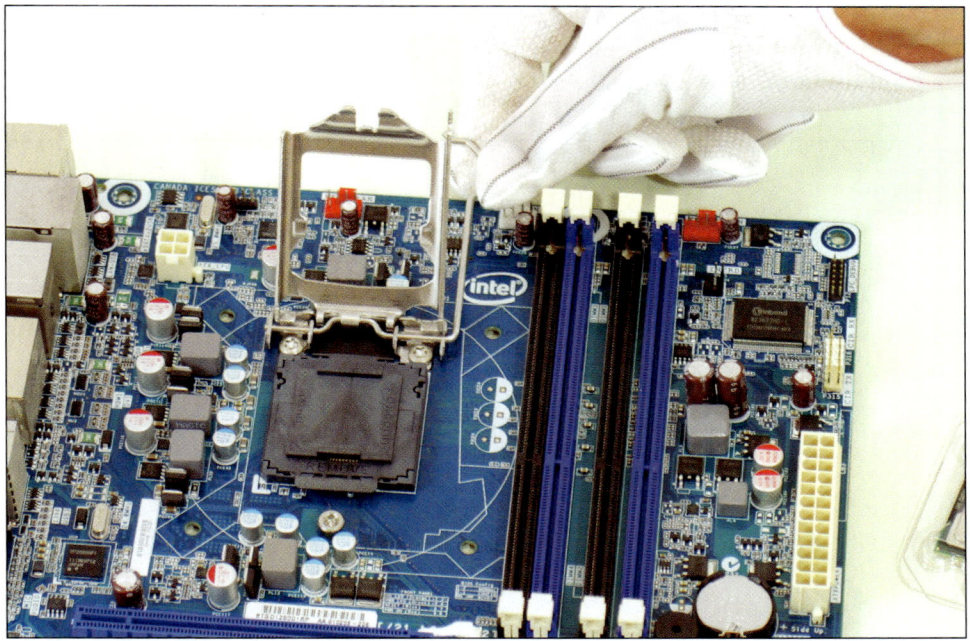

Figure 4-10 Lift the socket load plate

5. Remove the socket protective cover (see Figure 4-11). Keep this cover in a safe place. If you ever remove the processor, put the cover back in the socket to protect the socket. While the socket is exposed, be *very careful* to not touch the pins in the socket.

Figure 4-11 Remove the socket protective cover

150 | **CHAPTER 4** | Supporting Processors and Upgrading Memory

A+
220-801
1.6

6. Remove the protective cover from the processor. You can see the processor in this clear plastic cover on the right side of Figure 4-12, which also shows the open socket. While the processor contacts are exposed, take extreme care to not touch the bottom of the processor. Hold it only at its edges. (It's best to use antistatic gloves as you work, but the gloves make it difficult to handle the processor.) Put the processor cover in a safe place and use it to protect the processor if you ever remove the processor from the socket.

Figure 4-12 Open socket LGA1155 and processor in a protective cover

7. Hold the processor with your index finger and thumb and orient the processor so that the gold triangle on the corner of the processor lines up with the right-angle mark embedded on the motherboard just outside a corner of the socket (see Figure 4-13). Gently lower the processor straight down into the socket. Don't allow the processor to tilt, slide, or shift as you put it in the socket. To protect the pads, it needs to go straight down into the socket.

Figure 4-13 Align the processor in the socket using the gold triangle and the right-angle mark

8. Check carefully to make sure the processor is aligned correctly in the socket. Closing the socket without the processor fully seated can destroy the socket. Figure 4-14 shows the processor fully seated in the socket. Close the socket load plate so that it catches under the screw head at the front of the socket (see Figure 4-15).

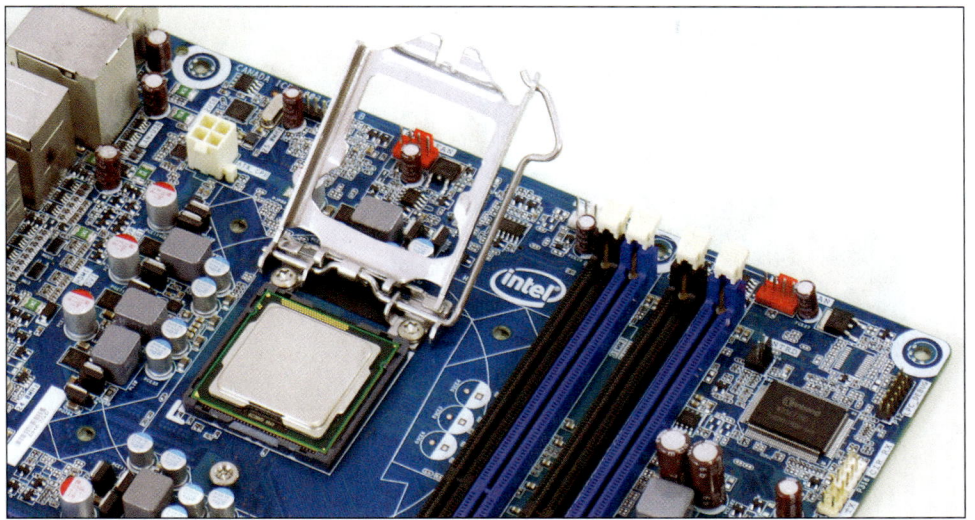

Figure 4-14 Processor in position ready to close the socket

Figure 4-15 The socket screw head secures the socket load plate

9. Push down on the lever and gently return it to its locked position (see Figure 4-16).

We are now ready to install the cooler. Before installing a cooler, read the directions carefully and make sure you understand them. Clips that hold the fan and heat sink to the processor frame or housing are sometimes difficult to install. The directions might give you important tips. Follow these general steps:

1. The motherboard has four holes to anchor the cooler. You can see them labeled in Figure 4-17. Examine the cooler posts that fit over these holes and the clips, screws, or wires that will hold the cooler firmly in place. Make sure you understand how this mechanism works.

A+ 220-801 1.6

Figure 4-16 Return the lever to its locked position

2. If the cooler has thermal compound preapplied, remove the plastic from the compound. If the cooler does not have thermal compound applied, put a small dot of compound (about the size of a small pea) in the center of the processor (see Figure 4-17). When the cooler is attached and the processor is running, the compound spreads over the surface. Don't use too much—just enough to later create a thin layer. If you use too much compound, it can slide off the housing and damage the processor or circuits on the motherboard. To get just the right amount, you can buy individual packets that each contain a single application of the thermal compound.

Figure 4-17 If the cooler does not have preapplied thermal compound, apply it on top of the processor

Notes: When removing and reinstalling a processor, use a soft dry cloth to carefully remove all the old thermal compound from both the processor and the cooler. Don't try to reuse the compound.

3. Verify the locking pins on the cooler are turned as far as they will go in a counter-clockwise direction. (Make sure the pins don't protrude into the hollow plastic posts that go down into the motherboard holes.) Align the cooler over the processor so that all four posts fit into the four holes on the motherboard and the fan power cord can reach the fan header on the motherboard (see Figure 4-18).

Figure 4-18 Align the cooler over the four holes in the motherboard

4. Push down on each locking pin until you hear it pop into the hole (see Figure 4-19). To help keep the cooler balanced and in position, push down two opposite pins and then push the remaining two pins in place. Using a flathead screwdriver, turn the locking pin clockwise to secure it. (Later, if you need to remove the cooler, turn each locking pin counterclockwise to release it from the hole.)

Figure 4-19 Push down on a locking pin to lock it into position

A+ 220-801 1.6

> **Notes** If you later notice the CPU fan is running far too often, you might need to tighten the connection between the cooler and the processor.

5. Connect the power cord from the cooler fan to the motherboard power connector near the processor, as shown in Figure 4-20.

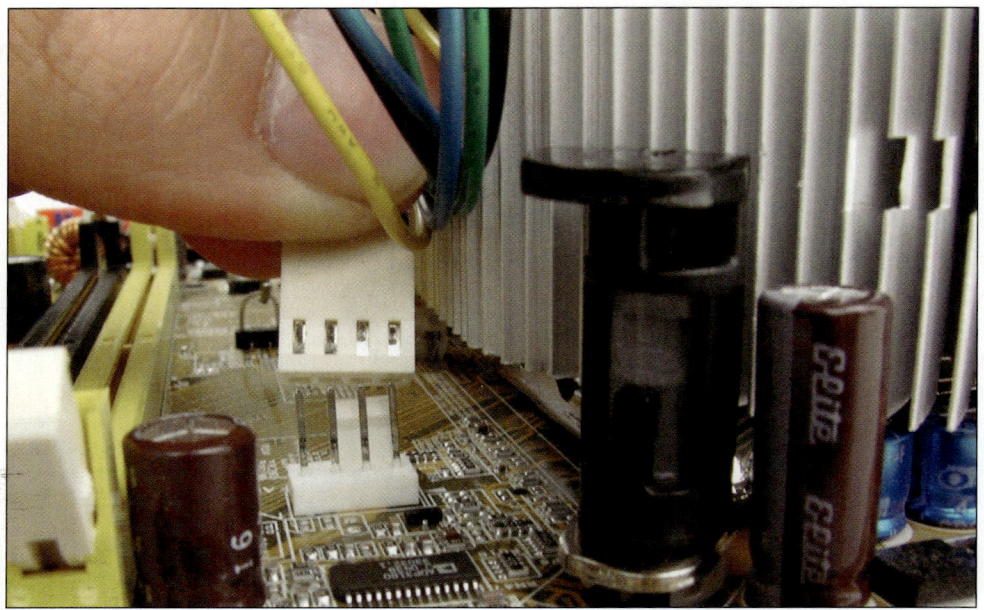

Figure 4-20 Connect the cooler fan power cord to the motherboard CPU fan header

After the processor and cooler are installed and the motherboard is installed in the case, make sure cables and cords don't obstruct fans or airflow, especially airflow around the processor and video card. Use cable ties to tie cords and cables up and out of the way.

Make one last check to verify all power connectors are in place and other cords and cables connected to the motherboard are correctly done. You are now ready to plug back up the system, turn it on, and verify all is working. If the power comes on (you hear the fan spinning and see lights), but the system fails to work, most likely the processor is not seated solidly in the socket or some power cord has not yet been connected or is not solidly connected. Turn everything off, unplug the power cord, press the power button to drain power, open the case, and recheck your installation. If the system comes up and begins the boot process, but suddenly turns off before the boot is complete, most likely the processor is overheating because the cooler is not installed correctly. Turn everything off, unplug the power cord, press the power button to drain power, open the case, and verify the cooler is securely seated and connected.

After the system is up and running, you can check BIOS setup to verify that the system recognized the processor correctly. The setup screen for one processor is shown in Figure 4-21. Look for items on the screen that manage processor features, and make sure each is set correctly. For example, in Figure 4-21, items listed in blue can be changed. Verify the two blue items that apply to the processor; verify that all processor cores are active and Hyper-Threading Technology is enabled.

**A+
220-801
1.6**

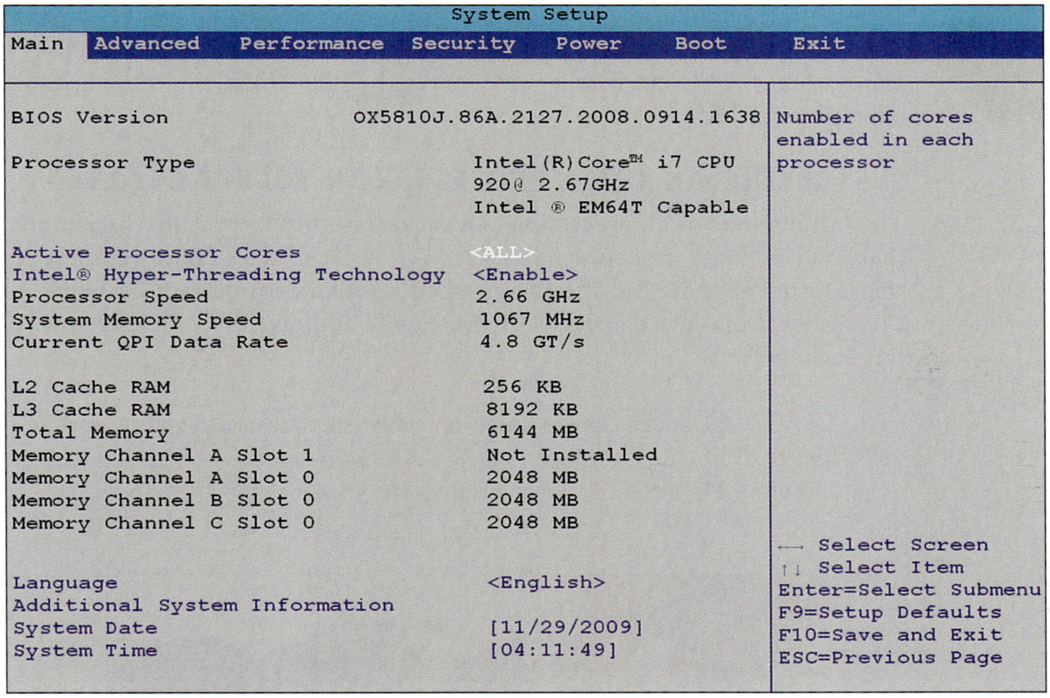

```
                            System Setup
Main   Advanced    Performance   Security    Power    Boot    Exit


BIOS Version                   0X5810J.86A.2127.2008.0914.1638   Number of cores
                                                                 enabled in each
Processor Type                 Intel(R)Core™ i7 CPU              processor
                               920@ 2.67GHz
                               Intel ® EM64T Capable

Active Processor Cores         <ALL>
Intel® Hyper-Threading Technology  <Enable>
Processor Speed                2.66 GHz
System Memory Speed            1067 MHz
Current QPI Data Rate          4.8 GT/s

L2 Cache RAM                   256 KB
L3 Cache RAM                   8192 KB
Total Memory                   6144 MB
Memory Channel A Slot 1        Not Installed
Memory Channel A Slot 0        2048 MB
Memory Channel B Slot 0        2048 MB
Memory Channel C Slot 0        2048 MB
                                                                 ⟶   Select Screen
                                                                 ↑↓  Select Item
Language                       <English>                         Enter=Select Submenu
Additional System Information                                    F9=Setup Defaults
System Date                    [11/29/2009]                      F10=Save and Exit
System Time                    [04:11:49]                        ESC=Previous Page
```
Source: Intel

Figure 4-21 Verify the CPU is recognized correctly by BIOS setup

Also check in BIOS setup the CPU and motherboard temperatures to verify the CPU is not overheating. For one BIOS setup in another system, this screen is under the Configuration menu, Fan Control & Real-Time Monitoring window, as shown in Figure 4-22.

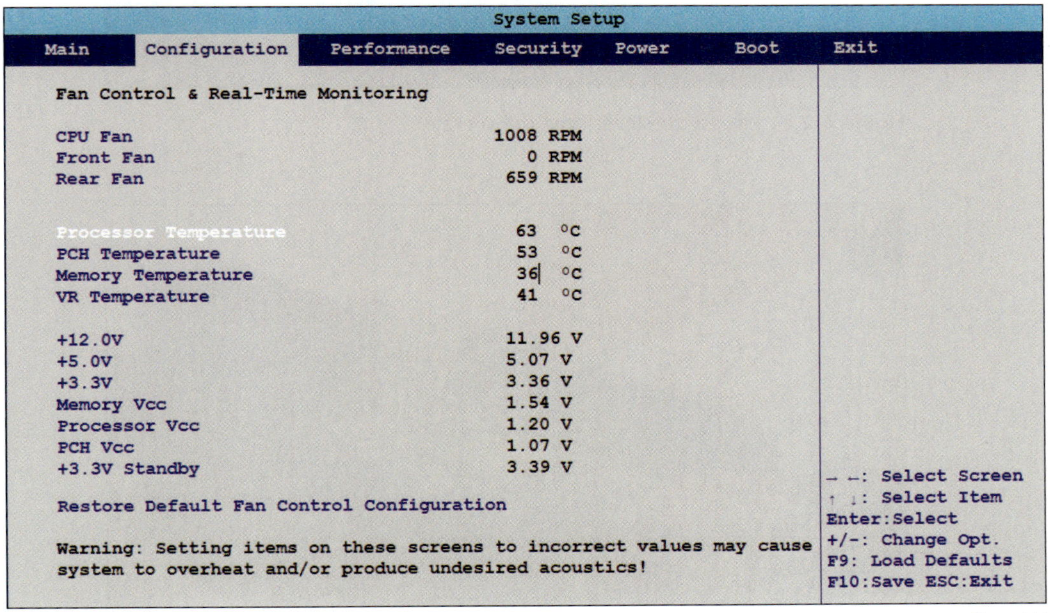

```
                            System Setup
Main   Configuration   Performance   Security    Power    Boot    Exit

  Fan Control & Real-Time Monitoring

  CPU Fan                             1008 RPM
  Front Fan                              0 RPM
  Rear Fan                             659 RPM

  Processor Temperature                 63  °C
  PCH Temperature                       53  °C
  Memory Temperature                    36  °C
  VR Temperature                        41  °C

  +12.0V                              11.96 V
  +5.0V                                5.07 V
  +3.3V                                3.36 V
  Memory Vcc                           1.54 V
  Processor Vcc                        1.20 V
  PCH Vcc                              1.07 V
  +3.3V Standby                        3.39 V
                                                           ← →: Select Screen
  Restore Default Fan Control Configuration                ↑ ↓: Select Item
                                                           Enter:Select
  Warning: Setting items on these screens to incorrect     +/-: Change Opt.
  values may cause system to overheat and/or produce       F9: Load Defaults
  undesired acoustics!                                     F10:Save ESC:Exit
```
Source: Intel

Figure 4-22 Verify the processor temperature is within an acceptable range

If you see the processor temperature rising and reaching 80 degrees, open the case cover and verify the processor fan is running. Perhaps a wire is in the way and preventing the fan from turning or the fan wire is not connected. Other troubleshooting tips for processors are covered in Chapter 8.

INSTALLING AN INTEL PROCESSOR IN SOCKET LGA1366

The installations of all processors and sockets in this part of the chapter are similar to that of installing a processor in Socket LGA1155, so we will not repeat many of those steps. Listed next are the differences when installing a processor in the LGA1366 socket. These socket pins are delicate, so work slowly and take care. Here is how to work with this socket:

1. To open the socket, press down on the socket lever and gently push it away from the socket to lift the lever (see Figure 4-23). You can then lift the socket load plate, as shown in Figure 4-24. Next, remove the socket protective cover.

Figure 4-23 Release the lever from the socket

Figure 4-24 Lift the socket load plate

2. To install the processor, hold the processor with your index finger and thumb and orient the processor so that the notches on the two edges of the processor line up with the two posts on the socket. You can see the notch and post on the right side of the processor and socket in Figure 4-25. Gently lower the processor straight down into the socket. Don't allow the processor to tilt, slide, or shift as you put it in the socket. To protect the pins, it needs to go straight down into the socket.

Figure 4-25 Orient the processor over the socket so that the notches on each side of the processor match the posts on each side of the socket

3. You can now lower the socket load plate and return the lever to its locked position (see Figure 4-26).

Figure 4-26 Return the lever to its locked position

INSTALLING AN INTEL PROCESSOR IN SOCKET LGA775

Socket LGA775 is shown in Figure 4-27 along with a Pentium processor and cooler. In the photo, the socket is open and the protective cover removed. The processor is lying upside down in front of the cooler.

Figure 4-27 A Pentium, cooler, and open socket 775

When installing a processor in socket LGA775, do the following:

1. Push down on the lever and gently push it away from the socket to lift it. Lift the socket load plate (see Figure 4-28). Remove the socket protective cover.

Figure 4-28 Lift the socket load plate

2. Orient the processor so that the notches on the two edges of the processor line up with the two notches on the socket (see Figure 4-29). Gently place the processor in the socket. Socket LGA775 doesn't have those delicate pins that Socket LGA1366 has, but you still need to be careful to not touch the top of the socket or the bottom of the processor as you work.

3. Close the socket cover. Push down on the lever and gently return it to its locked position.

Figure 4-29 Place the processor in the socket, orienting the notches on two sides

INSTALLING AN AMD PROCESSOR IN SOCKET AM2+

When installing an AMD processor in AMD socket AM2, AM2+, or other AMD sockets, do the following:

1. Open the socket lever. If there's a protective cover over the socket, remove it.//
2. Holding the processor very carefully so you don't touch the bottom, orient the four empty positions on the bottom with the four empty positions in the socket (see Figure 4-30). For some AMD sockets, a gold triangle on one corner of the processor matches up with a small triangle on a corner of the socket. Carefully lower the processor into the socket. Don't allow it to tilt or slide as it goes into the socket. The pins on the bottom of the processor are very delicate, so take care as you work.

Figure 4-30 Orient the four alignment positions on the bottom of the processor with those in the socket

160 | **CHAPTER 4** Supporting Processors and Upgrading Memory

A+
220-801
1.6

3. Check carefully to make sure the pins in the processor are sitting slightly into the holes. Make sure the pins are not offset from the holes. If you try to use the lever to put pressure on these pins and they are not aligned correctly, you can destroy the processor. You can actually feel the pins settle into place when you're lowering the processor into the socket correctly.

4. Press the lever down and gently into position (see Figure 4-31).

Figure 4-31 Lower the lever into place, which puts pressure on the processor

5. You are now ready to apply the thermal compound and install the cooler assembly. For one system, the black retention mechanism for the cooler is already installed on the motherboard (see Figure 4-32). Sit the cooler on top of the processor, aligning it inside the retention mechanism.

Black retention mechanism is preattached

Figure 4-32 Align the cooler over the retention mechanism

6. Next, clip into place the clipping mechanism on one side of the cooler. Then push down firmly on the clip on the opposite side of the cooler assembly; the clip will snap into place. Figure 4-33 shows the clip on one side in place for a system that has a yellow retention mechanism and a black cooler clip. Later, if you need to remove the cooler, use a Phillips screwdriver to remove the screws holding the retention mechanism in place. Then remove the retention mechanism along with the entire cooler assembly.

Figure 4-33 The clips on the cooler attach the cooler to the retention mechanism on the motherboard

7. Connect the power cord from the fan to the 4-pin fan header on the motherboard next to the CPU.

> **Notes** How to troubleshoot problems with the processor, motherboard, and RAM is covered in Chapter 8.

Hands-on Project 4-1 Research a Processor Upgrade or Replacement

To identify your motherboard and find out the processor and processor socket a motherboard is currently using, you can use BIOS setup, Windows utilities, or third-party software such as Speccy at *www.periform.com/speccy*. To research processors a board can support, you can use the motherboard user guide, the web site of the motherboard manufacturer, and for Intel processors, the Intel site at *ark.intel.com*. Research the current processor and processor socket of your computer's motherboard and which processors your board can support, and answer the following questions:

1. What is the brand and model of your motherboard? What processor socket does it use? How did you find your information?
2. Identify the currently installed processor, including its brand, model, speed, and other important characteristics. How did you find your information?
3. List three or more processors the board supports according to the motherboard documentation or web site.
4. Search the web for three or more processors that would match this board. Save or print three web pages showing the details and prices of a high-performing, moderately performing, and low-performing processor the board supports.
5. If your current processor fails, which processor would you recommend for this system? Explain your recommendation.

A+ 220-801 1.6

Now assume the Core i7 920 processor that you saw installed in the chapter in Figure 4-25 has gone bad. The motherboard in which it is installed is the Intel DX58SO desktop board. The owner of the motherboard has requested that you keep the replacement cost as low as possible. What processor would you recommend for the replacement? Save or print a web page showing the processor and its cost.

Hands-on Project 4-2 Insert and Remove a Processor

In this project, you remove and install a processor. As you work, be very careful to not bend pins on the processor or socket, and protect the processor and motherboard against ESD. Do the following:

1. Verify the computer is working. Turn off the system, unplug it, press the power button, and open the computer case. Put on your ground bracelet. Remove the cooler assembly and processor.
2. To best protect the processor, if you have thermal compound available, remove all the compound from the processor and cooler and replace it with new compound.
3. You are now ready to reinstall the processor and cooler. But first have your instructor check the thermal compound.
4. Reinstall the processor and cooler. Power up the system and verify all is working.

Now let's turn our attention to the various memory technologies used in personal computers, and how to upgrade memory.

MEMORY TECHNOLOGIES

A+ 220-801 1.2, 1.3

Recall that random access memory (RAM) temporarily holds data and instructions as the CPU processes them and that the memory modules used on a motherboard are made of dynamic RAM or DRAM. DRAM loses its data rapidly, and the memory controller must refresh it several thousand times a second. RAM is stored on memory modules, which are installed in memory slots on the motherboard (see Figure 4-34).

One populated black slot and one empty black slot

Two empty blue slots

© Cengage Learning 2014

Figure 4-34 RAM on motherboards today is stored in DIMMs

Memory Technologies

A+ 220-801 1.2, 1.3

> **A+ Exam Tip** The A+ 220-801 exam expects you to know the purposes and characteristics of the following memory technologies: DRAM, SRAM, SDRAM, DDR, DDR2, DDR3, and Rambus.

Several variations of DRAM have evolved over the years. Here are the four major categories of memory modules:

- All new motherboards for desktops sold today use a type of memory module called a **DIMM (dual inline memory module)**.
- Laptops use a smaller version of a DIMM called a **SO-DIMM (small outline DIMM** and pronounced "sew-dim"). MicroDIMMs are used on subnotebook computers and are smaller than SO-DIMMs. You learn about SO-DIMMs in Chapter 11.
- An older type of module is a **RIMM**, which is designed by Rambus, Inc.
- Really old computers used **SIMMs (single inline memory module)**. You're unlikely to ever see these modules in working computers.

The major differences among these modules are the width of the data path that each type of module accommodates and the way data moves from the system bus to the module. DIMMs have seen several evolutions. Four versions of DIMMs, one RIMM, and two types of SIMMs are shown in Table 4-3. Notice the notches on the modules, which prevent the wrong type of module from being inserted into a memory slot on the motherboard.

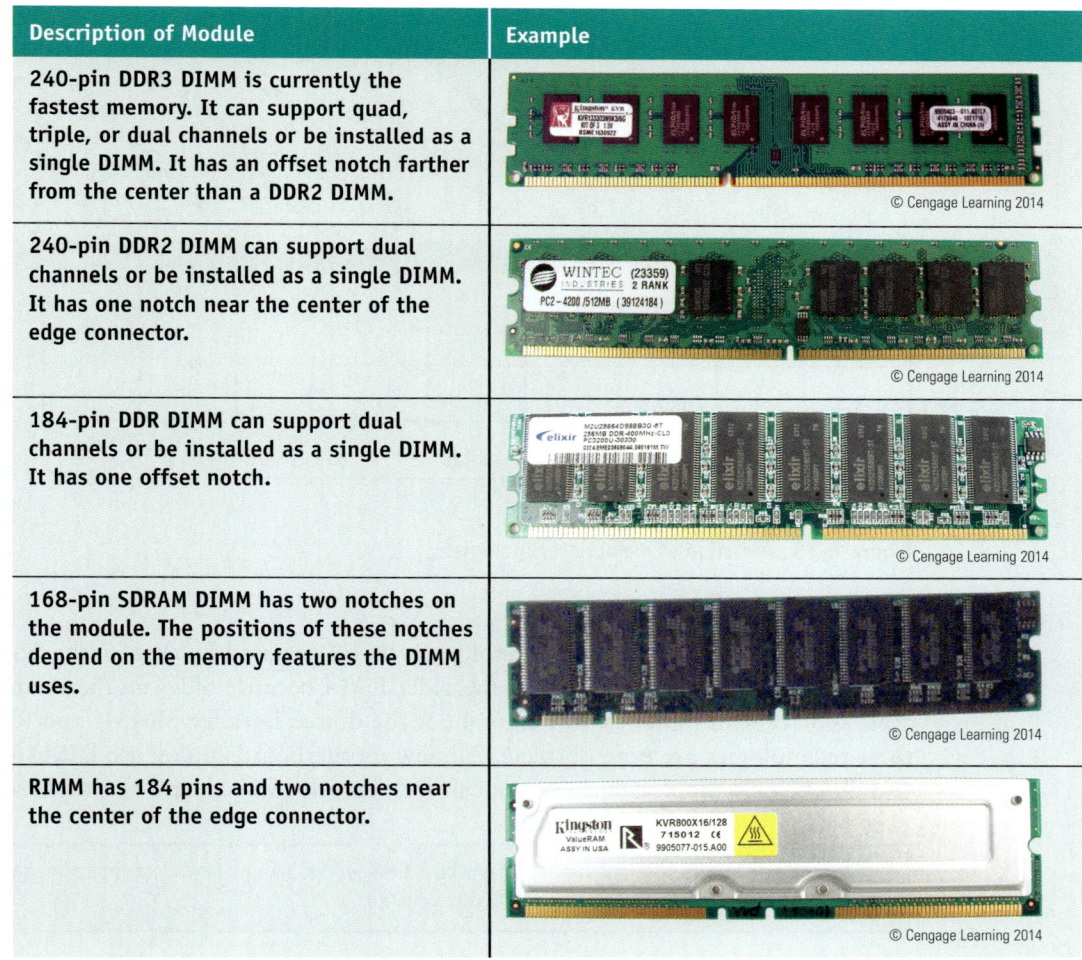

Description of Module	Example
240-pin DDR3 DIMM is currently the fastest memory. It can support quad, triple, or dual channels or be installed as a single DIMM. It has an offset notch farther from the center than a DDR2 DIMM.	© Cengage Learning 2014
240-pin DDR2 DIMM can support dual channels or be installed as a single DIMM. It has one notch near the center of the edge connector.	© Cengage Learning 2014
184-pin DDR DIMM can support dual channels or be installed as a single DIMM. It has one offset notch.	© Cengage Learning 2014
168-pin SDRAM DIMM has two notches on the module. The positions of these notches depend on the memory features the DIMM uses.	© Cengage Learning 2014
RIMM has 184 pins and two notches near the center of the edge connector.	© Cengage Learning 2014

Table 4-3 Types of memory modules (continues)

© Cengage Learning 2014

A+ 220-801 1.2, 1.3

Description of Module	Example
72-pin SIMMs were installed in groups of two modules to each bank of memory.	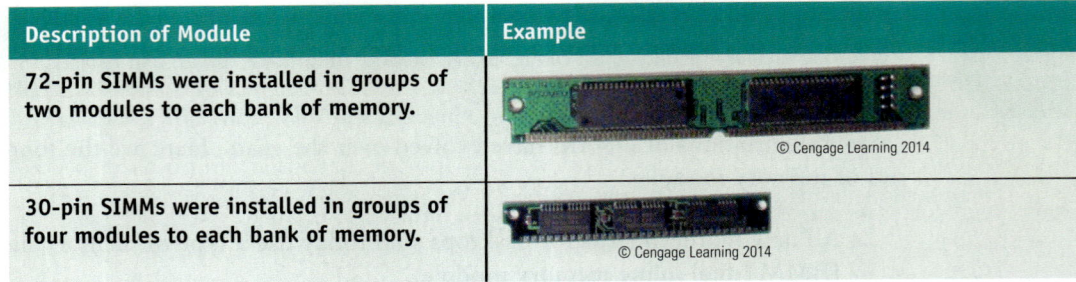
30-pin SIMMs were installed in groups of four modules to each bank of memory.	

Table 4-3 Types of memory modules (continued)

In this chapter, you'll see tons of different technologies used by RAM and so many can get a little overwhelming. You need to know about them because each motherboard you might support requires a specific type of RAM. Figure 4-35 is designed to help you keep all these technologies straight. You might find it a useful roadmap as you study each technology in the chapter. And who keeps up with all these technologies? JEDEC (*www.jedec.org*) is the organization responsible for standards used by solid-state devices, including RAM technologies. The goal of each new RAM technology approved by JEDEC is to increase speed and performance without greatly increasing the cost.

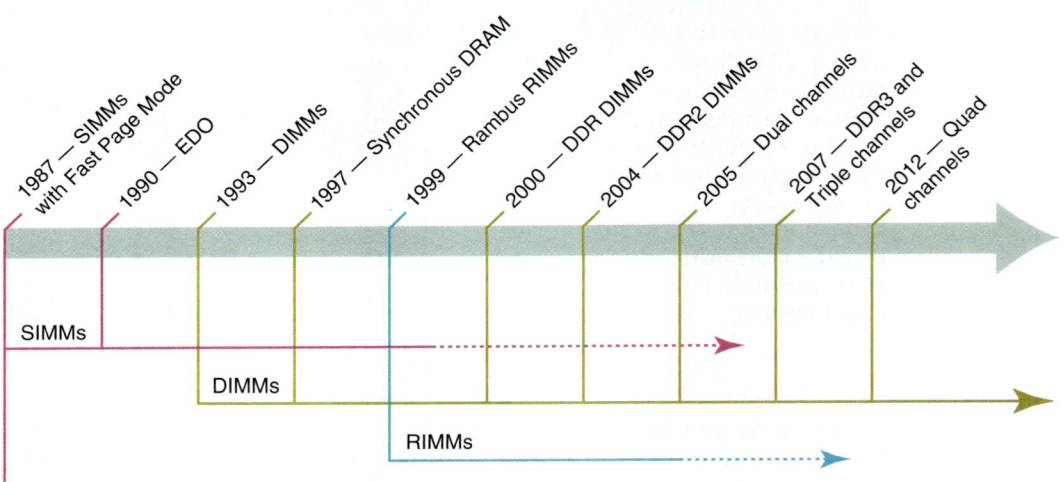

Figure 4-35 Timeline of memory technologies

Even though an older RAM technology is no longer used by new motherboards, RAM manufacturers continue to produce the older RAM because older motherboards require these replacement modules. In Figure 4-35, the dotted lines for SIMMs and RIMMs indicate these technologies are now obsolete. All new motherboards today use DIMMs. However, if you check some retail web sites, you can see that RIMMs can still be purchased.

> **Notes** For an interesting discussion on how RAM works, complete with animation, see the web site by HowStuffWorks, Inc. at *www.howstuffworks.com/ram.htm*.

DIMM TECHNOLOGIES

DIMMs use a 64-bit data path. (Some early DIMMs had a 128-bit data path, but they're now obsolete.) A DIMM (dual inline memory module) gets its name because it has independent pins on opposite sides of the module.

Early DIMMs did not run in sync with the system clock because they were too slow to keep up. Their speeds are measured in nanoseconds (ns), which is how long it takes for the module to read or write data. The first DIMM to run synchronized with the system clock was synchronous DRAM (SDRAM), which has two notches, and uses 168 pins. (Don't confuse SDRAM with SRAM. SRAM is static RAM used in processor memory caches, and SDRAM is dynamic RAM used on DIMMs.) Synchronized memory runs in step with the processor and system clock, and its speeds are measured just as processor and bus speeds are measured in MHz.

Double Data Rate SDRAM (DDR SDRAM, or SDRAM II, or simply DDR) is an improved version of SDRAM. DDR runs twice as fast as regular SDRAM, has one notch, and uses 184 pins. Instead of processing data for each beat of the system clock, as regular SDRAM does, it processes data when the beat rises and again when it falls, doubling the data rate of memory. If a motherboard runs at 200 MHz, DDR memory runs at 400 MHz. Two other improvements over DDR are DDR2 and DDR3. DDR2 is faster and uses less power than DDR. DDR3 is faster and uses less power than DDR2. Both DDR2 and DDR3 use 240 pins, although their notches are not in the same position. They are not compatible, and the different notch positions keep someone from installing a DDR2 or DDR3 DIMM in the wrong memory slot.

Factors that affect the capacity, features, and performance of DIMMs include the number of channels they use, how much RAM is on one DIMM, the speed, error-checking abilities, and buffering. All these factors are discussed next.

SINGLE, DUAL, TRIPLE, AND QUAD CHANNELS

When you look at a motherboard, you might notice the DIMM slots are different colors. This color coding is used to identify the channel each slot uses. Channels have to do with how many DIMM slots the memory controller can address at a time. Early DIMMs only used a single channel, which means the memory controller can access only one DIMM at a time. To improve overall memory performance, dual channels allow the memory controller to communicate with two DIMMs at the same time, effectively doubling the speed of memory access. A motherboard that supports triple channels can access three DIMMs at the same time. Sandy Bridge technology introduced quad channels where the processor can access four DIMMs at the same time. DDR, DDR2, and DDR3 DIMMs can use dual channels. DDR3 DIMMs can also use triple channels and quad channels. For dual, triple, or quad channels to work, the motherboard and the DIMM must support the technology.

Figure 4-36 shows how dual channeling works on a board with four DIMM slots. The board has two memory channels, Channel A and Channel B. With dual channeling, the two DIMMs installed in the two slots labeled Channel A can be addressed at the same time. If two more DIMMs are installed in the Channel B slots, they can be accessed at the same time.

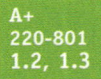

166 | **CHAPTER 4** Supporting Processors and Upgrading Memory

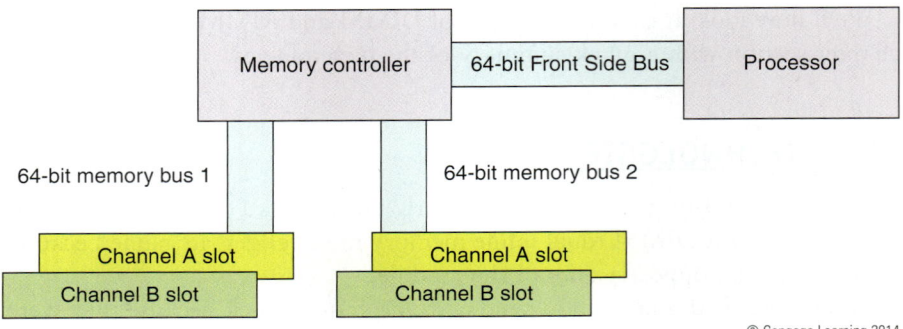

Figure 4-36 Using dual channels, the memory controller can read from two DIMMs at the same time

When setting up dual channeling, know that the pair of DIMMs in a channel must be equally matched in size, speed, and features, and it is recommended they come from the same manufacturer. A motherboard using dual channels was shown in Figure 4-34. The two black DIMM slots make up the first channel, and the two blue slots make up the second channel. To use dual channeling, matching DIMMs must be installed in the black slots and another matching pair in the blue slots, as shown in Figure 4-37. Know that the second pair of DIMMs does not have to match the first pair of DIMMs because the first channel runs independently of the second channel. If the two DIMM slots of a channel are not populated with matching pairs of DIMMs, the motherboard will revert to single channeling.

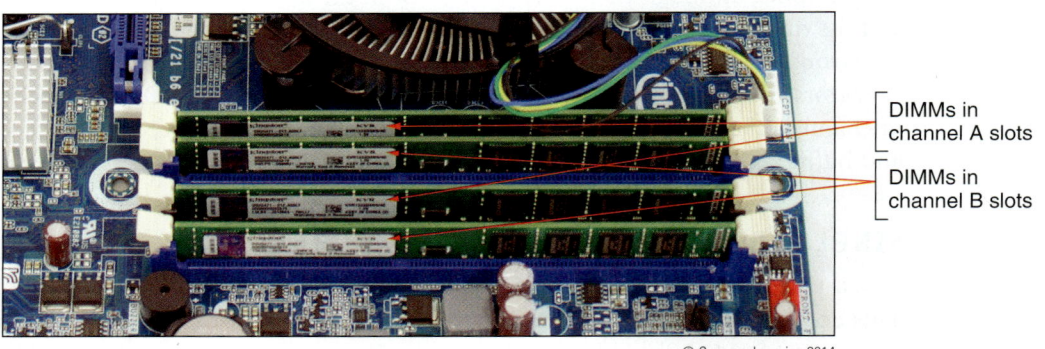

Figure 4-37 Matching pairs of DIMMs installed in four DIMM slots that support dual channeling

> **A+ Exam Tip** The A+ 220-801 exam expects you to be able to distinguish between single-channel, dual-channel, and triple-channel memory installations.

For a triple-channel installation, three DIMM slots must be populated with three matching DDR3 DIMMs (see Figure 4-38). The three DIMMs are installed in the three blue slots on the board. This motherboard has a fourth black DIMM slot. You can barely see this black slot behind the three filled slots in the photo. If the fourth slot is used, then triple channeling is disabled, which can slow down performance. If a matching pair of DIMMs is installed in the first two slots and another matching pair of DIMMs is installed in the third and fourth slots, then the memory controller will use dual channels. Dual channels are not as fast as triple channels, but certainly better than single channels.

Memory Technologies | 167

Figure 4-38 Three identical DDR3 DIMMs installed in a triple-channel configuration

The latest memory technology is quad channeling that was introduced with Intel Sandy Bridge chipsets and processors. Figure 4-39 shows an Intel motherboard that has the LGA2011 socket and eight memory slots. The processor can access four slots at the same time. The four black slots can be addressed by the processor on one memory channel and the four blue slots on another channel. Recall from Chapter 3 that Second Generation Sandy Bridge processors contain the memory controller within the processor package rather than on the chipset. To get the highest performance, memory slots are placed on either side of the processor in order to shorten the length of the memory bus. Because of the high performance of processors that use the LGA2011 socket, Intel recommends that systems using this socket use liquid cooling methods.

Figure 4-39 The Intel Desktop Board DX79TO has eight memory slots and supports two quad channels

DIMM SPEEDS

DIMM speeds are measured either in MHz (such as 1333 MHz or 800 MHz) or PC rating (such as PC6400). A PC rating is a measure of the total bandwidth of data moving between the module and the CPU. To understand PC ratings, let's take an example of a DDR DIMM module that runs at 800 MHz. The module has a 64-bit (8-byte) data path. Therefore, the transfer rate is 8 bytes multiplied by 800 MHz, which yields 6400 MB/second. This value equates to the PC rating of PC6400 for a DDR DIMM. A DDR2 PC rating is usually labeled PC2, and a DDR3 PC rating is labeled PC3. In Figure 4-40, this memory ad shows both the MHz and PC rating.

Some current PC ratings for DDR3 memory are PC3-16000 (2000 MHz), PC3-14400 (1800 MHz), PC3-12800 (1600 MHz), and PC3-10600 (1333 MHz). A couple of current

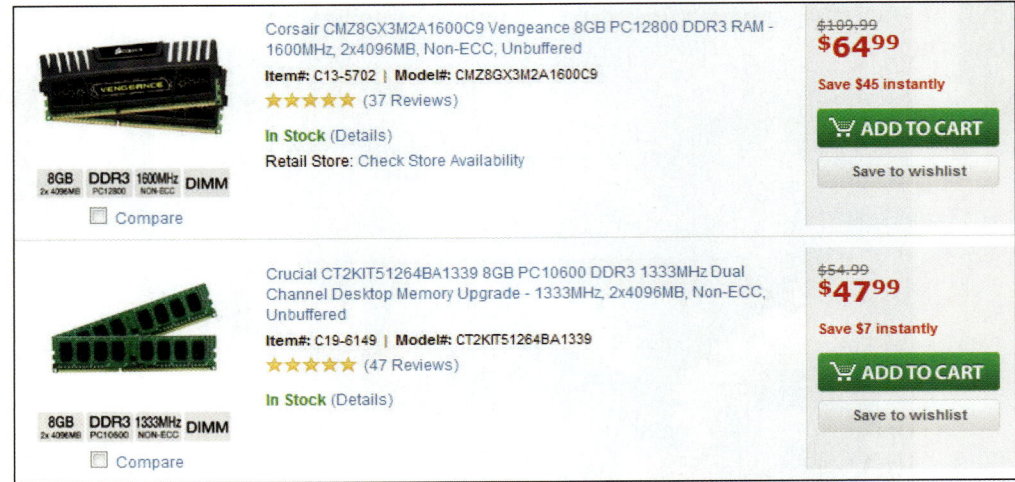

Figure 4-40 Memory speed is expressed in MHz and PC rating

Source: Tigerdirect.com

PC ratings for DDR2 memory are PC2-6400 (800 MHz) and PC2-5400 (667 MHz). DDR memory might be rated at PC6400 (800 MHz), PC4000 (500 MHz), PC3200 (400 MHz), or PC2700 (333 MHz). An older 168-pin SDRAM DIMM might run at PC100 or PC133.

SINGLE-SIDED AND DOUBLE-SIDED DIMMS

A DIMM can have memory chips installed on one side of the module (called *single-sided*) or both sides of the module (called *double-sided*). Most desktop and laptop processors address memory 64 bits at a time. A *memory bank* is the memory a processor addresses at one time and is 64 bits wide, and a DIMM slot provides a 64-bit data path. However, some double-sided DIMMs provide more than one bank, which means the chips on the DIMM are grouped so that the memory controller addresses one group and then addresses another. These DIMMs are said to be *dual ranked*, and don't perform as well as DIMMs where all the memory is addressed at one time. Notice in the memory ad in Figure 4-41 that the second item listed shows Dual Ranked as a feature.

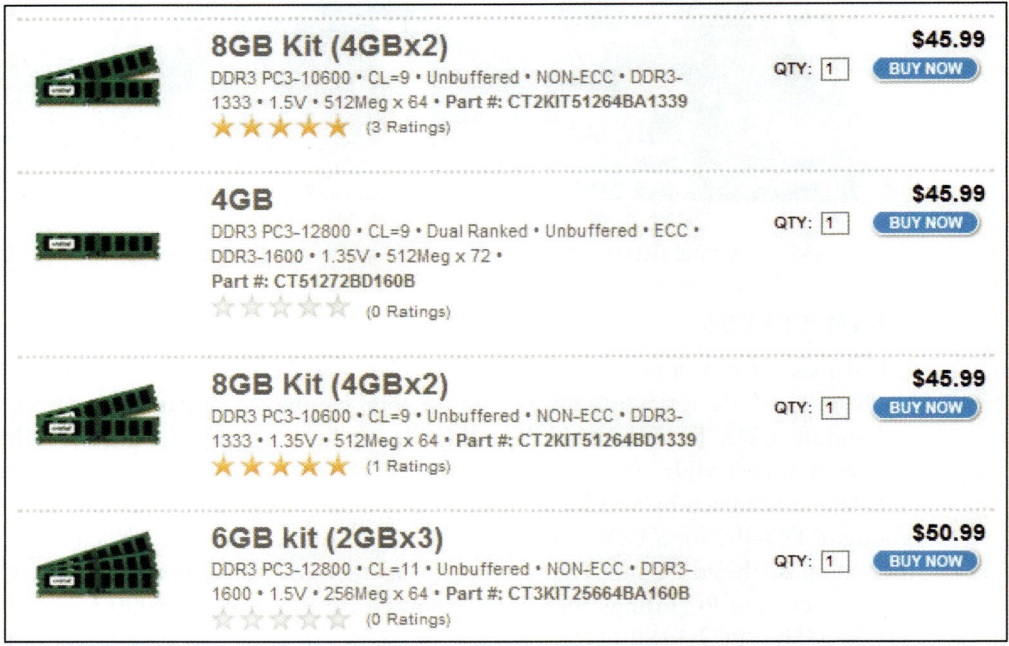

Figure 4-41 Memory ad lists dual ranked DDR3 memory

Source: Crucial.com

ERROR CHECKING AND PARITY

Because DIMMs intended to be used in servers must be extremely reliable, error-checking technology called **ECC (error-correcting code)** is sometimes used. Some SDRAM, DDR, DDR2, and DDR3 memory modules support ECC. A DIMM normally has an even number of chips on the module, but a DIMM that supports ECC has an odd number of chips on the module. The odd extra chip is the ECC chip. ECC compares bits written to the module to what is later read from the module, and it can detect and correct an error in a single bit of the byte. If there are errors in two bits of a byte, ECC can detect the error but cannot correct it. The data path width for DIMMs is normally 64 bits, but with ECC, the data path is 72 bits. The extra 8 bits are used for error checking. ECC memory costs more than non-ECC memory, but it is more reliable. For ECC to work, the motherboard and all installed modules must support it. Also, it's important to know that you cannot install a mix of ECC and non-ECC memory on the motherboard because such a mixture causes the system to not work.

As with most other memory technologies discussed in this chapter, when buying memory to add to a motherboard, match the type of memory to the type the board supports. To see if your motherboard supports ECC memory, look for the ability to enable or disable the feature in BIOS setup, or check the motherboard documentation. Figure 4-42 shows one ad for DIMMs. The first three items are non-ECC, and the last item is ECC memory. Also notice the first two items offer DIMMs in a kit of 4 DIMMs or 2 DIMMs.

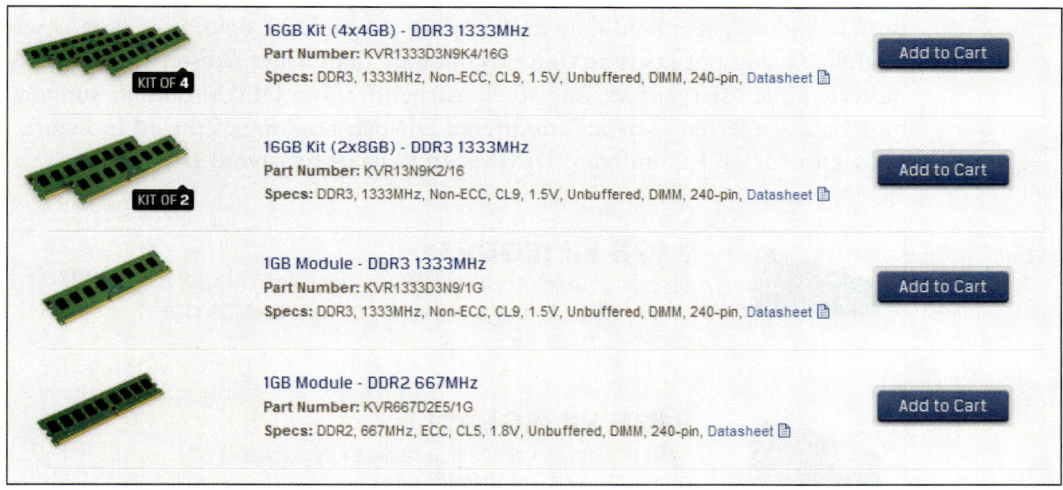

Source: Kingston.com

Figure 4-42 Memory ad for DDR3 and DDR2 memory

Refer back to the memory ad shown in Figure 4-41. The first item is non-ECC memory and has ×64 in the ad. The second item is ECC memory and has ×72 in the ad. The 64 or 72 is the width of the data path for non-ECC or ECC memory.

Older SIMMs used an error-checking technology called **parity**. Using parity checking, a ninth bit is stored with every 8 bits in a byte. If memory is using odd parity, it makes the ninth or parity bit either a 1 or a 0, to make the number of ones in the nine bits odd. If it uses even parity, it makes the parity bit a 1 or a 0 to make the number of ones in the 9 bits even.

> **A+ Exam Tip** The A+ 220-801 exam expects you to know that parity memory uses 9 bits (8 bits for data and 1 bit for parity). You also need to be familiar with ECC and non-ECC memory technologies.

Later, when the byte is read back, the memory controller checks the odd or even state. If the number of bits is not an odd number for odd parity or an even number for even parity, a **parity error** occurs. A parity error always causes the system to halt. On the screen, you see the error message "Parity Error 1" or "Parity Error 2" or a similar error message about parity. Parity Error 1 is a parity error on the motherboard; Parity Error 2 is a parity error on an expansion card.

Figure 4-43 shows a SIMM for sale. It's pricy because this old technology is hardly ever used. Notice the module is non-parity memory. In the ad, the SIMM is called EDO memory. EDO (extended data out) is a technology used by SIMMs.

Source: Crucial.com

Figure 4-43 A SIMM appears in a memory ad as EDO memory

> **Notes** RAM chips that have become undependable and cannot hold data reliably can cause errors. Sometimes this happens when chips overheat or power falters.

BUFFERED AND REGISTERED DIMMS

Buffers and registers hold data and amplify a signal just before the data is written to the module. (Using buffers is an older technology than using registers.) Some DIMMs use buffers, some use registers, and some use neither. If a DIMM doesn't support registers or buffers, it's referred to as an unbuffered DIMM. Looking at the ad in Figure 4-44, you can see a kit of DDR3 unbuffered DIMMs and kits of registered DIMMs.

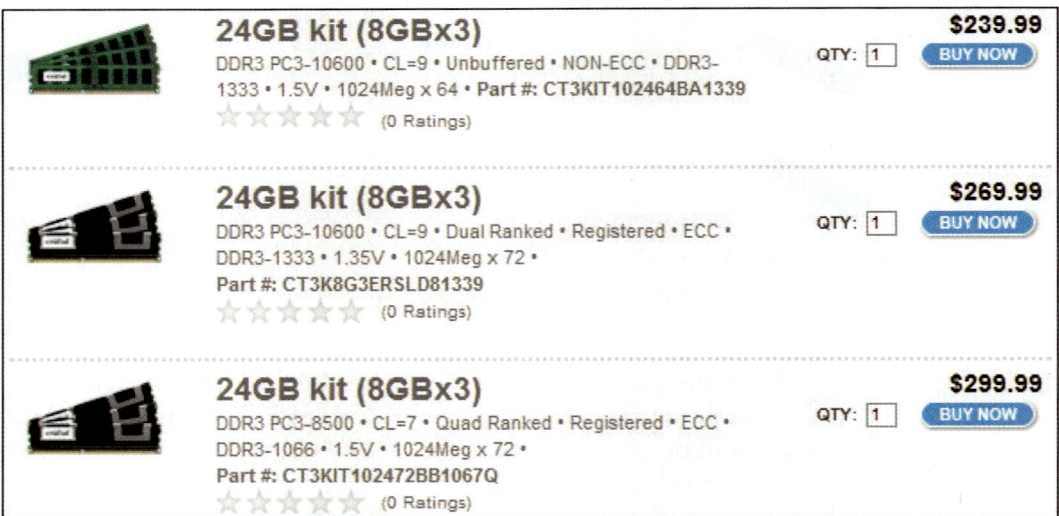

Source: Crucial.com

Figure 4-44 Kits of unbuffered or registered DIMMs

Notches on SDRAM DIMMs are positioned to identify the technologies that the module supports. In Figure 4-45, the position of the notch on the left identifies the module as registered (RFU), buffered, or unbuffered memory. The notch on the right identifies the voltage used by the module. The position of each notch not only helps identify the type of module but also prevents the wrong kind of module from being used on a motherboard.

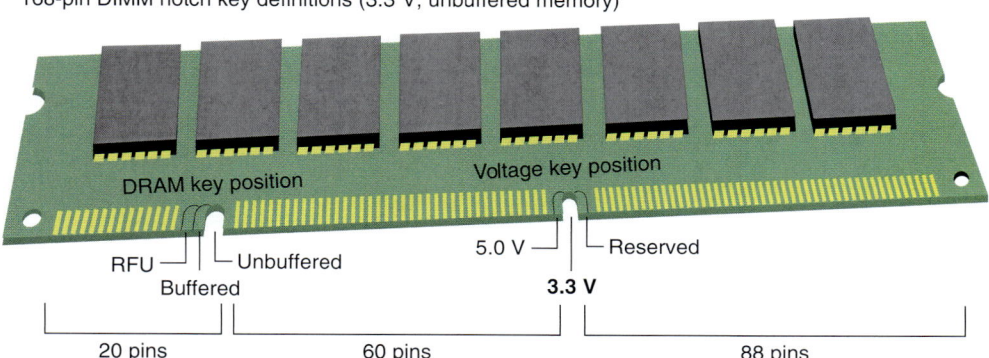

Figure 4-45 The positions of two notches on an SDRAM DIMM identify the type of DIMM and the voltage requirement and also prevent the wrong type from being installed on the motherboard

CAS LATENCY AND RAS LATENCY

Two other memory features are **CAS Latency** (CAS stands for "column access strobe") and **RAS Latency** (RAS stands for "row access strobe"), which are two ways of measuring access timing. Both features refer to the number of clock cycles it takes to write or read a column or row of data off a memory module. CAS Latency is used more than RAS Latency. Lower values are better than higher ones. For example, CL8 is a little faster than CL9.

> **Notes** In memory ads, CAS Latency is sometimes written as CL, and RAS Latency might be written as RL.

Ads for memory modules sometimes give the CAS Latency value within a series of timing numbers, such as 5-5-5-15. The first value is CAS Latency, which means the module is CL5. The second value is RAS Latency. Looking back at Figure 4-44 you can see two DDR3 DIMM kits are rated at CL9 and one is rated at CL7.

> **Notes** When selecting memory, use the memory type that the motherboard manufacturer recommends.

RIMM TECHNOLOGIES

Direct Rambus DRAM (sometimes called **RDRAM** or **Direct RDRAM** or simply **Rambus**) is named after Rambus, Inc., the company that developed it. A Rambus memory module is called a RIMM. RIMMs are expensive and are now slower than current DIMMs. No new motherboards are built to use RIMMs, but you might be called on to support an old motherboard that uses them.

RIMMs that use a 16-bit data bus have two notches and 184 pins (see Figure 4-46). RIMMs that use a 32-bit data bus have a single notch and 232 pins. The 232-pin RIMMs can support dual channels. RIMMs can be ECC or non-ECC and vary in size and speed. Size can vary from 64 MB to 512 MB, and speed ratings are 800 MHz or 1066 MHz.

With RIMMs, each memory slot on the motherboard must be filled to maintain continuity throughout all slots. If a slot does not hold a RIMM, it must hold a placeholder module called a **C-RIMM (Continuity RIMM)** to ensure continuity throughout all slots. The C-RIMM contains no memory chips. A C-RIMM is shown in Figure 4-46.

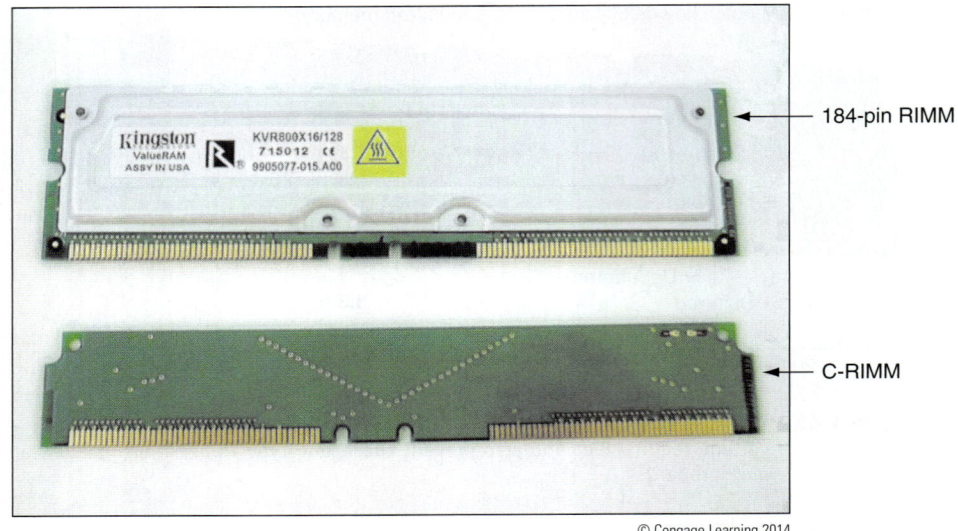

Figure 4-46 A RIMM or C-RIMM must be installed in every RIMM slot on the motherboard

MEMORY TECHNOLOGIES AND MEMORY PERFORMANCE

So now let's summarize the different memory technologies and consider how they affect overall memory performance. Factors to consider when looking at the overall performance of memory are listed below:

- *The total RAM installed.* The more memory there is, the faster the system. Generally use as much memory in a system as the motherboard and the OS can support and you can afford.
- *The memory technology used.* DDR3 is faster than DDR2. DDR2 is faster than DDR, and DDR is faster than SDRAM. When required by the motherboard, buffered or registered memory can improve performance. For all these technologies, use what the board supports.
- *The speed of memory in MHz or PC rating.* Use the fastest memory the motherboard supports. If you install modules of different speeds in the same system, the system will run at the slowest speed or might become unstable. Know that most computer ads give speeds in MHz or PC rating, but some ads give both values.
- *ECC or non-ECC.* Non-ECC is faster and less expensive, but might not be as reliable. Use what the board supports.
- *CL or RL rating.* The lower the better. Use what the board supports, although most boards don't specify a particular CL rating. The CL rating might be expressed as a series of timing numbers.
- *Single, dual, triple, or quad channeling.* DIMMs that differ in capacity or speed can function on a motherboard in single channels as long as you use DIMMs that the board supports and match ECC ratings. However, to improve performance, use dual, triple, or quad channeling if the board supports the feature. To use dual, triple, or quad channeling, install matching DIMMs from the same manufacturer in each group of channel slots. These matching modules are sometimes sold as memory kits.

**A+
220-801
1.2, 1.3**

When selecting memory, you need to know one more fact about memory technologies. On a motherboard, the connectors inside the memory slots are made of tin or gold, as are the edge connectors on the memory modules. It used to be that all memory sockets were made of tin, but now most are made of gold. You should match tin leads to tin connectors and gold leads to gold connectors to prevent a chemical reaction between the two metals, which can cause corrosion. Corrosion can create intermittent memory errors and even make the PC unable to boot.

HOW TO UPGRADE MEMORY

To upgrade memory means to add more RAM to a computer. Adding more RAM might solve a problem with slow performance, applications refusing to load, or an unstable system. When Windows does not have adequate memory to perform an operation, it gives an "Insufficient memory" error or it slows down to a painful crawl.

When first purchased, many computers have empty slots on the motherboard, allowing you to add DIMMs to increase the amount of RAM. Sometimes a memory module goes bad and must be replaced.

When you add more memory to your computer, you need answers to these questions:

- How much RAM do I need and how much is currently installed?
- How many and what kind of memory modules are currently installed on my motherboard?
- How many and what kind of modules can I fit on my motherboard?
- How do I select and purchase the right modules for my upgrade?
- How do I physically install the new modules?

All these questions are answered in the following sections.

HOW MUCH MEMORY DO I NEED AND HOW MUCH IS CURRENTLY INSTALLED?

With the demands today's software places on memory, the answer is probably, "All you can get." Windows 7 needs at least 2 GB, but more is better. The limit for a 32-bit OS is 4 GB installed RAM. A 64-bit Windows installation can handle more. For example, a 64-bit installation of Windows 7 Home Premium can use up to 16 GB of RAM.

> **APPLYING CONCEPTS** — **HOW MUCH MEMORY IS CURRENTLY INSTALLED?**
>
> In Windows, you can use the System Information window to report the amount of physical memory installed. Click **Start**, type **Msinfo32**, and press **Enter**. The System Information window shown in Figure 4-47 reports the amount of installed physical memory. Notice on the window that 16 GB is installed, but only 14 GB is available to Windows. The other 2 GB is used by BIOS and most of that is used for video memory.

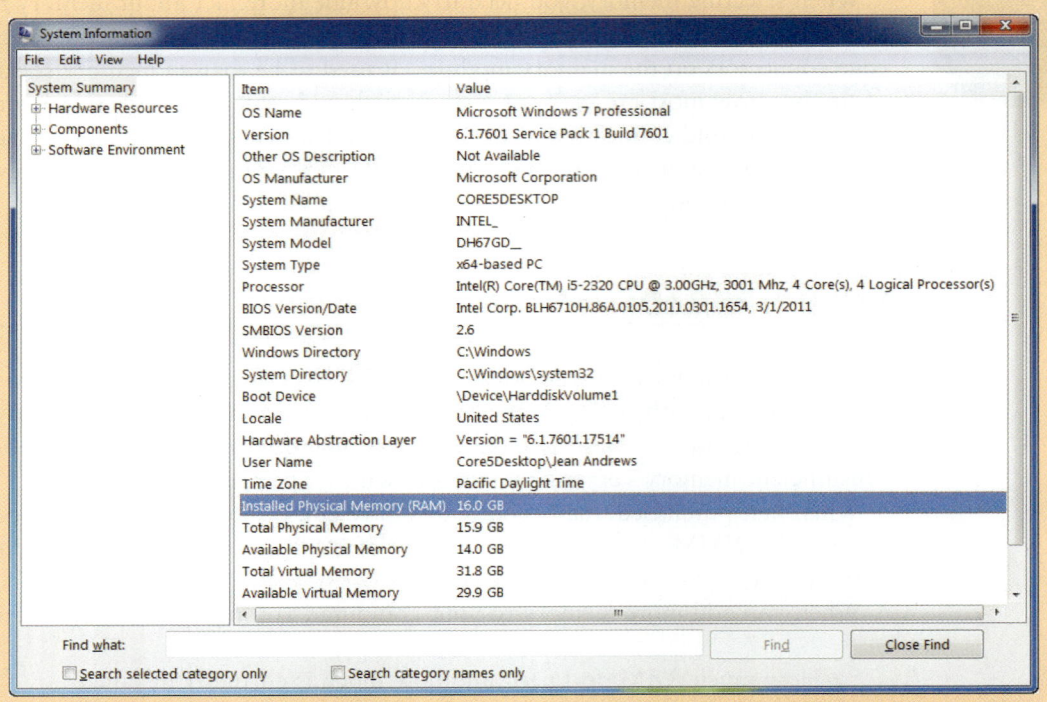

Figure 4-47 The System Information window reports installed physical memory

The BIOS setup screen shows more information about installed memory than does Windows. Reboot the computer and access BIOS setup (you learned how to do that in Chapter 3.) The BIOS setup main menu for one system is shown in Figure 4-48. This screen shows the number of memory slots and how much RAM is installed in each slot. Notice the system has two memory channels of two slots each. You can, therefore, conclude this system is using dual channels.

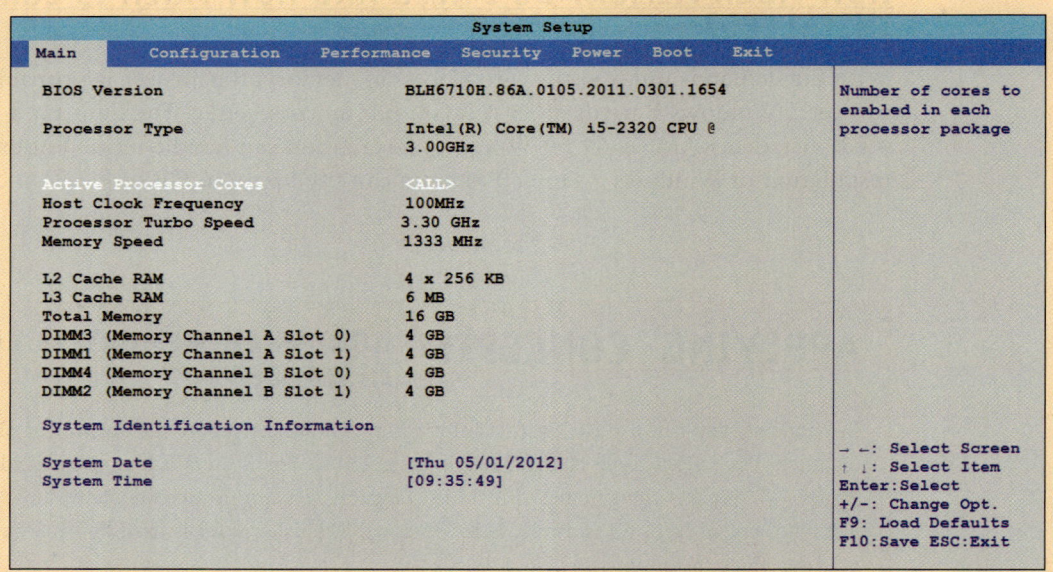

Figure 4-48 BIOS setup reports memory configuration and amount

HOW MANY AND WHAT KIND OF MEMORY MODULES ARE CURRENTLY INSTALLED?

The next step to upgrading memory is to determine what type of memory modules the motherboard is currently using. If the board already has memory installed, you want to do your best to match the new modules with whatever is already installed. To learn what type of memory modules are already installed, do the following:

▲ Open the case and look at the memory slots. How many slots do you have? How many are filled? Remove each module from its slot and look on it for imprinted type, size, and speed. For example, a module might say "PC2-4200/512MB." The PC2 tells you the memory is DDR2, the 4200 is the PC rating and tells you the speed, and the 512 MB is the size. This is not enough information to know exactly what modules to purchase, but it's a start.

▲ Examine the module for the physical size and position of the notches. Compare the notch positions to those in Table 4-3 and Figure 4-45.

▲ Read your motherboard documentation. If the documentation is not clear (and some is not) or you don't have the documentation, look on the motherboard for the imprinted manufacturer and model (see Figure 4-49). With this information, you can search a good memory web site such as Kingston (*www.kingston.com*) or Crucial (*www.crucial.com*), which can tell you what type of modules this board supports.

Figure 4-49 Look for the manufacturer and model of a motherboard imprinted somewhere on the board

▲ Look in the documentation to see if the board supports dual channel, triple channel, or quad channels. If it does, most likely the memory slots on the board will be color-coded in pairs (for dual channels) or groups of three slots (for triple channels) or four

A+
220-801
1.2, 1.3

slots (for quad channels). If the board supports multiple channels and modules are already installed, verify that matching DIMMs are installed in each channel.
▲ If you still have not identified the module type, you can take the motherboard and the old memory modules to a good computer parts store and they should be able to match it for you.

Hands-on | Project 4-3 Use an Online Memory Scanner

A great shortcut to research a memory upgrade is an online memory scanner. Go to *www.crucial.com/ systemscanner* by Crucial. Download and run the Crucial System Scanner, which scans your system and reports what type of memory is installed and can be installed. Using the Crucial report, answer these questions:

1. Which motherboard do you have installed? How much memory is installed? How many memory slots does the board have? How many are populated?
2. What is the maximum memory the board supports? What type of memory does the board support? What would be the total cost of the memory upgrade if you were to max out the total memory on the board?

HOW MANY AND WHAT KIND OF MODULES CAN FIT ON MY MOTHERBOARD?

Now that you know what memory modules are already installed, you're ready to decide how much and what kind of modules you can add to the board. Keep in mind that if all memory slots are full, sometimes you can take out small-capacity modules and replace them with larger-capacity modules, but you can only use the type, size, and speed of modules that the board can support. Also, if you must discard existing modules, the price of the upgrade increases.

To know how much memory your motherboard can physically hold, read the documentation that comes with the board. Next, let's look at what to consider when deciding how many and what kind of DIMMs or RIMMs to add to a system.

DIMM MODULES

You can always install DIMMs as single modules, but you might not get the best performance by doing so. For best performance, install matching DIMMs in all the slots (two, three, or four slots) on one channel. Now let's look at a few examples. The examples are ordered from a recent motherboard to an older motherboard. As you study these examples, notice that the older the board, the more complicated the configuration can be and the harder it is to understand the documentation. Is life with computers getting simpler or what?

Motherboard Using DDR3 Dual-Channel DIMMs

The Intel Desktop Board DH67GD shown earlier in Figure 4-12 has four memory slots that use dual channeling. These slots are numbered in the user guide, as shown in Figure 4-50. The slots can hold Dual Channel DDR3 1333 MHz and 1066 MHz non-ECC, 1.35 V modules for up to 32 GB of RAM on this board. To use four DIMMs and dual channeling, install matching DIMMs in the two blue slots and matching DIMMs in the two black slots.

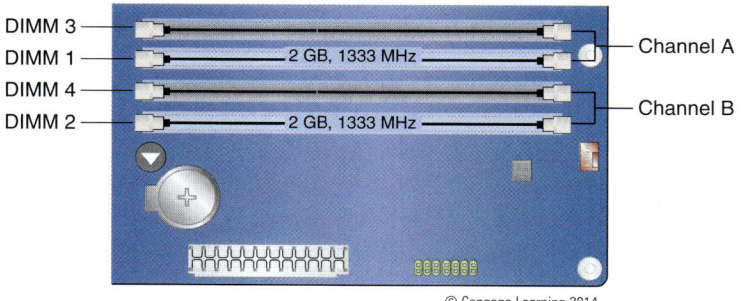

Figure 4-50 Documentation shows four DIMM slots that use dual channels

The mobo user guide says it is possible to use only three DIMMs and dual channeling if you install matching DIMMs in the two blue slots, and install a third DIMM in a black slot. This third DIMM must be equal in speed and total size of the DIMMs in the blue slots. For example, you can install two 4 GB DIMMs in the two blue slots and one 8 GB DIMM in a black slot for a total of 16 GB RAM. If you install only a single DIMM on this board, it must go in the first blue slot, which is the blue slot closest to the processor.

Motherboard Using DDR3 Triple-Channel DIMMs

The Intel motherboard shown earlier in Figure 4-38 has four DDR3 memory slots that can be configured for single, dual, or triple channeling. The four empty slots are shown in Figure 4-51. If triple channeling is used, three matching DIMMs are used in the three blue slots. If the fourth slot is populated, the board reverts to single channeling. For dual channeling, install two matching DIMMs in the two blue slots farthest from the processor and leave the other two slots empty. If only one DIMM is installed, it goes in the blue slot in the farthest position from the processor.

Figure 4-51 Four DDR3 slots on a motherboard

The motherboard documentation says that these types of DIMMs can be used:

- The DIMM voltage rating no higher than 1.6 V
- Non-ECC DDR3 memory
- Serial Presence Detect (SPD) memory only
- Gold-plated contacts (some modules use tin-plated contacts)
- 1333 MHz, 1066 MHz, or 800 MHz (best to match the system bus speed)
- Unbuffered, nonregistered single- or double-sided DIMMs
- Up to 16 GB total installed RAM

The third item in the list needs an explanation. Serial Presence Detect (SPD) is a DIMM technology that declares to system BIOS at startup the module's size, speed, voltage, and data path width. If the DIMM does not support SPD, the system might not boot or boot with errors. Today's memory always supports SPD.

Motherboard Using DDR DIMMs with Dual Channeling

Let's look at another example of a DIMM installation. The Pentium motherboard allows you to use three different speeds of DDR DIMMs in one to four sockets on the board. The board supports dual channeling and has two blue slots for one channel and two black slots for the other channel. For dual channeling to work, matching DIMMs must be installed in the two blue sockets. If two DIMMs are installed in the two black sockets, they must match each other.

This board supports up to 4 GB of unbuffered, 184-pin, non-ECC memory running at PC3200, PC2700, or PC2100. The documentation says the system bus can run at 800 MHz, 533 MHz, or 400 MHz, depending on the speed of the processor installed. Therefore, the speed of the processor determines the system bus speed, which determines the speed of memory modules.

Figure 4-52 outlines the possible configurations of these DIMM modules, showing that you can install one, two, or four DIMMs and which sockets should hold these DIMMs. To take advantage of dual channeling on this motherboard, you must populate the sockets according to Figure 4-52, so that identical DIMM pairs are working together in DIMM_A1 and DIMM_B1 sockets (the blue sockets), and another pair can work together in DIMM_A2 and DIMM_B2 sockets (the black sockets).

Mode		DIMM_A1	DIMM_A2	DIMM_B1	DIMM_B2
Single channel	(1)	Populated	—	—	—
	(2)	—	Populated	—	—
	(3)	—	—	Populated	—
	(4)	—	—	—	Populated
Dual channel*	(1)	Populated	—	Populated	—
	(2)	—	Populated	—	Populated
	(3)	Populated	Populated	Populated	Populated

*Use only identical DDR DIMM pairs

© Cengage Learning 2014

Figure 4-52 Motherboard documentation shows that one, two, or four DIMMs can be installed

A+ 220-801
1.2, 1.3

The board has two installed DDR DIMMs. The label on one of these DIMMs is shown in Figure 4-53. The important items on this label are the size (256 MB), the speed (400 MHz or 3200 PC rating), and the CAS Latency (CL3). With this information and knowledge about what the board can support, we are now ready to select and buy the memory for the upgrade. For example, if you decide to upgrade the system to 1 GB of memory, you would buy two DDR, 400 MHz, CL3 DIMMs that support dual channeling. For best results, you need to also match the manufacturer and buy Elixir memory.

Figure 4-53 Use the label on this DIMM to identify its features

Pentium Motherboard Using SDRAM DIMMs

Our last DIMM example uses older SDRAM DIMMs. The Pentium motherboard uses 168-pin single-sided DIMM modules, and the documentation says to use unbuffered, 3.3 V, ECC, PC100 DIMM SDRAM modules. The PC100 means that the modules should be rated to work with a motherboard that runs at 100 MHz. You can choose to use ECC modules. If you choose not to, BIOS setup should show the feature disabled. Three DIMM slots are on the board, which the motherboard documentation calls sockets. Each socket holds one bank of memory. Figure 4-54 shows the possible combinations of DIMMs that can be installed in these sockets.

DIMM Location	168-Pin DIMM		Total Memory
Socket 1 (Rows 0 & 1)	SDRAM 8, 16, 32, 64, 128, 256 MB	×1	
Socket 2 (Rows 2 & 3)	SDRAM 8, 16, 32, 64, 128, 256 MB	×1	
Socket 3 (Rows 4 & 5)	SDRAM 8, 16, 32, 64, 128, 256 MB	×1	
	Total System Memory (Max 768 MB)	=	

Figure 4-54 This table is part of the motherboard documentation and is used to show possible DIMM sizes and calculate total memory on the motherboard

RIMM MODULES

Systems using RIMMs are no longer made, but you might be called on to support one. Because RIMMs are obsolete, they are really expensive. Most likely you can purchase a comparable motherboard and processor that use DIMMs for less money than you can buy the RIMMs for one of these old systems. However, if you ever find yourself needing to replace or upgrade memory using RIMMs, if possible, match the new RIMMs with one already installed on the board. Be sure to follow guidelines given in the motherboard documentation for the capacity and speeds supported.

For example, suppose you see installed a RIMM like the one shown in Figure 4-55. The important information for us is "800X16/128." The value 128 is the size of the RIMM, 128 MB. The value 800 is the speed, 800 MHz. The value X16 tells us this RIMM is a non-ECC RIMM. (If it had been ECC compliant, the value would have been X18.) That's enough information to go find a RIMM for sale that matches this one.

Figure 4-55 Use the label on this RIMM to identify its features

Recall that all RIMM slots must be filled with either RIMMs or C-RIMMs. When you upgrade, you replace one or more C-RIMMs with RIMMs.

As you can see, the motherboard documentation is essential when selecting memory. If you can't find the motherboard manual, look on the motherboard manufacturer's web site.

HOW DO I SELECT AND PURCHASE THE RIGHT MEMORY MODULES?

You're now ready to make the purchase. As you select your memory, you might find it difficult to find an exact match to DIMMs or RIMMs already installed on the board. If necessary, here are some compromises you can not or can make:

▲ Mixing unbuffered memory with buffered or registered memory won't work.
▲ When matching memory, for best results, also match the module manufacturer. But in a pinch, you can try using memory from two different manufacturers.
▲ If you mix memory speeds, know that all modules will perform at the slowest speed.

Now let's look at how to use a web site or other computer ad to search for the right memory.

USING A WEB SITE TO RESEARCH YOUR PURCHASE

When purchasing memory from a web site such as Crucial Technology's site (*www.crucial.com*) or Kingston Technology's site (*www.kingston.com*), look for a search utility that will match memory modules to your motherboard (see Figure 4-56). These utilities are easy to

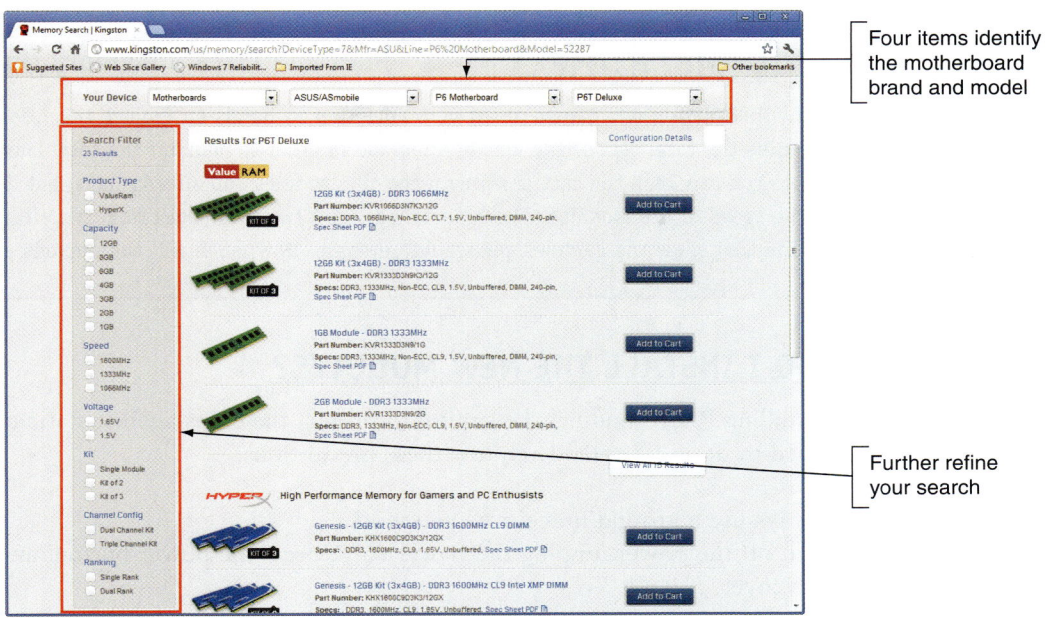

Figure 4-56 The Kingston web site DIMM recommendations for a particular motherboard

use and help you confirm you have made the right decisions about type, size, and speed to buy. They can also help if motherboard documentation is inadequate, and you're not exactly sure what memory to buy.

Let's look at one example on the Crucial site where we are looking to install memory in the Intel DH67GD motherboard discussed earlier in the chapter. The search results are shown in Figure 4-57. Modules faster than the board supports are listed. They will work on the board, running at a slower speed, but it's not necessary to spend the money for speed you won't use. The best buy is the second item listed; these DIMMs are rated at 1333 MHz, which is the maximum speed the board supports.

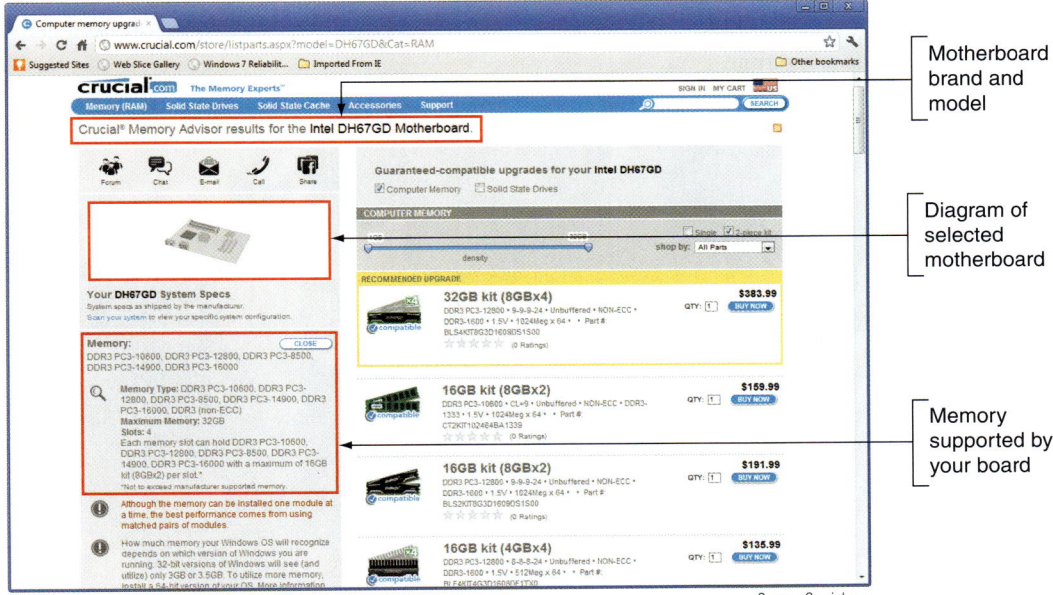

Figure 4-57 Selecting memory off the Crucial web site

A+ 220-801 1.2, 1.3

> **Hands-on | Project 4-4** Plan and Price a Memory Upgrade
>
> Using the information you gained about your computer in Hands-on Project 4-3, research the web to determine the total cost of the memory upgrade in order to max out the total memory on your computer. You can keep the cost down by using the modules you already have, but don't forget to match the speed of the modules already installed. Print two web pages from two sites other than the Crucial site that show the modules you would purchase. How much will the upgrade cost?

HOW DO I INSTALL THE NEW MODULES?

When installing RAM modules, be careful to protect the chips against static electricity, as you learned to do in Chapter 1. Follow these precautions:

- Always use a ground bracelet as you work.
- Turn off the power, unplug the power cord, press the power button, and remove the case cover.
- Handle memory modules with care.
- Don't touch the edge connectors on the memory module or on the memory slot.
- Don't stack cards or modules because you can loosen a chip.
- Usually modules pop into place easily and are secured by spring catches on both ends. Make sure that you look for the notches on one side or in the middle of the module that orient the module in the slot.

Let's now look at the details of installing a DIMM and a RIMM.

INSTALLING DIMMS

For DIMM modules, small clips latch into place on each side of the slot to hold the module in the slot, as shown in Figure 4-58. To install a DIMM, first pull the supporting arms on the sides of the slot outward. Look on the DIMM edge connector for the notches, which help you orient the DIMM correctly over the slot, and insert the DIMM straight down into the slot. When the DIMM is fully inserted, the supporting clips should pop back into place. Figure 4-59 shows a DIMM being inserted into a slot on a motherboard. Apply pressure on both ends of the DIMM at the same time.

Figure 4-58 Clips on each side of a slot hold a DIMM in place

Figure 4-59   Insert the DIMM into the slot by pressing down until the support clips lock into position

Most often, placing memory on the motherboard is all that is necessary for installation. When the computer powers up, it counts the memory present without any further instruction and senses the features that the modules support, such as ECC or buffering. For some really old computers, you must tell BIOS setup the amount of memory present. Read the motherboard documentation to determine what yours requires. If the new memory is not recognized, power down the system and reseat the module. Most likely it's not installed solidly in the slot.

INSTALLING RIMMs

For RIMM modules, install the RIMMs beginning with bank 0, followed by bank 1. (To know which slot is bank 0, see the motherboard documentation.) If a C-RIMM is already in the slot, remove the C-RIMM by pulling the supporting clips on the sides of the socket outward and pulling straight up on the C-RIMM. When installing the RIMM, notches on the edge of the RIMM module will help you orient it correctly in the socket. Insert the module straight down in the socket (see Figure 4-60). When it is fully inserted, the supporting clips should pop back into place.

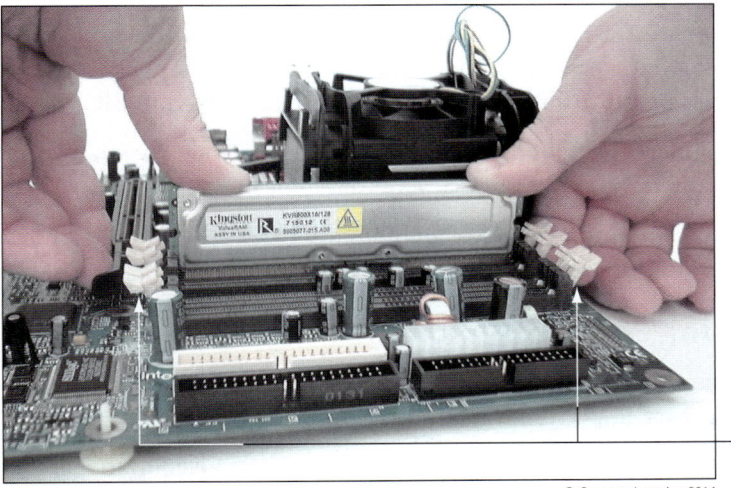

Figure 4-60   Install RIMM modules in banks beginning with bank 0

A+
220-801
1.2, 1.3

Hands-on Project 4-5 Examine BIOS Settings

On your home or lab computer, use BIOS setup to answer these questions:

1. Which processor is installed? What is the processor frequency?
2. What are the BIOS settings that apply to the processor and how is the processor configured?
3. What information does BIOS report about total memory installed and how each memory slot is populated? Does the board support dual, triple, or quad channelling? How do you know?

Hands-on Project 4-6 Upgrade Memory

To practice installing additional memory in a computer in a classroom environment, remove the DIMMs or RIMMs from one computer and place them in another computer. Boot the second computer and check that it counts the additional memory. When finished, return the borrowed modules to the original computer.

>> CHAPTER SUMMARY

Types and Characteristics of Processors

- The most important component on the motherboard is the processor, or central processing unit. The two major manufacturers of processors are Intel and AMD.

- Processors are rated by the speed of the system bus the processor can support, the processor speed, the socket and chipset the processor can use, processor architecture (32-bit or 64-bit), multi-core rating, how much internal memory cache the processor has, amount and type of RAM the processor can support, and the computing technologies the processor can use.

- A processor's memory cache inside the processor housing can be an L1 cache (contained on the processor die), L2 cache (off the die), and L3 cache (farther from the core than L2 cache).

- The core of a processor has two arithmetic logic units (ALUs). Multi-core processors have two, three, or more cores (called dual core, triple core, quad core, and so forth). Each core can process two threads at once if the feature is enabled in BIOS setup.

- The current families of Intel processors for desktops include the Core, Atom, Celeron, and Pentium families of processors. Several different processors are within each family.

- The current AMD desktop processor families are the FX, Phenom, Athlon, and Sempron. Several processors exist within each family.

Selecting and Installing a Processor

- Select a processor that the motherboard supports. A board is likely to support several processors that vary in performance and price.

- When installing a processor, always follow the directions given in the motherboard user guide and be careful to protect the board and processor against ESD. Current Intel sockets

LGA1155, LGA1366, and LGA775 use a socket lever and socket load plate. When opening these sockets, lift the socket lever and then the socket load plate, install the processor, and then close the socket. Many AMD sockets have a socket lever, but not a socket load plate.

Memory Technologies

- DRAM is stored on four kinds of modules: DIMM, SO-DIMM, RIMM, and SIMM modules.
- Types of DIMMs are DDR3 and DDR2 DIMMs that have 240 pins, DDR DIMMs with 184 pins, and SDRAM DIMMs with 168 pins. A RIMM has 184 or 232 pins, and RIMMs are outdated technologies.
- DIMMs can be single-sided or double-sided. Some double-sided DIMMs provide more than one memory bank and are called dual ranked or quad ranked. A memory bank has a 64-bit data path and is accessed by the processor independently of other banks.
- DIMMs can work together in dual channels, triple channels, and quad channels so that the memory controller can access more than one DIMM at a time to improve performance. In a channel, all DIMMs must match in size, speed, and features. DDR3 DIMMs can use dual, triple, or quad channeling, but DDR and DDR2 DIMMs can only use dual channels.
- DIMM and RIMM speeds are measured in MHz (for example, 1333 MHz) or PC rating (for example, PC3-10600).
- The memory controller can check memory for errors and possibly correct those errors using ECC (error-correcting code). Using parity, an older technology, the controller could only recognize an error had occurred, but not correct it.
- Buffers and registers are used to hold data and amplify a data signal. A DIMM is rated as a buffered, registered, or unbuffered DIMM.
- CAS Latency (CL) and RAS Latency (RL) measure access time to memory. The lower values are faster than the higher values.
- RIMMs require that every RIMM slot be populated. If a RIMM is not installed in the slot, install a placeholder module called a C-RIMM.

How to Upgrade Memory

- When upgrading memory, use the type, size, and speed the motherboard supports and match new modules to those already installed. Features to match include DDR3, DDR2, DDR, size in MB or GB, speed (MHz or PC rating), buffered, registered, unbuffered, single-sided, double-sided, CL rating, tin or gold connectors, support for dual, triple, or quad channeling, ECC, and non-ECC. Using memory made by the same manufacturer is recommended.

>> KEY TERMS

For explanations of key terms, see the Glossary near the end of the book.

CAS Latency
Centrino
C-RIMM (Continuity RIMM)
DDR
DDR2
DDR3
DIMM (dual inline memory module)
Direct Rambus DRAM
Direct RDRAM
Double Data Rate SDRAM (DDR SDRAM)
double-sided
dual channels
dual processors
dual ranked
dynamic RAM (DRAM)
ECC (error-correcting code)
graphics processing unit (GPU)
Hyper-Threading
HyperTransport
Level 1 cache (L1 cache)
Level 2 cache (L2 cache)
Level 3 cache (L3 cache)
memory bank
multi-core processing
multiplier

multiprocessing
multiprocessor platform
parity
parity error
processor frequency
quad channels
Rambus
RAS Latency
RDRAM
RIMM
SDRAM II
SIMM (single inline memory module)
single channel
single-sided
SO-DIMM (small outline DIMM)
static RAM (SRAM)
synchronous DRAM (SDRAM)
thread
triple channels
x86 processors
x86-64 bit processor

>> REVIEWING THE BASICS

1. Who are the two major manufacturers of processors?
2. What is the name of the memory cache that is on the same die as the processor?
3. What is the name of the memory cache that is closest to the processor die but is not housed on the die?
4. What is the name of the Intel technology that allows a processor to handle two threads at the same time?
5. How many threads can a quad-core processor handle at once?
6. Which Intel processor socket uses a screw head to hold down the socket load plate?
7. Which is faster, SRAM or DRAM? Why?
8. How many pins are on a DDR3 DIMM? DDR2 DIMM?
9. How many pins are on a DDR DIMM? SDRAM DIMM?
10. How many notches does a DDR3 DIMM have?
11. What was the first type of DIMM that ran synchronized with the system clock?
12. What major improvement did DDR make over regular SDRAM?
13. Which DIMM performs better, a double-sided dual-ranked DIMM or a double-sided single-ranked DIMM?
14. What prevents a DDR DIMM from being installed in a DDR2 DIMM slot on a motherboard?
15. Which module, a DDR3 or DDR2 DIMM, uses lower voltage?
16. In a memory ad for DIMMs, you notice 64Meg ×72 for one DIMM and 64Meg ×64 for another DIMM. What does the 72 tell you about the first DIMM?
17. A DIMM that contains memory chips in two memory banks on the module is said to be _____.
18. What type of DIMM supports triple channeling?
19. If two bits of a byte are in error when the byte is read from ECC memory, can ECC detect the error? Can it fix the error?
20. How many notches are on an SDRAM DIMM?
21. Looking at an SDRAM DIMM, how can you know for certain the voltage needed by the module?

22. A DIMM memory ad displays 5-5-5-15. What is the CAS Latency value of this DIMM?
23. What is the most amount of RAM that can be used by a 32-bit installation of Windows 7 Professional?
24. A motherboard uses dual channeling, but you have four DIMMs available that differ in size. The motherboard supports all four sizes. Can you install these DIMMs on the board? Will dual channeling be enabled?
25. You need to upgrade memory on a motherboard that uses RIMMs. You notice one RIMM and one C-RIMM module are already installed on the board. Which module should you replace?
26. What two types of memory can be used on a 100-MHz motherboard?
27. Which is faster, CL3 memory or CL5 memory?
28. You are looking to purchase two DIMMs running at 400 MHz. You find DIMMs advertised at PC4000 and PC3200. Which do you purchase?
29. You need to find out how much RAM is installed in a system. What command do you enter in the Search box to launch the System Information utility?
30. Although ECC memory costs more than non-ECC memory, why would you choose to use it? Which type of computer typically requires ECC memory?

>> THINKING CRITICALLY

1. You need to upgrade memory in a system but you don't have the motherboard documentation available. You open the case and notice that the board has four DIMM slots; three slots are colored yellow and one slot is black. What type of DIMM does the board likely use? How can you be sure?
2. If your motherboard supports DIMM memory, will RIMM memory still work on the board?
3. If your motherboard supports ECC SDRAM memory, can you substitute non-ECC SDRAM memory? If your motherboard supports buffered SDRAM memory, can you substitute unbuffered SDRAM modules?
4. You have just upgraded memory on a computer from 1 GB to 2 GB by adding one DIMM. When you first turn on the PC, the memory count shows only 1 GB. Select which of the following is most likely the source of the problem. What can you do to fix it?
    a. Windows is giving an error because it likely became corrupted while the PC was disassembled.
    b. The new DIMM you installed is faulty.
    c. The new DIMM is not properly seated.
    d. The DIMM is installed in the wrong slot.
5. Your motherboard supports dual channeling and you currently have two slots used in Channel A on the board; each module holds 1 GB. You want to install an additional 1 GB of RAM. Will your system run faster if you install two 512 MB DIMMs or one 1 GB DIMM? Explain your answer.

>> REAL PROBLEMS, REAL SOLUTIONS

REAL PROBLEM 4-1: Understanding Dual-Processor Motherboards

Print the web page of a picture of a motherboard that supports dual processors. Use one of these web sites to find the picture:

- ASUS at *www.asus.com*
- Intel at *www.intel.com*

Answer these questions about the motherboard:

1. What is the manufacturer and model number of the motherboard?
2. What type of memory and how much memory does the board support?
3. What operating systems does the board support?
4. What processors does the board support?

REAL PROBLEM 4-2: Troubleshooting Memory

Follow the rules outlined in Chapter 1 to protect the PC against ESD as you work. Remove the memory module in the first memory slot on a motherboard, and boot the PC. Did you get an error? Why or why not?

REAL PROBLEM 4-3: Memory Research Game

In a group of four players with Internet access and a fifth person who is the scorekeeper, play the Memory Research Game. The scorekeeper asks a question and then gives players one minute to find the best answer. Five points are awarded to the player who has the best answer at the end of each one-minute play. The scorekeeper can use these questions or make up his or her own. If you use these questions, mix up the order:

1. What is the fastest DDR3 DIMM sold today?
2. What is the lowest price for a 232-pin non-ECC Rambus RIMM?
3. What is the largest size DDR2 DIMM sold today?
4. What is the largest size fully buffered ECC 240-pin DDR2 DIMM sold today?
5. What is the lowest price for an 8 GB 240-pin ECC DDR3 DIMM?

CHAPTER 5

Supporting Hard Drives

In this chapter, you will learn:

- About the technologies used inside a hard drive and how a computer communicates with a hard drive
- How to select and install a hard drive
- About tape drives and floppy drives

The hard drive is the most important permanent storage device in a computer, and supporting hard drives is one of the more important tasks of a PC support technician. This chapter introduces the different kinds of hard drive technologies that have accounted for the continual upward increase in hard drive capacities and speeds over the past few years. The ways a computer interfaces with a hard drive have also changed several times over the years as the techniques for communication between the computer and hard drive continue to improve.

In this chapter, you will learn about past and present methods of communication between the computer and drive so that you can support both older and newer drives. You'll learn how to select and install the different types of hard drives and tape drives, and you'll learn enough about floppy drives so that you can support these really old storage devices.

HARD DRIVE TECHNOLOGIES AND INTERFACE STANDARDS

A+
220-801
1.5, 1.7,
1.11

A **hard disk drive (HDD)**, most often called a **hard drive**, comes in two sizes for personal computers: the 2.5" size is used for laptop computers and the 3.5" size is used for desktops. See Figure 5-1. In addition, a smaller 1.8" size hard drive (about the size of a credit card) is used in some low-end laptops and other equipment such as MP3 players.

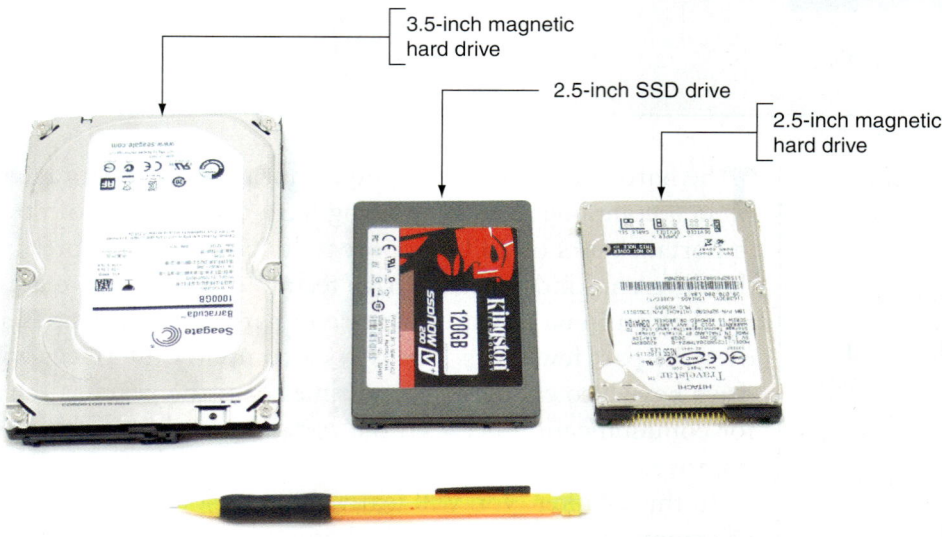

Figure 5-1 A hard drive for a desktop is larger than those used in laptops

In this part of the chapter, you learn about the technologies used inside a hard drive and about the various standards, cables, and connectors a drive might use to interface with the computer.

TECHNOLOGIES USED INSIDE A HARD DRIVE

The two types of hardware technologies used inside the drive are solid state and magnetic. In addition, some drives use a combination of both technologies. Here are important details about each:

- *Solid state drive.* A **solid state drive (SSD)**, also called a **solid state device (SSD)**, is called solid state because it has no moving parts. The drives are built using nonvolatile memory, which is similar to that used for USB flash drives. Recall this type of memory does not lose its data even after the power is turned off.

  In an SSD drive, flash memory is stored on EEPROM (Electronically Erasable Programmable Read Only Memory) chips inside the drive housing. The chips contain grids of rows and columns with two transistors at each intersection that hold a zero or one bit. One of these transistors is called a floating gate and accepts the zero or one state according to a logic test called NAND (stands for "Not AND"). Therefore, the memory in an SSD is called **NAND flash memory**. EEPROM chips are limited as to the number of times transistors can be reprogrammed. Therefore, the lifespan of an SSD drive is based on the number of write operations to the drive. (The number of read operations does not affect the lifespan.) For normal desktop or laptop computers, an SSD is rated to last for over 200 years. For high-use servers, the lifespan of an SSD is considerably shorter.

Because flash memory is expensive, solid-state drives are much more expensive than magnetic hard drives, but they are faster, more reliable, last longer, and use less power than magnetic drives. Figure 5-2 shows two sizes of solid state drives (2.5" and 1.8") and what the inside of an SSD hard drive looks like.

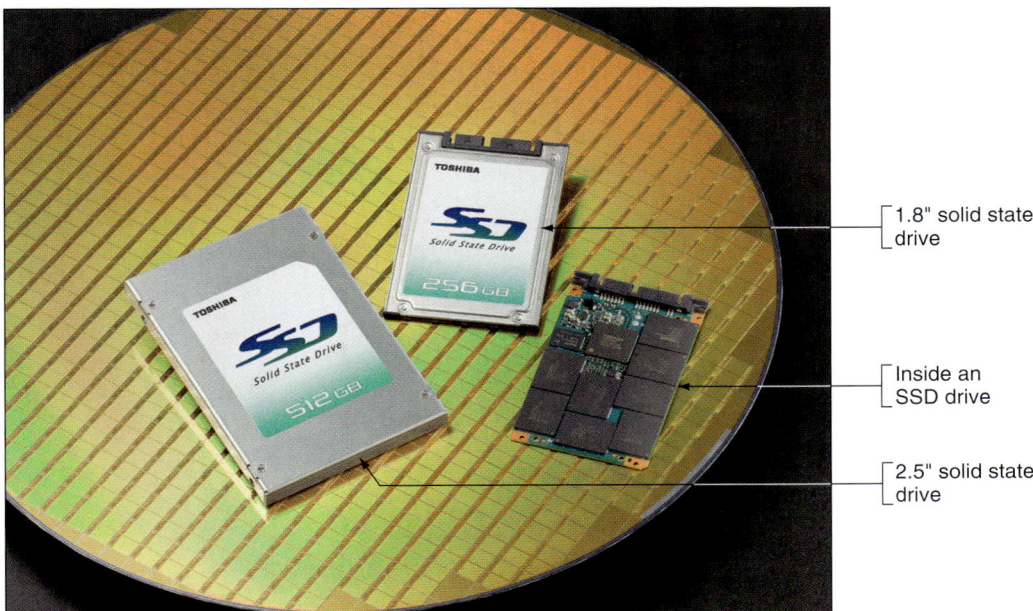

Figure 5-2 Solid-state drives by Toshiba

▲ *Magnetic hard drive*. A **magnetic hard drive** has one, two, or more platters, or disks, that stack together and spin in unison inside a sealed metal housing that contains firmware to control reading and writing data to the drive and to communicate with the motherboard. The top and bottom of each disk have a **read/write head** that moves across the disk surface as all the disks rotate on a spindle (see Figure 5-3). All the

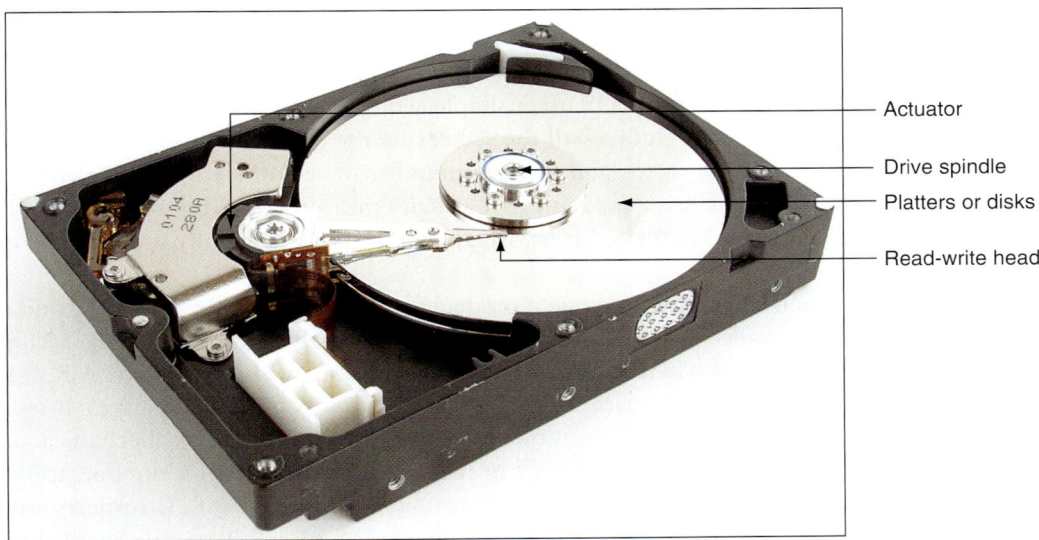

Figure 5-3 Inside a magnetic hard drive

read/write heads are controlled by an actuator, which moves the read/write heads across the disk surfaces in unison. The disk surfaces are covered with a magnetic medium that can hold data as magnetized spots. The spindle rotates at 5400, 7200, 10,000, or 15,000 RPM (revolutions per minute). The faster the spindle, the better performing the drive.

Data is organized on a magnetic hard drive in concentric circles, called tracks (see Figure 5-4). Each track is divided into segments called sectors (also called records). Older hard drives used sectors that contained 512 bytes. Most current hard drives use 4096-byte sectors.

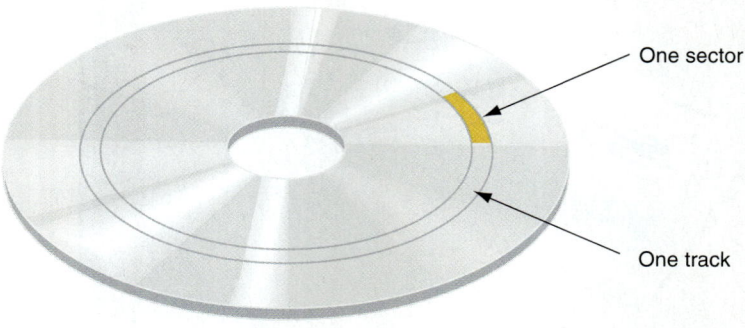

Figure 5-4 A hard drive or floppy disk is divided into tracks and sectors; several sectors make one cluster

▲ *Hybrid hard drives.* Some hard drives are **hybrid hard drives**, using both technologies. The flash component is used as a buffer to improve drive performance. Some hybrid drives perform just as well as an SSD drive. For a hybrid drive to function, the operating system must support it. Windows 7/Vista technology that supports a hybrid drive is called **ReadyDrive**.

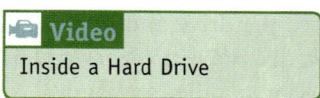

Before an SSD or magnetic drive leaves the factory, sector markings are written to it in a process called **low-level formatting**. (This formatting is different from the high-level formatting that Windows does after a drive is installed in a computer.) The hard drive firmware, BIOS, and the OS use a simple sequential numbering system called logical block addressing (LBA) to address all the sectors on the drive.

The size of each sector and the total number of sectors on the drive determine the drive capacity. Today's drive capacities are usually measured in GB (gigabytes) or TB (terabytes, each of which is 1024 gigabytes). Magnetic drives are generally much larger in capacity than SSD drives.

You need to be aware of one more technology supported by both SSD and magnetic hard drives called **S.M.A.R.T. (Self-Monitoring Analysis and Reporting Technology)**, which is used to predict when a drive is likely to fail. System BIOS uses S.M.A.R.T. to monitor drive performance, temperature, and other factors. For magnetic drives, it monitors disk spin-up time, distance between the head and the disk, and other mechanical activities of the drive. Many SSD drives report to the BIOS the number of write operations, which is the best measurement of when the drive might fail. If S.M.A.R.T. suspects a drive failure is about to happen, it displays a warning message. S.M.A.R.T. can be enabled and disabled in BIOS setup.

A+ 220-801
1.5, 1.7, 1.11

> **Notes** Malware has been known to give false S.M.A.R.T. alerts.

So now let's look at how the drive's firmware or controller communicates with the motherboard.

INTERFACE STANDARDS USED BY A HARD DRIVE

The interface standards between the hard drive and the motherboard have evolved over time, and there are competing standards, which can make for a confusing mess of standards. To help keep them all straight, use Figure 5-5 as your guideline for the standards used by internal drives.

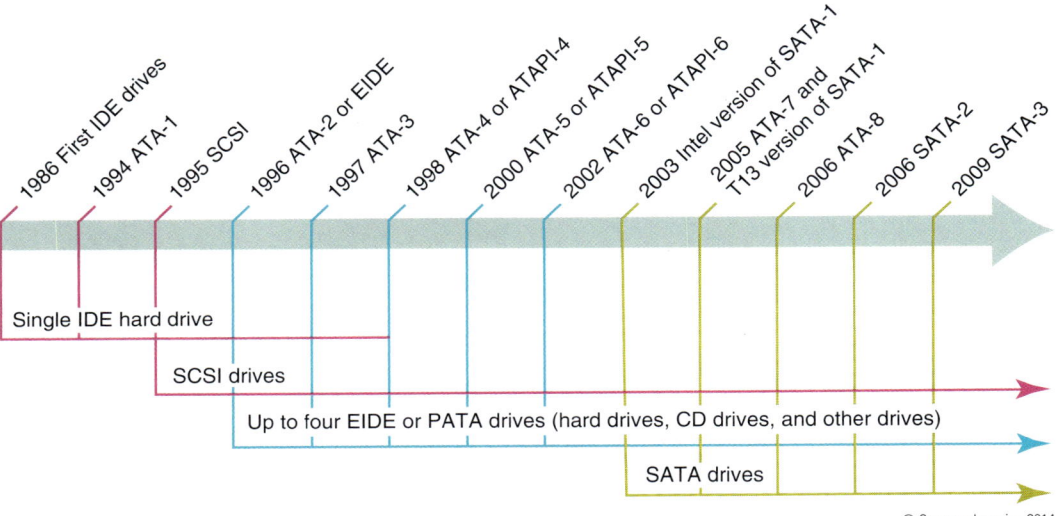

Figure 5-5 Timeline of interface standards used by internal drives

The two most popular internal drive interfaces are Parallel ATA (PATA) and Serial ATA (SATA). **Parallel ATA** or **PATA** (pronounced "pay-ta"), also called the **IDE (Integrated Drive Electronics)** standard, is older and slower than SATA. PATA allows for one or two IDE connectors on a motherboard, each using a 40-pin data cable (see Figure 5-6).

(A)

(B)

Floppy drive connector
Secondary IDE connector
Primary IDE connector

Figure 5-6 (a) A really old motherboard has two IDE connectors and one floppy drive connector, (b) A not-so-old motherboard with one IDE connector

**A+
220-801
1.5, 1.7,
1.11**

The **serial ATA or SATA** (pronounced "say-ta") standard uses a serial data path, and a SATA data cable can accommodate only a single SATA drive (see Figure 5-7). New motherboards sold today use only SATA connections, but you still might see many older boards that use a combination of SATA and IDE on the same board or use all IDE connections. A third internal interface standard is SCSI (pronounced "scuzzy").

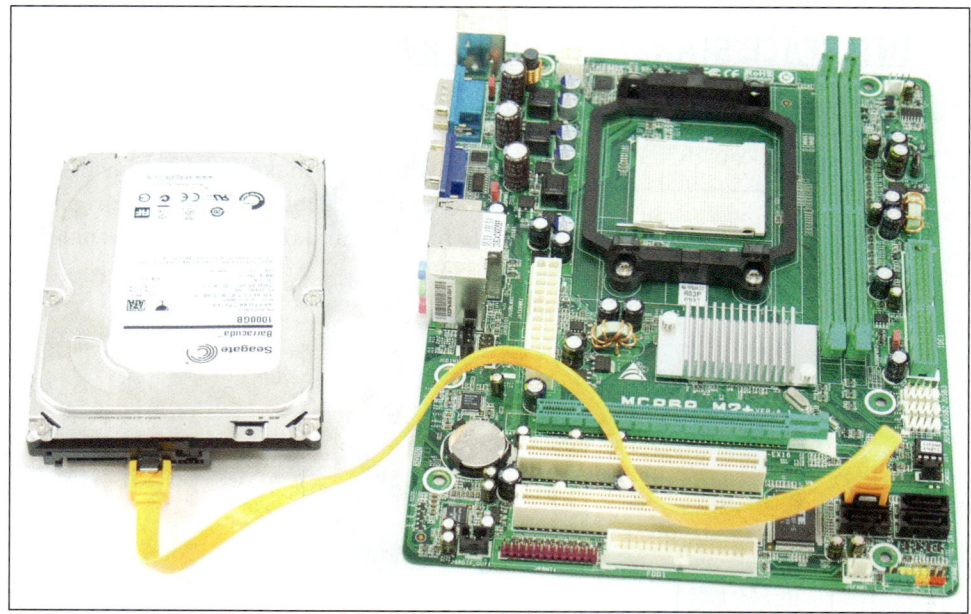

© Cengage Learning 2014

Figure 5-7 A SATA cable connects a single SATA drive to a motherboard SATA connector

External hard drives can connect to a computer by way of external SATA (eSATA), SCSI, FireWire, USB, or a variation of SCSI called Fibre Channel. The external standards are discussed in Chapter 6, and internal interface standards are covered in this chapter.

> **Notes** In technical documentation, you might see a hard drive abbreviated as HDD (hard disk drive). However, this chapter uses the term "hard drive."

Interface standards define data speeds and transfer methods between the drive controller, the BIOS, the chipset on the motherboard, and the OS. The standards also define the type of cables and connectors used by the drive and the motherboard or expansion cards.

The ATA standards are developed by Technical Committee T13 (*www.t13.org*) and published by **ANSI (American National Standards Institute**, *www.ansi.org*). As these standards developed, different drive manufacturers called them different names, which can be confusing when reading documentation or advertisements. The ATA standards have undergone several revisions, which are summarized in Table 5-1.

> **Notes** Remember from Chapter 4 that many memory standards exist because manufacturers and consortiums are always trying to come up with faster and more reliable technologies. The many ATA standards exist for the same reasons. It's unfortunate that you have to deal with so many technologies, but the old ones do stick around for many years after faster and better technologies are introduced.

A+ 220-801
1.5, 1.7, 1.11

Standard (Can Have More Than One Name)	Data Transfer Rate	Description
ATA* IDE/ATA	From 2.1 MB/sec to 8.3 MB/sec	The first T13 and ANSI standard for IDE hard drives. Limited to no more than 528 MB. Supports PIO modes 0-2.
ATA-2* ATAPI, Fast ATA, Parallel ATA (PATA), Enhanced IDE (EIDE)	Up to 16.6 MB/sec	Broke the 528-MB barrier. Allows up to four IDE devices; defines the EIDE standard. Supports PIO modes 3-4 and DMA modes 1-2.
ATA-3*	Up to 16.6 MB/sec (little speed increase)	Improved version of ATA-2 and introduced S.M.A.R.T.
ATA/ATAPI-4* Ultra ATA, Fast ATA-2, Ultra DMA Modes 0-2, DMA/33	Up to 33.3 MB/sec	Defined Ultra DMA modes 0-2 and an 80-conductor cable to improve signal integrity.
ATA/ATAPI-5* Ultra ATA/66, Ultra DMA/66	Up to 66.6 MB/sec	Defined Ultra DMA modes 3-4. To use these modes, an 80-conductor cable is required.
ATA/ATAPI-6* Ultra ATA/100, Ultra DMA/100	Up to 100 MB/sec	Requires the 80-conductor cable. Defined Ultra DMA mode 5 and supports drives larger than 137 GB.
ATA/ATAPI-7* Ultra ATA/133, SATA I, SAS STP	Parallel transfer speeds up to 133 MB/sec SATA transfer speeds up to 1.5 Gb/sec	Can use the 80-conductor cable or serial ATA cable. Defines Ultra DMA mode 6, serial ATA (SATA), and Serial Attached SCSI (SAS) coexisting with SATA by using STP (SATA Tunnelling Protocol).
ATA/ATAPI-8*	N/A	Defined hybrid drives and SATA II. No new revisions of ATA/ATAPI are expected because PATA is retired.

*Name assigned by the T13 Committee

Table 5-1 Summary of ATA interface standards for storage devices

© Cengage Learning 2014

A+ Exam Tip The A+ 220-801 exam expects you to know the speeds used by the IDE interfaces.

Let's now look first at the PATA or IDE standards and then we'll discuss the SATA standards. Finally, you'll learn about SCSI, a less used interface standard.

PARALLEL ATA OR EIDE DRIVE STANDARDS

PATA or IDE drives use ribbon cables that can accommodate one or two drives, as shown in Figure 5-8. A motherboard can have one or two IDE connectors for up to four PATA devices in the system using two data cables. All PATA standards since ATA-2 support this configuration of four IDE devices in a system, which is called the **Enhanced IDE (EIDE)** standard.

An optical drive must follow the **ATAPI (Advanced Technology Attachment Packet Interface)** standard in order to connect to a system using an IDE connector. Therefore, if you see ATAPI mentioned in an ad for a CD or DVD drive, know that the text means the drive connects to the motherboard using an IDE connector or header.

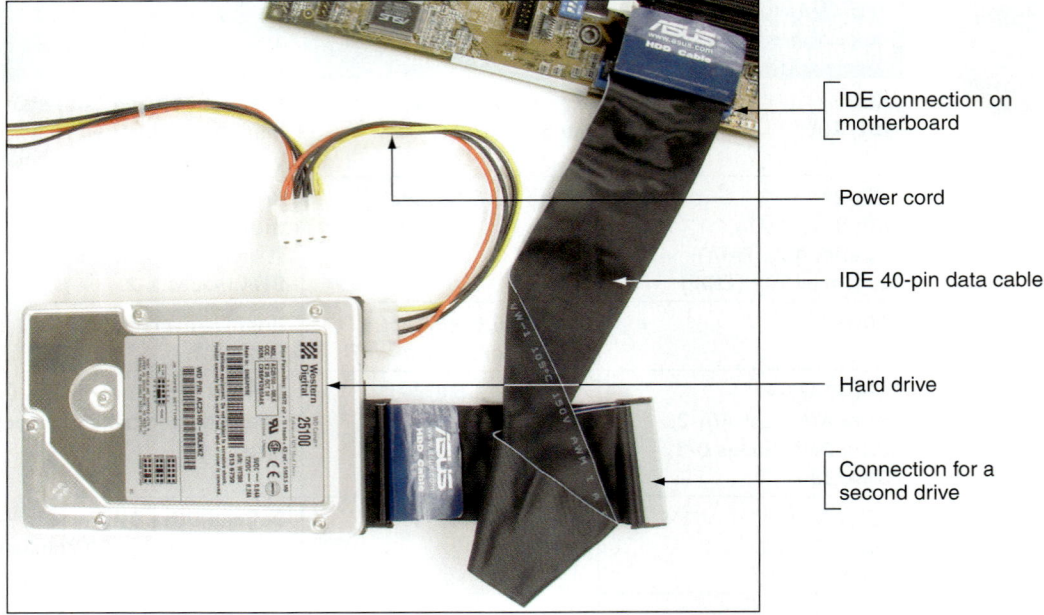

Figure 5-8 A PC's hard drive subsystem using parallel ATA

> **Notes** Acronyms sometimes change over time. Years ago, technicians knew *IDE* to mean *Integrated Drive Electronics*. As the term began to apply to other devices than hard drives, we renamed the acronym to become **Integrated Device Electronics**. Also, PATA and IDE are used interchangeably nowadays, although in the past, they had slightly different meanings. Currently, the term IDE is used more often than PATA to describe this interface standard.

Other technologies and changes mentioned in Table 5-1 that you need to be aware of are the two types of PATA data cables, DMA and PIO modes used by PATA, and Independent Device Timing. All these concerns are discussed next.

Two Types of PATA Ribbon Cables

Under parallel ATA, two types of ribbon cables are used. The older cable has 40 pins and 40 wires. The **80-conductor IDE cable** has 40 pins and 80 wires. Forty wires are used for communication and data, and an additional 40 ground wires reduce crosstalk on the cable. For maximum performance, an 80-conductor IDE cable is required by ATA/66 and above. Figure 5-9 shows a comparison between the two parallel cables. The 80-conductor cable is color-coded with the blue connector always connected to the motherboard. The connectors on each cable otherwise look the same, and you can use an 80-conductor cable in place of a 40-conductor cable in a system.

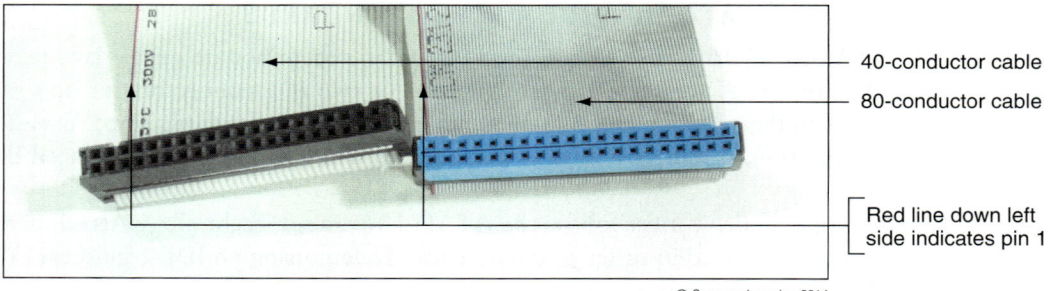

Figure 5-9 In comparing the 80-conductor cable to the 40-conductor cable, note they are about the same width, but the 80-conductor cable has many more and finer wires

A+
220-801
1.5, 1.7,
1.11

The maximum recommended length of both cables is 18", although it is possible to purchase 24" cables. A ribbon cable usually comes bundled with a motherboard that has an IDE header. Because ribbon cables can obstruct airflow inside a computer case, you can purchase a smaller round PATA cable that is less obstructive to the airflow inside the case (see Figure 5-10).

© Cengage Learning 2014

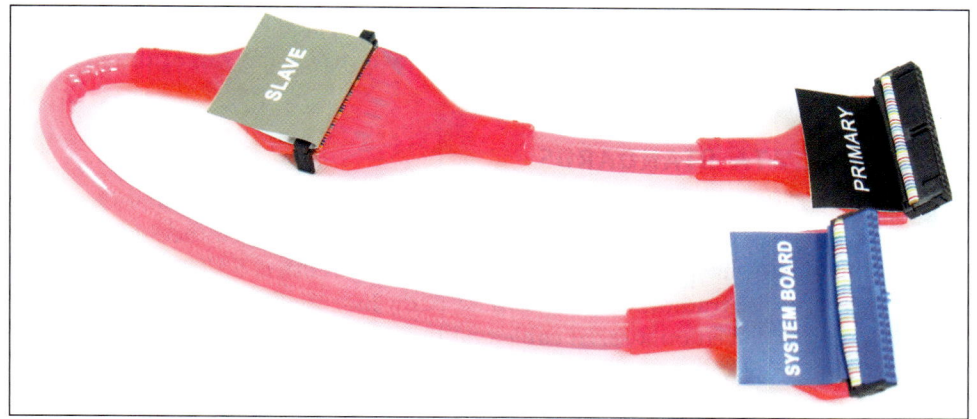

Figure 5-10 Use a smaller round PATA cable so as not to hinder air flow in a system

5

DMA or PIO Transfer Modes

A hard drive uses one of two methods to transfer data between the hard drive and memory: **DMA (direct memory access) transfer mode** or **PIO (Programmed Input/Output) transfer mode**. DMA transfers data directly from the drive to memory without involving the CPU. PIO mode involves the CPU and is slower and older than DMA mode.

There are different modes for PIO and DMA because both standards have evolved over the years. There are five PIO modes used by hard drives, from the slowest (PIO mode 0) to the fastest (PIO mode 4), and seven DMA modes from the slowest (DMA mode 0) to the fastest (DMA mode 6). All motherboards that use IDE today support Ultra DMA, which means that data is transferred twice for each clock beat, at the beginning and again at the end. Figure 5-11 shows a snip from an older Intel motherboard user guide that has two IDE headers. Because ATA-66/100 is mentioned rather than ATA/133, you can conclude the board supports ATA version 6 rather than version 7. (Refer to Table 5-1.)

PCI Enhanced IDE Interface

The ICH2's IDE interface handles the exchange of information between the processor and peripheral devices like hard disks, CD-ROM drives, and Iomega Zip† drives inside the computer. The interface supports:

- Up to four IDE devices (such as hard drives)
- ATAPI devices (such as CD-ROM drives)
- PIO Mode 3 and PIO Mode 4 devices
- Ultra DMA-33 and ATA-66/100 protocol
- Laser servo (LS-120) drives

Source: Intel

Figure 5-11 An older motherboard has two IDE headers using ATA-6 standards

A+
220-801
1.5, 1.7, 1.11

Most often, when installing an IDE drive, the startup BIOS autodetects the drive and selects the fastest mode that the drive and the BIOS support. After installation, you can go into BIOS setup and see which DMA mode is being used.

Independent Device Timing

As you saw in Table 5-1, there are different hard drive standards, each running at different speeds. If two hard drives share the same PATA cable but use different standards, both drives will run at the speed of the slower drive unless the motherboard chipset controlling the IDE connections supports a feature called Independent Device Timing. Most chipsets today support this feature, and with it, the two drives can run at different speeds as long as the motherboard supports those speeds.

SERIAL ATA STANDARDS

A consortium of manufacturers, called the Serial ATA International Organization (SATA-IO; see *www.sata-io.org*) and led by Intel, developed the SATA standards. These standards also have the oversight of the T13 Committee. SATA uses a serial data path rather than the traditional parallel data path. Essentially, the difference between the two is that data is placed on a serial cable one bit following the next, but with parallel cabling, all data in a byte is placed on the cable at one time. This fundamental difference is why transfer rates for PATA are expressed in bytes (MB/sec) and transfer rates for SATA are expressed in bits (Gb/sec). The three major revisions to SATA are summarized in Table 5-2.

SATA Standard	Data Transfer Rate	Comments
SATA Revision 1.x* SATA I or SATA1 Serial ATA-150 SATA/150 SATA-150	1.5 Gb/sec	First introduced with ATA/ATAPI-7.
SATA Revision 2.x* SATA II or SATA2 Serial ATA-300 SATA/300 SATA-300	3 Gb/sec	The first SATA II standards were published by the T13 Committee (t13.org) within ATA/ATAPI-8; later revisions of SATA II were published by SATA-IO (sata-io.org). The standard first came out in 2006. Most motherboards used it by 2010.
SATA Revision 3.x* SATA III or SATA3 Serial ATA-600 SATA/600 SATA-600	6 Gb/sec	SATA III was first published by SATA-IO in 2009. Most new motherboards today use this standard.

*Name assigned by the SATA-IO organization

© Cengage Learning 2014

Table 5-2 SATA standards

A+ Exam Tip The A+ 220-801 exam expects you to know the speeds used by SATA1, SATA2, and SATA3 also known as SATA I, SATA II, and SATA III. These speeds apply to internal (SATA) and external (eSATA) devices.

Hard Drive Technologies and Interface Standards | 199

**A+
220-801
1.5, 1.7,
1.11**

SATA interfaces are much faster than PATA interfaces and are used by all types of drives, including hard drives, CD, DVD, Blu-ray, and tape drives. Whereas PATA drives are not hot-swappable, SATA supports hot-swapping, also called hot-plugging. With **hot-swapping**, you can connect and disconnect a drive while the system is running. Hard drives that can be hot-swapped cost significantly more than regular hard drives.

SATA connections are much easier to configure and use than PATA connections. A SATA drive connects to one internal SATA connector on the motherboard by way of a 7-pin SATA data cable and uses a 15-pin SATA power connector (see Figure 5-12). An internal SATA data cable can be up to 1 meter in length, and is much narrower compared to the 40-pin PATA ribbon cable. The thinner SATA cables don't hinder airflow inside a case as much as the wide ribbon cables do. A motherboard might have two or more SATA connectors; use the connectors in the order recommended in the motherboard user guide. For example, for the four connectors shown in Figure 5-13, you are told to use the red ones before the black ones.

Figure 5-12 A SATA data cable and SATA power cable

Figure 5-13 This motherboard has two black and two red SATA II ports

In addition to internal SATA connectors, the motherboard or an expansion card can provide **external SATA (eSATA)** ports for external drives (see Figure 5-14). External SATA drives use a special external shielded SATA cable up to 2 meters long. Seven-pin eSATA ports run at the same speed as the internal ports using SATA I, II, or III standards. The eSATA port is shaped differently from an internal SATA connector so as to prevent people from using the unshielded internal SATA data cables with the eSATA port.

Figure 5-14 Two eSATA ports on a motherboard

When purchasing a SATA hard drive, keep in mind that the SATA standards for the drive and the motherboard need to match. If either the drive or the motherboard uses a slower SATA standard than the other device, the system will run at the slower speed. Other hard drive characteristics to consider when selecting a drive are covered later in the chapter.

SCSI TECHNOLOGY

Other than ATA, another interface standard for drives and other devices is SCSI, which is primarily used in servers. SCSI standards can be used by many internal and external devices, including hard drives, optical drives, printers, and scanners. **SCSI** (pronounced "scuzzy") stands for **Small Computer System Interface** and is a standard for communication between a subsystem of peripheral devices and the system bus. The SCSI bus can support up to 7 or 15 devices, depending on the SCSI standard. SCSI devices tend to be faster, more expensive, and more difficult to install than similar ATA devices. Because they are more expensive and more difficult to install, they are mostly used in corporate settings and are seldom seen in the small office or used on home PCs.

The SCSI Subsystem

If a motherboard does not have an embedded SCSI controller, the gateway from the SCSI bus to the system bus is the **SCSI host adapter card**, commonly called the **host adapter**. The host adapter is inserted into an expansion slot on the motherboard and is responsible for managing all devices on the SCSI bus. A host adapter can support both internal and external SCSI devices, using one connector on the card for a ribbon cable or round cable to connect to internal devices, and an external port that supports external devices (see Figure 5-15).

Hard Drive Technologies and Interface Standards   201

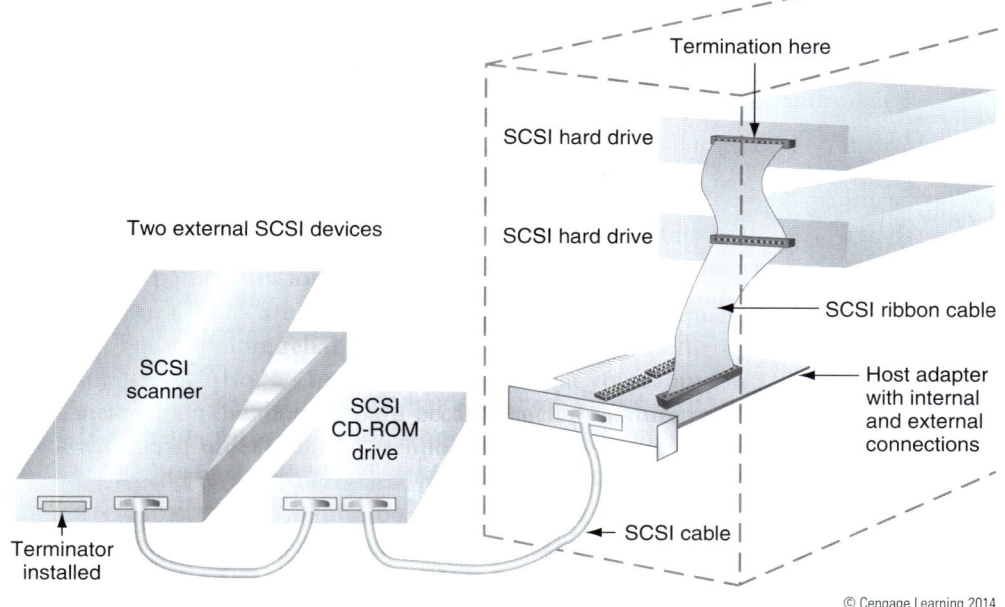

Figure 5-15 Using a SCSI bus, a SCSI host adapter card can support internal and external SCSI devices

All the devices and the host adapter form a single daisy chain. In Figure 5-15, this daisy chain has two internal devices and two external devices, with the SCSI host adapter in the middle of the chain. An example of a host adapter card is shown in Figure 5-16. It fits into a PCIe slot and provides one 68-pin internal SCSI connector and one external 68-pin connector. The host adapter manages all devices as a single SCSI chain and can support up to 15 devices.

> **A+ Exam Tip** The A+ 220-801 exam expects you to know that a motherboard might provide a SCSI controller and connector or that the SCSI host adapter can be a card installed in an expansion slot.

Courtesy of PMC-Sierra, Inc.

Figure 5-16 This Adaptec SCSI card uses a PCIe x1 slot and supports up to 15 devices and automatic termination

All devices go through the host adapter to communicate with the CPU or directly with each other without involving the CPU. Each device on the bus is assigned a number from 0 to 15 called the SCSI ID, by means of DIP switches, dials on the device, or software settings. The host adapter is assigned SCSI ID 7, which has the highest priority over all other devices. The priority order is 7, 6, 5, 4, 3, 2, 1, 0, 15, 14, 13, 12, 11, 10, 9, and 8. Cables connect the devices physically in a daisy chain, sometimes called a straight chain. The devices can be either internal or external, and the host adapter can be at either end of the chain or somewhere in the middle. The SCSI ID identifies the physical device, which can have several logical devices embedded in it. For example, a CD-ROM jukebox—a CD-ROM changer with trays for multiple CDs—might have seven trays. Each tray is considered a logical device and is assigned a Logical Unit Number (LUN) to identify it, such as 1 through 7 or 0 through 6. The ID and LUN are written as two numbers separated by a colon. For instance, if the SCSI ID is 5, the fourth tray in the jukebox is device 5:4.

To reduce the amount of electrical "noise," or interference, on a SCSI cable, each end of the SCSI chain has a terminating resistor. The terminating resistor can be a hardware device plugged into the last device on each end of the chain (see Figure 5-17), or the device can have firmware-controlled termination resistance, which makes installation simpler.

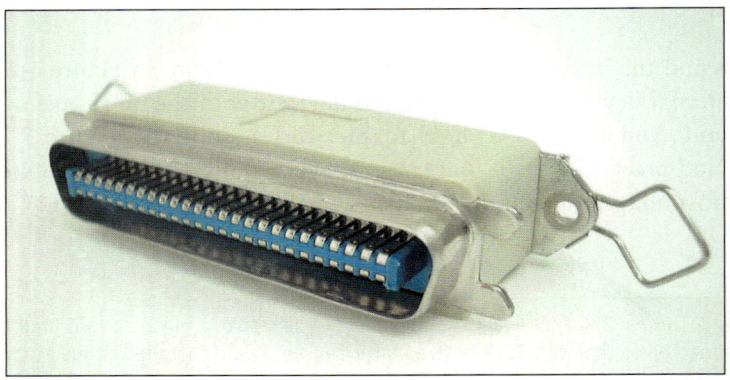

Figure 5-17 External SCSI terminator

© Cengage Learning 2014

Various SCSI Standards and Connectors

The two general categories of all SCSI standards used on PCs have to do with the width in bits of the SCSI data bus, either 8 bits (narrow SCSI) or 16 bits (wide SCSI). In almost every case, if the SCSI standard is 16 bits, the word "wide" is in the name for the standard. For 8-bit SCSI standards, the word "narrow" is usually not mentioned in names for the standard. Narrow SCSI uses a cable with a 50-pin SCSI connector (also called an A cable), and wide SCSI uses a cable with a 68-pin SCSI connector (also called a P cable). Narrow SCSI can also use a 25-pin SCSI connector that looks like a parallel port connector. Figure 5-18 shows five types of SCSI connectors. The 80-pin SCA (Single Connector Attachment) connector can provide power to a SCSI device.

A SCSI bus can support more than one type of connector, and you can use connector adapters to plug a cable with one type of connector into a port using another type of connector. Figure 5-19 shows a SCSI cable. One end of the cable attaches to the host adapter, and, for best results, you should always plug a device into the last connector on the cable.

The three major versions of SCSI are SCSI-1, SCSI-2, and SCSI-3, commonly known as Regular SCSI, Fast SCSI, and Ultra SCSI. A variation of SCSI is serial SCSI, also called

Hard Drive Technologies and Interface Standards

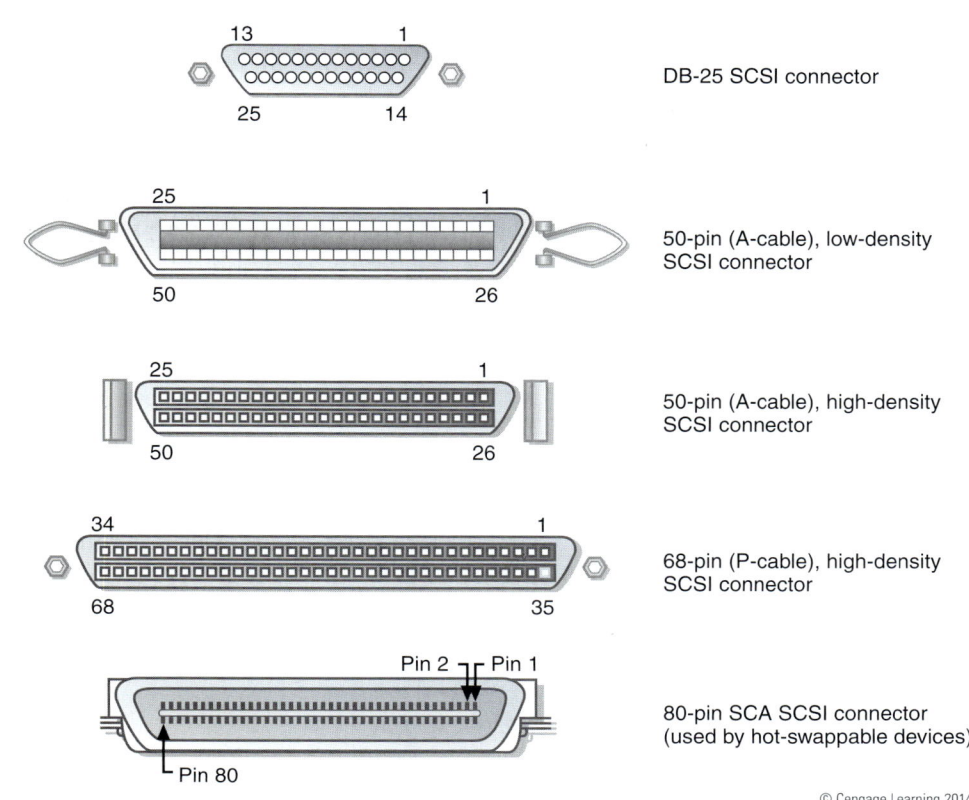

Figure 5-18 The most popular SCSI connectors are 50-pin, A-cable connectors for narrow SCSI and 68-pin, P-cable connectors for wide SCSI

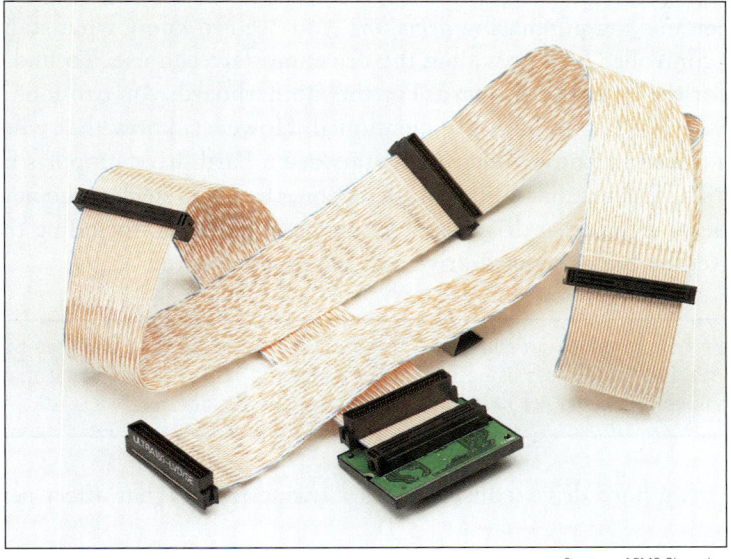

Figure 5-19 This 68-pin internal SCSI ribbon cable can connect several SCSI devices

serial attached SCSI (SAS), which allows for more than 15 devices on a single SCSI chain, uses smaller, longer, round cables, and uses smaller hard drive form factors that can support larger capacities than earlier versions of SCSI. SAS can be compatible with SATA drives in the same system and claims to be more reliable and better performing than SATA.

**A+
220-801
1.5, 1.7,
1.11**

Hands-on | Project 5-1 Examine BIOS Setting for a Hard Drive

Recall that in Chapter 3 you learned how to view and change BIOS settings on your motherboard. Following the directions given in Chapter 3, view the BIOS setup information on your computer, and write down all the BIOS settings that apply to your hard drive. Explain each setting that you can. What is the size of the installed drive? Does your system support S.M.A.R.T.? If so, is it enabled?

**A+
220-801
1.5**

Now that you know about the various hard drive technologies and interfaces, let's see how to select and install a hard drive.

HOW TO SELECT AND INSTALL HARD DRIVES

In this part of the chapter, you'll learn how to select a hard drive for your system. Then, you'll learn the details of installing a SATA drive and an IDE drive in a system. Next, you'll learn how to deal with using removable bays and the problem of installing a hard drive in a bay that is too wide for it. You'll also learn how to set up a RAID system.

SELECTING A HARD DRIVE

When selecting a hard drive, keep in mind that to get the best performance from the system, the system BIOS and the hard drive must support the same standard. If they don't support the same standard, they revert to the slower standard that both can use, or the drive will not work at all. There's no point in buying an expensive hard drive with features that your system cannot support.

Therefore, when making purchasing decisions, you need to know what standards the motherboard or controller card providing the drive interface can use. To find out, see the documentation for the board or the card. For the motherboard, you can look at BIOS setup screens to see which standards are mentioned. However, know that when installing a drive, you don't need to know which ATA standard a hard drive supports because the startup BIOS uses autodetection. With **autodetection**, the BIOS detects the new drive and automatically selects the correct drive capacity and configuration, including the best possible standard supported by both the hard drive and the motherboard.

> **Notes** To learn how to match up and install really old motherboards or drives, see the content "Selecting and Installing Hard Drives using Legacy Motherboards" in the online content at *cengagebrain.com* that accompanies this book. For more information, see the Preface.

When purchasing a hard drive, consider the following factors that affect performance, use, and price:

- *The capacity of the drive.* Today's hard drives for desktop systems are in the range of 60 GB for SSD drives to more than 2 TB for magnetic drives. The more gigabytes or terabytes, the higher the price. Magnetic drives have larger capacity for the money than solid state drives.
- *The spindle speed.* Magnetic hard drives for desktop systems run at 5400, 7200, 10,000, or 15,000 RPM (revolutions per minute). The most common is 7200 RPM. The higher the RPMs, the faster the drive.

A+ 220-801 1.5

- *The interface standard.* Use the standards your motherboard supports. For SATA, most likely that will be SATA II or SATA III. For a PATA IDE drive, most likely that will be Ultra ATA-100/133. For external drives, common standards are eSATA, FireWire 800 or 400, and SuperSpeed or Hi-Speed USB.
- *The cache or buffer size.* For magnetic hard drives, buffer memory improves hard drive performance and can range in size from 2 MB to 64 MB. The more the better, though the cost goes up as the size increases. A buffer helps because the hard drive reads ahead of the requested data and stores the extra data in the buffer. If the next read is already in the buffer, the controller does not need to return to the spinning platters for the data. Buffering especially improves performance when managing large files, such as when working with videos or movies.

A hard drive manufacturer might produce both magnetic drives and solid-state drives. Some hard drive manufacturers are listed in Table 5-3. Most manufacturers of memory also make solid state drives.

Manufacturer	Web Site
Crucial	www.crucial.com
Kingston Technology	www.kingston.com
Samsung	www.samsung.com
Seagate Technology and Maxtor	www.seagate.com or www.maxtor.com
Western Digital	www.wdc.com

© Cengage Learning 2014

Table 5-3 Hard drive manufacturers

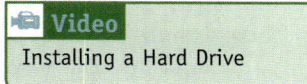
Video: Installing a Hard Drive

Now let's turn our attention to the step-by-step process of installing a Serial ATA drive.

STEPS TO INSTALL A SERIAL ATA DRIVE

A motherboard that has SATA connectors might have an IDE header, too. An IDE header can be used for an optical drive or some other EIDE drive, including a hard drive. But SATA drives are faster than PATA drives, so it's best to use the IDE header for other types of drives than the hard drive.

> **A+ Exam Tip** The A+ 220-801 exam expects you to know how to configure IDE and SATA devices in a system. What you learn in this chapter about installing an IDE or SATA hard drive in a system also applies to installing an IDE or SATA optical drive or tape drive. Hard drives, optical drives, and tape drives all use an IDE or SATA data connector and power connector.

In Figure 5-20, you can see the back of two hard drives; one uses a SATA interface and the other uses a PATA interface. Notice the PATA drive has a bank of jumpers. These jumpers are used to determine master or slave settings on the IDE channel. Because a serial data cable accommodates only a single drive, there is no need for jumpers on the drive for master or slave settings. However, a SATA drive might have jumpers used to set features such as the ability to power up from standby mode. Most likely, if jumpers are present on a SATA drive, the factory has set them as they should be and advises you not to change them.

Some SATA drives have two power connectors, as does the one in Figure 5-20. Choose between the SATA power connector (which is the preferred connector) or the legacy 5-pin

Figure 5-20 (A) Rear of a SATA drive and (B) rear of a PATA drive

Molex connector, but never install two power cords to the drive at the same time because this could damage the drive.

If you have a PATA drive and a SATA connector on the motherboard, or you have a SATA drive and a PATA connector on the motherboard, you can purchase an adapter to make the hard drive connector fit your motherboard connector. Figure 5-21 shows two converters: one converts SATA drives to PATA motherboards and the other converts PATA drives to SATA motherboards. When you use a converter, know that the drive will run at the slower PATA speed.

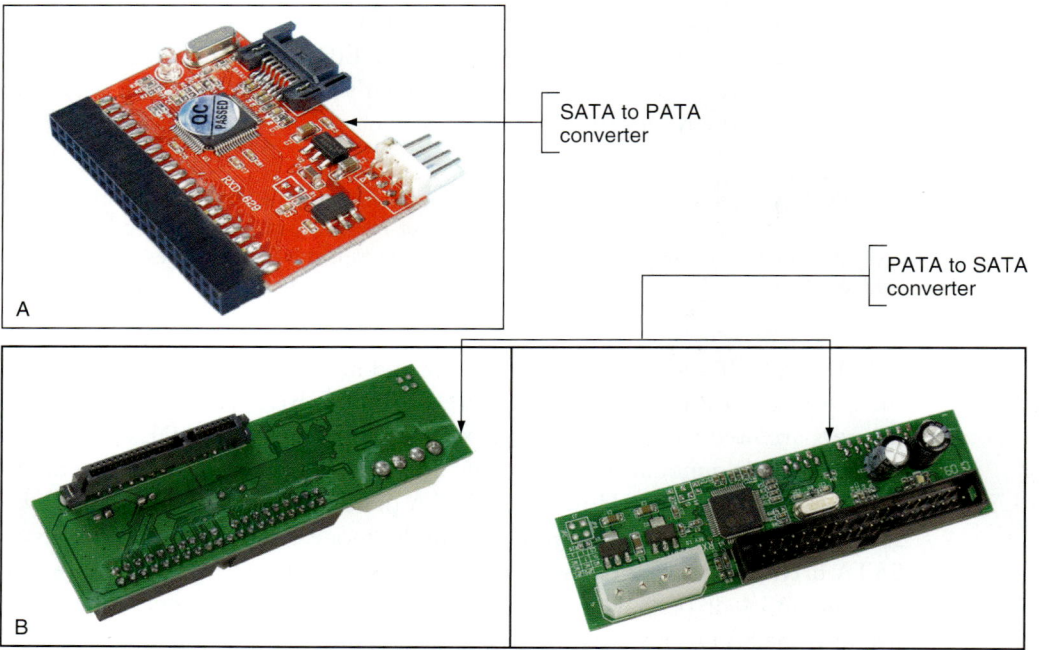

Figure 5-21 (A) SATA to PATA converter and (B) PATA to SATA converter

You can also purchase a SATA and/or PATA controller card that can provide internal PATA or SATA connectors and external eSATA connectors. You might want to use a controller card when (1) the motherboard drive connectors are not functioning, or (2) the motherboard does not support an ATA standard you want to implement (such as a SATA III drive). Figure 5-22 shows a storage controller card that offers one Ultra ATA-133/IDE connection, two internal SATA I connections, and one eSATA port.

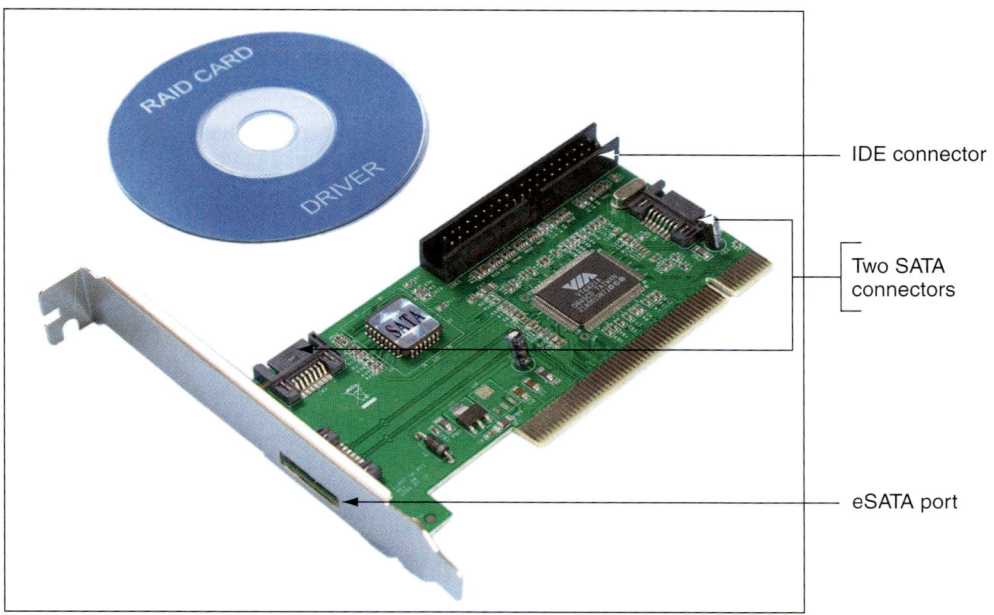

Figure 5-22 EIDE and SATA storage controller card

Now let's look at the step-by-step process of installing a SATA drive.

STEP 1: KNOW YOUR STARTING POINT

As with installing any other devices, before you begin installing your hard drive, make sure you know where your starting point is. Do this by answering these questions: How is your system configured? Is everything working properly? Verify which of your system's devices are working before installing a new one. Later, if a device does not work, the information will help you isolate the problem. Keeping notes is a good idea whenever you install new hardware or software or make any other changes to your computer system. Write down what you know about the system that might be important later.

> **Notes** When installing hardware and software, don't install too many things at once. If something goes wrong, you won't know what's causing the problem. Install one device, start the system, and confirm that the new device is working before installing another.

STEP 2: READ THE DOCUMENTATION AND PREPARE YOUR WORK AREA

Before you take anything apart, carefully read all the documentation for the drive and controller card, as well as the part of your motherboard documentation that covers hard drive installation. Make sure that you can visualize all the steps in the installation. If you have any questions, keep researching until you locate the answer. You can also call technical support,

A+ 220-801 1.5

or ask a knowledgeable friend for help. As you get your questions answered, you might discover that what you are installing will not work on your computer, but that is better than coping with hours of frustration and a disabled computer. You cannot always anticipate every problem, but at least you can know that you made your best effort to understand everything in advance. What you learn with thorough preparation pays off every time!

You're now ready to set out your tools, documentation, new hardware, and notebook. Remember the basic rules concerning static electricity, which you learned in Chapter 1. Be sure to protect against ESD by wearing a ground bracelet during the installation. You need to also avoid working on carpet in the winter when there's a lot of static electricity.

Some added precautions for working with a hard drive are as follows:

- Handle the drive carefully.
- Do not touch any exposed circuitry or chips.
- Prevent other people from touching exposed microchips on the drive.
- When you first take the drive out of the static-protective package, touch the package containing the drive to a screw holding an expansion card or cover, or to a metal part of the computer case, for at least two seconds. This drains the static electricity from the package and from your body.
- If you must set down the drive outside the static-protective package, place it component-side-up on a flat surface.
- Do not place the drive on the computer case cover or on a metal table.

If you're assembling a new system, it's best to install drives before you install the motherboard so that you will not accidentally bump sensitive motherboard components with the drives.

STEP 3: INSTALL THE DRIVE

So now you're ready to get started. Follow these steps to install the drive in the case:

1. Shut down the computer and unplug it. Then press the power button for three seconds to drain residual power. Remove the computer case cover. Check that you have an available power cord from the power supply for the drive.

> **Notes** If there are not enough power cords from a power supply, you can purchase a Y connector that can add an additional power cord.

2. Decide which bay will hold the drive. To do that, examine the locations of the drive bays and the length of the data cables and power cords. Bays designed for hard drives do not have access to the outside of the case, unlike bays for optical drives and other drives in which discs are inserted. Also, some bays are wider than others to accommodate wide drives such as a DVD drive. Will the data cable reach the drives and the motherboard connector? If not, rearrange your plan for locating the drive in a bay, or purchase a custom-length data cable. Some bays are stationary, meaning the drive is installed inside the bay as it stays in the case. Other bays are removable; you remove the bay and install the drive in the bay, and then return the bay to the case.

3. For a stationary bay, slide the drive in the bay, and secure one side of the drive with one or two short screws (see Figure 5-23). It's best to use two screws so the drive will not move in the bay, but sometimes a bay only provides a place for a single screw on each side. Some drive bays provide one or two tabs that you can pull out before you slide the drive in the bay and then push the tabs in to secure the drive. Another option

is a sliding tab (see Figure 5-24) that is used to secure the drive. Pull the tab back; slide in the drive, and push the tab forward to secure the drive.

Figure 5-23 Secure one side of the drive with one or two screws

> **Caution** Be sure the screws are not too long. If they are, you can screw too far into the drive housing, which will damage the drive itself.

Figure 5-24 This drive bay uses tabs to secure the drive

4. When using screws to secure the drive, carefully, without disturbing the drive, turn the case over and put one or two screws on the other side of the drive (see Figure 5-25). To best secure the drive in the case, use two screws on each side of the drive.

A+ 220-801 1.5

Figure 5-25 Secure the other side of the drive with one or two screws

> **Notes** Do not allow torque to stress the drive. In other words, don't force a drive into a space that is too small for it. Also, placing two screws in diagonal positions across the drive can place pressure diagonally on the drive.

5. Check the motherboard documentation to find out which SATA connectors on the board to use first. For example, five SATA connectors are shown in Figure 5-26. The documentation says the two blue SATA connectors support 6.0 Gb/s and slower speeds, and the two black and one red SATA connectors support 3.0 Gb/s and slower speeds. On this board, be sure to connect your fastest hard drive to a blue connector. For both the drive and the motherboard, you can only plug the cable into the connector in one direction. A SATA cable might provide a clip on the connector to secure it (see Figure 5-27).

Figure 5-26 Five SATA connectors support different SATA standards

A+ 220-801
1.5

Figure 5-27 A clip on a SATA connector secures the connection

6. Connect a 15-pin SATA power connector or 5-pin Molex power connector from the power supply to the drive (see Figure 5-28).

Figure 5-28 Connect the SATA power cord to the drive

7. Check all your connections and power up the system.

8. To verify the drive was recognized correctly, enter BIOS setup and look for the drive. Figure 5-29 shows a BIOS setup screen on one system that has two SATA connectors and one PATA connector. A hard drive is installed on one SATA connector and a CD drive is installed on the PATA connector.

Notes If the drive light on the front panel of the computer case does not work after you install a new drive, try reversing the LED wire on the motherboard pins.

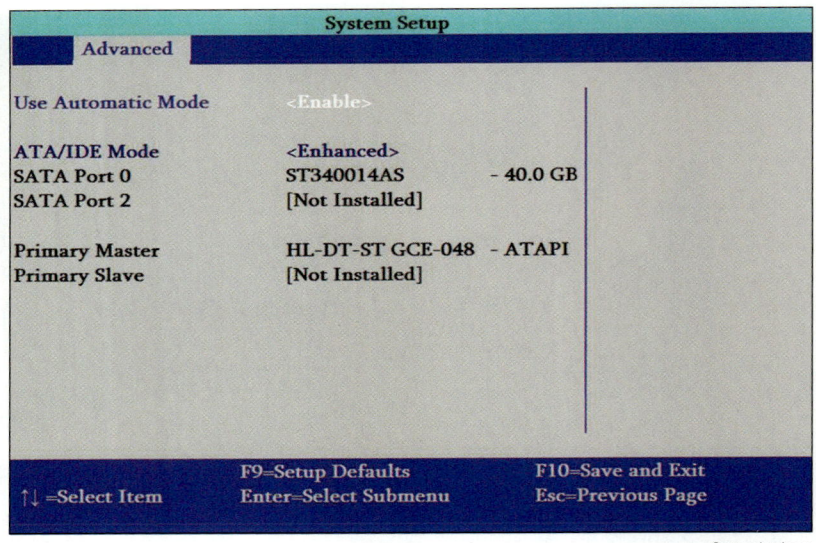

Source: Intel.com

Figure 5-29 BIOS setup screen showing a SATA hard drive and PATA CD drive installed

You are now ready to prepare the hard drive for first use. If you are installing a new hard drive in a system that is to be used for a new Windows installation, boot from the Windows setup DVD, and follow the directions on the screen to install Windows on the new drive. If you are installing a second hard drive in a system that already has Windows installed on the first hard drive, you use the Disk Management utility in Windows to prepare the drive for first use (called partitioning and formatting the drive). How to install Windows or to partition and format a second hard drive is not covered in this book.

INSTALLING A DRIVE IN A REMOVABLE BAY

Now let's see how a drive installation goes when you are dealing with a removable bay. Figure 5-30 shows a computer case with a removable bay that has a fan at the front of the bay to help keep the drives cool. (The case manufacturer calls the bay a fan cage.) The bay is anchored to the case with three black locking pins. The third locking pin from the bottom of the case is disconnected in the photo.

© Cengage Learning 2014

Figure 5-30 The removable bay has a fan in front and is anchored to the case with locking pins

How to Select and Install Hard Drives

A+ 220-801 1.5

Unplug the cage fan from its power source. Turn the handle on each locking pin counterclockwise to remove it. Then slide the bay to the front and out of the case. Insert the hard drive in the bay, and use two screws on each side to anchor the drive in the bay (see Figure 5-31). Slide the bay back into the case, and reinstall the locking pins. Plug in the cage fan power cord.

Figure 5-31 Install the hard drive in the bay using two screws on each side of the drive

INSTALLING A SMALL DRIVE IN A WIDE BAY

If you are mounting a hard drive into a bay that is too large, a universal bay kit can help you securely fit the drive into the bay. These inexpensive kits should create a tailor-made fit. In Figure 5-32, you can see how the universal bay kit adapter works. The adapter spans the

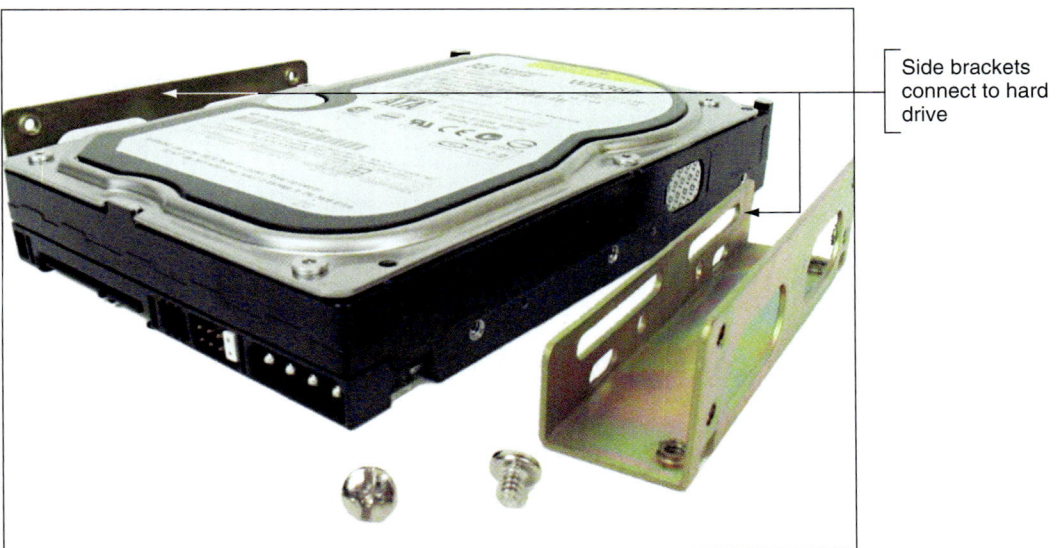

Figure 5-32 Use the universal bay kit to make the drive fit the bay

distance between the sides of the drive and the bay. Figure 5-33 shows a SATA SSD drive with the brackets connected, and Figure 5-34 shows a SATA magnetic drive installed in a wide bay. Because SSD drives are usually smaller than magnetic drives, you're likely to need a bay kit to fit these drives into most computer cases.

Figure 5-33 SSD drive with bay kit connected

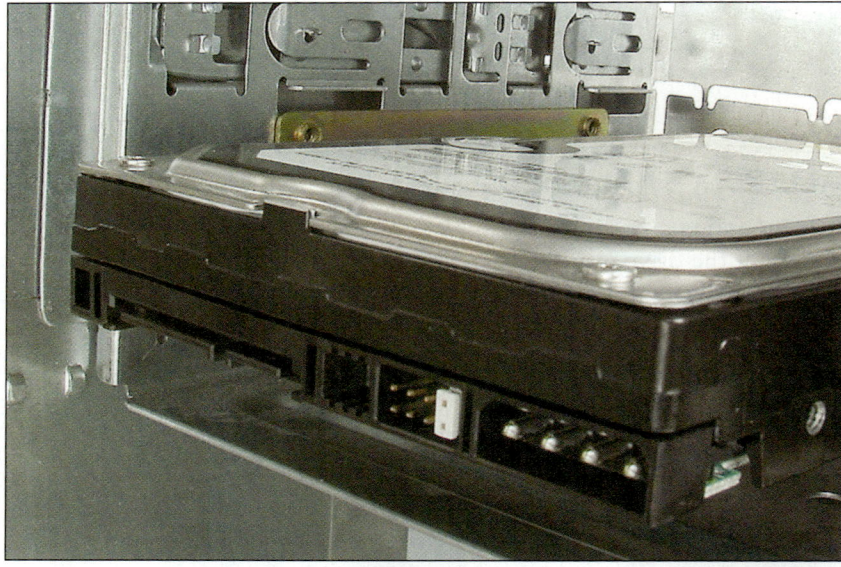

Figure 5-34 Hard drive installed in a wide bay using a universal bay kit adapter

STEPS TO CONFIGURE AND INSTALL A PARALLEL ATA DRIVE

Following the PATA or EIDE standard, a motherboard can support up to four EIDE devices using either 80-conductor or 40-conductor cables. A motherboard can have one or two IDE headers (see Figure 5-35). Each header or connector accommodates one IDE channel, and each channel can accommodate one or two IDE devices. One channel is called the primary channel, while the other channel is called the secondary channel. Each IDE connector uses one 40-pin cable. The cable has two connectors on it: one connector in the middle of the cable and one at the far end. An EIDE device can be a hard drive, DVD drive, CD drive, tape drive, or another type of drive. One device is configured to act as the master controlling the channel, and the other device on the channel is the slave. There are, therefore, four possible configurations for four EIDE devices in a system:

- Primary IDE channel, master device
- Primary IDE channel, slave device
- Secondary IDE channel, master device
- Secondary IDE channel, slave device

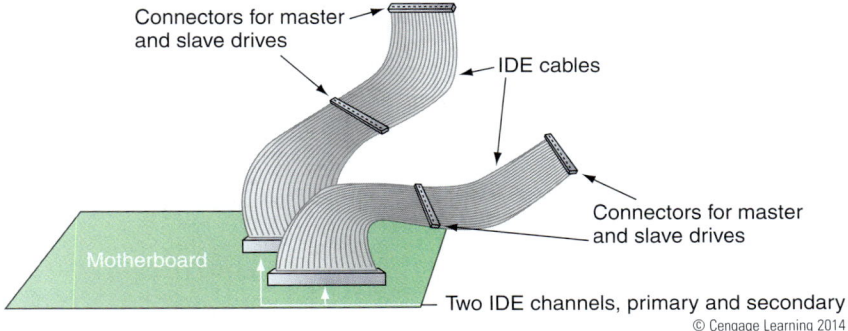

Figure 5-35 A motherboard supporting PATA has two IDE channels; each can support a master and slave drive using a single EIDE cable

The master or slave designations are made by setting jumpers or DIP switches on the devices, or by using a special cable-select data cable. Documentation can be tricky. Some hard drive documentation labels the master drive setting as the Drive 0 setting and the slave drive setting as the Drive 1 setting rather than using the terms master and slave. The connectors on a PATA 80-conductor cable are color-coded (see Figure 5-36). Use the blue end to connect to the motherboard; use the black end to connect to the drive. If you only have one drive connected to the cable, put it on the black connector at the end of the cable, not the gray connector in the middle.

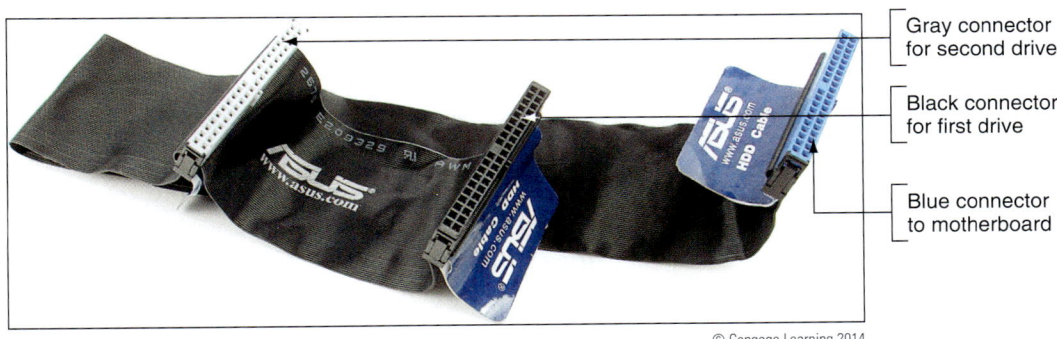

Figure 5-36 80-conductor cable connectors are color-coded

A+ 220-801 1.5

> **Notes** When installing a hard drive on the same channel with an ATAPI drive such as a CD drive, always make the hard drive the master and make the ATAPI drive the slave. An even better solution is to install the hard drive on the primary channel and the CD drive and any other drive on the secondary channel.

The motherboard might also be color-coded so that the primary channel connector is blue (see Figure 5-37) and the secondary channel connector is black. This color-coding is intended to ensure that the ATA/66/100/133 hard drive is installed on the primary IDE channel.

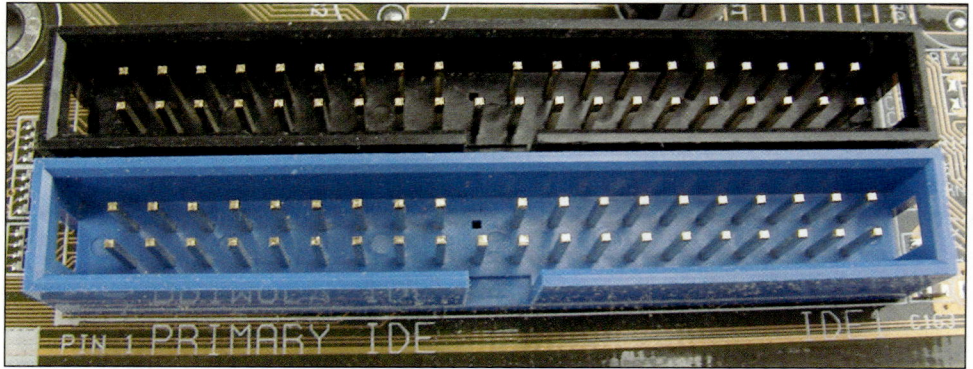

Figure 5-37 The primary IDE channel connector is often color-coded as blue
© Cengage Learning 2014

> **A+ Exam Tip** The A+ 220-801 exam expects you to know how to install a device such as a hard drive. Given a list of steps for the installation, you should be able to order the steps correctly or identify an error in a step.

As with installing SATA drives, know your starting point, read the documentation for the drive and the motherboard, prepare your work area, and be careful when handling the drive to protect it against ESD. Wear a ground bracelet as you work. Now let's look at the steps for installing a PATA drive.

STEP 1: OPEN THE CASE AND DECIDE HOW TO CONFIGURE THE DRIVES

Turn off the computer and unplug it. Press the power button to drain the power. Remove the computer case cover. Check that you have an available power cord from the power supply for the drive.

You must decide which IDE connector to use, and if another drive will share the same IDE data cable with your new drive. When possible, leave the hard drive as the single drive on one channel, so that it does not compete with another drive for access to the channel and possibly slow down performance. Use the primary channel before you use the secondary channel. Place the fastest devices on the primary channel and the slower devices on the secondary channel. This pairing helps keep a slow device from pulling down a faster device. As an example of this type of pairing, suppose you have a tape drive, CD drive, and two hard drives. Because the two hard drives are faster than the tape drive and CD drive, put the two hard drives on one channel and the tape drive and CD drive on the other.

A+ 220-801 1.5

> **Notes** If you have three or fewer devices, allow the fastest hard drive to be your boot device and the only device on the primary channel.

STEP 2: SET THE JUMPERS ON THE DRIVE

Often, diagrams of the jumper settings are printed on the top of the hard drive housing (see Figure 5-38). If they are not, see the documentation, or visit the web site of the drive manufacturer. (Hands-On Project 5-2 gives you practice researching jumper settings.)

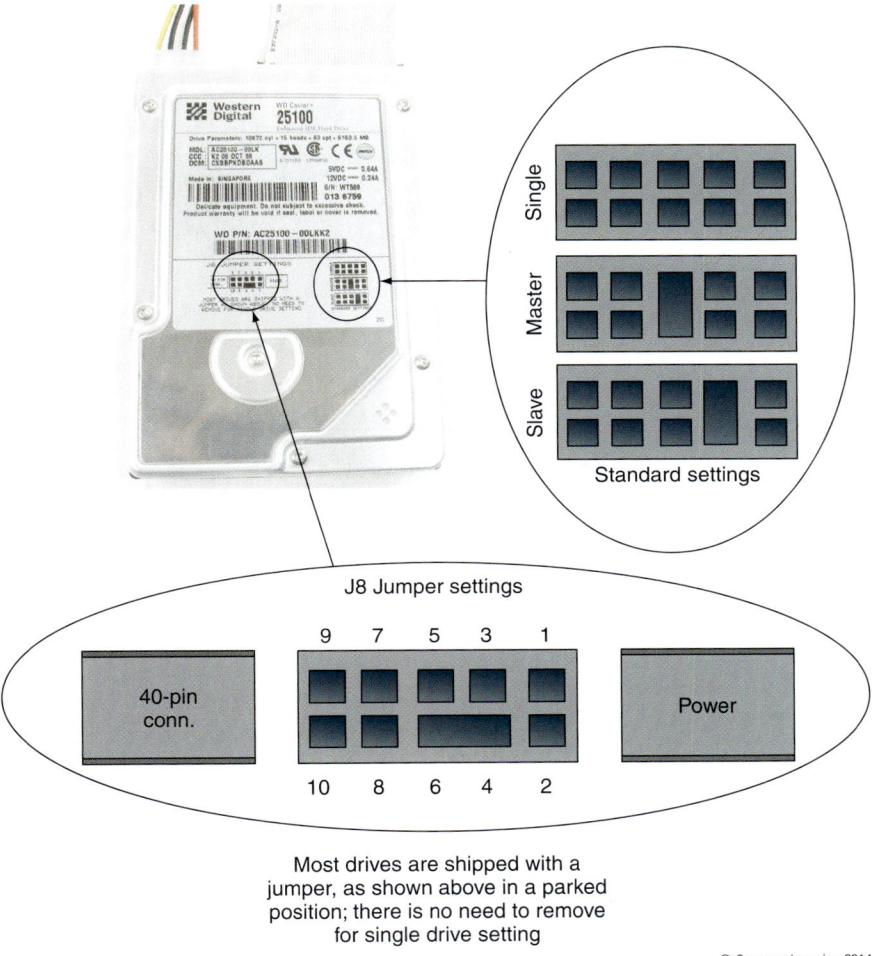

Figure 5-38 A PATA drive most likely will have diagrams of jumper settings for master and slave options printed on the drive housing

Table 5-4 lists the four choices for jumper settings, and Figure 5-39 shows a typical jumper arrangement for a drive that uses three of these settings. In Figures 5-38 and 5-39, note that a black square represents an empty pin and a black rectangle represents a pair of pins with a jumper in place. Know that your hard drive might not have the first configuration as an option, but it should have a way of indicating if the drive will be the master device. The factory default setting is usually correct for the drive to be the single drive on a system. Before you change any settings, write down the original ones. If things go wrong, you can revert to the original settings and begin again. If a drive is the only drive on a channel, set it to single. For two drives on a controller, set one to master and the other to slave.

Configuration	Description
Single-drive configuration	This is the only hard drive on this EIDE channel. (This is the standard setting.)
Master-drive configuration	This is the first of two drives; it most likely is the boot device.
Slave-drive configuration	This is the second drive using this channel or data cable.
Cable-select configuration	The cable-select (CS or CSEL) data cable determines which of the two drives is the master and which is the slave.

Table 5-4 Jumper settings on a PATA hard drive

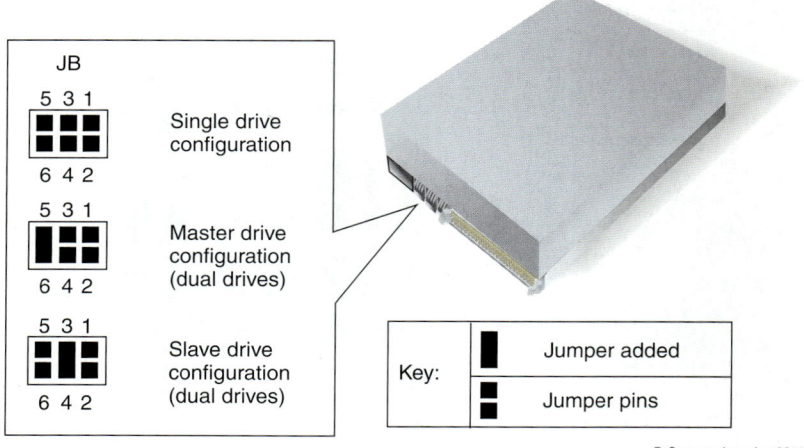

Figure 5-39 Jumper settings on a hard drive and their meanings

Some hard drives have a cable-select configuration option. If you choose this configuration, you must use a cable-select data cable and set both devices on the channel to cable-select. When using an 80-conductor cable-select cable, the drive nearest the motherboard is the master, and the drive farthest from the motherboard is the slave. You can recognize a cable-select cable by a small hole somewhere in the data cable or by labels (master or slave) on the connectors.

STEP 3: MOUNT THE DRIVE IN THE BAY

Now that you've set the jumpers, your next step is to look at the drive bay that you will use for the drive. The bay can be stationary or removable. You saw both types of bays earlier in the chapter. Follow these steps to install the drive:

1. Decide if it's best to connect the ribbon cable to the drive before or after you install the drive in the bay. Then install the drive in the bay and connect the cable in whichever order works best for your situation.

2. Connect the data cable to the IDE connector on the motherboard (see Figure 5-40). Make certain pin 1 and the edge color on the cable align correctly at both ends of the cable. Normally, pin 1 is closest to the power connection on the drive. Figure 5-41 shows three PATA drives installed in a system with data cables connected to the drives and the motherboard.

Figure 5-40 Floppy drive and two IDE connectors on the motherboard

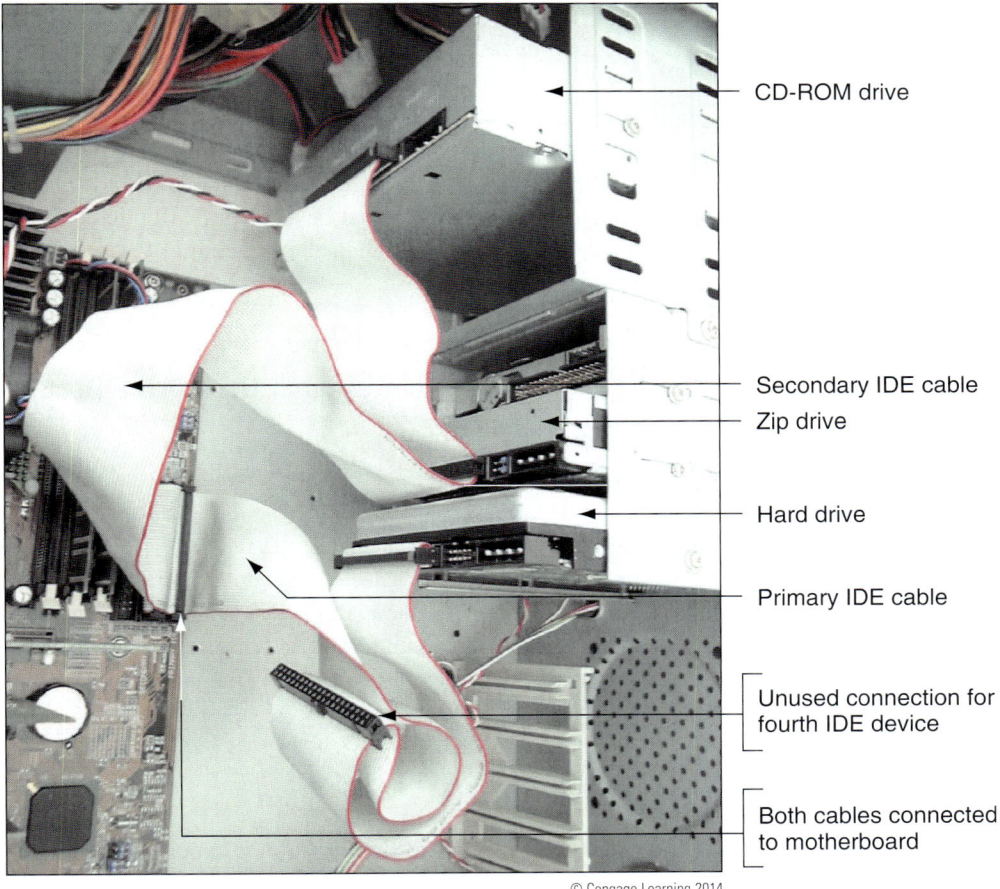

Figure 5-41 This system has a CD-ROM and a Zip drive sharing the secondary IDE cable and a hard drive using the primary IDE cable

3. You can now install a power connection to each drive (Figure 5-42). PATA drives use the Molex 5-pin power connector. The cord only goes into the connection one way.

Figure 5-42 Connect a power cord to each drive

4. Before you replace the case cover, plug in the monitor and turn on the computer. (On the other hand, some systems won't power up until the front panel is installed.) After you confirm that your drive is recognized, the size of the drive is detected correctly, and supported features are set to be automatically detected, power down the system and replace the case cover. Then the next thing to do is to use an operating system to prepare the drive for first use.

Hands-on | Project 5-2 Research Hard Drive Documentation

Suppose a friend has asked you to install an old hard drive in his computer. The drive is the Maxtor Quantum Fireball Plus AS 20.5-GB hard drive. You want the drive to be the slave drive, and you know that you must change the current jumper settings. The four jumpers on the drive are labeled DS, CS, PK, and Rsvd. The description of the jumpers doesn't tell you how to set the jumpers so the drive is the slave. The documentation is not available. What do you do?

The best solution is to use the Internet to access the drive manufacturer's web site for this information. In this case, the site is www.maxtor.com. Use this example or some other example given by your instructor to determine the correct settings for the jumpers.

SETTING UP HARDWARE RAID

For most personal computers, a single hard drive works independently of any other installed drives. A technology that configures two or more hard drives to work together as an array of drives is called RAID (redundant array of inexpensive disks or redundant array of independent disks). Two reasons you might consider using RAID are:

▲ To improve fault tolerance, which is a computer's ability to respond to a fault or catastrophe, such as a hardware failure or power outage, so that data is not lost. If data is important enough to justify the cost, you can protect the data by continuously writing two

copies of it, each to a different hard drive. This method is most often used on high-end, expensive file servers, but it is occasionally appropriate for a single-user workstation.
▲ To improve performance by writing data to two or more hard drives so that a single drive is not excessively used.

TYPES OF RAID

Several types of RAID exist; the four most commonly used are RAID 0, RAID 1, RAID 5, and RAID 10. Following is a brief description of each, including another method of two disks working together, called spanning. The first four methods are diagramed in Figure 5-43:

▲ **Spanning**, sometimes called JBOD (just a bunch of disks), uses two hard drives to hold a single Windows volume, such as drive E:. Data is written to the first drive, and, when it is full, the data continues to be written to the second.

▲ **RAID 0** also uses two or more physical disks to increase the disk space available for a single volume. RAID 0 writes to the physical disks evenly across all disks so that no one disk receives all the activity and therefore improves performance. Windows calls RAID 0 a **striped volume**. To understand that term, think of data striped—or written across—several hard drives. RAID 0 is preferred to spanning.

▲ **RAID 1** is a type of mirroring that duplicates data on one drive to another drive and is used for fault tolerance. Each drive has its own volume, and the two volumes are called mirrors. If one drive fails, the other continues to operate and data is not lost. Windows calls RAID 1 a **mirrored volume**.

> **Notes** In a SCSI implementation of RAID 1, if the two mirrored hard drives are sharing the same host adapter and the adapter fails, both drives go down together. To keep this from happening, each drive has its own host adapter, which is called RAID 1 with duplexing.

▲ **RAID 5** stripes data across three or more drives and uses parity checking, so that if one drive fails, the other drives can re-create the data stored on the failed drive by using the parity information. Data is not duplicated, and, therefore, RAID 5 makes better use of volume capacity. RAID 5 drives increase performance and provide fault tolerance. Windows calls these drives **RAID-5 volumes**.

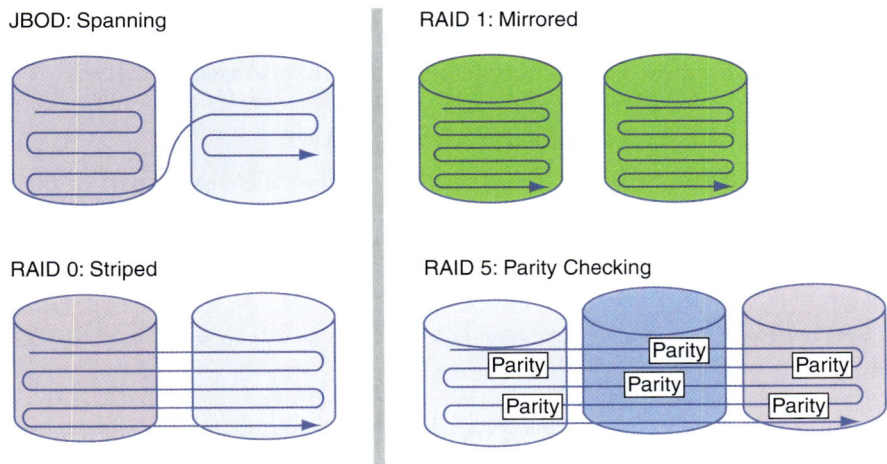

Figure 5-43 Ways that hard drives can work together

▲ **RAID 10**, also called **RAID 1+0** and pronounced "RAID one zero" (*not* "RAID ten"), is a combination of RAID 1 and RAID 0. It takes at least four disks for RAID 10. Data is mirrored across pairs of disks, as shown at the top of Figure 5-44. In addition, the two pairs of disks are striped, as shown at the bottom of Figure 5-44. To help you better understand RAID 10, in the figure notice the data labeled as A, A, B, B across the first stripe. RAID 10 is the most expensive solution that provides the best redundancy and performance.

RAID 1: Two pairs of mirrored disks

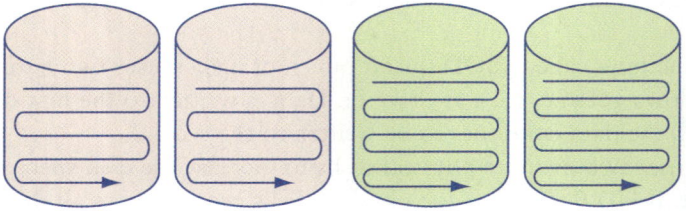

RAID 10: Mirrored and striped

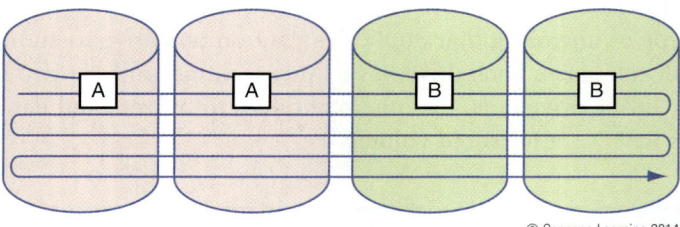

Figure 5-44   RAID 1 and RAID 10

© Cengage Learning 2014

> **A+ Exam Tip**   The A+ 220-801 exam expects you to be able to contrast RAID 0, RAID 1, RAID 5, and RAID 10.

All RAID configurations can be accomplished at the hardware level (called hardware RAID) or at the operating system level (called software RAID). Using Windows to implement software RAID, the Disk Management utility is used to configure a group of hard drives in a RAID array. However, software RAID is considered an unstable solution and not recommended by Microsoft. Configuring RAID at the hardware level is considered best practice because, if Windows gets corrupted, the hardware might still be able to protect the data. Also, hardware RAID is generally faster than software RAID.

HOW TO IMPLEMENT HARDWARE RAID

Hardware RAID can be set up by using a RAID controller that is part of the motherboard BIOS or by using a RAID controller expansion card. Figure 5-45 shows a RAID controller card by Sabrent that provides four SATA ports.

> **A+ Exam Tip**   The A+ 220-801 exam expects you to be able to set up hardware RAID.

When installing a hardware RAID system, for best performance, all hard drives in an array should be identical in brand, size, speed, and other features. Also, if Windows is to be installed on a hard drive that is part of a RAID array, RAID must be implemented

Figure 5-45 RAID controller card provides four SATA internal connectors

before Windows is installed. As with installing any hardware, first read the documentation that comes with the motherboard or RAID controller and follow those specific directions rather than the general guidelines given here. Make sure you understand which RAID configurations the board supports.

For one motherboard that has six SATA connectors that support RAID 0, 1, 5, and 10, here are the general directions to install the RAID array using three matching hard drives in a RAID 5 array:

1. Install the three SATA drives in the computer case and connect each drive to a SATA connector on the motherboard (see Figure 5-46). To help keep the drives cool, the drives are installed with an empty bay between each drive.

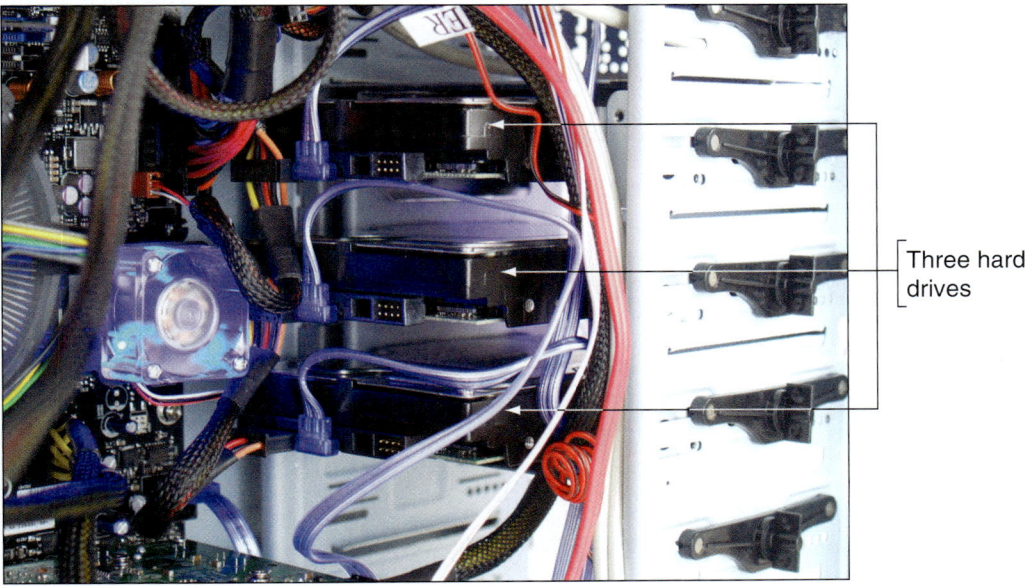

Figure 5-46 Install three matching hard drives in a system

2. Boot the system and enter BIOS setup. On the Advanced setup screen, verify the three drives are recognized. Select the option to configure SATA and then select RAID from the menu (see Figure 5-47).

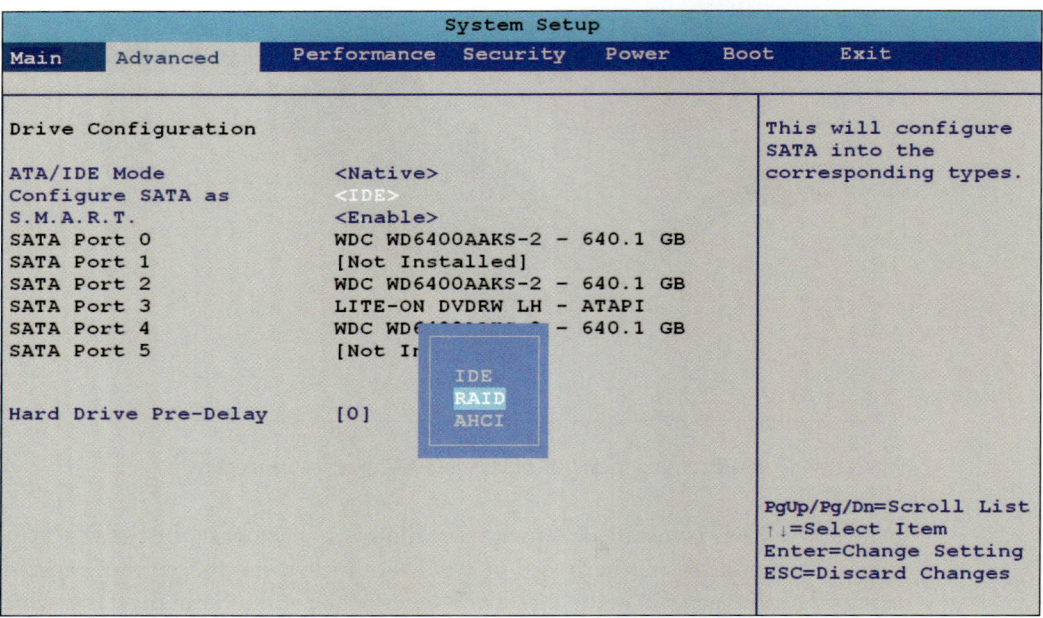

Figure 5-47 Configure SATA ports on the motherboard to enable RAID
Source: Intel

3. Reboot the system and a message is displayed on-screen: "Press <Ctrl+I> to enter the RAID Configuration Utility." Press **Ctrl** and **I** to enter the utility (see Figure 5-48). Notice in the information area that the three drives are recognized and their current status is Non-RAID Disk.

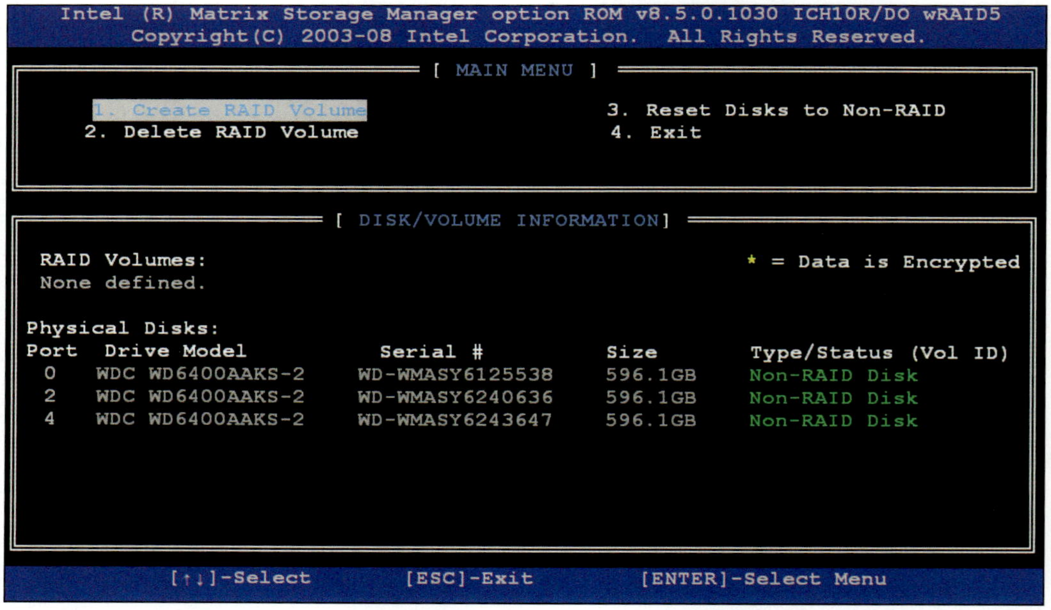

Figure 5-48 BIOS utility to configure a RAID array
Source: Intel

**A+
220-801
1.5**

4. Select option 1 to "**Create RAID Volume.**" On the next screen shown in Figure 5-49, enter a volume name (FileServer in our example).

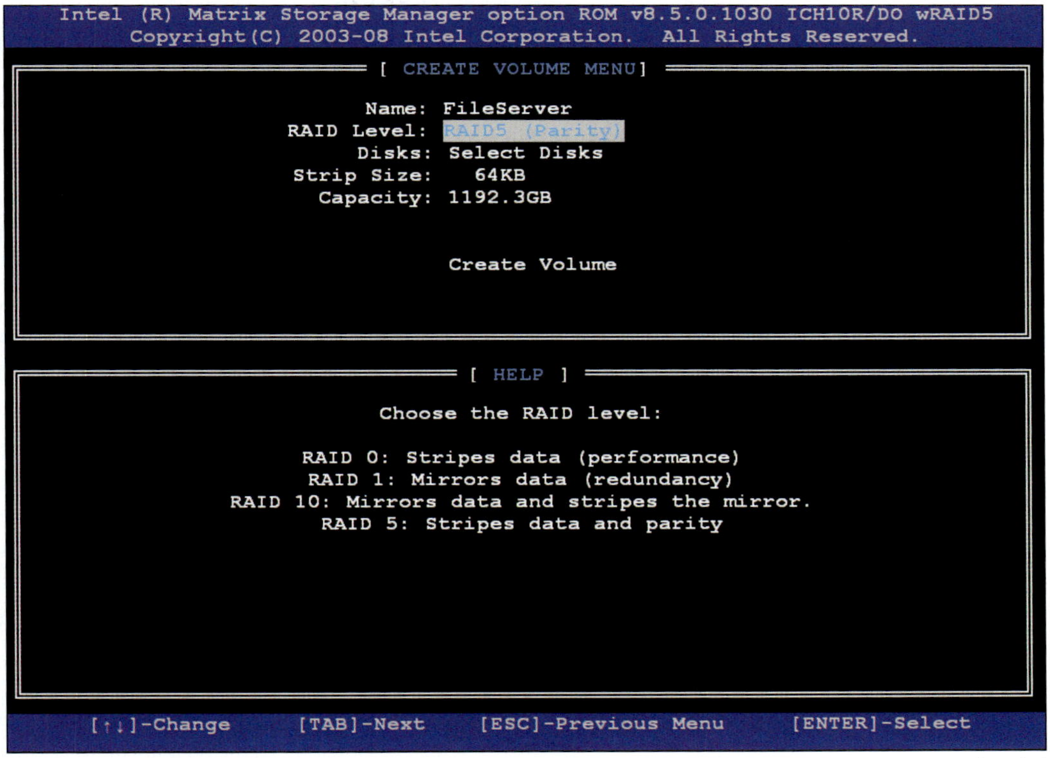

Figure 5-49 Make your choices for the RAID array

Source: Intel

5. Under RAID Level, select **RAID5 (Parity)**. Because we are using RAID 5, which requires three hard drives, the option to select the disks for the array is not available. All three disks will be used in the array.

6. Select the value for the Strip Size. (This is the amount of space devoted to one strip across the striped array. Choices are 32 KB, 64 KB, or 128 KB.)

7. Enter the size of the volume. The available size is shown in Figure 5-49 as 1192 GB, but you don't have to use all the available space. The space you don't use can later be configured as another array. (In this example, I entered 500 GB.)

8. Select **Create Volume** to complete the RAID configuration. A message appears warning you that if you proceed, all data on all three hard drives will be lost. Type **Y** to continue. The array is created and the system reboots.

You are now ready to install Windows. Windows 7/Vista automatically "sees" the RAID array as a single 500 GB hard drive because Windows 7/Vista has built-in hardware RAID drivers. For Windows XP, when you begin the XP installation, you must press F6 at the beginning of the installation to install RAID drivers. After Windows is installed on the drive, Windows will call it drive C:.

A+ 220-801 1.5

APPLYING CONCEPTS — TROUBLESHOOTING HARD DRIVE INSTALLATIONS

Sometimes, trouble crops up during an installation. Keeping a cool head, thinking things through carefully a second, third, and fourth time, and using all available resources will most likely get you out of any mess.

Installing a hard drive is not difficult, unless you have an unusually complex situation. For example, your first hard drive installation should not involve the intricacies of installing a second SCSI drive in a system that has two SCSI host adapters. Nor should you install a second drive in a system that uses an IDE connection for one drive on the motherboard and an adapter card in an expansion slot for the other drive. If a complicated installation is necessary and you have never installed a hard drive, ask for expert help.

The following list describes the errors that cropped up during a few hard drive installations; the list also includes the causes of the errors, and what was done about them. Everyone learns something new when making mistakes, and you probably will, too. You can then add your own experiences to this list.

- Shawn physically installed an IDE hard drive. He turned on the machine and accessed BIOS setup. The hard drive was not listed as an installed device. He checked and discovered that autodetection was not enabled. He enabled it and rebooted. Setup recognized the drive.
- When first turning on a previously working PC, John received the following error message: "Hard drive not found." He turned off the machine, checked all cables, and discovered that the data cable from the motherboard to the drive was loose. He reseated the cable and rebooted. POST found the drive.
- Lucia physically installed a new hard drive, replaced the cover on the computer case, and booted the PC with a Windows setup DVD in the drive. POST beeped three times and stopped. Recall that diagnostics during POST are often communicated by beeps if the tests take place before POST has checked video and made it available to display the messages. Three beeps on some computers signal a memory error. Lucia turned off the computer and checked the memory modules on the motherboard. A module positioned at the edge of the motherboard next to the cover had been bumped as she replaced the cover. She reseated the module and booted again, this time with the cover still off. The error disappeared.
- Jason physically installed a new hard drive and turned on the computer. He received the following error: "No boot device available." He forgot to insert a Windows setup DVD. He put the disc in the drive and rebooted the machine successfully.
- The hard drive did not physically fit into the bay. The screw holes did not line up. Juan got a bay kit, but it just didn't seem to work. He took a break, went to lunch, and came back to make a fresh start. Juan asked others to help view the brackets, holes, and screws from a fresh perspective. It didn't take long to discover that he had overlooked the correct position for the brackets in the bay.
- Maria set the jumpers on a PATA hard drive and physically installed the drive. She booted and received the error message "Hard drive not present." She rechecked all physical connections and found everything okay. After checking the jumper settings, she realized that she had set them as if this were the second drive of a two-drive system, when it was the only drive. She restored the jumpers to their original state. In this case, as in most cases, the jumpers were set at the factory to be correct when the drive is the only drive.

If BIOS setup does not recognize a newly installed hard drive, check the following:

- Has BIOS setup been correctly configured for autodetection?
- Are the jumpers on the drive set correctly?

A+ 220-801 1.5

- Have the power cord and data cable been properly connected? Verify that each is solidly connected at both ends.
- Check the web site of the drive manufacturer for suggestions if the above steps don't solve your problem. Look for diagnostic software that can be downloaded from the web site and used to check the drive.

> **Caution** When things are not going well, you can tense up and make mistakes more easily. Be certain to turn off the machine before doing anything inside! Not doing so can be a costly error. For example, a friend had been trying and retrying to boot for some time and got frustrated and careless. He plugged the power cord into the drive without turning the PC off. The machine began to smoke and everything went dead. The next thing he learned was how to replace a power supply!

Hands-on Project 5-3 Select a Replacement Hard Drive

Suppose the 640 GB Western Digital hard drive installed in the RAID array and shown in Figure 5-46 has failed. Search the Internet and find a replacement drive as close to this drive as possible. Print three web pages showing the sizes, features, and prices of three possible replacements. Which drive would you recommend as the replacement drive and why?

Hands-on Project 5-4 Prepare for Hard Drive Hardware Problems

1. Boot your PC and make certain that it works properly. Turn off your computer, remove the computer case, and disconnect the data cable to your hard drive. Turn on the computer again. Write down the message that you get.
2. Turn off the computer and reconnect the data cable. Reboot and make sure the system is working again.
3. Turn off the computer and disconnect the power supply cord to the hard drive. Turn on the computer. Write down the error that you get.
4. Turn off the computer, reconnect the power supply, and reboot the system. Verify the system is working again.

Hands-on Project 5-5 Install a Hard Drive

In a lab that has one hard drive per computer, you can practice installing a hard drive by removing a drive from one computer and installing it as a second drive in another computer. When you boot up the computer with two drives, verify that both drives are accessible in Windows Explorer. Then remove the second hard drive, and return it to its original computer. Verify that both computers and drives are working.

ABOUT TAPE DRIVES AND FLOPPY DRIVES

A+ 220-801 1.5, 1.11

Tape drives installed inside a computer case can use a SATA, PATA, or SCSI interface. Occasionally, you might be called on to support a computer with an old floppy drive. Both tape drives and floppy drives are covered in this part of the chapter.

INSTALLING TAPE DRIVES AND SELECTING TAPE MEDIA

Tape drives (see Figure 5-50) are an inexpensive way of backing up an entire hard drive or portions of it. Because tape drives are less expensive for backups than external hard drives, CDs, DVDs, or USB flash drives, they are still used for backups even though other methods are more convenient. Tapes currently have capacities up to 3.0 TB compressed and come in several types and formats. Some tape drives and tape cartridges support WORM (write once and read many). WORM drives and cartridges assure that data written on the tape will not be deleted or overwritten. Most tape drives come bundled with backup software to use them.

Courtesy of Quantum Corporation

Figure 5-50 The LTO-5 HH tape drive by Quantum writes to LTO Ultrium 5 and LTO Ultrium 4 tapes and reads from LTO Ultrium 5, LTO Ultrium 4, and LTO Ultrium 3 tapes. It provides AES 256-bit data encryption security, WORM functionality, and partitioning capability

> **A+ Exam Tip** The A+ 220-801 exam expects you to know how to install a tape drive and how to select the right tapes for the drive.

The biggest disadvantage of using tape drives is that data is stored on tape by **sequential access**; to read data from anywhere on the tape, you must start at the beginning of the tape and read until you come to the sought-after data. Sequential access makes recovering files slow and inconvenient, which is why tapes are not used for general-purpose data storage.

Tape drives accommodate one of two kinds of tapes: full-sized **data cartridges** are $4 \times 6 \times \frac{5}{8}$ inches, and the smaller **minicartridges**, like the one in Figure 5-51, are $3\frac{1}{4} \times 2\frac{1}{2} \times \frac{3}{5}$ inches. Minicartridges are more popular because their drives can fit into a standard 3-inch drive bay of a PC case.

Here is a list of some of the more common types of tape cartridges:

1. DDS-1, DDS-2, DDS-3, DDS-4, and DDS-5 are popular types. DDS-5 holds up to 36 GB native or 72 GB compressed data. DDS-5 is also called DAT72.

Figure 5-51 Minicartridge for a tape drive has a write-protect switch

2. LTO Ultrium 2, LTO Ultrium 3, LTO Ultrium 4, and LTO Ultrium 5 are sometimes referred to as LTO cartridges. LTO Ultrium 5 holds up to 1.5 TB native or 3.0 TB compressed data. Figure 5-52 shows an LTO Ultrium 3 tape.

3. DLT IV or DLT-4 holds up to 40 GB native or 80 GB compressed data.

4. Super DLTtape II holds up to 300 GB native or 600 GB compressed data.

5. Travan data types of cartridges vary from TR-1 through TR-7. The TR-7 holds 20 GB native and 40 GB compressed data.

6. AIT types have been around a long time and include AIT Turbo, AIT-1 through AIT-5, and S-AIT. S-AIT holds up to 1.3 TB compressed data.

7. SLR types include SLR1 through SLR140. SLR140 holds 70 GB native or 140 GB compressed data.

Figure 5-52 This Maxel LTO Ultrium 3 data tape cartridge can hold up to 800 GB of compressed data

When selecting a tape drive, consider how many and what type of cartridges the drive can use and how it interfaces with the computer. The drive might be able to read from more types of cartridges than it can write to. A tape drive can be external or internal. An external tape drive costs more but can be used by more than one computer. An internal tape drive can interface with a computer using a SCSI, PATA, or SATA connection. An external tape drive can connect to a computer using a USB, FireWire, SCSI, SAS, or eSATA port.

> **Notes** For an interesting photo gallery of tape media, see *www.backupworks.com*.

INSTALLING A FLOPPY DRIVE

Floppy drives: You almost never see them, but they're still covered on the A+ exam, so you need to know about them. We'll try to make this as brief and painless as possible. A 3½" high-density **floppy disk drive (FDD)** holds a mere 1.44 MB of data. When using floppy disks, know that to write to the disk, the write-protect notch must be closed (see Figure 5-53).

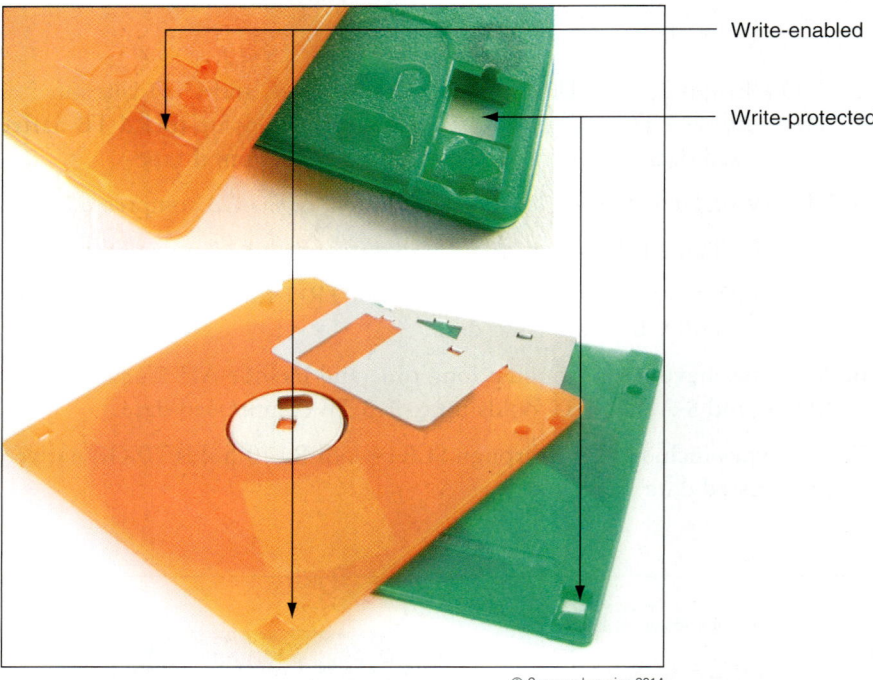

Figure 5-53 For you to write to a disk, the write-protect notch must be closed

> **Notes** One reason you still need to know about floppy disks and floppy disk drives is that Windows Server 2003 relies on floppy disks to recover from a failed installation, and Windows Server 2003 is still a popular server OS.

A floppy drive might be an external or internal device. Figure 5-54 shows a USB floppy drive. Figure 5-55 shows the floppy drive subsystem for an internal device, which consists of the floppy drive, its 34-pin ribbon cable, power cable, and connections. The Berg power connector has a small plastic latch that snaps in place when you connect it to the drive.

About Tape Drives and Floppy Drives | 231

A+ 220-801
1.5,
1.11

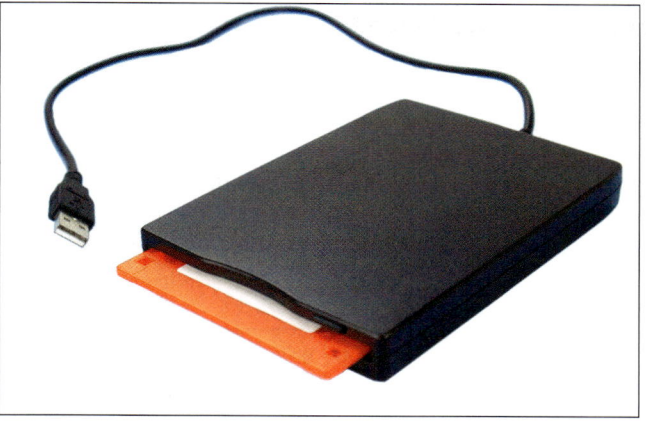

Figure 5-54 An external floppy drive uses a USB connection

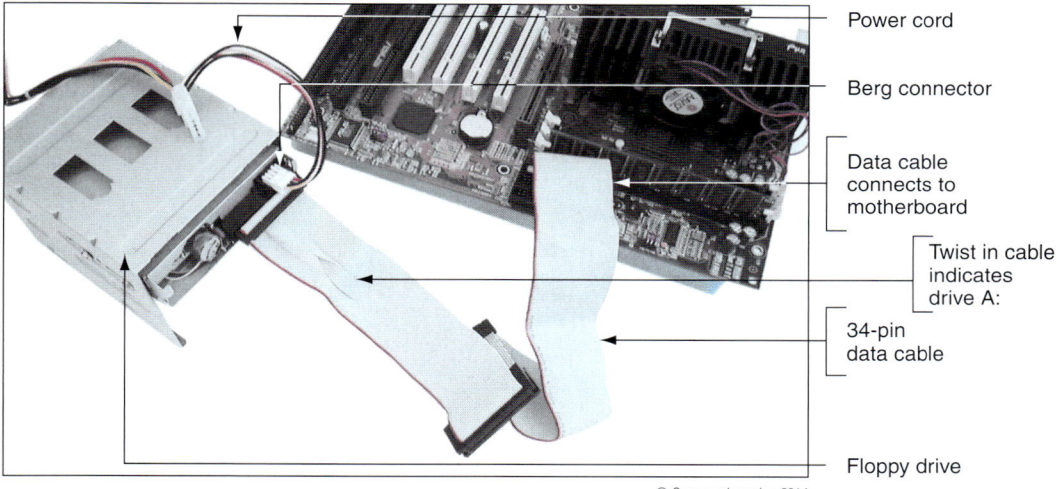

Figure 5-55 Floppy drive subsystem: floppy drive, 34-pin data cable, and power connector

Today's floppy drive cables have a connector at each end and accommodate a single drive, but older cables, like the one in Figure 5-55, have an extra connector or two in the middle of the cable for a second floppy drive. For these systems, you can install two floppy drives on the same cable, and the drives will be identified by BIOS as drive A: and drive B:. Notice in the figure the twist in the cable. The drive that has the twist between it and the controller is drive A:. The drive that does not have the twist between it and the controller is drive B:. Also notice in the figure the edge color down one side of the cable, which identifies the pin-1 side of the 34-pin connector.

> **A+ Exam Tip** The A+ 220-801 exam expects you to be able to install and configure a floppy disk drive (FDD).

When installing a floppy drive, install the drive in a bay as you would a hard drive and connect the data cable and power cord. When connecting the data cable, align the edge color of the ribbon cable with pin 1 on the motherboard connector. See Figure 5-56. If you connect the cable in the wrong direction, the floppy drive light stays lit continuously and the drive does not work. Some connectors allow you to insert the cable only in one direction. Be sure the end of the cable with the twist connects to the drive and the other end to the motherboard.

> **Notes** If your power supply doesn't have the smaller Berg connector for the floppy drive, you can buy a Molex-to-Berg converter to accommodate the floppy drive power connector.

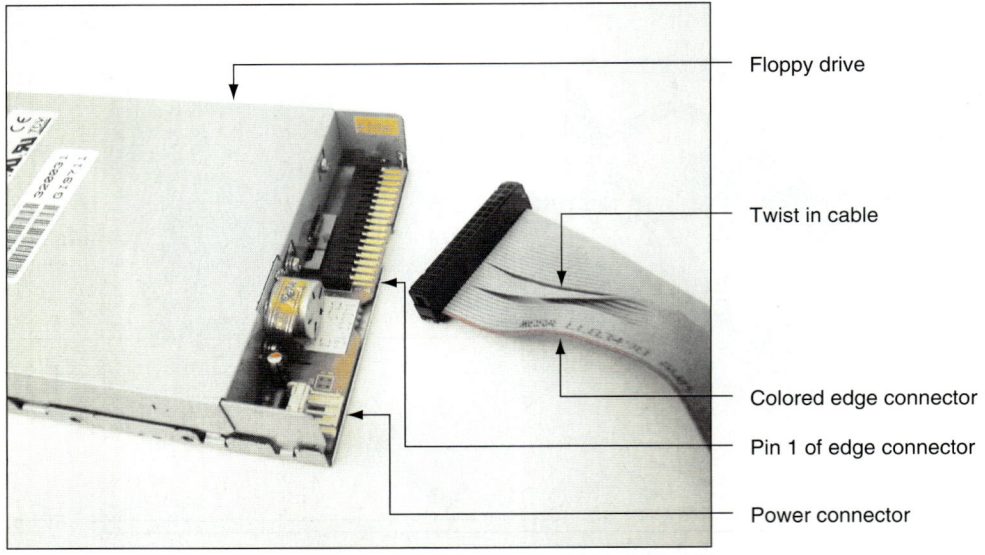

Figure 5-56 Connect colored edge of cable to pin 1

Replace the cover, turn on the computer, and enter BIOS setup to verify the drive is recognized with no errors. If you are adding (not replacing) a floppy drive, you must inform BIOS setup by accessing setup and changing the drive type. Boot to the Windows desktop and test the drive by formatting a disk or copying data to a disk.

> **Notes** Note that you can turn on the PC and test the drive before you replace the computer case cover. If the drive doesn't work, having the cover off makes it easier to turn off the computer, check connections, and try again. Just make certain that you don't touch anything inside the case while the computer is on. Leaving the computer on while you disconnect and reconnect a cable is very dangerous for the PC and will probably damage something—including you!

>> CHAPTER SUMMARY

Hard Drive Technologies and Interface Standards

- A hard disk drive (HDD) comes in two sizes: 3.5" for desktop computers and 2.5" for laptops.
- A hard drive can be a magnetic drive, a solid-state drive, or a hybrid drive. A solid-state drive contains flash memory and is more expensive, faster, more reliable, and uses less power than a magnetic drive.
- Most hard drives use the ATA interface standards. The two main categories of ATA are parallel ATA and serial ATA. Serial ATA is easier to configure and better performing than PATA. External SATA ports are called eSATA ports.
- S.M.A.R.T. is a self-monitoring technology whereby the BIOS monitors the health of the hard drive and warns of an impending failure.
- ATAPI standards are used by optical drives and other drives that use the ATA interface on a motherboard or controller card.
- Several PATA standards are Fast ATA, Ultra ATA, Ultra ATA/66, Ultra ATA/100, and Ultra ATA/133.
- Three SATA standards provide data transfer rates of 1.5 Gb/sec (using SATA I), 3.0 Gb/sec (using SATA II), and 6.0 Gb/sec (using SATA III).
- The SCSI interface standards include narrow and wide SCSI, and can use a variety of cables and connectors. Three connectors are a 50-pin, 68-pin, and 25-pin connector. A SCSI chain can contain up to 16 devices including the host adapter. Each device is identified by a SCSI ID, a number from 0 to 15.

How to Select and Install Hard Drives

- When selecting a hard drive, consider the storage capacity, technology (solid state or magnetic), spindle speed, interface standard, and buffer size (for hybrid drives).
- SATA drives require no configuration and are installed using a power cord and a single SATA data cable.
- PATA drives require you to set a jumper to determine if the drive will be the single drive, master, or slave on a single cable. The PATA cable can accommodate two drives. A PATA motherboard has one or two PATA connectors for up to four PATA drives in the system.
- RAID technology uses an array of hard drives to provide fault tolerance and/or improvement in performance. Choices for RAID are RAID 0 (striping using two drives), RAID 1 (mirroring using two drives), RAID 5 (parity checking using three drives), and RAID 10 (striping and mirroring combined using four drives).
- Hardware RAID is implemented using the motherboard BIOS or a RAID controller card. Software RAID is implemented in Windows. Best practice is to use hardware RAID rather than software RAID.

About Tape Drives and Floppy Drives

- Tape drives are an inexpensive way to back up an entire hard drive or portions of it. Tape drives are more convenient for backups than removable drives. The disadvantage of tape drives is that data can only be accessed sequentially.

- Today's floppy disks are 3½" high-density disks that hold 1.44 MB of data.
- After a floppy disk drive is installed, you must configure the drive in BIOS setup.

>> KEY TERMS

For explanations of key terms, see the Glossary near the end of the book.

25-pin SCSI connector
50-pin SCSI connector
68-pin SCSI connector
80-conductor IDE cable
ANSI (American National Standards Institute)
ATAPI (Advanced Technology Attachment Packet Interface)
autodetection
data cartridge
DMA (direct memory access) transfer mode
Enhanced IDE (EIDE)
external SATA (eSATA)
fault tolerance
floppy disk drive (FDD)
hard disk drive (HDD)
hard drive
host adapter
hot-swapping
hybrid hard drive
IDE (Integrated Drive Electronics)
Logical Unit Number (LUN)
low-level formatting
magnetic hard drive
minicartridge
mirrored volume
NAND flash memory
Parallel ATA (PATA)
PIO (Programmed Input/Output) transfer mode
RAID (redundant array of inexpensive disks or redundant array of independent disks)
RAID 0
RAID 1
RAID 1+0
RAID 10
RAID 5
RAID-5 volume
read/write head
ReadyDrive
S.M.A.R.T. (Self-Monitoring Analysis and Reporting Technology)
SCSI (Small Computer System Interface)
SCSI host adapter card
SCSI ID
sequential access
serial ATA (SATA)
solid state device (SSD)
solid state drive (SSD)
spanning
striped volume
terminating resistor

>> REVIEWING THE BASICS

1. What two types of technologies are used inside hard drives?
2. What four speeds in revolutions per minute might the spindle inside a hard drive rotate?
3. What is the name of the Windows technology that supports a memory buffer in a hybrid drive?
4. When the OS addresses the sectors on a hard drive as one long list of sequential sectors, what is this technology called?
5. A CD drive that uses a PATA connection must follow what standard?
6. How many pins does an 80-conductor IDE cable have? What is the maximum recommended length of an IDE cable?
7. What is the transfer speed of an IDE interface using the ATA-7 standard?
8. What is the transfer speed for SATA I? SATA II? SATA III?
9. How many pins does a SATA data cable have? How many pins does a SATA power cable have?

10. What term describes the technology that allows you to exchange a hard drive without powering down the system?

11. What are the four possible configurations for a PATA drive installed in a system?

12. Which SCSI ID is assigned to the SCSI host adapter?

13. Which two SCSI connectors might be used with narrow SCSI?

14. Which version of SCSI is known as Fast SCSI? Which version is known as Ultra SCSI?

15. Which RAID level mirrors one hard drive with a second drive so that the same data is written to both drives?

16. Which RAID level stripes data across multiple drives to improve performance and also provides fault tolerance?

17. How many hard drives does it take to implement RAID 10?

18. How many pins does a floppy drive connector have? What is the storage capacity of a 3½" high-density floppy disk?

19. If a motherboard has one blue IDE connector and one black IDE connector, which do you use to install a single drive?

20. When implementing RAID on a motherboard, where do you enable the feature?

>> THINKING CRITICALLY

1. You install an IDE hard drive and then turn on the PC for the first time. You access BIOS setup and see that the drive is not recognized. Which of the following do you do next?

    a. Turn off the PC, open the case, and verify that memory modules on the motherboard have not become loose.

    b. Turn off the PC, open the case, and verify that the data cable and power cable are connected correctly and jumpers on the drive are set correctly.

    c. Verify that BIOS autodetection is enabled.

    d. Reboot the PC and enter BIOS setup again to see if it now recognizes the drive.

2. You want to install an SSD drive in your desktop computer, but the drive is far too narrow to fit snugly into the bays of your computer case. Which of the following do you do?

    a. Install the SSD in a laptop computer.

    b. Buy a bay adapter that will allow you to install the narrow drive in a desktop case bay.

    c. This SSD is designed for a laptop. Flash BIOS so that your system will support a laptop hard drive.

    d. Use a special SATA controller card that will support the narrow hard drive.

3. Mark each statement as true or false:

   a. SATA 1 is about 10 times faster than IDE ATA/133.

   b. SATA 1 is about 100 times faster than IDE ATA/133.

   c. RAID 0 can be implemented using only a single hard drive.

   d. RAID 5 requires five hard drives working together at the same speed and capacity.

   e. You can use an internal SATA data cable with an eSATA port.

   f. A SATA data cable has 7 pins.

>> REAL PROBLEMS, REAL SOLUTIONS

REAL PROBLEM 5-1: Data Recovery Problem

Your friend has a Windows 7 desktop system that contains important data. He frantically calls you to say that when he turns on the computer, the lights on the front panel light up and he can hear the fan spin for a moment and then all goes dead. His most urgent problem is the data on his hard drive, which is not backed up. The data is located in several folders on the drive. What is the quickest and easiest way to solve the most urgent problem, recovering the data? List the major steps in that process.

REAL PROBLEM 5-2: Using Hardware RAID

You work as a PC technician for a boss who believes you are really bright and can solve just about any problem he throws at you. Folks in the company have complained one time too many that the file server downtime is just killing them, so he asks you to solve this problem. He wants you to figure out what hardware is needed to implement hardware RAID for fault tolerance.

You check the file server's configuration and discover it has a single hard drive using a SATA connection with Windows Server 2012 installed. There are four empty bays in the computer case and four extra SATA power cords. You also discover an empty PCIe x4 slot on the motherboard. BIOS setup does not offer the option to configure RAID, but you think the slot might accommodate a RAID controller.

Complete the investigation and do the following:

1. Decide what hardware you must purchase and print web pages showing the products and their cost.

2. What levels of RAID does the RAID controller card support? Which RAID level is best to use? Print any important information in the RAID controller documentation that supports your decisions.

3. What is the total hardware cost of implementing RAID? Estimate how much time you think it will take for you to install the devices and test the setup.

CHAPTER 6

Supporting I/O and Storage Devices

In this chapter, you will learn:

- About the general approaches you need to take when installing and supporting I/O and mass storage devices
- How to install and configure several I/O devices, such as barcode readers, biometric devices, digital cameras, webcams, graphic tablets, and touch screens
- How to install and configure adapter cards
- About supporting the video subsystem, including selecting a monitor and video card and supporting dual monitors and video memory
- How to support optical drives and flash memory devices

This chapter is packed full of details about the many I/O (input/output) and mass storage devices a PC support technician must be familiar with and must know how to install and support. Most of us learn about new technologies as we need to use a device or when a client or customer requests our help with purchasing decisions or solving a problem with a device. Good technicians soon develop the skills of searching the web for explanations, reviews, and ads about a device and can quickly turn to support web sites for how to install, configure, or troubleshoot a device. This chapter can serve as your jumpstart toward learning about many computer parts and devices used to enhance a system. It contains enough information to get you started toward becoming an expert at computer devices.

We begin with the basic skills common to supporting any device, including how to use Device Manager and how to select the right port for a new peripheral device. Then you'll learn to install I/O devices and adapter cards and to support the video subsystem. Finally, you'll learn to select and install an optical drive and enough about memory cards that you'll know which type of card to buy for a particular need.

BASIC PRINCIPLES FOR SUPPORTING DEVICES

> A+
> 220-801
> 1.5, 1.7,
> 1.10,
> 1.12

An I/O or storage device can be either internal (installed inside the computer case) or external (installed outside the case and called a peripheral device). These basic principles apply to supporting both internal and external devices:

- *Every device is controlled by software.* When you install a new device, such as a barcode reader or scanner, you must install both the device and the device drivers to control the device. These device drivers must be written for the OS you are using. Recall from earlier chapters that the exceptions to this principle are some simple devices, such as the keyboard, which are controlled by the system BIOS. Also, Windows has embedded device drivers for many devices. For example, when you install a video card, Windows can use its embedded drivers to communicate with the card, but to use all the features of the card, you can install the drivers that came bundled with it.
- *When it comes to installing or supporting a device, the manufacturer knows best.* In this chapter, you will learn a lot of principles and procedures for installing and supporting a device, but when you're on the job installing a device or fixing a broken one, read the manufacturer's documentation and follow those guidelines first. For example, for most installations, you install the device before you install the device driver. However, for some devices, such as a digital camera and a wireless keyboard, you might need to install the device driver first. Check the device documentation to know which to do first.
- *Some devices need application software to use the device.* For example, after you install a scanner and its device drivers, you might also need to install Adobe Photoshop to use the scanner.
- *A device is no faster than the port or slot it is designed to use.* When buying new external devices, pay attention to the type of port for which it is rated. For example, an external hard drive designed to use a USB 2.0 port will work at that speed even when it's connected to a faster USB 3.0 port. For another example, a TV tuner card in a PCI slot will not work as fast as a TV tuner card in a PCI Express slot because of the different speeds of the slots.
- *Use an administrator account in Windows.* When installing hardware devices under Windows, you need to be logged onto the system with a user account that has the highest level of privileges to change the system. This type of account is called an administrator account.
- *Problems with a device can sometimes be solved by updating the device drivers.* Device manufacturers often release updates to device drivers. Update the drivers to solve problems with the device or to add new features. You can use Device Manager in Windows to manage devices and their drivers.
- *Install only one device at a time.* If you have several devices to install, install one and restart the system. Make sure that device is working and all is well with the system before you move on to install another device.

> A+
> 220-802
> 1.7

Now let's see how to use the Windows 7 Action Center and Windows 7/Vista/XP Device Manager. These tools can help you solve problems with installed devices.

USING THE ACTION CENTER AND DEVICE MANAGER

If a problem occurs while Windows 7 is installing a device, it automatically launches the Action Center to help find a solution. For example, Figure 6-1 shows the error message window that appeared when a USB keyboard and USB printer were first connected to a computer. (Windows Vista and XP do not have an Action Center.)

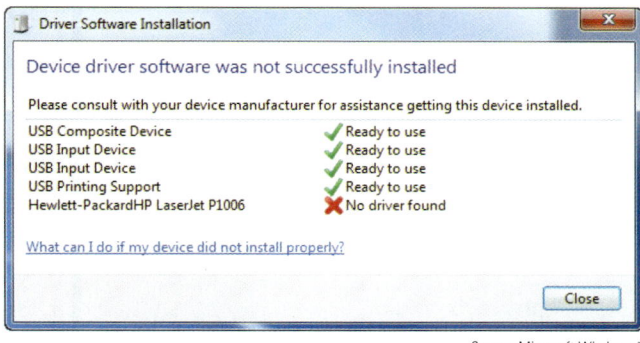

Source: Microsoft Windows 7

Figure 6-1 Windows 7 reports a problem with a driver for a USB printer

Immediately after this first window appeared, the Action Center provided the window shown in Figure 6-2. When the user clicked **Click to download and install the new driver from the Hewlett-Packard Company website**, the driver was immediately downloaded and installed with no errors.

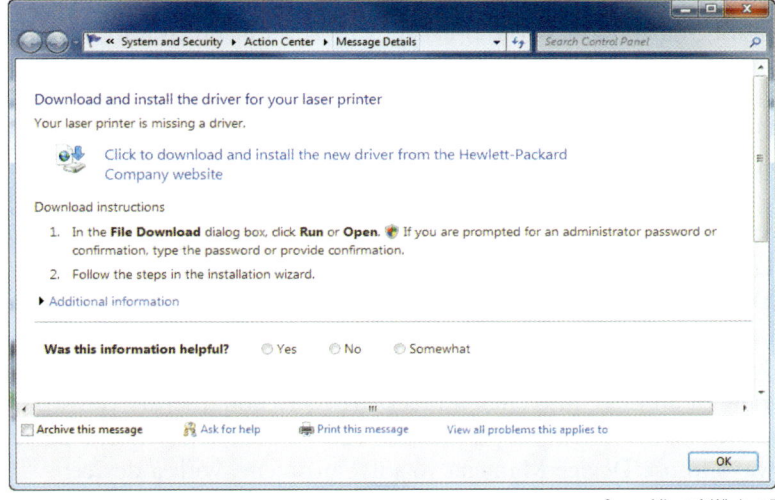

Source: Microsoft Windows 7

Figure 6-2 Windows offers to find the missing USB printer driver

You can also open the Action Center at any time to see a list of problems and solutions. To open the Action Center, click **Start**, right-click **Computer**, and click **Properties**. In the System window, click **Action Center**. For example, the Action Center in Figure 6-3 shows a problem with a media reader. (A media reader is a device that can read and write to memory cards such as an SD card.) When you click a problem, you can follow on-screen directions toward a solution. If the problem is still not resolved after following the solutions offered by the Action Center, turn to Device Manager.

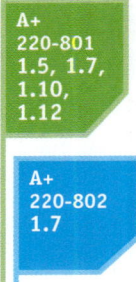

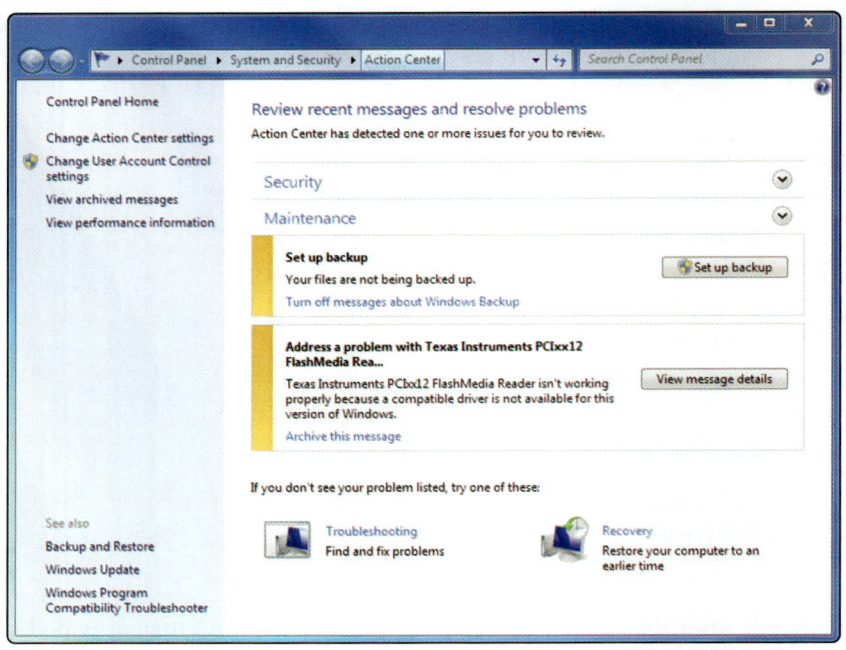

Figure 6-3 Use the Action Center to find a solution to a problem

Device Manager (its program file is named devmgmt.msc) is your primary Windows 7/Vista/XP tool for managing hardware. It lists almost all installed hardware devices and the drivers they use. (Printers and many USB devices are not listed in Device Manager.) Using Device Manager, you can disable or enable a device, update its drivers, uninstall a device, and undo a driver update (called a driver rollback).

To access Device Manager, use one of these methods:

- Click **Start**, right-click **Computer**, and select **Properties**. The System window appears. Click **Device Manager**. The Device Manager window opens.
- Enter **Device Manager** or **Devmgmt.msc** in the Search box and press **Enter**.

A Device Manager window is shown on the left side of Figure 6-4. Click a white arrow to expand the view of an item, and click a black arrow to collapse the view. Notice the yellow triangle beside the RAID controller, which indicates a problem with the device.

Here are ways to use Device Manager to solve problems with a device:

- **Look for error messages offered by Device Manager.** To find out more information about a device, right-click the device and select **Properties** on the shortcut menu. The right side of Figure 6-4 shows the properties box for the RAID controller. Many times, a message shows up in this box reporting the source of the problem and suggesting a solution.
- **Update the drivers or roll back (undo) a driver update.** Updating drivers can often solve a problem with a device. If a driver update creates a problem, you can roll back (undo) the driver update if the previous drivers were working. (Windows does

Basic Principles for Supporting Devices   241

A+
220-801
1.5, 1.7,
1.10,
1.12

A+
220-802
1.7

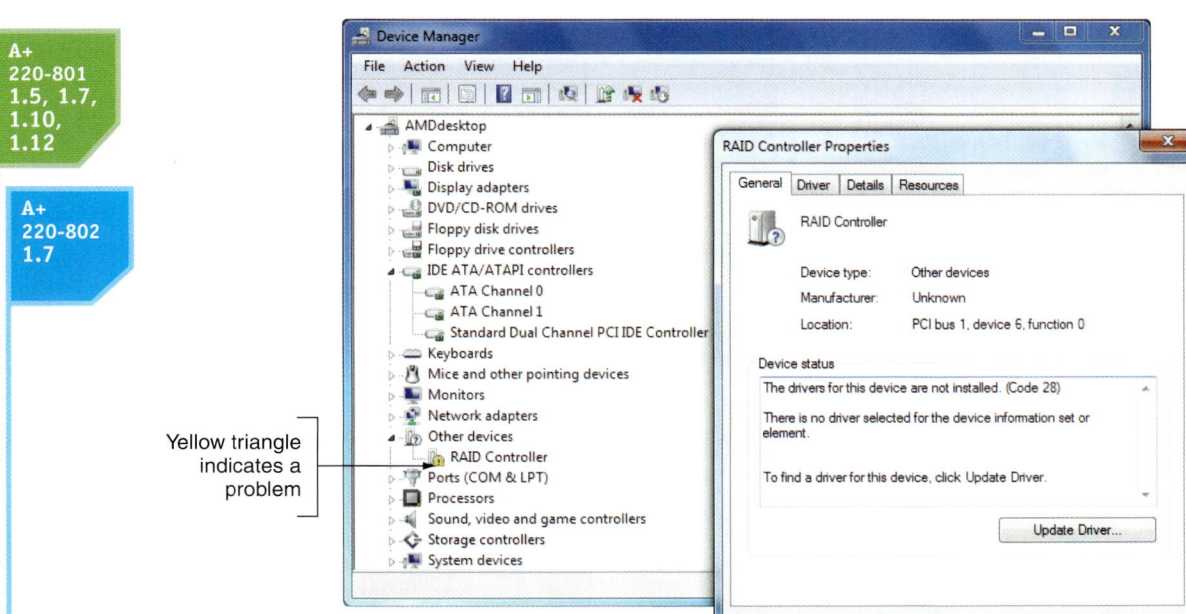

Yellow triangle indicates a problem

Figure 6-4 Use Device Manager to solve problems with hardware devices
Source: Microsoft Windows 7

not save drivers that were not working before the driver update.) Click the **Driver** tab. Figure 6-5 shows the Driver tab for one device. When you click **Update**, the box in Figure 6-6 appears.

To search the Internet for drivers, click **Search automatically for updated driver software**. (Windows 7/Vista searches the Microsoft web site and the manufacturer's

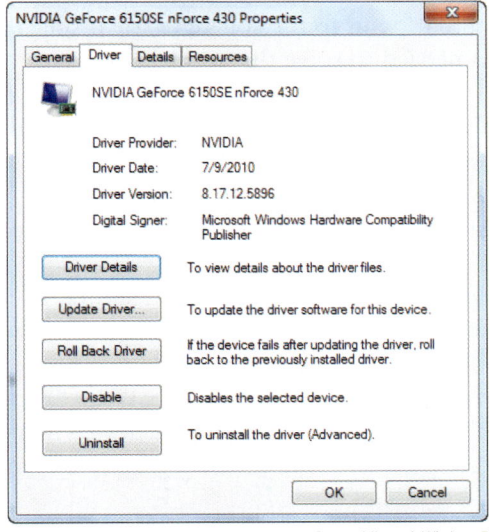

Source: Microsoft Windows 7

Figure 6-5 Update or roll back drivers for a device

A+ 220-801
1.5, 1.7, 1.10, 1.12

A+ 220-802
1.7

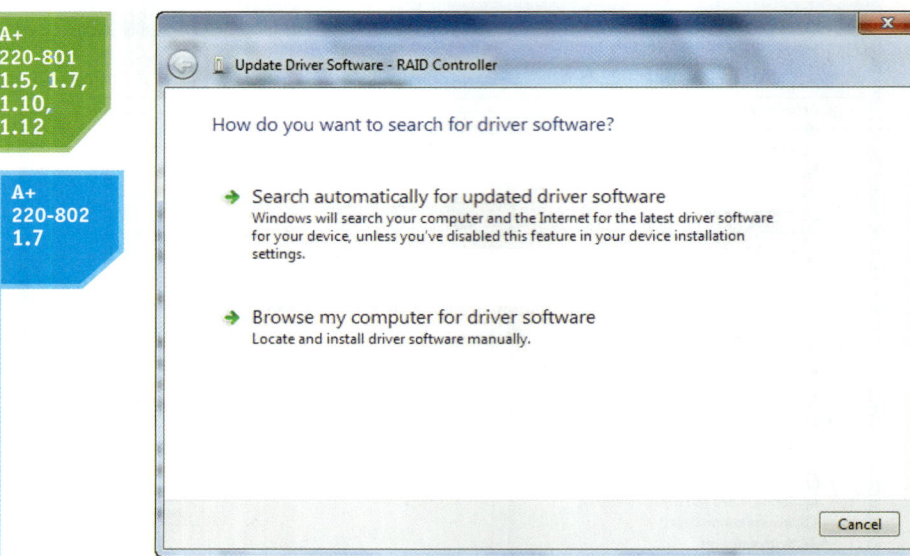

Source: Microsoft Windows 7

Figure 6-6 Decide where Windows should search to find the drivers

web site, but XP searches only the Microsoft web site for drivers.) If you have already downloaded drivers to your PC or you have the drivers on CD that came bundled with the device, click **Browse my computer for driver software,** and point to the downloaded files or to the CD. Note that Windows is looking for an .inf file to identify the drivers. Continue to follow the directions on-screen to complete the installation.

▲ **Try uninstalling and reinstalling the device.** If you are still having a problem with a device, try uninstalling it and installing it again. To uninstall the device, click **Uninstall** on the Driver tab (see Figure 6-5). Alternately, you can right-click the device and click Uninstall on the shortcut menu. Then reboot and reinstall the device, looking for problems during the installation that point to the source of the problem. Sometimes reinstalling a device is all that is needed to solve the problem.

If Windows is not able to locate new drivers for a device, locate and download the latest driver files from the manufacturer's web site to your hard drive. Be sure to use 64-bit drivers for a 64-bit OS and 32-bit drivers for a 32-bit OS. If possible, use Windows 7 drivers for Windows 7, and Vista drivers for Vista. You can double-click the downloaded driver files to launch the installation.

A few devices have firmware on the device that can be flashed similar to the way the BIOS on the motherboard is flashed. For example, after the RAID controller you saw in Figure 6-4 has its drivers installed, new tabs appear on the controller's properties box that are put there by the drivers (see Figure 6-7). To flash the firmware on this controller card, you first download the flash image file from the device manufacturer's web site. Then click **Browse** and locate the file. Next click **Program Flash** to begin the firmware update.

📝 **Notes** By default, Device Manager hides legacy devices that are not Plug and Play. To view installed legacy devices, click the **View** menu of Device Manager, and click **Show hidden devices** (see Figure 6-8).

Basic Principles for Supporting Devices 243

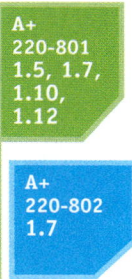

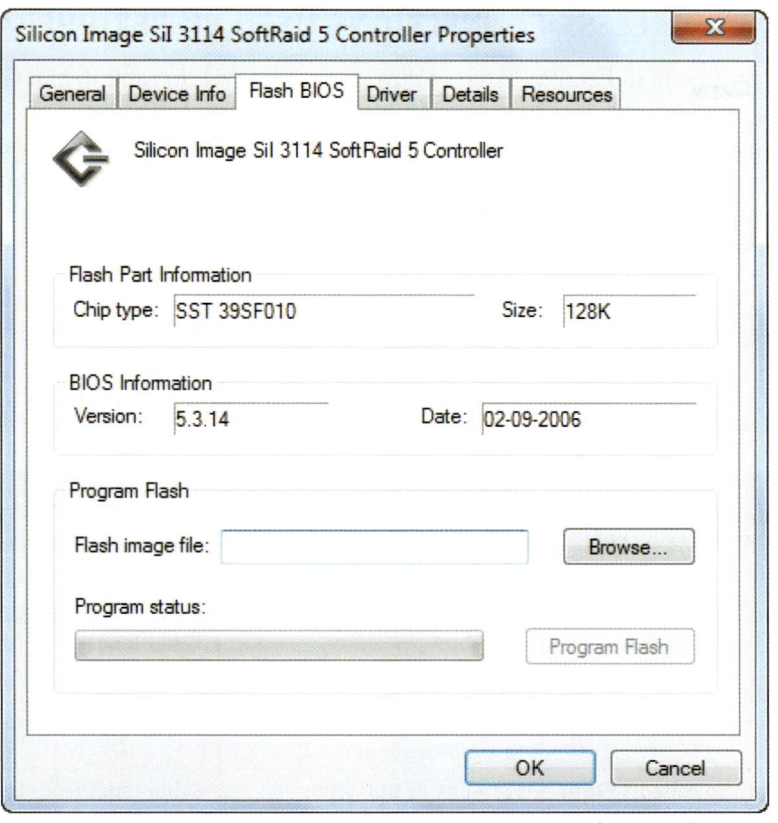

Figure 6-7 Use the device's properties box to flash the firmware on some devices
Source: Microsoft Windows 7

Figure 6-8 By default, Windows does not display legacy devices in Device Manager; you show these hidden devices by using the View menu
Source: Microsoft Windows 7

Before we move on to installing devices, you need to be familiar with the ports on a computer. When selecting a new device, to get the best performance, select one that uses the fastest port available on your computer.

PORTS AND WIRELESS CONNECTIONS USED BY PERIPHERAL DEVICES

A+
220-801
1.5, 1.7,
1.10,
1.12

Many ports used by peripheral or external devices are pictured in Table 1-1 in Chapter 1. When deciding what type of port a new device should use, the speed of the port is often a tiebreaker. Table 6-1 shows the speeds of various ports, from fastest to slowest. Because wireless connections are sometimes an option, they are also included in the table for comparison. For example, you might need to decide between a USB 2.0 printer connection and a Bluetooth wireless connection. This table can help you decide if speed should be a consideration.

> **A+ Exam Tip** The A+ 220-801 exam expects you to be able to compare the speeds and distances among USB (1.1, 2.0, and 3.0) and Firewire 400 and 800 ports and Bluetooth, Infrared, and RF wireless connections. The facts you need to know are found in Table 6-1.

Port or Wireless Type	Maximum Speed	Maximum Cable Length or Wireless Range
eSATA Version 3 (eSATA-600)	6.0 Gbps (gigabits per second)	Cable lengths up to 2 meters
SuperSpeed USB (USB 3.0)	5.0 Gbps	Cable lengths up to 3 meters
eSATA Version 2 (eSATA-300)	3.0 Gbps	Cable lengths up to 2 meters
eSATA Version 1 (eSATA-150)	1.5 Gbps or 1500 Mbps (megabits per second)	Cable lengths up to 2 meters
Firewire 800 (also called 1394b)	1.2 Gbps or 800 Mbps	Cable lengths up to 100 meters
Wi-Fi 802.11n RF (radio frequency) of 2.4 GHz or 5.0 GHz	Up to 500 Mbps	Range up to 70 meters
Hi-Speed USB (USB 2.0)	480 Mbps	Cable lengths up to 5 meters
FireWire 400 (also called 1394a)	400 Mbps	Cable lengths up to 4.5 meters
Original USB (USB 1.1)	12 Mbps or 1.5 Mbps	Cable lengths up to 3 meters
Parallel	1.5 Mbps	Cables up to 4.5 meters (15 feet)
Serial	115.2 Kbps (kilobits per second)	Cables up to 50 feet
Wi-Fi 802.11g RF of 2.4 GHz	Up to 54 Mbps	Range up to 100 meters
Wi-Fi 802.11a RF of 5.0 GHz	Up to 54 Mbps	Range up to 50 meters
Wi-Fi 802.11b RF of 2.4 GHz	Up to 11 Mbps	Range up to 100 meters
Bluetooth wireless RF of 2.4 GHz	Up to 3 Mbps	Range up to 10 meters
Infrared (IR) wireless Invisible light frequency range of 100 to 400 THz (terahertz or 1 trillion hertz) just above red light	Up to 4 Mbps for fast speed IR; up to 1.15 Mbps for medium speed IR, and up to 115 Kbps (kilobits per second) for slow speed IR	Range up to 5 meters

© Cengage Learning 2014

Table 6-1 Data transmission speeds for various port types and wireless connections

Basic Principles for Supporting Devices | 245

A+ 220-801
1.5, 1.7, 1.10, 1.12

> **A+ Exam Tip** The A+ 220-801 exam expects you to know about some old technologies, including serial and parallel ports and cables. For this reason, they are listed in Table 1-1 even though you are unlikely to be called on to support these outdated technologies.

USB CONNECTIONS

Here is a summary of important facts you need to know about USB connections:

- The USB Implementers Forum, Inc. (*www.usb.org*), the organization responsible for developing USB, uses the symbols shown in Figure 6-9 to indicate SuperSpeed USB (USB 3.0), Hi-Speed USB (USB 2.0), or Original USB (USB 1.1).

Source: USB Forum

Figure 6-9 SuperSpeed, Hi-Speed, and Original USB logos appear on products certified by the USB forum

- As many as 127 USB devices can be daisy chained together using USB cables. In a daisy chain, one device provides a USB port for the next device.
- USB uses serial transmissions, and USB devices are **hot-swappable**, meaning that you can plug or unplug one without first powering down the system.
- A USB cable has four wires, two for power and two for communication. The two power wires (one is hot and the other is ground) allow the host controller to provide power to a device. Table 6-2 shows the different USB connectors on USB cables.

Cable and Connectors	Description
A-Male to B-Male cable © Cengage Learning 2014	The **A Male connector** on the left is flat and wide and connects to an A-Male USB port on a computer or USB hub. The **B Male connector** on the right is square and connects to a USB 1.x or 2.0 device such as a printer.
Mini-B to A-Male cable © Cengage Learning 2014	The **Mini-B connector** has five pins and is often used to connect small electronic devices, such as a digital camera, to a computer.

© Cengage Learning 2014

Table 6-2 USB connectors (continues)

Cable and Connectors	Description
A-Male to Micro-B cable	The Micro-B connector has five pins and has a smaller height than the Mini-B connector. It's used on digital cameras, cell phones, and other small electronic devices.
A-Male to Micro-A cable	The Micro-A connector has five pins and is smaller than the Mini-B connector. It's used on digital cameras, cell phones, and other small electronic devices.
USB 3.0 A-Male to USB 3.0 B-Male cable	This USB 3.0 B-Male connector is used by SuperSpeed USB 3.0 devices such as printers or scanners. Devices that have this connection can also use regular B-Male connectors, but this USB 3.0 B-Male connector will not fit the connection on a USB 1.1 or 2.0 device. USB 3.0 A-Male and B-Male connectors and ports are blue.
USB 3.0 A-Male to USB 3.0 Micro-B cable	The USB 3.0 Micro-B connector is used by SuperSpeed USB 3.0 devices. The connectors are not compatible with regular Micro-B connectors.

Table 6-2 USB connectors (continued)

> **Notes** A USB 3.0 A-Male connector or port has additional pins compared to USB 1.1 or 2.0 ports and connectors, but still is backward compatible with USB 1.1 and 2.0 devices. A USB 3.0 A-Male or B-Male connector or port is usually blue. Take a close look at the blue and black USB ports shown in Figure 1-4 in Chapter 1.

FIREWIRE (IEEE 1394) CONNECTIONS

USB and FireWire competed as a solution for fast I/O connections for a few years, but USB clearly won that contest, and now FireWire is hardly used in new devices. FireWire standards are managed by the 1394 Trade Association (*www.1394ta.org*). The official name

Basic Principles for Supporting Devices

of these standards is IEEE 1394, and other names used are FireWire (first used by Apple) and i.LINK (first used by Sony). The most common name used today is FireWire. Here are the key facts you need to know about FireWire:

- FireWire uses serial transmissions, and Firewire devices are hot-swappable.
- **FireWire 800** (1394b) allows for up to 63 FireWire devices to be daisy chained together. FireWire 400 (1394a) allows for up to 16 daisy-chained devices.
- **FireWire 400** (1394a) supports two types of connectors and cables: a 4-pin connector that does not provide voltage to a device and a 6-pin connector that does. Figure 6-10 shows a cable that plugs into a 6-pin FireWire port to provide a 4-pin connector for a FireWire device.

> **Notes** IEEE 1394a ports with six pins are the most common FireWire ports on motherboards.

FireWire Ports

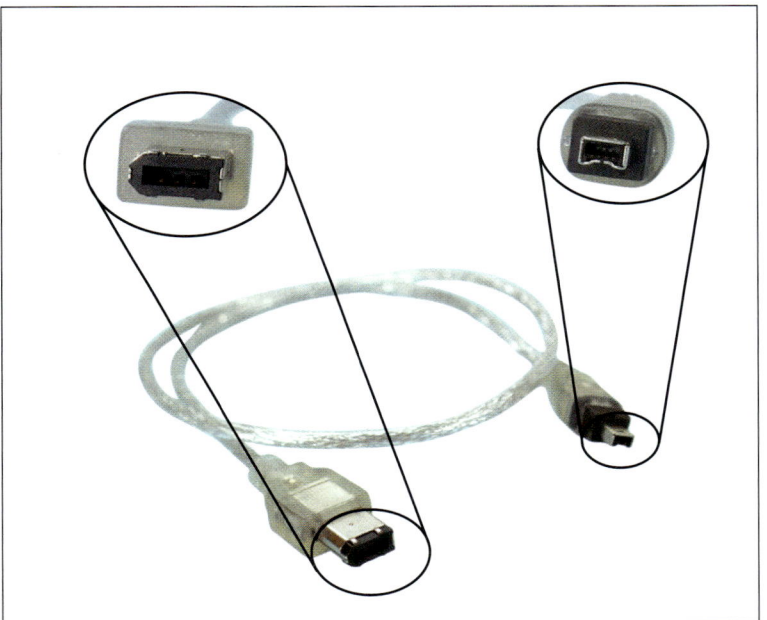

© Cengage Learning 2014

Figure 6-10 IEEE 1394a cable provides a smaller 4-pin and larger 6-pin connectors

- FireWire 800 (1394b) uses a 9-pin rectangular connector. Figure 6-11 shows a FireWire 800 adapter card that provides three 1394 ports: two 1394b 9-pin ports and one 1394a 6-pin port. The power cable connected to the card plugs into a 4-pin Molex power cable from the power supply to provide extra power to the card. The latest 1394 standard is 1394c, which allows FireWire 800 to use a standard network port and network cable.

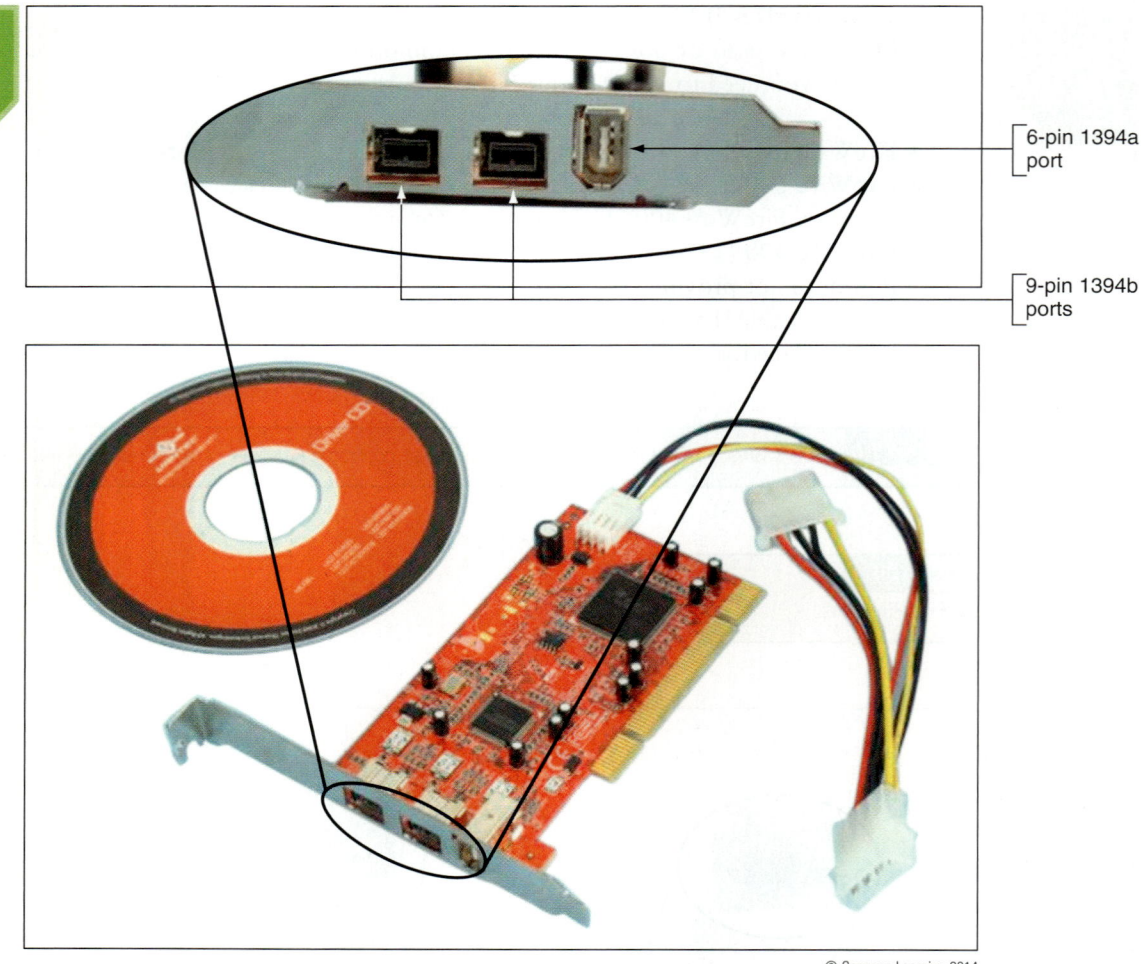

Figure 6-11 This 1394 adapter card supports both 1394a and 1394b and uses a 32-bit PCI slot

INFRARED CONNECTIONS

Infrared (IR) is an outdated wireless technology that has been mostly replaced by Bluetooth to connect personal devices. IR requires an unobstructed "line of sight" between the transmitter and receiver. Today, the most common use of Infrared is by remote controls. Figure 6-12 shows a remote control that can be used with multimedia applications installed on a notebook computer. The remote communicates with the notebook by way of an IR transceiver connected to a USB port. To use the remote, the device drivers that came bundled with the device are installed and then the IR transceiver is connected to the USB port.

> **Notes** Infrared standards are defined by the Infrared Data Association (IrDA). Its web site is *www.irda.org*.

A+ 220-801
1.5, 1.7, 1.10, 1.12

Figure 6-12 This remote control is an infrared device that uses an IR transceiver connected to a notebook by way of a USB port

Hands-on Project 6-1 Update Device Drivers

Using your home or lab computer connected to the Internet, go to Device Manager and attempt to update the drivers on all your installed devices. Which devices did Windows find newer drivers for?

Hands-on Project 6-2 Research Video Port Adapters

Research the web and find devices that can be used as solutions to these problems. Print or save the web page showing the device and price:

1. Find an adapter that allows you to connect a DisplayPort on a computer to a VGA monitor using a VGA cable.
2. Find an adapter that allows you to connect a Mini DisplayPort on your laptop to a DVI-D port on your monitor. Also find a cable that will work with the adapter.
3. Find an adapter that will allow you to connect a DVI-I port on your desktop to a VGA monitor, using a VGA cable.

Now that you know about the ports and wireless connections used for external devices, let's see how to install them.

INSTALLING I/O PERIPHERAL DEVICES

**A+
220-801
1.5, 1.7,
1.10,
1.12**

Installing peripheral or external devices is easy to do and usually goes without a hitch. All devices need device drivers or BIOS to control them and to interface with the operating system. Simple input devices, such as the mouse and keyboard, can be controlled by the BIOS or have embedded device drivers built into the OS. For these devices, you don't have to install additional device drivers.

Peripheral devices you might be called on to install include a keyboard, mouse, barcode reader, biometric device (for example, a fingerprint reader), touch screen, scanner, microphone, game pad, joystick, digitizer, digital camera, web cam, camcorder, MDI-enabled devices, speakers, and display devices. These installations are similar, so learning to do one will help you do another. Here are the general procedures to install any peripheral device:

1. **Read the manufacturer's directions.** I know you don't want to hear that again, but when you follow these directions, the installation goes better. If you later have a problem with the installation and you ask the manufacturer for help, being able to say you followed their directions exactly as stated goes a long way toward getting more enthusiastic help and cooperation.

2. **Make sure the drivers provided with the device are written for the OS you are using.** Recall that 64-bit drivers are required for a 64-bit operating system, and 32-bit drivers are required for a 32-bit OS. You can sometimes use drivers written for Vista in Windows 7, but for best results, use drivers written for the OS installed. You can download the drivers you need from the manufacturer's web site.

3. **Make sure the motherboard port you are using is enabled.** Most likely it is enabled, but if the device is not recognized when you plug it in, go into BIOS setup and make sure the port is enabled. In addition, BIOS setup might offer the option to configure a USB port to use SuperSpeed (USB 3.0), Hi-Speed USB (USB 2.0), or original USB (USB 1.1). Figure 6-13 shows the BIOS setup screen for one system where you can enable or disable onboard devices. In addition, if you are having problems with a motherboard port, don't forget to update the motherboard drivers that control the port.

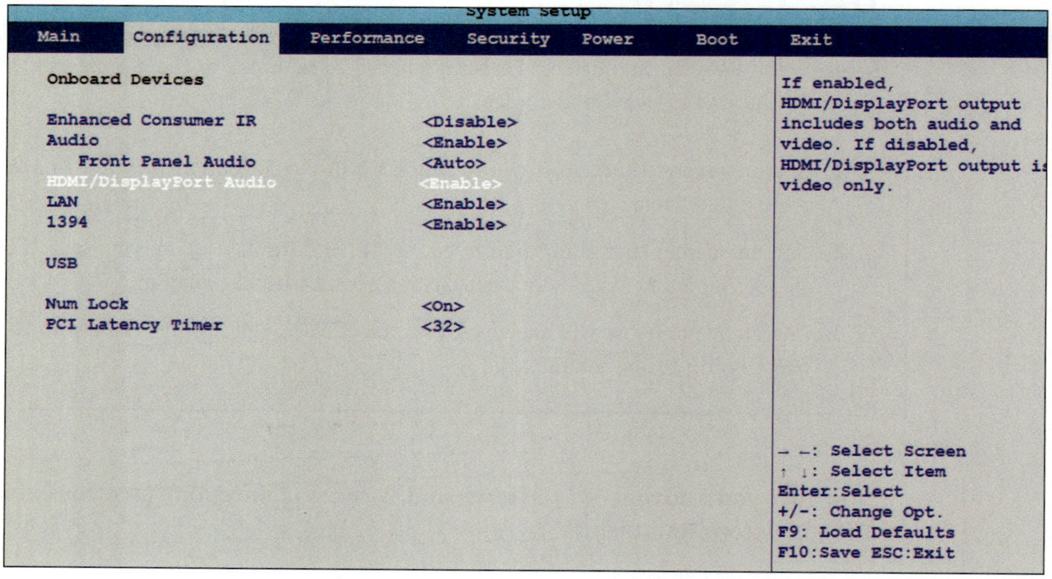

Figure 6-13 Use BIOS setup to enable or disable onboard ports

Source: Intel

Installing I/O Peripheral Devices

A+ 220-801
1.5, 1.7, 1.10, 1.12

4. **Install drivers or plug in the device.** Some devices, such as a USB printer, require that you plug in the device before installing the drivers, and some devices require you to install the drivers before plugging in the device. For some devices, it doesn't matter which is installed first. Carefully read and follow the device documentation. For example, the documentation for one digital camera says that if you install the camera before installing the driver, the drivers will not install properly.

If you plug in the device first, The Found New Hardware wizard appears and steps you through the installation of drivers (see Figure 6-14).

Source: Microsoft Windows 7

Figure 6-14 The Found New Hardware wizard begins installing a new device

If you need to install the drivers first, run the setup program on CD or DVD. If you downloaded drivers from the web, double-click the driver file and follow the directions on-screen. It might be necessary to restart the system after the installation. After the drivers are installed, plug the device into the port. The device should immediately be recognized by Windows. If you have problems using the device, turn to Device Manager or the Windows 7 Action Center for help.

5. **Install the application software to use the device.** For example, a FireWire camcorder is likely to come bundled with video-editing software. Run the software to use the device.

Now let's look at some key features and installation concerns for several peripheral devices.

MOUSE OR KEYBOARD

Plug a mouse or keyboard into a USB or older PS/2 port and Windows should immediately recognize it and install generic drivers. For keyboards with special features such as the one shown in Figure 6-15, you need to install the drivers that came with the keyboard before you can use these features.

You can later use Device Manager to uninstall, disable, or enable most devices. However, USB devices are managed differently. To uninstall a USB device such as the USB keyboard shown in Figure 6-15, in Control Panel, click **Uninstall a program**. In the Programs and Features window (see Figure 6-16), select the device and click **Change**. Follow the directions on-screen to uninstall the device.

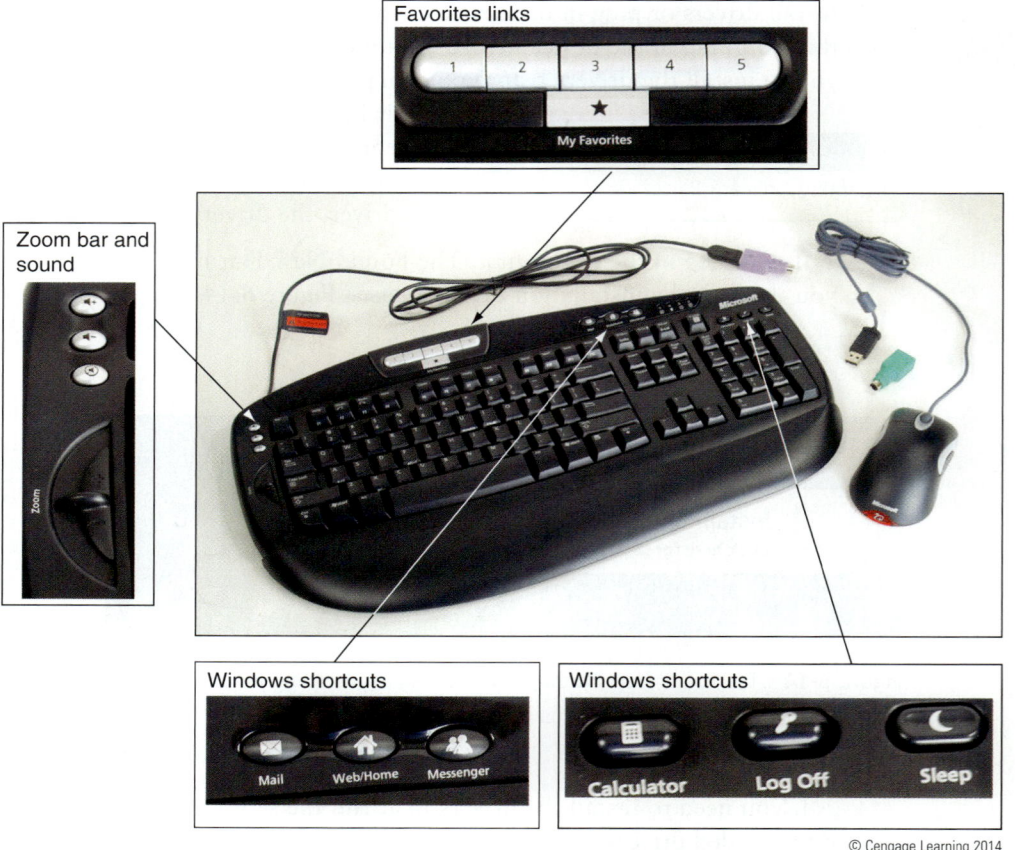

Figure 6-15 The mouse and keyboard require drivers to use the extra buttons and zoom bar

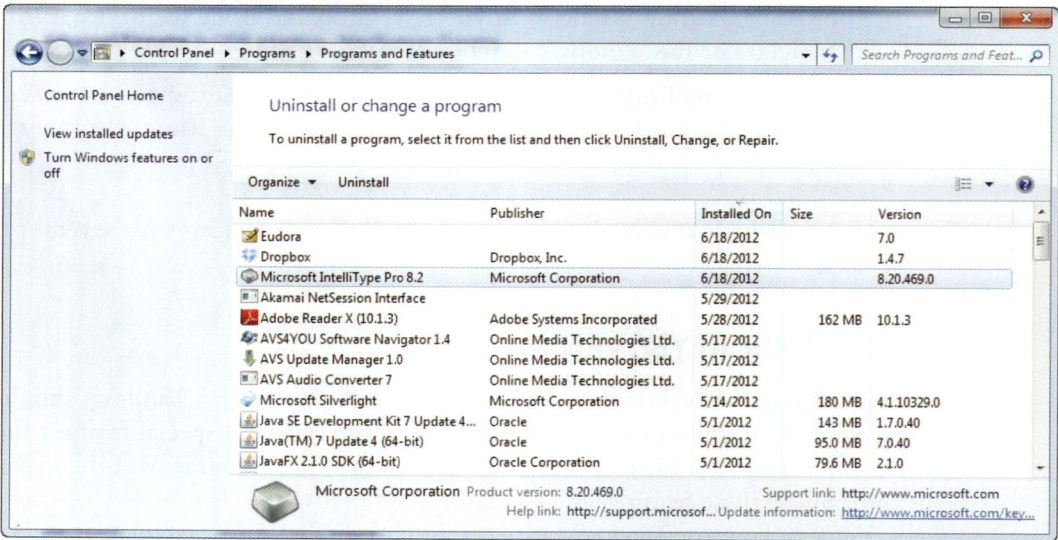

Figure 6-16 USB devices are listed as installed programs

BARCODE READERS

A **barcode reader** is used to scan barcodes on products at the point of sale (POS) or when taking inventory. The reader might use a wireless connection, a serial port, a USB port, or a keyboard port. If the reader uses a keyboard port, most likely it has a splitter (called a keyboard wedge) on it for the keyboard to use, and data read by the barcode reader is input into the system as though it were typed using the keyboard. Figure 6-17 shows a barcode reader by Intermec that is a laser scanner and uses Bluetooth to connect wirelessly to the PC.

Courtesy of Intermec Technologies

Figure 6-17 Handheld or hands-free barcode scanner by Intermec Technologies

BIOMETRIC DEVICES

A **biometric device** is an input device that inputs biological data about a person, which can be input data to identify a person's fingerprints, handprints, face, voice, eye, and handwritten signature. For example, you can use a fingerprint reader to log on to Windows. These fingerprint readers are not to be considered as the only authentication to control access to sensitive data: for that, use a strong password, which is a password that is not easy to guess.

Fingerprint readers can look like a mouse and use a wireless or USB connection, such as the one shown in Figure 6-18, or they can be embedded on a keyboard, flash drive, or laptop case. Most fingerprint readers that are not embedded in other devices use a USB connection. As with other USB devices, read the documentation to know if you should install the drivers first or the device first.

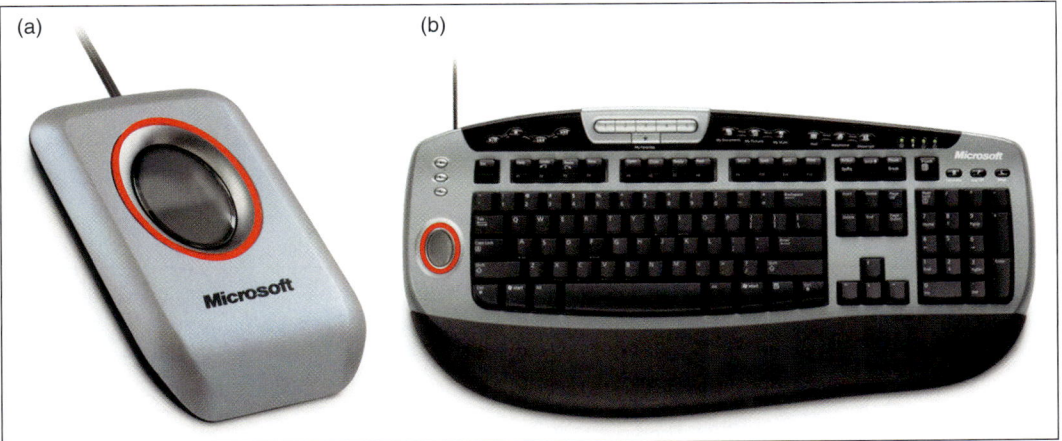

Courtesy of Microsoft

Figure 6-18 Fingerprint readers can (a) look like a mouse, but smaller, or (b) be embedded on a keyboard

DIGITAL CAMERAS AND CAMCORDERS

A+ 220-801
1.5, 1.7, 1.10, 1.12

A digital camera or camcorder can hold images and videos both in embedded memory that cannot be removed or exchanged and in removable flash memory cards. Both of these types of memory retain data without a battery. Here are two ways to transfer images from your camera or camcorder to the PC:

▲ *Connect the camera or camcorder to the PC using a cable.* Using embedded memory or flash memory cards, you can connect the device to your computer using a USB or FireWire port and cable. To connect the device to the PC, you might need to first install the software and then connect the device, or you might need to connect the device and then install the software. Read the camera or camcorder documentation to find out which order to use. After the device and software are installed, the software displays a menu to download images or video to your PC.

▲ *Install the memory card in the PC.* If images or video are stored on a flash memory card installed in your device, you can remove the card and then insert it in a flash memory card slot on your computer. Most laptop computers have one or more of these slots (see Figure 6-19).

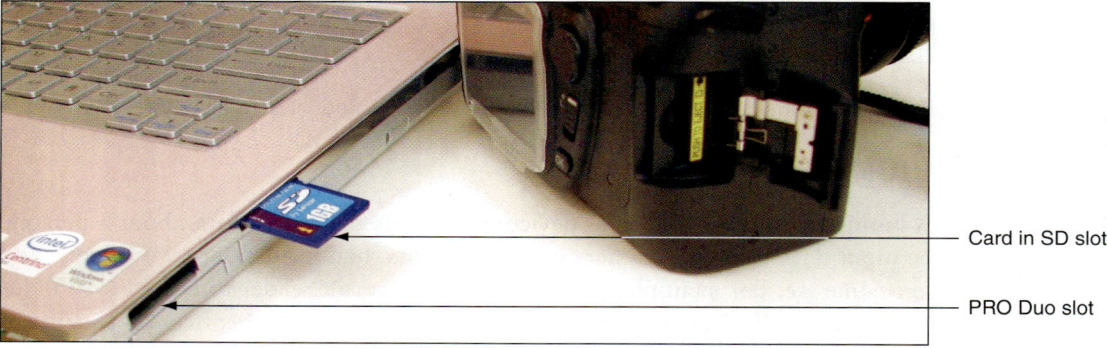

Figure 6-19 This laptop has two flash memory card slots

If your computer doesn't have this slot, or the slot is not compatible with the type of card you are using, you have two choices:

- Perhaps you can purchase an adapter so that your smaller memory card will fit into a larger memory slot. Figure 6-20 shows examples of these adapters.
- You can install a USB memory card reader that provides a memory card slot to fit your card. Figure 6-21 shows one reader that connects to a PC using a USB port.

When the memory card is recognized by Windows, it is assigned a drive letter and you can see it listed in Windows Explorer. Use Windows Explorer to copy, move, and delete files from the card.

> **Notes** It's interesting to know that TWAIN (Technology Without An Interesting Name) is a standard format used by scanners and digital cameras and other devices for transferring images.

> **A+ Exam Tip** The A+ 220-801 exam expects you to know how to install the software bundled with your digital camera before attaching the camera to your PC.

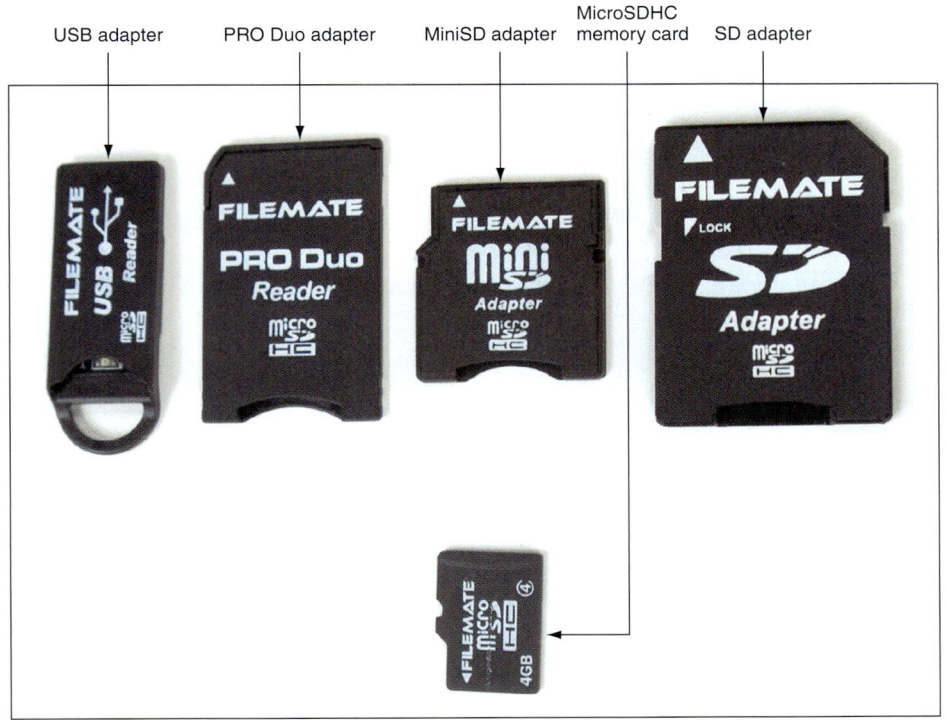

Figure 6-20 MicroSDHC card with four adapters

Figure 6-21 This Hi-Speed USB card reader/writer by Targus can read CompactFlash I and II, MicroDrive, SDHC, SD, MMC, xD, Memory Stick, PRO Duo, and Mini SD cards

WEBCAMS

A webcam (web camera) is embedded in most laptops and can also be installed as a peripheral device using a USB port or some other port. For example, the webcam shown in Figure 6-22 works well for personal chat sessions and videoconferencing and has a built-in microphone. First, use the setup CD to install the software and then plug in the webcam to a USB port.

A webcam comes with a built-in microphone. You can use this microphone or use the microphone port on the computer. Most software allows you to select these input devices. For example, Figure 6-23 shows the Tools Options box for Camtasia Recorder by TechSmith (*www.techsmith.com*).

© iStockphoto/Eric Ferfuson

Figure 6-22 This personal web camera clips to the top of your notebook and has a built-in microphone

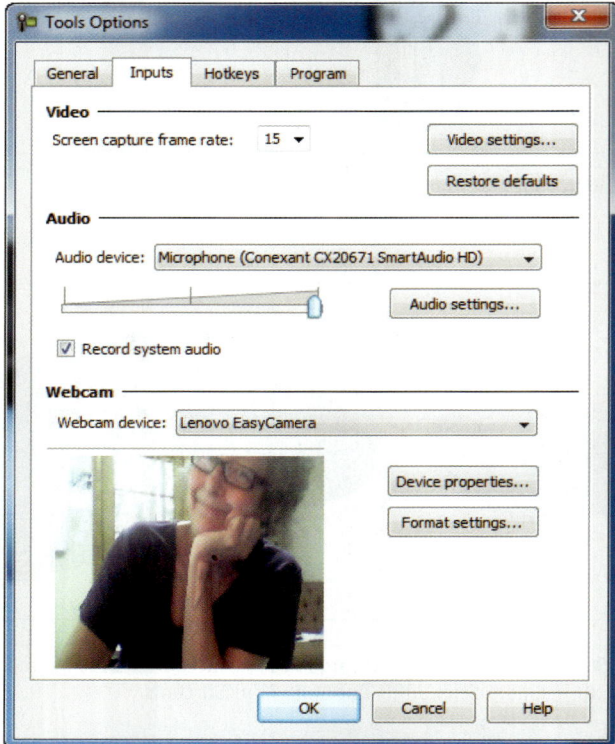

Source: Camtasia Recorder by TechSmith

Figure 6-23 The Camtasia Recorder application allows you to change the input devices used for video and sound

GRAPHICS TABLETS

Another input device is a **graphics tablet**, also called a **digitizing tablet** or **digitizer**, that is used to hand draw and is likely to connect by a USB port (see Figure 6-24). It comes with a **stylus** that works like a pencil on the tablet. The graphics tablet and stylus can be a replacement to a mouse or touch pad on a laptop, and some graphics tablets come with a mouse. Graphics tablets are popular with graphic artists and others who use desktop publishing applications.

Install the graphics tablet the same way you do other USB devices. Additional software might be bundled with the device to enhance its functions, such as inputting handwritten signatures into Microsoft Word documents.

Figure 6-24 A graphics tablet and stylus are used to digitize a hand drawing

MIDI DEVICES

MIDI (musical instrument digital interface), pronounced "middy," is a set of standards that are used to represent music in digital form. Using the MIDI format, each individual note played by each individual instrument is digitally stored. MIDI standards are used to connect electronic music equipment, such as musical keyboards and mixers, or to connect this equipment to a PC for input, output, and editing. Most sound cards can play MIDI files, and most electronic instruments have MIDI ports.

A MIDI port is a 5-pin DIN port that looks like a PS/2 keyboard port, only larger. Figure 6-25 shows MIDI ports on electronic drums. A MIDI port is either an input port

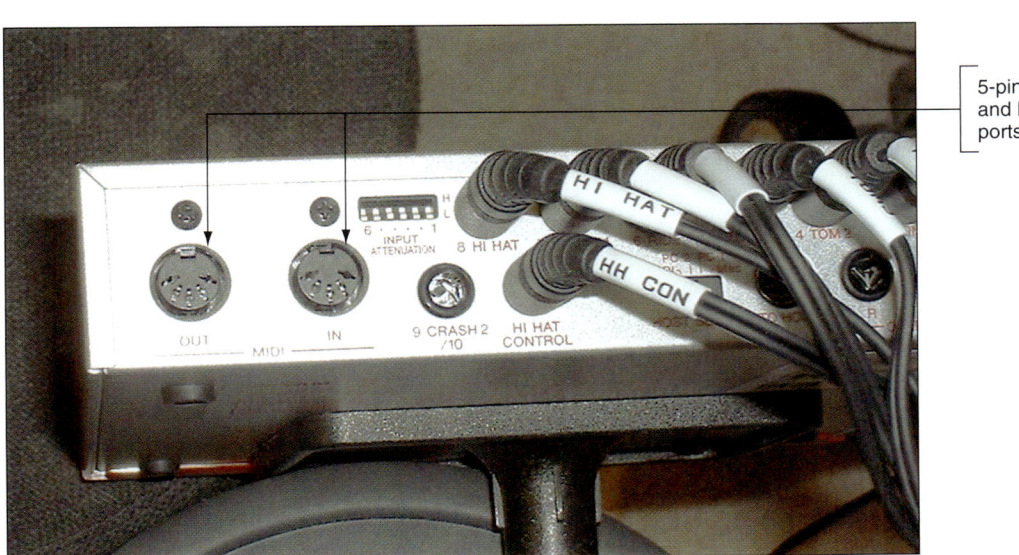

Figure 6-25 MIDI ports on an electronic drum set

or an output port, but not both. Normally, you would connect the MIDI output port to a mixer, but you can also use it to connect to a PC.

Here are ways to connect a musical instrument to a PC using the MIDI standards:

▲ *MIDI to MIDI:* A few sound cards provide MIDI ports. Use two MIDI cables to connect output jack to input jack and to connect input jack to output jack.
▲ *MIDI to USB:* If your PC does not have MIDI ports, you can use a MIDI-to-USB cable like the one in Figure 6-26. The two MIDI connectors on the cable are for input and output.
▲ *USB to USB:* Newer instruments have a USB port to interface with a PC using MIDI data transmissions.
▲ *USB to MIDI:* A USB port on an instrument can also connect to MIDI ports on a computer sound card.

> **A+ Exam Tip** The A+ 220-801 exam expects you to know how to install and configure MIDI devices.

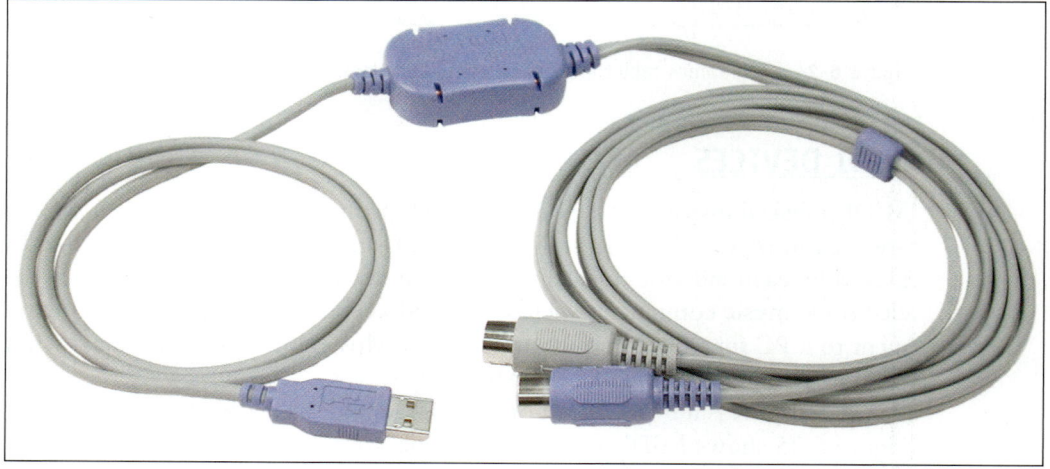

Figure 6-26 MIDI-to-USB cable lets you connect an electronic musical instrument to your computer

To mix and edit music using MIDI on your PC, you'll need MIDI editing software such as JAMMER Pro by SoundTrek (*www.soundtrek.com*). Before connecting the instrument to your PC, install the software that you intend to use to manage the music. Then, connect the instrument.

TOUCH SCREENS

A **touch screen** is an input device that uses a monitor or LCD panel as the backdrop for input options. In other words, the touch screen is a grid that senses taps, finger pinches, and slides and sends these events to the computer by way of a USB port or other type of connection. Some laptops have built-in touch screens, and you can also install a touch screen on top of a monitor screen as an add-on device. As an add-on device, the touch screen has its own AC adapter to power it. Some monitors for desktop systems have built-in touch screen capability.

For desktop monitors, clamp the touch screen over the monitor. For most installations, you install the drivers before you connect the touch screen to the computer by way of a USB port. After you install the drivers and the touch screen, you must use management software that came bundled with the device to decide how much of the monitor screen is taken up by the touch screen and to calibrate the touch screen. Later, if the monitor resolution is changed, the touch screen must be recalibrated.

KVM SWITCHES

A **KVM (Keyboard, Video, and Mouse) switch** allows you to use one keyboard, monitor, and mouse for multiple computers. A KVM switch can be useful in a server room or testing lab where you use more than one computer and want to keep desk space clear of multiple keyboards, mice, and monitors or you simply want to lower the cost of peripherals. Figure 6-27 shows a KVM switch that can connect a keyboard, monitor, mouse, microphone, and speakers to two computers. The device uses USB ports for the keyboard and mouse. Figure 6-28 shows a KVM switch that can connect up to four computers using VGA ports for the monitor and PS/2 ports for the keyboard and mouse connections. The setup for the four computers is shown in Figure 6-29.

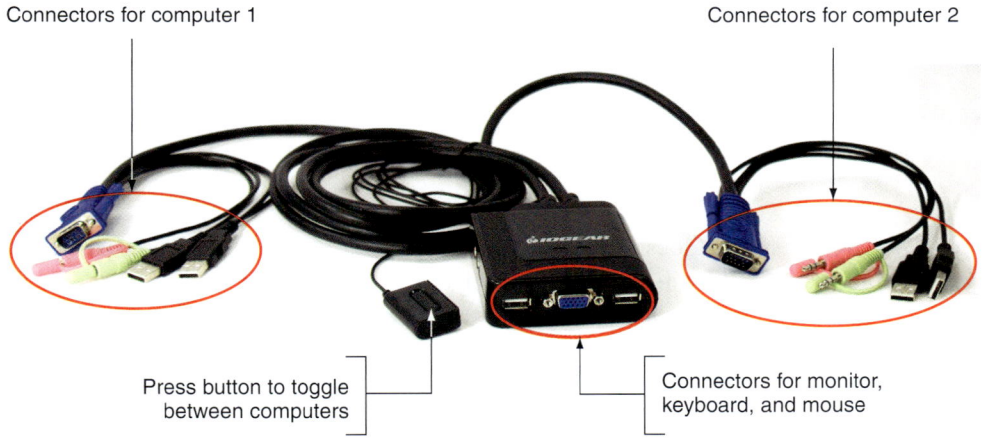

Figure 6-27 This KVM switch connects two computers to a keyboard, mouse, monitor, microphone, and speakers and uses USB for the keyboard and mouse

Figure 6-28 This KVM switch supports up to four computers, uses PS/2 ports for the keyboard and mouse, and provides microphone and speaker ports for sound

A+ 220-801
1.5, 1.7,
1.10,
1.12

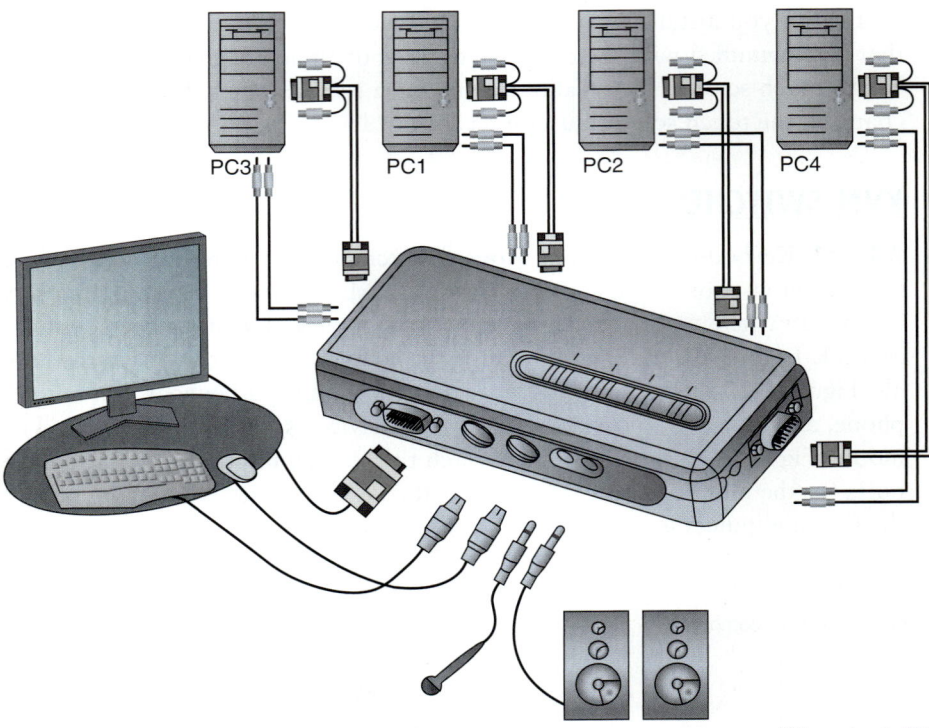

Figure 6-29 Hardware configuration for a four-port KVM switch that also supports audio

A KVM switch does not require that you install device drivers to use it. Just plug in the cables from each computer to the device. Also plug in the one monitor, mouse, keyboard, and possibly a microphone and speakers to the device. Switch between computers by using a hot key on the keyboard, buttons on the top of the KVM switch, or a wired remote such as the one shown in Figure 6-27.

INSTALLING AND CONFIGURING ADAPTER CARDS

A+ 220-801
1.4, 1.5,
1.7, 1.10,
1.12

In this part of the chapter, you will learn to install and configure adapter cards. These cards include a video card, sound card, storage controller card, serial and parallel port card, FireWire card, USB card, storage card, TV tuner card, and video capture card. The purpose of adding an adapter card to a system is to have available the external ports or internal connectors the card provides.

Regardless of the type of card you are installing, when preparing to install an adapter card, be sure to verify and do the following:

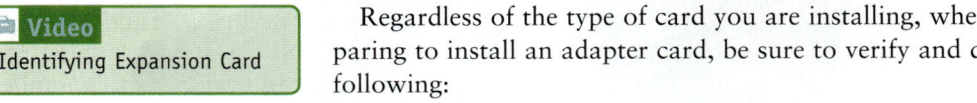
Video — Identifying Expansion Card

▲ *Verify the card fits an empty expansion slot.* Recall from Chapter 3 that there are several AGP, PCI, and PCI Express standards. Use the details in Chapter 3 to make sure the card will fit the slot. To help with airflow, try to leave an empty slot between cards. Especially try to leave an empty slot beside the video card, which puts off a lot of heat.

▲ *Verify the device drivers for your OS are available.* Check the card documentation and make sure you have the drivers for your OS. For example, you need to install 64-bit Windows 7 drivers in a 64-bit installation of Windows 7. It might be possible to download drivers for your OS from the web site of the card manufacturer.

A+ 220-801
1.4, 1.5, 1.7, 1.10, 1.12

- *Back up important data that is not already backed up.* Before you open the computer case, be sure to back up important data on the hard drive.
- *Know your starting point.* Know what works and doesn't work on the system. Can you connect to the network and the Internet, print, and use other installed adapter cards without errors?

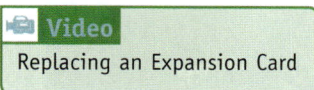
Video
Replacing an Expansion Card

Here are the general directions to install an adapter card. They apply to any type of card.

1. Read the documentation that came with the card. For most cards, you install the card first and then the drivers, but some adapter card installations might not work this way.

2. If you are installing a card to replace an onboard port, access BIOS setup and disable the port.

3. Wear a ground bracelet as you work to protect the card and the system against ESD. Shut down the system, unplug power cords and cables, and press the power button to drain the power. Remove the computer case cover.

4. Locate the slot you plan to use and remove the faceplate cover from the slot if one is installed. Sometimes a faceplate punches or snaps out, and sometimes you have to remove a faceplate screw to remove the faceplate. Remove the screw in the top of the expansion slot. Save the screw; you'll need it later.

5. Remove the card from its antistatic bag and insert it into the expansion slot. Be careful to push the card straight down into the slot, without rocking the card from side to side. Rocking it from side to side can widen the expansion slot, making it difficult to keep a good contact. If you have a problem getting the card into the slot, resist the temptation to push the front or rear of the card into the slot first. You should feel a slight snap as the card drops into the slot.

Recall from Chapter 2 that AGP and PCIe × 16 slots use a retention mechanism in the slot to help stabilize a heavy card (see Figure 6-30). For these slots, you might have to use one finger to push the stabilizer to the side as you push the card into the slot. Alternately, the card might snap into the slot and then the retention mechanism snaps into position. Figure 6-31 shows a PCIe video card installed in a PCIe x16 slot.

Figure 6-30 A white retention mechanism on a PCIe x16 slot pops into place to help stabilize a heavy video card

Figure 6-31 A PCIe video card installed in a PCIe x16 slot

6. Insert the screw that anchors the card to the top of the slot (see Figure 6-32). Be sure to use this screw. If it's not present, the card can creep out of the slot over time.

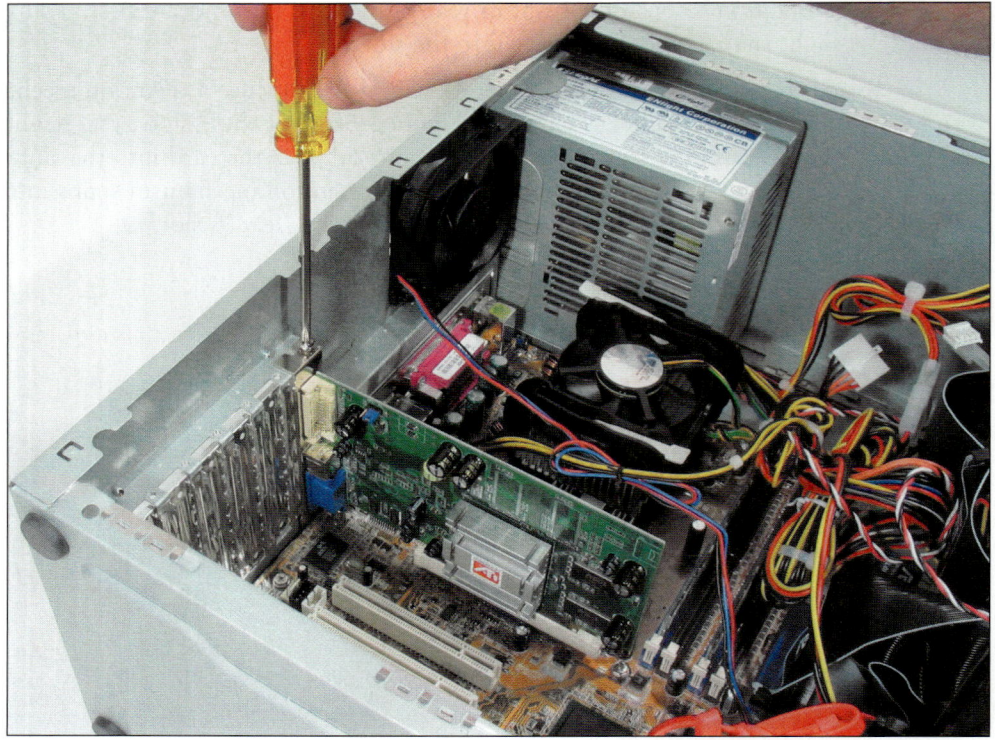

Figure 6-32 Secure the card to the case with a single screw

Installing and Configuring Adapter Cards | 263

**A+
220-801
1.4, 1.5,
1.7, 1.10,
1.12**

7. Connect any power cords or data cables the card might use. For example, a video card might have a 6-pin or 8-pin PCIe power connector for a power cord from the power supply to the card (see Figure 6-33). (If the power supply does not have the right connector, you can buy an inexpensive adapter to convert a 4-pin Molex connector to a PCIe connector.) In another example, look at Figure 6-11 shown earlier in the chapter. This FireWire card requires a power connection using a 4-pin Molex power cable from the power supply.

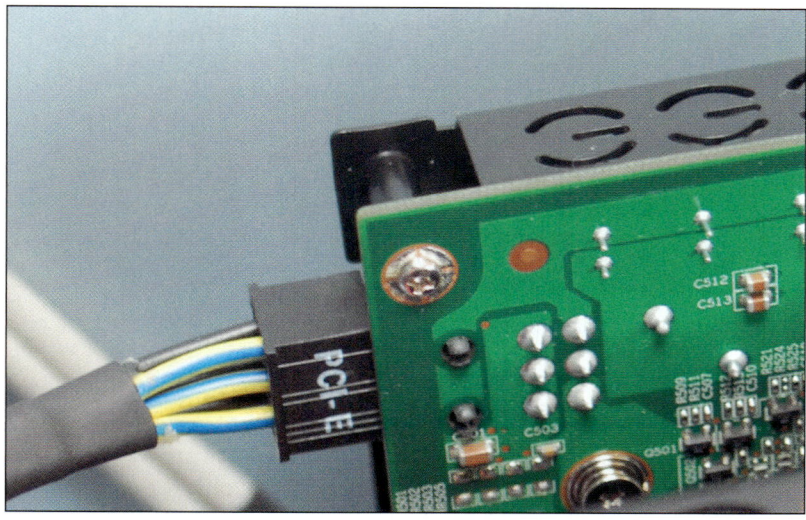

Source: Microsoft Windows 7

Figure 6-33 Connect a power cord to the PCIe power connector on the card

8. Make a quick check of all connections and cables, and then replace the case cover. (If you want, you can leave the case cover off until you've tested the card, in case it doesn't work and you need to reseat it.) Plug up the external power cable and essential peripherals.

9. Start the system. When Windows starts, it should detect a new hardware device is present and attempt to automatically install the drivers. As the drivers are installed, a message might appear above the taskbar (refer back to Figure 6-14). You can cancel the wizard and manually install the drivers.

10. Insert the CD that came bundled with the card and launch the setup program on the CD. The card documentation will tell you the name of the program (examples are Setup.exe and Autorun.exe). Figure 6-34 shows the opening menu for one setup program for a video card. Click **Install Video Drivers** and follow the on-screen instructions to install the drivers. If you are using downloaded driver files, double-click the file to begin the installation and follow the directions on-screen.

> **Notes** All 64-bit drivers must be certified by Microsoft to work in Windows. However, some 32-bit drivers might not be. During the driver installation, if you see a message that says 32-bit drivers have not been certified, go ahead and give permission to install the drivers if you obtained them from the manufacturer or another reliable source.

264 | **CHAPTER 6** Supporting I/O and Storage Devices

A+
220-801
1.4, 1.5,
1.7, 1.10,
1.12

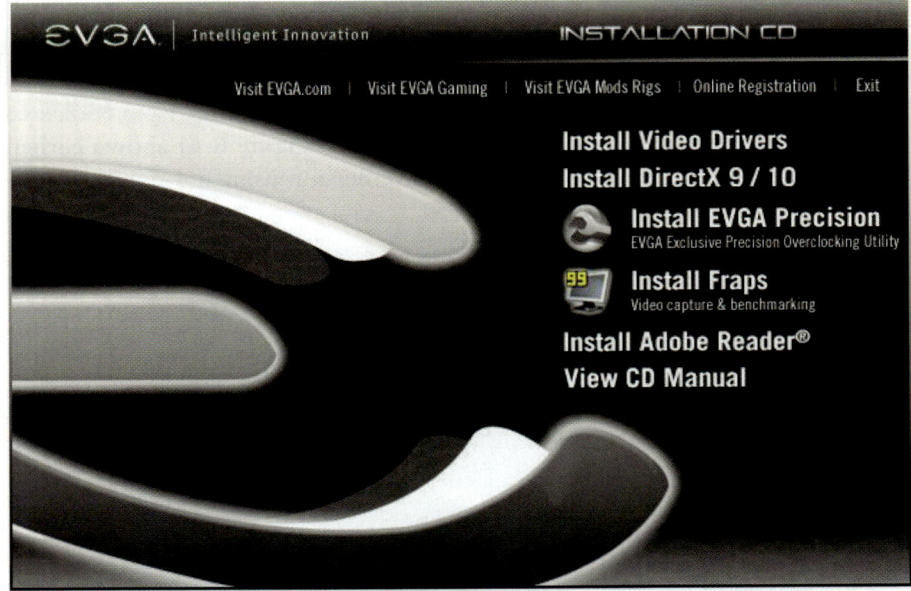

Figure 6-34 Opening menu to install video drivers

11. After the drivers are installed, you might be asked to restart the system. Then you can configure the card or use it with application software. If you have problems with the installation, turn to Device Manager and look for errors reported about the device. The card might not be properly seated in the slot.

> **Notes** Some motherboards provide extra ports that can be installed in faceplate openings off the back of the case. For example, Figure 6-35 shows a module that has a game port and two USB ports. To install the module, remove a faceplate and install the module in its place. Then connect the cables from the module to the appropriate connectors on the motherboard.

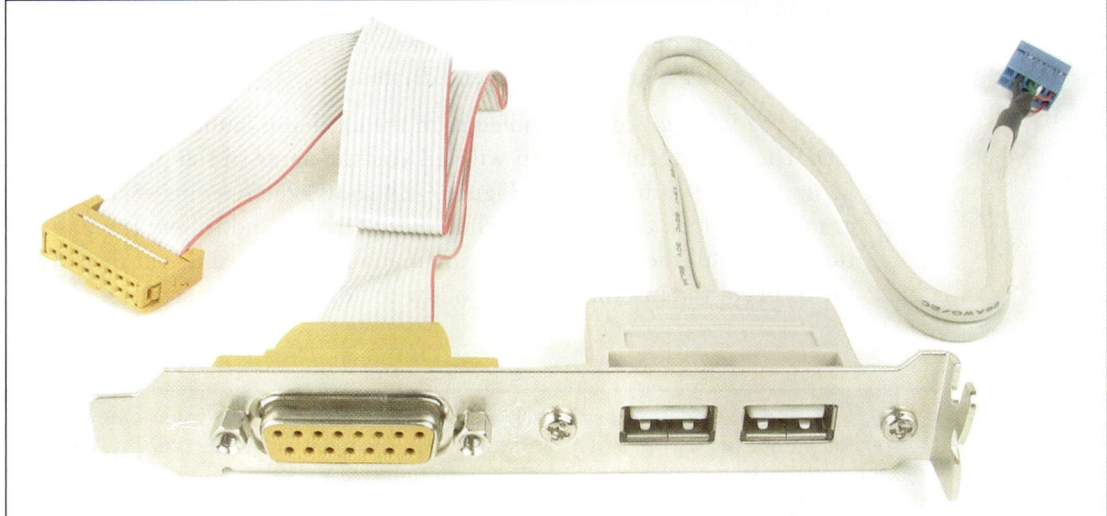

Figure 6-35 This I/O module provides two USB ports and one game port

Installing and Configuring Adapter Cards

A+ 220-801 1.4, 1.5, 1.7, 1.10, 1.12

Video
Installing a Video Card

When you install a video card, here is a list of things that can go wrong and what to do about them:

1. *When you first power up the system, you hear a whining sound.* This is caused by the card not getting enough power. Make sure a 6-pin or 8-pin power cord is connected to the card if it has this connector. The power supply might be inadequate.

2. *When you first start up the system, you see nothing but a black screen.* Most likely this is caused by the onboard video port not being disabled in BIOS setup. Disable the port.

3. *When you first start up the system, you hear a series of beeps.* BIOS cannot detect a video card. Make sure the card is securely seated. The video slot or video card might be bad.

4. *Error messages about video appear when Windows starts.* This can be caused by a conflict in onboard video and the video card. Try disabling onboard video in Device Manager.

5. *Games crash or lock up.* Try updating drivers for the motherboard, the video card, and the sound card. Also install the latest version of DirectX. (You learn about DirectX later in the chapter.) Then try uninstalling the game and installing it again. Then download all patches for the game.

Now let's turn our attention to a little information about three types of cards you might be called on to install. As with any adapter card you install, be sure to get familiar with the user guide before you start the installation so that you know the card's hardware and software requirements and what peripheral devices it supports.

SOUND CARDS AND ONBOARD SOUND

A **sound card** (an expansion card with sound ports) or onboard sound (sound ports embedded on a motherboard) can play and record sound, and save it in a file. Figure 6-36 shows a sound card by Creative (*us.creative.com*). This Sound Blaster card uses a PCIe x1 slot and supports up to eight surround sound version 7.1 speakers. The color-coded

Courtesy of Creative Technology Ltd.

Figure 6-36 Sound Blaster X-Fi Titanium sound card by Creative uses a PCIe x1 slot

speaker ports are for these speakers: front left and right, front center, rear left and right, subwoofer, and two additional rear speakers. The two S/PDIF (Sony/Philips Digital Interconnect Format) ports are used to connect to external sound equipment such as a CD or DVD player.

> **Notes** If you are using a single speaker or two speakers with a single sound cable, connect the cable to the lime green sound port on the motherboard, which is usually the middle port.

TV TUNER AND VIDEO CAPTURE CARDS

A **TV tuner card** can turn your computer into a television. A port on the card receives input from a TV cable and lets you view television on your computer monitor. If the TV signal is analog, the TV tuner card can convert it to digital. A **video capture card** lets you capture this video input and save it to a file on your hard drive. Some cards are a combination TV tuner card and video capture card, making it possible for you to receive television input and save that input to your hard drive (see Figure 6-37). A high-end TV tuner/video capture card might also serve as your video card. Also, some motherboards and notebook computers have onboard TV tuners and TV captures.

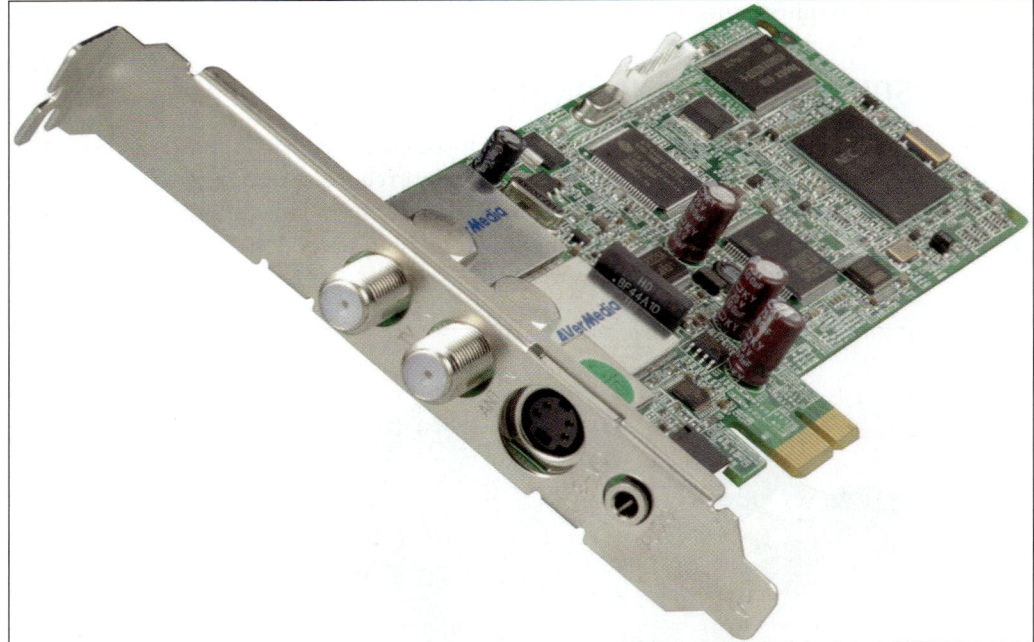

Courtesy of AVerMedia Technologies, Inc. USA.

Figure 6-37 The AVerMedia AVerTV PVR 150 Plus TV tuner and video capture card uses a PCIe x1 slot and works alongside a regular video card

When installing a TV tuner or capture card, most likely you will install the drivers, install the card, and then install the application software that comes bundled with the card. You can then configure and manage the card using the applications.

Hands-on Project 6-3 Install a Device

A+ 220-801 1.4, 1.5, 1.7, 1.10, 1.12

Install a device on a computer. If you are working in a classroom environment, you can simulate an installation by moving a device from one computer to another. Devices that you might consider installing are a video card, webcam, CD drive, or fingerprint reader.

Hands-on Project 6-4 Uninstall Devices Not Present

Device Manager shows only the devices that are currently present. If a device is no longer present, you cannot see the device listed in Device Manager in order to uninstall its drivers. To solve this problem, you can use an environmental variable that causes Device Manager to display devices no longer present. (An environmental variable is a name kept by Windows that has been assigned information, such as the path to a program file or a program setting, and is used by Windows and applications.) Do the following to practice these skills:

1. Install a USB flash drive in a system. Verify you can see the drive listed under Disk drives in Device Manager. Remove the flash drive from the system. Verify the drive is no longer listed in Device Manager even when you click **Show hidden devices** in the View menu of Device Manager.

2. Open the System window and click **Advanced system settings**. On the Advanced tab of the System Properties box, click **Environment Variables**. Add a new user variable named **devmgr_show_nonpresent_devices** and give the variable a value of **1** (see Figure 6-38). Log off and log back on the system.

3. Return to Device Manager. When you show hidden devices, the USB flash drive is listed. Uninstall its drivers. What other devices showed up in Device Manager that were not shown in Step 1?

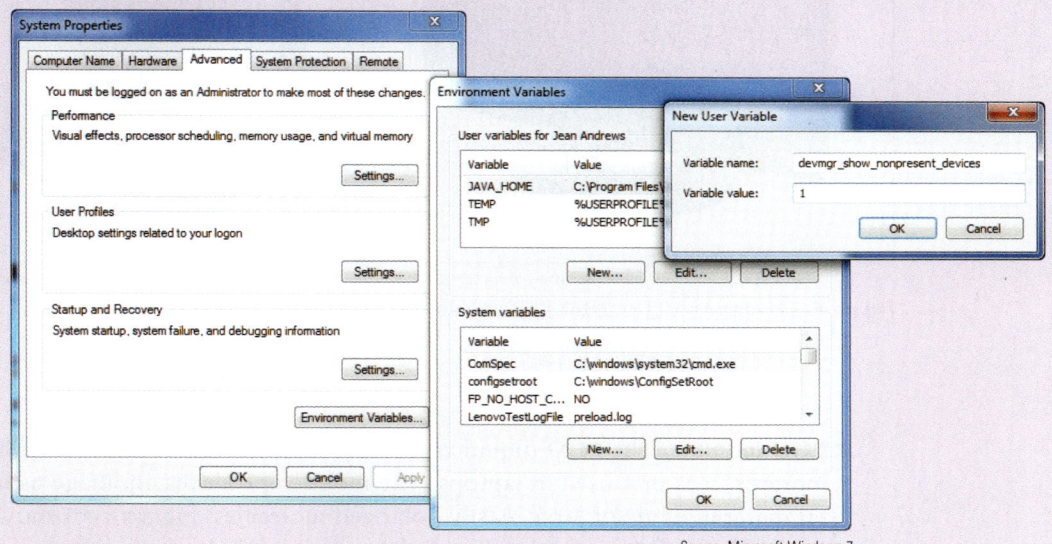

Source: Microsoft Windows 7

Figure 6-38 Set an environmental variable to cause Device Manager to display nonpresent devices

SUPPORTING THE VIDEO SUBSYSTEM

A+ 220-801 1.4, 1.5, 1.7, 1.10, 1.12

The primary output device of a computer is the monitor. The two necessary components for video output are the monitor and the video card (also called the video adapter and graphics adapter) or a video port on the motherboard. In this part of the chapter, you learn about monitors, video cards, the video connectors they use, and how to support the video subsystem.

MONITOR TECHNOLOGIES AND FEATURES

The most popular type of monitor for laptop and desktop systems is an LCD flat-screen monitor (see Figure 6-39), but you have other choices as well. Here is a list and description of each type of monitor:

▲ **CRT monitor.** The **CRT (cathode-ray tube) monitor** (see Figure 6-39) was first used in television sets, takes up a lot of desk space, and is largely obsolete. One reason to still use them is for children. The surface of a LCD monitor can easily be damaged, but CRT monitor surfaces can handle children touching them. CRT monitors use mercury, and, therefore, you must be careful when disposing of one to make sure the environment is not affected.

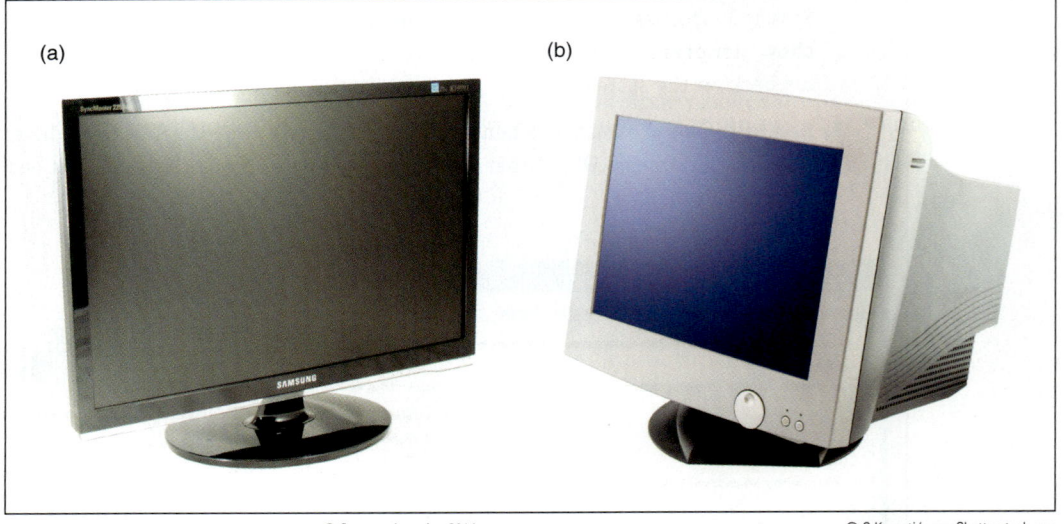

Figure 6-39 (a) An LCD monitor, (b) an older CRT monitor

▲ **LCD monitor.** The **LCD (liquid crystal display) monitor**, also called a **flat-panel monitor**, was first used in laptops. The monitor produces an image using a liquid crystal material made of large, easily polarized molecules. Figure 6-40 shows the layers of the LCD panel that together create the image. At the center of the layers is the liquid crystal material. Next to it is the layer responsible for providing color to the image. These two layers are sandwiched between two grids of electrodes forming columns and rows. Each intersection of a row electrode and a column electrode forms one **pixel** on the LCD panel. Software can address each pixel to create an image.

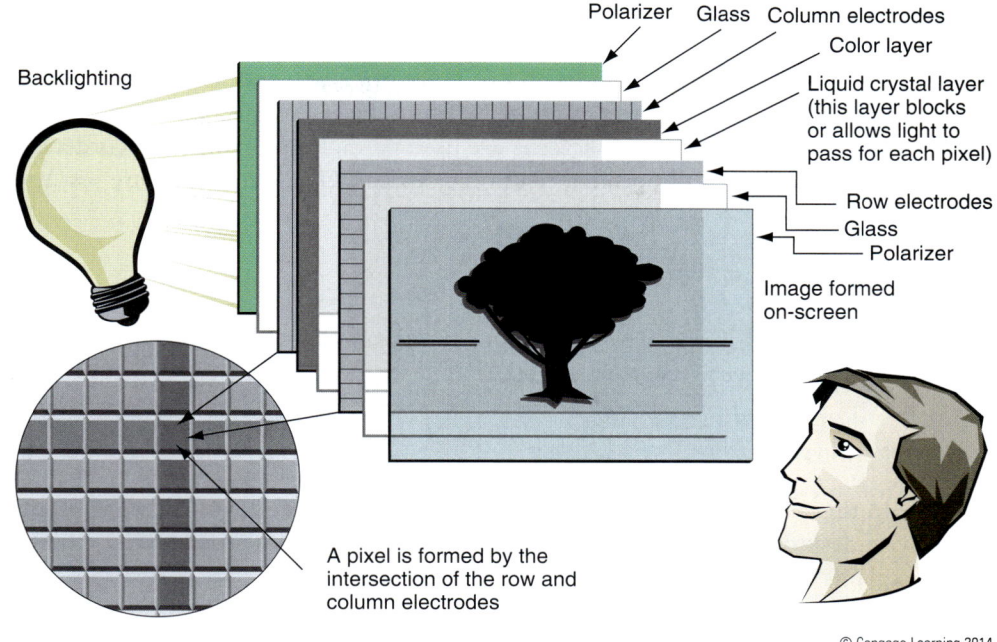

Figure 6-40 Layers of an LCD panel

Backlighting is used to light the LCD panel. The trend for most monitor manufacturers is to use LED backlighting, which provides a better range and accuracy of color and uses less power than earlier technologies. LED (Light-Emitting Diode) technology also uses less mercury, and is, therefore, kinder to the environment when an LCD monitor is disposed of. When you see a monitor advertised as an LED monitor, know the monitor is an LCD monitor that uses LED backlighting.

◂ Plasma monitor. A plasma monitor provides high contrast with better color than LCD monitors. They work by discharging xenon and neon plasma on flat glass, and don't contain mercury. Plasma monitors are expensive and heavy and are generally available only in large commercial sizes.

◂ Projector. A projector (see Figure 6-41) is used to shine a light that projects a transparent image onto a large screen and is often used in classrooms or with other large groups. Several types of technologies are used by projectors, including LCD. A projector is often installed on a computer as a dual monitor, which you learn how to do later in the chapter.

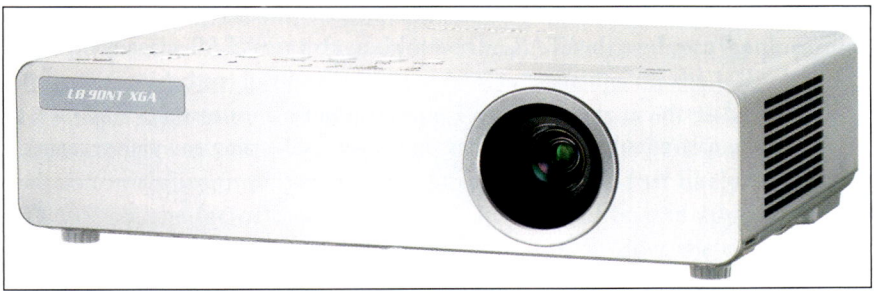

Figure 6-41 Portable XGA projector by Panasonic

▲ **OLED monitor.** An **OLED (Organic Light-emitting Diode) monitor** uses a thin LED layer or film between two grids of electrodes and does not use backlighting. It does not emit as much light as an LCD monitor does, and, therefore, can produce deeper blacks, provide better contrast, work in darker rooms, and use less power than can an LCD monitor. OLED screens are used by digital cameras, camcorders, mobile devices, and other small portable electronic devices. OLED monitors are just now appearing for desktop systems.

> **A+ Exam Tip** The A+220-801 exam expects you to know about these monitor types and technologies: CRT, LCD, LED, plasma, projector, and OLED.

In this chapter, we focus on LCD monitors—by far the most popular monitors used with desktop systems. Figure 6-42 shows an ad for one high-end LCD monitor. Table 6-3 explains the features mentioned in the ad.

Source: tigerdirect.com

Figure 6-42 An ad for a monitor lists cryptic monitor features

> **A+ Exam Tip** The A+ 220-801 exam expects you to know about these monitor features: refresh rate, resolution, native resolution, brightness in lumens, and analog and digital connectors used.

Supporting the Video Subsystem

A+ 220-801
1.4, 1.5, 1.7, 1.10, 1.12

Monitor Characteristic	Description
Screen size	Diagonal length of the screen surface in inches.
Refresh rate	The refresh rate, also called the response time, is the time it takes for a monitor to build one screen, measured in ms (milliseconds) or Hz(hertz). The lower the better. A monitor with a 12-ms response time can build 83 frames per second, and a 16-ms monitor can build 63 frames per second. The ad in Figure 6-42 shows a refresh rate of 6 ms.
Pixel pitch	A pixel is a spot or dot on the screen that can be addressed by software. The pixel pitch is the distance between adjacent pixels on the screen. An example of a pixel pitch is .283mm. The smaller the number, the better.
Resolution	The resolution is the number of spots or pixels on a screen that can be addressed by software. Values can range from 640 × 480 up to 1920 × 1200 for high-end monitors. Popular resolutions are 1920 × 1080 and 1366 × 768.
Native resolution	The native resolution is the number of pixels built into the LCD monitor. Using the native resolution usually gives the highest-quality image.
Contrast ratio	The contrast between true black and true white on the screen. The higher the contrast ratio the better. 1000:1 is better than 700:1. An advertised dynamic contrast ratio is much higher than the contrast ratio, but not a true measurement of contrast. Dynamic contrast adjusts the backlighting to give the effect of an overall brighter or darker image. For example, in Figure 6-42, the contrast ratio is 1000:1, and the dynamic ratio is 20,000,000:1. When comparing quality of monitors, pay attention to the contrast ratio, more so than the dynamic ratio.
Viewing angle	The angle of view when a monitor becomes difficult to see. A viewing angle of 170 degrees is better than 140 degrees.
Backlighting or brightness	Brightness is measured in cd/m^2 (candela per square meter), which is the same as $lumens/m^2$ (lumens per square meter). In addition, the best LED backlighting for viewing photography is class IPS (in-plane switching), which provides the most accurate color.
Connectors	Options for connectors are VGA, DVI-I, DVI-D, HDMI, DisplayPort, and Thunderbolt. Some monitors offer more than one connector (see Figure 6-43). These and other connectors used by video cards and monitors are discussed later in the chapter.
Other features	LCD monitors can also provide an antiglare surface, tilt screens, microphone input, speakers, USB ports, adjustable stands, and perhaps even a port for your iPod. Some monitors are also touch screens, so they can be used with a stylus or finger touch.

© Cengage Learning 2014

Table 6-3 Important features of a monitor

> **Caution** If you spend many hours in front of a computer, you may strain your eyes. To protect your eyes from strain, look away from the monitor into the distance every few minutes. Use a good monitor with a high refresh rate or response time. The lower rates that cause monitor flicker can tire and damage your eyes. When you first install a monitor, set the rate at the highest value the monitor can support.

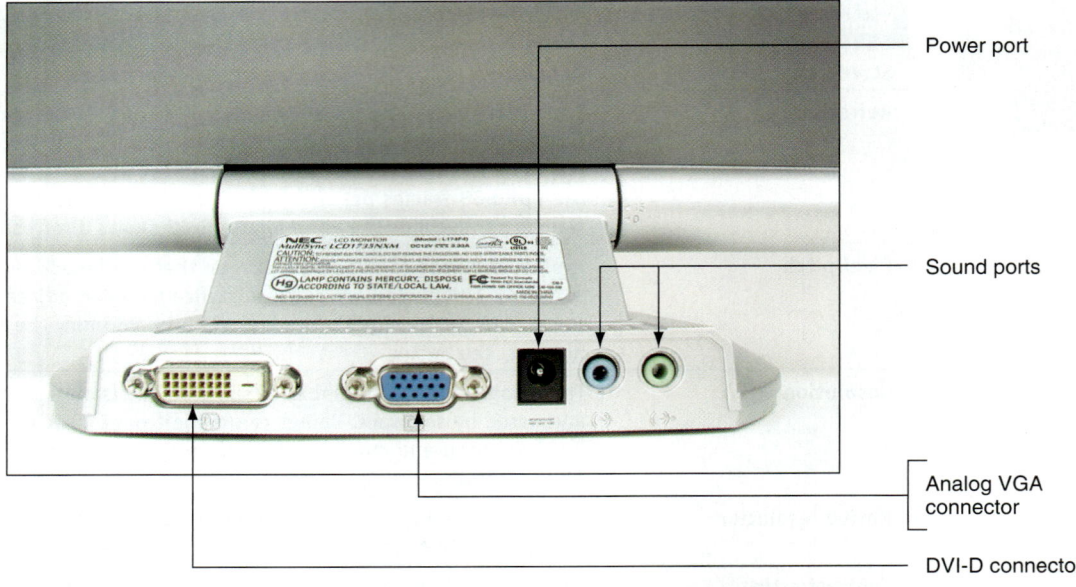

Figure 6-43 The rear of this LCD monitor shows digital and analog video ports to accommodate a video cable with either a 15-pin analog VGA connector or a digital DVI connector

VIDEO CARDS AND CONNECTORS

Video cards (see Figure 6-44) are sometimes called graphics adapters, graphics cards, or display cards. Most motherboards sold today have one or more video ports integrated into the motherboard. If you are buying a motherboard with a video port, make sure that you can disable the video port on the motherboard if it gives you trouble. You can then install a video card and use its video port rather than the port on the motherboard. Recall from Chapter 3 that a video card can use an AGP, PCI, or PCI Express slot on the motherboard. The fastest slot to use is a PCIe x16 slot.

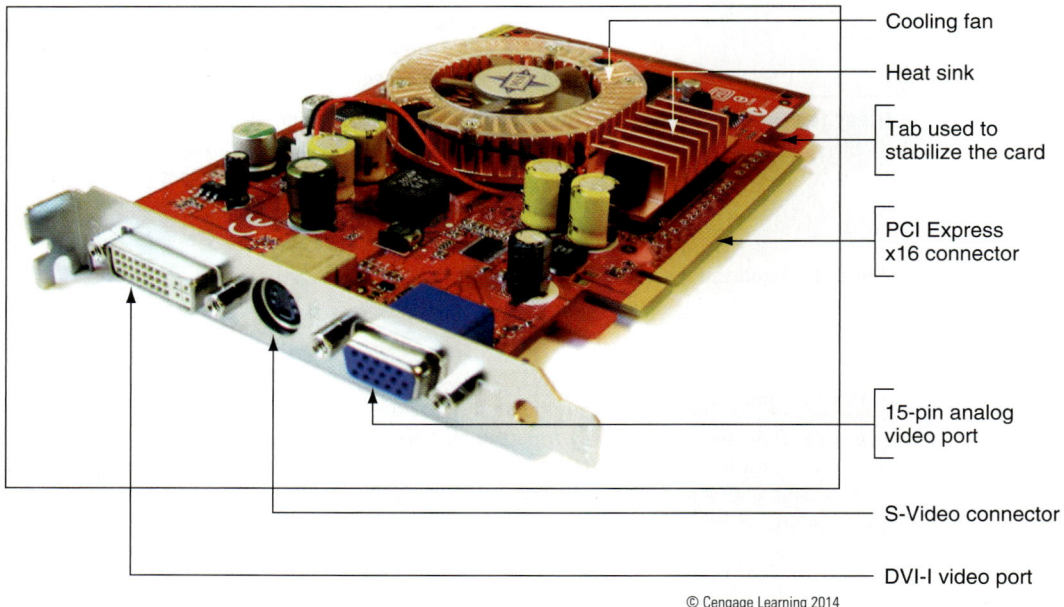

Figure 6-44 The PCX 5750 graphics card by MSI Computer Corporation uses the PCI Express x16 local bus

Supporting the Video Subsystem

A+
220-801
1.4, 1.5,
1.7, 1.10,
1.12

Recall from Chapter 1 that types of video ports include VGA, S-Video, DVI, DisplayPort, and HDMI connectors, which you can see in Table 1-1 in Chapter 1. In addition to these ports, you also need to know about a composite video, miniHDMI, miniDin-6, DVI-I, DVI-D, and DVI-A ports. All these ports are described here:

- *VGA.* The 15-pin VGA port is the standard analog video port and transmits three signals of red, green, and blue (RGB). A VGA port is sometimes called a DB-15 port.
- *DVI ports.* DVI ports were designed to replace VGA, and variations of DVI can transmit analog and/or digital data. The five DVI standards for pinouts are shown in Figure 6-45. Three DVI connectors are shown in Figure 6-46. The DVI standards specify the maximum length for DVI cables is 5 meters, although some video cards produce a strong enough signal to allow for longer DVI cables.

DVI-D (Digital Only)	DVI-I (Digital or Analog)	DVI-A (Analog Only)
DVI-D Single Link	DVI-I Single Link	DVI-A
DVI-D Dual Link	DVI-I Dual Link	

Figure 6-45 Five pinout arrangements for DVI ports and connectors

Figure 6-46 Three types of DVI connectors: (left) DVI-I, (middle) DVI-D, and (right) DVI-A

Here are the variations of DVI:

- *DVI-D.* The DVI-D port only transmits digital data. Using an adapter to convert a VGA cable to the port won't work. You can see a DVI-D port in Figure 6-47a.
- *DVI-I.* The DVI-I port (see Figure 6-47b) supports both analog and digital signals. If a computer has this type of port, you can use a digital-to-analog adapter to connect an older analog monitor to the port using a VGA cable (see Figure 6-48). If a video card has a DVI port, most likely it will be the DVI-I port (the one with the four extra holes) so that you can use an adapter to convert the port to a VGA port.

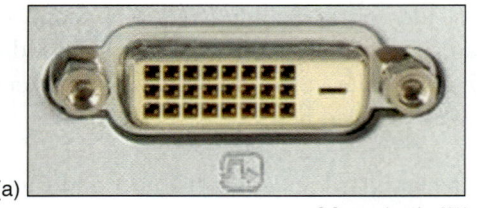

Figure 6-47 Two types of DVI ports: (a) DVI-D, (b) DVI-I

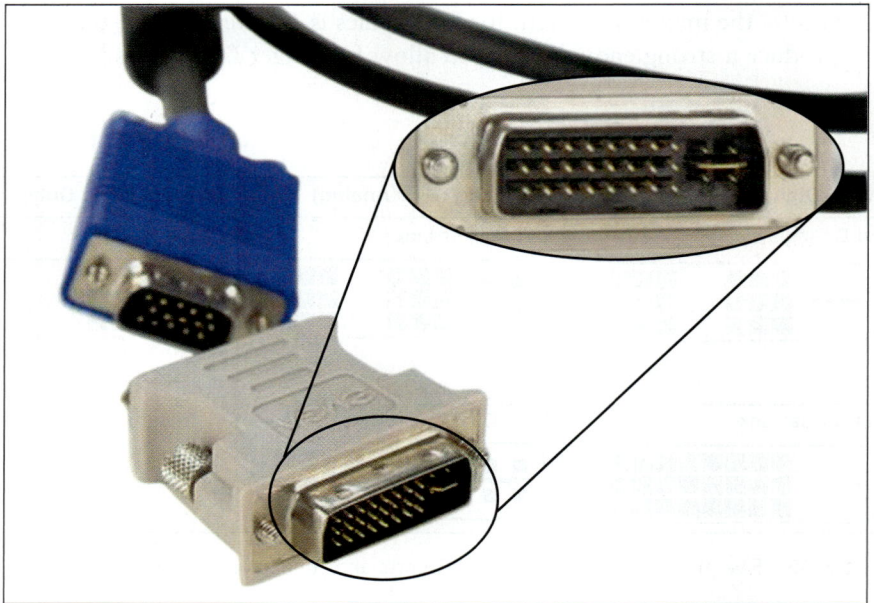

Figure 6-48 Digital to analog video port converter using DVI-I connector with extra four pins

- *DVI-A.* The DVI-A port only transmits analog data. You don't see them very often.
- *Single Link or Dual Link.* DVI digital transmissions can be Single Link or Dual Link. Dual Link transmissions double the power of the signal and can support higher screen resolutions (up to 2560 × 1600) than Single Link transmissions (up to 1920 × 1200). Most DVI-D or DVI-I ports are Dual Link.
- ▲ *Composite video.* Using a composite video port, also called an RGB port, the red, green, and blue (RGB) are mixed together in the same signal. This is the method used by television, and can be used by a video card that is designed to send output to a TV. A composite port is round and has only a single pin in the center of the port. Figure 6-49 shows a laptop that has a composite video input port so that you can use the laptop as your display for a game box. Composite video does not produce as sharp an image as VGA video or S-Video.
- ▲ *S-Video (Super-Video) ports.* An S-Video port is a 4-pin or 7-pin round port used by some televisions and video equipment. An S-Video cable is shown in Figure 6-50. A few older video cameras use a 6-pin variation of S-Video. The connector is called a MiniDin-6 connector and looks like a PS/2 connector used by a keyboard or mouse. (In general, a Din connector is always round with multiple pins in the connector.)

Supporting the Video Subsystem | 275

A+
220-801
1.4, 1.5,
1.7, 1.10,
1.12

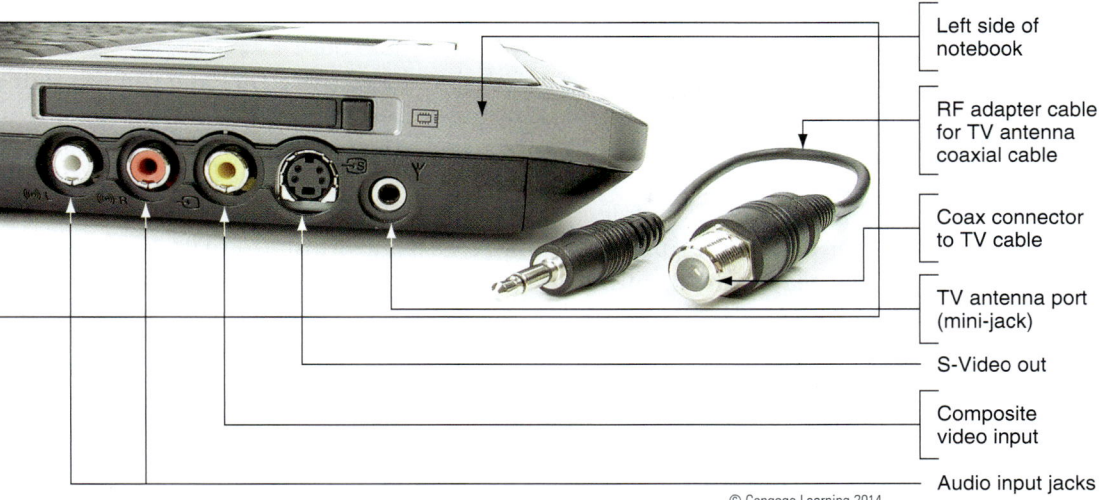

Figure 6-49 This laptop designed for multimedia applications has an embedded TV tuner and can also receive audio and video input from game boxes

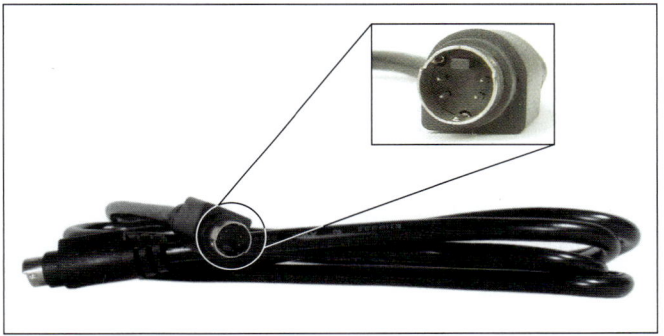

Figure 6-50 An S-Video cable used to connect a video card to an S-Video port on a television

▲ *Component video.* Whereas composite video has the red, green, and blue mixed in the same signal, component video has been split into different components and carried as separate signals. Figure 6-51 shows the connectors on one component video and audio

Figure 6-51 Component video and audio cable

cable. Three lines carry video (red, blue, and green), and the yellow and white connectors are used for audio (audio in and audio out).

- ▲ *DisplayPort.* DisplayPort was designed to replace DVI and can transmit digital (not analog) video and audio data. It uses data packet transmissions similar to those of Ethernet, USB, and PCI Express, and is expected to ultimately replace VGA, DVI, and HDMI on desktop and laptop computers. Besides the regular DisplayPort used on video cards and desktop computers, laptops might use the smaller Mini DisplayPort. Figure 6-52 shows a DisplayPort to Mini Display Port cable. Some DisplayPort controllers allow you to use a DisplayPort-to-HDMI adapter so the port can be used with an HDMI connection. Maximum length for DisplayPort cables is 15 meters.

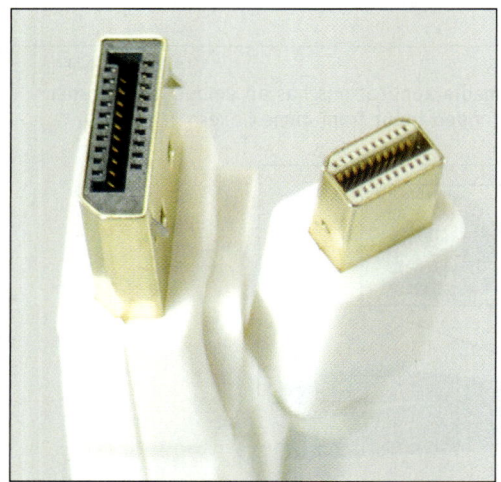

Figure 6-52 DisplayPort to Mini DisplayPort cable

BIOS setup can be used to manage onboard DisplayPort and HDMI ports. For example, look at Figure 6-13 shown earlier in the chapter, where you can enable or disable the audio transmissions of DisplayPort and HDMI ports, and still use these ports for video.

- ▲ *HDMI and HDMI mini connectors.* HDMI transmits both digital video and audio (not analog), and was designed to be used by home theater equipment. The HDMI standards allow for several types of HDMI connectors. The best known, which is used on most computers and televisions, is the Type A 19-pin **HDMI connector**. Small mobile devices can use the smaller Type C 19-pin **HDMI mini connector**, also called the **mini-HDMI connector**. Figure 6-53 shows a cable with both connectors that is useful when connecting some devices like a smartphone to a computer. Figure 6-54 shows an HDMI to DVI-D cable. Because HDMI does not transmit analog data, the connector works only on DVI-D ports, not DVI-I ports. The maximum length of an HDMI cable depends on the quality of the cable; no maximum length has been specified.

A+
220-801
1.4, 1.5,
1.7, 1.10,
1.12

Figure 6-53 HDMI to miniHDMI cable © Cengage Learning 2014

Courtesy of Belkin Corporation

Figure 6-54 An HDMI to DVI cable can be used to connect a PC that has a DVI port to home theater equipment that uses an HDMI port

> **A+ Exam Tip** The A+ 220-801 exam expects you to know about these video connector types: VGA (DB-15), HDMI, miniHDMI, DisplayPort, S-Video, miniDin-6, composite (RGB), component, DVI-D, DVI-I, and DVI-A connectors.

Now let's see how to configure a monitor or dual monitors connected to a Windows computer.

CHANGING MONITOR SETTINGS

A+
220-802
1.5

Settings that apply to the monitor can be managed by using the monitor buttons and Windows utilities. Using the monitor buttons, you can adjust the horizontal and vertical position of the screen on the monitor surface and change the brightness and contrast settings. For laptops, the brightness and contrast settings can be changed using function keys on the laptop.

A+ 220-801
1.4, 1.5,
1.7, 1.10,
1.12

A+ 220-802
1.5

APPLYING CONCEPTS | INSTALLING DUAL MONITORS

To increase the size of your Windows desktop, you can install more than one monitor for a single computer. To install dual monitors, you need two video ports on your system, which can come from motherboard video ports, a video card that provides two video ports, or two video cards.

To install a second monitor in a dual-monitor setup using two video cards, follow these steps:

1. Verify that the original video card works properly, determine whether it is PCIe or AGP (on really old computers), and decide whether it is to be the primary monitor.

2. Boot the PC and enter BIOS setup. If BIOS setup has the option to select the order in which video cards are initialized, verify that the currently installed card is configured to initialize first. If it does not initialize first, then, when you install the second card, video might not work at all when you first boot with two cards.

3. Install a second video card in an empty slot. A computer might have a second PCIe slot or an unused PCI slot you can use. (For a really old computer using an AGP slot, most likely you can install the second video card in an empty PCI slot.) Attach the second monitor.

4. Boot the system. Windows recognizes the new hardware and launches the Found New Hardware wizard. You can use the wizard to install the video card drivers or cancel the wizard and install them manually as you learned to do earlier in the chapter.

Here are the steps to configure dual monitors:

1. Connect two monitors to your system. Open **Control Panel**, and in the Appearance and Personalization group, click **Adjust screen resolution**. The Screen Resolution window appears (see Figure 6-55).

2. Notice the two numbered boxes that represent your two monitors. When you click one of these boxes, the drop-down menu changes to show the selected monitor, and the screen resolution and orientation (Landscape, Portrait, Landscape flipped, or Portrait flipped) follow the selected monitor. This lets you customize the settings for each monitor. If necessary, arrange the boxes so that they represent the physical arrangement of your monitors.

> **Notes** In Figure 6-55, if you arrange the two boxes side by side, your extended desktop will extend left or right. If you arrange the two boxes one on top of the other, your extended desktop will extend up and down.

3. Adjust the screen resolution according to your preferences. For the sharpest images, use the native resolution for each monitor. Most often, the native resolution is the highest resolution listed, but this is not always the case. To know for certain the native resolution, see the documentation that came with the monitor.

4. By default, Windows 7 extends your desktop onto the second monitor. However, in the Multiple displays drop-down list, you can select other options, as shown in Figure 6-55. To save the settings, click **Apply**. The second monitor should initialize and show the extended or duplicated desktop.

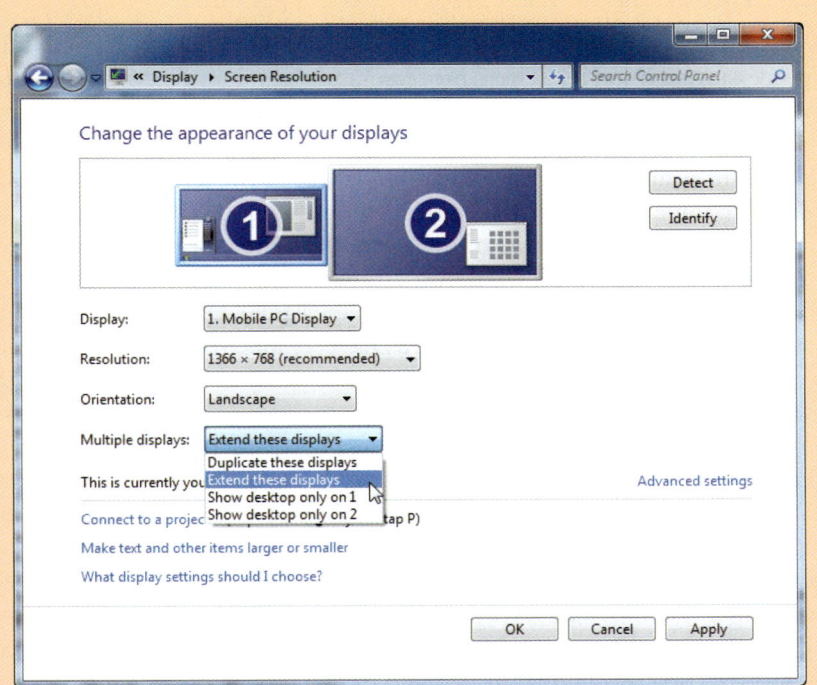

Figure 6-55 Configure each monitor in a dual monitor configuration

5. Close the **Screen Resolution** window. For an extended desktop, open an application and verify that you can use the second monitor by dragging the application window over to the second monitor's desktop.

After you add a second monitor to your system, you can move from one monitor to another simply by moving your mouse over the extended desktop. Switching from one monitor to the other does not require any special keystroke or menu option.

Most notebook computers are designed to be used with projectors and provide a VGA, DisplayPort, or HDMI port for this purpose. To use a projector, plug in the projector to the extra port and then turn it on. For a notebook computer, use a function key to activate the video port and toggle between extending the desktop to the projector, using only the projector, duplicating the screen on the projector, or not using the projector. When giving a presentation, most presenters prefer that they see their presentation duplicated on the LCD screen and the projector.

Notes For group presentations that require a projector, the software used for the presentations is likely to be Microsoft PowerPoint. If you configure your projector as a dual monitor, you can use PowerPoint to display a presentation to your audience on the projector at the same time you are using your LCD display to manage your PowerPoint slides. To do so, for PowerPoint 2007 and 2010, select the **Slide Show** tab. In the Set Up group, click **Set Up Slide Show**. In the Set Up Show box under Multiple monitors, check **Show Presenter View** and click **OK**.

VIDEO MEMORY AND WINDOWS 7/VISTA

Video cards have their own processor called a graphics processing unit (GPU) or visual processing unit (VPU). These processors use graphics RAM installed on the card so that RAM on the motherboard is not tied up with video data. (If a motherboard offers a video port rather than using a video card, the GPU is part of the onboard video controller and is called integrated video. For integrated video, RAM on the motherboard is used for video data, or some video RAM is embedded on the motherboard.)

The more RAM installed on the card, the better the performance. Most video cards used and sold today use DDR2, DDR3, Graphics DDR3 (GDDR3), GDDR4, or GDDR5 memory. Graphics DDR memory is faster than regular DDR memory and does a better job of storing 3D images. Some video cards have as much as 2 GB of graphics memory.

Most Windows 7/Vista editions offer the Aero user interface (also called Aero glass), which has a 3D appearance. The hardware must qualify for Aero glass before Windows can enable it. These requirements include onboard video or a video card that supports DirectX 9 or higher, has at least 128 MB of video memory, and uses the Windows Display Driver Model (WDDM). The Windows Display Driver Model is a Windows component that manages graphics. **DirectX** is a Microsoft software development tool that software developers can use to write multimedia applications such as games, video-editing software, and computer-aided design software. Components of DirectX include DirectDraw, DirectMusic, DirectPlay, and Direct3D. The video firmware on the video card or motherboard chipset can interpret DirectX commands to build 3D images as presented to them by the WDDM. In addition, Windows relies on DirectX and the WDDM to produce the Aero user interface.

If an application, such as a game or desktop publishing app, that relies heavily on graphics is not performing well or giving errors, the problem might be video memory or the version of DirectX the system is using. You can use the **dxdiag.exe** command to display information about hardware and diagnose problems with DirectX. To use the command, click **Start**, type **dxdiag.exe** in the search box, and press **Enter**. The first time you use the command, a message box appears asking if you want to check if your drivers are digitally signed. Then the opening window shown in Figure 6-56 appears. Look for the version of DirectX installed (version 11 in the figure).

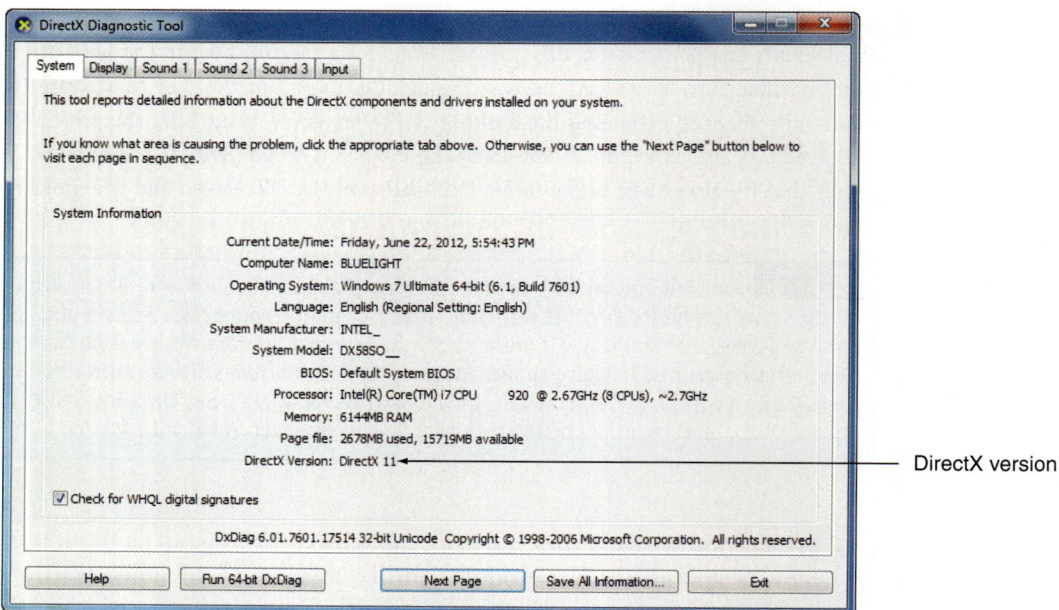

Source: Microsoft Windows 7

Figure 6-56 The DirectX Diagnostic tool reports information about DirectX components

To find out the latest version of DirectX published by Microsoft, go to *www.microsoft.com* and search on "DirectX End-User Runtime Web Installer." The download page in Figure 6-57 appears. If you want to install a new version of DirectX, click **Download** and follow the directions on-screen.

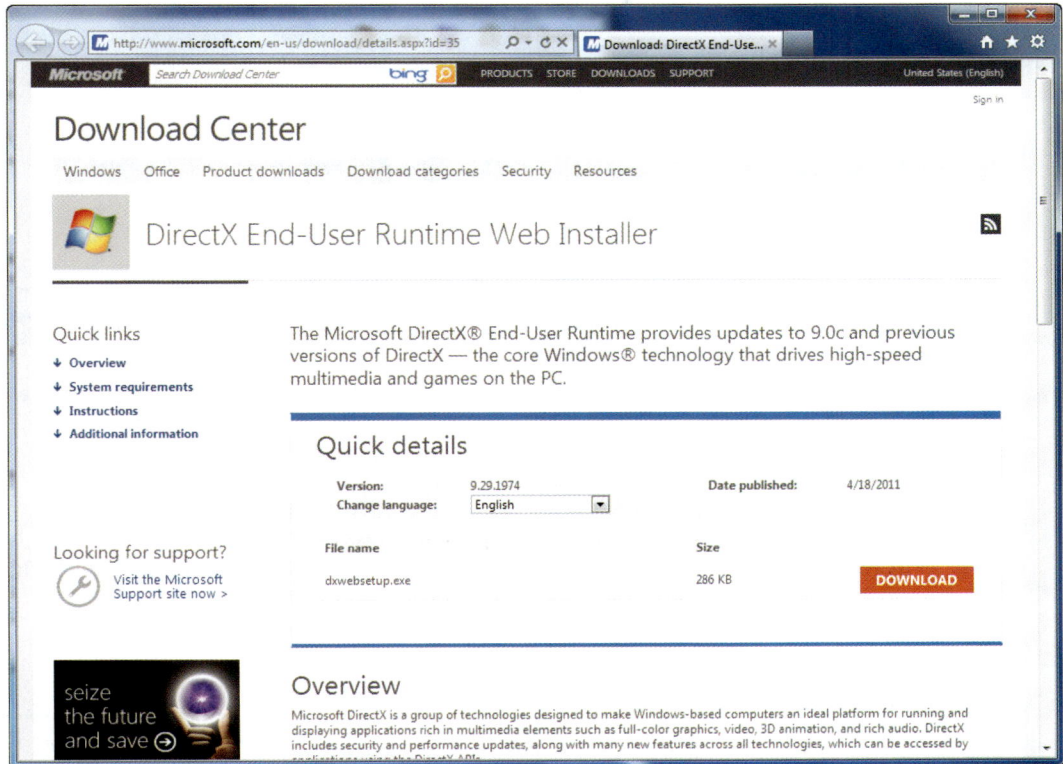

Figure 6-57 Download the latest version of DirectX

Source: Microsoft.com

Video memory available to the graphics processor can be the graphics memory embedded on the video card or on the motherboard, system memory, or a combination of both. To see the video memory available to Windows, click **Adjust Screen Resolution** in the Appearance and Personalization group in Control Panel. In the Screen Resolution window, click **Advanced settings**. The video properties box appears. Figure 6-58 shows two properties boxes for two systems. Figure 6-58a is for a notebook computer, and Figure 6-58b is for a desktop computer that has a video card.

Here is an explanation of the four entries in the dialog box that concern video memory:

▲ Total Available Graphics Memory is total memory that may be available to the video subsystem.
▲ Dedicated Video Memory is found on a video card or embedded on the motherboard. The motherboard in the notebook has 64 MB, and the video card in the desktop system has 512 MB of graphics memory.
▲ System Video Memory is system RAM dedicated to video. No other application or component can use it.
▲ Shared System Memory is system RAM that might be available to video if another application or component is not already using it.

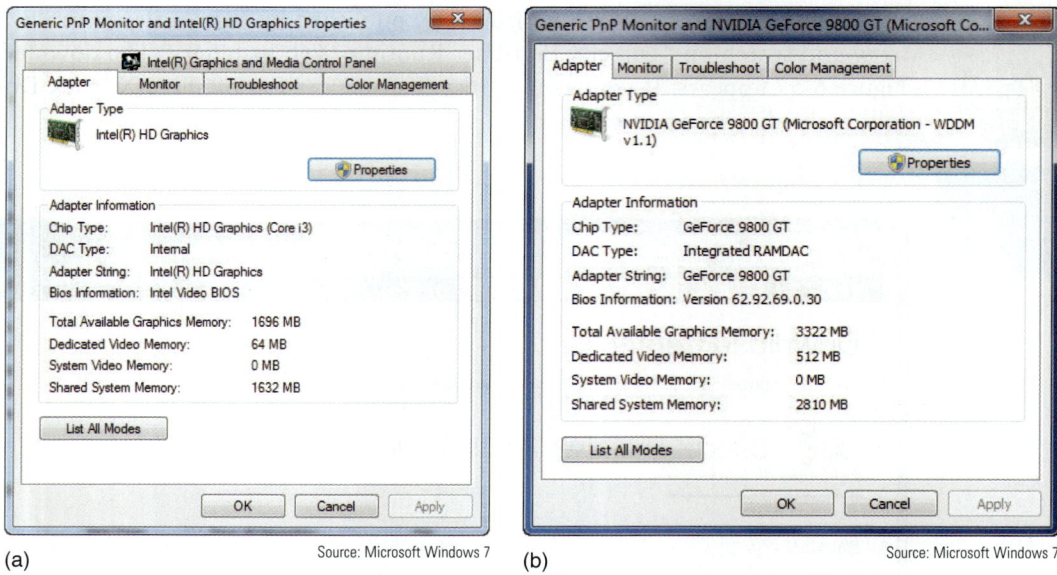

Figure 6-58 Memory allocated to video under Windows 7 (a) for a notebook computer, and (b) for a desktop computer with video card

For Windows to enable the Aero user interface, the video controller must have available at least 128 MB video memory. In other words, Total Available Graphics Memory must add up to at least 128 MB. This is true for both systems in Figure 6-58.

SUPPORTING STORAGE DEVICES

By now you must be thinking you've read in this chapter about every computer part there must be, but hold on; we have optical drives and flash memory still to go. Before we explore the details of several storage devices, including optical discs, USB flash drives, and memory cards, let's start with the file systems they might use.

FILE SYSTEMS USED BY STORAGE DEVICES

A storage device, such as a hard drive, CD, DVD, USB flash drive, or memory card, uses a file system to manage the data stored on the device. A **file system** is the overall structure the OS uses to name, store, and organize files on a drive. In Windows, each storage device is assigned a drive letter. In Windows Explorer, to see what file system a device is using, right-click the device and select **Properties** from the shortcut menu. The device Properties box appears, which shows the file system and storage capacity of the device (see Figure 6-59).

Installing a new file system on a device is called **formatting** the device, and the process erases all data on the device. One way to format a device is to right-click the device and select **Format** from the shortcut menu. In the box that appears, you can select the file system to use (see Figure 6-60). The NTFS file system (New Technology file system) is primarily used by hard drives. The exFAT file system is used by removable storage devices such as large-capacity USB flash drives and large-capacity memory cards. In addition, the older FAT32 and FAT file systems are used by smaller capacity devices.

Now let's look at the types of optical drives you might be called on to support.

Supporting Storage Devices 283

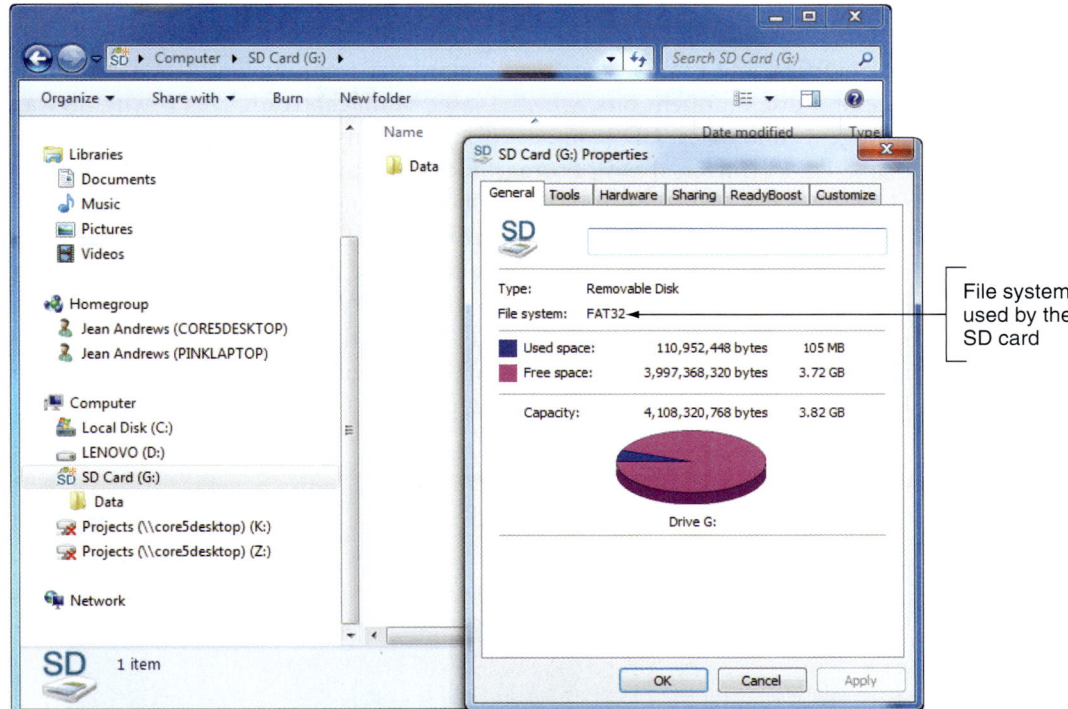

Figure 6-59 This 4 GB SD card is using the FAT32 file system

Source: Microsoft Windows 7

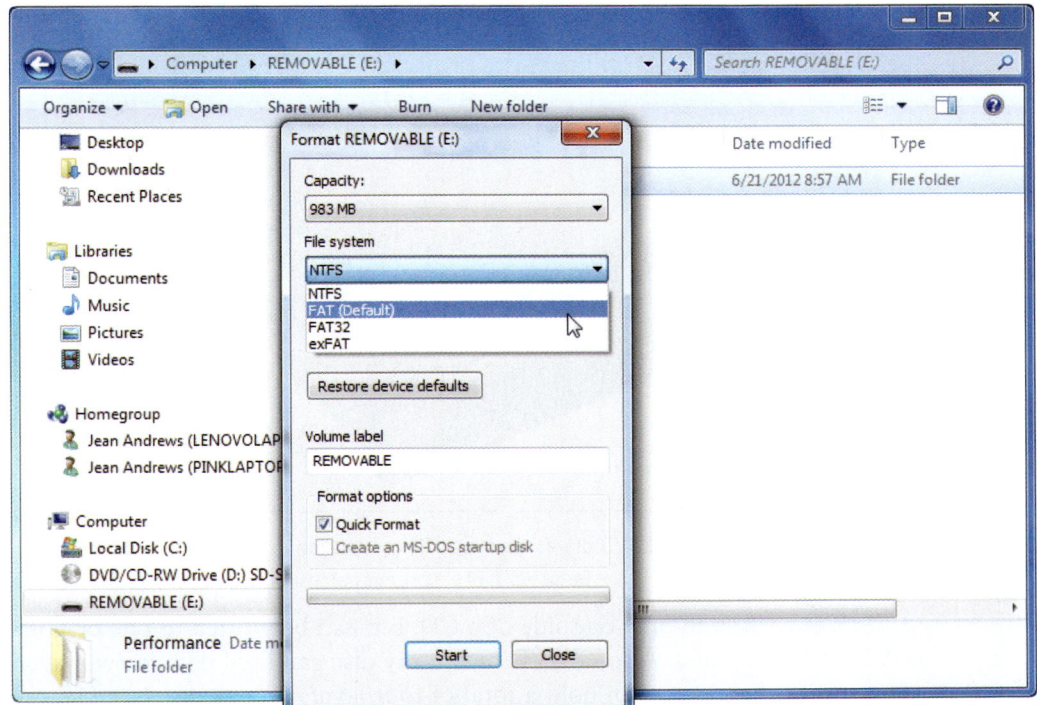

Figure 6-60 A storage device can be formatted using Windows Explorer

Source: Microsoft Windows 7

STANDARDS USED BY OPTICAL DRIVES AND DISCS

CDs, DVDs, and Blu-ray discs use similar laser technologies. Tiny lands and pits on the surface of a disc represent bits, which a laser beam can read. This is why they are called optical storage technologies. CD (compact disc) drives use the CDFS (Compact Disc File System) or the UDF (Universal Disk Format) file system, while DVD (digital versatile disc or digital video disc) drives and Blu-ray Disc (BD) drives use the newer UDF file system.

Blu-ray drives are backward compatible with DVD and CD technologies, and DVD drives are backward compatible with CD technologies. Depending on the drive features, an optical drive might be able to read and write to BDs, DVDs, and CDs. An internal optical drive can interface with the motherboard by way of an IDE or SATA connection. An external drive might use an eSATA, FireWire, or USB port. Figure 6-61 shows an internal DVD drive, and Figure 6-62 shows an external DVD drive.

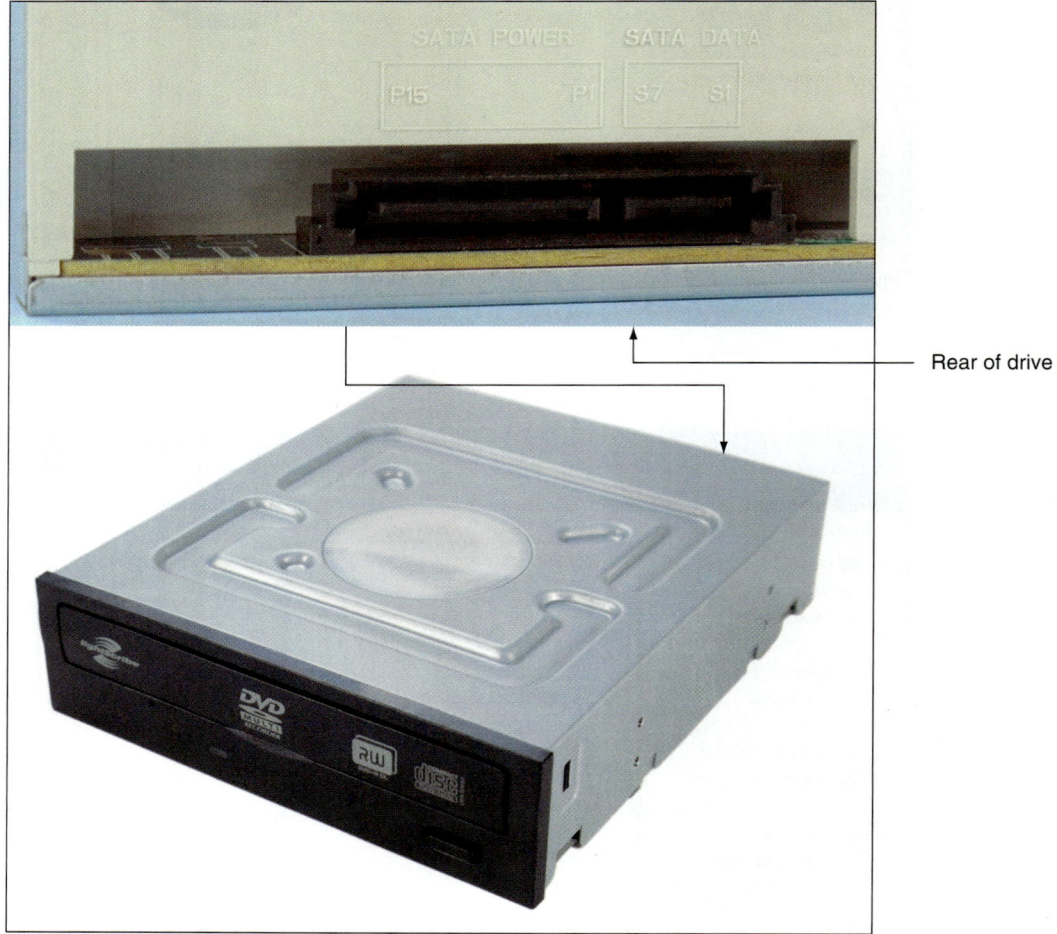

Figure 6-61 This internal DVD drives uses a SATA connection

Data is written to only one side of a CD, but can be written to one or both sides of a DVD or Blu-ray disc. Also, a DVD or Blu-ray disc can hold data in two layers on each side. This means these discs can hold a total of four layers on one disc (see Figure 6-63).

The breakdown of how much data can be held on CDs, DVDs, and BDs is shown in Figure 6-64. The capacities for DVDs and BDs depend on the sides and layers used to hold the data.

A+ 220-801
1.5, 1.7, 1.10

Figure 6-62   The PX-610U external DVD±RW drive by Plextor uses a USB 2.0 port

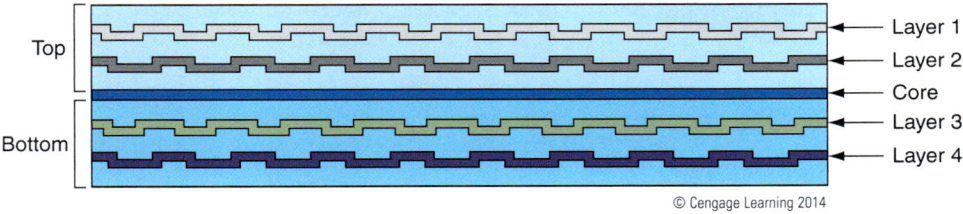

Figure 6-63   A DVD can hold data in double layers on both the top and bottom of the disc, yielding a maximum capacity of 17 GB

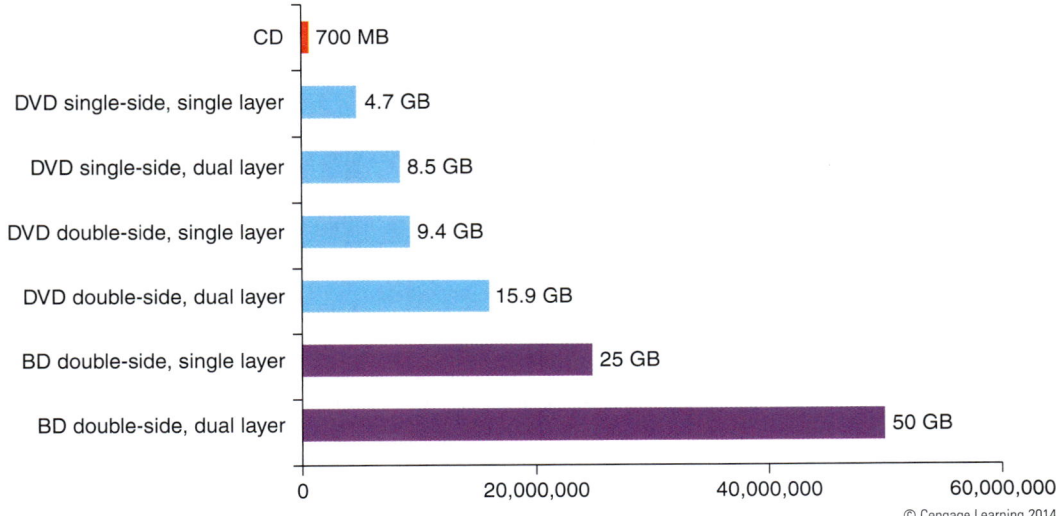

Figure 6-64   Storage capacities for CDs, DVDs, and BD discs

A+ Exam Tip   The A+ 220-801 exam expects you to know the capacities of CDs, DVDs, and Blu-ray discs. These capacities are all listed in Figure 6-64.

> **Notes** The discrepancy in the computer industry between one billion bytes (1,000,000,000 bytes) and 1 GB (1,073,741,824 bytes) exists because 1 KB equals 1024 bytes. Even though documentation might say that a DVD holds 17 GB, in fact, it holds 17 billion bytes, which is only 15.90 GB.

When shopping for an optical drive, suppose you see a couple of ads like those shown in Figure 6-65. To sort out the mix of disc standards, Table 6-4 can help. The table lists the popular CD, DVD, and Blu-ray disc standards.

Figure 6-65 Ads for internal and external DVD burners

Source: tigerdirect.com

Disc Standard	Description
CD-ROM disc or drive	*CD-read-only memory.* A CD-ROM disc burned at the factory can hold music, software, or other data. The bottom of a CD-ROM disc is silver. A CD-ROM drive can read CDs.
CD-R disc	*CD recordable.* A CD-R disc is a write-once CD.
CD-RW disc or drive	*CD rewriteable.* A CD-RW disc can be written to many times. A CD-RW drive can write to a CD-RW or CD-R disc and also overwrite a CD-RW disc.
DVD-ROM drive	*DVD read-only memory.* A DVD-ROM drive can also read CDs or DVDs.
DVD-R disc	*DVD recordable, single layer.* A DVD-R disc can hold up to 4.7 GB of data and is a write-once disc.
DVD-R DL disc	*DVD recordable in dual layers.* Doubles storage to 8.5 GB of data on one disc surface.
DVD-RW disc or drive	*DVD rewriteable.* Also known as an erasable, recordable drive or a write-many disc. The speeds in an ad for an optical drive indicate the maximum speed supported when burning this type of disc, for example, DVD-RW 6X.
DVD-RW DL disc or drive, a.k.a. DL DVD drive	*DVD rewriteable, dual layers.* Doubles disc storage capacity to 8.5 GB.
DVD+R disc or drive	*DVD recordable.* Similar to but faster than DVD-R. Discs hold about 4.7 GB of data.
DVD+R DL disc or drive	*DVD recordable, dual layers.* Doubles disc storage to 8.5 GB on one surface.

Table 6-4 Optical discs and drive standards (continues)

© Cengage Learning 2014

Disc Standard	Description
DVD+RW disc or drive	*DVD rewriteable.* Faster than DVD-RW.
DVD-RAM disc or drive	*DVD Random Access Memory.* Rewriteable and erasable. You can erase or rewrite certain sections of a DVD-RAM disc without disturbing other sections of the disc, and the discs can handle many times over the number of rewrites (around 100,000 rewrites), compared to about a thousand rewrites for DVD-RW and DVD+RW discs. DVD-RAM discs are popular media used in camcorders and set-top boxes.
BD-ROM drive	*BD read-only memory.* A BD-ROM drive can also read DVDs, and some can read CDs.
BD-R disc or drive	*BD recordable.* A BD-R drive might also write to DVDs or CDs.
BD-RE disc or drive	*BD rewriteable.* A BD-RE drive might also write to DVDs or CDs.

Table 6-4 Optical discs and drive standards (continued)

© Cengage Learning 2014

A+ Exam Tip The A+ 220-801 exam expects you to know about the combo optical drives and burners, including CD-RW, DVD-RW, Dual Layer DVD-RW, BD-R, and BD-RE combo drives.

One more feature that you might look for in an optical drive is the ability to burn labels on the top of a disc. Two competing technologies for this purpose are Labelflash and LightScribe. Using either technology, you flip a Labelflash or LightScribe CD or DVD upside down and insert it in the drive tray so that the drive can then burn a label on top of the disc. Both the drive and disc must support the technology for it to work, and the two technologies are not compatible. Figure 6-66 shows a LightScribe CD-R that was just labeled using LightScribe. Another way to print labels on a disc is to use special discs that have a white paper-like surface. Insert the disc into an ink-jet printer that will print the label. The printer has to be the type that will print on optical discs. It is not recommended that you glue paper labels on the top of discs because they can throw the disc off balance or clog up a drive if the labels come loose. You can use a permanent felt-tip marker to handwrite labels on a disc.

© Cengage Learning 2014

Figure 6-66 This disc label was written using a DVD burner that supports LightScribe

Notes CDs, DVDs, and BDs are expected to hold their data for many years; however, you can prolong the life of a disc by protecting it from exposure to light.

A+ 220-801 1.5, 1.7, 1.10

INSTALLING AN OPTICAL DRIVE

Internal optical drives use a SATA, IDE, or SCSI interface. You learned to install drives using these interfaces in Chapter 5. Figure 6-67 shows the front and rear of an EIDE DVD drive. Note the jumper bank that can be set to cable select, slave, or master. Figure 6-68 shows the rear of a SATA optical drive.

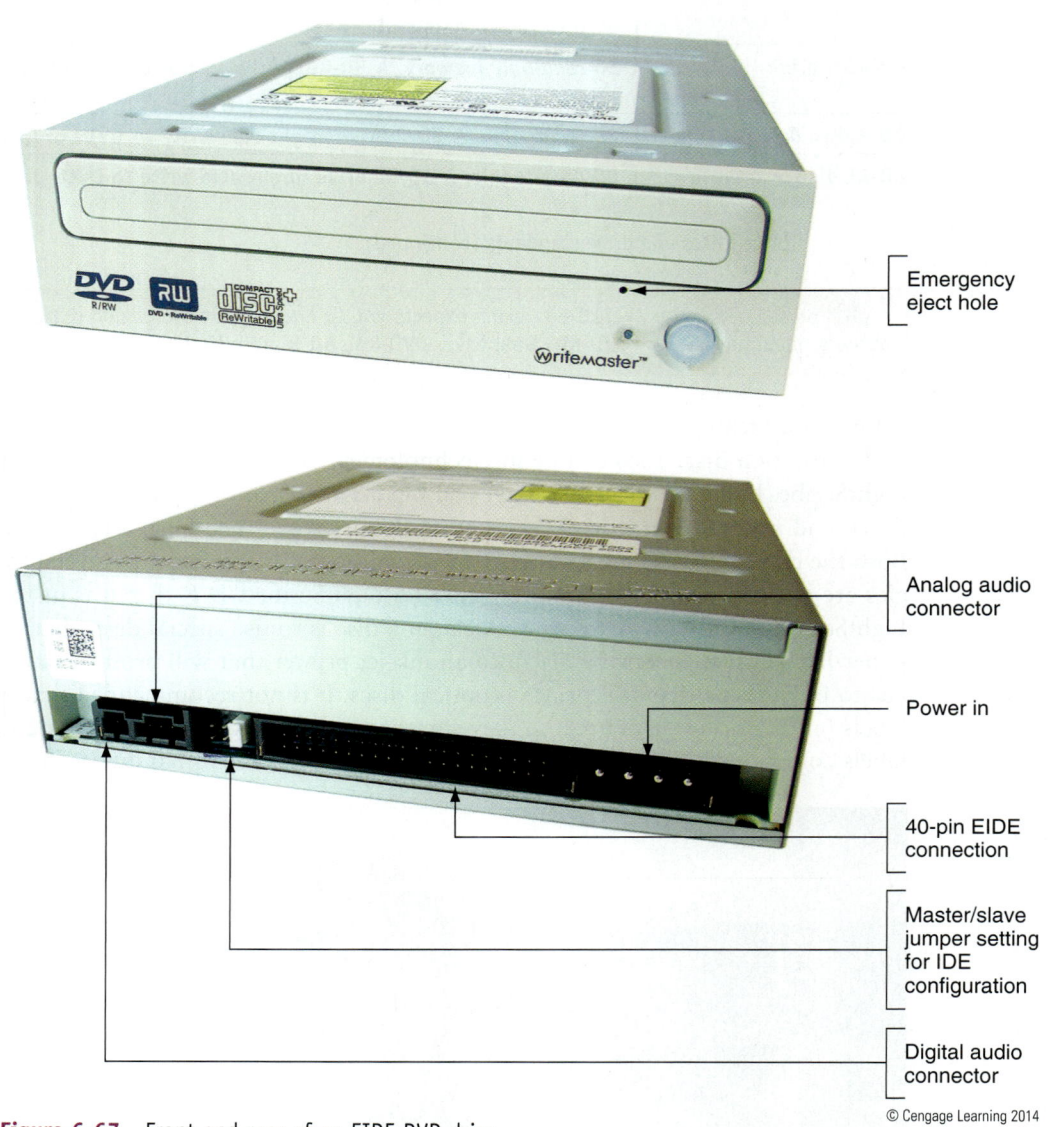

Figure 6-67 Front and rear of an EIDE DVD drive

© Cengage Learning 2014

> **A+ Exam Tip** The A+ 220-801 exam expects you to know how to install a CD, DVD, or Blu-ray drive.

When given the choice of putting an IDE optical drive on the same cable with an IDE hard drive or on its own cable, choose to use its own cable. An optical drive that shares a cable with a hard drive can slow down the hard drive's performance. If you must, however,

A+
220-801
1.5, 1.7,
1.10

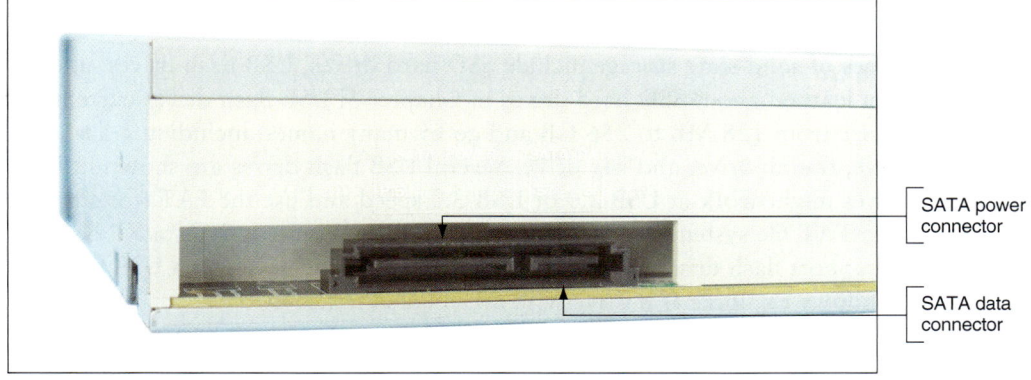

Figure 6-68 Rear of a SATA optical drive

put the optical drive and hard drive on the same IDE channel, make the hard drive the master and the optical drive the slave.

Some motherboards have one SATA connection and one IDE connection. Use SATA connections for all hard drives. The optical drive can use the one IDE connection or a SATA connection. An optical drive is usually installed in the drive bay at the top of a desktop case (see Figure 6-69). After the drive is installed in the bay, connect the data and power cables.

Optical drives might also have a connection for an audio port so that sound from audio CDs can be sent directly to the audio controller. The DVD drive in Figure 6-67 has two connectors for audio. The 4-pin connector is used for analog sound, and the 2-pin connector is used for digital sound. These connections are no longer needed because Windows 7/Vista/XP transfers digital sound from the drive to the sound card without the use of a direct cable connection.

Figure 6-69 Slide the drive into the bay flush with the front panel

Windows 7/Vista/XP supports optical drives using its own embedded drivers without add-on drivers. Therefore, after the Found New Hardware Wizard completes, Windows should recognize the drive.

And now, moving onward to solid-state storage. . . . You're almost done!

SOLID-STATE STORAGE

A+
220-801
1.5, 1.7,
1.10

Types of solid-state storage include SSD hard drives, USB flash drives, and memory cards. You learned about SSD hard drives in Chapter 5. USB flash drives currently for sale range in size from 128 MB to 256 GB and go by many names, including a flash pen drive, jump drive, thumb drive, and key drive. Several USB flash drives are shown in Figure 6-70. Flash drives might work at USB 2.0 or USB 3.0 speed and use the FAT (for small-capacity drives) or exFAT file system (for large-capacity drives). Windows 7/Vista/XP has embedded drivers to support flash drives. To use one, simply insert the device in a USB port. It then shows in Windows Explorer as a drive with an assigned letter.

Figure 6-70 USB flash drives come in a variety of styles and sizes

To make sure that data written to a flash drive is properly saved before you remove the flash drive from the PC, double-click the **Safely Remove Hardware** icon in the notification area (see Figure 6-71). The Safely Remove Hardware box opens, also shown in Figure 6-71. After you click the device listed, it is then safe to remove it.

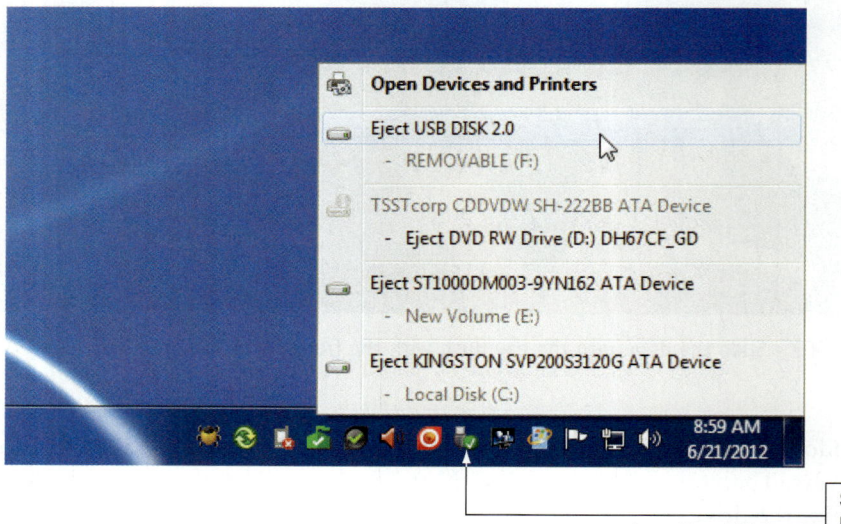

Figure 6-71 Safely Remove Hardware icon and dialog box

A+ 220-801
1.5, 1.7, 1.10

Memory cards might be used in digital cameras, tablets, cell phones, MP3 players, digital camcorders, and other portable devices, and most laptops have memory card slots. The SD Association (www.sdcard.org) is responsible for standards used by the **Secure Digital (SD) cards** shown in Table 6-5. The three standards used by SD cards are 1.x (regular SD), 2.x (SD High Capacity or SDHC), and 3.x (SD eXtended Capacity or SDXC). In addition, these cards come in three physical sizes.

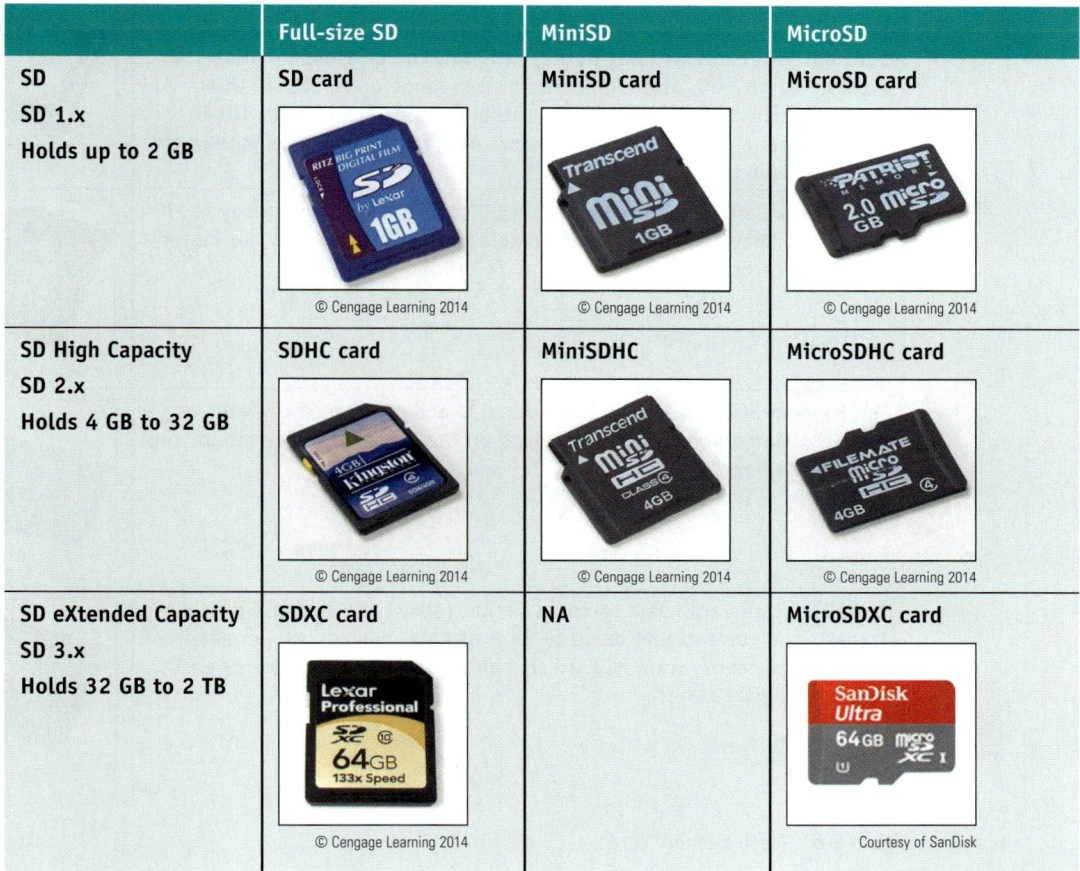

Table 6-5 Flash memory cards that follow the SD Association standards

SDHC and SDXC slots are backward compatible with earlier standards for SD cards. However, you cannot use an SDHC card in an SD slot, and you cannot use an SDXC card in an SDHC slot or SD slot. Only use SDXC cards in SDXC slots.

SD and SDHC cards use the FAT file system, and SDXC cards use the exFAT file system. Windows 7/Vista supports both file systems, so you should be able to install an SD, SDHC, or SDXC card in an SD slot on a Windows 7/Vista laptop with no problems (assuming the slot supports the SDHC or SDXC card you are using). Windows XP can use the exFAT file system only when exFAT drivers are installed. For information about these drivers, see *support.microsoft.com/kb/955704*.

Memory cards other than SD cards are shown in Table 6-6. Some of the cards in Table 6-6 are now obsolete.

292 | **CHAPTER 6** Supporting I/O and Storage Devices

A+ 220-801
1.5, 1.7, 1.10

Flash Memory Device	Example
The Sony Memory Stick PRO Duo is about half the size of the Memory Stick PRO, but is faster and has a higher storage capacity (up to 2 GB). You can use an adapter to insert the Memory Stick PRO Duo in a regular Memory Stick slot.	 © Cengage Learning 2014
CompactFlash (CF) cards come in two types, Type I (CFI) and Type II (CFII). Type II cards are slightly thicker. CFI cards will fit a Type II slot, but CFII cards will not fit a Type I slot. The CF standard allows for sizes up to 137 GB, although current sizes range up to 32 GB. UDMA CompactFlash cards are faster than other CompactFlash cards. UDMA (Ultra Direct Memory Access) transfers data from the device to memory without involving the CPU.	 © Cengage Learning 2014
MultiMedia Card (MMC) looks like an SD card, but the technology is different and they are not interchangeable. Generally, SD cards are faster than MMC cards.	 © Cengage Learning 2014
The Memory Stick is used in Sony cameras and camcorders. A later version, the Memory Stick PRO, improved on the slower transfer rate of the original Memory Stick.	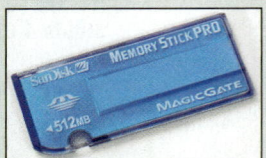 © Cengage Learning 2014
The xD-Picture Card has a compact design (about the size of a postage stamp), and currently holds up to 8 GB of data. You can use an adapter to insert this card into a PC Card slot on a notebook computer or a CF slot on a digital camera.	 © Cengage Learning 2014

© Cengage Learning 2014

Table 6-6 Flash memory cards

> **A+ Exam Tip** The A+ 220-801 exam expects you to know about SD, MicroSD, MiniSD, CompactFlash, and xD memory cards

Sometimes a memory card is bundled with one or more adapters so that a smaller card will fit a larger card slot. Earlier in the chapter, Figure 6-20 shows a MicroSDHC card that came packaged with four adapters, which are labeled in the figure. Figure 6-72 shows several flash memory cards together so you can get an idea of their relative sizes.

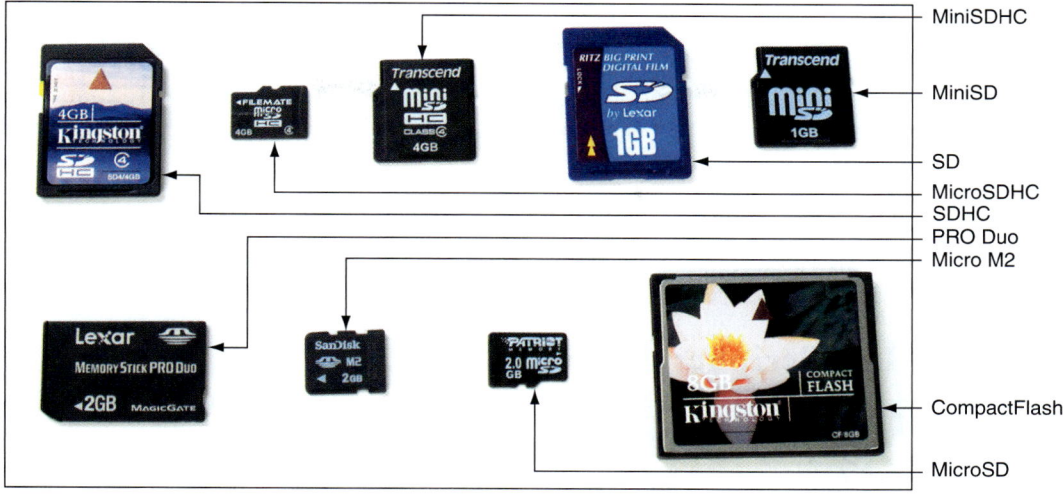

Figure 6-72 Flash memory cards

Hands-on Project 6-3 Learn How Optical Drives Work

Optical drives and other removable storage technologies are interesting to study. Check out the animated explanation at the web site of HowStuffWorks, Inc. (*www.howstuffworks.com*). Search on "How Removable Storage Works." List 10 facts you learned about optical drives.

Hands-on Project 6-4 Shop for Storage Media

Shop online and print or save web pages showing the following devices. Two online sites you can use are Micro Center (*microcenter.com*) and TigerDirect (*tigerdirect.com*):

1. DVD+R DL discs, which are usually sold in packs. What is the storage capacity of each disc? How many discs are in the pack? What is the price per disc?
2. DVD+RW disc, which is usually sold as a single. What is the price per disc? How many more times expensive is a DVD+RW disc than a DVD+R disc?
3. The largest capacity USB flash drive you can find. What is its capacity and price?
4. The eight types of SD memory cards in Table 6-5. What is the storage capacity and price of each card? Which type of SD card gives you the most storage per dollar?

>> CHAPTER SUMMARY

Basic Principles for Supporting Devices

▲ Adding new devices to a computer requires installing hardware and software. Even if you know how to generally install an I/O device, always follow the specific instructions of the product manufacturer.

- Use Device Manager under Windows to manage hardware devices and to solve problems with them. The Windows 7 Action Center can also help with problem solving.
- Popular I/O ports on a motherboard include eSATA (Versions 1, 2, and 3), FireWire 800 and 400, and USB (Versions 1, 2, and 3). Older ports include parallel, serial, and PS/2 ports.
- Wireless connections can use Wi-Fi 802.11a/b/g/n, Bluetooth, and Infrared standards.
- USB connectors include the A-Male, B-Male, Mini-B, Micro-B, Micro-A, USB 3.0 B-Male, and USB 3.0 Micro-B connectors.

Installing I/O Peripheral Devices

- When installing devices, use 32-bit drivers for a 32-bit OS and 64-bit drivers for a 64-bit OS.
- A touch screen is likely to use a USB port. Software is installed to calibrate the touch screen to the monitor screen and receive data input.
- Biometric input devices, such as a fingerprint reader, collect biological data and compare it to that recorded about the person to authenticate the person's access to a system.
- A KVM switch lets you use one keyboard, monitor, and mouse with multiple computers.

Installing and Configuring Adapter Cards

- Generally, when an adapter card is physically installed in a system and Windows starts up, it detects the card and then you install the drivers using the Windows wizard. However, always follow specific instructions from the device manufacturer when installing an adapter card because the order of installing the card and drivers might be different.
- A TV tuner card turns your PC or notebook into a television. A video capture card allows you to capture input from a camcorder or directly from TV. Combo cards have both abilities.

Supporting the Video Subsystem

- Types of monitors include CRT monitor, LCD monitor, plasma monitor, projector, and OLED monitor.
- Technologies and features of LCD monitors include screen size, refresh rate, pixel pitch, resolution, native resolution, contrast ratio, viewing angle, backlighting, and connectors that a monitor uses.
- Video ports that a video card or motherboard might provide are VGA, DVI-I, DVI-D, DVI-A, composite video, S-Video, component video, DisplayPort, HDMI, and HDMI mini ports.
- Use the Screen Resolution window in Windows 7/Vista to configure a monitor resolution and configure dual monitors.
- To use the Aero user interface, Windows 7/Vista requires a video card or onboard video to have at least 128 MB of video RAM, support DirectX version 9 or higher, and use the Windows Display Driver Model (WDDM).
- The dxdiag.exe command is used to report information about hardware, including the video card and which version of DirectX it is using.

Supporting Storage Devices

▲ File systems a storage device might use in Windows include NTFS, exFAT, and FAT.

▲ CDs, DVDs, and BDs are optical devices with data physically embedded into the surface of the disc. Laser beams are used to read data off the disc by measuring light reflection.

▲ Optical discs can be recordable (such as a CD-R disc) or rewriteable (such as a DVD-RW disc).

▲ Types of flash memory card standards by the SD Association include SD, MiniSD, MicroSD, SDHC, MiniSDHC, MicroSDHC, SDXC, and MicroSDXC. Other memory cards include Memory Stick PRO Duo, Memory Stick PRO, Sony Memory Stick Micro M2, CompactFlash I and II, and xD-Picture Card.

>> KEY TERMS

For explanations of key terms, see the Glossary near the end of the book.

1394a	DVI-D	MiniDin-6 connector
1394b	DVI-I	mini-HDMI connector
A Male connector	dxdiag.exe	native resolution
B Male connector	file system	OLED (Organic Light-emitting Diode) monitor
barcode reader	FireWire 400	pixel
biometric device	FireWire 800	pixel pitch
Blu-ray Disc (BD)	flat panel monitor	plasma monitor
CD (compact disc)	formatting	projector
CDFS (Compact Disc File System)	graphics tablet	refresh rate
	HDMI connector	resolution
CompactFlash (CF) card	HDMI mini connector	RGB port
composite video port	hot-swappable	Secure Digital (SD) card
contrast ratio	Infrared (IR)	sound card
CRT (cathode-ray tube) monitor	KVM (Keyboard, Video, and Mouse) switch	stylus
DB-15	LCD (Liquid Crystal Display) monitor	touch screen
Device Manager		TV tuner card
digitizer	LED (Light-Emitting Diode)	UDF (Universal Disk Format) file system
digitizing tablet	Micro-A connector	
DirectX	Micro-B connector	USB 3.0 B-Male connector
DVD (digital versatile disc or digital video disc)	MIDI (musical instrument digital interface)	USB 3.0 Micro-B connector
		video capture card
DVI-A	Mini-B connector	xD-Picture Card

>> REVIEWING THE BASICS

1. What command can you enter in the Search box to launch Device Manager?

2. Which is faster, an eSATA-600 port or a FireWire 800 port?

3. What is the speed for Hi-Speed USB?

4. How many times faster is a Hi-Speed USB port than an Original USB port running at 12 Mbps?

5. Which is faster, USB 3.0 or eSATA 600?

6. Which is faster, Wi-Fi 802.11n or Bluetooth?
7. How many pins does a FireWire 800 port have?
8. What type of wireless transmission requires a line-of-sight clearance?
9. Will a printer rated to use USB 3.0 work when you connect the printer's USB cable into a USB 2.0 port on your computer?
10. What is the easiest way to tell if a USB port on a notebook computer is using the USB 3.0 standard?
11. For an LCD monitor, what is the best resolution to use?
12. Which gives a better measurement for the quality of an LCD monitor, the contrast ratio or the dynamic contrast ratio?
13. Which type of port gives the best output, a composite out port or an S-Video port?
14. What command do you use to find out what version of DirectX your video card is using?
15. Name two types of ports a keyboard might use.
16. Which Windows utility is most likely the one to use when uninstalling an expansion card?
17. Would you expect all the devices listed in BIOS setup to also be listed in Device Manager? Would you expect all devices listed in Device Manager to also be listed in BIOS setup?
18. Why is it best to leave a slot empty between two expansion cards?
19. Which speaker port should you use when connecting a single speaker to a PC?
20. What type of adapter card allows you to watch TV using your computer?
21. What type of file system is used by Blu-ray discs?
22. What type of file system is used by SDXC memory cards?
23. What two types of interfaces might be used by an internal DVD drive?
24. How much data can a CD hold?
25. How much data can a double-sided, dual-layer DVD hold?
26. How much data can a double-sided, single-layer BD hold?
27. Which costs more, a CD-R or a CD-RW disc?
28. Which type of flash memory card is currently the smallest type of card?
29. What are the group of standards that are used to represent music in digital form?
30. Why might a musical keyboard have two MIDI ports?

>> THINKING CRITICALLY

1. If a PS/2 keyboard does not work on your system and yet you know the keyboard is good, what is the best solution?
    a. Disable the PS/2 port in BIOS setup and use a PS/2 splitter to install a keyboard and mouse using the PS/2 mouse port.
    b. Install a USB keyboard on a USB port.

c. Exchange the PS/2 port on your motherboard.

d. Replace the motherboard.

2. You plug a new scanner into a USB port on your Windows 7 system. When you first turn on the scanner, what should you expect to see?

   a. A message displayed by the scanner software telling you to reboot your system.

   b. You see the Found New Hardware Wizard launch.

   c. Your system automatically reboots.

   d. An error message from the USB controller.

3. You turn on your Windows 7 computer and see the system display POST messages. Then the screen turns blue with no text. Which of the following items could be the source of the problem?

   a. The video card

   b. The monitor

   c. Windows

   d. Microsoft Word software installed on the system

4. You have just installed a new sound card in your system, and Windows says the card installed with no errors. When you plug up the speakers and try to play a music CD, you hear no sound. What is the first thing you should do? The second thing?

   a. Check Device Manager to see if the sound card is recognized and has no errors.

   b. Reinstall Windows 7.

   c. Use Device Manager to uninstall the sound card.

   d. Identify your sound card by opening the case and looking on the card for manufacturer and model.

   e. Verify the volume is turned up in Windows and on the speakers.

   f. Use Device Manager to update the sound card drivers.

5. You have just installed a new DVD drive and its drivers under Windows 7. The drive will read a CD but not a DVD. You decide to reinstall the device drivers. What is the first thing you do?

   a. Open Control Panel and launch the Add New Hardware Wizard.

   b. Open Device Manager and choose Update Driver.

   c. Remove the data cable from the DVD drive so Windows will no longer recognize the drive and allow you to reinstall the drivers.

   d. Open Device Manager and uninstall the drive.

6. Match the following ports to the diagrams in Figure 6-73. Note that some ports are not used: Dual Link DVI-I, Single Link DVI-D, parallel, USB Type A, USB Type B, FireWire 400, VGA, DisplayPort, Mini Display Port, 4-pin S-Video, HDMI, PS/2, and serial.

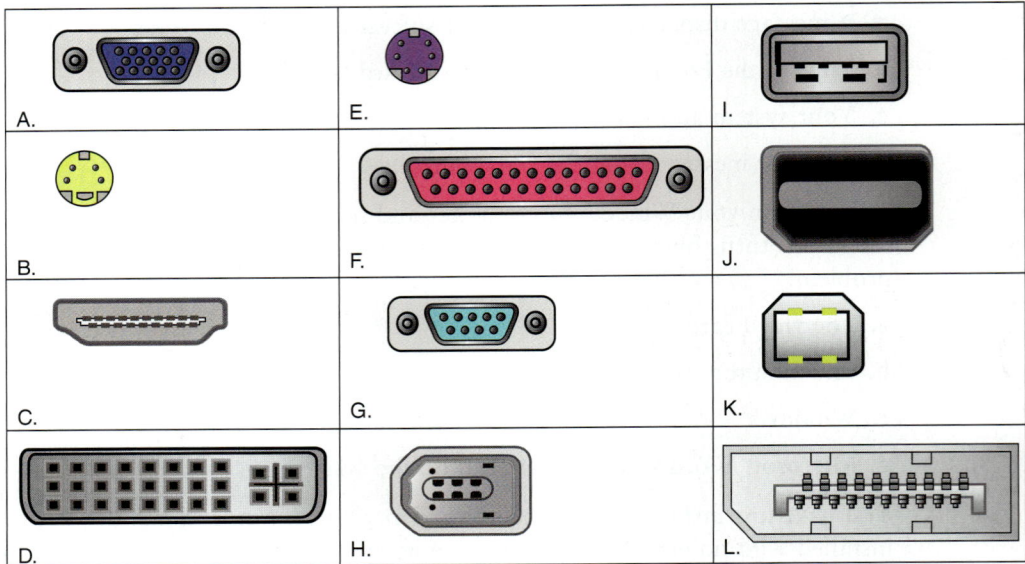

Figure 6-73 Identify ports

>> REAL PROBLEMS, REAL SOLUTIONS

REAL PROBLEM 6-1: Helping with Upgrade Decisions

Upgrading an existing system can sometimes be a wise thing to do, but sometimes the upgrade costs more than the system is worth. Also, if existing components are old, they might not be compatible with components you want to use for the upgrade. A friend, Renata, asks your advice about several upgrades she is considering. Answer these questions:

1. Renata has a four-year-old desktop computer that has a Core2 Duo processor and 2 GB memory. It does not have a FireWire port. She wants to use a camcorder that has a FireWire 400 interface to a PC. How would she perform the upgrade, and what is the cost? Save or print web pages to support your answers.

2. Her computer has one USB port, but she wants to use her USB printer at the same time she uses her USB scanner. How can she do this, and how much will it cost? Save or print web pages to support your answers.

3. Renata also uses her Windows 7 computer for gaming and wants to get a better gaming experience. The computer is using onboard video and has an empty PCI Express video slot. What is the fastest and best graphics card she can buy? How much does it cost? Save or print web pages to support your answer.

4. What is the total cost of all the upgrades Renata wants? Do you think it is wise for her to make these upgrades or purchase a new system? How would you explain your recommendation to her?

REAL PROBLEM 6-2: Using Input Director

Input Director is software that lets you use one keyboard and mouse to control two or more computers that are networked together. You can download the free software from *www.inputdirector.com*. To use the software, you need to know the host name of each computer that will share the keyboard and mouse. To find out the host name, right-click **Computer** (**My Computer** in Windows XP) and select **Properties**. The host name is listed in Windows 7/Vista as the Computer name and in XP as Full computer name.

Working with a partner, download and install Input Director and configure it so that you and your partner are using the same keyboard and mouse for your computers.

REAL PROBLEM 6-3: Researching a Computer Ad

Pick a current web site or magazine ad for a complete, working desktop computer system, including computer, monitor, keyboard, and software, together with extra devices such as a mouse or printer. Research the details of the ad and write a two- to four-page report describing and explaining these details. This project provides a good opportunity to learn about the latest offerings on the market as well as current pricing.

REAL PROBLEM 6-4: Working with a Monitor

Do the following to practice changing monitor settings and troubleshooting monitor problems:

1. Practice changing the display settings, including the wallpaper, screen saver, and appearance. If you are not using your own computer, be sure to restore each setting after making changes.

2. Pretend you have made a mistake and selected a combination of foreground and background colors that makes reading the screen impossible. Solve the problem by booting Windows into Safe Mode. Correct the problem and then reboot.

3. Change the monitor resolution. Try several resolutions. Make a change and then make the change permanent. You can go back and adjust it later if you want.

4. Work with a partner who is using a different computer. Unplug the monitor in the computer lab or classroom, loosen or disconnect the computer monitor cable, or turn the contrast and brightness all the way down while your partner does something similar to the other PC. Trade PCs and troubleshoot the problems.

5. Wear a ground bracelet. Turn off the PC, press the power button, remove the case cover, and loosen the video card. Turn on the PC and write down the problem as a user would describe it. Turn off the PC, reseat the card, and verify that everything works.

6. Turn off your system. Insert into the system a defective video card provided by your instructor. Turn on the system. Describe the resulting problem in writing, as a user would.

CHAPTER 7

Satisfying Customer Needs

In this chapter, you will learn:

- About some job roles and responsibilities of those who sell, fix, or support personal computers
- What customers want and expect beyond your technical abilities
- How to interact with customers when selling, servicing, and supporting personal computers
- How to customize a computer system to meet customer needs

In this chapter, the focus is on relating to people and your career as a professional PC support technician. As a professional PC technician, you can manage your career by staying abreast of new technology, using every available resource to do your job well, and striving for top professional certifications. There was a time when most PC support jobs had to do with simply working with hardware and software, and the perception was that people skills were not that important. But times have changed and our vocation has become much more service oriented.

Knowing how to effectively work with people in a technical world is one of the most sought-after skills in today's service-oriented work environments. Just before writing this chapter, an employer told me, "It's not hard to find technically proficient people these days. But it's next to impossible to find people who know how to get along with others and can be counted on when managers are not looking over their shoulders." I could sense his frustration, but I also felt encouraged to know that good social skills and good work ethics can take you far in today's world. My advice to you is to take this chapter seriously. It's important to be technically proficient, but the skills learned in this chapter just might be the ones that make you stand out above the crowd to land that new job or promotion.

In this chapter, you'll learn about the job roles of a professional PC support technician, including the certifications and record-keeping and informational tools you might use. Then we focus on interpersonal skills (people skills, sometimes called soft skills) needed by a technical support technician. Finally, you learn how to select appropriate parts for a customized computer system to satisfy the specifications given by your customer.

> **Notes** People respond in kind to the position of facial muscles presented to them. Try smiling when you first greet someone and watch to see what happens.

JOB ROLES AND RESPONSIBILITIES

A+ 220-801 5.3

As a PC troubleshooter, you might have to solve a problem on your own PC or for someone else. As a PC technician, you might fulfill several different job roles:

Figure 7-1 Picture yourself here and think about your job role in this position

- *PC support technician.* A PC support technician works on site, closely interacting with users, and is responsible for ongoing PC maintenance. Of the job roles in this list, a PC support technician is the only one responsible for the PC before trouble occurs. Therefore, you are able to prepare for a problem by performing routine preventive maintenance, keeping good records, and making backups of important data (or teaching users how to do so). You might also be expected to provide desk-side support, helping computer users with all sorts of hardware and application concerns. Some job titles that fall into this category include enterprise technician, IT administrator, PC technician, support technician, PC support specialist, and desk-side support technician.
- *PC service technician.* A PC service technician goes to a customer site in response to a service call and, if possible, repairs the PC on site. PC service technicians are usually not responsible for ongoing PC maintenance but usually do interact with users. Other job titles might include computer repair technician, field technician, or field service technician.
- *Technical retail associate.* Those responsible for selling computers and related equipment are often expected to have technical knowledge about the products they sell. These salespeople work in somewhat of a consulting role and are expected to advise customers about the best technology to meet their needs, how to apply the technology, and maybe even how to configure entire networks and interconnected applications and equipment. Sometimes job roles involve only one stage of the sale. For instance, less technical people might make the initial contact with the customer and begin the sales process, and those who are more technically knowledgeable can act as technical sales consultants to complete the details of the sale.

- *Bench technician.* A bench technician works in a lab environment, might not interact with users of the PCs being repaired, and is not permanently responsible for them. (The job title bench technician can also apply to someone who repairs any type of electronic equipment.) Bench technicians probably don't work at the site where the PC is kept. They might be able to interview the user to get information about the problem, or they might simply receive a PC to repair without being able to talk to the user. A bench technician who repairs computers rather than any type of electronic equipment is sometimes called a depot technician.
- *Help-desk technician.* A help-desk technician provides telephone or online support. Help-desk technicians, who do not have physical access to the PC, are at the greatest disadvantage of the types of technicians listed. They can interact with users over the phone, by a chat session, or by remote control of the user's computer and must obviously use different tools and approaches than technicians who are at the PC. Other job titles in this category include remote support technician, service desk technician, and call center technician.

Now let's turn our attention to the need to be certified, and then we'll look at the record-keeping and information tools needed by a technician.

© iStockphoto

Figure 7-2 PC support technicians might have limited contact with users

CERTIFICATION AND PROFESSIONAL ORGANIZATIONS

Many people work as PC technicians without any formal classroom training or certification. However, by having certification or an advanced technical degree, you prove to yourself, your customers, and your employers that you are prepared to do the work and are committed to being educated in your chosen profession. Certification and advanced degrees serve as recognized proof of competence and achievement, improve your job opportunities, create a higher level of customer confidence, and often qualify you for promotions and other training or degrees.

The most significant certifying organization for PC technicians is the Computing Technology Industry Association (CompTIA, pronounced "comp-TEE-a"). CompTIA sponsors the A+ Certification Program, and manages the exams. **A+ Certification** has industry recognition, so it should be your first choice for certification as a PC technician. CompTIA has more than 13,000 members from every major company that manufactures, distributes, or publishes computer-related products and services.

Go to the CompTIA home page at **www.comptia.org** and drill down to the information about A+ Certification, shown in Figure 7-3. Follow the *See what the exam covers* link on the page to get the list of objectives for the latest exams, which are currently the A+ 2012 exams. To become certified, you must pass the A+ 220-801 exam that covers content on hardware, soft skills (working with people), and networking and the A+ 220-802 exam that covers operating systems, security, networking, and troubleshooting hardware and software. This book primarily covers the content on the A+ 220-801 exam plus hardware troubleshooting on the A+ 220-802 exam, and its companion book, *A+ Guide to Software*, covers the remaining content on the A+ 220-802 exam that focuses on software.

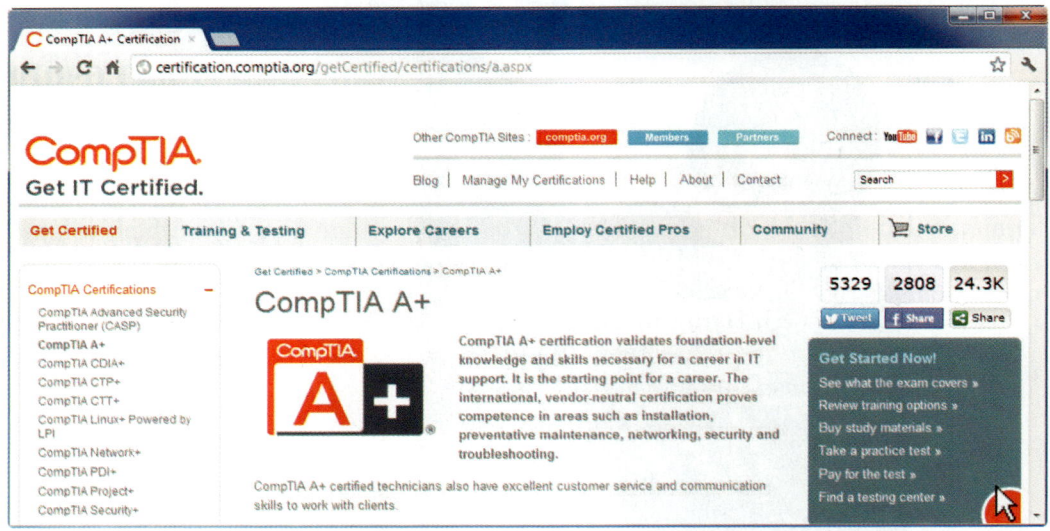

Figure 7-3 CompTIA A+ Certification web page

Source: comptia.org

Other certifications are more vendor specific. For example, Microsoft and Cisco offer certifications to use and support their products. These are excellent choices for additional certifications when your career plan is to focus on these products.

In addition to becoming certified and seeking advanced degrees, the professional PC technician must continually learn about new technologies. Helpful resources include on-the-job training, books, magazines, the Internet, trade shows, and interaction with colleagues, seminars, and workshops. Using the Internet, a convenient and inexpensive way to keep up with the latest technologies is to subscribe to newsletters by email. Newsletters I read regularly are those published by LAPTOP at *www.laptopmag.com*, *PC World* at *www.pcworld.com,* and PCstats at *www.pcstats.com*. Also, the Experts Exchange site (*www.experts-exchange.com*) is an excellent tool for learning and sharing about tech solutions.

A+ 220-801 5.3

It's important to build your professional network of technicians, co-workers, and potential employers. Focus on building good relationships on the job and maintaining these contacts even when you have moved on to another job. Trade shows, job fairs, seminars, and workshops are excellent opportunities for networking. On the web, take advantage of Facebook (*www.facebook.com*) and LinkedIn (*www.linkedin.com*) to help develop your online network.

> **Notes** Statistics show that more than 50 percent of potential employers check a person's online presence as part of the hiring process. Make sure your Facebook, blogs, and forum entries and photos present you in a favorable light. For example, don't complain online about your current job. Keep your online presence upbeat, friendly, and positive.

RECORD-KEEPING AND INFORMATION TOOLS

If you work for a service organization, it will probably have most of the tools you need to do your job, including printed forms, online record-keeping, procedures, and manuals. In some cases, help-desk support personnel might have software to help them do their jobs, such as programs that support the remote control of customers' PCs. Examples of this type of software are GoToAssist by CiTRIX at *www.netviewer.com* and LogMeIn Rescue by LogMeIn at *secure.logmeinrescue.com*.

Other types of resources, records, and information tools that can help you support PCs are:

- *Tool 1*. The specific application, operating system, or hardware you support must be available to you to test, observe, and study and to use to re-create a customer's problem whenever possible.
- *Tool 2*. You need a digital or printed copy of the same documentation the user sees, and should be familiar with that documentation.
- *Tool 3*. Hardware and software products generally have more technical documentation than just a user manual. A company should make this technical documentation available to you when you support its product. If you don't find it on hand, know that you are likely to find user manuals and technical support manuals as .pdf files that can be downloaded from the product manufacturers' web sites.
- *Tool 4*. Online help targeted to field technicians and help-desk technicians is often available for a product. This online help will probably include a search engine that searches by topics, words, error messages, and the like.
- *Tool 5*. An expert system is software that is designed and written to help solve problems. It uses databases of known facts and rules to simulate human experts' reasoning and decision making. Expert systems for PC technicians work by posing questions about a problem to be answered by the technician or the customer. The response to each question triggers another question from the software until the expert system arrives at a possible solution or solutions. Many expert systems are "intelligent," meaning the system will record your input and use it in subsequent sessions to select more questions to ask and approaches to try. Therefore, future troubleshooting sessions on this same type of problem tend to zero in more quickly toward a solution.
- *Tool 6*. When someone initiates a call for help, the technician starts the process by creating a ticket, which is a record of the request and what is happening to resolve it. In the past, a technician kept these records on paper, but most organizations today use call tracking software to track the progress and resolution of a ticket. The software

might track: (1) the date, time, and length of help-desk or on-site calls, (2) causes of and solutions to problems already addressed, (3) who is currently assigned to the ticket and who has already worked on it, (4) who did what and when, and (5) how each call was officially resolved. The ticket is entered into the call tracking system and stays open until the issue is resolved. Figure 7-4 shows a new ticket being created in Spiceworks (*www.spiceworks.com*), free help desk call tracking software. Support staff assigned to the ticket document their progress under this ticket in the call tracking system. As an open ticket ages, more attention and resources are assigned to it, and the ticket might be escalated, which is to assign the ticket to those higher up in the support chain until the problem is finally resolved and the ticket closed. Help-desk personnel and managers acknowledge and sometimes even celebrate those who consistently close the most tickets!

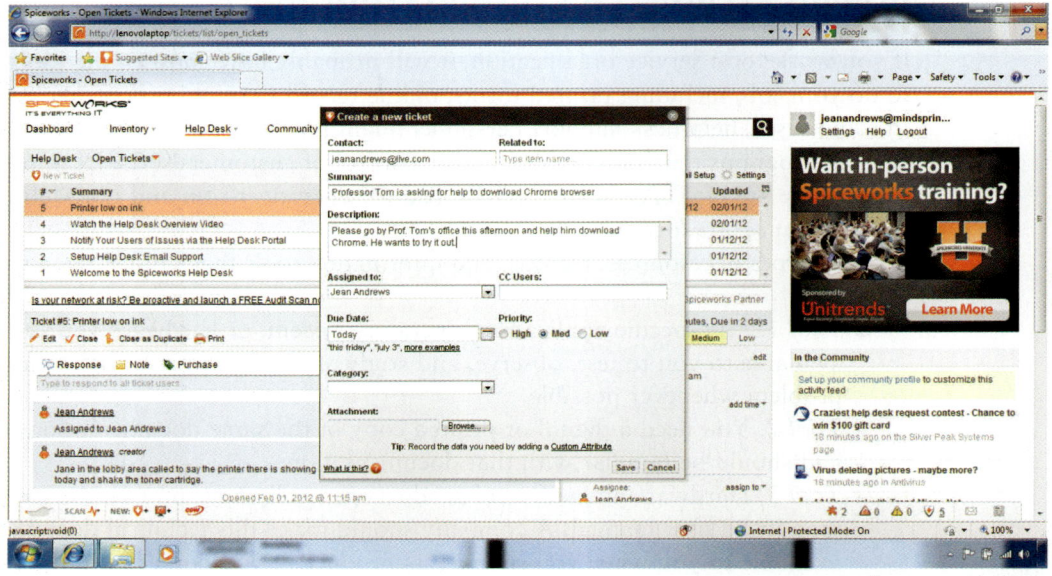

Source: www.spiceworks.com

Figure 7-4 Spiceworks Help Desk Software allows you to create, edit, and close tickets used by technicians

Now let's focus on our customers and what they expect from us beyond our technical knowledge.

WHAT CUSTOMERS WANT: BEYOND TECHNICAL KNOW-HOW

Probably the most significant indication that a PC technician is doing a good job is that customers are consistently satisfied. In your career as a support technician, commit to providing excellent service and to treating customers as you would want to be treated in a similar situation. One of the most important ways to achieve customer satisfaction is to do your best by being prepared, both technically and personally. Being prepared includes knowing what customers want, what they don't like, and what they expect from a PC technician.

Your customers can be "internal" (you both work for the same company, in which case you might consider the customer your colleague) or "external" (your customers come to you or your company for service). Customers can be highly technical or

A+ 220-801 5.3

technically naive, represent a large company or simply own a home PC, be prompt or slow at paying their bills, want only the best (and be willing to pay for it) or be searching for bargain service, be friendly and easy to work with or demanding and condescending. In each situation, the key to success is always the same: don't allow circumstances or personalities to affect your commitment to excellence and to treating the customer as you would want to be treated.

The following traits distinguish a competent and helpful technician from a technician who is incompetent or unhelpful in the eyes of the customer:

▲ *Trait 1.* ***A positive and helpful attitude.*** This helps establish good customer relationships. You communicate your attitude in your tone of voice, the words you choose, how you use eye contact, your facial expressions, how you dress, and in many other subjective and subtle ways. Generally, your attitudes toward your customers stem from how you see people, how you see yourself, and how you see your job. Your attitude is a heart issue, not a head issue. To improve your attitude, you must do it from your heart. That's pretty subjective and cannot be defined with a set of rules, but it always begins with a decision to change. As you work with customers or users, make it a habit to not talk down to or patronize them. Don't make the customers or users feel inferior. People appreciate it when they feel your respect for them, even when they have made a mistake or are not knowledgeable. If a problem is simple to solve, don't make the other person feel he or she has wasted your time. Your customer or user should always be made to feel that the problem is important to you.

APPLYING CONCEPTS Josie walked into a computer parts store and wandered over to the cleaning supplies looking for Ace monitor wipes. She saw another brand of wipes, but not the ones she wanted. Looking around for help, she noticed Mary stocking software on the shelves in the next aisle. She walked over to Mary and asked her if she could help her find Ace monitor wipes. Mary put down her box, walked over to the cleaning supply aisle without speaking, picked up a can of wipes and handed them to Josie, still without speaking a word. Josie explained she was looking for Ace wipes. Mary yells over three aisles to a co-worker in the back room, "Hey, Billy! This lady says she wants Ace monitor wipes. We got any?" Billy comes from the back room and says, "No, we only carry those," pointing to the wipes in Mary's hand, and returns to the back room. Mary turns to Josie and says, "We only carry these," and puts the wipes back on the shelf. She turns to walk back to her aisle when Josie says to Mary, "Well, those Ace wipes are great wipes. You might want to consider carrying them." Mary says, "I'm only responsible for software." Josie leaves the store.

Discuss this situation in a small group of students and answer the following questions:

1. If you were Josie, how would you feel about the service in this store?
2. What would you have expected to happen that did not happen?
3. If you were Mary, how could you have provided better service?
4. If you were Billy, is there anything more you could have done to help?
5. If you were the store manager, what principles of good customer service would you want Billy and Mary to know that would have helped them in this situation?

▲ *Trait 2. Listening without interrupting your customer.* When you're working with or talking to a customer, focus on him or her. Don't assume you know what your customer is about to say. Let her say it, listen carefully, and don't interrupt. Make it your job to satisfy this person, not just your organization, your boss, your bank account, or the customer's boss.

Figure 7-5 Learn to listen before you decide what a user needs or wants

▲ *Trait 3. Proper and polite language.* Speak politely and use language that won't confuse your customer. Avoid using slang or jargon (technical language that only technical people can understand). Avoid acronyms (initial letters that stand for words). For example, don't say to a nontechnical customer, "I need to ditch your KVM switch," when you could explain yourself better by saying to the customer, "I need to replace that little switch box on your desk that controls your keyboard, monitor, and mouse."

▲ *Trait 4. Sensitivity to cultural differences.* Cultural differences happen because we are from different countries and societies or because of physical disabilities. Culture can cause us to differ in how we define or judge good service. For example, culture can affect our degree of tolerance for uncertainty. Some cultures are willing to embrace uncertainty, and others strive to avoid it. Those who tend to avoid uncertainty can easily get upset when the unexpected happens. For these people, you need to make special efforts to communicate early and often when things are not going as expected. For the physically disabled, especially the deaf or sight-impaired, communication can be more difficult. It's your responsibility in these situations to do whatever is necessary to find a way to communicate. And it's especially important to have an attitude that expresses honor and patience, which you will unconsciously express in your tone of voice, your choice of words, and your actions.

▲ *Trait 5. Taking ownership of the problem.* Taking ownership of the customer's problem means to accept the customer's problem as your own problem. Doing that builds trust and loyalty because the customer knows you can be counted on. Taking ownership of a problem also increases your value in the eyes of your co-workers and boss. People who don't take ownership of the problem at hand are likely to be viewed as lazy, uncommitted, and uncaring. One way to take ownership of a problem is to not engage your boss in unproductive discussions about a situation that he expects you to handle on your own.

▲ *Trait 6.* ***Dependability and reliability.*** Customers appreciate and respect those who do as they say. If you promise to be back at 10:00 the next morning, be back at 10:00 the next morning. If you cannot keep your appointment, never ignore your promise. Call, apologize, let the customer know what happened, and reschedule your appointment. Also, do your best to return phone calls the same day and email within two days.

Figure 7-6 When talking with customers, make sure they understand what to expect from you
© iStockphoto

APPLYING CONCEPTS Jack had had a bad day on the phones at the networking help desk in Atlanta. An electrical outage coupled with a generator failure had caused servers in San Francisco to be down most of the day. The entire help-desk team had been fielding calls all day explaining to customers why they did not have service and about expected recovery times. The servers were finally online, but it was taking hours to get everything reset and functioning. No one had taken a break all afternoon, but the call queue was still running about 20 minutes behind. Todd, the boss, had asked the team to work late until the queue was empty. It was Jack's son's birthday and his family was expecting Jack home on time. Jack moaned as he realized he might be late for Tyler's party. Everyone pushed hard to empty the queue. As Jack watched the last call leave the queue, he logged off, stood up, and reached for his coat.

And then the call came. Jack was tempted to ignore it, but decided it had to be answered. It was Lacy. Lacy was the executive secretary to the CEO (Chief Executive Officer over the entire company) and when Lacy calls, all priorities yield to Lacy, and Lacy knows it. The CEO was having problems printing to the laser printer in his office. Would Jack please walk down to his office and fix the problem? Jack asks Lacy to check the simple things like, "Is the printer turned on? Is it plugged in?" Lacy gets huffy and says, "Of course, I've checked that. Now come right now. I need to go." Jack walks down to the CEO's office, takes one look at the printer, and turns it on.

> **A+ 220-801 5.3**
>
> He turns to Lacy and says, "I suppose the on/off button was just too technical for you." Lacy glares at him in disbelief. Jack says, "I'll be leaving now." As he walks out, he begins to form a plan as to how he'll defend himself to his boss in the morning, knowing the inevitable call to Todd's office will come.
>
> In a group of two or four students, role-play Jack and Todd and discuss these questions:
>
> 1. Todd is informed the next morning of Jack's behavior. Todd calls Jack into his office. He likes Jack and wants him to be successful in the company. Jack is resistant and feels justified in what he did. As Todd, what do you think is important that Jack understand? How can you explain this to Jack so he can accept it? What would you advise Jack to do? In role-play, one student plays the role of Jack, and another the role of Todd.
>
> 2. Switch roles or switch team members and replay the roles.
>
> 3. What are three principles of relating to people that would be helpful for Jack to keep in mind?

- *Trait 7. **Credibility**.* Convey confidence to your customers. Don't allow yourself to appear confused, afraid, or befuddled. Troubleshoot the problem in a systematic way that portrays confidence and credibility. Get the job done, and do it with excellence. Credible technicians also know when the job is beyond their expertise and when to ask for help.
- *Trait 8. **Integrity and honesty**.* Don't try to hide your mistakes from your customer or your boss. Everyone makes mistakes, but don't compound them by a lack of integrity. Accept responsibility and do what you can to correct the error.
- *Trait 9. **Know the law with respect to your work**.* For instance, observe the laws concerning the use of software. Don't use or install pirated software.
- *Trait 10. **Looking and behaving professionally**.* A professional at work knows to not allow his emotions to interfere with business relationships. If a customer is angry, allow the customer to vent, keeping your own professional distance (You do, however, have the right to expect a customer not to talk to you in an abusive way.) Dress appropriately for the environment. Take a shower each day, and brush your teeth after each meal. Use mouthwash. Iron your shirt. If you're not in good health, try as best you can to take care of the problem. Your appearance matters. And finally—don't use rough language. It is *never* appropriate.

> **Notes** Your customers might never remember what you said or what you did, but they will always remember how you made them feel.

PLANNING FOR GOOD SERVICE

Customers want good service. And to provide good service, you need to have a good plan when servicing customers on the phone or online, on site, or in a shop. This section surveys the entire service situation, from the first contact with the customer to closing the call. We begin with the first contact you have with the customer.

> **A+ Exam Tip** The A+ 220-801 exam expects you to know that when servicing a customer, you should be on time, avoid distractions, set and meet expectations and timelines, communicate the status of the solution with the customer, and deal appropriately with customer confidential materials.

A+ 220-801 5.3

INITIAL CONTACT WITH A CUSTOMER

Your initial contact with a customer might be when the customer comes to you, such as in a retail setting, when you go to the customer's site, when the customer calls you on the phone, or when the customer reaches you by chat or email. In each situation, always follow the specific guidelines of your employer. Let's look at some general guidelines when you go to the customer's site and when the customer calls you on the phone.

BEGINNING A SITE VISIT PROFESSIONALLY

When a technician makes an on-site service call, customers expect him or her to have both technical and interpersonal skills. Prepare for an on-site visit by reviewing information given you by whoever took the call. Know the problem you are going to address, the urgency of the situation, and what computer, software, and hardware need servicing. Arrive with a complete set of equipment appropriate to the visit, which might include a tool kit, flashlight, multimeter, grounding strap and mat, and bootable CDs and DVDs.

When you arrive at the customer's site, greet the customer in a friendly manner and shake his or her hand. Use Mr. or Ms. and last names or Sir or Ma'am rather than first names when addressing the customer, unless you are certain the customer expects you to use a first name. If the site is a residence, know that you should never stay at a site when only a minor is present. If a minor child answers the door, ask to speak with an adult and don't allow the adult to leave the house with only you and the child present.

Figure 7-7 If a customer permits it, begin each new relationship with a handshake

After initial greetings, the first thing you should do is listen and ask questions. As you listen, it's fine to take notes, but don't start the visit by filling out your paperwork. Save the paperwork for later, or have the essentials already filled out before you reach the site.

Figure 7-8 A frustrated customer will appreciate your confidence and friendly attitude

BEGINNING A PHONE CALL PROFESSIONALLY

When you answer the phone, identify yourself and your organization. (Follow the guidelines of your employer on what to say.) Then ask for and write down the name and phone number of the caller. Ask for spelling if necessary. If your help desk supports businesses, get the name of the business the caller represents.

Follow company policies to obtain other specific information you should take when answering an initial call. For example, your company might require that you obtain a licensing or warranty number to determine whether the customer is entitled to receive your support. Be familiar with your company's customer service policies. You might need to refer questions about warranties, licenses, documentation, or procedures to other support personnel or customer relations personnel. After you have obtained all the information you need to know that you are authorized to help the customer, open up the conversation for the caller to describe the problem.

> **Notes** If you spend many hours on the phone at a help desk, use a headset instead of a regular phone to reduce strain on your ears and neck. Investing in a high-quality headset will be worth the money.

INTERVIEW THE CUSTOMER

Troubleshooting begins by interviewing the user. As you ask the user questions, take notes and keep asking questions until you thoroughly understand the problem. Have the customer reproduce the problem, and carefully note each step taken and its results. This process gives

**A+
220-801
5.3**

you clues about the problem and about the customer's technical proficiency, which helps you know how to communicate with the customer.

Here are some questions that can help you learn as much as you can about the problem and its root cause:

1. Please describe the problem. What error messages, unusual displays, or failures did you see? (Possible answer: I see this blue screen with a funny-looking message on it that makes no sense to me.)

2. When did the problem start? (Possible answer: When I first booted after loading this neat little screensaver I downloaded from the web.)

3. What was the situation when the problem occurred? (Possible answers: I was trying to start up my PC. I was opening a document in MS Word. I was using the web to research a project.)

4. What programs or software were you using? (Possible answer: I was using Internet Explorer.)

5. Did you move your computer system recently? (Possible answer: Well, yes. Yesterday I moved the computer case across the room.)

6. Has there been a recent thunderstorm or electrical problem? (Possible answer: Yes, last night. Then when I tried to turn on my PC this morning, nothing happened.)

7. Have you made any hardware, software, or configuration changes? (Possible answer: No, but I think my sister might have.)

8. Has someone else used your computer recently? (Possible answer: Sure, my son uses it all the time.)

9. Is there some valuable data on your system that is not backed up that I should know about before I start working on the problem? (Possible answer: Yes! Yes! My term paper! It's not backed up! You gotta save that!)

10. Can you show me how to reproduce the problem? (Possible answers: Yes, let me show you what to do.)

After you have interviewed the user, ask him to listen while you repeat the problem to make sure you understand it correctly. If you don't understand what the customer is telling you, ask open-ended questions to try to narrow down the specifics of the problem. Re-create the circumstances that existed when the problem occurred in as much detail as you can. Make no assumptions. All users make simple mistakes and then overlook them. And before you begin work, be sure to ask the very important Question 9 listed above, "Does the system hold important data that is not backed up?" Then watch the user reproduce the problem. Or, if the user is not at the computer and you are at the computer, follow his directions to reproduce the problem yourself.

Use diplomacy and good manners when you work with a user to solve a problem. For example, if you suspect that the user dropped the PC, don't ask, "Did you drop the PC?" Put the question in a less accusatory manner: "Could the PC have been dropped?"

> **A+ Exam Tip** The A+ 220-801 exam expects you to be able to clarify customer statements by asking open-ended questions to narrow the scope of the problem and by restating the issue or question.

SET AND MEET CUSTOMER EXPECTATIONS

A+ 220-801 5.3

A professional technician knows that it is his responsibility to set and meet expectations with a customer. It's important to create an expectation of certainty with customers so that they are not left hanging and don't know what will happen next.

Part of setting expectations is to establish a timeline with your customer for the completion of a project. If you cannot solve the problem immediately, explain to the customer what needs to happen and the timeline that she should expect for a solution. Then keep the customer informed about the progress of the solution. For example, you can say to a customer, "I need to return to the office and research the cost of parts that need replacing. I'll call you tomorrow before 10:00 AM with an estimate." If later you find out you need more time, call the customer before 10:00 AM, explain your problem, and give her a new time to expect your call. This kind of service is very much appreciated by customers and, if you are consistent, you will quickly gain their confidence.

Another way to set expectations is to give the customer an opportunity to make decisions about repairs to the customer's equipment. When explaining to the customer what needs to be done to fix a problem, offer repair or replacement options if they apply. Don't make decisions for your customer. Explain the problem and what you must do to fix it, giving as many details as the customer wants. When a customer must make a choice, state the options in a way that does not unfairly favor the solution that makes the most money for you as the technician or for your company. For example, if you must replace a motherboard (a costly repair in parts and labor), explain to the customer the total cost of repairs and then help her decide if it is to her advantage to purchase a new system or repair this one.

© iStockphoto

Figure 7-9 Advise and then allow a customer to make purchasing decisions

WORKING WITH A CUSTOMER ON SITE

As you work with a customer on site, avoid distractions as you work. Don't accept personal calls on your cell phone. Most organizations require that you answer calls from work, but keep the calls to a minimum. Be aware that the customer might be listening, so be careful to not discuss problems with co-workers, the boss, or other situations that might put the company, its employees, or products in a bad light with the customer. If you absolutely must excuse yourself from the on-site visit for personal reasons, explain to the customer the situation and return as soon as possible.

Figure 7-10 Consider yourself a guest at the customer's site

© iStockphoto

As you work, be as unobtrusive as possible. Consider yourself a guest in the customer's office or residence. Don't make a big mess. Keep your tools and papers out of the customer's way. Don't use the phone or sit in the customer's desk chair without permission. If the customer needs to work while you are present, do whatever is necessary to accommodate that.

Protect the customer's confidential materials. Don't read these materials. For example, if you are working on the printer and discover a budget report in the out tray, quickly turn it over so you can't read it, and hand it to the customer. If you notice a financial spreadsheet is displayed on the customer's computer screen, step away and ask the user if she wants to first close the spreadsheet before you work with the computer. If sensitive documents are lying on the customer's desk, you might let him know and ask if he would like to put them out of your view or in a safe place.

When working at a user's desk, follow these general guidelines:

1. Don't take over the mouse or keyboard from the user without permission.
2. Ask permission again before you use the printer or other equipment.
3. Don't use the phone without permission.
4. Don't pile your belongings and tools on top of the user's papers, books, and so forth.
5. Accept personal inconvenience to accommodate the user's urgent business needs. For example, if the user gets an important call while you are working, don't allow your work to interfere. You might need to stop work and perhaps leave the room.
6. Also, if the user is present, ask permission before you make a software or hardware change, even if the user has just given you permission to interact with the PC.

Figure 7-11 Teaching a user how to fix her problem can prevent it from reoccurring

In some PC support situations, it is appropriate to consider yourself a support to the user as well as to the PC. Your goals can include educating the user, as well as repairing the computer. If you want users to learn something from a problem they caused, explain how to fix the problem and walk them through the process if necessary. Don't fix the problem yourself unless they ask you to. It takes a little longer to train the user, but it is more productive in the end because the user learns more and is less likely to repeat the mistake.

WORKING WITH A CUSTOMER ON THE PHONE

Phone support requires more interaction with customers than any other type of PC support. To understand the problem and also give clear instructions, you must be able to visualize what the customer sees at his or her PC. Patience is required if the customer must be told each key to press or command button to click. Help-desk support requires excellent communication skills, good phone manners, and lots of patience. As your help-desk skills improve,

Figure 7-12 Allow an irate customer to vent, and then speak calmly

© iStockphoto

you will learn to think through the process as though you were sitting in front of the PC yourself. Drawing diagrams and taking notes as you talk can be very helpful.

If your call is accidentally disconnected, call back immediately. Don't eat or drink while on the phone. If you must put callers on hold, tell them how long it will be before you get back to them. Speak clearly and don't talk too fast. Don't complain about your job, your boss or co-workers, your company, or other companies or products to your customers. A little small talk is okay and is sometimes beneficial in easing a tense situation, but keep it upbeat and positive.

APPLYING CONCEPTS Julie and James were good friends who worked together at the corporate help desk for internal customers. Staying on the phones all day can be tense and demanding and they had learned that good humor and occasional chit-chat can break up the day. Julie was on a long troubleshooting call and the call queue was getting backed up. James was answering one call after another trying to keep up. Julie says to her customer, "I have to check with another technician. I'll be right back," and puts the customer on hold. She turns to James and says, "You gonna go to that new movie on Saturday?" James puts his caller on hold and answers, "I sure want to. Wonder what times it's showing. Let me see." James and Julie browse through the movie listings and decide when to meet for the movie and where to eat later. About 10 minutes later, Julie and James return to their callers. Julie says to her caller, "Okay, I have the information I need. Let's continue."

In a small group, discuss this situation and answer the following questions:

1. If you were Julie's caller, how would you feel about being left on hold for 10 minutes in the middle of a long call?

2. What principles of customer service do you think Julie and James need to reconsider?

3. If you were Julie or James, how do you think you would handle this situation?

DEALING WITH DIFFICULT CUSTOMERS

Most customers are polite and appreciate your help. And, if you make it a habit to treat others as you want to be treated, you'll find that most of your customers will tend to treat you well, too. However, occasionally you'll have to deal with a difficult customer. In this part of the chapter, you'll learn how to work with customers who are not knowledgeable, who are overly confident, and who complain.

WHEN THE CUSTOMER IS NOT KNOWLEDGEABLE

A help-desk call with a customer who is not knowledgeable about how to use a computer is the most difficult situation to handle. When on site, you can put a PC in good repair without depending on a customer to help you, but when you are trying to solve a problem over the phone, with a customer as your only eyes, ears, and hands, a computer-illiterate user can present a challenge. Here are some tips for handling this situation:

▲ *Tip 1.* Be specific with your instructions. For example, instead of saying, "Open Windows Explorer," say, "Using your mouse, right-click the Start button and select Open Windows Explorer from the menu."

Figure 7-13 Learn to be patient and friendly when helping users

▲ *Tip 2.* Don't ask the customer to do something that might destroy settings or files without first having the customer back them up carefully. If you think the customer can't handle your request, ask for some on-site help.
▲ *Tip 3.* Frequently ask the customer what is displayed on the screen to help you track the keystrokes and action.
▲ *Tip 4.* Follow along at your own PC. It's easier to direct the customer, keystroke by keystroke, if you are doing the same things.
▲ *Tip 5.* Give the customer plenty of opportunity to ask questions.
▲ *Tip 6.* Compliment the customer whenever you can to help the customer gain confidence.
▲ *Tip 7.* If you determine that the customer cannot help you solve the problem without a lot of coaching, you might need to tactfully request that the caller have someone with more experience call you. The customer will most likely breathe a sigh of relief and have someone take over the problem.

A+
220-801
5.3

> **Notes** When solving computer problems in an organization other than your own, check with technical support within that organization instead of working only with the PC user. The user might not be aware of policies that have been set on the PC to prevent changes to the OS, hardware, or applications.

WHEN THE CUSTOMER IS OVERLY CONFIDENT

Sometimes customers are proud of their computer knowledge. Such customers might want to give advice, take charge of a call, withhold information they think you don't need to know, or execute commands at the computer without letting you know, so you don't have enough information to follow along. A situation like this must be handled with tact and respect for the customer. Here are a few tips:

- *Tip 1*. When you can, compliment the customer's knowledge, experience, or insight.
- *Tip 2*. Slow the conversation down. You can say, "Please slow down. You're moving too fast for me to follow. Help me catch up."
- *Tip 3*. Don't back off from using problem-solving skills. You must still have the customer check the simple things, but direct the conversation with tact. For example, you can say, "I know you've probably already gone over these simple things, but could we just do them again together?"
- *Tip 4*. Be careful not to accuse the customer of making a mistake.
- *Tip 5*. Even though the customer might be using technical jargon, keep to your policy of not using jargon back to the customer unless you're convinced he truly understands you.

> **A+ Exam Tip** The A+ 220-801 exam expects you to know that it is important to not minimize a customer's problem and to not be judgmental toward a customer.

WHEN THE CUSTOMER COMPLAINS

When you are on site or on the phone, a customer might complain to you about your organization, products, or service or the service and product of another company. Consider the complaint to be helpful feedback that can lead to a better product or service and better customer relationships. Here are a few suggestions that can help you handle complaints and defuse customer anger:

- *Suggestion 1*. Be an active listener, and let customers know they are not being ignored. Look for the underlying problem. Don't take the complaint or the anger personally.
- *Suggestion 2*. Give the customer a little time to vent, and apologize when you can. Then start the conversation from the beginning, asking questions, taking notes, and solving problems. Unless you must have the information for problem solving, don't spend a lot of time finding out exactly whom the customer dealt with and what happened to upset the customer.
- *Suggestion 3*. Don't be defensive. It's better to leave the customer with the impression that you and your company are listening and willing to admit mistakes. No matter how much anger is expressed, resist the temptation to argue or become defensive.
- *Suggestion 4*. Know how your employer wants you to handle a situation where you are verbally abused. If this type of language is happening, you might say something like this in a very calm tone of voice: "I'm sorry, but my employer does not require me to accept this kind of talk."

▲ *Suggestion 5.* If the customer is complaining about a product or service that is not from your company, don't start off by saying, "That's not our problem." Instead, listen to the customer complain. Don't appear as though you don't care.

▲ *Suggestion 6.* If the complaint is against you or your product, identify the underlying problem if you can. Ask questions and take notes. Then pass these notes on to people in your organization who need to know.

▲ *Suggestion 7.* Sometimes simply making progress or reducing the problem to a manageable state reduces the customer's anxiety. As you are talking to a customer, summarize what you have both agreed on or observed so far in the conversation.

▲ *Suggestion 8.* Point out ways that *you* think communication could be improved. For example, you might say, "I'm sorry, but I'm having trouble understanding what you want. Could you please slow down, and let's take this one step at a time."

Figure 7-14 When a customer is upset, try to find a place of agreement

APPLYING CONCEPTS Andy was one of the most intelligent and knowledgeable support technicians in his group working for CloudPool, Inc. He was about to be promoted to software engineer and today was his last day on the help desk. Sarah, a potential customer with little computer experience, calls asking for help accessing the company web site. Andy says, "The URL is www dot cloud pool dot com." Sarah responds, "What's a URL?" Andy's patience grows thin. He's thinking to himself, "Oh, help! Just two more hours and I'm off these darn phones." He answers Sarah in a tone of voice that says, hey, I really think you're an idiot! He says to her, "You know, lady! That address box at the top of your browser. Now enter www dot cloud pool dot com!" Sarah gets all flustered and intimidated and doesn't know what to say next. She really wants to know what a browser is, but instead she says, "Wait. I'll just ask someone in the office to help me," and hangs up the phone.

A+ 220-801 5.3

> Discuss the situation with others in a small group and answer these questions:
>
> 1. If you were Andy's manager and overheard this call, how would you handle the situation?
> 2. What principles of working with customers does Andy need to keep in mind?
>
> Two students sit back-to-back, one playing the role of Andy and the other playing the role of Sarah. Play out the entire conversation. Others in the group can offer suggestions and constructive criticism.

THE CUSTOMER DECIDES WHEN THE WORK IS DONE

When you think you've solved the problem, allow the customer to decide when the service is finished to his or her satisfaction. For remote support, generally, the customer ends the call or chat session, not the technician. If you end the call too soon and the problem is not completely resolved, the customer can be frustrated, especially if it is difficult to contact you again.

For on-site work, after you have solved the problem, complete these tasks before you close the call:

1. If you changed anything on the PC after you booted it, reboot one more time to make sure you have not caused a problem with the boot.

2. Allow the customer enough time to be fully satisfied that all is working. Does the printer work? Print a test page. Does the network connection work? Can the customer log on to the network and access data on it?

3. If you backed up data before working on the problem and then restored the data from backups, ask the user to verify that the data is fully restored.

4. Review the service call with the customer. Summarize the instructions and explanations you have given during the call. This is an appropriate time to fill out your paperwork and explain to the customer what you have written. Then ask if she has any questions.

5. Explain preventive maintenance to the customer (such as deleting temporary files from the hard drive or cleaning the mouse). Most customers don't have preventive maintenance contracts for their PCs and appreciate the time you take to show them how they can take better care of their computers. One technician keeps a pack of monitor wipes in his tool kit and ends each call by cleaning the customer's monitor screen.

It's a good idea to follow up later with the customer and ask if he is still satisfied with your work and if he has any more questions. For example, you can say to the customer, "I'll call you on Monday to make sure everything is working and you're still satisfied with the work." And then on Monday make that call.

> **A+ Exam Tip** The A+ 220-801 exam expects you to know to follow up with the customer at a later date to verify his or her satisfaction.

SOMETIMES YOU MUST ESCALATE A PROBLEM

You are not going to solve every computer problem you encounter. Knowing how to **escalate** properly so the problem is assigned to those higher in the support chain is one of the first things you should learn on a new job. Know your company's policy for escalation. What documents or entries in the ticket-tracking software do you use? Who do you contact? How do you pass the problem on (email, phone call, or an online entry in a database)? Do you remain the responsible "support" party, or does the person now addressing the problem become the new contact? Are you expected to keep in touch with the customer and the problem, or are you totally out of the picture?

For help-desk support, escalation is most likely done in the call-tracking system where you keep your call notes. It's very important to include detailed information in your notes so that the next person can pick up the call without having to waste time finding out information you already knew.

When you escalate, let the customer know. Tell the customer you are passing the problem on to someone who is more experienced or has access to more extensive resources. In most cases, the person who receives the escalation will immediately contact the customer and assume responsibility for the problem. However, in some situations you should follow through, at least to confirm that the new person and the customer have made contact.

If you check back with the customer only to find out that the other support person has not called or followed through to the customer's satisfaction, don't lay blame or point fingers. Just do whatever you can to help within your company guidelines. Your call to the customer will go a long way toward helping the situation.

THE JOB ISN'T FINISHED UNTIL THE PAPERWORK IS DONE

For on-site support, a customer expects documentation about your services. Include in the documentation sufficient details broken down by cost of individual parts, hours worked, and cost per hour. Give the documentation to the customer at the end of the service and keep a copy for yourself. For phone support, the documentation stays in-house.

If your organization is using an electronic tracking system and you're providing phone support, most likely you're typing notes as the call happens. Be clear with your notes, especially if others must handle the problem. If you cannot solve the problem on this one call, the next time you talk with the customer, you'll be dependent on your notes to remember the details of the previous call. You'll also want to use the solution to help build your knowledge base about this type of problem. Make the notes detailed enough so that you can use them later when solving similar problems. Also, know that tracking-system notes are sometimes audited.

If you don't have an electronic tracking system, after the call, create a written or digital record to build your own knowledge base. Record the initial symptoms of the problem, the source of the problem you actually discovered, how you made that discovery, and how the problem was finally solved. File your documentation according to symptoms or according to solutions.

> **APPLYING CONCEPTS** Daniel had not been a good note taker in school, and this lack of skill was affecting his work. His manager, Jonathan, had been watching Daniel's notes in the ticketing system at the help desk he worked on, and was not happy with what he saw. Jonathan had pointed out to Daniel more than once that his cryptic notes with sketchy information would one day cause major problems. On Monday

A+ 220-801 5.3

morning, calls were hammering the help desk because a server had gone down over the weekend and many internal customers were not able to get to their data. Daniel escalated one call from a customer named Matt to a tier-two help desk. Later that day, Sandra, a tier-two technician, received the escalated ticket, and to her dismay the phone number of the customer was missing. She called Daniel. "How am I to call this customer? You only have his first name, and these notes about the problem don't even make sense!" Daniel apologized to Sandra, but the damage was done.

Two days later, an angry Matt calls the manager of the help desk to complain that his problem is still not solved. Jonathan listens to Matt vent and apologizes for the problem his help desk has caused. It's a little embarrassing to Jonathan to have to ask Matt for his call-back information and to repeat the details of the problem. He gives the information to Sandra and the problem gets a quick resolution.

Discuss this situation in a small group and answer the following questions:

1. If you were Daniel, what could you do to improve note taking in the ticketing system?
2. After Sandra called, do you think Daniel should have told Jonathan about the problem? Why or why not?
3. If you were Jonathan, how would you handle the situation with Daniel?

Two students play the role of Daniel and Jonathan when Jonathan calls Daniel into his office to discuss the call he just received from Matt. The other students in the group can watch and make suggestions as to how to improve the conversation.

WORKING WITH CO-WORKERS

Learn to be a professional when working with co-workers. A professional at work is someone who puts business matters above personal matters. In big bold letters I can say **the key to being professional is to learn to not be personally offended when someone lets you down or does not please you.** Remember, most people do the best they can considering the business and personal constraints they're up against. Getting offended leads to becoming bitter about others and about your job. Learn to keep negative opinions to yourself, and to expect the best of others. When a co-worker starts to gossip, try to politely change the subject.

Practice good organizational skills. Clean your desk before you leave work each day. Put things away. Use a good filing system. If you don't know how to organize your things, ask someone in the office for advice. Organize your time by making to-do lists and sticking with them as best you can. It's amazing the positive impression good organization makes with co-workers and the boss.

Know your limitations and be willing to admit when you can't do something. For example, Larry's boss stops by his desk and asks him to accept one more project. Larry already is working many hours overtime just to keep up. He needs to politely say to his boss, "I can accept this new project only if you relieve me of some of these tasks."

Learn how to handle conflict at work. Few of us have enough social skills to be able to effectively confront a co-worker about his faults. In almost every situation, when a co-worker disappoints us, the appropriate response is to shake it off, to not gossip to other co-workers about the problem, and move on. If you can't do that, the next best thing is to go to your boss or the co-worker's boss with the problem. Hopefully your boss has been trained in handling conflict and will take care of the problem. If you do find yourself in a situation where you want to help a co-worker with his problem, go to the co-worker with a good attitude and a sincere offer to help resolve the problem. And one more tip: Never give bad news or point out

Figure 7-15 Co-workers who act professionally are fun to work with

a fault by email. Using email, you are not able to communicate your tone of voice or read the facial expression of the other person. And, if miscommunication happens, you will not be able to immediately clear it up. Speak face to face, and if that is not possible, speak by telephone.

APPLYING CONCEPTS Ray was new at the corporate help desk that supported hospitals across the nation. He had only had a couple weeks of training before he was turned loose on the phones. He was a little nervous the first day he took calls without a mentor sitting beside him. His first call came from Fernanda, a radiology technician who was trying to log onto her computer system to start the day. When Fernanda entered her user account and passcode, an error message appeared saying her user account was not valid. She told Ray she had tried it several times on two different computers. Ray checked his database and found her account, which appeared to be in good order. He asked her to try it again. She did and got the same results. In his two weeks of training, this problem had never occurred. He told her, "I'm sorry, I don't know how to solve this problem." She said, "Okay, well, thank you anyway," and hung up. She immediately called the help desk number back and the call was answered by Jackie, who sits across the room from Ray. Fernanda said, "The other guy couldn't fix my problem. Can you help me?"

"What other guy?" Jackie asks. "I think his name was Ray." "Oh, him! He's new and he doesn't know much and besides that he should have asked for help. Tell me the problem." Jackie resets the account and the problem is solved.

In a group of three or more students, discuss and answer the following questions:

1. What mistake did Ray make? What should he have done or said?

2. What mistake did Jackie make? What should she have done or said?

3. What three principles of relating to customers and co-workers would be helpful for Ray and Jackie to keep in mind?

Hands-on Project 7-1 Evaluating Your Own Interpersonal Skills with Customers and Co-workers

A+ 220-801 5.3

Assume that you are working as a PC support technician for a corporation. Your job requires you to give desk-side support to users, answer the phone at the help desk, and make an occasional on-site call at corporate branches. Answer the following questions:

1. In the role of desk-side support to users, what do you think is your strongest social skill that would help you succeed in this role?
2. What is likely to be your greatest interpersonal weakness that might present a challenge to you in this role?
3. What is one change you might consider making that will help you to improve on this weakness?
4. In the role of phone support at the help desk, what part of that job would you enjoy the most? What part would give you the greatest challenge?
5. When making on-site calls to corporate branches, what part of this job would you enjoy the most? What interpersonal skills, if any, would you need to develop so that you could do your best in this role?

Hands-on Project 7-2 The Johari Window Online Game

The Johari (pronounced "Joe-Harry" after the two men who created it) window reveals an interesting view of how we relate to others. Sometimes when we evaluate our own interpersonal skills, we overlook our greatest assets that others can see. This project is designed to help others reveal to you those assets. The house in Figure 7-16 represents who we are. Room 1 is what we know about ourselves that we allow others to see. Room 2 is what others see about us that we don't see ourselves (our blind spots). Room 3 is what we see about ourselves that we hide from others. And Room 4 contains traits in us that we don't know about and neither do others see—traits yet to be discovered.

As we move Bar A to the right, we are making a conscious decision to reveal more about ourselves to others, which is a technique successful salespeople often use to immediately connect with their customers. The theory is that if you move Bar A to the right, not only are you choosing to reveal what you normally would hide, but you are also moving the bar so that more of Room 4 can be seen in Room 2. This means that others can see more about you that you don't see. When we allow others to tell us something about ourselves, we are moving Bar B away from us, which, in effect, allows us to see more of who we really are. Therefore, to learn more about yourself, you can do two things: Reveal more of yourself to others and allow others to tell you more about yourself. Try playing the Interactive Johari Window game at *www.kevan.org/johari* by Kevan Davis. Then answer the following questions:

1. What five or six descriptive words did you use to describe yourself at the beginning of the game?
2. What words did others use to describe you?

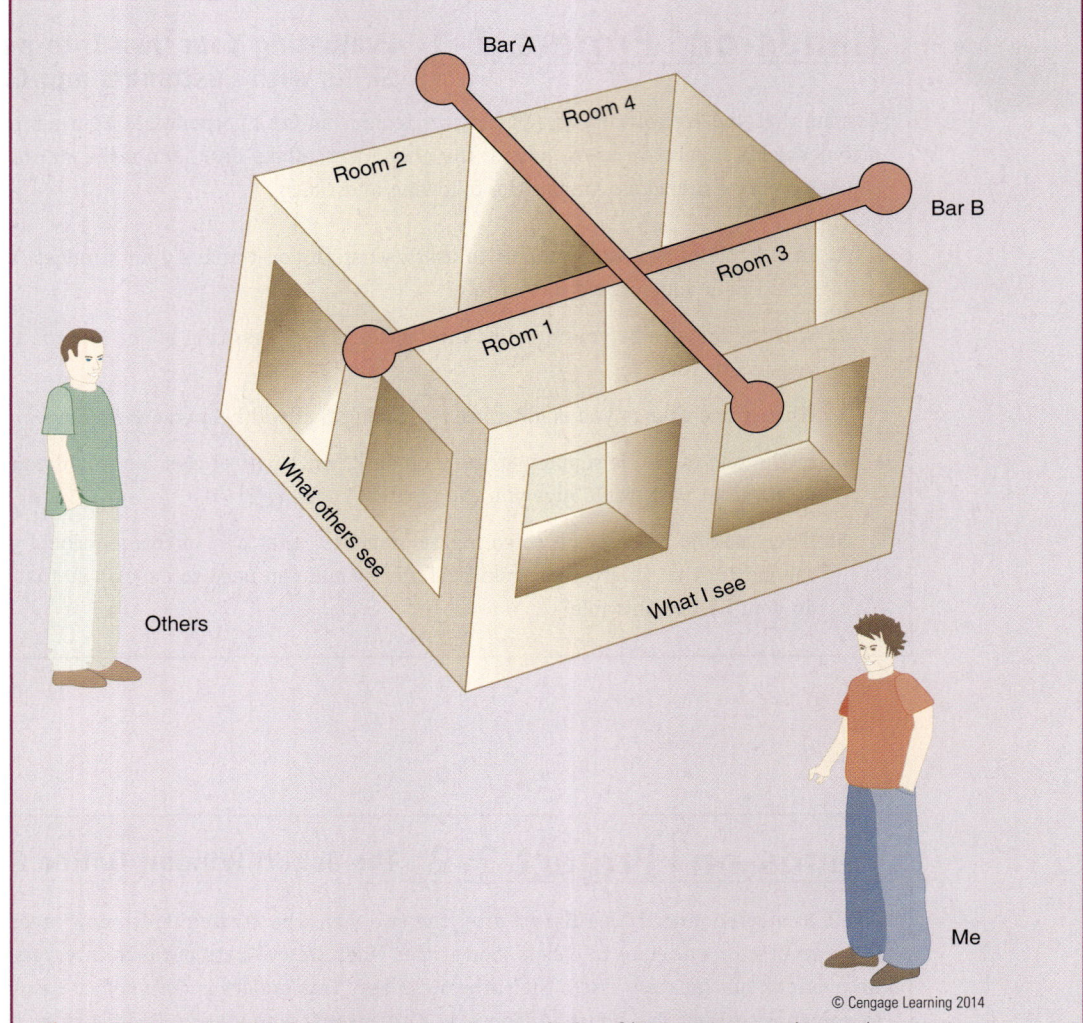

Figure 7-16 Johari Window demonstrates the complexity of how we see ourselves and how others see us

3. How has input from your friends adjusted how you see yourself?

4. How might this adjustment affect the way you will relate to customers and co-workers on the job?

5. If you were to play the Interactive Johari Window game a second time, would you still use the same five or six descriptive words you used the first time? If your answer is no, what new words would you use?

Hands-on | Project 7-3 Handling Conflict at Work

Jenny works with a team of seven other professionals. Linda, a team member, is a very close personal friend of the boss. With the boss's approval, Linda took a sudden and unexpected two-week vacation to go on a cruise during the team's most difficult month of the year. One team member, Jason, had to work 16 days nonstop, without a day off during Linda's vacation. Other team members

A+ 220-801 5.3

soon began complaining and resenting Linda for the unbearable workload her vacation caused them. A few weeks back from vacation, Linda began to notice that she was being excluded from informal luncheons and after-work gatherings. She confided in Jenny that she could not understand why everyone seemed to be mad at her. Jenny, not wanting to cause trouble, said nothing to Linda. In a group of four or five classmates, discuss the answers to the following questions:

1. If you were Jenny, what would you do?
2. What would you do if you were Linda?
3. What would you do if you were Jason?
4. What would you do if you were another team member?
5. If you were the boss and got wind of the resentment against Linda, what would you do?

Hands-on Project 7-4 Learning to Be a Good Communicator

Working with a partner, discuss ways to respond to the following statements made by a customer. Then decide on your best response.

1. My computer is all dark.
2. I got so mad at my laptop, I threw it to the floor. Now it won't start. I think it's still under warranty.
3. My dog chewed the mouse cord and now nothing works.
4. I heard you tell that other customer that your product stinks. I came here to buy one. Now what am I to do?
5. I don't see the "any" key. Where is it?

Hands-on Project 7-5 Interacting with the User

Rob, a PC service technician, has been called on site to repair a PC. He has not spoken directly with the user, Lisa, but he knows the floor of the building where she works and can look for her name on her cubicle. The following is a description of his actions. Create a table with two columns. List in one column the mistakes he made in the following description and in the next column the correct action he should have taken.

Rob's company promised that a service technician would come some time during the next business day after the call was received. Rob was given the name and address of the user and the problem, which was stated as "PC will not boot." Rob arrived the following day at about 10 AM. He found Lisa's cubicle, but she was not present. Because Lisa was not present, Rob decided not to disturb the papers all over her desk, so he laid his notebooks and tools on top of her work.

Rob tried to boot the PC, and it gave errors indicating a corrupted file system on the hard drive. He successfully booted from a CD and was able to access a directory list of drive C. The list was corrupted and jumbled and he realized most of the files were corrupted. Next, Rob used a recovery utility to try to recover the files and directories but was unable to do so. He began to suspect that a virus had caused the problem, so he ran a virus scan program that did not find the suspected virus.

A+ 220-801 5.3

He made a call to his technical support to ask for suggestions. Technical support suggested he try erasing everything on the hard drive to remove any possible viruses and then reinstall Windows. Rob cleaned everything off the hard drive and was on the phone with technical support, in the process of reloading Windows from the company's file server, when Lisa arrived.

Lisa took one look at her PC and gasped. She caught her breath and asked where her data was. Rob replied, "A virus destroyed your hard drive. I had to reformat."

Lisa tried to explain the importance of the destroyed data. Rob replied, "Guess you'll learn to make backups now." Lisa left to find her manager.

Hands-on | Project 7-6   Learn from the Best

Relate a first hand experience when a technician, co-worker, help-desk personnel, or salesperson followed best practices while helping a customer or co-worker. What is a principle this person applied that could help you when working with your own customers or co-workers?

DEALING WITH PROHIBITED CONTENT AND ACTIVITY

A+ 220-801 5.4

Many organizations have documented a code of conduct that applies to its employees and/or customers. As an employee, you need to be aware of these codes of conduct and the procedures to follow when you believe these rules have been broken. Examples of prohibited content or activity might be when an employee saves pornographic photos to company computers, uses company computers and time for personal shopping, or installs pirated software on these computers.

As a PC support technician, you need to be especially aware of the issues surrounding software copyrights. When someone purchases software from a software vendor, that person has only purchased a **license** for the software, which is the right to use it. The buyer does not legally *own* the software and, therefore, does not have the right to distribute it. The right to copy the work, called a **copyright**, belongs to the creator of the work or others to whom the creator transfers this right. Copyrights are intended to legally protect the intellectual property rights of organizations or individuals to creative works, which include books, images, and software.

Making unauthorized copies of original software violates the Federal Copyright Act of 1976 and is called **software piracy** or, more officially, software copyright infringement. (This act allows for one backup copy of software to be made.) Making a copy of software and then selling it or giving it away is a violation of the law. Because it is so easy to do, and because so many people do it, many people don't realize that it's illegal. Normally, only the employee who violated the copyright law is liable for infringement; however, in some cases, an employer or supervisor is also held responsible, even when the copies were made without the employer's knowledge.

> **Notes** By purchasing a **site license**, a company can obtain the right to use multiple copies of software.

> **A+ Exam Tip** The A+ 220-801 exam expects you to know how to report prohibited content or activity through the proper channels and about a chain-of-custody document you might be called on to sign.

**A+
220-801
5.4**

When you start a new job, find out from your employer how to deal with prohibited content or activity. Here are some things you need to know:

- When you identify what you believe to be an infringement of the law or the company's code of conduct, where do you turn to report the issue? Make sure you go only through proper channels; don't spread rumors or accusations with those who are not in these channels.
- What data or device should you immediately preserve as evidence for what you believe has happened? For example, if you believe you have witnessed a customer or employee using a company computer for a crime, should you remove and secure the hard drive from the computer or should you remove and secure the entire computer?
- Proper documentation surrounding the evidence of a crime is crucial to a criminal investigation. What documentation are you expected to submit and to whom is it submitted? This documentation might track the chain of custody for the evidence, which includes exactly what, when, and from whom evidence was collected, the condition of this evidence, and how the evidence was secured while it was in your possession. It also includes a paper trail of exactly to whom the evidence has been passed on and when. For example, suppose you suspect that a criminal act has happened and you hold a CD that you believe contains evidence of this crime. You need to carefully document exactly when and how you received the CD. Also, don't pass it on to someone else in your organization unless you have this person's signature on a chain-of-custody document so that you can later prove you handled the evidence appropriately. You don't want the evidence to not be allowed in a court of law because you have been accused of misconduct or there are allegations of tampering with the evidence.

Now let's turn our attention to a happier topic: customizing computer systems.

CUSTOMIZING COMPUTER SYSTEMS

**A+
220-801
1.9**

Many computer vendors and manufacturers offer to build customized systems to meet specific needs of their customers. As a technical retail associate, you need to know how to recommend to a customer which computer components are needed for his or her specific needs. You also might be called on to select and purchase components for a customized system and perhaps even build this system from parts. In this part of the chapter, we focus on several types of customized systems you might be expected to know how to configure and what parts to consider when configuring these systems.

Here are important principles to keep in mind when customizing a system to meet customer needs:

- **Meet applications requirements.** Consider the applications the customer will use and make sure the hardware meets or exceeds the recommended requirements for these applications. Consider any special hardware the applications might require such as a joystick for gaming or a digital tablet for graphics applications.
- **Balance functionality and budget.** When working with a customer's budget, put the most money on the hardware components that are most needed for the primary intended purposes of the system. For example, if you are building a customized gaming PC, a RAID hard drive configuration is not nearly as important as the quality of the video subsystem.
- **Consider hardware compatibility.** When selecting hardware, start with the motherboard and processor. Then select other components that are compatible with this motherboard.

A+ 220-801 1.9

Now let's look at the components you need to consider when building these eight types of customized systems: graphics or CAD/CAM workstation, audio- and video-editing workstation, virtualization workstation, gaming PC, Home Theater PC, home server PC, thick client, and thin client.

> **A+ Exam Tip** The A+ 220-801 exam expects you to know how to customize each of the eight types of computers covered in this part of the chapter.

GRAPHICS OR CAD/CAM WORKSTATION

You might be called on to configure a graphics or CAD/CAM (computer-aided design/computer-aided manufacturing) workstation. People who use these systems might be an engineer working with CAD software to design bridges, an architect who designs skyscrapers, a graphics designer who creates artistic pages for children's books, or a landscape designer who creates lawn and garden plans. Examples of the applications these people might use include AutoCAD Design Suite by Autodesk (*usa.autodesk.com*) or Adobe Illustrator by Adobe Systems (*www.adobe.com*).

These graphics-intensive, advanced applications perform complex calculations, use large and complex files, and can benefit from the most powerful of workstations. Because rendering 3D graphics is a requirement, a high-end or ultra-high-end video card is needed. Figure 7-17 shows one ultra-high-end customized CAD workstation by CAD Computers (*www.cadcomputers.com*).

Source: cadcomputers.com

Figure 7-17 A high-end CAD workstation customized for maximum performance

Here is a breakdown of the requirements for these high-end workstations:

▲ *Use a motherboard that provides quad channels for memory and plenty of memory slots and install a generous amount of RAM.* In the ad shown in Figure 7-17,

A+ 220-801 1.9

the motherboard has 12 memory slots, and the system has 48 GB installed RAM. Notice the board can support up to 192 GB RAM, so there's room for upgrading RAM. For best performance, you can install the maximum amount of RAM the board supports. The board also has two processor slots, so you can install a second processor to further improve performance.

▲ *Use a powerful multicore processor with a large CPU cache.* In the ad shown in Figure 7-17, the Intel Second Generation Xeon processor, which is rated for high-end workstations and servers, has six cores and a 12 MB cache. This processor can handle the high demands of complex calculations performed by advanced software.

▲ *Use fast hard drives with plenty of capacity.* Notice the system in Figure 7-17 has two hard drives. The faster hard drive runs at 10 K RPM and holds the Windows installation. The moderately fast second hard drive has a capacity of 2 TB to accommodate large amounts of data. For best hard drive performance in any system, be sure the motherboard and hard drives are all using SATA III.

▲ *Use a high-end video card.* To provide the best 3D graphics experience, use a high-end video card. Probably the best chipset manufacturer for high-end video cards is NVIDIA (*www.nvidia.com*). The ad in Figure 7-17 mentions the Quadro 6000. The Quadro family of graphics processors has the best performing GPUs on the market, and the Quadro 6000 is the best Quadro currently sold (see Figure 7-18). It uses a PCIe ×16 slot and has 6 GB of GDDR5 video memory using a 384-bit video bus. The card can support a native screen resolution of 2560 × 1600. The card alone cost almost $4,000 and accounts for a major portion of the total system cost, which is almost $10,000.

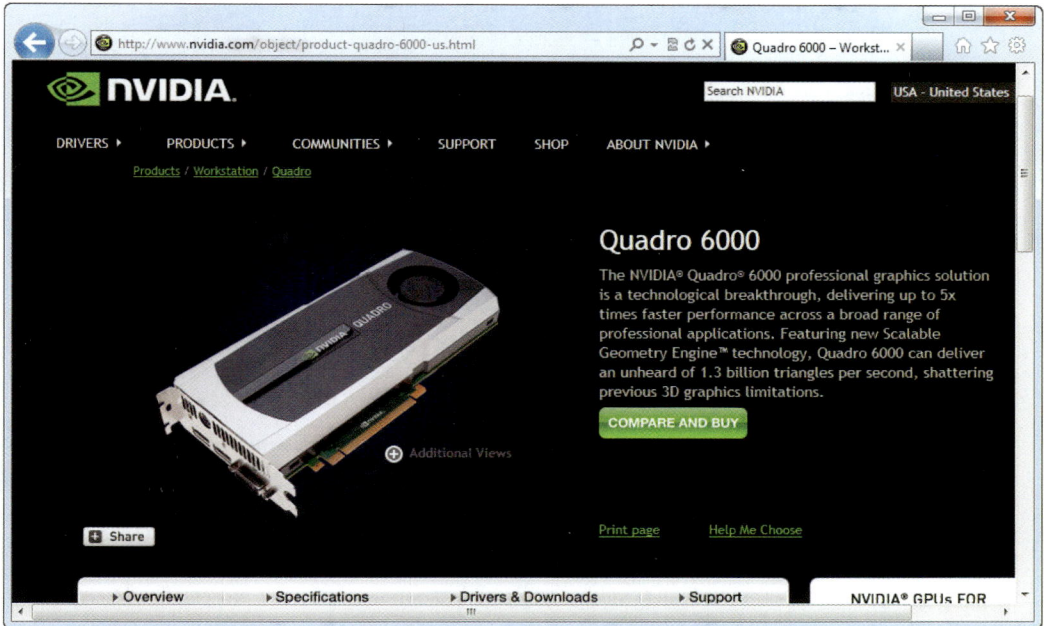

Source: www.nvidia.com

Figure 7-18 This ultra-high-end video card by NVIDIA costs almost $4,000

Wouldn't it be fun to build this system! However, not all graphics workstations need to be this powerful or this expensive. You can still get adequate performance in a system for less than half the cost if you drop the processor down to an Intel Core i7, drop RAM down to 16 GB, and use an NVIDIA Quadro 2000 GPU on the video card along with a motherboard that supports dual-channel memory.

AUDIO AND VIDEO EDITING WORKSTATION

Examples of professional applications software used to edit music, audio, video, and movies include Camtasia by TechSmith (*techsmith.com*), Adobe Production Premium by Adobe Systems (*adobe.com*), Media Composer by Avid (*avid.com*), and Final Cut Pro by Apple Computers (*apple.com*). (Final Cut Pro is used only on Macs, which are popular computers in the video editing industry.) Audio and video editing applications are not usually as power-hungry as CAD/CAM and graphics applications. The major difference in requirements is that most audio and video editing does not require rendering 3D graphics; therefore, you can get by with a not-so-expensive graphics card and processor. Customers might require a Blu-ray drive and dual monitors. Recall from Chapter 6 that the best LCD monitors that provide the most accurate color are LED monitors with a class IPS rating. Figure 7-19 shows one customized video editing workstation by ADK Media Group (*adkvideoediting.com*).

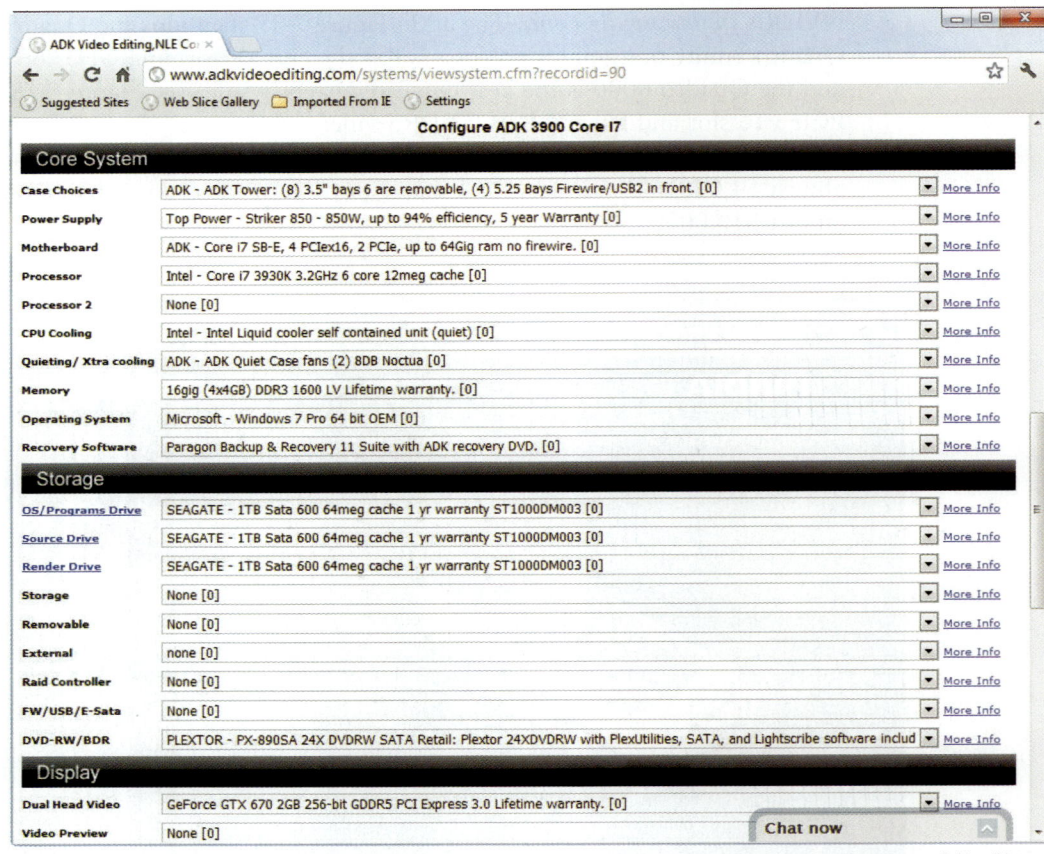

Source: www.adkvideoediting.com

Figure 7-19 This mid-range video editing workstation uses a Core i7 processor and GeForce graphics processor

Here is what you need for a mid-range to high-end audio/video editing workstation:

▲ Use a motherboard that supports dual, triple, or quad channel memory running at least at 1600 MHz RAM speed.
▲ Use a Core i7 or higher processor.
▲ Install at least 16 GB RAM; more is better.

A+ 220-801 1.9

▲ Select a good video card that has a GeForce GTX graphics processor or better. GeForce is a family of graphics processors designed by NVIDIA that is not as high end as the Quadro graphics processors, but still gives good video performance. Most users will require dual or triple monitors. You might need to consider dual video cards for optimum video performance or for more than two video ports.
▲ Use a double-sided, dual layer DVD burner and possibly a Blu-ray burner.
▲ Install one or more fast and large hard drives, running at least 7200 RPM.

VIRTUALIZATION WORKSTATION

Virtualization is when one physical machine hosts multiple activities that are normally done on multiple machines. One way to implement virtualization is to use virtual machine management software to create a virtual machine (VM) that uses simulated hardware. Each virtual machine has its own virtual hardware (virtual motherboard, processor, RAM, hard drive, and so forth) and can act like a physical computer. You can install an OS in each VM and then install applications in the VM. A program that manages VMs is called a **hypervisor**. Examples of hypervisors used on a desktop computer include XenClient by Citrix, Windows Virtual PC by Microsoft, and Oracle VirtualBox. Figure 7-20 shows a Windows 7 Professional desktop with two virtual machines running that were created by Windows Virtual PC. One VM is running Windows 7 Home Premium, and the other VM is running Windows XP.

Source: Windows 7 and Windows Virtual PC, both by Microsoft

Figure 7-20 Two virtual machines running, each with its own virtual hardware and OS installed

Here are the requirements for a desktop computer that will be used to run multiple virtual machines:

▲ Each VM has its own virtual processor, so it's important the processor is a multicore processor. All dual core or higher processors and all motherboards sold today support **hardware-assisted virtualization (HAV)**. This technology enhances the processor support for virtual machines and must be enabled in BIOS setup.

A+ 220-801 1.9

▲ Some virtual machine management programs are designed so that each VM that is running ties up all the RAM assigned to it. Therefore, you need extra amounts of RAM when a computer is running several VMs.

▲ Each VM must have an operating system installed, and it takes about 20 GB for a Windows 7 installation. In addition, you need hard drive space for each application installed in each VM. Make sure you have adequate hard drive space for each VM.

When deciding how to use the overall budget for a virtualization workstation, maximize the number of CPU cores and the amount of installed RAM.

GAMING PC

Gaming computers benefit from a powerful processor and a high-end video card and sound card. Gamers who are also computer hobbyists might want to overclock their CPUs or use dual video cards for extra video performance. Take extra care to make sure the cooling methods are adequate. Because of the heat generated by multiple video cards and overclocking, liquid cooling is sometimes preferred. Also recall from Chapter 4 that when using the LGA2011 socket, liquid cooling is a Microsoft recommendation. Most gaming PCs use onboard surround sound, or you can use a sound card to improve sound. A lighted case with a clear plastic side makes for a great look.

Figure 7-21 shows a group of gaming PCs built by iBUYPOWER (*ibuypower.com*). Notice several of the PCs use liquid cooling, and all use a powerful processor with at least 8 GB of RAM. The video card uses a GeForce GTX or GT graphics processor or an AMD Radeon HD graphics processor. The Radeon line of graphics processors by AMD are comparable to the NVIDIA GeForce graphics processors.

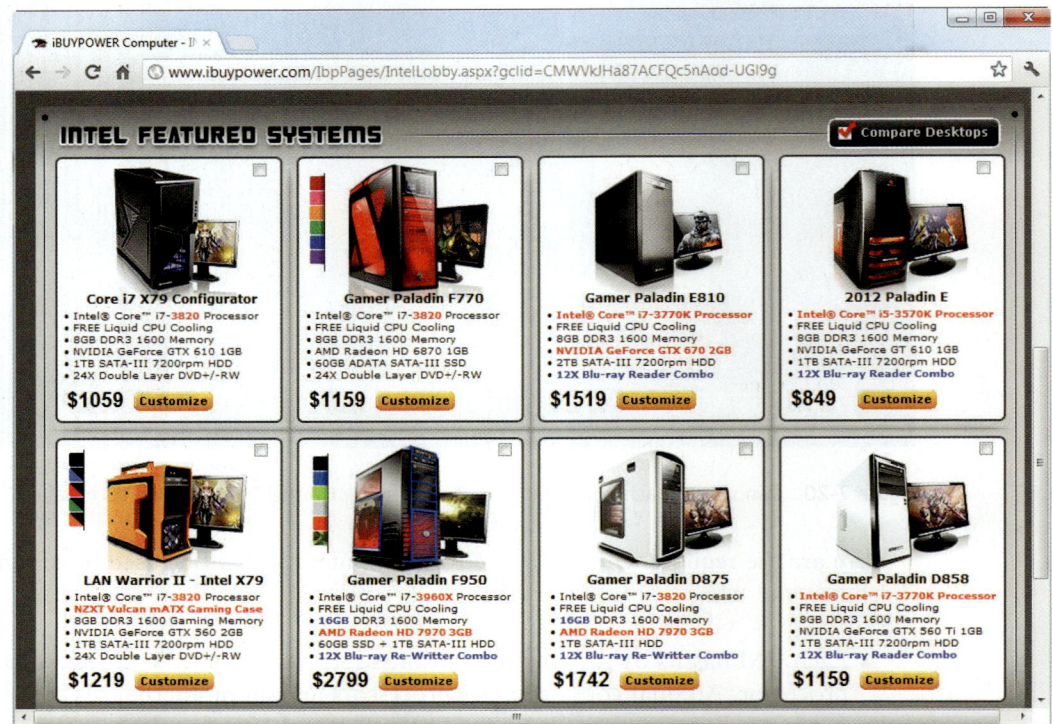

Source: www.ibuypower.com

Figure 7-21 A group of Intel Core i5 or Core i7 gaming PCs

Customizing Computer Systems

A+ 220-801 1.9

HOME THEATER PC

A **Home Theater PC (HTPC)** is designed to play and possibly record music, photos, movies, and video on a television or extra-large monitor screen. Because these large screens are usually viewed from across the room, applications software is used to control output display menus and other clickable items in fonts large enough to read at a distance of 10 feet. This interface is called a **10-foot user interface**. Manufacturers such as Roku (*roku.com*) sell HTPCs as a set-top box complete with a remote control. In addition, some televisions have a built-in HTPC. An HTPC is also known as a media center appliance.

A custom-built HTPC needs to include these features:

- *Applications software.* The application controls the user interface and plays and records music and video. Examples of HTPC software include Windows Media Center, which is integrated into Windows, XBMC Media Center (*xbmc.org*), and Plex Media Center (*plexapp.com*).
- *HDMI port to connect video output to television.* And be sure to use a high-quality HDMI cable.
- *Cable TV input.* The best solution is to use a TV tuner card to connect the TV coax cable directly to the computer. Most TV tuner cards include a remote (see Figure 7-22). Some TV tuner cards are also video capture cards that offer the ability to record video and audio input. If the customer plans to use a TV cable box between the TV coax cable and the HTPC, you need to provide a way to make the connection. Most TV cable boxes have an HDMI output port. Realize this won't work with the HDMI port on a motherboard because these ports are output ports and you need an input port. To input to the PC using an HDMI port, you can use a video capture card that has an HDMI input port (see Figure 7-23).

Courtesy of Hauppauge Computer Works Inc.

Figure 7-22 Dual TV tuner card with IR remote lets you watch and record two TV programs at the same time

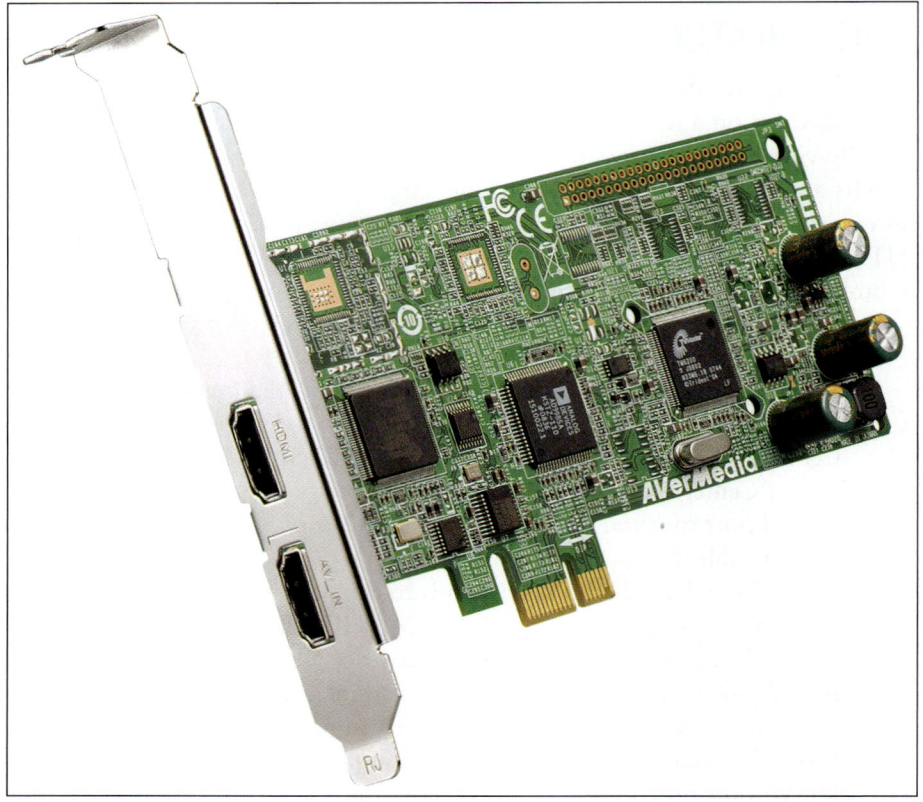

Courtesy of AVerMedia

Figure 7-23 The AVerMedia AVerTV HD DVR (C027) video capture card has two HDMI input ports and uses a PCIe ×1 expansion slot

- *Satellite TV input.* This setup requires a satellite set-top box supplied by the company providing the satellite TV service. The best solution is to use a TV tuner card to receive input from the satellite set-top box. Make sure the types of ports on the computer and the box match up.
- *Internet access.* A way to receive streaming video from the Internet. To connect to the Internet, use a Gigabit Ethernet port or Wi-Fi connection.
- *Remote control.* A way to remotely control the HTPC because most likely the user will be sitting across the room from the computer. You can use a wireless keyboard and mouse, although the range for these devices might be too short. Some TV tuner cards include a remote. Also consider an app you can download to a smart phone to make it work as the remote.
- *Low background noise.* Because these computers don't perform complex calculations, you don't need as much processor or RAM power as in other systems. For example, you can use the small Intel Atom processor with 4 GB of RAM. Therefore, you won't need an extensive cooling system. You do, however, want a system that runs quietly. You can reduce noise by using SSD hard drives and low-speed fans or no fans at all.
- *Surround sound.* The system should support surround sound using at least six speakers located around the room. In Figure 7-24, you can see the preferred location for six speakers. Three popular variations of surround sound are 5.1 (uses up to six channels and speakers), 7.1 (uses up to eight channels and speakers), and 9.1 (uses up to 10 channels and speakers). Most sound cards and motherboards support six channels or ports for sound.

Customizing Computer Systems   337

A+ 220-801 1.9

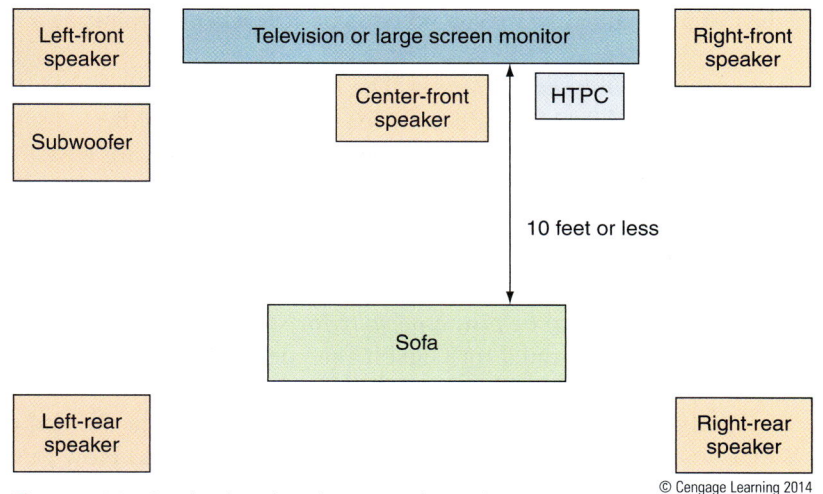

Figure 7-24 Speaker locations for surround sound

▲ *Case form factor.* An HTPC should be small enough to fit on a shelf in an entertainment center, and several companies make **HTPC cases** specifically for this purpose. The HTPC case shown in Figure 7-25 accommodates a MicroATX, mini-ITX, or mini-DTX motherboard and power supply. (A mini-DTX motherboard is slightly wider than the mini-ITX board.) The case has drive bays for 3.5 inch and 2.5 inch drives.

Courtesy of Silverstone Technology Co. Ltd.

Figure 7-25 The HTPC case by Silverstone is less than six inches high and has three silent fans

HOME SERVER PC

A home server PC is useful when you have several computers on a small home network and want to share files among them. You can use the PC to serve up these files and to stream video files and movies to client computers. One popular type of home server PC is Slingbox by Sling Media (*slingbox.com*). The device can serve up streaming media that you have stored on it not only to other computers in your home but also to a client computer anywhere on the Internet.

Here are the features and hardware you need to consider when customizing a home server PC:

- *Use a processor with moderate power.* The Intel Core i5 or Core i3 works well. A moderate amount of RAM is sufficient, for example, 6 to 8 GB.
- *Storage speed and capacity need to be maximized.* Use hardware RAID implemented on the motherboard to provide fault tolerance and high performance. Make sure the motherboard supports hardware RAID. Use fast hard drives (at least 7200 RPM) with plenty of storage capacity. Make sure the case has plenty of room for all the hard drives a customer might require.
- *Network transfers need to be fast, especially for streaming videos and movies.* Make sure the network port is rated for Gigabit Ethernet (1000 Mbps). All other devices and computers on the LAN should also use Gigabit Ethernet.
- *Printer sharing.* A USB printer can be connected directly to the PC and then you can use Windows to share the printer with others on the network. How to share printers is covered in Chapter 12. Alternately, some routers and switches provide a USB port that can be used to connect a USB printer to other computers on the network.
- *Onboard video works well.* Recall that onboard video is a video port embedded on the motherboard and does not perform as well as a good video card. Because the PC is not likely to be used as a workstation, you don't need powerful video.
- *Windows 7 can be used as the OS, but Windows Home Server 2011 provides the additional security features needed to better secure a home network.* In addition, if the customer plans to use the PC to back up files on client computers, know that Windows Home Server provides a more robust backup utility than does Windows 7.

THICK CLIENT AND THIN CLIENT

Recall that a desktop computer can use virtual machine management software (called a hypervisor) to provide one or more VMs, and in this situation the computer is called a virtualization workstation. In a corporate environment, the VM can also be provided by a virtualization server, which serves up a virtual machine to a client computer. The **virtualization server** provides a virtual desktop for users on multiple client machines. Most, if not all, processing is done on the server, which provides to the client the Virtual Desktop Infrastructure (VDI). See Figure 7-26.

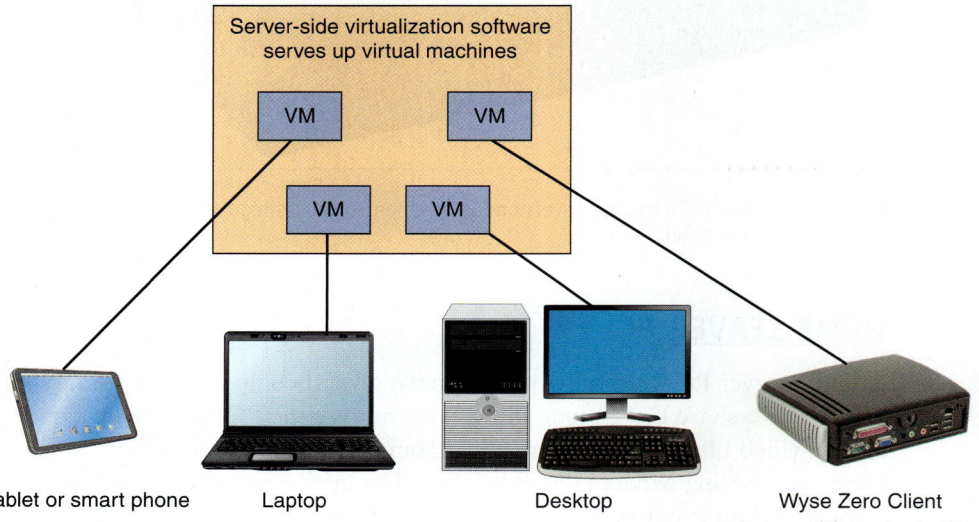

Figure 7-26 A virtualization server provides a desktop to each client computer or appliance

A+ 220-801 1.9

These VM clients that receive the virtual desktop from the server can be a thick client, thin client, or zero client. You might be called on to customize a thick client or thin client computer for a customer. (A zero client, also called a dumb terminal, is built by the manufacturer. It does not have an OS and is little more than an interface to the network with a keyboard, monitor, and mouse.) Here are the details for a thick client and thin client computer:

- A **thick client**, also called a fat client, is a regular desktop computer or laptop that is sometimes used as a client by a virtualization server. It can be a low-end or high-end desktop or laptop. It should meet the recommended requirements to run Windows 7 and any applications the user might require when it is being used as a stand-alone computer rather than a VM client. Table 7-1 lists the hardware requirements for Windows 7.
- A **thin client** is a computer that has an operating system, but has little computer power and might only need to support a browser used to communicate with the server. The server does most of the processing for the thin client. To reduce the cost of the computer, configure it to meet only the minimum requirements for Windows.

Hardware	For 32-bit Windows 7	For 64-bit Windows 7
Processor	1 GHz or faster	1 GHz or faster
Memory	1 GB	2 GB
Free hard drive space	16 GB	20 GB
Video device and driver	Direct X 9 device with WDDM 1.0 or higher driver	Direct X 9 device with WDDM 1.0 or higher driver

Table 7-1 Minimum and recommended hardware requirements for Windows 7

© Cengage Learning 2014

Hands-on | Project 7-7   Research a Customized System

Working with a partner, design a gaming PC or a Home Theater PC by doing the following:

1. Search the web for a prebuilt system that you like. Print or save the web page showing the detailed specifications for the system and its price. Which parts in the system do you plan to use for your system? Which parts would you not use or upgrade for your own system?

2. Search the web for the individual parts for your system. Save or print web pages showing all the parts you need to build this computer. Don't forget the case, power supply, motherboard, processor, RAM, hard drive, and other specialized components.

3. Make a list of each part with links to the web page that shows the part for sale. What is the total cost of all parts?

4. Exchange your list and web pages with a partner and have your partner check your work to make sure each part is compatible with the entire system and nothing is missing. Do the same for your partner's list of parts.

5. After you are both convinced your list of parts is compatible and nothing is missing, submit your work to your instructor.

>> CHAPTER SUMMARY

Job Roles and Responsibilities

- Five key job roles of a PC technician include PC support technician, PC service technician, technical retail associate, bench technician, and help-desk technician.

- A+ Certification by CompTIA is the most significant and most recognized certification for PC repair technicians.

- Learning about new technology can be done by attending trade shows, reading trade magazines, researching on the web, subscribing to email newsletters, and attending seminars and workshops.

What Customers Want: Beyond Technical Know-how

- Customers want more than just technical know-how. They want a positive and helpful attitude, respect, good communication, sensitivity to their needs, ownership of their problem, dependability, credibility, integrity, honesty, and professionalism.

Planning for Good Service

- Customers expect their first contact with you to be professional and friendly, and they want you to put listening to their problem or request as your first priority.

- Know how to ask penetrating questions when interviewing a customer about a problem or request.

- Set and meet customer expectations by good communication about what you are doing or intending to do and allowing the customer to make decisions where appropriate.

- Deal confidently and gracefully with customers who are difficult, including those who are not knowledgeable, are overly confident, or complain.

- When you first start a new job, find out how to escalate a problem you cannot solve.

Dealing with Prohibited Content and Activity

- Be aware of the documented code of conduct for your organization as it applies to any prohibited content or activity. As a PC support technician, you need to especially be aware of the problem of software piracy.

- A chain-of-custody document provides a paper trail of how evidence in a criminal case is handled and includes how, when, where, and by whom evidence was preserved and secured.

Customizing Computer Systems

- As a technician, you might be called on to customize a system for a customer including a graphics or CAD/CAM workstation, audio and video editing workstation, virtualization workstation, gaming PC, Home Theater PC (HTPC), home server PC, thick client, or thin client.

- A high-end video card is a requirement in a graphics, CAD/CAM, or video editing workstation or a gaming PC. These systems also need powerful processors and ample RAM.

- A TV tuner card is needed in a Home Theater PC.

▲ A thick client needs to meet recommended requirements for Windows and applications, and a thin client is a low-end computer that only needs to meet the minimum requirements for Windows.

>> KEY TERMS

For explanations of key terms, see the Glossary near the end of the book.

- 10-foot user interface
- A+ Certification
- call tracking
- chain of custody
- copyright
- escalate
- expert system
- hardware-assisted virtualization (HAV)
- Home Theater PC (HTPC)
- HTPC case
- hypervisor
- license
- site license
- software piracy
- technical documentation
- thick client
- thin client
- ticket
- virtualization server

>> REVIEWING THE BASICS

1. Name five job roles that can all be categorized as a PC technician.
2. Of the five jobs in Question 1, which one job might never include interacting with the PC's primary user?
3. Assume that you are a customer who wants to have a PC repaired. List five main characteristics that you would want to see in your PC repair person.
4. What is one thing you should do when you receive a phone call requesting on-site support, before you make an appointment?
5. You make an appointment to do an on-site repair, but you are detained and find out that you will be late. What is the best thing to do?
6. When you arrive for an on-site service call, how important is your greeting? What would be a good greeting to start off a good business relationship?
7. When making an on-site service call, what should you do before making any changes to software or before taking the case cover off a computer?
8. What should you do after finishing your PC repair?
9. What is a good strategy to follow if a conflict arises between you and your customer?
10. If you are about to make an on-site service call to a large financial organization, is it appropriate to show up in shorts and a T-shirt? Why or why not?
11. You have exhausted your knowledge of a problem and it still is not solved. Before you escalate it, what else can you do?
12. If you need to make a phone call while on a customer's site and your cell phone is not working, what do you do?
13. When someone calls your help desk, what is the first thing you should do?
14. What is one thing you can do to help a caller who needs phone support and is not a competent computer user?

15. Describe what you should do when a customer complains to you about a product or service that your company provides.

16. What are some things you can do to make your work at a help desk easier?

17. When applying for a position as a help desk technician, you discover the job interview will happen by telephone. Why do you think the employer has chosen this method for the interview?

18. What is the primary importance of a chain-of-custody document?

19. In a Home Theater PC, what is the purpose of an HDMI output port?

20. In a Home Theater PC, why might you need an HDMI input port? Which type of adapter card might provide this port?

21. Which system requires the best graphics card, a CAD workstation or a virtualization workstation?

22. Which is generally a better GPU, one in the NVIDIA Quadro family or one in the NVIDIA GeForce family?

23. Which socket does Intel recommend you use with liquid cooling?

24. How many speakers or sound channels does surround sound version 5.1 use?

25. Why is it important that a virtualization workstation have a lot of RAM?

>> THINKING CRITICALLY

1. You own a small PC repair company and a customer comes to you with a PC that will not boot. After investigating, you discover the hard drive has crashed. What should you do first?

   a. Install a hard drive the same size and speed as the original.

   b. Ask the customer's advice about the size drive to install, but select a drive the same speed as the original drive.

   c. Ask the customer's advice about the size and speed of the new drive to install.

   d. If the customer looks like he can afford it, install the largest and fastest drive the system can support.

2. You have repaired a broken LCD panel in a notebook computer. However, when you disassembled the notebook, you bent the hinge on the notebook lid so that it now does not latch solidly. When the customer receives the notebook, he notices the bent hinge and begins shouting at you. What do you do first? Second?

   a. Explain to the customer you are sorry but you did the best you could.

   b. Listen carefully to the customer and don't get defensive.

   c. Apologize and offer to replace the bent hinge.

   d. Tell the customer he is not allowed to speak to you like that.

>> REAL PROBLEMS, REAL SOLUTIONS

REAL PROBLEM 7-1: Looking for a PC Support Job

Suppose you've finished your PC repair curriculum and have achieved A+ Certification. Now it's time to find a job. Research the online job sites and newspapers for PC support jobs in your area. Look for jobs that require A+ Certification and also look for PC support-related jobs that don't require certification. Don't forget to check out retail jobs selling computers and computer parts. Find at least three job ads. If you can't find ads in your immediate area, branch out into nearby cites. Make printouts or copies of the three job ads and answer these questions:

1. What source (newspaper, web site, or other source) did you use to find the job?
2. What is the job title?
3. What are the qualifications of the job?
4. What is the salary?
5. What additional experience or certification do you need to qualify for the job?
6. If you were actually looking for a PC support-related job, which of the three jobs would be your first choice? Why?

REAL PROBLEM 7-2: Write Your Own Scenario for Developing Interpersonal Social Skills

In the chapter, you read several scenarios where technical support people failed to serve their customers well or failed to relate professionally with co-workers. Recall a similar situation where you observed poor service from a technician or salesperson. Write the scenario using fictitious names. Then write three questions to cause other students to think through what went wrong, what should have happened, and what are some principles of relating to customers or co-workers that could have helped if they had been applied. Present your scenario in class or with a student group for discussion.

REAL PROBLEM 7-3: Volunteer to Help a Local Public School with Technical Support

To improve your customer service and technical skills, volunteer to work at a local elementary school, middle school, house of worship, or other nonprofit organization to provide instruction, tutoring, or deskside support. Perhaps you can teach a class how to solve common and easy computer problems or work two hours a week helping students in a computer lab or helping faculty learn new computer skills.

REAL PROBLEM 7-4: Install and Use Help Desk Software

Go to *www.spiceworks.com* and watch a few of the videos about Spiceworks Help Desk Software. Then download, install, and run the software. Practice using the software to add help desk workers, open a ticket, assign a worker to a ticket, and resolve and close the ticket.

Consider setting up a PC repair help desk where your PC repair classmates can provide end-user support to other students and instructors at your school as they have problems with their personal computers. One computer in the class would be designated the help desk computer that holds the Spiceworks Help Desk Software for the entire class. Classmates are entered in Spiceworks as help desk workers and are assigned tickets as users request help.

Spiceworks can be set up to receive requests for help through an email account, and you can advertise the email address as a way to offer support for students and instructors on campus. What other ways can you use to advertise your help desk and provide a way for your customers to contact the help desk? Some PC repair classes have run extremely successful help desks and have received a small donation for services.

CHAPTER 8

Troubleshooting Hardware Problems

In this chapter, you will learn:

- How to approach and solve a computer problem related to hardware, especially when the problem occurs during the boot
- How to troubleshoot problems with the electrical system
- How to troubleshoot problems that occur during POST before video is active
- How to troubleshoot error messages that occur during the POST
- How to troubleshoot problems with the motherboard, processor, and RAM
- How to troubleshoot hard drive problems
- How to troubleshoot problems with the monitor and video
- About protecting a computer and the environment

In the last several chapters, you have learned much about the hardware components of a system, including features and characteristics of the power supply, motherboard, processor, RAM, hard drive, I/O devices, and storage devices. You've learned how to select, install, and configure each device.

This chapter focuses on troubleshooting these various hardware subsystems and components. I've gathered troubleshooting techniques and procedures into a single chapter so you can get the full picture of what it's like to have the tools and knowledge in hand to solve any computer hardware-related problem. By the end of this chapter, you should feel confident that you can face a problem with hardware and understand how to zero in on the source of the problem and its solution. The best support technicians are good at preventing a problem from happening in the first place, so in this chapter, you'll learn some tips for protecting a computer from damage.

We begin the chapter with a general strategy for facing a computer problem and a strategy for quickly isolating the source of a problem related to booting up a computer. Then we tackle the problems and solutions for each major hardware component and subsystem.

HOW TO APPROACH A HARDWARE PROBLEM

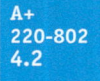

When an end user brings any computer problem to you, begin the troubleshooting process by interviewing the user. When you interview the user, you might want to include these questions:

- Can you describe the problem and describe when the problem first started and when it occurs?
- Was the computer recently moved?
- Was any new hardware or software recently installed?
- Was any software recently reconfigured or upgraded?
- Did someone else use your computer recently?
- Does the computer have a history of similar problems?
- Is there important data on the drive that is not backed up?
- Can you show me how to reproduce the problem?

After you gather this basic information, you can prioritize what to do and begin diagnosing and addressing the problem. If the computer will not start or starts with errors so that you cannot reach the Windows desktop, setting priorities helps focus your work. For most users, data is the first priority unless they have a recent backup.

A good PC technician builds over time a strong network of resources he or she can count on when solving computer problems. Here are some resources to help you get started with your own list of reliable and time-tested sources of help:

- *User manuals* often list error messages and their meanings. They also might contain a troubleshooting section and list any diagnostic tools available.
- *The web* can also help you diagnose computer problems. Go to the web site of the product manufacturer, and search for a support forum. It's likely that others have encountered the same problem and posted the question and answer. If you search and cannot find your answer, you can post a new question. Use a search engine such as *www.google.com* to search for the error, the hardware device, the problem, the technology used, and other keywords that can help you find useful information. Youtube.com videos might help. Many technicians enjoy sharing what they know online, and the web can be a rich source of all kinds of technical information and advice. Be careful, however. Not all technical advice is correct or well intentioned.
- *Chat, telephone, or email technical support* from the hardware and software manufacturers can help you interpret an error message, or it can provide general support in diagnosing a problem. Most technical support is available during working hours by way of an online chat session.
- *Manufacturer's diagnostic software* is available for download from the web sites of many hardware device manufacturers. For example, you can download SeaTools for Windows (must be installed in Windows) or SeaTools for DOS (used to create a bootable CD that contains the software) and use the software to diagnose problems with Seagate and Maxtor drives. See Figure 8-1. Search the support section of a manufacturer's web site to find diagnostic software and guidelines for using it.

> **Notes** Always check compatibility between utility software and the operating system with which you plan to use it.

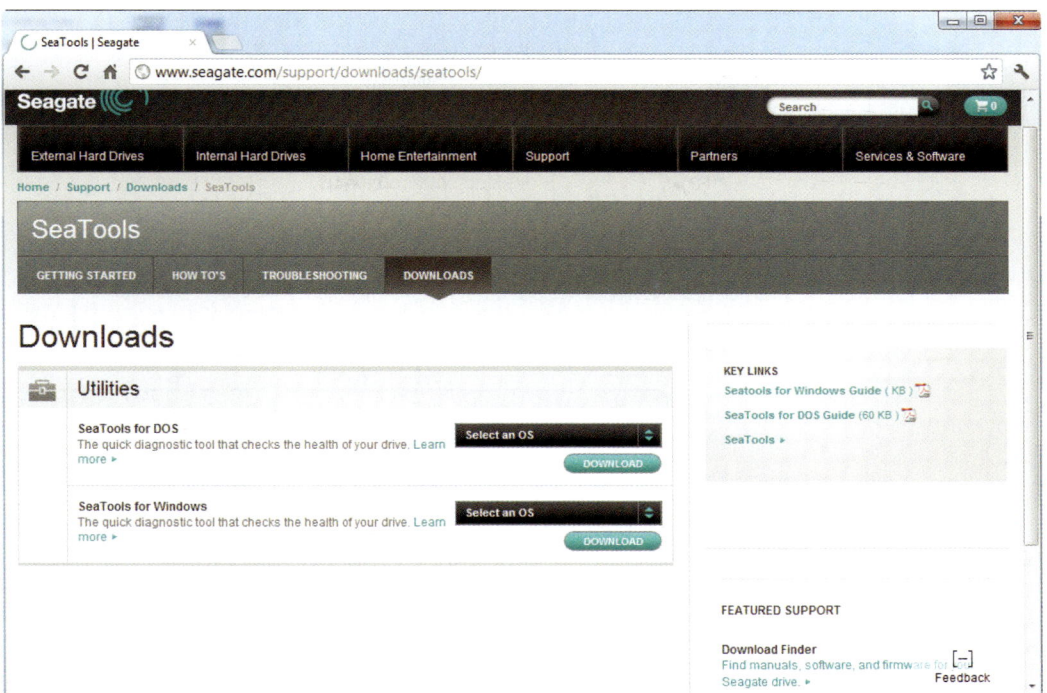

Source: Seagate at www.seagate.com

Figure 8-1   Download diagnostic software from a manufacturer's web site

▲ *Technical associates in your organization can help.* Be sure to ask for advice when you're stuck. Also, after making a reasonable and diligent effort to resolve a problem, getting the problem fixed could become more important than resolving it yourself. There comes a time when you might need to turn the problem over to a more experienced technician. (In an organization, this process is called escalating the problem.)

Most PC problems are simple and can be simply solved, but you do need a game plan. That's how Figure 8-2 can help. The flowchart focuses on problems that affect the boot. As we work our way through it, you're eliminating one major computer subsystem after another until you zero in on the problem. After you've discovered the problem, many times the solution is obvious.

As Figure 8-2 indicates, troubleshooting a computer problem is divided into problems that occur during the boot and those that occur after the Windows desktop has successfully loaded. Problems that occur during the boot might happen before Windows starts to load or during Windows startup. Read the flowchart in Figure 8-2 very carefully to get an idea of the symptoms you might be faced with that would cause you to suspect each subsystem. Also, Table 8-1 can help as a general guideline for the primary symptoms and what are likely to be the source of a problem.

A+ Exam Tip   The A+ 220-802 exam might give you a symptom and expect you to select a probable source of a problem from a list of sources. These examples of what can go wrong can help you connect problem sources to symptoms.

A+
220-802
4.2

© Cengage Learning 2014

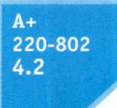

Figure 8-2 Use this flowchart when first facing a computer problem

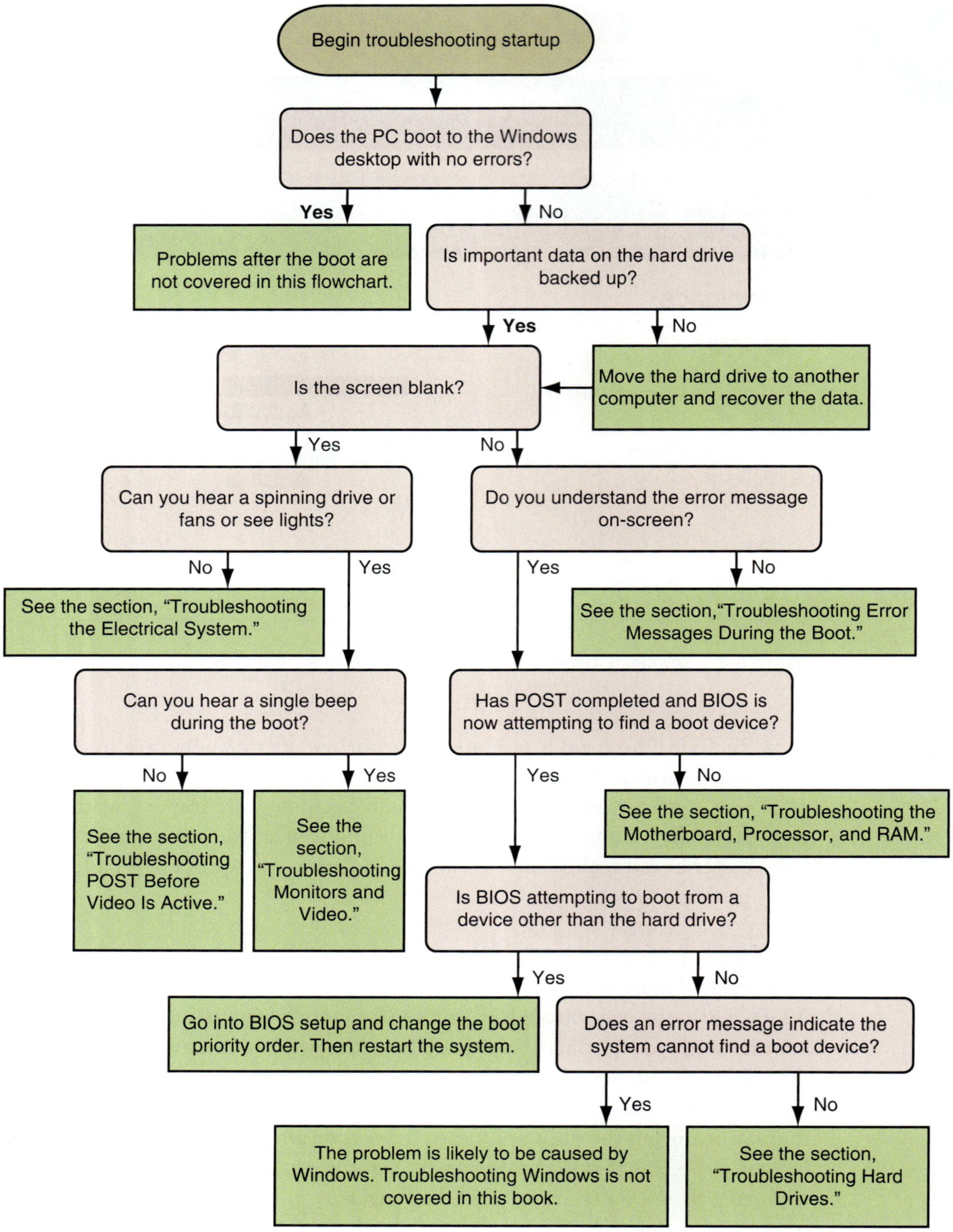

If the hard drive has important data on it that has not been backed up, your first priority is most likely to recover the data. If a system won't boot from the hard drive, consider removing the drive and installing it as a second drive in a working system. If the file system on the problem drive is intact, you might be able to copy data from the drive to the primary drive in the working system.

A+ 220-802 4.2

Symptom or Error Message	What to Do About the Problem
The system shuts down unexpectedly	Try to find out what was happening at the time of the shutdowns to zero in on an application or device causing the problem. Possible sources of the problem are overheating or faulty RAM, motherboard, or processor.
Error messages appear on a blue screen called a **blue screen of death (BSOD)**	Figure 8-3 shows an example of a BSOD error screen. These Windows errors are caused by problems with devices, device drivers, or a corrupted Windows installation. Begin troubleshooting by searching the Microsoft web site for the error message and a description of the problem.
Error messages on a black screen	These error messages, such as the one shown in Figure 8-4, are most likely caused by an error at POST. Begin by troubleshooting the device mentioned in the error message.
The system freezes or locks up	If the system locks up immediately after a BSOD error screen, begin troubleshooting by investigating the error messages on the blue screen. If the system freezes while still displaying the Windows desktop, the problem is most likely caused by Windows or an application.
POST code beeps	Startup BIOS communicates POST errors as a series of beeps before it tests video. Search the web site of the motherboard or BIOS manufacturer to know how to interpret a series of beep codes.
Blank screen when you first power up the computer, and no noise or indicator lights	Is power getting to the system? If power is getting to the computer, address the problem as an electrical problem with the computer. Make sure the power supply is good and power supply connectors are securely connected.
Blank screen when you first power up the computer, and you can hear the fans spinning and see indicator lights	Troubleshoot the video subsystem. Is the monitor turned on? Is the monitor data cable securely connected at both ends? Is the indicator light on the front of the monitor on?
BIOS loses its time and date settings	This problem happens when the CMOS battery fails. Replace the battery.
The system attempts to boot to the wrong boot device	Go into BIOS setup and change the boot device priority order.
Continuous reboots	Continuous reboots can be caused by overheating, a failing processor, motherboard, or RAM, or a corrupted Windows installation. Begin by checking the system for overheating. Is the processor cooler fan working? Go to BIOS setup and check the temperature of the processor.
No power	If you see no lights on the computer case and hear no spinning fans, make sure the surge protector or wall outlet has power. Is the switch on the rear of the case on? Is the dual voltage selector switch set correctly? Are power supply connectors securely connected? Is the power supply bad?

© Cengage Learning 2014

Table 8-1 Symptoms or error messages caused by hardware problems and what to do about them (continues)

A+ 220-802 4.2

Symptom or Error Message	What to Do About the Problem
Fans spin but no power gets to other devices	Begin by checking the power supply. Are connectors securely connected? Use a power supply tester to check for correct voltage outputs.
Smoke or burning smell	Consider this a serious electrical problem. Immediately unplug the computer.
Loud whining noise	Most likely the noise is made by the power supply or a failing hard drive. There might be a short. The power supply might be going bad or is underrated for the system.
Intermittent device failures	Failures that come and go might be caused by overheating or failing RAM, the motherboard, processor, or hard drive. Begin by checking the processor temperature for overheating. Then check RAM for errors and run diagnostics on the hard drive.

© Cengage Learning 2014

Table 8-1 Symptoms or error messages caused by hardware problems and what to do about them (continued)

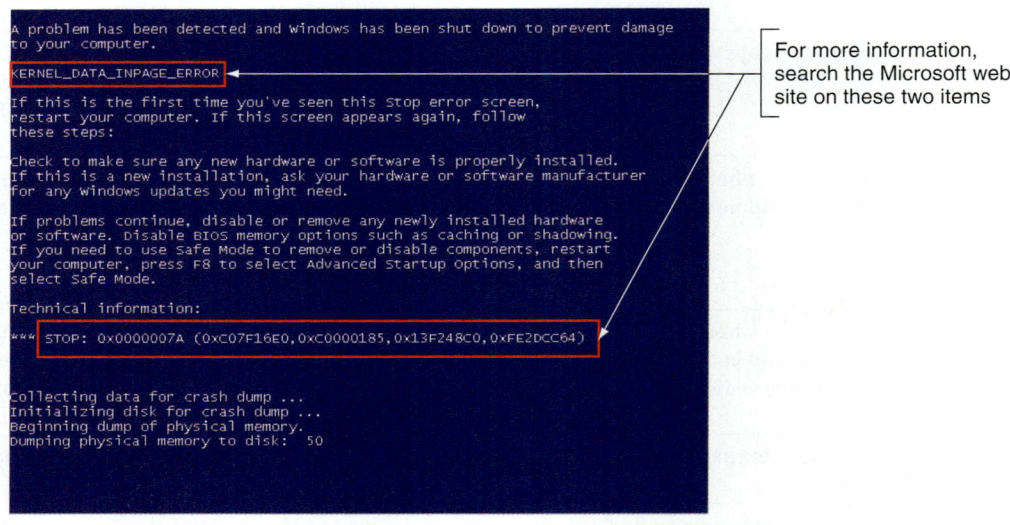

Source: Microsoft Windows 7

Figure 8-3 Search the Microsoft web site for information about a BSOD error

To move the hard drive to a working computer, you don't need to physically install the drive in the drive bay. Open the computer case. Carefully lay the drive on the case and connect a power cord and data cable (see Figure 8-5). Then turn on the PC. While you have the PC turned on, be *very careful* to not touch the drive or touch inside the case. Also, while a tower case is lying on its side like the one in Figure 8-5, don't use the optical drive.

Start the computer and log onto Windows using an Administrator account. (If you don't sign in with an Administrator account, you must provide the password to an Administrator account before you can access the files on the newly connected hard drive.) When Windows finds the new drive, it assigns it a drive letter. Use Windows Explorer to copy files from this drive to the primary hard drive in this system or to another storage media. Then return the drive to the original system and turn your attention to solving the original problem.

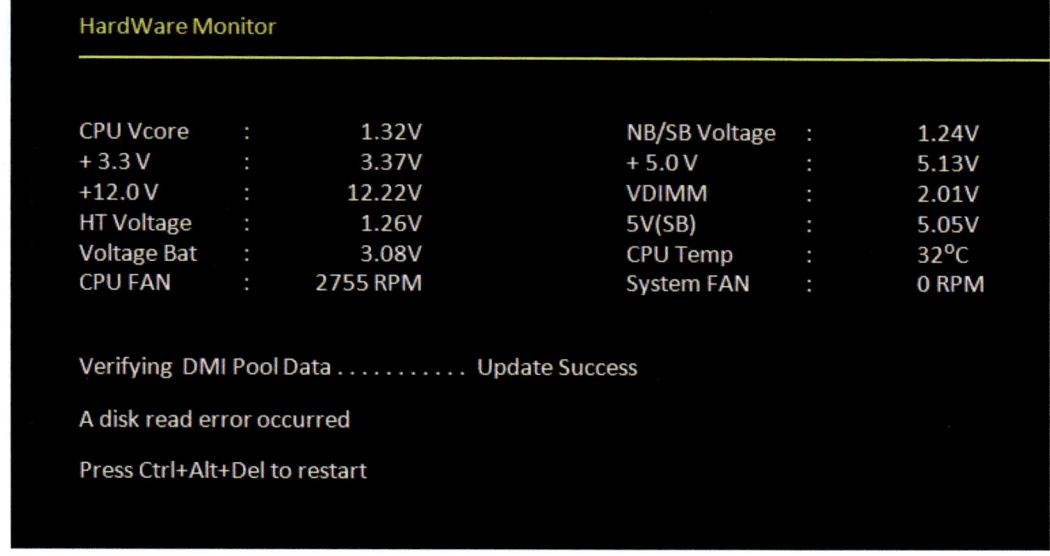

Figure 8-4 A POST error message on a black screen shown early in the boot

Source: Intel

Figure 8-5 Move a hard drive to a working computer to recover data on the drive

© Cengage Learning 2014

> **Notes** An easier way to temporarily install a hard drive in a system is to use a USB port. For a PATA hard drive, use a PATA-to-USB converter. The converter kit in Figure 8-6 includes a converter for a PATA desktop and PATA laptop hard drive. Figure 8-7 shows a SATA-to-USB converter kit. The SATA connector can be used for desktop or laptop hard drives because a SATA connector is the same for both. These ATA-to-USB converters are really handy when recovering data and troubleshooting problems with hard drives that refuse to boot.

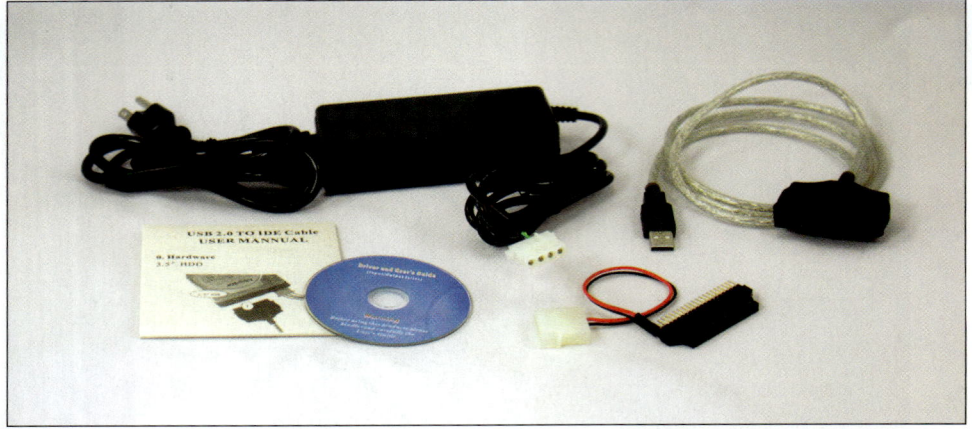

Figure 8-6 Use an IDE-to-USB converter for diagnostic testing and to recover data from a failing PATA hard drive

Figure 8-7 Use a USB-to-SATA converter to recover data from a drive using a SATA connector

Now that you have a general idea as to how to troubleshoot hardware errors during the boot, you're ready to look at how to troubleshoot each subsystem that is critical to booting up the computer. We begin with the electrical system.

TROUBLESHOOTING THE ELECTRICAL SYSTEM

Electrical problems can occur before or after the boot and can be consistent or intermittent. Many times PC repair technicians don't recognize the cause of a problem to be electrical because of the intermittent nature of some electrical problems. In these situations, the hard drive, memory, the OS, or even user error might be suspected as the source of the problem and then systematically eliminated before the electrical system is suspected. This section will help you to be aware of symptoms of electrical problems so that you can zero in on the source of an electrical problem as quickly as possible.

APPLYING CONCEPTS — FOUR TROUBLESHOOTING RULES

Here are four important rules that can help you solve many hardware problems:

Rule 1: Check the Obvious and Check Simple Things First

Check for obvious and simple solutions first. Here are some tips:

- Is the external device plugged in and turned on? Are the data cable connections solid at both ends? Is there a wall light switch controlling the power, and is it turned on? Is the power strip you're using plugged in and turned on?
- For expansion cards and memory modules, are they seated solidly in their slots? For sound, is the volume knob turned up? For video, is the monitor getting power, turned on, connected, and is the screen resolution correct?
- Consider the application using the device. For example, if you are having problems trying to use a USB scanner, try scanning using a different application.

Rule 2: Trade Known Good for Suspected Bad

When diagnosing hardware problems, this method works well if you can draw from a group of parts that you know work correctly. Suppose, for example, video does not work. The parts of the video subsystem are the video card, the power cord to the monitor, the cord from the monitor to the PC case, and the monitor itself. Also, don't forget that the video card is inserted into an expansion slot on the motherboard, and the monitor depends on electrical power. As you suspect each of these five components to be bad, you can try them one at a time beginning with the easiest one to replace: the monitor. Trade the monitor for one that you know works. If this theory fails, trade the power cord, trade the cord to the PC video port, move the video card to a new slot, and trade the video card. When you're trading a good component for a suspected bad one, work methodically by eliminating one component at a time.

Rule 3: Trade Suspected Bad for Known Good

An alternate approach works well in certain situations. If you have a working computer that is configured similarly to the one you are troubleshooting (a common situation in many corporate or educational environments), rather than trading good for suspected bad, you can trade suspected bad for good. Take each component that you suspect is bad and install it in the working computer. If the component works on the good computer, then you have eliminated it as a suspect. If the working computer breaks down, then you have probably identified the bad component.

Rule 4: Divide and Conquer

Isolate the problem. In the overall system, remove one hardware or software component after another, until the problem is isolated to a small part of the whole system. As you divide a large problem into smaller components, you can analyze each component separately. You can use one or more of the following to help you divide and conquer on your own system:

- In Windows, stop all nonessential services running in the background to eliminate them as the problem.
- Boot from a bootable CD or DVD to eliminate the OS and startup files on the hard drive as the problem.
- Remove any unnecessary hardware devices, such as a second video card, optical drive, and even the hard drive.

Once down to the essentials, start exchanging components you know are good for those you suspect are bad, until the problem goes away. You don't need to physically remove the optical drive or hard drive from the bays inside the case. Simply disconnect the data cable and the power cable.

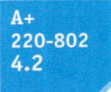

APPLYING CONCEPTS Your friend Sharon calls to ask for your help with a computer problem. Her system has been working fine for over a year, but now strange things are happening. Sometimes the system powers down for no apparent reason while she is working, and sometimes Windows locks up. As you read this section, look for clues as to what the problem might be. Also, as you read, think of questions to ask your friend that will help you.

Possible symptoms of a problem with the electrical system are:

- The PC appears "dead"—no indicator lights and no spinning drive or fan.
- The PC sometimes locks up during booting. After several tries, it boots successfully.
- Error codes or beeps occur during booting, but they come and go.
- You smell burnt parts or odors. (Definitely not a good sign!)
- The PC powers down at unexpected times.
- The PC appears dead except you hear a whine coming from the power supply.

Without opening the computer case, the following list contains some questions you can ask and things you can do to solve a problem with the electrical system. The rule of thumb is "try the simple things first." Most PC problems have simple solutions.

- If you smell any burnt parts or odors, don't try to turn the system on. Identify the component that is fried and replace it.
- When you first plug up power to a system and hear a whine coming from the power supply, the power supply might be inadequate for the system or there might be a short. Don't press the power button to start up the system. Unplug the power cord so that the power supply will not be damaged. The next step is to open the case and search for a short. If you don't find a short, consider upgrading the power supply.
- Is the power cord plugged in? If it is plugged into a power strip or surge suppressor, is the device turned on and also plugged in?
- Is the power outlet controlled by a wall switch? If so, is the switch turned on?
- Are any cable connections loose?
- Is the circuit breaker blown? Is the house circuit overloaded?
- Are all switches on the system turned on? Computer? Monitor? Surge suppressor or UPS (uninterruptible power supply)?
- Is there a possibility the system has overheated? If so, wait awhile and try again. If the system comes on, but later turns itself off, you might need additional cooling fans inside the unit. How to solve problems with overheating is covered later in the chapter.
- Older computers might be affected by electromagnetic interference (EMI). Check for sources of electrical or magnetic interference such as fluorescent lighting or an electric fan or copier sitting near the computer case.

The next step is to open the computer case and then do the following:

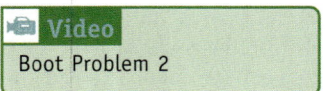

- Turn off the computer, unplug it, press the power button to drain residual power, and open the case. Check all power connections from the power supply to the motherboard and drives. Also, some cases require the case's front panel be in place before the power-on button will work. Are all cards securely seated?

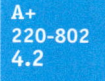

▲ If you smell burnt parts, carefully search for shorts and frayed and burnt wires. Disassemble the parts until you find the one that is damaged.
▲ If you suspect the power supply is bad, test it with a power supply tester.

> **Caution** Before opening the case of a brand name computer, such as a Gateway or Dell, consider the warranty. If the system is still under warranty, sometimes the warranty is voided if the case is opened. If the warranty prevents you from opening the case, you might need to return the system to a manufacturer's service center for repairs.

PROBLEMS THAT COME AND GO

If a system boots successfully to the Windows desktop, you still might have a power system problem. Some problems are intermittent; that is, they come and go. Generally, intermittent problems are more difficult to solve than a dead system. There can be many causes of intermittent problems, such as an inadequate power supply, overheating, and devices and components damaged by ESD. Here are some symptoms that might indicate an intermittent problem with the electrical system after the boot:

▲ The computer stops or hangs for no reason. Sometimes it might even reboot itself.
▲ Memory errors appear intermittently.
▲ Data is written incorrectly to the hard drive.
▲ The keyboard stops working at odd times.
▲ The motherboard fails or is damaged.
▲ The power supply overheats and becomes hot to the touch.
▲ The power supply fan whines and becomes very noisy or stops.

Here is what to do to eliminate the electrical system as the source of an intermittent problem:

1. **Consider the power supply is inadequate.** If the power supply is grossly inadequate, it will whine when you first plug up the power. If you have just installed new devices that are drawing additional power, follow the directions given in Chapter 2 to make sure the wattage rating of the power supply is adequate for the system.

    You can also test the system to make sure you don't have power problems by making all the devices in your system work at the same time. For instance, you can make two hard drives and the DVD drive work at the same time by copying files from one hard drive to the other while playing a movie on the DVD. If the new drive and the other drives each work independently, but data errors occur when all work at the same time, suspect a shortage of electrical power.

2. **Suspect the power supply is faulty.** You can test it using either a power supply tester (the easier method) or a multimeter (the more tedious method). However, know that a power supply that gives correct voltages when you measure it might still be the source of problems because power problems can be intermittent. Also be aware that an ATX power supply monitors the range of voltages provided to the motherboard and halts the motherboard if voltages are inadequate. Therefore, if the power supply appears "dead," your best action is to replace it.

3. **The power supply fan might not work.** Don't operate the PC if the fan does not work because computers without cooling fans can quickly overheat. Usually just before a fan stops working, it hums or whines, especially when the PC is first turned on. If this has just happened, replace the power supply. After you replace the power supply, if the new fan does not work, you have to dig deeper to find the source of the problem.

You can now assume the problem wasn't the original fan. A short somewhere else in the system drawing too much power might cause the problem. To troubleshoot a non-functional fan, which might be a symptom of another problem and not a problem of the fan itself, follow these steps:

   a. Turn off the power and remove all power cord connections to all components except the motherboard. Turn the power back on. If the fan works, the problem is with one of the systems you disconnected, not with the power supply, the fan, or the motherboard.

   b. Turn off the power and reconnect one card or drive at a time until you identify the device with the short.

   c. If the fan does not work when all devices except the motherboard are disconnected, the problem is the motherboard or the power supply. Because you have already replaced the power supply, you can assume the problem is the motherboard and it's time to replace it.

POWER PROBLEMS WITH THE MOTHERBOARD

A short might occur if some component on the motherboard makes improper contact with the chassis. This short can seriously damage the motherboard. For some cases, check for missing standoffs (small plastic or metal spacers that hold the motherboard a short distance away from the bottom of the case). A missing standoff most often causes these improper connections. Also check for loose standoffs or screws under the board that might be touching a wire on the bottom of the board and causing a short.

Shorts in the circuits on the motherboard might also cause problems. Look for damage on the bottom of the motherboard. These circuits are coated with plastic, and quite often damage is difficult to spot. Also look for burned-out capacitors that are spotted brown or corroded. You'll see examples of burned out capacitors later in the chapter.

> **APPLYING CONCEPTS** Back to Sharon's computer problem. Here are some questions that will help you identify the source of the problem:
>
> ▲ Have you added new devices to your system? (These new devices might be drawing too much power from an overworked power supply.)
> ▲ Have you moved your computer recently? (It might be sitting beside a heat vent or electrical equipment.)
> ▲ Does the system power down or hang after you have been working for some time? (This symptom might have more than one cause, such as overheating or a power supply, processor, memory, or motherboard about to fail.)
> ▲ Has the computer case been opened recently? (Someone working inside the case might not have used a ground bracelet and components are now failing because of ESD damage.)
> ▲ Are case vents free so that air can flow? (The case might be close to a curtain covering the vents.)
>
> Intermittent problems like the one Sharon described are often heat related. If the system only hangs but does not power off, the problem might be caused by faulty memory or bad software, but because it actually powers down, you can assume the problem is related to power or heat.
>
> If Sharon tells you that the system powers down after she's been working for several hours, you can probably assume overheating. Check that first. If that's not the problem, the next thing to do is replace the power supply.
>
> **Caution** Never replace a damaged motherboard with a good one without first testing or replacing the power supply. You don't want to subject another good board to possible damage.

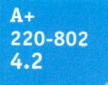

A+
220-802
4.2

PROBLEMS WITH OVERHEATING

As a PC repair technician, you're sure to eventually face problems with computers overheating. Overheating can happen as soon as you turn on the computer or after the computer has been working awhile. Overheating can cause intermittent errors, the system to hang, or components to fail or not last as long as they normally would. (Overheating can significantly shorten the lifespan of the CPU and memory.) Overheating happens for many reasons, including improper installations of the CPU cooler or fans, overclocking, poor air flow inside the case, underrated power supply, a component going bad, or the computer's environment (for example, heat or dust).

Here are some symptoms that a system is overheating:

▲ The system hangs or freezes at odd times or freezes just a few moments after the boot starts.
▲ A Windows BSOD error occurs during the boot.
▲ You cannot hear a fan running or the fan makes a whining sound.
▲ You cannot feel air being pulled into or out of the case.

If you suspect overheating, know that processors can sense their operating temperatures and report that information to BIOS. You can view that information in BIOS setup. To protect the expensive processor and other components, you can also purchase a temperature sensor. The sensor plugs into a power connection coming from the power supply and mounts on the side of the case or in a drive bay. The sensor sounds an alarm when the inside of the case becomes too hot. To decide which temperature sensor to buy, use one recommended by the case manufacturer. You can also install utility software that can monitor the system temperatures. For example, SpeedFan by Alfredo Comparetti is freeware that can monitor fan speeds and temperatures (see Figure 8-8). A good web site to download the freeware is *www.filehippo.com/download_speedfan*.

Here are some simple things you can do to solve an overheating problem:

1. If the system refuses to boot or hangs after a period of activity, suspect overheating. Immediately after the system hangs, go into BIOS setup and find the CPU screen that reports the temperature. The temperature should not exceed 38 degrees C.

2. Use compressed air, a blower, or an antistatic vacuum to remove dust from the power supply, the vents over the entire computer, and the processor cooler fan (see Figure 8-9). Excessive dust insulates components and causes them to overheat.

3. Check airflow inside the case. Are all fans running? You might need to replace a fan. Is there an empty fan slot on the rear of the case? If so, install a case fan in the slot (see Figure 8-10). Orient the fan so that it blows air out of the case. The power cord to the fan can connect to a fan header on the motherboard or to a power connector coming directly from the power supply.

4. If there are other fan slots on the side or front of the case, you can also install fans in these slots. However, don't install more fans than the case is designed to use.

5. Can the side of the case hold a chassis air guide that guides outside air to the processor? If it has a slot for the guide and the guide is missing, install one. However, don't install a guide that obstructs the CPU cooler. How to install an air guide is covered later in this section.

6. A case is generally designed for optimal airflow when slot openings on the front and rear of the case are covered and when the case cover is securely in place. To improve airflow, replace missing faceplates over empty drive bays and replace missing slot covers over empty expansion slots. See Figure 8-11.

358 | **CHAPTER 8** Troubleshooting Hardware Problems

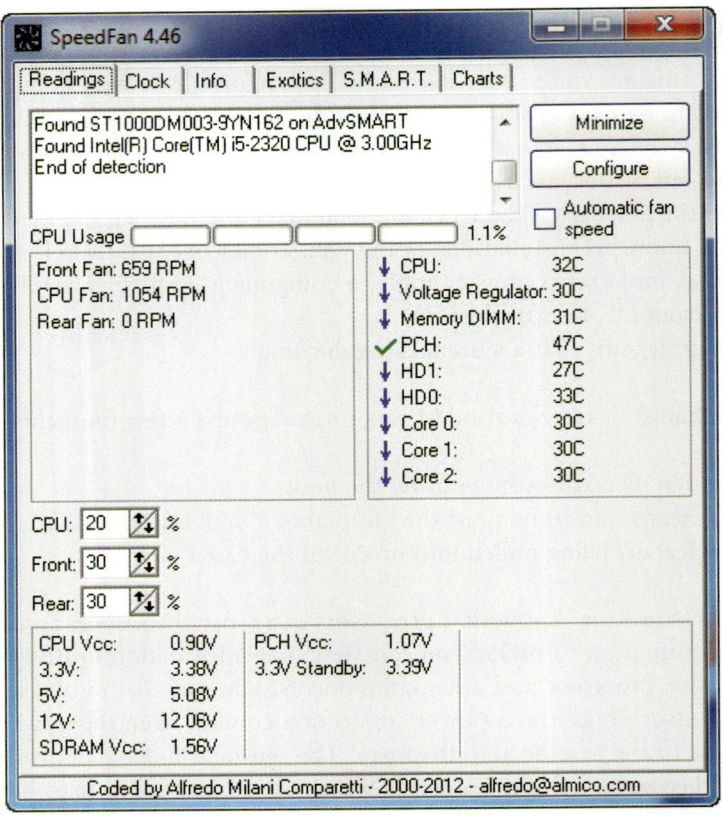

Source: SpeedFan by Alfredo Milani Comparetti

Figure 8-8 SpeedFan monitors fan speeds and system temperatures

© Cengage Learning 2014

Figure 8-9 Dust in this cooler fan can cause the fan to fail and the processor to overheat

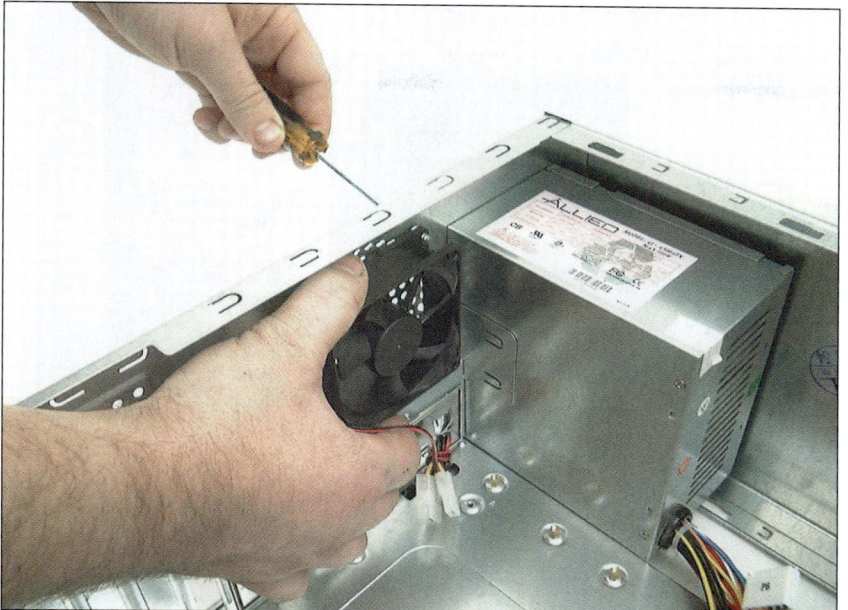

Figure 8-10 Install one exhaust fan on the rear of the case to help pull air through the case

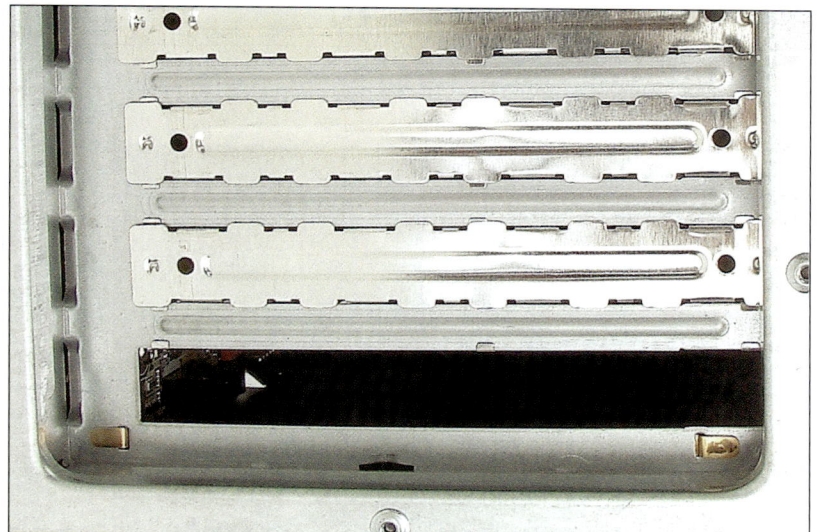

Figure 8-11 For optimum airflow, don't leave empty expansion slots and bays uncovered

7. Are cables in the way of airflow? Use tie wraps to secure cables and cords so that they don't block airflow across the processor or get in the way of fans turning. Figure 8-12 shows the inside of a case where cables are tied up and neatly out of the way of air flow from the front to the rear of the case.

8. A case needs some room to breathe. Place it so there are at least a few inches of space on both sides and the top of the case. If the case is sitting on carpet, put it on a computer stand so that air can circulate under the case and also to reduce carpet dust inside the case. Many

360 | **CHAPTER 8** Troubleshooting Hardware Problems

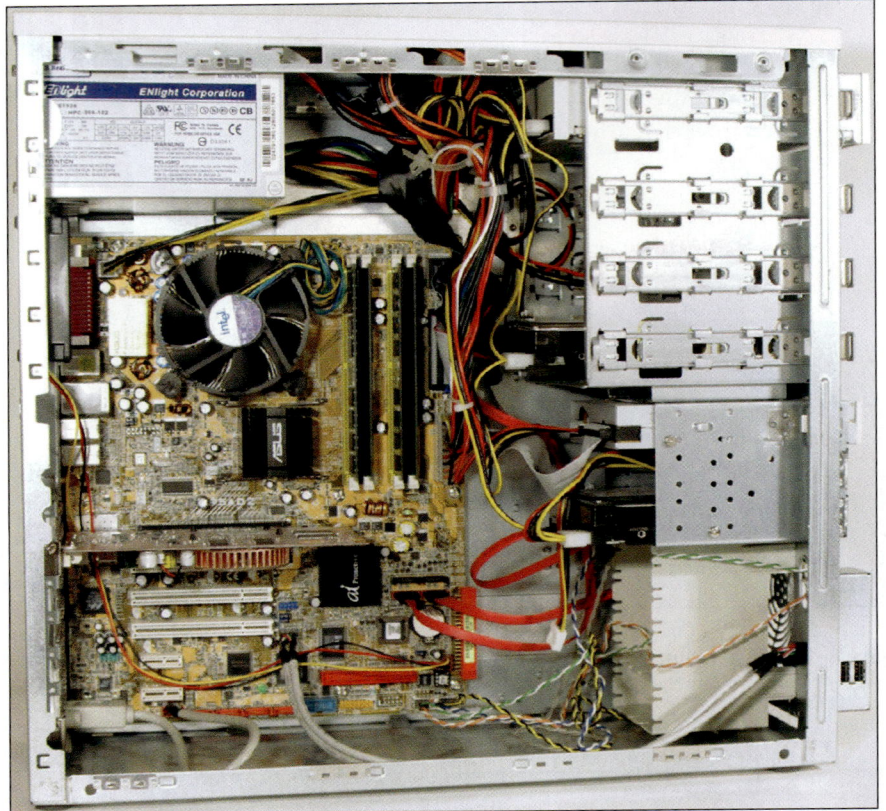

Figure 8-12 Use cable ties to hold cables out of the way of fans and airflow

Figure 8-13 Keep a tower case off carpet to allow air to flow into the bottom air vent

cases have a vent on the bottom front of the case and carpet can obstruct airflow into this vent (see Figure 8-13). Make sure drapes are not hanging too close to fan openings.

9. Verify the cooler is connected properly to the processor. If it doesn't fit well, the system might not boot and certainly the processor will overheat. If the cooler is not tightly connected to the motherboard and processor or the cooler fan is not working,

the processor will quickly overheat as soon as the computer is turned on. Has thermal compound been installed between the cooler and processor?

10. After you close the case, leave your system off for at least 30 minutes. When you power up the computer again, let it run for 10 minutes, go into BIOS setup, check the temperature readings, and reboot. Next, let your system run until it shuts down. Power it up again and check the temperature in BIOS setup again. A significant difference in this reading and the first one you took after running the computer for 10 minutes indicates an overheating problem.

11. Check BIOS setup to see if the processor is being overclocked. Overclocking can cause a system to overheat. Try restoring the processor and system bus frequencies to default values.

12. Have too many peripherals been installed inside the case? Is the case too small for all these peripherals? Larger tower cases are better designed for good airflow than smaller slimline cases. Also, when installing cards, try to leave an empty slot between each card for better airflow. The same goes for drives. Try not to install a group of drives in adjacent drive bays. For better airflow, leave empty bays between drives. Take a close look at Figure 8-12, where you can see space between each drive installed in the system.

13. Flash BIOS to update the firmware on the motherboard. How to flash BIOS is covered in Chapter 3.

14. Thermal compound should last for years, but eventually it will harden and need replacing. If the system is several years old, replace the thermal compound.

> **A+ Exam Tip** The A+ 220-802 exam expects you to recognize that a given symptom is possibly power or heat related.

If you try the above list of things to do and still have an overheating problem, it's time to move on to more drastic solutions. Consider the case design is not appropriate for good airflow, and the problem might be caused by poor air circulation inside the case. The power supply fan in ATX cases blows air out of the case, pulling outside air from the vents in the front of the case across the processor to help keep it cool. Another exhaust fan is usually installed on the back of the case to help the power supply fan pull air through the case. In addition, most processors require a cooler with a fan installed on top of the processor. Figure 8-14 shows a good arrangement of vents and fans for proper airflow and a poor arrangement.

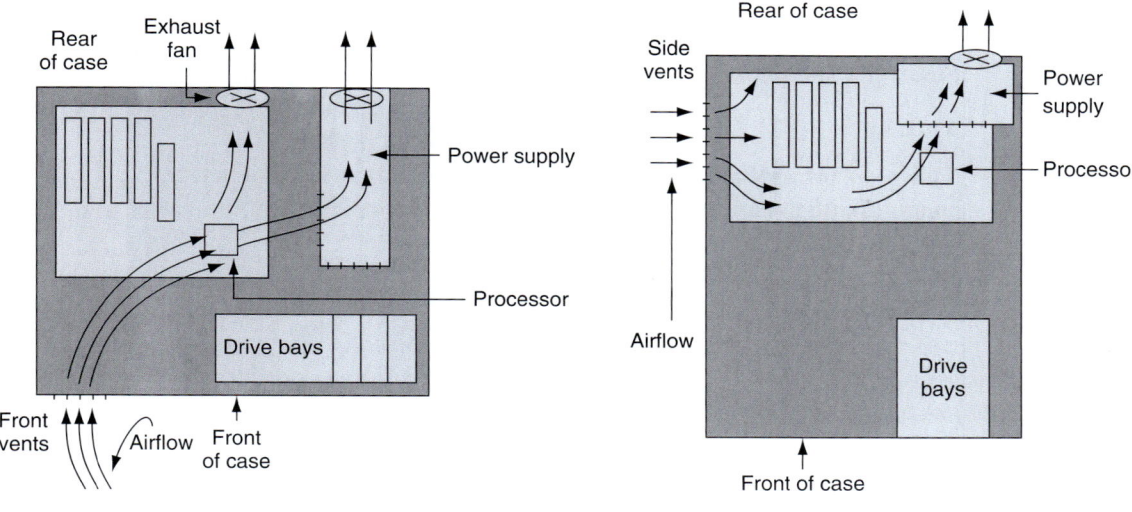

Figure 8-14 Vents and fans need to be arranged for best airflow

For better ventilation, use a power supply that has vents on the bottom and front of the power supply. Note in Figure 8-15 airflow is coming into the bottom of the power supply because of these bottom vents. The power supply in Figure 8-10 has vents only on the front and not on the bottom. Compare that to the power supply in Figure 8-15, which has vents on both the front and bottom.

An intake fan on the front of the case might help pull air into the case. Intel recommends you use a front intake fan for high-end systems, but AMD says a front fan for ATX systems is not necessary. Check with the processor and case manufacturers for specific instructions as to the placement of fans and what type of fan and heat sink to use.

Intel and AMD both recommend a **chassis air guide (CAG)** as part of the case design. This air guide is a round air duct that helps to pull and direct fresh air from outside the case to the cooler and processor (see Figure 8-16). The guide should reach inside the case very close to the cooler, but not touch it. Intel recommends the clearance be no greater than

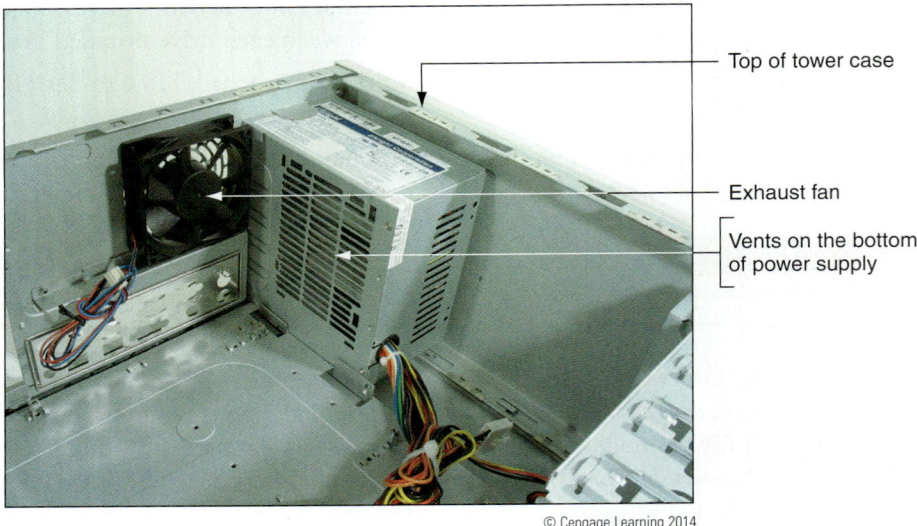

Figure 8-15 This power supply has vents on the bottom to provide better airflow inside the case

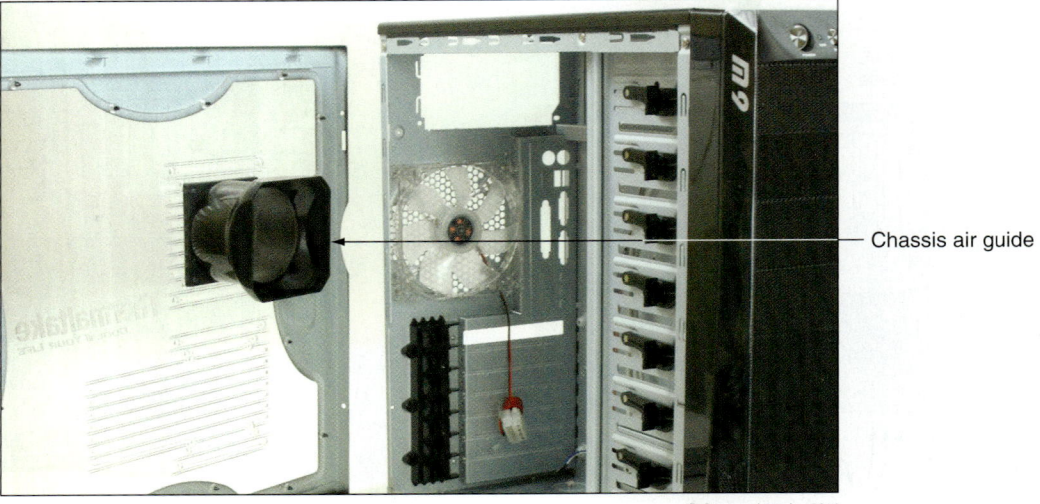

Figure 8-16 Use a chassis air guide to direct outside air over the cooler

20 mm and no less than 12 mm. If the guide obstructs the cooler, you can remove the guide, but optimum airflow will not be achieved.

Be careful when trying to solve an overheating problem. Excessive heat can damage the CPU and the motherboard. Never operate a system if the case fan, power-supply fan, or cooler fan is not working.

TROUBLESHOOTING POST BEFORE VIDEO IS ACTIVE

Error messages on the screen indicate that video and the electrical system are working. If you observe that power is getting to the system (you see lights and hear fans or beeps) but the screen is blank, turn off the system and turn it back on and carefully listen to any beep codes or BIOS speech messages. Recall that, before BIOS checks video, POST reports any error messages as beep codes. When a PC boots, one beep or no beep indicates that all is well after POST. If you hear more than one beep, look up the beep code in the motherboard or BIOS documentation or on the web sites of these manufacturers. Each BIOS manufacturer has its own beep codes, and Table 8-2 lists the more common meanings.

Beeps During POST	Description
One short beep or no beep	The computer passed all POST tests
1 long and 2 short beeps	Award BIOS: A video problem, no video card, bad video memory Intel BIOS: A video problem
Continuous short beeps	Award BIOS: A memory error Intel BIOS: A loose card or short
1 long and 1 short beep	Intel BIOS: Motherboard problem
1 long and 3 short beeps	Intel BIOS: A video problem
3 long beeps	Intel BIOS: A keyboard controller problem
Continuous 2 short beeps and then a pause	Intel BIOS: A video card problem
Continuous 3 short beeps and then a pause	Intel BIOS: A memory error
8 beeps followed by a system shutdown	Intel BIOS: The system has overheated
Continuous high and low beeps	Intel BIOS: CPU problem

Table 8-2 Common beep codes and their meanings for Intel and Award BIOS

© Cengage Learning 2014

Hands-on | Project 8-1 Research Beep Codes

Identify the motherboard and BIOS version installed in your computer. Locate the motherboard user guide on the web and find the list of beep codes that the BIOS might give at POST. If the manual doesn't give this information, search the support section on the web site of the motherboard manufacturer or search the web site of the BIOS manufacturer. List the beep codes and their meanings for your motherboard.

TROUBLESHOOTING ERROR MESSAGES DURING THE BOOT

A+ 220-802 4.2

If video and the electrical systems are working, then most boot problems show up as an error message displayed on-screen. These error messages that occur before Windows starts to load apply to hardware components that are required to boot the system. Some possible error messages are listed in Table 8-3, along with their meanings. For other error messages, look in your motherboard user guide or the manufacturer's web site. You can also search the web on the motherboard brand and model and the error message.

Error Message Before Windows Starts	Meaning of the Error Message
CMOS battery low	The CMOS battery needs replacing.
CMOS checksum bad	CMOS RAM might be corrupted. Run BIOS setup and reset BIOS to default settings. If the problem occurs again, try flashing the BIOS.
Memory size decreased	Startup BIOS recognized that the amount of installed RAM is less than that of the previous boot. A memory module might be bad. Begin troubleshooting memory.
Processor thermal trip error	The processor overheated and the system has restarted.
Intruder detection error	An intrusion detection device installed on the motherboard has detected that the computer case was opened.
Overclocking failed. Please enter setup to reconfigure your system.	Overclocking should be discontinued. However, this error might not be related to overclocking; it can occur when the power supply is failing.
No boot device available Hard drive not found Fixed disk error Invalid boot disk Inaccessible boot device or drive Invalid drive specification	Startup BIOS did not find a device to use to load the operating system. Make sure the boot device priority order is correct in BIOS setup. Then begin troubleshooting the hard drive.
Missing BOOTMGR Missing NTLDR Missing operating system Error loading operating system	The Windows program needed to start Windows is missing or corrupted. This program is called the OS boot manager program.

© Cengage Learning 2014

Table 8-3 Error messages that occur before Windows starts

If the Windows boot manager program has problems loading Windows, it gives a different set of error messages than the ones listed in Table 8-3. For example, a Windows error that occurred early in the boot is shown in Figure 8-17.

When these errors are related to hardware that is necessary for the boot, they are likely to be a BSOD error message on a blue screen such as the one shown earlier in Figure 8-3. Sometimes Windows is configured to restart immediately after a BSOD. This setting can lead to continuous reboots, and the error message might fly by so fast you can't read it. To disable these automatic restarts, press **F8** as Windows starts up. The Advanced Boot Options menu appears. Figure 8-18 shows the Windows 7 menu; the Vista and XP menus are similar.

Troubleshooting Error Messages During the Boot | 365

A+ 220-802
4.2

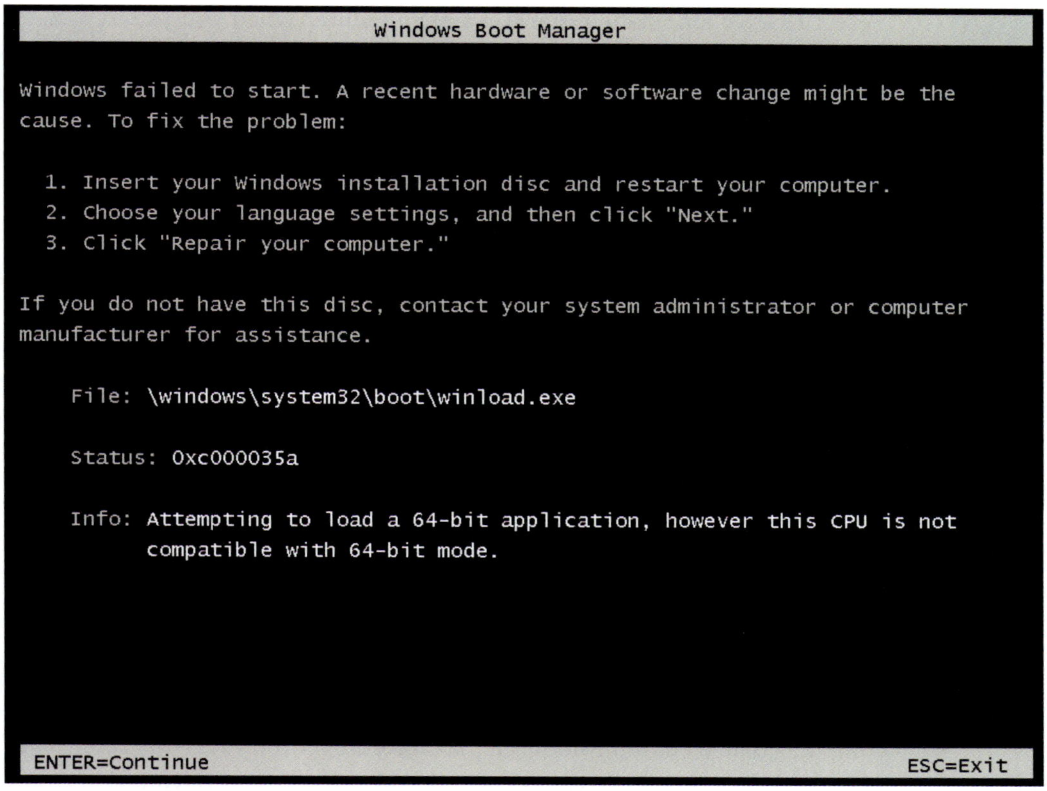

```
                    Windows Boot Manager
Windows failed to start. A recent hardware or software change might be the
cause. To fix the problem:

  1. Insert your Windows installation disc and restart your computer.
  2. Choose your language settings, and then click "Next."
  3. Click "Repair your computer."

If you do not have this disc, contact your system administrator or computer
manufacturer for assistance.

    File: \windows\system32\boot\winload.exe

    Status: 0xc000035a

    Info: Attempting to load a 64-bit application, however this CPU is not
          compatible with 64-bit mode.




ENTER=Continue                                                      ESC=Exit
```

Source: Microsoft Windows 7

Figure 8-17 A Windows error early in the boot that is related to software

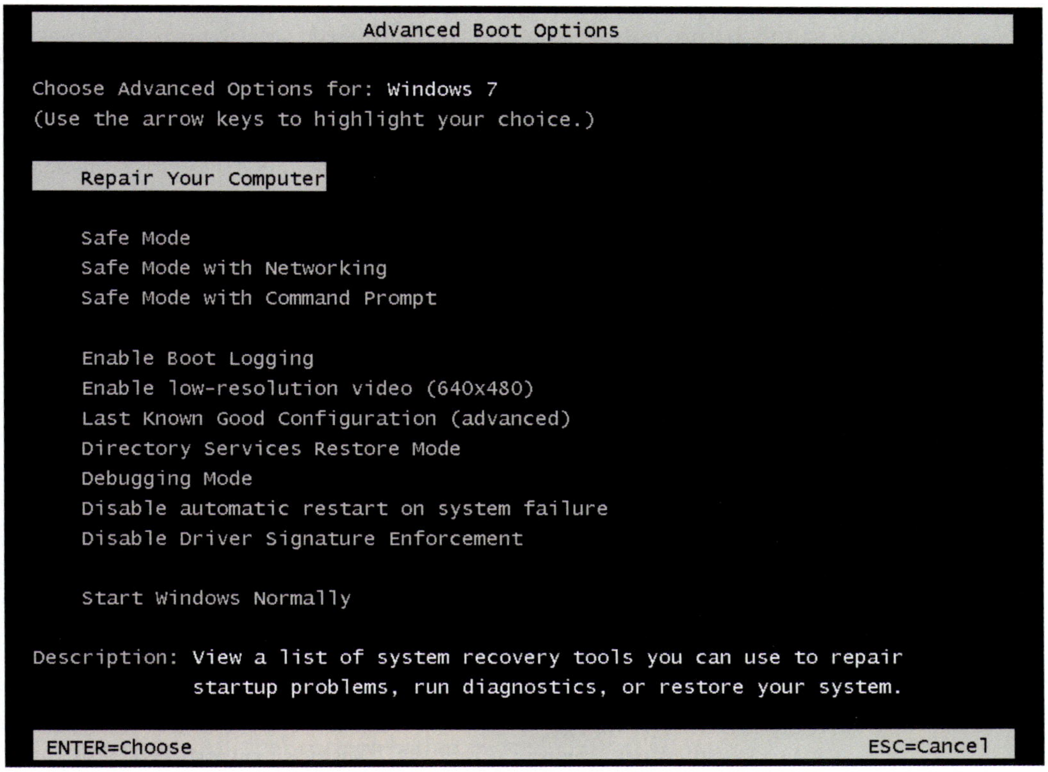

```
                    Advanced Boot Options

Choose Advanced Options for: Windows 7
(Use the arrow keys to highlight your choice.)

    Repair Your Computer

    Safe Mode
    Safe Mode with Networking
    Safe Mode with Command Prompt

    Enable Boot Logging
    Enable low-resolution video (640x480)
    Last Known Good Configuration (advanced)
    Directory Services Restore Mode
    Debugging Mode
    Disable automatic restart on system failure
    Disable Driver Signature Enforcement

    Start Windows Normally

Description: View a list of system recovery tools you can use to repair
             startup problems, run diagnostics, or restore your system.

ENTER=Choose                                                      ESC=Cancel
```

Source: Microsoft Windows 7

Figure 8-18 Press F8 during the boot to see the Advanced Boot Options menu

Select **Disable automatic restart on system failure**. When you restart Windows, the error message stays on-screen long enough for you to read it. Search the Microsoft web sites (*support.microsoft.com* and *technet.microsoft.com*) for information about the hardware component causing the problem and what to do about it. BSOD errors might apply to the motherboard, video card, RAM, processor, hard drive, or some other device for which Windows is trying to load device drivers.

TROUBLESHOOTING THE MOTHERBOARD, PROCESSOR, AND RAM

The field replaceable units (FRUs) on a motherboard are the processor, the processor cooler assembly, RAM, and the CMOS battery. Also, the motherboard itself is an FRU. As you troubleshoot the motherboard and discover that some component is not working, such as a network port, you might be able to disable that component in BIOS setup and install a card to take its place.

> **A+ Exam Tip** The A+ 220-802 exam expects you to know how to troubleshoot problems with motherboards, processors, and RAM.

When you suspect a bad component, a good troubleshooting technique is to substitute a known-good component for the one you suspect is bad. Be cautious here. A friend once had a computer that would not boot. He replaced the hard drive, with no change. He replaced the motherboard next. The computer booted up with no problem; he was delighted, until it failed again. Later he discovered that a faulty power supply had damaged his original motherboard. When he traded the bad one for a good one, the new motherboard also got zapped! If you suspect problems with the power supply, check the voltage coming from the power supply before putting in a new motherboard.

Symptoms that a motherboard, processor, or memory module is failing can appear as:

- The system begins to boot but then powers down.
- An error message is displayed during the boot. Investigate this message.
- The system becomes unstable, hangs, or freezes at odd times. (This symptom can have multiple causes, including a failing power supply, RAM, hard drive, motherboard or processor, Windows errors, and overheating.)
- Intermittent Windows or hard drive errors occur.
- Components on the motherboard or devices connected to it don't work.

Remember the troubleshooting principle to check the simple things first. The motherboard and processor are expensive and time consuming to replace. Unless you're certain the problem is one of these two components, don't replace either until you first eliminate other components as the source of the problem.

If you can boot the system, follow these steps to eliminate Windows, software, RAM, BIOS settings, and other software and hardware components as the source of the problem:

1. The problem might be a virus. If you can boot the system, run a current version of antivirus software to check for viruses.

2. A memory module might be failing. In Windows 7/Vista, use the **Memory Diagnostics** tool to test memory. Even if Windows 7/Vista is not installed, you can still run the tool by booting the system from the Windows setup DVD. How to use the Memory Diagnostics tool is coming up later in the chapter.

Troubleshooting the Motherboard, Processor, and RAM

A+ 220-802 4.2

> **Notes** Other than the Windows 7/Vista Memory Diagnostics tool, you can use the Memtest86 utility to test installed memory modules. Check the site *www.memtest86.com* to download this program.

3. Suspect the problem is caused by an application or by Windows. In Windows, the best tool to check for potential hardware problems is Device Manager.

4. In Windows, download and install any Windows updates or patches. These updates might solve a hardware or application problem.

> **Notes** Another useful Windows tool for troubleshooting hardware problems that reports logs of hardware and applications errors is Event Viewer. For a thorough discussion of how to use Event Viewer, open Windows Help and Support and search on "How to use Event Viewer." Alternately, you can look in the companion book, *A+ Guide to Software*. A Real Problems, Real Solutions activity at the end of this chapter helps you learn to use Event Viewer.

5. Ask yourself what has changed since the problem began. If the problem began immediately after installing a new device or application, uninstall the device or applications.

6. A system that does not have enough RAM can sometimes appear to be unstable. Using the System window, find out how much RAM is installed, and compare that to the recommended amounts. Consider upgrading RAM.

7. The BIOS might be corrupted or have wrong settings. Check BIOS setup. Have settings been tampered with? Is the system bus speed set incorrectly or is it overclocked? Reset BIOS setup to restore default settings.

8. Disable any quick booting features in BIOS so that you get a thorough report of POST. Then look for errors reported on the screen during the boot.

9. Following the procedures in Chapter 3, flash BIOS to update the firmware on the board.

10. Look on the CD that came bundled with the motherboard. It might have diagnostic tests on it that might identify a problem with the motherboard.

11. Update all drivers of motherboard components that are not working. For example, if the USB ports are not working, try updating the USB drivers with those downloaded from the motherboard manufacturer's web site. This process can also update the chipset drivers. For example, for one Intel motherboard, Figure 8-19 shows updates available for the board.

12. If an onboard port or connector isn't working, but the motherboard is stable, follow these steps:

    a. Verify the problem is not with the device using the port. Try moving the device to another port on the same computer or move the device to another computer. If it works there, return it to this port. The problem might have been a bad connection.

    b. Go into BIOS setup and verify the port is enabled.

    c. Check Device Manager and verify Windows recognizes the port with no errors. For example, Device Manager shown in Figure 8-20 reports a problem with the onboard Wi-Fi adapter. Uninstall and reinstall the drivers for the device using the port.

    d. Update the motherboard drivers for this port from the motherboard manufacturer's web site.

    e. If you have a loop-back plug, use it to test the port.

    f. If the problem is still not solved, disable the port in BIOS setup and install an expansion card to provide the same type of port or connector.

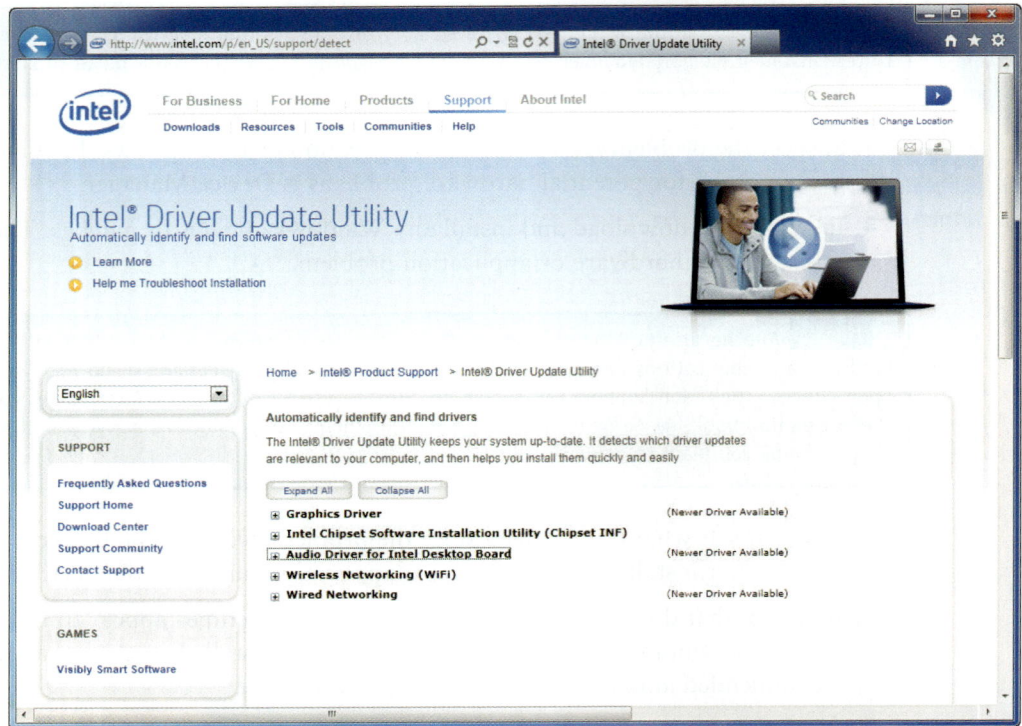

Figure 8-19 Update all motherboard drivers using the motherboard manufacturer's web site

Source: Intel at www.intel.com

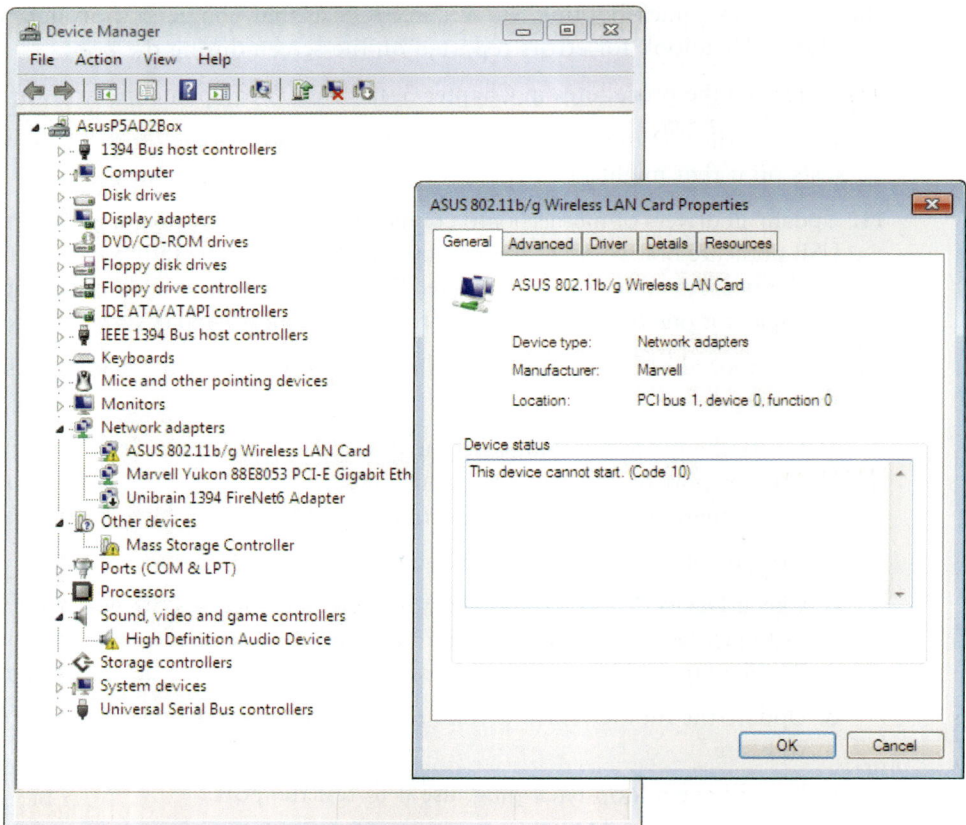

Figure 8-20 Device Manager reports a problem with an onboard port

Source: Microsoft Windows 7

13. Suspect the problem is caused by a failing hard drive. How to troubleshoot a failing drive is covered later in the chapter.

14. Suspect the problem is caused by overheating. How to check for overheating is covered earlier in the chapter.

15. Search the support section of the web sites of the motherboard and processor manufacturers for things to do and try. Then do a general search of the web using a search engine such as *www.google.com*. Search on the error message, symptom, motherboard model, processor model, or other text related to the problem. Most likely, you'll find a forum where someone else has posted the same problem, and others have posted a solution.

16. Verify the installed processor is supported by the motherboard. Perhaps someone has installed the wrong processor.

APPLYING CONCEPTS — HOW TO USE WINDOWS MEMORY DIAGNOSTICS

Errors with memory are often difficult to diagnose because they can appear intermittently and might be mistaken as application errors, user errors, or other hardware component errors. Sometimes these errors cause the system to hang, a blue screen error might occur, or the system continues to function with applications giving errors or data getting corrupted. You can quickly identify a problem with memory or eliminate memory as the source of a problem by using the Windows 7/Vista Memory Diagnostics tool. It tests memory for errors and works before Windows is loaded and can be used on computers that don't have Windows 7 or Vista installed. Use one of these three methods to start the utility:

▲ *Method 1:* In a command prompt window, enter **mdsched.exe** and press **Enter**. A dialog box appears (see Figure 8-21) asking if you want to run the test now or on the next restart.

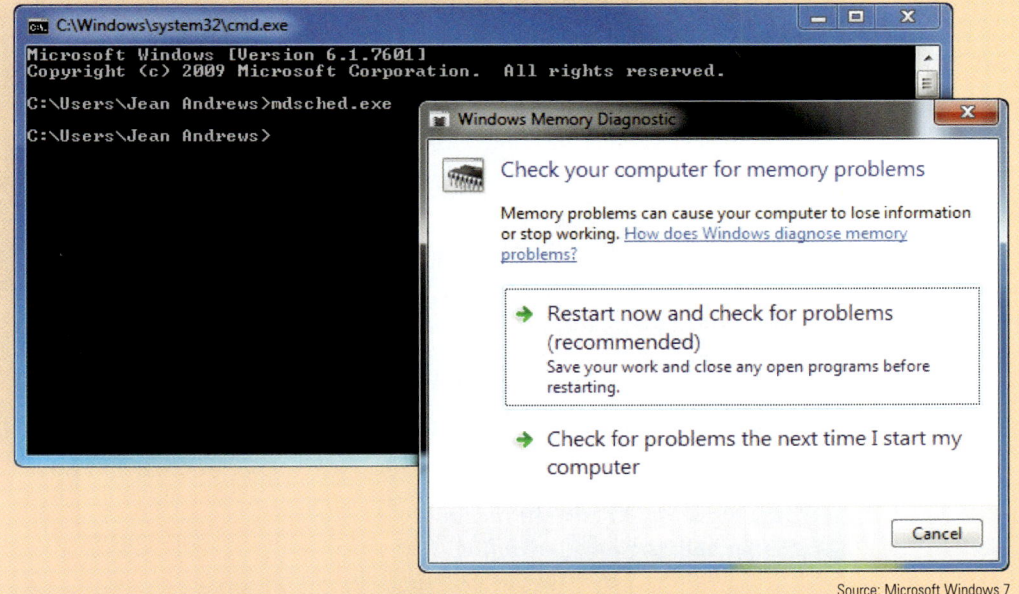

Figure 8-21 Use the mdsched.exe command to test memory

▲ *Method 2:* If you cannot load the Windows desktop, press the Spacebar during the boot. The Windows Boot Manager screen appears (see Figure 8-22). Select **Windows Memory Diagnostic** and press **Enter**.

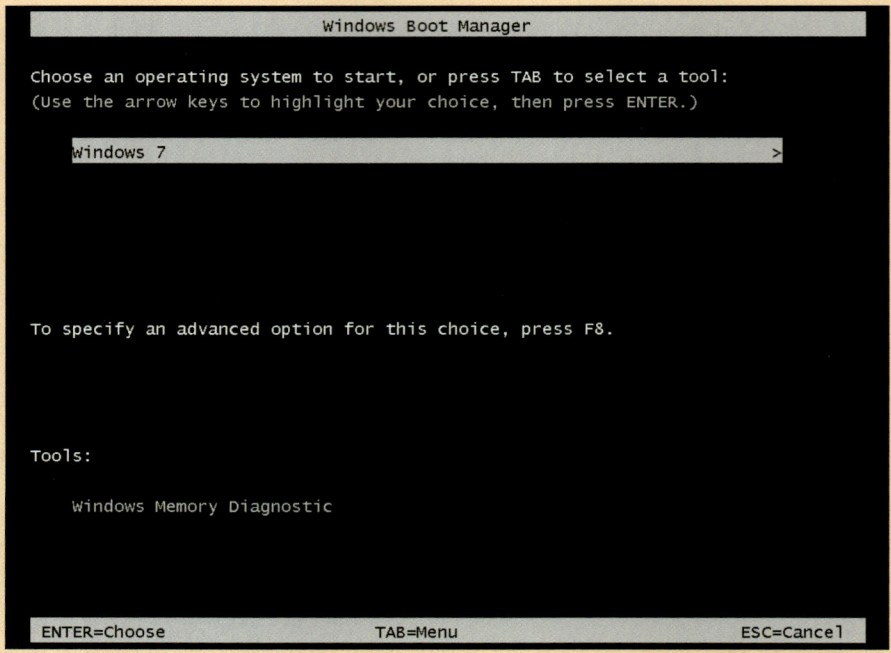

Source: Microsoft Windows 7

Figure 8-22 Force the Windows Boot Manager menu to display by pressing the Spacebar during the boot

▲ *Method 3:* If you cannot boot from the hard drive, boot the computer from the Windows setup DVD. On the opening screen, select your language. On the next screen (see Figure 8-23), click **Repair your computer**. In the next box, select the Windows installation

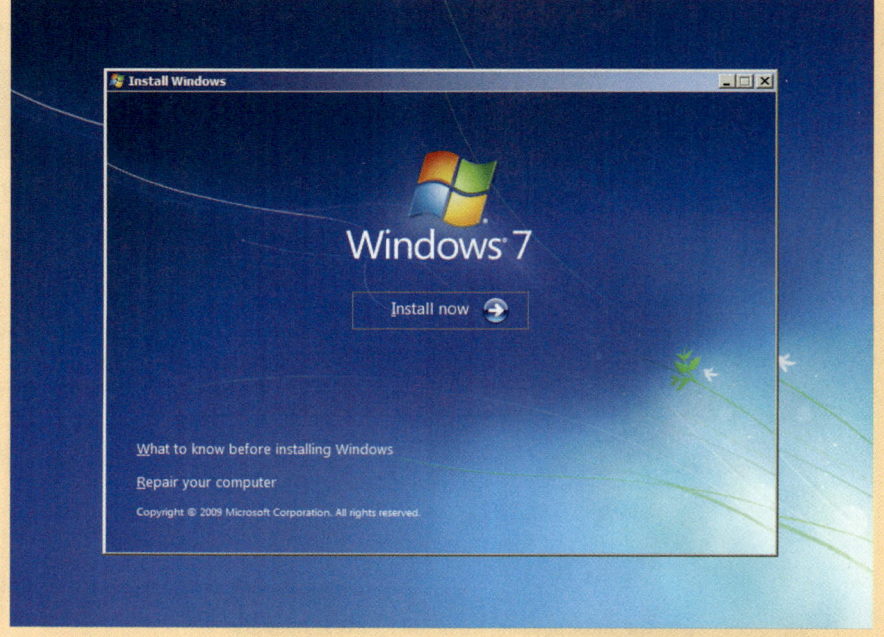

Source: Microsoft Windows 7

Figure 8-23 Opening menu when you boot from the Windows 7 setup DVD

to repair. The System Recovery Options window appears (see Figure 8-24). Click **Windows Memory Diagnostic** and follow the directions on-screen.

If the tool reports memory errors, replace all memory modules installed on the motherboard.

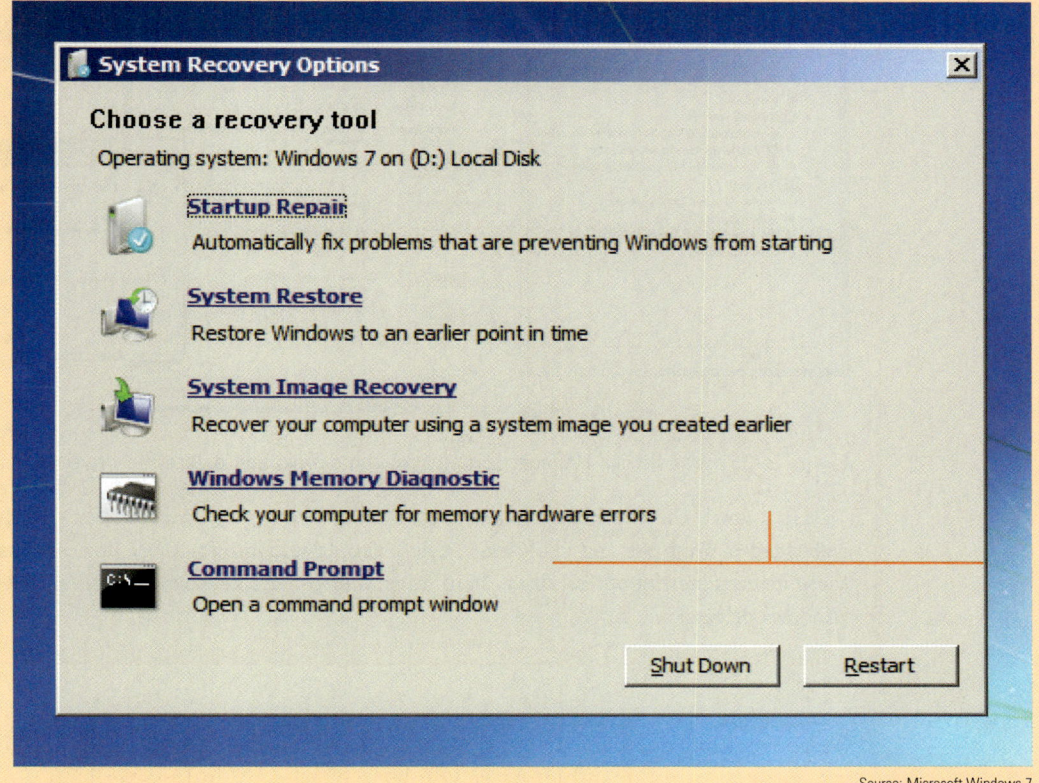

Figure 8-24 Test memory using the System Recovery Options menu

Source: Microsoft Windows 7

APPLYING CONCEPTS — USE DEVICE MANAGER TO DELETE THE DRIVER STORE

One thing you can do to solve a problem with a device is to uninstall and reinstall the device. When you first install a device, Windows stores a copy of the driver software in a **driver store**. When you uninstall the device, you can tell Windows to also delete the driver store. If you don't delete the driver store, Windows uses it when you install the device again. That's why the second time you install the same device Windows does not ask you for the location of the drivers. Windows might also use the driver store to automatically install the device on the next reboot without your involvement.

All this is convenient unless there is a problem with the driver store. To get a true fresh start with an installation, you need to delete the driver store. To do that in Device Manager, open the **Properties** box for the device, click the **Driver** tab, and click **Uninstall**. In the Confirm Device Uninstall box (see Figure 8-25), check **Delete the driver software for this device**, and click **OK**. The installed drivers and the driver store are both deleted. When you reinstall the device, you'll need the drivers on CD or downloaded from the web.

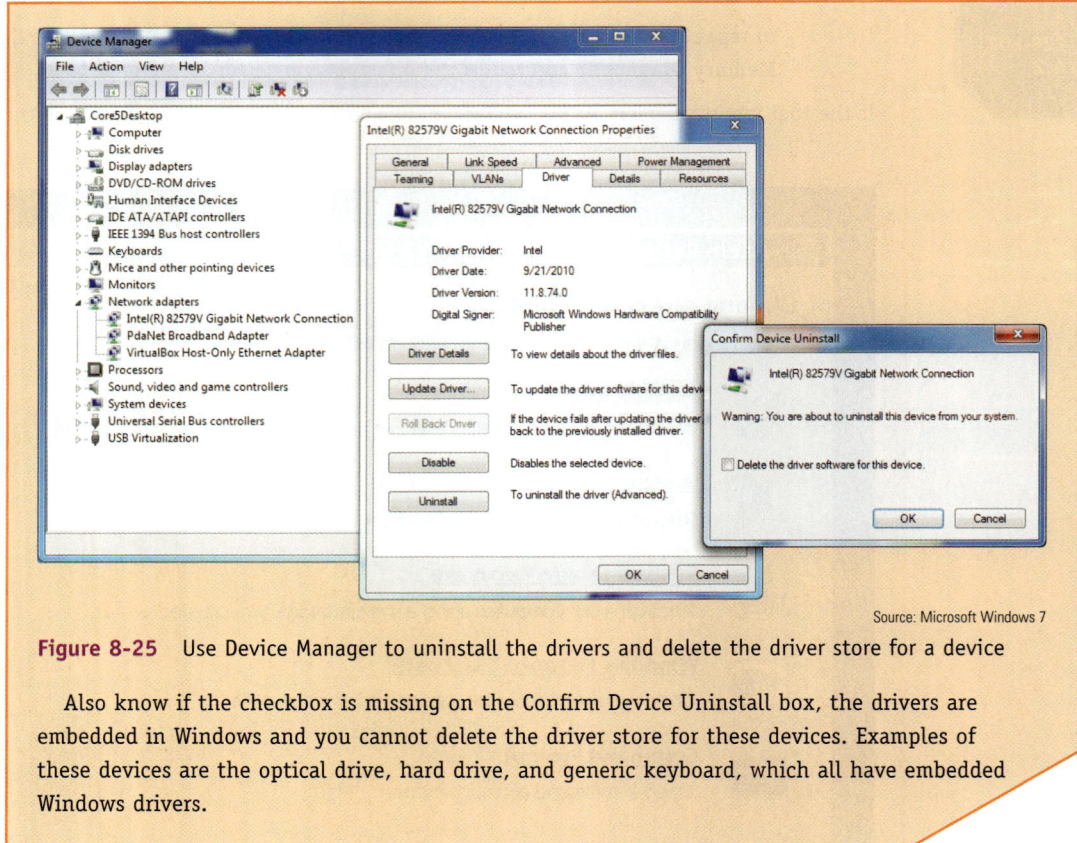

Figure 8-25 Use Device Manager to uninstall the drivers and delete the driver store for a device

Also know if the checkbox is missing on the Confirm Device Uninstall box, the drivers are embedded in Windows and you cannot delete the driver store for these devices. Examples of these devices are the optical drive, hard drive, and generic keyboard, which all have embedded Windows drivers.

We're working our way through what to do when the system locks up, gives errors, or generally appears unstable. After you have checked Windows and BIOS settings and searched the web for help and still not identified the source of the problem, it's time to open the case and check inside. As you do so, be sure to use an antistatic bracelet and follow other procedures to protect the system against ESD. With the case open, follow these steps:

1. Check that all the power and data cables the system is using are securely connected. Try reseating all expansion cards and DIMM modules.

2. Look for physical damage on the motherboard. Look for frayed traces on the bottom of the board or brown or burnt capacitors on the board.

3. Reduce the system to essentials. Remove any unnecessary hardware, such as expansion cards, and then watch to see if the problem goes away. If the problem goes away, replace one component at a time until the problem returns and you have identified the component causing the trouble.

4. Try using a POST diagnostic card. It might offer you a clue as to which component is giving a problem.

5. Suspect the problem is caused by a failing power supply. It's less expensive and easier to replace than the motherboard or processor, so eliminate it before you move on to the motherboard or processor.

6. Exchange the processor.

7. Exchange the motherboard, but before you do, measure the voltage output of the power supply or simply replace it, in case it is producing too much power and has damaged the board.

APPLYING CONCEPTS

Jessica complained to Wally, her PC support technician, that Windows was occasionally giving errors, data would get corrupted, or an application would not work as it should. At first, Wally suspected Jessica might need a little more training in how to open and close an application or save a file, but he discovered user error was not the problem. He tried reinstalling the application software Jessica most often used, and even reinstalled Windows, but the problems persisted.

> **Notes** Catastrophic errors (errors that cause the system to not boot or a device to not work) are much easier to resolve than intermittent errors (errors that come and go).

Then he began to suspect a hardware problem. Carefully examining the motherboard revealed the source of the problem: failing capacitors. Look carefully at Figure 8-26 and you can see five bad capacitors with bulging and discolored heads. (Know that sometimes a leaking capacitor can also show crusty corrosion at the base of the capacitor.) When Wally replaced the motherboard, the problems went away.

Figure 8-26 These five bad capacitors have bulging and discolored heads

PROBLEMS WITH INSTALLATIONS

If you have just installed a new processor, DIMM, or other component and the system does not boot, do the following:

1. When troubleshooting an installation, it's easy to forget to check the simple things first. Are the system and monitor plugged in and turned on? Are the monitor, keyboard, and mouse connected to the system? Is the case front cover securely in place?

2. As you work inside the case, don't forget to use your antistatic bracelet. Open the case and check the installation of the new component:

   ▲ When installing DIMMs, verify each DIMM is securely seated in the memory socket. Make sure a new DIMM sits in the socket at the same height as other modules and clips on each side of the slot are in latched positions.

A+ 220-802 4.2

- ▲ For a new processor, did you install thermal compound between the processor and the heat sink? Is the cooler securely fastened to the frame on the motherboard? If the cooler and thermal compound are not installed correctly, the CPU can overheat during the boot, causing BIOS to immediately power down the system. Is the power cable from the cooler fan connected to the correct fan header on the motherboard? Look in the motherboard documentation for the correct header.
- ▲ For all types of installations, did other components or connectors become dislodged during the installation? Check memory modules, the P1 power connector, the 4-pin CPU auxiliary power connector, hard drive connectors, and auxiliary PCIe power connectors.

3. Try rebooting the system. If you still have a problem, verify you have installed a component that is compatible with the system. For a processor, double-check that the motherboard supports the processor installed. For memory, check that you have the right memory modules supported by your motherboard. Can your OS support all the memory installed?

4. For a processor installation, remove the processor from its socket and look for bent or damaged pins or lands on the socket and processor. For memory, remove the newly installed memory and check whether the error message disappears. Try the memory in different sockets. Try installing the new memory without the old installed. If the new memory works without the old, the problem is that the modules are not compatible.

5. Consider whether the case does not have enough cooling. Is a case fan installed and running at the rear of the case? Are cables and cords tied up out of the way of airflow?

6. For memory modules or expansion cards, clean the edge connectors with a soft cloth or contact cleaner. Blow or vacuum dust from the slot. Don't touch the edge connectors or the slot.

7. When upgrading a processor, reinstall the old processor, flash BIOS, and then try the new processor again.

Here are additional things to check if you have just installed a new motherboard that is not working:

1. If the system can boot into Windows, install all motherboard drivers on the CD that came bundled with the board.
2. Open the computer case and check the following:
   - ▲ Study the motherboard documentation and verify all connections are correct. Most likely this is the problem. Remember the Power Switch lead from the front of the case must be connected to the header on the motherboard. Check all connectors from the front of the case to the front panel header.
   - ▲ Is the BIOS jumper group set for a normal boot?
   - ▲ Are cards seated firmly in their slots? Is the screw in place that holds the card to the back of the case?
   - ▲ Are DIMMs seated firmly in their slots? Remove the DIMMs and reseat them.
   - ▲ Are all I/O cables from the front panel connected to the right connector on the motherboard? Check the USB cable and the audio cable.
   - ▲ Verify the processor, thermal compound, and cooler are all installed correctly.
   - ▲ Are standoffs or spacers in place? Verify that a standoff that is not being used by the motherboard is not under the motherboard and causing a short.
3. Check the motherboard web site for other things you can check or try.

APPLYING CONCEPTS Lance is putting together a computer from parts for the first time. He has decided to keep costs low and is installing an AMD processor on a microATX motherboard, using all low-cost parts. He installed the hard drive, optical drive, and power supply in the computer case. Then he installed the motherboard in the case, followed by the processor, cooler, and memory. Before powering up the system, he checked all connections to make sure they were solid and read through the motherboard documentation to make sure he did not forget anything important. Next, he plugs in the monitor to the onboard video port and then plugs in the keyboard and power cord. He takes a deep breath and turns on the power switch on the back of the computer. Immediately, he hears a faint whine, but he's not sure what is making the noise. When he presses the power button on the front of the case, nothing happens. No fans, no lights. Here are the steps Lance takes to troubleshoot the problem:

1. He turns off the power switch and unplugs the power cord. He remembers to put on his ground bracelet and carefully checks all power connections. Everything looks okay.

2. He plugs in the system and presses the power button again. Still all he hears is the faint whine.

3. He presses the power button a second and third time. Suddenly a loud pop followed by smoke comes from the power supply, and the strong smell of electronics fills the room! Lance jumps back in dismay.

4. He removes a known-good power supply from another computer, disconnects the blown power supply, and connects the good one to the computer. When he turns on the power switch, he hears that same faint whine. Quickly he turns off the switch and unplugs the power cord. He does not want to lose another power supply!

5. Next, Lance calls technical support of the company that sold him the computer parts. A very helpful technician listens carefully to the details and tells Lance that the problem sounds like a short in the system. He explains that a power supply might whine if too much power is being drawn. As Lance hangs up the phone, he begins to think that the problem might be with the motherboard installation.

6. He removes the motherboard from the case, and the source of the problem is evident: he forgot to install spacers between the board and the case. The board was sitting directly on the bottom of the case, which had caused the short.

7. Lance installs the spacers and reinstalls the motherboard. Using the good power supply, he turns on the system. The whine is gone, but the system is dead.

8. Lance purchases a new power supply and motherboard, and this time, carefully uses spacers in every hole used by the motherboard screws. Figure 8-27 shows one installed spacer and one ready to be installed. The system comes up without a problem.

In evaluating his experience with his first computer build, Lance declares the project a success. He was grateful he had decided to use low-cost parts for his first build. He learned much from the experience and will never, ever forget to use spacers. He told a friend, "I made a serious mistake, but I learned from it. I feel confident I know how to put a system together now, and I'm ready to tackle another build. When you make mistakes and get past them, your confidence level actually grows because you learn you can face a serious problem and solve it."

Figure 8-27 Spacers installed in case holes keep the motherboard from causing a short

Hands-on Project 8-2 Troubleshoot Memory

Do the following to troubleshoot memory:

1. Open the Windows System window and record the amount of memory in your system.

2. Follow the rules outlined in Chapter 1 to protect a computer against ESD as you work. Remove the memory module in the first memory slot on the motherboard, and boot the PC. Did you get an error? Why or why not? Replace the module and verify the system starts with no errors and that the full amount of memory is recognized by Windows.

3. Use the Windows 7/Vista Memory Diagnostics tool to test memory. About how long did the test take? Were any errors reported?

Hands-on Project 8-3 Sabotage and Repair a Computer

Open the computer case and create a hardware problem with your computer that prevents the system from booting without damaging a component. For example, you can disconnect a data cable or power cable or loosen a DIMM in a memory slot. Close the computer case and restart the system. Describe the problem as a user would describe it who does not know much about computer hardware. Power down the system and fix the problem. Boot up the system and verify all is well.

TROUBLESHOOTING HARD DRIVES

In this part of the chapter, you'll learn how to troubleshoot problems with hard drives. Problems caused by the hard drive during the boot can be caused by the hard drive subsystem, by the file system on the drive, or by files required by Windows when it begins to load. When trying to solve a problem with the boot, you need to decide if the problem is caused by hardware or software. All the problems discussed in this section are caused by hardware.

Hardware problems usually show up at POST, unless there is physical damage to an area of the hard drive that is not accessed during POST. Hardware problems often make the

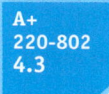

hard drive totally inaccessible. If BIOS cannot find a hard drive at POST, it displays an error message similar to these:

```
No boot device available
Hard drive not found
Fixed disk error
Invalid boot disk
Inaccessible boot device
Inaccessible boot drive
Numeric error codes in the 1700s or 10400s
```

The reasons BIOS cannot access the drive can be caused by the drive, the data cable, the electrical system, the motherboard, the SCSI host adapter (if one is present), or a loose connection. Here is a list of things to do and check before you open the case:

1. If BIOS displays numeric error codes or cryptic messages during POST, check the Web site of the BIOS manufacturer for explanations of these codes or messages.

2. Check BIOS setup for errors in the hard drive configuration. If you suspect an error, set BIOS to default settings, make sure autodetection is turned on, and reboot the system.

3. Try booting from another bootable media such as the Windows setup DVD or a USB flash drive or CD with the Linux OS and diagnostics software installed (for example, Hiren's BootCD software at *www.hirensbootcd.org*). If you can boot using another media, you have proven that the problem is isolated to the hard drive subsystem. You can also use the bootable media to access the hard drive, run diagnostics on the drive, and possibly recover its data. A Hands-on Project later in the chapter gives you practice doing that.

4. For a RAID array, use the firmware utility to check the status of each disk in the array and to check for errors. Recall from Chapter 5 that you press a key at startup to access the RAID BIOS utility. This utility lists each disk in the array and its status. You can search the web site of the motherboard or RAID controller manufacturer for an interpretation of the messages on this screen and what to do about them. If one of the disks in the array has gone bad, it might take some time for the array to rebuild using data on the other disks. In this situation, the status for the array is likely to show as Caution.

   After the array has rebuilt, your data should be available. However, if one of the hard drives in the array has gone bad, you need to replace the hard drive. After you have replaced the failed drive, you must add it back to the RAID array. This process is called rebuilding a RAID volume. How to do this depends on the RAID hardware you are using. For some motherboards or RAID controller cards, you use the RAID firmware. For others, you use the RAID management software that came bundled with the motherboard or controller. You install this software in Windows and use the software to rebuild the RAID volume using the new hard drive.

If the problem is still not solved, open the case and check these things. Be sure to protect the system against ESD as you work:

1. Remove and reattach all drive cables. For IDE drives, check for correct pin-1 orientation.

2. If you're using a RAID, SATA, PATA, or SCSI controller card, remove and reseat it or place it in a different slot. Check the documentation for the card, looking for directions for troubleshooting.

3. For new installations, check the jumper settings on an IDE drive.

4. Inspect the drive for damage, such as bent pins on the connection for the cable.

5. Determine if the hard drive is spinning by listening to it or lightly touching the metal drive (with the power on).

6. Check the cable for frayed edges or other damage.

7. Check the installation manual for things you might have overlooked. Look for a section about system setup, and carefully follow all directions that apply.

8. Windows includes several tools for checking a hard drive for errors and repairing a corrupted Windows installation that are not covered in this book. Without getting into these details of supporting Windows, here are a few simple things you can try:

   a. Following directions given earlier in the chapter, boot from the Windows setup DVD and load the System Recovery Options menu shown earlier in Figure 8-24. Select Startup Repair. This option restores many of the Windows files needed for a successful boot.

   b. To make sure the hard drive does not have bad sectors that can corrupt the file system, you can use the chkdsk command. To use the command, select Command Prompt from the System Recovery Options menu. At the command prompt that appears, enter the **chkdsk C: /r** command to search for and recover data from bad sectors on drive C:.

9. Check the drive manufacturer's web site for diagnostic software. Sometimes this software can be run from a bootable CD. Run the software to test the drive for errors.

10. If it is not convenient to create a bootable CD with hard drive diagnostic software installed, you can move the drive to a working computer and install it as a second drive in the system. Then you can use the diagnostic software installed on the primary hard drive to test the problem drive. While you have the drive installed in a working computer, be sure to find out if you can copy data from it to the good drive, so that you can recover any data not backed up. Remember that you sit the drive on the open computer case (see Figure 8-28) or use a PATA-to-USB converter or SATA-to-USB

Figure 8-28 Temporarily connect a faulty hard drive to another system to diagnose the problem and try to recover data

converter to connect the drive to a USB port. If you have the case open with the PC turned on, be *very careful* to not touch the drive or touch inside the case.

11. If the drive still does not boot, exchange the three field replaceable units—the data cable, the adapter card (optional), and the hard drive itself—for a hard drive subsystem. Do the following, in order:

    a. Reconnect or swap the drive data cable.

    b. Reseat or exchange the drive controller card, if one is present.

    c. Exchange the hard drive for a known good drive.

12. Sometimes older drives refuse to spin at POST. Drives that have trouble spinning often whine at startup for several months before they finally refuse to spin altogether. If your drive whines loudly when you first turn on the computer, never turn off the computer and replace the drive as soon as possible. One of the worst things you can do for a drive that is having difficulty starting up is to leave the computer turned off for an extended period of time. Some drives, like old cars, refuse to start if they are unused for a long time.

13. A bad power supply or a bad motherboard also might cause a disk boot failure.

If the problem is solved by exchanging the hard drive, take the extra time to reinstall the old hard drive to verify that the problem was not caused by a bad connection.

Hard drives are sometimes stored in external enclosures such as the one shown in Figure 8-29. These enclosures make it easy to expand the storage capacity of a single computer or to make available hard drive storage to an entire network. For network attached storage (NAS), the enclosure connects to the network using an Ethernet port. When the

Courtesy of D-Link Corporation

Figure 8-29 The NAS ShareCenter Pro 1100 by D-Link can hold four hot-swappable SATA hard drives totalling 12 TB storage, has a dual core processor and 512 MB RAM, and supports RAID

storage is used by a single computer, the connection is made using a USB or eSATA port. Regardless of how the enclosure connects to a computer or network, the hard drives inside the enclosure might use a SATA or PATA connection.

Here is what you need to know about supporting these external enclosures:

1. An enclosure might contain firmware that supports RAID. For example, a switch on the rear of one enclosure for two hard drives can be set for RAID 0, RAID 1, or stand-alone drives. Read the documentation for the enclosure to find out how to manage the RAID volumes.

2. To replace a hard drive in an enclosure, see the documentation for the enclosure to find out how to open the enclosure and replace the drive.

3. If a computer case is overheating, one way to solve this problem is to remove the hard drives from the case and install them in an external enclosure. However, it's better to leave in the case the hard drive that contains the Windows installation.

TROUBLESHOOTING MONITORS AND VIDEO

For monitor and video problems, as with other devices, if you have problems, try doing the easy things first. For instance, try to make simple hardware and software adjustments. Many monitor problems are caused by poor cable connections or bad contrast/brightness adjustments. Typical monitor and video problems and how to troubleshoot them are described next. In Chapter 11, you learn more about troubleshooting video problems on notebook computers.

> **Notes** A user very much appreciates a PC support technician who takes a little extra time to clean a system being serviced. When servicing a monitor, take the time to clean the screen with a soft dry cloth or monitor wipe.

MONITOR INDICATOR LIGHT IS NOT ON; NO IMAGE ON-SCREEN

If you hear one beep during the boot and you see a blank screen, then BIOS has successfully completed POST, which includes a test of the video card or onboard video. You can then assume the problem must be with the monitor or the monitor cable. Ask these questions and try these things:

1. Is the monitor power cable plugged in?

2. Is the monitor turned on? Try pushing the power button on the front of the monitor. An indicator light on the front of the monitor should turn on, indicating the monitor has power.

3. Is the monitor cable plugged into the video port at the back of the PC and the connector on the rear of the monitor?

4. Try a different monitor and a different monitor cable that you know are working.

> **Notes** When you turn on your computer, the first thing you see on the screen is the firmware on the video card identifying itself. You can use this information to search the web, especially the manufacturer's web site, for troubleshooting information about the card.

MONITOR INDICATOR LIGHT IS ON; NO IMAGE ON-SCREEN

For this problem, try the following:

1. Make sure the video cable is securely connected at the computer and the monitor. Most likely the problem is a bad cable connection.

2. If the monitor displays POST but goes blank when Windows starts to load, the problem is Windows and not the monitor or video. Try booting Windows in Safe Mode, which you learned to do earlier in the chapter. Safe Mode allows the OS to select a generic display driver and low resolution. If this works, change the driver and resolution.

3. The monitor might have a switch on the back for choosing between 110 volts and 220 volts. Check that the switch is in the right position.

4. The problem might be with the video card. If you have just installed the card and the motherboard has onboard video, go into BIOS setup and disable the video port on the motherboard.

5. Verify that the video cable is connected to the video port on the video card and not to a disabled onboard video port.

6. Using buttons on the front of the monitor, check the contrast adjustment. If there's no change, leave it at a middle setting.

7. Check the brightness or backlight adjustment. If there's no change, leave it at a middle setting.

8. If the monitor-to-computer cable detaches from the monitor, exchange it for a cable you know is good, or check the cable for continuity. If this solves the problem, reattach the old cable to verify that the problem was not simply a bad connection.

9. Test a monitor you know is good on the computer you suspect to be bad. If you think the monitor is bad, make sure that it also fails to work on a good computer.

10. Open the computer case and reseat the video card. If possible, move the card to a different expansion slot. Clean the card's edge connectors, using a contact cleaner purchased from a computer supply store.

11. If there are socketed chips on the video card, remove the card from the expansion slot and then use a screwdriver to press down firmly on each corner of each socketed chip on the card. Chips sometimes loosen because of temperature changes; this condition is called chip creep.

12. Trade a good video card for the video card you suspect is bad. Test the video card you think is bad on a computer that works. Test a video card you know is good on the computer that you suspect is bad. Whenever possible, do both.

13. Test the RAM on the motherboard with memory diagnostic software.

14. For a motherboard that is using a PCI-Express or AGP video card, try using a PCI video card in a PCI slot or a PCIe ×1 video card in a PCIe ×1 slot. A good repair technician keeps an extra PCI video card around for this purpose.

15. Trade the motherboard for one you know is good. Sometimes, though rarely, a peripheral chip on the motherboard can cause the problem.

16. For notebook computers, is the LCD switch turned on? Function keys are sometimes used for this purpose.

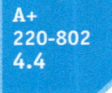

A+
220-802
4.4

17. For notebook computers, try connecting a second monitor to the notebook and use the function key to toggle between the LCD panel and the second monitor. If the second monitor works, but the LCD panel does not work, the problem might be with the LCD panel hardware. How to solve problems with notebook computers is covered in Chapter 11.

SCREEN GOES BLANK 30 SECONDS OR ONE MINUTE AFTER THE KEYBOARD IS LEFT UNTOUCHED

A Green motherboard (one that follows energy-saving standards) used with an Energy Saver monitor can be configured to go into standby or sleep mode after a period of inactivity. To wake up the computer, press any key on the keyboard or press the power button. How to configure sleep mode settings is covered in Chapter 11.

> **Notes** Problems might occur if the motherboard power-saving features are turning off the monitor, and Windows screen saver is also turning off the monitor. If the system hangs when you try to get the monitor going again, try disabling one or the other. If this doesn't work, disable both.

POOR DISPLAY

In general, you can solve problems with poor display by using controls on the monitor and using Windows settings. Do the following:

- ▲ *LCD monitor controls.* Use buttons on the front of an LCD monitor to adjust color, brightness, contrast, focus, and horizontal and vertical positions.
- ▲ *Windows display settings.* Use Windows settings to adjust font size, screen resolution, brightness, color, and Clear Type text. Open Control Panel and in the Appearance and Personalization group, click **Display**. Use these settings to adjust the display:
  - To make sure Clear Type text is selected, click **Adjust ClearType text** and turn on ClearType (see Figure 8-30). Then follow the steps in the wizard to improve the quality of text displayed on the screen.

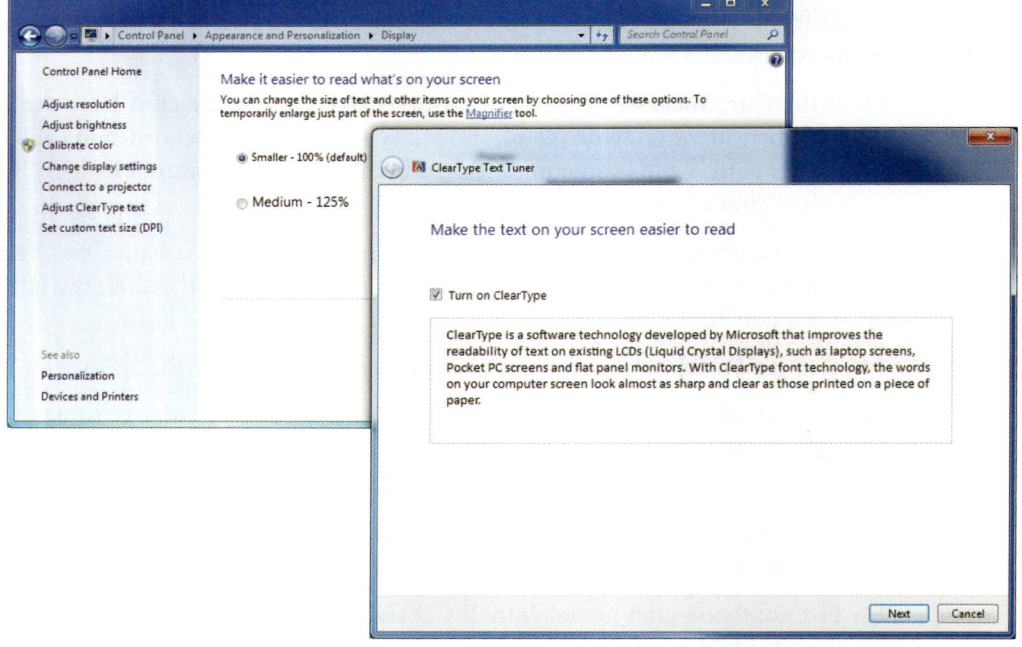

Figure 8-30 ClearType in Windows improves the display of text on the screen

Source: Microsoft Windows 7

Troubleshooting Monitors and Video | 383

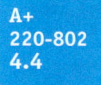
A+ 220-802 4.4

- To adjust screen resolution, click **Change display settings** in the Display window.
- To calibrate colors, click **Calibrate color** and follow the directions on-screen. As you do so, color patterns appear (see Figure 8-31). Use these screens to adjust the gamma settings, which define the relationships among red, green, and blue as well as other settings that affect the display.

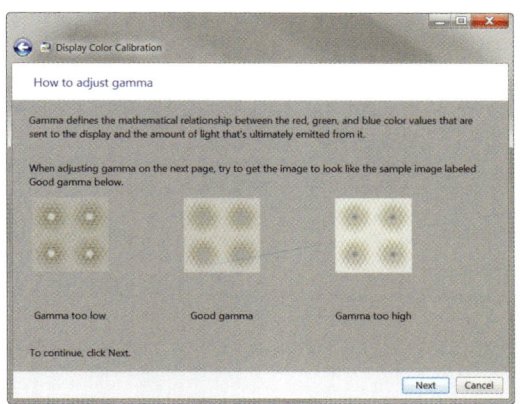
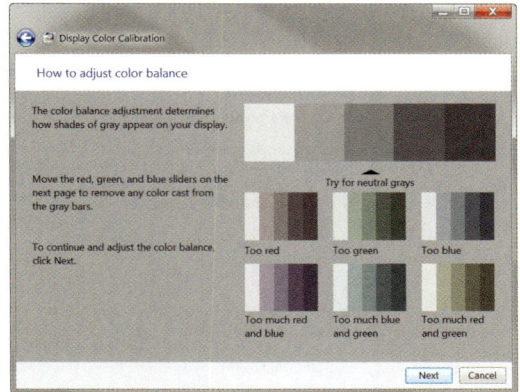

Source: Microsoft Windows 7

Figure 8-31 Two screens in the Windows 7 color calibration wizard

▲ *Update the video drivers.* How to do that is covered in Chapter 6. The latest video drivers can solve various problems with the video subsystem, including poor display.

Here are a few other display problems and their solutions:

▲ *Dead pixels.* An LCD monitor might have pixels that are not working called **dead pixels**, which can appear as small white, black, or colored spots on your screen. A black or white pixel is likely to be a broken transistor, which cannot be fixed. Having a few dead pixels on an LCD monitor screen is considered acceptable and usually not covered under the manufacturer's warranty.

> **Notes** A pixel might not be a dead pixel (a hardware problem), but only a stuck pixel (a software problem). You might be able to use software to fix stuck pixels. For example, run the online software at www.flexcode.org/lcd2.html to fix stuck pixels. The software works by rapidly changing all the pixels on the screen. (Be aware the screen flashes rapidly during the fix.)

▲ *Dim image.* A notebook computer dims the LCD screen when the computer is running on battery to conserve the charge. You can brighten the screen using the Windows display settings. To do so, open **Control Panel**, and click **Display** in the Appearance and Personalization group and then click **Adjust brightness** (see Figure 8-32). To check if settings to conserve power are affecting screen brightness, note the power plan that is selected. Click **Change plan settings** for this power plan. On the next screen, you can adjust when or if the screen will dim (see Figure 8-33). If the problem is still not resolved, it might be a hardware problem. How to troubleshoot hardware in laptops is covered in Chapter 11.

A dim image in a desktop monitor might be caused by a faulty video card or a faulty monitor. To find out which is the problem, connect a different monitor. If the monitor is the problem, most likely the backlighting in the LCD monitor is faulty and the monitor needs replacing.

▲ *Artifacts.* Horizontally torn images on-screen are called **artifacts** (see Figure 8-34), and happen when the video feed from the video controller gets out of sync with the refresh

8

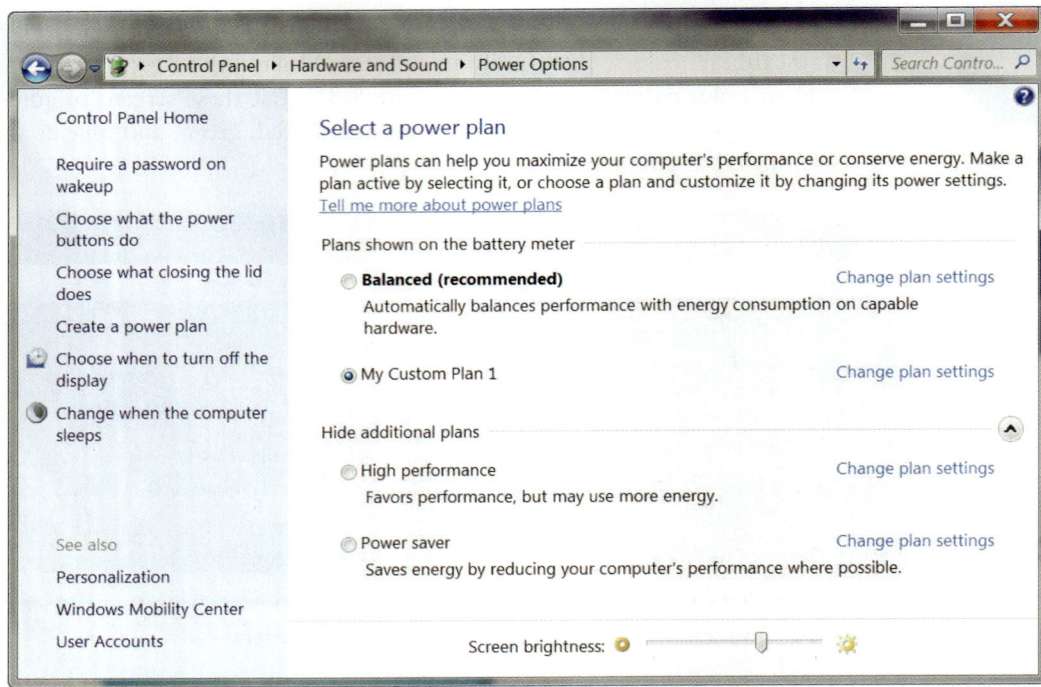

Figure 8-32 Adjust screen brightness

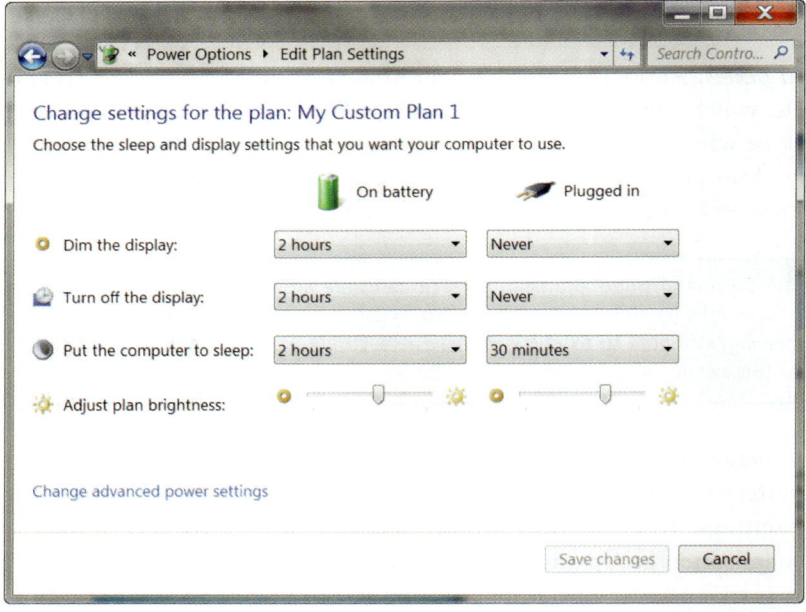

Figure 8-33 Change power plan options to affect how or if the screen dims

of the monitor screen. The problem can be caused by hardware or software. A common cause is when the GPU on the video card overheats. You can test that possibility by downloading and running freeware to monitor the temperature of the CPU and the GPU while you're playing a video game. If you notice the problem occurs when the GPU temp is high, install extra fans around the video card to keep it cool. Two freeware programs to monitor temperatures are CPU-Z by CPUID (*www.cpuid.com/softwares/cpu-z.html*) and GPU-Z by TechPowerUp (*www.techpowerup.com/gpuz*). See Figure 8-35.

Figure 8-34 A simulation of horizontal tears on an image called artifacts

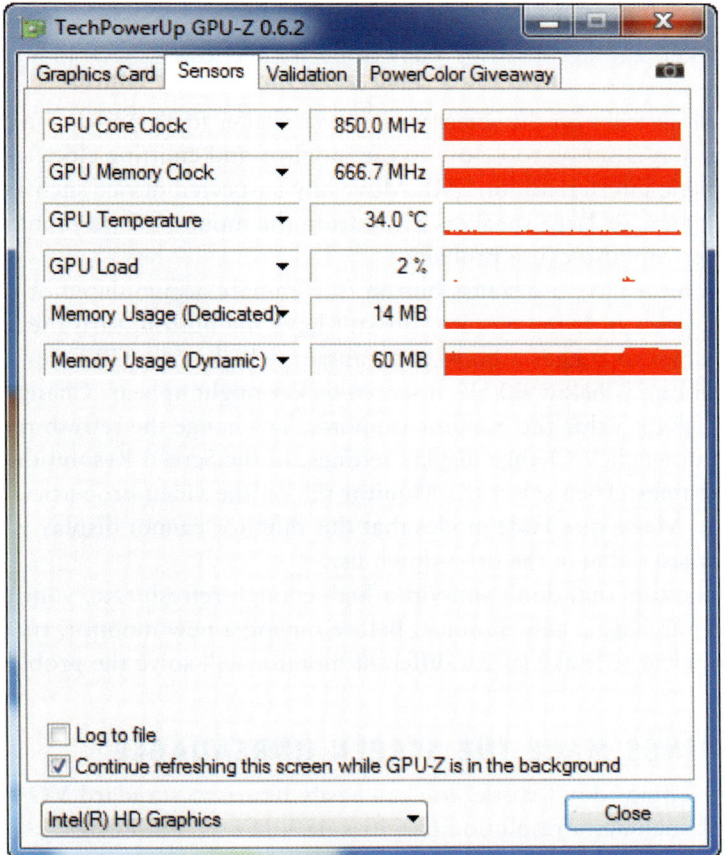

Figure 8-35 GPU-Z monitors the GPU temperature

A+ 220-802 4.4

> **Notes** In this book, I've given several options for various freeware utilities. It's a good idea to know about your options for several reasons. Each freeware utility has different options; owners of freeware might not update their utility in a timely manner, and web sites might decide to include adware with their downloads.

Try updating the video drivers. However, if you see artifacts on the screen before Windows loads, then you know the problem is not caused by the drivers. The problem might be caused by the monitor. Try using a different monitor to see if the problem goes away. If so, replace the monitor.

Overclocking can cause artifacts. Other causes of artifacts are the motherboard or video card going bad, which can happen if the system has been overheating or video RAM on the card is faulty. Try replacing the video card. The power supply also might be the problem.

In general, to improve video quality, upgrade the video card and/or monitor. Poor display might be caused by inadequate video RAM. Your video card might allow you to install additional video RAM. See the card's documentation.

PROBLEMS WITH CRT MONITORS

If a CRT monitor makes a crackling sound, dirt or dust inside the monitor might be the cause. Someone at a computer monitor service center trained to work on the inside of the monitor can vacuum inside it. Recall from Chapter 1 that a monitor holds a dangerous charge of electricity, and you should not open one unless trained to do so.

If the monitor flickers or has wavy lines, a distorted image, or discoloration, try the following:

- Monitor flicker can be caused by poor cable connections. Check that the cable connections are snug.
- Odd-colored blotches on the screen or a screen flicker might indicate a device such as a speaker or fan is sitting too close to the monitor and emitting electrical noise called electromagnetic interference or EMI. Move any suspected device such as a fan, bad fluorescent lights, or large speakers away from the monitor. Two monitors placed very close together can also cause problems.
- Does the monitor have a **degauss button** to eliminate accumulated or stray magnetic fields? If so, press it. If the monitor doesn't have the button, turn the monitor on and off several times to trigger a built-in degausser, which some CRT monitors have.
- If the refresh rate is below 60 Hz, a screen flicker might appear. Change the refresh rate to the highest value the monitor supports. To change the refresh rate, in the Display window, click **Change display settings**. In the Screen Resolution window, click **Advanced settings**. Then select the **Monitor** tab on the video properties box (see Figure 8-36). Make sure **Hide modes that this monitor cannot display** is selected. Then select the largest value in the drop-down list.
- For older monitors that don't support a high enough refresh rate, your only cure might be to purchase a new monitor. Before buying a new monitor, try a second available monitor to make sure a different monitor will solve the problem.

DISPLAY SETTINGS MAKE THE SCREEN UNREADABLE

When the display settings don't work, you can easily return to standard VGA settings called **VGA mode**, which includes a resolution of 640 × 480. Do the following:

A+ 220-802 4.4

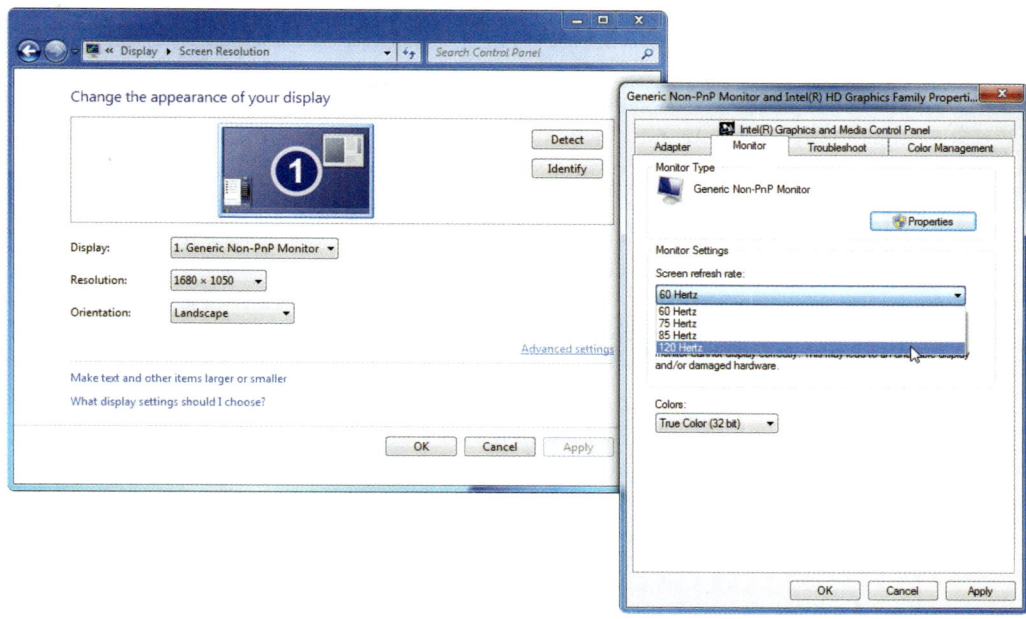

Figure 8-36 Set the refresh rate high to avoid screen flicker

Source: Microsoft Windows 7

- Reboot the system and press the **F8** key after the first beep. The Advanced Boot Options menu appears (refer to Figure 8-18).
- Select **Safe Mode** to boot up with minimal configurations of Windows, which includes standard VGA mode. To boot to the regular Windows environment and use VGA mode, select **Enable low-resolution video (640 × 480)**.
- After you have changed the display settings, restart Windows.

Hands-on Project 8-4 Adjust Windows Display Settings

A support technician needs to be able to instruct others how to change their display settings. To practice this skill, do the following:

1. Using the Windows 7 Display window, calibrate the color displayed on your monitor screen. Verify that ClearType text is enabled.

2. Try different screen resolutions supported by your monitor. On the Display window, click **Set custom text size (DPI)** and adjust font size. Verify the monitor is set to use the highest refresh rate it supports.

3. To view your Windows desktop in VGA mode, boot to the Advanced Boot Options menu and select **Enable low-resolution video (640 × 480)**. Then restart Windows and return your system to normal Windows display settings.

Now let's turn our attention to the final topic of this chapter: protecting a computer and the environment.

PROTECTING A COMPUTER AND THE ENVIRONMENT

**A+
220-801
5.1, 5.2**

As you learn to troubleshoot and solve computer problems, you gradually begin to realize that many problems you face could have been avoided by good computer maintenance that includes protecting the computer against environmental factors such as humidity, dust, and out-of-control electricity. In addition, computer technicians need to be aware that we can do damage to the environment if we carelessly dispose of used computer equipment improperly. Both these concerns are covered in this part of the chapter.

PHYSICALLY PROTECT YOUR EQUIPMENT

Preventive maintenance can prevent certain computer problems from occurring in the first place. The more preventive maintenance work you do initially, the fewer problems you are likely to have later, and the less troubleshooting and repair you will have to do. Here is my list of dos and don'ts (you can probably add your own tips to the list) that you can do to physically protect a computer:

▲ *Don't move or jar your desktop computer while the hard drive is working.* Don't put the computer case under your desk where it might get bumped or kicked. Although modern hard drives are tougher than earlier ones, it's still possible to crash a drive by banging into it while it's reading or writing data.

> **Notes** The read/write heads on a hard drive get extremely close to the platters, but do not actually touch them. A "hard drive crash" can happen when a computer is bumped while the hard drive is operating, and a head bumps against the platter and scratches the surface. Most likely, this hard drive is now unusable.

▲ *Protect a computer against dust and other airborne particles.* Here are some things you can do to protect a computer when it must sit in a dusty environment, around those who smoke, or where pets might leave hair:
- You can purchase a plastic keyboard cover to protect the keyboard. When the computer is turned off, cover the entire system with a protective cover or enclosure.
- Install air filters over the front or side vents of the case where air flows into the case. Put your hand over the case of a running computer to feel where the air flows in. For most systems, air flows in from the front vents (refer to Figure 8-14) or vents on the side of the case that is near the processor cooler (refer to Figure 8-16). The air filter shown in Figure 8-37 has magnets that hold the filter to the case when screw holes are not available.
- Whenever you have the case cover open, be sure to use compressed air or an antistatic vacuum (see Figure 8-38) to remove dust from inside the case. Figure 8-39 shows a case fan that jammed because of dust and caused a system to overheat. And while you're cleaning up dust, don't forget to blow or vacuum out the keyboard.

> **Notes** When working at a customer site, be sure to clean up any mess you created by blowing dust out of a computer case or keyboard.

Figure 8-37 This air filter is designed to fit over a case fan, power supply fan, or panel vent on the case

Courtesy of Metropolitan Vacuum Cleaner

Figure 8-38 An antistatic vacuum designed to work inside sensitive electronic equipment such as computers and printers

▲ *Allow for good ventilation inside and outside the system.* Proper air circulation is essential to keeping a system cool. Don't block air vents on the front and rear of the computer case or on the monitor. Inside the case, make sure cables are tied up and out of the way so as to allow for air flow and not obstruct fans from turning. Put covers on expansion slot openings on the rear of the case and put faceplates over empty bays on the front of the case. Don't set a tower case directly on thick carpet because the air vent on the bottom front of the case can be blocked. If you are concerned about overheating, monitor temperatures inside and outside the case.

A+ 220-801 5.1, 5.2

Figure 8-39 This dust-jammed case fan caused a system to overheat

> **A+ Exam Tip** The A+ 220-801 exam expects you to know how to keep computers and monitors well ventilated and to use protective enclosures and air filters to protect the equipment from airborne particles.

▲ *High temperatures and humidity can be dangerous for hard drives.* I once worked in a basement with PCs, and hard drives failed much too often. After we installed dehumidifiers, the hard drives became more reliable. If you suspect a problem with humidity, you can use a hygrometer to monitor the humidity in a room. High temperatures can also damage computer equipment, and you should take precautions to not allow a computer to overheat.

> **Notes** A server room where computers stay and people generally don't stay for long hours is set to balance what is good for the equipment and to conserve energy. Low temperature and moderate humidity are best for the equipment, although no set standards exist for either. Temperatures might be set from 65 to 70 degrees F, and humidity between 30 percent and 50 percent, although some companies keep their server rooms at 80 degrees F to conserve energy. A data center where both computers and people stay is usually kept at a comfortable temperature and humidity for humans.

▲ *In BIOS setup, disable the ability to write to the boot sector of the hard drive.* This alone can keep boot viruses at bay. However, before you upgrade your OS, such as when you upgrade Windows XP to Windows 7, be sure to enable writing to the boot sector, which the OS setup will want to do.

▲ *Protect your CDs, DVDs, BDs, and other storage media.* To protect discs, keep them away from direct sunlight, heat, and extreme cold. Don't allow a disc to be scratched.

▲ *Don't leave a computer turned off for weeks or months at a time.* Once my daughter left her computer turned off for an entire summer. At the beginning of the new school term, the computer wouldn't boot. We discovered that the boot record at the beginning of the hard drive had become corrupted. PCs, like old cars, can give you problems after long spans of inactivity.

▲ *Don't unpack and turn on a computer that has just come in from the cold.* If your new laptop has just arrived and sat on your doorstep in freezing weather, don't bring it in and immediately unpack it and turn it on. Wait until a computer has had time to reach room temperature to prevent damage from condensation and static electricity. In addition, when unpacking hardware or software, to help protect against static electricity, remove the packing tape and cellophane from the work area as soon as possible.

▲ *Protect electrical equipment from power surges.* Lightning and other electrical power surges can destroy computers and other electrical equipment. If the house or office building does not have surge protection equipment installed at the breaker box, be sure to install a protective device at each computer. The least expensive device is a power strip that is also a surge protector, although you might want to use a line conditioner or UPS for added protection.

Lightning can also get to your equipment across network cabling coming in through your Internet connection. To protect against lightning, use a surge protector such as the one shown in Figure 8-40 in line between the DSL modem or cable modem and the computer or home router to protect it from spikes across the network cables. Notice the cord on the surge protector, which connects it to ground.

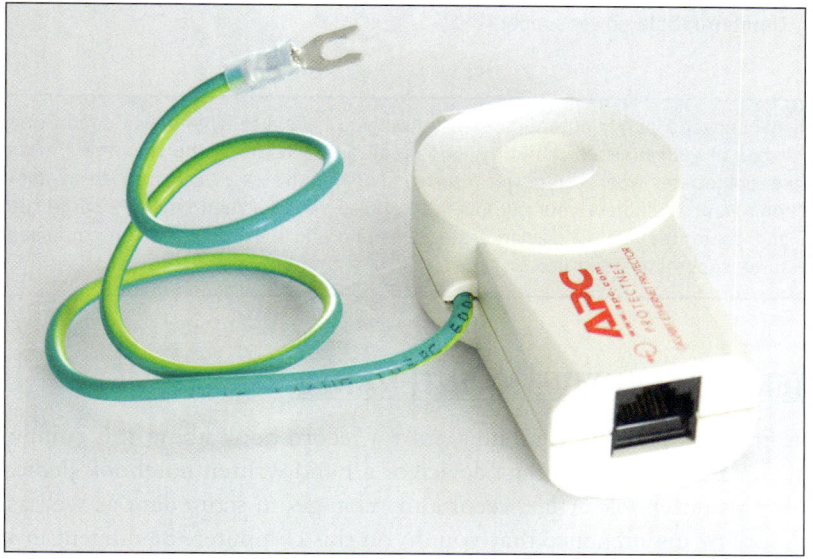

© Cengage Learning 2014

Figure 8-40 Surge protector by APC for Ethernet lines

An **uninterruptible power supply (UPS)** is a device that raises the voltage when it drops during **brownouts** or **sags** (temporary voltage reductions). A UPS also does double duty as a surge protector to protect the system against power surges or spikes. In addition, a UPS can provide power for a brief time during a total blackout long enough for you to save your work and shut down the system. A UPS is not as essential for a laptop computer as it is for a desktop because a laptop has a battery that can sustain it during a blackout.

A common UPS device is a rather heavy box that plugs into an AC outlet and provides one or more outlets for the computer and the monitor (see Figure 8-41). It has an on/off switch, requires no maintenance, and is very simple to install. Use it to provide uninterruptible power to your desktop computer and monitor. It's best not to connect it to nonessential devices such as a laser printer or scanner.

Courtesy of American Power Conversion Corp.   Source: Courtesy of American Power Conversion Corp.

Figure 8-41 Uninterruptible power supply (UPS)

> **Notes** Whenever a power outage occurs, unless you have a reliable power conditioner installed at the breaker box in your house or building, unplug all power cords to the computers, printers, monitors, and the like. Sometimes when the power returns, sudden spikes are accompanied by another brief outage. You don't want to subject your equipment to these surges. When buying a surge suppressor, look for those that guarantee against damage from lightning and that reimburse for equipment destroyed while the surge suppressor is in use.

DOCUMENT PREVENTIVE MAINTENANCE

When you first set up a new computer, start a record book about this computer, using either a file on a removable storage device or a hand written notebook dedicated to this machine. In this notebook or file, record any changes in setup data as well as any problems you experience or maintenance that you do on this computer. Be diligent in keeping this notebook up to date because it will be invaluable in diagnosing problems and upgrading equipment. Keep a printed or handwritten record of all changes to BIOS setup data and jumpers on the motherboard, and store the record with the hardware and software documentation.

If you are not the primary user of the computer, you might want to keep the hardware documentation separate from the computer itself. Label the documentation so that you can easily identify that it belongs to this computer. Keep this hardware documentation and your notes in a safe place. Some support people tape a large envelope inside the computer case; the envelope contains important documentation and records specific to that computer. On the other hand, if you're also responsible for software reference manuals, know that these manuals need to be kept in a location that is convenient for users.

HOW TO DISPOSE OF USED EQUIPMENT

> **Notes** We've provided the document, "Computer Inventory and Maintenance," that you can use to take an inventory of the hardware and software installed on a computer and record the ongoing maintenance, upgrades, and troubleshooting you do to the computer. To download the document, go to *www.cengagebrain.com*. For more information, see the Preface.

As a PC technician, one day you're sure to face an assortment of useless equipment and consumables (see Figure 8-42). Before you decide to trash it all, take a moment and ask yourself if some of the equipment can be donated or at least recycled. Think about fixing up an old computer and donating it to a needy middle school student. If you don't have the time for that, consider donating to the local computer repair class. The class can fix the computers up as a class project and donate them to young students.

© iStockphoto

Figure 8-42 Keep, trash, recycle, or donate?

If you do decide to give away a computer, first uninstall any applications software that you intend to use on another computer and delete any private data. To completely wipe a hard drive clean without destroying it, you can use a **zero-fill utility** downloaded from the hard drive manufacturer. For Windows or other software still installed on the drive, be sure to include documentation and installation CDs or DVDs with the computer.

If you're trashing a computer or hard drive, you can use special equipment called a degausser to erase *everything* on a magnetic hard drive or you can do physical damage (such as drilling holes through the drive). For SSD drives, download and use a Secure Erase utility from the drive manufacturer. When disposing of any type of equipment or consumables, make sure to comply with local government environmental regulations. Table 8-4 lists some items and how to dispose of them.

Part	How to Dispose
Alkaline batteries, including AAA, AA, A, C, D, and 9-volt	Dispose of these batteries in the regular trash. First check to see if there are recycling facilities in your area.
Button batteries used in digital cameras and other small equipment; battery packs used in notebooks	These batteries can contain silver oxide, mercury, lithium, or cadmium and are considered hazardous waste. Dispose of them by returning them to the original dealer or by taking them to a recycling center. To recycle, pack them separately from other items. If you don't have a recycling center nearby, contact your county for local regulations for disposal.
Laser printer toner cartridges	Return these to the manufacturer or dealer to be recycled.
Ink-jet printer cartridges, computer cases, power supplies, and other computer parts, monitors, chemical solvents, and their containers	Check with local county or environmental officials for laws and regulations in your area for proper disposal of these items. The county might have a recycling center that will receive them. Discharge a CRT monitor before disposing of it. See the MSDS documents for chemicals to know how to dispose of them.
Storage media such as hard drives, CDs, DVDs, and BDs	Do physical damage to the device so it is not possible for sensitive data to be stolen. Then the device can be recycled or put in the trash. Your organization might be required to meet legal requirements to destroy data. If so, make sure you understand these requirements and how to comply with them.

Table 8-4 Computer parts and how to dispose of them

© Cengage Learning 2014

A+ Exam Tip The A+ 220-801 exam expects you to know to follow environmental guidelines to dispose of batteries, CRTs, chemical solvents, and containers. If you're not certain how to dispose of a product, see its MSDS document.

Hands-on Project 8-5 Safely Clean Computer Equipment

Practice some preventive maintenance tasks by following these steps to clean a computer:

1. Shut down the computer and unplug it. Press the power button to drain power.
2. Clean the keyboard, monitor, and mouse. For a wheel mouse, remove the ball and clean the wheels. Clean the outside of the computer case. Don't forget to clean the mouse pad.
3. Open the case and using a ground bracelet, clean the dust from the case. Make sure all fans move freely.
4. Verify the cables are out of the way of airflow. Use cable ties as necessary.
5. Check that each expansion card and memory module is securely seated in its slot.
6. Power up the system and make sure all is working.
7. Clean up around your work area. If you left dust on the floor as you blew it out of the computer case, be sure to clean it up.

A+ 220-801 5.1, 5.2

Hands-on Project 8-6 Research Disposal Rules

Research the laws and regulations in your community concerning the disposal of batteries and old computer parts. Answer these questions regarding your community:

1. How do you properly dispose of a monitor?
2. How do you properly dispose of a battery pack used by a notebook computer?
3. How do you properly dispose of a large box of assorted computer parts, including hard drives, optical drives, computer cases, and circuit boards?

>> CHAPTER SUMMARY

How to Approach a Hardware Problem

- If possible, always begin troubleshooting a computer problem by interviewing the user. Find out when the problem started and what happened about the time it started. You also need to know if important data on the computer is not backed up. When troubleshooting, set your priorities based on user needs.
- Sources that can help with hardware troubleshooting are user manuals, the web, online technical support and forums, diagnostic software, and your network of technical associates.
- Decide if a computer problem occurs before or after a successful boot and if it is caused by hardware or software.

Troubleshooting the Electrical System

- To determine if a system is getting power, listen for spinning fans or drives and look for indicator lights.
- Use a power supply tester to test the power supply.
- Intermittent problems that come and go are the most difficult to solve and can be caused by hardware or software. The power supply, motherboard, RAM, processor, hard drive, and overheating can cause intermittent problems.
- Removing dust from a system, providing for proper ventilation, and installing extra fans can help to keep a system from overheating.

Troubleshooting POST Before Video Is Active

- BIOS gives beep codes when a POST error occurs during the boot before it tests video.

Troubleshooting Error Messages During the Boot

- Error messages on a black screen during the boot are usually put there by startup BIOS during the POST.
- Error messages on a blue screen during or after the boot are put there by Windows and are called the blue screen of death (BSOD).
- Search the web site of the BIOS or motherboard manufacturer or the Microsoft web site to find an error message and what to do about it.

Troubleshooting the Motherboard, Processor, and RAM

▲ The motherboard, processor, RAM, processor cooler assembly, and CMOS battery are field replaceable units.

▲ An unstable system that freezes or hangs at odd times can be caused by a faulty power supply, RAM, hard drive, motherboard, or processor, Windows error, or overheating.

▲ When troubleshooting, check the simple things first. For example, you can scan for viruses, test RAM, and run diagnostic software before you begin the process of replacing expensive components.

▲ A POST diagnostic card can troubleshoot problems with the motherboard.

Troubleshooting Hard Drives

▲ Problems caused by the hard drive during the boot can be caused by the hard drive subsystem, by the file system on the drive, or by files required by Windows when it begins to load. After the boot, bad sectors on a drive can cause problems with corrupted files.

▲ To determine if the hard drive is the problem when booting, try to boot from another media, such as the Windows setup DVD.

▲ For problems with a RAID volume, use the RAID controller firmware (on the motherboard or on the RAID controller card) or RAID management software installed in Windows to report the status of the array and to rebuild the RAID volume.

▲ To determine if a drive has bad sectors, use the chkdsk command. You can run the command after booting to the System Recovery Options menu using the Windows setup DVD.

Troubleshooting Monitors and Video

▲ Video problems can be caused by the monitor, video cable, video card, onboard video, video drivers, or Windows display settings.

▲ To bypass Windows display settings, boot the system to the Advanced Boot Options menu and select Safe Mode or Enable low-resolution video (640 × 480).

▲ A few dead pixels on an LCD monitor screen are considered acceptable by the manufacturer.

▲ Artifacts on the monitor screen can be caused by hardware, software, overheating, or overclocking. Try updating video drivers and checking for high temperatures.

▲ A CRT monitor might have a degauss button to eliminate stray EMI.

Protecting a Computer and the Environment

▲ Protect a computer against dust and other airborne particles using protective enclosures and air filters, and ridding the inside of a computer from dust.

▲ To further protect a computer, use good ventilation, keep temperatures and humidity from getting too high, and use a surge protector or UPS. To conserve energy, a company keeps a balance between cool temperatures and the cost of air conditioning.

▲ To protect the environment, make sure you dispose of used equipment and consumables, including batteries, printer toner cartridges, hard drives, and monitors, according to local government environmental guidelines.

>> KEY TERMS

For explanations of key terms, see the Glossary near the end of the book.

artifacts	degauss button	sags
blue screen of death (BSOD)	dead pixel	uninterruptible power supply (UPS)
brownouts	driver store	VGA mode
chassis air guide (CAG)	Memory Diagnostics	zero-fill utility

>> REVIEWING THE BASICS

1. When you first turn on a computer and you don't hear a spinning drive or fan or see indicator lights, is the problem hardware or software related?
2. What is a Windows error message called that appears on a blue screen?
3. How many beeps does startup BIOS give to indicate a successful POST?
4. Which two components in a system might give out a loud whining noise?
5. What Windows utility can you use to test RAM?
6. What is the purpose of standoffs installed between the bottom of the case and the motherboard?
7. If a system hangs after being used for several hours and you suspect overheating, what can you do to easily monitor the CPU and system temperature?
8. What are two reasons to tie cables up and out of the way inside a computer case?
9. Why should a tower case not sit on thick carpet?
10. For most computer cases, does air flow from front to rear or rear to front?
11. What should you do if you get the POST error "CMOS checksum bad"?
12. What can you do if a port on the motherboard is faulty and a device requires this type of port?
13. If you see artifacts on the screen before Windows loads, why can you eliminate the video drivers as the source of the problem?
14. What can you do to stop a computer from repeatedly restarting in a continuous loop?
15. What is the screen resolution used by VGA mode?
16. What can you do to protect a keyboard that is used in an extremely dusty area?
17. Why is not a good practice to unpack computer parts immediately after they have been delivered on a cold day?
18. Why is it not a good idea to throw used button batteries in the trash?
19. What device can keep a computer running during a brownout?
20. What is the best way to get rid of laser printer toner cartridges?

>> THINKING CRITICALLY

1. You upgrade a faulty PCIe video card to a recently released higher-performing card. Now the user complains that Windows 7 hangs a lot and gives errors. Which is the most likely source of the problem? Which is the least likely source?

   a. Overheating

   b. Windows does not support the new card.

   c. The drivers for the card need updating.

   d. Memory is faulty.

2. What should you immediately do if you turn on a PC and smell smoke or a burning odor?

   a. Unplug the computer.

   b. Dial 911.

   c. Find a fire extinguisher.

   d. Press a key on the keyboard to enter BIOS setup.

3. When you boot up a computer and hear a single beep, but the screen is blank, what can you assume is the source of the problem?

   a. The video card or onboard video

   b. The monitor or monitor cable

   c. Windows startup

   d. The processor

4. You suspect that a power supply is faulty, but you use a power supply tester to measure its voltage output and find it to be acceptable. Why is it still possible that the power supply may be faulty?

5. Someone asks you for help with a computer that hangs at odd times. You turn it on and work for about 15 minutes, and then the computer freezes and powers down. What do you do first?

   a. Replace the surge protector.

   b. Replace the power supply.

   c. Wait about 30 minutes for the system to cool down and try again.

   d. Install an additional fan.

>> REAL PROBLEMS, REAL SOLUTIONS

REAL PROBLEM 8-1: Using Event Viewer to Troubleshoot a Hardware Problem

Just about anything that happens in Windows is recorded in Event Viewer (Eventvwr.msc). You can find events such as a hardware or network failure, OS error messages, or a device that has failed to start. When you first encounter a Windows, hardware, application, or security problem, get in the habit of checking Event Viewer as one of your first steps toward investigating the problem. To save time, first check the Administrative Events log because it filters out all events except Warning and Error events, which are the most useful for troubleshooting. Do the following to practice using Event Viewer:

1. Enter **eventvwr.msc** in the search box to open Event Viewer. Drill down into the **Custom Views** list in the left pane and click **Administrative Events**. Scroll through the list of Error or Warning events and list any that indicate a possible hardware problem. Make note of the first event in the list.

2. Disconnect the network cable.

3. In the Event Viewer menu bar, click **Action** and **Refresh** to refresh the list of events. How many new events do you see? Click each new event to see its details below the list of events until you find the event that tells you the network cable was unplugged. See Figure 8-43. Describe the details of the event about the network cable.

4. Tinker around with other hardware on your computer. What actions did you take that triggered a Warning or Error event in Event Viewer?

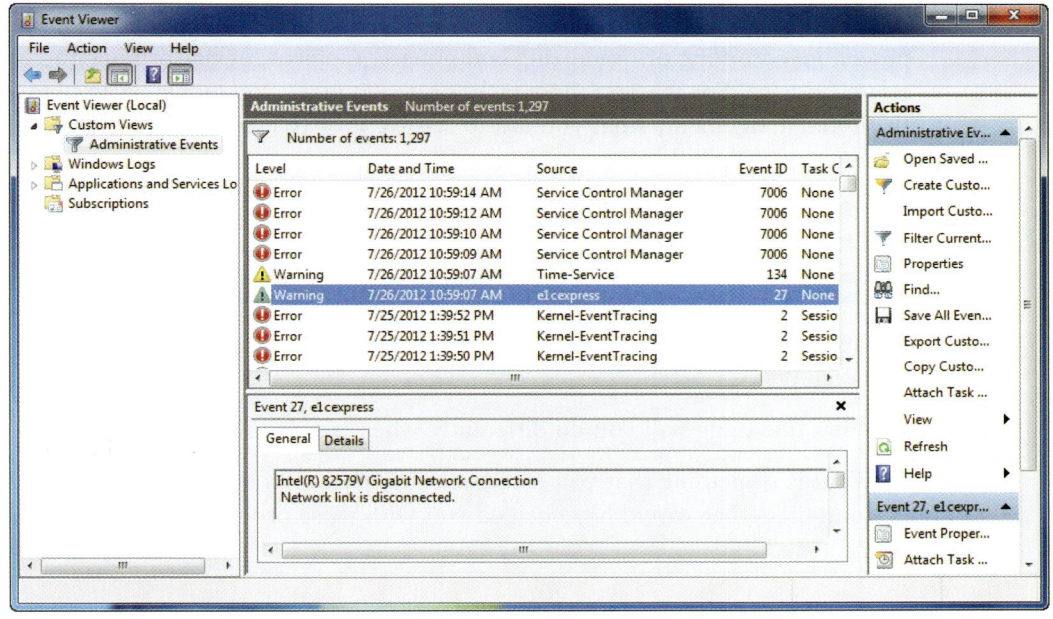

Source: Microsoft Windows 7

Figure 8-43 Use Event Viewer to find logs that can help with troubleshooting hardware problems

REAL PROBLEM 8-2: Troubleshooting a Hung System

A user complains to you that her system hangs for no known reason. After asking her a few questions, you identify these symptoms:

▲ The system hangs after about 15–20 minutes of operation.

▲ When the system hangs, it doesn't matter what application is open or how many applications are open.

▲ When the system hangs, it appears as though power is turned off: there are no lights, spinning drives, or other evidence of power.

You suspect overheating might be the problem. To test your theory, you decide to do the following:

1. You want to verify that the user has not overclocked the system. How do you do that?

2. You decide to check for overheating by examining the temperature of the system immediately after the system is powered up and then again immediately after the system hangs. Describe the steps you take to do this.

3. After doing the first two steps, you decide overheating is the cause of the problem. What are four things you can do to fix the problem?

REAL PROBLEM 8-3: Serving Others with Your Computer Skills

You have learned much about PC troubleshooting and repair already in this book. Now it's time to try your hand at some real-life troubleshooting and help someone else with what you know. Donate a few hours of service to help an elementary school, middle school, or other nonprofit organization with its computer needs. You can help by troubleshooting computer problems, teaching someone how to use a computer, researching equipment the organization wants to buy, disposing of used equipment, cleaning and maintaining the computers, inventorying or organizing computer equipment, or performing any other computer-related service. For the first three tasks or assignments you tackle, keep notes that describe the initial assignment, what you did to resolve it or to escalate it to others, and the outcome. Then answer the following questions:

1. List three assignments or tasks you performed. If one of these tasks was troubleshooting a PC problem, describe the problem, what you did to solve it, and the outcome.

2. List what you learned about technology from these three assignments.

3. List what you learned about working with people when helping them with these three assignments.

4. What one thing will you do differently when faced with similar tasks?

5. What is something that you recognize you need to know, that you don't yet know, about computers that would have helped you with these problems?

CHAPTER 9

Connecting to and Setting Up a Network

In this chapter, you will learn:

- About the TCP/IP protocols and standards Windows uses for networking
- How to connect a computer to a network
- How to configure and secure a multifunction router on a local network

In this chapter, you'll learn how Windows uses TCP/IP protocols and standards to create and manage network connections, including how computers are identified and addressed on a network. You'll also learn to connect a computer to a network and how to set up and secure a small wired or wireless network.

This chapter prepares you to assume total responsibility for supporting both wired and wireless networks in a small-office-home-office (SOHO) environment. In the next chapter, you learn more about the hardware used in networking, including network devices, connectors, and cabling, networking tools, and the types of networks used for Internet connections. So let's get started by looking at how TCP/IP works in the world of Windows networking.

A+ Exam Tip Much of the content in this chapter applies to both the A+ 220-801 exam and the A+ 220-802 exam.

UNDERSTANDING TCP/IP AND WINDOWS NETWORKING

When two computers communicate using a local network or the Internet, communication happens at three levels (hardware, operating system, and application). The first step in communication is one computer must find the other computer. The second step is both computers must agree on the methods and rules for communication (called **protocols**). Then one computer takes on the role of making requests from the other computer. A computer making a request from another is called the client and the one answering the request is called the server. Most communication between computers on a network or the Internet uses this **client/server** model. For example, in Figure 9-1, someone uses a web browser to request a web page from a web server. To handle this request, the client computer must first find the web server, the protocols for communication are established, and then the request is made and answered. Hardware, the OS, and the applications on both computers are all involved in this process.

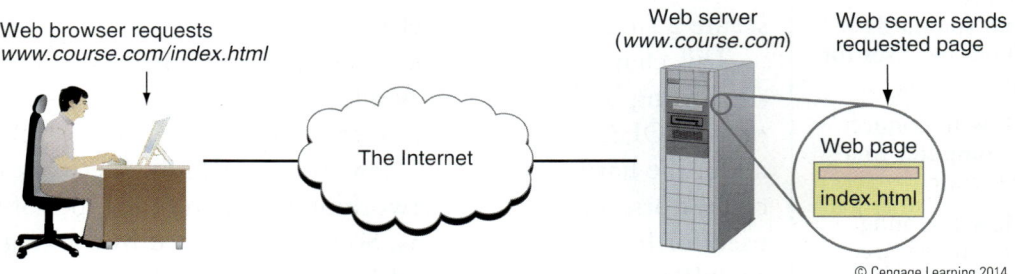

Figure 9-1 A web browser (client software) requests a web page from a web server (server software); the web server returns the requested data to the client

Let's first look at the layers of communication that involve hardware, the OS, and applications and then see how computers are addressed and found on a network or the Internet. Then we'll see how a client/server request is made by the client and answered by the server.

LAYERS OF NETWORK COMMUNICATION

When your computer at home is connected to your Internet Service Provider (ISP) off somewhere in the distance, your computer and a computer on the Internet must be able to communicate. When two devices communicate, they must use the same protocols so that the communication makes sense. For almost all networks today, including the Internet, the group or suite of protocols used is called **TCP/IP (Transmission Control Protocol/Internet Protocol)**.

Before data is transmitted on a network, it is first broken up into segments. Each data segment is put into a **packet**. The packet contains the data (called the payload) and information at the beginning of the packet (called the IP header) that identifies the type of data, where it came from, and where it's going. If the data to be sent is large, it is first divided into several packets, each small enough to travel on the network.

Part of the information included in a packet header is the address information needed to find the computer that is to receive the packet. The address information includes three levels: the address at the hardware level (called a MAC address), the address at the OS level (called an IP address), and the address at the application level (called a port address).

Communication between two computers happens in layers. In Figure 9-2, you can see how communication starts with an application (browser) passing a request to the OS, which passes the request to the network card and then onto the network. When the request reaches the network card on the server, the network card passes it on to the OS and then the OS passes it on to the application (the web server).

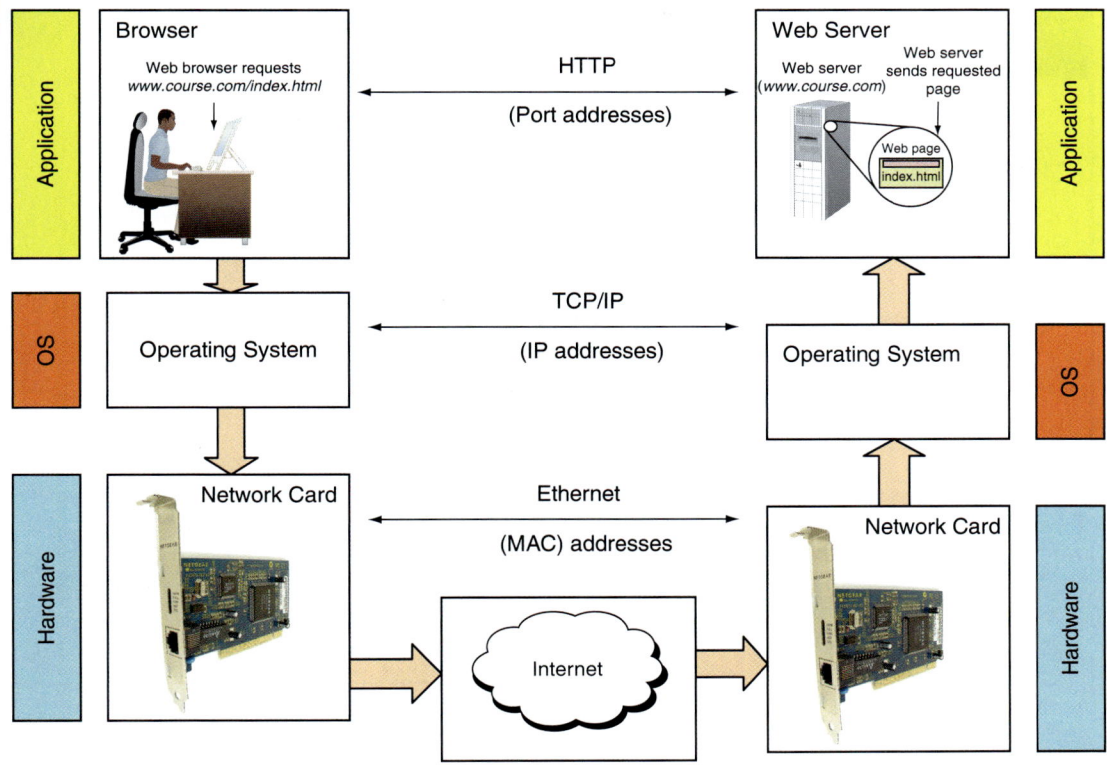

Figure 9-2 Network communication happens in layers

Listed next is a description of each level of communication:

- *Level 1: Hardware level.* At the root level of communication is hardware. The hardware or physical connection might be wireless or might use network cables, phone lines (for DSL or dial-up), or TV cable lines (for a cable modem). For local wired or wireless networks, a **network adapter** (also called a network card, a network interface card, or a NIC) inside your computer is part of this physical network. Every network adapter (including a network card, network port on a motherboard, onboard wireless, or wireless NIC) has a 48-bit (6-byte) number hard-coded on the card by its manufacturer that is unique for that device (see Figure 9-3). The number is written in hex, and is called the **MAC (Media Access Control) address**, **hardware address**, **physical address**, **adapter address**, or Ethernet address. Part of the MAC address identifies the manufacturer that is responsible for making sure that no two network adapters have the same MAC address. MAC addresses are used to locate a computer on a local area network (LAN). A **local area network (LAN)** is a network bound by routers or other gateway devices. A **router** is a device that manages traffic between two or more networks and can help find the best path for traffic to get from one network to another. A **gateway** is any device or computer that network traffic can use to leave one network and go to a different network.

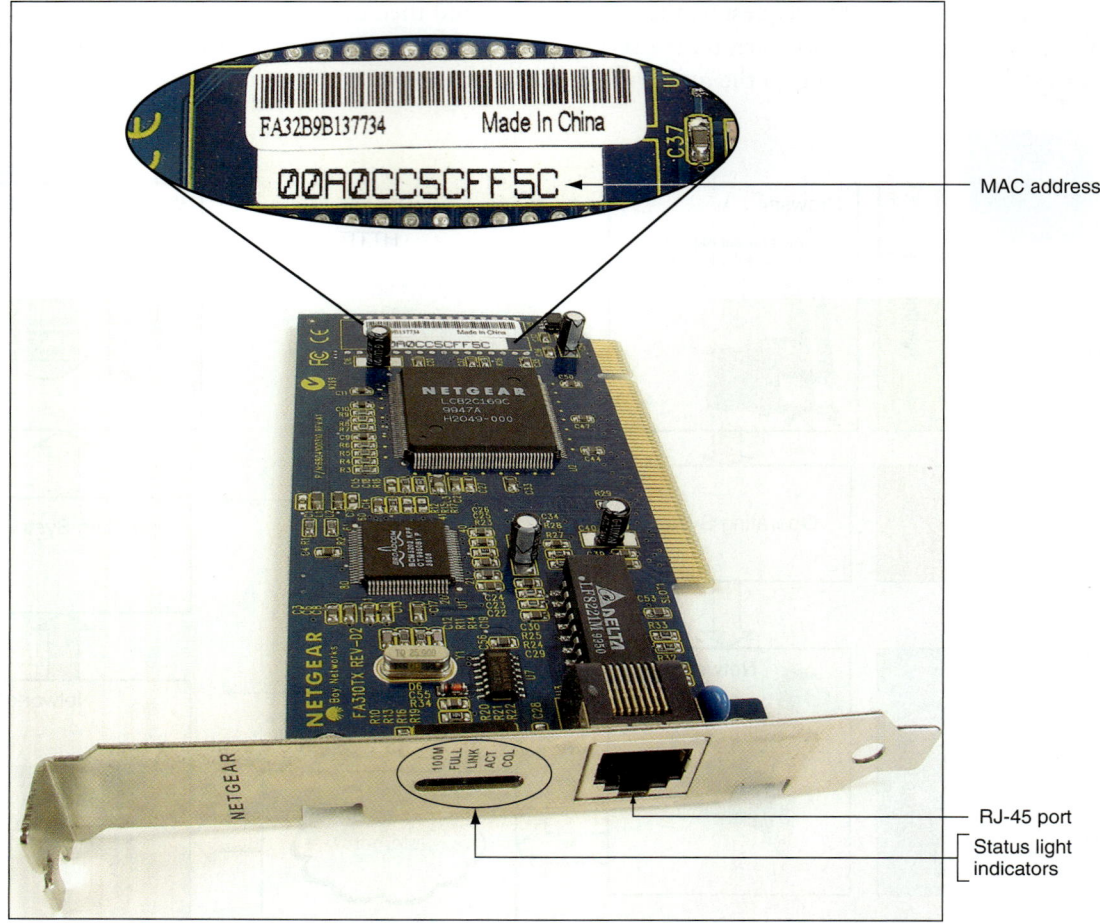

Figure 9-3 Ethernet network card showing its MAC address

▲ *Level 2: Operating system level.* Operating systems use IP addresses to find other computers on a network. An **IP address** is a 32-bit or 128-bit string that is assigned to a network connection when the connection is first made. Whereas a MAC address is only used to find a computer on a local network, an IP address can be used to find a computer anywhere on the Internet (see Figure 9-4) or on an intranet. An **intranet** is

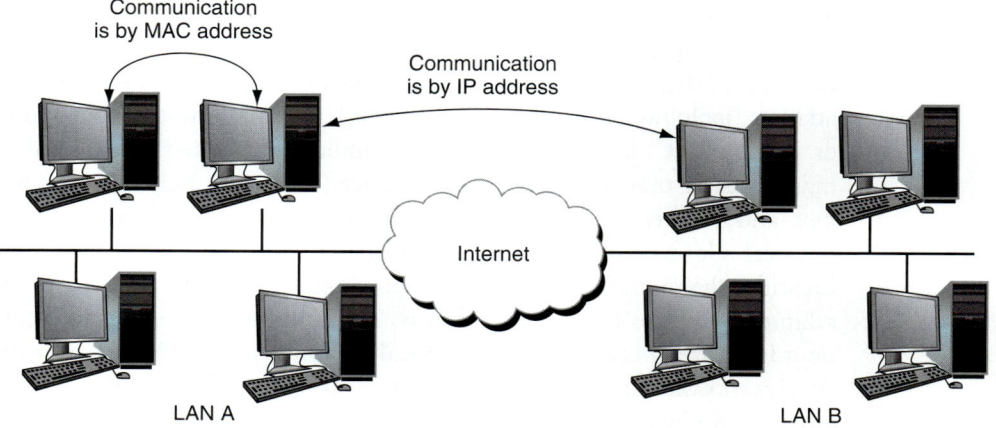

Figure 9-4 Computers on the same LAN use MAC addresses to communicate, but computers on different LANs use IP addresses to communicate over the Internet

any private network that uses TCP/IP protocols. A large enterprise might support an intranet that is made up of several local networks. When several local networks are tied together in a subsystem of the larger intranet, this group of small local networks is called a subnetwork or **subnet**. IP addresses are used to find computers on subnets, an intranet, or the Internet.

▲ *Level 3: Application level.* Most applications used on the Internet or a local network are client/server applications. Client applications, such as Internet Explorer, Google Chrome, or Outlook, communicate with server applications such as a web server or email server. Each client and server application installed on a computer listens at a predetermined address that uniquely identifies the application on the computer. This address is a number and is called a **port number**, **port**, or **port address**. For example, you can address a web server by entering into a browser address box an IP address followed by a colon and then the port number. These values are known as a socket. For example, an email server waiting to send email to a client listens at port 25, and a web server listens at port 80. Suppose a computer with an IP address of 136.60.30.5 is running both an email server and a web server application. If a client computer sends a request to 136.60.30.5:25, the email server that is listening at that port responds. On the other hand, if a request is sent to 136.60.30.5:80, the web server listening at port 80 responds (see Figure 9-5).

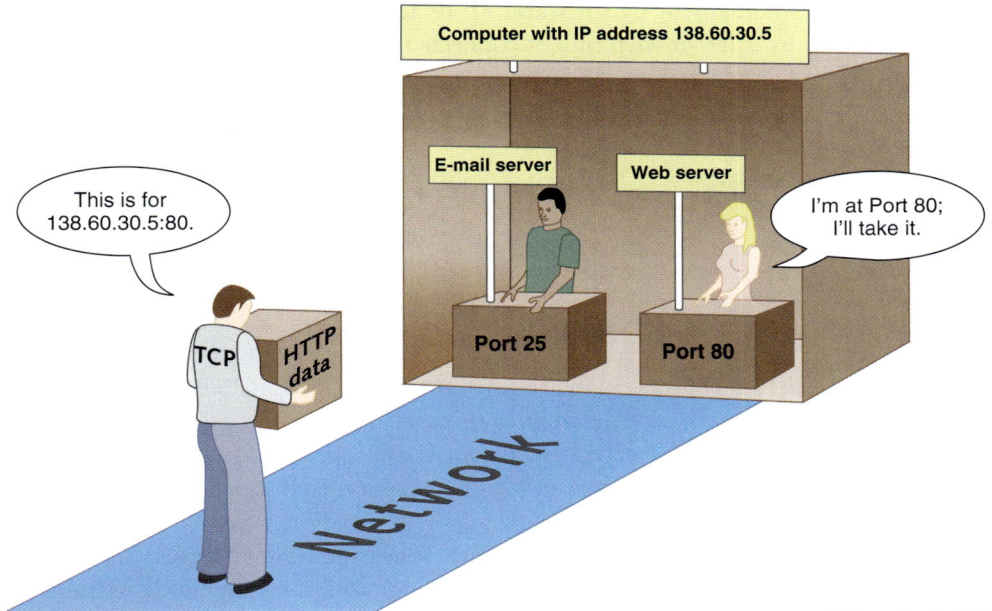

Figure 9-5 Each server running on a computer is addressed by a unique port number

Figure 9-6 shows how communication moves from a browser to the OS to the hardware on one computer and on to the hardware, OS, and web server on a remote computer. As you connect a computer to a network, keep in mind that the connection must work at all three levels. And when things don't work right, it helps to understand that you must solve the problem at one or more levels. In other words, the problem might be with the physical equipment, with the OS, or with the application.

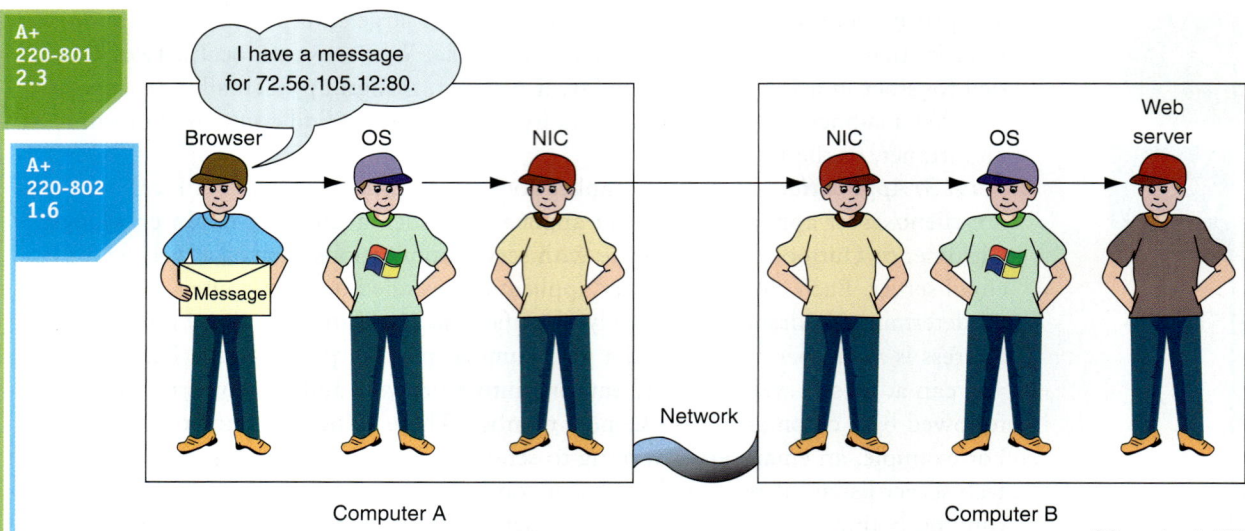

Figure 9-6 How a message gets from a browser to a web server using three levels of communication

HOW IP ADDRESSES GET ASSIGNED

A MAC address is embedded on a network adapter at the factory, but IP addresses are assigned manually or by software. An IP address can be a **dynamic IP address** (IP address is assigned by a server each time it connects to the network) or a **static IP address** (IP address is permanently assigned to the computer or device).

> **A+ Exam Tip** The A+ 220-801 and A+ 220-802 exams expect you to know what a DHCP server is and understand how to use static and dynamic IP addressing.

For dynamic IP addresses, a **DHCP (dynamic host configuration protocol)** server gives an IP address to a computer when it first attempts to initiate a connection to the network and requests an IP address. A computer or other device (such as a network printer) that requests address from a DHCP server is called a **DHCP client**. It is said that the client is leasing an IP address. How to configure a Windows computer to use dynamic or static IP addressing is covered later in the chapter.

An IP address has 32 bits or 128 bits. When the Internet and TCP/IP were first invented, it seemed that 32 bits were more than enough to satisfy any needs we might have for IP addresses because this standard, called **Internet Protocol version 4 (IPv4)**, created about four billion potential IP addresses. Today we need many more than four billion IP addresses over the world. Partly because of a shortage of 32-bit IP addresses, **Internet Protocol version 6 (IPv6)**, which uses an IP address with 128 bits, was developed. Currently, the Internet uses a mix of 32-bit and 128-bit IP addresses. The Internet Assigned Numbers Authority (IANA at *iana.org*) is responsible for keeping track of assigned IP addresses and has already released all its available 32-bit IP addresses. IP addresses leased from IANA today are all 128-bit addresses.

A+ 220-801 2.3

A+ 220-802 1.6

> **Notes** Now that all of the four billion IPv4 addresses are leased, companies that own these addresses are selling them. Recently, Microsoft purchased over 600,000 IP addresses from Nortel for 7.5 million dollars.

Next let's see how IPv4 IP addresses are used, and then you'll learn about IPv6 addresses.

HOW IPV4 IP ADDRESSES ARE USED

A 32-bit IP address is organized into four groups of eight bits each, which are presented as four decimal numbers separated by periods, such as 72.56.105.12. The largest possible 8-bit number is 11111111, which is equal to 255 in decimal, so the largest possible IP address in decimal is 255.255.255.255, which in binary is 11111111.11111111.11111111 .11111111. Each of the four numbers separated by periods is called an octet (for 8 bits) and can be any number from 0 to 255, making a total of about 4.3 billion IP addresses (256 × 256 × 256 × 256). Some IP addresses are reserved, so these numbers are approximations.

The first part of an IP address identifies the network, and the last part identifies the host. When data is routed over the Internet, the network portion of the IP address is used to locate the right network. After the data arrives at the local network, the host portion of the IP address is used to identify the one computer on the network that is to receive the data. Finally, the IP address of the host must be used to identify its MAC address so the data can travel on the host's LAN to that host. The next section explains this in detail.

CLASSES OF IP ADDRESSES

IPv4 IP addresses are divided into three classes: Class A, Class B, and Class C. IP addresses belong in each class according to the scheme outlined in Table 9-1. When IPv4 addresses were available from IANA, a company would lease a Class A, Class B, or Class C license from IANA and from this license could generate multiple IP addresses.

Class	Network Octets*	Approximate Number of Possible Networks or Licenses	Total Number of Possible IP Addresses in Each Network
A	1.x.y.z to 126.x.y.z	126	16 million
B	128.0.x.y to 191.255.x.y	16,000	65,000
C	192.0.0.x to 223.255.255.x	2 million	254

*An x, y, or z in the IP address stands for an octet used to identify hosts.

© Cengage Learning 2014

Table 9-1 Classes of IP addresses

Recall that the first part of an IP address identifies the network, and the last part identifies the host. Figure 9-7 shows how each class of IP addresses is divided into the network and host portions.

Looking back at Table 9-1, you can see that a **Class A** license is for a single octet, which is the network portion of the IP addresses in that license. The remaining octets can be used for host addresses or to identify subnetworks in the larger network. For example, if a company is assigned 87 as its Class A license, then 87 is the network address and is used as the first octet for every host using this license (87.0.0.1, 87.0.0.2, 87.0.0.3, and so forth).

Figure 9-7 The network portion and host portion for each class of IP addresses

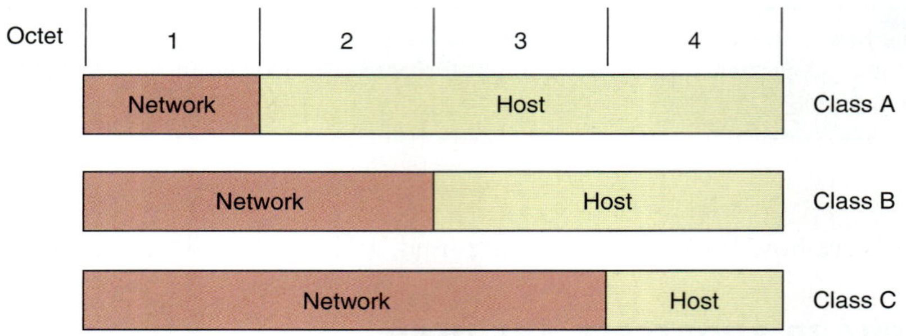

(In practice, such a large network is divided into subnets.) Because three octets can be used for Class A host addresses, one Class A license can have approximately 256 × 256 × 254 host addresses, or about 16 million IP addresses. Only very large corporations with heavy communication needs were able to obtain a Class A license.

> **A+ Exam Tip** The A+ 220-801 exam expects you to know how to identify the class of any given IP address. For the exam, memorize these facts: IP addresses that begin with 1 through 126 are class A addresses; addresses that begin with 128 through 191 are class B addresses, and addresses that begin with 192 through 223 are class C addresses.

A **Class B** license leases the first two octets, and these first two octets are used for the network portion and the last two can be used for the host address or for subnetting the network. An example of a Class B license is 150.35, and examples of IP addresses in this network are 150.35.0.1, 150.35.0.2, and 150.35.0.3. How many host addresses are there in one Class B license? The number of possible values for two octets is about 256 × 254, or about 65,000 host addresses in a single Class B license.

A **Class C** license assigns three octets as the network address. With only one octet used for the host addresses, there can be only 254 host addresses on a Class C network or its subnetworks. For example, if a company is assigned a Class C license for its network with a network address of 200.80.15, some IP addresses on the network would be 200.80.15.1, 200.80.15.2, and 200.80.15.3.

Class D and Class E IP addresses are not available for general use. Class D addresses begin with octets 224 through 239 and are used for **multicasting**, in which one host sends messages to multiple hosts, such as when the host transmits a video conference over the Internet. Class E addresses begin with 240 through 254 and are reserved for research.

In addition to classes of IP addresses, a few IP addresses were reserved for special use by TCP/IP and should not be assigned to a device on a network. Table 9-2 lists these reserved IP addresses.

IP Address	How It Is Used
255.255.255.255	Used for broadcast messages by TCP/IP background processes
0.0.0.0	Currently unassigned IP address
127.0.0.1	Indicates your own computer and is called the loopback address

Table 9-2 Reserved IP addresses

SUBNETS USING IPV4

Looking back at Table 9-1, you can see that a single class license network might have millions of hosts. Managing a network with so many hosts is not practical unless you divide the network into subnets. To divide a network into subnets, you designate part of the host portion of the IP address as a subnet. For example, suppose you have a Class A license of 69. Without using subnets, you have one network: the first octet of all the IP addresses in this network is 69; the last three octets are used for host addresses; and the number of hosts in this one network is about 16 million. Suppose you divide this one network into 256 subnets by using the second octet for the subnet address. (The subnets are 69.0.x.y through 69.255.x.y.) The last two octets are used for host addresses in each subnet with a potential of about 65,000 hosts in each subnet (256 x 254).

The **subnet mask** used with IPv4 identifies which part of an IP address is the network portion and which part is the host portion. Using a subnet mask, a computer or other device can know if an IP address of another computer is on its network or another network (see Figure 9-8).

Figure 9-8 A host (router, in this case) can always determine if an IP address is on its network

A subnet mask is a string of ones followed by a string of zeros. The ones in a subnet mask say, "On our network, this part of an IP address is the network part," and the group of zeros says, "On our network, this part of an IP address is the host part."

If you don't divide a network into subnets, the default subnet mask is used, which is called a **classful subnet mask** because the network portion of the IP address aligns with the class license. For example, Table 9-3 shows the default subnet masks used for three IP addresses. In the table, the green numbers identify the network and the red numbers identify the host.

A+ 220-801 2.3

A+ 220-802 1.6

Class	Subnet Mask	Address	Network ID	Host ID
Class A	11111111.00000000.00000000.00000000	89.100.13.78	89	100.13.78
Class B	11111111.11111111.00000000.00000000	190.78.13.250	190.78	13.250
Class C	11111111.11111111.11111111.00000000	201.18.20.208	201.18.20	208

Table 9-3 Default subnet masks for classes of IP addresses

© Cengage Learning 2014

These three subnet masks would be displayed in a TCP/IP configuration window like this:

▲ Subnet mask of 11111111.00000000.00000000.00000000 is displayed as 255.0.0.0
▲ Subnet mask of 11111111.11111111.00000000.00000000 is displayed as 255.255.0.0
▲ Subnet mask of 11111111.11111111.11111111.00000000 is displayed as 255.255.255.0

A network is divided into subnets when the subnet mask takes some of the host portion of the IP address for the network ID. This **classless subnet mask** does not align the network ID with the network octets assigned by the class license. Using our earlier example, the classless subnet mask for a Class A license of 69 that uses two octets for the network ID rather than the one octet assigned by the class license would be 11111111.11111111.00000000.00000000 or 255.255.0.0. A classless subnet mask can also have a mix of zeros and ones in one octet such as 11111111.11111111.11110000.00000000, which can be written as 255.255.240.0. These classless subnet masks are used to subnet large corporate networks.

APPLYING CONCEPTS Larry is setting up a new computer on a network. He creates TCP/IP settings to use static IP addressing. He assigns a subnet mask of 255.255.240.0 and an IP address of 15.50.212.59 to this computer. Suppose this computer wants to communicate with a computer assigned an IP address of 15.50.235.80. Are these two computers in the same subnet? To find out, you can first compare the binary values of the first two octets and determine if they match. Then compare the binary values of the third octet, like this:

```
212 = 11010100
235 = 11101011
```

To be in the same subnet, the first four bits must match, which they don't. Therefore, these two computers are not in the same subnet. However, an IP address that is in the same subnet as 15.50.212.59 is 15.50.220.100 because the first two octets match and the first four bits of the third octet match (comparing 11010100 to 11011100).

Notes Sometimes an IP address and subnet mask are written using a shorthand notation like 15.50.212.59/20, where the /20 means that the subnet mask is written as 20 ones followed by enough zeros to complete the full 32 bits.

A+
220-801
2.3

A+
220-802
1.6

That brings us to a fun way of explaining subnet masks. Suppose all the tall sticks shown in Figure 9-9 belong to the same network, and the short stick is the subnet mask for this network. How many subnets are in the network? Which sticks belong in the same subnet as Stick 5? As Stick 6?

Figure 9-9 The short stick represents a subnet mask for a network of sticks

PUBLIC, PRIVATE, AND AUTOMATIC PRIVATE IP ADDRESSES

When a company applied for a Class A, B, or C license, it was assigned a group of IP addresses that are different from all other IP addresses and are available for use on the Internet. The IP addresses available to the Internet are called **public IP addresses**.

A company conserves its public IP addresses by using **private IP addresses** that are not allowed on the Internet. Within the company network, computers communicate with one another using these private IP addresses. A computer using a private IP address on a private network can still access the Internet if a router or other device that stands between the network and the Internet is using **NAT (Network Address Translation)**. NAT is a TCP/IP protocol that substitutes the public IP address of the router for the private IP address of the other computer when these computers need to communicate on the Internet.

Because of NAT, a small company can rely solely on private IP addresses for its internal network and use only the one public IP address assigned to it by its ISP for Internet communication. IEEE recommends that the following IP addresses be used for private networks:

- 10.0.0.0 through 10.255.255.255
- 172.16.0.0 through 172.31.255.255
- 192.168.0.0 through 192.168.255.255

> **Notes** IEEE, a nonprofit organization, is responsible for many Internet standards. Standards are proposed to the networking community in the form of an RFC (Request for Comment). RFC 1918 outlines recommendations for private IP addresses. To view an RFC, visit the web site www.rfc-editor.org.

If a computer first connects to the network and is unable to lease an IP address from the DHCP server, it uses an **Automatic Private IP Address (APIPA)** in the address range 169.254.*x.y*.

HOW IPV6 IP ADDRESSES ARE USED

Using the IPv6 standards, more has changed than just the number of bits in an IP address. To improve routing capabilities and speed of communication, IPv6 changed the way IP addresses are used to find computers on the Internet. Let's begin our discussion of IPv6 by looking at how IPv6 IP addresses are written and displayed:

- An IPv6 address has 128 bits that are written as 8 blocks of hexadecimal numbers separated by colons, like this: 2001:0000:0B80:0000:0000:00D3:9C5A:00CC.
- Each block is 16 bits. For example, the first block in the address above is 2001 in hex, which can be written as 0010 0000 0000 0001 in binary.
- Leading zeros in a 4-character hex block can be eliminated. For example, the IP address above can be written as 2001:0000:B80:0000:0000:D3:9C5A:CC.
- If blocks contain all zeros, they can be written as double colons (::). The IP address above can be written two ways:
  - 2001::B80:0000:0000:D3:9C5A:CC
  - 2001:0000:B80::D3:9C5A:CC

To avoid confusion, only one set of double colons is used in an IP address. In this example, the preferred method is the second one: 2001:0000:B80::D3:9C5A:CC because the address is written with the fewest zeros.

The way computers communicate using IPv6 has changed the terminology used to describe TCP/IP communication. Here are a few terms used in the IPv6 standards:

- A **link**, sometimes called the **local link**, is a local area network (LAN) or wide area network (WAN) bounded by routers.
- An **interface** is a node's attachment to a link. The attachment can be a logical attachment or a physical attachment using a network adapter or wireless connection. For example, a logical attachment can be used for tunneling. Tunnels are used by IPv6 to transport IPv6 packets over an IPv4 network.
- The last 64 bits or 4 blocks of an IP address identify the interface and are called the **interface ID** or interface identifier. These 64 bits uniquely identify an interface on the local link.
- **Neighbors** are two or more nodes on the same link.

Three tunneling protocols have been developed for IPv6 packets to travel over an IPv4 network:

- **ISATAP** (pronounced "eye-sa-tap") stands for Intra-Site Automatic Tunnel Addressing Protocol).
- **Teredo** (pronounced "ter-EE-do") is named after the Teredo worm that bores holes in wood. IPv6 addresses intended to be used by this protocol always begin with the same

32 bit-prefix (called fixed bits). Teredo IP addresses begin with 2001, and the prefix is written as 2001::/32.
- **6TO4** is an older tunneling protocol being replaced by the more powerful Teredo or ISATAP protocols.

IPv6 classifies IP addresses differently from that of IPv4. IPv6 supports these three types of IP addresses:

- Using a **unicast address**, packets are delivered to a single node on a network.
- Using a **multicast address**, packets are delivered to all nodes on a network.
- An **anycast address** is used by routers. The address identifies multiple destinations, and packets are delivered to the closest destination.

A unicast address identifies a single interface on a network. The three types of unicast addresses are global, link-local, and unique local addresses, which are graphically shown in Figure 9-10.

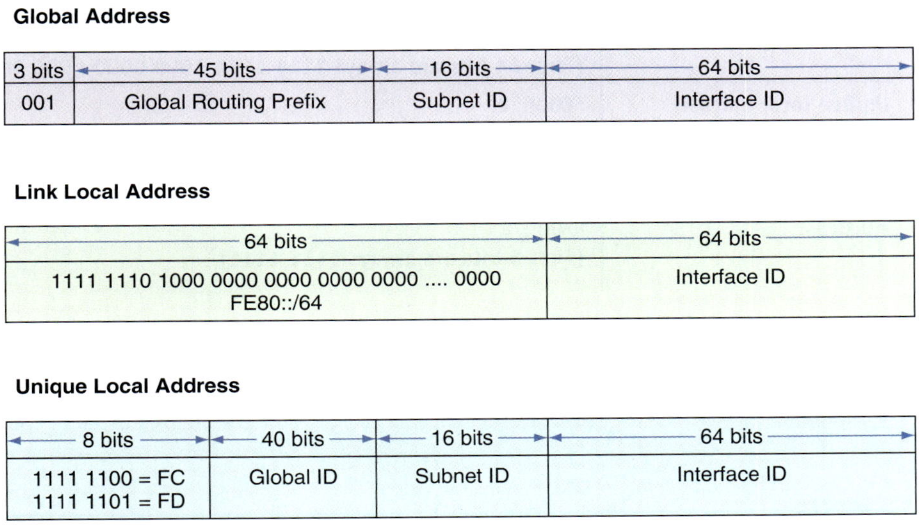

Global Address

3 bits	45 bits	16 bits	64 bits
001	Global Routing Prefix	Subnet ID	Interface ID

Link Local Address

64 bits	64 bits
1111 1110 1000 0000 0000 0000 0000 .... 0000 FE80::/64	Interface ID

Unique Local Address

8 bits	40 bits	16 bits	64 bits
1111 1100 = FC 1111 1101 = FD	Global ID	Subnet ID	Interface ID

Figure 9-10 Three types of IPv6 addresses

Here is a description of each of the three types:

- A **global unicast address**, also called a **global address**, can be routed on the Internet. These addresses are similar to IPv4 public IP addresses. Most global addresses begin with the prefix 2000::/3, although other prefixes are being released. The /3 indicates that the first three bits are fixed and are always 001.
- A **link-local unicast address**, also called a **link-local address** or local address, can be used for communicating with nodes in the same link. These addresses are similar to IPv4 private IP addresses and are sometimes called link-local addresses or local addresses and most begin with FE80::/64. (This prefix notation means the address begins with FE80 followed by enough zeros to make 64 bits.) Link-local addresses are not allowed on the Internet.
- A **unique local unicast address**, also called a **unique local address (ULA)**, is used to identify a specific site within a large organization. For example, an organization might have these two sites: employee.mycompany.com and support.mycompany.com.

The address prefixes used for unique local addresses are FC00::/7 and FD00::/8. The Global ID portion of the address is assigned by the organization. Unique local addresses are not allowed on the Internet. They are hybrid addresses between a global unicast address that works on the Internet and a link-local address that works on only one link.

Notice in Figure 9-10 that global and unique local addresses contain a block labeled the **Subnet ID**, which is the last block in the 64-bit prefix of an IP address. Recall that when using IPv4, the subnet could be identified by any number of bits at the beginning of the IP address. Using IPv6, a subnet is identified using some or all of the 16 bits in the Subnet ID block. Using IPv6, a subnet is, therefore, identified as one or more links that have the same 64 bits in the IP address prefix. This definition implies that a local link is itself a subnet.

Table 9-4 lists the currently used address prefixes for these types of IP addresses. In the future, we can expect more prefixes to be assigned as they are needed.

IP Address Type	Address Prefix
Global unicast	2000::/3 (First 3 bits are always 001)
Link-local unicast	FE80::/64 (First 64 bits are always 1111 1110 1000 0000 0000 0000 ..... 0000)
Unique local unicast	FC00::/7 (First 7 bits are always 1111 110) FD00::/8 (First 8 bits are always 1111 1101)
Multicast	FF00::/8 (First 8 bits are always 1111 1111)

Table 9-4 Address prefixes for types of IPv6 addresses

© Cengage Learning 2014

A+ Exam Tip The A+ 220-801 exam expects you to know the prefixes listed in Table 9-4.

Notes An excellent resource for learning more about IPv6 and how it works is the ebook, *TCP/IP Fundamentals for Microsoft Windows*. To download the free PDF, search for it at *www.microsoft.com/download*.

VIEW IP ADDRESS SETTINGS

The Ipconfig command can be used in a command prompt window to show the IPv4 and IPv6 IP addresses assigned to all network connections (see Figure 9-11).

Notice in the figure the four IP addresses that have been assigned to the physical connections:

 Windows has assigned the wireless connection two IP addresses, one using IPv4 and one using IPv6.
 The Ethernet LAN connection has also been assigned an IPv4 address and an IPv6 address.

The IPv6 addresses are followed by a % sign and a number; for example, %13 follows the first IP address. This number is called the zone ID or scope ID and is used to identify the interface in a list of interfaces for this computer.

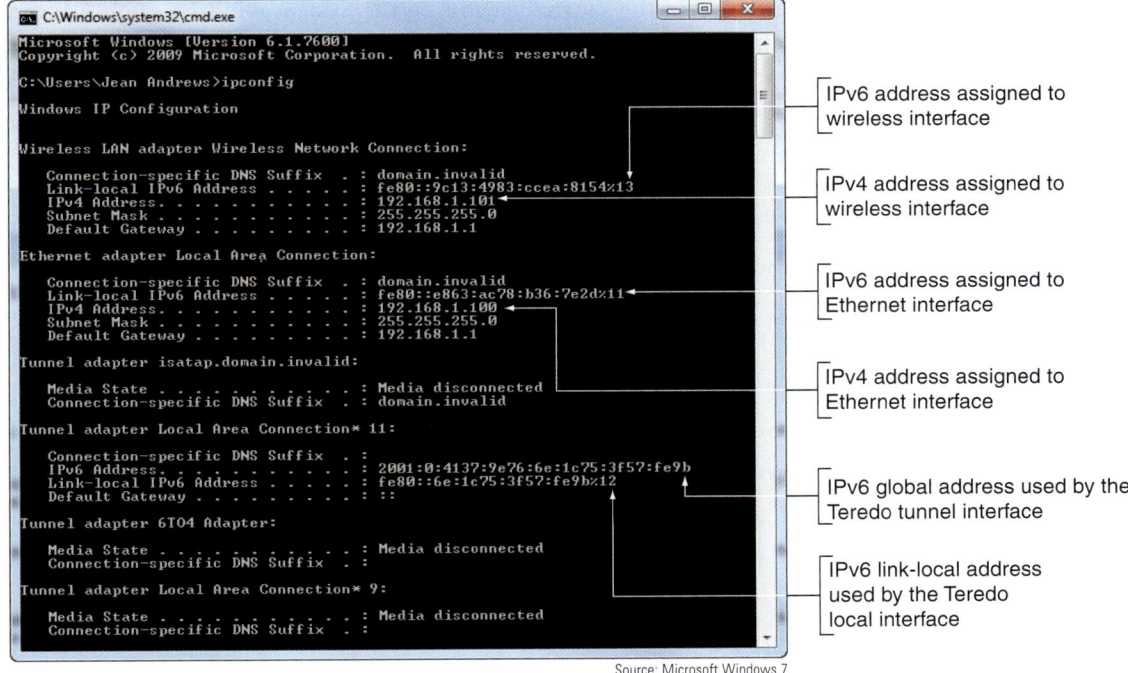

Source: Microsoft Windows 7

Figure 9-11 The ipconfig command showing IPv4 and IPv6 addresses assigned to this computer

IPv6 addressing is designed so that a computer can autoconfigure its own link-local IP address, which is similar to how IPv4 uses an Automatic Private IP Address (APIPA). Here's what happens when a computer using IPv6 first makes a network connection:

1. The computer creates its IPv6 address by using the FE80::/64 prefix and randomly generating an Interface ID for the last 64 bits.

2. It then performs a duplicate address detection process to make sure its IP address is unique on the network.

3. Next, it asks if a router is present on the network to provide configuration information. If a router responds with DHCP information, the computer uses whatever information this might be, such as the IP addresses of DNS servers or its own IP address. Because a computer can generate its own link-local IP address, a DHCPv6 server usually serves up only global IPv6 addresses.

CHARACTER-BASED NAMES IDENTIFY COMPUTERS AND NETWORKS

Remembering an IP address is not always easy, so character-based names are used to substitute for IP addresses. Here are the possibilities:

▲ A *host name*, also called a *computer name*, is the name of a computer and can be used in place of its IP address. Examples of host names are www, ftp, Jean's Computer, TestBox3, and PinkLaptop. You assign a host name to a computer when you first configure it for a network connection. The name can have up to 63 characters, including letters, numbers, and special characters. On a local network, you can use the computer name in the place of an IP address to identify a computer. To find out and change the computer name in Windows 7/Vista, click **Start**, right-click **Computer**, and select

**A+
220-801
2.4**

Properties from the shortcut menu. In the System window, click **Advanced system settings**. In the System Properties box, click the **Computer Name** tab (see Figure 9-12). To rename a computer, click **Change**. (For XP, click **Start**, right-click **My Computer**, and select **Properties** from the shortcut menu. Then click the **Computer Name** tab.)

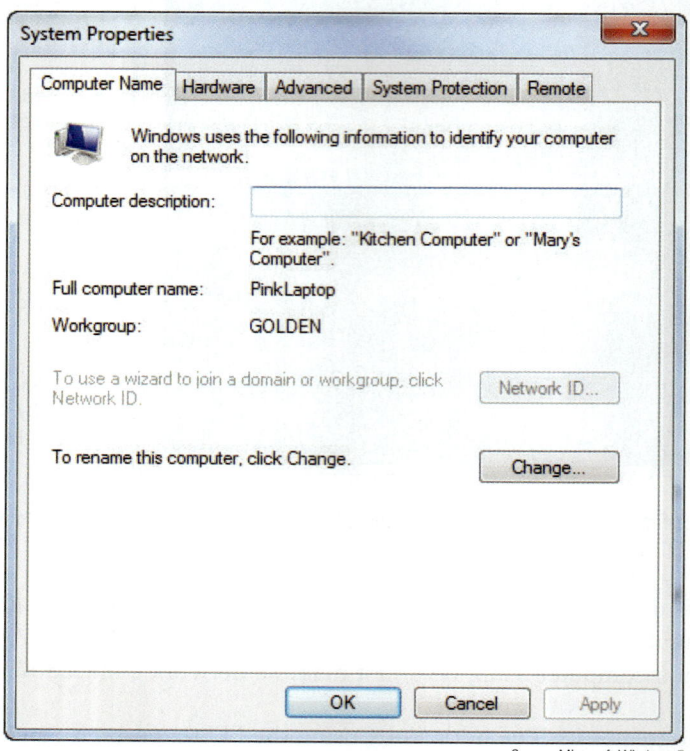

Source: Microsoft Windows 7

Figure 9-12 View and change the computer name

- A workgroup is a group of computers on a peer-to-peer network that are sharing resources. The workgroup name assigned to this group is only recognized within the local network.
- A **domain name** identifies a network. Examples of domain names are the names that appear before the period in microsoft.com, course.com, and mycompany.com. The letters after the period are called the top-level domain and tell you something about the domain. Examples are .com (commercial), .org (nonprofit), .gov (government), and .info (general use).
- A **fully qualified domain name (FQDN)** identifies a computer and the network to which it belongs. An example of an FQDN is www.course.com. The host name is *www* (a web server), *course* is the domain name, and *com* is the top-level domain name of the Course Technology network. Another FQDN is *joesmith.mycompany.com*.

On the Internet, a fully qualified domain name must be associated with an IP address before this computer can be found. This process of associating a character-based name with an IP address is called **name resolution**. The **DNS (Domain Name System or Domain Name Service)** protocol is used by a **DNS server** to find an IP address for a computer when the fully qualified domain name is known. Your ISP is responsible for providing you access to one or more DNS servers as part of the service it provides for Internet access. When a web-hosting site first sets up your web site, IP address, and domain name, it is responsible for entering the name resolution information into its primary DNS server. This server can present the information to other DNS servers on the web and is called the authoritative name server for your site.

> **A+ Exam Tip** The A+ 220-802 exam expects you to be familiar with client-side DNS.

> **Notes** When you enter a fully qualified domain name such as *www.cengage.com* in a browser address bar, that name is translated into an IP address followed by a port number. It's interesting to know that you can skip the translation step and enter the IP address and port number in the address box. See Figure 9-13.

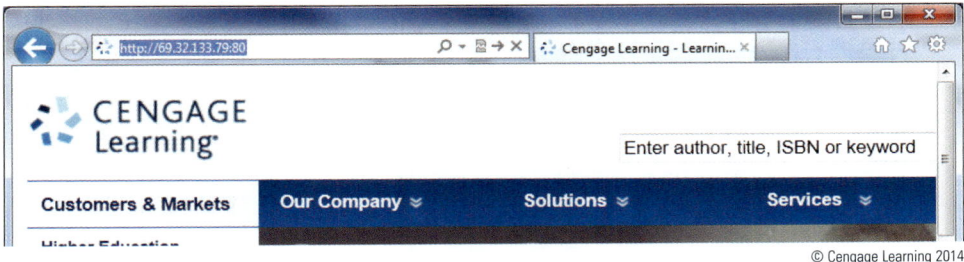

Figure 9-13 A web site can be accessed by its IP address and port number: http://69.32.133.79:80

When Windows is trying to resolve a computer name to an IP address, it first looks in the DNS cache it holds in memory. Information in this cache includes what it loaded at startup from the **Hosts file** in the C:\Windows\System32\drivers\etc folder. This file, which has no file extension, contains computer names and their associated IP addresses on the local network. An administrator is responsible for manually editing the hosts file when the association is needed on the local network. If the computer name is not found in the hosts file, Windows then turns to a DNS server if it has the IP address of the server. When Windows queries the DNS server for a name resolution, it is called the **DNS client**.

> **Notes** For an entry in the Hosts file to work, the remote computer must always use the same IP address. One way to accomplish this is to assign a static IP address to the computer. Alternately, if your DHCP server supports this feature, you can configure it to assign the same IP address to this computer each time if you tell the DHCP server the computer's MAC address. This method of computer name resolution is often used for intranet web servers, Telnet servers, and other servers.

TCP/IP PROTOCOL LAYERS

Recall that a protocol is an agreed-to set of rules for communication between two parties. Operating systems and client/server applications on the Internet all use protocols that are supported by TCP/IP. The left side of Figure 9-14 shows these different layers of protocols and how they relate to one another. As you read this section, this figure can serve as your road map to the different protocols.

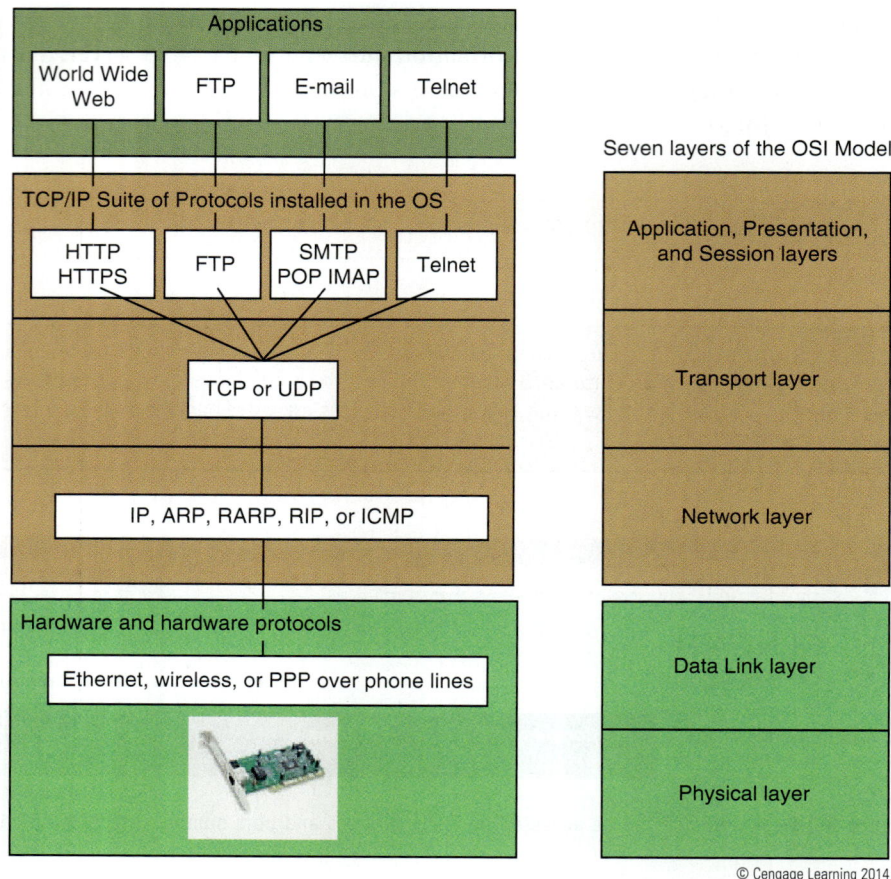

Figure 9-14 How software, protocols, and technology on a TCP/IP network relate to each other

> **Notes** When studying networking theory, the OSI Model is used, which divides network communication into seven layers. In the OSI Model, protocols used by hardware are divided into two layers (data link and physical), and TCP/IP protocols used by the OS are divided into five layers (network, transport, session, presentation, and application). These seven layers are shown on the right side of Figure 9-14.

In the following sections, the more significant applications and operating system protocols are introduced. However, you should know that the TCP/IP protocol suite includes more protocols than just those mentioned in this chapter; only some of them are shown in Figure 9-14.

TCP/IP PROTOCOLS USED BY THE OS

Looking back at Figure 9-14, you can see three layers of protocols between the applications and the hardware protocols. These three layers make up the heart of TCP/IP communication. In the figure, TCP or UDP manages communication with the applications protocols above them as well as the protocols shown underneath TCP and UDP, which control communication on the network.

Remember that all communication on a network happens by way of packets delivered from one location on the network to another. In TCP/IP, the protocol that guarantees packet delivery is **TCP (Transmission Control Protocol)**. TCP makes a connection, checks whether the data is received, and resends it if it is not. TCP is, therefore, called a **connection-oriented protocol**. TCP is used by applications such as web browsers and email. Guaranteed delivery takes longer and is used when it is important to know that the data reached its destination.

For TCP to guarantee delivery, it uses protocols at the IP layer to establish a session between client and server to verify that communication has taken place. When a TCP packet reaches its destination, an acknowledgment is sent back to the source (see Figure 9-15). If the source TCP does not receive the acknowledgment, it resends the data or passes an error message back to the higher-level application protocol.

Figure 9-15 TCP guarantees delivery by requesting an acknowledgment

> **A+ Exam Tip** The A+ 220-801 exam expects you to be able to contrast the TCP and UDP protocols.

On the other hand, **UDP (User Datagram Protocol)** does not guarantee delivery by first connecting and checking whether data is received; thus, UDP is called a **connectionless protocol** or **best-effort protocol**. UDP is used for broadcasting, such as streaming video or sound over the web, where guaranteed delivery is not as important as fast transmission. UDP is also used to monitor network traffic.

TCP/IP PROTOCOLS USED BY APPLICATIONS

Some common applications that use the Internet are web browsers, email, chat, FTP, Telnet, Remote Desktop, and Remote Assistance. Here is a bit of information about several of the protocols used by these and other applications:

- *HTTP.* **HTTP (Hypertext Transfer Protocol)** is the protocol used for the World Wide Web and used by web browsers and web servers to communicate. You can see when a browser is using this protocol by looking for http at the beginning of a URL in the address bar of a browser, such as *http://www.microsoft.com*.
- *HTTPS.* **HTTPS (HTTP secure)** is the HTTP protocol working with a security protocol such as Secure Sockets Layer (SSL) or Transport Layer Security (TLS), which is better than SSL, to create a secured socket. HTTPS is used by web browsers and servers to encrypt the data before it is sent and then decrypt it before the data is processed. To know a secured protocol is being used, look for https in the URL, as in *https://www.wellsfargo.com*.
- *SMTP.* **SMTP (Simple Mail Transfer Protocol)** is used to send an email message to its destination (see Figure 9-16). An improved version of SMTP is **SMTP AUTH (SMTP Authentication)**. This protocol is used to authenticate a user to an email server when the

email client first tries to connect to the email server to send email. Using SMTP AUTH, an extra dialogue between the client and server happens before the client can fully connect that proves the client is authorized to use the service. After authentication, the client can then send email to the email server. The email server that takes care of sending email messages (using the SMTP protocol) is often referred to as the SMTP server.

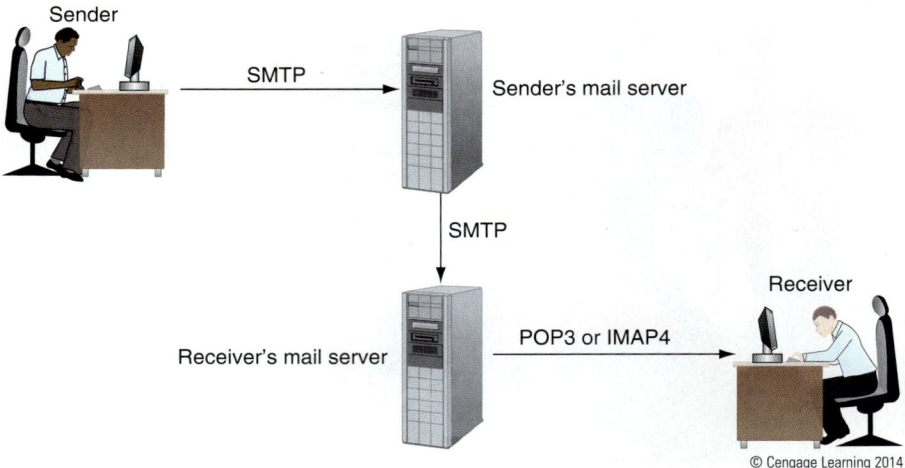

Figure 9-16 The SMTP protocol is used to send email to a recipient's mail server, and the POP3 or IMAP4 protocol is used by the client to receive email

- ▲ *POP and IMAP.* After an email message arrives at the destination email server, it remains there until the recipient requests delivery. The recipient's email server uses one of two protocols to deliver the message: **POP3 (Post Office Protocol, version 3)** or **IMAP4 (Internet Message Access Protocol, version 4)**. Using POP, email is downloaded to the client computer. Using IMAP, the client application manages the email stored on the server.
- ▲ *Telnet.* The **Telnet** protocol is used by the Telnet client/server applications to allow an administrator or other user to control a computer remotely. Telnet is not considered secure because transmissions in Telnet are not encrypted.
- ▲ *LDAP.* **Lightweight Directory Access Protocol (LDAP)** is used by various client applications when the application needs to query a database. For example, an email client on a corporate network might query a database that contains the email addresses for all employees. Another example is when an application looks for a printer by querying a database of printers supported by an organization on the corporate network or Internet. Data sent and received using the LDAP protocol is not encrypted; therefore, an encryption layer is sometimes added to LDAP transmissions.
- ▲ *SMB.* **Server Message Block (SMB)** is the protocol used by Windows to share files and printers on a network.
- ▲ *FTP.* **FTP (File Transfer Protocol)** is used to transfer files between two computers. Web browsers can use the protocol. Also, special FTP client software such as CuteFTP by GlobalSCAPE (*www.cuteftp.com*), can be used, which offers more features for file transfer than does a browser. To use FTP in Internet Explorer version 9, enter the address of an FTP site in the address box, for example, *ftp.cengage.com*. A logon dialog box appears where you can enter a username and password (see Figure 9-17). When you click **Log on**, you can see folders on the

Understanding TCP/IP and Windows Networking

A+ 220-801 2.4

FTP site and the FTP protocol displays in the address bar, as in *ftp://ftp.cengage.com*. It's easier to use Windows Explorer to transfer files rather than Internet Explorer. After you have located the FTP site, to use Windows Explorer for file transfers, press **Alt**, which causes the menu bar to appear. In the menu bar, click **View, Open FTP site in Windows Explorer** (see Figure 9-18). Then click **Allow** in the Internet Explorer Security box. Windows Explorer opens, showing files and folders on the FTP site. You can copy and paste files and folders from your computer to the site.

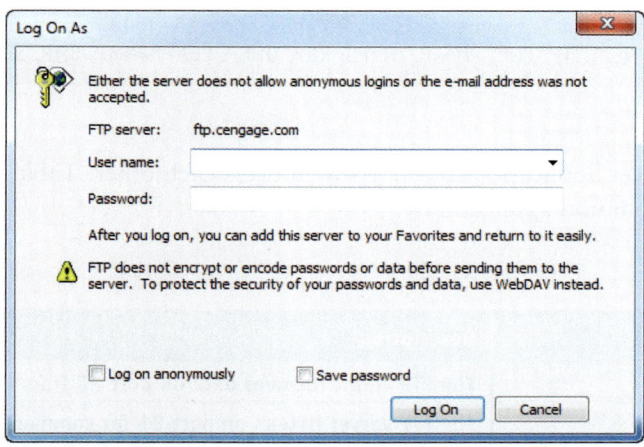

Source: Microsoft Windows 7

Figure 9-17 Log on to an FTP site

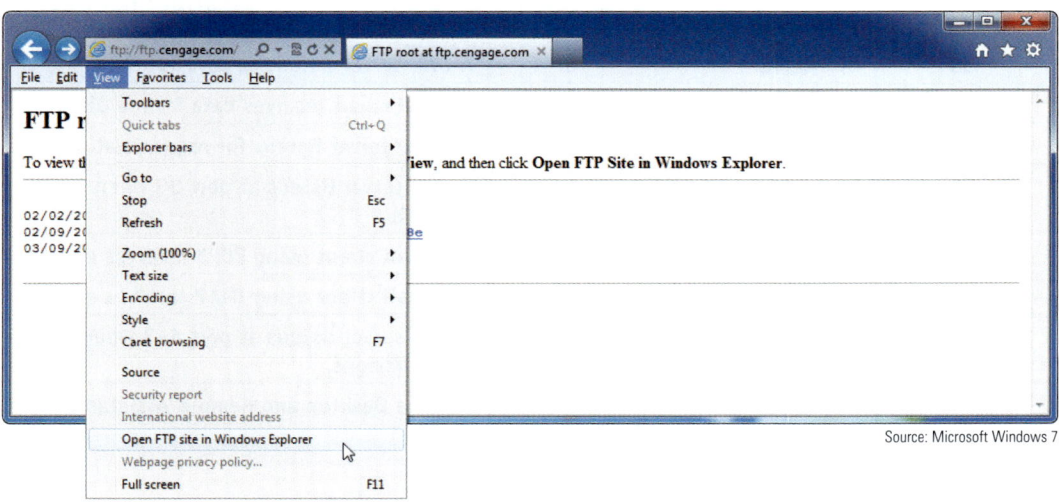

Source: Microsoft Windows 7

Figure 9-18 Use Windows Explorer to transfer files using the FTP protocol

▲ *SSH.* The **Secure Shell (SSH)** protocol is used to pass login information to a remote computer and control that computer over a network. Transmissions are encrypted so they cannot be intercepted by a hacker.

A+ 220-801 2.4

- *SFTP.* **Secure FTP (SFTP)** is used to transfer files from an FTP server to an FTP client using encryption. The encryption layer of the protocol used by Secure FTP is a variation of the SSH (Secure Shell) protocol.
- *SNMP.* **Simple Network Management Protocol (SNMP)** is used to monitor network traffic. It is used by the Microsoft SNMP Agent application that monitors traffic on a network and helps balance that traffic.
- *RDP.* **Remote Desktop Protocol (RDP)** is used by the Windows Remote Desktop and Remote Assistance utilities to connect to and control a remote computer.

> **A+ Exam Tip** The A+ 220-801 exam expects you to know about the following application protocols: FTP, Telnet, SMTP, DNS, HTTP, POP3, IMAP, HTTPS, RDP, DHCP, LDAP, SNMP, SMB, SSH, and SFTP.

Recall that client/server applications use ports to address each other. Table 9-5 lists the port assignments for common applications.

Port	Protocol and App	Description
20	FTP client	The FTP client receives data on port 20 from the FTP server.
21	FTP server	The FTP server listens on port 21 for commands from an FTP client.
22	SSH server	A server using the SSH protocol listens at port 22.
23	Telnet server	A Telnet server listens at port 23.
25	SMTP email server	An email server listens at port 25 to receive email from a client computer.
53	DNS server	A DNS server listens at port 53.
67	DHCP client	A DHCP client receives data from a DHCP server at port 67.
68	DHCP server	A DHCP server listens for requests at port 68.
80	Web server using HTTP	A web server listens at port 80 when receiving HTTP requests.
110	POP3 email client	An email client using POP3 receives email at port 110.
143	IMAP email client	An email client using IMAP receives email at port 143.
443	Web server using HTTPS	A web server listens at port 443 when receiving HTTPS transmissions.
3389	RDP apps, including Remote Desktop and Remote Assistance	Remote Desktop and Remote Assistance listen at port 3389.

© Cengage Learning 2014

Table 9-5 Common TCP/IP port assignments for client/server applications

> **A+ Exam Tip** The A+ 220-801 expects you to know the common port assignments of the FTP, Telnet, SMTP, DNS, HTTP, POP3, IMAP, HTTPS, and RDP protocols. Before sitting for this exam, be sure to memorize the ports listed in Table 9-5.

A+ 220-801 2.4

Hands-on | Project 9-1   Practice Using FTP

Practice using FTP by downloading the latest version of Firefox, a web browser, using these methods. Do the following:

1. Using your current browser, go to the Mozilla web site at *www.mozilla.org* and download the latest version of Firefox. What is the version number? What is the name of the downloaded file? In what folder on your hard drive did you put the file?

2. Using your current browser as an FTP client, locate the same version of Firefox and the same file at the Mozilla FTP site (*ftp.mozilla.org*) and download it to your PC. What is the path to the Firefox file on the FTP site? In what folder on your hard drive did you put the file?

Now that you have an understanding of TCP/IP and Windows networking, let's apply that knowledge to making network connections.

CONNECTING A COMPUTER TO A NETWORK

A+ 220-802 1.5, 1.6

Connecting a computer to a network is quick and easy in most situations. In this part of the chapter, you'll learn to connect a computer to a network using Ethernet, wireless, and dial-up connections.

CONNECT TO A WIRED NETWORK

To connect a computer to a network using a wired (Ethernet) connection, follow these steps:

1. If the network adapter is not yet installed, install it now. These steps include physically installing the card, installing drivers, and using Device Manager to verify that Windows recognizes the adapter without errors.

2. Connect a network cable to the Ethernet port (called an RJ-45 port) and to the network wall jack or directly to a switch or router. Indicator lights near the network port should light up to indicate connectivity and activity. If you connected the cable directly to a switch or router, verify the light at that port is also lit.

3. By default, Windows assumes dynamic IP addressing and automatically configures the network connection. To find out if the connection is working, open Windows Explorer and drill down into the Network group (see Figure 9-19). (For Windows XP, click **Start, My Network Places** to open the My Network Places window.) You should see icons that represent other computers on the network. Double-click a computer and drill down to shared folders and files to verify you can access these resources.

4. To verify you have Internet connectivity, open Internet Explorer and browse to a few web sites.

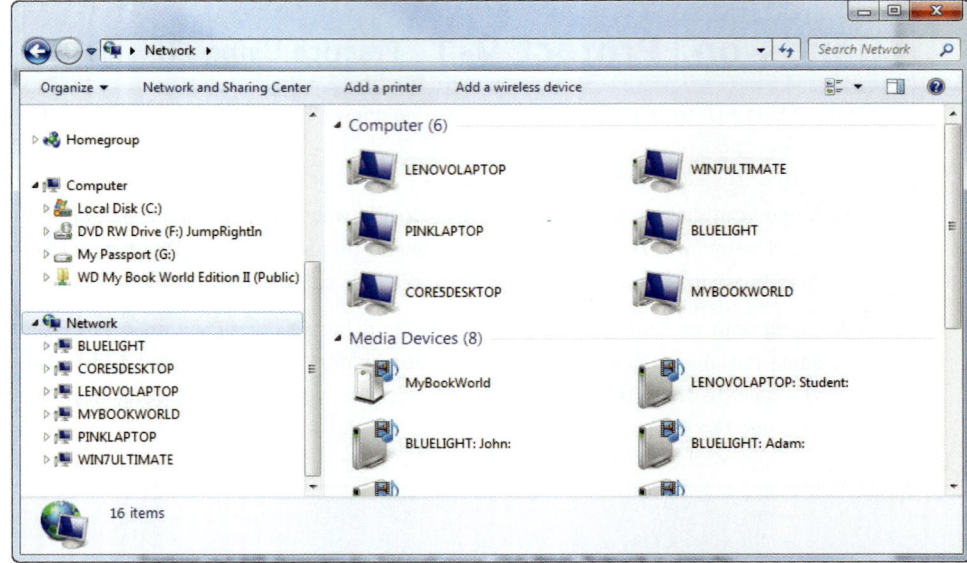

Figure 9-19 Windows Explorer shows resources on the network

If the connection does not work, it's time to verify that network settings are configured correctly. Follow these steps using Windows 7:

1. Verify that Device Manager recognizes the network adapter without errors. If you find an error, try updating the network adapter drivers. If that doesn't work, then try uninstalling and reinstalling the drivers. Make sure Device Manager recognizes the network adapter without errors before you move on to the next step.

2. To open the Network and Sharing Center, open **Control Panel** and click **Network and Sharing Center**. (You can also click the network icon in the taskbar.) The Network and Sharing Center window opens (see Figure 9-20).

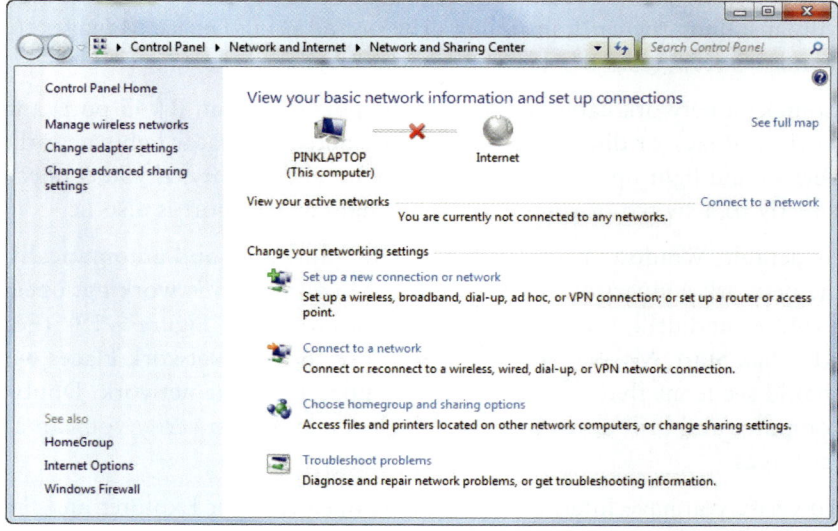

Figure 9-20 The Network and Sharing Center reports a problem connecting to the network

A+
220-802
1.5, 1.6

3. A red X indicates a problem. Click the **X** to get help and resolve the problem. Windows Network Diagnostics starts looking for problems, applying solutions, and making suggestions. You can also check these things:

- Is the network cable connected?
- Are status light indicators on the network port and router or switch lit or blinking appropriately to indicate connectivity and activity?

4. After Windows has resolved the problem, you should see a clear path from the computer to the Internet, as shown in Figure 9-21. Use Windows Explorer to try again to access resources on the local network, and use Internet Explorer to try to access the Internet.

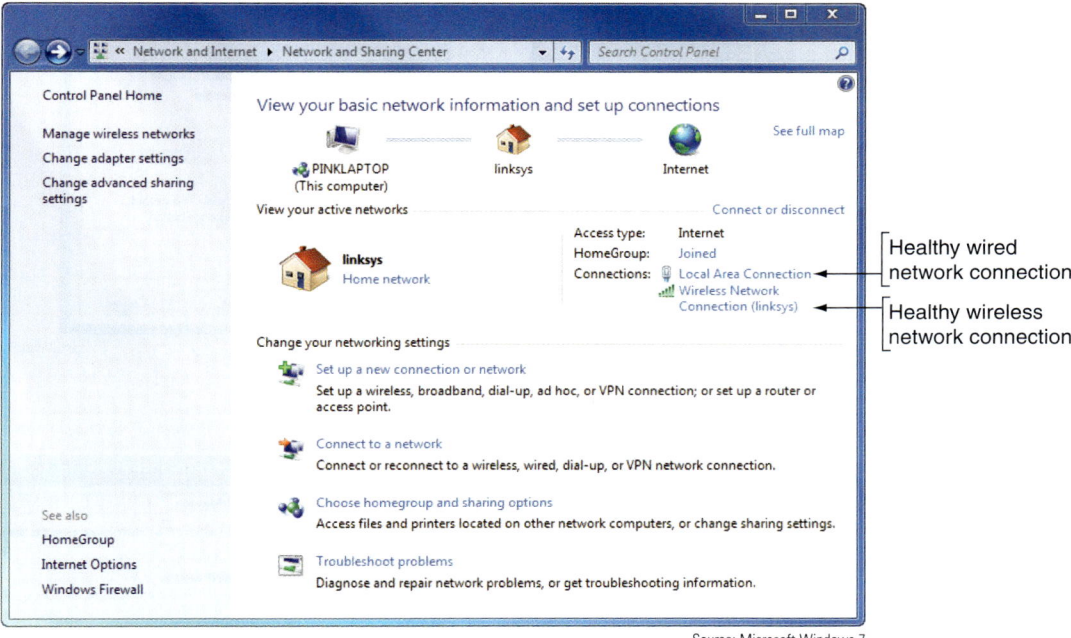

Source: Microsoft Windows 7

Figure 9-21 The Network and Sharing Center reports two healthy network connections

If you still do not have connectivity, follow these steps to verify and change TCP/IP settings:

1. In the Network and Sharing Center, click **Change adapter settings**. In the Network Connections window, right-click the local area connection and select **Properties** from the shortcut menu. The properties box appears (see Figure 9-22).

2. Select **Internet Protocol Version 4 (TCP/IPv4)** and click **Properties**. The properties box shown in Figure 9-23 (a) appears. Settings are correct for dynamic IP addressing.

Notes Notice in Figure 9-22 that you can uncheck Internet Protocol Version 6 (TCP/IPv6) to disable it. For most situations, you need to leave it enabled. A bug in Windows 7 prevents you from joining a homegroup if IPv6 is disabled.

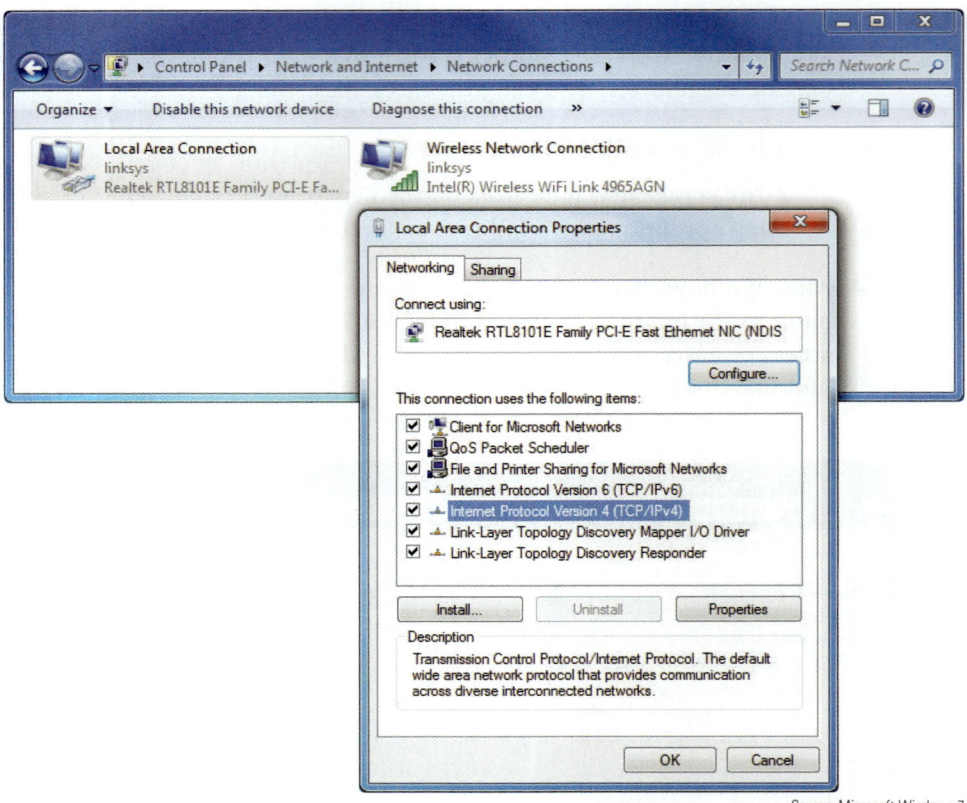

Figure 9-22 Verify and change TCP/IP settings

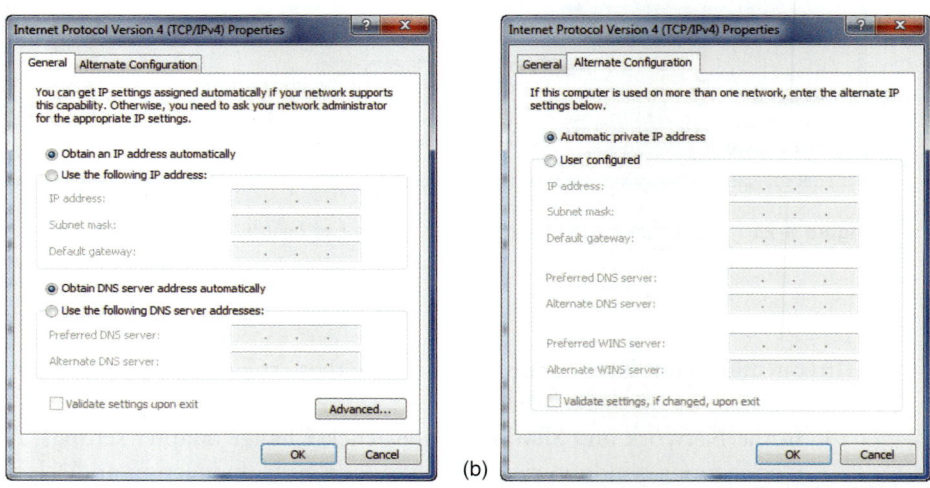

Figure 9-23 Configure TCP/IP settings

3. To change the settings to static IP addressing, select **Use the following IP address**. Then enter the IP address, subnet mask, and default gateway. (A **default gateway** is the gateway a computer uses to access another network if it does not have a better option.)

4. If you have been given the IP addresses of DNS servers, check **Use the following DNS server** addresses and enter up to two IP addresses. If you have other DNS IP addresses, click **Advanced** and enter them on the **DNS** tab of the Advanced TCP/IP Settings box.

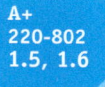

5. If the computer you are using is a laptop that moves from one network to another and one network uses static IP addressing, you can click the **Alternate Configuration** tab and configure an alternate IP address (see Figure 9-23 [b]). On this tab, select **User configured**. Then enter a static IP address, subnet mask, default gateway, and DNS server addresses. When you configure the General tab to use dynamic IP addressing, the computer will first try to use dynamic IP addressing. If that is not available on the network, it then applies the static IP address settings entered on the Alternate Configuration tab. If static IP address settings are not available on this tab, the computer uses an automatic private IP address (APIPA). This setup works well for a computer to receive a dynamic IP address while traveling, but use a static IP address when connected to the company network that uses static IP addressing.

A+ Exam Tip The A+ 220-802 exam expects you to know how to configure an alternate IP address, including setting the static IP address, subnet mask, DNS addresses, and gateway.

6. Close all boxes and windows and again try to access network resources. If you still don't have connectivity, try to disable and enable the network connection. To do that, right-click the connection in the Network Connections window and select **Disable** (see Figure 9-24). For dynamic IP addressing, the IP address is released. Then right-click again and select **Enable**. The connection is remade and a new IP address is leased.

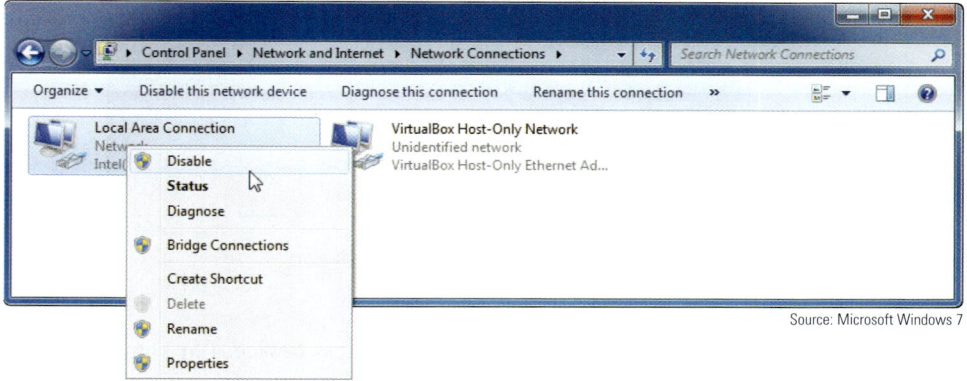

Figure 9-24 To reset a network connection, disable and enable the connection

If you still don't have local or Internet access, it's time to dig a little deeper into the source of the problem.

Do the following:

▲ Verify Device Manager recognizes the network adapter with no errors.
▲ Determine if other computers on the network are having trouble with their connections. If the entire network is down, the problem is not isolated to the computer you are working on.

A+ 220-802 1.5, 1.6

CONNECT TO A WIRELESS NETWORK

Wireless networks are either unsecured public hotspots or secured private hotspots. Even if you connect to a secured private hotspot, still be careful to protect your data and other Windows resources from attack. In this part of the chapter, you learn how to connect to unsecured and secured wireless networks.

Here are the steps to connect to a wireless network using Windows 7 and how to protect your computer on that network:

1. If necessary, install the wireless adapter. For external adapters such as the one shown in Figure 9-25, be sure to follow the manufacturer's instructions for the installation. Most likely you'll be asked to first install the software before installing the device. During the installation process, you will be given the opportunity to use the manufacturer's configuration utility to manage the wireless adapter or to use Windows to do the job. For best results, use the utility provided by the manufacturer. In the following steps, we're using the Windows utility.

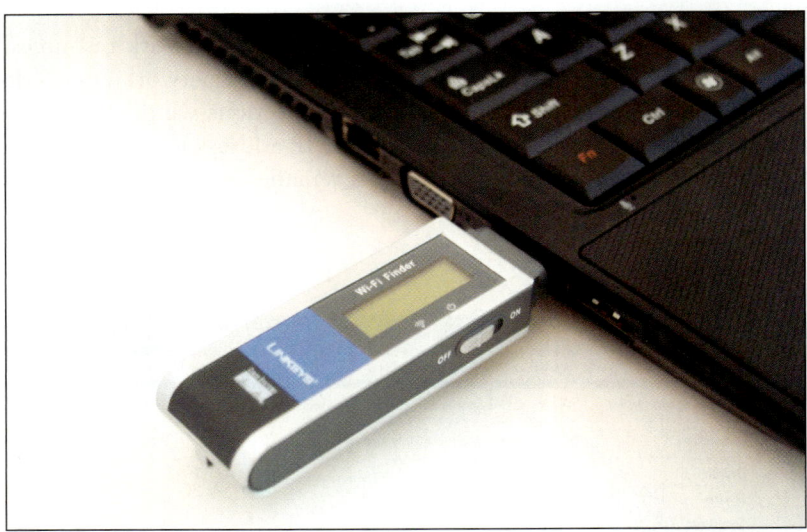

© Cengage Learning 2014

Figure 9-25 Plug the wireless USB adapter into the USB port

2. For embedded wireless, turn on your wireless device. For some laptops, that's done by a switch on the keyboard (see Figure 9-26) or on the side of the laptop. The wireless antenna is usually in the lid of a notebook and gives best performance when the lid is fully raised. For a desktop computer, make sure the antenna is in an upright position (see Figure 9-27).

3. A yellow star in the network icon in the taskbar indicates hotspots are available. Double-click the network icon to see a list of networks. Click one to select it and then click **Connect** (see Figure 9-28).

4. If the network is secured, Windows asks for the security key the first time you connect (see Figure 9-29). Enter the security key or password to the network and click **OK**.

5. If the network is unsecured or you don't trust all the users of the network, verify that Windows has configured the network as a Public network. To do so, open the Network and Sharing Center window (see Figure 9-30). If the network location says

Figure 9-26 Turn on the wireless switch on your laptop

Figure 9-27 Raise the antenna on a NIC to an upright position

Home network or Work network, click it. The Set Network Location box appears (see Figure 9-31). Click **Public network** and click **Close**. The Network and Sharing Center reports the network location as Public network.

6. Open your browser to test the connection. For some hotspots, a home page appears and you must enter a code or agree to the terms of use before you can use the network.

In addition to a security key used to access a secured wireless network, the network might be set up for even more security. A wireless network is created by a wireless device known

430 | **CHAPTER 9**   Connecting to and Setting Up a Network

A+
220-802
1.5, 1.6

Figure 9-28 Windows orders the list of wireless networks in the area from strongest to weakest signals

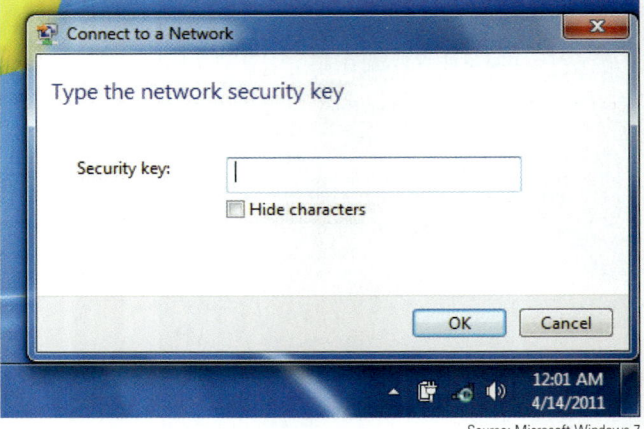

Figure 9-29 Enter the security key to connect to a secured wireless network

as the **wireless access point**. Here is a list of methods that the wireless access point might use to secure the wireless network:

- ▲ *A security key is required.* This is the most common method of securing a wireless network. A network that uses a security key encrypts data on the network using an encryption standard. You learn about these standards later in the chapter.
- ▲ *The SSID is not broadcasted.* The wireless device might not be broadcasting its name, which is called the **Service Set Identifier (SSID)**. If the SSID is not broadcasting, the

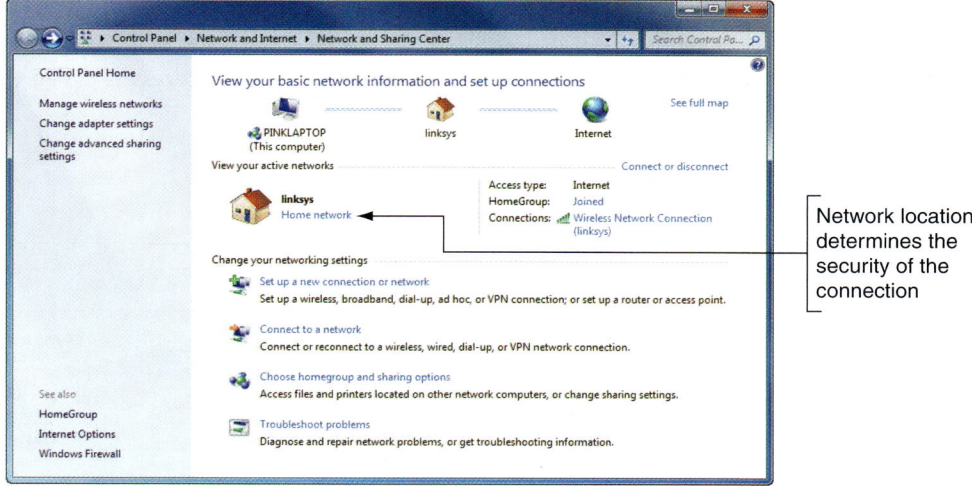

Figure 9-30 Verify that your connection is secure

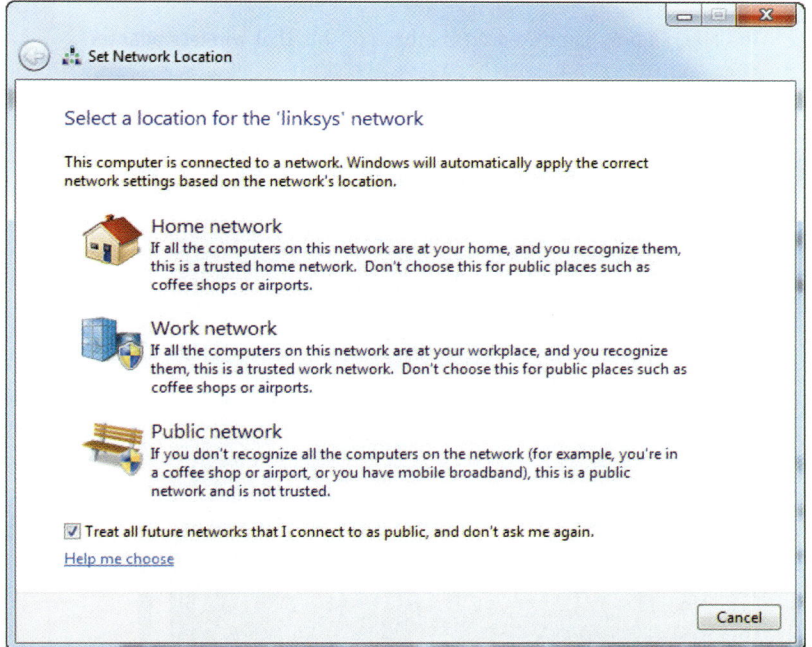

Figure 9-31 For best protection on a network, use the Public network location

name of the wireless network will appear as Unnamed or Unknown Network. When you select this network, you are given the opportunity to enter the name. If you don't enter the name correctly, you will not be able to connect.

▲ *Only computers with registered MAC addresses are allowed to connect.* If MAC address filtering is used, you must give the network administrator the MAC address of your wireless adapter. This address is entered into a table of acceptable MAC addresses kept by the wireless access point.

To know the MAC address of your wireless adapter, for an external adapter, you can look on the back of the adapter itself (see Figure 9-32) or in the adapter documentation.

A+ 220-802 1.5, 1.6

Also, if the adapter is installed on your computer, you can open a command prompt window and enter the command **ipconfig /all**, which displays your TCP/IP configuration for all network connections. In the results displayed, the MAC address is called the Physical Address (see Figure 9-33).

Figure 9-32 The MAC address is printed on the back of this USB wireless adapter

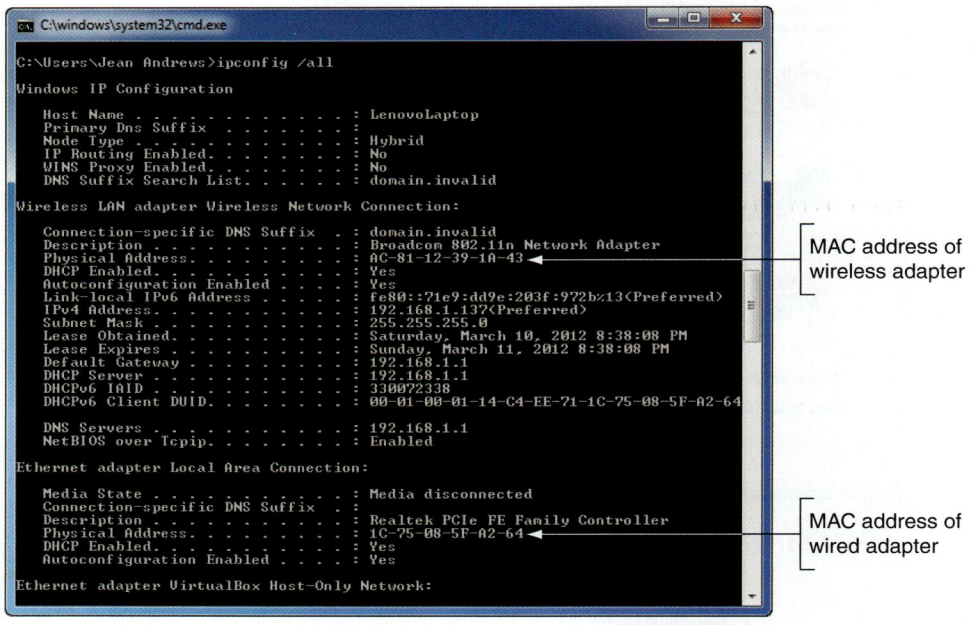

Figure 9-33 Use the ipconfig /all command to display TCP/IP configuration data

If you have problems connecting to a wireless network, here are the steps to follow to verify the network settings:

1. In the left pane of the Network and Sharing Center, click **Manage wireless networks**. The Manage Wireless Networks window appears (see the left side of Figure 9-34).

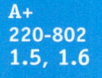
A+
220-802
1.5, 1.6

2. Using this window, you can change the order of networks that Windows uses to try to make a wireless connection. To view security settings, double-click a network in the list. The Properties box for the wireless network appears.

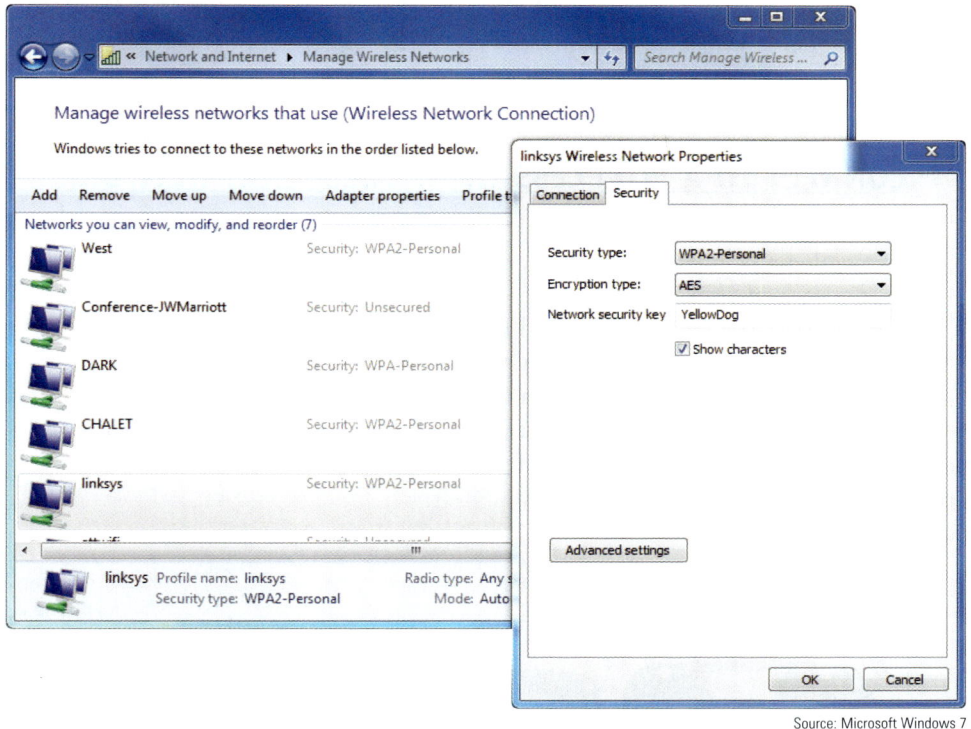

Figure 9-34 Verify the Network security key for the wireless network is correct

3. On the Properties box, click the **Security** tab, which is shown in the right side of Figure 9-34. Check **Show characters** so that you can verify the Network security key is correct. Windows 7 should automatically sense the Security type and Encryption type for the wireless network, and these values should be correct. Change the Network security key if necessary.

4. Click **OK** to close the Properties box. Windows should automatically connect to the network.

Hands-on | Project 9-2 Investigate a Wireless Connection

Using a computer connected to a wireless network, do the following:

1. In the Network and Sharing Center, click **Manage wireless networks**. Right-click the wireless connection and click Properties to view the Properties box for the wireless network. Is the network secured? If so, what is the security type? What is the encryption type?

A+ 220-802 1.5, 1.6

2. Open the Properties box for the Wireless Network Connection. Is the connection using TCP/IPv4? TCP/IPv6?

3. View the TCP/IPv4 settings for the wireless adapter. Is the wireless connection using static or dynamic IP addressing?

4. Using the Ipconfig command, what is the IPv4 IP address for the wireless connection? What is the MAC address of the wireless adapter?

CONNECT TO A WIRELESS WAN (CELLULAR) NETWORK

To connect a computer using mobile broadband to a **wireless wide area network (WWAN)**, also called a cellular network, such as those provided by Verizon or AT&T, you need the hardware and software to connect and a SIM card. A **SIM (Subscriber Identification Module) card** is a small flash memory card that contains all the information you need to connect to a cellular network, including a password and other authentication information needed to access the network, encryption standards used, and the services that your subscription includes. SIM cards are used in cell phones, mobile broadband modems, and other devices that use a cellular network (see Figure 9-35).

Figure 9-35 A SIM card contains proof that your device can use a cellular network

Here are your options for hardware and software:

▲ *Use an embedded mobile broadband modem.* A laptop might have an embedded broadband modem. In this situation, you still need to subscribe to a mobile operator, which will provide you with a SIM card for your laptop.

▲ *Tether your cell phone to your computer.* You can tether your cell phone to your computer by way of a cable that connects your cell phone to a USB port. See Figure 9-36. (Some cell phones don't have a USB port; in this situation, you have to purchase a special cable that works with your proprietary phone connector and a USB port on your computer.) A cell phone with Wi-Fi capabilities can be used to provide a Wi-Fi hotspot that your computer and other devices can connect to. In this situation, the cell phone acts like a wireless router. An app installed on the phone is used to configure the WLAN created by the phone.

Figure 9-36 Tether your cell phone to your laptop using a USB cable

▲ *Use a USB broadband modem.* For any computer, you can use a USB broadband modem (sometimes called an air card), such as the one shown in Figure 9-37. If you purchase the device from your mobile operator, a SIM card is included. If you purchase the modem from another source, you need to go to your mobile operator (for example, AT&T, Verizon, or Sprint) to obtain the SIM card the device will use to verify your subscription to the cellular network. A USB broadband modem is likely to give you access to a cellular network as well as a Wi-Fi network.

Mobile operators and laptop manufacturers with embedded modems provide software and instructions for connecting to the cellular network. Follow those instructions rather than the generic ones presented here. Generally, here's how you can connect to a cellular network:

▲ *Using an embedded broadband modem.* For a laptop with an embedded broadband modem, you must insert the SIM card provided by your mobile operator in the SIM card slot on the laptop. For some laptops, this slot might be in the battery bay, and you must remove the battery to find the slot. Then use a program installed on the

Figure 9-37 A USB broadband modem by Sierra Wireless

laptop by the laptop manufacturer to connect to the cellular network. Look for a shortcut on the desktop or a program in the Start menu. In addition, the mobile operator might provide software for you to use.
- *Using your cell phone.* To tether your cell phone to your computer to use a cellular network, know that you need a subscription from your mobile operator to use this service. The mobile operator is likely to provide you software on CD, or you can download the software from the operator's web site. Install the software first and then tether your cell phone to your computer. Use the software to make the connection.
- *Use a USB broadband modem.* When using a USB broadband modem, make sure the SIM card is inserted in the device (see Figure 9-38). When you insert the modem into a USB port, Windows finds the device, and the software stored on the device automatically installs and runs. A window then appears provided by the software that allows you to connect to the cellular network.

Here are more details of how to connect to a WWAN. In this example, we are using the Sierra Wireless modem shown earlier in Figure 9-37. Do the following to make the connection:

1. For best results, connect your computer to a wired network during the first part of the installation.

2. Insert the device into the USB port, and Windows automatically installs the device drivers stored on the device as well as the management software to use the device. Then the management software launches where you must accept the licensing agreement. A shortcut is added to your desktop and programs in the Start menu.

3. You must go to the web site of your mobile operator (AT&T in our example) and activate the phone number used by the modem. Then for best results, remove the modem and restart your computer.

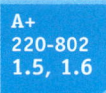

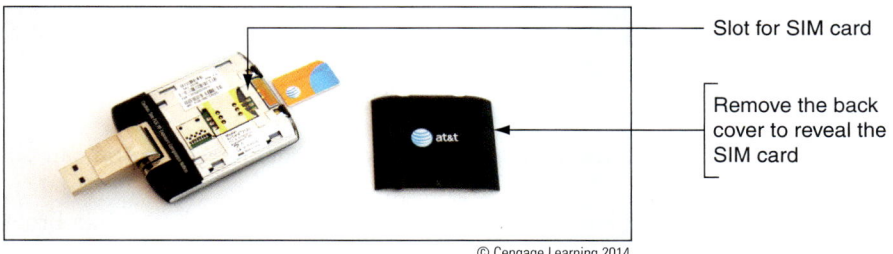

Figure 9-38 A SIM card with subscription information on it is required to use a cellular network

4. After your computer restarts, plug in the modem. Wait until LED lights on the modem indicate the modem has found a network and is ready to connect. For this device, a solid blue light on the left indicates power is on, and a blinking green light on the right indicates the device has found a network and is ready to connect.

5. Start the Communication Manager software. When the software starts, it automatically connects to the network (see Figure 9-39). Note that if your computer is connected to a cellular network, it disconnects from a Wi-Fi network.

Source: AT&T Communication Manager

Figure 9-39 Use the management software to connect and disconnect from the Mobile (cellular) or Wi-Fi network

6. To test the connection, unplug your network cable and try to surf the web. The speed of the connection depends on the type of cellular network you are using, 2G, 3G, or 4G. The 4G networks are the fastest. For the device we are using, the color of the LED indicates the type of network (solid amber is 2G, solid blue is 3G or 4G, solid green is 4G LTE, which currently is the fastest type of cellular network).

> **A+ Exam Tip** The A+ 220-802 exam expects you to know how to connect to a cellular network.

To manage the broadband modem and the WWAN connection, you can do the following:

1. Open the **Network and Sharing Center**. You should see the Mobile Broadband Connection (see Figure 9-40). Make sure the network location is set to Public network.
2. Use Ipconfig to see the IP address assigned to the connection. In Figure 9-41, you can see the IPv4 IP address is a public IP address.

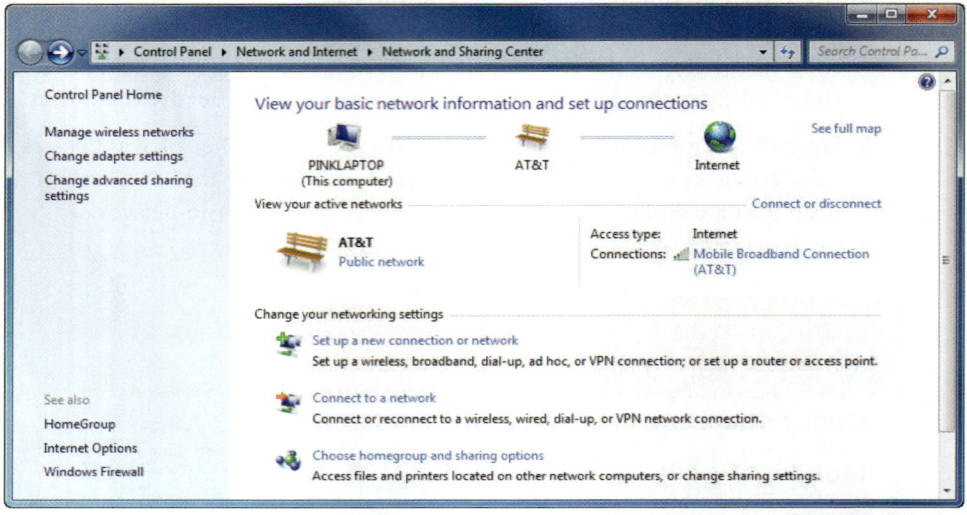

Source: Microsoft Windows 7

Figure 9-40 Make sure your WWAN connection is secured with a Public network location

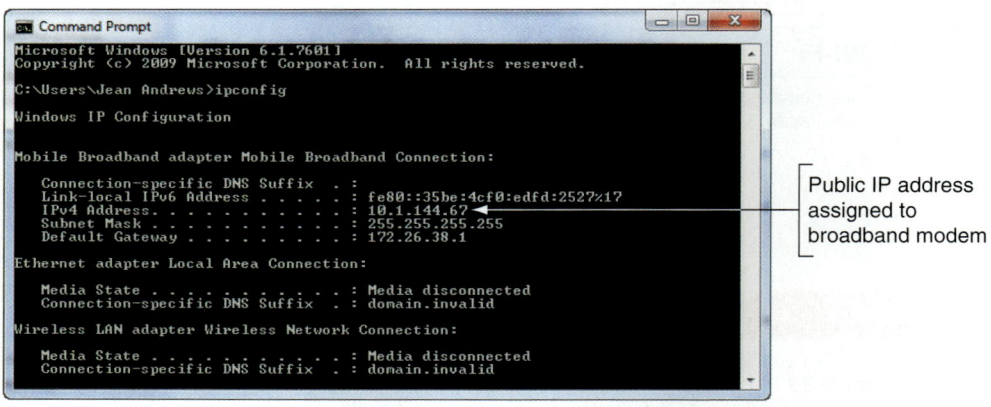

Source: Microsoft Windows 7

Figure 9-41 View the IP address assigned to the WWAN connection by the mobile operator

3. Device Manager should report the modem is installed with no errors. If you are having problems making the connection, start by checking Device Manager. If errors are reported here, update the device drivers.

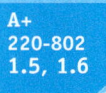

CREATE A DIAL-UP CONNECTION

You never know when you might be called on to support an older dial-up connection. Here are the bare-bones steps you need to set up and support this type of connection:

1. Install an internal or external dial-up modem. Make sure Device Manager recognizes the card without errors.
2. Plug the phone line into the modem port on your computer and into the wall jack.
3. Open the Network and Sharing Center window and click **Set up a new connection or network**. In the dialog box that appears, select **Set up a dial-up connection** and click **Next**.
4. In the next box (see Figure 9-42), enter the phone number to your ISP, your ISP username and password, and the name you decide to give the dial-up connection, such as the name and city of your ISP. Then click **Connect**.

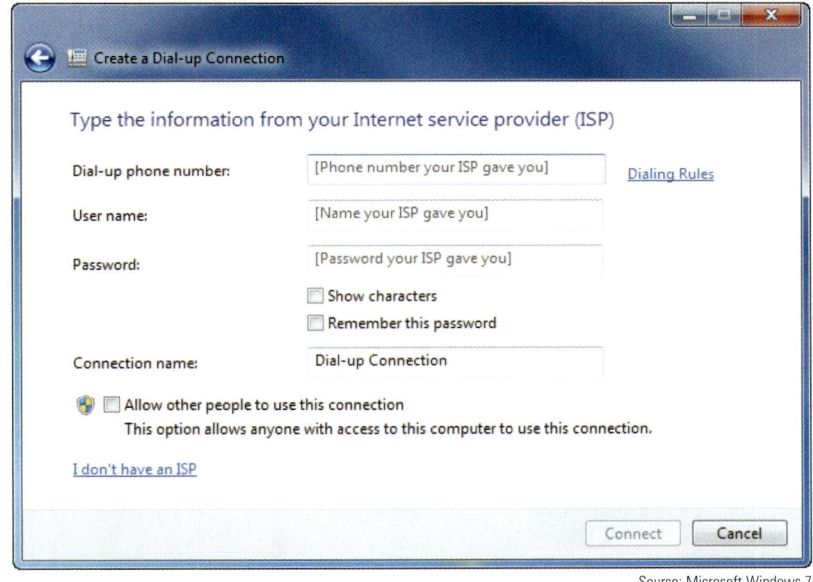

Figure 9-42 Configure a dial-up connection

To use the connection, go to the Network and Sharing Center and click **Connect to a network** (see Figure 9-40). Alternately, you can click your network icon in the taskbar. A bubble appears above your taskbar (see Figure 9-43). Select the dial-up connection, and click **Connect**. The Connect dialog box appears, where you can enter your password (see Figure 9-44). Click **Dial**. You will hear the modem dial up the ISP and make the connection. (For XP, double-click the connection icon in the Network Connections window, and then click **Dial**.)

A+
220-802
1.5, 1.6

Source: Microsoft Windows 7

Figure 9-43 Select the dial-up connection and then click the Connect button that appears

Source: Microsoft Windows 7

Figure 9-44 Enter the password to your ISP

Setting Up a Multifunction Router for a SOHO Network | 441

**A+ 220-802
1.5, 1.6**

> **A+ Exam Tip** The A+ 220-802 exam expects you to be able to establish a dial-up connection.

If the dial-up connection won't work, here are some things you can try:

- Is the phone line working? Plug in a regular phone and check for a dial tone. Is the phone cord securely connected to the computer and the wall jack?
- Does the modem work? Check Device Manager for reported errors about the modem. Does the modem work when making a call to another phone number (not your ISP)?
- Check the Dial-up Connection Properties box for errors. To do so, click **Change adapter settings** in the Network and Sharing Center, and then right-click the dial-up connection and select **Properties** from the shortcut menu. Is the phone number correct? Does the number need to include a 9 to get an outside line? Has a 1 been added in front of the number by mistake? If you need to add a 9, you can put a comma in the field like this "9,4045661200", which causes a slight pause after the 9 is dialed.
- Try dialing the number manually from a phone. Do you hear beeps on the other end? Try another phone number.
- When you try to connect, do you hear the number being dialed? If so, the problem is most likely with the phone number, the phone line, or the username and password.
- Try removing and reinstalling the dial-up connection.

Hands-on | Project 9-3 Investigate TCP/IP Settings

Using a computer connected to a network, answer these questions:

1. What is the hardware device used to make this connection (network card, onboard port, wireless)? List the device's name as Windows sees it in the Device Manager window.
2. What is the MAC address of the wired or wireless network adapter? What command or window did you use to get your answer?
3. What is the IPv4 IP address of the network connection?
4. Are your TCP/IP version 4 settings using static or dynamic IP addressing?
5. What is the IPv6 IP address of your network connection?
6. Disable and enable your network connection. Now what is your IPv4 IP address?

SETTING UP A MULTIFUNCTION ROUTER FOR A SOHO NETWORK

**A+ 220-801
2.6**

**A+ 220-802
2.5**

A PC support technician is likely to be called on to set up a small office or home office network. As part of setting up a small network, you need to know how to configure a multipurpose router to stand between the network and the Internet. You also need to know how to set up and secure a wireless access point. Most SOHO routers are also a wireless access point.

> **A+ Exam Tip** The A+ 220-801 and A+ 220-802 exams expect you to be able to install, configure, and secure a SOHO wired and wireless router.

FUNCTIONS OF A SOHO ROUTER

Routers can range from small ones designed to manage a SOHO network connecting to an ISP (costing around $75 to $150) to those that manage multiple networks and extensive traffic (costing several thousand dollars). On a small office or home network, a router stands between the ISP network and the local network (see Figure 9-45), and the router is the gateway to the Internet. Note in the figure that computers can connect to the router using wired or wireless connections.

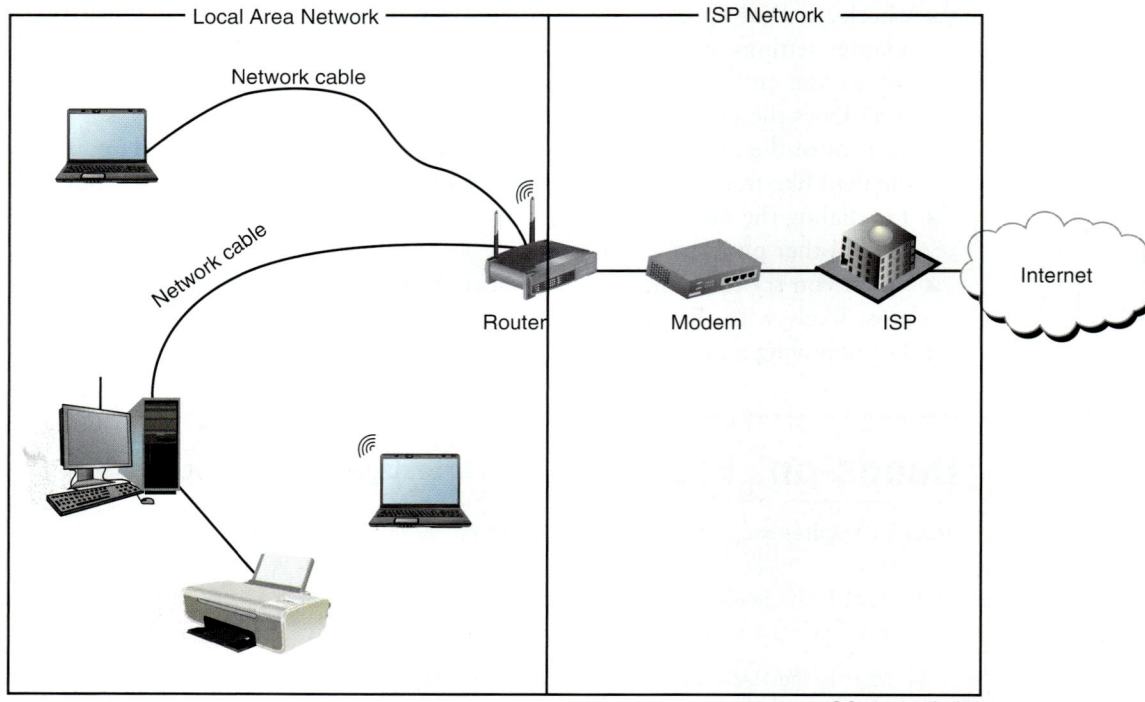

Figure 9-45 A router stands between a local network and the ISP network and manages traffic between them

This router is typical of many SOHO routers and is several devices in one:

▲ *Function 1:* As a router, it stands between the ISP network and the local network, routing traffic between the two networks.
▲ *Function 2:* As a switch, it manages several network ports that can be connected to wired computers or to a switch that provides more ports for more computers.
▲ *Function 3:* As a DHCP server, all computers can receive their IP address from this server.
▲ *Function 4:* As a wireless access point, a wireless computer can connect to the network. This wireless connection can be secured using wireless security features.
▲ *Function 5:* As a firewall, it blocks unwanted traffic initiated from the Internet and provides Network Address Translation (NAT) so that computers on the LAN can use private or link local IP addresses. Another firewall feature is to restrict Internet access for computers behind the firewall. Restrictions can apply to days of the week, time of day, keywords used, or certain web sites.
▲ *Function 6:* As an FTP server, you can connect an external hard drive to the router, and the FTP firmware on the router can be used to share files with network users.

Setting Up a Multifunction Router for a SOHO Network

A+ 220-801 2.6

A+ 220-802 2.5

> **Notes** The speed of a network depends on the speed of each device on the network and how well a router manages that traffic. Routers, switches, and network adapters currently run at three speeds: Gigabit Ethernet (1000 Mbps or 1 Gbps), Fast Ethernet (100 Mbps), or Ethernet (10 Mbps). If you want your entire network to run at the fastest speed, make sure all your devices are rated for Gigabit Ethernet.

An example of a multifunction router is the Linksys E4200 by Cisco shown in Figures 9-46 and 9-47. It has one port for the broadband modem (cable modem or DSL modem) and four ports for computers on the network. The USB port can be used to plug in a USB external hard drive for use by any computer on the network. The router is also a wireless access point having multiple antennas to increase speed and range using Multiple In, Multiple Out (MIMO) technology. The antennas are built in.

Figure 9-46 The Linksys E4200 router by Cisco has built-in wireless antennas and can be used with a DSL or cable modem Internet connection

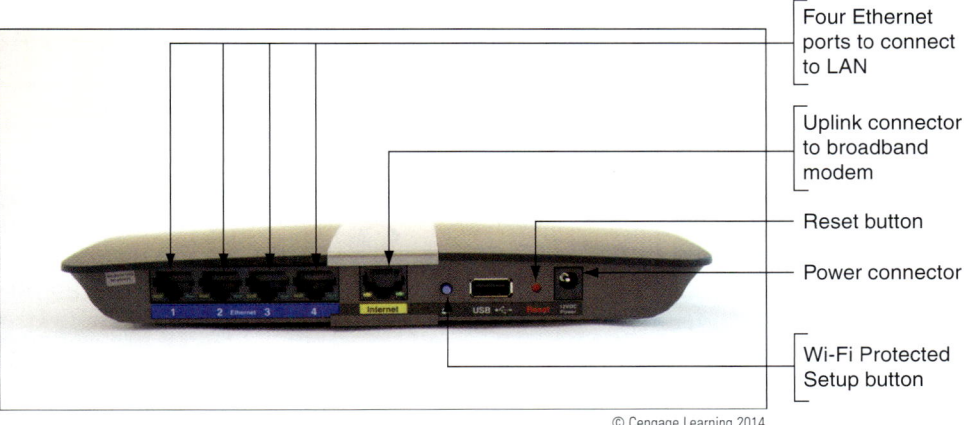

Figure 9-47 Connectors and ports on the back of the Cisco router

A+ 220-801 2.6

A+ 220-802 2.5

INSTALL AND CONFIGURE THE ROUTER ON THE NETWORK

To install a router on the network, always follow the directions of the manufacturer rather than the general directions given here. Using the Linksys E4200 as our example router, here is how to install it on the network:

1. On one of your computers on the network (it doesn't matter which one), launch the setup program on the CD that came bundled with the router. The setup program instructs you to use one network cable to connect the computer to the router and a second network cable to connect the router to the DSL or cable modem box using the Internet port on the router. After you have made the connections, click **Next** on the setup screen.

2. On the next screen, you are given the opportunity to change the SSID and password to the router. Be sure to change the password. On the next screen, you can decide to allow or not allow the router to receive automatic updates from Cisco.

3. The setup program says you should be connected to the Internet. Verify the connection by opening your browser and surfing the web. You can then close the router setup program.

> **Caution** Changing the router password is especially important if the router is a wireless router. Unless you have disabled or secured the wireless access point, anyone outside your building can use your wireless network. If they guess the default password to the router, they can change the password to hijack your router. Also, your wireless network can be used for criminal activity. When you first install a router, before you do anything else, change your router password and disable the wireless network until you have time to set up and test the wireless security. And, to give even more security, change the default name to another name if the router utility allows that option.

Using any computer on the network, you can use your browser and the firmware on the router to configure it at any time. To do so, follow these steps:

1. Open your browser and enter the IP address of the router, 192.168.1.1, in the address box. The Windows Security box appears (see Figure 9-48). Enter **admin** as the username and the password is the one you set up when installing the router.

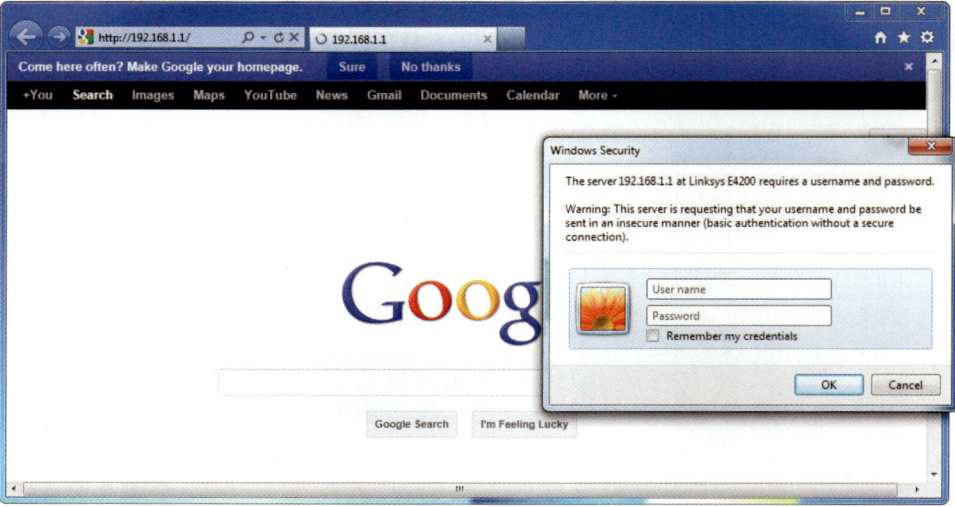

Source: Microsoft Windows 7

Figure 9-48 Enter the username and password to your router firmware utility

2. The main setup page of the router firmware appears in your browser window (see Figure 9-49). Use the menus near the top of the screen and items on each menu to change your router's configuration. Each router utility is different, but you should be able to poke around and find the setting you need. When finished, click **Save Settings** and close the browser window.

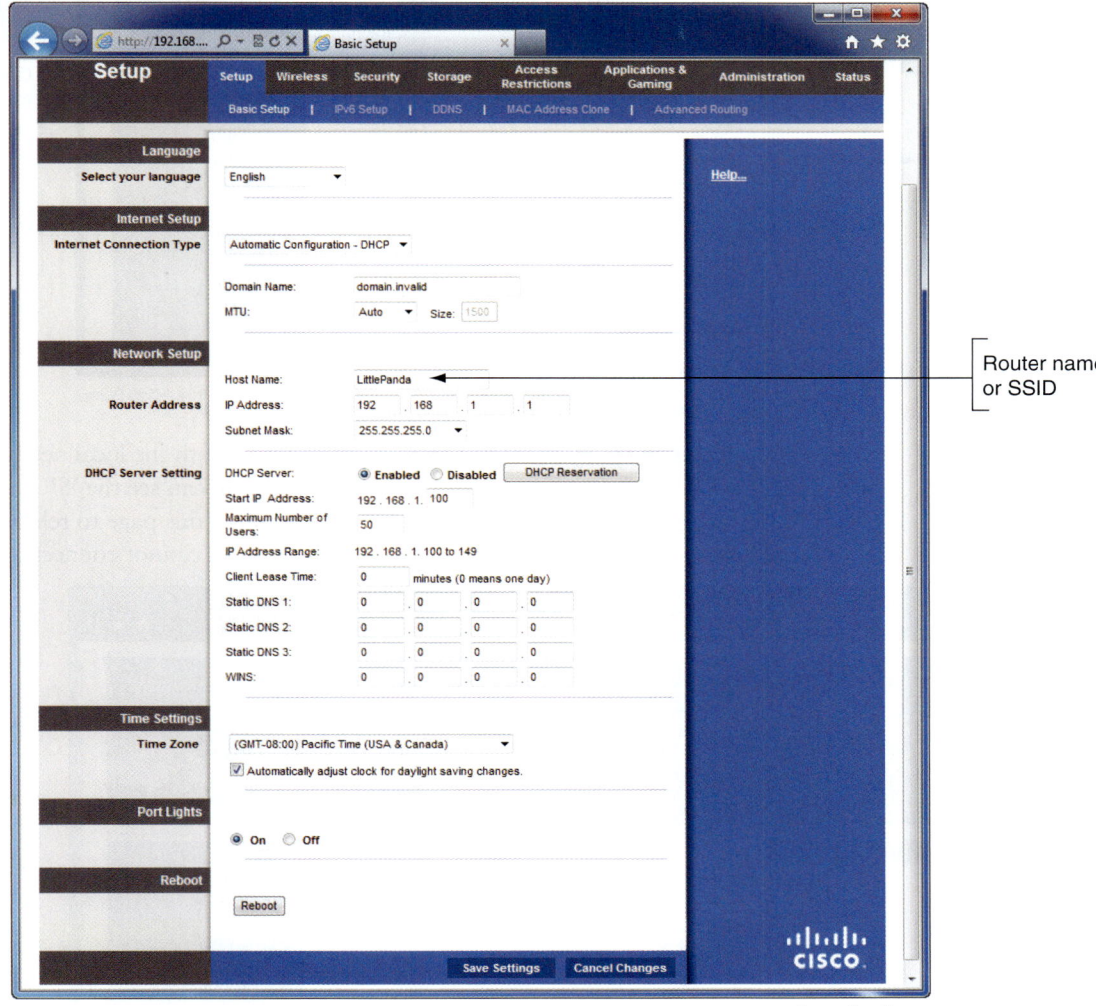

Figure 9-49 Use menus on the router firmware utility screens to configure your router

Source: Cisco Systems

Following are some changes that you might need to make to the router's configuration. If you make changes on a page, be sure to click **Save Settings** to save your changes. The first setting should always be done:

▲ *Change the router password.* It's extremely important to protect access to your network and prevent others from hijacking your router. If you have not already done so, change the default password to your router firmware. If the firmware offers the option, disable the ability to configure the router from over the wireless network (see Figure 9-50).

▲ *Change the SSID and configure the DHCP server.* On the Basic Setup menu shown earlier in Figure 9-49, you can change the name of the router (the SSID), and you can enable or disable the DHCP server. For the DHCP server, you set the start IP address and set the number of IP addresses DHCP can serve up.

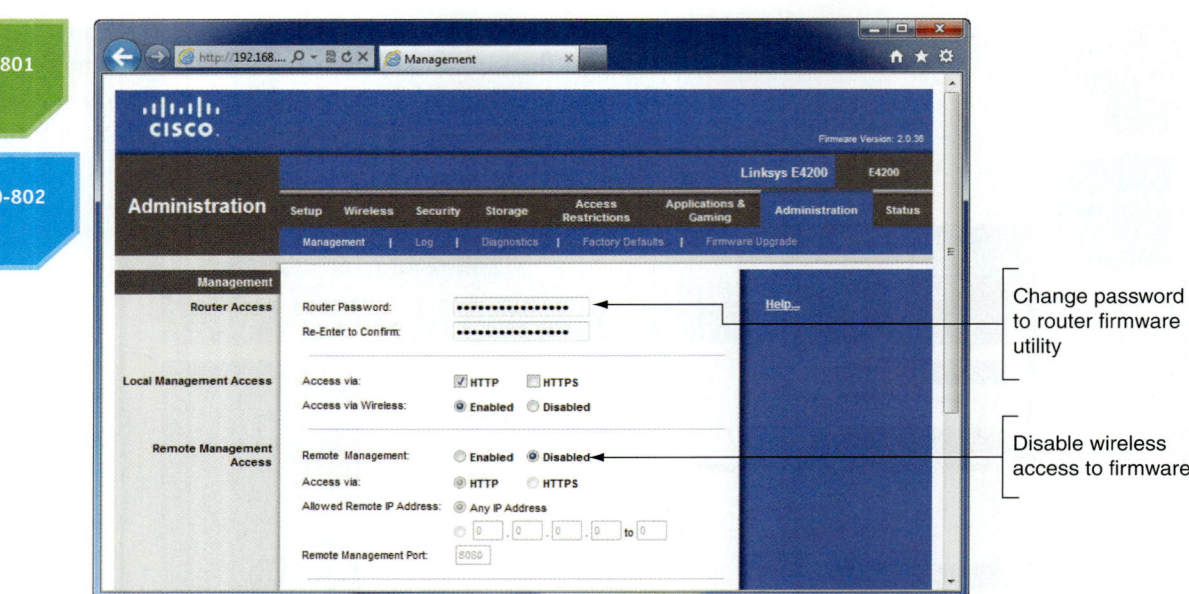

Figure 9-50 Prevent others from hijacking your router

▲ *View assignments made by the ISP.* The router belongs to both the local network and the ISP network. On the Status page shown in Figure 9-51, you can see the ISP has assigned the router a private IP address on its network. You can also use this page to release and renew this IP address, which might help solve a problem when you cannot connect to the ISP.

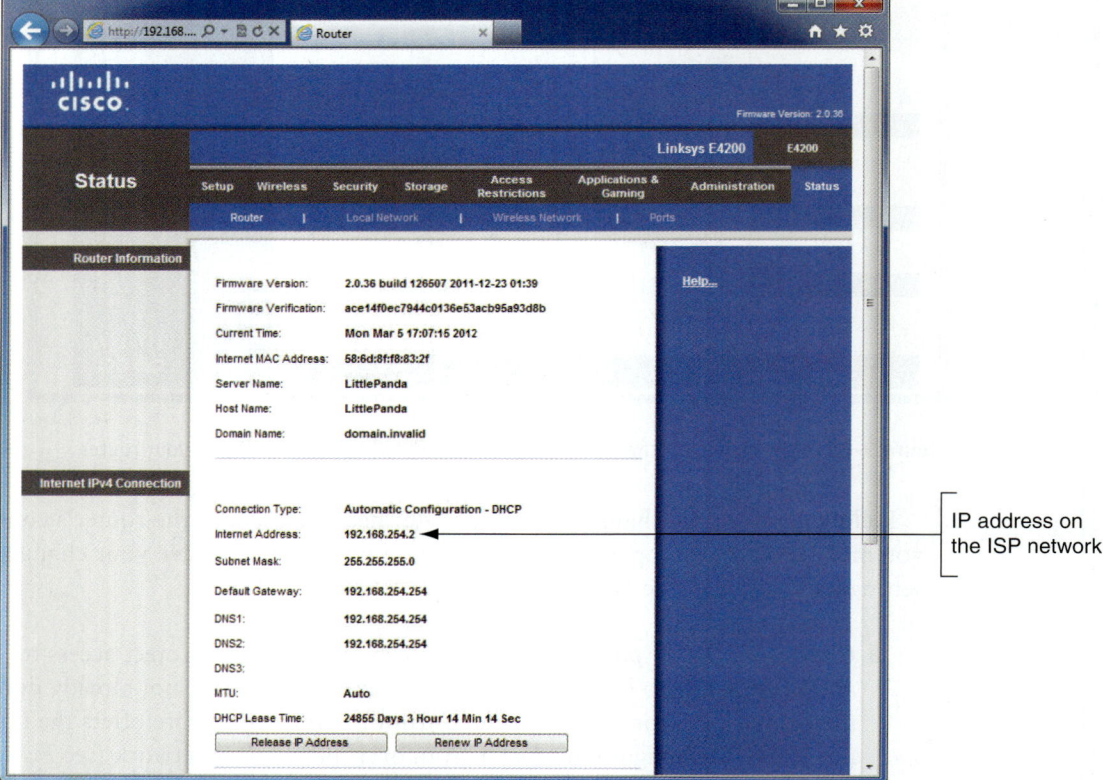

Figure 9-51 The ISP has assigned the router a private IP address

> **Notes** If you are running a web server on the Internet, the web server must use a public and static IP address. For this situation, you can lease a public IP address from your ISP at an additional cost.

Setting Up a Multifunction Router for a SOHO Network

A+
220-801
2.6

A+
220-802
2.5

▲ *Assign static IP addresses.* A computer or network printer might require a static IP address. For example, when a computer is running a web server on the local network, it needs a static IP address that you can add to the Hosts file for each computer on the network that needs to access this intranet web site. A network printer also needs a static IP address so computers will always be able to find the printer. To assign a static IP address to a client, click **DHCP Reservation** on the Setup page shown earlier in Figure 9-49. In the DHCP Reservation box, select a client from the DHCP table and click **Add Clients**. Then click **Save Settings**. In Figure 9-52, a Canon network printer is set to receive the IP address 192.168.1.118 each time it connects to the network.

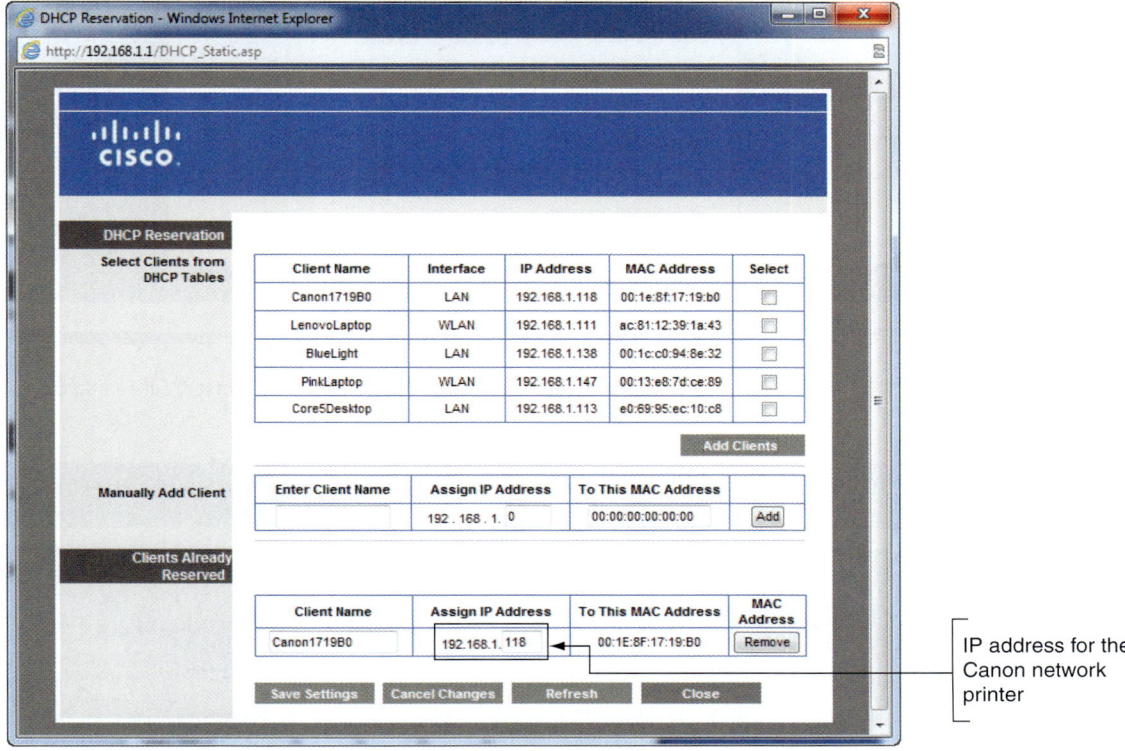

Source: Cisco Systems

Figure 9-52 Assign a static IP address to a network printer

▲ *Configure the firewall to disable all ports.* On the Security page, you can enable SPI Firewall Protection (see Figure 9-53). SPI (stateful packet inspection) examines each data packet and rejects those unsolicited by the local network. Using this setting, all ports are disabled (closed) and no activity initiated from the Internet can get in. You can allow exceptions to this firewall rule by using port forwarding, port triggering, or a DMZ. How to do so is coming up in the next section.

▲ *Improve QoS for an application.* As you use your network and notice that one application is not getting the best service, you can improve network performance for this application using the **Quality of Service (QoS)** feature. For example, suppose you routinely use Skype to share your desktop with collaborators over the Internet. To assign a high priority to Skype, go to the **Applications & Gaming** tab (see Figure 9-54). Under Internet Access Priority, select **Enabled**. Under Category, in the drop-down list of Applications, select **Skype**. Under Priority, select **High** and click **Apply**. Skype is added in the Summary area. If you don't see your application listed, you can click **Add a New Application** in the drop-down list of applications and enter its name.

Now let's look at the concepts and steps to allow certain activity initiated from the Internet past your firewall. Then we'll look at how to set up a wireless network.

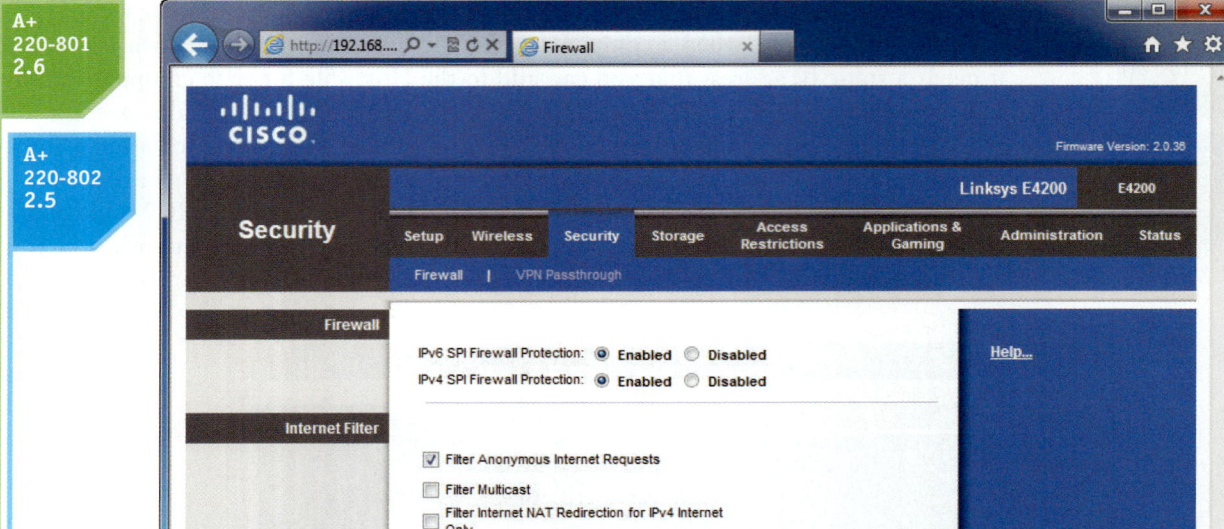

Figure 9-53 Configure the router's firewall to prevent others on the Internet from seeing or accessing your network

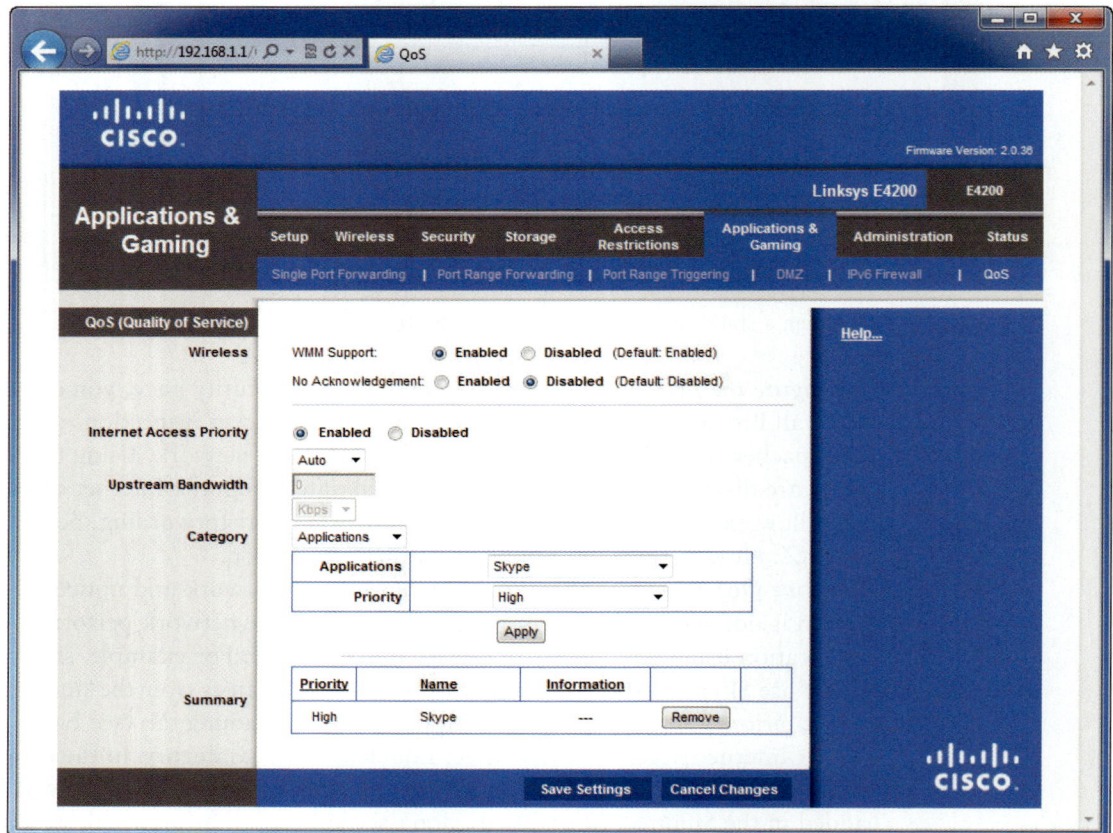

Figure 9-54 Use the QoS feature to assign a high priority to an application to improve its network service

PORT FORWARDING, PORT TRIGGERING, AND A DMZ

Suppose you're hosting an Internet game or want to use Remote Desktop to access your home computer from the Internet. In both situations, you need to enable (open) certain ports so that activity initiated from the Internet can get past your firewall.

Recall that a router uses NAT redirection to present its own IP address to the Internet in place of IP addresses of computers on the local network. The NAT protocol is also responsible for passing communication to the correct port on the correct local computer.

Here are the ways a router can use NAT to open or close certain ports:

- **Port filtering** is used to open or close certain ports so they can or cannot be used. Remember that applications are assigned these ports. Therefore, in effect, you are filtering or controlling what applications can or cannot get through the firewall. For example, in Figure 9-55a, all requests from the Internet to ports 20, 443, 450, and 3389 are filtered or disabled. These ports are closed.
- **Port forwarding** means that when the firewall receives a request for communication from the Internet to a specific computer and port, the request will be allowed and forwarded to that computer on the network. The computer is defined to the router by its static IP address. For example, in Figure 9-55a, port 80 is open and requests to

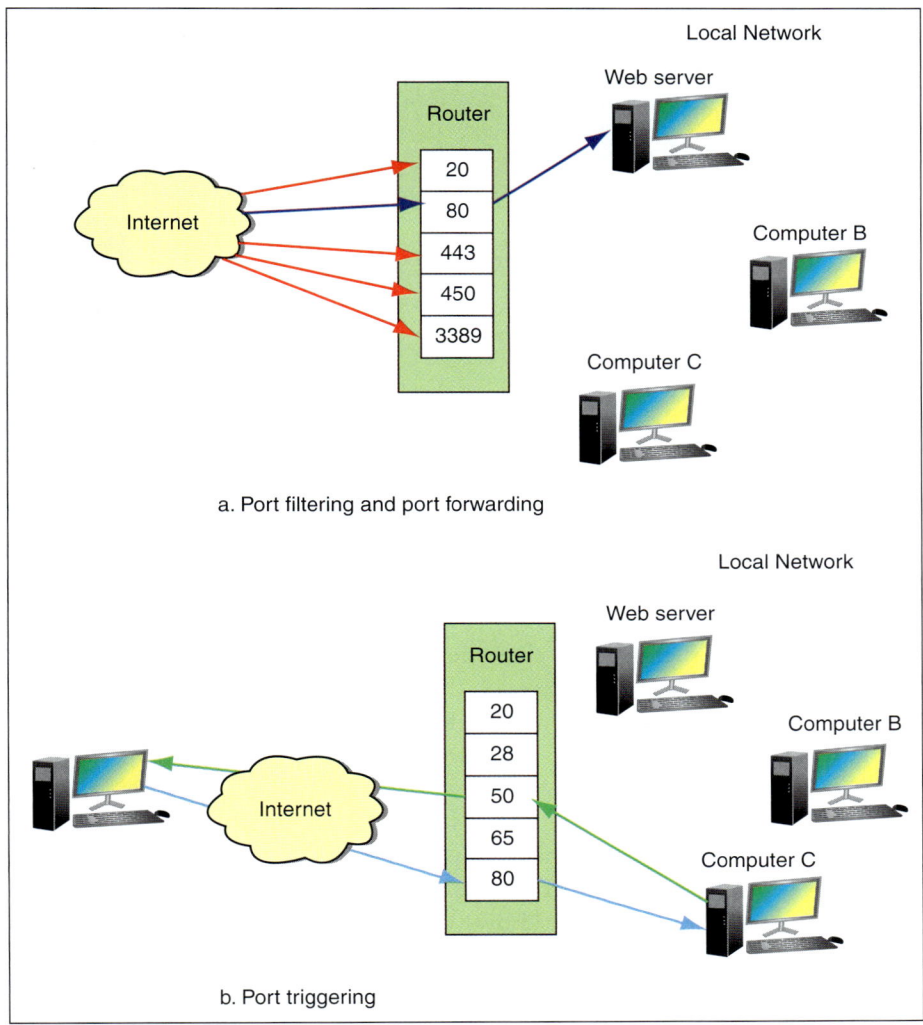

a. Port filtering and port forwarding

b. Port triggering

Figure 9-55 Port filtering, port forwarding, and port triggering

port 80 are forwarded to the web server that is listening at that port. This one computer on the network is the only one allowed to receive requests at port 80.

▲ **Port triggering** opens a port when a PC on the network initiates communication through another port. For example, in Figure 9-55b, Computer C sends data to port 50 to a computer on the Internet. The router is configured to open port 80 for communication from this remote computer. Port 80 is closed until this trigger occurs. Port triggering does not require a static IP address for the computer inside the network, and any computer can initiate port triggering. The router will leave port 80 open for a time. If no more data is received from port 50, then it closes port 80.

> **A+ Exam Tip** The A+ 220-801 exam expects you to know how to implement port forwarding and port triggering.

To configure port forwarding or port triggering, use the Applications & Gaming tab shown in Figure 9-56. In the figure, the Remote Desktop application outside the network can use port forwarding to communicate with the computer whose IP address is 192.168.1.90 using port 3389. The situation is illustrated in Figure 9-57. This computer is set to support the Remote Desktop server application.

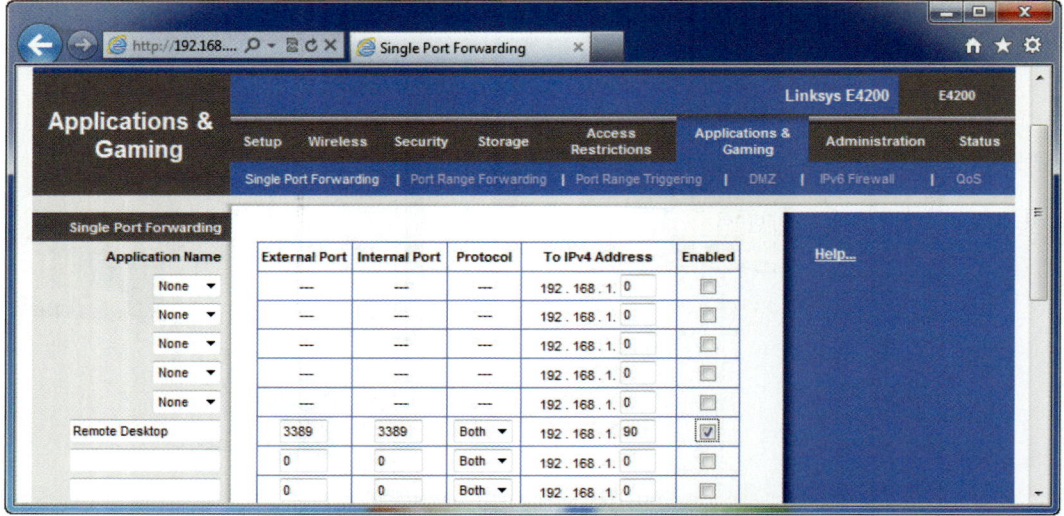

Source: Cisco Systems

Figure 9-56 Using port forwarding, activity initiated from the Internet is allowed access to a computer on the network

To configure port triggering, click the **Port Range Triggering** tab and enter the two ranges of ports. For example, in Figure 9-58, the Triggered Range of ports will trigger the event to open the ports listed under Forwarded Range.

Here are some tips to keep in mind when using port forwarding or port triggering:

▲ You must lease a static IP address from your ISP so that people on the Internet can find you. Most ISPs will provide you a static IP address for an additional monthly fee.

▲ For port forwarding to work, the computer on your network must have a static IP address so that the router knows where to send the communication.

▲ If the computer using port triggering stops sending data, the router might close the triggered port before communication is complete. Also, if two computers on the network attempt to trigger the same port, the router will not allow data to pass to either computer.

Setting Up a Multifunction Router for a SOHO Network

Figure 9-57 With port forwarding, a router allows requests initiated outside the network

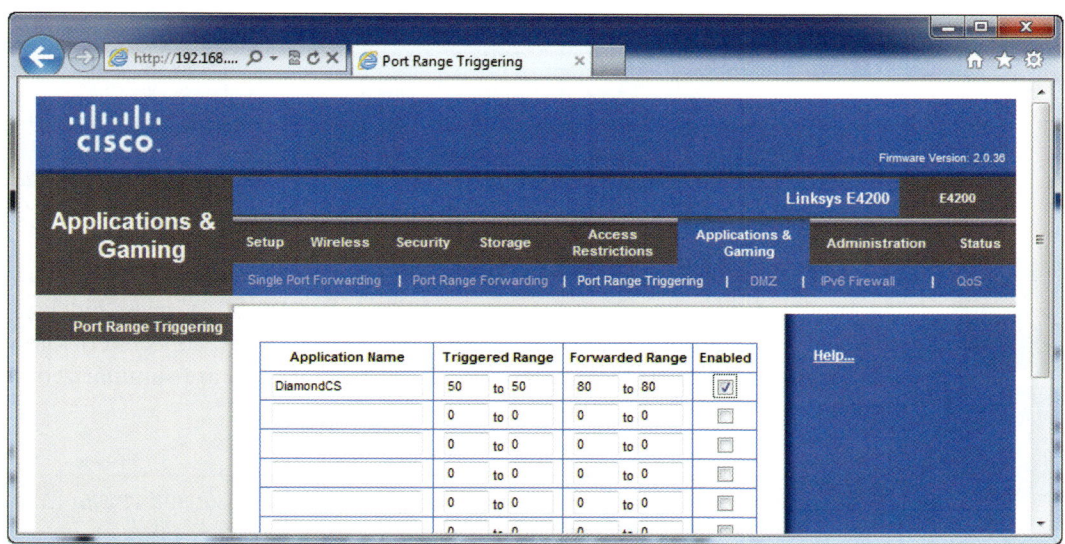

Figure 9-58 Port triggering opens a range of ports when data is sent from inside the network

▲ Using port forwarding, your computer and network are more vulnerable because you are allowing external users directly into your private network. For better security, turn on port forwarding only when you know it's being used.

A **demilitarized zone (DMZ)** in networking is a computer or network that is not protected by a firewall. You can drop all your shields protecting a computer by putting it in a **DMZ** and the firewall no longer protects it. If you are having problems getting port forwarding or port triggering to work, putting your computer in a DMZ can free it to receive any communication from the Internet. Enter its IP address or MAC address on the DMZ page of the router utility (see Figure 9-59) under Destination. You can also specify that any IP address on the Internet is allowed access or you can limit access to a specific IP address. It goes without saying to not leave the DMZ enabled unless you are using it.

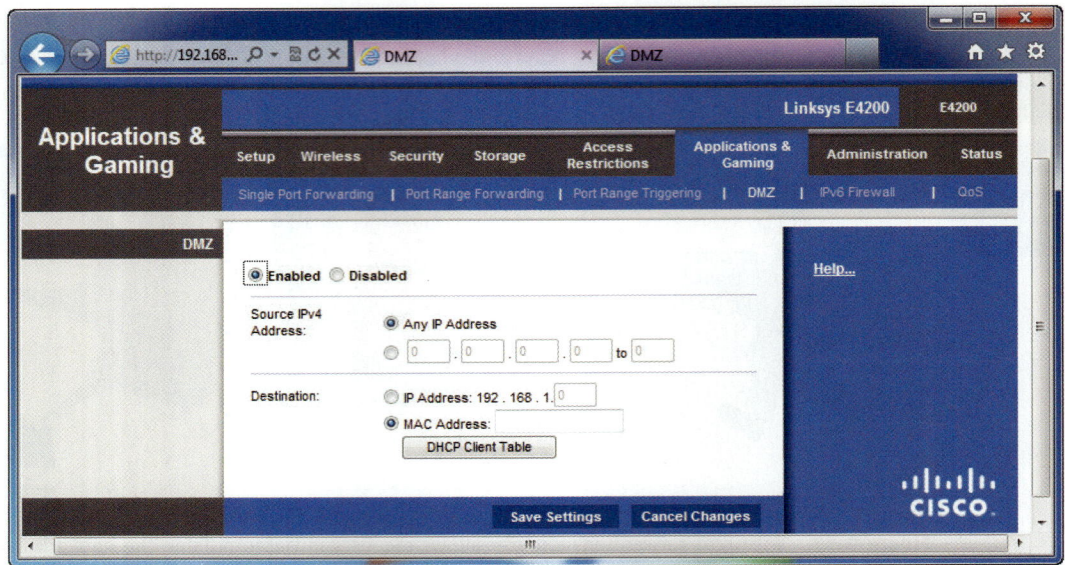

Source: Cisco Systems

Figure 9-59 Put a computer in a DMZ so that the router firewall does not prevent it from receiving communication from the Internet

Notes By the way, if you want to use a domain name rather than an IP address to access a computer on your network from the Internet, you'll need to purchase the domain name and register it in the Internet name space to associate it with your static IP address assigned by your ISP. Several web sites on the Internet let you do both; one site is by Network Solutions at *www.networksolutions.com*.

SET UP A WIRELESS NETWORK

The standards for a local wireless network are called **Wi-Fi (Wireless Fidelity)**, and their technical name is IEEE 802.11. The IEEE 802.11 standards, collectively known as the **802.11 a/b/g/n** standards, have evolved over the years and are summarized in Table 9-6.

A+ Exam Tip The A+ 220-801 exam expects you to know about 802.11 a/b/g/n standards, their speeds, distances, and frequencies.

Wi-Fi Standard	Speeds, Distances, and Frequencies
IEEE 802.11a	• Speeds up to 54 Mbps (megabits per second). • Short range up to 50 meters with radio frequency of 5.0 GHz. • 802.11a is no longer used.
IEEE 802.11b	• Up to 11 Mbps with a range of up to 100 meters. (Indoor ranges are less than outdoor ranges.) • The radio frequency of 2.4 GHz experienced interference from cordless phones and microwaves.
IEEE 802.11g	• Same as 802.11b, but with a speed up to 54 Mbps.
IEEE 802.11n	• Up to 500 Mbps depending on the configuration. • Indoor range up to 70 meters and outdoor range up to 250 meters. • Can use either 5.0 GHz or 2.4 GHz radio frequency.

© Cengage Learning 2014

Table 9-6 Older and current Wi-Fi standards

The latest Wi-Fi standard, 802.11n, uses **multiple input/multiple output (MIMO)**, which means a device can use two or more antennas to improve performance (see Figure 9-60). Most wireless devices today are 802.11 b/g/n compatible.

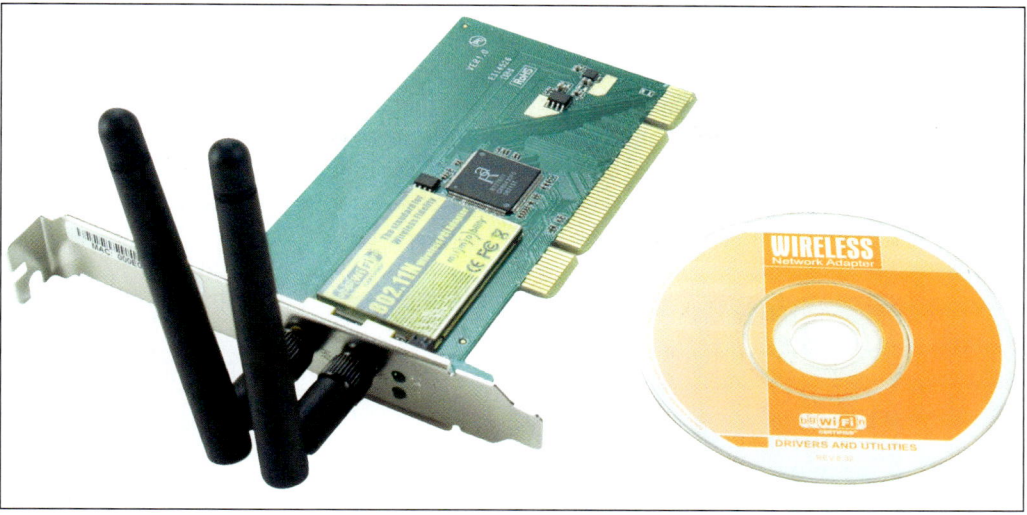

Figure 9-60 Wireless network adapter with two antennas supports 802.11 b/g/n Wi-Fi standards

When setting up a wireless network, position your router or the stand-alone wireless access point in the center of where you want your hotspot and know that a higher position (near the ceiling) works better than a lower position (on the floor). Be sure to set the device in a physically secure place and not in a public area where it can be stolen.

When configuring an 802.11n network, consider these options:

- *The radio frequency (RF) the network will use.* Choices for **radio frequency (RF)** are 5 GHz and 2.4 GHz. The 5 GHz frequency yields faster speeds than the 2.4 GHz frequency, but the range is shorter. For best performance in a small space, use 5 GHz. Use 2.4 GHz if your hotspot must reach a longer distance. Use both frequencies so they can share the network traffic.
- *The older wireless devices that will use the network.* If your network must support older 802.11 b/g wireless devices, you must support the 2.4 GHz frequency.
- *The RF interference the network will experience.* Interference for 2.4 GHz frequency might come from cordless phones, microwaves, and other Wi-Fi networks. The 5 GHz frequency is less likely to experience this interference.
- *The channel the network will use.* A **channel** is a specific radio frequency within a broader frequency. For example, two channels in the 5 GHz band are 5.180 GHz and 5.200 GHz channels. In the United States, eleven channels are allowed for 5 GHz or 2.4 GHz bands (Channels 1 through 11). For most networks, you can allow auto channel selection so that any channel in the frequency range (5 GHz or 2.4 GHz) will work. The device scans for the least-busy channel. However, if you are trying to solve a problem with interference from a nearby wireless network, you can set each network to a different channel; make the channels far apart to reduce interference. For example, set one network to Channel 1 and set the other to Channel 11.
- *The channel width the network will use.* For a 5 GHz network, choices are 40 MHz and 20 MHz channel widths. For best performance, use 40 MHz. For less interference, use 20 MHz.

▲ *The radio power level the device will use.* Some high-end access points allow you to adjust the radio power levels the device can use. To reduce interference, limit the range of the network, or to save on electricity, reduce the power level.

For the firmware utility of the Linksys E4200 wireless router, you can change wireless settings on the Wireless tab when you click **Manual** (see Figure 9-61). Notice in the figure the two wireless setting groups; one is for the 5 GHz range and the other is for the 2.4 GHz range. Unless you have a reason to do otherwise, you can leave the Network Mode for each group set to Mixed, which allows 801.11 b/g/n connections in the 5 GHz or 2.4 GHz band. Notice in the figure that the Channel and Channel Width for each band are set to Auto. If necessary, you can specify a channel or channel width. To force a device to use one band or the other, set a different passphrase for each band.

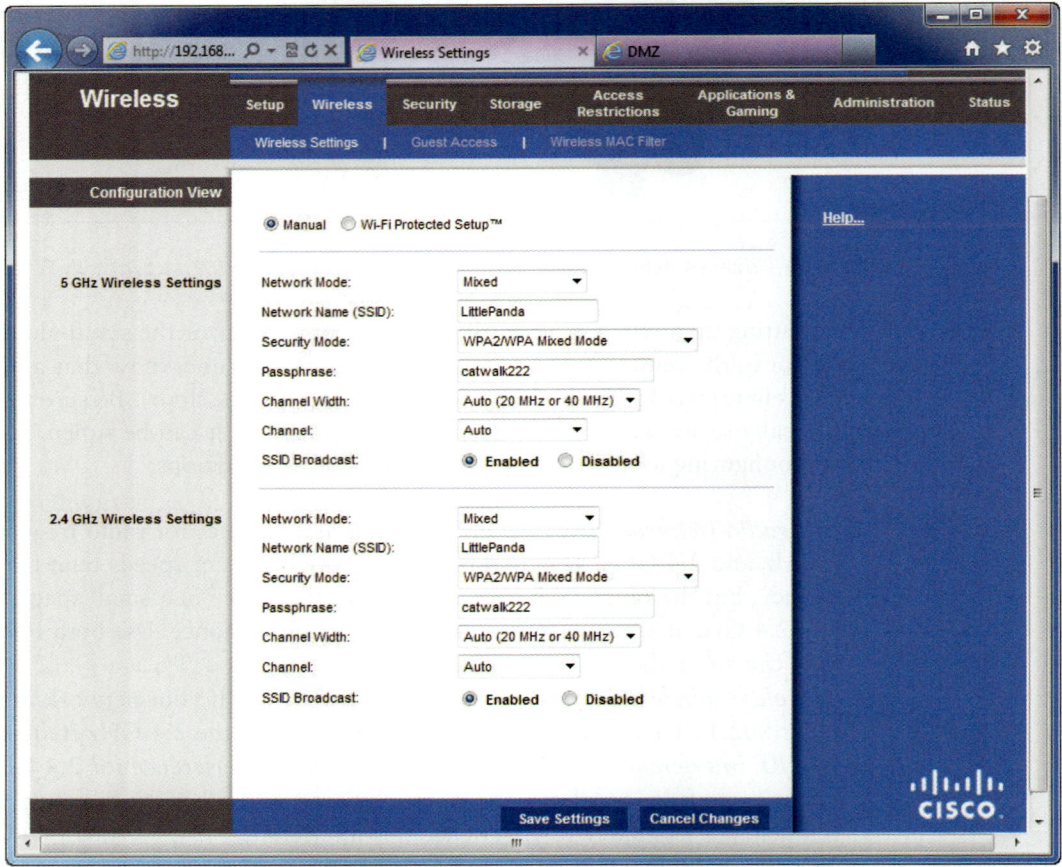

Source: Cisco Systems

Figure 9-61 Configure settings for the wireless network

It is important to secure a wireless network from outside attack. Recall that securing a wireless network is generally done in three ways:

▲ *Method 1: Requiring a security key and using data encryption*—If encryption is used when you connect to a wireless network, a security key is required. If no security key is required, the data on the wireless network is not encrypted. The three main protocols for encryption for 802.11 wireless networks are:

   o **WEP. WEP (Wired Equivalent Privacy)** is no longer considered secure because the key used for encryption is static (it doesn't change).

- o **WPA.** **WPA (Wi-Fi Protected Access)** also called **TKIP (Temporal Key Integrity Protocol)** encryption, is stronger than WEP and was designed to replace it. With WPA encryption, encryption keys are constantly changing.
- o **WPA2.** **WPA2 (Wi-Fi Protected Access 2)**, also called the 802.11i standard, is the latest and best wireless encryption standard. It is based on the **AES (Advanced Encryption Standard)**, which improved on the way TKIP generated encryption keys. All wireless devices sold today support the WPA2 standard.

To configure encryption for the Cisco router, select **Manual** in the Wireless Settings page shown in Figure 9-61 and select the Security Mode from the drop-down menu. For best security, enter a passphrase (security key) to the wireless network that is different from the password you use to the router utility.

> **Notes** To make the strongest passphrase or security key, use a random group of numbers, uppercase and lowercase letters, and, if allowed, at least one symbol. Also use at least eight characters in the passphrase.

▲ *Method 2: Disable SSID broadcasting*—You can disable SSID broadcasting and change the SSID on the Wireless page shown in Figure 9-61. This security method is not considered strong security because software can be used to discovery an SSID that is not broadcasted.

▲ *Method 3: Filter MAC addresses*—A wireless access point can filter the MAC addresses of wireless adapters to either allow or not allow these MAC addresses access to the wireless network (see Figure 9-62). MAC address filtering is considered a weak security measure and does not use encryption.

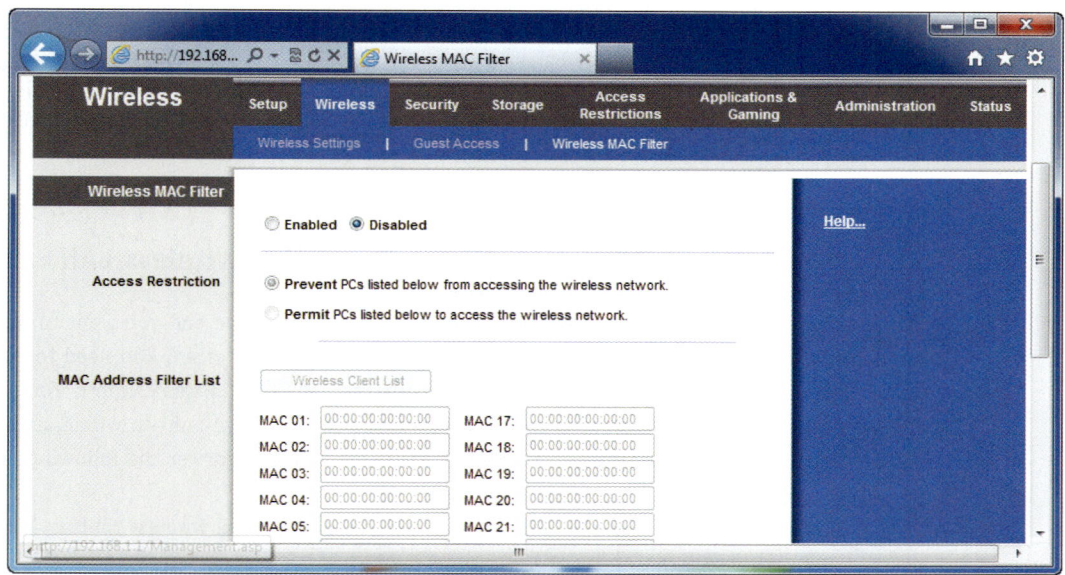

Source: Cisco Systems

Figure 9-62 Configure how the router will filter MAC addresses

You also need to know about **Wi-Fi Protected Setup (WPS)**, which is designed to make it easier for users to connect their computers to a wireless network when a hard-to-remember SSID and security key are used. WPS generates the SSID and security key using a random string of hard-to-guess letters and numbers. The SSID is not broadcasted, so both the SSID and security key must be entered to connect. Rather than having to enter these difficult strings, a user presses a button on a wireless computer or the router's PIN or computer's PIN is used. All computers on the wireless network must support WPS for it to be used. WPS is enabled on the Wireless page of the router utility shown in Figure 9-63.

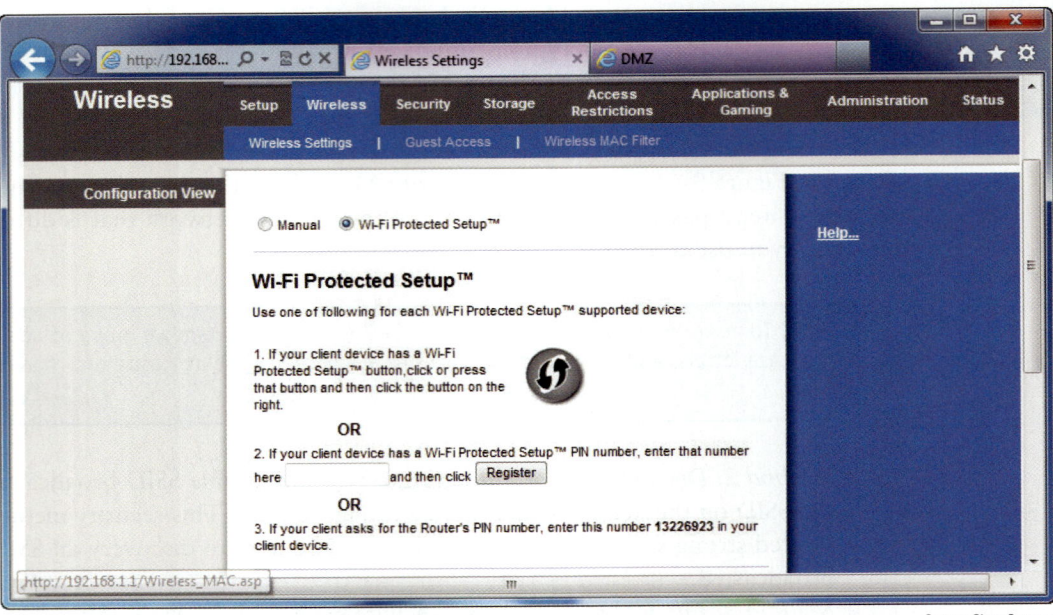

Source: Cisco Systems

Figure 9-63 Using WPS, it is easy for users to connect to a wireless network with strong security

> **A+ Exam Tip** The A+ 220-801 exam expects you to know about installing and configuring a wireless network, including MAC filtering, Wi-Fi channels (1–11), SSID broadcasting, WEP, WPA, WPA2, TKIP, AES, and WPS.
>
> The A+ 220-802 exam expects you to know about installing and configuring a wireless network, including changing default usernames and passwords, disabling and changing the SSID, using MAC filtering, antenna and access point placements, radio power levels, and assigning static IP addresses.

Hands-on Project 9-4 Research a Wireless LAN

Suppose you have a DSL connection to the Internet in your home and you want to connect two laptops and a desktop computer in a wireless network to the Internet. You need to purchase a multifunction wireless router like the one you learned to configure in this chapter. You also need a wireless adapter for the desktop computer. (The two laptops have built-in wireless.) Use the web to research the equipment needed to create the wireless LAN and answer the following:

1. Print two web pages showing two different multifunctional wireless routers. What are the brand, model, and price of each router?

2. Print two web pages showing two different wireless adapters a desktop computer can use to connect to the wireless network. Include one external device that uses a USB port and one internal device. What are the brand, model, and price of each device?

3. Which router and wireless adapter would you select for your home network? What is the total cost of both devices?

>> CHAPTER SUMMARY

Understanding TCP/IP and Windows Networking

- Networking communication happens at three levels: hardware, operating system, and application levels.

- At the hardware level, a network adapter has a MAC address that uniquely identifies it on the network.

- Using the TCP/IP protocols, the OS identifies a network connection by an IP address. At the application level, a port address identifies an application.

- IP addresses can be dynamic or static. A dynamic IP address is assigned by a DHCP server when the computer first connects to a network. A static IP address is manually assigned.

- An IP address using IPv4 has 32 bits, and an IP address using IPv6 has 128 bits.

- Classes of IPv4 IP addresses used by the public are Class A, Class B, and Class C addresses. Some IP addresses are private IP addresses that can be used only on intranets.

- If a computer is unable to obtain an IP address from a DHCP server, Windows uses Automatic Private IP Addressing (APIPA) to assign the computer an IP address unless an alternate static IP address has been configured for the computer.

- Using IPv6, three types of IP addresses are a unicast address (used by a single node on a network), multicast address (used for one-to-many transmissions), and anycast address (used by routers).

- Three types of unicast addresses are a global unicast address (used on the Internet), a link local unicast address (used on a private network), and a unique local unicast address (used on subnets in a large enterprise).

- A computer can be assigned a computer name (also called a host name), and a network can be assigned a domain name. A fully qualified domain name (FQDN) includes the computer name and the domain name. An FQDN can be used to find a computer on the Internet if this name is associated with an IP address kept by DNS servers.

- TCP/IP uses protocols at the application level (such as FTP, HTTP, and Telnet) and at the operating system level (such as TCP and UDP).

Connecting a Computer to a Network

- A PC support person needs to know how to configure TCP/IP settings and make a wired or wireless connection to an existing network.

- The best method to secure a wireless network is to use encryption (which requires you enter a security key to connect). Two other methods that are sometimes used to secure a network are to not broadcast the SSID (which requires you enter the SSID to connect) and MAC address filtering (which requires the network administrator enter the MAC address of your wireless adapter in a table). These last two methods provide weak security and are not recommended.

- To connect to a wireless WAN or cellular network, you need a mobile broadband modem, a SIM card, and a subscription to the cellular network. The mobile operator provides you a SIM card with your subscription. Your cell phone can serve as the mobile broadband modem when you tether it to your computer.

- A dial-up connection uses a telephone modem to make a connection to an ISP.

Setting Up a Multifunction Router for a SOHO Network

▲ A multifunction router for a small-office-home-office network might serve several functions, including a router, a switch, a DHCP server, a wireless access point, a firewall using NAT, and an FTP server.

▲ It's extremely important to change the password to configure your router as soon as you install it, especially if the router is also a wireless access point.

▲ To allow certain network traffic initiated on the Internet past your firewall, you can use port forwarding, port triggering, and a DMZ.

▲ To secure a wireless access point, you can enable MAC address filtering, disable SSID broadcasting, and enable encryption (WPA2, WPA, or WEP).

>> KEY TERMS

6TO4
802.11 a/b/g/n
adapter address
AES (Advanced Encryption Standard)
alternate IP address
anycast address
Automatic Private IP Address (APIPA)
best-effort protocol
channel
Class A
Class B
Class C
classful subnet mask
classless subnet mask
client/server
computer name
connectionless protocol
connection-oriented protocol
default gateway
DHCP (dynamic host configuration protocol)
DHCP client
DMZ
DNS (Domain Name System or Domain Name Service)
DNS client
DNS server
domain name
dynamic IP address
FTP (File Transfer Protocol)
fully qualified domain name (FQDN)
gateway
global address
global unicast address
hardware address

host name
Hosts file
HTTP (Hypertext Transfer Protocol)
HTTPS (HTTP secure)
IMAP4 (Internet Message Access Protocol, version 4)
interface
interface ID
Internet Protocol version 4 (IPv4)
Internet Protocol version 6 (IPv6)
intranet
IP address
ISATAP
Lightweight Directory Access Protocol (LDAP)
link
link-local address
link-local unicast address
local area network (LAN)
local link
loopback address
MAC (Media Access Control) address
multicast address
multicasting
multiple input/multiple output (MIMO)
name resolution
NAT (Network Address Translation)
neighbors
network adapter
octet
packet
physical address

POP3 (Post Office Protocol, version 3)
port
port address
port filtering
port forwarding
port number
port triggering
private IP addresses
protocols
public IP addresses
Quality of Service (QoS)
radio frequency (RF)
Remote Desktop Protocol (RDP)
router
Secure FTP (SFTP)
Secure Shell (SSH)
Server Message Block (SMB)
Service Set Identifier (SSID)
SIM (Subscriber Identification Module) card
Simple Network Management Protocol (SNMP)
SMTP (Simple Mail Transfer Protocol)
SMTP AUTH (SMTP Authentication)
static IP address
subnet
subnet ID
subnet mask
TCP (Transmission Control Protocol)
TCP/IP (Transmission Control Protocol/Internet Protocol)
Telnet

Teredo
TKIP (Temporal Key Integrity Protocol)
UDP (User Datagram Protocol)
unicast address
unique local address (ULA)
unique local unicast address
WEP (Wired Equivalent Privacy)
Wi-Fi (Wireless Fidelity)
Wi-Fi Protected Setup (WPS)
wireless access point
wireless wide area network (WWAN)
WPA (Wi-Fi Protected Access)
WPA2 (Wi-Fi Protected Access 2)

>> REVIEWING THE BASICS

1. How many bits are in a MAC address?
2. How many bits are in an IPv4 IP address? In an IPv6 IP address?
3. How does a client application identify a server application on another computer on the network?
4. What are IP addresses called that begin with 10, 172.16, or 192.168?
5. In what class is the IP address 185.75.255.10?
6. In what class is the IP address 193.200.30.5?
7. Describe the difference between public and private IP addresses. If a network is using private IP addresses, how can the computers on that network access the Internet?
8. Why is it unlikely that you will find the IP address 192.168.250.10 on the Internet?
9. In Figure 9-9, the subnet mask is four notches tall and is considered a classless subnet mask for this network of sticks. How many notches tall would be a classful subnet mask for the same network?
10. If no DHCP server is available when a computer configured for dynamic IP addressing connects to the network, what type of IP address is assigned to the computer?
11. If a computer is found to have an IP address of 169.254.1.1, what can you assume about how it received that IP address?
12. What are the last 64 bits of a IPv6 IP address called? How are these bits used?
13. Name at least three tunneling protocols that are used for IPv6 packets to travel over an IPv4 network.
14. How is an IPv6 IP address used that begins with 2000::? That begins with FE80::?
15. How many bits are in the Subnet ID block? What are the values of these bits for a link-local IP address?
16. Which type of IPv6 address is used to create multiple sites within a large organization?
17. What type of server serves up IP addresses to computers on a network?
18. Which TCP/IP protocol that manages packet delivery guarantees that delivery? Which protocol does not guarantee delivery, but is faster?
19. At what port does an SMTP email server listen to receive email from a client computer?
20. Which protocol does a web server use when transmissions are encrypted for security?
21. What type of server resolves fully qualified domain names to IP addresses?

22. Which email protocol allows a client application to manage email stored on an email server?

23. What type of protocol is used to present a public IP address to computers outside the LAN to handle requests to use the Internet from computers inside the LAN?

24. Which protocol is used when an application queries a database on a corporate network such as a database of printers?

25. What type of encryption protocol does Secure FTP (SFTP) use to secure FTP transmissions?

26. What two Windows applications use the RDP protocol and port 3389?

27. Which version of 802.11 technologies can use two antennas at both the access point and the network adapter?

28. Which wireless encryption standard is stronger, WEP or WPA?

29. When securing a Wi-Fi wireless network, which is considered better security: to filter MAC addresses, use encryption, or not broadcast the SSID?

30. Would you expect WPS to be used when a wireless network is using strong security, weak security, or no security (as in a public hotspot)?

>> THINKING CRITICALLY

1. You have just installed a network adapter and have booted up the system, installing the drivers. You open Windows Explorer on a remote computer and don't see the computer on which you just installed the NIC. What is the first thing you check?

    a. Has TCP/IPv6 been enabled?

    b. Is the computer using dynamic or static IP addressing?

    c. Are the lights on the adapter functioning correctly?

    d. Has the computer been assigned a computer name?

2. Your boss asks you to transmit a small file that includes sensitive personnel data to a server on the network. The server is running a Telnet server and an FTP server. Why is it not a good idea to use Telnet to reach the remote computer?

    a. Telnet transmissions are not encrypted.

    b. Telnet is not reliable and the file might arrive corrupted.

    c. FTP is faster than Telnet.

    d. FTP running on the same computer as Telnet causes Telnet to not work.

3. Your job is to support the desktop computers in a small company of 32 employees. A consulting firm is setting up a private web server to be used internally by company employees. The static IP address of the server is 192.168.45.200. Employees will open their web browser and enter *personnel.mycompany.com* in the URL address box to browse this web site. What steps do you take so that each computer in the company can browse the site using this URL?

>> REAL PROBLEMS, REAL SOLUTIONS

REAL PROBLEM 9-1: Setting Up a Small Network

The simplest possible wired network is two computers connected together using a crossover cable. In a crossover cable, the send and receive wires are crossed so that one computer can send and the other computer receive on the same wire. At first glance, a crossover cable looks just like a regular network cable (also called a patch cable) except for the labeling (see Figure 9-64). (In Chapter 10, you learn how to distinguish between the cables by examining their connectors.)

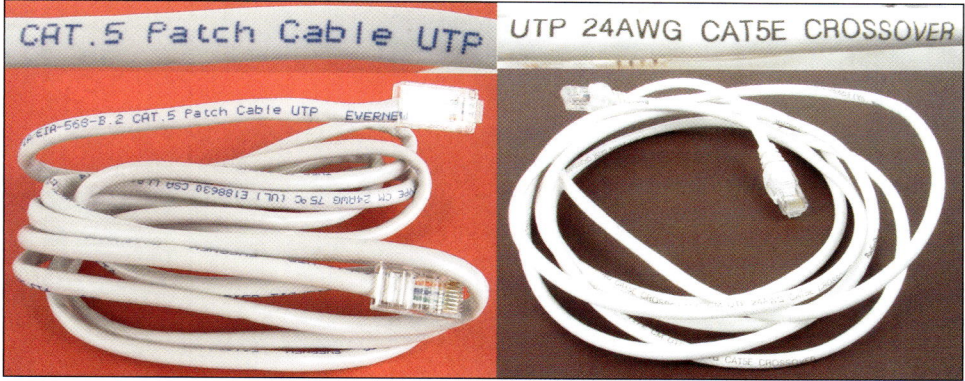

© Cengage Learning 2014

Figure 9-64 A patch cable and crossover cable look the same but are labeled differently

Do the following to set up and test the network:

1. Connect two computers using a crossover cable. Using the Network and Sharing Center, verify your network is up. What is the IP address of Computer A? Of Computer B?

2. Join the two computers to the same homegroup. Then use Windows Explorer to view the files on the other computer shared with the homegroup.

3. Convert the TCP/IP configuration to static IP addressing. Assign a private IP address to each computer. What is the IP address of Computer A? Of Computer B?

4. Verify you can still see files shared with the homegroup on each computer.

CHAPTER 10

Networking Types, Devices, and Cabling

In this chapter, you will learn:

- About network types and topologies
- About the hardware used to build local networks
- How to set up and troubleshoot the wiring in a small network

In the last chapter, you learned how to connect a computer to a network and how to set up and secure a wired and wireless router for a small network. This chapter takes you one step further in supporting networks. You'll learn about the types of networks and the technologies used to build these networks. You'll also learn about the hardware devices, cables, and connectors used to construct a network. Finally, you'll learn about networking tools, how to terminate network cables, and how to troubleshoot problems with network hardware.

NETWORK TYPES AND TOPOLOGIES

> A+ 220-801
> 2.7, 2.8

A computer network is created when two or more computers can communicate with each other. Networks can be categorized by several methods, including the technology used and the size of the network. When networks are categorized by size or physical area they cover, these are the categories used:

- *PAN.* A PAN (personal area network) consists of personal devices communicating at close range such as a cell phone and notebook computer. PANs can use wired connections (such as USB or FireWire) or wireless connections (such as Bluetooth or infrared).
- *LAN.* A LAN (local area network) covers a small local area such as a home, office, other building, or small group of buildings. LANs can use wired (most likely Ethernet) or wireless (most likely Wi-Fi, also called 802.11) technologies. A LAN is used for workstations, servers, printers, and other devices to communicate and share resources.
- *Wireless LAN.* A wireless LAN (WLAN) covers a limited geographical area, and is popular in places where networking cables are difficult to install, such as outdoors, in public places, and in homes that are not wired for networks. They are also useful in hotel rooms.
- *MAN.* A MAN (metropolitan area network) covers a large campus or city. (A small MAN is sometimes called a CAN or campus area network.) Network technologies used can be wireless (most likely LTE or WiMAX) and/or wired (for example, Ethernet with fiber-optic cabling).
- *WAN.* A WAN (wide area network) covers a large geographical area and is made up of many smaller networks. The best-known WAN is the Internet. Some technologies used to connect a single computer or LAN to the Internet include DSL, cable Internet, satellite, cellular WAN, and fiber optic.

> **A+ Exam Tip** The A+ 220-801 exam expects you to know about a LAN, WAN, PAN, and MAN.

The physical arrangement of the connections between computers is called the network topology or the physical topology. Here are the possibilities:

- **A mesh network.** In a mesh network, each node (a computer or other device that uses the network) on the network is responsible for sending and receiving transmissions to any other node to which it wants to communicate without a central point of communication. Figure 10-1a shows one configuration for a mesh network. Notice there might be more than one path from one node to another. One example of a wireless mesh network is when wireless computers connect to each other in ad hoc mode. In ad hoc mode, each wireless computer serves as its own wireless access point and is responsible for securing each connection. When several wireless computers each set up their own ad hoc mode network, the group of networked computers are a mesh network. When each node connects to every node on the network, the network is called a fully connected mesh topology (see Figure 10-1b).
- **A ring network.** In a ring network (see Figure 10-1c), nodes form a ring. Really old IBM Token Ring networks worked by passing a token around the ring. This topology is seldom used today because one down computer or a broken cable can halt all communication on the ring.

▲ **A bus network.** Another really old topology is a bus network (see Figure 10-1d) whereby all computers are connected in a sequential line. The bus network worked better than a ring network because one down computer does not prevent other computers from communicating on the bus. However, a broken cable can still bring down an entire bus network.

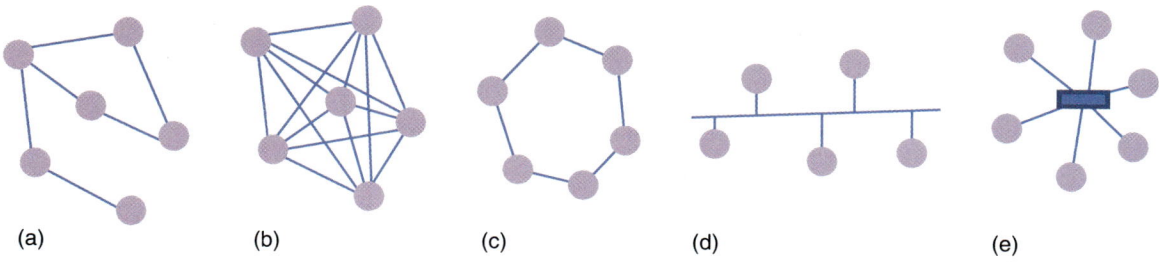

(a)　　　(b)　　　(c)　　　(d)　　　(e)

Figure 10-1 Network topologies: (a) mesh, (b) fully connected mesh, (c) ring, (d) bus, and (e) star

▲ **A star network.** A star network uses a centralized device to manage traffic on the network (see Figure 10-1e). This centralized device can be a switch or hub that offers multiple network ports or wireless connections. (Hubs are not as efficient as switches and no longer sold even though you might still see a hub in use.) Star networks are almost totally used for LANs today. An advantage of a star network is that one down computer or one broken cable does not bring down the entire network. When a star network uses multiple switches in sequence, the switches form a bus network, and the network topology is called a star bus network or a hybrid network (see Figure 10-2).

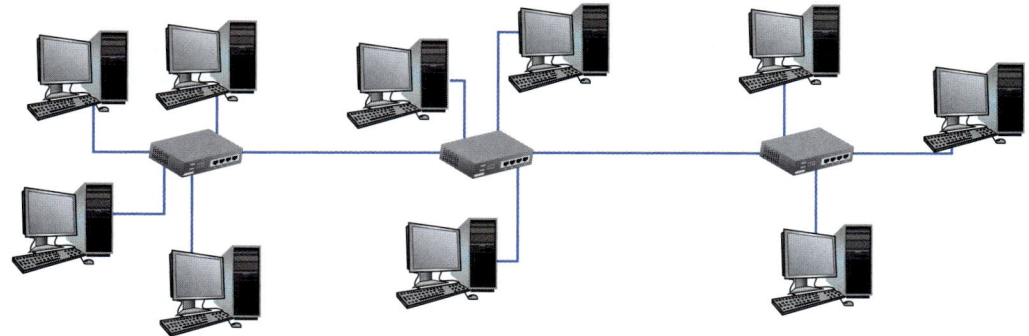

Figure 10-2 A hybrid network formed by nodes connected to multiple switches

APPLYING | CONCEPTS   SET UP AN AD HOC NETWORK

Suppose you are sitting in a meeting with a friend and you want to share some files on your laptops but you are not within range of a public Wi-Fi hotspot. If the two laptops are within 30 feet of each other, one of you can set up an ad hoc network so the two laptops can communicate wirelessly. Do the following:

1. Open the Network and Sharing Center. Click **Set up a new connection or network**. Then click **Set up a wireless ad hoc (computer-to-computer) network** and click **Next**.

A+ 220-801 2.7, 2.8

2. If a message appears saying you are already connected to the Internet (for example, when your cell phone is tethered to your laptop and the cell phone is providing an Internet connection), click **Set up a new connection anyway** and then click **Wireless**.

3. You can then give the network a name and select a security type and security key (see Figure 10-3). Recall from Chapter 9 that the best security is WPA2-Personal.

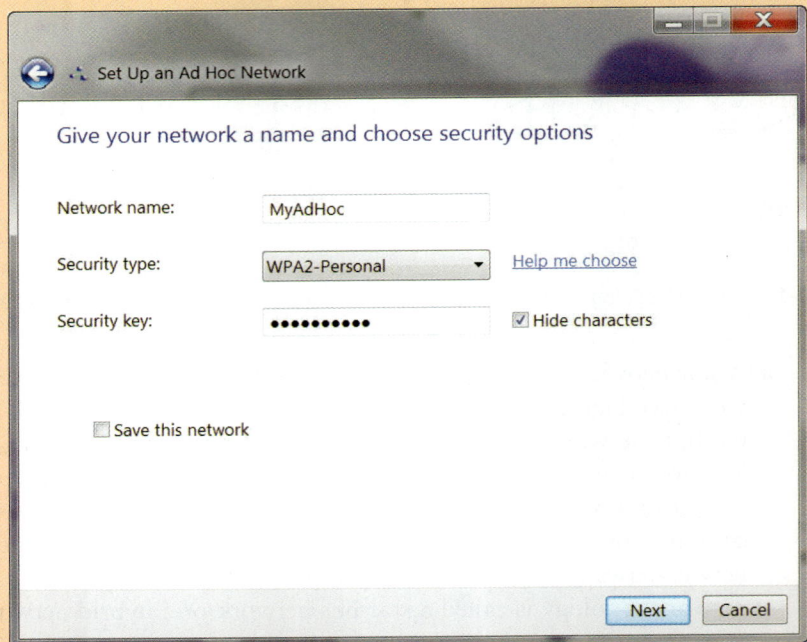

Source: Microsoft Windows 7

Figure 10-3 Set up security for the ad hoc network

4. The next box (see Figure 10-4) asks if you want to share your Internet connection with others on the ad hoc network. If so, click **Turn on Internet connection sharing**. Click **Close**.

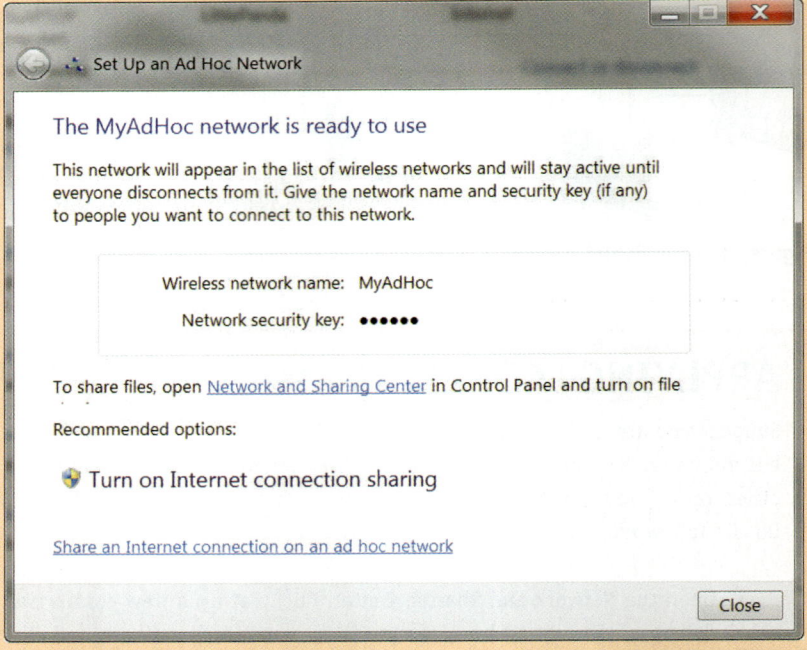

Source: Microsoft Windows 7

Figure 10-4 You can share an Internet connection with others on your ad hoc network

A+ 220-801 2.7, 2.8

5. On the other computer, the new network is listed when the user clicks the network icon in the taskbar (see Figure 10-5). The user must enter your security key to connect.

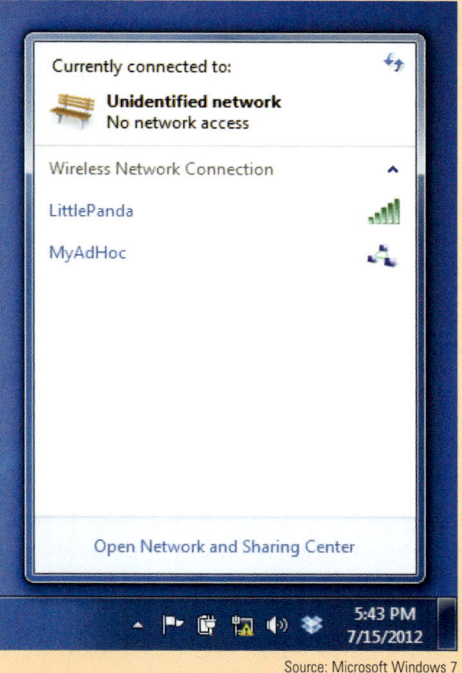

Figure 10-5 Other users can see and connect to your ad hoc network

By default, an ad hoc network is deleted after you or all users disconnect from the network.

Now let's look at network technologies used for Internet connections.

NETWORK TECHNOLOGIES USED FOR INTERNET CONNECTIONS

To connect to the Internet, a network first connects to an **Internet Service Provider (ISP)**, such as Earthlink or Comcast. The most common type of connections are DSL and cable Internet (commonly called cable or cable modem). See Figure 10-6. When connecting to an ISP, know that upload speeds are generally slower than download speeds. These rates differ because users generally download more data than they upload. Therefore, an ISP devotes more of the available bandwidth to downloading and less of it to uploading.

Networks are built using one or more technologies that provide varying degrees of bandwidth. **Bandwidth** (the width of the band) is the theoretical number of bits that can be transmitted over a network at one time, similar to the number of lanes on a highway. In practice, however, the networking industry refers to bandwidth as a measure of the maximum rate of data transmission in bits per second (bps), thousands of bits per second (Kbps), millions of bits per second (Mbps), or billions of bits per second (Gbps). Bandwidth is the theoretical or potential speed of a network, whereas **data throughput** is the average of the actual speed. In practice, network transmissions experience delays that result in slower network performance. These delays in network transmissions are

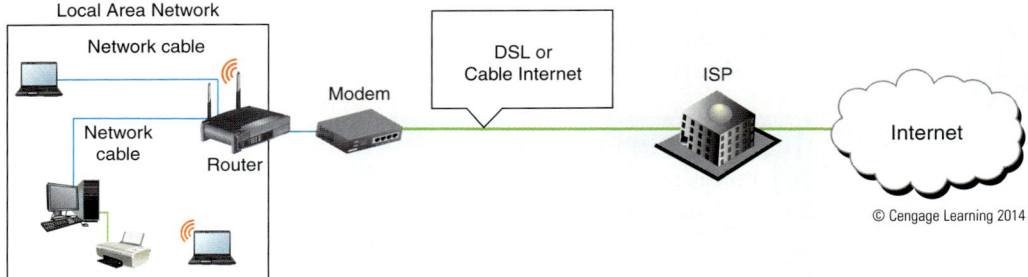

Figure 10-6 An ISP stands between a LAN and the Internet

called **latency**. Latency is measured by the round-trip time it takes for a data packet to travel from source to destination and back to source.

Table 10-1 lists network technologies used to connect to the Internet. The table is more or less ordered from slowest to fastest maximum bandwidth, although latency (time delays) can affect the actual bandwidth of a particular network. For comparison, the table includes the more common Ethernet and Wi-Fi standards used for LANs as well as the faster technologies used for Internet backbones.

Currently, cable Internet and DSL are the two most popular ways to make an Internet connection. Let's first compare these two technologies and then we'll look at satellite, fiber-optic dedicated lines, WiMAX, and cellular WANs.

Technology Wireless or Wired	Maximum Speed	Common Uses
2G cellular (second generation cellular) ✓ Wireless	Up to 50 Kbps	Uses the mobile phone service on a cellular network for voice and data (digital) transmissions. Most 2G networks use an improved version of the GSM mobile phone service although some use CDMA, which is a competing service.
Dial-up or regular telephone (POTS, for plain old telephone service) ✓ Wired	Up to 56 Kbps	Slow access to an ISP using a modem and dial-up connection over phone lines.
ISDN ✓ Wired	64 Kbps or 128 Kbps	**ISDN (Integrated Services Digital Network)** is an outdated business-use access to an ISP over dial-up phone lines.
2G EDGE or 2G E cellular ✓ Wireless	Up to 230 Kbps	Improved over 2G and uses the GSM mobile phone service. (EDGE stands for Enhanced Data for GSM Evolution.)
3G cellular (third-generation cellular) ✓ Wireless	At least 200 Kbps, but can be up to 2.4 Mbps	Improved over 2G EDGE and allows for transmitting data and video. Uses either CDMA or GSM mobile phone services. Speeds vary widely according to the revision standards used.
Satellite ✓ Wireless	Up to 1.5 Mbps	Requires a dish to send and receive from a satellite, which is in a relative fixed position with earth.

Table 10-1 Networking technologies (continues)

Technology Wireless or Wired	Maximum Speed	Common Uses
SDSL (Symmetric Digital Subscriber Line) ✓ Wired	Up to 2.3 Mbps	Equal bandwidth in both directions. SDSL is a type of broadband technology. (Broadband refers to a networking technology that carries more than one type of signal, such as DSL and telephone or cable Internet and TV.) DSL uses regular phone lines and is an always-up or always-on connection that does not require a dial-up.
ADSL (Asymmetric DSL) ✓ Wired	640 Kbps upstream and up to 24 Mbps downstream	Most bandwidth is from ISP to user. Slower versions of ADSL are called ADSL Lite or DSL Lite. ISP customers pay according to a bandwidth scale.
Cable Internet ✓ Wired	Up to 30 Mbps, depends on the type of cable	Connects a home or small business to an ISP, and usually comes with a cable television subscription and shares cable TV lines. Fiber-optic cable gives highest speeds.
T3 ✓ Wired	44 Mbps	Dedicated lines used by large companies that require a lot of bandwidth.
Dedicated line using fiber optic ✓ Wired	Up to 20 Mbps upstream and 50 Mbps downstream	Dedicated line from ISP to business or home. Speeds vary with price.
VDSL (very-high-bit-rate DSL) ✓ Wired	Up to 52 Mbps	A type of asymmetric DSL that works only a short distance.
Wi-Fi 802.11g wireless ✓ Wireless	Up to 54 Mbps	Compatible with and has replaced 802.11b.
802.16 wireless (WiMAX) WiMAX 2.0 ✓ Wireless	Up to 75 Mbps Up to 1 Gbps	Ranges up to 6 miles and is used to provide wireless access to an ISP in rural areas.
Fast Ethernet (100BaseT) ✓ Wired	100 Mbps	Used for local networks.
802.11n wireless ✓ Wireless	Up to 160 Mbps	Latest Wi-Fi technology.
4G cellular (fourth-generation cellular) ✓ Wireless	100 Mbps to 1 Gbps	Higher speeds are achieved when the client stays in a fixed position. A 4G network uses either LTE (Long Term Evolution) or WiMAX technology. LTE is more popular and faster.
Gigabit Ethernet (1000BaseT) ✓ Wired	1000 Mbps or 1 Gbps	Fastest Ethernet standard for a local network.
OC-1, OC-3, OC-24, up to OC-3072 ✓ Wired	52 Mbps, 155 Mbps, 1.23 Gbps, 160 Gbps	Optical Carrier levels (OCx) used for Internet backbones; they use fiber-optic cabling.

Table 10-1 Networking technologies (continues)

Technology Wireless or Wired	Maximum Speed	Common Uses
10-gigabit Ethernet (10GBaseT) ✓ Wired	10 Gbps	Newest Ethernet standard expected to largely replace SONET, OC, and ATM because of its speed, simplicity, and lower cost.
SONET (Synchronous Optical Network) ✓ Wired	Up to 160 Gbps	Major backbones built using fiber-optic cabling make use of different OC levels.

Table 10-1 Networking technologies (continued)

> **A+ Exam Tip** The A+ 220-801 exam expects you to be able to compare these network types used for Internet connections: Cable, dial-up, DSL, fiber, satellite, ISDN, cellular (mobile hotspot), and WiMAX.

COMPARE CABLE INTERNET AND DSL

Here are the important facts about cable Internet and DSL:

- **Cable Internet** is a broadband technology that uses cable TV lines and is always connected (always up). With cable Internet, the TV signal to your television and the data signals to your PC or LAN share the same coaxial (coax) cable. The cable modem converts a computer's digital signals to analog when sending them and converts incoming analog data to digital.
- **DSL (Digital Subscriber Line)** is a group of broadband technologies that covers a wide range of speeds. DSL uses ordinary copper phone lines and a range of frequencies on the copper wire that are not used by voice, making it possible for you to use the same phone line for voice and DSL at the same time. When you make a regular phone call, you dial in as usual. However, the DSL part of the line is always connected (always up) for most DSL services.

When deciding between cable Internet and DSL, consider these points:

- Both cable Internet and DSL can sometimes be purchased on a sliding scale, depending on the bandwidth you want to buy. Subscriptions offer residential and the more-expensive business plans. Business plans are likely to have increased bandwidth and better support when problems arise.
- With cable Internet, you share the TV cable infrastructure with your neighbors, which can result in service becoming degraded if many people in your neighborhood are using cable Internet at the same time. I once used cable Internet in a neighborhood where I found I needed to avoid web surfing between 5:00 and 7:00 P.M. when folks were just coming in from work and using the Internet. With DSL, you're using a dedicated phone line, so your neighbors' surfing habits are not important.
- With DSL, static over phone lines in your house can be a problem. The DSL company provides filters to install at each phone jack (see Figure 10-7), but still the problem might not be fully solved. Also, your phone line must qualify for DSL; some lines are too dirty (too much static or noise) to support DSL.
- Setup of cable and DSL works about the same way, using either a cable modem or a DSL modem for the interface between the broadband jack (TV jack or phone jack) and the computer. Figure 10-8 shows a DSL modem. In most cases, cable Internet and DSL

use a network port or a USB port on the computer to connect to the cable modem or DSL modem. Alternately, you can use a small router between the modem and the LAN (refer to Figure 10-6), such as the one you learned to configure in Chapter 9.

Figure 10-7 When DSL is used in your home, filters are needed on every phone jack except the one used by the DSL modem

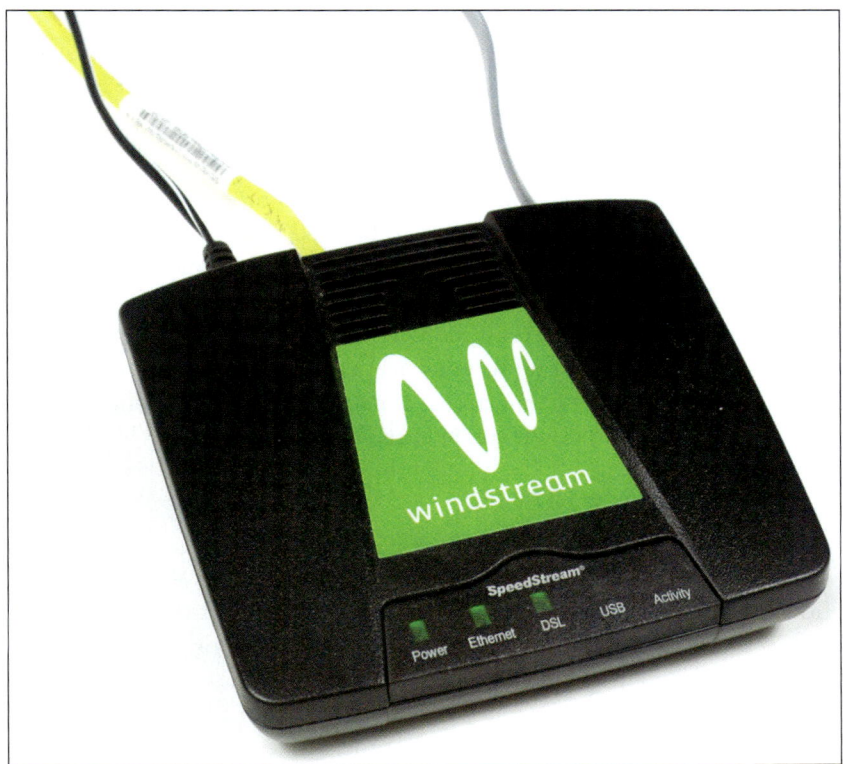

Figure 10-8 This DSL modem connects to a phone jack and a computer or router to provide a broadband connection to an ISP

SATELLITE

People who live in remote areas and want high-speed Internet connections often are limited in their choices. DSL and cable options might not be available where they live, but satellite access is available from pretty much anywhere. Internet access by satellite is available even on airplanes. Passengers can connect to the Internet using a wireless hotspot and satellite dish on the plane. A satellite dish mounted on top of your house or office building communicates with a satellite used by an ISP offering the satellite service (see Figure 10-9). One disadvantage of satellite is that it requires **line-of-sight connectivity** without obstruction from mountains, trees, and tall buildings. Another disadvantage is that it experiences delays in transmission (called latency), especially when uploading, and is, therefore, not a good solution for an Internet connection that is to be used for video conferencing or voice over Internet.

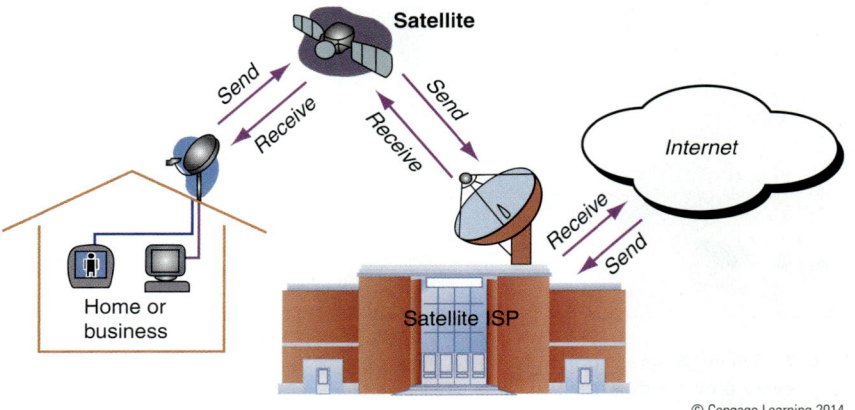

Figure 10-9 Communication by satellite can include television and Internet access

DEDICATED LINE USING FIBER OPTIC

Another broadband technology used for Internet access is **fiber optic.** The technology uses a dedicated line from your ISP to your place of business or residence. This dedicated line is called a point-to-point (PTP) connection because no other business or residence shares the line with you. Many types of cabling can be used for dedicated lines, but fiber-optic cabling is becoming popular. Television, Internet data, and voice communication all share the broadband **fiber-optic cable.** Verizon calls the technology FiOS (Fiber Optic Service), and the fiber-optic cabling is used all the way from the ISP to your home. Other providers can provide fiber-optic cabling up to your neighborhood and then use coaxial cable (similar to that used in cable Internet connections) for the last leg of the connection to your business or residence. Upstream and downstream speeds and prices vary.

WIMAX OR 802.16 WIRELESS

WiMAX is defined under IEEE 802.16d and 802.16e. WiMAX supports up to 75 Mbps with a range up to several miles and uses 2- to 11-GHz frequency. WiMAX version 2.0, defined under IEEE 802.16m, is not widely available and can support up to 1 Gbps for fixed-position users and up to 100 Mbps for mobile users. The WiMAX range in miles depends on many factors. For a wide-area network, WiMAX cellular towers are generally placed 1.5 miles apart to assure complete coverage. It is sometimes used as a last-mile solution for DSL and cable Internet technologies, which means that the DSL or cable connection goes into a central point in an area, and WiMAX is used for the final leg to the consumer. WiMAX was first used for 4G transmissions in cell phones, but LTE has taken over this market. Some laptops have a built-in WiMAX modem to connect to 4G networks that use WiMAX.

Figure 10-10 shows a WiMAX external modem used to create an Internet connection for a single computer or LAN. The modem communicates wirelessly with a WiMAX tower within range. You connect the computer or local network to the modem using its one Ethernet port. To configure the modem, enter its IP address (192.168.15.1) in your browser address box and enter its default password. The firmware page that appears in your browser is used to configure the modem. You must have a subscription with the WiMAX carrier to use the modem.

© Cengage Learning 2014

Figure 10-10 WiMAX modem by Motorola used to create a WiMAX Internet connection for a computer or network

CELLULAR WAN

A **cellular network** or **cellular WAN** consists of cells, and each cell is controlled by a base station (see Figure 10-11). The **base station** might include more than one transceiver and antenna on the same tower to support multiple technologies (such as WiMAX, LTE, and GSM). Cell phones are called that because they use a cellular network.

Cell phone networks use one of these two competing technologies:

▲ **GSM (Global System for Mobile Communications)** is an open standard that uses digital communication of data, and is accepted and used worldwide. GSM networks require that a cellular device have a **SIM (Subscriber Identity Module) card** that contains a microchip to hold data about the subscription you have with your cellular carrier. Figure 10-12 shows the slot on the side of an iPad where you can insert a SIM card.

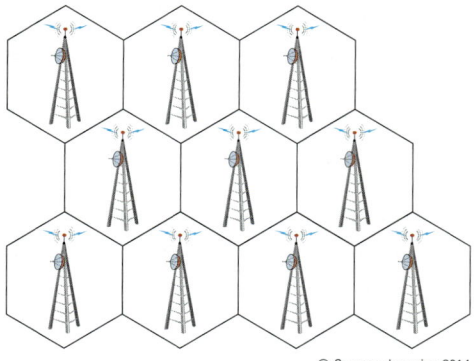

Figure 10-11 A cellular WAN is made up of many cells that provide coverage over a wide area

▲ **CDMA (Code Division Multiple Access)** was more popular than GSM in the United States for many years, but GSM is overtaking the market. CDMA networks do not require a SIM card in a cellular device.

Figure 10-12 A SIM card is required for a device to use a GSM cellular network

The ability to use your cell phone to browse the web, stream music and video, play online games, and use instant messaging and video conferencing is called 2G, 3G, or 4G. **4G (Fourth Generation)** offers the fastest speeds for cellular data. To use 2G, 3G, or 4G, both the client and cellular network must support it, and you must have a subscription for data transmissions.

Look back at Table 10-1 to see where 4G cellular fits in the list of technologies ordered from slow to fast; 4G is faster than both DSL and cable. 4G is not yet widely available but is expected to ultimately replace both DSL and cable as a solution for connecting homes and small businesses to the Internet. Where 4G coverage is available, you can use it to connect a mobile computer, desktop computer, or network to the Internet, and this connection is faster than DSL or cable.

Some laptops and tablets have embedded broadband modems. Figure 10-13 shows four other ways a computer or network can connect to the Internet by way of a cellular network connection.

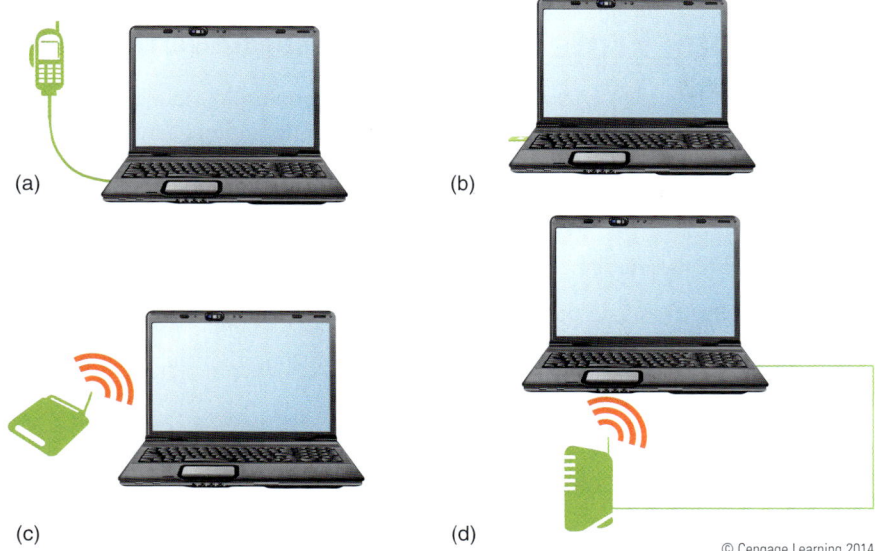

Figure 10-13 Four external devices a computer or network can use to make a cellular Internet connection

Here is an explanation of the four methods shown in Figure 10-13:

- **Cell phone tethered to computer.** A cell phone connected to a computer by way of a USB port (see Figure 10-13a) communicates with the cellular network. Software must be installed on the computer to use the connection and your subscription with the cellular carrier must include the option to tether your phone.
- **Mobile broadband modem.** An external mobile broadband modem, also called an Internet card or air card, can be a small USB device (see Figure 10-13b), a Wi-Fi portable broadband modem that creates a Wi-Fi hotspot for one or more computers (see Figure 10-13c), or a wired stationary broadband modem that is part of a wired LAN (see Figure 10-13d). Figure 10-14 shows a USB broadband modem that you learned to configure in Chapter 9. An example of a stationary wired broadband modem is the WiMAX modem shown in Figure 10-10.

Figure 10-14 A USB broadband modem by Sierra Wireless

A+ 220-801 2.7, 2.8

Hands-on | Project 10-1 Investigate Verizon FiOS

Verizon (*www.verizon.com*) offers, FiOS, an alternative to DSL and cable for wired broadband Internet access to a residence or small business. FiOS is a fiber-optic Internet service that uses fiber-optic cable all the way to your house or business for both your telephone service and Internet access. Search the web for answers to these questions about FiOS:

1. Give a brief description of FiOS and how it is used for Internet access.
2. What downstream and upstream speeds can FiOS support?
3. When using FiOS, does your telephone voice communication share the fiber-optic cable with Internet data?
4. What does Verizon say about FiOS cabling used for television?
5. Is FiOS available in your area?

HARDWARE USED BY LOCAL NETWORKS

A+ 220-801 1.4, 1.11, 2.1, 2.2, 2.9

In this part of the chapter, you will learn about the hardware devices that create and connect to networks. In Chapter 9, you learned about routers, firewalls, and wireless access points. In the following subsections, we discuss desktop and laptop devices, hubs, switches, bridges, and other network devices, and the cables and connectors these devices use.

A+ 220-802 1.6

WIRED AND WIRELESS NETWORK ADAPTERS

A PC makes a direct connection to a local wired network by way of a **network adapter**, which might be a network port embedded on the motherboard or a **network interface card (NIC)** installed in an expansion slot on the motherboard. In addition, the adapter might also be an external device plugged into a USB port (see Figure 10-15). The wired network adapter provides an **RJ-45** port (RJ stands for registered jack) that looks like a large phone jack.

Figure 10-15 USB device provides an Ethernet port

© Cengage Learning 2014

A+ Exam Tip The A+ 220-801 exam expects you to know the features of a network adapter, including the slot it uses, speeds, half duplex, full duplex, MAC address, status indicator lights, Wake on LAN, QoS, and PoE.

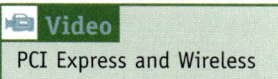

Here are the features you need to be aware of that might be included with a network adapter. You learned about several of these features in Chapter 9:

- *The slot a NIC uses.* For expansion cards, consider the slot (PCI Express or PCI) the network adapter card uses. Figure 10-16 shows a network adapter that uses a PCI Express ×1 slot. Before installing a network adapter, be sure to first go to Device Manager and uninstall any network adapters already present. You might also need to go to BIOS setup and disable an onboard network port.

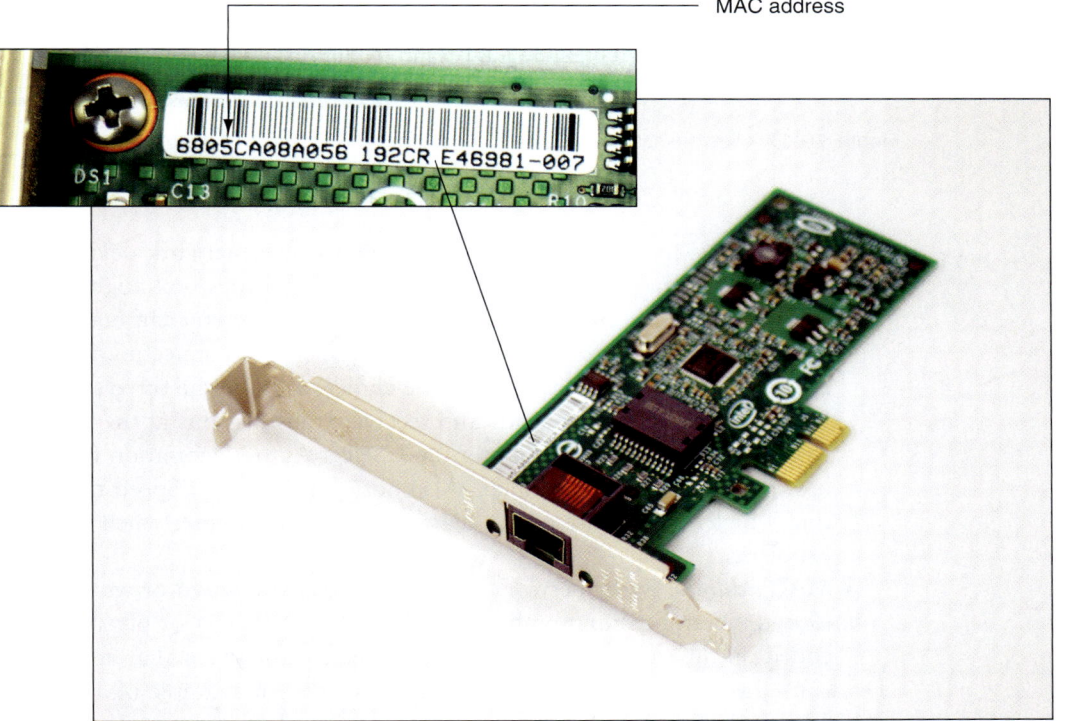

Figure 10-16 Gigabit Ethernet adapter by Intel uses a PCIe ×1 slot

- *Ethernet speeds.* For wired networks, the four speeds for Ethernet are 10 Mbps, 100 Mbps (Fast Ethernet or 100BaseT), 1 Gbps (Gigabit Ethernet or 1000BaseT), and 10 Gbps (10-gigabit Ethernet or 10GBaseT). Most network cards sold today for local networks use Gigabit Ethernet and also support the two slower speeds. To see the speeds supported, open the network adapter's properties box in Device Manager. The speed is usually included in the name of the adapter (see the left side of

A+
220-801
1.4, 1.11,
2.1, 2.2,
2.9

A+
220-802
1.6

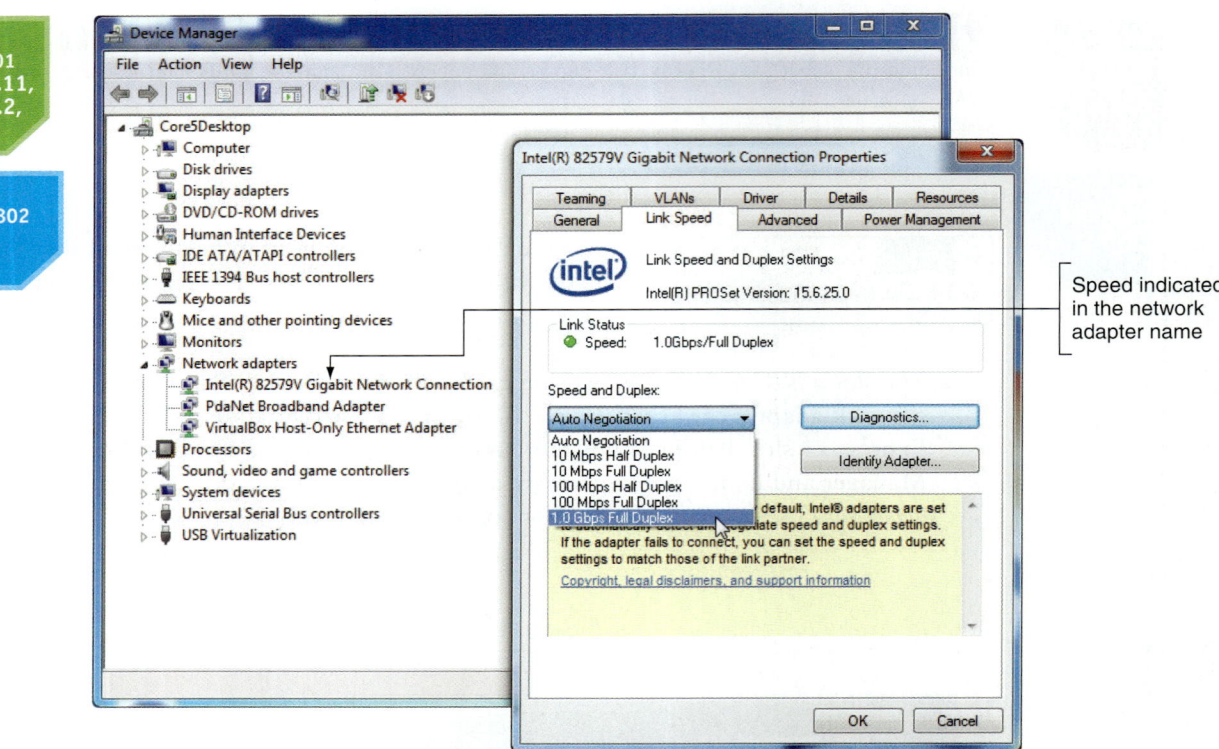

Figure 10-17 Set the speed and duplex for the network adapter

Source: Microsoft Windows 7

Figure 10-17). If the adapter connects with slower network devices on the network, the adapter works at the slower speed. The properties box might offer the Link Speed tab (see the right side of Figure 10-17) where you can manually adjust the speed to correct a problem when the adapter is not connecting to an older device. Notice in the drop-down list that the choices include the three speeds at half duplex or full duplex. **Full duplex** sends and receives transmissions at the same time. **Half duplex** works in only one direction at a time. Select Auto Negotiation for Windows to use the best possible speed and duplex. Also notice on the Link Speed tab the Diagnostics button, which you can use to run diagnostics on the adapter when you suspect it's giving problems.

▲ *MAC address.* Every network adapter (including a wired or wireless) has a 48-bit (6-byte) identification number, called the MAC address or physical address, hard-coded on the card by its manufacturer that is unique for that adapter, and this number is used to identify the adapter on the network. An example of a MAC address is 00-0C-6E-4E-AB-A5. Most likely the MAC address is printed on the device. You can also have Windows tell you the MAC address by entering the **ipconfig /all** command in a command prompt window (see Figure 10-18).

▲ *Status indicator lights.* A wired network adapter might provide indicator lights on the side of the RJ-45 port that indicate connectivity and activity (see Figure 10-19). When you first discover you have a problem with a computer not connecting to a network, be sure to check the status indicator lights to verify you have connectivity and activity. If not, then the problem is related to hardware. Next, check the cable connections to make sure they are solid.

Hardware Used by Local Networks

**A+
220-801
1.4, 1.11,
2.1, 2.2,
2.9**

**A+
220-802
1.6**

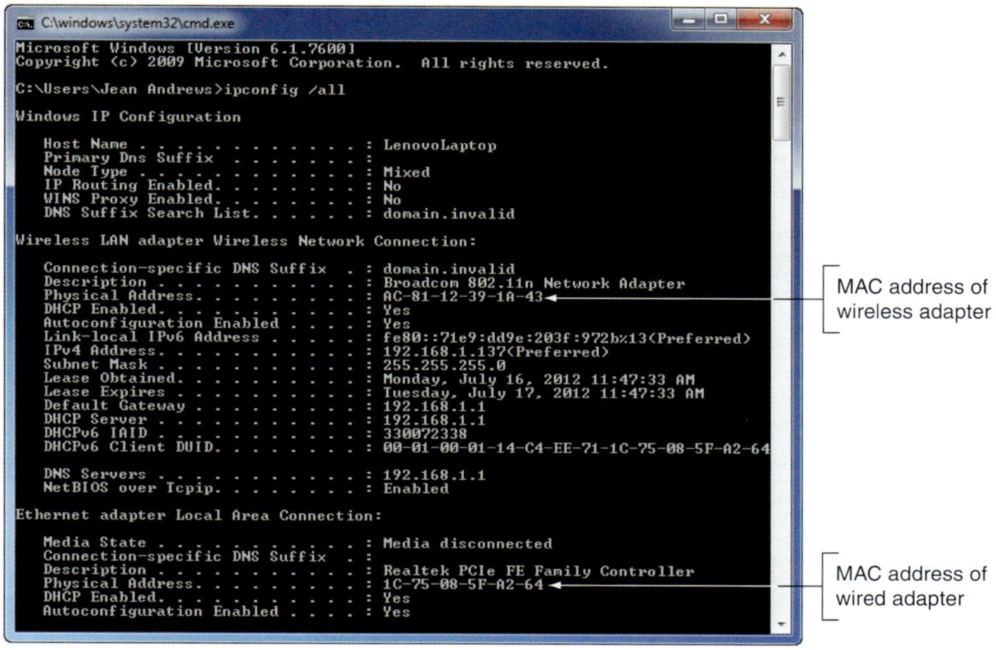

Figure 10-18 Use the ipconfig /all command to show the MAC address of a network adapter

Figure 10-19 Status indicator lights for the embedded network port

▲ *Wake-on-LAN.* A network adapter might support Wake-on-LAN, which allows the adapter to wake up the computer when it receives certain communication on the network. To use the feature, it must be enabled on the network adapter. To do that, use the Power Management tab on the network adapter properties box (see Figure 10-20). It is not recommended that you enable Wake on LAN for a wireless network adapter.

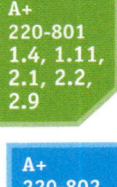

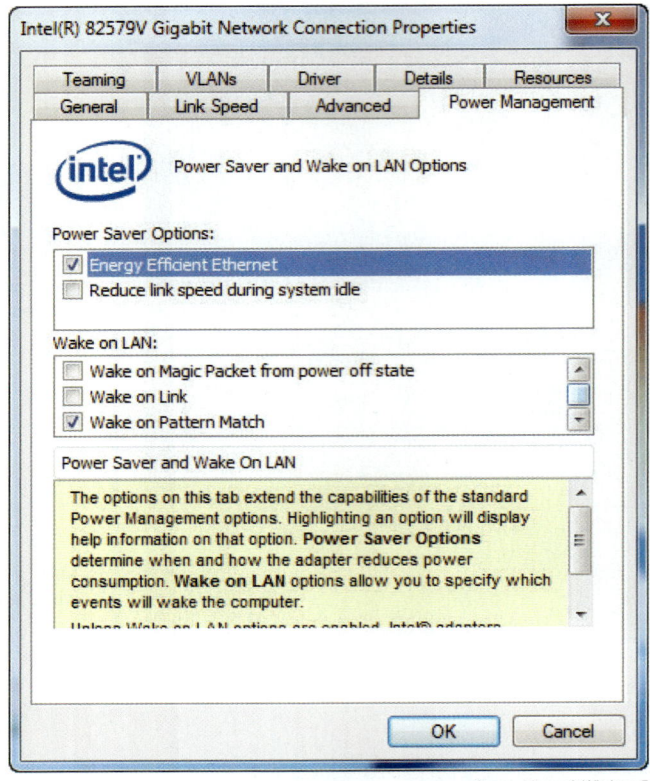

Source: Microsoft Windows 7

Figure 10-20 Enable variations of Wake on LAN based on what type of software is allowed to wake up the computer

▲ *Quality of Service (QoS).* Another feature of a network adapter is the ability to control which applications have priority on the network. The feature must be enabled and configured on the router and also enabled on the network adapters and configured in Windows for every computer on the network using the high-priority applications. To enable the network adapter to use QoS, use the Advanced tab on the network adapter properties box (see Figure 10-21). Make sure **Priority Enabled** is selected. (If the option is not listed, the adapter does not support QoS.) In Chapter 9, you learned how to configure a router to use QoS. How to configure Windows to prioritize an application on the network is not covered in this book.

▲ *Power over Ethernet (PoE).* **Power over Ethernet (PoE)** is a feature that might be available on high-end wired network adapters that allows power to be transmitted over Ethernet cable. Using this feature, you can place a wireless access point, webcam, IP phone, or other device that needs power, in a position in a building where you don't have an electrical outlet. The Ethernet cable to the device provides both power and data transmissions. Some devices, such as a webcam, are designed to receive both power and data from the Ethernet cable. For other devices, you must use a splitter that splits the data transmission and the power transmission. Then use both a power cable and Ethernet data cable to run from the splitter to the device. PoE can provide up to 25.5 W from a single Ethernet port.

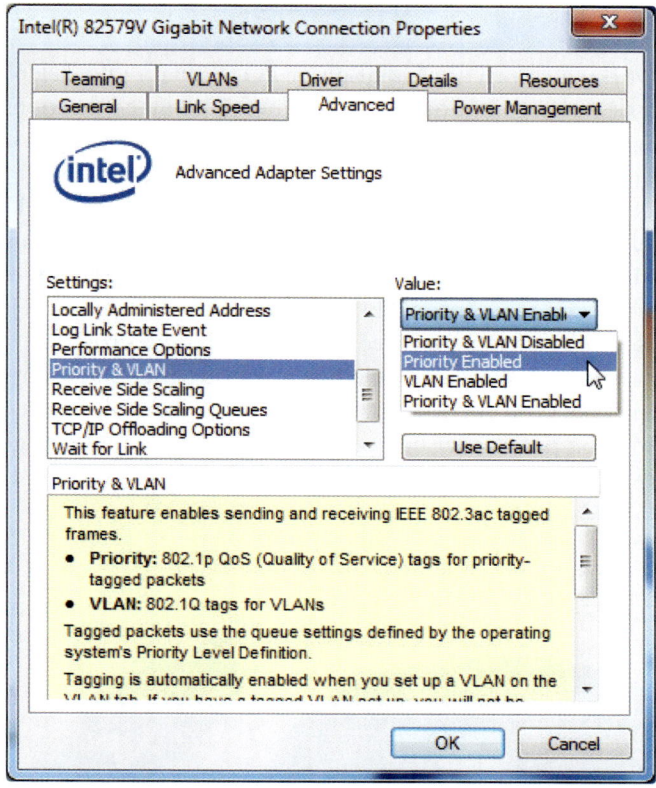

Source: Microsoft Windows 7

Figure 10-21 Select Priority Enabled to allow the network adapter to support QoS on the network

The amount of power that reaches a device degrades with the length of the cable. Most high-quality switches provide PoE. Figure 10-22 shows a PoE switch and a splitter used to provide power to a non-PoE access point. When setting up a device to receive power by PoE, make sure the device sending the power, the splitter, and the device receiving the power are all compatible. Pay special attention to the voltage and wattage requirements and the type of power connector of the receiving device.

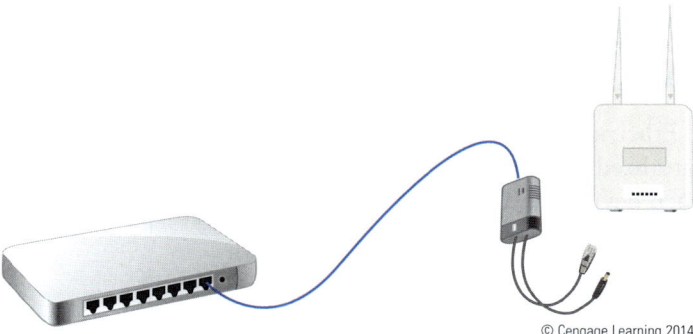

© Cengage Learning 2014

Figure 10-22 Use a PoE splitter if the receiving device is not PoE compatible

DIAL-UP MODEMS

A+
220-801
1.4, 1.11,
2.1, 2.2,
2.9

Of all the types of networking connections, dial-up or POTS (Plain Old Telephone Service) is the least expensive and slowest connection to the Internet. Dial-up connections are painfully slow, but many times we still need them when traveling, and they're good at home when our broadband connection is down or when we just plain want to save money.

Modem cards in desktop computers provide two phone jacks, called **RJ-11 jacks**, so that one can be used for dial-up networking and the other jack can be used to plug in an extension telephone. Figure 10-23 shows a modem card that comes bundled with drivers on CD and a phone cord. Phone cords are a type of twisted-pair cable and use an RJ-11 connector. **Twisted-pair cabling** uses pairs of wires twisted together to reduce crosstalk. The RJ-11 jack has four connectors, and a phone cord can have one or two twisted pairs for a total of two or four wires in the cord. The cord carries power on the lines that can be used to power a simple telephone. Laptop computers that have embedded modem capability generally have only a single phone jack. Dial-up standards are no longer being revised, and the last dial-up modem standard is the V.92 standard.

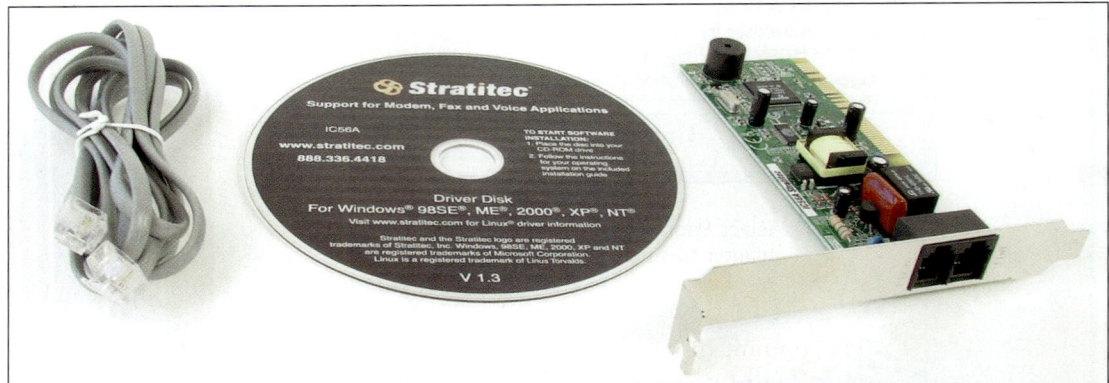

Figure 10-23 This 56K V.92 PCI modem card comes bundled with a phone cord and setup CD

When installing a modem card, be sure to follow manufacturer directions. Most directions say to install the drivers on CD before you physically install the modem. How to configure a modem card and set up a dial-up connection are covered in Chapter 9.

SWITCHES AND HUBS

A+
220-801
1.11,
2.1, 2.2,
2.9

Recall that today's Ethernet networks use a star bus topology whereby nodes are connected to one or more centralized devices (refer to Figure 10-2). This centralized device can be a switch or a hub. Each device handles a network packet or frame differently.

> **Notes** In Chapter 9, you learned about packets, which are segments of data sent over a TCP/IP network with IP address header information added. Just before a packet is put on the network, the network adapter adds additional information to the beginning and end of the packet, and this information includes the source and destination MAC addresses. The packet, with this additional information is now called a frame.

Here are the differences between a hub and a switch:

▲ An Ethernet **hub** transmits the data frame to every device, except the device that sent the frame, as shown in Figure 10-24. A hub is just a pass-through and distribution point for every device connected to it, without regard for what kind of data is passing through and where the data might be going. Hubs are outdated technology, having been replaced by switches. Figure 10-25 shows a hub that supports 10 Mbps and 100 Mbps Ethernet speeds.

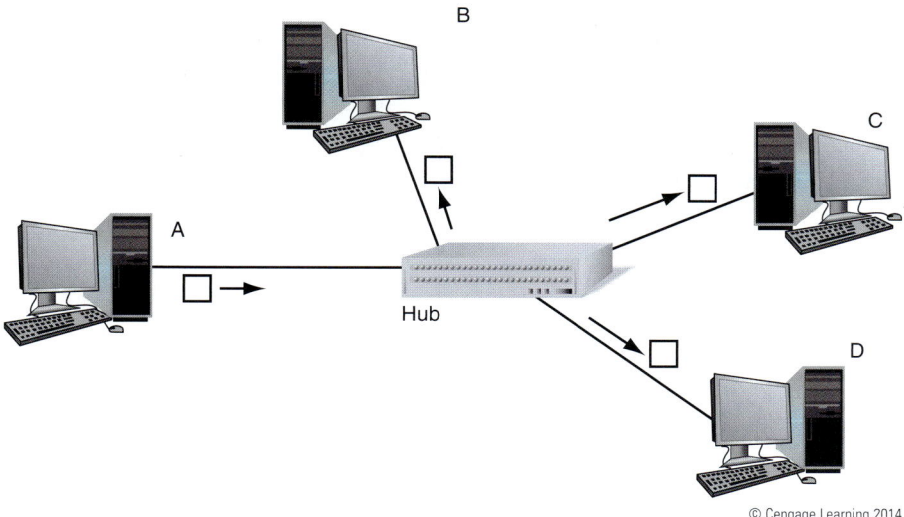

Figure 10-24 Any data received by a hub is replicated and passed on to all other devices connected to it

Figure 10-25 A hub is a pass-through device to connect nodes on a network

▲ A **switch** (see Figure 10-26) is smarter and more efficient than a hub because it keeps a table of all the MAC addresses for devices connected to it. When the switch receives a frame, it searches its MAC address table for the destination MAC address of the frame and sends the frame only to the device or interface using this MAC address. At first, a switch does not know the MAC addresses of every device connected to it. It learns this information as it receives frames and records the source MAC addresses in its MAC address table. When it receives a frame destined to a MAC address not in its table, the switch acts like a hub and broadcasts the frame to all devices except the one that sent it.

across the bridge if it knows that the frame is addressed to a destination on its own segment. Figure 10-28 demonstrates the concept of a network bridge. (Logically, you can think of a switch as a multi port bridge.)

Figure 10-28 A bridge is an intelligent device making decisions concerning network traffic

Similar to a switch, a bridge at first does not know which nodes are on each network segment. It learns that information by maintaining a table of MAC addresses from information it collects from each frame that arrives at the bridge. Eventually, it learns which nodes are on which network segment and becomes more efficient at preventing frames from getting on the wrong segment, which can bog down network traffic.

> **A+ Exam Tip** The A+ 220-801 exam expects you to know the functions and features of a hub, switch, router, access point, bridge, modem, NAS, firewall, VoIP phone, and Internet appliance.

OTHER NETWORK DEVICES

Here are a few more network devices that you might encounter as you support small networks:

- *Network Attached Storage (NAS) device.* You saw an example of a Network Attached Storage (NAS) device in Chapter 8 in Figure 8-29. The enclosure provides four bays for hard drives and an Ethernet port to connect to the network and supports RAID. NAS enclosures might provide many more drive bays and almost always support RAID.
- *VoIP phone.* VoIP (Voice over Internet Protocol) is a TCP/IP protocol that manages voice communication over the Internet. A VoIP phone connects directly to a network by way of an Ethernet port or an embedded Ethernet cable (see Figure 10-29). A VoIP phone uses firmware to configure its TCP/IP settings (including its IP address) and the phone number assigned to the phone.
- *Internet appliance.* An Internet appliance is a type of thin client that is designed to make it easy for a user to connect to the Internet, browse the web, use email, and perform other simple chores on the Internet. They were sold several years ago, but hard to find today, primarily because a low-end netbook or tablet doesn't cost that much compared to what an Internet appliance would cost today.

Figure 10-29 This VoIP digital telephone connects to a local network and on to the Internet by way of a network cable

ETHERNET CABLES AND CONNECTORS

Several variations of Ethernet cables and connectors have evolved over the years and are primarily identified by their speeds and the types of connectors used to wire these networks. Table 10-2 compares cable types and Ethernet versions.

> **A+ Exam Tip** The A+ 220-801 exam expects you to know the details shown in Table 10-2.

Cable System	Speed	Cables and Connectors	Example of Connectors	Maximum Cable Length
10Base2 (ThinNet)	10 Mbps	Coaxial cable uses a BNC connector.		185 meters or 607 feet
10Base5 (ThickNet)	10 Mbps	Coaxial uses an AUI 15-pin D-shaped connector.		500 meters or 1,640 feet
10BaseT, 100BaseT (Fast Ethernet), 1000BaseT (Gigabit Ethernet), and 10GBaseT (10-Gigabit Ethernet)	10 Mbps, 100 Mbps, 1 Gbps, or 10 Gbps	Twisted pair (UTP or STP) uses an RJ-45 connector.		100 meters or 328 feet

Table 10-2 Variations of Ethernet and Ethernet cabling (continues)

Hardware Used by Local Networks

Cable System	Speed	Cables and Connectors	Example of Connectors	Maximum Cable Length
10BaseF, 10BaseFL, 100BaseFL, 100BaseFX, 1000BaseFX, or 1000BaseX (fiber optic)	10 Mbps, 100 Mbps, 1 Gbps, or 10 Gbps	Fiber-optic cable uses ST or SC connectors (shown to the right) or LC and MT-RJ connectors (not shown).	Courtesy of Black Box Corporation	Up to 2 kilometers (6,562 feet)

Table 10-2 Variations of Ethernet and Ethernet cabling (continued)

As you can see from Table 10-2, the three main types of cabling used by Ethernet are twisted-pair, coaxial, and fiber optic. Coaxial cable is older and almost never used today. Within each category, there are several variations:

▲ *Twisted-pair cable*. Twisted-pair cable is the most popular cabling method for local networks, and uses an RJ-45 connector. The cable comes in two varieties: **unshielded twisted pair (UTP) cable** and **shielded twisted pair (STP) cable**. UTP cable is the least expensive and is commonly used on LANs. UTP is rated by category: **CAT-3 (Category 3)** is less expensive than the more popular **CAT-5** cable or **enhanced CAT-5 (CAT-5e)**. **CAT-6** has less crosstalk than CAT-5 or CAT-5e because it has a plastic core that keeps the twisted pairs separated. Always use CAT-5e or CAT-6 for Gigabit Ethernet. **CAT-6a** is thicker than CAT-6 and used by 10GBase-T (10-Gigabit Ethernet).

Figure 10-30 shows unshielded twisted pair cables and the RJ-45 connector. Twisted-pair cable has four pairs of twisted wires for a total of eight wires. You learn more about how the eight wires are arranged later in the chapter.

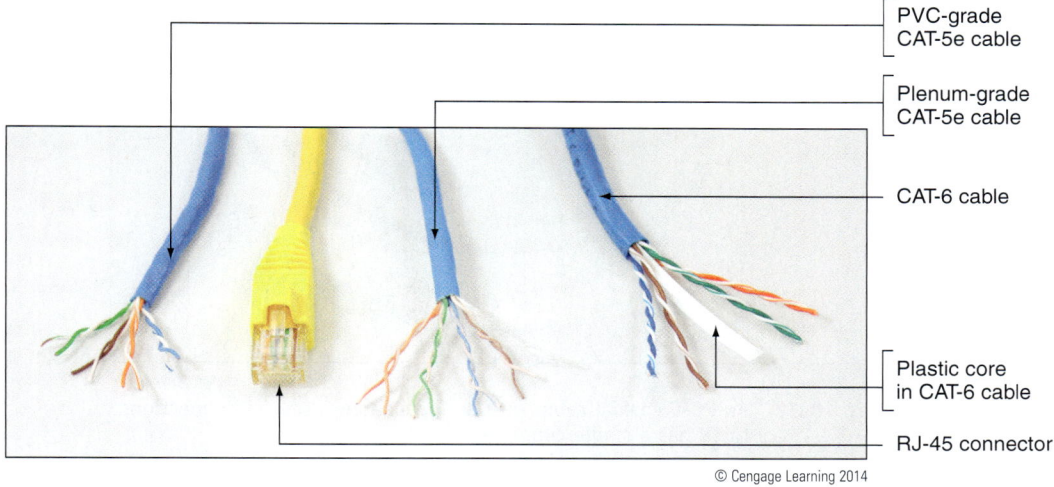

Figure 10-30 Unshielded twisted-pair cables and RJ-45 connector used for local wired networks

STP cable uses a covering or shield around each pair of wires inside the cable that protects it from electromagnetic interference caused by electrical motors, transmitters, or high-tension lines. It costs more than unshielded cable, so it's used only when the situation demands it.

> **Notes** Normally, the plastic covering of a cable is made of PVC (polyvinyl chloride), which is not safe when used inside plenums (areas between the floors of buildings). In these situations, plenum cable covered with Teflon is used because it does not give off toxic fumes when burned. Plenum cable is two or three times more expensive than PVC cable. Figure 10-30 shows plenum cable and PVC cable, which are unshielded twisted pair cables.

▲ *Coaxial cable.* Coaxial cable has a single copper wire down the middle and a braided shield around it (see Figure 10-31). The cable is stiff and difficult to manage, and is no longer used for networking. RG-6 coaxial cable is used for cable TV, having replaced the older and thinner RG-59 coaxial cable once used for cable TV. RG-6 cables use an F connector shown in Figure 10-32.

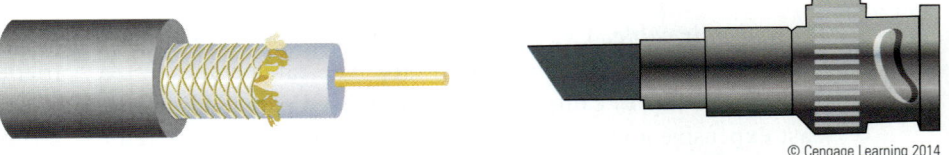

Figure 10-31 Coaxial cable and a BNC connector are used with ThinNet Ethernet

Figure 10-32 An RG-6 coaxial cable with an F connector used for connections to TV has a single copper wire

> **A+ Exam Tip** The A+ 220-801 exam expects you to know about these cables and connectors: BNC, RJ-45, coaxial, SC, ST, LC, RJ-11, F-connector, STP, UTP, CAT-3, CAT-5, CAT-5e, CAT-6, plenum, PVC, RG-6, and RG-59.

▲ *Fiber optic.* **Fiber-optic cables** transmit signals as pulses of light over glass or plastic strands inside protected tubing, as illustrated in Figure 10-33. Fiber-optic cable comes in two types: single-mode (thin, difficult to connect, expensive, and best performing) and multimode (most popular). A single-mode cable uses a single path for light to travel in the cable and multimode cable uses multiple paths for light. Both single-mode and multimode fiber-optic cables can be constructed as loose-tube cables for outdoor use or tight-buffered cables for indoor or outdoor use. Loose-tube cables are filled with gel to prevent water from soaking into the cable, and tight-buffered cables are filled with yarn to protect the fiber-optic strands, as shown in Figure 10-33.

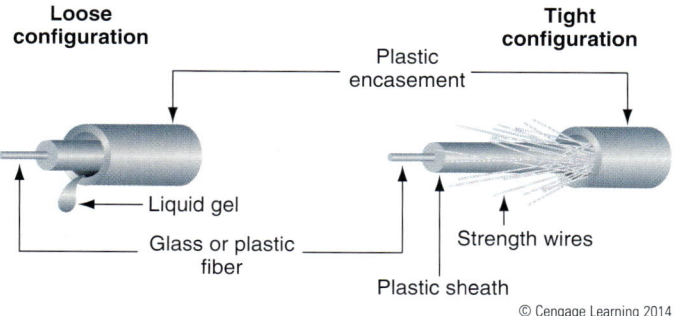

Figure 10-33 Fiber-optic cables contain a glass or plastic core for transmitting light

Fiber-optic cables can use one of four connectors, all shown in Figure 10-34. The two older types are **ST (straight tip) connectors** and **SC (subscriber connector or standard connector) connectors**. Two newer types are **LC (local connector) connectors** and **MT-RJ (mechanical transfer registered jack) connectors**. Any one of the four connectors can be used with either single-mode or multimode fiber-optic cable.

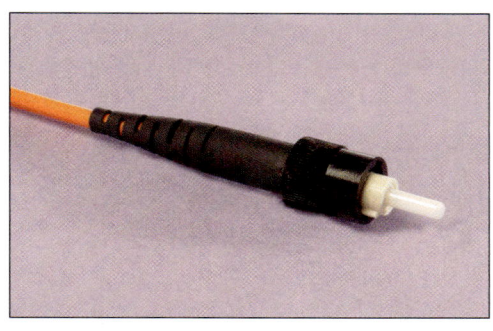

(a) ST (straight tip)

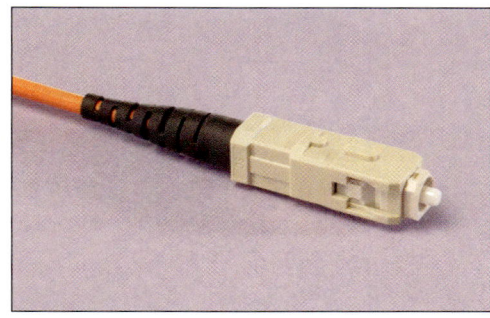

(b) SC (standard connector)

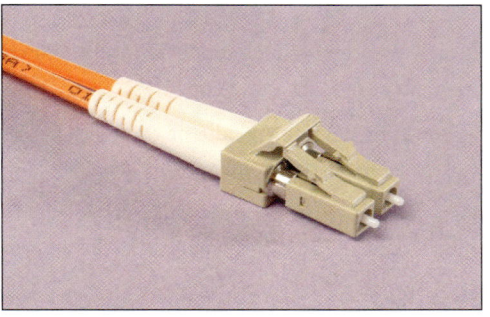

(c) LC (local connector)

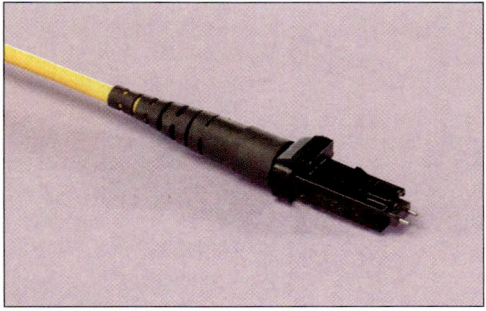

(d) MT-RJ (mechanical transfer RJ)

Courtesy Fiber Communications, Inc.

Figure 10-34 Four types of fiber-optic connectors: (a) ST, (b) SC, (c) LC, and (d) MT-RJ

A+
220-801
1.11,
2.1, 2.2,
2.9

Recall that Ethernet can run at four speeds. Each version of Ethernet can use more than one cabling method. Here is a brief description of the transmission speeds and the cabling methods they use:

- *10-Mbps Ethernet.* This first Ethernet specification was invented by Xerox Corporation in the 1970s, and later became known as Ethernet.
- *100-Mbps Ethernet or Fast Ethernet.* This improved version of Ethernet (sometimes called **100BaseT** or **Fast Ethernet**) operates at 100 Mbps and uses STP or UTP cabling rated CAT-5 or higher. 100BaseT networks can support slower speeds of 10 Mbps so that devices that run at either 10 Mbps or 100 Mbps can coexist on the same LAN. Two variations of 100BaseT are 100BaseTX and 100BaseFX. The most popular variation is 100BaseTX. 100BaseFX uses fiber-optic cable.
- *1000-Mbps Ethernet or Gigabit Ethernet.* This version of Ethernet operates at 1000 Mbps and uses twisted-pair cable and fiber-optic cable. **Gigabit Ethernet** is becoming the most popular choice for LAN technology. Because it can use the same cabling and connectors as Fast Ethernet, a company can upgrade from Fast Ethernet to Gigabit without rewiring the network.
- *10-Gigabit Ethernet.* This version of Ethernet operates at 10 billion bits per second (10 Gbps) and uses fiber-optic cable. It can be used on LANs, MANs, and WANs, and is also a good choice for backbone networks. (A backbone network is a channel whereby local networks can connect to wide area networks or to each other.)

Hands-on | Project 10-2   Research a Network Upgrade

A PC support technician is often called on to research equipment to maintain or improve a computer or network and make recommendations for purchase. Suppose you are asked to upgrade a small network that consists of one switch and four computers from 100BaseT to Gigabit Ethernet. The switch connects to a router that already supports Gigabit Ethernet. Do the following to price the hardware needed for this upgrade:

1. Find three switches by different manufacturers that support Gigabit Ethernet and have at least five ports. Save or print the web pages describing each switch.
2. Compare the features and prices of the three switches. What additional information might you want to know before you make your recommendation for a small business network?
3. Find three network adapters by different manufacturers to install in the desktop computers to support Gigabit Ethernet. Save or print web pages for each NIC.
4. Compare features of the three network adapters. What additional information do you need to know before you make your recommendation?
5. Make your recommendations based on the moderate (middle of the road) choices. What is the total price of the upgrade, including one switch and four network adapters?
6. What is one more question you need to have answered about other equipment before you can complete the price of the upgrade? Explain how you would find the answer to your question.

SETTING UP AND TROUBLESHOOTING NETWORK WIRING

**A+ 220-801
1.11, 2.1, 2.10**

**A+ 220-802
4.5**

To set up a small network, you'll need computers, switches, network cables, a router, and whatever device (for example, a DSL or cable modem) that provides Internet access. Some network cables might be wired inside walls of your building with wall jacks that use RJ-45 ports. These cables might converge in an electrical closet or server room. If network cables are lying on the floor, be sure to install them against the wall so they won't be a trip hazard. Take care that cables don't exceed the recommended length (100 meters for twisted pair). For best results, always use twisted-pair cables rated at CAT-5e or higher. (CAT-6 gives better performance than CAT-5e for Gigabit Ethernet, but it is a lot harder to wire and also more expensive.) To connect multiple computers, use switches rated at the same speed as your router and network adapters. For Gigabit speed on the entire network, you need to use all Gigabit switches and network adapters and a Gigabit router. However, if some devices run at slower speeds, most likely a switch or router can still support the higher speeds for other devices on the network.

If your router is also your wireless access point, take care in planning where to place it. Place the wireless access point near the center of the area where you want your wireless hotspot. The router also needs to have access to your cable modem or DSL modem. The modem needs access to the cable TV or phone jack where it receives service. Figure 10-35 shows a possible inexpensive wiring job where two switches and a router are used to wire two rooms for five workstations and a network printer. The only inside-wall wiring that is required is two back-to-back RJ-45 wall jacks on either side of the wall between the two rooms. The plan allows for all five desktop computers and a network printer to be wired with cabling neatly attached to the baseboards of the office without being a trip hazard.

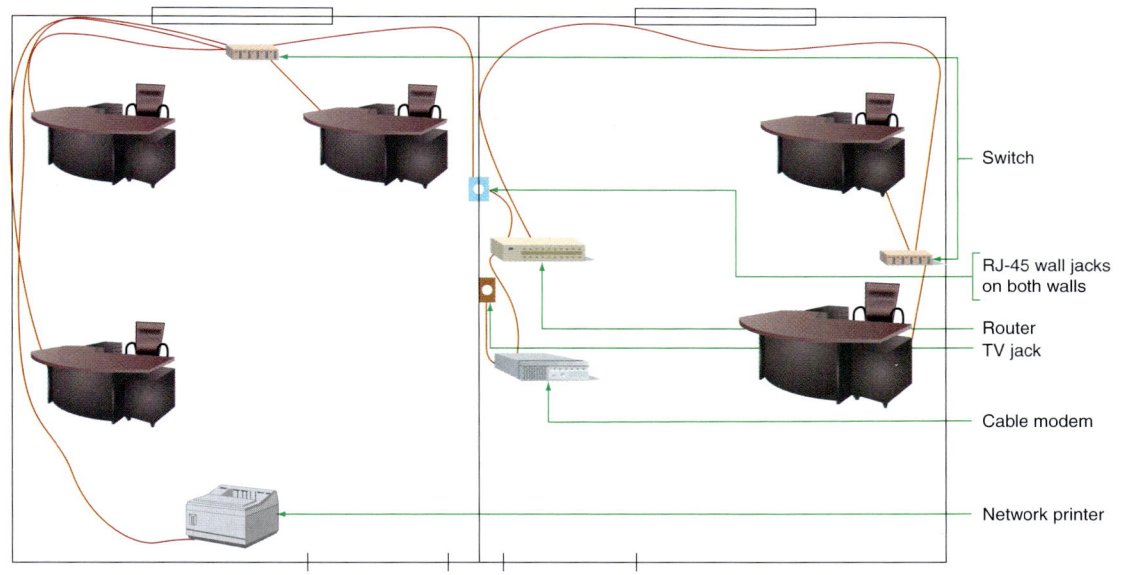

Figure 10-35 Plan the physical configuration of a small network

Let's look at the tools you need to solve problems with network cabling, the details of how a network cable is wired, and how you can create your own network cables by installing RJ-45 connectors on twisted-pair cables.

TOOLS USED BY NETWORK TECHNICIANS

Here's a list of tools a network technician might want in his or her toolbox:

▲ *Loopback plug.* A loopback plug can be used to test a network cable or port. To test a port or cable, connect one end of the cable to a network port on a computer or other device, and connect the loopback plug to the other end of the cable (see Figure 10-36). If the LED light on the loopback plug lights up, the cable and port are good. Another way to use a loopback plug is to find out which port on a switch in an electrical closet matches up with a wall jack. Plug the loopback plug into the wall jack. The connecting port on the switch in the closet lights up. When buying a loopback plug, pay attention to the Ethernet speeds it supports. Some only support 100 Mbps; others support 100 Mbps and 1000 Mbps.

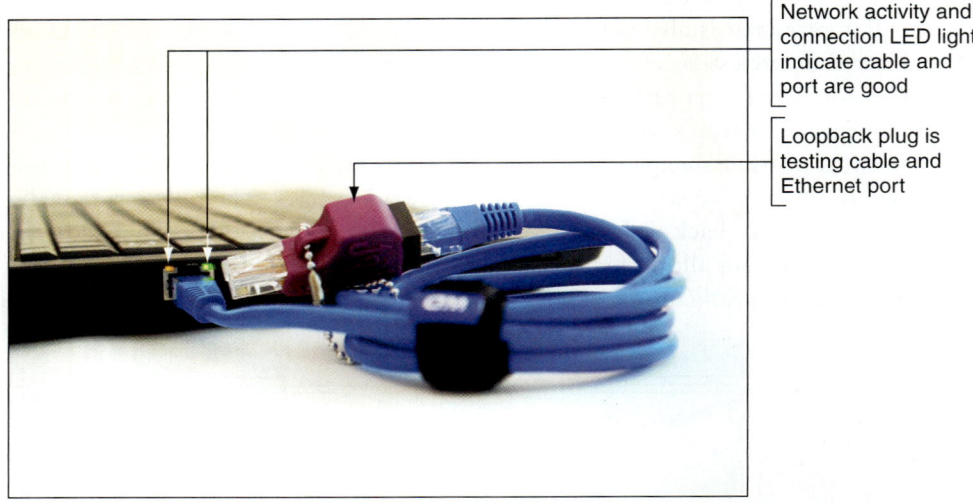

Figure 10-36 A loopback plug verifies the cable and network port are good

▲ *Cable tester.* A cable tester is used to test a cable to find out if it is good or to find out what type of cable it is if the cable is not labeled. You can also use a cable tester to locate the ends of a network cable in a building. A cable tester has two components, the remote and the base (see Figure 10-37).

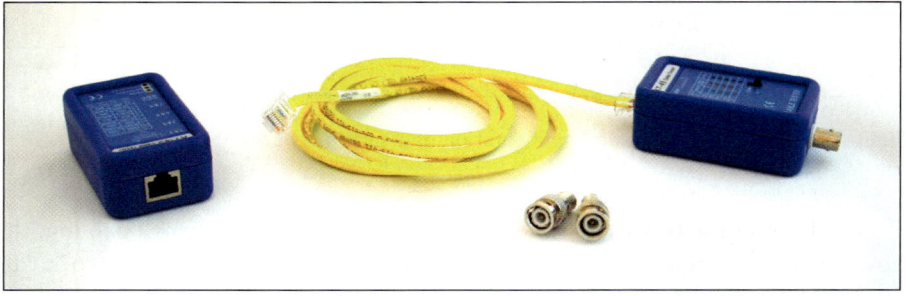

Figure 10-37 Use a cable tester pair to determine the type of cable and/or if the cable is good

A+ 220-801
1.11,
2.1, 2.10

A+ 220-802
4.5

To test a cable, connect each component to the ends of the cable and turn on the tester. Lights on the tester will show you if the cable is good and what type of cable you have. You'll need to read the user manual that comes with the cable tester to know how to interpret the lights.

You can also use the cable tester to find the two ends of a network cable installed in a building. Suppose you see several network jacks on walls in a building, but you don't know which jacks connect. Install a short cable in each of the two jacks or a jack and a port in a patch panel. Then use the cable tester base and remote to test the continuity, as shown in Figure 10-38. Whereas a loopback plug works with live cables and ports, a cable tester works on cables that are not live. You might damage a cable tester if you connect it to a live circuit, so before you start connecting the cable tester to wall jacks, be sure that you turn off all devices on the network.

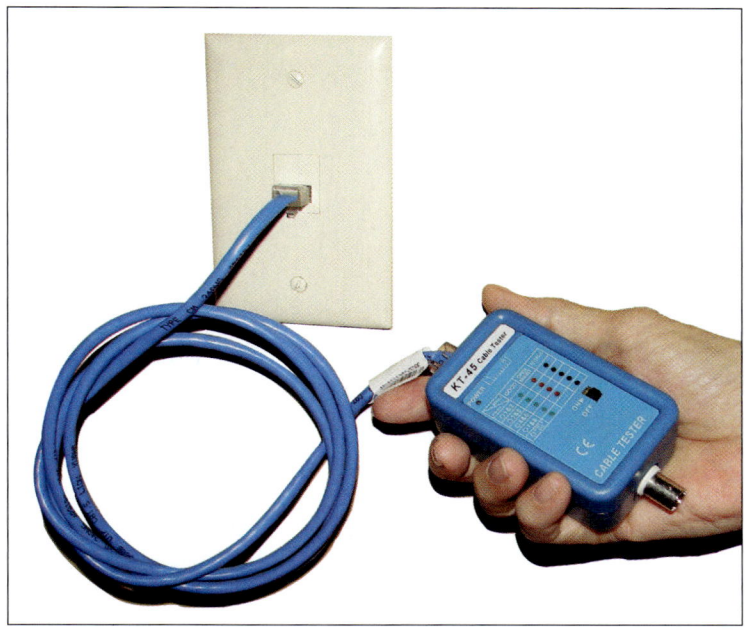

© Cengage Learning 2014

Figure 10-38 Use cable testers to find the two ends of a network cable in a building

▲ *Network multimeter.* You learned about multimeters in Chapter 1. A **network multimeter** (see Figure 10-39) is a multifunctional tool that can test cables, ports, and network adapters. When you connect it to your network, it can also detect the Ethernet speed, duplex status, default router on the network, length of a cable, voltage levels of PoE, and other network statistics and details. Many network multimeters can document test results and upload results to a PC. Good network multimeters can cost several hundred dollars.

▲ *Toner probe.* A **toner probe**, sometimes called a **tone probe**, is a two-part kit that is used to find cables in the walls of a building. See Figure 10-40. The toner connects to one end of the cable and puts out a continuous or pulsating tone on the cable. While the toner is putting out the tone, you use the probe to search the walls for the tone. The probe amplifies the tone so you hear it as a continuous or pulsating beep. The beeps get louder when you are close to the cable and weaker when you move the probe away from the cable. With a little patience, you can trace the cable through the walls. Some toners can put out tones up to 10 miles on a cable, and offer a variety of ways to connect to the cable, such as clips and RJ-45 and RJ-11 connectors.

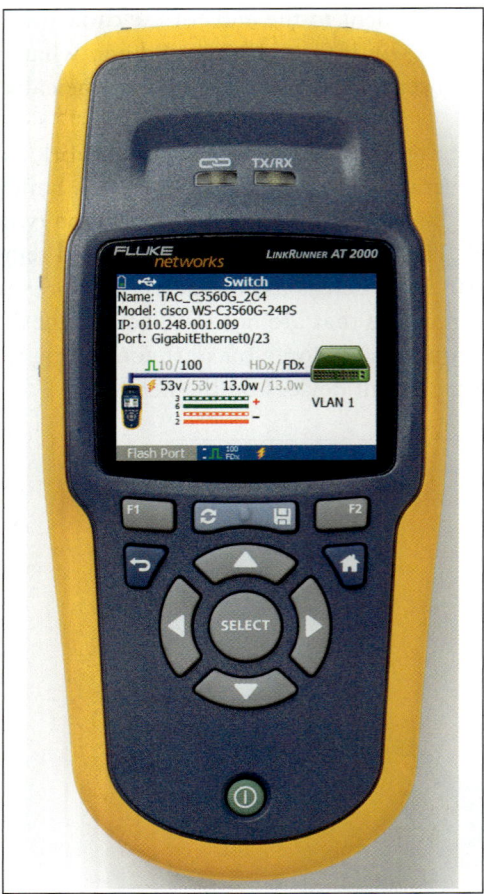

Courtesy of Fluke Corporation

Figure 10-39 The LinkRunner Pro network multimeter by Fluke Corporation works on Gigabit Ethernet networks using twisted-pair copper cabling

Figure 10-40 A toner probe kit by Fluke Corporation

Setting Up and Troubleshooting Network Wiring 495

- *Wire stripper.* A wire stripper is used to build your own network cable or repair a cable. Use the wire stripper to cut away the plastic jacket or coating around the wires inside a twisted-pair cable so that you can install a connector on the end of the cable. How to use wire strippers is covered later in the chapter.
- *Crimper.* A crimper is used to attach a terminator or connector to the end of a cable. It applies force to pinch the connector to the wires in the cable to securely make a solid connection. Figure 10-41 shows a multifunctional crimper that can crimp a RJ-45 or RJ-11 connector. It also serves double-duty as a wire cutter and wire stripper.

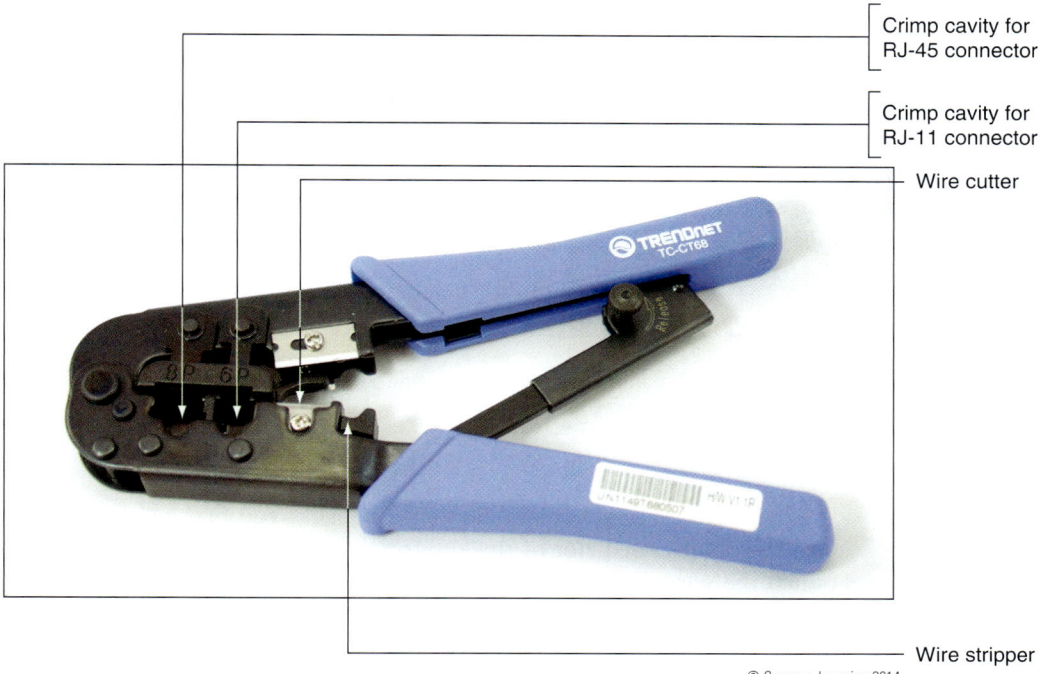

Figure 10-41 This crimper can crimp RJ-45 and RJ-11 connectors

- *Punchdown tool.* A punchdown tool, also called an impact tool (see Figure 10-42), is used to punch individual wires in a network cable into their slots in a keystone RJ-45 jack that is used in an RJ-45 wall jack. Later in the chapter, you'll learn how to use the tool with a keystone jack.

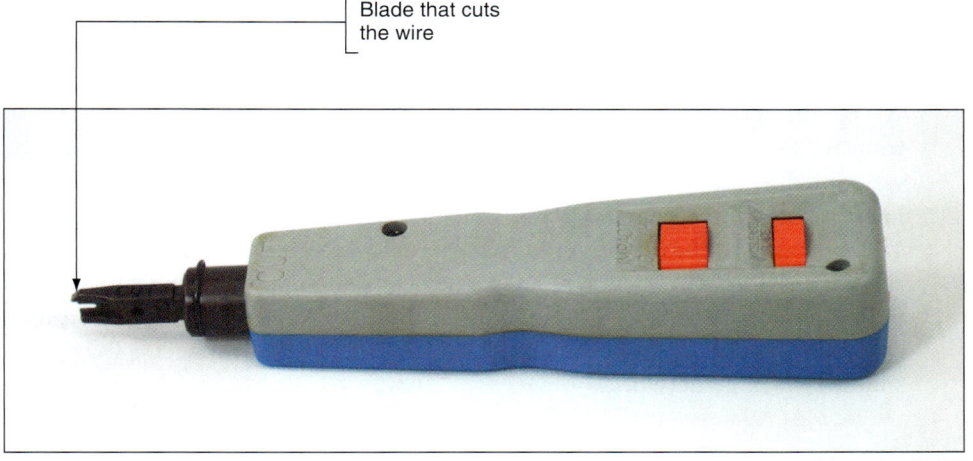

Figure 10-42 A punchdown tool forces a wire into a slot and cuts off the wire

Another use of a punchdown tool is to terminate network cables in a patch panel. A **patch panel** (see Figure 10-43) provides multiple network ports for cables that converge in one location such as an electrical closet or server room. Each port is numbered on the front of the panel. On the back side, keystone jacks are color-coded for the wires to be inserted.

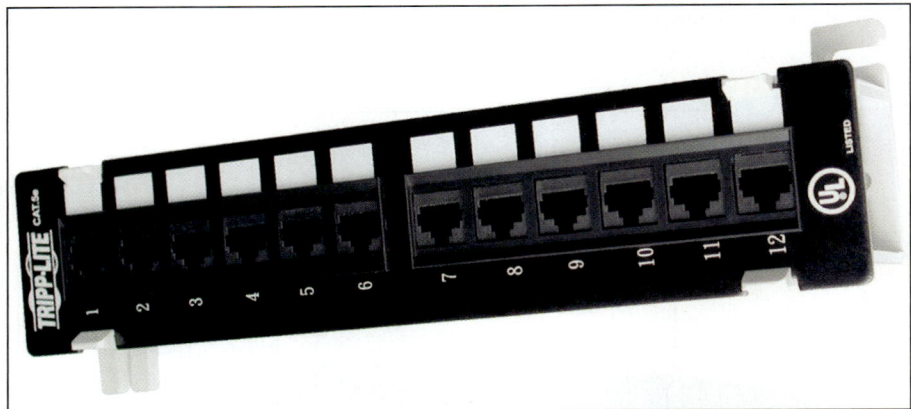

Courtesy of Tripp Lite

Figure 10-43 A patch panel provides Ethernet ports for cables converging in an electrical closet

When terminating a cable in a keystone jack, you first gently push each wire down into the color-coded slot of the keystone jack and then you use the punchdown tool to punch the wire down all the way into the slot. A small blade on the tip of one prong cuts off the wire at the side of the slot.

Now that you know about the tools you'll need to wire networks, let's see how the cables and connectors are wired.

HOW TWISTED-PAIR CABLES AND CONNECTORS ARE WIRED

Recall from Chapter 9 that two types of network cables can be used when building a network: a straight-through cable and a crossover cable. A **straight-through cable** (also called a **patch cable**) is used to connect a computer to a switch or other network device. A **crossover cable** is used to connect two like devices such as a hub to a hub or a PC to a PC (to make the simplest network of all).

The difference between a straight-through cable and a crossover cable is the way the transmit and receive lines are wired in the connectors at each end of the cables. A crossover cable has the transmit and receive lines reversed so that one device receives off the line to which the other device transmits. Before the introduction of Gigabit Ethernet, 10BaseT and 100BaseT required that a crossover cable be used to connect two like devices such as a switch to a switch. Today's devices that support Gigabit Ethernet use auto-uplinking, which means you can connect a switch to a switch using a straight-through cable. Crossover cables are seldom used today except to connect a PC to a PC to create this simple two-node network.

Twisted-pair copper wire cabling uses an RJ-45 connector that has eight pins, as shown in Figure 10-44. 10BaseT and 100BaseT Ethernet use only four of these pins: pins 1 and 2 for transmitting data and pins 3 and 6 for receiving data. The other pins can be used for phone lines or for power (PoE). Gigabit Ethernet uses all eight pins to transmit and receive data and can also transmit power on these same lines.

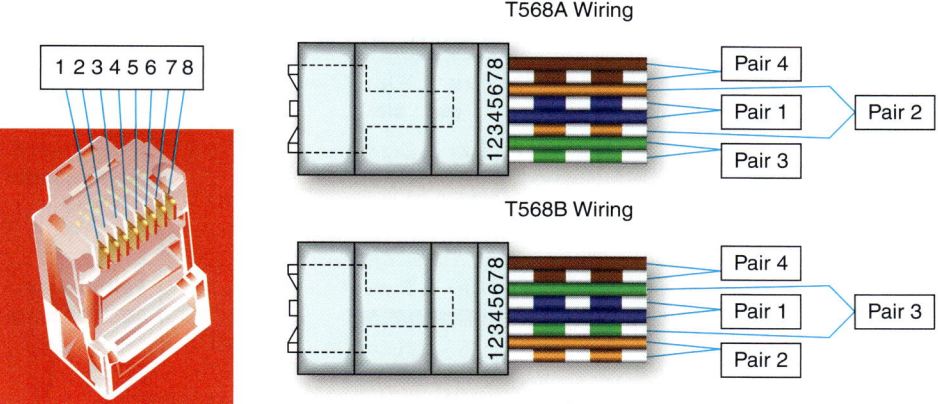

Figure 10-44 Pinouts for an RJ-45 connector

Twisted-pair cabling used with RJ-45 connectors is color-coded in four pairs, as shown in Figure 10-44. Pair 1 is blue; pair 2 is orange; pair 3 is green, and pair 4 is brown. Each pair has one solid wire and one striped wire. Two standards have been established in the industry for wiring twisted-pair cabling and RJ-45 connectors: T568A and T568B standards. Both are diagrammed in Figure 10-44 and listed in Table 10-3. The T568A standard has the green pair connected to pins 1 and 2 and the orange pair connected to pins 3 and 6. The T568B standard has the orange pair using pins 1 and 2 and the green pair using pins 3 and 6, as shown in the diagram and the table. For both standards, the blue pair uses pins 4 and 5, and the brown pair uses pins 7 and 8.

It doesn't matter which standard you use so long as you're *consistent*. The important thing is that the wiring on one end of the cable match the wiring on the other end, be it T568A or T568B standards. Either way, you have a straight-through cable.

> **Notes** The T568A and T568B standards as well as other network wiring standards and recommendations are overseen by the Telecommunications Industry Association (TIA), Electronics Industries Alliance (EIA), and American National Standards Institute (ANSI).

For 10BaseT and 100BaseT networks, if you use T568A wiring on one end of the cable and T568B on the other end of the cable, you have a crossover cable (see the diagram on the left side of Figure 10-45). For Gigabit Ethernet (1000BaseT) that transmits data on all four pairs, you must not only cross the green and orange pairs but also cross the blue and brown pairs to make a crossover cable (see the diagram on the right

Pin	100BaseT Purpose	T568A Wiring	T568B Wiring
1	Transmit+	Pair 3: White/green	Pair 2: White/orange
2	Transmit-	Pair 3: Green	Pair 2: Orange
3	Receive+	Pair 2: White/orange	Pair 3: White/green
4	(Used only on Gigabit Ethernet)	Pair 1: Blue	Pair 1: Blue
5	(Used only on Gigabit Ethernet)	Pair 1: White/blue	Pair 1: White/blue
6	Receive-	Pair 2: Orange	Pair 3: Green
7	(Used only on Gigabit Ethernet)	Pair 4: White/brown	Pair 4: White/brown
8	(Used only on Gigabit Ethernet)	Pair 4: Brown	Pair 4: Brown

Table 10-3   The T568A and T568B Ethernet standards for wiring RJ-45 connectors

side of Figure 10-45). Recall, however, that crossover cables are seldom used on Gigabit Ethernet. When you buy a crossover cable, most likely it is wired only for 10BaseT or 100BaseT networks. If you ever find yourself needing to make a crossover cable, be sure to cross all four pairs so the cable will work on 10BaseT, 100BaseT, and 1000BaseT networks. You can also buy an adapter to convert a straight-through cable to a crossover cable. But most likely the adapter only crosses two pairs and works only for 10BaseT or 100BaseT networks, such as the adapter shown in Figure 10-46.

When you are wiring a network in a building that already has network wiring, be sure to find out if the wiring is using T568A or T568B. And then be sure you always use that standard. If you don't know which to use, use T568B because it's the most common, unless, however, you are working for the U.S. government, which requires T568A for all its networking needs.

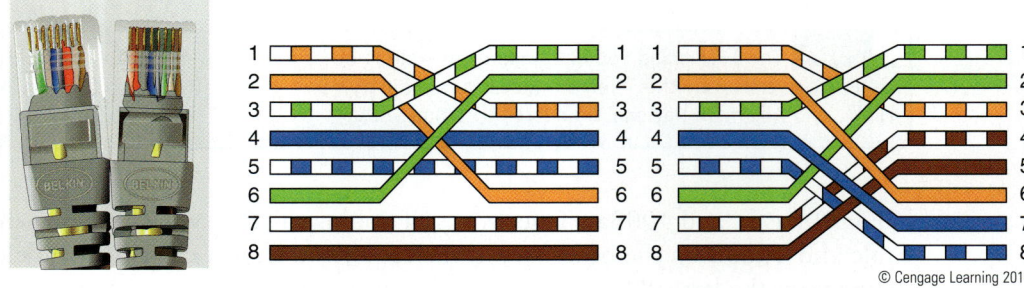

Figure 10-45   Two crossed pairs in a crossover cable is compatible with 10BaseT or 100BaseT Ethernet; four crossed pairs in a crossover cable is compatible with Gigabit Ethernet

A+
220-801
1.11,
2.1, 2.10

A+
220-802
4.5

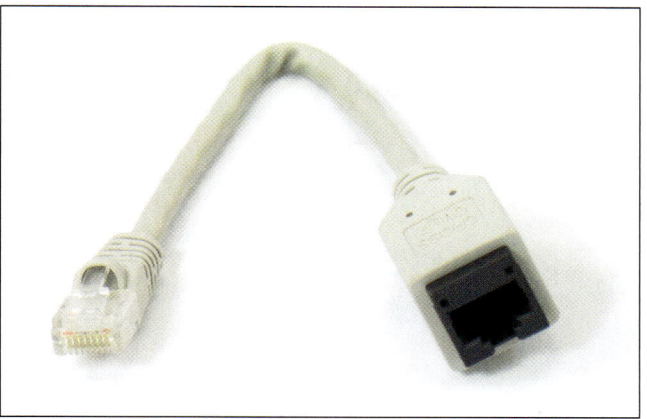

Figure 10-46 A crossover adapter converts a patch cable to a crossover cable for a 10BaseT or 100BaseT network

---

APPLYING CONCEPTS — **MAKE A STRAIGHT-THROUGH CABLE USING T568B WIRING**

It takes a little practice to make a good network straight-through cable, but you'll get the hang of it after doing only a couple of cables. Figure 10-47 shows the materials and tools you'll need to make a network cable.

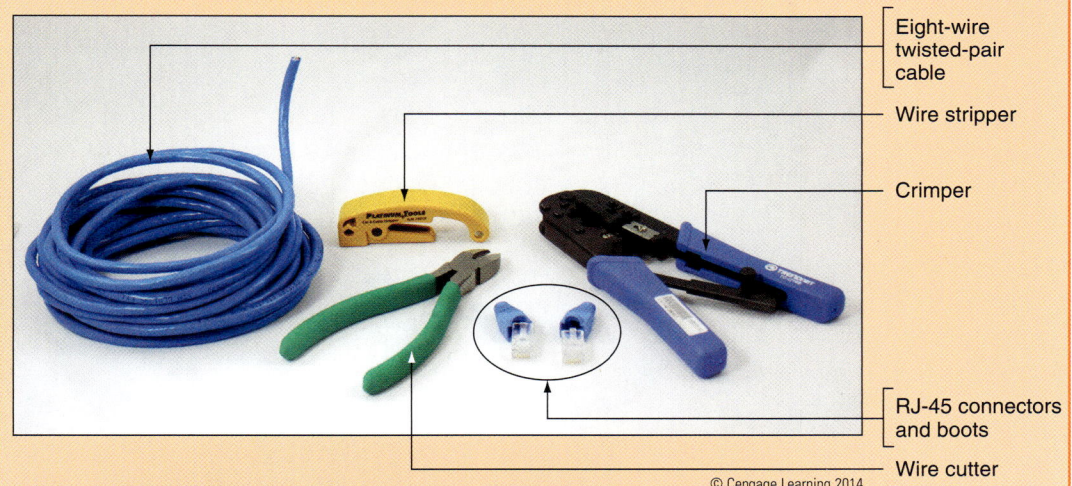

Figure 10-47 Tools and materials to make a network cable

Here are the steps to make a straight-through cable using the T568B standard.

1. Use wire cutters to cut the twisted-pair cable the correct length plus a few extra inches.
2. If your RJ-45 connectors include boots, slide two boots onto the cable.
3. Use wire strippers to strip off about two inches of the plastic jacket from the end of the wire. To do that, put the wire in the stripper and rotate the stripper around the wire to score the jacket (see Figure 10-48). You can then pull off the jacket.

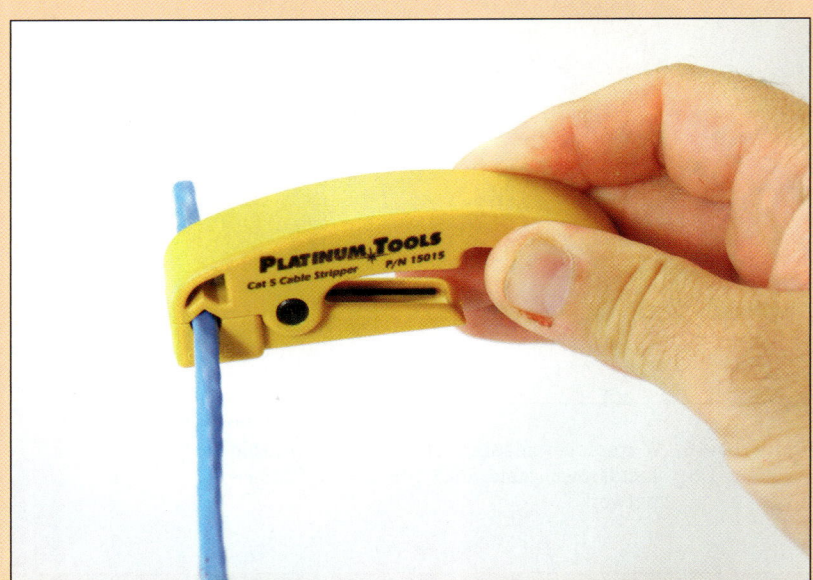

Figure 10-48 Rotate a wire stripper around the jacket to score it so you can slide it off the wire

4. Use wire cutters to start a cut into the jacket, and then use the rip cord to pull the jacket back a couple of inches (see Figure 10-49). Next, cut off the rip cord and the jacket. You take this extra precaution of removing the jacket because you might have nicked the wires with the wire strippers.

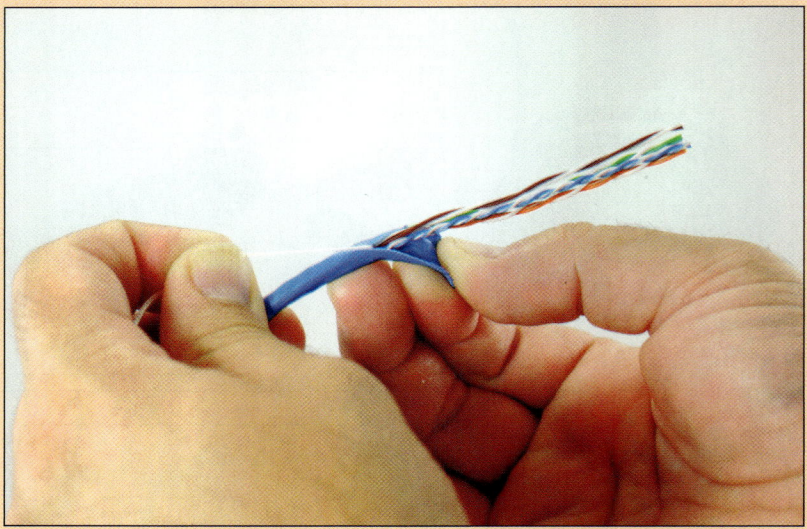

Figure 10-49 Rip back the jacket, and then cut off the extra jacket and rip cord

5. Untwist each pair of wires so you have the eight separate wires. Smooth each wire out, straightening out the kinks. Line up the wires in the T568B configuration (refer to Table 10-3).

6. Holding the tightly lined-up wires between your fingers, use wire cutters to cut the wires off evenly, leaving a little over an inch of wire. See Figure 10-50. To know how short to cut the wires, hold the RJ-45 connector up to the wires. The wires must go all the way to the front of the connector. The jacket must go far enough into the connector so that the crimp at the back of the connector will be able to solidly pinch the jacket.

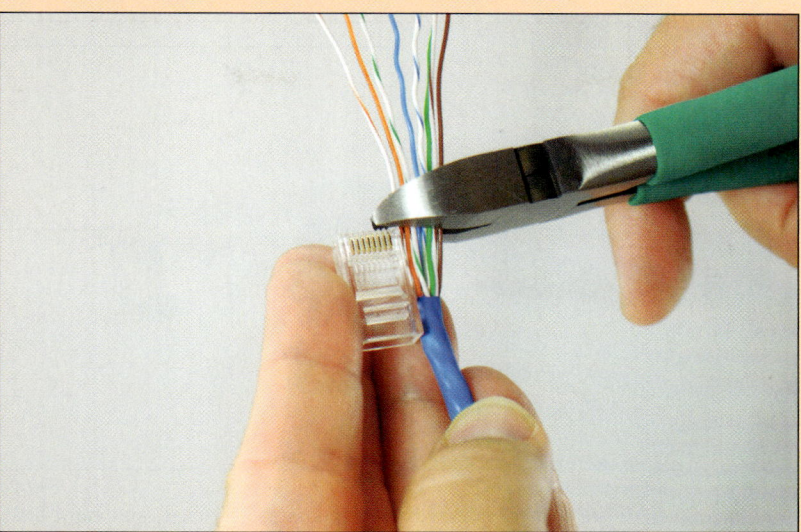

Figure 10-50   Evenly cut off wires measured to fit in the RJ-45 connector with the jacket protruding into the connector

7. Be sure you have pin 1 of the connector lined up with the orange and white wire. Then insert the eight wires in the RJ-45 connector. Guide the wires into the connector, making sure they reach all the way to the front. (It helps to push up a bit as you push the wires into the connector.) You can jam the jacket firmly into the connector. Look through the clear plastic connector to make sure the wires are lined up correctly and they all reach the front and that the jacket goes past the crimp.

8. Insert the connector into the crimper tool. Use one hand to push the connector firmly into the crimper as you use the other hand to crimp the connector. See Figure 10-51. Use plenty of force to crimp. The eight blades at the front of the connector must pierce through to each copper wire to complete each of the eight connections, and the crimp at the back of the connector must solidly crimp the cable jacket to secure the cable to the connector (see Figure 10-52). Remove the connector from the crimper and make sure you can't pull the connector off the wire.

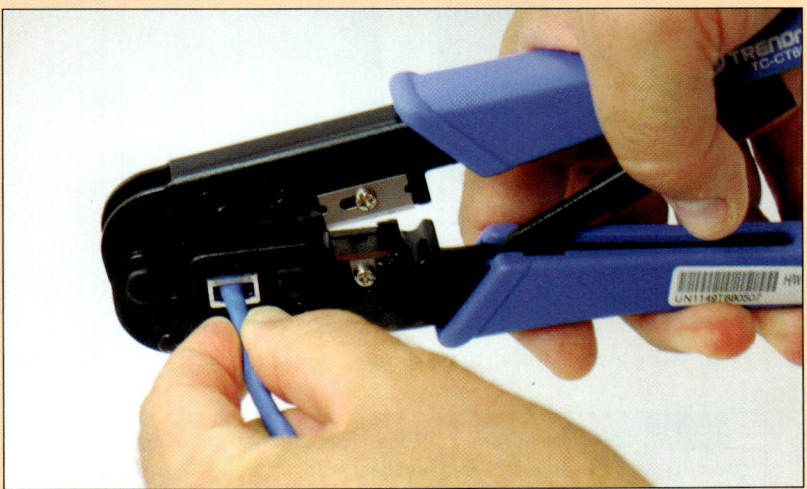

Figure 10-51   Use the crimper to crimp the connector to the cable

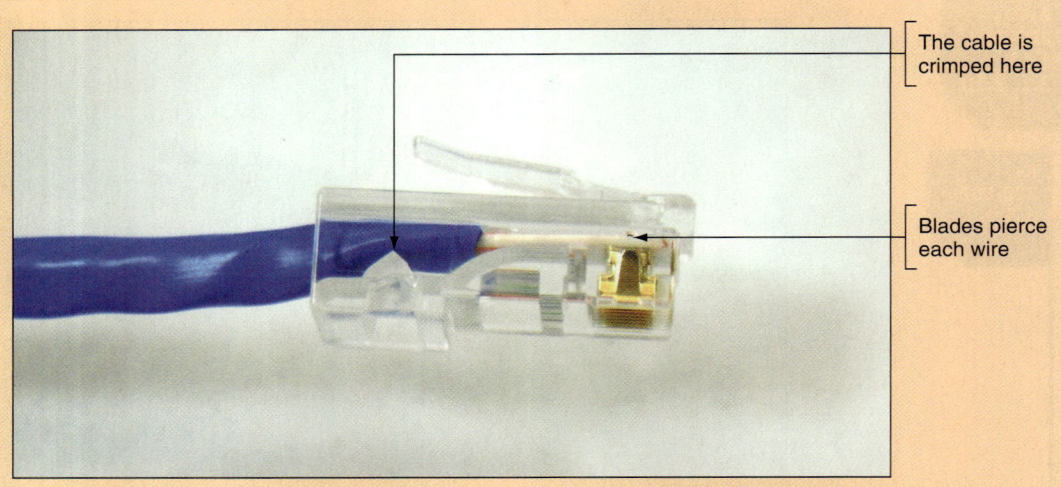

Figure 10-52 The crimper crimps the cable and cable jacket, and eight blades pierce the jacket of each individual copper wire

9. Slide the boot into place over the connector. Now you're ready to terminate the other end of the cable. Configure it to also use the T568B wiring arrangement. Figure 10-53 shows the straight-through cable with only one boot in place.

Figure 10-53 Finished patch cable with one boot in place

10. Use a cable tester to make sure the cable is good.

> **Notes** You'll find several YouTube videos on network wiring. An excellent one of making a straight-through cable by CableSupply.com is posted at *www.youtube.com/watch?v=h7TjqnRl3QQ*.

Setting Up and Troubleshooting Network Wiring

Notes Networking standards that apply to wiring a keystone RJ-45 jack and a straight-through panel say that, to avoid crosstalk, the cable jacket should be removed to expose no more than three inches of twisted pair wires, and that exposed twisted-pair wires should be untwisted no more than a half inch.

APPLYING CONCEPTS — WIRE A KEYSTONE JACK

A keystone RJ-45 jack is used in a network wall jack. Here are the instructions to wire one:

1. Using a wire stripper and wire cutter, strip and trim back the jacket from the twisted-pair wire, leaving about two inches of wire exposed. Untwist the wires only so far as necessary so each wire can be inserted in the color-coded slot in the jack. The twists are needed to prevent crosstalk, and the untwisted wire should be no longer than a half inch. Figure 10-54 shows the wires in position for T568B wiring. Notice how the cable jacket goes into the keystone jack.

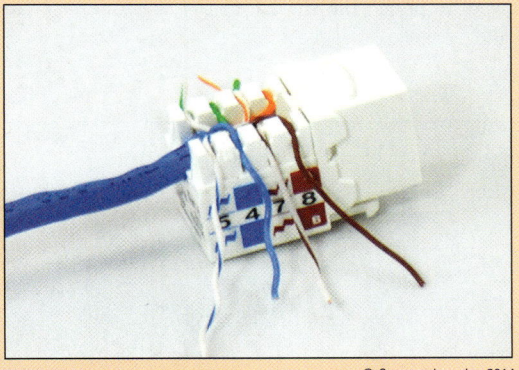 

Figure 10-54 Eight wires are in position in a keystone jack for T568B wiring

2. Using the punchdown tool, make sure the blade side of the tool is on the outside of the jack. (The punchdown tool has Cut embedded on the blade side of the tool.) Push down with force to punch each wire into its slot and cut off the wire on the outside edge of the slot. It might take a couple of punches to do the job. See the left side of Figure 10-55. Place the jack cover over the jack, as shown in the right side of Figure 10-55.

3. The jack can now be inserted into the back side of a wall faceplate (see Figure 10-56). Make sure the wires in the jack are at the top of the jack. If you look closely at the faceplate, you can see the arrow pointing up. It's important the wires in the jack be at the top so that over the years dust doesn't settle on these wires. Use screws to secure the faceplate to the wall receptacle. Be sure to use a cable tester to check the network cable from its jack to the other end to make sure the wiring is good. When wiring a building, testing the cable and its two connections is called certifying the cable.

A+ 220-801 1.11, 2.1, 2.10

A+ 220-802 4.5

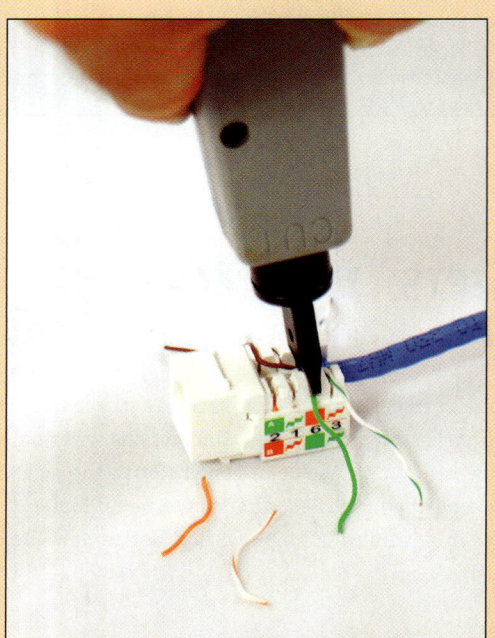
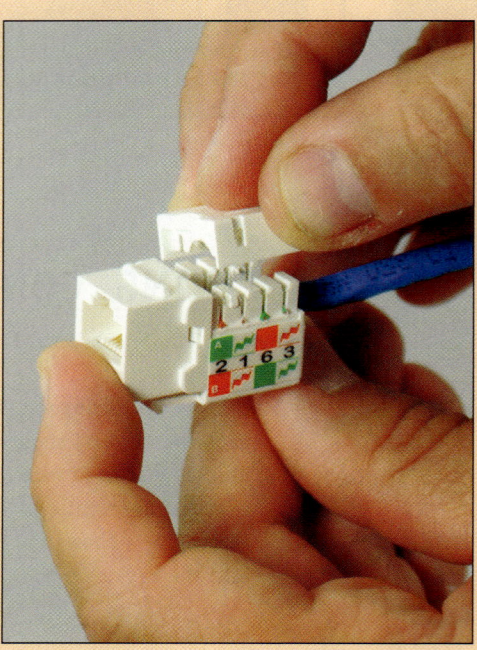

Figure 10-55 Use a punchdown tool to punch the wires into the keystone jack, and then place the cover in position

Figure 10-56 Insert the jack in the faceplate, making sure the wire connectors are at the top of the jack

> **Notes** To see a video by CableSupply.com of using a punchdown tool to make an RJ-45 keystone jack, see *www.youtube.com/watch?v=sHy8mtW9eak*.

Setting Up and Troubleshooting Network Wiring

Let's wrap up the chapter with some guidelines to follow when troubleshooting a network problem related to hardware. The process is outlined in Figure 10-57 and listed here:

1. First check the status indicator lights on the network ports for connectivity and activity.
2. Use a loopback plug to verify each port. The loopback plug can work on ports provided by a computer, wall jack, patch panel, switch, router, or other device that is turned on. If you find a bad port, try a different port on a switch, router, or patch panel. You might need to replace the device.

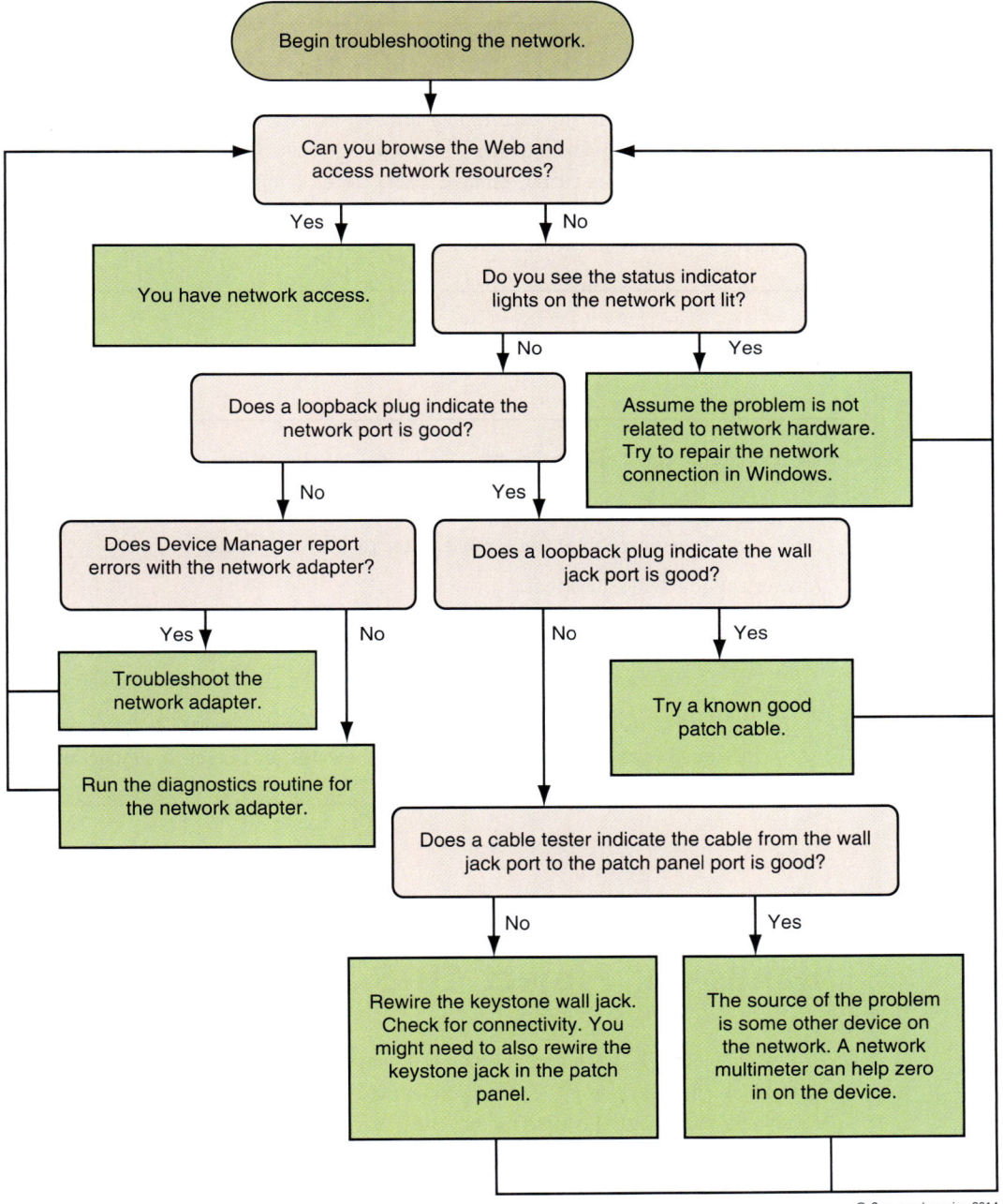

Figure 10-57 Flowchart to troubleshoot networking problems related to hardware

A+
220-801
1.11,
2.1, 2.10

A+
220-802
4.5

3. For short straight-through cables connecting a computer to a wall jack or other nearby device, exchanging the straight-through cable for a known good one is easier and quicker than using a cable tester to test the cable.

4. Use a cable tester to verify a cable permanently installed alongside or inside a wall is good. To test the cable, you have to first disconnect it from a computer, patch panel, switch, or other device at both ends of the cable. Common problems with networks are poorly wired termination in patch panels and wall jacks. If the cable proves bad, first try reinstalling the two jacks before you replace the cable.

Hands-on | Project 10-3   Research Network Tools

Use the web to research the features and prices for the network tools you learned about in this chapter that you can include among your PC repair tools. Suppose you have a budget of $200 to buy a wire stripper, wire cutter, crimper, cable tester, loopback plug, punchdown tool, toner probe, and/or network multimeter. Save or print web pages showing the features and price of each tool you select for your toolkit. Which, if any tools, did you decide to not purchase? Why?

Hands-on | Project 10-4   Make Network Cables

Using the tools and skills you learned about in this chapter, practice making a straight-through cable and a crossover cable. Use a cable tester to test both cables.

Answer the following questions:

1. Which wiring standard did you use for the straight-through cable? List the pinouts (pin number and wire color) for each of the eight pins on each connector.

2. Will your crossover cable work on a Gigabit Ethernet network? List the pinouts (pin number and wire color) for each of the eight pins on each connector.

Hands-on | Project 10-5   Network Two Computers Using a Crossover Cable

In Real Problem 9-1 at the end of Chapter 9, you used a crossover cable to connect two computers in a simple network. Using the skills you learned in Chapter 9, again connect two computers in a simple network, but this time use the crossover cable you just made. What are the Ethernet speeds that each computer supports? Which speed is the network using? Verify the network connectivity by copying a file from one computer to the other.

>> CHAPTER SUMMARY

Network Types and Topologies

- Networks are categorized in size as a PAN, LAN, Wireless LAN, MAN, or WAN.
- Topologies used by a network include a mesh, ring, bus, star, and hybrid network topology. Ethernet that is used to create a LAN uses the star or hybrid (star bus) topology.
- Performance of a network technology is measured in bandwidth and latency.
- The two most popular ways to connect to the Internet are cable Internet and DSL. Other methods used include satellite, dedicated fiber optic, dial-up, and wireless technologies (a cellular WAN using 2G, 3G, 4G, WiMAX, and/or LTE).
- Technology used by cell phones that allows us to browse the web, stream music and video, play online games, and use chat and video conferencing is called 3G or 4G.

Hardware Used by Local Networks

- Networking hardware used on local networks includes network adapters, dial-up modems, hubs, switches, routers, wireless access points, bridges, cables, and connectors.
- Features used and supported by a network adapter include the slot a NIC uses, Ethernet speeds, MAC address, status indicator lights, Wake on LAN, Quality of Service (QoS), and Power over Ethernet (PoE).
- The most popular Ethernet cable is twisted pair using an RJ-45 connector. Phone lines use an RJ-11 connector.
- Switches and older hubs are used as a centralized connection for devices on a wired network. A bridge stands between two network segments and controls traffic between them.
- Other network devices include a NAS (Network Attached Storage), a VoIP phone, and older and outdated Internet appliances.
- Most wired local networks use twisted-pair cabling that can be unshielded twisted pair (UTP) cable or shielded twisted pair (STP) cable. UTP is rated by category: CAT-3, CAT-5, CAT-5e, CAT-6, and CAT-6a.

Setting Up and Troubleshooting a Small Network

- Tools used to manage and troubleshoot network wiring and connectors are a loopback plug, cable tester, multimeter, tone probe, wire stripper, crimper, and punchdown tool.
- The RJ-45 connector has eight pins. Four pins (pins 1, 2, 3, and 6) are used to transmit and send data using the 10BaseT and 100BaseT speeds. Using 1000BaseT speed, all eight pins are used for transmissions.
- Two standards used to wire network cables are T568A and T568B. The difference between the T568A and T568B standards is the orange twisted-pair wires are reversed in the RJ-45 connector from the green twisted-pair wires.
- A straight-through cable uses the T568A or T568B standard on both connectors. A crossover cable for 10BaseT or 100BaseT uses T568A for one connector and T568B for the other connector. Crossover cables are generally not used on Gigabit Ethernet networks.
- Either T568A or T568B can be used to wire a network. To avoid confusion, don't mix the two standards in a building.

- Use wire strippers, wire cutters, and a crimper to make network cables. A punchdown tool is used to terminate cables in a patch panel or keystone RJ-45 jack. Be sure to use a cable tester to test or certify a cable you have just made.

- When troubleshooting network wiring, tools that can help are status indicator lights, loopback plug, cable testers, and a network multimeter.

>> KEY TERMS

For explanations of key terms, see the Glossary near the end of the book.

100BaseT
4G (Fourth Generation)
ad hoc mode
bandwidth
base station
BNC connector
bridge
broadband
bus network
cable Internet
cable tester
CAT-3 (Category 3)
CAT-5 (Category 5)
CAT-6
CAT-6a
CDMA (Code Division Multiple Access)
coaxial cable
cellular network
cellular WAN
crimper
crossover cable
data throughput
DSL (Digital Subscriber Line)
enhanced CAT-5 (CAT-5e)
F connector
Fast Ethernet
fiber optic
fiber-optic cable
full duplex
fully connected mesh topology
Gigabit Ethernet
GSM (Global System for Mobile Communications)
half duplex
hub
hybrid network
Internet appliance
Internet Service Provider (ISP)
ISDN (Integrated Services Digital Network)
keystone RJ-45 jack
LAN (local area network)
latency
LC (local connector) connector
line-of-sight connectivity
loopback plug
MAN (metropolitan area network)
mesh network
MT-RJ (mechanical transfer registered jack) connector
network adapter
Network Attached Storage (NAS)
network interface card (NIC)
network multimeter
PAN (personal area network)
patch cable
patch panel
Power over Ethernet (PoE)
punchdown tool
RG-6 coaxial cable
RG-59 coaxial cable
ring network
RJ-11 jack
RJ-45
SC (subscriber connector or standard connector) connector
shielded twisted pair (STP) cable
SIM (Subscriber Identity Module) card
ST (straight tip) connector
star network
straight-through cable
switch
T568A
T568B
tone probe
toner probe
topology
twisted-pair cabling
unshielded twisted pair (UTP) cable
VoIP (Voice over Internet Protocol)
VoIP phone
WAN (wide area network)
wire stripper
wireless LAN (WLAN)

>> REVIEWING THE BASICS

1. What type of network topology is used when five switches are used on a small LAN and each switch connects to multiple computers on the LAN?

2. Place the following networking technologies in the order of their highest speed, from slowest to fastest: WiMAX, dial-up networking, cable Internet, Fast Ethernet, 3G

3. What is the difference between ADSL and SDSL?

4. Among satellite, cable Internet, and DSL, which technology experiences more latency?

5. When using DSL to connect to the Internet, the data transmission shares the cabling with what other technology?
6. When using cable Internet, the data transmission shares the cabling with what other technology?
7. What is the name of the port used by an Ethernet cable? What is the name of the port used by a dial-up modem?
8. If you want to upgrade your 100BaseT Ethernet network so that it will run about 10 times the current speed, what technology would you use?
9. What is the maximum length of a cable on a 100BaseT network?
10. What does the 100 in the name 100BaseT indicate?
11. Which type of networking cable is more reliable, STP or UTP? Which is used on LANs?
12. Which is more expensive, UTP CAT-5e cabling or STP CAT-5e cabling?
13. When looking at a network cable that is not labeled, describe how you can tell if the cable is a straight-through cable or a crossover cable.
14. What technology is used when power is transmitted on a network cable?
15. Describe the difference between a hub and a switch.
16. How is a wireless access point that is also a bridge more efficient in handling network traffic than a wireless access point that is not a bridge?
17. What type of cable uses an F connector?
18. Why does a CAT-6 cable have a plastic core? Which two types of cabling are recommended for Gigabit Ethernet?
19. How many wires does a CAT-5 cable have? A CAT-5e cable? A coaxial cable?
20. Which tool can you use to verify that a network port on a computer is good?
21. After making a straight-through cable, which tool can you use to certify the cable?
22. Which tool can help you find a network cable in the walls of a building?
23. Which tool is used to firmly attach an RJ-45 connector to a network cable?
24. Which tool can help you find out which wall jack connects to which port on a switch in an electrical closet?
25. Name two places where you might find a keystone RJ-45 jack in a building.
26. List the number assigned to each pair and the color of each pair used in twisted-pair networking cables.
27. What two standards are used to wire networking cables?
28. Of the two standards in Question 27, which standard is the most common? Which is required for all U.S. government installations?
29. Using either of the two wiring standards, what are the colors of the two pairs used to send and/or receive data on a 100BaseT network?
30. How many pairs of wires are crossed in a crossover cable that will work on a 100BaseT network? On a 1000BaseT network?
31. To prevent crosstalk in a keystone RJ-45 jack, what is the minimum length of wire that should be untwisted?

>> THINKING CRITICALLY

1. Linda has been assigned the job of connecting five computers to a network. The room holding the five computers has three network jacks that connect to a switch in an electrical closet down the hallway. Linda decides to install a second switch in the room. The new switch has four network ports. She uses one port to connect the switch to a wall jack. Now she has five ports available (two wall jacks and three switch ports). While installing and configuring the NICs in the five computers, she discovers that the PCs connected to the two wall jacks work fine, but the three connected to the switch refuse to communicate with the network. What could be wrong and what should she try next?

2. If a Gigabit Ethernet NIC is having a problem communicating with a 100BaseT switch that only supports half duplex, what steps can you take to manually set the NIC to the speed and duplex used by the switch? Which speed and duplex should you choose?

3. You connect a computer to an RJ-45 wall jack using a straight-through cable. When you first open the browser on the computer, you discover it does not have Internet access. Put the following steps in the correct order to troubleshoot the problem.

    a. Use a loopback plug to verify the network port on the computer.

    b. Rewire the keystone RJ-45 wall jack.

    c. Use a loopback plug to verify the network port in the wall jack.

    d. Exchange the straight-through cable for a known good one.

    e. Verify the status indicator lights on the NIC.

    f. Use a cable tester to test the network cable and termination from the switch in the electrical closet to the wall jack.

>> REAL PROBLEMS, REAL SOLUTIONS

REAL PROBLEM 10-1: Setting Up a Wireless Access Point

As a computer and networking consultant to small businesses, you are frequently asked to find solutions to increasing demands for network and Internet access at a business. One business rents offices in a historical building that has strict rules for wiring. They have come to you asking for a solution for providing Wi-Fi access to their guests in the lobby of the building. Research options for a solution and answer the following questions:

1. Print or save web pages showing two options for a Wi-Fi wireless access point that can mount on the wall or ceiling. For one option, select a device that can receive its power by PoE from the network cable run to the device. For the other option, select a device that requires an electrical cable to the device as well as a network cable.

2. Print or save two web pages for a splitter that can be mounted near the second wireless access point that splits the power from data on the network cable. Make sure the power connectors for the splitter and the access point can work together.

3. To provide PoE from the electrical closet on the network cable to the wireless access point, print or save the web page for an injector that injects power into a network cable. Make sure the voltage and wattage output for the injector are compatible with the needs of both wireless access points.

4. You estimate the distance for network cabling from the switch to the wireless access point is about 200 feet. What is the cost of 200 feet of PVC CAT-5e cabling? For 200 feet of plenum CAT-5e cabling? For 200 feet of plenum CAT-6 cabling?

5. Of the options you researched, which option do you recommend? Using this option, what is the total cost of the Wi-Fi hotspot?

CHAPTER 11

Supporting Notebooks

In this chapter, you will learn:

- About special considerations when supporting notebooks that are different from supporting desktop computers
- How to configure, optimize, and troubleshoot slots, ports, and peripheral devices used with notebooks
- How to replace and upgrade internal components in a notebook and all-in-one computer
- How to troubleshoot hardware problems with notebooks

More than half of personal computers purchased today are notebook computers, and almost 30 percent of personal computers currently in use are notebooks. As a PC service technician, you need to know how to support notebooks. In this chapter, you'll learn about supporting, upgrading, and troubleshooting notebooks and all-in-one computers.

There was a time that a notebook was considered a "black box" to PC support technicians. If it needed servicing inside, the notebook was taken to an authorized service center supported by the notebook manufacturer. These technicians were all trained by the manufacturer to service its products. However, taking apart and servicing a notebook computer are now seen as tasks that every A+ certified technician needs to know how to do. As part of your preparation to be A+ certified, try to find an old notebook computer you can take apart. If you can locate the service manual, you should be able to take it apart, repair it (assuming the parts are still available and don't cost more than the notebook is worth), and get it up and running again. Have fun with this chapter and enjoy tinkering with that old notebook!

SPECIAL CONSIDERATIONS WHEN SUPPORTING NOTEBOOKS

A **notebook**, also called a **laptop**, is designed for portability (see Figure 11-1 a and b) and can be just as powerful as a desktop computer. Notebooks use the same technology as desktops, but with modifications to use less power, take up less space, and operate on the move. Notebooks come in several varieties, including tablet PCs and netbooks. A tablet PC has more features than a notebook, including a touch screen that also allows you to handwrite on it with a stylus. Another variation of a notebook is a **netbook** that is smaller and less expensive than a notebook and has fewer features. An **all-in-one computer** (Figure 11-1c) has the monitor and computer case built together and uses components that are common to both a notebook and a desktop computer. Because all-in-one computers use many notebook components and are serviced in similar ways, we include them in this chapter.

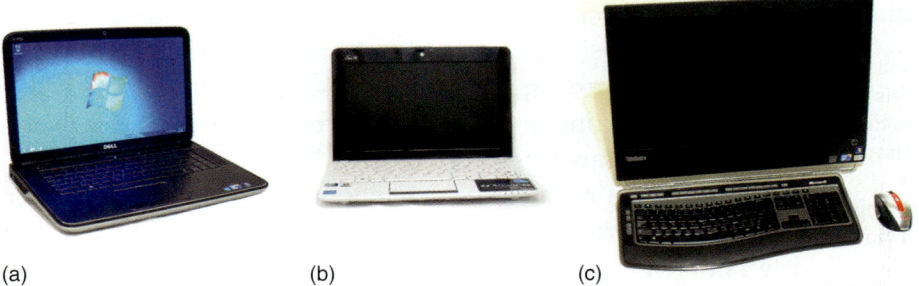

(a)　(b)　(c)

Figure 11-1 A laptop, netbook, and all-in-one computer

A notebook provides ports on its sides, back, or front for connecting peripherals (see Figure 11-2). Ports common to notebooks as well as desktop systems include USB (A male and/or B male), FireWire, network, dial-up modem (seldom seen on newer

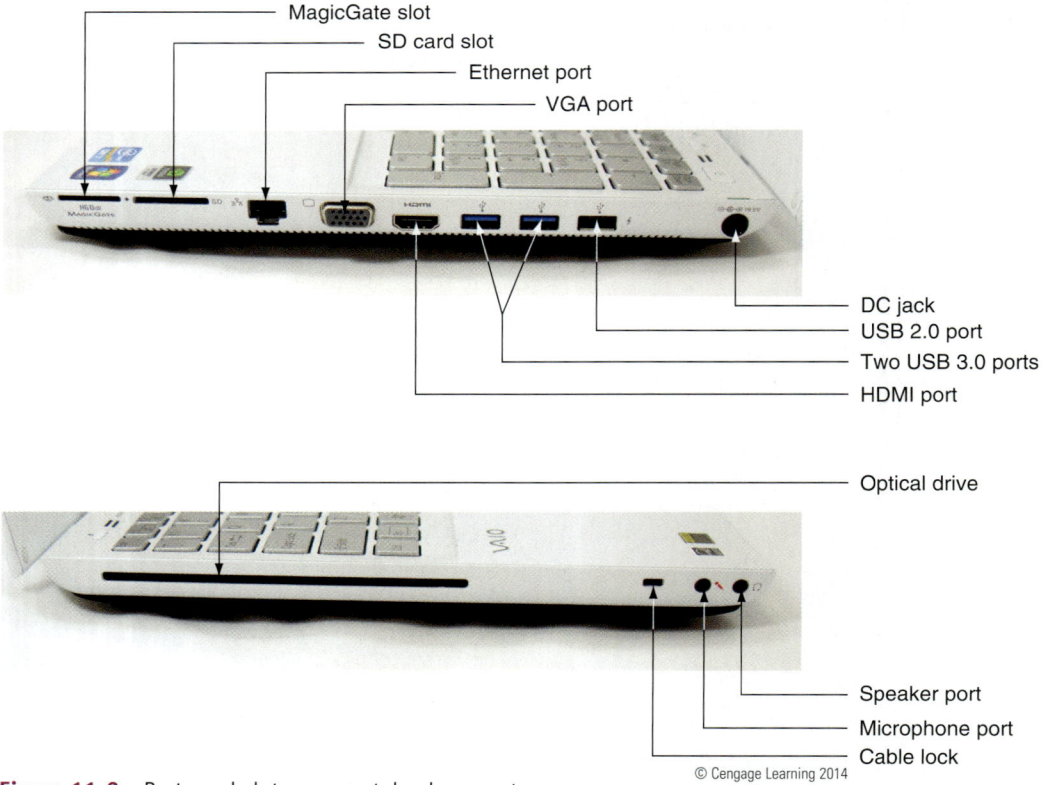

Figure 11-2 Ports and slots on a notebook computer

A+ 220-801 3.3

notebooks), and audio ports (for a microphone, headset, or external speakers). Video ports might include one or more VGA, HDMI, DisplayPort, or S-Video ports to connect to a projector, second monitor, or television. On the side or back of the notebook, you'll see a lock connector that's used to physically secure the laptop with a cable lock (see Figure 11-3) and a DC jack to receive power from the AC adapter.

Slots you might find on a notebook include one or more flash memory and ExpressCard slots. Also, a notebook is likely to have an optical drive, but netbooks usually don't have optical drives. The notebook shown in Figure 11-2 has two slots for flash memory: a MagicGate slot and an SD slot. The MagicGate slot is used for memory sticks and can support Memory Stick Duo, Memory Stick PRO Duo, Memory Stick PRO-HG Duo, and Memory Stick Micro. The SD slot supports SD, SDHC, and SDXC cards. Be sure the flash memory slots on a notebook support the type of card you're trying to use in a slot.

Notebooks and their replacement parts cost more than desktop PCs with similar features because their components are designed to be more compact and stand up to travel. They use compact hard drives, small memory modules, and CPUs that require less power than regular components. Whereas a desktop computer is often assembled from parts made by a variety of manufacturers, notebook computers are almost always sold by a vendor that either manufactured the notebook or had it manufactured as a consolidated system. Factors to consider that generally apply more to notebook computers than desktop computers are the original equipment manufacturer's warranty, the service manuals and diagnostic software provided by the manufacturer, the customized installation of the OS that is unique to notebooks, and the advantage of ordering replacement parts directly from the notebook manufacturer or other source authorized by the manufacturer.

In many situations, the tasks of maintaining, upgrading, and troubleshooting a notebook require the same skills, knowledge, and procedures as when servicing a desktop computer.

Source: Kensington Technology Group

Figure 11-3 Use a cable lock system to secure a notebook computer to a desk to help prevent it from being stolen

A+ 220-801 3.3

However, you should take some special considerations into account when caring for, supporting, upgrading, and troubleshooting notebooks. These same concerns apply to netbooks and all-in-one computers. Let's begin with warranty concerns.

WARRANTY CONCERNS

Most manufacturers or retailers of notebooks offer at least a one-year warranty and the option to purchase an extended warranty. Therefore, when problems arise while the notebook is under warranty, you are dealing with a single manufacturer or retailer to get support or parts. After the notebook is out of warranty, this manufacturer or retailer can still be your one-stop shop for support and parts.

> **Caution** The warranty often applies to all components in the system, but it can be voided if someone other than an authorized service center services the notebook. Therefore, you, as a service technician, must be very careful not to void a warranty that the customer has purchased. Warranties can be voided by opening the case, removing part labels, installing other-vendor parts, upgrading the OS, or disassembling the system unless directly instructed to do so by the authorized service center help desk personnel.

Before you begin servicing a notebook, to avoid problems with a warranty, always ask the customer, "Is the notebook under warranty?" If the notebook is under warranty, look at the documentation to find out how to get technical support. Options are chat sessions on the web, phone numbers, and email. Use the most appropriate option. Before you contact technical support, have the notebook model and serial number ready (see Figure 11-4).

© Cengage Learning 2014

Figure 11-4 The model and serial number stamped on the bottom of a notebook are used to identify the notebook to service desk personnel

Special Considerations when Supporting Notebooks

A+ 220-801 3.3

You'll also need the name, phone number, and address of the person or company that made the purchase. Consider asking the customer for a copy of the receipt and warranty so that you'll have the information you need to talk with support personnel.

Based on the type of warranty purchased by the notebook's owner, the manufacturer might send an on-site service technician, ask you to ship or take the notebook to an authorized service center, or help you solve the problem by an online chat session or over the phone. Table 11-1 lists some popular manufacturers of notebooks, netbooks, tablet PCs, and all-in-ones. Manufacturers of notebooks typically also produce all-in-ones because of the features they have in common.

Manufacturer	Web Site
Acer	*us.acer.com* and *support.acer.com*
Apple Computer	*www.apple.com* and *www.apple.com/support*
ASUS	*usa.asus.com* and *www.service.asus.com*
Dell Computer	*www.dell.com* and *support.dell.com*
Fujitsu/Fuji	*www.fujitsu.com* and *www.fujitsu.com/support*
Gateway	*www.gateway.com* and *support.gateway.com*
Hewlett Packard (HP)	*www.hp.com* *www8.hp.com/us/en/support-drivers.html*
Lenovo (formerly IBM ThinkPads)	*www.lenovo.com* and *support.lenovo.com*
Samsung	*www.samsung.com* and *www.samsung.com/support*
Sony (VAIO)	*store.sony.com* and *esupport.sony.com*
Toshiba America	*www.csd.toshiba.com*

Table 11-1 Notebook, netbook, tablet PC, and all-in-one manufacturers

© Cengage Learning 2014

SERVICE MANUALS AND OTHER SOURCES OF INFORMATION

Desktop computer cases tend to be similar to one another, and components in desktop systems tend to be interchangeable among manufacturers. Not so with notebooks. Notebook manufacturers tend to take great liberty in creating their own unique computer cases, buses, cables, connectors, drives, circuit boards, fans, and even screws, all of which are likely to be proprietary in design.

Every notebook model has a unique case. Components are installed in unique ways and opening the case for each notebook model is done differently. Because of these differences, servicing notebooks can be very complicated and time consuming. For example, a hard drive on one notebook is accessed by popping open a side panel and sliding the drive out of its bay. However, to access the hard drive on another model notebook, you must remove the keyboard. If you are not familiar with a particular notebook model, you can damage the case as you pry and push trying to open it. Trial and error is likely to damage a case. Even though you might successfully replace a broken component, the damaged case will result in an unhappy customer.

Fortunately, a notebook service manual can save you much time and effort—if you can locate one (see Figure 11-5). Most notebook manufacturers closely guard these service manuals and release them only to authorized service centers. Two notebook manufacturers, Lenovo (formally IBM ThinkPad) and Dell, provide their service manuals online free of charge. HP also does an excellent job of offering online support. For example, in Figure 11-6, you can see a video in progress showing you the steps to replace the optical drive in an HP notebook. I applaud Lenovo, Dell, and HP for the generous documentation

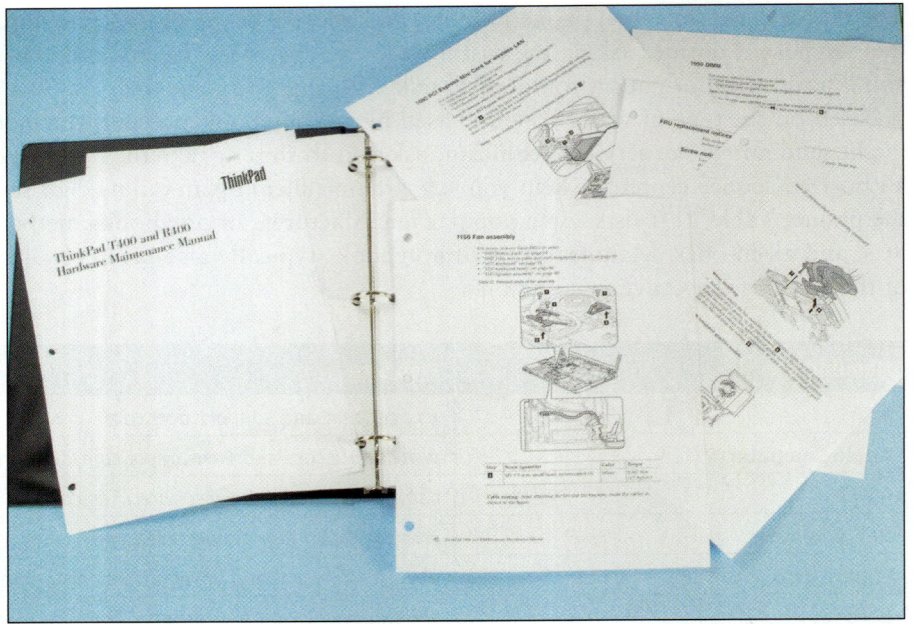

Figure 11-5 A notebook service manual tells you how to use diagnostic tools, troubleshoot a notebook, and replace components

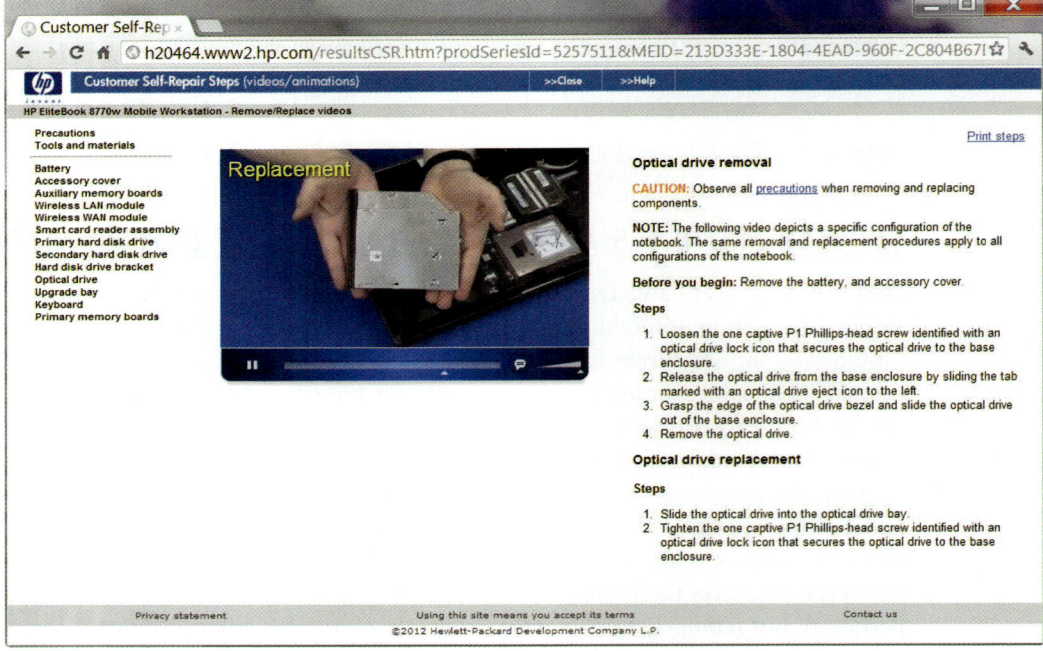

Figure 11-6 The HP web site (*www.hp.com*) provides detailed instructions and videos for troubleshooting and replacing components

about how their notebooks are disassembled and the options to purchase proprietary parts without first being an authorized service center.

For all notebook manufacturers, check the Support or FAQ pages of their web sites for help in tasks such as opening a case without damaging it and locating and replacing a component. Be aware that some manufacturers offer almost no help at all. Sometimes, you can

recovery partition. Notice in the figure the 596 GB hard drive is labeled Disk 0. Most of the space on the hard drive is used by drive C:.

To know how to access the recovery tools stored on a recovery partition, see the user manual. Most likely, you'll see a message at the beginning of the boot, such as "Press ESC for diagnostics" or "Press F12 to recover the system." For one Sony laptop, you press the red **Assist** button during the boot (see Figure 11-9). When you press the key or button, a menu appears giving you options to diagnose the problem, to repair the current OS installation, or to completely rebuild the entire hard drive to its state when the notebook was first purchased.

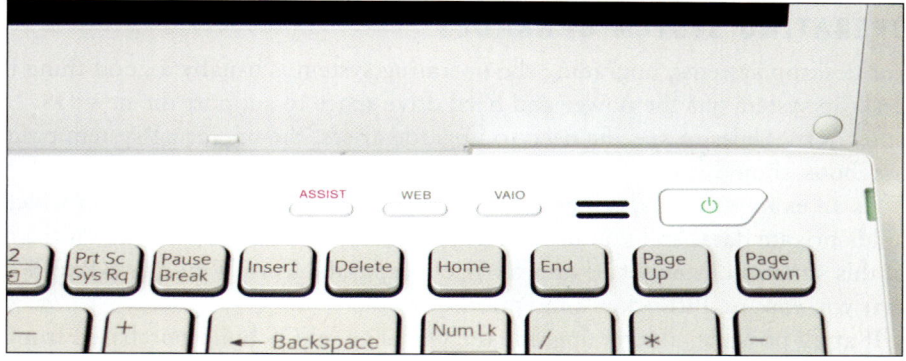

Figure 11-9 For this laptop, press the Assist button during the boot to launch programs on the recovery partition

The recovery partition won't be any help at all if the hard drive is broken or corrupted. In this situation, you're dependent on other recovery media. Older laptops came bundled with the full recovery on CDs, but today's laptops only provide a way for you to create the recovery media. It's important to create the recovery media *before* a problem occurs. To do so, you launch a program preinstalled in Windows. For one Lenovo laptop, the program's window is shown in Figure 11-10. When you click Create Recovery Disc, you are given the option to create recovery discs using the current system or the factory default recovery.

Figure 11-10 Create recovery discs *before* a problem occurs

A+ 220-801 3.3

> **Notes** When you first become responsible for a notebook, make sure you have recovery discs containing the installed OS so you can recover from a failed hard drive. If you cannot create them, you can purchase the discs from the notebook manufacturer. (The price should be less than $30.) Do this before problems arise. If the notebook is more than three years old, the manufacturer might no longer provide the recovery media.
>
> You can also download all the device drivers for the notebook from the manufacturer's web site and burn them to CD.

OPERATING SYSTEM UPGRADES

For desktop systems, upgrading the operating system is usually a good thing to do if the desktop system has the power and hard drive space to support the new OS. Not so with notebooks. Unless a specific need to upgrade arises, the operating system preinstalled on the notebook should last the life of the notebook.

As an example of a specific reason to upgrade, consider a situation in which a notebook holds private data, and you need to provide the best possible security on the notebook. In this situation, it might be appropriate to upgrade from Windows XP to Windows 7 so that you can use BitLocker Encryption.

If at all possible, always upgrade the OS using an OS build purchased from the notebook manufacturer, which should include the OS and device drivers specific to your notebook. In addition, carefully follow their specific instructions for the installation.

If you decide to upgrade the OS using an off-the-shelf version of Windows, first determine that all components in the system are compatible with the upgrade. Be certain to have available all the device drivers you need for the new OS before you upgrade. Download the drivers from the notebook manufacturer's web site and store them in a folder on the hard drive. After you upgrade the OS, install the drivers from this folder. The notebook manufacturer might also suggest you first flash the BIOS before you perform the upgrade. And, if applications are installed on the notebook, find out if you have the applications' setup CDs, and if they will install under the new OS.

Now let's turn our attention to how to maintain a notebook.

Hands-on | Project 11-1 Research Notebook Service Manuals

Do the following to find a service manual for a notebook that you have access to, such as one you or a friend own:

1. What are the brand, model, and serial number of the notebook?
2. What is the web site of the notebook manufacturer? Print a web page on that site that shows the documentation and/or drivers available for this notebook.
3. If the web site provides a service manual for disassembling the notebook, download the manual. Print two or three pages from the manual showing the title page and table of contents for the manual.
4. If the web site does not provide a service manual, search the Internet for the manual. If you find it, download it and print the title page and table of contents.

MAINTAINING NOTEBOOKS AND NOTEBOOK COMPONENTS

A+ 220-801 3.1, 3.3

Notebook computers tend to not last as long as desktop computers because they are portable and, therefore, subjected to more wear and tear. A notebook's user manual gives specific instructions on how to care for the notebook. Those instructions follow these general guidelines:

- LCD panels on notebooks are fragile and can be damaged fairly easily. Take precautions against damaging a notebook's LCD panel. Don't touch it with sharp objects like ballpoint pens.
- Don't pick up or hold the notebook by the lid. Pick it up and hold it by the bottom. Keep the lid closed when the notebook is not in use.
- Only use battery packs recommended by the notebook manufacturer. Keep the battery pack away from moisture or heat, and don't attempt to take the pack apart. When it no longer works, dispose of it correctly. Chapter 8 covers how to dispose of batteries.
- Don't tightly pack the notebook in a suitcase because the LCD panel might get damaged. Use a good-quality carrying case and make it a habit of always transporting the notebook in the carrying case. Don't place heavy objects on top of the notebook case.
- Don't move the notebook while the hard drive is being accessed (the drive indicator light is on). Wait until the light goes off.
- Don't put the notebook close to an appliance such as a TV, large audio speakers, or refrigerator that generates a strong magnetic field, and don't place your cell phone on a notebook while the phone is in use.
- Never, ever connect to the Internet using a public network without setting the network location to a Public network or using a software firewall.
- Always use passwords with each Windows user account so that the laptop is better protected when connected to a public network, stolen, or used by an unauthorized person.
- Keep your notebook at room temperature. For example, never leave it in a car overnight when it is cold, and don't leave it in a car during the day when it's hot. Don't expose your notebook to direct sunlight for an extended time.
- Don't leave the notebook in a dusty or smoke-filled area. Don't use it in a wet area such as near a swimming pool or in the bathtub. Don't use it at the beach where sand can get in it.
- Don't power it up and down unnecessarily.
- Protect the notebook from overheating by not running it when it's still inside the case, resting on a pillow, or partially covered with a blanket or anything else that would prevent proper air circulation around it.
- If a notebook has just come indoors from the cold, don't turn it on until it reaches room temperature. In some cases, condensation can cause problems. Some manufacturers recommend that when you receive a new notebook shipped to you during the winter, you should leave it in its shipping carton for several hours before you open the carton to prevent subjecting the notebook to a temperature shock.
- Protect a notebook against ESD. If you have just come in from the cold on a low-humidity day when there is the possibility that you are carrying ESD, don't touch the notebook until you have grounded yourself.
- Before placing a notebook in a carrying case for travel, remove any CDs, DVDs, or USB flash drives, and put them in protective covers. Verify that the system is powered down and not in suspend or standby mode.

**A+
220-801
3.1, 3.3**

- If a notebook gets wet, you can follow steps given later in the chapter to partially disassemble it to allow internal components to dry. Give the notebook several days to dry before attempting to turn it on. Don't use heat to speed up the drying time.
- When you first become responsible for a notebook, take the time to locate or create the recovery media in case the hard drive ever crashes and needs replacing.

A well-used notebook, especially one that is used in dusty or dirty areas, needs cleaning occasionally. Here are some cleaning tips:

- Clean the LCD panel with a soft dry cloth. If the panel is very dirty, you can use monitor wipes to clean it or dampen the cloth with water. Some manufacturers recommend using a mixture of isopropyl alcohol and water to clean an LCD panel. Be sure the LCD panel is dry before you close the lid.
- Use a can of compressed air meant to be used on computer equipment to blow dust and small particles out of the keyboard, track ball, and touchpad. Turn the notebook at an angle and direct the air into the sides of the keyboard. Then use a soft, damp cloth to clean the key caps and touch pad.
- Use compressed air to blow out all air vents on the notebook to make sure they are clean and unobstructed.
- If keys are sticking, remove the keyboard so you can better spray under the key with compressed air. If you can remove the key cap, remove it and clean the key contact area with contact cleaner. One example of a contact cleaner you can use for this purpose is Stabilant 22 (*www.stabilant.com*). Reinstall the keyboard and test it. If the key still sticks, replace the keyboard.
- Remove the battery and clean the battery connections with a contact cleaner.

Now let's look at the special keys and buttons a notebook might have, how to support the slots and peripherals used on notebooks, how to manage power on a notebook, and how to use port replicators or docking stations.

**A+
220-802
1.5**

SPECIAL KEYS, BUTTONS, AND INPUT DEVICES ON A NOTEBOOK

Buttons or switches might be found above the keyboard, and a **keyboard backlight** might light up the keyboard. Here are the purposes of a few keys and buttons. Some of them change Windows settings. Know that these same settings can also be changed using Windows tools:

- *Volume setting.* You can set the volume using the volume icon in the Windows taskbar. In addition, some notebooks offer buttons or function keys to control the volume (see Figure 11-11).
- *Screen brightness.* The Fn key and F5 or F6 control the screen brightness on many notebooks. Screen brightness can also be controlled in Windows display settings.
- *Dual displays.* Most laptops use a function key to control dual displays. For example, for one laptop, the combination of the Fn key and the F7 key (see Figure 11-11) displays the box shown in Figure 11-12. Use arrow keys to use only the LCD panel, duplicate or extend output to the external monitor, or use only the external monitor. Dual displays can also be managed using Windows display settings.
- *Bluetooth or Wi-Fi on or off.* Some notebooks use function keys such as Fn with F5 or F6 to toggle Bluetooth or Wi-Fi on or off, or a notebook might have a switch for this purpose. You can also control Bluetooth and Wi-Fi using Windows settings or software utilities provided by the manufacturer.

A+ 220-801
3.1, 3.3

A+ 220-802
1.5

Figure 11-11 Use the Fn and the F2, F3, or F4 key to control volume; use the Fn key and the F5 or F6 key to control screen brightness; and use the Fn key and the F7 key to manage dual displays

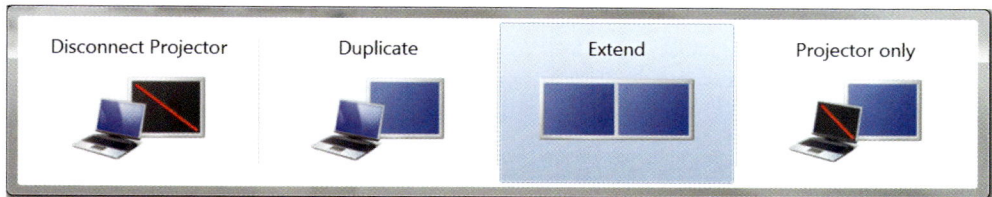

Figure 11-12 Control dual monitors on a laptop

> **Notes** Later in the chapter, you learn how to exchange a notebook keyboard. If the keyboard fails and you're not able to immediately exchange it, know that you can plug in an external keyboard to a USB port to use in the meantime.

The most common pointing device on a notebook is a touchpad (see Figure 11-13). IBM and Lenovo ThinkPad notebooks use a unique and popular pointing device embedded in the keyboard (see Figure 11-14) called a TrackPoint or pointing stick. Some people prefer to use a USB wired or wireless mouse instead of a touchpad or TrackPoint.

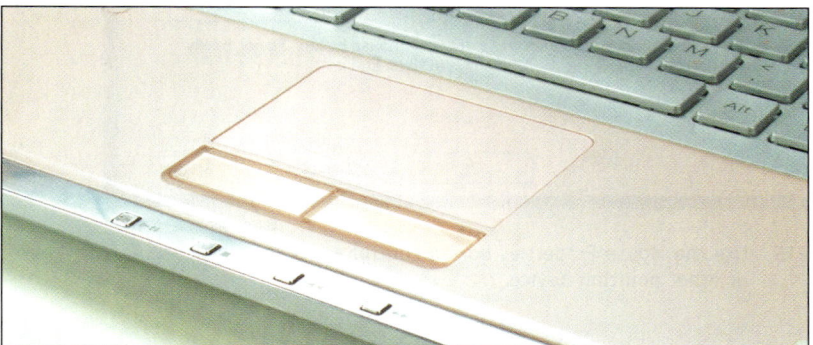

Figure 11-13 The touch pad is the most common pointing device on a notebook

A+ 220-801
3.1, 3.3

A+ 220-802
1.5

Figure 11-14 An IBM ThinkPad TrackPoint

© Cengage Learning 2014

You can adjust the way the touchpad or TrackPoint works on a laptop using the Mouse Properties box. Click **Mouse** in the Hardware and Sound group of Control Panel to open the box shown in Figure 11-15. The tabs on this box vary depending on the pointing devices installed. Use the Mouse Properties box to adjust pointer speed, mouse trails, pointer size, how the touchpad buttons work, and other settings for pointing devices.

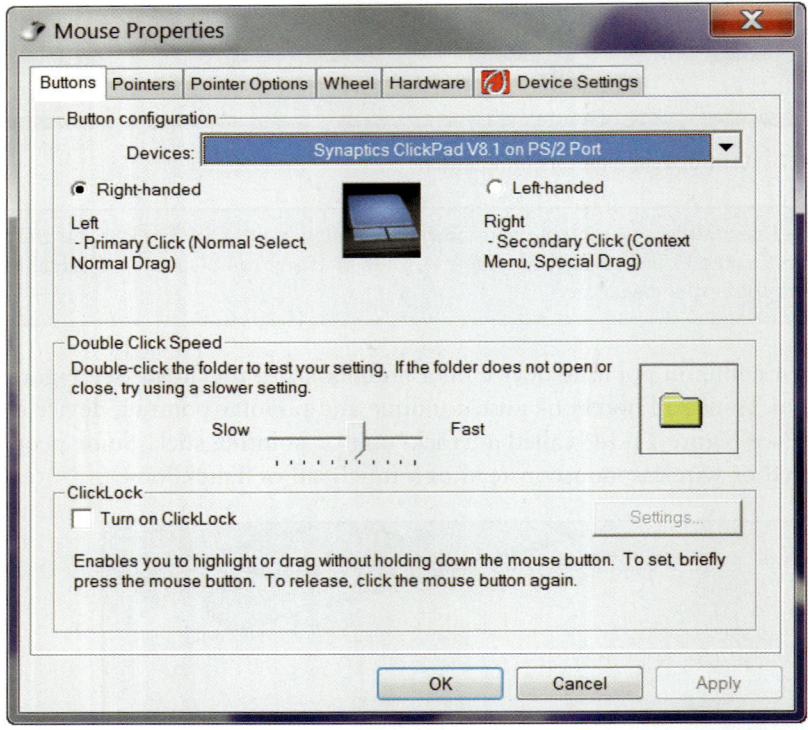

Source: Microsoft Windows 7

Figure 11-15 Use the Mouse Properties box to control a mouse, touch pad, or other pointing device

For tablet PCs, the stylus can be controlled from the Pen and Input Devices box. The box can be accessed from Control Panel, and allows you to control stylus clicks and motion.

PCMCIA AND EXPRESSCARD SLOTS

A+
220-801
3.1, 3.3

Most peripheral devices on today's notebooks use a USB port to connect to the notebook. Before USB devices became so popular, a notebook offered ExpressCard slots and even older PC Card and CardBus slots to connect peripheral devices. These slot and card standards were designed and supported by the PCMCIA (Personal Computer Memory Card International Association). **PCMCIA cards** include one or more variations of PC Card, CardBus, and ExpressCard. The cards were used by many devices, including modems, network cards for wired or wireless networks, sound cards, SCSI host adapters, FireWire (IEEE 1394) controllers, USB controllers, flash memory adapters, TV tuners, and hard disks. Most new notebooks don't have these slots, but you still need to know how to support them because you'll see them on older notebooks.

You need to be aware of the different standards for PCMCIA cards, which are summarized here, listed in the order they were introduced into the market:

1. A **PC Card** that uses a PC Card slot is about the size of a credit card, but thicker. The slot used a 16-bit bus called the ISA bus. Originally, PC Cards were called PCMCIA Cards and the first of these cards were used to add memory to a notebook. Figure 11-16 shows a PC Card being inserted into a PC Card slot. Three standards for PC Cards and PC Card slots that pertain to size are Type I, Type II, and Type III. Generally, the thicker the PC Card or slot, the higher the standard. You're unlikely to see PC Card slots on notebooks today.

Figure 11-16 Many peripheral devices are added to a notebook using a PC Card slot; here, a Microdrive (a tiny hard drive) adapter PC Card is inserted in a PC Card slot

2. **CardBus** slots improved PC Card slots by increasing the bus width to 32 bits, while maintaining backward compatibility with earlier standards. The slot uses the 32-bit PCI bus standards. CardBus slots can support the older 16-bit PC Card devices. You cannot, however, insert a CardBus card into an older 16-bit PC Card slot. A PC Card has a smooth edge, and a CardBus has a bumpy strip on the edge. This bumpy strip prevents a CardBus card from being inserted into a 16-bit PC Card slot.

Figure 11-17 shows a TV tuner CardBus card. If you look closely at the edge, you can see the gold, bumpy strip that prevents a CardBus card from being inserted into an older PC Card slot. PC Card and CardBus slots look alike on a notebook computer, and you can recognize these slots by the eject button on the side of the slot (see Figure 11-18). One way to know which type of slot you have is to look in Device Manager. If Device Manager shows a controller with "CardBus" in the controller title, then the slot is a 32-bit CardBus slot (see Figure 11-19).

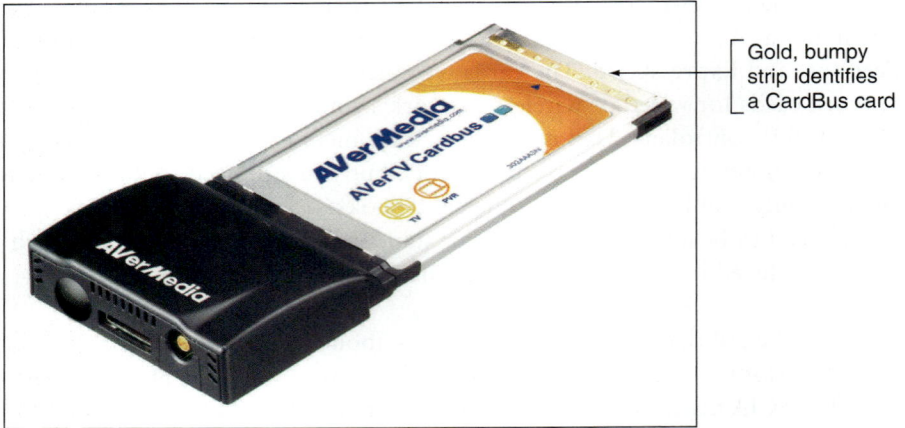

Source: AVerMedia Technologies, Inc. USA

Figure 11-17 AVerMedia AVerTV CardBus Plus (E501R) TV tuner card connects to a notebook by way of a PCMCIA CardBus slot

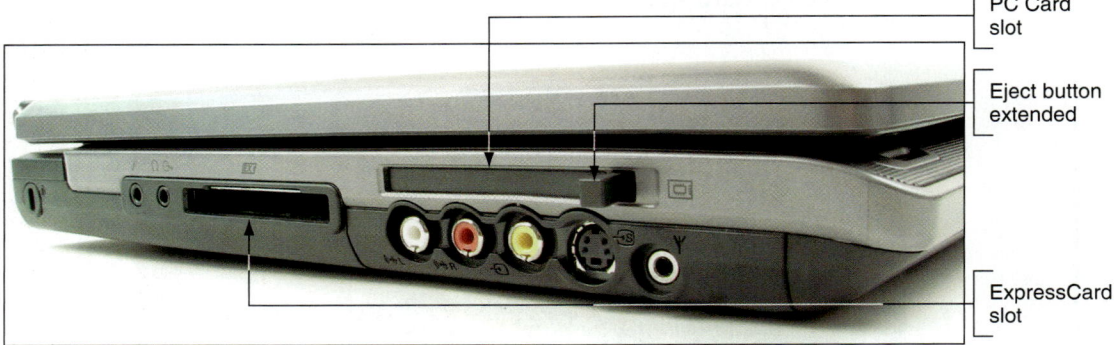

© Cengage Learning 2014

Figure 11-18 This notebook has one CardBus slot and one ExpressCard slot

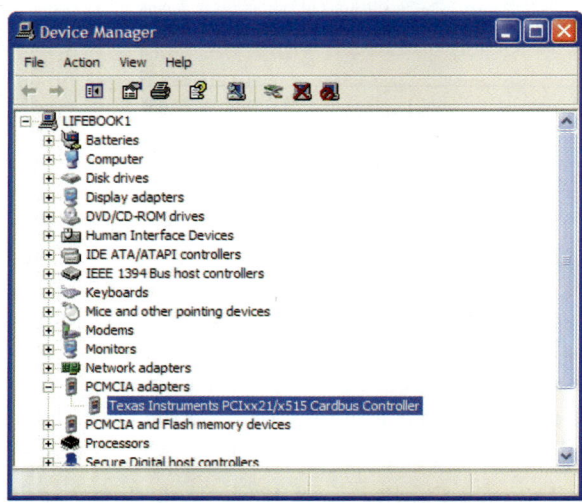

Source: Microsoft Windows XP

Figure 11-19 Device Manager recognizes a PCMCIA slot as a CardBus slot

> **A+ Exam Tip** The A+ 220-801 exam expects you to know about PCMCIA cards and slots and ExpressCard/34 and ExpressCard/54 cards and slots.

3. The last PCMCIA standard is ExpressCard, which uses the PCI Express bus standard or the USB 2.0 standard. Two sizes of ExpressCards exist: **ExpressCard/34** is 34mm wide and **ExpressCard/54** is 54mm wide. Both of these types of cards are 75mm long and 5mm high. Figure 11-20 compares a CardBus card to each of the two ExpressCard cards. An ExpressCard/34 card can fit into an ExpressCard/54 slot, but not vice versa. ExpressCard slots are not backward compatible with PC Card or CardBus cards. An ExpressCard slot is fully hot-pluggable (add a card while the system is on), hot-swappable (exchange or add a card while the system is on), and supports autoconfiguration, just as does a USB port. Figure 11-21 shows an ExpressCard/54 card that provides two eSATA ports for external SATA drives.

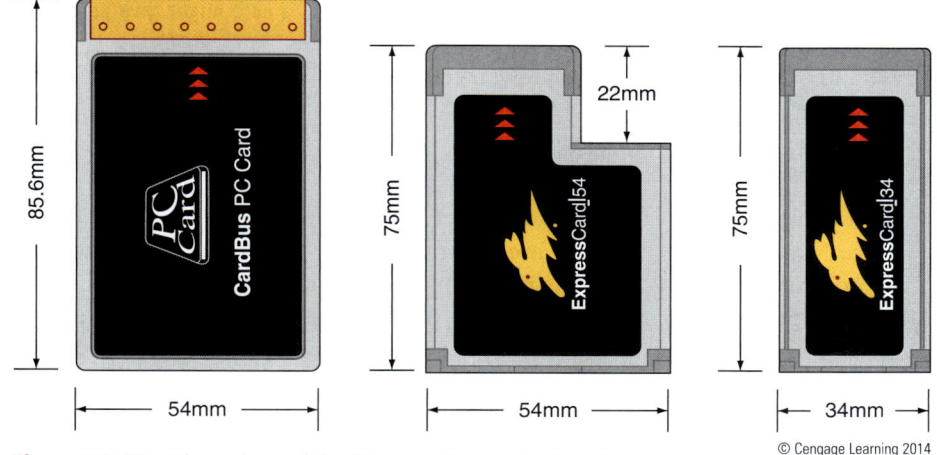

Figure 11-20   Dimensions of CardBus and ExpressCard cards

Figure 11-21   This ExpressCard/54 card supports two eSATA drives

Windows must provide two services for a PC Card or ExpressCard: a socket service and a card service. The socket service establishes communication between the card and the notebook when the card is first inserted. The card service provides the device driver to interface with the card after the socket is created.

The first time you insert a PCMCIA card in a notebook, the Found New Hardware Wizard starts and guides you through the installation steps in which you can use the drivers provided by the hardware manufacturer or use Windows drivers. The next time you insert the card in the notebook, the card is detected and starts without help.

ExpressCards and PC Cards can be hot-swapped (inserted or removed while the system is on), but you must stop one card before inserting another. To stop the card, use the Safely Remove Hardware icon in the notification area, which is similar to how you stop a USB device before unplugging it.

After you have stopped the card, press the eject button beside the PC Card slot, which causes the button to pop out. You can then press the button again to eject the card. For an ExpressCard, push on the card, which causes it to pop out of the slot. Then you can remove the card.

> **Caution** Inserting a card in a PCMCIA slot while the notebook is shutting down or booting up can cause damage to the card and/or to the notebook. Also, a card might give problems when you insert or remove the card while the system is in hibernation or sleep mode.

UPDATING PORT OR SLOT DRIVERS

If you ever have a problem with a port or slot on a notebook not working, first turn to Device Manager to see if errors are reported and to update the drivers for the port or slot. The notebook manufacturer has probably stored backups of the drivers on the hard drive under support tools and on the recovery media if the recovery media is available. You can also download the latest drivers from the manufacturer's web site. For some laptops, you can launch the support tools from the Windows **Start, All Programs** menu. Figure 11-22 shows a dialog box available in the support tools for one laptop where you select which drivers to update. If the problem is still not solved after updating the drivers, try using Device Manager to uninstall the port or slot drivers and then use the support tools to reinstall the drivers.

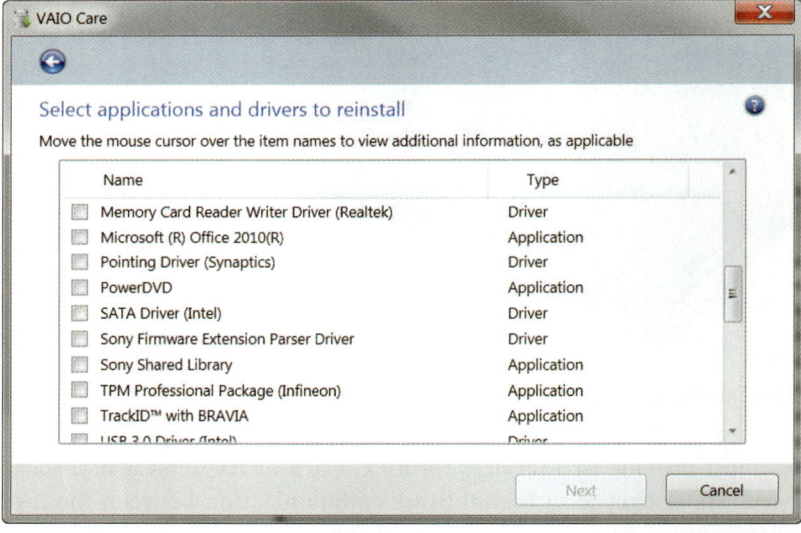

Source: Sony

Figure 11-22 Update drivers to solve a problem with a port or slot not working

POWER AND ELECTRICAL DEVICES

A+ 220-801 3.1, 3.3

A notebook can be powered by an **AC adapter** (which uses regular house current to power the notebook) or an installed battery pack. Battery packs today use **Lithium Ion** technology. Most AC adapters today are capable of **auto-switching** from 110 V to 220 V AC power. Figure 11-23 shows an AC adapter that has a green light that indicates the adapter is receiving power.

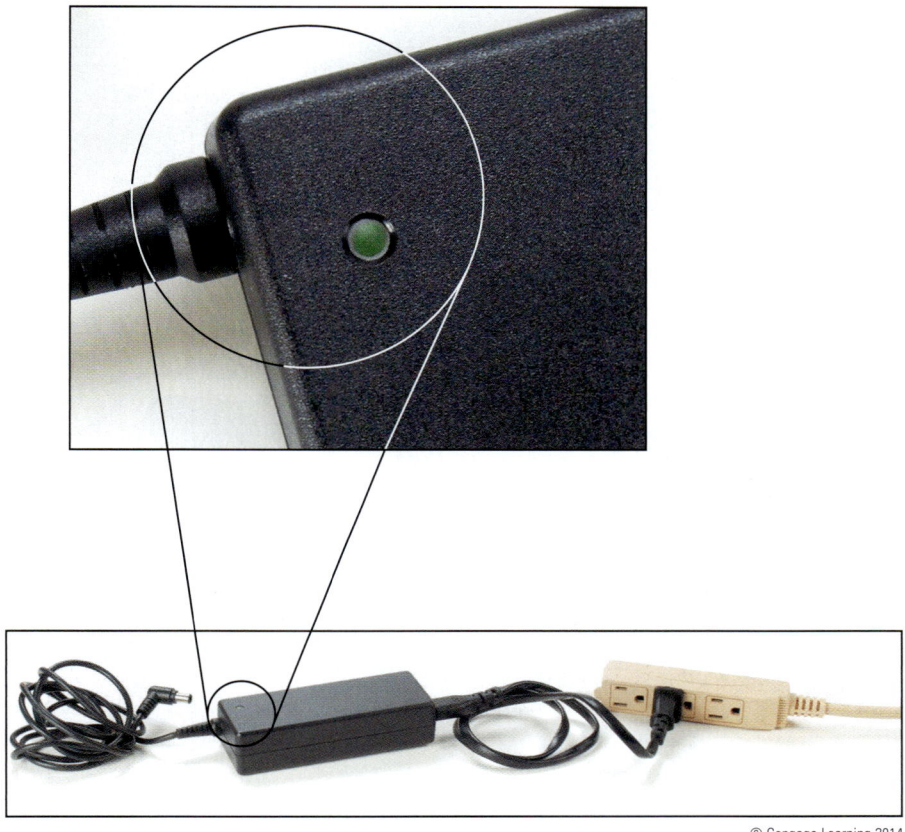

Figure 11-23 AC adapter for a notebook uses a green light to indicate power

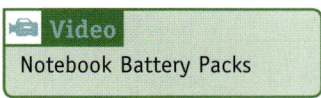

Some mobile users like to keep an extra battery on hand in case the first one uses up its charge. When the notebook signals that power is low, shut down the system, remove the old battery and replace it with a charged one. To remove a battery, generally, you release a latch and then remove the battery, as shown in Figure 11-24.

For best battery charge times, some notebooks can use two batteries. For example, the notebook in Figure 11-25 uses a second battery called a **sheet battery** that fits on the bottom of the notebook. The two batteries together give about 12 hours of use between charges. The sheet battery comes with an adapter so you can charge it when it's disconnected from the notebook.

A DC adapter to provide power while in a car can be handy. Figure 11-26 shows an inexpensive one that plugs into a cigarette lighter in a vehicle to provide AC power. The device is a type of inverter. (An **inverter** is an electrical device that changes DC to AC.) You can plug your AC adapter into the inverter to power a laptop in your car. If you are using an inverter, be sure to purchase one that supplies enough power (measured in watts) to meet the needs of your notebook.

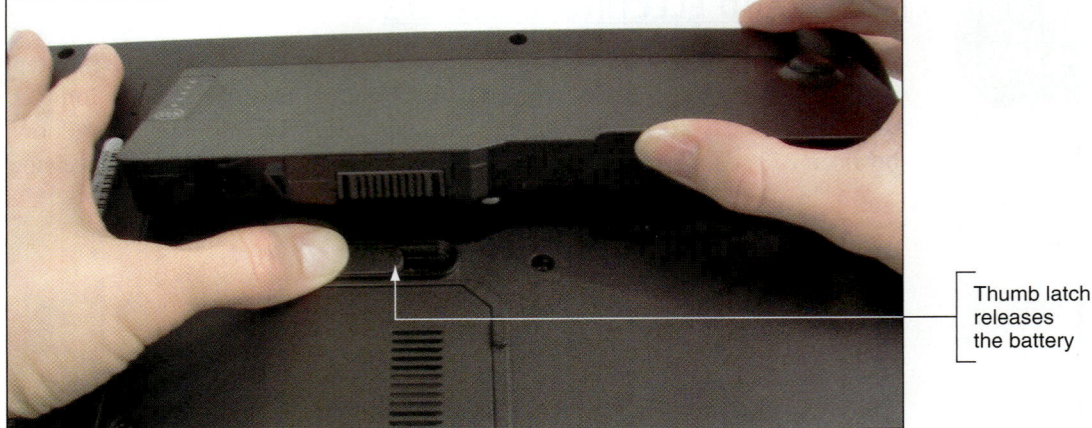

Figure 11-24 Release a latch to remove the battery from a notebook

Figure 11-25 The second battery for this notebook is a sheet battery that attaches to the bottom of the notebook and adds up to six hours to the battery charge

Figure 11-26 An inverter changes DC to AC and provides an outlet for your laptop's AC adapter

Maintaining Notebooks and Notebook Components | 533

A+ 220-801 3.1, 3.3

> **Notes** If you're using the AC adapter to power your notebook when the power goes out, the installed battery serves as a built-in UPS. The battery immediately takes over as your uninterruptible power supply (UPS). Also, a notebook has an internal surge protector. However, for extra protection, you might want to use a power strip that provides surge protection.

A+ 220-802 1.5

POWER MANAGEMENT

Use power management settings to conserve power and to increase the time before a battery pack needs recharging. Power is managed by putting the computer into varying degrees of suspend or sleep modes.

> **A+ Exam Tip** The A+ 220-801 exam expects you to know how to manage power, including using sleep (suspend), hibernate, and standby modes.

Here are the different power-saving states:

▲ *Sleep mode.* Using Windows 7/Vista, you can put the computer into **sleep mode**, also called **suspend mode**, to save power when you're not using the computer. If applications are open or other work is in progress, Windows first saves the current state including open files to memory and saves some of the work to the hard drive. Then everything is shut down except memory and enough of the system to respond to a wake-up. In sleep mode, the power light on the notebook might blink from time to time. (A notebook generally uses about 1 to 2 percent of battery power for each hour in sleep mode.) To wake up the computer, press the power button or, for some computers, press a key or touch the touchpad. Windows wakes up in about two seconds. When Windows is in sleep mode, it can still perform Windows updates and scheduled tasks. Windows can be configured to go to sleep after a period of inactivity, or you can manually put it to sleep. To put the system to sleep manually, click **Start**, click the arrow to the right of Shut down, and then click **Sleep** (see Figure 11-27). Notebooks are usually configured to go to sleep when you close the lid.

> **Notes** In Windows XP, **standby mode** is similar to Windows 7/Vista sleep mode. Work is saved to memory and a trickle of power preserves that memory. In hibernation, all work in memory is saved to the hard drive and then the power is turned off.

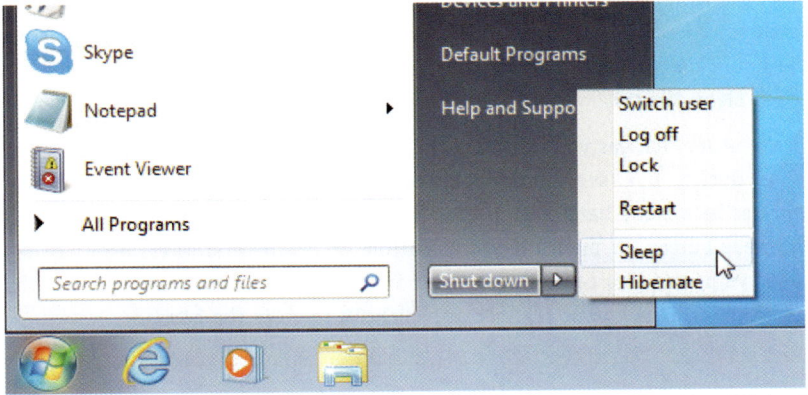

Source: Microsoft Windows 7

Figure 11-27 Put Windows to sleep using the Start menu

▸ *Hibernation.* **Hibernation** saves all work to the hard drive and powers down the system. When you press the power button, Windows reloads its state, including all open applications and documents. When Windows is in sleep mode on a notebook and senses the battery is critically low, it will put the system into hibernation.

> **Notes** Recall that hard drives are permanent or nonvolatile storage and memory is temporary or volatile storage. A hard drive does not require power to hold its contents, but memory, on the other hand, is volatile and loses its contents when it has no power. In hibernation, the computer has no power and everything must, therefore, be stored on the hard drive.

APPLYING CONCEPTS: CONFIGURE WINDOWS POWER MANAGEMENT SETTINGS

Follow these steps to configure power in Windows 7:

1. In Control Panel, click **Power Options** in the Hardware and Sound group. The Power Options window opens. Figure 11-28 shows the window for one laptop. The plans might be different for other laptops.

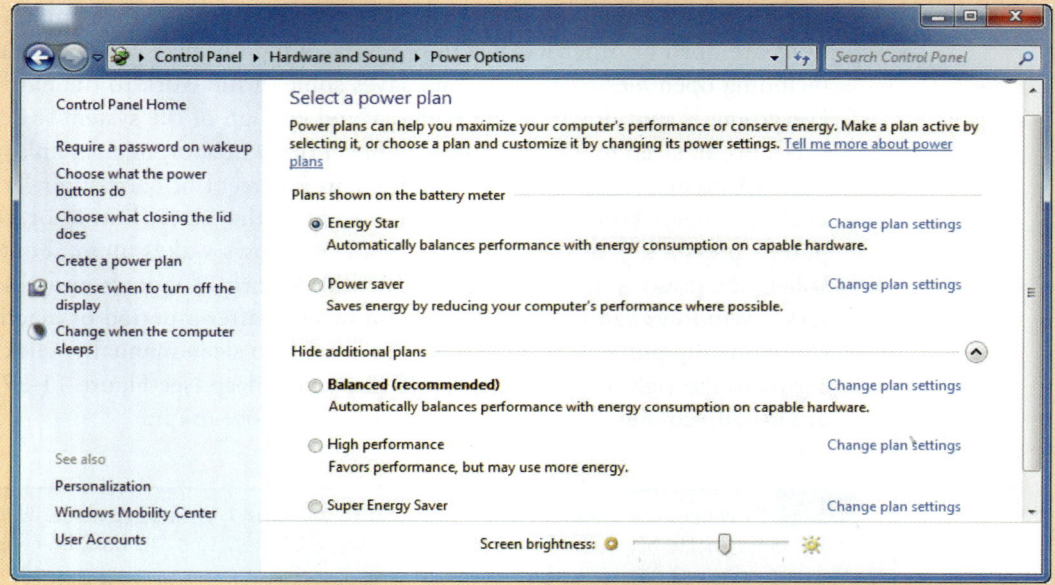

Figure 11-28 Power-saving plans in Windows 7
Source: Microsoft Windows 7

2. You can customize each plan. For example, under Balanced (recommended), click **Change plan settings**. The Edit Plan Settings window appears (see the left side of Figure 11-29). Notice in the figure the various times of inactivity before the computer goes into sleep mode, which are called **sleep timers**.

3. To see other changes you can make, click **Change advanced power settings**. Using this Power Options box (see the right side of Figure 11-29), you can do such things as control the minutes before the hard drive turns off, control what happens when you close the lid, press the sleep button, or press the power button, or set the brightness level of the LCD panel to conserve power. You can also use this box to set what happens when the battery gets low or critically low. Make your changes and click **OK** to close the box.

Maintaining Notebooks and Notebook Components   535

A+
220-801
3.1, 3.3

A+
220-802
1.5

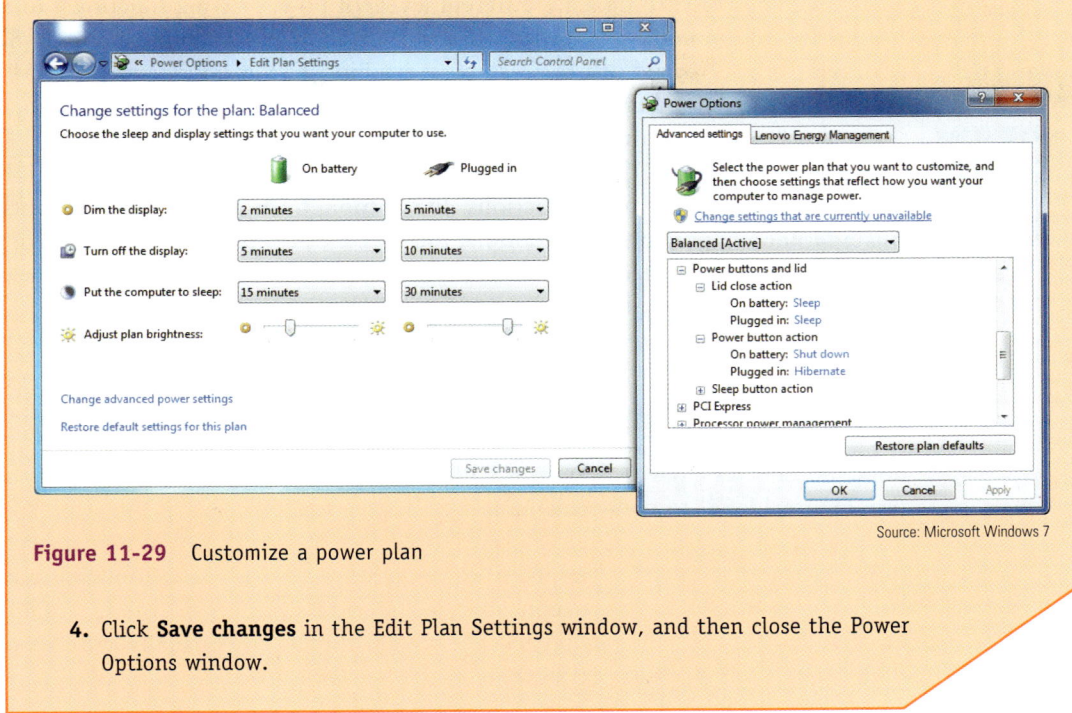

Figure 11-29   Customize a power plan

Source: Microsoft Windows 7

4. Click **Save changes** in the Edit Plan Settings window, and then close the Power Options window.

With older computers, power settings could be configured in Windows and in BIOS setup and the two settings could create a conflict. Newer BIOS does not control power settings that might be in conflict with Windows settings, such as when the computer goes to sleep. If you are having a problem with a computer refusing to go into sleep mode or hibernation or to wake up from sleep mode, check the BIOS power settings. Figure 11-30 shows the BIOS Power screen for one newer system. These settings apply primarily to how or when the system can wake up.

Let's cover a little of what you might see on the BIOS power screen. Using the **Advanced Configuration and Power Interface (ACPI)** power standards, BIOS might refer to five S states,

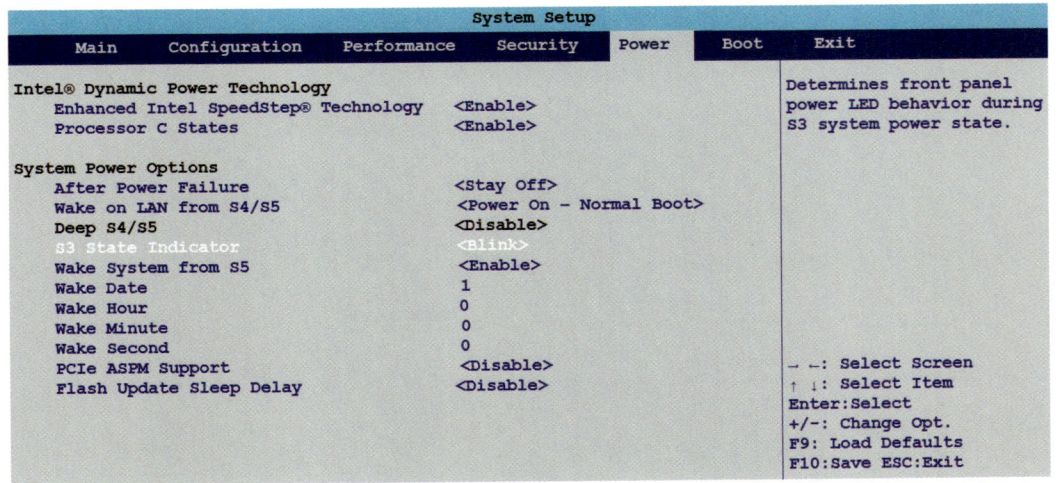

Figure 11-30   BIOS setup screen to configure power options

Source: Intel

536 | **CHAPTER 11** Supporting Notebooks

> A+
> 220-801
> 3.1, 3.3
>
> A+
> 220-802
> 1.5

S1 through S5, used to indicate different levels of power-saving functions. In S1 state, the hard drive and monitor are turned off and everything else runs normally. In S2 state, the processor is also turned off. In S3 state, everything is shut down except RAM and enough of the system to respond to a wake-up. S3 state is sleep mode. S4 state is hibernation. S5 state is the power off state after a normal shutdown.

C states in setup BIOS refer to various degrees of shutting down the CPU. In C0 state, a CPU can work, executing instructions. In C1 though C6 states, the CPU shuts down various internal components (for example, the core clock, buffers, cache, and core voltage) to conserve power. The deeper the C state, the longer it takes for the processor to wake up. Mobile processors usually offer more C states than desktop processors.

So, onward to port replicators and docking stations.

PORT REPLICATORS AND DOCKING STATIONS

Some notebooks have a connector, called a **docking port**, on the bottom of the notebook (see Figure 11-31) to connect to a port replicator or docking station. A **port replicator** provides ports to allow a notebook to easily connect to a full-sized monitor, keyboard, AC power adapter, and other peripheral devices. See Figure 11-32. A **docking station** provides the same functions as a port replicator but provides additional slots for adding secondary storage devices and expansion cards. Laptop manufacturers usually offer a port replicator or docking station as additional options.

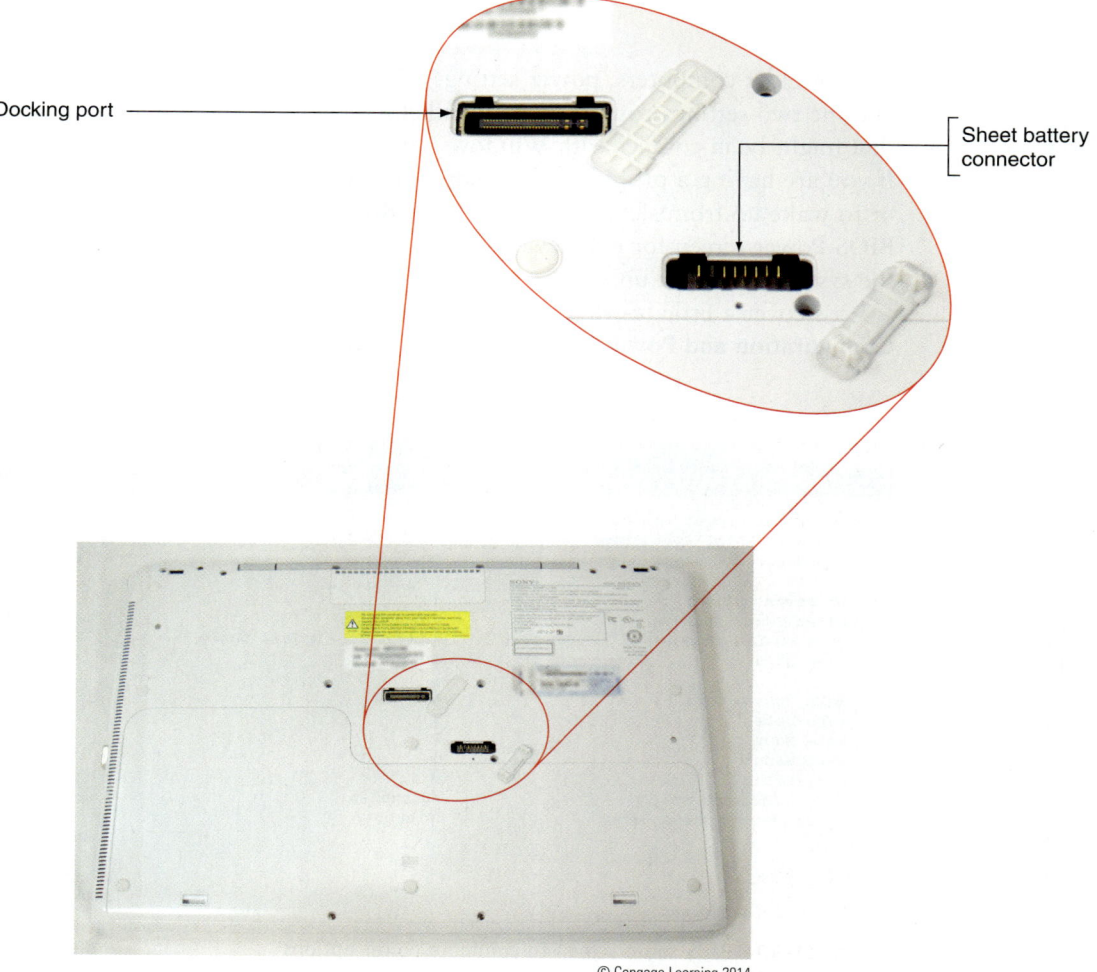

© Cengage Learning 2014

Figure 11-31 The docking port and sheet battery connector on the bottom of a laptop

Figure 11-32 Port replicator for a Lenovo ThinkPad — Courtesy of Lenovo

To use a port replicator or docking station, plug all the peripherals into the port replicator or docking station. Then connect your notebook to the device. No software needs installing. When you need to travel with your notebook, rather than having to unplug all the peripherals, all you have to do is disconnect the notebook from the port replicator or docking station.

> **A+ Exam Tip** The A+ 220-801 exam expects you to know the difference between a port replicator and a docking station.

APPLYING CONCEPTS — HARDWARE PROFILES AND WINDOWS XP

A **hardware profile** is a group of settings that Windows keeps about a specific hardware configuration. If a notebook using Windows XP has a docking station, you can set up one hardware profile to use the docking station and another when you are on the road and don't have access to the docking station. Windows 7/Vista doesn't require you to set up hardware profiles, because it automatically senses when a docking station is present.

> **A+ Exam Tip** The A+ 220-802 exam expects you to know about Windows XP hardware profiles and how to use Control Panel to create one.

To create a hardware profile in Windows XP, do the following:

1. Open the **System Properties** window and click the **Hardware** tab.
2. Click the **Hardware Profiles** button at the bottom of the Hardware tab. The Hardware Profiles dialog box opens (Figure 11-33).
3. Select a profile from the list of available hardware profiles, and then click the **Copy** button.
4. Type a new name for the profile, and then click **OK**.

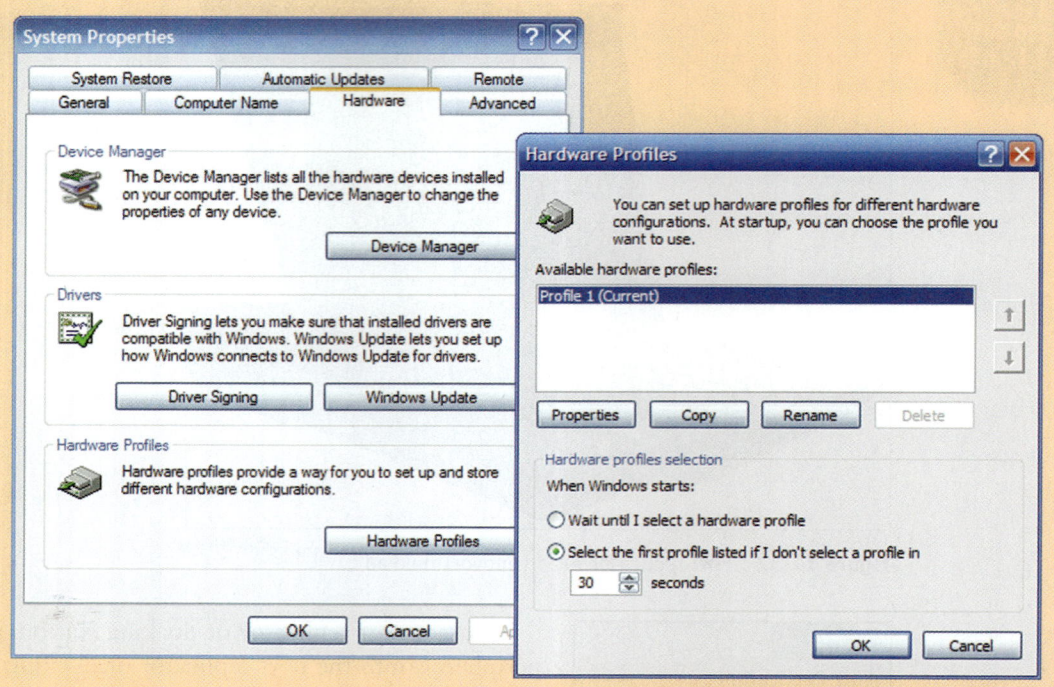

Figure 11-33 Windows XP allows you to set a hardware profile for different hardware configurations

5. Under *When Windows starts*, select either the option for Windows to wait for you to select a hardware profile or the option for Windows to start with the first profile listed if you don't select one in the specified number of seconds. Close all open windows.

6. Restart the computer and, when prompted, select the new hardware profile.

7. Open the **System Properties** dialog box. Click the **Hardware** tab, click **Device Manager**, and then double-click the icon for a device that you want enabled or disabled in the new profile. For example, you might set one profile to access a second hard drive that is installed on the docking station, which is not available when traveling.

8. Click the **General** tab in the Properties dialog box for the device. In the area for Device usage, select the option to enable or disable the device for the current profile or for all hardware profiles. Close all open dialog boxes.

Hands-on | Project 11-2 Update Device Drivers

Do the following to investigate and perform driver updates for a notebook:

1. Using a notebook computer, locate any support software installed on the notebook. List the devices for which the software can provide device driver updates.

2. Using Device Manager, list the embedded devices on the notebook that might benefit from a driver update (for example, the touchpad, display adapter, and Bluetooth device). Perform a driver update for each of these devices. For which devices did Windows find driver updates?

REPLACING AND UPGRADING INTERNAL PARTS

A+
220-801
3.1

A+
220-802
4.8

Sometimes it is necessary to open a notebook case so you can upgrade memory, exchange a hard drive, or replace a failed component such as the LCD panel, video inverter, keyboard, touchpad, processor, optical drive, DC jack, fan, motherboard, CMOS battery, Mini-PCIe card, wireless card, or speaker. Most notebooks sold today are designed so that you can easily purchase and exchange memory modules or hard drives. However, replacing a broken LCD panel or motherboard can be a complex process, taking several hours. In this section, we'll first look at the alternatives you need to consider before you decide to take on complex repair projects, and then we'll look at how to upgrade memory, exchange a drive, and perform other complex repair projects, such as exchanging an LCD panel or motherboard.

THREE APPROACHES TO DEALING WITH A BROKEN INTERNAL DEVICE

When a component on a notebook needs replacing or upgrading, first you need to consider the warranty and how much time the repair will take. Before you decide to upgrade or repair an internal component, take into consideration these three alternatives:

- *Return the notebook to the manufacturer or another service center for repair.* If the notebook is under warranty, you need to return it to the manufacturer to do any serious repair work such as fixing a broken LCD panel. However, for simple repair and upgrade tasks, such as upgrading memory or exchanging a hard drive, most likely you can do these simple jobs by yourself without concern for voiding a warranty. Manufacturers allow a user to exchange the hard drive or memory when these components are accessible by way of a door or cover on the bottom of the notebook and it's not necessary to open the case. If you're not sure about the possibility of voiding the warranty, check with the manufacturer before you begin working on the notebook. If the notebook is not under warranty and you don't have the experience or time to fix a broken component, find out how much the manufacturer will charge to do the job. Also, consider using a generic notebook repair service. Know that some notebook manufacturers refuse to sell internal components or service manuals that explain how to take the notebook apart except to authorized service centers. In this case, you have few options but to use the service center for repairs.

> **Caution** Before you send a notebook for repairs, if possible, back up any important data on the hard drive. It's possible the service center will format the hard drive or install a new drive.

- *Substitute an external component for an internal component.* As you'll see later in the chapter, replacing components on notebooks can be time consuming and require a lot of patience. If the notebook is not under warranty, sometimes it's wiser to simply avoid opening the case and working inside it. Instead, you could simply use BIOS setup to disable an internal component and then use an external device in its place. For example, if a keyboard fails, you can use a wireless keyboard with an access point connected to the USB port. Also, if the Ethernet port fails, the simplest solution might be to disable the port and use a USB network adapter to provide the Ethernet port.

A+ 220-801 3.1

A+ 220-802 4.8

▲ *Replace the internal device.* Before deciding to replace an internal device that is not easy to get to, such as an LCD panel, first find out if you can get the manufacturer documentation necessary to know how to open the notebook case and exchange the component. How to find this documentation was discussed earlier in the chapter. Without the instructions or a lot of experience servicing notebooks, the project could be very frustrating and result in a notebook useful only as a paperweight. Also consider if the cost of parts and labor is worth more than the value of the notebook. Buying a new notebook might be the best solution.

> **Notes** Before making the decision to replace an internal part, ask the question, "Can an external device substitute?" Many customers appreciate these solutions because most often they are much less labor intensive and less costly.

Before attempting to replace or upgrade a component installed in a notebook, always do the following:

1. If the computer is working, have the user back up any important data stored on the notebook.
2. Ground yourself by using an antistatic ground strap.
3. Remove any ExpressCards, CDs, DVDs, flash memory cards, or USB devices and then shut down the notebook.
4. Disconnect the AC adapter from the computer and from the electrical outlet.
5. If the notebook is attached to a port replicator or docking station, release it to undock the computer.
6. Remove the battery pack.

> **Caution** It is very important to unplug the AC adapter and remove the battery pack before working inside a notebook case. If the battery is still in the notebook, power provided by the battery could damage components as you work on them.

You are now ready to follow specific instructions for your particular notebook model to replace or upgrade an internal component. Some components can easily be accessed by either removing a panel to expose the component or by removing a screw or two and then sliding the component out the side of the case. When a component can be accessed this easily, most users can do the job if given detailed instructions.

Now let's see how to upgrade memory and exchange a hard drive. Then we'll look at more complicated replacements that require you to disassemble the notebook.

UPGRADING MEMORY

In this section, you'll learn about the different types of memory modules used with notebook computers and how to upgrade memory.

TYPES OF MEMORY USED IN NOTEBOOKS

Today's notebooks all use DDR3 or DDR2 SO-DIMM (small outline DIMM) memory. You might encounter older notebooks that use SO-RIMM (small outline RIMM) memory. Table 11-2 lists current and outdated SO-DIMMs and SO-RIMMs. All of these memory modules are smaller than regular DIMMs or RIMMs.

Replacing and Upgrading Internal Parts

A+ 220-801 3.1

> 💡 **A+ Exam Tip** The A+ 220-801 exam expects you to know that DDR3, DDR2, DDR, and SDRAM memory can be found on SO-DIMMs. You also need to be aware of SO-RIMMs by Rambus.

A+ 220-802 4.8

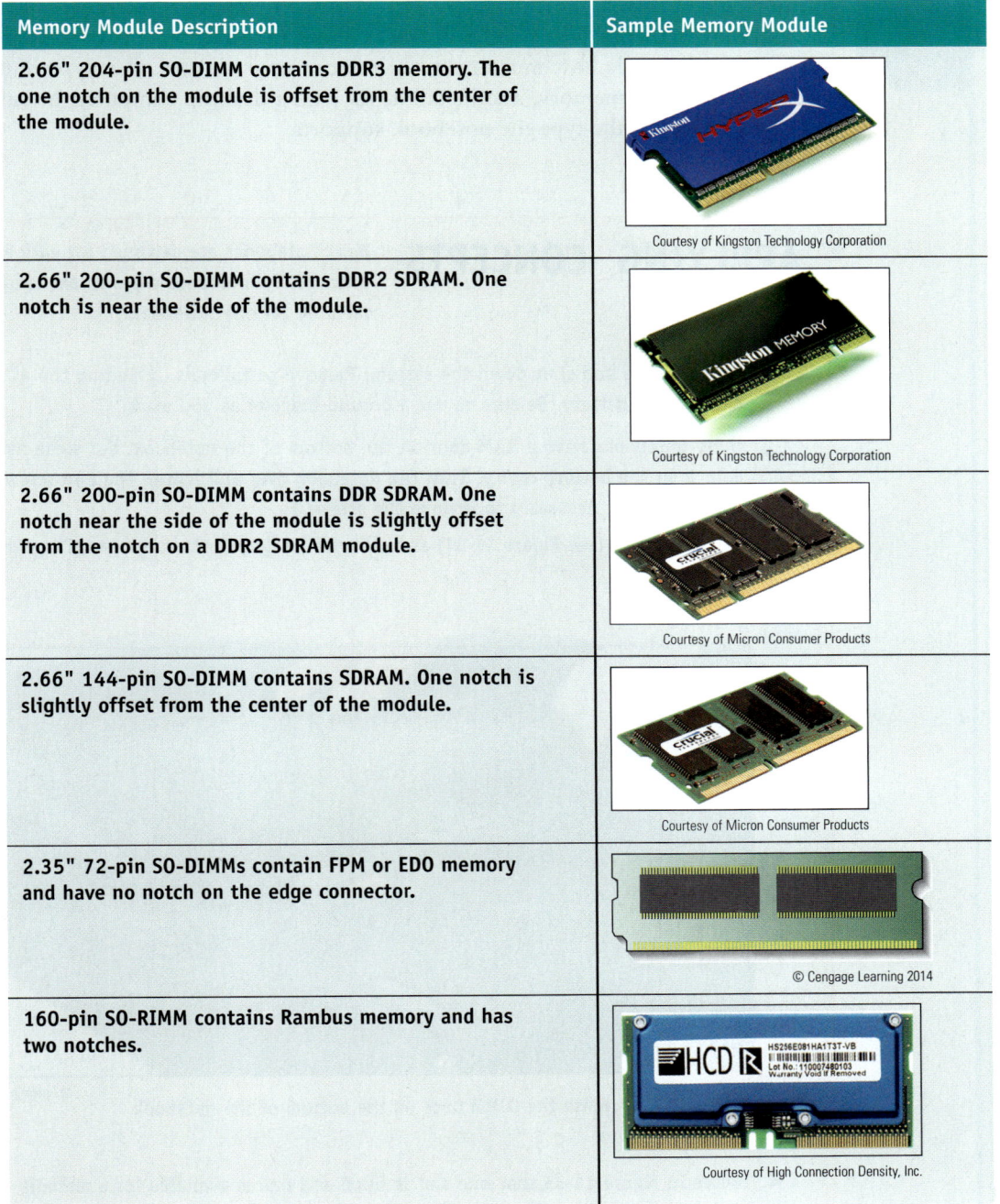

Memory Module Description	Sample Memory Module
2.66" 204-pin SO-DIMM contains DDR3 memory. The one notch on the module is offset from the center of the module.	Courtesy of Kingston Technology Corporation
2.66" 200-pin SO-DIMM contains DDR2 SDRAM. One notch is near the side of the module.	Courtesy of Kingston Technology Corporation
2.66" 200-pin SO-DIMM contains DDR SDRAM. One notch near the side of the module is slightly offset from the notch on a DDR2 SDRAM module.	Courtesy of Micron Consumer Products
2.66" 144-pin SO-DIMM contains SDRAM. One notch is slightly offset from the center of the module.	Courtesy of Micron Consumer Products
2.35" 72-pin SO-DIMMs contain FPM or EDO memory and have no notch on the edge connector.	© Cengage Learning 2014
160-pin SO-RIMM contains Rambus memory and has two notches.	Courtesy of High Connection Density, Inc.

Table 11-2 Memory modules used in notebook computers

© Cengage Learning 2014

Just as with memory modules used in desktop computers, you can only use the type of memory the notebook is designed to support. The number of pins and the position of the notches on a SO-DIMM keep you from inserting the wrong module in a memory slot.

A+ 220-801 3.1

A+ 220-802 4.8

HOW TO UPGRADE MEMORY ON A NOTEBOOK

Before upgrading memory, make sure you are not voiding your warranty. Search for the best buy, but make sure you use memory modules made by or authorized by your notebook's manufacturer and designed for the exact model of your notebook. Installing generic memory might save money but might also void the notebook's warranty.

Upgrading memory on a notebook works about the same way as with upgrading memory on a desktop: Decide how much memory you can upgrade and what type of memory you need, purchase the memory, and install it. As with a desktop computer, be sure to match the type of memory to the type the notebook supports.

APPLYING CONCEPTS Most notebooks are designed for easy access to memory. Follow these steps to exchange or upgrade memory for one notebook.

1. Back up data and shut down the system. Remove peripherals, including the AC adapter. Remove the battery. Be sure to use a ground bracelet as you work.

2. Many notebooks have a RAM door on the bottom of the notebook. For some notebooks, this door is in the battery cavity. Turn the notebook over and loosen the two screws on the RAM door. (It is not necessary to remove the screws.)

3. Raise the door (see Figure 11-34) and remove the door from its hinges. The two memory slots are exposed.

Figure 11-34 Raise the DIMM door on the bottom of the notebook

© Cengage Learning 2014

4. Notice in Figure 11-35 that one slot is filled and one is available for a memory upgrade. Also notice in the figure that when you remove the RAM door, the CMOS battery is exposed. This easy access to the battery makes exchanging it very easy. To remove a SO-DIMM, pull the clips on the side of the memory slot apart slightly (see Figure 11-36). The SO-DIMM will pop up out of the slot and can then be removed. If it does not pop up, you can hold the clips apart as you pull the module up and out of the slot.

A+ 220-801 3.1

A+ 220-802 4.8

Figure 11-35 SO-DIMM slots, one installed SO-DIMM, and the CMOS battery are exposed

Figure 11-36 Pull apart the clips on the memory slot to release the SO-DIMM

5. To install a new SO-DIMM, insert the module at an angle into the slot (see Figure 11-37) and gently push it down until it snaps into the clips (see Figure 11-38). Replace the RAM door.

Figure 11-37 Insert a new SO-DIMM into a memory slot

Figure 11-38 Push down on the SO-DIMM until it pops into the clips

REPLACING A HARD DRIVE

When purchasing and installing an internal hard drive or optical drive, see the notebook manufacturer's documentation about specific sizes and connectors that will fit the notebook. Also be aware of voiding a warranty if you don't follow the notebook manufacturer's directions. Here is what you need to know when shopping for a notebook hard drive:

- ▲ A desktop hard drive is 3.5 inches wide and a notebook drive is 2.5 inches wide. Because the form factor of a notebook drive is more compact, it costs more than a desktop drive holding the same amount of data. Some notebook hard drives use SSD (solid state device) technology.
- ▲ Notebook hard drives use either a SATA or PATA interface. A SATA connector on a notebook looks the same as that on a desktop. PATA or IDE connectors on a desktop

motherboard use 40 pins, but notebook IDE connectors use 44 pins. Figure 11-39 shows interfaces for IDE and SATA drives for desktop and notebook systems. Check your notebook manual to know which type of hard drive to buy, or remove the old drive and see which interface it uses.

Figure 11-39 SATA and IDE interfaces used by drives in notebook and desktop systems

- For IDE drives, some notebooks use an adapter to interface between the 44-pin IDE connector on the hard drive and a proprietary connector on the notebook motherboard. You'll need to remove the old drive and see how it's connected to know if an adapter is used. If you find an adapter, you can remove it from the old hard drive and connect it to the new drive.

Before deciding to replace a hard drive, consider these issues:
- If the old drive has crashed, you'll need the recovery media to reinstall Windows and the drivers. Make sure you have the recovery media before you start.
- If you are upgrading from a low-capacity drive to a higher-capacity drive, you need to consider how you will transfer data from the old drive to the new one. One way to do that is to use a USB-to-IDE or USB-to-SATA converter that you first learned about in Chapter 8 (refer back to Figures 8-6 and 8-7). Using this converter, both drives can be up and working on the notebook at the same time, so you can copy files.

To replace a hard drive, older notebook computers required that you disassemble the notebook. With newer notebooks, you should be able to easily replace a drive. For example, for one notebook, first power down the system, remove peripherals, including the AC adapter, and remove the battery pack. Then remove a screw that holds the drive in place (see Figure 11-40). Open the lid of the notebook slightly so that the lid doesn't obstruct your removing the drive. Turn the notebook on its side and push the drive out of its bay (see Figure 11-41). Then remove the plastic cover from the drive. Move the cover to the new drive, and insert the new drive in the bay. Next, replace the screw and power up the system.

When the system boots up, if BIOS setup is set to autodetect hard drives, BIOS recognizes the new drive and searches for an operating system. If the drive is new, boot from the Windows recovery DVD and install the OS.

546 | CHAPTER 11 Supporting Notebooks

Figure 11-40 This one screw holds the hard drive in position

Figure 11-41 Push the drive out of its bay

> **Notes** In other chapters, it is possible to give general directions on PC repair that apply to all kinds of brands, models, and systems. Not so with notebooks. Learning to repair notebooks involves learning unique ways to assemble, disassemble, and repair notebook components for specific brands and models of notebooks.

For some laptops, such as the one shown in Figure 11-42, you remove a cover on the bottom of the computer to expose the hard drive. Then remove one screw that anchors the drive. You can then remove the drive.

DISASSEMBLING AND REASSEMBLING A NOTEBOOK COMPUTER

Working on notebooks requires special tools and extra patience. Just as when you are working with desktop systems, before opening the case of a notebook or touching sensitive components, you should always use a ground strap to protect the system against ESD. You can attach the alligator clip end of the ground strap to an unpainted metallic surface on the notebook. This surface could be, for instance, a port on the back of the notebook (see Figure 11-43). If a ground strap is not available, first dissipate any ESD between you and the notebook by touching a metallic unpainted part of the notebook, such as a port on the back, before you touch a component inside the case.

Figure 11-42 Remove a cover on the bottom of the laptop to exchange the hard drive, which is attached to a proprietary bracket

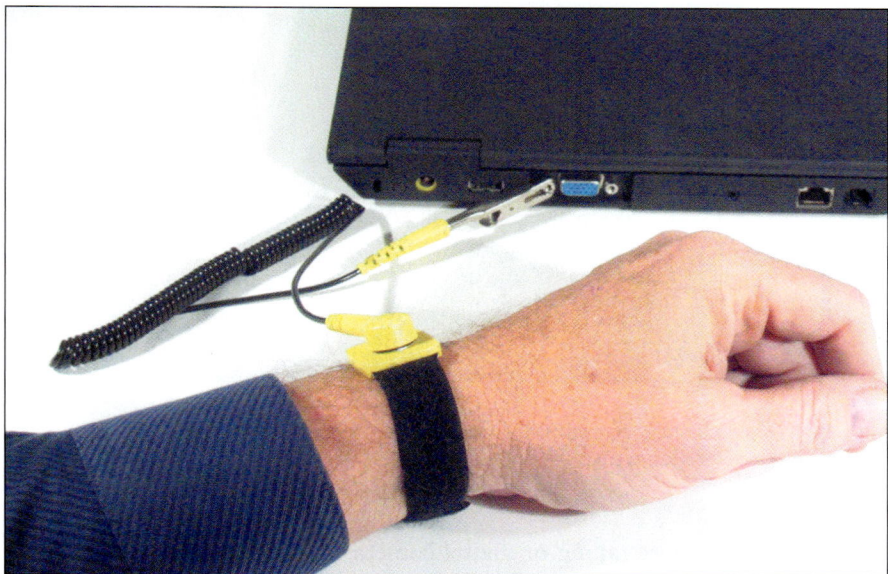

Figure 11-43 To protect the system against ESD, attach the alligator clip of a ground strap to an I/O port on the back of the notebook

Screws and nuts on a notebook are smaller than a desktop system and therefore require smaller tools. Figure 11-44 shows a display of several tools used to disassemble a notebook, although you can get by without several of them. Here's the list:

- Antistatic ground strap
- Small flat-head screwdriver
- Number 1 Phillips-head screwdriver
- Dental pick (useful for prying without damaging plastic cases, connectors, and screw covers such as the one in Figure 11-45)
- Torx screwdriver set, particularly size T5
- Something such as a pillbox to keep screws and small parts organized

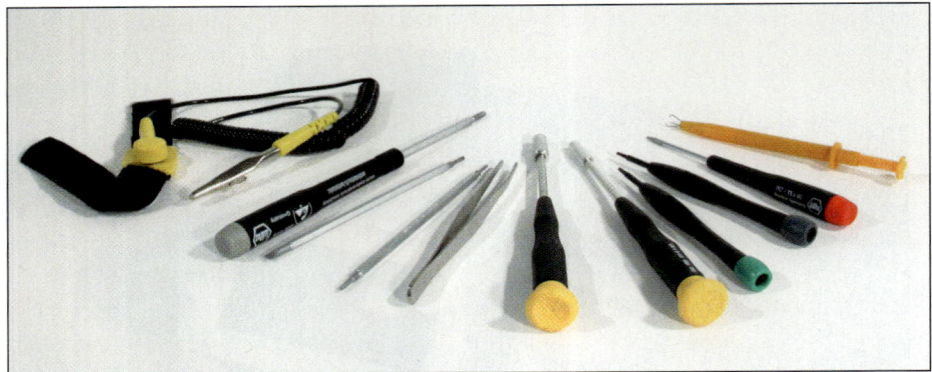

Figure 11-44 Tools for disassembling a notebook computer

Figure 11-45 Use a small screwdriver or dental pick to pry up the plastic cover hiding a screw

- Notepad for note taking or digital camera (optional)
- Flashlight (optional)
- Three-prong extractor to pick up tiny screws (optional)

Notebooks contain many small screws of various sizes and lengths. When reassembling, put screws back where they came from so that when you reassemble the system, you won't use screws that are too long and that can protrude into a sensitive component and damage it. As you remove a screw, store or label it so you know where it goes when reassembling. One way to do that is to place screws in a pillbox with each compartment labeled. Another way is to place screws on a soft padded work surface and use white labeling tape to label each set of screws. A third way to organize screws is to put them on notebook paper and write beside them where the screw belongs (see Figure 11-46). My favorite method of keeping up with all those screws is to tape the screw beside the manufacturer documentation that I'm following to disassemble the notebook (see Figure 11-47). Whatever method you use, work methodically to keep screws and components organized so you know what goes where when reassembling.

Figure 11-46 Using a notepad can help you organize screws so you know which screw goes where when reassembling

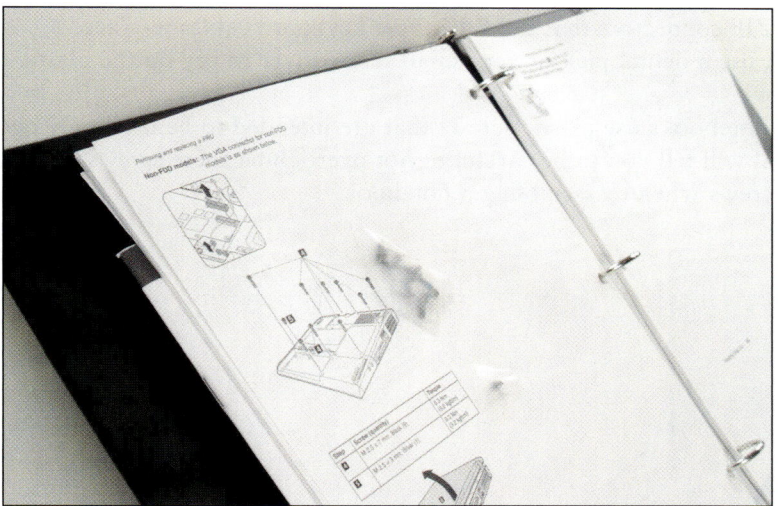

Figure 11-47 Tape screws beside the step in the manufacturer documentation that told you to remove the screw

> **A+ Exam Tip** The A+ 220-802 exam expects you to know the importance of keeping parts organized when disassembling a notebook as well as the importance of having manufacturer documentation to know the steps to disassembly.

As you disassemble the computer, if you are not following directions from a service manual, keep notes as you work to help you reassemble later. Draw diagrams and label things carefully. Include in your drawings cable orientations and screw locations. You might consider using a digital camera. Photos that you take at each step in the disassembly process will be a great help when it's time to put the notebook back together.

When disassembling a notebook, consider the following tips:

▲ Make your best effort to find the hardware service manual for the particular notebook model you are servicing. The manual should include all the detailed steps to disassemble the notebook and a parts list of components that can be ordered from the notebook manufacturer. If you don't have this manual, your chances of successfully replacing an internal component are greatly reduced! And, if you don't have much experience disassembling a notebook, it is not wise to attempt to do so without this manual.

▲ Consider the warranty that might still apply to the notebook. Remember that opening the case of a notebook under warranty most likely will void the warranty. Make certain that any component you have purchased to replace an internal component will work in the model of notebook you are servicing.

▲ Take your time. Patience is needed to keep from scratching or marring plastic screw covers, hinges, and the case.

▲ As you work, don't force anything. If you find yourself forcing something, you're likely to break it.

▲ Always wear a ground strap or use other protection against ESD.

▲ When removing cables, know that sometimes cable connectors are ZIF connectors. To disconnect a cable from a ZIF connector, first pull up on the connector and then remove the cable, as shown in Figure 11-48. Figure 11-49 shows a notebook using three ZIF connectors that hold the three keyboard cables in place.

▲ Again, use a dental pick or very small screwdriver to pry up the plastic cover hiding a screw.

▲ Some notebooks use plastic screws that are intended to be used only once. The service manual will tell you to be careful to not overtighten these screws and to always use new screws when reassembling a notebook.

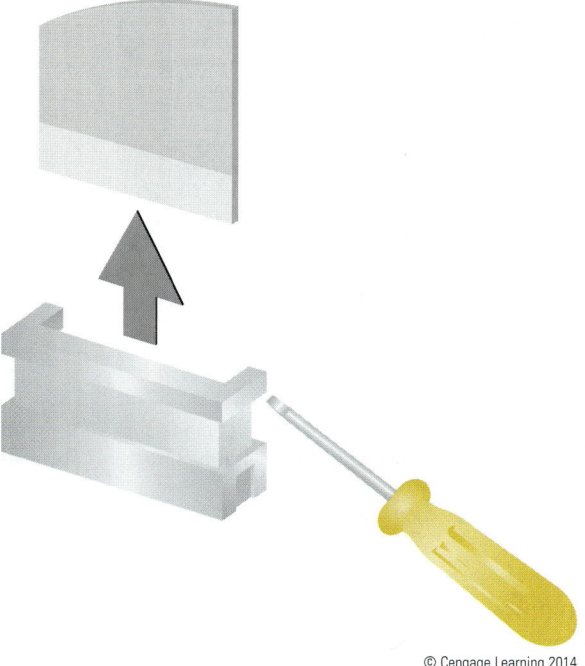

Figure 11-48 To disconnect a ZIF connector, first push up on the connector to release the latch, and then remove the cable

Replacing and Upgrading Internal Parts 551

A+ 220-801 3.1

A+ 220-802 4.8

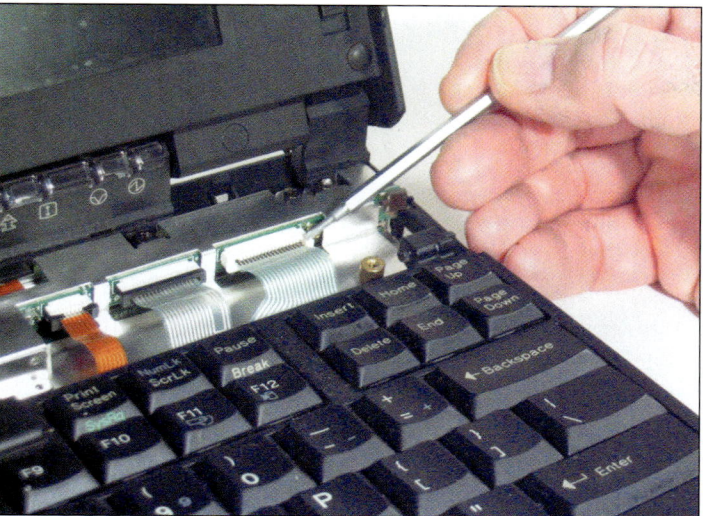

Figure 11-49 Three ZIF connectors hold the three keyboard cables in place
© Cengage Learning 2014

- Disassemble the notebook by removing each field replaceable unit (FRU) in the order given by the service manual for your notebook. For example, one manufacturer says that to replace the motherboard for a notebook, remove components in this order: battery pack, RAM door, keyboard, middle cover, hinge cover, DVD drive and bracket, mini PCIe adapter, keyboard bezel assembly, fan assembly, CPU, CPU fixture, and DVD drive bracket. After all these components are removed, you can then remove the motherboard. Follow the steps to remove each component in the right order.

When reassembling a notebook, consider these general tips:

- Reassemble the notebook in the reverse order of the way you disassembled it. Follow each step carefully.
- Be sure to tighten, but not overtighten, all screws. Loose screws or metal fragments in a notebook can be dangerous; they might cause a short as they shift about inside the notebook.
- Before you install the battery or AC adapter, verify there are no loose parts inside the notebook. Pick it up and shake it. If you hear anything loose, open the case and find the loose component, screw, spring, or metal flake, and fix the problem.

Now let's look at the specific situations where you are disassembling a notebook to replace an LCD panel, mini PCIe card, and other internal components.

REPLACING THE KEYBOARD AND TOUCHPAD

Replacing the keyboard is pretty easy to do. Here are typical steps that are similar to many models of notebooks:

1. Power down the notebook and remove the AC adapter and the battery pack.
2. Remove two or more screws on the bottom of the notebook (see Figure 11-50). (Only the documentation can tell you which ones because there are probably several of them used to hold various components in place.)
3. Turn the notebook over and open the lid. Gently push the keyboard toward the lid while pulling it up to release it from the case (see Figure 11-51).

11

Figure 11-50 Remove screws on the bottom of the notebook

Figure 11-51 Pry up and lift the keyboard out of the notebook case

4. Bring the keyboard out of the case and forward to expose the keyboard ribbon cable attached underneath the board. Use a screwdriver to lift the cable connector up and out of its socket (see Figure 11-52).

5. Replace the keyboard following the steps in reverse order.

Figure 11-52 Disconnect the keyboard cable from the motherboard

Sometimes the touchpad and keyboard are one complete field replaceable unit. If the touchpad is a separate component, if might be part of the keyboard bezel, also called the palm rest. This bezel is the flat cover that surrounds the keyboard. Most likely you have to remove the keyboard before you can remove the keyboard bezel.

REPLACING OPTICAL DRIVES

For some systems you'll need to first remove the keyboard to expose an optical drive. Follow along as we remove the DVD drive from one system:

1. Remove the keyboard.
2. Remove the screw that holds the DVD drive to the notebook (see Figure 11-53).
3. Slide the drive out of the bay (see Figure 11-54).

Figure 11-53 Remove the screw that holds the DVD drive

© Cengage Learning 2014

Figure 11-54 Slide the drive out of the bay

© Cengage Learning 2014

4. When you slide the new drive into the bay, make sure you push it far enough into the bay that it solidly connects with the drive connector at the back of the bay. Replace the screw.

For other systems, the optical drive can be removed by first removing a cover from the bottom of the notebook. Then you remove one screw that secures the drive. Next, push the optical drive out of the case (see Figure 11-55).

A+ 220-801 3.1

A+ 220-802 4.8

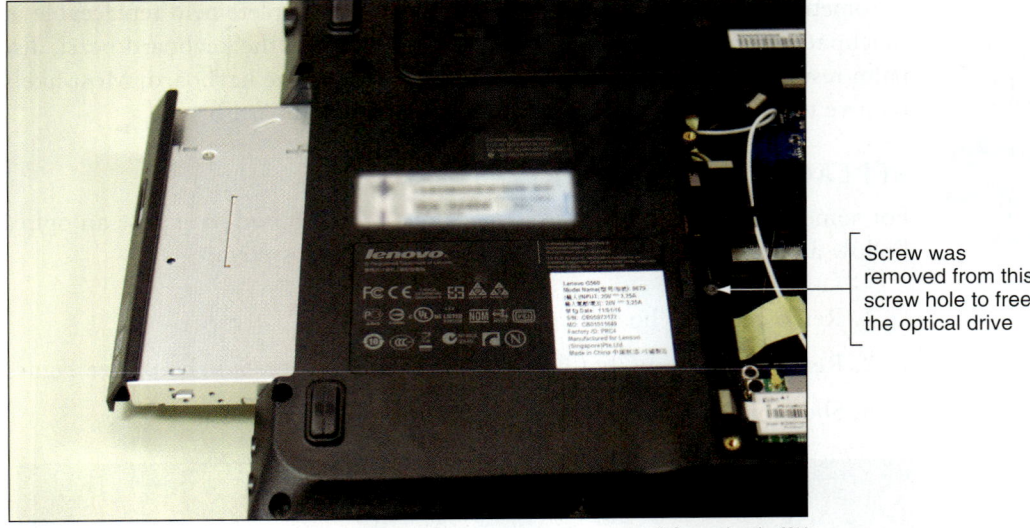

Figure 11-55 Push the optical drive out the side of the case

REPLACING EXPANSION CARDS

A notebook does not contain the normal PCI Express or PCI slots found in desktop systems. Newer notebooks are likely to use the **Mini PCI Express** slots (also called **Mini PCIe** slots) that use the PCI Express standards applied to notebooks. Mini PCI Express slots use 52 pins on the edge connector. These slots can be used by many kinds of Mini PCIe cards. These cards are often used to enhance communications options for a notebook, including Wi-Fi wireless, cellular WAN, and Bluetooth Mini PCIe cards. Figure 11-56 shows a Mini PCI

Figure 11-56 MC8775 PCI Express Mini card by Sierra Wireless used for voice and data transmissions on 3G networks

Express Sierra Wireless mobile broadband Internet card. Older notebooks use a **Mini PCI** slot (see Figure 11-57), which uses PCI standards. Mini PCI cards are about twice the size of Mini PCI Express cards. Figure 11-58 shows a Wi-Fi Mini PCI card by MikroTik.

Figure 11-57 A Mini PCI slot follows PCI standards applied to notebooks

Figure 11-58 Wireless IEEE 802.11a/b/g/n Mini PCI card by MikroTik

For many laptops, you can remove a cover on the bottom of the laptop to expose expansion cards so that you can exchange them without an extensive disassemble. For example, to remove the cover on the bottom of one Lenovo laptop, first remove several screws and then lift the laptop cover up and out. Several internal components are exposed, as shown in Figure 11-59.

The half-size Mini PCIe wireless Wi-Fi card shown in Figure 11-60 has two antennas. To remove the card, first remove the one screw shown in the photo and disconnect the two black and white antenna wires. Then slide the card forward and out of the slot. You can then install a new card.

Figure 11-59 Removing the cover from the bottom of a laptop exposes several internal components

Figure 11-60 This half-size Mini PCIe wireless card is anchored in the expansion slot with one screw

Figure 11-61 shows a full-size Mini PCIe card installed in a different laptop. First disconnect the one antenna and remove the one screw at the top of the card, and then pull the card forward and out of the slot.

A+ 220-801
3.1

A+ 220-802
4.8

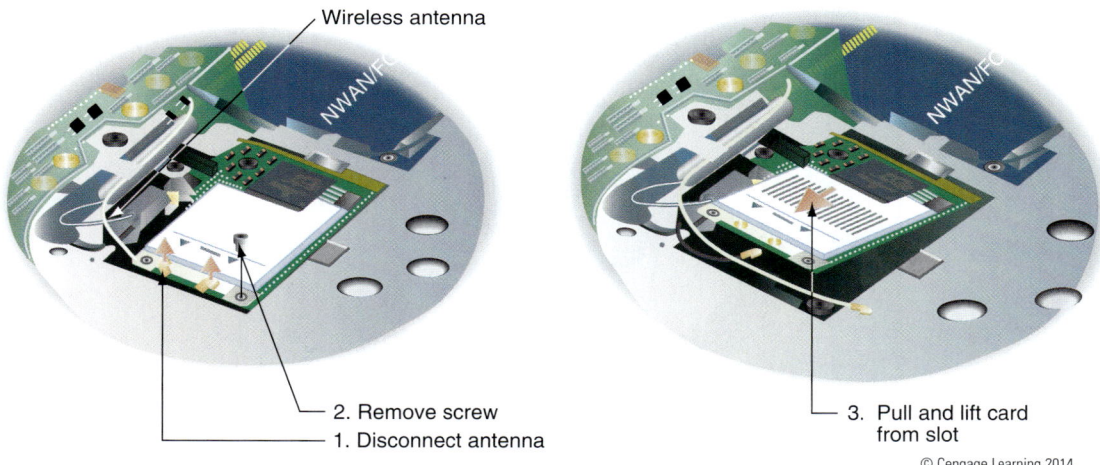

Figure 11-61 How to remove a Mini PCI Express card

© Cengage Learning 2014

> **A+ Exam Tip** The A+ 220-801 exam expects you to be able to replace a Mini PCIe card in a notebook.

After you have installed a Mini PCIe card that is a Bluetooth, cellular WAN, or other wireless adapter, try to connect the notebook to the wireless network. If you have problems making a connection, verify that Device Manager reports the device is working properly and that Event Viewer has not reported error events about the device.

REPLACING THE PROCESSOR

When replacing or upgrading the processor in a laptop, be sure to select a processor supported by the notebook manufacturer for this particular notebook. The range of processors supported by a notebook does not usually include as many options as those supported by a desktop motherboard. Some significant Intel mobile processor sockets include FCPGA988, PPGA988, and the older PPGA478. Currently the FCPGA988 is the most popular Intel mobile socket. AMD sockets for mobile processors include sockets S1, AM2+, and ASB1. By far, the most used AMD mobile socket is the 638-pin S1 socket.

For many laptops, removing the cover on the bottom of a laptop exposes the processor fan and heat sink assembly. When you remove this assembly, you can then open the socket and remove the processor. For example, looking back at the laptop shown in Figure 11-59, you can see the processor heat sink and fan assembly exposed. To remove the assembly, remove the seven screws and the fan power connector (see Figure 11-62). Then lift the assembly straight up, being careful not to damage the processor underneath.

For another laptop, the heat sink and fan assembly is also exposed when you remove the cover on the bottom of the laptop (see Figure 11-63). Notice the heat sink on this laptop extends to the processor and chipset. You remove several screws and then lift the entire assembly out as a unit. For both laptops, the heat sink fits on top of the processor and the fan sits to the side of the processor. This design is typical of many laptops. However, some laptops require you to remove the keyboard and the keyboard bezel to reach the fan assembly and processor under the bezel.

Figure 11-64 shows the heat sink and fan assembly removed in one laptop, exposing the processor. Notice the thermal compound on the processor. To remove the processor, turn the CPU socket screw 90 degrees to open the socket, as shown in the figure. Most Intel and AMD sockets have this socket screw on the side of the socket, as shown in Figure 11-64, although other sockets have the screw on the corner of the socket.

Figure 11-62 Seven screws hold the processor heat sink and fan assembly in place

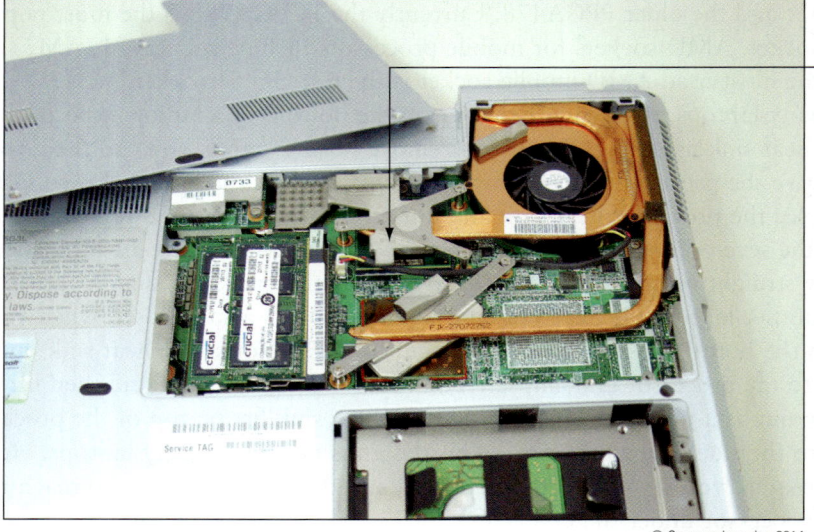

Figure 11-63 Remove the cover from the bottom of the laptop to expose the heat sink and fan assembly and to reach the processor

Figure 11-64 Open the CPU socket

Lift the CPU from the socket. Be careful to lift straight up without bending the CPU pins. Figure 11-65 shows the processor out of the socket. If you look carefully, you can see the missing pins on one corner of the processor and socket. This corner is used to correctly orient the processor in the socket, which is socket 478B.

Figure 11-65 The processor removed from socket 478B

Before you place the new processor into the socket, be sure the socket screw is in the open position. Then delicately place the processor into its socket. If it does not drop in completely, consider that the screw might not be in the full open position. Be sure to use thermal compound on top of the processor. Intel recommends 0.2 grams of compound, which is about the size of a small pea. To make sure you use just the right amount of compound, consider buying it in individual packets that are measured for a single application.

REPLACING THE MOTHERBOARD

Replacing the motherboard probably means you'll need to fully disassemble the entire notebook except the LCD assembly. Therefore, before you tackle the job, consider alternatives. If a port or component on the motherboard fails, consider installing an external device rather than replacing the motherboard (also called the system board). Also, before you decide to replace the motherboard, check if the notebook manufacturer has diagnostic software you can download and use to verify the problem is the motherboard. Search the site for information about the error message or symptom. Replacing the motherboard is a big deal, so consider that the cost of repair, including parts and labor, might be more than the laptop is worth. A new laptop might be your best solution.

Here is the general procedure for replacing the motherboard in one notebook:

1. Remove the keyboard, optical drive, and mini PCIe card.

2. The next step is to remove the notebook lid and keyboard bezel assembly. To do this, first remove two screws on the back of the notebook (see Figure 11-66) and the screws on the bottom of the notebook. You can then crack the case by lifting the notebook lid and keyboard bezel from the case (see Figure 11-67).

Figure 11-66 Remove two screws on the back of the notebook

Figure 11-67 Cracking the notebook case

Replacing and Upgrading Internal Parts | 561

A+ 220-801 3.1

A+ 220-802 4.8

3. Lift up the assembly and look underneath to see two cables connecting the assembly to the motherboard (see Figure 11-68). Disconnect these two cables and set the assembly aside.

4. Figure 11-69 shows the open case. To remove the CPU fan assembly, remove screws (see Figure 11-70) and then lift the fan assembly up. Then open the CPU socket and remove the CPU.

Figure 11-68 Lift the assembly to locate the two cable connections © Cengage Learning 2014

Figure 11-69 Components inside the open case © Cengage Learning 2014

Figure 11-70 Remove the screws holding the CPU fan assembly in place

5. The DVD drive can now be removed, and the motherboard is fully exposed.
6. Remove a single screw that holds the motherboard in place (see Figure 11-71) and lift the board out of the case. Figure 11-72 shows the top of the board, and Figure 11-73 shows the bottom. Both top and bottom are packed with components. When reassembling the system, all steps are done in reverse.

Figure 11-71 Remove the single screw attaching the motherboard to the case

Replacing and Upgrading Internal Parts 563

A+
220-801
3.1

A+
220-802
4.8

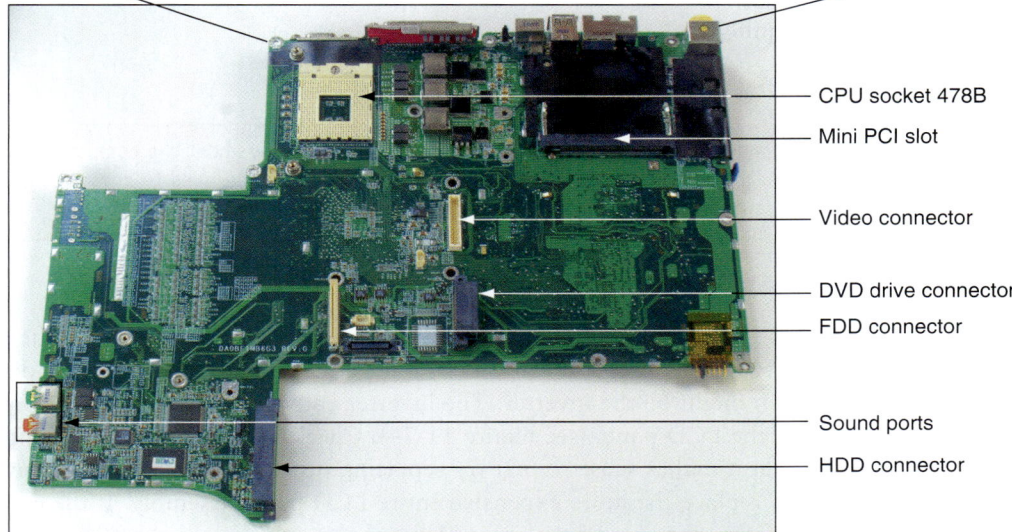

Figure 11-72 Top of the motherboard

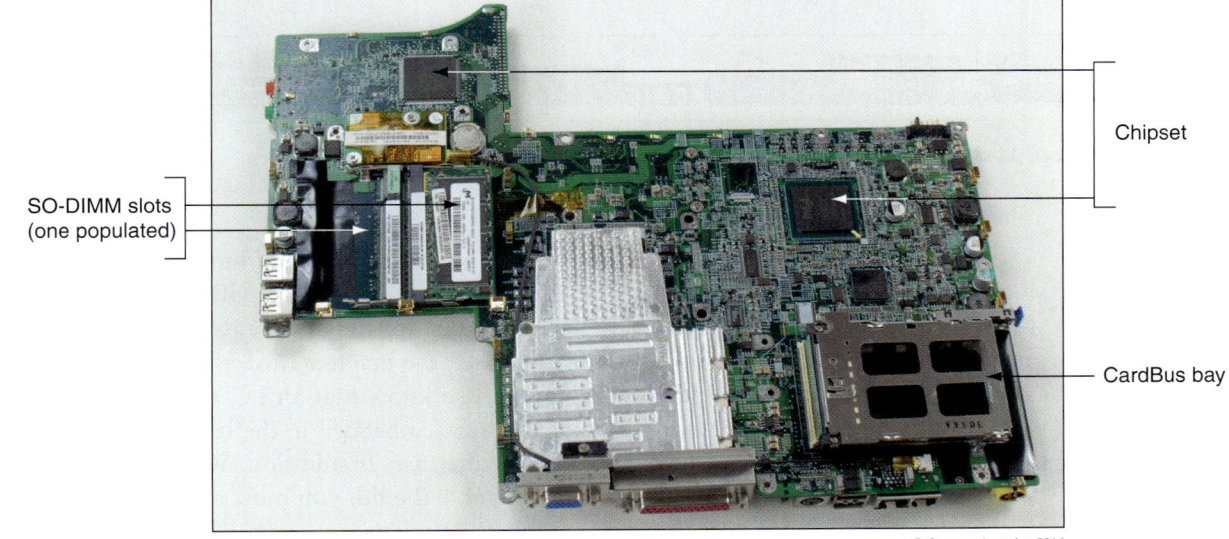

Figure 11-73 Bottom of the motherboard

REPLACING THE LCD PANEL

A notebook display almost always uses LCD technology, although Samsung recently released a notebook that uses OLED display. It is expected that laptops will one day use plasma display because plasma is expected to use only about 20 percent as much power as LCD and gives better quality display than LCD. Some laptop LCD panels use LED backlighting to improve display quality and conserve power.

Because the LCD panel is so fragile, it is one component that is likely to be broken when a notebook is not handled properly. If the LCD panel is dim or black when the notebook is running, first try to use the video port on the notebook to connect it to an external monitor. After you connect the monitor, use a function key to toggle between the LCD panel, the external monitor, and both the panel and monitor. If the external monitor works, but the LCD panel does not work, then most likely the problem is with the LCD panel assembly.

> **A+ Exam Tip** The A+ 220-801 exam expects you to know about the components within the display of a laptop, including LCD, LED, OLED, and plasma types. You also need to know about backlighting and the function of an inverter.

If the LCD display is entirely black, most likely you'll have to replace the entire LCD assembly. However, if the screen is dim, but you can make out that some display is present, the problem might be the inverter. The inverter converts DC to AC used to power the backlighting of the LCD panel (see Figure 11-74). Check with the notebook manufacturer to confirm that it makes sense to first try replacing just the relatively inexpensive inverter board before you replace the more expensive entire LCD panel assembly. If the entire assembly needs replacing, the cost of the assembly might exceed the value of the notebook. You also need to know that LCD panels that use LED backlighting don't use an inverter because the LED backlight uses DC power directly from the motherboard.

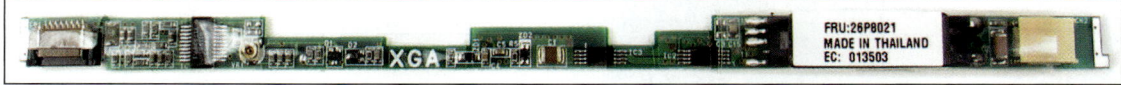

Figure 11-74   A ThinkPad inverter board

Sometimes, a notebook LCD panel, including the entire cover and hinges, is considered a single field replaceable unit, and sometimes components within the LCD assembly are considered FRUs. For example, the field replaceable units for the display panel in Figure 11-75 are the LCD front bezel, the hinges, the LCD panel, the inverter card, the LCD interface cables, the LCD USB cover, and the rear cover. Also know that an LCD assembly might include a microphone, webcam, or speakers that are embedded in the laptop lid. For other laptops, the microphone and speakers are inside the case. In addition, Wi-Fi antenna might be in the lid of the notebook. When you disassemble the lid, you must disconnect the antenna from the bottom part of the notebook.

Some high-end notebooks contain a video card that has embedded video memory. This video card might also need replacing. In most cases, you would replace only the LCD panel and perhaps the inverter card.

Replacing and Upgrading Internal Parts | 565

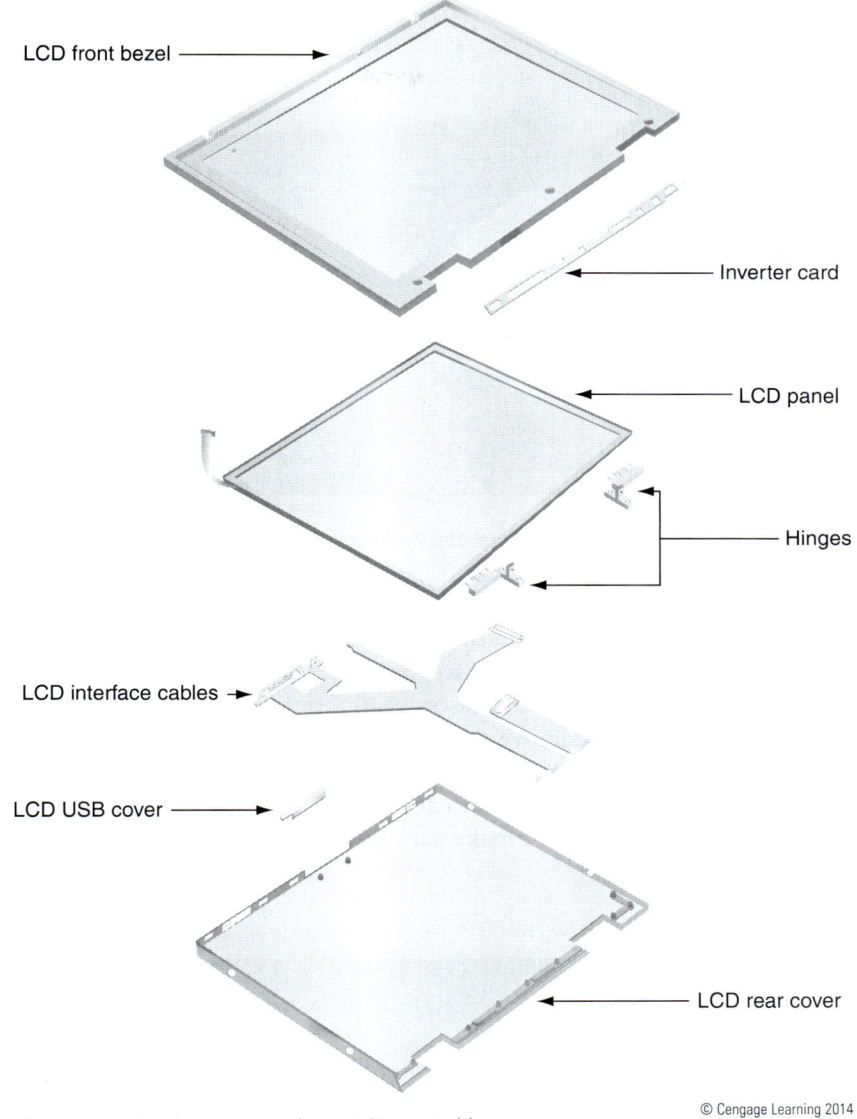

Figure 11-75 Components in an LCD assembly

The following are some general directions to replace an LCD panel:

1. Remove the AC adapter and the battery pack.
2. Remove the keyboard.
3. Remove the screws holding the hinge in place and remove the hinge cover. Figure 11-76 shows a notebook with a metal hinge cover, but some notebooks use plastic covers that you can easily break as you remove them. Be careful with the plastic ones.
4. Remove the screws holding the LCD panel to the notebook.
5. You're now ready to remove the LCD panel from the notebook. Be aware there might be wires running through the hinge assembly, cables, or a pin connector. Cables might be connected to the motherboard using ZIF connectors. As you remove the LCD top cover, be careful to watch for how the panel is connected. Don't pull on wires or cables as you remove the cover, but first carefully disconnect them.

Figure 11-76 Remove the hinge cover from the notebook hinge

6. Next, remove screws that hold the top cover and LCD panel together. Sometimes, these screws are covered with plastic or rubber circles or pads that match the color of the case. First use a dental pick or small screwdriver to pick off these covers. You should then be able to remove the front bezel and separate the rear cover from the LCD panel. For one LCD panel, when you separate the LCD assembly from the lid cover, you can see the inverter card. Figure 11-77 shows the inverter card being compared to the new one to make sure they match. The match is not identical but should work.

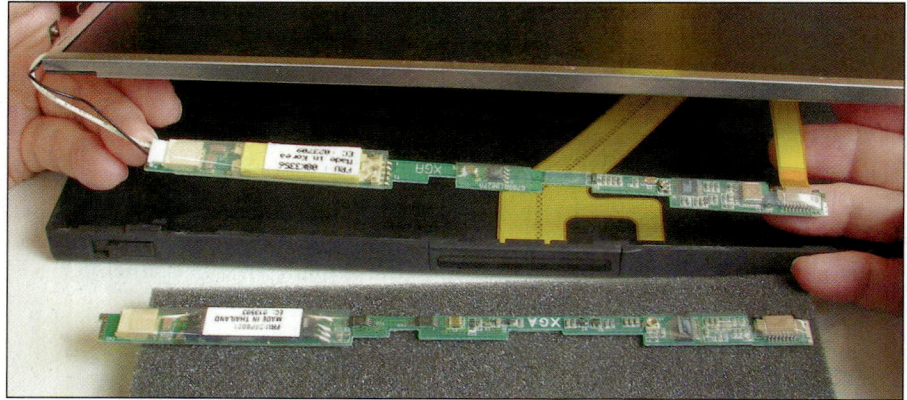

Figure 11-77 The inverter is exposed and is compared to the new one

7. Disconnect the old inverter and install the new one. When disconnecting the ribbon cable from the old inverter, notice you must first lift up on the lock holding the ZIF connector in place, as shown in Figure 11-78.

8. Install the new inverter. Reassemble the LCD panel assembly. Make sure the assembly is put together with a tight fit so that all screws line up well.

9. Reattach the LCD panel assembly to the notebook.

Replacing and Upgrading Internal Parts | 567

A+ 220-801 3.1, 3.2

A+ 220-802 4.8

Figure 11-78 Lift up on the ZIF connector locking mechanism before removing the ribbon cable

A+ 220-801 3.1

WORKING INSIDE AN ALL-IN-ONE COMPUTER

An all-in-one computer uses a mix of components sized for a desktop computer and a notebook. Just as with notebooks, you'll need the service manual to know how to crack the case and replace internal components. Also, for some components, such as the motherboard and power supply, you'll need to buy the replacement component from the all-in-one manufacturer because these components are likely to be proprietary as with many notebook components.

For specific directions about replacing parts in an all-in-one, see the service manual. Let's get the general idea by looking inside the case of the Lenovo ThinkCentre all-in-one shown earlier in Figure 11-1. First remove all discs and other devices, shut down the computer, and disconnect all cables. Lay the computer flat with the LCD panel down on a soft cloth or other surface that will not scratch the screen. An antistatic pad works well. To open the case, push the two clips on either side of the case cover outward as you push the back of the case upward toward the top of the computer. See Figure 11-79. The case cover can then be removed and laid to the side.

Figure 11-80 shows the computer with the case cover removed. Notice in the figure the hard drive is a 3.5 inch drive appropriate for a desktop system, and the memory modules

Figure 11-79 Push back on release tabs to open the case of an all-in-one computer

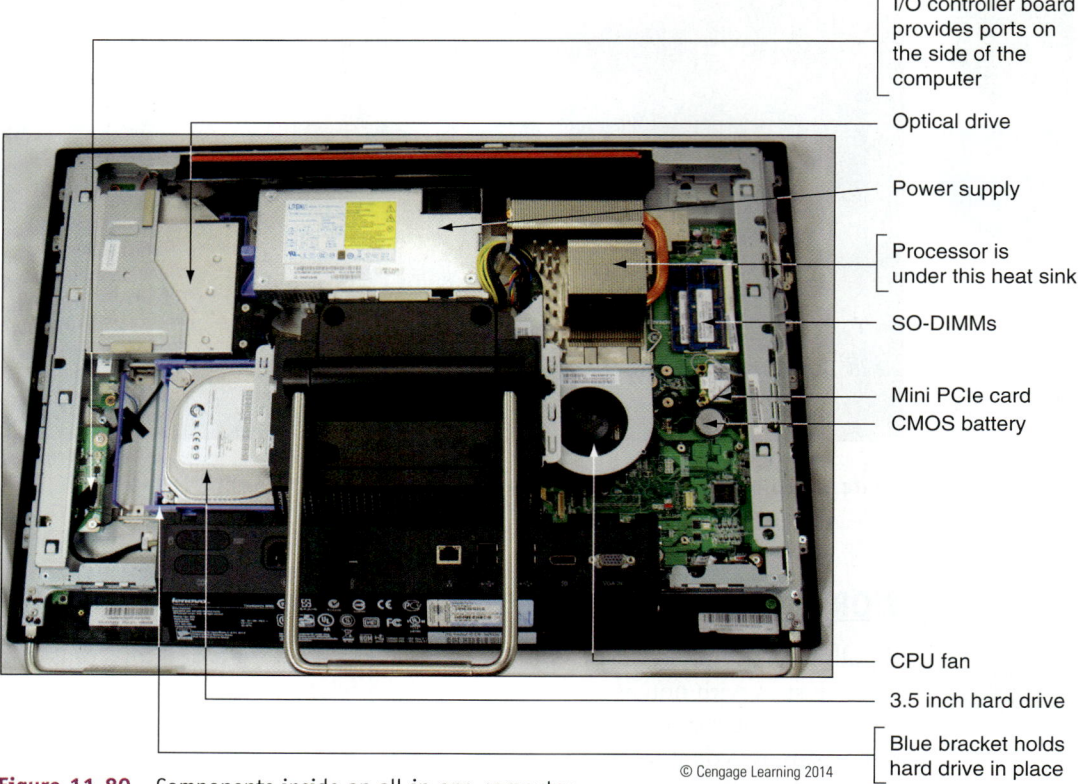

Figure 11-80 Components inside an all-in-one computer

are SO-DIMMs appropriate for a notebook. So goes the hybrid nature of an all-in-one. The fan and heat sink look more like that of a notebook computer, but the processor socket on the motherboard is a desktop processor socket, another hybrid design.

Several components are easy to exchange in this all-in-one without further disassembly. For example, the Mini PCIe card for wireless connectivity, shown in Figure 11-81, is easy to get to as is the CMOS battery that you can see to the left of the card.

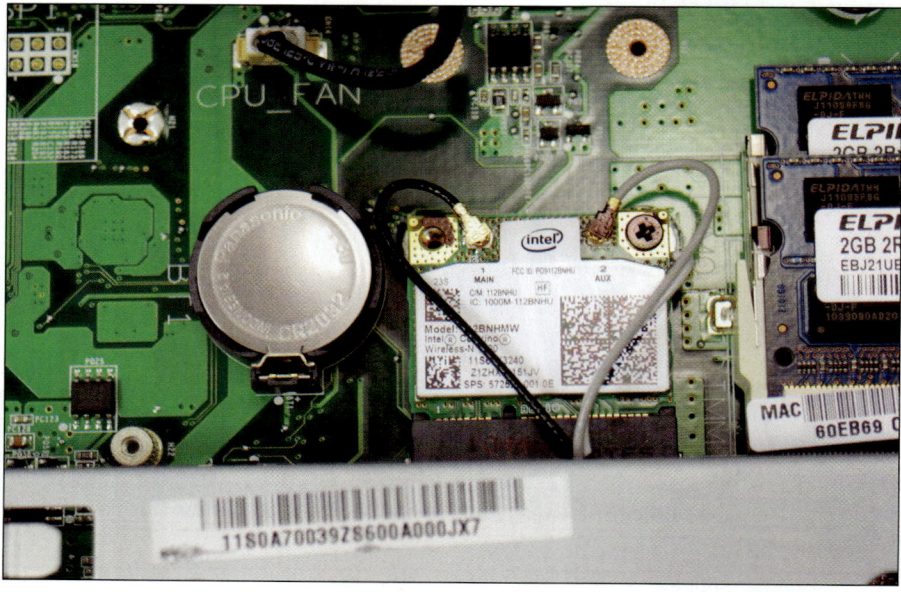

Figure 11-81 CMOS battery and Mini PCIe wireless card

To remove the hard drive, simply lift up on the blue handle shown in Figure 11-82 and slide the drive attached to the blue bracket out of the case. You then have to remove the bracket from the old drive, install it on the new drive, and reinsert the bracket with the new drive.

Figure 11-82 Lift up on the blue handle to release the 3.5 inch hard drive

The optical drive is removed by pressing a release button at the back of the optical drive and then sliding it out of the case. After the hard drive and optical drive are removed, you can get to the video inverter, which is secured to the case with two screws (see Figure 11-83).

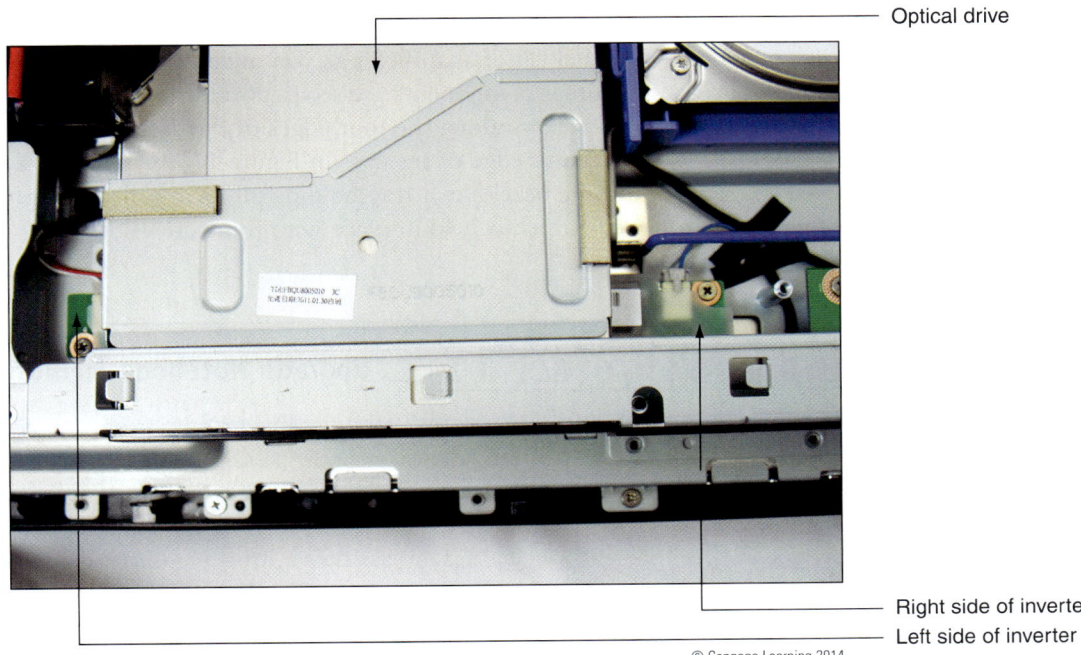

Figure 11-83 Optical drive above the inverter

The SO-DIMMs shown in Figure 11-84 are to the right of the Mini PCIe card. The processor is underneath the heat sink, and the heat sink is held in place with four screws shown in Figure 11-84. Remove the four screws and lift the heat sink up and out exposing the processor. The desktop processor socket works like the ones you saw in Chapter 4.

Figure 11-84 SO-DIMMs, CPU fan, and heat sink

To exchange the LCD panel is not as difficult as you might expect. The motherboard, power supply, drives, and other components are secured to a front bezel. This bezel is secured to the case with 13 screws along the four edges of the case. You can see several of these screws just inside the outer edge of the case in Figure 11-80. When you remove the 13 screws, you can lift out the bezel like a tray holding all its installed components. The LCD panel is then exposed, which is held in place with four screws.

Hands-on Project 11-3 Upgrade Notebook Memory

A friend has a Lenovo ThinkPad X200 notebook and is looking for ways to improve its performance. He's cleaned up the hard drive and is now considering the possibility of upgrading memory. Windows reports the system has 2 GB of RAM. He opens the cover on the bottom of the case and discovers that both SO-DIMM slots are filled. How much will the upgrade cost to bring total RAM in the system to 4 GB? Print the web page to support your answer. What type and speed of SO-DIMMs does this notebook use?

A+ 220-801
3.1

A+ 220-802
4.8

Hands-on | Project 11-4   Observe Notebook Features

Examine a notebook, its documentation, and the manufacturer's web site, and then answer these questions:

1. How do you exchange the battery pack on the notebook?
2. How many SO-DIMMs are installed? What type of SO-DIMM does the notebook use? What is the size and speed of each SO-DIMM?
3. How much total RAM is currently installed? How much total RAM can the system hold?
4. What is the capacity of the hard drive?
5. What OS is installed?
6. What processor is installed?
7. What ports are on the notebook?
8. What type of PC Card or ExpressCard slots does the notebook have?
9. What type of memory slots does the notebook have?
10. How much does the notebook weigh?
11. What is the cost of a new battery pack?
12. Search for SO-DIMMs the notebook can use. How much would it cost to upgrade the notebook's memory to full capacity? When doing so, will you be able to use existing SO-DIMMs or must you replace these?

TROUBLESHOOTING NOTEBOOKS

When troubleshooting problems with notebook ports, slots, or other devices, don't forget to use the diagnostics software installed on the hard drive or available on the notebook manufacturer's web site to help with troubleshooting components. Now let's look at some common problems with notebooks and how to solve them.

Video
Troubleshooting Notebooks

PROBLEMS LOGGING ONTO WINDOWS

If a user complains she cannot log onto Windows even when she's certain she is entering the correct password, ask her to make sure the NumLock key is off. Notebooks use this key to toggle between the keys interpreted as letters and numbers. Most notebooks have a NumLock indicator light near the keyboard.

NO WIRELESS CONNECTIVITY

In a notebook, an internal wireless adapter uses an internal antenna, and the notebook might have a switch to turn on the internal wireless adapter or might use a key combination for that purpose. Look for the switch near the keyboard or on the side of the notebook

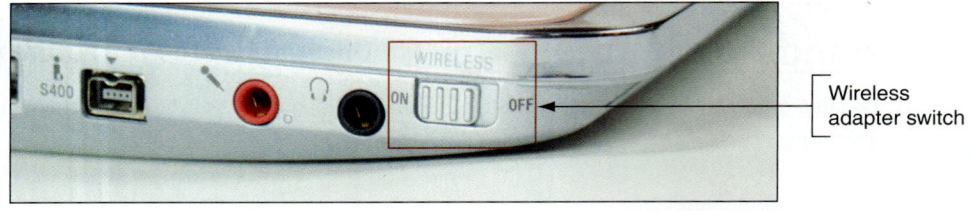

Figure 11-85 This switch controls an internal wireless adapter

(see Figure 11-85). Make sure the switch is set to the on position when you want to use wireless. The internal antenna might be embedded in the lid of the notebook. Raising the lid to a vertical position can sometimes improve the signal and solve a problem with intermittent connectivity. For intermittent wireless connectivity, check that the laptop is within range of the wireless access point.

If your notebook supports Bluetooth, you need to read the documentation for configuring the Bluetooth connection that came with the notebook because Bluetooth setups differ from one notebook to another. Following the directions for your notebook, turn on Bluetooth. After Bluetooth is turned on, you should be able to make a connection with your Bluetooth device when it is set close to the notebook.

If you are having problems getting the Bluetooth connection to work, try the following:

- Make sure Bluetooth is turned on (for some notebooks, Bluetooth and Wi-Fi wireless is controlled by a function key or a wireless switch).
- Verify that Windows sees Bluetooth enabled. You might do this by using an applet in Control Panel, by using a program on the Start menu, or by using the Bluetooth icon in the notification area of the taskbar.

Notes Be aware that a notebook might show the Bluetooth icon in the taskbar even when the notebook does not support Bluetooth.

- Be sure you have downloaded all Windows updates. (Windows XP Service Pack 2 is required for Bluetooth.)
- Look in Device Manager to make sure the Bluetooth component is recognized with no errors. For some notebooks, even though the component is an internal device, it is seen in Device Manager as a USB device.
- Make sure the other device has Bluetooth turned on. For example, when trying to communicate with a cell phone, you must use the menu on the phone to activate Bluetooth connections. Windows should see the Bluetooth device when you use the Bluetooth icon in the taskbar and then click **Add a device,** as shown in Figure 11-86.
- The Bluetooth software on the notebook might have a high level of security enabled. If so, you can lower the security mode or follow directions in the documentation to pair up the two devices. Pairing up is the term used to allow the other device to use your secured Bluetooth connection and involves entering a password before the connection is established.
- You can also try uninstalling and reinstalling the Bluetooth drivers that come bundled with your notebook.
- You can also try uninstalling and reinstalling the drivers for your Bluetooth device. For example, if you are trying to connect to a printer using a Bluetooth wireless connection, try first turning on Bluetooth and then uninstalling and reinstalling the printer. During the printer installation, select the Bluetooth connection for the printer port, which might be called Bluetooth COM or something similar.

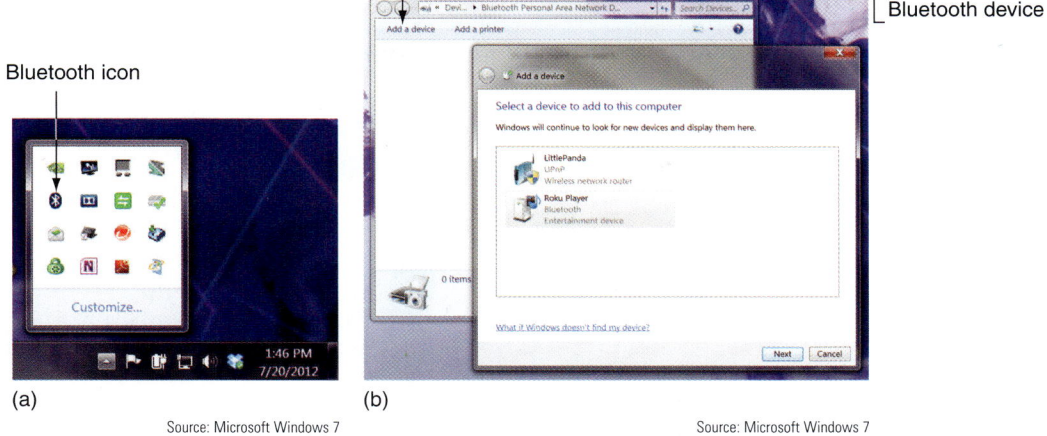

Figure 11-86 (a) Bluetooth icon used to control Bluetooth devices and settings, and (b) connect to a Bluetooth device

For more ideas for solving a Bluetooth problem, try the web site of the notebook manufacturer or the web site of the device you are trying to connect to your notebook using Bluetooth.

POWER OR BATTERY PROBLEMS

If power is not getting to the system or the battery indicator light is lit when the AC adapter should be supplying power, verify the AC adapter is plugged into a live electrical outlet. Is the light on the AC adapter lit? Check if the AC adapter's plug is secure in the electrical outlet. Check the connections on both sides of the AC adapter transformer. Check the connection at the notebook. Try exchanging the AC adapter for one you know is good.

If the battery is not charging when the AC adapter is plugged in, the problem might be with the battery or the motherboard. A hot battery might not charge until it cools down. If the battery is hot, remove it from the computer and allow it to cool to room temperature. Then try to recharge it.

APPLYING CONCEPTS — TEST AN AC ADAPTER

If the system fails only when the AC adapter is connected, it might be defective. Try a new AC adapter, or, if you have a multimeter, use it to verify the voltage output of the adapter. Do the following for an adapter with a single center pin connector:

1. Unplug the AC adapter from the computer, but leave it plugged into the electrical outlet.

2. Using a multimeter set to measure voltage in the 1 to 20 V DC range, place the red probe of the multimeter in the center of the DC connector that would normally plug into the DC outlet on the notebook. Place the black probe on the outside cylinder of the DC connector (see Figure 11-87).

3. The voltage range should be plus or minus 5 percent of the accepted voltage. For example, if a notebook is designed to use 16 V, the voltage should measure somewhere between 15.2 and 16.8 V DC.

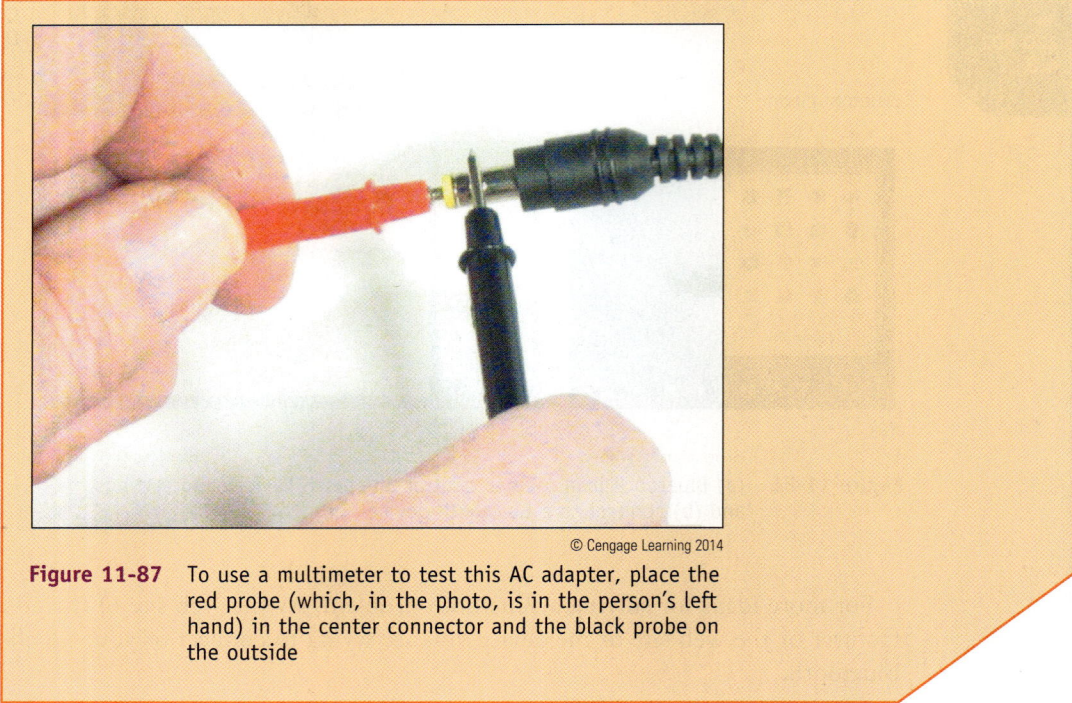

Figure 11-87 To use a multimeter to test this AC adapter, place the red probe (which, in the photo, is in the person's left hand) in the center connector and the black probe on the outside

NO DISPLAY

If the LCD panel shows a black screen, but the power light indicates that power is getting to the system, the video subsystem might be the source of the problem. Do the following:

1. Look for an LCD cutoff switch or button on the laptop (see Figure 11-88). The switch must be on for the LCD panel to work.

Figure 11-88 LCD cutoff button on a laptop

2. Try to use the video port on the notebook to connect it to an external monitor. After you connect the monitor, use a function key to toggle between the LCD panel, the external monitor, and both the panel and monitor. If the external monitor works, but the LCD panel does not work, try these things using the external monitor:

   ▲ Check Device Manager for warnings about the video controller and to update the video drivers. See Figure 11-89 for an example of the dedicated video card installed on the motherboard of one laptop.

   ▲ Check Event Viewer for reported problems with the video subsystem.

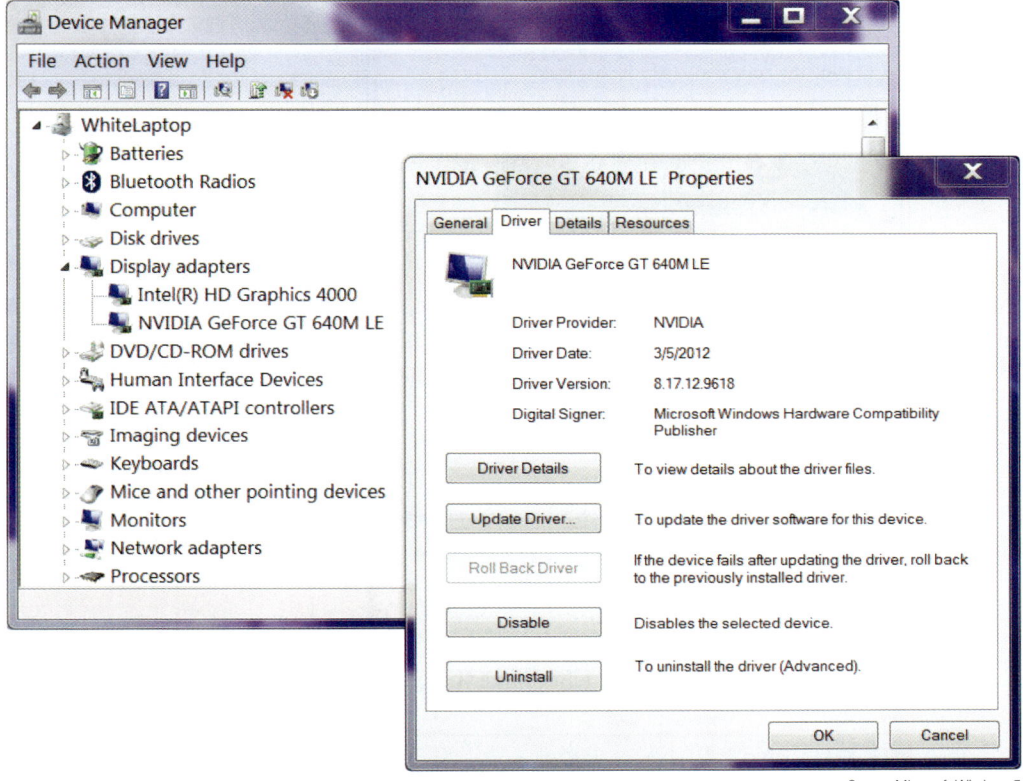

Source: Microsoft Windows 7

Figure 11-89 Use Device Manager to check for errors and update the video drivers

3. If you still can't get the LCD panel to work, but the external monitor does work, you have proven the problem is with the LCD panel assembly. Recall from earlier in the chapter, a dim screen or no display can be caused by a bad inverter. If replacing the inverter does not help, the next task is to replace the LCD panel. Be aware the replacement components might cost more than the laptop is worth.

FLICKERING, DIM, OR OTHERWISE POOR VIDEO

Use these tips to solve problems with bad video:

▲ Verify Windows display settings. Try using the native resolution for the LCD panel. This resolution will be the highest resolution available unless the wrong video drivers are installed.

▲ Try adjusting the brightness, which is a function of the backlight component of the LCD panel.

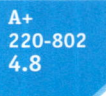
A+
220-802
4.8

▲ Try updating the video drivers. Download the latest drivers from the notebook manufacturer's web site. Bad drivers can cause an occasional ghost cursor on-screen. A **ghost cursor** is a trail left behind when you move the mouse.

▲ A flickering screen can be caused by bad video drivers, a low refresh rate, a bad inverter, or loose connections inside the laptop. To adjust the refresh rate, use Control Panel to open the Display window. In the Display window, click **Change display settings**. In the Screen Resolution window, click **Advanced settings**. On the Monitor tab, select the highest refresh rate available (see Figure 11-90).

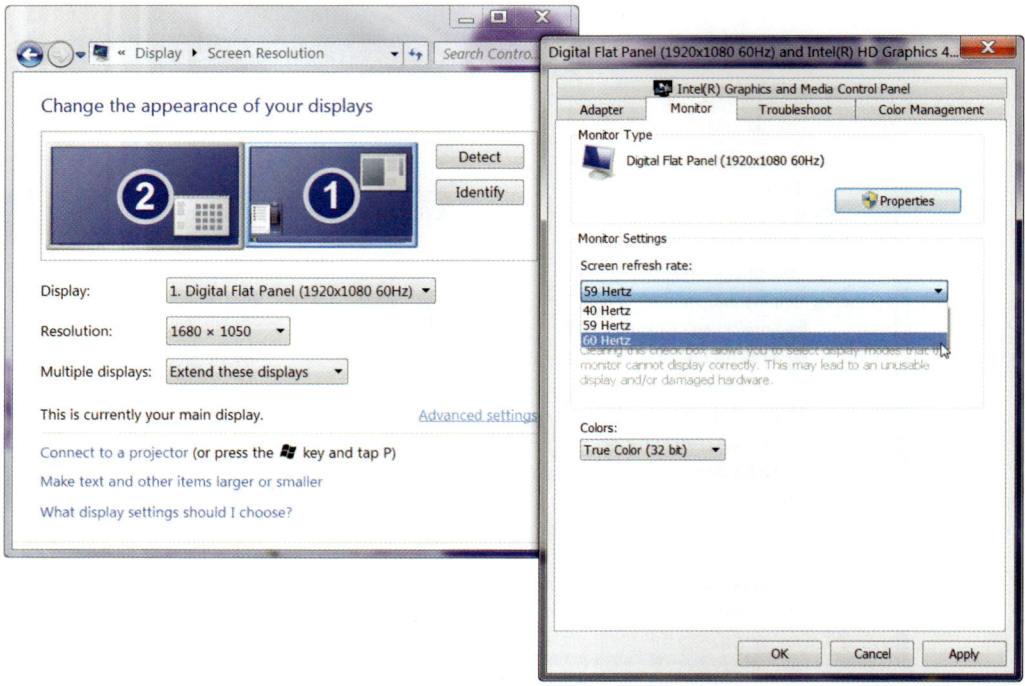

Figure 11-90 Use the highest refresh rate the system supports

Source: Microsoft Windows 7

Hands-on | Project 11-5 POST Diagnostics Cards for Notebooks

Suppose you spend much of your day diagnosing problems with notebook computers. Notebooks have a Mini PCI or Mini PCIe slot that works in a similar way to PCI and PCIe slots on desktop systems. Search the web for diagnostic cards that you can use in a mini PCI or mini PCIe slot that can help you diagnose hardware problems with notebooks. Print the web pages showing your findings. Which diagnostic card would you choose to buy and why?

>> CHAPTER SUMMARY

Special Considerations when Supporting Notebooks

▲ Notebook computers are designed for travel. They use the same technology as desktop computers, with modifications for space, portability, and power conservation. A notebook generally costs more than a desktop with comparable power and features. Special concerns when supporting a notebook also apply to supporting a netbook or all-in-one computer.

- When supporting notebooks, pay careful attention to what the warranty allows you to change on the computer.

- The notebook manufacturer documentation, including the service manual, diagnostic software, and recovery media are useful when disassembling, troubleshooting, and repairing a notebook.

- A notebook uses a customized installation of the Windows OS, customized by the notebook manufacturer. For most situations, the OS does not need upgrading for the life of the notebook unless you need to use features of a new OS. To perform an upgrade, you might need to obtain a customized version of the new OS from the notebook manufacturer.

- A notebook hard drive is likely to contain a recovery partition or the notebook might come bundled with recovery CDs. You might be able to create recovery media by using a program installed on the hard drive. Use the media to diagnose problems with the notebook, create system backups, and reimage the hard drive if the hard drive is replaced or becomes corrupted.

Maintaining Notebooks and Notebook Components

- Use special keys or buttons on a notebook to manage volume, dual displays, screen brightness, and Bluetooth.

- PC Cards, CardBus, and ExpressCard slots are a popular way to add peripheral devices to notebooks. ExpressCard slots are faster and newer than PC Card or CardBus slots. All three slots are sometimes called PCMCIA slots. ExpressCard/34 and ExpressCard/54 cards do not work in PC Card slots.

- Updating the drivers for a port or slot can sometimes solve problems with the port or slot.

- A notebook can be powered by its battery pack or by an AC adapter connected to a power source. Some notebooks have two battery packs, one of which can be a sheet battery.

- Windows 7/Vista uses sleep mode and hibernation to conserve power. Windows XP uses standby mode and hibernation. Use Control Panel to change power settings for a notebook to conserve power and make the battery charge last longer.

- Port replicators and docking stations can make it easier to connect a notebook to peripherals. Docking stations can provide additional slots and bays for components.

Replacing and Upgrading Internal Parts

- Field replaceable units in a notebook can include the memory modules, hard drive, LCD panel, video inverter, keyboard, touchpad, processor, optical drive, DC jack, fan, motherboard, CMOS battery, Mini-PCIe card, wireless card, or speakers.

- When an internal component needs replacing, consider the possibility of disabling the component and using an external peripheral device in its place. Don't jeopardize the warranty on a notebook by opening the case or using components not authorized by the manufacturer.

- When disassembling a notebook, the manufacturer's service manual is essential.

- Current notebooks use SO-DIMMs for memory. SO-DIMMs can have DDR, DDR2, or DDR3 memory. An older notebook might use SO-RIMMs.

- When upgrading components on a notebook, including memory, use components that are the same brand as the notebook, or use only components recommended by the notebook's manufacturer.

- Hard drives use a SATA or 44-pin IDE connection on a notebook. Notebooks use 2.5 inch magnetic or SSD hard drives.

- Follow the directions in a service manual to disassemble a notebook. Keep small screws organized as you disassemble a notebook because the notebook will have a variety of sizes and lengths of screws. Some manufacturers use plastic screws and require you to use new screws rather than reuse the old ones.

Troubleshooting Notebooks

- Use diagnostics software from the notebook manufacturer to troubleshoot problems with notebook slots, ports, or devices.

- Use a multimeter to check the voltage output of an AC adapter.

- Use an external monitor to verify that a video problem is with the LCD panel rather than the internal video card or motherboard.

>> KEY TERMS

For explanations of key terms, see the Glossary near the end of the book.

AC adapter	inverter	S1 state
Advanced Configuration and Power Interface (ACPI)	keyboard backlight	S2 state
	laptop	S3 state
all-in-one computer	Lithium Ion	S4 state
auto-switching	Mini PCI	S5 state
CardBus	Mini PCIe	sheet battery
docking port	Mini PCI Express	sleep mode
docking station	netbook	sleep timers
ExpressCard/34	notebook	standby mode
ExpressCard/54	PC Card	suspend mode
ghost cursor	PCMCIA card	touchpad
hardware profile	pointing stick	TrackPoint
hibernation	port replicator	

>> REVIEWING THE BASICS

1. Why are notebooks usually more expensive than desktop computers with comparable power and features?

2. Why is the service manual so important to have when you disassemble a notebook?

3. Why is it important to reinstall the OS on a notebook from the recovery media rather than use a retail version of the OS?

4. Which has more features, a port replicator or a docking station?

5. What type of bus is used by ExpressCard slots?

6. Can you use an ExpressCard card in a CardBus slot? In a PC Card slot?
7. What prevents a CardBus card from being inserted in a 16-bit PC Card slot?
8. What type of technology is used by battery packs for notebooks?
9. To what ACPI mode does Windows 7 sleep mode correspond? Windows 7 hibernation?
10. Which port do you use to connect a docking station to a notebook?
11. Why is it not necessary to set up two hardware profiles in Windows 7 for a notebook to use or not use a docking station?
12. How many pins does a DDR3 SO-DIMM have? A DDR2 SO-DIMM?
13. When a notebook internal device fails, what three options can you use to deal with the problem?
14. How many pins does a notebook IDE connector have? A desktop IDE connector?
15. When an LCD panel is very dim and brightness adjustments don't help, what component is likely to be the problem?
16. After you have removed the AC adapter and all peripherals, what is the next component you should always remove before servicing any internal notebook components?
17. How many pins does a Mini PCIe card have?
18. What three wireless technologies might be provided by a Mini PCIe card?
19. Which mobile processor socket is currently the most popular by Intel? By AMD?
20. What is one cause of a ghost cursor on an LCD screen?

>> THINKING CRITICALLY

1. Your friend has a Windows XP notebook computer and has purchased Windows 7 and installed it as an upgrade on his notebook. He calls to tell you about the upgrade and says that he cannot connect to the Internet. His notebook has an embedded Ethernet port that he uses for communication. What do you tell him to do?
    a. Reinstall Windows XP.
    b. Using another computer, download and install the Windows 7 Ethernet drivers from the notebook manufacturer's web site.
    c. Search the CDs that came with the notebook for Windows 7 Ethernet drivers and install them.
    d. Perform a clean install of Windows 7.
2. A friend asks you for help in determining the best product to buy: a notebook, tablet PC, or smartphone. She is a paralegal and spends a lot of time at the courthouse researching real estate titles. She wants a device to take notes with as she works. List three questions you would ask her to help her make her decision.
3. What type of computer is likely to use SO-DIMMs, have an internal power supply, and use a desktop processor socket?

>> REAL PROBLEMS, REAL SOLUTIONS

REAL PROBLEM 11-1: Setting Up a Service Center for Notebooks

If you ever intend to set up your own PC Repair Shop, you might want to consider becoming a service center for a few brands of the more popular notebooks. Reasons to become an authorized service center are that you have access to service manuals, parts lists, and wholesale parts for notebooks. Do the following to research becoming an authorized service center:

1. Select a brand of notebooks that you think you would like to service.
2. Research the web site of this manufacturer and answer these questions:
   a. Where is the closest authorized service center for this brand of notebooks?
   b. What are the requirements to become an authorized service center? Print the web page showing the requirements.
   c. Is A+ certification one of those requirements?
   d. Some notebook manufacturers offer a program that falls short of becoming an authorized service center but does provide support for IT professionals so that repair technicians can order notebook parts. Does the manufacturer offer this service? If so, what must you do to qualify?

If you try one brand of notebook and can't find the information you need, try another brand. Sometimes this information can only be obtained by contacting the manufacturer directly. And one more hint: To use *www.google.com* to search a particular site, begin the search string with *site:hostname.com*.

REAL PROBLEM 11-2: Notebook Keyboard Replacement

Xavier's Lenovo G560 notebook keyboard no longer works, and the notebook is not under warranty. Because Xavier travels a lot, he does not want to rely on a USB external keyboard. He has come to you for help replacing the keyboard and is interested in replacing it with a Spanish keyboard. Download the hardware maintenance manual for his notebook from *www.lenovo.com* and find the pages that show how to replace the keyboard. Describe the steps in detail. After the cover on the bottom of the notebook is removed, how many screws must be removed before you can remove the keyboard? What is the part number of an English keyboard? What is the part number for a Spanish keyboard?

REAL PROBLEM 11-3: Taking Apart a Notebook

If you enjoy putting together a thousand-piece jigsaw puzzle, you'll probably enjoy working on notebook computers. With desktop systems, replacing a component is not a time-consuming task, but with notebooks, the job could take half a day. If you take the time to carefully examine the notebook's case before attempting to open it, you will probably find markings provided by the manufacturer to assist you in locating components that are commonly upgraded. If you have a service manual, your work will be much easier than without one.

The best way to learn to disassemble a notebook is to practice on an old one that you can afford to break. Find an old Dell or Lenovo or IBM ThinkPad for which you can download the service manual from the Dell or Lenovo web site. Then carefully and patiently follow the disassembly instructions and then reassemble it. When done, you can congratulate yourself and move on to newer notebooks.

CHAPTER 12

Supporting Printers

In this chapter, you will learn:

- About printer types and features
- How to install and share printers and how to manage printer features, add-on devices, and the printer queue
- About routine maintenance tasks necessary to support printers
- How to troubleshoot printer problems

This chapter discusses the most popular types of printers and how to support them. As you work through the chapter, you'll learn about printer types and features, how to install a local or network printer, and how to share a printer with others on a network. You'll learn how to manage printer features, add-on devices, shared printers, and print jobs. Then, you'll learn about maintaining and troubleshooting printers.

PRINTER TYPES AND FEATURES

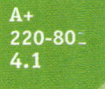

You need to be aware of the types of printers and know about features a printer might have that you could be called on to configure, repair, or maintain. We begin with a discussion of how data is sent from Windows to a printer and then how each type of printer works. Understanding how a printer works will help you fix printer problems when they arise.

PRINTER LANGUAGES

The language or method that Windows uses to send a page to a printer depends on what the printer is designed to support and the printer drivers installed. If the printer has sophisticated firmware, it might be able to support more than one method. In this case, the installed printer drivers determine which methods can be used:

- ▲ *The printer uses PostScript commands to build the page.* Windows can send the commands and data needed to build a page to the printer using the PostScript language by Adobe Systems. The printer firmware then interprets and processes these commands to produce a bitmap of the page, which is stored in the printer memory. (A bitmap is just a bunch of bits in rows and columns. Each row in the bitmap is called a raster line.) PostScript is popular with desktop publishing, the typesetting industry, and the Mac OS.
- ▲ *The printer uses PCL commands to build the page.* A printer language that competes with PostScript is PCL (Printer Control Language). PCL was developed by Hewlett-Packard but is considered a de facto standard in the printing industry. Many printer manufacturers use PCL.
- ▲ *The Windows GDI builds the page and then sends it to the printer.* A less-sophisticated method of communicating to a printer is to use the GDI (Graphics Device Interface) component of Windows. GDI draws and formats the page, converting it to bitmap form, and then sends the almost-ready-to-print bitmap to the printer. Because Windows, rather than the printer, does most of the work of building the page, a GDI printer needs less firmware and memory, and, therefore, generally costs less than a PCL or PostScript printer. The downside of using the GDI method is that Windows performance can suffer when printing a lot of complicated pages. Most low-end inkjet and laser printers are GDI printers. If the printer specifications don't say PCL or PostScript, you can assume it's a GDI printer.
- ▲ *Windows 7/Vista uses XML Paper Specification (XPS) to build the page and then sends it to the printer.* XPS (XML Paper Specification) was introduced with Windows Vista and was designed to ultimately replace GDI as the method Windows uses to prepare (render) the page before sending it to the printer. Windows 7/Vista uses either GDI or XPS for rendering based on the type of printer driver installed. Generally, PostScript and PCL are used with high-end printers, and GDI and XPS are used with low-end printers. Many high-end printers support more than one protocol and can handle GDI, XPS, PCL, or PostScript printing.
- ▲ *Raw data is printed with little-to-no formatting.* Text data that contains no graphics or embedded control characters is sent to the printer as is, and the printer can print it without any processing. The data is called raw data.

TYPES OF PRINTERS

A+ 220-801 4.1

The major categories of printer types include laser, inkjet (ink dispersion), thermal printers, and impact printers. In the following sections, we'll look at the different types of printers for desktop computing.

> **Notes** For heavy business use, the best practice is to purchase one machine for one purpose, instead of bundling many functions into a single machine. For example, if you need a scanner and a printer, purchase a good printer and a good scanner rather than a combo machine. Routine maintenance and troubleshooting are easier and less expensive on single-purpose machines, although the initial cost is higher. On the other hand, for home or small office use, a combo device can save money and counter space.

LASER PRINTERS

A **laser printer** is a type of electrophotographic printer that can range from a small, personal desktop model to a large, network printer capable of handling and printing large volumes continuously. Figure 12-1 shows an example of a typical laser printer for a small office.

Figure 12-1 Oki Data C3200n color laser printer

© Cengage Learning 2014

> **A+ Exam Tip** The A+ 220-801 exam expects you to be familiar with these types of printers: laser, inkjet, thermal, and impact.

Laser printers require the interaction of mechanical, electrical, and optical technologies to work. Laser printers work by placing toner on an electrically charged rotating drum (sometimes called the **imaging drum**) and then depositing the toner on paper as the paper moves through the system at the same speed the drum is turning. Figure 12-2 shows the seven steps of laser printing.

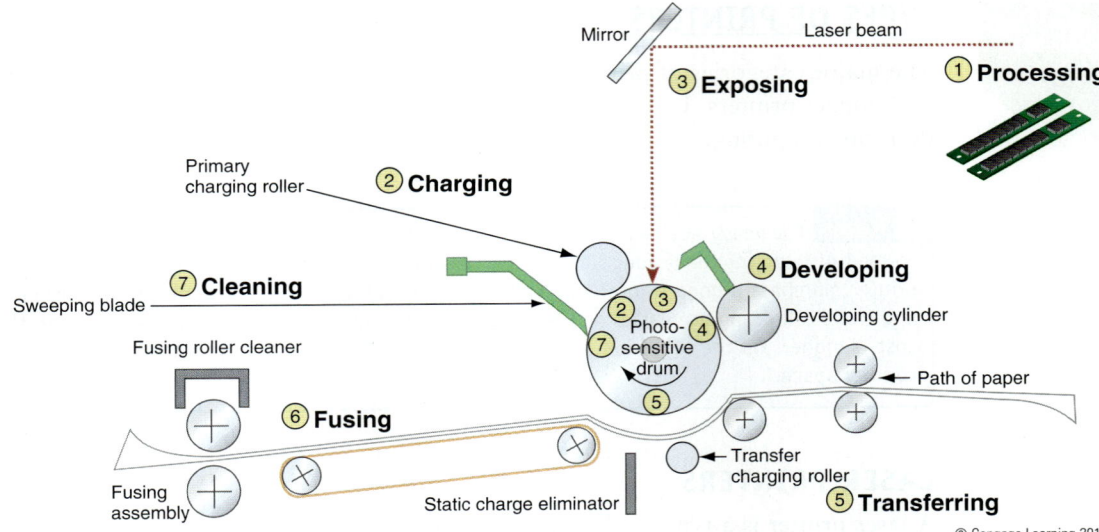

Figure 12-2 The seven progressive steps of laser printing

Note that Figure 12-2 shows only a cross-section of the drum, mechanisms, and paper. Remember that the drum is as wide as a sheet of paper. The mirror, blades, and rollers in the drawing are also as wide as paper. Also know that toner responds to a charge and moves from one surface to another if the second surface has a more positive charge than the first.

> **A+ Exam Tip** The A+ 220-801 exam expects you to know the seven steps of laser printing.

The seven steps of laser printing are listed next:

1. *Processing the image.* A laser printer processes and prints an entire page at one time. The page comes to the printer encoded in a printer language and the firmware inside the printer processes the incoming data to produce a bitmap of the final page, which is stored in the printer's memory. One bitmap image is produced for monochrome images. For color images, one bitmap is produced for each of four colors. (The colors are blue, red, yellow, and black, better known as cyan, magenta, yellow, and black, and sometimes written as CMYK.)

2. *Charging or conditioning.* The drum is conditioned by a roller that places a high uniform electrical charge of −600 V on the surface of the drum. The roller is called the primary charging roller or primary corona, which is charged by a high-voltage power supply assembly. For some printers, a corona wire is used instead of the charging roller to charge the drum.

3. *Exposing or writing.* A laser beam controlled by motors and a mirror scans across the drum until it completes the correct number of passes. The laser beam is turned on and off continually as it makes a single pass down the length of the drum, once for each raster line, so that dots are exposed only where toner should go to print the image. For example, for a 1200 dots per inch (dpi) printer, the beam makes 1200 passes for every one inch of the drum circumference. For a 1200-dpi printer, 1200 dots are exposed or not exposed along the drum for every inch of linear pass. The 1200 dots per inch down this single pass, combined with 1200 passes per inch of drum circumference, accomplish the resolution of 1200 × 1200 dots per square inch of many laser printers. The laser beam writes an image to the drum surface as a −100 V charge. The −100 V charge on this image area will be used in the developing stage to transmit toner to the drum surface.

> **Notes** A laser printer can produce better quality printouts than a dot matrix printer, even when printing at the same dpi, because it can vary the size of the dots it prints, creating a sharp, clear image. Hewlett-Packard (HP) calls this technology of varying the size of dots **REt (Resolution Enhancement technology)**.

4. *Developing.* The developing cylinder applies toner to the surface of the drum. The toner is charged and sticks to the developing cylinder because of a magnet inside the cylinder. A control blade prevents too much toner from sticking to the cylinder surface. As the cylinder rotates very close to the drum, the toner is attracted to the part of the surface of the drum that has a −100 V charge and repelled from the −600 V part of the drum surface. The result is that toner sticks to the drum where the laser beam has hit and is repelled from the area where the laser beam has not hit.

5. *Transferring.* In the transferring step (shown in Figure 12-2), a strong electrical charge draws the toner off the drum onto the paper. This is the first step that takes place outside the cartridge and the first step that involves the paper. The soft, black **transfer roller** puts a positive charge on the paper to pull the toner from the drum onto the paper. Then the static charge eliminator (refer again to Figure 12-2) weakens the charges on both the paper and the drum so that the paper does not stick to the drum. The stiffness of the paper and the small radius of the drum also help the paper move away from the drum and toward the fusing assembly. Very thin paper can wrap around the drum, which is why printer manuals usually instruct you to use only paper designated for laser printers.

6. *Fusing.* The **fuser assembly** uses heat and pressure to fuse the toner to the paper. Up to this point, the toner is merely sitting on the paper. The fusing rollers apply heat to the paper, which causes the toner to melt, and the rollers apply pressure to bond the melted toner into the paper. The temperature of the rollers is monitored by the printer. If the temperature exceeds an allowed maximum value (410 degrees F for some printers), the printer shuts down.

7. *Cleaning.* A sweeper strip cleans the drum of any residual toner, which is swept away by a sweeping blade. The charge left on the drum is then neutralized. Some printers use erase lamps in the top cover of the printer for this purpose. The lamps use red light so as not to damage the photosensitive drum.

For color laser printers, the writing process repeats four times, one for each toner color of cyan, magenta, yellow, and black. Each color requires a separate image drum. Then, the paper passes to the fusing stage, when the fuser bonds all toner to the paper and aids in blending the four tones to form specific colors.

The charging, exposing, developing, and cleaning steps use the printer components that undergo the most wear. To make the printer last longer, these steps are done inside removable cartridges that can be replaced. For older printers, all four steps were done inside one cartridge. For newer printers, the cleaning, charging, and exposing steps are done inside the image drum cartridge. The developing cylinder is located inside the toner cartridge. The transferring is done using a **transfer belt** that can be replaced, and the fusing is done inside a fuser cartridge. By using these multiple cartridges inside laser printers, the cost of maintaining a printer is reduced. You can replace one cartridge without having to replace them all. The toner cartridge needs replacing the most often, followed by the image drum, the fuser cartridge, and the transfer assembly, in that order.

Other printer parts that might need replacing include the **pickup roller** that pushes forward a sheet of paper from the paper tray and the **separation pad** that keeps more than one sheet of paper from moving forward. If the pickup roller is worn, paper misfeeds into the printer. If the separation pad is worn, multiple sheets of paper will be drawn into the printer. Sometimes you can clean a pickup roller or separation pad to prolong its life before it needs replacing.

A+ 220-801 4.1

> **Notes** Before replacing expensive parts in a printer, consider whether a new printer might be more cost effective than repairing the old one.

A printer that is able to print on both sides of the paper is called a **duplex printer** or a double-sided printer. After the front of the paper is printed, a **duplexing assembly**, which contains several rollers, turns the paper around and draws it back through the print process to print on the back of the paper. Alternately, some high-end printers have two print engines so that both sides of the paper are printed at the same time.

INKJET PRINTERS

An **inkjet printer** (see Figure 12-3) uses a type of ink-dispersion printing and doesn't normally provide the high-quality resolution of laser printers. Inkjet printers are popular because they are small and can print color inexpensively. Most inkjet printers today can print high-quality photos, especially when used with photo-quality paper.

Courtesy of EPSON America, Inc.

Figure 12-3 An example of an inkjet printer

An inkjet printer contains firmware that processes the image. The more expensive inkjet printers can process PostScript or PCL, and the less expensive ones can process GDI and XPS print jobs. An inkjet printer uses a **print head** that moves across the paper, creating one line of the image with each pass. The printer puts ink on the paper using a matrix of small dots. Different types of inkjet printers form their droplets of ink in different ways. Printer manufacturers use several technologies, but the most popular is the bubble-jet. Bubble-jet printers use tubes of ink that have tiny resistors near the end of each tube. These resistors heat up and cause the ink to boil. Then, a tiny air bubble of ionized ink (ink with an electrical charge) is ejected onto the paper. A typical bubble-jet print head has 64 or 128 tiny nozzles, all of which can fire a droplet simultaneously. (High-end printers can have as many as 3,000 nozzles.) Plates carrying a magnetic charge direct the path of ink onto the paper to form shapes.

Inkjet printers include one or more **ink cartridges** to hold the different colors of ink for the printer. Figure 12-4 shows two ink cartridges. A black cartridge is on the left and a three-color cartridge is on the right. For this printer, a print head is built into each ink cartridge.

A stepper motor moves the print head and ink cartridges across the paper using a belt to move the assembly and a stabilizing bar to control the movement (see Figure 12-5). A paper tray can hold a stack of paper, or a paper feeder on the back of the printer can hold a few

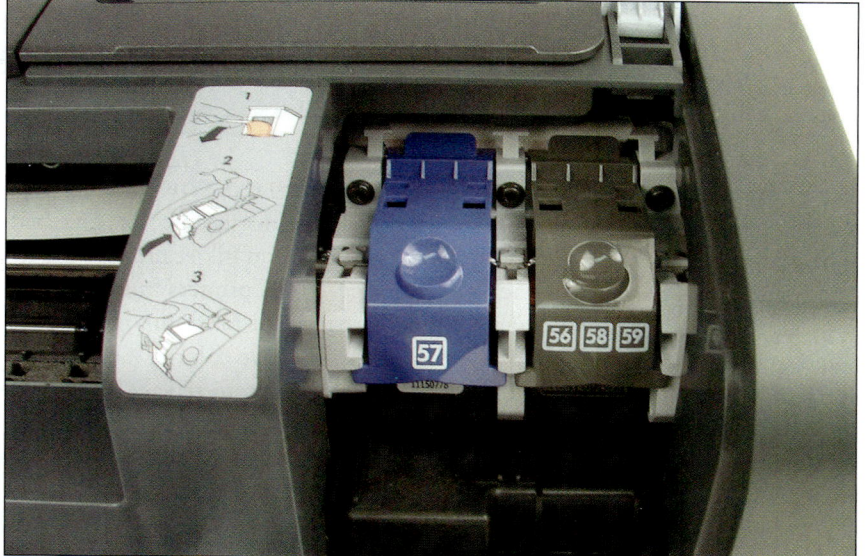

Figure 12-4 The ink cartridges of an inkjet printer

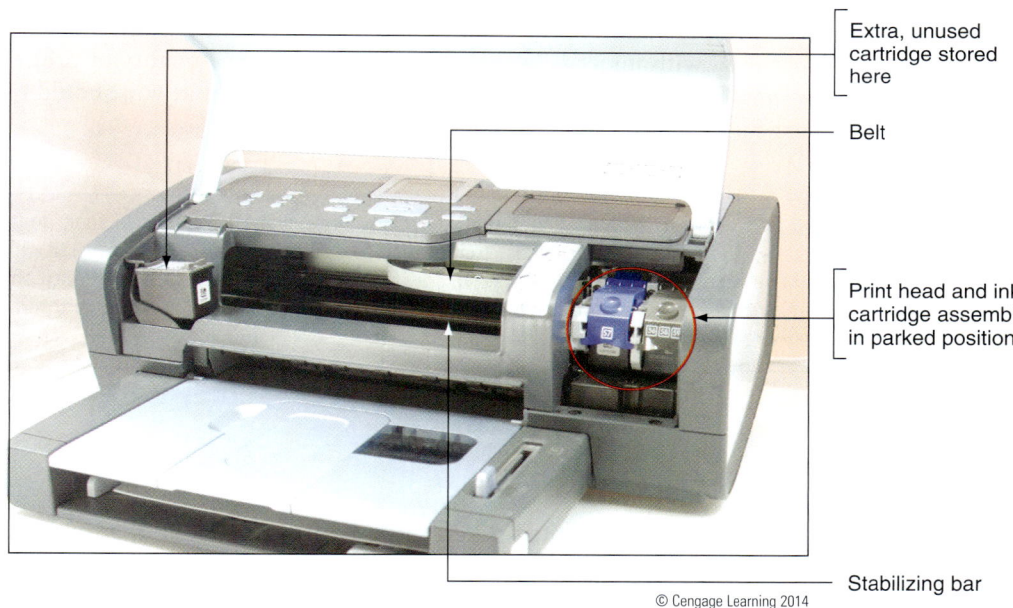

Figure 12-5 The belt and stabilizing bar used to move the print head across the page

sheets of paper. The sheets stand up in the feeder and are dispensed one at a time. Rollers pull a single sheet into the printer from the paper tray or paper feeder. A motor powers these rollers and times the sheet going through the printer in the increments needed to print the image. When the printer is not in use, the assemblage sits in the far-right position shown in Figure 12-4, which is called the home position or parked position. This position helps protect the ink in the cartridges from drying out.

Some inkjet printers offer duplex printing. These printers are larger than normal inkjet printers because of the added space required for the duplexing assembly. For duplex printing, be sure to use heavy paper (rated at 24-pound paper or higher) so the ink doesn't bleed through.

A+ 220-801 4.1

> **Notes** Weight and brightness are the two primary ways of measuring paper quality. The rated weight of paper (for example, 20 pounds to 32 pounds) determines the thickness of the paper. Brightness is measured on a scale of 92 to 100.

When purchasing an inkjet printer, look for the kind that uses two or four separate cartridges. One cartridge is used for black ink. Three cartridges, one for each color, give better quality color than one cartridge that holds all three colors. Some low-end inkjet printers use a single three-color cartridge and don't have a black ink cartridge. These printers must combine all colors of ink to produce a dull black. Having a separate cartridge for black ink means that it prints true black and, more important, does not use the more expensive colored ink. To save money, you should be able to replace an empty cartridge without having to replace all cartridges.

> **Notes** To save money, you can refill an ink cartridge, and many companies will sell you the tools and ink you need as well as show you how to do it. You can also purchase refilled cartridges at reduced prices. When you purchase ink cartridges, make sure you know if they are new or refilled. Also, for best results, don't refill a cartridge more than three times.

Inkjet printers tend to smudge on inexpensive paper, and they are slower than laser printers. If a printed page later gets damp, the ink can run and get quite messy. The quality of the paper used with inkjet printers significantly affects the quality of printed output. You should use only paper that is designed for an inkjet printer, and you should use a high-grade paper to get the best results.

> **Notes** Photos printed on an inkjet printer tend to fade over time, more so than photos produced professionally. To make your photos last longer, use high-quality paper (rated at high gloss or studio gloss) and use fade-resistant ink (such as Vivera ink by HP). Then protect these photos from exposure to light, heat, humidity, and polluted air. To best protect photos made by an inkjet printer, keep them in a photo album rather than displayed and exposed to light.

IMPACT PRINTERS

An **impact printer** creates a printed page by using some mechanism that touches or hits the paper. The best-known impact printer is a dot matrix printer, which prints only text that it receives as raw data. It has a print head that moves across the width of the paper, using pins to print a matrix of dots on the page. The pins shoot against a cloth ribbon, which hits the paper, depositing the ink. The ribbon provides both the ink for printing and the lubrication for the pinheads. The quality of the print is poor compared to other printer types. However, three reasons you see impact printers still in use are: (1) they use continuous **tractor feeds** and fanfold paper (also called computer paper) rather than individual sheets of paper, making them useful for logging ongoing events or data, (2) they can use carbon paper to print multiple copies at the same time, and (3) they are extremely durable, give little trouble, and seem to last forever.

Maintaining a dot matrix impact printer is easy to do. The **impact paper** used by impact printers comes as a box of fanfold paper or in rolls (used with receipt printers). When the paper is nearing the end of the stack or roll, a color on the edge alerts you to replace the paper. Occasionally, you should replace the ribbon of a dot matrix printer. If the print head fails, check on the cost of replacing the head versus the cost of buying a new printer. Sometimes, the cost of the head is so high it's best to just buy a new printer. Overheating can damage a print head (see Figure 12-6), so keep it as cool as possible to make it last longer. Keep the printer in a cool, well-ventilated area, and don't use it to print more than 50 to 75 pages without allowing the head to cool down.

Figure 12-6 Keep the print head of a dot matrix printer as cool as possible so that it will last longer

THERMAL PRINTERS

Thermal printers use heat to create an image. Two types of thermal printers are a direct thermal printer and a thermal transfer printer. The older **direct thermal printer** burns dots onto special coated paper, called **thermal paper**, as was done by older fax machines. The process requires no ink and does not use a ribbon. Direct thermal printers are often used as receipt printers that use rolls of thermal paper (see Figure 12-7). The printed image can fade over time.

Figure 12-7 The TM-T88V direct thermal printer by EPSON

A **thermal transfer printer** uses a ribbon that contains wax-based ink. The heating element melts the ribbon (also called foil) onto special thermal paper so that it stays glued to the paper as the feeder assembly moves the paper through the printer. Thermal transfer printers are used to print receipts, bar code labels, clothing labels, or container labels. Figure 12-8 shows a thermal transfer printer used to make bar codes and other labels.

Courtesy of Zebra Technologies

Figure 12-8 The GC420 printer by Zebra is both a thermal transfer printer and a direct thermal printer

Thermal printers are reliable and easy to maintain. When you're responsible for a thermal printer, you know it's time to replace the paper roll when the roll shows the color down one edge. It's important to regularly clean the print head because build-up can harden over time and permanently damage the head. Follow the printer manufacturer's directions to clean the print head. Some thermal printer ribbons have a print head cleaning stripe at the end of the ribbon, and it's a good idea to clean the head each time you replace the ribbon. Additionally, some manufacturers suggest cleaning the head with isopropyl alcohol wipes.

When cleaning, remove any dust and debris that gets down in the print head assembly. As you work, ground yourself to protect the sensitive heating element against static electricity. Don't touch the heating element with your fingers. Also, to prolong the life of the print head, use the lowest heat setting for the heating element that still gives good printing results.

Table 12-1 lists some printer manufacturers.

Printer Manufacturer	Web Site
Brother	www.brother-usa.com
Canon	usa.canon.com
Hewlett-Packard	www.hp.com
Konica Minolta	kmbs.konicaminolta.us
Lexmark	www.lexmark.com
Oki Data	www.okidata.com
Samsung	www.samsung.com
Seiko Epson	www.epson.com
Xerox	www.xerox.com
Zebra Technologies	www.zebra.com

© Cengage Learning 2014

Table 12-1 Printer manufacturers

Hands-on Project 12-1 Research Printer Web Sites

A+ 220-801 4.1

Your company plans to purchase a new printer, and you want to evaluate the printer manufacturers' web sites to determine which site offers the best support. Research three web sites listed in Table 12-1 and answer these questions, supporting your answers with pages that you have saved or printed from the web site:

1. Which web site made it easiest for you to select a new printer, based on your criteria for its use?
2. Which web site made it easiest for you to find help for troubleshooting printer problems?
3. Which web site gave you the best information about routine maintenance for its printers?
4. Which web site gave you the best information about how to clean its printers?

Now let's turn our attention to using Windows to install, share, and manage printers.

USING WINDOWS TO INSTALL, SHARE, AND MANAGE PRINTERS

A+ 220-801 1.11, 1.12, 4.2

A printer connects to a single computer or to the network. A **local printer** connects directly to a computer by way of a USB port, parallel port, serial port, or wireless connection (Bluetooth, infrared, or Wi-Fi). Some printers support more than one method. A **network printer** has an Ethernet port to connect directly to the network or uses Wi-Fi to connect to a wireless access point. Some printers have both an Ethernet port and a USB port (see Figure 12-9).

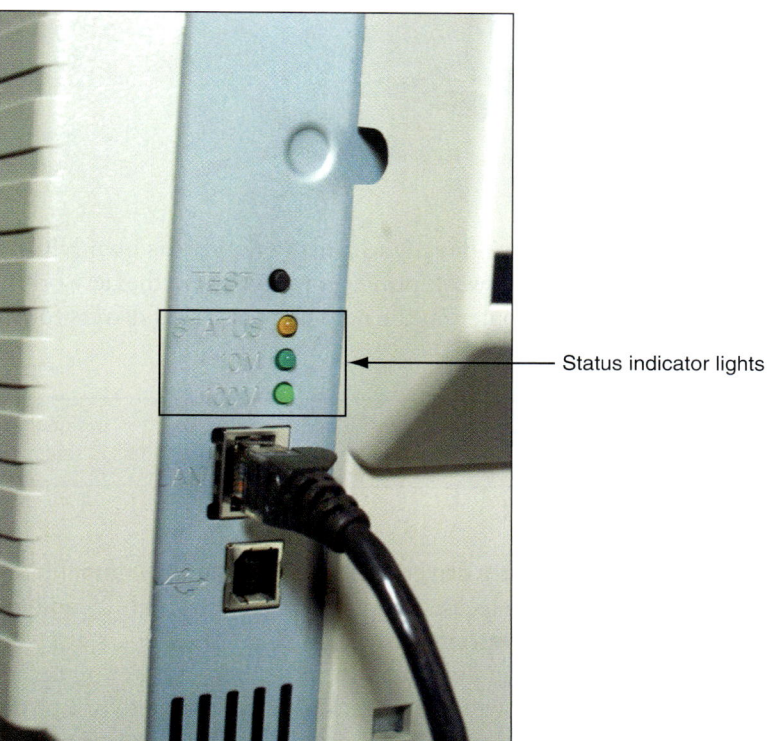

Figure 12-9 This printer has an Ethernet and USB port

These printers can be installed as either a network printer (connecting directly to the network) or a local printer (connecting directly to a computer) depending on which port you use.

The two ways to install a printer and make it available on a network are listed here:

▲ A local printer can be attached to a computer using a port (for example, USB, parallel, or wireless) on the computer (see Computer A in Figure 12-10). The printer can be dedicated to only this one computer, or you can share the printer for network users. For a shared local printer to be available to other computers on the network, the host computer must be turned on and not in sleep or standby mode. For another computer on the network to use the shared printer, the printer drivers must be installed on the remote computer.

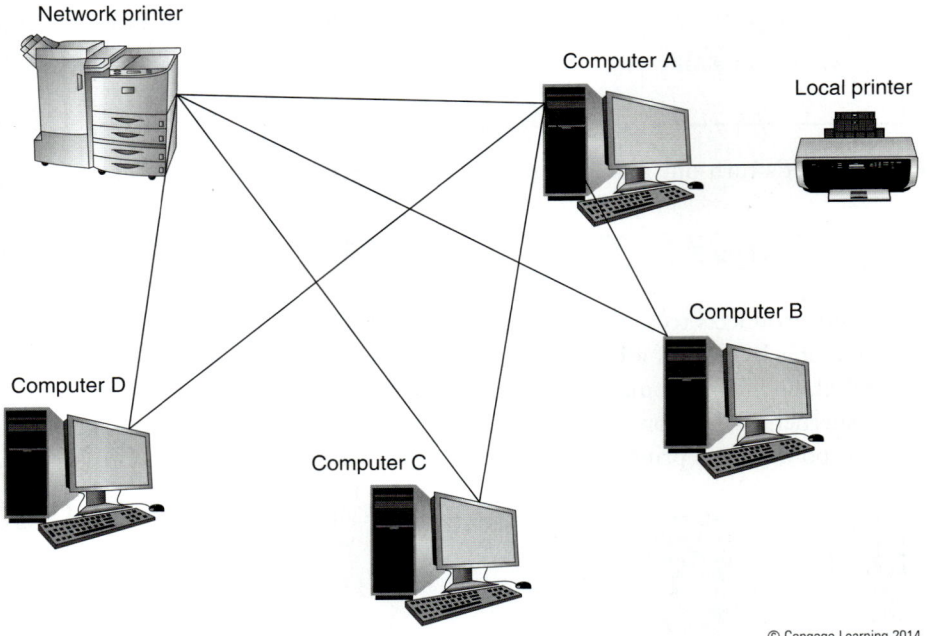

Figure 12-10 A shared local printer and a network printer

▲ A network printer can connect directly to a network with its own NIC (see the network printer in Figure 12-10). A network printer is identified on the network by its IP address. To use the printer, any computer on the network can install drivers for this printer.

> **Notes** A computer can have several printers installed. Of these, Windows designates one printer to be the **default printer**, which is the one Windows prints to unless another is selected.

When you install a printer, printer drivers are required that are compatible with the installed operating system. Be sure to use 32-bit drivers for a 32-bit OS and 64-bit drivers for a 64-bit OS. Windows 7 has many printer drivers built in. The drivers also come on a CD bundled with the printer or you can download them from the printer manufacturer's web site.

In this part of the chapter, you will learn to install local and network printers, share an installed printer, and remotely use a shared printer. You'll also learn how to configure printer add-ons and features and to manage the printer queue in Windows. We begin with learning how to install a printer under Windows 7 or Vista.

INSTALLING A LOCAL OR NETWORK PRINTER

To install a local USB printer, all you have to do is plug in the USB printer and Windows 7/Vista installs the printer automatically. Also, for some types of printers, you can launch the installation program that came bundled on CD with the printer or downloaded from the printer manufacturer's web site. On the other hand, you can use the Windows 7 **Devices and Printers window,** the Vista **Printers window,** or the XP **Printers and Faxes window** to install a printer. These windows are also used to manage and uninstall printers. Printer installations in Windows 7/Vista work differently than XP installations. You first learn how to install a printer in Windows 7/Vista and then in XP.

INSTALL A PRINTER USING WINDOWS 7/VISTA

Follow these steps to use Windows 7 or Vista to install a non-USB local printer or a network printer:

1. For a network printer, make sure the printer is connected to the network and turned on. For a wireless printer, turn on the printer and set the printer within range of the access point or computer. For a parallel port or serial port printer, connect the printer to the computer and turn it on.
2. In the Windows 7 Control Panel, using the Large or Small icon view, click **Devices and Printers**. (Alternately, you can click Start, Devices and Printers.) The Devices and Printers window opens, as shown on the left side of Figure 12-11. (For Windows Vista, in Control Panel, click **Printers** to open the Printers window, which works the same as the Windows 7 Devices and Printers window.)

> **Notes** By default, the Devices and Printers option is listed in the Start menu. If you don't find it there, you can add it by right-clicking the taskbar and selecting **Properties**. In the Taskbar and Start Menu Properties box, click the **Start Menu** tab and then click **Customize**. Check **Devices and Printers** and click **OK** twice.

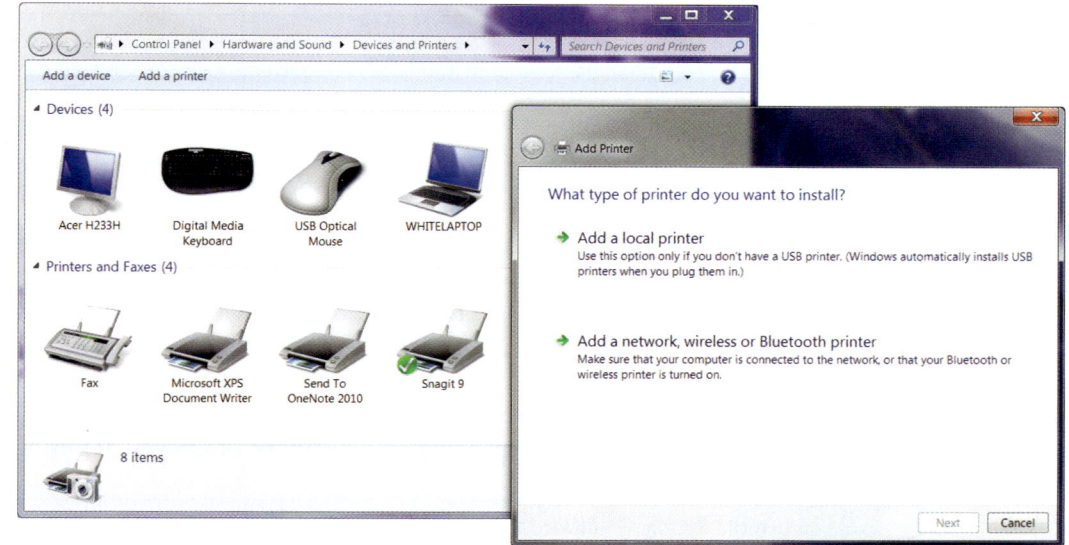

Source: Microsoft Windows 7

Figure 12-11 Use the Devices and Printers window to install a printer

Notes Notice in Figure 12-11 that Windows includes the Microsoft XPS Document Writer as an installed printer. When you print to this printer, the **XPS Document Writer** creates an .xps file. The file is similar to a .pdf file and can be viewed, edited, printed, faxed, emailed, or posted on web sites. In Windows, the file is viewed in a browser window.

3. Click **Add a printer**. In the Add Printer window that appears (see the right side of Figure 12-11), select the type of printer.

4. Windows searches for available printers and lists them. Figure 12-12 shows a list when installing a network printer. Select the printer from the list and click **Next**. If your printer is not listed, click **The printer that I want isn't listed**, and, on the next screen, point to the port or IP address of the printer. In Figure 12-12, we are installing a network printer identified by its IP address, which is 192.168.1.101.

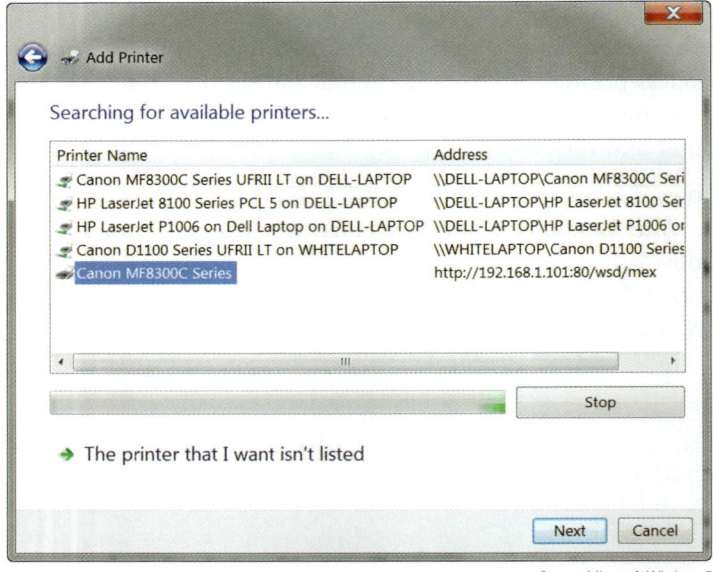

Source: Microsoft Windows 7

Figure 12-12 Select the printer from the list of available printers

Notes To know the IP address of a network printer, direct the printer to print a configuration page, which should include its IP address. To print the page, use buttons, keys, or other controls on the front of the printer. The printer documentation shows you how to use these controls. Some printers have a control panel on the front of the printer. For these printers, scroll through the menu to display the IP address in the panel window.

5. In the next box (see the far left of Figure 12-13), you tell Windows where to find the printer drivers. To select the drivers kept by Windows, select the printer brand and model. To use drivers stored on CD or previously downloaded from the web, click **Have Disk**. The Install From Disk box appears (see the middle of Figure 12-13). Click **Browse** to locate the drivers; Windows is looking for an .inf file. Notice the choice of folders for this particular printer listed in the Locate File box on the far right side of Figure 12-13. Use the 32bit or x64 folder depending on which type of OS you are using.

Notes Use the System window to find out if a 32-bit or 64-bit OS is installed. To open the System window, click **Start**, right-click **Computer**, and select **Properties**.

Using Windows to Install, Share, and Manage Printers 595

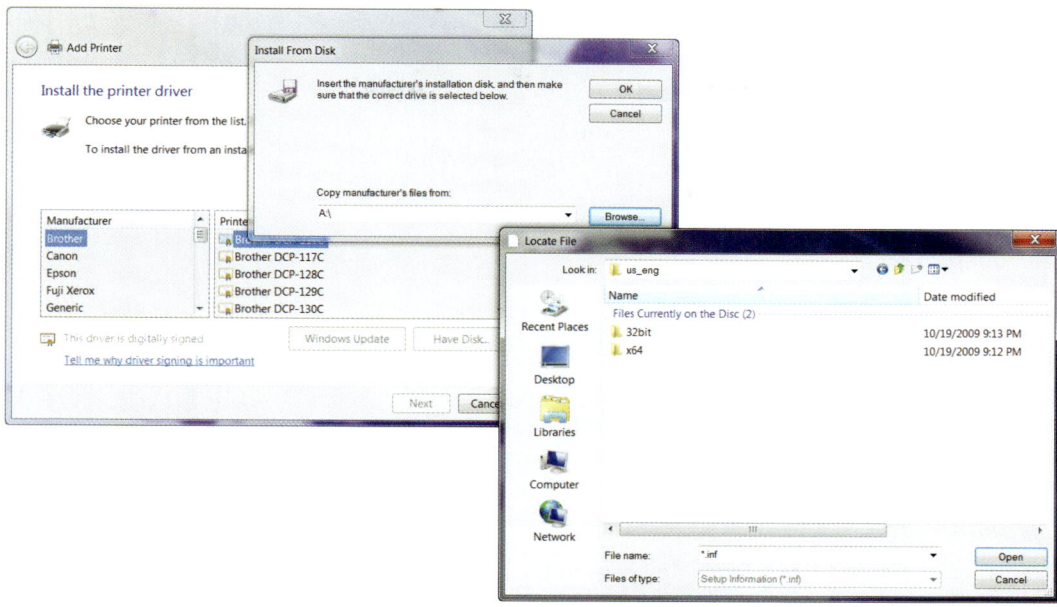

Figure 12-13 Locate printer drivers on CD or downloaded from the web

Source: Microsoft Windows 7

6. Continue to follow the wizard to install the printer. Dialog boxes give you the opportunity to change the name of the printer and designate the printer as the default printer. You are also given the opportunity to test the printer. It's always a good idea to print a test page when you install a printer to verify the installation works.

You can also send a test page to the printer at any time. To do so, right-click the printer in the Devices and Printers window and select **Printer properties**. See Figure 12-14. On the General tab of the Properties box, click **Print Test Page** (see Figure 12-15).

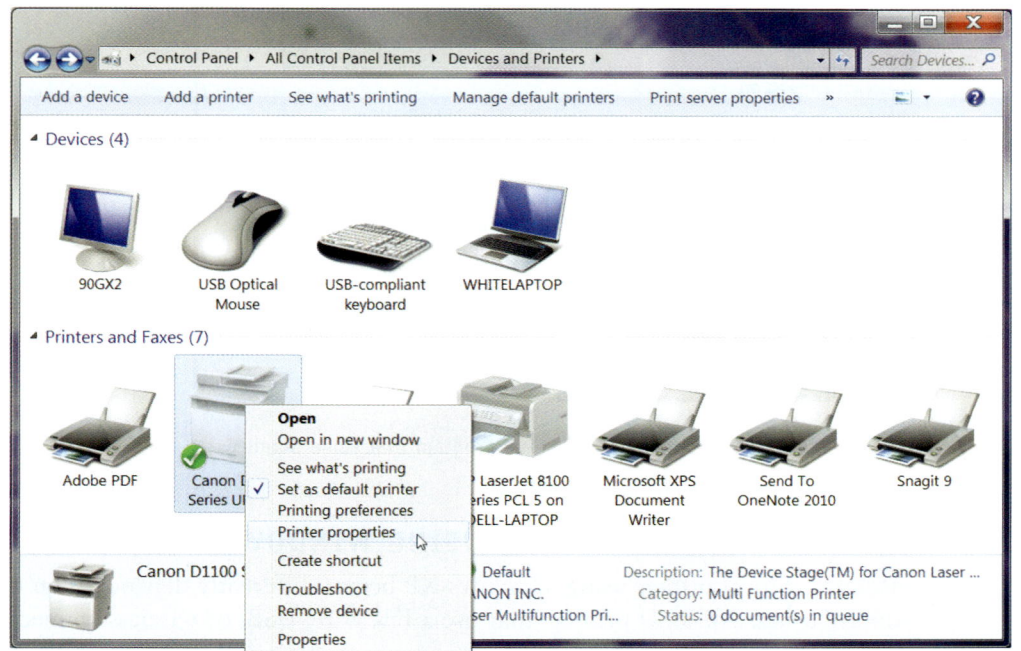

Figure 12-14 Select Printer properties to open the printer Properties box

Source: Microsoft Windows 7

596   **CHAPTER 12**   **Supporting Printers**

A+
220-801
1.11,
1.12,
4.2

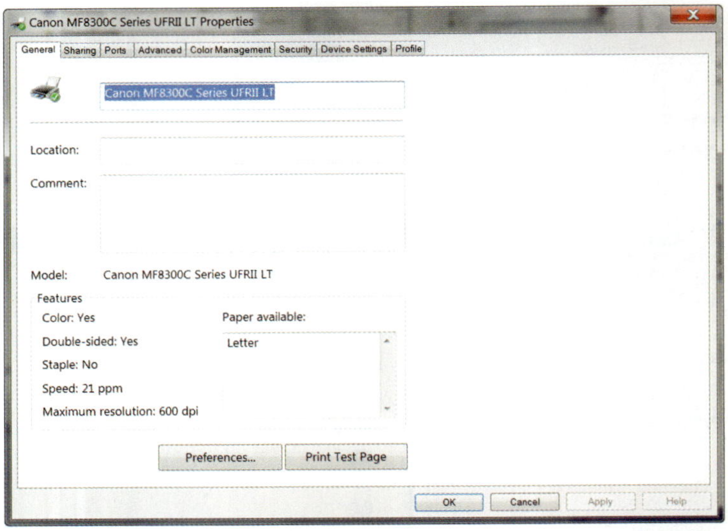

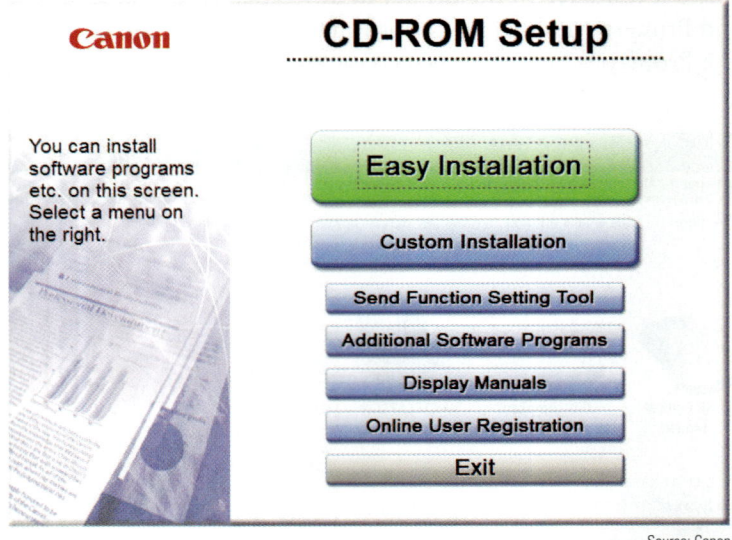

Source: Canon

Figure 12-15 Send a test page to the printer to test connectivity to the printer, the printer, and the printer installation

Rather than using the Windows Devices and Printers window to start a printer installation, you can also start the installation using the setup program on the CD that came bundled with the printer or using the setup program downloaded from the printer manufacturer's web site. For one Canon printer, when you launch that setup program, the menu shown in Figure 12-16 appears. Follow the directions to install the printer. This method might work when the first method fails.

Source: Canon

Figure 12-16 Menu provided by a setup program that came bundled with a printer

INSTALL A LOCAL PRINTER USING WINDOWS XP

Installing a local printer using Windows XP begins differently depending on the type of port you are using. For local printers that use a FireWire, USB, or wireless connection, you might need to first install the software before connecting the printer or connect the printer before installing the software. See the documentation to know which order to use.

Using Windows to Install, Share, and Manage Printers

A+ 220-801
1.11, 1.12, 4.2

> **A+ Exam Tip** The A+ 220-801 exam expects you to know how to install a local and network printer using Windows 7, Vista, or XP.

Follow these steps to install a local printer using FireWire, USB, or a wireless connection:

1. Log onto the system as an administrator. Run the setup program stored on CD or downloaded from the printer manufacturer's web site before you install the printer. The setup program installs the drivers.

2. At one point in the setup, you will be told to connect the printer. Figure 12-17 shows this step for one HP printer installation routine. Connect the printer to the port. For this printer, a USB port is used. For wireless printers, verify the wireless connection is enabled. For infrared wireless printers, place the printer in the line of sight of the infrared port on the computer. (Most wireless printers have a status light that stays lit when a wireless connection is active.) Turn on the printer.

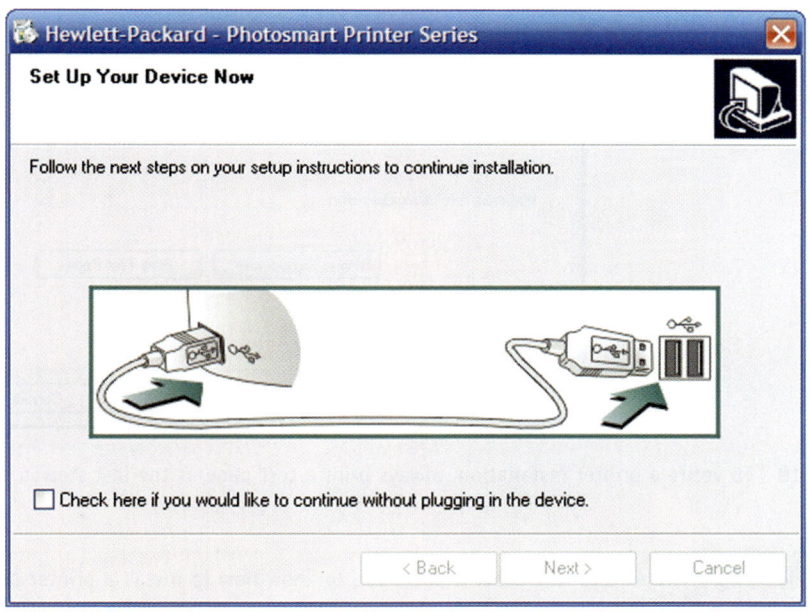

Source: Hewlett-Packard

Figure 12-17 The printer setup program tells you when to connect the printer

3. The setup program detects the printer. If Windows launches the Found New Hardware Wizard, it should close quickly. If not, cancel the wizard.

4. The setup program asks if you want this printer to be the default printer. Click Yes or No to make your selection. The setup program finishes the installation.

5. You can now test the printer. Open the Printers and Faxes window by clicking **Start**, **Control Panel**, and **Printers and Faxes** (in Classic view). For Category view, click **Printers and Other Hardware** and then click **Printers and Faxes**. Either way, the Printers and Faxes window opens (see the top of Figure 12-18). Right-click the printer and select **Properties** from the shortcut menu. Click the **General** tab and then click the **Print Test Page** button, as shown in Figure 12-18.

A+
220-801
1.11,
1.12,
4.2

Source: Microsoft Windows 7 and Hewlett-Packard

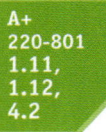

Figure 12-18 To verify a printer installation, always print a test page as the last step in the installation

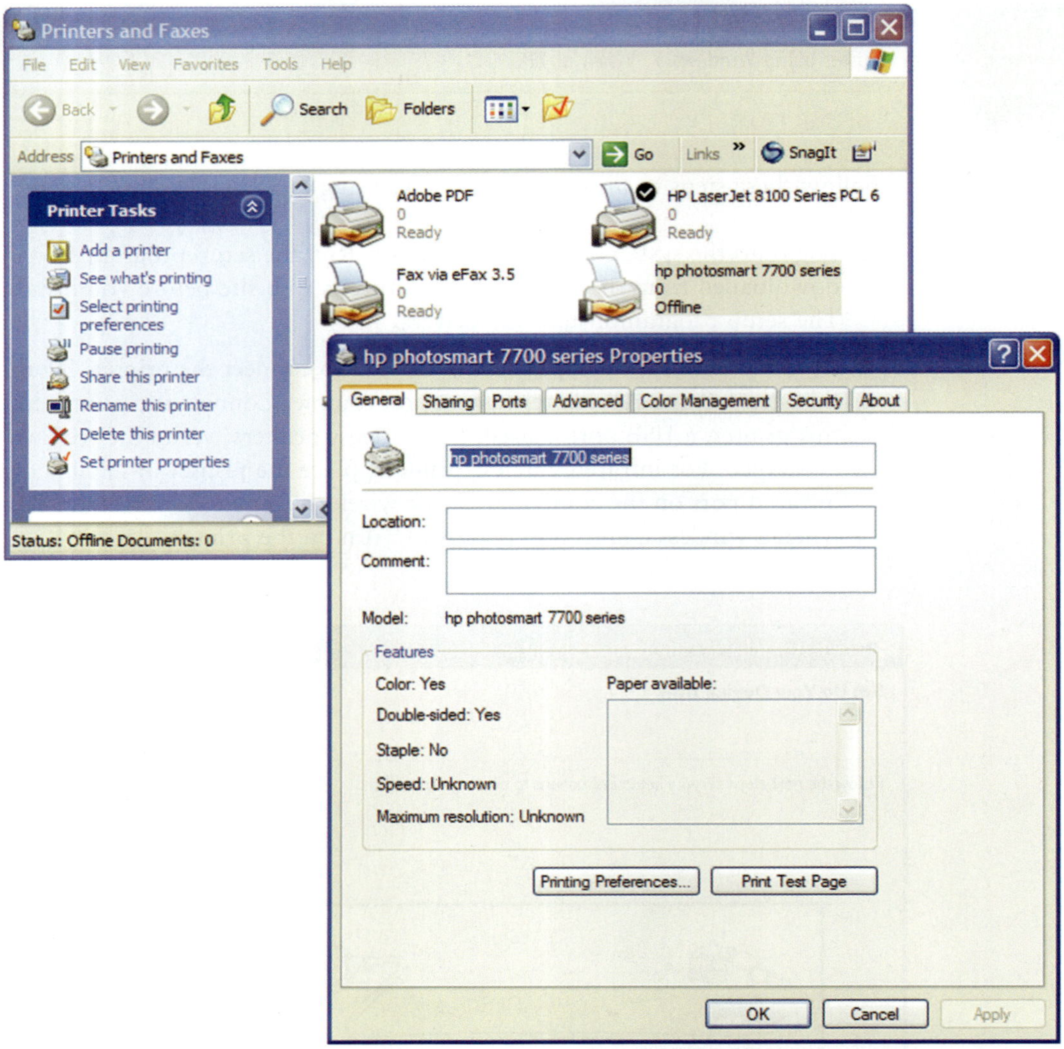

> **A+ Exam Tip** The A+ 220-801 exam expects you to know how to install a printer using older technologies, including how to install a local printer using a serial or parallel port in Windows XP.

PRINTER INSTALLATIONS USING A PARALLEL PORT

Serial and parallel printer ports are not hot pluggable. Here are the directions to install a local printer using a serial or parallel port in Windows XP:

1. Plug in the printer to the port and turn on the printer. Now, you must decide how you want to install the drivers. You can use the setup program from the printer manufacturer or use the Windows installation process. First try using the setup program that came on the printer's setup CD or downloaded from the manufacturer's web site. If you have problems with the installation, you can then try the Windows approach.
2. To use the printer's setup program, launch the program and follow the directions on-screen to install the printer.

**A+
220-801
1.11,
1.12,
4.2**

3. Alternately, you can use the Windows installation process to install the printer drivers. Open the Printers and Faxes window and click **Add a printer**. The Add Printer Wizard launches, as shown in Figure 12-19. Follow the directions on-screen to install the printer drivers. After the printer is installed, print a test page to verify the installation works.

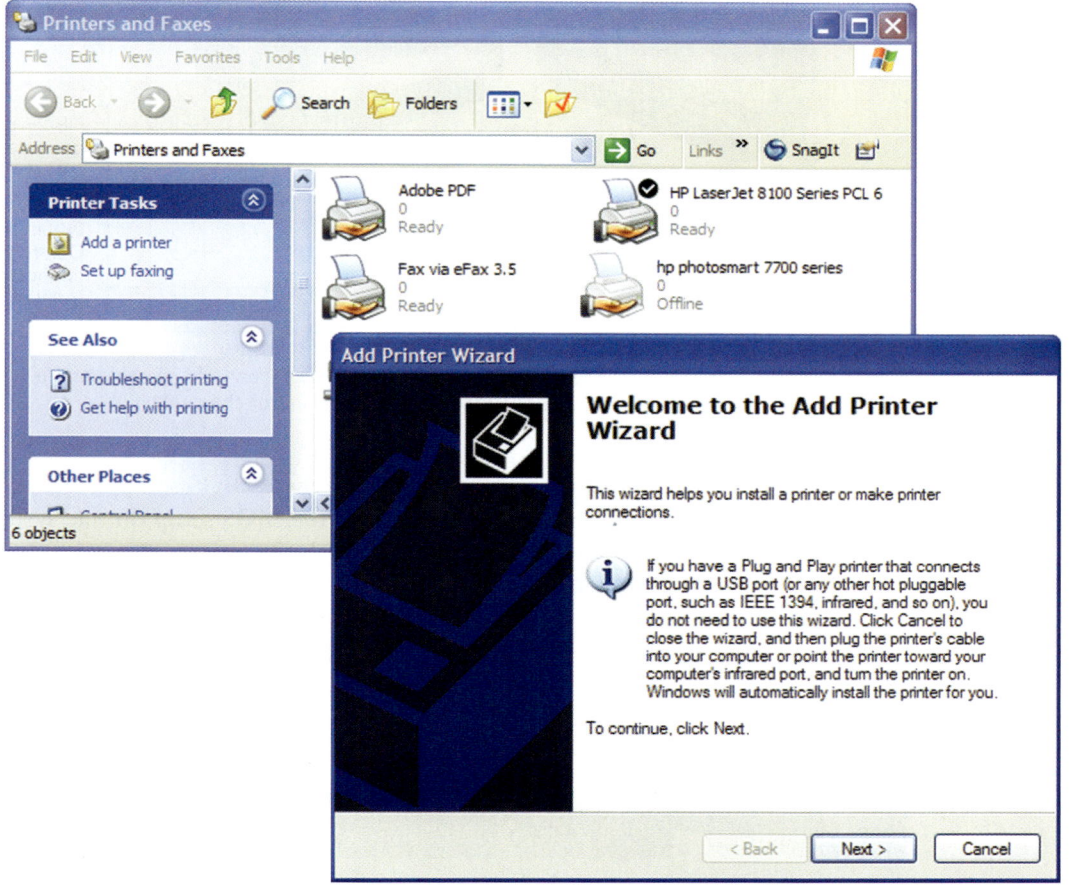

Figure 12-19 Use the Add Printer Wizard to install a printer

Source: Microsoft Windows 7

> **A+ Exam Tip** The A+ 220-801 exam expects you to be able to configure a parallel port and install a printer that uses a parallel port.

If you have a problem with the installation that is using a parallel port, consider the port might not be configured correctly in BIOS setup or there is a problem with the parallel cable.

Parallel ports, commonly used by older printers, transmit data in parallel, eight bits at a time. Parallel ports fall into three categories: **Standard Parallel Port (SPP)** that transmits in only one direction (the computer can communicate with the printer, but the printer cannot communicate with the computer), **EPP (Enhanced Parallel Port)** that transmits in both directions, and **ECP (Extended Capabilities Port)** that is faster than an EPP port. A parallel port is sometimes called a Centronics port, named after the 36-pin Centronics connection used by printers (see Figure 12-20). Both EPP and ECP are covered under the **IEEE 1284** specifications of the Institute of Electrical and Electronics Engineers (IEEE). A parallel cable should not exceed 10 feet and should be IEEE 1284 compliant; look for the IEEE 1284 label on the cable.

Figure 12-20 A parallel cable has a DB25 connection at the PC end of the cable and a 36-pin Centronics connection at the printer end of the cable

If you're having a problem with a parallel port, check BIOS setup to make sure the port is enabled and configured correctly. For example, the BIOS setup on one system is shown in Figure 12-21. Unless you are having a problem with the port or suspect a conflict with other hardware, keep the default setting of ECP.

Also check Device Manager to make sure it recognizes the port without an error. In Device Manager, a parallel port is known as LPT1: or LPT2:. The **LPT (Line Printer Terminal)** assignments refer to the system resources a parallel port will use to manage a print job.

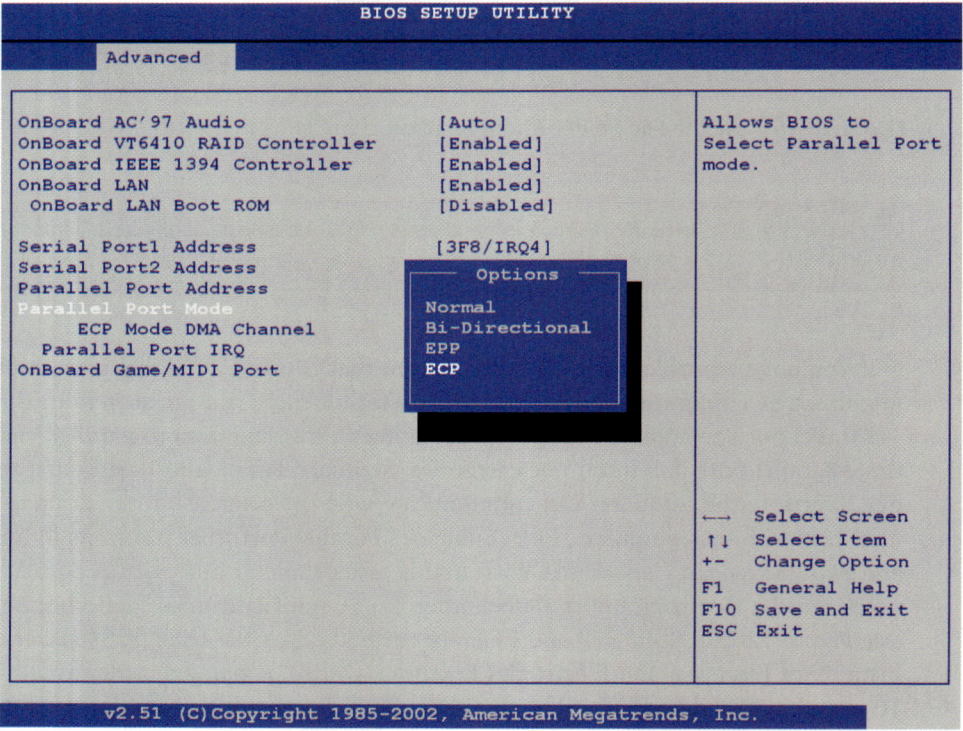

Figure 12-21 BIOS settings for a parallel port on one motherboard

STEPS TO INSTALL A NETWORK PRINTER USING WINDOWS XP

Always follow the manufacturer's directions when installing a printer. If you don't have these instructions, here are the general steps to install a network printer using Windows XP:

1. Open the XP Printers and Faxes window and start the wizard to add a new printer. Select the option to install a local printer but do not ask Windows to automatically detect the printer.

2. On the next window shown in Figure 12-22, choose **Create a new port**. From the list of port types, select **Standard TCP/IP Port**. Click **Next** twice.

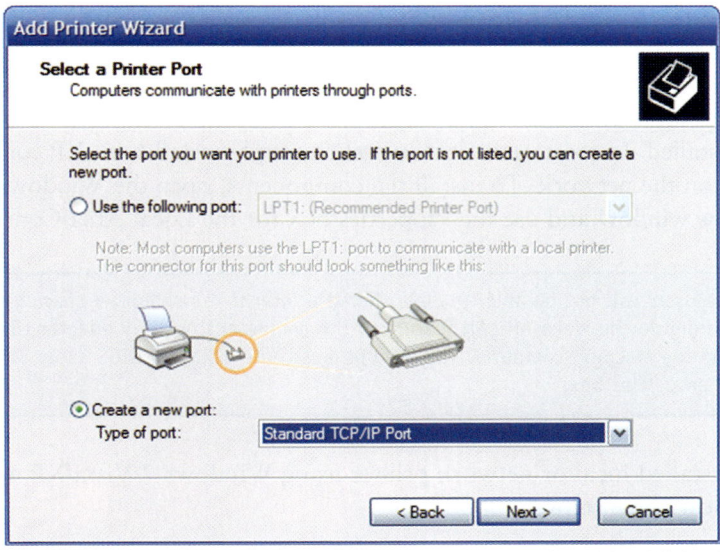

Source: Microsoft Windows 7

Figure 12-22 Configure a local printer to use a standard TCP/IP port

3. On the next window shown in Figure 12-23, you need to identify the printer on the network. If you know the IP address of the printer, enter it in the first box on this window and click **Next**. Alternately, you can enter the printer name.

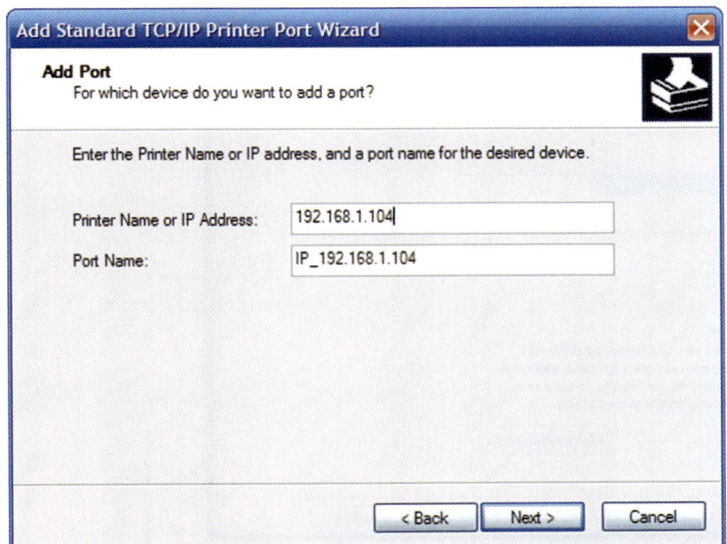

Source: Microsoft Windows 7

Figure 12-23 Enter the printer name or IP address to identify the printer on the network

4. On the next window, click **Have Disk** so you can point to and use the downloaded driver files that will then be used to complete the printer installation.

SHARING AN INSTALLED PRINTER

Before you share an installed local or network printer, verify these Windows settings for shared resources:

▲ Using Windows 7, make sure **Turn on file and printer sharing** is selected, which is the default setting for a Home or Work network. To check the setting, click **Change advanced sharing settings** in the Network and Sharing Center.
▲ Using Windows Vista, Printer sharing must be turned on in the Network and Sharing Center.
▲ Using Windows XP, to share an installed printer, File and Printer Sharing must be installed. To use a printer shared by a remote computer, Client for Microsoft Networks must be installed. In most cases, it is easiest to simply install both XP components on all computers on the network. To install the components, open the Windows XP Network Connections window and use the Properties box for the Local Area Connection icon.

> **Notes** Remote users will not be able to use a shared printer if the computer sharing the printer is asleep. You can configure the Wake-on-LAN feature of the computer's network adapter to cause network activity to wake up the sleeping computer. The feature must be enabled in BIOS setup and also in the network adapter's properties box.

To share an installed local or network printer using Windows 7/Vista/XP with others on the network, follow these steps:

1. In the printer Properties box, click the **Sharing** tab. Check **Share this printer**, as shown in Figure 12-24 for Windows 7. (For Vista or XP, you must click the **Change sharing options** button on the Sharing tab before you can make changes. This button is missing in Windows 7.)

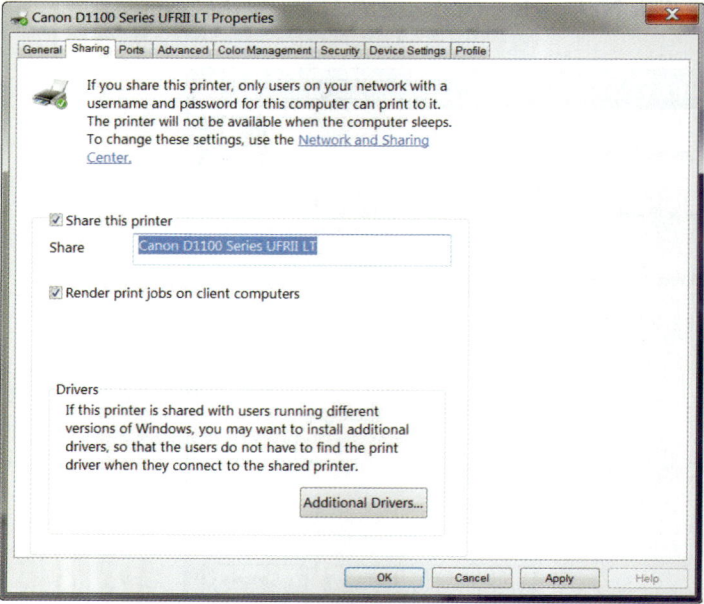

Source: Canon

Figure 12-24 Share the printer and make decisions as to how printer sharing is handled

2. You can then change the share name of the printer. Notice in Figure 12-24 the option to control where print jobs are rendered. A print job can be prepared (rendered) on the remote computer (client computer) or this computer (print server). Your choice depends on which computer you think should carry this burden. You can test several print jobs on remote computers with rendering done at either location and see which method best uses computing resources on the network.

> **Notes** Group Policy under Windows 7/Vista can be used to limit and control all kinds of printer-related tasks, including the number of printers that can be installed, how print jobs are sent to print servers (rendered or not rendered), which print servers the computer can use, and which printers on a network the computer can use.

3. If you want to make drivers for the printer available to remote users who are using an operating system other than the OS on this computer, click **Additional Drivers**.

4. The Additional Drivers box opens, as shown in Figure 12-25. For 32-bit operating systems, select **x86**. For 64-bit operating systems, select **x64**. Click **OK** to close the box. You might be asked for the Windows setup DVD or other access to the installation files. (For Windows XP, the Additional Drivers box lists specific operating systems for drivers to be made available to remote computers.)

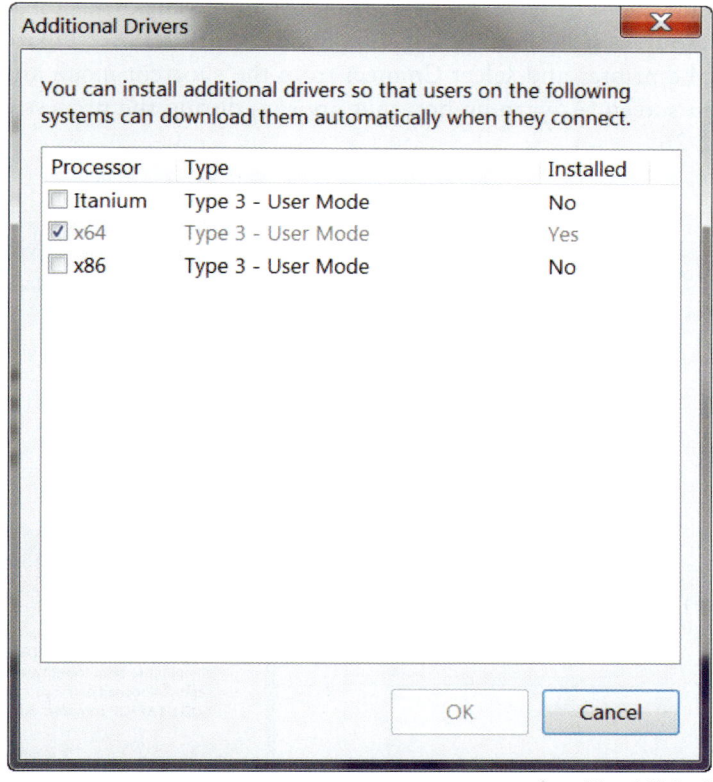

Source: Microsoft Windows 7

Figure 12-25 Select additional drivers you want available for other operating systems that will use the shared printer

5. Click **OK** to close the Properties box. A shared printer shows a two-friends icon (for Windows 7/Vista) or a hand icon (for XP) under it in the Devices and Printers window, and the printer is listed in the Network windows of other computers on the network.

INSTALLING A SHARED PRINTER

A+
220-801
1.11,
1.12,
4.2

You can install a shared printer on a remote computer using one of two methods: (1) Use the Windows 7 Devices and Printers window, the Vista Printer window, or the XP Printers and Faxes window, or (2) use Windows Explorer or the Network or My Network Places window. Here are the general steps to follow when using the first method:

1. On a remote computer, open the Windows 7 Devices and Printers window, the Vista Printer window, or the XP Printers and Faxes window. Click **Add a printer** and follow the directions on-screen to add a network printer.

2. As you follow the wizard, select the shared printer from the list of available printers. Windows attempts to use printer drivers found on the host computer. If it doesn't find the drivers, you will be given the opportunity to provide them on CD or another media. Follow the directions on-screen to complete the installation wizard.

Another way to install a shared printer is to first use Windows Explorer or the Network window or XP My Network Places to locate the printer on the network. Do the following:

1. On a remote computer, open **Windows Explorer**. In the Network resources, select the computer that is sharing the printer. Double-click the computer to reveal the resources it is sharing, which include the printer. See Figure 12-26. Right-click the printer and select **Connect** from the shortcut menu and follow the directions on-screen. A warning box that appears during the process is shown in Figure 12-26.

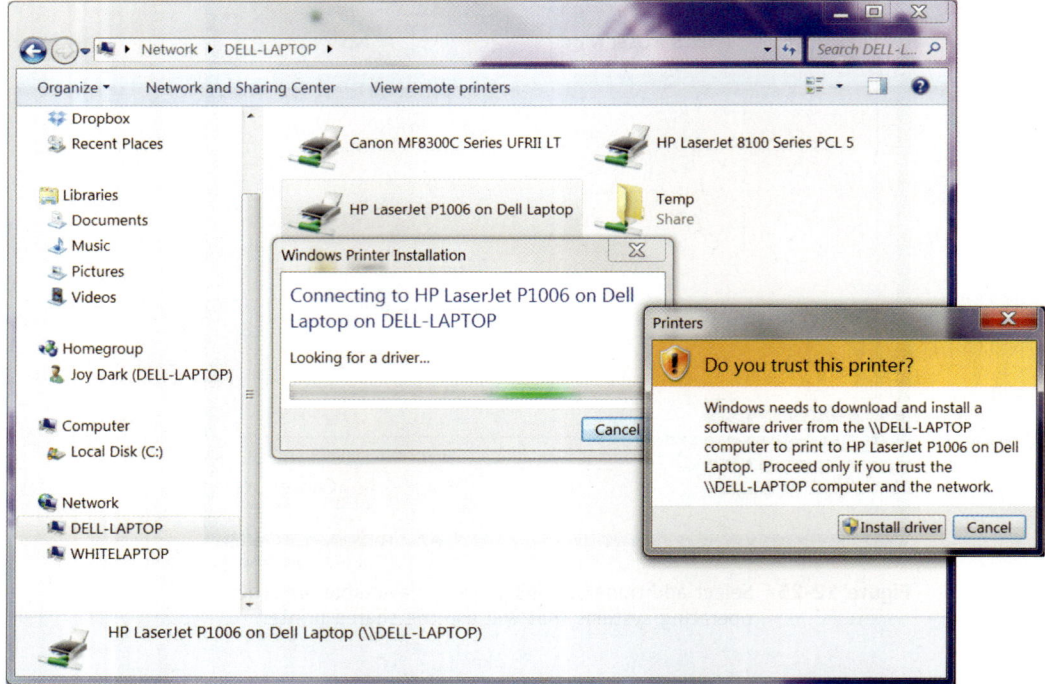

Figure 12-26 Install a shared printer using Windows Explorer

Source: Microsoft Windows 7

Using Windows to Install, Share, and Manage Printers

A+ 220-801 1.11, 1.12, 4.2

2. If the host computer is sharing the right drivers, you can use those drivers for the installation. If Windows cannot find the right drivers, it sends you an error message and gives you the opportunity to install the drivers using the printer manufacturer's CD or downloaded from the web. Be sure to send a test page to the printer to verify the installation is successful.

MANAGING PRINTER FEATURES AND ADD-ON DEVICES

After the printer is installed, use the printer Properties box to manage printer features and hardware devices installed on the printer. To open the box, right-click the printer and choose **Printer properties**. On the Properties box, click the **Device Settings** tab. The options on this tab depend on the installed printer. Figure 12-27 shows the box for an HP printer, and the box for a Canon printer is shown in Figure 12-28. For the printer in Figure 12-27, duplex printing is available, as shown in the figure. You can also control the size of the paper installed in each input tray bin and various add-on devices for this printer, such as a stapler or stacker unit.

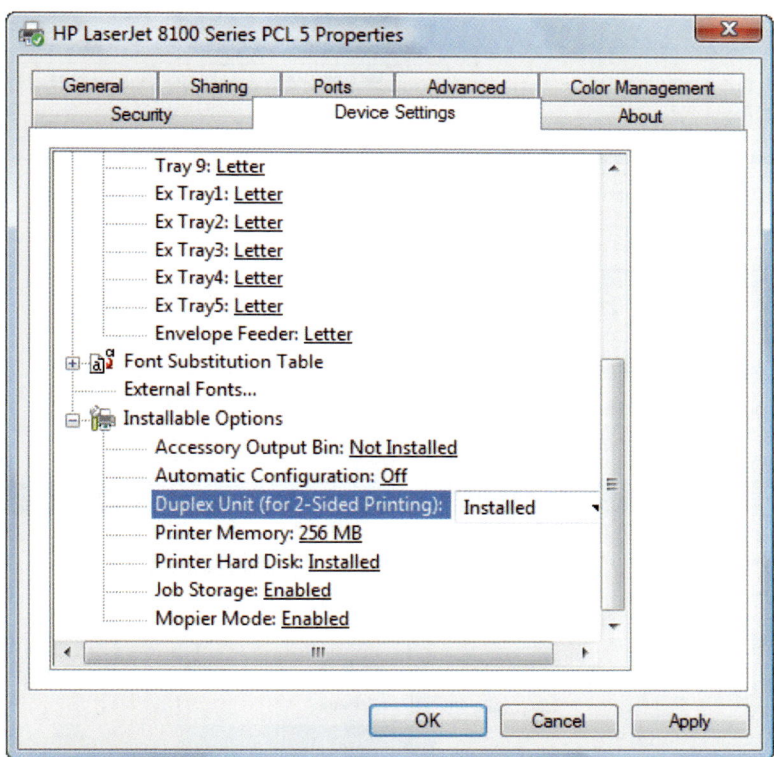

Source: Microsoft Windows 7

Figure 12-27 The Device Settings for an HP printer

After you have installed new printer add-on equipment or a feature, the equipment or feature is listed as an option in the Printing Preferences box when a user is printing a document. The users of this printer need to know how to use the option. For example, if you install duplexing and a user attempts to print from an application, the user needs to know how to print on both sides of the paper. When printing from Notepad, the Print window shown on the left side of Figure 12-29 appears. To print on both sides of the paper, the user can select the printer and click **Preferences**, select the **Finishing** tab in the Printing Preferences box, and select **2-sided Printing** from the drop-down list (see the right side of Figure 12-29).

606 | **CHAPTER 12** Supporting Printers

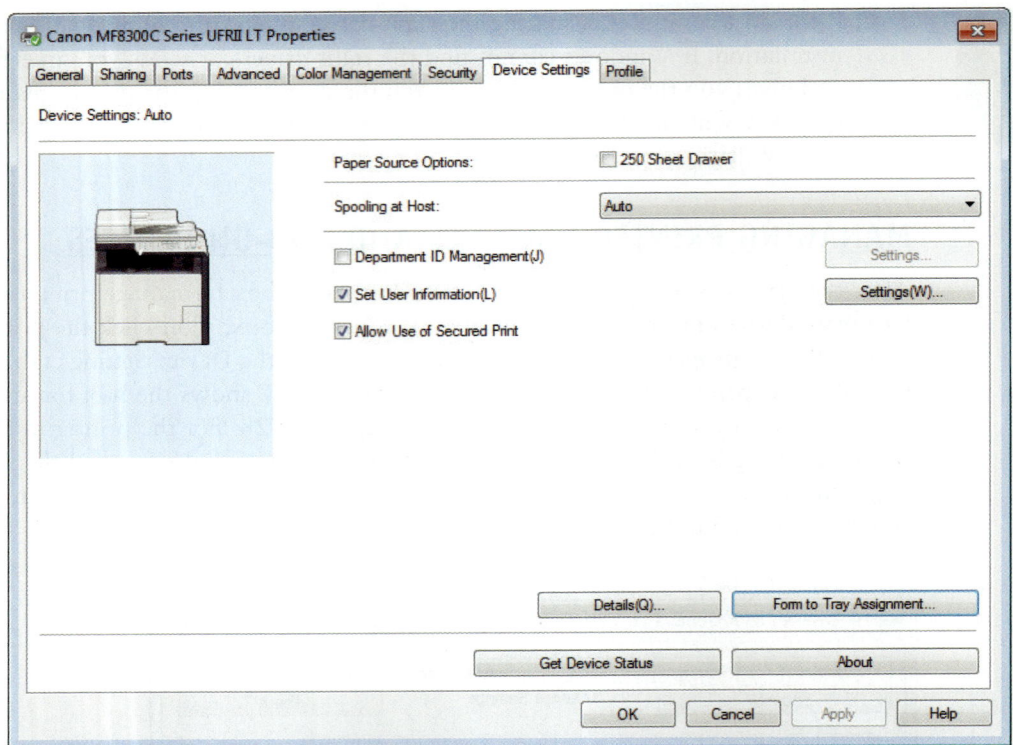

Figure 12-28 The Device Settings for a Canon printer

Source: Canon

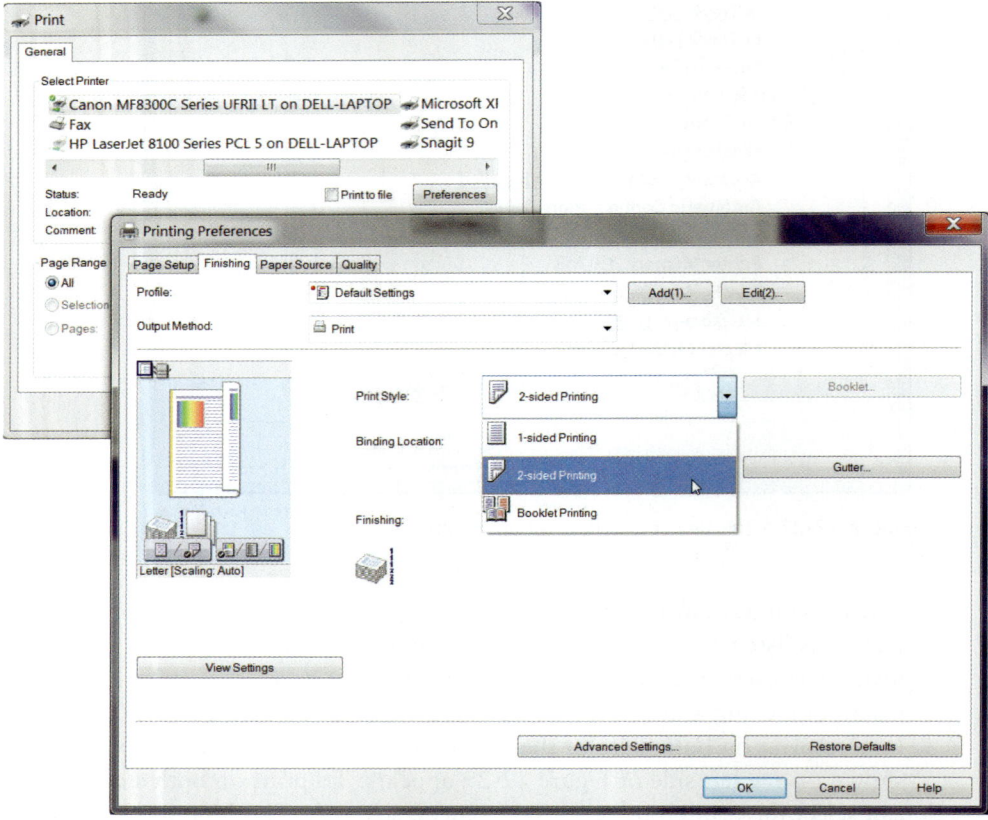

Figure 12-29 Printing on both sides of the paper

Source: Microsoft Windows 7

Using Windows to Install, Share, and Manage Printers

> **Notes** You might be expected to train a user how to install paper and envelopes in the various paper trays. Let the user know whom to contact if printer problems arise. You might also consider providing a means for the user to record problems with the printer that don't require immediate attention. For example, you can hang a clipboard and paper close to the printer for the user to write questions and comments that you can address at a later time.

MANAGING THE PRINTER QUEUE

Normally, when Windows receives a print job from an application, it places the job in a queue and prints from the queue, so that the application is released from the printing process as soon as possible. Several print jobs can accumulate in the queue, and the process is called **spooling**. (The word *spool* is an acronym for *s*imultaneous *p*eripheral *o*perations *online*.) The print queue is sometimes called the **print spooler**. Most printing from Windows uses spooling.

To manage the printer queue, double-click the printer icon in the Windows 7 Devices and Printers window. The printer status window that appears for one printer is showing in Figure 12-30. Other printer status windows might be organized slightly differently. From this window, you can see the status and order of the print jobs. If the printer reports a problem with printing, it will be displayed as the status for the first job in the print queue. To cancel a single print job, right-click the job and select **Cancel** from the shortcut menu. See Figure 12-30. To cancel all print jobs, click **Printer** on the menu and select **Cancel All Documents**. If you still can't get the printer moving again, try pressing a Cancel or Reset button on the printer or turning the printer off and on. To verify that the problem with printing is solved, print a test page using the printer Properties box.

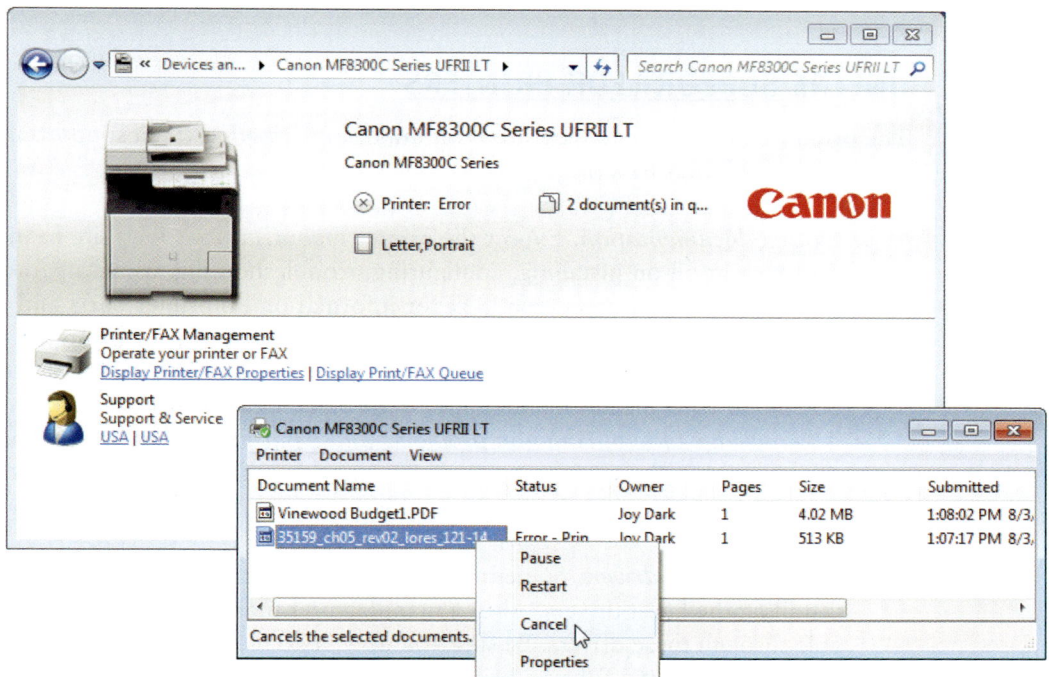

Figure 12-30 Manage the printer queue

Source: Microsoft Windows 7

> **Notes** If the printer queue is backed up, try deleting the first job in the queue (the one listed last.) If you are having a problem deleting all jobs in the queue, you can stop and restart the Windows print spooler service. How to do that is covered later in the chapter.

> **Hands-on | Project 12-2** Share a Local Printer
>
> Practice printer sharing skills using Windows and a printer:
>
> 1. Install and share a local printer with others on the network.
> 2. Install a shared printer on a remote computer. Verify that you can print to the printer from the remote computer.
> 3. Turn off the shared printer. Print again from the remote computer. On which computer is the print job queued? Cancel this print job.

Now let's turn our attention to tasks you might be called on to do when maintaining and upgrading a printer.

PRINTER MAINTENANCE AND UPGRADES

Printers generally last for years if they are properly used and maintained. To get the most out of a printer, it's important to follow the manufacturer's directions when using the device and to perform the necessary routine maintenance. For example, the life of a printer can be shortened if you allow the printer to overheat, don't use approved paper, or don't install consumable maintenance kits when they are required.

ONLINE SUPPORT FOR PRINTERS

The printer manufacturer's web site is an important resource when supporting printers. Here are some things to look for:

- *Online documentation.* Expect the printer manufacturer's web site to include documentation on installing, configuring, troubleshooting, using, upgrading, and maintaining the printer. Also look for information on printer parts and warranty, compatibility information, specifications and features of your printer, a way to register your printer, and how to recycle or dispose of a printer. You might also be able to download your printer manual in PDF format.
- *A knowledge base of common problems and what to do about them.* Some web sites offer a forum where you can communicate with others responsible for supporting a particular printer. Also look for an online chat link or email address for technical support.
- *Updated device drivers.* Sometimes you can solve printer problems by downloading and installing the latest drivers. Also, a manufacturer makes new features and options available through these drivers. Be sure you download files for the correct printer and OS.
- *Replacement parts.* When a printer part breaks, buy only parts made by or approved by the printer manufacturer. Manufacturers also sell consumable supplies such as toner and ink cartridges.
- *Printer maintenance kits.* The best practice is to buy everything you need for routine maintenance either from the printer manufacturer or an approved vendor. If you buy from a nonapproved vendor, you risk damaging the printer, voiding its warranty, or shortening its lifespan.

A+ 220-801 4.3

▲ *Firmware updates.* Some high-end printers have firmware that can be flashed to solve problems and add features. Be careful to download the correct update for your printer.

For now, let's focus on how to protect yourself when working inside a printer. Some laser printer parts can get hot enough to burn you while in operation. So before you work inside a laser printer, turn it off, unplug it, and wait about 30 minutes for it to cool down. Printer parts that get hot might have one of the symbols in Figure 12-31 imprinted on or near them. Also notice in the figure other symbols that indicate danger. If you see these symbols on parts or in documentation, pay attention to them and stay safe.

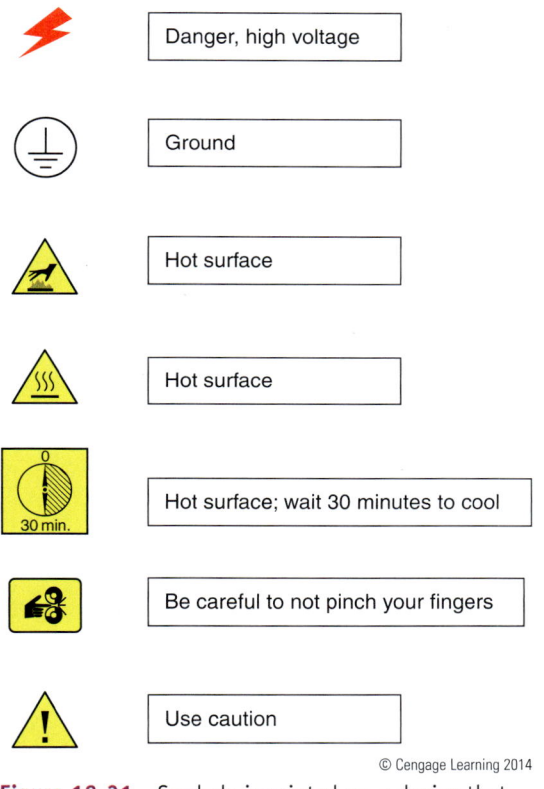

© Cengage Learning 2014

Figure 12-31 Symbols imprinted on a device that indicate danger

Also know that a printer might still keep power even when the printer on/off switch is turned off. To ensure that the printer has no power, unplug it. Even when a laser printer is unplugged, internal components might still hold a dangerous electrical charge for some time. For your protection, laser printers use a laser beam that is always enclosed inside a protective case inside the printer. Therefore, when servicing a laser printer, you should never have to look at the laser beam, which can damage your eyes.

To protect memory modules and hard drives inside printers, be sure to use an antistatic ground bracelet to protect these sensitive components when installing them. It is not necessary or recommended that you wear the ground bracelet when exchanging consumables such as toner cartridges, fuser assembles, or image drums.

Here's one more tip to stay safe, but I don't want it to frighten you: When you work inside high-voltage equipment such as a laser printer, don't do it when no one else is around. If you have an emergency, someone needs to be close by to help you.

> **Notes** When working with laser printer toner cartridges, if you get toner dust on your clothes or hands while exchanging the cartridge, don't use hot water to clean it up. Remember that heat sets the toner. Go outdoors and use a can of compressed air to blow off the toner. Then use cold water to clean your hands and clothes. It's a good idea to wear a smock or apron when working on printers.

Figure 12-32 shows an ink cartridge being installed in an inkjet printer. To replace a cartridge, turn on the printer and open the front cover. The printer releases the cartridges. You can then open the latch on top of the cartridge and remove it. Install the new cartridge as shown in the figure.

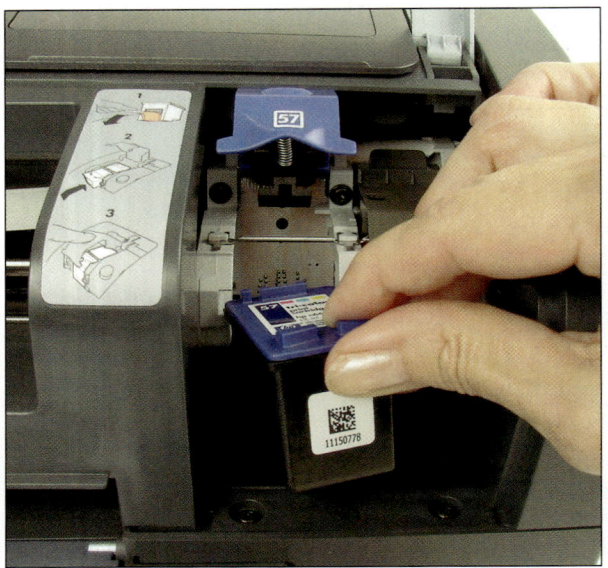

Figure 12-32 Installing an ink cartridge in an inkjet printer

CLEANING A PRINTER

A printer gets dirty inside and outside as stray toner, ink, dust, and bits of paper accumulate. As part of routine printer maintenance, you need to regularly clean the printer. How often depends on how much the printer is used and the work environment. Some manufacturers suggest a heavily used printer be cleaned weekly, and others suggest you clean it whenever you exchange the toner, ink cartridges, or ribbon.

Clean the outside of the printer with a damp cloth. Don't use ammonia-based cleaners. Clean the inside of the printer with a dry cloth and remove dust, bits of paper, and stray toner. Picking up stray toner can be a problem. Don't try to blow it out with compressed air because you don't want the toner in the air. Also, don't use an antistatic vacuum cleaner. You can, however, use a vacuum cleaner designed to pick up toner, called a **toner vacuum**. This type of vacuum does not allow the toner that it picks up to touch any conductive surface. Some printer manufacturers also suggest you use an **extension magnet brush**. The long-handled brush is made of nylon fibers that are charged with static electricity and easily attract the toner like a magnet. For a laser printer, wipe the rollers from side to side with a dry cloth to remove loose dirt and toner. Don't touch the soft black roller (the transfer roller), or you might affect the print quality. You can find specific instructions for cleaning a printer on the printer manufacturer's web site.

An inkjet printer might require **calibration** to align and/or clean the inkjet nozzles, which can solve a problem when colors appear streaked or out of alignment. To calibrate the printer, you might use the menu on the control panel of the printer or use software that came bundled with the printer. How to access these tools differs from one printer to another. See the printer manual to learn how to perform the calibration. For some printers, a Services tab is added to the printer Properties window. Other printer installations might put utility programs in the Start menu. The first time you turn on a printer after installing ink cartridges, it's a good idea to calibrate the printer.

If an inkjet printer still does not print after calibrating it, you can try to manually clean the cartridge nozzles. Check the printer manufacturer's web site for directions. For most inkjet printers, you are directed to use clean, distilled water and cotton swabs to clean the face of the ink cartridge, being careful not to touch the nozzle plate. To prevent the inkjet nozzles from drying out, don't leave the ink cartridges out of their cradle for longer than 30 minutes. Here are some general directions:

1. Following the manufacturer's directions, remove the inkjet cartridges from the printer and lay them on their sides on a paper towel.

2. Dip a cotton swab in distilled water (not tap water) and squeeze out any excess water.

3. Hold an ink cartridge so that the nozzle plate faces up and use the swab to wipe clean the area around the nozzle plate, as shown in Figure 12-33. Do not clean the plate itself.

Figure 12-33 Clean the area around the nozzle plate with a damp cotton swab

4. Hold the cartridge up to the light and make sure that no dust, dirt, ink, or cotton fibers are left around the face of the nozzle plate. Make sure the area is clean.

5. Clean all the ink cartridges the same way and replace the cartridges in the printer.

6. Print a test page. If print quality is still poor, try calibrating the printer again.

7. If you still have problems, you need to replace the ink cartridges.

Laser printers automatically calibrate themselves periodically. You can instruct a laser printer to calibrate at any time by using the controls on the front of the printer or the browser-based utility program that is included in the firmware of a network printer. To access the utility, enter the IP address of the printer in the browser address box.

PRINTER MAINTENANCE KITS

Manufacturers of high-end printers provide **printer maintenance kits**, which include specific printer components, step-by-step instructions for performing maintenance, and any special tools or equipment you need to do maintenance. For example, the maintenance plan for the HP Color LaserJet 4600 printer says to replace the transfer roller assembly after printing 120,000 pages and replace the fusing assembly after 150,000 pages. The plan also says the black ink cartridge should last for about 9,000 pages and the color ink cartridge for about 8,000 pages. HP sells the image transfer kit, the image fuser kit, and the ink cartridges designed for this printer.

> **A+ Exam Tip** The A+ 220-801 exam expects you to know about the importance of resetting the page count after installing a printer maintenance kit.

To find out how many pages a printer has printed so that you know if you need to do the maintenance, you need to have the printer give you the page count since the last maintenance. You can tell the printer to display the information or print a status report by using buttons on the front of the printer (see Figure 12-34) or you can use utility software from a computer connected to the printer. See the printer documentation to know how to get this report. For network printers that offer a browser-based utility, enter the IP address of the printer in your browser and use the utility to find the counters (Figure 12-35 shows such a utility for a Canon network printer).

After you have performed the maintenance, be sure to reset the page count so it will be accurate to tell you when you need to do the next routine maintenance. Keep a written record of the maintenance and other service done. If a printer gives problems, one of the first things you can do is check this service documentation to find out if maintenance is due. You can also check for a history of prior problems and how they were resolved.

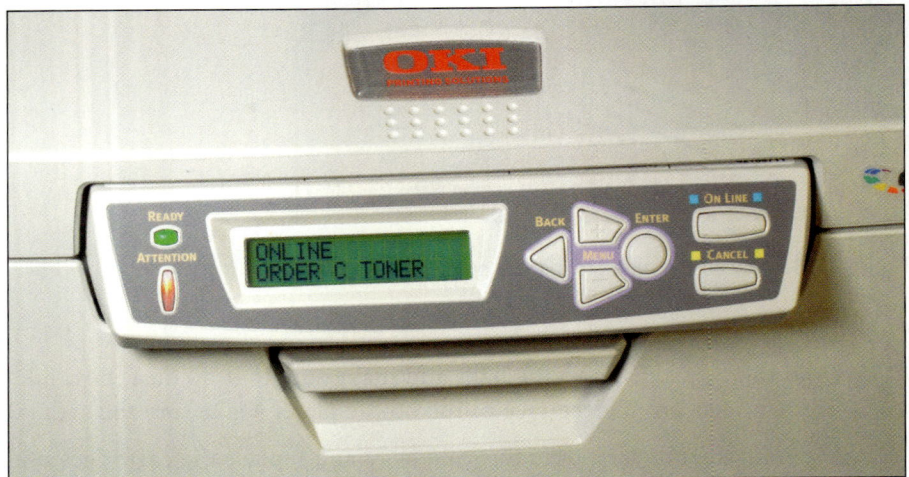

Figure 12-34 Use buttons on the front of the printer to display information, including the page count

Printer Maintenance and Upgrades | 613

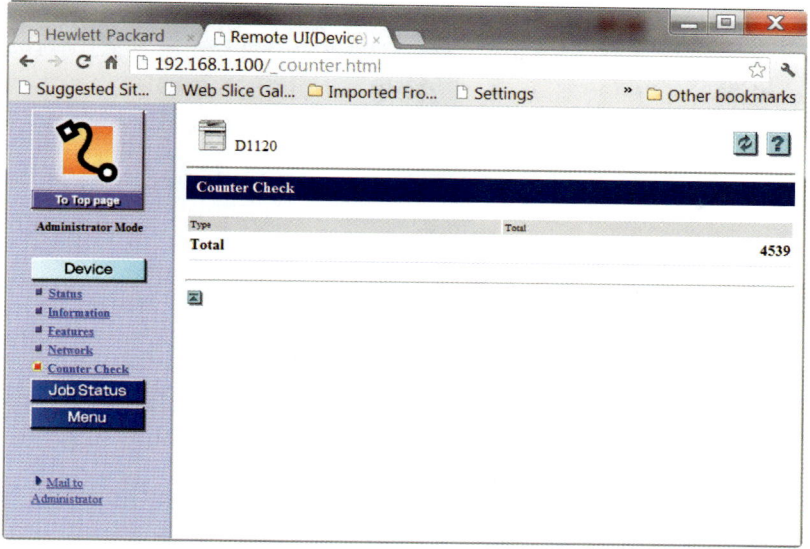

Source: Canon

Figure 12-35 Use the web-based printer utility to read the printer counters

As examples of replacing printer consumables, let's look at how to replace a toner cartridge, image drum, and fuser for the Oki Data color laser printer shown earlier in Figure 12-1.

> **A+ Exam Tip** The A+ 220-801 exam expects you to know how to replace a toner cartridge and apply a maintenance kit that can include an image drum or a fuser assembly.

A toner cartridge for this printer generally lasts for about 1,500 pages. Here are the steps to replace a color toner cartridge:

1. Turn off and unplug the printer. Press the cover release button on the top-left corner of the printer and open the printer cover (see Figure 12-36).

2. Figure 12-37 shows the cover up. Notice the four erase lamps on the inside of the cover. Look inside the printer for the four toner cartridges and the fuser assembly labeled in Figure 12-38. Pull the blue toner cartridge release button forward to release the cartridge from the image drum below it and to which it is connected (see Figure 12-39).

© Cengage Learning 2014

Figure 12-36 Open the printer cover

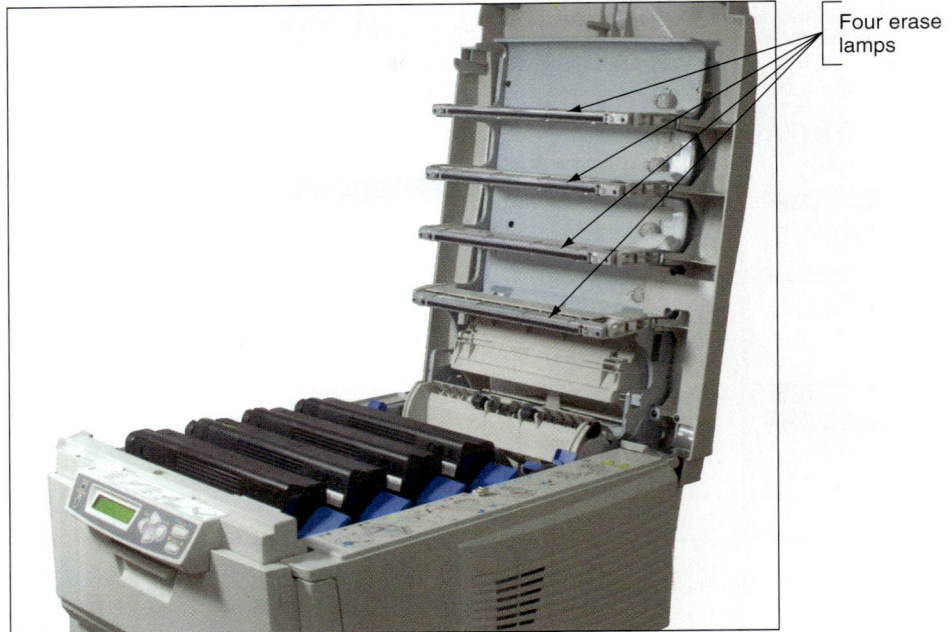

Figure 12-37 Cover lifted

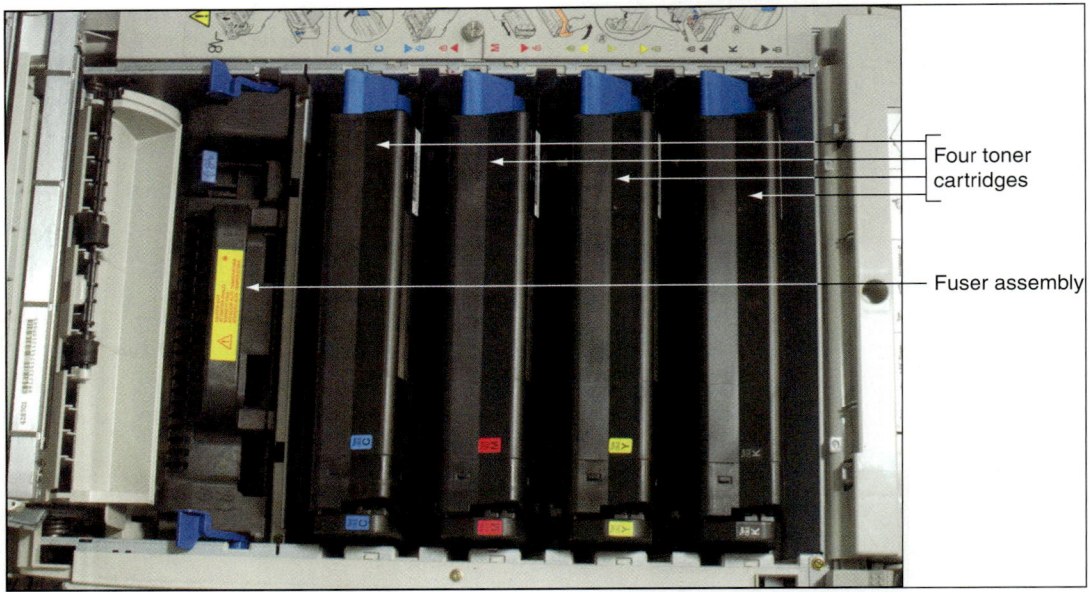

Figure 12-38 Inside the Oki Data printer

3. Lift the cartridge out of the printer, lifting up on the right side first and then removing the left side (see Figure 12-40). Be careful not to spill loose toner.

4. Unpack the new cartridge. Gently shake it from side to side to loosen the toner. Remove the tape from underneath the cartridge, and place the cartridge in the printer by inserting the left side first and then the right side. Push the cartridge lever back into position to lock the cartridge in place. Close the printer cover.

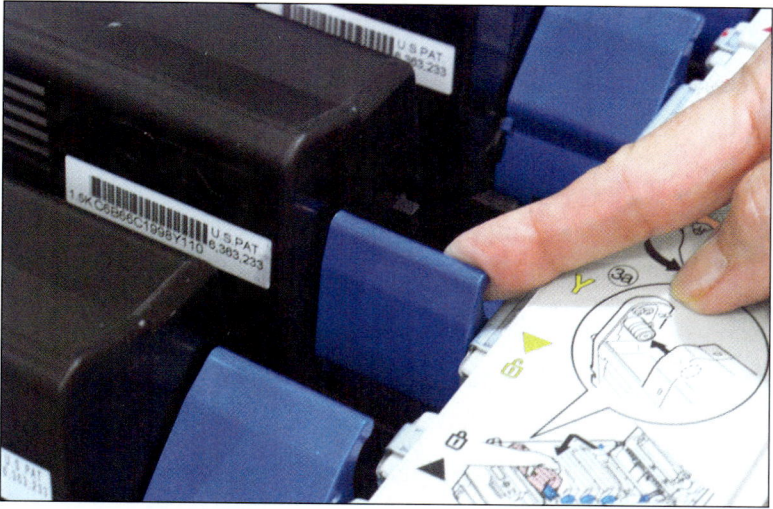

Figure 12-39 Push the blue lever forward to release the toner cartridge

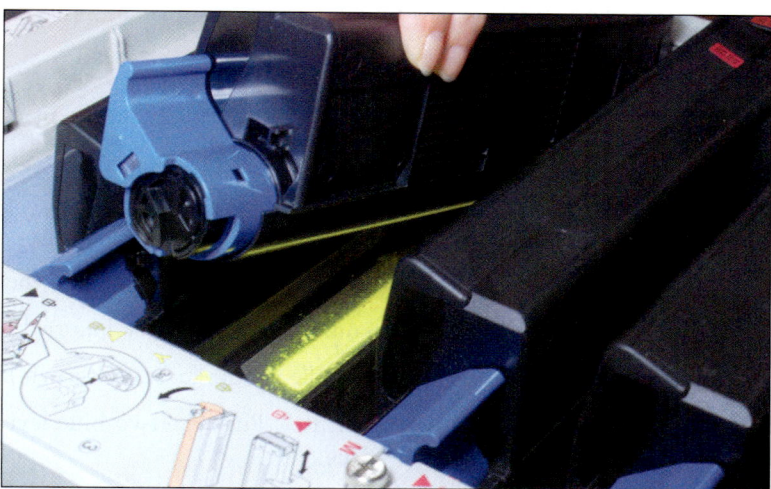

Figure 12-40 Remove the toner cartridge

The printer has four image drums, one for each color. The drums are expected to last for about 15,000 pages. When you purchase a new drum, the kit comes with a new color toner cartridge. Follow these steps to replace the cartridge and image drum. In these steps, we are using the yellow drum and cartridge:

1. Turn off and unplug the printer. Wait about 30 minutes after you have turned off the printer for it to cool down. Then open the printer cover. The toner cartridge is inserted into the image drum. Lift the drum together with the toner cartridge out of the printer (see Figure 12-41). Be sure to dispose of the drum and cartridge according to local regulations.

2. Unpack the new image drum. Peel the tape off the drum and remove the plastic film around it. As you work, be careful to keep the drum upright so as not to spill the toner. Because the drum is sensitive to light, don't allow the drum to be exposed to bright light or direct sunlight. Don't expose it to normal room lighting for longer than five minutes.

Figure 12-41 Remove the image drum and toner cartridge as one unit

3. Place the drum in the printer. Install the new toner cartridge in the printer. Close the printer cover.

The fuser should last for about 45,000 pages. To replace the fuser, follow these steps:

1. Turn off and unplug the printer. Allow the printer to cool and open the cover.
2. Pull the two blue fuser levers forward to unlock the fuser (see Figure 12-42).
3. Lift the fuser out of the printer using the handle on the fuser, as shown in Figure 12-43.
4. Unpack the new fuser and place it in the printer. Push the two blue levers toward the back of the printer to lock the fuser in place.

Figure 12-42 Pull the two fuser levers forward to release the fuser

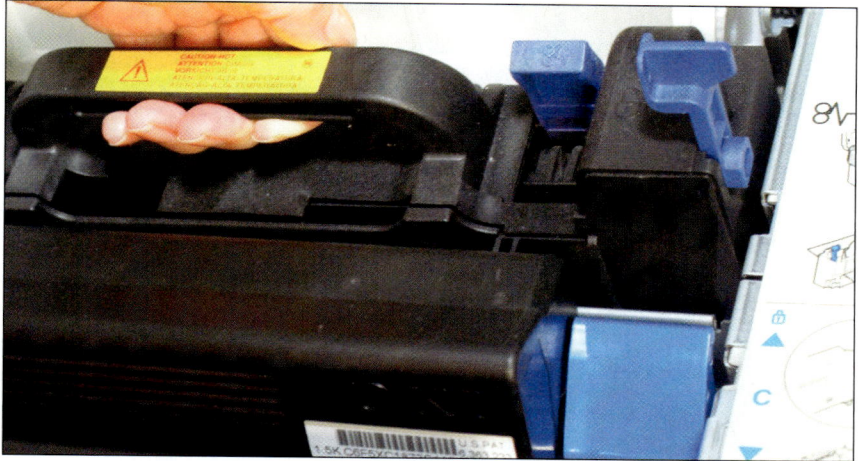

Figure 12-43 Remove the fuser

Whenever you service the inside of this printer, as a last step always carefully clean the LED erase lamps on the inside of the top cover (see Figure 12-44). The printer maintenance kits you've just learned to use all include a wipe to clean these strips.

Figure 12-44 Clean the LED strips on the inside top cover

UPGRADE THE PRINTER MEMORY OR HARD DRIVE

Some printers have internal hard drives to hold print jobs and fonts, and printers might also give you the option to install additional memory in the printer. Extra memory can speed up memory performance, reduce print errors, and prevent Out of Memory errors. Check the user guide to determine how much memory the printer can support and what kind of memory to buy or what kind of internal hard drive the printer might support.

As you work with printer hardware, be sure you turn off the printer and disconnect it from the power source. Also, use an antistatic ground bracelet to protect memory modules from static electricity. Most likely, you will use a screwdriver to remove a cover plate on the printer to expose a cavity where memory or a drive can be installed. To access memory on one printer, you remove thumbscrews on the back of the printer and then pull out the formatter board shown in Figure 12-45. Memory modules are installed on this board (see Figure 12-46). You can also install a hard drive in one of the two empty bays on the board. The hard drive comes embedded on a proprietary board that fits in the bay.

Figure 12-45 Remove the formatter board from the printer

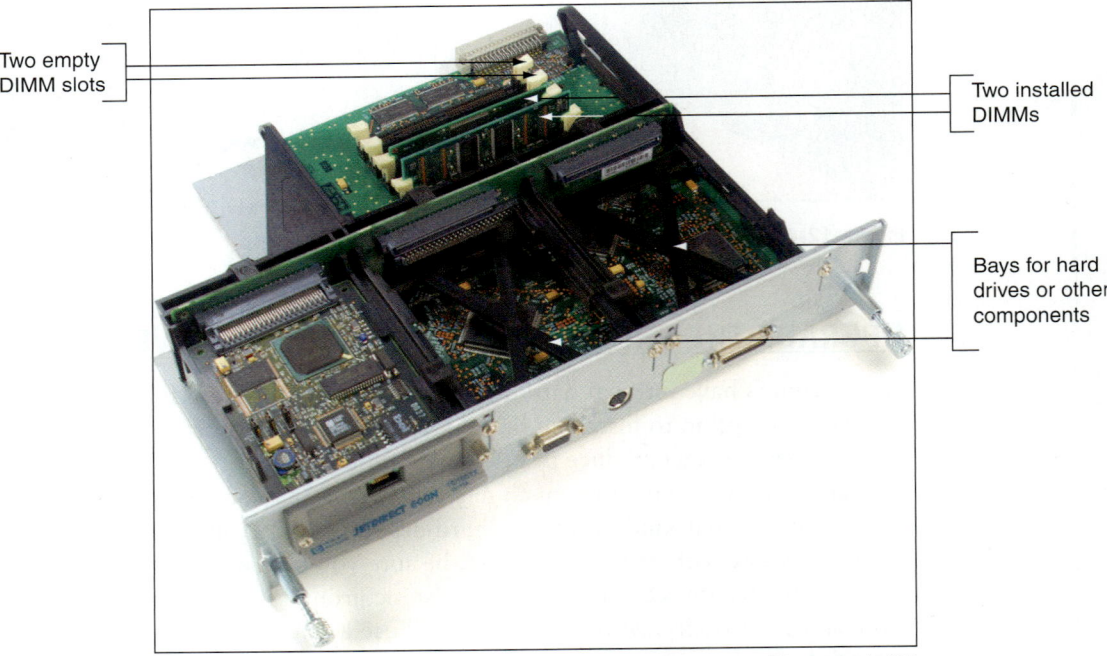

Figure 12-46 Memory is installed on the formatter board

After this equipment is installed, you must enable and configure it using the printer Properties window. For example, for the HP 8100 printer, use the Device Settings tab of the printer Properties box (see Figure 12-47). You can then set the hard drive as Installed or change the amount of Printer Memory that is installed. Some printers also give you the option to set the size of the hard drive.

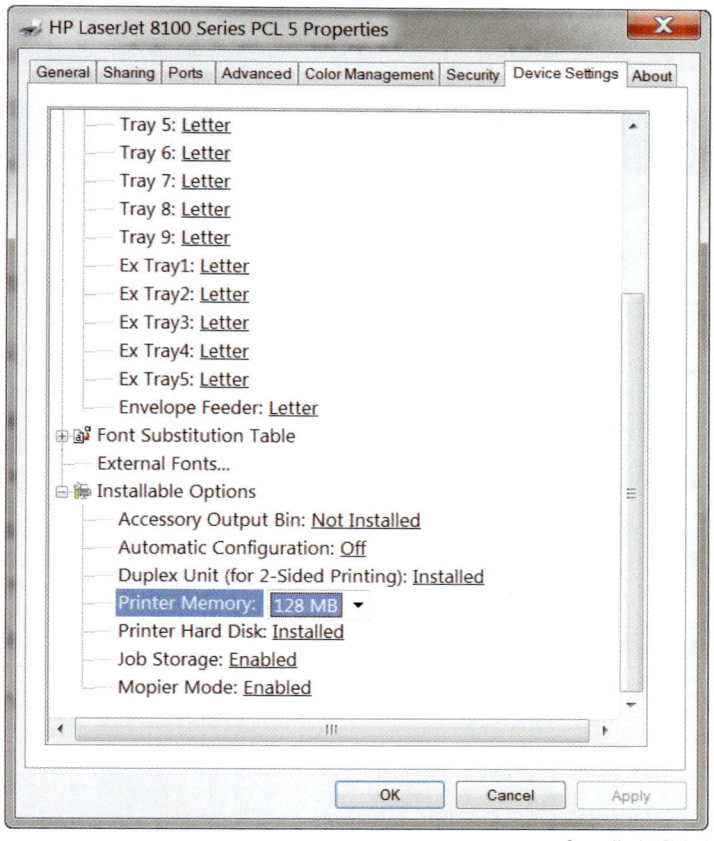

Source: Hewlett-Packard

Figure 12-47 Configure the printer for newly installed hardware

PRINT SERVERS AND THE PRINT MANAGEMENT TOOL

A **print server** is hardware or software that manages the print jobs sent to one or more printers on a network. The server receives print jobs from computers on the network and sends these jobs to the appropriate printer. A print server can be: (1) A dedicated hardware device, (2) software, such as Print Queue Manager by AMT Software, which is installed on a computer on the network, or (3) programs embedded in firmware on a printer, such as HP JetDirect, which is used by many HP printers.

Let's take a look at printer firmware used as a print server and at Print Management, a Windows 7 utility that you can use to manage printers on a network.

EMBEDDED FIRMWARE PRINT SERVER

Most high-quality printers offer a utility embedded in the firmware that you can use to manage print jobs, view the status of the printer, see a job history, and check counters, such as the number of pages printed. These utilities are accessed through a browser. For one Canon printer, when you enter the IP address of the printer in a browser window and log on to the firmware utility, the window in Figure 12-48 appears.

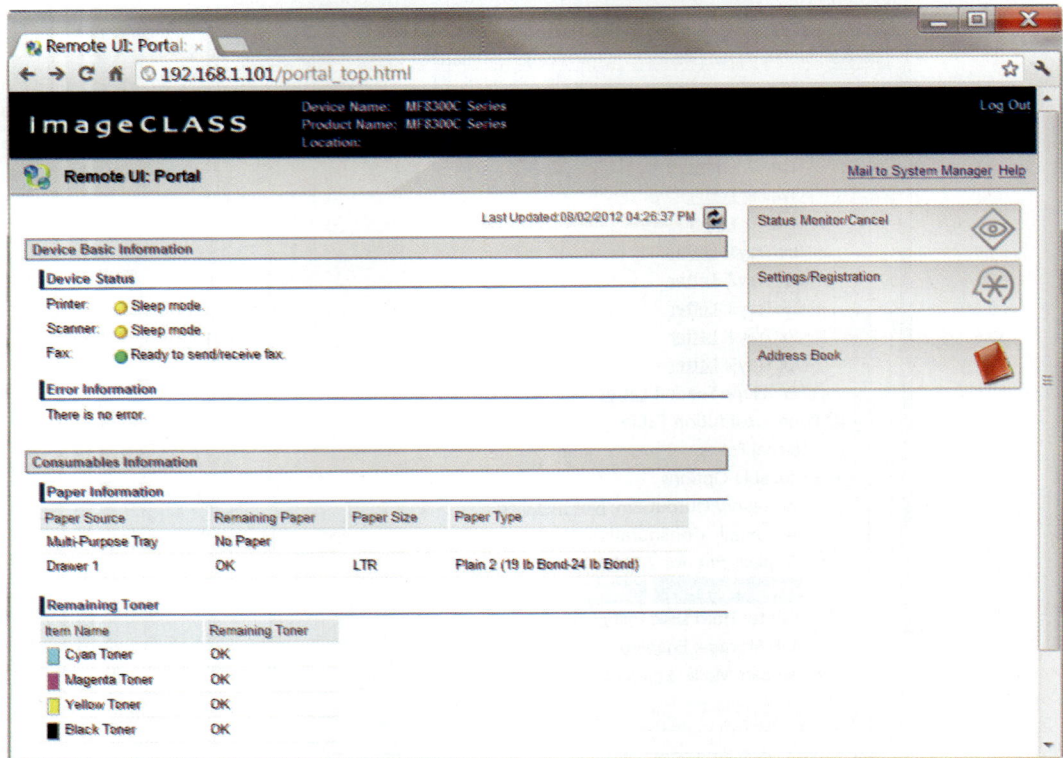

Source: Canon

Figure 12-48 Use the printer's web-based utility to view the printer status and manage print jobs

More advanced print server firmware programs allow you more control over how the printer is used. Using the print server, you can manage print protocols, start or stop jobs in the print queue, reorder jobs in the queue, cancel specific jobs coming from a particular computer on the network, and set up your email address so the printer alerts you by email when it has a problem.

WINDOWS PRINT MANAGEMENT

Windows 7/Vista professional and business editions offer the **Print Management** utility in the Administrative Tools group of Control Panel. (Home editions don't provide the Print Management tool.) You can use it to monitor and manage printer queues for all printers on the network. In Print Management, each computer on the network that shares a printer is considered a print server.

Printer Maintenance and Upgrades | 621

A+ 220-801 4.2

A+ 220-802 1.4

APPLYING | CONCEPTS LEARN TO USE PRINT MANAGEMENT

Follow these steps to learn to use Print Management:

1. In Control Panel, click **Administrative Tools** in the System and Security group. In the list of administrative tools, double-click **Print Management**. The Print Management window appears.

2. In the Print Servers group, drill down to your local computer and click **Printers**. The list of printers installed on your computer appears, as shown in Figure 12-49.

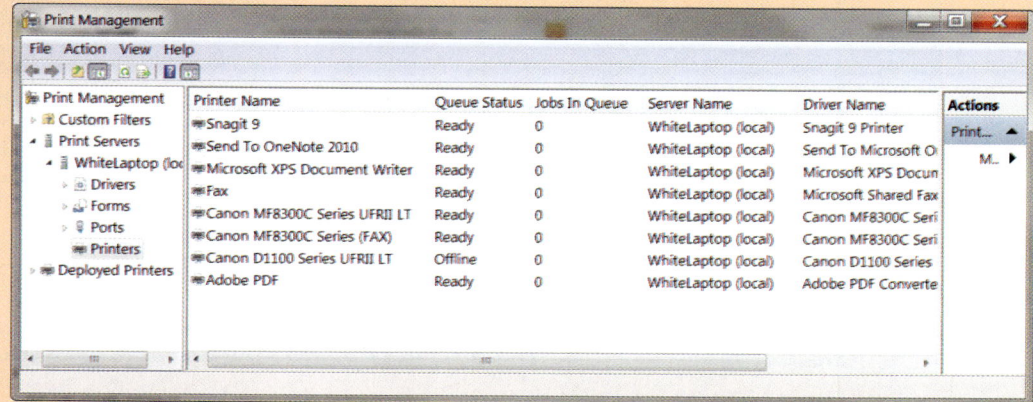

Source: Microsoft Windows 7

Figure 12-49 Use Print Management to monitor and manage printers on the network

3. To add other print servers to the list, right-click **Print Servers** in the left pane and click **Add/Remove Servers**. In the Add/Remove Servers box (see the left side of Figure 12-50), click **Browse**. Locate the computer (see the right side of Figure 12-50) and click **Select Server**. The computer is now listed under Add servers in the Add/Remove Servers box. Click **Add to List**. The computer is listed in the Print servers area. Click **OK** to close the Add/Remove Servers box.

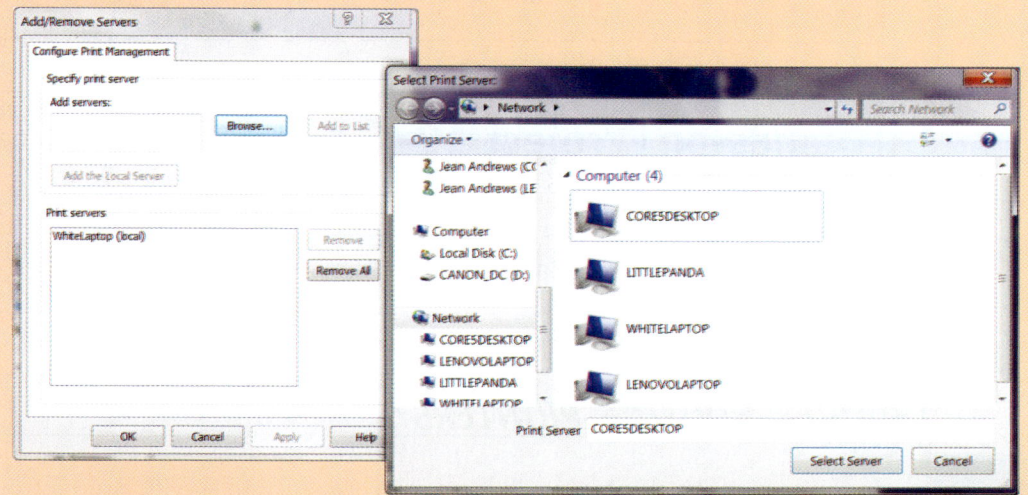

Source: Microsoft Windows 7

Figure 12-50 Select a print server to monitor and manage

A+ 220-801 4.2

A+ 220-802 1.4

4. The computer is now listed as a print server in the left pane of the Print Management window. Notice in Figure 12-51, you can view a computer on the network that has its printer offline and one job in the queue. Right-click this printer to see a menu with options shown in the figure that you can use to manage the printer and its printer queue.

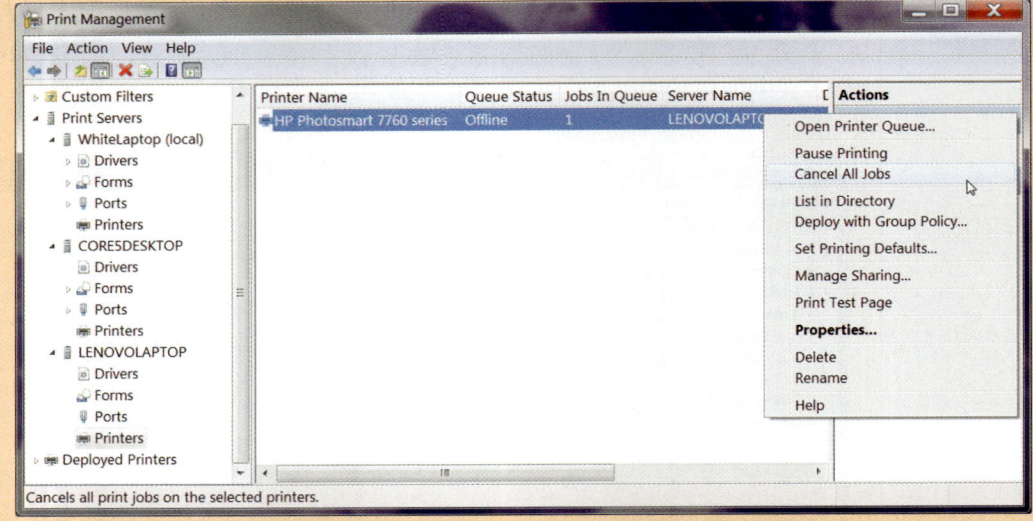

Source: Microsoft Windows 7

Figure 12-51 Manage print servers, printers, and printer queues on the network

Hands-on | Project 12-3 Research a Printer Maintenance Plan

You have been asked to recommend a maintenance plan for a laser printer. Search the manufacturer's web site for information, and then write a maintenance plan. Include in the plan the tasks that need to be done, how often they need doing, and what tools and components are needed to perform the tasks. Use the Hewlett-Packard LaserJet CP2025dn printer unless your instructor tells you to use a different printer, perhaps one that is available in your lab.

Hands-on | Project 12-4 Practice Printer Maintenance

For an inkjet printer, follow the procedures in the printer's user guide to clean the printer nozzles and ink cartridges. For a laser printer, follow the procedures in its user guide to clean the inside of the printer where the toner cartridge is installed.

TROUBLESHOOTING PRINTERS

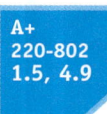

In this part of the chapter, you'll learn some general and specific printer troubleshooting tips. If you need more help with a printer problem, turn to the manufacturer's web site for additional information and support.

**A+
220-802
1.5, 4.9**

APPLYING | CONCEPTS Jill is the computer support technician responsible for supporting 10 users, their peer-to-peer network, printers, and computers. Everything was working fine when Jill left work one evening, but the next morning three users meet her at the door, complaining that they cannot print to the network printer and that important work must be printed by noon. What do you think are the first three things Jill should check?

As with all computer problems, begin troubleshooting by interviewing the user, finding out what works and doesn't work, and making an initial determination of the problem. When you think the problem is solved, ask the user to check things out to make sure he is satisfied with your work. And, after the problem is solved, be sure to document the symptoms of the problem and what you did to solve it.

PRINTER DOES NOT PRINT

When a printer does not print, the problem can be caused by the printer, the computer hardware or Windows, the application using the printer, the printer cable, or the network. Follow the steps in Figure 12-52 to isolate the problem.

As you can see in the figure, the problem can be isolated to one of the following areas:

- The printer itself
- Connectivity between the computer and its local printer
- Connectivity between the computer and a network printer
- The OS and printer drivers
- The application attempting to use the printer

In addition, if this is the first time you have tried to print after installing the printer, the printer drivers or the printer installation might be the problem. The following sections address printer problems caused by all of these categories, starting with hardware.

PROBLEMS WITH THE PRINTER ITSELF

To eliminate the printer as the problem, first check that the printer is on, and then print a **printer self-test page** by using controls at the printer. For directions to print a self-test page, see the printer's user guide. For example, you might need to hold down a button or buttons on the printer's front panel. If this test page prints correctly, then the printer is working.

A printer self-test page generally prints some text, some graphics, and some information about the printer, such as the printer resolution and how much memory is installed. Verify that the information on the test page is correct. For example, if you know that the printer should have 2 MB of onboard printer memory, but the test only reports 1 MB, then there is a problem with memory. If the information reported is not correct and the printer allows you to upgrade firmware on the printer, try doing that next.

If the self-test page does not print or prints incorrectly (for example, it has missing dots or smudged streaks through the page), then troubleshoot the printer until it prints correctly. When the printer self-test page does not print, check the following:

- Does the printer have paper? Is the paper installed correctly? Are the printer cover and rear access doors properly closed and locked? Is there a paper jam?

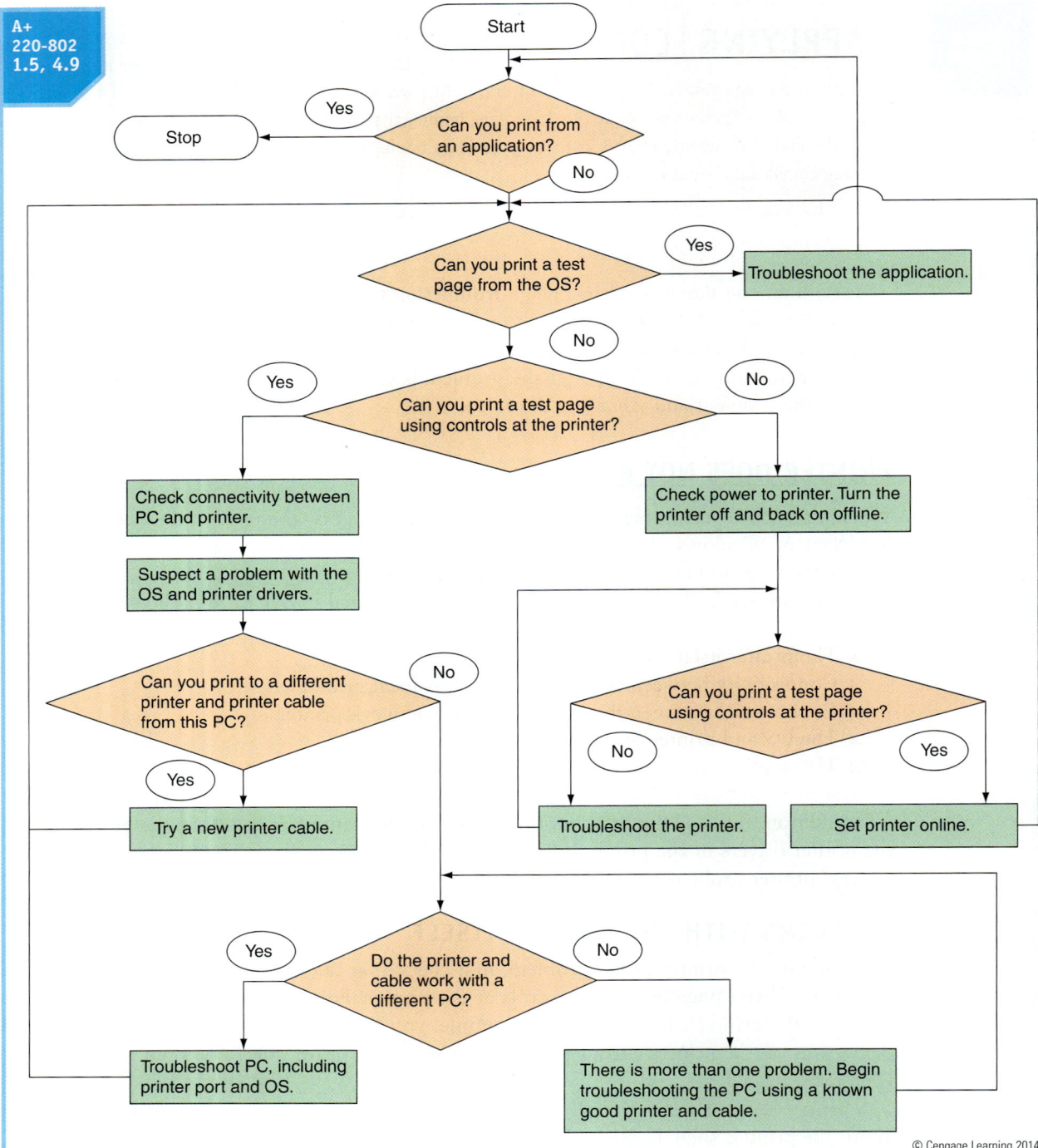

Figure 12-52 How to isolate a printer problem

Video: Clearing a Paper Jam

▲ If paper is jammed inside the printer, follow the directions in the printer documentation to remove the paper. Don't jerk the paper from the printer mechanism, but pull evenly on the paper, with care. You don't want to leave pieces of paper behind. Check for jammed paper from both the input tray and the output bin. Check both sides. An inkjet printer is likely to have a door in the back that you can open to gently remove the jammed paper, as shown in Figure 12-53.

Figure 12-53 Open the door on the back of an inkjet printer to remove jammed paper

▲ Is the paper not feeding? Remove the paper tray and check the metal plate at the bottom of the tray. Can it move up and down freely? If not, replace the tray. When you insert the tray in the printer, does the printer lift the plate as the tray is inserted? If not, the lift mechanism might need repair.

▲ Damp paper can cause paper jams or the printer to refuse to feed the paper or to wrinkle or crease the paper. Be sure to only use dry paper in a printer. Paper that is too thin can also crease or wrinkle in the printer.

▲ Look for an error message or error code in the control panel on the front of the printer. You might need to search the printer documentation or web site to find out the meaning of a code. For example, error codes in the 79.xx range for HP printers can indicate a variety of problems from a print job with characters it does not understand to a failed memory module in the printer.

▲ For some error codes, the problem might be with a print job the printer cannot process. Cancel all print jobs and disconnect the printer from the network. If the control panel reports "Ready," then you can assume the problem is with the network, computers, or print jobs, and not with the printer. If the error code is still displayed, the problem is with the printer. Follow the directions on the printer manufacturer's web site to address the error code.

▲ Try resetting the printer (for some printers, press the Reset button on the printer). Try powering down or unplugging the printer and starting it again. Check that power is getting to the printer. Try another power source.

▲ For an inkjet printer, check if nozzles are clogged. Sometimes, leaving the printer on for a while will heat up the ink nozzles and unclog them.

▲ For an impact printer, if the print head moves back and forth but nothing prints, check the ribbon. Is it installed correctly between the plate and print head? Is it jammed? If the ribbon is dried out, it needs to be replaced.

▲ Check the service documentation and printer page count to find out if routine maintenance is due or if the printer has a history of similar problems. Check the user guide for the printer and the printer manufacturer's web site for other troubleshooting suggestions.

A+ 220-802 1.5, 4.9

If you still cannot get a printer to work, you might need to take the printer to a certified repair shop. Before you do, though, try contacting the manufacturer. You might also be able to open a chat session on the printer manufacturer's web site.

> **APPLYING CONCEPTS** Now back to Jill and her company's network printer problem. Generally, Jill should focus on finding out what works and what doesn't work, always remembering to check the simple things first. Jill should first go to the printer and check that the printer is online and has no error messages, such as a Paper Out message. Then, Jill should ask, "Can anyone print to this printer?" To find out, she should go to the closest computer and try to print a Windows test page. If the test page prints, she should next go to one of the three computers that do not print and begin troubleshooting that computer's connection to the network. If the test page did not print at the closest computer, the problem is still not necessarily the printer. To eliminate the printer as the problem, the next step is to print a self-test page at the printer. If that self-test page prints, then Jill should check other computers on the network. Is the entire network down? Can one computer see another computer on the network? Perhaps part of the network is down (maybe because of a switch serving one part of the network).

PROBLEMS WITH A LOCAL PRINTER CABLE OR PORT

If the printer self-test did work, but the Windows printer test did not work, check for connectivity problems between the printer and the computer. For a local printer connected directly to a computer, the problem might be with the printer cable or the port the printer is using. Do the following:

- Check that the cable is firmly connected at both ends. For a USB port, try a different port. For some parallel ports, you can use a screwdriver to securely anchor the cable to the parallel port with two screws on each side of the port. If you suspect the cable is bad, you can use a multimeter to check the cable.
- Try a different cable. For older parallel cables, make sure the cable is no longer than 10 feet and verify that the cable is IEEE 1284-compliant.
- Try printing using the same printer and printer cable but a different computer.
- Use Device Manager to verify the port the printer is using is enabled and working properly. Try another device on the same port to verify the problem is not with the port.
- Use BIOS setup to check how the port is configured. Is it enabled? For a parallel port, is the port set to ECP or bidirectional?
- If you have access to a port tester device, test the port.

PROBLEMS WITH CONNECTIVITY FOR A NETWORK PRINTER OR SHARED PRINTER

If the self-test page prints but the Windows test page does not print and the printer is a network printer or shared printer, the problem might be with connectivity between the computer and the network printer or with the host computer that is sharing the printer.

> **A+ Exam Tip** The A+ 220-802 exam expects you to know how to determine if connectivity between the printer and the computer is the problem when troubleshooting printer issues.

Troubleshooting Printers | 627

A+ 220-802 1.5, 4.9

Follow these steps to solve problems with network printers:

- Is the printer online?
- Turn the printer off and back on. Try rebooting the computer.
- Verify that the correct default printer is selected.
- Consider the IP address of the printer might have changed, which can happen if the printer is receiving a dynamic IP address. Using Windows, delete the printer, and then install the printer again. If this solves the problem, assign a static IP address to the printer to keep the problem from reoccurring.
- Can you print to another network printer? If so, there might be a problem with the printer. Look at the printer's configuration.
- Try pinging the printer. To do that, open a command prompt window and enter **ping 192.168.1.100** (substitute the IP address of your printer). If the printer replies (see Figure 12-54), the problem is not network connectivity.

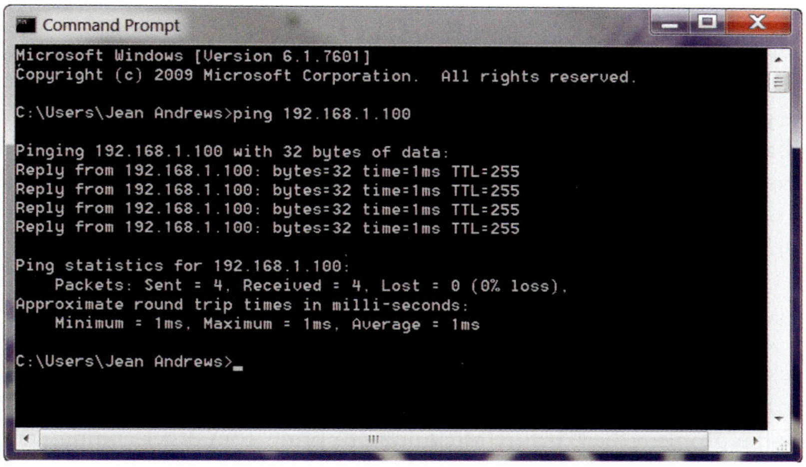

Source: Microsoft Windows 7

Figure 12-54 Use the ping command to determine if you have network connectivity with the printer

- If pinging doesn't work, try using another network cable for the printer. Check status indicator lights on the printer network port and on the switch or router to which the printer connects.
- Use the printer's browser-based utility and check for status reports and error messages. Run diagnostic software that might be available on the utility menu.
- Try flashing the network printer's firmware.

Even though you are using a network printer, the printer might have been installed as a shared printer. Let's look at an example of this situation. Figure 12-55 shows a Devices and Printers window with several installed printers. Notice the two installations of the HP LaserJet 8100 printer. The first installation was done installing the LaserJet 8100 as a network printer addressed by its IP address. The second installation was done by using a shared printer that was shared by another computer on the network named DELL-LAPTOP. When you print using the first installation of the LaserJet 8100, you print directly over the network to the printer. But when you print to the second installation of the LaserJet 8100, you print by way of the DELL-LAPTOP computer. If this computer is offline, the print jobs back up in the print queue until the computer is available.

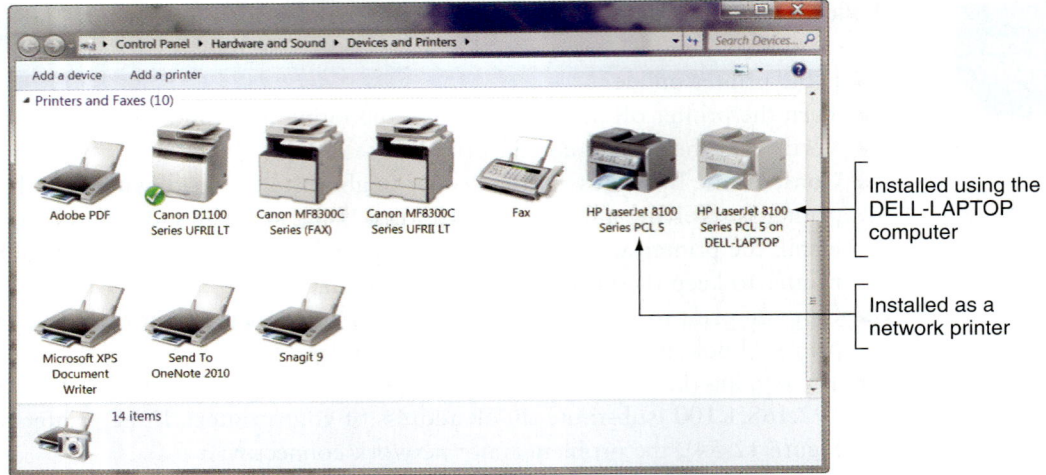

Figure 12-55 A network printer installed using two methods

Source: Microsoft Windows 7

When all users on a network are responsible for managing their own network resources, you should not install a network printer by using another computer on the network that has shared the printer. However, to get centralized control of a printer and its print queue, you can install a network printer on one computer, share it, and then install this shared printer on other computers on the network. Using this scenario, all print jobs must go through this one host computer, which becomes the print server for this printer. In this scenario, you can manage all print jobs to the printer from this one computer.

When a computer has shared a local or network printer with others on the network, follow these steps to solve problems with these shared printers:

▲ Check that you can print a test page from the computer that has the printer attached to it locally or is sharing a network printer. If you cannot print from the host computer, solve the problem there before attempting to print from other computers on the network.
▲ Is enough hard drive space available on the client or host computer?
▲ Did you get an "Access denied" message when you tried to print from the remote computer? If so, you might not have access to the host computer. On the remote computer, go to Windows Explorer or the Network window and attempt to open shared folders on the printer's computer. Perhaps you have not entered a correct user account and password to access this computer; if so, you will be unable to use the computer's resources. Make sure you have a matching Windows user account and password on each computer.
▲ On the host computer, open the printer's Properties box and click the **Security** tab. Select **Everyone** and make sure Permissions for Everyone includes permission to print, as shown in Figure 12-56. Notice you can use this Security tab to control other things a user can do with the shared printer.
▲ Using Windows on the remote computer, delete the printer, and then install the printer again. Watch for and address any error messages that might appear.

PROBLEMS PRINTING FROM WINDOWS

If a self-test page works and you have already stepped through checking the printer connectivity, but you still cannot print a test page from Windows, try the following:

▲ The print spool might be stalled. Try deleting all print jobs in the printer's queue. Recall you can do that using the Windows 7 Devices and Printers window, the Vista Printers window, or the XP Printers and Faxes window. If the printer is still hung, try using buttons on the front of the printer to cancel print jobs. You can also power cycle the printer (turn it off and back on). Some printers have a Reset button for this purpose.

A+
220-802
1.5, 4.9

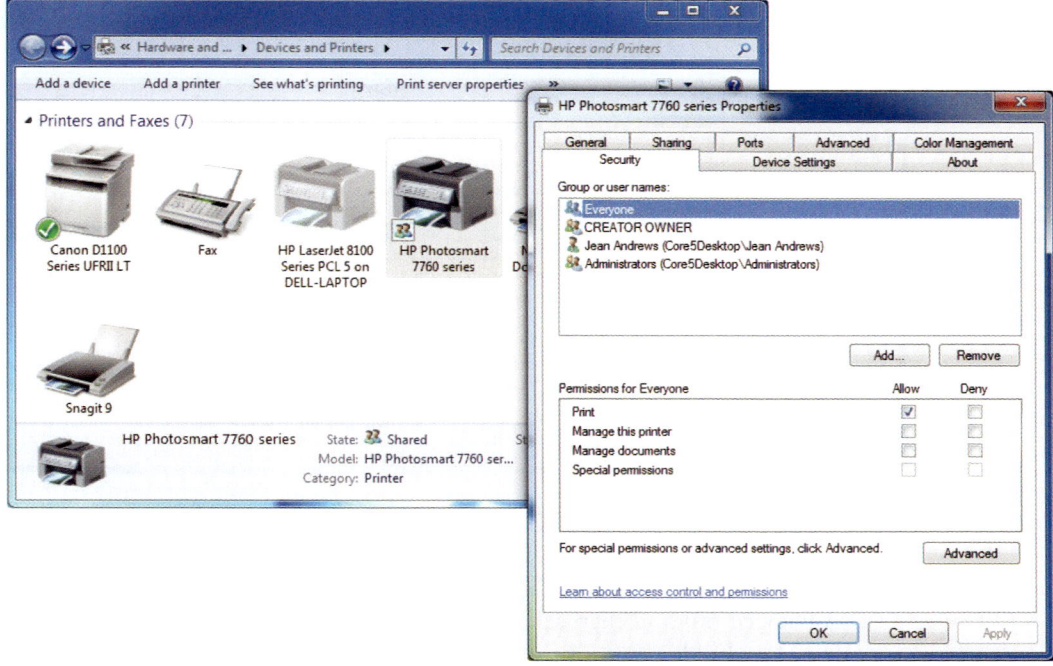

Figure 12-56 Give permission to everyone to print using this shared printer

Source: Microsoft Windows 7

> **A+ Exam Tip** The A+ 220-802 exam expects you to know how to solve problems with the print spool.

- Verify that the correct printer is used.
- Verify that the printer is online. See the printer documentation for information on how to determine the status from the control panel of the printer. For many printers, "Ready" appears in this control panel.
- Verify that the printer cable or cable connections are solid.
- Stop and restart the Windows Print Spooler service. Windows uses the **Services console** to stop, start, and manage background services used by Windows and applications. Do the following:

  1. To stop the service, click **Start**, type **Services** in the search box, and press **Enter**. The Services console opens. Scroll down to and select **Print Spooler** (see Figure 12-57). Click **Stop** to stop the service.

  2. To delete any print jobs left in the queue, open Windows Explorer and delete all files in the C:\Windows\System32\spool\PRINTERS folder.

  3. Start the print spooler back up. To start up the print spooler, return to the Services console. With Print Spooler selected, click **Restart**. Close the Services console window.

- If you still cannot print, reboot the computer. Try deleting the printer and then reinstalling it.
- Check the printer manufacturer's web site for an updated printer driver. Download and install the correct driver.

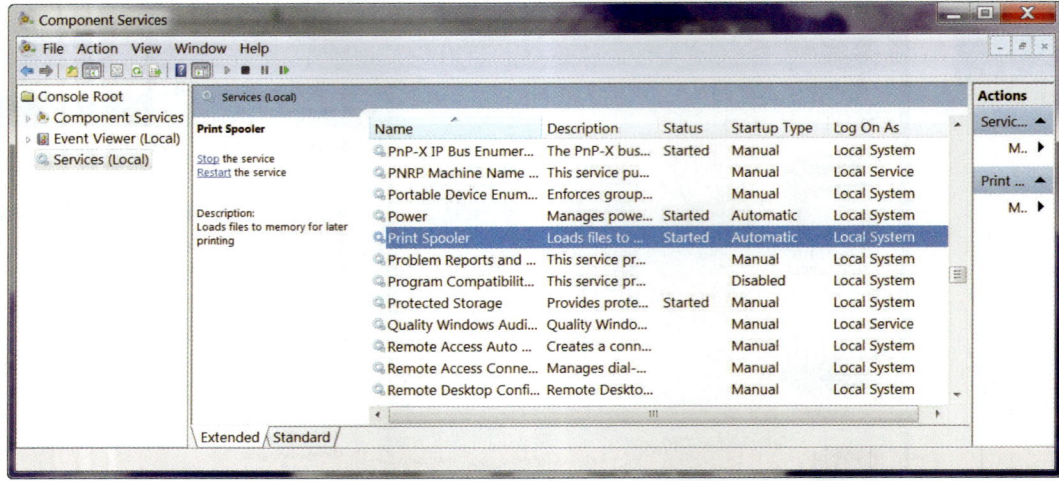

Figure 12-57 Use the Services console to stop and start the print spooler

Source: Microsoft Windows 7

▲ Try disabling printer spooling. On the printer's Properties dialog box, select the **Advanced** tab and then select **Print directly to the printer** (see Figure 12-58). Click **OK**. Spooling holds print jobs in a queue for printing, so if spooling is disabled, printing from an application can be slower.

▲ If you have trouble printing from an application, try to print to a file. For example, you can print to an XPS document by selecting **Microsoft XPS Document Writer** in the list of installed printers. Then you can double-click the .xps file, which opens in the XPS Viewer window, and you can print from this window.

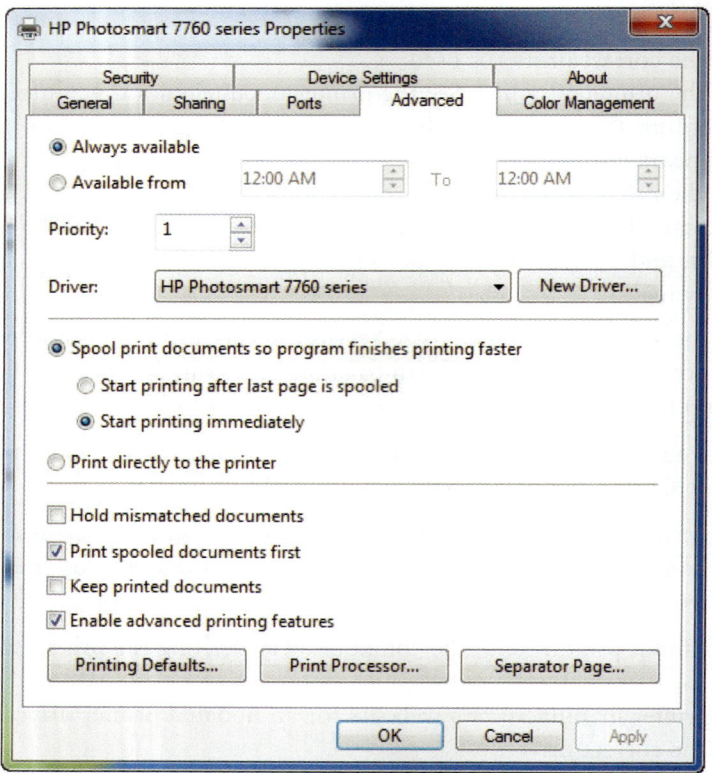

Figure 12-58 Disable printer spooling

Source: Hewlett-Packard

A+ 220-802 1.5, 4.9

- Verify that enough hard drive space is available for the OS to create temporary print files.
- Boot Windows into Safe Mode and attempt to print. If this step works, there might be a conflict between the printer driver and another driver or application.
- Run diagnostic software downloaded from the printer manufacturer's web site or diagnostic routines you can run from the printer's browser-based utility menu.

APPLYING CONCEPTS — **SOLVING PROBLEMS WITH PRINTER INSTALLATIONS**

Here are some steps you can take if the printer installation fails or installs with errors:

1. If you still have problems, consider that Windows might be using the wrong or corrupted printer drivers. Try removing the printer and then installing it again. To remove a printer, right-click the printer in the Devices and Printers window and click **Remove device** (refer to Figure 12-14). Try to install the printer again.

2. If the problem is still not solved, completely remove the printer drivers by using the printui command. The Printer User Interface command, **printui**, is used by administrators to manage printers and printer drivers on remote computers. You can also use it to delete drivers on the local computer. Follow these steps:

   a. If the printer is listed in the Devices and Printers window, remove it. (Sometimes Windows automatically puts a printer there when it finds printer drivers are installed.)

   b. Before you can delete printer drivers, you must stop the print spooler service. Open the Services console and use it to stop the Print Spooler (refer to Figure 12-57). To delete any print jobs left in the queue, open Windows Explorer and delete all files in the C:\Windows\System32\spool\PRINTERS folder.

   c. You can now start the print spooler back up. Because the printer is no longer listed in the Devices and Printers window, starting the spooler will not tie up these drivers.

> **Notes** If you ever have a problem clearing the printer queue, one thing you can do is stop and restart the print spooler.

   d. Open an **elevated command prompt window**, which is a window used to enter commands that have administrator privileges. To open the window, click **Start**, **All Programs**, **Accessories**. Right-click **Command prompt** and click **Run as administrator**. Respond to the User Account Control box. To get past the UAC security box, you must be logged on as an administrator or enter an administrator password. The Administrator: Command Prompt window then opens, as shown on the left side of Figure 12-59.

   e. At the command prompt, enter the command:

   ```
   printui /s /t2
   ```

   (In the command line, the /s causes the Print Server Properties box to open and the /t2 causes the Drivers tab to be the selected tab.)

   f. The Print Server Properties box opens, as shown in the middle of Figure 12-59. Select the printer and click **Remove**. In the Remove Driver And Package box, select **Remove driver only** and click **OK**. It is not necessary to remove the driver package. (This driver package, also called the driver store, can be installed on this computer or a remote computer and holds a backup of the printer drivers.)

   g. When a warning box appears, click **Yes**. Close all windows.

A+
220-802
1.5, 4.9

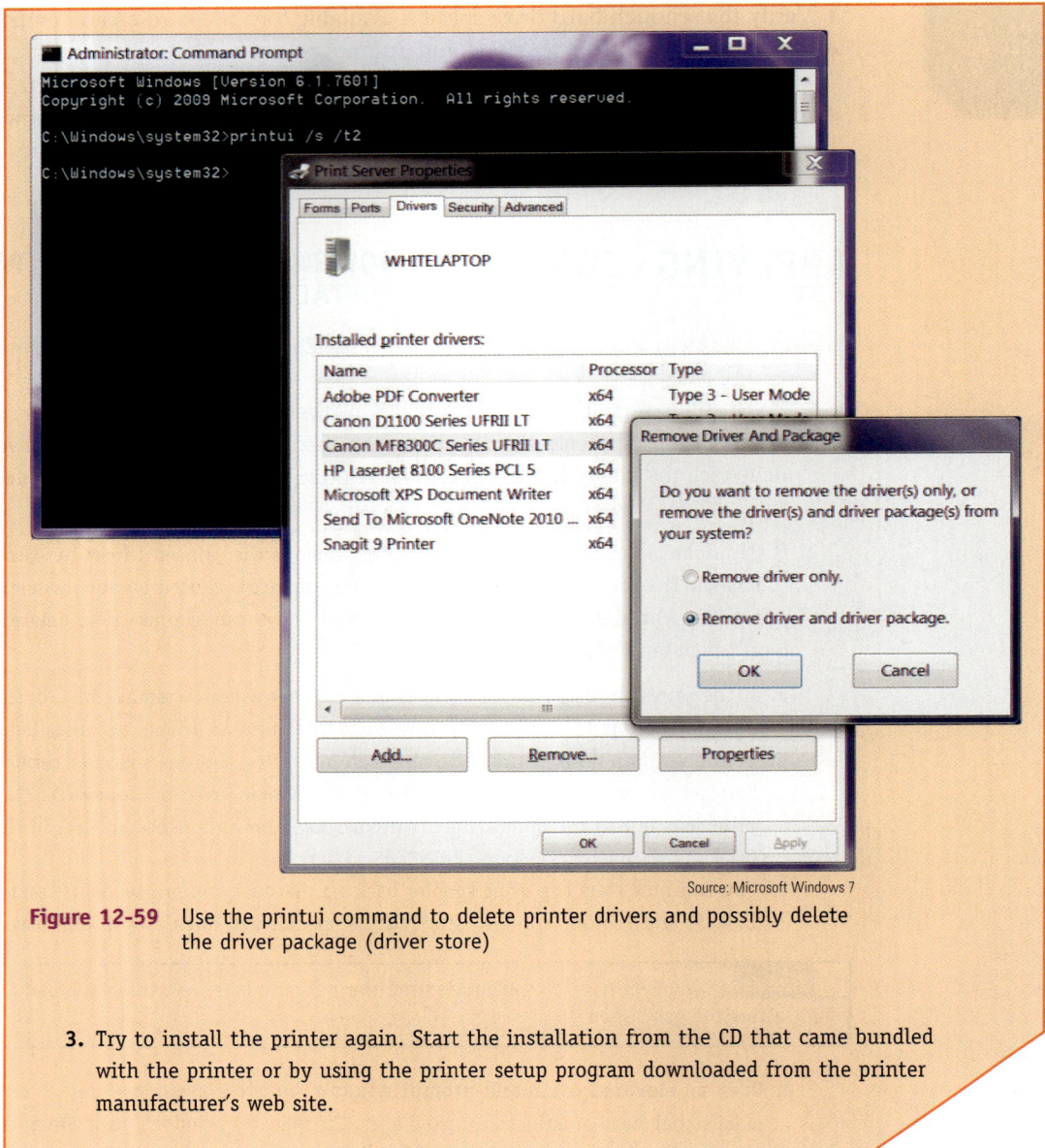

Source: Microsoft Windows 7

Figure 12-59 Use the printui command to delete printer drivers and possibly delete the driver package (driver store)

3. Try to install the printer again. Start the installation from the CD that came bundled with the printer or by using the printer setup program downloaded from the printer manufacturer's web site.

PROBLEMS PRINTING FROM APPLICATIONS

If you can print a Windows test page, but you cannot print from an application, try the following:

- Verify that the correct printer is selected in the application.
- Try printing a different file within the same application.
- Cancel all print jobs in the print queue and then reboot the computer. Reopen the application giving the print error and attempt to print again.
- Try creating data in a new file and printing it. Keep the data simple.
- Try printing from another application.
- If you can print from other applications, consider reinstalling the problem application.
- Close any applications that are not being used.
- Add more memory to the printer.

Hands-on Project 12-5: Configure a Static IP Address for a Printer

A+ 220-802 1.5, 4.9

A network printer needs a static IP address so that computers can always find the printer each time it restarts. Some printers can be assigned a static IP address using firmware on the printer; other printers receive their IP address from the DHCP server on the network each time the printer is started. If the printer receives an IP address from a DHCP server, the server needs to be configured to serve up a static IP address to the printer. Answer the following questions:

1. Investigate the situation in your school lab or home network. What is the brand and model of the network printer you are using?

2. Go online and locate the user manual for this printer. Can the printer be configured to use a static IP address or does it use an IP address received from a DHCP server? Figure 12-60 shows a browser-based utility for one printer where you can set a static IP address for this printer.

3. Research the router or other DHCP server you are using. Can you configure this device to serve up a static IP address to the printer?

4. A DHCP server uses a MAC address to identify a device that requires a static IP address. What is the MAC address of your printer?

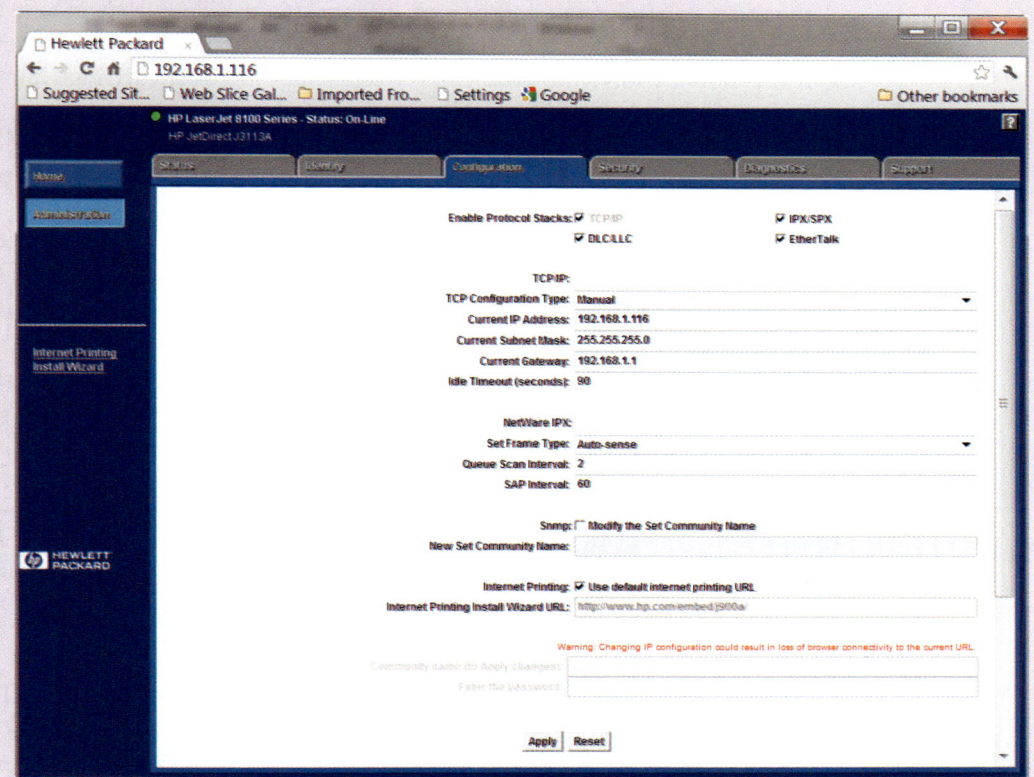

Figure 12-60 Configure a network printer for static IP addressing

Source: Hewlett-Packard

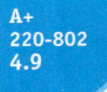
A+
220-802
4.9

POOR PRINT QUALITY

Poor print quality can be caused by the printer drivers, the application, Windows, or the printer. Let's start by looking at what can cause poor print quality with laser printers and then move on to other problems that affect printouts.

> **A+ Exam Tip** The A+ 220-802 exam expects you to know how to resolve problems with streaks, faded prints, ghost images, garbled characters on a page, vertical lines, low memory errors, and wrong print colors. All these problems are covered in this part of the chapter.

POOR PRINT QUALITY FOR LASER PRINTERS

For laser printers, poor print quality, including faded, smeared, wavy, speckled, or streaked printouts, often indicates that the toner is low. All major mechanical printer components that normally create problems are conveniently contained within the replaceable toner cartridge. In most cases, the solution to poor-quality printing is to replace this cartridge.

Follow these general guidelines to fix poor print quality with laser printers:

- If you suspect the printer is overheated, unplug it and allow it to cool for 30 minutes.
- The toner cartridge might be low on toner or might not be installed correctly. Remove the toner cartridge and gently rock it from side to side to redistribute the toner. Replace the cartridge. To avoid flying toner, don't shake the cartridge too hard.
- If this doesn't solve the problem, try replacing the toner cartridge immediately.
- EconoMode (a mode that uses less toner) might be on; turn it off.
- The paper quality might not be high enough. Try a different brand of paper. Only use paper recommended for use with a laser printer. Also, some types of paper can receive print only on one side.
- The printer might need cleaning. Clean the inside of the printer with a dry, lint-free cloth. Don't touch the transfer roller, which is the soft, spongy black roller.
- If the transfer roller is dirty, the problem will probably correct itself after several sheets print. If not, take the printer to an authorized service center.
- Does the printer require routine maintenance? Check the web site of the printer's manufacturer for how often to perform the maintenance and to purchase the required printer maintenance kit.

> **Notes** Extreme humidity can cause the toner to clump in the cartridge and give a Toner Low message. If this is a consistent problem in your location, you might want to invest in a dehumidifier for the room where your printer is located.

- Streaking is usually caused by a dirty developer unit or corona wire. The developer unit is contained in the toner cartridge. Replace the cartridge or check the printer documentation for directions on how to remove and clean the developer unit. Allow the corona wire to cool and clean it with a lint-free swab.
- Speckled printouts can be caused by the laser drum. If cleaning the printer and replacing the toner cartridge don't solve the problem, replace the laser drum.

> **Notes** If loose toner comes out with your printout, the fuser is not reaching the proper temperature. Professional service is required.

▲ Distorted images can be caused by foreign material inside the printer that might be interfering with the mechanical components. Check for debris that might be interfering with the printer operation.

▲ If the page has a gray background or gray print, the image drum is worn out and needs to be replaced.

▲ A ghosted image appears a few inches below the actual darker image on the page. Ghosted images are usually caused by a problem with the image drum or toner cartridge. The drum is not fully cleaned in the cleaning stage, and toner left on it causes the ghost image. If the printer utility installed with the printer offers the option to clean the drum, try that first. The next solution is to replace the less expensive toner cartridge. If the problem is still not solved, replace the image drum.

POOR PRINT QUALITY FOR INKJET PRINTERS

To troubleshoot poor print quality for an inkjet printer, check the following:

1. Is the correct paper for inkjet printers being used?
   The quality of paper determines the final print quality, especially with inkjet printers. In general, the better the quality of the paper used with an inkjet printer, the better the print quality. Don't use less than 20-pound paper in any type of printer, unless the printer documentation specifically says that a lower weight is satisfactory.

2. Is the ink supply low, or is there a partially clogged nozzle?

3. Remove and reinstall the cartridge.

4. Follow the printer's documentation to clean each nozzle. Is the print head too close to or too far from the paper?

5. There is a little sponge in some printers near the carriage rest that can become clogged with ink. It should be removed and cleaned.

6. If you are printing transparencies, try changing the fill pattern in your application.

7. Missing lines or dots on the printed page can be caused by the ink nozzles drying out, especially when the printer sits unused for a long time. Follow the directions given earlier in the chapter for cleaning inkjet nozzles.

8. Streaks or lines down the page can be caused by dust or dirt in the print head assemblage. Follow the manufacturer's directions to clean the inkjet nozzles.

POOR PRINT QUALITY FOR IMPACT PRINTERS

For an impact printer that is printing with poor print quality, do the following:

1. Begin with the ribbon. Does it advance normally while the carriage moves back and forth? If not, replace the ribbon. If the new ribbon still does not advance properly, check the printer's advance mechanism.

2. Adjust the print head spacing. Look for a lever adjustment you can use to change the distance between the print head and plate.

3. Check the print head for dirt. Make sure it's not hot before you touch it. If debris has built up, wipe each wire with a cotton swab dipped in alcohol or contact cleaner.

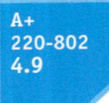

A+
220-802
4.9

GARBLED CHARACTERS ON PAPER

If scrambled or garbled characters print on all or part of a page, the problem can be caused by the document being printed, the application, connectivity between the computer and the printer, or the printer. Follow these steps to zero in on the problem:

1. First, cancel all print jobs in the print queue. Then try printing a different document from the same application. If the second document prints correctly, the problem is with the original document.

2. Try printing using a different application. If the problem is resolved, try repairing or reinstalling the application.

3. For a USB printer, the problem might be with a USB hub, port, or cable. Is the USB cable securely connected at both ends? If you are using a USB hub, remove the hub, connecting the printer directly to the computer. Try a different USB cable or USB port.

4. Recycle the printer by powering it down and back up or pressing a Reset button.

5. Update the printer drivers. To do that, go to the web site of the printer manufacturer to find the latest drivers and follow their directions to install the drivers.

6. If the problem is still not solved, the printer might need servicing. Does the printer need maintenance? Search the web site of the printer manufacturer for other solutions.

LOW MEMORY ERRORS

For some printers, an error occurs if the printer does not have enough memory to hold the entire page. For other printers, only a part of the page prints. Some might signal this problem by flashing a light or displaying an error message on their display panels, such as "20 Mem Overflow," "Out of memory," or "Low Memory." The solution is to install more memory or to print only simple pages with few graphics. Print a self-test page to verify how much memory is installed. Some printers give you the option to install a hard drive in the printer to give additional printer storage space.

WRONG PRINT COLORS

For a printer that is printing the wrong colors, do the following:

1. Some paper is designed to print on only one side. You might need to flip the paper in the printer.

2. Try adjusting the quality of print. How to do so varies by printer. For one color laser printer, open the **Printing Preferences** box and click the **Quality** tab (see the left side of Figure 12-61). You can try different selections on this box. To manually adjust the color, check **Manual Color Settings** and then click **Color Settings**. The box on the right side of Figure 12-61 appears.

3. For an inkjet printer, try cleaning the ink cartridges and calibrating the printer. One step in doing that prints a self-test page. If the self-test page shows missing or wrong colors, the problem is with the ink cartridges. Try cleaning the ink nozzles. If that doesn't work, replace the ink cartridges.

4. For a laser printer, try calibrating the printer.

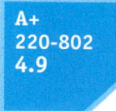
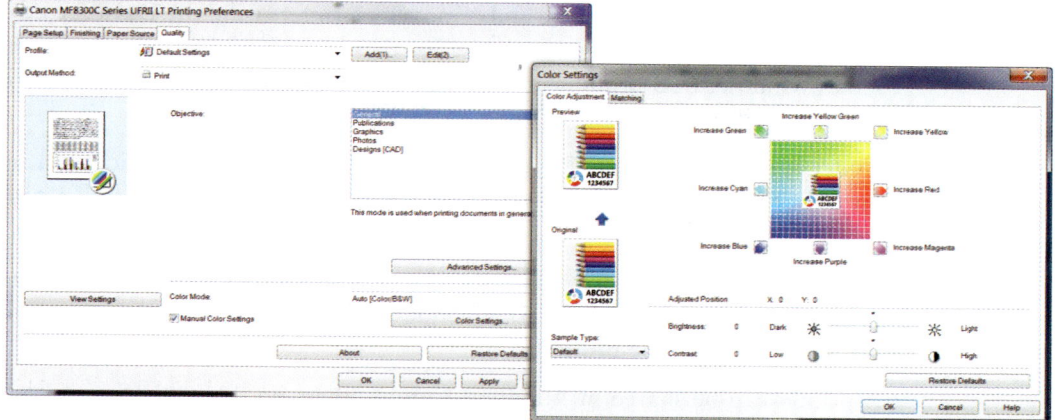

Figure 12-61 Adjust printing quality and color

Source: Canon

>> CHAPTER SUMMARY

Printer Types and Features

▲ The languages that Windows can use when it sends print jobs to a printer are PostScript, PCL, GDI, and XPS. In addition, Windows can send raw data to a printer. The printer converts the page into a bitmap, which it stores in the printer's memory before it prints.

▲ The two most popular types of printers are laser and inkjet. Other types of printers are thermal printers and impact printers (dot matrix). Laser printers produce the highest quality, followed by inkjet printers. Dot matrix printers have the advantage of being able to print multicopy documents.

▲ The seven steps that a laser printer performs to print are processing, charging, exposing, developing, transferring, fusing, and cleaning. The charging, exposing, developing, and cleaning steps take place inside removable cartridges, which makes the printer easier to maintain.

▲ Inkjet printers print by shooting ionized ink at a sheet of paper. The quality of the printout largely depends on the quality of paper used with the printer.

▲ Dot matrix printers are a type of impact printer. They print by projecting pins from the print head against an inked ribbon that deposits ink on the paper.

▲ Direct thermal printers use heat to burn dots into special paper, and thermal transfer printers melt the ribbon or foil during printing.

Using Windows to Install, Share, and Manage Printers

▲ A printer is installed as a local printer connected directly to a computer or a network printer that works as a device on the network. A computer can share a printer so that others can use it as a resource on the network.

- Windows 7 installs, manages, and removes a printer using the Devices and Printers windows; Vista uses the Printers window for these purposes, and XP uses the Printers and Faxes window. USB printers are installed automatically with Windows 7/Vista and by using the printer setup CD in XP.

- Under Windows 7/Vista/XP, you can also install a printer by launching a setup program on the CD that came bundled with the printer. The last step to install a printer is to print a printer test page.

- You can share an installed printer on the network so that other users can access the printer through the computer to which it connects. The host computer must be on and awake to serve up the printer.

- A printer can be shared in Windows so that others on the network can use it. To use a shared printer, the printer drivers must be installed on the remote computer.

- Network printers are usually identified on the network by their IP address.

- The Windows print queue is managed from the Windows 7 Devices and Printers window, the Vista Printers window, or the XP Printers and Faxes window.

Printer Maintenance and Upgrades

- An inkjet or laser printer can be calibrated to align the color on the page. The nozzles of an inkjet printer tend to clog or dry out, especially when the printer remains unused. The nozzles can be cleaned automatically by means of printer software or buttons on the front panel of the printer.

- Check the page count of the printer to know when service is due and you need to order the printer maintenance kit.

- Memory and a hard drive can be added to a printer to improve performance and prevent errors.

- Use a print server to manage printers on a network. Three types of print servers are a dedicated hardware device, software installed on a computer on the network, or programs embedded in firmware on a printer.

- The Print Management tool is a Windows Administrative Tool that can be used to manage printers and print servers on a network.

Troubleshooting Printers

- When troubleshooting printers, first isolate the problem. Narrow the source to the printer, connectivity between the computer and its local printer, the network, Windows, printer drivers, the application using the printer, or the printer installation. Test pages printed directly at the printer or within Windows can help narrow down the source of the problem.

- Poor print quality can be caused by the printer drivers, the application, Windows, or the printer. For a laser printer, consider that low toner can be the problem. For an inkjet printer, consider that the ink cartridges need cleaning or replacing. The quality of paper can also be a problem.

- A printer needs memory to render a print job. Low memory can cause part of the page not to print or a printer error.

>> KEY TERMS

For explanations of key terms, see the Glossary near the end of the book.

bitmap	impact printer	printui
calibration	ink cartridge	raster line
default printer	inkjet printer	raw data
Devices and Printers window	laser printer	REt (Resolution Enhancement technology)
direct thermal printer	local printer	
duplex printer	LPT (Line Printer Terminal)	separation pad
duplexing assembly	network printer	Services console
elevated command prompt window	PCL (Printer Control Language)	spooling
		Standard Parallel Port (SPP)
Enhanced Parallel Port (EPP)	pickup roller	thermal paper
Extended Capabilities Port (ECP)	PostScript	thermal printer
	Print Management	thermal transfer printer
extension magnet brush	Printers window	toner vacuum
fuser assembly	Printers and Faxes window	tractor feed
GDI (Graphics Device Interface)	print head	transfer belt
	print server	transfer roller
IEEE 1284	print spooler	XPS Document Writer
imaging drum	printer maintenance kit	XPS (XML Paper Specification)
impact paper	printer self test page	

>> REVIEWING THE BASICS

1. Which two methods of rendering a print job are done in Windows before the page is sent to the printer? Which of these two methods was introduced with Windows Vista?

2. Which two printing languages are used to send a print job to a printer where the printer uses these languages to render a print job before it is printed?

3. List the seven steps used by a laser printer to print a page.

4. Which document exhibits better quality, one printed with 600 dpi or one printed with 1200 dpi? Why?

5. During the laser printing process, what determines when the toner sticks to the drum and when it does not stick to the drum?

6. What type of printer is most dependent on the quality of paper it uses to get the best printing results?

7. What should you do if an inkjet printer prints with missing dots or lines on the page?

8. What can you do to help a dot matrix printer last longer?

9. What feature on a printer must be enabled so that a printer can automatically print on both sides of the paper?

10. What two Windows XP components are used to share resources on a network and access those shared resources?

11. Using Windows 7, how do you share a local printer with others on the network?

12. What is likely to be the problem when a laser printer consistently produces pages with gray print?

13. What kind of printer is assigned an IP address?

14. What two tools can you use to remove loose toner from inside a printer?

15. Where is the best place to look for a firmware upgrade for a printer?

16. How can you prove a printer problem is not with the printer itself, but lies with the network, computer, OS, or application?

17. When you get a toner-low message, what can you do to extend the life of the toner cartridge before you replace the cartridge?

18. What causes a ghosted image on a printout?

19. What is likely the problem when a portion of a complicated page does not print?

20. What can you do to verify a printing problem is with an application or a document and not with Windows?

>> THINKING CRITICALLY

1. You are not able to print a Word document on a Windows 7 computer to a network printer. The network printer is connected directly to the network, but when you look at the Devices and Printers window, you see the name of the printer as \\SMITH\HP LaserJet 8100. In the following list, select the possible sources of the problem.

   a. The SMITH computer is not turned on.

   b. The HP LaserJet 8100 printer is not online.

   c. The SMITH printer is not online.

   d. The Windows 7 computer has a stalled print spool.

   e. The HP LaserJet 8100 computer is not logged on to the workgroup.

2. You are not able to print a test page from your Windows 7 computer to your USB local HP DeskJet printer. Which of the following are possible causes of the problem?

   a. The network is down.

   b. The printer cable is not connected properly.

   c. The Windows print spool is stalled.

   d. You have the wrong printer drivers installed.

   e. File and Printer Sharing is not enabled.

>> REAL PROBLEMS, REAL SOLUTIONS

REAL PROBLEM 12-1: Selecting a Color Printer for a Small Business

Jack owns a small real estate firm and has come to you asking for help with his printing needs. Currently, he has a color inkjet printer that he is using to print flyers, business cards, brochures, and other marketing materials. However, he is not satisfied with the print quality and wants to invest in a printer that produces more professional-looking hard copy. He expects to print no more than 8,000 sheets per month and needs the ability to print envelopes, letter-size and legal-size pages, and business cards. He wants to be able to automatically print on both sides of a legal-size page to produce a three-column brochure. Research printer solutions and do the following:

1. Save or print web pages showing three printers to present to Jack that satisfy his needs. Include at least one laser printer and at least one printer technology other than laser in your selections.

2. Save or print web pages showing the routine maintenance requirements of these printers.

3. Save or print web pages showing all the consumable products (other than paper) that Jack should expect to have to purchase in the first year of use.

4. Calculate the initial cost of the equipment and the total cost of consumables for one year (other than paper) for each printer solution.

5. Prepare a list of advantages and disadvantages for each solution.

6. Based on your research, which of the three solutions do you recommend? Why?

APPENDIX A: Keystroke Shortcuts in Windows

This appendix lists a few handy keystrokes to use when working with Windows, including the function keys you can use during startup. You can also use the mouse to do some of these same things, but keystrokes are sometimes faster. Also, in some troubleshooting situations, the mouse is not usable. At those times, knowing these keystrokes can get you out of a jam.

General Action	Keystrokes	Description
While loading Windows	F8	To display the Advanced Boot Options menu.
	Spacebar	To display the Windows boot menu.
Managing Windows and applications	F1	To display Help.
	Alt+Tab	To move from one loaded application to another.
	Ctrl+Tab and Ctrl+Shift+Tab	To move through tabbed pages in a dialog box.
	Alt+Esc	To cycle through items in the order they were opened.
	F6	To cycle through screen elements in a window or on the desktop.
	Win or Ctrl+Esc	Display Start menu. Use arrow keys to move over the menu. (The Win key is the one labeled with the Windows flag icon.)
	Win+E	Start Windows Explorer.
	Win+M	Minimize all windows.
	Win+Tab	Move through items on the taskbar.
	Win+R	Display the Run dialog box.
	Win+Break	Display the Windows 7/Vista System window or the XP System Properties window.
	F5	Refresh the contents of a window.
	Alt+F4	Close the active application window, or, if no window is open, shut down Windows.
	Ctrl+F4	Close the active document window.
	Alt+Spacebar	To display the System menu for the active window. To close this window, you can then use the arrow key to step down to Close.
	Alt+M	First, put the focus on the Start menu (use Win or Ctrl+Esc) and then press Alt+M to minimize all windows and move the focus to the desktop.
	F10 or Alt	Activate the menu bar in the active program.
	Ctrl+Alt+Del	Display the Task List, which you can use to switch to another application, end a task, or shut down Windows.
	Application	When an item is selected, display its shortcut menu. (The Application key is labeled with a box and an arrow.)
Working with text anywhere in Windows	Ctrl+C	Shortcut for Copy.
	Ctrl+V	Shortcut for Paste.
	Ctrl+A	Shortcut for selecting all text.
	Ctrl+X	Shortcut for Cut.
	Ctrl+Z	Shortcut for Undo.
	Ctrl+Y	Shortcut for Repeat/Redo.
	Shift+arrow keys	To select text, character by character.

© Cengage Learning 2014

General Action	Keystrokes	Description
Managing files, folders, icons, and shortcuts	Ctrl+Shift while dragging a file	Create a shortcut.
	Ctrl while dragging a file	Copy a file.
	Shift+Delete	Delete a file without placing it in the Recycle Bin.
	F2	Rename an item.
	Alt+Enter	Display an item's Properties window.
Selecting items	Shift+click	To select multiple entries in a list (such as filenames in Explorer), click the first item, hold down the Shift key, and click the last item you want to select in the list. All items between the first and last are selected.
	Ctrl+click	To select several nonsequential items in a list, click the first item to select it. Hold down the Ctrl key and click other items anywhere in the list. All items you click are selected.
Using menus	Alt	Press the Alt key to activate the menu bar.
	Alt, letter	After the menu bar is activated, press a letter to select a menu option. The letter must be underlined in the menu.
	Alt, arrow keys, Enter	In a window, use the Alt key to make the menu bar active. Then use the arrow keys to move over the menu tree and highlight the correct option. Use the Enter key to select that option.
	Esc	Press Esc to exit a menu without making a selection.
Copying to the Clipboard	Print Screen	Copy the desktop to the Clipboard.
	Alt+Print Screen	Copy the active window to the Clipboard.

© Cengage Learning 2014

APPENDIX B: CompTIA A+ Acronyms

CompTIA provides a list of acronyms that you need to know before you sit for the A+ exams. You can download the list from the CompTIA web site at *www.comptia.org*. The list is included here for your convenience. However, CompTIA occasionally updates the list, so be sure to check the CompTIA web site for the latest version.

APPENDIX B CompTIA A+ Acronyms

Acronym	Spelled Out
A/V	Audio Video
AC	alternating current
ACL	access control list
ACPI	advanced configuration power interface
ACT	activity
ADSL	asymmetrical digital subscriber line
AGP	accelerated graphics port
AMD	advanced micro devices
APIPA	automatic private internet protocol addressing
APM	advanced power management
ARP	address resolution protocol
ASR	automated system recovery
ATA	advanced technology attachment
ATAPI	advanced technology attachment packet interface
ATM	asynchronous transfer mode
ATX	advanced technology extended
BIOS	basic input/output system
BNC	Bayonet-Neill-Concelman or British Naval Connector
BTX	balanced technology extended
CAPTCHA	Completely Automated Public Turing Test To Tell Computers and Humans Apart
CCFL	Cold Cathode Fluorescent Lamp
CD	compact disc
CDFS	compact disc file system
CD-ROM	compact disc-read-only memory
CD-RW	compact disc-rewritable
CFS	Central File System, Common File System, Command File System
CMOS	complementary metal-oxide semiconductor
CNR	Communications and Networking Riser
COMx	communication port (x=port number)
CPU	central processing unit
CRIMM	Continuity Rambus Inline Memory Mode
CRT	cathode-ray tube
DAC	discretionary access control
DB-25	serial communications D-shell connector, 25 pins
DB-9	9-pin D shell connector
DC	direct current
DDOS	distributed denial of service
DDR	double data-rate
DDR RAM	double data-rate random access memory
DDR SDRAM	double data-rate synchronous dynamic random access memory

Acronym	Spelled Out
DFS	distributed file system
DHCP	dynamic host configuration protocol
DIMM	dual inline memory module
DIN	Deutsche Industrie Norm
DIP	dual inline package
DLP	digital light processing
DLT	digital linear tape
DMA	direct memory access
DMZ	demilitarized zone
DNS	domain name service or domain name server
DOS	denial of service
DRAM	dynamic random access memory
DSL	digital subscriber line
DVD	digital video disc or digital versatile disc
DVD-R	digital video disc-recordable
DVD-RAM	digital video disc-random access memory
DVD-ROM	digital video disc-read only memory
DVD-RW	digital video disc-rewritable
DVI	digital visual interface
ECC	error correction code
ECP	extended capabilities port
EEPROM	electrically erasable programmable read-only memory
EFS	encrypting file system
EIDE	enhanced integrated drive electronics
EMI	electromagnetic interference
EMP	electromagnetic pulse
EPP	enhanced parallel port
EPROM	erasable programmable read-only memory
ERD	emergency repair disk
ESD	electrostatic discharge
EVDO	evolution data optimized or evolution data only
EVGA	extended video graphics adapter/array
FAT	file allocation table
FAT12	12-bit file allocation table
FAT16	16-bit file allocation table
FAT32	32-bit file allocation table
FDD	floppy disk drive
Fn	Function (referring to the function key on a laptop)
FPM	fast page-mode
FQDN	fully qualified domain name

© Cengage Learning 2014

Acronym	Spelled Out
FRU	field replaceable unit
FSB	Front Side Bus
FTP	file transfer protocol
Gb	gigabit
GB	gigabyte
GDI	graphics device interface
GHz	gigahertz
GPS	global positioning system
GSM	global system for mobile communications
GUI	graphical user interface
HAL	hardware abstraction layer
HAV	Hardware Assisted Virtualization
HCL	hardware compatibility list
HDD	hard disk drive
HDMI	high definition media interface
HPFS	high performance file system
HTML	hypertext markup language
HTPC	Home Theater PC
HTTP	hypertext transfer protocol
HTTPS	hypertext transfer protocol over secure sockets layer
I/O	input/output
ICMP	internet control message protocol
ICR	intelligent character recognition
IDE	integrated drive electronics
IDS	Intrusion Detection System
IEEE	Institute of Electrical and Electronics Engineers
IIS	Internet Information Services
IMAP	internet mail access protocol
IP	internet protocol
IPCONFIG	internet protocol configuration
IPP	internet printing protocol
IPSEC	internet protocol security
IR	infrared
IrDA	Infrared Data Association
IRQ	interrupt request
ISA	industry standard architecture
ISDN	integrated services digital network
ISO	Industry Standards Organization
ISP	internet service provider
JBOD	just a bunch of disks

Acronym	Spelled Out
Kb	kilobit
KB	Kilobyte or knowledge base
LAN	local area network
LBA	logical block addressing
LC	Lucent connector
LCD	liquid crystal display
LDAP	lightweight directory access protocol
LED	light emitting diode
Li-on	lithium-ion
LPD/LPR	line printer daemon / line printer remote
LPT	line printer terminal
LVD	low voltage differential
MAC	media access control / mandatory access control
MAPI	messaging application programming interface
MAU	media access unit, media attachment unit
Mb	megabit
MB	megabyte
MBR	master boot record
MBSA	Microsoft Baseline Security Analyzer
MFD	multi-function device
MFP	multi-function product
MHz	megahertz
MicroDIMM	micro dual inline memory module
MIDI	musical instrument digital interface
MIME	multipurpose internet mail extension
MIMO	Multiple Input Multiple Output
MMC	Microsoft management console
MMX	multimedia extensions
MP3	Moving Picture Experts Group Layer 3 Audio
MP4	Moving Picture Experts Group Layer 4
MPEG	Moving Picture Experts Group
MSCONFIG	Microsoft configuration
MSDS	material safety data sheet
MUI	multilingual user interface
NAC	network access control
NAS	network-attached storage
NAT	network address translation
NetBEUI	networked basic input/output system extended user interface
NetBIOS	networked basic input/output system
NFS	network file system

Acronym	Spelled Out
NIC	network interface card
NiCd	nickel cadmium
NiMH	nickel metal hydride
NLX	new low-profile extended
NNTP	network news transfer protocol
NTFS	new technology file system
NTLDR	new technology loader
NTP	Network Time Protocol
OCR	optical character recognition
OEM	original equipment manufacturer
OLED	Organic Light Emitting Diode
OS	operating system
PAN	personal area network
PATA	parallel advanced technology attachment
PC	personal computer
PCI	peripheral component interconnect
PCIe	peripheral component interconnect express
PCIX	peripheral component interconnect extended
PCL	printer control language
PCMCIA	Personal Computer Memory Card International Association
PDA	personal digital assistant
PGA	pin grid array
PGA2	pin grid array 2
PII	Personally Identifiable Information
PIN	personal identification number
PKI	public key infrastructure
PnP	plug and play
POP3	post office protocol 3
PoS	Point of Sale
POST	power-on self test
POTS	plain old telephone service
PPP	point-to-point protocol
PPTP	point-to-point tunneling protocol
PRI	primary rate interface
PROM	programmable read-only memory
PS/2	personal system/2 connector
PSTN	public switched telephone network
PSU	power supply unit
PVC	permanent virtual circuit
PXE	preboot execution environment

Acronym	Spelled Out
QoS	quality of service
RAID	redundant array of independent (or inexpensive) discs
RAM	random access memory
RAS	remote access service
RDP	Remote Desktop Protocol
RDRAM	RAMBUS® dynamic random access memory
RF	radio frequency
RFI	radio frequency interference
RGB	red green blue
RIMM	RAMBUS® inline memory module
RIP	routing information protocol
RIS	remote installation service
RISC	reduced instruction set computer
RJ	registered jack
RJ-11	registered jack function 11
RJ-45	registered jack function 45
RMA	returned materials authorization
ROM	read only memory
RS-232 or RS-232C	recommended standard 232
RTC	real-time clock
S.M.A.R.T.	self-monitoring, analysis, and reporting technology
SAN	storage area network
SAS	Serial Attached SCSI
SATA	serial advanced technology attachment
SC	subscription channel
SCP	secure copy protection
SCSI	small computer system interface
SCSI ID	small computer system interface identifier
SD card	secure digital card
SDRAM	synchronous dynamic random access memory
SEC	single edge connector
SFC	system file checker
SFF	Small Form Factor
SGRAM	synchronous graphics random access memory
SIMM	single inline memory module
SLI	scalable link interface or system level integration or scanline interleave mode
SMB	server message block or small to midsize business
SMTP	simple mail transfer protocol
SNMP	simple network management protocol
SoDIMM	small outline dual inline memory module

Acronym	Spelled Out
SOHO	small office/home office
SP	service pack
SP1	service pack 1
SP2	service pack 2
SP3	service pack 3
SP4	service pack 4
SPDIF	Sony-Philips digital interface format
SPGA	staggered pin grid array
SRAM	static random access memory
SSH	secure shell
SSID	service set identifier
SSL	secure sockets layer
ST	straight tip
STP	shielded twisted pair
SVGA	super video graphics array
SXGA	super extended graphics array
TB	terabyte
TCP	transmission control protocol
TCP/IP	transmission control protocol/internet protocol
TDR	time domain reflectometer
TFTP	trivial file transfer protocol
TKIP	Temporal Key Integrity Protocol
TPM	trusted platform module
UAC	user account control
UART	universal asynchronous receiver transmitter
UDF	user defined functions or universal disk format or universal data format
UDMA	ultra direct memory access
UDP	user datagram protocol
UNC	universal naming convention
UPS	uninterruptible power supply
URL	uniform resource locator
USB	universal serial bus
USMT	user state migration tool
UTP	unshielded twisted pair
UXGA	ultra extended graphics array
VESA	Video Electronics Standards Association
VFAT	virtual file allocation table
VGA	video graphics array
VM	Virtual Machine
VoIP	voice over internet protocol

© Cengage Learning 2014

Acronym	Spelled Out
VPN	virtual private network
VRAM	video random access memory
WAN	wide area network
WAP	wireless application protocol
WEP	wired equivalent privacy
WIFI	wireless fidelity
WINS	windows internet name service
WLAN	wireless local area network
WPA	wireless protected access
WUXGA	wide ultra extended graphics array
XGA	extended graphics array
ZIF	zero-insertion-force
ZIP	zigzag inline package

© Cengage Learning 2014

GLOSSARY

This glossary defines terms related to managing and maintaining a personal computer.

100BaseT An Ethernet standard that operates at 100Mbps and uses twisted-pair cabling up to 100 meters (328 feet). *Also called* Fast Ethernet. Variations of 100BaseT are 100BaseTX and 100BaseFX.

4-pin motherboard auxiliary connector A connector on the motherboard used to provide additional power to the processor other than that provided by the P1 connector.

8-pin motherboard auxiliary connector A connector on the motherboard used to provide additional power to the processor other than that provided by the P1 connector or the earlier 4-pin auxiliary connector.

10-foot user interface Applications software used on large screens to control output display menus and other clickable items in fonts large enough to read at a distance of 10 feet.

20-pin P1 connector Used by an older ATX power supply and motherboard and provided +3.3 volts, +5 volts, +12 volts, −12 volts, and an optional and rarely used −5 volts.

24-pin P1 connector Used by ATX Version 2.2 power supply and motherboard and provides additional power for PCI Express slots.

1394a *See* FireWire 400.

1394b *See* FireWire 800.

25-pin SCSI connector A SCSI connector used by narrow SCSI that looks like a parallel port connector.

4G (Fourth Generation) The ability to use a cell phone to browse the web, stream music and video, play online games, and use instant messaging and video conferencing. 4G offers the fastest speed for cellular data.

50-pin SCSI connector A type of SCSI connector, *also called* an A connector, used by narrow SCSI.

68-pin SCSI connector A type of SCSI connector, *also called* a P connector, used by wide SCSI.

6TO4 In TCP/IP version 6, an older tunneling protocol being replaced by the more powerful Teredo or ISATAP protocols. Tunnels are used by IPv6 to transport IPv6 packets over an IPv4 network.

802.11 a/b/g/n The collective name for the IEEE 802.11 standards for local wireless networking, which is the technical name for Wi-Fi.

A+ Certification A certification awarded by CompTIA (The Computer Technology Industry Association) that measures a PC technician's knowledge and skills.

AC adapter A device that converts AC to DC and can use regular house current to power a notebook computer.

Accelerated Graphics Port (AGP) A 32-bit wide bus standard developed specifically for video cards that includes AGP 1x, 2x, 3x, 4x, and 8x standards. AGP has been replaced by the PCI Express standards.

adapter address *See* MAC (Media Access Control) address.

ad hoc mode A type of physical arrangement of the connection between computers where each wireless computer serves as its own wireless access point and is responsible for securing each connection.

Advanced Configuration and Power Interface (ACPI) Standards used by system BIOS and other components that define power states for the system and processor used to conserve power when the system is not in full use.

AES (Advanced Encryption Standard) The basis for wireless encryption standards and improve the way TKIP generated encryption keys.

all-in-one computer A computer that has the monitor and computer case built together and uses components that are common to both a notebook and a desktop computer.

alternate IP address A setting that allows a computer to first try using dynamic IP addressing when a laptop moves from one network to another. If dynamic IP addressing is not available on the network, it then applies the static IP address setting entered on the Alternate Configuration tab.

alternating current (AC) Current that cycles back and forth rather than traveling in only one direction. In the United States, the AC voltage from a standard wall outlet is normally between 110 and 115V. In Europe, the standard AC voltage from a wall outlet is 220V.

A Male connector A common type of USB connector that is flat and wide and connects an A Male USB port on a computer or USB hub.

amp A measure of electrical current.

ANSI (American National Standards Institute) A nonprofit organization dedicated to creating trade and communications standards.

antistatic bags Static shielding bags that new computer components are shipped in.

antistatic gloves Gloves designed to prevent an ESD discharge between you and a device, as you pick it up and handle it.

antistatic wrist strap See ground bracelet.

anycast address Using TCP/IP version 6, a type of IP address used by routers and identifies multiple destinations. Packets are delivered to the closest destination.

artifacts Horizontally torn images on a computer screen.

ATAPI (Advanced Technology Attachment Packet Interface) An interface standard, part of the IDE/ATA standards, that allows tape drives, optical drives, and other drives to be treated like an IDE hard drive by the system.

ATX (Advanced Technology Extended) The most common form factor for PC systems presently in use, originally introduced by Intel in 1995. ATX motherboards and cases make better use of space and resources than did the earlier AT form factor.

ATX12V power supply An ATX Version 2.1 power supply that provides a 12V power cord with a 4-pin connector to be used by the auxiliary 4-pin power connector on motherboards used to provide extra power for processors.

Automatic Private IP Address (APIPA) In TCP/IP Version 4, an IP address that is assigned to a computer when the computer is not able to lease a dynamic IP address from a DHCP server.

auto-switching A function of a laptop computer AC adapter that is able to automatically switch between 110 V and 220 V AC power.

ball grid array (BGA) A connection via a processor that is soldered to the motherboard, and the two are always purchased as a unit.

bandwidth In relation to analog communication, the range of frequencies that a communications channel or cable can carry. In general use, the term refers to the volume of data that can travel on a bus or over a cable stated in bits per second (bps), kilobits per second (Kbps), or megabits per second (Mbps). *Also called* data throughput or line speed.

barcode reader Used to scan barcodes on products at the points of sale or when taking inventory.

base station A fixed transceiver and antenna used to create one cell within a cellular network.

Berg power connector A type of power connector used by a power cord to provide power to a floppy disk drive.

best-effort protocol See connectionless protocol.

biometric device An input device that inputs biological data about a person; the data can identify a person's fingerprints, handprints, face, voice, eye, and handwriting.

BIOS (basic input/output system) Firmware that can control much of a computer's input/output functions, such as communication with the keyboard and the monitor.

BIOS setup The program in system BIOS that can change the values in CMOS RAM. *Also called* CMOS setup.

bitmap A bunch of bits in rows and columns.

B Male connector A USB connector that connects a USB 1.x or 2.0 device such as a printer.

blue screen of death (BSOD) An error screen on a blue background indicating Windows errors that are caused by problems with devices, device drivers, or a corrupted Windows installation.

Blu-ray Disc (BD) An optical disc technology that uses the UDF version 2.5 file system and a blue laser beam, which is shorter than any red beam used by DVD or CD discs. The shorter blue laser beam allows Blu-ray discs to store more data than a DVD.

BNC connector A connector used with thin coaxial cable. Some BNC connectors are T-shaped and called T-connectors. One end of the T connects to the NIC, and the two other ends can connect to cables or end a bus formation with a terminator.

bridge A device that stands between two segments of a network and manages network traffic between them.

broadband A transmission technique that carries more than one type of transmission on the same medium, such as voice and DSL on a regular telephone line.

brownouts Temporary reductions in voltage, which can sometimes cause data loss. *Also called* sags.

bus The paths, or lines, on the motherboard on which data, instructions, and electrical power move from component to component.

bus network An older topology whereby all computers are connected in a sequential line.

cable Internet A broadband technology that uses cable TV lines and is always connected (always up).

cable tester Used to test a cable to find out if it is good or to find out what type of cable it is if the cable is not labeled.

calibration The process of checking and correcting the graduations of an instrument or device such as an inkjet printer.

call tracking A system that tracks the dates, times, and transactions of help-desk or on-site PC support calls, including the problem presented, the issues addressed, who did what, and when and how each call was resolved.

CardBus A PCMCIA specification that improved on the earlier PC Card standards. It improved I/O speed, increased the bus width to 32 bits, and supported lower-voltage PC Cards, while maintaining backward compatibility with earlier standards. CardBus has been replaced with ExpressCard specifications.

CAS Latency A method of measuring access timing to memory, which is the number of clock cycles required to write or read a column of data off a memory module. CAS stands for Column Access Strobe. *Compare to* RAS Latency.

case fan A fan inside a computer case used to draw air out of or into the case.

CAT-3 (Category 3) A rating used for UTP cables that is less expensive than the more popular CAT-5 cables.

CAT-5 (Category 5) A rating used for UTP cables. CAT-5 or higher cabling is required for Fast Ethernet.

CAT-6 A rating used for UTP cables that has less crosstalk than CAT-5 or CAT-5e cables. CAT-6 cables contain a plastic cord down the center of the cable that helps to prevent crosstalk.

CAT-6a A rating used for UTP cables that is thicker than CAT-6 and used by 10GBase-T (10-Gigabit Ethernet.

CD (compact disc) An optical disc technology that uses a red laser beam and can hold up to 700 MB of data.

CDFS (Compact Disc File System) The 32-bit file system for CD discs and some CD-R and CD-RW discs. *See also* Universal Disk Format (UDF).

CDMA (Code Division Multiple Access) A protocol standard used by cellular WANs and cell phones.

cellular network A network that can be used when a wireless network must cover a wide area. The network is made up of cells, each controlled by a base station. *Also called* a cellular WAN.

cellular WAN *See* cellular network.

central processing unit (CPU) *Also called* a microprocessor or processor. The component where almost all processing of data and instructions takes place. The CPU receives data input, processes information, and executes instructions.

Centrino A technology used by Intel whereby the processor, chipset, and wireless network adapter are all interconnected as a unit, which improves laptop performance.

chain of custody Documentation that tracks evidence used in an investigation and includes exactly what, when, and from whom the evidence was collected, the condition of the evidence, and how the evidence was secured while in possession of a responsible party.

channel A specific radio frequency within a broader frequency.

chassis air guide (CAG) A round air duct that helps to pull and direct fresh air from outside a computer case to the cooler and processor.

chipset A group of chips on the motherboard that controls the timing and flow of data and instructions to and from the CPU.

Class A A class of IPv4 IP address that is for a single octet, which is the network portion of the IP addresses in that license.

Class B A class of IPv4 IP address that leases the first two octets, and these first two octets are used for the network portion and the last two can be used for the host address or for subnetting the network.

Class C A class of IPv4 IP address that assigns three octets as the network address.

Class C fire extinguisher A fire extinguisher rated to put out electrical fires.

classful subnet mask In TCP/IP Version 4, the default subnet mask that is used if a network is not divided into subnets. It is called a classful subnet mask because the network portion of the IP address aligns with the class license.

classless subnet mask In TCP/IP Version 4, the subnet mask takes some bits of the host portion of the IP address for the network ID and does not align the network portion of the IP address with the network octets assigned by the class license.

client/server Two computers communicating using a local network or the Internet. One computer takes on the role of making requests from the other computer. A computer making a request from another is called the client and the one answering the request is called the server.

CMOS (complementary metal-oxide semiconductor) The technology used to manufacture microchips. CMOS chips require less electricity, hold data longer after the electricity is turned off, and produce less heat than earlier technologies. The configuration or setup chip is a CMOS chip.

CMOS battery The battery on the motherboard used to power the CMOS chip that holds BIOS setup data so that the data is retained when the computer is unplugged.

CMOS RAM Memory contained on the CMOS configuration chip.

CMOS setup *See* BIOS setup.

coaxial cable A cable that has a single copper wire down the middle and a braided shield around it.

CompactFlash (CF) card A flash memory device that allows for sizes up to 137 GB, although current sizes range up to 32 GB.

computer name *See* host name.

connectionless protocol A TCP/IP protocol that works at the OSI Transport layer and does not guarantee delivery by first connecting and checking where data is received. It might be used for broadcasting, such as streaming video or sound over the web, where guaranteed delivery is not as important as fast transmission. *Also see* UDP (User Datagram Protocol).

connection-oriented protocol A connection, such as that made by the TCP protocol, which checks whether data is received, and resends it if it is not.

composite video port A port used by television or by a video card that is designed to send output to a TV. A composite port is round and has only a single pin in the center of the port.

contrast ratio The contrast between true black and true white on a screen.

cooler A cooling system that sits on top of a processor and consists of a fan and a heat sink.

copyright The right to copy the work that belongs to the creators of the works or others to whom the creator transfers this right.

C-RIMM (Continuity RIMM) A placeholder module that fills a memory slot on the motherboard when the slot does not hold a RIMM in order to maintain continuity.

crimper A tool used to attach a terminator or connector to the end of a cable.

crossover cable A cable used to connect two like devices such as a hub to a hub or a PC to a PC (to make the simplest network of all).

CRT (cathode-ray tube) monitor A type of monitor first used in older television sets.

data bus Lines of the bus, a system of pathway used for communication on the motherboard, used for data.

data cartridge A full-sized cartridge that holds data and is used in a tape drive.

data path size The number of lines on a bus that can hold data, for example, 8, 16, 32, and 64 lines, which can accommodate 8, 16, 32, and 64 bits at a time.

data throughput *See* bandwidth.

DB-15 port A 15-pin female port that transmits analog video.

DDR *See* Double Data Rate SDRAM.

dead pixel A pixel on an LCD monitor that is not working and can appear as small white, black, or colored spots on the computer screen.

default gateway The gateway a computer uses to access another network if it does not have a better option.

default printer The designated printer to which Windows prints unless another printer is selected.

degauss button A button on some older CRT monitors used to eliminate accumulated or stray magnetic fields.

desktop case A computer case that lies flat and sometimes serves double-duty as a monitor stand.

device driver Small programs stored on the hard drive and installed in Windows that tell Windows how to communicate with a specific hardware device such as a printer, network, port on the motherboard, or scanner.

Device Manager Primary Windows 7/Vista/XP tool for managing hardware.

Devices and Printers window A window used in Windows 7 to manage and uninstall printers.

DHCP (dynamic host configuration protocol) A server that gives an IP address to a computer when it first attempts to initiate a connection to the network and requests an IP address.

DHCP client A computer of other device (such as a network printer) that requests an IP address from a DHCP server.

digitizer *See* graphics tablet.

digitizing tablet *See* graphics tablet.

DIMM (dual inline memory module) A miniature circuit board installed on a motherboard to hold memory. DIMMs can hold up to 16 GB of RAM on a single module.

direct current (DC) Current that travels in only one direction (the type of electricity provided by batteries). Computer power supplies transform AC to low DC.

Direct Rambus DRAM A memory technology by Rambus and Intel that uses a narrow network-type system bus. Memory is stored on a RIMM module. *Also called* RDRAM, Rambus, or Direct RDRAM.

Direct RDRAM *See* Direct Rambus DRAM.

direct thermal printer A type of thermal printer that burns dots onto special coated paper as was done by older fax machines.

DirectX A Microsoft software development tool that software developers can use to write multimedia applications such as games, video-editing software, and computer-aided design software.

DisplayPort A port that transmits digital video and audio (not analog transmissions) and is slowly replacing VGA and DVI ports on personal computers.

DMA (direct memory access) transfer mode A transfer mode used by devices, including the hard drive, to transfer data to memory without involving the CPU.

DMZ A demilitarized zone in networking is a computer or network that is not protected by a firewall.

DNS (Domain Name System or Domain Name Service) A protocol used by a DNS server to find an IP address for a computer when the fully qualified domain name is known.

DNS client When Windows queries the DNS server for a name resolution.

DNS server A Doman Name Service server that uses a DNS protocol to find an IP address for a computer when the fully qualified domain name is known. An Internet Service Provider is responsible for providing access to one or more DNS servers as part of the service it provides for Internet access.

docking port A connector on the bottom of the notebook to connect to a port replicator or docking station.

docking station A device that receives a notebook computer and provides additional secondary storage and easy connection to peripheral devices.

domain name A name that identifies a network and appears before the period in a website address such as microsoft.com.

Double Data Rate SDRAM (DDR SDRAM) A type of memory technology used on DIMMs that runs at twice the speed of the system clock. *Also called* DDR SDRAM, SDRAM II, and DDR.

double-sided A DIMM feature whereby memory chips are installed on both sides of a DIMM.

driver store The location where Windows stores a copy of the driver software when first installing a device.

DSL (Digital Subscriber Line) A telephone line that carries digital data from end to end, and is used as a type of broadband Internet access.

dual channels A motherboard feature that improves memory performance by providing two 64-bit channels between memory and the chipset. DDR, DDR2, and DDR3 DIMMs can use dual channels.

dual processors Two processor sockets on a server motherboard.

dual ranked Double-sided DIMMs that provide two 64-bit banks. The memory controller accesses first one bank and then the other. Dual-ranked DIMMs do not perform as well as single-ranked DIMMs.

dual voltage selector switch A switch on the back of the computer case where you can switch the input voltage to the power supply to 115 V used in the United States or 220 V used in other countries.

duplexing assembly Used in a duplex printer, a duplexing assembly contains several rollers, turns the paper around and draws it back through the print process to print on the back of the paper.

duplex printer A printer that is able to print on both sides of the paper.

DVD (digital versatile disc or digital video disc) A technology used by optical discs that uses a red laser beam and can hold up to 17 GB of data.

DVI-A A DVI (Digital Visual Interface) video port that only transmits analog data.

DVI-D A DVI (Digital Visual Interface) video port that works only with digital monitors.

DVI-I A DVI (Digital Visual Interface) video port that supports both analog and digital monitors.

DVI (Digital Video Interface) port A port that transmits digital or analog video.

dynamic IP address An IP address assigned by a DHCP server when the computer first connects to a network, whereas a static IP address is manually assigned.

dynamic RAM (DRAM) The most common type of system memory, it requires refreshing every few milliseconds.

dxdiag.exe A command used to display information about hardware and diagnose problems with DirectX.

ECC (error-correcting code) A chipset feature on a motherboard that checks the integrity of data stored on DIMMs or RIMMs and can correct single-bit errors in a byte. More advanced ECC schemas can detect, but not correct, double-bit errors in a byte.

electrostatic discharge (ESD) Another name for static electricity, which can damage chips and destroy motherboards, even though it might not be felt or seen with the naked eye.

elevated command prompt window A Windows command prompt window that allows commands that require administrative privileges.

enhanced CAT-5 (CAT-5e) A improved version of CAT-5 cable that reduces crosstalk.

Enhanced IDE (EIDE) PATA standard that supports the configuration of four IDE devices in a system.

Enhanced Parallel Port (EPP) A type of parallel port that transmits data in both directions.

escalate When a technician passes a customer's problem to higher organizational levels because he or she cannot solve the problem.

ESD gloves *See* antistatic gloves.

ESD mat *See* ground mat.

ESD strap *See* ground bracelet.

Ethernet port *See* network port.

expansion card A circuit board inserted into a slot on the motherboard to enhance the capability of the computer.

expert system Software that uses a database of known facts and rules to simulate a human expert's reasoning and decision-making processes.

ExpressCard The latest PCMCIA standard for notebook I/O cards that uses the PCI Express and USB 2.0 data transfer standards. Two types of Express-Cards are ExpressCard/34 (34mm wide) and ExpressCard/54 (54mm wide).

Extended Capabilities Port (ECP) A type of parallel port that is faster than an EPP port.

extension magnet brush A long-handled brush made of nylon fibers that are charged with static electricity to pick up stray toner inside a printer.

external SATA (eSATA) A standard for external drives based on SATA that uses a special external shielded SATA cable up to 2 meters long. eSATA is up to six times faster than USB or FireWire.

Fast Ethernet *See* 100BaseT.

fault tolerance The degree to which a system can tolerate failures. Adding redundant components, such as disk mirroring or disk duplexing, is a way to build in fault tolerance.

F connector A connector used with an RG-6 coaxial cable and is used for connections to a TV and has a single copper wire.

fiber optic A dedicated, leased line used for Internet access that uses fiber-optic cable from the ISP to a residence or place of business.

fiber-optic cable Cable that transmits signals as pulses of light over glass or plastic strands inside protected tubing.

field replaceable unit (FRU) A component in a computer or device that can be replaced with a new component without sending the computer or device back to the manufacturer. Examples: power supply, DIMM, motherboard, hard disk drive.

file system The overall structure that an OS uses to name, store, and organize files on a disk. Examples of file systems are NTFS and FAT32.

FireWire 400 A data transmission standard used by computers and peripherals (for example, a video camera) that transmits at 400 Mbps. *Also called* 1394a.

FireWire 800 A data transmission standard used by computers and peripherals (for example, a video camera) that transmits at 800 Mbps. *Also called* 1394b.

FireWire port A port used for high-speed multimedia devices such as camcorders. *Also called an* IEEE 1394 port.

firmware Software that is permanently stored in a chip. The BIOS on a motherboard is an example of firmware.

flashing BIOS The process of upgrading or refreshing the programming stored on a firmware chip.

flat panel monitor *See* LCD (Liquid Crystal Display) monitor.

flip-chip land grid array (FCLGA) A type of socket used by processors that has blunt protruding pins on the socket that connect with lands or pads on the bottom of the processor. The chips in the processor package are flipped over so that the top of the chip makes contact with the socket.

flip-chip pin grid array (FCPGA) A type of socket used by processors that has holes aligned in rows to receive pins on the bottom of the processor. The chips in the processor are flipped over so that the top of the chip makes contact with the socket.

floppy disk drive (FDD) A drive that can hold either a 5½ inch or 3¼ inch floppy disk. *Also called* floppy drive.

floppy drive *See* floppy disk drive (FDD).

form factor A set of specifications on the size, shape, and configuration of a computer hardware component such as a case, power supply, or motherboard.

formatting Preparing a hard drive volume, logical drive, or USB flash drive for use by placing tracks and sectors on its surface to store information (for example, FORMAT D:).

front panel connectors A group of wires running from the front of the computer case to the motherboard.

front panel header A group of pins on a motherboard that connect to wires that are connected to the front panel of the computer case.

Front Side Bus (FSB) *See* system bus.

FTP (File Transfer Protocol) A common application that uses the Internet to transfer files between two computers.

full duplex Communication that happens in two directions at the same time.

fully connected mesh topology A network where each node connects to every node on the network.

fully qualified domain name (FQDN) Identifies a computer and the network to which it belongs and includes the computer name and domain name.

fuser assembly A component in laser printing that uses heat and pressure to fuse the toner to paper.

gateway Any device or computer that network traffic can use to leave one network and go to a different network.

GDI (Graphics Device Interface) A component of Windows that uses a less-sophisticated method of communicating with a printer than other methods. GDI draws and formats the page, converting it to bitmap form, and then sends the almost-ready-to-print bitmap to the printer.

ghost cursor A trail on the screen left behind when you move the mouse.

Gigabit Ethernet A version of Ethernet that supports rates of data transfer up to 1 gigabit per second.

gigahertz (GHz) One thousand MHz, or one billion cycles per second.

global address *See* global unicast address.

global unicast address In TCP/IP Version 6, an IP address that can be routed on the Internet. *Also called* global address.

graphics processing unit (GPU) A processor that manipulates graphic data to form the images on a monitor screen. A GPU can be embedded on a video card or on the motherboard or integrated within the processor.

graphics tablet An input device that can use a stylus to hand draw. It works like a pencil on the tablet and uses a USB port.

ground bracelet A strap you wear around your wrist that is attached to the computer case, ground mat, or another ground so that ESD is discharged from your body before you touch sensitive components inside a computer. *Also called* static strap, ground strap, ESD bracelet.

ground mat A mat that dissipates ESD and is commonly used by technicians who repair and assemble computers at their workbenches or in an assembly line.

GSM (Global System for Mobile Communications) An open standard for cellular WANs and cell phones that uses digital communication of data and is accepted and used worldwide.

half duplex Communication between two devices whereby transmission takes place in only one direction at a time.

hard disk drive (HDD) *See* hard drive.

hard drive The main secondary storage device of a computer. Two technologies are currently used by hard drives: magnetic and solid state. *Also called* hard disk drive (HDD).

hardware address *See* MAC (Media Access Control) address.

hardware-assisted virtualization (HAV) A feature of a processor whereby it can provide enhanced support for virtual machines running in a system. The feature must be enabled in BIOS setup.

hardware profile A group of settings that Windows keeps about a specific hardware configuration. A hardware profile can be manually configured in Windows XP, but Windows 7 and Vista automatically configure hardware profiles.

HDMI (High Definition Multimedia Interface) port A digital audio and video interface standard currently used on televisions and other home theater equipment and expected to ultimately replace DVI.

HDMI connector A connector that transmits both digital video and audio and is used on most computers and televisions.

HDMI mini connector A smaller type of HDMI connector used for connecting some devices such as a smartphone to a computer.

heat sink A piece of metal, with cooling fins, that can be attached to or mounted on an integrated chip (such as the CPU) to dissipate heat.

hertz (Hz) Unit of measurement for frequency, calculated in terms of vibrations, or cycles per second. For example, for 16-bit stereo sound, a frequency of 44,000Hz is used. *See also* megahertz.

hibernation A power-saving state that saves all work to the hard drive and powers down the system.

Home Theater PC (HTPC) A PC that is designed to play and possibly record music, photos, movies, and video on a television or extra-large monitor screen.

host adapter The circuit board that controls a SCSI bus supporting as many as seven or fifteen separate devices. The host adapter controls communication between the SCSI bus and the computer.

host name The name of a computer and can be used in place of its IP address.

Hosts file A file, which has no file extension, and contains computer names and their associated IP addresses on the local network.

hot-plugging Plugging in a device while the computer is turned on. The computer will sense the device and configure it without rebooting. In addition, the device can be unplugged without an OS error. *Also called* hot-swapping.

hot swappable The ability to plug or unplug devices without first powering down the system. USB devices are hot swappable.

hot-swapping Allows you to connect and disconnect a device while the system is running.

HTPC case A case used to accommodate a home theater PC and must be small enough to fit on a shelf in an entertainment center.

HTTP (Hypertext Transfer Protocol) The protocol used for the World Wide Web and used by web browsers and web servers to communicate.

HTTPS (HTTP secure) The HTTP protocol working with a security protocol such as Secure Sockets Layer (SSL) or Transport Layer Security (TLS), which is better than SSL, to create a secured socket.

hub A network device or box that provides a central location to connect cables and distributes incoming data packets to all other devices connected to it. *Compare to* switch.

hybrid hard drive A hard drive that uses both magnetic and SSD technologies. The bulk of storage uses the magnetic component, and a storage buffer on the drive is made of an SSD component. Windows ReadyDrive supports hybrid hard drives.

hybrid network A network where a star network uses multiple switches in sequence, and the switches form a bus network.

Hyper-Threading The Intel technology that allows each logical processor within the processor package to handle an individual thread in parallel with other threads being handled by other processors within the package.

HyperTransport The AMD technology that allows each logical processor within the processor package to handle an individual thread in parallel with other threads being handled by other processors within the package.

hypervisor Virtual machine software that can provide one or more virtual machines.

I/O shield A plate installed on the rear of a computer case that provides holes for I/O ports coming off the motherboard.

IDE (Integrated Drive Electronics or Integrated Device Electronics) A hard drive whose disk controller is integrated into the drive, eliminating the need for a controller cable and thus increasing speed, as well as reducing price. *See also* EIDE.

IEEE 1284 A standard for parallel ports and cables developed by the Institute for Electrical and Electronics Engineers and supported by hardware manufacturers.

IEEE1394 port *See* FireWire port.

imaging drum An electrically charged rotating drum found in laser printers.

IMAP4 (Internet Message Access Protocol, version 4) A protocol used by a recipient's email server to deliver messages. Using IMAP, the client application manages the email stored on the server. *Compare to* POP3.

impact paper Paper used by impact printers and comes as a box of fanfold paper or in rolls (used with receipt printers).

impact printer A type of printer that creates a printed page by using a mechanism that touches or hits the paper.

Infrared (IR) An outdated wireless technology that has been mostly replaced by Bluetooth to connect personal computing devices.

ink cartridge Cartridge in inkjet printers that holds the different colors of ink for the printer.

inkjet printer A type of ink dispersion printer that uses cartridges of ink. The ink is heated to a boiling point and then ejected onto the paper through tiny nozzles.

interface In TCP/IP Version 6, a node's attachment to a link.

interface ID In TCP/IP Version 6, the last 64 bits or 4 blocks of an IP address that identify the interface.

internal components The main components installed in a computer case.

Internet appliance A type of thin client that is designed to make it easy for a user to connect to the Internet, browse the web, use email, and perform other simple chores on the Internet.

Internet Protocol version 4 (IPv4) An IP address with 32 bits that created about four billion potential IP addresses. Used by TCP/IP Version 4.

Internet Protocol version 6 (IPv6) An IP address with 128 bits used by TCP/IP Version 6.

Internet Service Provider (ISP) A commercial group that provides Internet access for a monthly fee; AOL, Earthlink, and Comcast are large ISPs.

intranet Any private network that uses TCP/IP protocols. A large enterprise might support an intranet that is made up of several local networks.

inverter A device that converts DC to AC.

IP address Used to find computers on subnets, an intranet, or on the Internet.

ISATAP In TCP/IP Version 6, a tunneling protocol that has been developed for IPv6 packets to travel over an IPv4 network and stands for Intra-Site Automatic Tunnel Addressing Protocol.

ISDN (Integrated Services Digital Network) A broadband telephone line that can carry data at about five times the speed of regular telephone lines. Two channels (telephone numbers) share a single pair of wires. ISDN has been replaced by DSL.

ISO image A file format that has an .iso file extension and holds an image of all the data, including the file system that is stored on an optical disc.

joule A measure of work or energy. One joule of energy produces one watt of power for one second.

jumper Two wires that stick up side by side on the motherboard or other device and are used to hold configuration information. The jumper is considered closed if a cover is over the wires, and open if the cover is missing.

keyboard backlight A feature on some keyboards where the keys light up on the keyboard.

keystone RJ-45 jack A jack that is used in an RJ-45 wall jack.

KVM (Keyboard, Video, and Mouse) switch A switch that allows you to use one keyboard, mouse, and monitor for multiple computers. Some KVM switches also include sound ports so that speakers and a microphone can be shared among multiple computers.

LAN (local area network) A computer network that covers only a small area, usually within one building.

land grid array (LGA) A feature of a CPU socket whereby pads, called lands, are used to make contact in uniform rows over the socket. *Compare to* pin grid array (PGA).

laptop *See* notebook.

laser printer A type of printer that uses a laser beam to control how toner is placed on the page and then uses heat to fuse the toner to the page.

latency Delays in network transmissions resulting in slower network performance. Latency is measured by the round-trip time it takes for a data packet to travel from source to destination and back to source.

LC (local connector) connector A newer type of connector used by fiber-optic cables and can be used with either single-mode or multimode fiber-optic cables.

LCD (Liquid Crystal Display) monitor A monitor that uses LCD technology. LCD produces an image using a liquid crystal material made of large, easily polarized molecules. LCD monitors are flatter than CRT monitors and take up less desk space. *Also called* a flat-panel monitor.

LED (Light-Emitting Diode) A technology used in an LCD monitor that uses less mercury than earlier technologies.

Level 1 cache (L1 cache) Memory on the processor die used as a cache to improve processor performance.

Level 2 cache (L2 cache) Memory in the processor package but not on the processor die. The memory is used as a cache or buffer to improve processor performance. *Also see* Level 1 (L1) cache.

Level 3 cache (L3 cache) Cache memory further from the processor core than Level 2 cache, but still in the processor package.

license Permission for an individual to use a product or service. A manufacturer's method of maintaining ownership while granting permission for use to others.

Lightweight Directory Access Protocol (LDAP) A protocol used by various client applications when the application needs to query a database.

line-of-sight connectivity A connection used by satellites that requires no obstruction from mountains, trees, and tall buildings from the satellite dish to the satellite.

link In TCP/IP Version 6, a local area network or wide area network bounded by routers.

link-local address *See* link-local unicast address.

link-local unicast address In TCP/IP Version 6, an IP address used for communicating with nodes in the same link. *Also called* local address.

Lithium Ion Currently the most popular type of battery popular with notebook computers that is more efficient than earlier types. Sometimes abbreviated as "Li-Ion" battery.

local area network (LAN) A network bound by routers or other gateway devices.

local link *See* link.

local printer A printer connected to a computer by way of a port on the computer. *Compare to* network printer.

Logical Unit Number (LUN) A number assigned to a logical device (such as a tray in a CD changer) that is part of a physical SCSI device, which is assigned a SCSI ID.

LoJack Technology embedded in the BIOS of many laptops to protect a system against theft.

loopback address An IP address that indicates your own computer.

loopback plug A device used to test a port in a computer or other device to make sure the port is working and might also test the throughput or speed of the port.

low-level formatting A process (usually performed at the factory) that electronically creates the hard drive tracks and sectors and tests for bad spots on the disk surface.

LPT (Line Printer Terminal) Assignments of system resources that are made to a parallel port and that are used to manage a print job. Two possible LPT configurations are referred to as LPT1: and LPT2:.

MAC (Media Access Control) address A 48-bit (6-byte) number hard-coded on a network adapter by its manufacturer that is unique for that device. *Also called* hardware address, physical address, or adapter address.

magnetic hard drive One of two technologies used by hard drives where data is stored as magnetic spots on disks that rotate at a high speed. The other technology is solid state drive (SSD).

main board *See* motherboard.

MAN (metropolitan area network) A type of network that covers a large city or campus.

Material Safety Data Sheet (MSDS) A document that explains how to properly handle substances such as chemical solvents; it includes information such as physical data, toxicity, health effects, first aid, storage, disposal, and spill procedures.

megahertz (MHz) One million Hz, or one million cycles per second. *See* hertz (Hz).

memory bank The memory a processor addresses at one time. Today's desktop and notebook processors use a memory bank that is 64 bits wide.

Memory Diagnostics (mdsched.exe) A Windows 7/Vista utility used to test memory.

mesh network Each node (a computer or other device) that uses the network is responsible for sending and receiving transmissions to any other node to which it wants to communicate with a central point of communication.

MicroATX (MATX) A version of the ATX form factor. MicroATX addresses some new technologies that were developed after the original introduction of ATX.

Micro-A connector A USB connector that has five pins and is smaller than the Mini-B connector. It is used on digital cameras, cell phones, and other small electronic devices.

Micro-B connector A USB connector that has five pins and has a smaller height than the Mini-B connector. It is used on digital cameras, cell phones, and other small electronic devices.

microprocessor *See* central processing unit (CPU).

MIDI (musical instrument digital interface) A set of standards that are used to represent music in digital form. A MIDI port is a 5-pin DIN port that looks like a keyboard port, only larger.

Mini-B connector A USB connector that has five pins and is often used to connect small electronic devices, such as a digital camera, to a computer.

MiniDin-6 connector A 6-pin variation of the S-Video port and looks like a PS/2 connector used by a keyboard or mouse.

mini-HDMI connector *See* HDMI mini connector.

Mini PCI The PCI industry standard for desktop computer expansion cards, applied to a much smaller form factor for notebook expansion cards.

Mini PCI Express A standard used for notebook internal expansion slots that follows the PCI Express standards applied to notebooks. *Also called* Mini PCIe.

Mini PCIe *See* Mini PCI Express.

minicartridge A tape drive cartridge that is only 3¼ × 2½ × 3/5. It is small enough to allow two drives to fit into a standard 5 inch drive bay of a PC case.

mirrored volume The term used by Windows for the RAID 1 level that duplicates data on one drive to another drive and is used for fault tolerance.

modem port A port used to connect dial-up phone lines to computers.

Molex power connector A 4-pin power connector used to provide power to a PATA hard drive or optical drive.

motherboard The main board in the computer, *also called* the system board. The CPU, ROM chips, DIMMs, RIMMs, and interface cards are plugged into the motherboard.

MT-RJ (mechanical transfer registered jack) connector A newer type of connector used by fiber-optic cables and can be used with either single-mode or multimode fiber-optic cables.

multicast address An IPv6 address where packets are delivered to all nodes on a network.

multicasting One host sends messages to multiple hosts, such as when the host transmits a video conference over the Internet.

multi-core processing A processor technology whereby the processor housing contains two or more processor cores that operate at the same frequency but independently of each other.

multimeter A device used to measure the various attributes of an electrical circuit. The most common measurements are voltage, current, and resistance.

multiple input/multiple output (MIMO) Used by the latest Wi-Fi standard, 802.11n, and allows a device to use two or more antennas to improve performance.

multiplier The factor by which the bus speed or frequency is multiplied to get the CPU clock speed.

multiprocessing Two processing units installed within a single processor and first used by the Pentium processor.

multiprocessor platform A system that contains more than one processor. The motherboard has more than one processor socket and the processors must be rated to work in this multiprocessor environment.

name resolution The process of associating a character-based name with an IP address.

NAND flash memory The type of memory used in SSD drives. NAND stands for "Not AND" and refers to the logic used when storing a one or zero in the grid of rows and columns on the memory chip.

NAT (Network Address Translation) A TCP/IP protocol that substitutes the public IP address of the router for the private IP address of the other computer when these computers need to communicate on the Internet.

native resolution The actual (and fixed) number of pixels built into an LCD monitor. For the clearest display, always set the resolution to the native resolution.

neighbors In TCP/IP Version 6, two or more nodes on the same link.

netbook A low-end, inexpensive laptop with a small 9 or 10 inch screen and no optical drive that is generally used for Web browsing, email, and word processing by users on the go.

network adapter Part of the physical network inside a computer. The network adapter has a 48-bit number hard-coded on the card by its manufacturer that is unique for that device and called the MAC address.

Network Attached Storage (NAS) A device that provides multiple bays for hard drives and an Ethernet port to connect to the network. The device is likely to support RAID.

network adapter *See* network interface card.

network interface card (NIC) An expansion card that plugs into a computer's motherboard and provides a port on the back of the card to connect a computer to a network. *Also called* a network adapter.

network multimeter A multifunctional tool that can test network connections, cables, ports, and network adapters.

network port A port used by a network cable to connect to the wired network.

network printer A printer that any user on the network can access, through its own network card and connection to the network, through a connection to a stand-alone print server, or through a connection to a computer as a local printer, which is shared on the network.

North Bridge That portion of the chipset hub that connects faster I/O buses (for example, the video bus) to the system bus. *Compare to* South Bridge.

notebook A portable computer that is designed for travel and mobility. Notebooks use the same technology as desktop PCs, with modifications for conserving voltage, taking up less space, and operating while on the move. *Also called* a laptop computer.

octet In TCP/IP Version 4, each of the four numbers in an IP address separated by periods and can be any number from 0 to 255, making a total of about 4.3 billion IP addresses.

ohm (Ω) The standard unit of measurement for electrical resistance. Resistors are rated in ohms.

OLED (Organic Light-emitting Diode) monitor A type of monitor that uses a thin LED layer or film between two grids of electrodes and does not use backlighting.

on-board ports Ports that are directly on the motherboard, such as a built-in keyboard port or on-board network port.

overclocking Running a processor at a higher frequency than is recommended by the manufacturer, which can result in an unstable system, but is a popular thing to do when a computer is used for gaming.

packet A segment of data sent over a network that contains the data and information at the beginning of the segment that identifies the type of data, where it came from, and where it's going.

PAN (personal area network) A small network consisting of personal devices at close range; the devices can include cell phones, PDAs, and notebook computers.

parallel ATA (PATA) An older IDE cabling method that uses a 40-pin flat or round data cable or an 80-conductor cable and a 40-pin IDE connector. *See also* serial ATA.

parallel port An outdated female 25-pin port on a computer that transmitted data in parallel, 8 bits at a time, and was usually used with a printer. The names for parallel ports are LPT1 and LPT2. Parallel ports have been replaced by USB ports.

parity An error-checking scheme in which a ninth, or "parity," bit is added. The value of the parity bit is set to either 0 or 1 to provide an even number of ones for even parity and an odd number of ones for odd parity.

parity error An error that occurs when the number of 1s in the byte is not in agreement with the expected number.

patch cable *See* straight-through cable.

patch panel A device that provides multiple network ports for cables that converge in one location such as an electrical closet or server room.

PC Card A card that uses a PC Card slot on a notebook and provides a port for peripheral devices or adds memory to the notebook. A PC Card is about the size of a credit card, but thicker.

PCI (Peripheral Component Interconnect) A bus common to desktop computers that uses a 32-bit wide or a 64-bit data path. Several variations of PCI exist. One or more notches on a PCI slot keep the wrong PCI cards from being inserted in the PCI slot.

PCI Express (PCIe) The latest evolution of PCI, which is not backward-compatible with earlier PCI slots and cards. PCIe slots come in several sizes, including PCIe x1, PCIe x4, PCIe x8, and PCIe x16.

PCL (Printer Control Language) A printer language developed by Hewlett-Packard that communicates to a printer how to print a page.

PCMCIA card Includes one or more variations of a PC Card to add memory to a notebook or provide ports for peripheral devices. For example, modem cards, network cards for wired or wireless network, sound cards, SCSI host adapters, FireWire controllers, USB controllers, flash memory adapter, TV tuner, and hard disks.

physical address *See* MAC (Media Access Control) address.

pickup roller A part in a printer that pushes forward a sheet of paper from the paper tray.

pin grid array (PGA) A socket that has holes aligned in uniform rows around the socket to receive the pins on the bottom of the processor.

PIO (Programmed Input/Output) transfer mode A transfer mode that uses the CPU to transfer data from the hard drive to memory. PIO mode is slower than DMA mode.

pixel A small spot on a fine horizontal scan line. Pixels are illuminated to create an image on the monitor.

plasma monitor A type of monitor that provides high contrast with better color than LCD monitors. They work by discharging xenon and neon plasma on flat glass, and don't contain mercury.

pointing stick *See* TrackPoint.

POP3 (Post Office Protocol, version 3) A protocol used by a recipient's email server to deliver messages. Using POP, email is downloaded to the client computer. *Compare to* IMAP4.

port (1) As applied to services running on a computer, a number assigned to a process on a computer so that the process can be found by TCP/IP. *Also called* a port address or port number. (2) A physical connector, usually at the back of a computer, that allows a cable from a peripheral device, such as a printer, mouse, or modem, to be attached.

port address *See* port.

port filtering To open or close certain ports so they can or cannot be used. A firewall uses port filtering to protect a network from unwanted communication.

port forwarding A technique that allows a computer on the Internet to reach a computer on a private network using a certain port when the private network is protected by a firewall device using NAT. When the firewall receives a request for communication from the Internet to a specific computer and port, the request will be allowed and forwarded to that computer on the network. *Also called* tunneling.

port number *See* port.

port replicator A device designed to connect to a notebook computer in order to make it easy to connect the notebook to peripheral devices such as a full-sized monitor, keyboard, and AC power adapter.

port triggering When a firewall opens a port because a computer behind the firewall initiates communication on another port.

POST (power-on self test) A self-diagnostic program used to perform a simple test of the CPU, RAM, and various I/O devices. The POST is performed by startup BIOS when the computer is first turned on, and is stored in ROM-BIOS.

POST card A test card installed in a slot on the motherboard that is used to help discover and report computer errors and conflicts that occur when a computer is first turned on and before the operating system is launched.

POST diagnostic card *See* POST card.

PostScript A printer language developed by Adobe Systems that tells a printer how to print a page.

Power over Ethernet (PoE) A feature that might be available on high-end wired network adapters that allows power to be transmitted over Ethernet cable to remote devices.

power supply A box inside the computer case that receives power and converts it to provide power to the motherboard and other installed devices. Power supplies provide 3.3, 5, and 12 volts DC. *Also called* a power supply unit (PSU).

power supply tester A device that can test the output of each power cord coming from a power supply.

power supply unit (PSU) *See* power supply.

Print Management A utility located in the Administrative Tool group in Windows 7/ Vista professional and business editions that allow you to monitor and manage printer queues for all printers on the network.

Printers window A window used in Windows Vista to manage and uninstall printers.

Printers and Faxes window A window used in XP to manage and uninstall printers.

print head The part in an inkjet or impact printer that moves across the paper, creating one line of the image with each pass.

print server Hardware or software that manages the print jobs sent to one or more printers on a network.

print spooler A queue for print jobs.

printer maintenance kit A kit purchased from a printer manufacturer that contains the parts, tools, and instructions needed to perform routine printer maintenance.

printer self-test page A test page that prints by using controls at the printer. The page allows you to eliminate a printer as a problem and usually prints test, graphics, and information about the printer such as the printer resolution and how much memory is installed.

printui The Printer User Interface command used by administrators to manage printers on the local and remote computers.

private IP addresses In TCP/IP Version 4, IP addresses that are not allowed on the Internet used by a company conserving its public IP address. Within the company network, computers communicate with one another using private IP addresses.

processor *See* central processing unit (CPU).

processor frequency The frequency at which the CPU operates. Usually expressed in GHz.

projector Used to shine a light that projects a transparent image onto a large screen and is often used in classrooms or with other large groups.

protocol A set of rules and standards that two entities use for communication.

PS/2 port A round 6-pin port used by a keyboard or mouse.

public IP addresses In TCP/IP Version 4, IP addresses available to the Internet.

punchdown tool A tool used to punch individual wires from a network cable into their slots to terminate the cable.

quad channels Technology used by a motherboard and DIMMs that allows the memory controller to access four DIMMS at the same time.

Quality of Service (QoS) A feature used by Windows and network hardware devices to improve network performance for an application that is not getting the best network performance.

QuickPath Interconnect The technology used first by the Intel X58 chipset for communication between the chipset and the processor using 16 serial lanes similar to that used by PCI Express. Replaced the 64-bit wide Front Side Bus used by previous chipsets.

radio frequency (RF) A rate or range of rates of oscillation used for wireless communication. For example, Wi-Fi 802.11n can use either 5.0 GHz or 2.4 GHz radio frequency (RF).

RAID (redundant array of inexpensive disks or redundant array of independent disks) Several methods of configuring multiple hard drives to store data to increase logical volume size and improve performance, or to ensure that if one hard drive fails, the data is still available from another hard drive.

RAID 0 Using space from two or more physical disks to increase the disk space available for a single volume. Performance improves because data is written evenly across all disks. Windows calls RAID 0 a striped volume.

RAID 1 A type of drive imaging that duplicates data on one drive to another drive and is used for fault tolerance. Windows calls RAID 1 a mirrored volume.

RAID 1+0 *See* RAID 10.

RAID 10 A combination of RAID 1 and RAID 0 that requires at least four disks to work as an array of drives and provides the best redundancy and performance.

RAID 5 A technique that stripes data across three or more drives and uses parity checking, so that if one drive fails, the other drives can re-create the data stored on the failed drive. RAID 5 drives increase performance and provide fault tolerance. Windows calls these drives RAID-5 volumes.

RAID-5 volume *See* RAID 5.

RAM (random access memory) Memory modules on the motherboard containing microchips used to temporarily hold data and programs while the CPU processes both. Information in RAM is lost when the PC is turned off.

Rambus *See* Direct Rambus DRAM.

RAS Latency A method of measuring access timing to memory, which is the number of clock cycles required to write or read a row of data off a memory module. RAS stands for Row Access Strobe. *Compare to* CAS Latency.

raster line A row in the bitmap that represents a page that has been rendered and is ready for printing.

raw data Data sent to a printer without any formatting or processing.

RDRAM *See* Direct Rambus DRAM.

read/write head A sealed, magnetic coil device that moves across the surface of a disk in a hard disk drive (HDD) either reading data from or writing data to the disk.

ReadyDrive The Windows 7/Vista technology that supports a hybrid hard drive.

rectifier An electrical device that converts AC to DC. A computer power supply contains a rectifier.

refresh rate As applied to monitors, the number of times in one second the monitor can fill the screen with lines from top to bottom. *Also called* vertical scan rate.

Remote Desktop Protocol (RDP) The protocol used by Windows Remote Desktop and Remote Assistance utilities to connect to and control a remote computer.

resolution The number of pixels on a monitor screen that are addressable by software (example: 1024 × 768 pixels).

REt (Resolution Enhancement technology) The term used by Hewlett-Packard to describe the way a laser printer varies the size of the dots used to create an image. This technology partly accounts for the sharp, clear image created by a laser printer.

RG-59 coaxial cable An older and thinner coaxial cable once used for cable TV.

RG-6 coaxial cable A coaxial cable used for cable TV and replaced the older and thinner RG-59 coaxial cable.

RGB port *See* composite video port.

RIMM A type of memory module developed by Rambus, Inc.

ring network A type of network where nodes form a ring.

riser card A card that plugs into a motherboard and allows for expansion cards to be mounted parallel to the motherboard. Expansion cards are plugged into slots on the riser card.

RJ-11 *See* RJ-11 jack.

RJ-11 jack A phone line connection or port found on modems, telephones, and house phone outlets.

RJ-45 A port that looks like a large phone jack and is used by twisted-pair cable to connect to a wired network adapter or other hardware device. RJ stands for registered jack.

router A device that manages traffic between two or more networks and can help find the best path for traffic to get from one network to another.

S1 state On the BIOS power screen, one of the five S states used by ACPI power saving mode to indicate different levels of power-savings functions. In the S1 state, the hard drive and monitor are turned off and everything else runs normally.

S2 state On the BIOS power screen, one of the five S states used by ACPI power saving mode to indicate different levels of power-savings functions. In S2 state, the hard drive and monitor are turned off and everything else runs normally. In addition, the processor is also turned off.

S3 state On the BIOS power screen, one of the five S states used by ACPI power-saving mode to indicate different levels of power-savings functions. In S3 state, everything is shut down except RAM and enough of the system to respond to a wake-up. S3 is sleep mode.

S4 state On the BIOS power screen, one of the five S states used by ACPI power-saving mode to indicate different levels of power-savings functions. In S4 state, everything in RAM is copied to a file on the hard drive and the system is shut down. When the system is turned on, the file is used to restore the system to its state before shut down. S4 is hibernation.

S5 state On the BIOS power screen, one of the five S states used by ACPI power-saving mode to indicate different levels of power-savings functions. S5 state is the power off state after a normal shutdown.

SDRAM II *See* Double Data Rate SDRAM.

Secure Digital (SD) card A type of memory card used in digital cameras, tablets, cell phones, MP3 players, digital camcorders, and other portable devices. The three standards used by SD cards are 1.x (regular SD), 2.x (SD High Capacity or SDHC), and 3.x (SD eXtended Capacity or SDXC).

separation pad A printer part that keeps more than one sheet of paper from moving forward.

Services console A console used by Windows to stop, start, and manage background services used by Windows and applications.

S.M.A.R.T. (Self-Monitoring Analysis and Reporting Technology) A system BIOS and hard drive feature that monitors hard drive performance, disk spin up time, temperature, distance between the head and the disk, and other mechanical activities of the drive in order to predict when the drive is likely to fail.

sags *See* brownouts.

SATA power connector A 15-pin flat power connector that provides power to SATA drives.

SC (subscriber connector or standard connector) connector A type of connector used by fiber-optic cables and can be used with either single-mode or multimode fiber-optic cables.

SCSI (Small Computer System Interface) A fast interface between a host adapter and the CPU that can daisy chain as many as 7 or 15 devices on a single bus.

SCSI host adapter card A card that manages the SCSI bus and serves as the gateway to the system bus. *Also called* the host adapter.

SCSI ID A number from 0 to 15 assigned to each SCSI device attached to the daisy chain.

Secure FTP (SFTP) A file transfer protocol used to transfer files between an FTP server and client using encryption.

Secure Shell (SSH) A secure protocol that is used to pass encrypted login information to a remote computer and control that computer over a network.

self-grounding A method to safeguard against ESD that involves touching the computer case or power supply before touching a component in the computer case.

sequential access A method of data access used by tape drives, whereby data is written or read sequentially from the beginning to the end of the tape or until the desired data is found.

serial ATA (SATA) An ATAPI interface standard that uses a narrower and more reliable cable than the 80-conductor cable and is easier to configure than PATA systems. *See also* parallel ATA.

serial port A male 9-pin or 25-pin port on a computer system used by slower I/O devices such as a mouse or modem. Data travels serially, one bit at a time, through the port. Serial ports are sometimes configured as COM1, COM2, COM3, or COM4.

Server Message Block (SMB) The protocol used by Windows to share files and printers on a network.

Service Set Identifier (SSID) The name of a wireless network.

sheet battery A secondary battery that fits on the bottom of a notebook to provide additional battery charge time.

shielded twisted pair (STP) cable A cable that is made of one or more twisted pairs of wires and is surrounded by a metal shield.

SIM (Subscriber Identity Module) card A small flash memory card that contains all the information a device needs to connect to a cellular network, including a password and other authentication information needed to access the network, encryption standards used, and the services that a subscription includes.

SIMM (single inline memory module) An outdated miniature circuit board used to hold RAM. SIMMs held 8, 16, 32, or 64 MB on a single module. SIMMs have been replaced by DIMMs.

Simple Network Management Protocol (SNMP) A protocol used to monitor network traffic.

single channel The memory controller on a motherboard that can access only one DIMM at a time. *Compare to* dual channel and triple channel.

single-sided A DIMM that has memory chips installed on one side of the module.

site license A license that allows a company to install multiple copies of software, or to allow multiple employees to execute the software from a file server.

sleep mode A power-saving state for a computer used to save power when not using the computer. *Also see* S3 state.

sleep timers The number of minutes of inactivity before a computer goes into a power-saving state such as sleep mode.

SMTP (Simple Mail Transfer Protocol) A protocol used to send an email message to its destination.

SMTP AUTH (SMTP Authentication) An improved version of SMTP and used to authenticate a user to an email server when the email client first tries to connect to the email server to send email.

SO-DIMM (small outline DIMM) A type of memory module used in notebook computers that uses DIMM technology. A DDR3 SO-DIMM has 204 pins. A DDR2 or DDR SO-DIMM has 200 pins. Older, outdated SO-DIMMs can have 72 pins or 144 pins.

software piracy The act of making unauthorized copies of original software, which violates the Federal Copyright Act of 1976.

solid state device (SSD) An electronic device with no moving parts. A storage device that uses memory chips to store data instead of spinning disks (such as those used by magnetic hard drives and CD drives). Examples of solid state devices are jump drives (*also called* key drives or thumb drives), flash memory cards, and solid state disks used as hard drives in notebook computers designed for the most rugged uses. *Also called* solid state disk (SSD) or solid state drive (SSD).

solid state drive (SSD) A hard drive that has no moving parts. *Also see* solid state device (SSD).

South Bridge That portion of the chipset hub that connects slower I/O buses (for example, a PCI bus) to the system bus. *Compare to* North Bridge.

spacers *See* standoffs.

spanning Using a spanned volume to increase the size of a volume.

S/PDIF (Sony-Phillips Digital Interface) sound port A port that connects to an external home theater audio system, providing digital audio output and the nest signal quality.

spooling Placing print jobs in a print queue so that an application can be released from the printing process before printing is completed. Spooling is an acronym for simultaneous peripheral operations online.

staggered pin grid array (SPGA) A feature of a CPU socket whereby the pins are staggered over the socket in order to squeeze more pins into a small space.

Standard Parallel Port (SPP) An outdated parallel port that allows data to flow in only one direction and is the slowest of the three types of parallel ports. *Also called* a Centronics port. *Compare to* EPP (Enhanced Parallel Port) and ECP (Extended Capabilities Port).

standby mode In Windows XP, standby mode is similar to Windows 7/Vista sleep mode where work is saved to memory and a trickle of power preserves that memory.

standoffs Round plastic or metal pegs that separate the motherboard from the case, so that components on the back of the motherboard do not touch the case.

startup BIOS Part of system BIOS that is responsible for controlling the computer when it is first turned on. Startup BIOS gives control over to the OS once it is loaded.

static IP address An IP address that is permanently assigned to a computer or device.

static RAM (SRAM) RAM chips that retain information without the need for refreshing, as long as the computer's power is on. They are more expensive than traditional DRAM.

ST (straight tip) connector A type of connector used by fiber-optic cables and can be used with either single-mode or multimode fiber-optic cables.

star network A network configuration that uses a centralized device such as a switch or hub to manage traffic on the network.

straight-through cable A cable used to connect a computer to a switch or other network device. *Also called* a patch cable.

striped volume A type of dynamic volume used for two or more hard drives that writes to the disks evenly rather than filling up allotted space on one and then moving on to the next. *Compare to* spanned volume.

stylus A device that is included with a graphics tablet that works like a pencil on the tablet.

subnet The small group of local networks when several networks are tied together in a subsystem of the larger intranet. In TCP/IP Version 6, one or more links that have the same 64 bits in the first part of the IP address (called the prefix).

subnet ID In TCP/IP Version 6, the last block (16 bits) in the 64-bit prefix of an IP address. The subnet is identified using some or all of these 16 bits.

subnet mask Used with IPv4 and identifies which part of an IP address is the network portion and which part is the host portion.

suspend mode *See* sleep mode.

S-Video port A 4-pin or 7-pin round video port that sends two signals over the cable, one for color and the other for brightness, and is used by some high-end TVs and video equipment.

switch A device used to connect nodes on a network in a star network topology. It also segments the network to improve network performance by deciding which network segment is to receive a packet, on the basis of the packet's destination MAC address.

system board *See* motherboard.

system bus The bus between the CPU and memory on the motherboard. The bus frequency in documentation is called the system speed, such as 400 MHz. *Also called* the memory bus, front-side bus, local bus, or host bus.

system clock A line on a bus that is dedicated to timing the activities of components connected to it. The system clock provides a continuous pulse that other devices use to time themselves.

T568A Standards for wiring twisted-pair network cabling and RJ-45 connectors and have the green pair connected to pins 1 and 2 and the orange pair connected to pins 3 and 6.

T568B Standards for wiring twisted-pair network cabling and RJ-45 connectors and have the orange pair using pins 1 and 2 and the green pair connected to pins 3 and 6.

TCP (Transmission Control Protocol) The protocol in the TCP/IP suite of protocols that works at the OSI Transport layer and guarantees packet delivery.

TCP/IP (Transmission Control Protocol/Internet Protocol) The group or suite of protocols used for almost all networks, including the Internet.

technical documentation The technical reference manuals, included with software packages and hardware, that provide directions for installation, usage, and troubleshooting. The information extends beyond that given in user manuals.

Telnet A TCP/IP protocol used by the Telnet client/server applications to allow an administrator or other user to control a computer remotely.

Teredo In TCP/IP Version 6, a tunneling protocol named after the Teredo worm that bores holes in wood. IPv6 addresses intended to be used by this protocol always begin with the same 32 bit-prefix. Teredo IP addresses begin with 2001, and the prefix is written as 2001::/32.

terminating resistor The resistor added at the end of a SCSI chain to dampen the voltage at the end of the chain.

thermal compound A creamlike substance that is placed between the bottom of the cooler heatsink and the top of the processor to eliminate air pockets and to help to draw heat off the processor.

thermal paper Special coated paper used by thermal printers.

thermal printer A type of line printer that uses wax-based ink, which is heated by heat pins that melt the ink onto paper.

thermal transfer printer A type of thermal printer that uses a ribbon that contains wax-based ink. The heating element melts the ribbon onto special thermal paper so that it stays glued to the paper as the feeder assembly moves the paper through the printer.

thick client A regular desktop computer or laptop that is sometimes used as a client by a virtualization server.

thin client A computer that has an operating system, but has little computer power and might only need to support a browser used to communicate with a virtualization server.

thread Each process that the CPU is aware of; a single task that is part of a longer task or program.

Thunderbolt A port that transmits both video and data on the same port and cable. The port is shaped the same as the DisplayPort and is compatible with DisplayPort devices.

ticket An entry in a call-tracking system made by whoever receives a call for help and used to track and document actions taken. The ticket stays open until the issue is resolved.

TKIP (Temporal Key Integrity Protocol) See WPA (Wi-Fi Protected Access).

tone probe A two-part kit that is used to find cables in the walls of a building. *Also called* a toner probe.

toner probe *See* tone probe.

toner vacuum A vacuum cleaner designed to pick up toner used in laser printers and does not allow it to touch any conductive surface.

topology The physical arrangement of the connections between computers in a network.

touchpad A common pointing device on a notebook computer.

touch screen An input device that uses a monitor or LCD panel as a backdrop for user options. Touch screens can be embedded in a monitor or LCD panel or installed as an add-on device over the monitor screen.

tower case The largest type of personal computer case. Tower cases stand vertically and can be as high as two feet tall. They have more drive bays and are a good choice for computer users who anticipate making significant upgrades.

TPM (Trusted Platform Module) chip A chip on a motherboard that holds an encryption key required at startup to access encrypted data on the hard drive. Windows 7/Vista BitLocker Encryption can use the TPM chip.

traces A wire on a circuit board that connects two components or devices.

TrackPoint Similar to a touchpad, a unique and popular pointing device embedded in the keyboard of some IBM and Lenovo ThinkPad notebooks.

tractor feed A continuous feed within an impact printer that feeds fanfold paper through the printer rather than individual sheets, making them useful for logging ongoing events or data.

transfer belt A laser printer component that completes the transferring step in the printer.

transfer roller A soft, black roller in a laser printer that puts a positive charge on the paper. The charge pulls the toner from the drum onto the paper.

transformer An electrical device that changes the ratio of current to voltage. A computer power supply is basically a transformer and a rectifier.

trip hazard Loose cables or cords in a traffic area where people can trip over them.

triple channels When the memory controller accesses three DIMMs at the same time. DDR3 DIMMs support triple channeling.

TV tuner card An adapter card that receives a TV signal and displays TV on the computer screen.

twisted-pair cabling Cabling, such as a network cable, that uses pairs of wires twisted together to reduce crosstalk.

UDP (User Datagram Protocol) A connectionless protocol that works at the OSI Transport layer and is commonly used for broadcasting to multiple nodes on a network or the Internet.

unicast address In TCP/IP Version 6, an IP address where packets are delivered to a single node on a network.

Unified Extensible Firmware Interface (UEFI) An interface between firmware on the motherboard and the operating system and improves on legacy BIOS processes for booting, handing over the boot to the OS, and loading device drivers and applications before the OS loads.

uninterruptible power supply (UPS) A device that raises the voltage when it drops brownouts.

unique local address (ULA) *See* unique local unicast address.

unique local unicast address In TCP/IP Version 6, an address used to identify a specific site within a large organization. It can work on multiple links within the same organization. The address is a hybrid between a global unicast address that works on the Internet and a link-local unicast address that works on only one link.

UDF (Universal Disk Format) file system A file system for optical media used by all DVD discs and some CD-R and CD-RW discs.

unshielded twisted pair (UTP) cable The most popular cabling method for local networks and is the least expensive and is commonly used on LANs. The cable is made of twisted pairs of wires and is not surrounded by shielding.

USB 3.0 B-Male connector A USB connector used by SuperSpeed USB 3.0 devices such as printers or scanners.

USB 3.0 Micro-B connector A small USB connector used by SuperSpeed USB 3.0 devices. The connectors are not compatible with regular Micro-B connectors.

USB (Universal Serial Bus) port A type of port designed to make installation and configuration of I/O devices easy, providing room for as many as 127 devices daisy-chained together.

VGA (Video Graphics Adapter) port A 15-pin analog video port popular for many years.

VGA mode Standard VGA settings, which include a resolution of 640 × 480.

video capture card An adapter card that captures video input and saves it to a file on the hard drive.

video memory Memory used by the video controller. The memory might be contained on a video card or be part of system memory. When part of system memory, the memory is dedicated by Windows to video.

virtualization When one physical machine hosts multiple activities that are normally done on multiple machines.

virtualization server A computer that serves up virtual machines to multiple client computers and provides a virtual desktop for users on these client machines.

virtual machine (VM) One or more logical machines created within one physical machine.

VoIP (Voice over Internet Protocol) A TCP/IP protocol and an application that provides voice communication over a network. *Also called* Internet telephone.

VoIP phone A telephone that connects to a network and uses the VoIP TCP/IP protocol for voice communication over the network or the Internet.

volt A measure of potential difference in an electrical circuit. A computer ATX power supply usually provides five separate voltages: +12V, −12V, +5V, −5V, and +3.3V.

wait state A clock tick in which nothing happens, used to ensure that the microprocessor isn't getting ahead of slower components. A 0-wait state is preferable to a 1-wait state. Too many wait states can slow down a system.

WAN (wide area network) A network or group of networks that span a large geographical area.

watt The unit of electricity used to measure power. A typical computer may use a power supply that provides 500W.

WEP (Wired Equivalent Privacy) An encryption protocol used to secure transmissions on a Wi-Fi wireless network; however, it is no longer considered secure because the key used for encryption is static (it doesn't change).

Wi-Fi (Wireless Fidelity) The common name for standards for a local wireless network as defined by IEEE 802.11. *Also see* 802.11 a/b/g/n.

Wi-Fi Protected Setup (WPS) A method used to secure a wireless network from an outside attack and was designed to make it easier for users to connect their computers to a wireless network when a hard-to-remember SSID and security key are used.

wireless access point A wireless device that is used to create and manage a wireless network.

wireless LAN (WLAN) A type of LAN that does not use wires or cables to create connections but instead transmits data over radio or infrared waves.

wireless wide area network (WWAN) A network for a computer using mobile broadband; *also called* a cellular network.

wire stripper A tool used when terminating a cable. The tool cuts away the plastic jacket or coating around the wires in a cable so that a connector can be installed on the end of the cable.

WPA (Wi-Fi Protected Access) An encryption protocol used with Wi-Fi networks and is stronger than WEP because the encryption keys are constantly changing.

WPA2 (Wi-Fi Protected Access 2) An improved version of the WPA protocol and is considered the latest and best encryption standard for Wi-Fi.

x86 processor An older processor that first used the number 86 in the model number and processes 32 bits at a time.

x86-64 bit processor Hybrid processors that can process 32 bits or 64 bits.

xD-Picture Card A type of flash memory device that has a compact design and currently holds up to 8 GB of data.

XPS (XML Paper Specification) A standard introduced with Windows Vista and designed to ultimately replace GDI as the method Windows uses to render a printed page before sending it to the printer.

XPS Document Writer A Windows 7/Vista feature that creates a file with an .xps file extension. The file is similar to a .pdf file and can be viewed, edited, printed, faxed, emailed, or posted on Web sites.

zero insertion force (ZIF) socket A socket that uses a small lever to apply even force when you install the processor into the socket.

zero-fill utility A hard drive utility that fills every sector on the drive with zeroes.

INDEX

4G (Fourth Generation) cellular connections, 474
4-pin auxiliary connector, 12
4-pin motherboard auxiliary connector, 12
6-pin PCIe connectors, 16
6TO4 tunneling protocol, 413
8-pin auxiliary connector, 12
8-pin motherboard auxiliary connector, 12
10-foot user interface, 335
10-Gigabit Ethernet, 490, 497
20+4-pin P1 connector, 13
20-pin P1 connector, 12
24-pin P1 connector, 13
25-pin SCSI connector, 202
32-bit processor architecture, 138, 141
40-pin ribbon cable and connector, 20
50-pin SCSI connector, 202
64-bit processor architecture, 138
68-pin SCSI connector, 202
100BaseT Ethernet, 490, 497
1394 Trade Association, 246

A

Absolute.com, 117
A cable (50-pin SCSI connector), 202
AC adapter, 531, 573–574
AC (alternating current) and DC (direct current), 25
Accelerated Graphics Port (AGP) buses, 101–104
Accelerated Hub Architecture, in Intel chipset, 90
AC outlet ground tester, 34
ACPI (Advanced Configuration and Power Interface), 535
Acronyms list, 647–655
Action Center, 238–243
Actuator, on read/write head, 192
Adapter address, 403
Adapter cards, 260–267
    overview, 260–265
    sound cards and onboard sound, 265–266
    TV tuner and video capture cards, 266–267
Ad hoc mode, in wireless mesh network, 464–467
ADK Media Group, 332
Adobe Systems, 330, 332, 582
ADSL (Asymmetric DSL), 469
Advanced Configuration and Power Interface (ACPI), 535
Advanced Encryption Standard (AES), 455
Advanced Technology Attachment Packet Interface (ATAPI) standard, 195
Advanced Technology Extended (ATX) form factor, 10–16, 74, 82–83
AES (Advanced Encryption Standard), 455
AGP (Accelerated Graphics Port) buses, 101–104
Alfredo Comparetti, 115
All-in-one computer, 514, 567–571
Alternate IP addresses, 427
ALU (arithmetic logic units), 141
A Male connectors, 245
AMD (Advanced Micro Devices, Inc.)
    Athlon 64-bit processors, 141
    chassis air guide (CAG) recommendations, 362
    chipset, 90
    Hyper-Transport technology, 139
    mobile processor sockets, 557
    overview, 75
    processors
        installing in Socket AM2+, 159–162
        overview, 145–146

AMD (*continued*)
  Raedeon graphics, 334
  sockets for, 88–89
Amperes (amps), 24
ANSI (American National Standards Institute), 18, 194, 497
Antec, Inc., 76
Antistatic bags, 31, 35
Antistatic gloves, 32, 34
Antistatic grounding bracelet, 28, 30
Anycast addresses, 413
APIPA (Automatic Private IP Address), 411–412, 415, 427
A+ Certification Program (CompTIA), 304
A+ Guide to Software, Managing and Troubleshooting, 6th ed., 1
Apple Computers, 332
Application level, communication at, 405–406
Arithmetic logic units (ALUs), 141
Artifacts ("torn" screen images), 383–386
ASRock, 108
ASUS, 108, 147
Asymmetric DSL (ADSL), 469
ATAPI (Advanced Technology Attachment Packet Interface) standard, 195
Athlon processors (AMD), 145
ATI Technologies, 93
Atom processors (Intel), 142–143, 145
AT&T, Inc., 434
ATX (Advanced Technology Extended) form factor, 10–16, 74, 82–83
ATX12 power supply, 12
Audio and video editing workstation, 332–333
Audio ports, 4
Authoritative name server, 417
AutoCAD Design Suite (Autodesk), 330
Autodetection, 204
Automatic Private IP Address (APIPA), 411–412, 415, 427
Auto-switching, in AC adapters, 531
Avid.com, 332

B
Backing up data, 47
Ball grid array (BGA) connection, 87
Bandwidth, 96, 467
Barcode readers, 252–253
Base station, in cellular WAN, 473
Batteries, notebook, 531, 573–574

Bench technicians, 31, 303
Berg power connector, 21
Best-effort protocols, 419
Biometric devices, 253
BIOS (basic input/output system) setup for configuring motherboards, 110–121
  accessing, 111–112
  boot sequence changing, 112–113
  drive encryption and password protection, 118
  exiting, 121–122
  hard drive and optical drive, 113–114
  intrusion detection, 115–116
  LoJack technology, 117
  onboard device configuration, 113
  power-on passwords, 116–117
  processor and clock speeds, 114
  temperature, fan, and voltage monitoring, 115
  TPM chip, 118–120
  virtualization, 120–121
  flashing, 124–125
  overheating checked in, 155
  overview, 35–36
BIOSTAR Group, 108
BitLocker Encryption, 118, 522
Bitmap, 582
Blue screen of death (BSOD), 349
Bluetooth connections, 248, 572
Blu-ray Disc (BD), 284
B Male connectors, 245
Boot sequence, 112–113, 364–366
Boxed processor, 143–144
Bridges, wireless, 484–485
Broadband technology, 469, 474–475
Brownouts, 391
BSOD (blue screen of death), 349
BTX form factor, 83
Bubble-jet print head, in inkjet printers, 586
Buffer, in hard drive selection, 205
Buffered DIMMs, 170–171
Bus/core ratio, 114
Buses, 141, 465
Buses and expansion slots, on motherboards, 94–104
  AGP buses, 101–104
  conventional PCI, 97–98
  overview, 94–97
  PCI Express, 99–101
  PCI riser cards, 101
  PCI-X, 98–99

C

Cable Internet connection, 470–471
Cables
   connection diagram for, 52
   drive, 18–23
   as trip hazards, 40
Cable tester, 492–493, 506
Cable ties, 34
Cache, 139–142, 205
CAD/CAM workstation, 330–331
Calibration, of inkjet printers, 610
Call tracking, 305
Camcorders, 254–255
CAN (campus area network), 464
Capacitors, 28, 46, 373
CardBus slots, 527
Case cover, 48
Case fans, 69–71
Case form factor, 337
CAS (column access strobe) latency, 171
CAT-3 (Category 3) cable, 487
CAT-5 (Category 5) cable, 487
CAT-5e (enhanced CAT 5) cable, 487
CAT-6 (Category 6) cable, 487
CAT-6a (Category 6a) cable, 487
CD (compact disc) drives, 2, 58, 284
CDFS (Compact Disc File System), 284
CDMA (Code Division Multiple Access), 474
CD-ROM jukebox, 202
CDs, recovery, 520–522
Celeron processors (Intel), 142–143
Cell phones, tethering, 434, 436
Cellular network, 434–438
Cellular WAN connection, 473–476
Central processing unit (CPU), 6
Centrino processor technology (Intel), 145
Centronics Port, 599
Certification, 303–305
Chain of custody documentation, 329
Channels, 453
Chassis, computer, 1–5
Chip extractor, 35
Chipset, 89–94, 96, 138
Cisco Systems, Inc., 443
CiTRIX, 305, 333
Class A IP addresses, 407–408
Class B IP addresses, 408
Class C IP addresses, 408
Class D IP addresses, 408
Class E IP addresses, 408
Classful subnet mask, 410

Classless subnet mask, 410
Cleaning pads and solutions, 34, 39–40
Cleaning printers, 610–612
Clear Type screen text, 382
Client/server model, 402
Clock speed, 114, 138
CL rating, 172
CMOS (complementary metal-oxide
      semiconductor) battery, 125–126
CMOS (complementary metal-oxide
      semiconductor) RAM, 35, 106
CMOS (complementary metal-oxide
      semiconductor) setup, 36, 106
Coaxial cable, 488
Code Division Multiple Access (CDMA), 474
Colors, print, 636–637
Comcast.com, 467
CompactFlash (CF) cards, 292
Component video ports, 275
Composite video ports, 274
Compressed air, 34
CompTIA (Computing Technology Industry
      Association), 304
Computers
   all-in-one, 567–571
   character-based name of, 415
   disposal of, 393–395
   gaming, 71, 75, 93, 334
   physical protection of, 388–392
   tethering cellphone to, 434, 436, 475
Computer parts and tools
   chassis, 1–5
   drive cables and connectors, 18–23
   drives, 8
   electrical dangers, 23–33
      AC and DC, 25
      electrical measures and properties, 24–25
      hot, neutral, and ground, 26–27
      protection against, 28–29
      static electricity, 29–33
   expansion cards, 6–7
   form factors, 9–18
      ATX, 10–16
      MicroATX, 16–18
   memory modules, 7
   motherboard, processor, and cooler, 6
   power supply, 8–9
   repair tools, 33–41
      cleaning pads and solutions, 39–40
      lifting heavy objects, 40–41
      loopback plugs, 37–38

Computer parts and tools (*continued*)
    multimeter, 37
    POST diagnostic cards, 35–37
    power supply tester, 37
Computers, working inside, 45–80
    case fans and other fans and heat sinks, 69–71
    dust, 72–73
    expansion card removal, 52–54
    liquid cooling systems, 71
    motherboard, power supply, and drive removal, 55–59
    opening and examining, 46–52
    planning and organizing, 46
    power supply selection, 73–77
    processor coolers, fans, and heat sinks, 67–69
    reassembling, 60–67
Computrace Agent software (Absolute.com), 117
Configuring motherboards, 106–122
    jumpers for, 108–110
    overview, 106–108
    setup BIOS for, 110–121
        accessing, 111–112
        boot sequence changing, 112–113
        drive encryption and password protection, 118
        exiting, 121–122
        hard drive and optical drive, 113–114
        intrusion detection, 115–116
        LoJack technology, 117
        onboard device configuration, 113
        power-on passwords, 116–117
        processor and clock speeds, 114
        temperature, fan, and voltage monitoring, 115
        TPM chip, 118–120
        virtualization, 120–121
Connectionless protocols, 419
Connection-oriented protocols, 418
Connectivity problems in network printers, 626–628
Connectors
    drive, 18–23
    front panel, 55
    on-board, 104–106
    in power supplies, 74
Continuity RIMM (C-RIMM), 171–172
Contrast ratio, of monitors, 271
Conventional PCI expansion slots, 97–98
Cooler Master, Inc., 76
Cooling
    boxed processor for, 143–144
    case fans and other fans and heat sinks, 69–71
    installing, 151, 160
    liquid, 71, 334
    overview, 6
    processor, 57, 67–69
Copyright, 328
Core Max Multiplier, 114
Core processors (Intel), 142–143
Corrosion, fingerprints and, 46
Coworkers, working with, 323–328
Creative.com, 265
C-RIMM (Continuity RIMM), 171–172
Crimpers, 495
Crossfire (AMD), 75
Crossover cable, 496
Crosstalk, 482
CRT (cathode-ray tube) monitors
    discharging, 28, 32
    overview, 268
    troubleshooting, 386
Crucial Technology, 175, 180–181, 205
Cultural differences, sensitivity to, 308
Cursor, ghost, 576
Customers, satisfying needs of, 301–344
    coworkers, working with, 323–328
    customizing systems for, 329–339
        audio and video editing workstation, 332–333
        gaming PC, 334
        graphics or CAD/CAM workstation, 330–331
        home server PC, 337–338
        home theater PC, 335–337
        thick client and thin client, 338–339
        virtualization workstation, 333–334
    difficult, 318–321
    escalating problems, 322
    expectations of, 314
    initial contact with, 311–312
    interviewing, 312–313
    job completion and, 321
    job responsibilities, 302–306
    paperwork, 322–323
    prohibited content and activity, 328–329
    technical knowledge and beyond, 306–310
    working on phone, 316–317
    working on site, 315–316
CuteFTP (GlobalSCAPE), 420

D

Data bus, 94
Data cartridges, 228
Data path size, 95
Data throughput, 467
DB-15 port, 3, 273
DB-9 port, 4
DC (direct current) and AC (alternating current), 25
DDR SDRAM (Double Data Rate SDRAM), 165
Dead pixels, 383
Default gateway, 426
Default printer, 591
Degausser, 386, 393
Dell, Inc., 37, 76, 517
Depot technicians, 31
Desktop case, 2
Device drivers, 122
Device Manager, 238–243, 371–372, 423
Devices and Printers window, in Windows 7, 593
Device support, 237–300
   Action Center and Device Manager, 238–243
   adapter cards, 260–267
      overview, 260–265
      sound cards and onboard sound, 265–266
      TV tuner and video capture cards, 266–267
   peripheral device installation, 250–260
      barcode readers, 252–253
      biometric devices, 253
      digital cameras and camcorders, 254–255
      graphics tablets, 256–257
      KVM switches, 259–260
      MIDI devices, 257–258
      mouse or keyboard, 251–252
      overview, 250–251
      touch screens, 258–259
      webcams, 255–256
   ports and wireless connections, 244–250
      Firewire, 246–248
      infrared, 248–249
      USB, 245–246
   storage devices, 282
      file systems of, 282–283
      optical drive and disc standards, 284–287
      optical drive installation, 288–289
      solid state, 290–293
   video subsystem, 268–282
      monitor, 268–272
      monitor settings, 277–279
      video cards and connectors, 272–277
      video memory, 280–282
DHCP (dynamic host configuration protocol), 406
DHCP client, 406
Diagnostic testing converters, 351–352
Diagnostic tools, 519–520
Dial-up connections, 438–441, 482
Digital cameras, 254–255
Digital Subscriber Line (DSL), 470–471
Digital video interface (DVI) ports, 3, 273–274
Digitizing tablet, 256
DIMM (dual inline memory module)
   buffered and registered, 170–171
   installing, 176–179, 182–183
   on motherboard, 163
   overview, 7–8, 165–171
   single-sided and double-sided, 168
   speeds of, 167–168
Dimming screens, 383
Direct memory access (DMA) transfer mode, 197
Direct Rambus DRAM (RDRAM), 171
Direct thermal printers, 589
DirectX software development tool, 280
Disk Management utility, in Windows, 212, 222
Display, notebook, 574–575. *See also* Video
DisplayPort, 3, 276
Disposal of equipment, 393–395
DMZ (demilitarized zone), 448–452
DNS (Domain Name System), 416
DNS client, 417
DNS server addresses, 426
Docking stations, 536–538
Documentation
   Asus motherboards, 147
   Bluetooth, 572
   chain of custody, 329
   hardware and software product, 305
   motherboard, 107–108, 175
   online, 608
   preventive maintenance, 392–393
   serial ATA drive installation, 207–208
   service, 322
   warranty, 516
Domain name, 416
Domain Name System (DNS), 416
Dot matrix printers, 588
Double Data Rate SDRAM (DDR SDRAM), 165

Double-sided printers, 586
DRAM (dynamic RAM), 140
Drivers, 122–124, 608
Driver Store, 371–372
Drives. *See also* Hard drives
   cables and connectors, 18–23
   CD, 2, 58, 284
   DVD, 2
   encryption of, 118
   overview, 8
   removing, 55–59
   viewing hard and optical, 113–114
DSL Internet connection, 470–471
Dual channel DIMMs, 165–166, 172
Dual monitors, 269, 278–279
Dual processors, 139
Dual ranked DIMMs, 168
Dual-voltage selector switch, 8
Dumb terminal, 339
Duplex printers, 586–587
Dust removal, 72–73
DVD drives, 2
DVDs (digital versatile disc), 284
DVI (digital video interface) ports, 3, 273–274
dxdiag.exe command, 280
Dynamic contrast ratio, of monitors, 271
Dynamic host configuration protocol (DCHP), 406
Dynamic IP addresses, 406
Dynamic RAM (DRAM), 140

E

Earthlink.net, 467
ECC (error-correcting code), 169
ECP (Extended Capabilities Port), 599
EEPROM (Electronically Erasable Programmable Read-Only Memory), 190
EIA (Electronic Industries Alliance), 497
EIDE (Enhanced IDE) drives, 195–198
Electrical dangers, 23–33
   AC and DC, 25
   electrical measures and properties, 24–25
   hot, neutral, and ground, 26–27
   protection against, 28–29
   static electricity, 29–33
Electrical system, 352–363
   intermittent problems, 355–356
   motherboard problems, 356
   notebook, 531–533
   overheating problems, 357–363
   overview, 352–355
Electronic Industries Alliance (EIA), 497
Electrostatic discharge (ESD), 29, 87
Elston Systems, Inc., 36
Embedded broadband modems, 474–475
Embedded firmware print servers, 620
Embedded mobile broadband modem, 434–436
Employment. *See* Customers, satisfying needs of
Energy Saver monitor, 382
Enhanced ATX boards, 14
Enhanced CAT-5 (CAT 5e) cable, 487
Enhanced IDE (EIDE) standards, 21–22
ENLight Corporation, 76
EPP (Enhanced Parallel Port), 599
Equipment disposal, 393–395
Error-correcting code (ECC), 169, 172
Error messages
   boot, 364–366
   troubleshooting, 349–351
eSATA (external SATA) ports, 104, 200
Escalating problems, 322
ESD gloves, 32
ESD mat, 31
ESD strap, 30
Ethernet
   cables and connectors for, 486–491
   hub for, 483
   port, 3, 423
   power over, 480–481
   speeds of, 477–478, 490
Ethernet address, 403
Evga.com, 108
exFAT file system, 282
Expansion bus, 96
Expansion cards
   in notebooks, 554–557
   overview, 6–7
   removing, 52–54
   20-pin P1 connector to power, 12
Expansion slots. *See* Buses and expansion slots, on motherboards
Experts Exchange web site, 304
Expert system software, 305
Expresscard slots, 527–530
Extended Capabilities Port (ECP), 599
Extension magnet brush, for printers, 610
External hard drives, 194
External SATA (eSATA) ports, 4, 200
Extractor, 34

F

Facebook.com, 305
Fanfold paper, 588
Fans, cooling
   case, 69–71
     monitoring, 115
     in power supplies, 74
     processor, 67–69
Faraday cage, 31, 35
Fast Ethernet, 490
FAT file system, 282
FAT32 file system, 282
Fault tolerance, 220–221
Fax machines, 589
F connector, 488
Federal Copyright Act of 1976, 328
Fiber optics, 469, 472, 489
Fibre Channel, 194
Field replaceable units (FRUs), 28, 81, 137, 366
File systems of storage devices, 282–283
File transfer protocol (FTP), 420–421
Final Cut Pro (Apple Computers), 332
Fingerprints, corrosion from, 46
FiOS (Fiber Optic Service, Verizon, Inc.), 472, 476
Fire extinguishers, 29
Firewalls, 4, 442, 447
FireWire, 194
FireWire (IEEE 1394) ports, 104, 246–248
Firmware updates, for printers, 608, 620
Flashing BIOS, 124–125
Flashlights, 34
Flash memory, 190, 292
Flash ROM, 35
Flat-panel monitor, 268
Flip-chip land grid array (FCLGA) socket, 87
Flip-chip pin grid array (FCPGA) socket, 87
Floating gate transistor, 190
Floppy disk drive (FDD), 21–23, 228–232
Flowchart, for hardware troubleshooting, 348
Formatting devices, 282
Form factors, 9–18
   ATX, 10–16
   case, 337
   MicroATX, 16–18
   motherboard, 82–84
   of power supply, 74
FQDN (fully qualified domain name), 416–417
Frequency, processor, 141
Front panel connectors, 55
Front panel header, 53, 64–65
Front Side Bus (FSB), 90, 96, 114, 141
FRUs (field replaceable units), 28, 81, 137, 366
FTP (file transfer protocol), 420–421
Fujitsu notebooks, 520
Full duplex Ethernet speed, 478
Fully connected mesh topology, in networks, 464
Fully qualified domain name (FQDN), 416–417
Fuser assembly, in laser printers, 585
FX processors (AMD), 145–146

G

Gaming computers, 71, 75, 93, 334
Garbled characters, printing, 636
Gateway, 403, 426
GDI (Graphics Device Interface), 582
GeForce GTX graphics processor (NVIDIA), 333–334
Ghost cursor, 576
Gigabit Ethernet, 490, 497
Gigabyte Technology Co., Ltd., 108
Gigahertz (GHz), 96
GlobalSCAPE, 420
Global System for Mobile Communication (GSM), 473
Global unicast addresses, 413
GoToAssist software (CiTRIX), 305
GPU (Graphics processing unit), 140
Graphics Device Interface (GDI), 582
Graphics processors, 331
Graphics tablets, 256–257
Graphics workstation, 330–331
Green motherboard, 382
Ground bracelet, 30, 32, 34, 51
Grounding, in electricity, 26–28
Ground mats, 31–32, 34
Group Policy, 603
GSM (Global System for Mobile Communication), 473

H

Half duplex Ethernet speed, 478
Hard disk drive (HDD), 8, 113–114, 190
Hard drives, 189–236
   hardware RAID, 220–227
     implementing, 222–227
     types of, 221–222

Hard drives, (continued)
  interface standards for, 193–204
    overview, 193–195
    parallel ATA or EIDE, 195–198
    SCSI technology, 200–204
    serial ATA, 198–200
  notebook replacement, 544–546
  parallel ATA drive installation, 214–220
    configuring, 216–217
    jumper setting, 217–218
    mounting, 218–220
    overview, 214–216
  printer upgrades of, 617–619
  selecting, 204–205
  serial ATA drive installation, 205–214
    documentation, 207–208
    overview, 205–207
    process of, 208–212
    in removable bay, 212–213
    starting point for, 207
    in wide bay, 213–214
  tape and floppy drives, 228–232
  technologies in, 190–193
  troubleshooting, 376–380
Hardware address, 403
Hardware-assisted virtualization (HAV), 333
Hardware level, communication at, 403–404
Hardware profile, 537–538
Hardware RAID, 220–227
  implementing, 222–227
  troubleshooting, 377–378
  types of, 221–222
Hardware troubleshooting, 345–400
  approaches, 346–352
    diagnostic testing converters, 351–352
    error messages, 349–351
    flowchart, 348
  documenting preventative maintenance, 392–393
  electrical system, 352–363
    intermittent problems, 355–356
    motherboard problems, 356
    overheating problems, 357–363
    overview, 352–355
  equipment disposal, 393–395
  error messages during boot, 364–366
  hard drives, 376–380
  monitors and video, 380–387
    CRT monitors, 386
    no image, 380–382
    poor display, 382–386
    sleep mode settings, 382
    VGA mode resolution, 386–387
  motherboard, processor, and RAM, 366–376
    capacitor failure, 373
    Device Manager to delete Driver Store, 371–372
    installations, 373–376
    overview, 366–369
    Windows Memory Diagnostics tool, 369–371
  physical protection of computer, 388–392
  POST before video active, 363
HDMI (high-definition multimedia interface), 3, 276, 335
Headers, on motherboard, 53
Heat sinks, 6, 67–71
Heavy objects, lifting, 40–41
Help-desk technician, 303
Hertz (Hz), 96
Hewlett-Packard (HP) Corp., 517–518, 520, 582
Hibernation, for notebooks, 533, 536
Home server PC, 337–338
Home theater systems, 87, 335–337
Host adapter, SCSI, 200
Host Clock Frequency, 114
Host name, 415
Hosts file, 417
Hot lines, in electricity, 26–27
Hot-swapping, 199, 245, 529–530
HP (Hewlett-Packard) Corp., 517–518, 520, 582
HTPC cases, 337
HTTP (Hypertext Transfer Protocol), 419
HTTPS (HTTP secure), 419
Hub, Ethernet, 483
Hub architecture, in Intel chipset, 90
Hubs and switches, 482–484
Hybrid hard drives, 192
Hybrid networks, 465
Hyper-Threading, 139
Hyper-Transport, 139
Hypervisor, 333

I

IANA (Internet Assigned Numbers Authority), 406
IBM, Inc., 517
IDE (Integrated Drive Electronics) standard, 20, 106, 193

IDE-to-USB converter, 352
IEEE (Institute of Electrical and Electronics Engineers), 411–412, 599
IEEE 802.11 standard, 452
IEEE 802.16d and 802.16e standards, 472
IEEE 1284 specifications, 599
IEEE 1394 ports, 4, 104, 247
Imaging drum, in laser printers, 583
IMAP4 (Internet Message Access Protocol, version 4), 420
Impact printers, 588–589, 635
Impact tool, 495
Independent device timing, 198
Infrared ports and wireless connections, 248–249
Infrared wireless connections, 248–249
Ink cartridges, in inkjet printers, 586
Inkjet printers, 586–588, 635
Installations, troubleshooting, 373–376
Installing processors, 147–162
    Intel in Socket LGA775, 157–159
    Intel in Socket LGA1155, 147–156
    Intel in Socket LGA1366, 156–157
Institute of Electrical and Electronics Engineers (IEEE), 411–412, 599
Integrated Drive Electronics (IDE) standard, 193
Integrated Services Digital Network (ISDN), 468
Intel chipset, 89–93
Intel Corp., 16
    chassis air guide (CAG) recommendations, 362
    Hyper-Threading technology, 139
    mobile processor sockets, 557
    motherboard manufacturing, 108
    processors
        installing in Socket LGA775, 157–159
        installing in Socket LGA1155, 147–156
        installing in Socket LGA1366, 156–157
        overview, 82, 142–145
        64-bit, 141
        sockets for, 85–88
    quad channel DIMMs, 167
    in serial ATA International Organization (SATA-IO), 198
Intel VT, 120
Interface, in IPv standards, 412
Interface ID, in IPv standards, 412
Interface standards for hard drives, 193–204
    drive selection and, 205
    overview, 193–195
    parallel ATA or EIDE, 195–198
    SCSI technology, 200–204
    serial ATA, 198–200
Internal device replacement, in notebooks, 539–540
Internal memory caches, 141
Internet, printer support on, 608–610
Internet appliance, 485
Internet Assigned Numbers Authority (IANA), 406
Internet connection technology
    cable Internet *versus* DSL, 470–471
    cellular WAN connection, 473–476
    fiber-optic Internet connection, 472
    overview, 467–470
    satellite Internet connection, 472
    WiMAX connection, 472–473
Internet Message Access Protocol, version 4 (IMAP4), 420
Internet Service Provider (ISP), 467
Intranet, 404–405
Intrusion detection, 115–116
Inverters, 25, 531
I/O controller hub (ICH), 90
I/O shield, 105
IP addresses
    assignment of, 406–407
    description of, 402, 404–405
    IPv4, 406–412
    IPv6, 406, 412–414
IP headers, 402
ISATAP (Intra-Site Automatic Tunnel Addressing Protocol), 412–413
ISDN (Integrated Services Digital Network), 468
ISP (Internet Service Provider), 467
Itanium 64 bit processors, 141
Ivy Bridge chipsets, 93

J

JBOD (just a bunch of disks), 221
JEDEC standards organization, 164
Jobs. *See* Customers, satisfying needs of
Johari Window, 326
Joules, 24
Jumpers, 108–110, 217–218

K

Keyboard
   backlight for, 524
   installing, 251–252
   notebook, 551–553
Keyboard, Video, and Mouse (KVM) switch, 259–260
Keystone jack wiring, 503–504
Keystone RJ-45 jack, 495–496, 503–504
Keystroke shortcuts, Windows, 643–646
Kingston Technology, 175, 180–181, 205
KVM switches, 259–260

L

Labelflash technology, 287
LAN (local area networks), 403, 464, 479, 490
Land grid array (LGA) socket, 86–88
Languages, printer, 582
LAPTOP newsletter, 304
Laptops. *See* Notebooks
Laser printers, 583–586, 610, 634–635
Latency, 468, 472
LBA (logical block addressing), on drives, 192
LC (local connector) connectors, 489
LCD (liquid crystal display) monitor, 268
LCD panel replacement, in notebooks, 564–567
LDAP (Lightweight Directory Access Protocol), 420
LED (Light-Emitting Diode) technology, 269
Lenovo notebooks, 517, 520–521, 537
Level 1 cache, 139
Level 2 cache, 139
Level 3 cache, 139
License, software, 328
LightScribe technology, 287
Lightweight Directory Access Protocol (LDAP), 420
Line-of-sight connectivity, for satellite connections, 472
Line Printer Terminal (LPT) assignments, 600
LinkedIn.com, 305
Link-local unicast addresses, 413
Links, in IPv standards, 412
Liquid cooling, 71, 334
Lithium Ion technology, for notebooks, 531
Local area networks (LANs), 464, 479, 490
Local bus, 96
Local links, in IPv standards, 412
Local printers, 591

Logical block addressing (LBA), on drives, 192
Logical Unit Number (LUN), 202
LogMeIn Rescue (LogMeIn), 305
LoJack technology, 117
Loopback address, 408
Loopback plugs, 35, 37–38, 492, 505
Low-level formatting, on drives, 192
LPT (Line Printer Terminal) assignments, 600
LUN (Logical Unit Number), 202

M

MAC (Media Access Control) address, 402–403, 455, 478–479, 483
MagicGate slot, 515
Magnetic hard drive, 191–192
Main board, 6
Maintenance kits for printers, 612–617
MAN (metropolitan area network), 464
Maxtor BlackArmor (Seagate Corp.), 118, 205
Media Access Control (MAC) address, 402–403, 455, 478–479, 483
Media center appliance, 335
Media Composer (Avid), 332
Megahertz (MHz), 96
Memory, 162–184. *See also* Processors; RAM (random access memory)
   cache on processor, 139–142
   DIMM technologies, 165–171
   EEPROM (Electronically Erasable Programmable Read Only Memory), 190
   flash, 190
   low memory errors, 636
   memory modules, 7
   Nehalem chipsets with, 91
   notebook upgrade, 540–544
   overview, 162–165
   performance, 172–173
   printer upgrades of, 617–619
   RAM (random access memory), 7, 71
   RIMM technologies, 171–172
   ROM (read-only memory), 35
   troubleshooting, 376
   upgrading, 173–184
      module installation, 182–184
      modules currently installed, 175–176
      module selection and purchase, 180–182
      motherboard slots for, 176–180
      needed *versus* installed, 173–174
   video, 7, 280–282

Memory bank, 168
Mesh network, 464
Metropolitan area network (MAN), 464
Micro-A connectors, 246
MicroATX form factor, 16–18, 74, 82–83
Micro-B connectors, 246
MicroBTX form factor, 84
MicroDIMM memory modules, 163
Microprocessor, 6
Microsoft Corporation, 333, 407. *See also* Windows
Micro-Start International (MSI), 108
Microsystem Development, Inc., 36
MIDI devices, 257–258
MIMO (Multiple In, Multiple Out) technology, 443, 453
Mini-B connectors, 245
Minicartridges, 228
MiniDin-6 connector, 274
Mini-DIN port, 4
Mini-HDMI connectors, 276
Mini-ITX form factor, 83, 87
Mini PCI Express slots, 554–555
Mirrored volume (RAID 1), 221
Mobile broadband modem, 475
Modem ports, 5, 104
Molex connectors, 62
Molex power connector, 20
Monitors, 380–387
   CRT, 386
   no image on, 380–382
   overview, 268–272
   poor display on, 382–386
   settings, 277–279
   sleep mode settings, 382
   VGA mode resolution, 386–387
Motherboards, 6, 81–136
   BIOS (basic input/output system) programs on, 35
   buses and expansion slots, 94–104
      AGP buses, 101–104
      conventional PCI, 97–98
      overview, 94–97
      PCI Express, 99–101
      PCI riser cards, 101
      PCI-X, 98–99
   chipset, 89–94
   CMOS battery replacement, 125–126
   configuring, 106–122
      jumpers for, 108–110
      overview, 106–108
      setup BIOS for, 110–121
   DDR dual-channel DIMMs on, 178–179
   DDR3 dual-channel DIMMs on, 176–177
   DDR3 triple-channel DIMMs on, 177–178
   documentation, 147, 175
   drive connections to, 8
   driver updating, 122–124
   electrical system problems, 356
   extra ports, 264
   flashing BIOS, 124–125
   form factors, 10, 82–84
   green, 382
   headers on, 53
   installing or replacing, 126–131
   notebook replacement, 559–563
   on-board ports and connectors, 104–106
   processor sockets, 84–89
   removing, 55–59
   SDRAM DIMMs on Pentium, 179
   troubleshooting, 366–376
      capacitor failure, 373
      Device Manager to delete Driver Store, 371–372
      installations, 373–376
      overview, 366–369
      Windows Memory Diagnostics tool, 369–371
   upgrading memory and, 176–180
Mouse, 251–252, 524
MSDS (Material Safety Data Sheet), 39
MT-RJ (mechanical transfer registered jack) connectors, 489
Multicast addresses, 413
Multi-core processing, 139
MultiMedia (MMC) cards, 292
Multimeter, 30, 34, 37
Multiple In, Multiple Out (MIMO) technology, 443, 453
Multiplier, 141
Multiprocessing abilities, 139
Multithreading, 139
Musical instrument digital interface (MIDI), 257–258

N

Name resolution, 416
NAND (Not AND logic test), 190
NAS (Network Attached Storage) device, 485
NAT (Network Address Translation), 411
Native resolution, of monitors, 271
Needle-nose pliers, 34
Negative wires, 65
Nehalem chipsets, 91
Neighbors, in IPv standards, 412
Netbook, 514
Networks, 401–462
    dial-up connections, 438–441
    printer connectivity problems in, 626–628
    printer installation with Windows XP on, 601–602
    SOHO router functions, 442–443
    SOHO router installation, 444–456
        overview, 444–448
        port forwarding, port triggering, and DMZ, 448–452
        wireless network with, 452–456
    TCP/IP, 402–423
        character-based names in, 415–417
        IP address assignment, 406–407
        IP address settings, 414–415
        IPv4 IP address use, 407–412
        IPv6 IP address use, 412–414
        layers in, 402–406
        protocol layers in, 417–423
    wired connections, 423–427
    wireless, 428–434
    wireless WAN (cellular), 434–438
Network adapters, 403, 476–481
Network Address Translation (NAT), 442, 449
Network and Sharing Center, 424
Network Attached Storage (NAS) device, 485
Network cable tester, 34
Networking types, devices, and cabling, 463–512
    local network hardware, 476–490
        dial-up modems, 482
        Ethernet cables and connectors, 486–491
        switches and hubs, 482–484
        wired and wireless network adapters, 476–481
        wireless access points and bridges, 484–485
    tools used with, 492–496
    types and topologies, 464–476
        cable Internet *versus* DSL, 470–471
        cellular WAN connection, 473–476
        fiber-optic Internet connection, 472
        Internet connection technology overview, 467–470
        overview, 464–467
        satellite Internet connection, 472
        WiMAX connection, 472–473
    wiring twisted-pair cables and connectors, 496–506
        keystone jack wiring, 503–504
        overview, 496–499
        straight-through cable with T568B wiring, 499–502
        troubleshooting, 505–506
Network interface card (NIC), 476–477, 591
Network multimeter, 493–494
Network ports, 3, 104
Neutral lines, in electricity, 26–27
nForce chipset, 93
NIC (network interface card), 476–477, 591
NLX form factor, 84
Nortel, Inc., 407
North Bridge, in Intel Accelerated Hub Architecture, 90
Notebooks, 513–580
    disassembling and reassembling, 546–567
        all-in-one computer, 567–571
        expansion card replacement, 554–557
        keyboard and touchpad, 551–553
        LCD panel replacement, 564–567
        motherboard replacement, 559–563
        optical drives, 553–554
        overview, 546–551
        processor replacement, 557–559
    hard drive replacement, 544–546
    internal device replacement, 539–540
    maintaining, 523–538
        keys, buttons, and input devices, 524–526
        PCMCIA and Expresscard slots, 527–530
        port or slot driver updates, 530
        port replicators and docking stations, 536–538
        power and electrical devices, 531–533
        power management, 533–536
    memory upgrade, 540–544
    supporting, 514–522
        diagnostic tools, 519–520
        OEM operating system build, 520–522
        service manuals, 517–519
        warranties, 516–517

troubleshooting, 571–576
  display, 574–575
  power or battery problems, 573–574
  video flickering or dim, 575–576
  Windows logon, 571
  wireless connectivity, 571–573
NTFS (New Technology file system), 282
NVIDIA chipset, 90, 93
NVIDIA processors, 75
NVIDIA video cards, 331, 333–334

O

Octets, in IP addresses, 407
OCx (Optical Carrier levels), 469
OEM operating system, in notebooks, 520–522
Ohms, 24
OLED (Organic Light-emitting Diode) monitor, 270, 564
Onboard sound, 265–266
Operating system, 404–405, 522. *See also* Windows
Optical Carrier levels (OCx), 469
Optical drives and discs
  installation, 288–289
  in notebooks, 553–554
  overview, 113–114
  standards for, 284–287
Oracle Virtual Box, 120, 333
OSI Model, in networking theory, 418
Overclocking, 71, 114
Overheating problems, 357–363

P

Packets, 402
PAN (personal area network), 464
Paper. *See also* Printers
  garbled characters on, 636
  impact, 588
  thermal, 589
Parallel ATA (PATA) connectors, 106
Parallel ATA (PATA) drives
  installation of, 214–220
    configuring, 216–217
    jumper setting, 217–218
    mounting, 218–220
    overview, 214–216
  interface standards for, 195–198
  standard, 18, 20

Parallel ports, 5, 104, 598–600
Parity, 221
Parity errors, 169–170
Partition, recovery, 520–522
Passwords, 116–118
PATA-to-USB converter, 351
Patch cable, 496
Patch panel, 496
P cable (68-pin SCSI connector), 202
PC Card, 527
PC-Doctor, 520
PCIe power connector, 16
PCIe video cards, 63
PCI (Peripheral Component Interconnect) expansion slots, 12
PCI Express bus standard, 529
PCI Express (PCIe) expansion slots, 13, 99–101
PCI Express standards, 554
PCI riser cards, 101
PCI-X expansion slots, 98–99
PCL (Printer Control Language), 582, 586
PCMCIA slots, notebook, 527–530
PC Power and Cooling, Inc., 76
PC service technician, 302
PC support technician, 302
PC World, 304
Pentium processors, 140, 142–143
Performance, memory, 172–173
Peripheral devices, 250–260
  barcode readers, 252–253
  biometric devices, 253
  digital cameras and camcorders, 254–255
  graphics tablets, 256–257
  KVM switches, 259–260
  MIDI devices, 257–258
  mouse or keyboard, 251–252
  overview, 250–251
  touch screens, 258–259
  webcams, 255–256
Personal area network (PAN), 464
Personal Computer Memory Card (PCMCIA), 527–530
Phenom processors (AMD), 145
Physical address, 403
Pickup roller, in laser printers, 585
PicoBTX form factor, 84
Pin grid array (PGA) socket, 86, 88
PIO (Programmed Input/Output) transfer mode, 197
Pixel pitch, of monitors, 271

Pixels, 268, 383
Plain Old Telephone Service (POTS), 482
Plasma monitor, 269
Plex Media Center, 335
Pliers, 34
Plug and Play devices, 242
PoE (Power over Ethernet), 480–481
Pointing stick, on notebooks, 524
Point-to-Point (PTP) connections, 472
POP3 (Post Office Protocol, version 3), 420
Port addresses, 402, 405
Port filtering, 449
Port forwarding, 448–452
Port number, 405
Port replicators, in notebooks, 536–538
Ports
    notebook, 530
    on-board, 104–106
    overview, 2–3
Ports and wireless connections, 244–250
    Firewire, 246–248
    infrared, 248–249
    USB, 245–246
Port triggering, 448–452
Positive wires, 65
POST before video active, 363
POST (power-on self test) diagnostic cards, 35–37
Post Office Protocol, version 3 (POP3), 420
PostScript commands, for printers, 582, 586
POTS (Plain Old Telephone Service), 482
Power
    ATX form factor, 10–12
    notebook, 531–533
    notebook management, 533–536
    notebook problems with, 573–574
    overview, 8–9
    power supply tester, 34, 37
    as rectifier and transformer, 25
    removing, 55–59
    selecting, 73–77
    surges in, 391
    troubleshooting, 355–356
Powering down, 47
Power-on passwords, 116–117
Power over Ethernet (PoE), 480–481
PowerPoint software, 279
Preventive maintenance, 392–393
Printer Control Language (PCL), 582, 586
Printers, 581–642
    cleaning, 610–612
    impact, 588–589
    inkjet, 586–588
    languages of, 582
    laser, 583–586
    maintenance kits for, 612–617
    online support for, 608–610
    servers and print management tool, 619–622
    thermal, 589–591
    troubleshooting, 622–637
        applications problems, 632–634
        connectivity problems in network printers, 626–628
        hardware problems, 623–626
        local cable or port problems, 626
        quality problems, 634–637
        Windows problems, 628–632
    upgrading memory or hard drive of, 617–619
    Windows for, 591–608
        installing local printer with Windows XP, 596–598
        installing network printer with Windows XP, 601–602
        installing with parallel port, 598–600
        installing with Windows 7/Vista, 593–596
        managing printers and add-on devices, 605–607
        overview, 591–593
        printer queue, 607–608
        sharing printers, 602–605
Print head, in inkjet printers, 586
Print spooler, 607, 628
Private IP addresses, 411–412
Processors, 137–162. *See also* Memory
    AMD, 145–146
    cooling assemblies for, 57
    graphics, 331
    installing, 147–162
        AMD in Socket AM2+, 159–162
        Intel in Socket LGA775, 157–159
        Intel in Socket LGA1155, 147–156
        Intel in Socket LGA1366, 156–157
    Intel, 142–145
    matching system needs with, 146–147
    mobile, 557
    notebook replacement, 557–559
    operations of, 140–142
    overview, 6, 138–140
    sockets for, 84–89
    speed of, 114

troubleshooting
  capacitor failure, 373
  Device Manager to delete Driver Store, 371–372
  installations, 373–376
  overview, 366–369
  Windows Memory Diagnostics tool, 369–371
Programmed Input/Output (PIO) transfer mode, 197
Prohibited content and activity, 328–329
Projector technologies, 269, 279
Protocols
  connectionless or best-effort, 419
  connection-oriented, 418
  overview, 94, 402
  TCP/IP, 419–423
  in TCP/IP network layers, 417–423
  tunneling, 412–413
PS/2j ports, 4
PS/2 ports, 104
PSU (power supply unit), 8
PTP (Point-to-Point) connections, 472
Public IP addresses, 411–412
Punchdown tool, 495
PWM (pulse width modulation), 68–69

Q

QoS (Quality of Service) feature, 447, 480
Quad channel DIMMs, 165, 167, 172
Quadro graphics processors, 331
Queue, printer, 607–608
QuickPath Interconnect (QPI) technology, 91–92, 114

R

Radio frequency (RF), 453
Raedeon graphics processors (AMD), 334
RAID (redundant array of inexpensive disks). *See* Hardware RAID
RAID 5 volumes, 221
RAID 1+0, 222
Rails, in power supplies, 74
RAM (random access memory), 7. *See also* Memory
  cooling, 71
  troubleshooting
    capacitor failure, 373
    Device Manager to delete Driver Store, 371–372
    installations, 373–376
    overview, 366–369
    Windows Memory Diagnostics tool, 369–371
Rambus, Inc., 163, 171
RAS (row access strobe) latency, 171
Raster lines, 582
Raw data, printing, 582
RDP (Remote Desktop Protocol), 422
RDRAM (direct Rambus DRAM), 171
Read/write head, on magnetic hard drive, 191–192
ReadyDrive technology, 192
Reassembling computers, 60–67
Receptacle tester, 26–27
Recovery partition and CDs, 520–522
Recovery software, 34
Rectifier, 25
Refresh rate, of monitors, 271
Registered DIMMs (RFU), 170–171
Registered jack-45 (RJ-45) port, 476, 478, 487, 495
Registers, 141
Remote Assistance utilities, 422
Remote Desktop Protocol (RDP), 422
Repair tools, 33–41
  cleaning pads and solutions, 39–40
  lifting heavy objects, 40–41
  loopback plugs, 37–38
  multimeter, 37
  post diagnostic cards, 35–37
  power supply tester, 37
Residual power, 47
Resolution, of monitors, 271
REt (Resolution Enhancement technology), 585
RexATX form factor, 83
RF (radio frequency), 453
RFC (Request for Comment) on Internet standards, 412
RFU (registered DIMMs), 170–171
RGB ports, 274
RG-6 coaxial cable, 488
RG-59 coaxial cable, 488
Ribbon cables, PATA, 196–197
RIMM memory modules
  description of, 163
  installing, 179–180, 183–184
  motherboard slots for, 171–172

Ring networks, 464
Riser cards, 101
RJ-11 jacks, 482
RJ-11 port, 5
RJ-45 port, 3, 476, 478, 487, 495
RL rating, 172
Roku.com, 335
ROM (read-only) memory chip, 35
Rosewill, Inc., 76
Router, 403. *See also* SOHO (small office home office) router

S

Sags (voltage reductions), 391
Samsung Corp., 205, 564
Sandy Bridge chipsets, 92–93
S1 state, in power saving, 536
S2 state, in power saving, 536
S3 state, in power saving, 536
S4 state, in power saving, 536
S5 state, in power saving, 536
SATA power connector, 18
Satellite Internet connection, 472
Satellite TV input, 336
SC (subscriber or standard connector) connectors, 489
Screwdrivers, 34
SCSI technology, 106, 200–204
SD (Secure Digital) cards, 291
SDRAM (synchronous DRAM), 165
SD slot, 515
Seagate Corp., 118, 205
Sectors, on read/write head, 192
Secure Digital (SD) cards, 291
Secure Erase utility, 393
Secure FTP (SFTP), 422
Secure Shell (SSH) protocol, 421
Secure Sockets Layer (SSL), 419
Self-grounding, 32
Self-Monitoring Analysis and Reporting Technology (S.M.A.R.T.), 192
Self-test page, printer, 623
Sempron processors (AMD), 145
Separation pad, in laser printers, 585
Sequential access, in tape drives, 228
Serial ATA (SATA) drives
    connectors, 106
    installation of, 205–214
        documentation, 207–208
        overview, 205–207
        process of, 208–212
        in removable bay, 212–213
        starting point for, 207
        in wide bay, 213–214
    interface standards for, 18, 198–200
Serial ATA International Organization (SATA-IO), 198
Serial ports, 4, 104
Servers, printer, 619–622
Service manuals, 517–519, 550
Service Set Identifier (SSID), 430, 455
Sharing printers, 602–605
Sheet battery, 531
Shielded twisted-pair (STP) cabling, 487–488
Silverstone, Inc., 76
SIM (Subscriber Identification Module) card, 434, 473
SIMM (single inline memory module), 163–164
Simple Mail Transfer Protocol (SMTP), 419
Simple Network Management Protocol (SNMP), 422
Single channel DIMMs, 165, 172
Single link or dual link DVI transmissions, 274
SiS chipset, 90, 93
Site license, 328
Sleep mode, 382, 533, 536, 602
Sleep timers, for notebooks, 533
SLI method, for multiple video cards, 93
Sling Media, 337
Slot drivers, updating, 530
Small Computer System Interface (SCSI) technology, 200–204
S.M.A.R.T. (Self-Monitoring Analysis and Reporting Technology), 192
SMB (Server Message Block), 420
SMTP (Simple Mail Transfer Protocol), 419
SMTP AUTH (SMTP Authentication), 419
SNMP (Simple Network Management Protocol), 422
Sockets, 84–89, 405. *See also* Processors
SO-DIMM (small outline DIMM), 163, 540–541, 568, 570
Software license, 328
Software piracy, 328
Software RAID, 222

SOHO (small office home office) router
  functions of, 442–443
  installation of, 444–456
    overview, 444–448
    port forwarding, port triggering, and DMZ, 448–452
    wireless network with, 452–456
Solid state drive (SSD), 190, 192
Solid state storage devices, 290–293
SONET (Synchronous Optical Network), 470
Sony laptops, 521
SO-RIMM (small outline RIMM) memory, 540
Sound cards, 265–266
Sound ports, 104
South Bridge, in Intel Accelerated Hub Architecture, 90
Spacers, for motherboard, 56
Spanning (JBOD, just a bunch of disks), 221
S/PDIF (Sony/Philips Digital Interconnect Format), 266
S/PDIF (Sony-Philips Digital Interface) sound port, 4
Speed. *See also* Ethernet
  clock, 138
  processor, 138
  spindle, 204
  USB connection, 245
  wireless connection, 244
SpeedFan, Alfredo Comparetti, 115
Spindle speed, 204
Spooling, in printer queue, 607, 628
SPP (Standard Parallel Port), 599
SRAM (static RAM), 140, 165
SSH (Secure Shell) protocol, 421
SSID (Service Set Identifier), 430, 455
SSL (Secure Sockets Layer), 419
Staggered pin grid array (SPGA) socket, 87
Standard Parallel Port (SPP), 599
Standby mode, for notebooks, 533
Standoffs, for motherboard, 56
Star networks, 465
StarTech.com, 36
Startup BIOS (basic input/output system), 36
Static electricity, 29–33, 46, 87
Static IP addresses, 406, 417, 633
Static RAM (SRAM), 140, 165
Static shielding bags, 31
ST (straight tip) connectors, 489

Storage devices
  file systems of, 282–283
  optical drive and disc standards, 284–287
  optical drive installation, 288–289
  solid state, 290–293
STP (shielded twisted-pair) cabling, 487–488
Straight-through cable, 496, 499–502
Striped volume (RAID 0), 221
Stylus, for graphics tablet, 256
Subnet ID, 414
Subnet mask, 409–411
Subnets, 405, 409–411
Subscriber Identification Module (SIM) card, 434, 473
Sunus Suntek, Inc., 76
Super Micro Computer, Inc., 108
SuperSpeed USB 3.0 devices, 245–246
Super-Video (S-Video) ports, 274
Surge protectors, 391
Surge suppresser, 24
Surround sound, 336
Suspend mode, for notebooks, 533
S-Video (Super-Video) ports, 3, 274
Switches and hubs, 482–484
Synchronous DRAM (SDRAM), 165
Synchronous Optical Network (SONET), 470
System BIOS (basic input/output system), 36
System board, 6
System clock, 96

T

Tape drives, 228–230
TCP (Transmission Control Protocol), 418
TCP/IP Fundamentals for Microsoft Windows, 414
TCP/IP networks, 402–423
  character-based names in, 415–417
  IP address assignment, 406–407
  IPv4 IP address use, 407–412
  IPv6 IP address use, 412–414
  layers in, 402–406
  protocol layers in, 417–423
Technical Committee T13, 194
Technical retail associate, 302
TechSmith.com, 255, 332
Telecommunications Industry Association (TIA), 497
Telnet protocol, 420
Temperature monitoring, 115

Teredo tunneling protocol, 412–413
Terminating resistor, 202
Tethering cellphone to computer, 434, 436, 475
T568A standard, 497
T568B standard, 497, 499–502
T568B wiring, 499–502
Thermal compound, 68–69, 152, 160
Thermal printers, 589–591
Thermaltake, Inc., 68, 76
Thermal transfer printers, 590
Thick client and thin client, 338–339, 485
Thread, 139
Thunderbolt port, 3
TIA (Telecommunications Industry Association), 497
Ticket record, 305
TLS (Transport Layer Security), 419
Toner probe, 493–494
Toner vacuum, for printers, 610
Topology, network, 464
Torx screwdriver set, 34
Touchpad, notebook, 524, 551–553
Touch screens, 258–259
Tower case, 2
TPM (Trusted Platform Module) chip, 118–120
Traces, on motherboards, 94
TrackPoint, on notebooks, 524
Tracks, on read/write head, 192
Tractor feeds, in dot matrix printers, 588
Transfer belt, in laser printers, 585
Transformer, 25
Transmission Control Protocol/Internet Protocol (TCP/IP). *See* TCP/IP networks
Transport Layer Security (TLS), 419
Trip hazards, 40
Triple channel DIMMs, 165–166, 172
Troubleshooting. *See also* Hardware troubleshooting
   notebooks, 571–576
      display, 574–575
      power or battery problems, 573–574
      video flickering or dim, 575–576
      Windows logon, 571
      wireless connectivity, 571–573
   printers
      applications problems, 632–634
      connectivity problems in network printers, 626–628
      hardware problems, 623–626
      local cable or port problems, 626
      quality problems, 634–637
      Windows problems, 628–632
   twisted-pair cables and connectors, 505–506
Tunneling protocols, 412–413
Turion processors (AMD), 145
TV tuner, 266–267
Tweezers, 34
Twisted-pair cables and connectors, 496–506
   crosstalk reduced by, 482
   for Ethernet, 487
   keystone jack wiring, 503–504
   overview, 496–499
   straight-through cable with T568B wiring, 499–502
   troubleshooting, 505–506

U

UDF (Universal Disk Format), 284
UDP (User Datagram Protocol), 419
UEFI (Unified Extensible Firmware Interface) Boot, 112–113
Unicast addresses, 413
Uninterruptible power supply (UPS), 391–392
Unique local unicast addresses (ULA), 413
Unshielded twisted-pair (UTP) cabling, 487
Upgrading memory, 173–184
   module installation, 182–184
   modules currently installed, 175–176
   module selection and purchase, 180–182
   motherboard slots for, 176–180
   needed *versus* installed, 173–174
USB Implementers Forum, 245
USB 3.0 Micro-B connectors, 246
USB (Universal Serial Bus) ports
   broadband modem, 435–436
   connections, 245
   on motherboards, 104, 106
   overview, 4, 194
   USB loopback tester for, 37
   wireless connections and, 245–246
USB-to-SATA converter, 352
User Datagram Protocol (UDP), 419
UTP (unshielded twisted-pair) cabling, 487

V

Vantec PCI fan card, 70
VDI (Virtual Desktop Infrastructure), 338
VDSL (very-high-bit-rate DSL), 469

Verizon, Inc., 434, 472, 476
VGA mode resolution, 386–387
VGA (video graphics array) port, 3, 273
VIA chipset, 90, 93
Video. *See also* Monitors
    audio and video editing workstation, 332–333
    memory for, 7
    ports for, 104
    POST before active, 363
    troubleshooting notebook, 575–576
Video capture cards, 266–267
Video cards
    for graphics workstation, 331
    latches for, 54
    PCIe x 16, 15–16
    power needs for, 75
    support for multiple, 63
    in video subsystem, 272–277
Video conferencing, 472
Video subsystem
    memory, 280–282
    monitor, 268–272
    monitor settings, 277–279
Virtual Desktop Infrastructure (VDI), 338
Virtualization
    overview, 120–121
    processor support for, 140
    virtualization server, 338–339
    workstation for, 333–334
Virtual machine (VM), 120
Vista Printers window, 593
VoIP (voice over Internet protocol), 472, 485
Volatile memory, 140
Voltage, 24–25, 115
Voltage reductions (sags), 391
V Series processors (AMD), 145

W

Wait state, 96
Wake-on LAN feature, 479, 602
WAN (wide area network), 464, 473–476
Warranties, 355, 516–517, 542
Wattage ratings, for power supplies, 24, 74–77
Webcams, 255–256
WEP (Wired Equivalent Privacy) security, 454
Western Digital, 205
Wide area network (WAN), 464

Wi-Fi (Wireless Fidelity), 452
Wi-Fi Protected Access (WPA) security, 455
Wi-Fi Protected Access 2 (WPA2) security, 455
Wi-Fi Protected Setup (WPS), 455
WiMAX connection, 472–473
Windows. *See also* Networks
    Disk Management utility in, 212, 222
    GDI (Graphics Device Interface) of, 582
    keystroke shortcuts in, 643–646
    for printer installation and management, 591–608
        managing printers and add-on devices, 605–607
        network printer with Windows XP, 601–602
        overview, 591–593
        parallel port, 598–600
        printer queue, 607–608
        sharing printers, 602–605
        Windows 7/Vista, 593–596
        Windows XP, 596–598
    printer problems with, 628–632
Windows Display Driver Model, 280
Windows logon, 571
Windows Media Center, 335
Windows Memory Diagnostics tool, 369–371
Windows Remote Desktop, 422
Windows 7
    installing printers with, 593–596
    operating system, 8, 118
    processor architecture in, 138
    ReadyDrive technology, 192
    video memory and, 280–282
    XML Paper Specification (XPS) in, 582
Windows Virtual PC, 120, 333
Windows Vista
    installing printers with, 593–596
    video memory and, 280–282
    XML Paper Specification (XPS) in, 582
Windows XP
    hardware profiles and, 537–538
    network printer installation with, 601–602
    for printer installation and management, 596–598
Wired and wireless network adapters, 476–481
Wired connections, to networks, 423–427
Wired Equivalent Privacy (WEP) security, 454

Wireless access points and bridges, 430, 442, 484–485
Wireless antenna, port for, 104
Wireless connections
　in notebooks, 571–573
　types of, 244–250
Wireless LAN (WLAN), 464
Wireless mouse, 524
Wireless networks
　connecting to, 428–434
Wireless networks (*continued*)
　SOHO (small office home office) router and, 452–456
　WAN (cellular), 434–438
　wide area (WWAN), 434, 436
　wireless network adapter, 145
Wire stripper, 495
WLAN (wireless LAN), 464
Workgroup, 416
Working inside computers. *See* Computers, working inside
Working professionally. *See* Customers, satisfying needs of
WORM (write once and read many), 228
WPA (Wi-Fi Protected Access) security, 455
WPA2 (Wi-Fi Protected Access 2) security, 455
WPS (Wi-Fi Protected Setup), 455
WWAN (wireless wide area network), 434, 436

X

XBMC Media Center, 335
xD-Picture cards, 292
x86 processors, 141
x86-64 bit processors, 141
XenClient (CiTRIX), 333
Xeon processors, 139
Xeon 64-bit processors, 141
XML Paper Specification (XPS), 582
XP Printers and Faxes window, 593
XPS (XML Paper Specification), 582

Z

Zalman, Inc., 76
Zero client, 339
Zero-fill utility, 393
Zero insertion force (ZIF) sockets, 88